Also by Robert A. Caro

The Power Broker:
Robert Moses and the Fall of New York
(1974)

THE PATH TO POWER

THE YEARS OF
LYNDON
JOHNSON

THE
PATH TO
POWER

ROBERT A. CARO

Alfred A. Knopf   New York   1982

THIS IS A BORZOI BOOK
PUBLISHED BY ALFRED A. KNOPF, INC.

Portions of this book have appeared in *The Atlantic Monthly*.

Grateful acknowledgment is made to the following for permission to reprint from previously published material:

Harcourt Brace Jovanovich, Inc.: From *Roosevelt: The Lion and the Fox* by James MacGregor Burns. Used with permission of Harcourt Brace Jovanovich, Inc.

Macmillan Publishing Co., Inc., and Scott Meredith Literary Agency, Inc.: From *Lone Star: A History of Texas and the Texans* by T. R. Fehrenbach. Copyright © 1968 by T. R. Fehrenbach. Reprinted with permission of Macmillan Publishing Co., Inc., and Scott Meredith Literary Agency, Inc.

McGraw-Hill, Inc.: From *A Family Album* by Rebekah Johnson. Copyright © 1965 by Rebekah Johnson. Used with permission of McGraw-Hill, Inc.

Simon & Schuster, Inc.: From *Secret Diary,* Volume II, by Harold Ickes. Copyright © 1953 by Simon & Schuster, Inc. Renewed © 1981 by Harold M. and Elizabeth Ickes. Reprinted with permission of Simon & Schuster, Inc., a Division of Gulf & Western Corporation.

Library of Congress Cataloging in Publication Data

Caro, Robert A.   The years of Lyndon Johnson.

Bibliography: v. 1, p.
Includes index.
Contents: v. 1. The path to power.
1. Johnson, Lyndon B. (Lyndon Baines), 1908–1973.
2. United States—Politics and government—1945–   .
3. Presidents—United States—Biography.   I. Title.
E847.C34   1982   973.923′092′4   [B]   82-47811
ISBN 0–394–49973–5 (v. 1)

Manufactured in the United States of America

FIRST EDITION

For Ina

"More is thy due than more than all can pay."

—Shakespeare

Contents

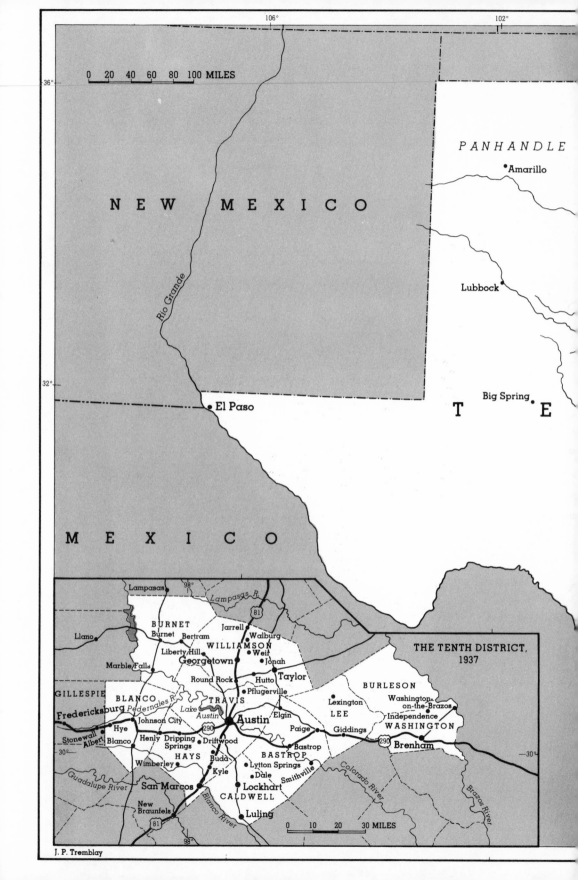

0 20 40 60 80 100 MILES

36°

106°   102°

PANHANDLE

•Amarillo

N E W   M E X I C O

Rio Grande

Lubbock•

32°

•El Paso   T   E

Big Spring•

M E X I C O

THE TENTH DISTRICT, 1937

Lampasas•   98°
                    Lampasas R.
        B U R N E T   81
        Burnet• Jarrell• Walburg•
Llano• •Burnet •Bertram W I L L I A M S O N
            Liberty Hill• •Weir
        •Marble Falls Georgetown •Jonah
                    Round Rock• Hutto• •Taylor
G I L L E S P I E   Pflugerville•   B U R L E S O N
        B L A N C O   T R A V I S   Lexington•   Washington-
Fredericksburg *Pedernales R.* Lake   L E E   on-the-Brazos•
            Johnson City• Austin Austin Elgin•   Independence•
Stonewall• •Hye   •290 •   Paige• Giddings•   W A S H I N G T O N
•Albert Blanco• Henly• Dripping •Driftwood   290   Brenham•
30°   Springs   Bastrop•
        H A Y S   Buda• B A S T R O P
        Wimberley• Kyle• •Lytton Springs *Colorado River*   30°
                    •Dale •Smithville
        San Marcos• Lockhart•
                C A L D W E L L
        New   •Luling
        Braunfels•
Guadalupe River   *Blanco River*   0 10 20 30 MILES   *Brazos River*
            81
                98°

J. P. Tremblay

INTRODUCTION

Patterns

TWO OF THE MEN lying on the blanket that day in 1940 were rich. The third was poor—so poor that he had only recently purchased the first suit he had ever owned that fit correctly—and desperately anxious not to be: thirty-two-year-old Congressman Lyndon Johnson had been pleading with one of the other two men, George Brown, to find him a business in which he could make a little money. So when Brown, relaxing in the still-warm Autumn sun at the luxurious Greenbrier Hotel in the mountains of West Virginia, heard the third man, Charles Marsh, make his offer to Lyndon Johnson, he felt sure he knew what the answer would be.

Brown wasn't surprised by the offer. The fifty-three-year-old Marsh, a tall, imperious man whose profile and arrogance reminded friends of a Roman emperor, was addicted to the grandiose gesture, particularly toward young men in whom he took a paternal interest: only recently, pleased with a reporter's work, he had told him he deserved a "tip"—and had thereupon given him a newspaper; some years earlier, his sympathies having been engaged by the story of a young oil wildcatter reduced by a series of dry wells to pawning his hunting rifle for room and board, he had agreed, in return for a share of the wildcatter's future profits (profits he believed would never materialize), to guarantee bank loans to enable young Sid Richardson to continue drilling. And Marsh's feelings toward Lyndon Johnson, whose control of his Texas congressional district was cemented by the support of Marsh's influential Austin newspaper, were particularly warm; "Charles loved Lyndon like a son," Brown says.

Brown wasn't even surprised by the size of the offer. A rich man himself by most standards, he knew how far from rich he was by Marsh's. The newspaper Marsh had so casually given away was only one of a dozen he owned; and he held—and collected interest on—the notes on a dozen more. In Austin alone, his possessions included not only the city's largest newspaper, but much of the stock in its largest bank, all of the stock in its streetcar franchise, and vast tracts of its most valuable real estate. And these were only minor items on Marsh's balance sheet, for his partnership with Richardson was not his only venture in the fabulous oil fields of West Texas; forests of derricks pumped black gold out of the earth for his sole profit. So Brown listened with interest but not astonishment when Marsh explained that he no longer was getting along with Richardson, and that he had one inflexible rule: if he didn't like a partner, he got out of the partnership. This partnership, he said, hadn't cost him a dime anyway—he had obtained his share in Richardson's wells just by guaranteeing those bank loans years before. He would sell his share to Johnson at a low price, he said, and, he said, using a characteristic phrase: "I'll sell it to you in a way you can buy it." There was only one such way for a young man without resources, and that was the way Marsh was proposing: he offered to let the young Congressman buy his share in the Richardson enterprises without a down payment. "He told Lyndon he could pay for it out of his profits each year," Brown explains. The share was probably not worth a million dollars, says Brown, who had seen the partnership's balance sheets—but it was worth "close to" a million, "certainly three-quarters of a million." Marsh was offering to make Lyndon Johnson rich, without Johnson investing even a dollar of his own.

But though George Brown wasn't surprised by Marsh's offer, he was surprised by the response it received. Johnson thanked Marsh, polite, ingratiating and deferential as he always was with the older man. But he was also, Brown recalls, quite firm. He would like to think the offer over, he said, but he felt almost certain he was going to have to decline with thanks. I can't be an oil man, he said; if the public knew I had oil interests, it would kill me politically.

All that week, Lyndon Johnson considered the offer—in a setting that emphasized what he would be giving up if he declined it. The Greenbrier— with its immense, colonnaded Main House rearing up, gleaming white, in the midst of 6,500 acres of lush lawns and serene gardens, its vast, marble-floored ballroom in which guests danced under huge cut-glass chandeliers, its cupolaed Spring House, around which, every afternoon, chilled champagne was served at canopied tables, its arcade lined with expensive shops, its indoor swimming pool as big as a lake, its battalions of green-liveried servants, its fleet of limousines which met guests arriving at a nearby station in their private railroad cars—was, as *Holiday* magazine put it, "opulent America at its richest," the distillation of all that was available in the United States to the wealthy, and not to others. As the three men lay every morning on their blanket, which had been spread on a slope in front of their accommodations—a row of white cottages, set away from the main building for privacy, which were the resort's most expensive—Johnson discussed the offer with Brown, telling him details of his life he had often told him before: about the terrible poverty of his youth, about his struggle to go to college—and about the fact (which, Brown felt, preyed con-

stantly on his mind) that after three years in Congress, three years, moreover, in which he had accumulated, thanks to President Roosevelt's friendship, far more than three years' worth of power, he still had nothing—not
a thousand dollars, he said—in the bank. Again and again he spoke to
Brown of his fear (a fear which, Brown believed, tormented him) of ending
up like his father, who had also been an elected official—six times elected
to the Texas State Legislature—but had died penniless. He talked repeatedly
about his realization that a seat in Congress was no hedge against that fate;
so many times since he had come to Washington, he said, he had seen former
Congressmen, men who had once sat in the great Chamber as he was sitting
now, but who had lost their seats—as, he said, he himself would inevitably
one day lose his—working in poorly paid or humiliating jobs. Again and
again, he harked back to one particular incident he could not get out of his
mind: while riding an elevator in the Capitol one day, he had struck up a
conversation with the elevator operator—who had said that *he* had once
been a Congressman, too. He didn't want to end up an elevator operator,
Johnson said. Accepting Marsh's offer would free him from such fears forever—Brown could see that Johnson had not misunderstood the offer, that
he was aware he had been offered great wealth. But again and again Johnson
returned to the statement he had made when Marsh had first made the offer:
"it would kill me politically."

George Brown had been working closely with Johnson for three years;
Johnson's initial nomination to Congress, in 1937, had, in fact, been brought
about to ensure an immensely complicated transaction with a very simple
central point: the firm in which George and his brother Herman were the
principals—Brown & Root, Inc.—was building a dam near Austin under an
unauthorized arrangement with the federal government, and it needed a Congressman who could get the arrangement authorized. Johnson had succeeded
in doing so—the Browns made millions of dollars from that federal contract
—and ever since he had been trying to make them more, an effort that had
recently been crowned with success by the award to Brown & Root of the
contract for a gigantic United States Navy base at Corpus Christi. Having
worked with Johnson so long, Brown felt he knew him—and knew how important money was to him, how anxious he was to obtain it. He sensed,
moreover, that this anxiety was increasing, a belief nurtured not only by
the growing intensity of Johnson's pleas that the Browns find him a business
of his own, but by a story circulating among Johnson's intimates: several
months before, at a party, Johnson had introduced two men, and one of
them had later purchased a piece of Austin real estate from the other. The
seller, a local businessman, had been astonished when the Congressman approached him one evening and asked for a "finder's fee" for the "role" he
had played in the transaction. Telling Johnson that he hadn't played any role
beyond the social introduction, he had refused to give him anything, and
had considered the matter closed; the transaction, he recalls, was small, and

the finder's fee would not have amounted to "more than a thousand dollars, if that." When, therefore, he opened the front door of his home at seven the next morning to pick up his newspaper, he was astonished to see his Congressman sitting on the curb, waiting to ask him again for the money. And when he again explained to Johnson that he wasn't entitled to a fee, "Lyndon started—well, really, to beg me for it—and when I refused, I thought he was going to cry." Brown, knowing how desperate Johnson had recently been over a thousand dollars, was surprised to see him hesitating over three-quarters of a million.

He was surprised also by Johnson's reason for hesitating. *It would kill me politically*—what "politically" was Johnson talking about? Until that week at the Greenbrier, Brown had thought he had measured Johnson's political ambition—had measured it easily, he thought, for Johnson talked so incessantly about what he wanted out of politics. He was always saying that he wanted to stay in Congress until a Senate seat opened up, and then run for the Senate. Well, his congressional district was absolutely safe; being an oil man couldn't hurt him there. And when he ran for the Senate, he would be running in Texas, and being an oil man wouldn't hurt him in Texas. For what office, then, would Johnson be "killed" by being an "oil man"?

Only when he asked himself that question, George Brown recalls, did he finally realize, after three years of intimate association with Lyndon Johnson, what Johnson really wanted. And only when, at the end of that week, Johnson firmly refused Marsh's offer did Brown realize how much Johnson wanted it.

GEORGE BROWN, who had thought he knew Lyndon Johnson so well, realized during that week at the Greenbrier that he didn't know him at all. Their lives would be entwined for thirty more years: as Brown & Root became, thanks to Johnson, an industrial colossus, one of the largest construction companies—and shipbuilding companies and oil-pipeline companies—in the world, holder of Johnson-arranged government contracts and receiver of Johnson-arranged government favors amounting to billions of dollars, suave George Brown and his fierce brother Herman became, in return, the principal financiers of Johnson's rise to national power. But at the end of those thirty years—on the day Lyndon Johnson died—George Brown still felt that to some extent he didn't really know him.

KNOWING LYNDON BAINES JOHNSON—understanding the character of the thirty-sixth President of the United States—is essential to understanding the history of the United States in the twentieth century. During his Presidency, his Great Society, with its education acts and civil-rights acts and anti-poverty acts, brought to crest tides of social change that had begun flowing during the New Deal a quarter of a century before; after his Presidency, the currents of social change were to flow—abruptly—in a very different course. When he became President, 16,000 American advisors were serving in Vietnam—in a war that was essentially a Vietnamese war. When he left the Presidency, 536,000 American combat troops were fighting in Vietnam's jungles, 30,000 Americans had died there, and the war had been "Americanized"—transformed into a war that would, before it was ended, exhaust America financially and soak up the blood of thousands upon thousands of its young men; into a war abroad that at home caused civil disobedience that verged on civil insurrection; into a war that transformed America's image of itself as well as its image in the eyes of the world. Lyndon Johnson's full term as President began in triumph: the 1964 landslide that Theodore H. White calls "the greatest electoral victory that any man ever won in an election of free peoples." It ended—to the chant, "Hey, hey, LBJ, how many kids did you kill today?" from a generation to whom he was the hated war maker—with his announcement that he would not again ask the nation to elect him its leader. The Great Society; Vietnam—the Presidency of Lyndon Johnson, only five years in span, was nonetheless a watershed in America's history, one of the great divides in the evolution of its foreign and domestic policies. And in this evolution, Johnson's personality bore, in relation to other factors, an unusually heavy weight, both because of its overpowering, elemental force—he seemed at times to brood, big-eared, big-nosed, huge, over the entire American political landscape—and because of the unusual degree to which the workings of that personality were (perhaps not on the surface, but in reality) unencumbered by philosophy or ideology. It was also during Johnson's Presidency that there developed the widespread mistrust of the President that was symbolized by the phrase, coined during his administration, "credibility gap." And if, during the long evolution from a "constitutional" to an "imperial" Presidency, there was a single administration in which the balance tipped decisively, it was the Presidency of Lyndon Johnson. Both these latter developments, which were to affect the nation's history profoundly, were to a considerable extent a function of this one man's personality.

Knowledge of the inner workings of Lyndon Johnson's character illuminates a Presidency; knowledge of the broader outlines of his life illuminates far more. For the drama of his life—and of the lives, so inextricably linked with his, of his father and grandfather—was played out against a panorama vast in scope: the panorama of the westward movement in America, and particularly in America's Southwest. The story of Lyndon Johnson is the story of the slow settlement of endless, empty, fearsomely hostile plains and hills with the "dog-run" log cabins of families who would for generations that added up to a century remain not only poor—bereft of modern machinery, of electricity, of a thousand amenities urban America took for granted—but isolated: cut off from the rest of America. Lyndon Johnson grew up

in the Hill Country of Texas during the 1920s, the Age of Radio, the Age
of the Movies. But there were few movies, and almost no radios—and
no paved roads and no electricity and so little money that the economy
was basically an agricultural barter economy—in the Hill Country during
the 1920s, or, indeed, during the 1930s. And the story of Lyndon Johnson
is, in microcosm, the story of how, at last, government, deaf for generations,
finally, during the New Deal, during the Age of Roosevelt, answered the
pleas of impoverished farmers for help in fighting forces too big for them to
fight alone. The story of Lyndon Johnson is the story of the great dams
that tamed the rivers of the West, and turned their waters into electric
power—for it was because of Lyndon Johnson that great dams were built in
the Hill Country. And the story of Lyndon Johnson is the story of the electric
wires, gleaming silver across dun-brown plains and hills, which linked the
life of the West, as railroads had linked its commerce, to the rest of America
—for it was Lyndon Johnson who brought those wires to the Hill Country.
When, in 1937, at the age of twenty-eight, Johnson became their Congressman, Hill Country farmers were still plowing their fields with mules because
they could not afford tractors. Because they had no electricity, they were
still doing every chore by hand, while trying to scratch a living from soil
from which the fertility had been drained decades before. They were still
watching their wives made stooped and old before their time by a life of
terrible drudgery, a life that seemed, as one Hill Country woman put it, "out
of the Middle Ages." Four years later, the people of the Hill Country were
living in the twentieth century. Lyndon Johnson had brought them there.

ESSENTIAL THOUGH it may be to understand Lyndon Johnson—his character and his career—this understanding is hard to acquire. He made it hard.
Enlisting all his energy and all his cunning in a lifelong attempt to obscure
not only the true facts of his rise to power and his use of power but even of
his youth, he succeeded well. He told stories readily and repeatedly (filling
them with vivid, convincing, detail) about the year he spent in California as
a teenager, about his college girlfriend and the denouement of their relationship, about his father, whom he often sought to portray as a drunken
ne'er-do-well—about, in fact, a hundred aspects of his youth. And not
merely many but most of these stories were false. Aiding in his success,
moreover, was an aspect of his temperament with which, during his Presidency, Washington was to become familiar: an extraordinary preoccupation
with, and talent for, secrecy. This talent was striking even in his youth, and
in the concealment of his own life story the President outdid himself. On
innocuous personal letters written while he was still a young congressional
assistant, he wrote: "Burn this." His years at college provide a vivid illus-
tration of his efforts at concealment, and of their success. While still an undergraduate at Southwest Texas State Teachers College, in San Marcos, he

arranged to have excised (literally cut out) from hundreds of copies of the college yearbook certain pages that gave clues to his years there (luckily, other copies escaped the scissors). Issues of the college newspaper that chronicle certain crucial episodes in his college career are missing from the college library. A ruthless use thereafter of political power in San Marcos made faculty members and classmates reluctant to discuss those aspects of his career. And college is merely one example. In a sense, Lyndon Johnson not only attempted to create, and leave for history, his own legend, but to ensure that it could never be disproven.

WHAT DUMAS MALONE wrote of Thomas Jefferson, however, is true of Lyndon Johnson: "He loses none of his fascination but he does lose much of his elusiveness when one follows him through life the way he himself went through it, that is, chronologically." In this three-volume work, Johnson's life will be told as in fact it unfolded.

The more one thus follows his life, the more apparent it becomes that alongside the thread of achievement running through it runs another thread, as dark as the other is bright, and as fraught with consequences for history: a hunger for power in its most naked form, for power not to improve the lives of others, but to manipulate and dominate them, to bend them to his will. For the more one learns—from his family, his childhood playmates, his college classmates, his first assistants, his congressional colleagues— about Lyndon Johnson, the more it becomes apparent not only that this hunger was a constant throughout his life but that it was a hunger so fierce and consuming that no consideration of morality or ethics, no cost to himself—or to anyone else—could stand before it.

It, too, can be seen in college. There he obtained his first power. "San Marcos," as it was called, was a school that represented for most of its students their only chance to escape from a life of poverty and brutal physical toil. And for many of these students, their only chance of staying in college was to secure campus jobs. Lyndon Johnson obtained the power to give out these jobs, and once he had it, he used it—exacting deference, a face-to-face acknowledgment of this power, from his classmates. His years at college made clear not only this hunger but a willingness to do whatever was necessary to temporarily satisfy it (in the final analysis, it was insatiable). To obtain the power that he wanted, Lyndon Johnson, who was alleged to have won his seat in the United States Senate in a stolen election in 1948, stole his first election at college, in 1930. He won another campus election by the use against a young woman of what his lieutenants call "blackmail." And a score of political tricks on the same moral level earned him a reputation on campus as a man who was not "straight," not honest. He was, in fact, so deeply and widely mistrusted at college that the nickname he bore during all his years there was "Bull" (for "Bullshit") Johnson. Most significant, perhaps, the dislike and distrust of him extended beyond politics. As President, Lyndon Johnson would be accused of lying to the American people. When he was a college student, his fellow students (who used his nickname to his face: "Hiya, Bull," "Howya doin', Bull?") believed not only that he lied to them—lied to them constantly, lied about big matters and small, lied so incessantly that he was, in a widely used phrase, "the biggest liar on campus" —but also that some psychological element *impelled* him to lie, made him, in one classmate's words, "a man who just could not tell the truth." Credibility gap as well as Great Society are foreshadowed in this volume.

The dark thread was still present after college. It would be present throughout his life. *The Path to Power*, the first of three volumes that will constitute *The Years of Lyndon Johnson*, ends in 1941, when Johnson is only thirty-two years old. But by 1941, the first major stage of his life is over. A young man—desperately poor, possessed of an education mediocre at best, from one of the most isolated and backward areas of the United States—has attained the national power he craved. He has won not only a seat in Congress but influence that reaches far beyond his district's borders. And by 1941, also, the major patterns of his entire life are established and clear. In attaining this influence, he has displayed a genius for discerning a path to power, an utter ruthlessness in destroying obstacles in that path, and a seemingly bottomless capacity for deceit, deception and betrayal in moving along it. In every election in which he ran—not only in college, but thereafter—he displayed a willingness to do whatever was necessary to win: a willingness so complete that even in the generous terms of political morality, it amounted to amorality.

ANOTHER PATTERN with significant implications is established in this volume: Lyndon Johnson's use of money as a lever to move the political world.

Johnson came to the use of money in elections very early. While he was still a congressional assistant, he sat in a San Antonio hotel room buying votes with five-dollar bills. An extravagant use of this lever characterized his own campaigns from the first: his initial race for Congress, in 1937, was one of the most expensive congressional campaigns in Texas political history. During his first Senate campaign, in 1941, men handed him (or handed to his aides, for his use) checks or envelopes stuffed with cash—checks and cash in amounts unprecedented even in the free-spending world of Texas politics—and with these campaign contributions, which totaled hundreds of thousands of dollars, he waged the most expensive senatorial campaign in Texas political history, a campaign so expensive that it amounted to an attempt to buy a state. It was not, however, the use of money in his own campaigns that was to have the deepest significance for Lyndon Johnson's political career—and for American political history—but his use of money in the campaigns of others. At the beginning of October, 1940, not long after his refusal of Marsh's offer at the Greenbrier, Johnson was merely a junior Congressman, a rather unpopular one at that, with neither power nor influence on Capitol Hill. During that month, however, as a result of his maneuverings, men came to him bearing checks and envelopes containing cash for him to dole out—at his discretion—to scores of other congressional candidates. By Election Day, 1940, just a month later, Lyndon Johnson was a Congressman with considerable influence—as a colleague put it, "a guy you couldn't deny any more." This inpouring of campaign contributions was re-enacted in 1942 (when in a private letter Johnson flatly spelled out, with no circumlocutions, the philosophy which he felt should motivate campaign contributions: money should be given, he wrote, because of "the wealth and consideration that has been extended" to favored oil men and contractors by the federal government). It was to be re-enacted over and over—on a larger and larger scale—in years to come. These later contributions—and their impact on American politics—will be detailed in chronological sequence in the last two volumes. But by 1941, the pattern of such contributions, and of Lyndon Johnson's use of them, had been firmly established. Congressmen who were worried about money to ensure their return to Capitol Hill had learned that all the money they needed was available from Texas—from Texas and from the new industrial order of the Southwest, of which Texas was the heart—and that Lyndon Johnson, more than any other single figure, controlled it.

This money was the basic source of Johnson's power on Capitol Hill. Lyndon Johnson has been described as a legislative genius, a reader of men, a leader of men—countless articles described how he could grasp men's lapels, peer into their eyes, and talk them around, how he could create consensus out of disparity. Lyndon Johnson *was* all these things, but his genius would have had far less impact without the money to back it up, without the knowledge on the part of the legislator being approached that the man grasping his lapel possessed the power to advance his political career or—by aiding his opponent—to end it. The "Johnson Treatment"—his blend of threats and pleading, of curses and cajolery—became a staple of the national political folklore. But the picturesque elements of the Johnson Treatment were only tassels on the bludgeon of power.

BECAUSE THIS MONEY came from Texas, the rise of Lyndon Johnson sheds light on the new economic forces that surged out of the Southwest in the middle of the twentieth century, on the immense influence exerted over America's politics, its governmental institutions, its foreign and domestic policies by these forces: the oil and sulphur and gas and defense barons of the Southwest. As the robber barons of the last century looted the nation's earth of its wealth—its coal and coke, its oil and ore, its iron, its forests, the very surface of its earth to provide a footing for the rails of their railroads—and used part of that wealth to ensure that the nation's government would not force them to give more than a pittance of their loot back to the nation's people, so the robber barons of this century have drained the earth of the Southwest of its riches and have used those riches to bend government to their ends.

Lyndon Johnson was not the architect of their ascendancy, but he was its embodiment and its instrument—its most effective instrument. It was these new economic forces—the oil, gas, defense, space and other new industries of the Southwest—that raised him to power, and, once he was in power, helped him to extend it. They placed at his disposal sums of money whose dimensions were extraordinary in politics, and he used this money to force other politicians to do his bidding. By 1941, the influence of these new forces on national policy would only be beginning to be felt, but the pattern had been established.

ONLY ONE PATTERN in Johnson's later life would be substantially different—the change began in late 1942, a year after this book's conclusion—and this difference must be mentioned here briefly, even if it cannot be detailed until later volumes, since otherwise this book would leave an incorrect impression of the overall shape of his life.

If at the Greenbrier Johnson subordinated his desire for personal wealth to his desire to become President, he found, in 1942, a way to reconcile his two ambitions—and in years to come he found a dozen ways, and he entered the Oval Office perhaps the richest man ever to occupy it. Shortly after he assumed the Presidency, *Life* magazine, in the most detailed contemporary analysis of his wealth, estimated his "family's" fortune at $14 million; Johnson's representatives protested publicly that that estimate was far too high; privately, one of his key advisors now admits that it was far too low. Even had his wealth been no greater than $14 million, that means that during the twenty-one years between 1942 and his assumption of the Presidency in 1963—twenty-one years during which Johnson continually held public office—the Johnson fortune increased at a rate of well over half a million dollars a year.

Although from time to time dedicated investigative journalists produced articles detailing one or another episode in that accumulation, these episodes were never linked to reveal the overall pattern, in large part because of Johnson's genius for secrecy. The one aspect of his fortune that was explored in depth was the Johnson radio and television interests, which were in his wife's name (although, as these articles show, the carefully nurtured legend that he had nothing to do with them was largely fiction). There existed a vague public awareness that Federal Communications Commission actions had favored the Johnson radio station and, later, the Johnson television station in Austin. There were jokes—bitter in Austin, knowing in Washington—about the fact that the capital of Texas had to make do with a single television channel. But little public understanding existed of the fact that the FCC not only created the Johnson broadcasting monopoly and insulated it against would-be competitors, but steadily expanded its sphere until it was a radio-television empire that was not limited to Austin or even to Texas. This empire grew from a radio station that was purchased in 1942 for $17,500. By the time Lyndon Johnson entered the Presidency, it was worth $7 million—and was producing profits of $10,000 per week. And the growth of this radio-television empire was only part of the history of his accumulation of wealth. Nor does any detailed exploration exist of the economic fate of those men who, owning their own television stations (or banks, or ranches), tried to compete with Lyndon Johnson, or simply to hold on, against his wishes, to their property—men who were broken financially on the wheel of his power.

According to attorneys close to him, attainment of the Presidency did not slake Lyndon Johnson's thirst for money. Upon assuming the office, he announced that he was immediately placing all his business affairs in a "blind trust," of whose activities, he said, he would not even be kept informed. But these attorneys say that the establishment of the trust was virtually simultaneous with the installation in the White House of private telephone lines to Texas lawyers associated with the administration of the trust —and they say that during the entire five years of his Presidency, Johnson personally directed his business affairs, down to the most minute details. Of this there was virtually no public awareness, and Lyndon Johnson left the Presidency, and lived out his life, and died, with the American people still ignorant not only of the dimensions of his greed but of its intensity.

IT IS NOT MERELY his skill at a secrecy that makes understanding Lyndon Johnson so difficult. It is a lack of knowledge about the land in which he was born and raised: the Hill Country of Texas. For all the patterns of his life have their roots in that land.

Stella Gliddon, editor of the local newspaper in the remote Hill Country town called Johnson City and, for almost fifty years, the little town's historian, said not long before she died, "So much has been written about Lyndon, but the thing is that none of it explains what it meant to grow up in a place like this.

"And without understanding that, no one will ever understand Lyndon Johnson."

Part I

THE
TRAP

1

The Bunton Strain

ON THE DAY HE WAS BORN, he would say, his white-haired grandfather leaped onto his big black stallion and thundered across the Texas Hill Country, reining in at every farm to shout: "A United States Senator was born this morning!" Nobody in the Hill Country remembers that ride or that shout, but they do remember the baby's relatives saying something else about him, something which to them was more significant. An old aunt, Kate Bunton Keale, said it first, bending over the cradle, and as soon as she said it, everyone saw it was true, and repeated it: "He has the Bunton strain." And to understand Lyndon Johnson it is necessary to understand the Bunton strain, and to understand what happened to it when it was mixed with the Johnson strain—and, most important, to understand what the Hill Country did to those who possessed it.

So strong were its outward marks that pictures of generations of Bunton men might, except for different hair styles and clothing, almost be pictures of the same man—a tall man, always over six feet, with heavily waved coal-black hair and dramatic features: large nose, very large ears, heavy black eyebrows and, underneath the eyebrows, the most striking of all the Bunton physical characteristics, the "Bunton eye." The Bunton skin was milky white—"magnolia white," the Hill Country called it—and out of that whiteness shone eyes so dark a brown that they seemed black, so bright that they glittered, so piercing that they often seemed to be glaring. "When my mother and father came back from seeing the baby and said he had the Bunton eye, I knew exactly what they meant," says Lyndon's cousin Ava. "Because Grandmother Bunton had the Bunton eye. If you talked to her, you never had to wonder if the answer was yes or no. Those eyes told you. Those eyes talked. They spit fire."

If the Bunton eye was famed throughout the Hill Country, so was the Bunton personality. The Bunton temper was fierce and flaring, and the Bunton pride was so strong that some called it arrogance—although a writer describing one of the family notes that the arrogance was softened by a "shadow of sadness running through his features," and pictures of Buntons in middle and old age invariably show men whose mouths are pulled grimly tight and down.

The first Bunton in Texas was a hero, with a personality so striking that a man who met him only casually—encountering him among a group of riders on the great plains south of Bastrop in 1835—never forgot him, and years later would recall: "There were several men in the party, but Mr. Bunton's personality attracted me. [He] had an air of a man of breeding and boldness. While our meeting was casual, he asked me a number of questions [and] I was greatly impressed by his manly bearing." John Wheeler Bunton, a six-foot-four-inch Tennesseean, had come to Texas only that year, but apparently he impressed others as he impressed that rider: when the settlers of the Bastrop area met the next year to elect a delegate to the constitutional convention that would, in defiance of Mexico, create the Republic of Texas, he was elected—at the age of twenty-eight, the same age at which Lyndon Johnson would be elected to Congress. He was one of the signers of the Texas Declaration of Independence and a member of the committee that wrote the constitution of the new Republic. In the war between Texas and Mexico, he was at the first major battle—the three bloody days of house-to-house fighting that began when an old frontiersman, refusing to obey his officer's order to retreat, shouted, "Who will go with old Ben Milam into San Antonio?" and led a wild charge into the city—and he was at the last: in the great charge at the San Jacinto when Sam Houston waved his 800 ragged men forward against the entire Mexican Army (the Texans marched side by side in a single line half a mile long; before them floated a white silk flag bearing a lone star; beside the flag rode Houston on his great white stallion, Saracen; for a while the Texans advanced in silence; then someone shouted, "Remember the Alamo!"). At San Jacinto, a fellow officer wrote, Bunton's "towering form could be seen amidst the thickest of the fight. He penetrated so far into the ranks of the defenders of the breastworks that it is miraculous that he was not killed." According to one account, he was the leader of the seven-man patrol that the next day captured Santa Anna, who was trying to escape in a private's uniform, and brought "the Napoleon of the West" before Houston. Of his deeds as an Indian-fighter, a friend wrote years later: "To the present generation of Texans the name of this honored man is, perhaps, but little known; but in the day long gone by, it was a household word in all the scattered log cabins that dotted the woods and prairies of Texas." Returning to Tennessee after the war to claim his sweetheart, he brought her to Texas—on a wild journey during which their ship was captured by a Mexican man-of-war and they were imprisoned for three months—and was elected to the new Republic's first Congress, where he quickly demonstrated an ability to lead legislators: observers wrote of his "commanding presence" and "eloquent tongue"; among the bills in whose passage he played a prominent role was the one that established the Texas

Rangers. He was re-elected, seemed on the road to political prominence—and then, without a word of explanation, abruptly retired from public life forever.

Whatever the reasons for Bunton's retirement from politics, they did not include lack of ambition: ambition—ambition on the grand scale—was, in fact, perhaps the most vivid of all the vivid Bunton characteristics. While some of the men who came to Texas—that vast and empty land—in the mid-nineteenth century were fleeing from the law or from debts, many of the thousands and tens of thousands who chalked GTT ("Gone to Texas") on the doors of their homes in the Southern states were not fleeing from, but searching for something. "Big country . . . fed big dreams," as one historian put it, and Texas, with its huge tracts of land free for the taking—in 1838, it enacted the first homestead legislation in America (and a man's homestead, the legislation also provided, could never be seized for debt)—fed the biggest dreams of all. And judging from the actions of John Wheeler Bunton and his brothers, no dreams were bigger than theirs.

These were years when the frontier, the edge of settlement in central Texas, was terrible in its isolation, separated as it was by hundreds of miles from the state's more populated areas near the Louisiana and Arkansas borders; families which moved to the edge of settlement in the 1830's and '40s and '50s, says Texas historian T. R. Fehrenbach, "left 19th century civilization far behind." And because central Texas was the hunting ground of the Apaches and the fierce Penetaka Comanches, masters of human torture, it was, in Fehrenbach's words, "a genuine frontier of war." Men who went—and took their families—to the edge of settlement had to be driven, or lured, by big dreams indeed. Each farmer who did so, Fehrenbach says, did so "yearning for his own small kingdom, willing to suffer hardships beyond counting while he carved it out with his own hands." The Buntons went to the *very* edge. John Wheeler Bunton, the hero, came from a wealthy family in Tennessee but wanted something more and went west to Texas, then after the war with Mexico moved west within Texas, and then west again. His first homestead was on the plains below Brenham, when those plains were the edge of the frontier. About 1840, despite the hammerblows of the Apaches and Penetakas, the frontier edged west to the Colorado River; Bunton about 1840 moved beyond the Colorado, settling near Bastrop. During the 1850's, settlers pushed about fifty miles farther west, to the 98th meridian, where the plains ended and the Texas Hill Country (a highland known to geologists as the "Edwards Plateau") began, and along that meridian, Fehrenbach says, for two decades, "the frontier wavered, now forward, now back, locked in bitter battle"; during 1858 and 1859, two of the "bloodiest years in Texas history," the dead of that frontier would be numbered in the hundreds; in the isolated log cabins that dotted the hills, settlers huddled in fear during the nights of the full moon, the "Comanche moon." But during the 1850's, near the 98th meridian, in the plains at the edge of the Hill Country, John Bunton

built not a cabin but a graceful two-story plantation house with three veran-
das, surrounded by cotton fields and pastures in which grazed not only sheep
and cattle but the finest Tennessee thoroughbreds, and staffed with Negro
slaves dressed in black trousers and white waistcoats—the great plantation
of which he had dreamed. And although Indians still roamed the area (twice
his wife, in his absence, scared off threatening bands with a rifle), when a
log-cabin church was founded in nearby Mountain City in 1857, the Buntons
would arrive at it on Sundays in an elegant sulky driven by an elderly retainer named Uncle Ranch. The Bunton plantation (named Rancho Rambouillet after a French breed of sheep John was trying to raise there) may
have been the westernmost cotton plantation—and plantation house—on
such a scale in all Texas.

West and west and west again, pursuing a big dream—John was not the
only Bunton who took that course. So did the three brothers who followed
him to Texas, one of whom, Robert Holmes Bunton—"a large impressive
man, standing six feet and three inches in height and weighing about two
hundred and sixty pounds . . . with fair skin, coal-black hair and piercing
eyes"—was Lyndon Johnson's great-grandfather.

Very little is known about Robert Bunton. He first moved from Tennessee to Kentucky, where he became a "substantial planter." Nevertheless,
in 1858, at the age of forty, he moved to Texas, near Bastrop; and then he,
too, moved west, to Lockhart, in the plains just below the Hill Country. He
fought in the Lost Cause (as did his sons and six grandsons, all of whom,
a family historian noted, were over six feet tall), enlisting as a private and
within a year being promoted twice, to sergeant and lieutenant. After the
war, he raised cattle and sent them up the Chisholm Trail to Abilene—huge
herds raised on a huge ranch, for with the profits of each drive he bought
more land.

Dreamers of big dreams, the Buntons were also, to an extent somewhat
unusual among Texas frontier families, interested in ideas and abstractions.
John Bunton was one of the founders of the short-lived Philosophical Society
of Texas, which was formed in 1837 to explore "topics of interest which our
new and rising republic unfolds to the philosopher, the scholar and the man
of the world." No such details exist about Robert, but his descendants recall
hearing that he had a reputation for being "absolutely truthful" and "an
excellent conversationalist, and greatly interested in government and politics." If, in his old age, he found someone at Weinheimer's Store to talk with
when he went shopping, he would sit and talk all day and into the night,
although, unlike most of those with whom he talked, he preferred to discuss
not "practical" politics but theories of government; he was regarded by the
other men, says a descendant of one of them, as "an idealist."

Idealists, romantics, dreamers of big dreams though they may have
been, there was nonetheless a hard, tough, practical side to the Buntons.

Neighbors remember them as canny traders, and remember, too, their favorite saying: "Charity begins at home." And while their dreams were big, in the face of necessity they had the strength to scale them down, to adapt to reality.

The dreams of John Wheeler Bunton proved too big for the land to support: cotton could not be grown profitably enough in central Texas to support a huge, elegant plantation, and the showy French sheep didn't produce enough wool or mutton. But he experimented with new breeds, and although he lost some of the "thousands of acres" Rancho Rambouillet had originally covered, he held on to enough so that he died "leaving a handsome estate" to his son, Desha. Desha drove cattle north and, making money, bought large tracts of land near Austin. When cattle-driving turned unprofitable he had to sell those tracts—but he managed to hold on to what he had started with. He held on to it and turned it into a farm, its hogs (if cattle weren't profitable, the Buntons would raise an animal that was) producing sausage that he sold in Austin, acquiring as he did so a reputation as a hard, shrewd businessman. As late as 1930, Desha's son and daughter were running the same ranch their hero grandfather had left—and the hero's house still stood. ("The Buntons were very proud people," a neighbor recalls. "They had elegant parties in that beautiful yard. They were really striking, the way they looked. Tall and straight. Their ears were big and their noses— and they had those piercing Bunton eyes.") And although during the Depression they were forced to sell off first one piece and then another, they held on grimly to as much as possible—so that as late as 1981, more than a century after its founding, the ranch, reduced to perhaps 200 acres, was still in the family.

Robert Holmes Bunton, Lyndon Johnson's great-grandfather, sent big herds up to Abilene with his sons. Cattle prices began to fall, and from one drive his sons returned all but penniless. Then, together with another brother, Robert mustered up a herd of 1,500 head and sent them up the trail with one of the brother's sons. The young man returned home without a dime, having apparently fallen into the hands of cardsharps in Abilene; Robert, it is related, "said not one word of reproach." But while other men persisted in making drives that grew steadily less profitable, the two Bunton brothers all but stopped raising cattle themselves, and instead rented out their pastures as grazing land for herds from South Texas that were passing through and needed to rest for a few days on the way north. Many of the men who owned those herds made no money from them—but the Buntons did. Robert Bunton made enough so that he was able to retire comfortably, and to give his six children a start in life when they married: money to his daughters—one of whom, Eliza Bunton, was Lyndon Johnson's grandmother —and land to his sons. And the sons made successes of their land—one becoming one of the biggest ranchers in the big ranch country of West Texas.

The Buntons, then, while never as successful as they had dreamed of becoming, were more successful than the run of ranchers in central Texas: in a land in which economic survival was very difficult, they survived. Central Texans often judged their neighbors by whether or not they "left something for their children." The Buntons left something for theirs, and the children made something out of what they were left. It was only when, in Lyndon Johnson's father, the Bunton strain became mixed with the Johnson strain that the Bunton temper and pride, ambition and dreams, and interest in ideas and abstractions brought disaster, for the Johnsons were not only also dreamers, romantics, and idealists, not only had a fierce pride and flaring temper of their own, and physical characteristics which greatly resembled those of the Buntons, they also resembled the Buntons in their passion for ideas and abstractions—without resembling them at all in shrewdness and toughness. They had all the impractical side of the Buntons—and none of the practical side. Big as were the Buntons' dreams, moreover, the Johnsons' dreams were even bigger. Their dreams lured them beyond even that far point to which the Buntons had ventured. The Buntons stopped just before the edge of the Hill Country; the Johnsons pushed forward—into its heart.

And the Hill Country was hard on dreams.

THE HILL COUNTRY was a trap—a trap baited with grass.

To men who had lived in the damp, windless forests of Alabama or East Texas and then had trudged across 250 miles of featureless Texas plains— walking for hours alongside their wagons across the flat land toward a low rise, and then, when they reached the top of the rise, seeing before them just more flatness, until at the top of one rise they saw, in the distance, something different: a low line that, as they toiled toward it, gradually became hills, hills stretching across the entire horizon—to these men the hills were beautiful. From the crest of the first ones they climbed, they could see that this wasn't an isolated line of higher ground, but the beginning of a different kind of country—from that crest, range after range of hills rolled away into the distance. And from every new hill they climbed, the hills stretched away farther; according to these early settlers, every time they thought they were seeing the last range of hills, there would be another crest, and when they climbed it, they would see more ranges ahead, until the hills seemed endless—the Hill Country, they said, was a land of "false horizons." They were, in fact, at the eastern edge of a highland that covered 24,000 square miles.

The air of the highland was drier and clearer than the air on the plains below; it felt clean and cool on the skin. The sky, in that clear air, was a blue so brilliant that one of the early settlers called it a "sapphire sky." Beneath that sky the leaves of Spanish oaks, ancient and huge, and of elms and cedars sparkled in the sun; the leaves of the trees in the hills looked different from the leaves of the scattered trees on the plains below, where the settlers' wagons still stood—a darker, lush green, a green with depths and cool shadows.

Beneath the trees, the Hill Country was carpeted with wildflowers, in the Spring, bluebonnets, buttercups, the gold-and-burgundy Indian paintbrush and the white-flowered wild plum, in Fall, the goldeneye and the goldenmane and the golden evening primrose. And in the Fall, the sugar maples and sumac blazed red in the valleys.

Springs gushed out of the hillsides, and streams ran through the hills— springs that formed deep, cold holes, streams that raced cool and clear over gravel and sand and white rock, streams lined so thickly with willows and sycamores and tall cypresses that they seemed to be running through a shadowy tunnel of dark leaves. The streams had cut the hills into a thousand shapes: after crossing 250 miles of flat sameness, these men had suddenly found a landscape that was new at every turn.

And the streams, these men discovered, were full of fish. The hills were full of game. There were, to their experienced eyes, all the sign of bear, and you didn't need sign to know about the deer—they were so numerous that when riders crested a hill, a whole herd might leap away in the valley below, white tails flashing. There were other white tails, too: rabbits in abundance. And as the men sat their horses, staring, flocks of wild turkeys strutted in silhouette along the ridges. Honeybees buzzed in the glades, and honey hung in the trees for the taking. Wild mustang grapes, plump and purple, hung down for making wine. Wrote one of the first men to come to the Hill Country: "It is a Paradise."

But most of all, to the men who moved into it first, the Hill Country was beautiful because of its grass.

These first settlers were not Southern aristocrats or "substantial planters"—substantial planters had money to buy good, easily accessible land, and slaves to work it; when they came to Texas, they settled on the rich river bottoms of the coastal plains; by 1850 they had re-created a Southern Plantation economy, complete with mansions, near the Gulf. The men who came to the Hill Country were not from the Plantation South but from the hill and forest sections of the South; they were small farmers, and they were poor. These were the men who had fled the furnishing merchant, who furnished the farmer with supplies and clothing for the year on credit, and the crop lien, which the merchant took on the farmer's cotton to make sure he "paid out" the debt. And they had fled the eroded, gullied, worn-out, used-up land of the Old South that would not let them grow enough cotton or graze enough livestock ever to pay it out. Land was something these men and their families had to live off—and that was why the grass of the Hill Country was what filled their eye. These were the men who had come farther even than the Buntons. Their numbers were small. Thousands of rural Southern families heard the news of San Jacinto in 1836, took one last look at their eroded, exhausted soil, chalked GTT on their gates and headed for a new land and a new start. In 1846, statehood, which had been pushed by the new President, increased the flood of migration; tens of thousands of Southern families painted POLK AND TEXAS on their wagon canvas and headed down the plank roads of the South, through its weary towns—as bystanders cheered—and westward across the Mississippi and the Sabine into Texas. In 1837, the population of Texas was 40,000. In 1847, it was 140,000. By 1860, it would be 600,000. But the flood crested near the Sabine, and flowed south toward the Gulf; most of the newcomers settled in the "piney woods" of East Texas and the coastal plains. Only a shallow stream flowed west across the 250 miles of prairie blacklands. And by the time the stream reached the Edwards Plateau in the center of Texas, at whose edge the Buntons stopped, it was no more than a trickle—and only a very thin trickle indeed climbed up into the hills. Although Austin, almost on the plateau's edge, was the state capital, it was still a frontier town; in 1850, people were still being killed on its outskirts and its population was only 600. Beyond, in the Hill Country, the dreaded Comanches ruled—and during this era the population of the typical Hill Country county is counted not in thousands or in hundreds but in scores. "The cabins became more distant, separated by miles and miles," Fehrenbach has written, "and the settlements significantly were no longer called towns, but forts. If the lights in the [eastern] Texas forest by the middle of the 19th century were still few, in the middle of the state, . . . the lights . . . were swallowed in vastness." Trying to explain why men, often with their families, would trade civilization for terror, Fehrenbach notes that this was the part of Texas in which dreams seemed nearest to realization. "A man could see far and smell winds that coursed down from Canada across a thousand miles of plains. There was an apparently endless, rolling vista north and west and south. The small woodchopper, with an axe and a couple of brawny sons, could catch a scent of landed empire and dream of possibilities to come." There were many reasons bound up with these— but whatever the reasons, whatever the dreams or fears that pulled or drove hundreds of thousands of men into Texas, few had made a journey as long or as hard as these men. But when they saw the grass, they felt the journey had been worth it. "Grass knee high!" one wrote home. "Grass as high as my stirrups!" wrote another.

The tall grass of the Hill Country stretched as far as the eye could see, covering valleys and hillsides alike. It was so high that a man couldn't see the roots or the bottoms of the big oaks; their dark trunks seemed to be rising out of a rippling, pale green sea. There was almost no brush, and few small trees—only the big oaks and the grass, as if the Hill Country were a landscaped park. But a park wasn't what these men thought of when they saw the grass of the Hill Country. To these men the grass was proof that their dreams would come true. In country where grass grew like that, cotton would surely grow tall, and cattle fat—and men rich. In country where grass grew like that, they thought, *anything* would grow.

How could they know about the grass?

THE GRASS HAD GROWN not over a season but over centuries. It wouldn't have grown at all had it not been for fire—prairie fires set by lightning and driven by wind across tens of thousands of acres, and fires set by Indians to stampede game into their ambushes or over cliffs—for fire clears the land of underbrush, relentless enemy of grass. The roots of brush are merciless, spreading and seeking out all available moisture, and so are the leaves of brush, which cast on grass the shade that kills it, so if brush and grass are left alone in a field, the grass will be destroyed by the brush. But grass grows much faster than brush, so fire gives grass the head start it needs to survive; after a fire, grass would re-enter the burned-over land first—one good rain and among the ashes would be new green shoots—and by the time the brush arrived, the grass would be thick and strong enough to stand it off.

Even with the aid of fire, the grass had grown slowly—agonizingly slowly. Some years most of it died, some years all. But in other years, it grew, and after a while it had a base to grow in, for even in the years when most of it died, some residue remained. This base built up gradually until there was, at last, atop the soil a padding to protect the soil from rain and add to the fertility with which it fed the next growth of grass—at first a thin pad and then a thicker one, and finally a lush, diverse carpet in which could grow the big grass, the stirrup-high grass, that dominated the beautiful Hill Country meadows that the first settlers saw. The big grass had big roots; every time fire came to help it—natural fire or Indian-set—it grew back faster. As it got taller, it grew faster still, for it held more and more moisture and thus could survive dry spells better. But even so, it had taken a very long time to grow.

It had grown so slowly because the soil beneath it was so thin. The Hill Country was limestone country, and while the mineral richness of limestone makes the soil produced by its crumbling very fertile, the hardness of limestone makes it produce that soil slowly. There was only a narrow, thin, layer of soil atop the Hill Country limestone, a layer as fragile as it was fertile, vulnerable to wind and rain—and especially vulnerable because it lay not on level ground but on hillsides: rain running down hillsides washes the soil on those slopes away. The very hills that made the Hill Country so picturesque also made it a country in which it was difficult for soil to hold. The grass of the Hill Country, then, was rich only because it had had centuries in which to build up, centuries in which nothing had disturbed it. It was rich only because it was virgin. And it could be virgin only once.

.   .   .

THE HILL COUNTRY was a trap baited with water.

The men toiling toward that country saw the hills as a low line on the horizon. There was another line in the same place, right along those first ridges, in fact, but the men couldn't see that line. It was invisible. It was a line that would be drawn only on maps, and it wasn't drawn on any map then, and wouldn't be for another fifty years. But the line was there—and it would determine their fate.

There were clues to tell them it was there. Some of the first men to enter the Hill Country noted the remarkable resemblance of a small shrub they found there to the tall walnut trees of the Atlantic coast they had left behind them; even its nuts were similar, except, of course, they were so much smaller—no larger, one early observer wrote, than a musket ball. There was a reason the little shrub resembled the big walnut tree—it *was* the tree, the tall tree shrunken into a small bush. Some of the settlers commented on bushes they found along the streams of the Hill Country, bushes which looked exactly like the mulberry bushes along the streams and rivers in the Old South—except that they were a quarter the size. There were many other trees and shrubs that resembled, in miniature, trees and shrubs in the states from which the settlers had come.

There were other clues: the way the settlers' campfires burned so brightly in the Hill Country—because the wood in this new country was so dense and hard; the way the branches of even living trees were so rigid that they snapped at a touch; the stiffness and smallness of the leaves—even the somber darkness of their green, the darkness that added so much to the beauty of the Hill Country. And in the fields of the Hill Country there was, all but hidden in the tall grass, a rather large amount of a plant whose presence was surprising in such a lush, rich land: cactus. There were plenty of clues—plenty of warnings—to tell the settlers the line was there, but none of the settlers understood them.

The line was an "isohyet" (from the Greek: *isos*, equal; *hyetos*, rain) —a line drawn on a map so that all points along it have equal rainfall. This particular isohyet showed the westernmost limits in the United States along which the annual rainfall averages thirty inches; and a rainfall of thirty inches, when combined with two other factors—rate of evaporation (very high in the Hill Country), and seasonal distribution of rainfall (very uneven in the Hill Country, since most of it comes in spring or autumn thundershowers)—is the bare minimum needed to grow crops successfully. Even this amount of rainfall, "especially with its irregular seasonal distribution," is, the United States Department of Agriculture would later state, "too low" for that purpose. East of that line, in other words, farmers could prosper; west of it, they couldn't. And when, in the twentieth century, meteorologists began charting isohyets, they would draw the crucial thirty-inch isohyet along the 98th meridian—almost exactly the border of the Hill Country. At the very moment in which settlers entered that country in pursuit of their dream, they unknowingly crossed a line which made the realization of that dream impossible. And since rainfall diminishes quite rapidly westward, with every step they took into the Hill Country, the dream became more impossible still.

Agricultural experts would later understand the line's significance. There is a "well-defined division" between the fertile east and the arid western regions of Texas, one expert would write in 1905: "An average line of change can be traced across the state . . . approximately where the annual rainfall diminishes to below 30 inches, or near the 98th meridian." That line, another expert could say in 1921, runs down the entire United States: "the United States may be divided into an eastern half and a western half, characterized, broadly speaking, one by a sufficient and the other by an insufficient amount of rainfall for the successful production of crops by ordinary farming methods." Historians, too, would come to understand it. One would sum up the Hill Country simply as "west of 98, west of thirty inches of rain." The Western historian Walter Prescott Webb says that the line amounts to "an institutional fault" (comparable to a geological fault) at which "the ways of life and living changed." But this understanding would come later—much later. At the time the Hill Country was being settled, there was no understanding at all—not of the climatic conditions and certainly not of their consequences. "When people first crossed this line," as Webb states, "they did not immediately realize the imperceptible change that had taken place in their environment, nor, more is the tragedy, did they foresee the full consequences which that change was to bring in their own characters and in their modes of life." This lack of understanding was demonstrated during the years leading up to the Civil War, when North and South argued over whether or not to prohibit slavery in areas that included western Texas and New Mexico. "In all this sound and fury," as Fehrenbach points out, "there was no real understanding that slavery, based on cotton agriculture, had reached its natural limits. It had no future west of the 98th meridian; where the [Edwards Plateau] began in Texas, the rainfall, and the plantation system of the 19th-century South, abruptly ended. From the middle of the state, on a line almost even with Austin, the rainfall dribbled away from 30 inches annually to 15 or less across the vast plateaus. The farm line halted in crippled agony."

The trap was baited by man as well as by nature. The government of Texas, eager to encourage immigration to strengthen the Indian-riddled frontier, plastered the South with billboards proclaiming Texas advantages, and was joined in boosterism by the state's press. In an overstatement that nonetheless has some truth in it, Fehrenbach writes that "There was almost a conspiracy to conceal the fact that in the West there was little water and rain. . . . Official pressure even caused regions where rainfall was fifteen inches annually to be described as 'less humid' in reports and geography

books. The term 'arid' was angrily avoided." Boosterism was just as strong
in the Hill Country: George Wilkins Kendall, who began sheep-ranching
there in 1857, was soon trying to sell off land in Blanco County by firing off
enthusiastic letters to the *New Orleans Picayune* exhorting others to follow
his example. "Those who failed in the venture," notes a Hill Country resident, "were called 'Kendall's victims.' "

But when the first settlers came to the Hill Country, no one was calling
them "victims," least of all themselves. If someone had told them the truth,
in fact, they might not have listened. For the trap was baited well. Who,
entering this land after a rainy April, when "the springs are flowing, the
streams are rushing, the live oaks spread green canopies, and the field flowers wave in widespread beauty," would believe it was not in a "less humid"
but an "arid" zone? Moreover, as to the adequacy of rainfall, the evidence
of the settlers' own eyes was often misleading, for one aspect of the trap was
especially convincing—and especially cruel. Meteorologists would later conclude that rainfall over the entire Edwards Plateau is characterized by the
most irregular and dramatic cycles. Even modern meteorology cannot fathom
their mysteries; in the 1950's, during a searing, parching dry spell that lasted
for seven consecutive years, the United States Weather Bureau would confess
that it had been unable to find any logical rhythm in Hill Country weather;
"just when the cycle seems sure enough for planning, nature makes one of
her erratic moves in the other direction." Rain can be plentiful in the Hill
Country not just for one year, but for two or three—or more—in a row.
Men, even cautious men, therefore could arrive during a wet cycle and conclude—and write home confidently—that rainfall was adequate, even abun-
dant. And when, suddenly, the cycle shifted—and the shift could be very
sudden; during the 1950's, it rained forty-one inches one year, eleven the
next—who could blame these men for being sure that the dry spell was an
aberration; that it would surely rain the next year—or the next? It had to,
they felt; there was plenty of rain in the Hill Country—hadn't they seen it
with their own eyes?

The first settlers did not realize they were crossing a significant line.
They came into the new land blithely. After all those years in which they had
feared their fate was poverty, they saw at last the glimmerings of a new hope.
But in reality, from the moment they first decided to settle in this new land,
their fate was sealed. Dreaming of cotton and cattle kingdoms, or merely of
lush fields of corn and wheat, they went back for their families and brought
them in, not knowing that they were bringing them into a land which would
adequately support neither cattle nor cotton—nor even corn or wheat. Fleeing the crop lien and the furnishing merchant, hundreds of thousands of
Southerners came to Texas. Of all those hundreds of thousands, few had
come as far as these men who came to the Hill Country. And they had come
too far.

. . .

THE BUNTONS HAD STOPPED just before the Hill Country. The Johnsons had headed into it, to become, they boasted, "the richest men in Texas."

They were descended from a John Johnson. Some family historians say he was "of English descent," but they don't know this for certain. The few known facts of his life, and of the life of his son, Jesse, fit the pattern—of migration into newly opened, fertile land, the using up of the land and the move west again—that underlay so much of the westward movement in America; and the Johnsons' route was the route many followed. Georgia, the most sparsely populated of the original thirteen colonies, wanted settlers, particularly settlers who could shoot, and it was the most generous of the colonies in offering land to Revolutionary War veterans. The first time the name of Lyndon Johnson's great-great-grandfather, John Johnson, who was a veteran, appears in an official record is in 1795, when he was paying taxes on land in Georgia's Oglethorpe County; by his death in 1827, he owned land in three other counties as well—but little else.

As Georgia's land wore out under repeated cotton crops, men searched for new land on which to plant it, and when, after the War of 1812, Georgia's western territories were cleared of Indians, settlers poured into them in a "Great Migration." John's son, Jesse, who was Lyndon Johnson's great-grandfather, was part of that migration. He was a "first settler" of Henry County. Few facts are known about Jesse's life, but from those few it is possible to theorize about big dreams—which, unlike the dreams of the Buntons, ended in failure. For a time, for example, Jesse Johnson appears to have been a respected and prosperous farmer in Henry County. He served as its sheriff from 1822 to 1835, and also as a judge. But by 1838, he was no longer living in Henry County; he and his wife, Lucy, and their ten children, had moved west again—into Alabama. There, in the records of Randolph County, appear again hints of transient success. The 1840 census lists only two persons in the entire county engaged in "commerce": Jesse and one of his sons. A local historian "guesses" that "they operated a stagecoach line or were in the banking business. They were prosperous." Jesse owned seventeen slaves. But by 1846, Jesse was GTT—to Lockhart, on the plains near the Hill Country. In the Lockhart courthouse are records showing that in 1850 Jesse Johnson owned 332 acres, 250 head of cattle and 21 horses, and there exists also a will drawn up, in 1854, as if Jesse believed he was leaving a substantial estate to his family. One of its clauses, for example, provides that at his wife's death, the estate is to be equally divided among his children, excepting the heirs of one who had died, "who I will to have one thousand dollars more than my other heirs." But the reality was that there was no thousand dollars "more"—or at all. When, after his death in 1856, his sons sold their father's assets, they didn't realize enough even to pay their father's debts. In 1858, two of them—Tom, then twenty-two years old, and Samuel Ealy Johnson, Lyndon Johnson's grandfather, then twenty—headed west into the hills, making their boast.

To GO INTO THAT LAND took courage.

The Spanish and Mexicans had not dared to go. As early as 1730, they had built three presidios, or forts, in the Hill Country. But down from the Great Plains to the north swept the Lipan Apaches—"the terror," in the words of one early commentator, "of all whites and most Indians." The presidios lasted one year, then the Spanish pulled out their garrisons and retreated to San Antonio, the city below the Edwards Plateau. In 1757, lured by the Apaches' protestations that they were now ready to be converted to Christianity—and by Apache hints of fabulously rich silver mines—the Spaniards built a fort and a mission deep within the Hill Country, at San Sabá. But the Apaches had only lured the Spaniards north—because pressing down into their territory were the Comanches, who rode to war with their faces painted black and whom even the Apaches feared; they had decided to let their two foes fight each other. The Spaniards believed that Comanche territory was far to the north; not knowing the Comanches, they didn't know that the only limit to the range of a Comanche war party was light for it to ride by or grass for its horses to feed on—and that when the grass was tall and the moon was full, Comanche warriors could range a thousand miles. On the morning of March 16, 1758, there was a shout outside the San Sabá mission walls; priests and soldiers looked out—and there, in barbaric splendor, wearing buffalo horns and eagle plumes, stood 2,000 Comanche braves.

When word of the San Sabá massacre reached San Antonio, the Spaniards sent out a punitive expedition—600 men armed with two field guns and a long supply train, the greatest Spanish expedition ever mounted in Texas. Its commander chased the Comanches all the way to the Red River—and then he caught them. He lost his cannon, all his supplies, and was lucky to get back to San Antonio with the remnants of his force—and thereafter the Hill Country, and all central Texas, was Comanchería, a fastness into which Spanish soldiers would not venture even in company strength. It wasn't until half a century later—in 1807—that the next attempt would be made to penetrate the Hill Country: a walled Spanish town, complete with houses and cattle, was built on a bluff near the present site of San Marcos. That lasted four years; when, during the 1820's, settlers from young Stephen Austin's colony in South Texas began to push up the Lower Colorado River, the only traces of the town were some remnants of cattle running with the buffalo. In 1839, the dashing President-elect of the three-year-old Republic of Texas, Mirabeau Buonaparte Lamar, hunting buffalo on the edge of the Hill Country, looked out to the beautiful hills and exclaimed: "This should be the seat of future empire!" The capital of the new Republic, Austin, was founded the next year on the spot where Lamar had stood. But Austin was still in Comanche country; from the surrounding hills, parties of mounted Penetaka Comanches watched the settlement being built; it wasn't until the 1850's that the town's slow, steady growth, combined with the success of the Republic's "ranging forces," forced the Indians to retreat.

Where they retreated to was the Hill Country. This was their stronghold. Writes a Texas historian: "They lived along the clear streams in the wooded valleys, venturing out to raid the white settlements, and ambushing any who were hardy enough to follow them into the hills."

But men followed them. Even as Austin was being built, pushing beyond it—into this country which Spanish soldiers wouldn't enter even in force—were men who entered it alone, or with their wives and children. As early as the 1840's, there were cabins in the Hill Country.

After Texas became one of the united states—in 1846—border defense became a federal responsibility, and the United States Army established a north-south line of forts in Texas about seventy-five miles deep in the Hill Country. But these forts were scattered, and their garrisons were tiny. They were ill-equipped with horses—at the time the forts were built, the Army did not even have a formal cavalry branch, and some of the first troops sent out to fight the fleet Comanches were infantry mounted on mules. For some years, moreover, they were not permitted to pursue Indians; they could fight only if attacked—which made them all but useless against the hit-and-run Indian raiders. But they did provide a little encouragement for settlement, and a little encouragement was all these men needed. Behind the fort line, Americans crept slowly up the valleys of the Hill Country. By 1853, there were thirty-six families along the Blanco River, and thirty-four along the Pedernales.

This was the very edge of the frontier. These families had left civilization as far behind as safety. Their homes were log cabins—generally small and shabby cabins, too. Shocked travelers found conditions in Texas rougher and more primitive than in other states. One traveler "just from the 'States,' " directed to a certain home in the Blanco Valley, thought as he neared it that it "must be one of the outhouses." Inside, however, he found eight people living—in a single room fourteen by sixteen feet. (Outhouses were, as a matter of fact, not common in the Hill Country; said Frederick Law Olmsted, who traveled through it in 1857: "It would appear that water-closets are of recent introduction in Texas"; he told of staying at one house where "there was no other water-closet than the back of a bush or the broad prairie.") The home of the ordinary Hill Country family, often set in a fire-blackened clearing still dotted with tree stumps, was a "dog-run"—two separate rooms or cabins connected under a continuous roof, with an open corridor left between for ventilation; the dog-run acquired its name, Fehrenbach notes, "from its most popular use, and the corridor was hardly the most sanitary of spots." The walls of these cabins, visitors complained, were so full of holes that they did little to keep the wind out; Rutherford Hayes wrote that he slept in one through whose walls a cat could be hurled "at random." The cabins were surrounded with tools, plows, pigs and hungry hounds. There were few amenities: "This life," Fehrenbach says, "was hardy, dirty, terribly monotonous, lonely, and damagingly narrow. . . . Few of the Americans who later eulogized it would care to relive it." The only thing plentiful was terror. This frontier was, for forty years, "a frontier of continual war." Indian wars raged for decades in many states, Fehrenbach notes, "but there was a difference to the Anglo frontier in Texas that colored the whole struggle, that embued it with virulent bitterness rare in any time or place. The Anglo frontier in Texas was not a frontier of traders, trappers and soldiers, as in most other states. It was a frontier of farming families, with women and small children, encroaching and colliding with a long-ranging, barbaric, war-making race."

Remington paintings—lines of mounted men charging on horseback—came to life on that frontier. The first battle in which Texas Rangers were armed with the new Colt revolver which was to equalize warfare with the Comanches—previously, one of these savage Cossacks of the Plains could charge 300 yards and shoot twenty arrows in the time it took a frontiersman to reload his single-shot rifle—took place, in 1842, on the Pedernales; Captain Jack Hays' Rangers routed the Comanches, whose war chief said: "I will never again fight Jack Hays, who has a shot for every finger on his hand." As late as 1849, at least 149 white men, women and children—the figures are incomplete—were killed on the Texas frontier. During a two-year period a decade later, hundreds died.

And those who died were luckier than those who were captured. The Comanches were masters of human torture for its own sake; many Hill Country families saw with their own eyes—and the rest heard about—the results of Comanche raids: women impaled on fenceposts and burned; men staked out to die under the blazing sun with eyelids removed, or with burning coals heaped on their genitals. Many women captured by the Comanches were raped,* and afterward they might be scalped but left alive—so the Comanches could hold red-hot tomahawks against their naked skulls. For the Hill Country, the full moon—"the Comanche moon"—meant terror. Recalling her girlhood, one pioneer woman remembered how "people were always on the alert and watching for the red men. If we children went to the spring to get a bucket of water, we watched all the time to see if an Indian came out of the brush or from behind a tree. We lived in constant dread and fear. . . . If the dogs barked we thought of Indians at once. . . . My mother said she had suffered a thousand deaths at that place." One night, she recalled, her

---

* Fehrenbach says that "There was never to be a single case of a white woman being taken by Southern Plains Indians without rape."

father saw a light in a nearby valley and, leaving her mother, her brother and her alone, went to investigate. He didn't come back for a long time, and then the three of them heard the footsteps of several men approaching—and sixty years later, she still remembered how they waited to see who would open the door, and what their fate would be. Fortunately, it was her father with some white men who had been camped in the valley, but sixty years later she could still remember "the agonizing fear we had." And she adds a poignant note: "Why men would take their families out in such danger, I can't understand."

Nonetheless, whatever the terrors of the land, white men, believing in its promise of wealth, came to claim it. In 1858, there were enough—perhaps a thousand—people along the Blanco and Pedernales rivers and their tributary streams to form a county (Blanco County, after the white Hill Country limestone), and to build a church and a school (in which, along a wall, lay long logs the length of the building, to hold the shutters in place in case of Indian attack). And for two men who came to Blanco County in 1858, young Tom and Sam Johnson, it appeared for a while as if the promise would be fulfilled.

When, after the Civil War, in which both brothers fought (Private Sam Johnson had a horse shot from under him at the Battle of Pleasant Hill; under fire, he carried a wounded companion from the battlefield), they returned to the Hill Country, they found that their small herd of cattle had multiplied—as had the cattle left to run wild by other men; before the war, with prices low and markets and transportation uncertain, cattle had not been valuable. The hills were swarming with steers—longhorns unbranded and free for the taking; Texas law made unbranded stock public property.

And now, suddenly, cattle were very valuable. Giant cities were rising in the North, cities hungry for meat. And there was, all at once, a means of getting the meat to the cities—the railroads pushing west.

In 1867, the rails reached Abilene, Kansas, and about that same year, lured by rumors of high prices—the price of a cow in Texas was still only three or four dollars—the first drives began to head out of the Hill Country: east to Austin to get out of the hills and then north up the Chisholm Trail, across the Red River and up to the boomtown railhead on the Kansas plains. The men who drove those first herds must have wondered—as on their journey of over a thousand miles they battled stampedes, outlaws, Indians and hysterical Kansas mobs afraid the cattle were carrying "Texas fever"—if the trip would be worth it. But when they reached Abilene they stopped wondering. The price of a longhorn there in 1867 was between forty and fifty dollars. Men who had left penniless returned to the Hill Country carrying pouches of gold. Forty dollars for four-dollar steers! Forty dollars for steers you could get for *nothing!* All you needed was land rich in grass and water to graze your herds on, and the Hill Country had all the grass and water a man could want. They rounded up the cows in the hills, and brought more in from the southern plains—huge herds of them—to graze on that rich Hill Country grass.

The Johnson brothers were among those first trail drivers. In 1867, they bought a ranch on the Pedernales; by 1869, their corrals stretched along the river for miles; by 1870, they were, one of their riders said, the "largest individual trail drivers operating in Blanco, Gillespie, Llano, Hays, Comal and Kendall Counties"; during that year, they drove 7,000 longhorns north on the Chisholm Trail to Abilene. Tom led the last drive; "on his return from Kansas," one of his cowboys recalled, "his saddlebags were full of gold coins." Sitting at a table in the brothers' ramshackle ranchhouse, he "placed the saddlebags and a Colt's revolver on the table, and counted out the money—$100,000."

Riding beside Sam on those drives was his wife. She was Eliza Bunton, the daughter of Robert Holmes Bunton, the successful Lockhart rancher, and she had the Bunton looks (a relative described her as "tall, with patrician bearing, high-bred features, raven hair, piercing black eyes, and magnolia-white skin") and the Bunton pride ("She loved to talk of her" hero uncle, John Wheeler Bunton, and of other ancestors, a cousin who had been Governor of Kentucky, for example, and a brother who was fighting with the Texas Rangers; "she admonished her children to be worthy of their glorious heritage"). Sam, a dashing, gallant, handsome young man with black hair and the soft blue-gray eyes, shaded by long eyelashes, that were characteristic of the Johnsons, married her following the successful drive in 1867 and brought her to the ranchhouse on the Pedernales—but she refused to stay there.

Describing those early cattle drives, one historian writes of "the months of grinding, 18-hour days in the saddle, the misery of rainstorms and endless dust clouds, the fright of Indian or cattle rustler attack, the sheer terror of a night stampede when lightning sparked across the plains." Few women rode on those early drives. But Eliza rode (one historian says she was the only Hill Country wife who did)—not only rode but, astride a fleet Kentucky-bred mare that her father had given her, rode out ahead of the herd to scout.* "Gently reared," wrote an historian of Eliza Bunton Johnson, "she took to the frontier life like the heroine she was."

It was still the era when the full moon brought terror to the Hill Country—it was the worst of the era, in fact, for just the year before, while the families in the lonely cabins in the hills raged helplessly at the government in faraway Washington that didn't understand (or understood all too well, some said: however unfounded, suspicion existed in the Hill Country that

---

* "I am the hero of our camp," wrote one of the Johnsons' cowboys, Horace M. Hall, in 1871. "Riding out with Mrs. Johnson some 8 miles in advance of the train, . . . I shot a deer."

Washington was deliberately trying to punish the ex-Rebs), the government had withdrawn the troops from its forts. In July, 1869, it brought terror to Eliza. A young couple who lived not far from the Johnsons was caught and killed by Comanches; the man who found them could tell that the woman had been scalped while still alive. Sam was one of the men who rode out on the Indians' trail—and while he was gone, and Eliza, alone except for her baby daughter, Mary, was drawing water from a spring near her cabin, she saw Comanches riding toward her through the woods. The Indians hadn't noticed her yet; running to her cabin, she snatched up the baby, and crawled down into the root cellar. She closed the trapdoor, and then stuck a stick through a crack in it, and inched a braided rug over the trapdoor so that it couldn't be seen. As she heard the Indians approaching, she tied a diaper over Mary's mouth—published accounts say it was an "extra diaper," but that is a cleaned-up story: it was the dirty diaper the baby had been wearing—to keep her from making a sound. The Indians burst into the cabin, and as she crouched in the dark, Eliza heard them smashing the wedding gifts she and Sam had brought from Lockhart. Then they went outside and she heard them stealing horses from the corral and riding away. She didn't come out of the cellar until, after dark, Sam came home.

But 1869 was the last year of heavy Comanche raids. Far north of the Hill Country, in the Comanche homeland, white men were decimating the buffalo, which was food, clothing and shelter to the Indians, and thus were forcing them to move onto reservations or starve. Not for some years would the Hill Country be finally freed from the fear of the Comanche moon—the last Indian raid in Blanco County took place in 1875—but beginning in 1870, the raids became noticeably fewer, and finally faded away. The Johnson brothers—and the other men, and women, who had settled the land—had won it.

AND THEN THEY BEGAN to find out about the land.

All the time they had been winning the fight with the Comanches, they had, without knowing it, been engaged in another fight—a fight in which courage didn't count, a fight which they couldn't win. From the first day on which huge herds of cattle had been brought in to graze on that lush Hill Country grass, the trap had been closing around them. And now, with the Indians gone, and settlement increasing—and the size of the herds increasing, too, year by year—it began to close faster.

The grass the cattle were eating was the grass that had been holding that thin Hill Country soil in place and shielding it from the beating rain. The cattle ate the grass—and then there was no longer anything holding or shielding the soil.

In that arid climate, grass grew slowly, and as fast as it grew, new herds of cattle ate it. They ate it closer and closer to the ground, ate it right down into the matted turf—the soil's last protection. Then rain came—the heavy, pounding Hill Country thunderstorms. The soil lay naked beneath the pounding of the rain—this soil which lay so precariously on steep hillsides.

The soil began to wash away.

It washed faster and faster; the Hill Country storms had always been fierce, but the grass had not only shielded the soil from the rain but had caught the rain and fed it out slowly, gently, down the hillsides into the streams. Now, with less grass to hold it, the rain ran off faster and faster, eating into the soil, cutting gullies into it.

And there was so little soil. From one Spring to the next, landscape changed. One year, a rancher would be looking contentedly at hills covered with grass—green, lush. The next Spring, he would keep waiting for those hills to turn green, but they stayed brown—little grass, and that parched, and bare soil showing through. And the next, he would suddenly realize that there was white on them, white visible through the brown—chalky white, limestone white: the bare rock was showing through. Not only was the grass gone, in many places so was the soil in which new grass could grow. Flash floods roared down the gullies now (men called them "gully-washers" or "stump-jumpers"); they raced down the sheer, slippery limestone hard enough to rip away even tree stumps and carried the soil away faster and faster. Sometimes it happened almost before a man's eyes; one afternoon, there would be soil on a hill, soil in which he hoped that next year at least grass would grow and he could graze stock there; then a thunderstorm, and the next morning when he looked at the hill he would see a hill of bare white rock. The steep hills went first, of course, but even shallower slopes washed fairly soon—it all happened so fast. That rock was the reality of the Hill Country. It had taken centuries to disguise it with grass, but it took only a very few years for that disguise to be ripped away. Even on the shallowest slopes, on which grass remained, in a very short time the richness of the land was gone.

Then the brush came.

Fire had held it back—fires set by lightning and Indians—fire and grass. But now the Indians were gone, and when lightning started a prairie fire, men hurried to put it out, not understanding that it was a friend and not a foe. And what was left of the grass wasn't the tall, strong bluestem and Indian grass but shorter, delicate strains.

So the brush began to move up out of the ravines and off the rocky cliff-faces to which it had been confined. It began to creep into the meadows: small, low, dense shrubs and bushes and stunted trees, catclaw and prickly pear and Spanish dagger, shrub oak and juniper—and mesquite, mesquite with its lacy leaves so delicate in the sun, and, hidden in the earth, its monstrous, voracious taproot that reached and reached through thin soil, searching for more and more water and nourishment. Finally, even cedar came, cedar that can grow in the driest, thinnest soil, cedar whose fierce, aggressive roots are strong enough to rip through rock to find moisture, and which therefore can grow where there is *no* soil—cedar that grows so fast that it seems to gobble up the ground. The brush came first in long tentacles pushing hesitantly forward into a grassy meadow, and then in a thin line, and then the line becoming thicker, solid, so that sometimes a rancher could see a mass of rough, ragged, thorny brush moving implacably toward the delicate green of a grassy meadow and then, in huge bites, devouring it. Or there would be a meadow that a rancher was sure was safe—no brush anywhere near it, a perfect place for his cattle if only the grass would come back—and one morning he would suddenly notice one shrub pushing up in it, and even if he pulled it up, its seeds would already be thrown, and the next year there would be a dozen bushes in its place.

The early settlers in the Hill Country couldn't believe how fast the brush spread. In the early days, it seemed to cowboys that, from one year to the next, whole sections of land changed; one year, they would be riding untrammeled across open meadows; the next year, in the same meadows, their horses had to step cautiously through scrub a foot or two high; the next year, the scrub was up to a rider's shins as he sat his horse—they called these scrub jungles "shinnery"—and horses couldn't get through it any more. When white men first came into the Hill Country, there was little cedar there. Twenty years later, cedar covered whole areas of the country as far as the eye could see; by 1904, a single cedar brake reaching northwest from Austin covered 500 square miles—and was growing, faster and faster, every year. And every acre of brush meant an acre less of grass.

AT FIRST, it didn't seem to matter so much, because in about 1870 cotton began to be raised in the Hill Country and for a few years it prospered, the Hill Country earth producing a bale or more per acre. A Hill Country historian writes, "That king cash crop was . . . being sowed wherever there was enough dirt to sprout a seed, . . . wherever their mules could tug a plow, whether in the valleys, in the slopes, or atop the hills."

But cotton was worse for this country than cattle, which, through their manure, put back into the soil between thirty and forty percent of the nutrients their grazing removed from it. Cotton put back nothing, and as each crop fed upon the soil, the soil grew poorer, thinner, more powdery. Cattle ate the grass down, but at least left the roots underneath. The steel blades of the plows used in cotton-planting ripped through the roots and killed them. Moreover, cotton was a seasonal crop, and, not knowing the science of crop rotation and continuous cover—no one knew it, of course, until the 1880's—the Hill Country farmers didn't plant anything in their cotton fields after harvest, which meant that for months of each year, including the entire winter, the land lay naked and defenseless, no roots within it to strengthen it, no grass atop it to shield it.

Inevitably, drought came. The land burned beneath the blazing Hill Country sun, what was left of its nutrients scorching away, what was left of the roots within it starving and shriveling. Winds—those continual Hill Country breezes that help make the climate so delightful, and the winter northers that come sweeping down off the Great Plains—blew the soil away in swirls of dust, blew it, as one bitter Hill Country farmer put it, into "the next county, the next region, the next state." And when the heavy, hammering rains came, they washed the soil away, down the steep hillsides and along the furrows of the cotton fields (which the farmers all too often cut up and down the slope instead of across it) into the creeks and rivers, cutting gullies in the ground that the next rain would make even deeper, so that the rain would run down that land even faster. Water poured down the hillsides and into the creeks in a torrent, and flash floods roared down the creeks' slick limestone beds, sweeping away the fertile land on their banks that was the only truly fertile land in the Hill Country. The rivers rose, and, when they receded, sucked more of the fertile soil back down with them, to run down the Pedernales to the Colorado, down the Colorado to the Gulf. And all the time, in the places too steep for mules to pull a plow, men, remembering the trail drives and the pouches of gold, persisted in grazing cattle, who kept "eating down the grass as fast as it could grow and faster, leaving nude soil in those places, too, to blow and wash away."

It had taken centuries to create the richness of the Hill Country. In two decades or three after man came into it, the richness was gone. In the early 1870's, the first few years of cotton-planting there, an acre produced a bale or more of cotton; by 1890, it took more than three acres to produce that bale; by 1900, it took eleven acres.

The Hill Country had been a beautiful trap. It was still beautiful—even more beautiful, perhaps, because woods covered so much more of it now, and there were still the river-carved landscapes, the dry climate, the clear blue sky—but it was possible now to see the jaws of the trap. No longer, in fact, was it even necessary to look beneath the surface of the country to see the jaws. On tens of thousands of acres the reality was visible right on the surface. These acres—hundreds of square miles of the Hill Country—had once been thickly covered with grass. Now they were covered with what from a distance appeared to be debris. Up close, it became apparent that the debris was actually rocks—from small, whitish pebbles to stones the size of fists—that littered entire meadows. A farmer might think when he first saw them that these rocks were lying on top of the soil, but if he tried to clear away a portion of the field and dig down, he found that there was no soil—none at all, or at most an inch or two—beneath those rocks. Those rocks *were* the soil—they were the topmost layer of the limestone of which the Hill Country was formed. The Hill Country was down to reality now—and the reality was rock. It was a land of stone, that fact was plain now, and the implications of that fact had become clear. The men who had come into the Hill Country had hoped to grow rich from the land, or at least to make a living from it. But there were only two ways farmers or ranchers can make a living from land: plow it or graze cattle on it. And if either of those things was done to this land, the land would blow or wash away.

THE JOHNSON BROTHERS appear not to have recognized the trap—not to have recognized the reality of the Hill Country. Their grandiose dreams were nourished and protected by the nature of their occupation. "The terms used to describe the cattle explosion were always kingdom or empire, never the cattle business or the cattle industry," Fehrenbach points out. Its grandeur—the herds that stretched as far as the eye could see; the endless drives across the immense, empty land; the shower of golden eagles—fed big dreams, and in Abilene the brothers had met, or at least heard about, men who had proved that such dreams could come true, men who had started out as cattle-drivers but had become much more—John Chisum, Charles Goodnight, Richard King, the Rio Grande steamboat captain who had gone into cattle-driving not so long before they did and was now becoming a king indeed, with a ranch that, men whispered, covered more than a million acres ("The sun's done riz, and the sun's done set, And I ain't off'n the King Ranch yet"). The Johnson brothers weren't content to be merely cattle-drivers. Land in the Hill Country, which for so long had been free, was beginning to be bought up now, and the Johnson boys, while continuing to graze most of their cattle on land still vacant, bought a lot of it: 640 acres in Blanco County to add to the 320 they had started with, and then 1,280 acres more; 170 acres in Hays County and then 533 more—they bought both these tracts in 1870, plunking down in payment $10,925 in gold coins; and then far bigger ranches, unsurveyed and still measured in leagues, in Gillespie County. The most valuable real estate in the Hill Country was in its leading "city," Fredericksburg—the Johnsons bought real estate in Fredericksburg. They even bought a large, valuable tract in south Austin. They "made a market for almost everything: corn, bacon, labor, and cow ponies," John Speer writes—labor because the Johnsons needed all the men the Hill Country could supply for their drives north. By 1871, the Johnson brothers weren't merely the largest trail-drivers in the Hill Country; they were probably the largest landowners, too. To help them run things, they brought in three nephews—Jesse, John and James Johnson—and a cousin, Richard; soon Sam and Tom bought a busy mill, the Action Mill in Fredericksburg, and started making plans to open a store.

The Johnsons were building an empire up in the hills.

. . .

BUT THE LAND WAS DOMINANT, and while the Hill Country may have seemed
a place of free range and free grass, in the Hill Country nothing was free.
Success—or even survival—in so hard a land demanded a price that was
hard to pay. It required an end to everything not germane to the task at hand.
It required an end to illusions, to dreams, to flights into the imagination—to
all the escapes from reality that comfort men—for in a land so merciless,
the faintest romantic tinge to a view of life might result not just in hardship
but in doom. Principles, noble purposes, high aims—these were luxuries that
would not be tolerated in a land of rock. Only material considerations
counted; the spiritual and intellectual did not; the only art that mattered in
the Hill Country was the art of the possible. Success in such a land required
not a partial but a total sacrifice of idealism; it required not merely pragmatism but a pragmatism almost terrifying in its absolutely uncompromising
starkness. It required a willingness to face the hills head-on in all their grimness, to come to terms with their unyielding reality with a realism just as
unyielding—a willingness, in other words, not only to accept sacrifices but
to be as cruel and hard and ruthless as this cruel and hard and ruthless land.
Fehrenbach, writing about Texas as a whole but in words that apply with
particular force to the Hill Country, says that because of the "harshness" of
the "pressing realities" of the land,

> Inner convictions, developed in more rarified civilizations, could
> not stand unless they were practical. . . . The man who held to a
> preconceived attitude toward Indians, and could not learn the
> Comanche reality, often saw his family killed; or he himself died
> in his own homestead's ashes. A little-noted but obvious fact of
> the Texas frontier was that some men lived and some families
> prospered on the edge of Comanchería, while many others failed.
> And chance was not the major determining factor. *Eternal vig-
> ilance, eternal hardness, was the price of success.* . . . A Charles
> Goodnight could move early onto the far edge of nowhere, and
> hold his new range against all comers. Some men could not.

The Johnsons could not. They were, in fact, particularly unsuited to
such a land, and not just because they were, in the sense that mattered in
the Hill Country, unrealistic—as, in failing to understand the reality of the
land, they grazed their herds on the same meadows every year. Noting that
"the best-adapted Westerner was keenly intelligent and observant but at the
same time highly unintellectual," Fehrenbach points out that "Table talk, as
writer after American writer has recorded, was of crops and cattle, markets
and weather, never some remote realm of ideas." Table talk at the Johnsons'

was quite often of ideas. Sam Johnson, who had nine children, encouraged them to discuss "serious issues" at the table for the same reason he encouraged them to play whist, a relative recalls: "He encouraged his children to engage in games that required them to think." After dinner, he would often have them engage in impromptu debates. Two of his three sons became teachers: one attended the University of Michigan—possibly the first Hill Country boy to travel out of Texas for an education. Sam was interested not just in politics but in government; at a time when few people in the Hill Country got newspapers—and when those who did, got them, by freight wagon, a week or two late—he subscribed to an Austin daily and arranged to have it delivered every other day to Weinheimer's General Store in the nearby town of Stonewall—even though he had to ford the Pedernales to pick it up. His politics, moreover, were less practical than idealistic. One of his key beliefs was in a "tenant purchase program" that would enable tenant farmers to buy their farms: men, he said, should not have to work land they did not own; when asked for details of the program, he was a little vague. Every available description of Samuel Ealy Johnson emphasizes his interest in philosophy and theology, not just in the Fundamentalist religion of the Hill Country but in deeper religious questions. He was a Baptist, but once a minister of a sect called the Christadelphians stopped at the Johnson house, and Sam welcomed the opportunity to debate with him. All through dinner and into the evening, they discussed the Bible. Because the minister raised questions he couldn't answer, Sam arranged for him to debate the local Baptist preacher. And because Sam felt that the Christadelphian had won the debate, he changed his membership to that church.

The Johnsons were dreamers. There was a streak of romanticism in them—of extravagance, a gift for the grandiose gesture. When Sam married Eliza, Tom gave his brother's bride a carriage with trappings of silver and, to pull it, a matched span of magnificent Kentucky-born thoroughbreds, named Sam Bass and Coreen—a gift not only unheard of in the Hill Country but, in that country, incredibly expensive.

The Johnsons were impractical. Eliza, a Bunton, was not; she was known for the shrewd bargaining with which she sold her eggs, and for repeating the family saying: "Charity begins at home." But her husband and his brother, lulled, no doubt, by the sweep and grandeur of the cattle business, and by the ease with which money was made in it, acted as if they couldn't be bothered with mundane details—as if, for example, haggling and bargaining were beneath them. When Tom returned from Abilene in 1870 with the $100,000 in twenty-dollar gold double eagles, the men—many of them German businessmen from Fredericksburg, businessmen whose penuriousness is legendary in Texas—who had given the Johnsons their cattle on credit came in to be paid. The Johnsons took receipts for the money they paid out, but not in a very orderly way. Relates Speer:

They took receipts and soon had a large carpetbag full, and in
such a shape that there is no doubt in my mind that a good many
beeves were paid for twice, and some of them several times. . . .

As Fehrenbach points out, for all the romance of the Cattle Kingdom, the
men who became its barons—the Goodnights and Chisums and Kings—
were, above all else, businessmen. The Johnson brothers were not. When
they had finished paying for the beeves, they had made many people in the
Hill Country happy, Speer notes; "$20 gold pieces were about as plentiful
as 50-cent pieces are now." But while the Johnsons still had a lot of money
left—it was the following month that they paid the $10,000 in gold for the
Hays County land—they had less than they had expected to—and not enough
when measured against their dreams.

They were guilty of wishful thinking. "Cowmen in whom wishful thinking was . . . dominant," Fehrenbach says, could not survive. Sam Johnson
was, a relative says, "a man of great optimism," and his brother apparently
shared the trait. Every trail drive was in a way a gamble, a gamble that
while you were on the trail, you wouldn't lose your herd to floods or
Indians or disease; a gamble that when you reached trail's end, prices would
still be high. Eventually, a gambler will lose at least some rolls of the dice—
in terms of poker, for the Johnson boys loved to play poker, at least some
hands. A prudent, practical gambler keeps a reserve to tide him over the
inevitable runs of bad luck. The Johnsons were not prudent and practical.
They had gambled in 1867 and 1868 and 1869 and 1870, and had won
each time, and they seemed to think they could not lose, for they kept
nothing back as a hedge against disaster. No matter how successful they
were, they bet everything they had made on the next year's drive. Each
year, the poker-playing Johnsons shoved into the pot their whole pile.

After they had finished paying out the gold pieces in 1870, they spent
those remaining on land. They owned that land free and clear—but only
for a few months, for they wanted more land, much more, and to get it,
they mortgaged to the hilt what they already owned. To get cattle for the
1871 drives, they bought as many head on credit as they could, promising
as usual to pay for them on their return, and then borrowed $10,000 from
eight Fredericksburg Germans, giving the Action Mill as collateral, to buy
more. The brothers had taken 7,000 head north to Abilene in 1870, their
biggest year up to that time; in 1871, they assembled in the milling corrals
along the Pedernales several times 7,000—one of their drivers, Horace Hall,
was to say that "The Johnson boys have brought up 25 herds this season,
the smallest of which was 1500." They had assembled a fortune on the hoof.
They had bet everything they owned and everything they could borrow on
another successful year.

And in the Hill Country, that was a bad bet to make.

. . .

"THE YEAR 1871 set in cold, sleety and disagreeable," Speer recounts. There had been only mild winters in the Hill Country since the Civil War, but now howling northers swept down from the Great Plains one after another. Solid ice three inches thick covered the hills. Cattle died.

The richness of the land had been going. There had been a warning on July 7, 1869: a flood that, Speer said, "did great damage to farms along the creeks and branches." A stagecoach was swept away in the Blanco River; several passengers were drowned. A mill was washed off the banks and found two miles downstream, hanging in a tree. Speer had lived in the Hill Country for ten years; this was "the first overflow," he said. "The Blanco was higher than it had ever been before." He displays a light-hearted attitude: "It was really grand to stand off at a safe distance and see the Blanco on a grand tear." But the second overflow came the very next year. Speer didn't laugh this time; he called it "terrible." People began to wonder; "all the old inhabitants were hunted up and interviewed, but not one of them had ever seen anything like it," Speer wrote. And no one understood its significance. Nonetheless, in 1871, the meadows along the Pedernales were no longer so thick with grass to make cattle fat. Spring came, but rain didn't —the Hill Country had had half a dozen wet years; now it had drought. The Johnsons' cattle were thin when they set out on the long trail.

When the first of the Johnson herds reached the Red River ford that they always used, they found other herds lined up before them for miles. And when they finally got to Abilene, they saw, "for miles around the chief shipping points, the stock herded awaiting a chance to sell or ship. From any knoll could be seen thousands of sleek beeves, their branching horns glistening in the sunlight." Over twice as many cattle as in any previous year —a million longhorns—were driven north from Texas in 1871, and they glutted the market. There was, moreover, a recession in the Northeast, and an end to a railroad rate war which had previously benefited the cattlemen. Prices plummeted. In hopes that prices would rise, and that their thin beeves would fatten, the Johnsons bought Northern corn and kept their herds off the market, but prices only fell further. "Half the cattle brought from Texas [in 1871] remained unsold and had to be wintered . . . on the plains of Kansas," Webb states. The Johnsons might have wanted to winter their stock in Kansas, but they couldn't; their $10,000 note fell due on December 15. About November 15, selling at the very bottom of the market, they headed home.

The trip home was bleak. Winter had come early that year; "the winds cut a fellow through and through," Horace Hall wrote his mother. Arriving at the Arkansas River, they had a long delay because there were so many other wagons ahead of them waiting for the ferry. Their reception at home was even bleaker, for they were returning to a country that had been depending on them, a country whose prosperity was tied up with theirs. Moreover, in order to make even a token payment on the $10,000 note and keep the mill, they had to default on many of their smaller debts, "which," Speer says, "was a great loss to the people and destroyed confidence. Some were disposed to say, and no doubt believe, hard things about [Tom] Johnson, but in justice . . . I will say that while he prospered no one condemned him." The Johnsons' arrogance—their inability to excuse and explain, to plead for time —made the situation worse. Mortgages were foreclosed, lawsuits begun—the brothers lost the land in Austin, the land in Fredericksburg, the land in Gillespie County measured in leagues, most of the land in Blanco County. And then, after struggling to make a few more token payments on the $10,000 debt, they could make no more—and they lost the mill anyway. They had been building an empire; a single disastrous year, and it was gone.

THEY WERE REDUCED to frantic maneuverings. To avoid a court-ordered sale of a tract of land to satisfy a debt, they hurriedly sold it to one of their nephews, James Polk Johnson. On another occasion, a creditor secured a court order to have another tract auctioned by the Blanco County sheriff on the steps of the county courthouse; however, there were only two bidders and the land was sold for a fraction of its value—to a man who promptly sold it right back to the Johnsons.

Trying to recoup, the brothers put together another—much smaller— herd in 1872. (Some indication of the distrust in which they were now held is a condition of the credit extended: a lawyer, one "Mr. Louis of Fredericksburg," had to be taken along on the drive.) But the drought in 1872 was terrible. The blazing Hill Country sun seared the grass brown and then burned the soil beneath—it was so thin now—all the way through. Creeks dried up; the Pedernales ran sluggish and low. So intense was the heat that branding and other round-up activities had to be halted; on July 22, Horace Hall wrote his mother that "It has been so hot that we can do nothing working with the stock for the flies blow wherever blood is drawn." That Summer the Comanches raided, killing or kidnapping several persons, and running off between 250 and 300 horses which the Johnsons had been preparing to drive north and sell, a considerable loss since a good cow pony was then worth eighty dollars. The precise results of the 1872 drive are not known, but late in that year another lawsuit was filed against the Johnsons, and in 1873 the last of their land in Blanco County was sold by the sheriff on the courthouse steps—this time without any maneuvering. In 1871, Tom Johnson had paid taxes in Blanco County on property worth $16,000; in 1872, on property worth $6,000; in 1873, on property worth $180. He is not listed on any tax roll in 1874 or 1875 or 1876; no detail of his life is available. In 1877, he drowned in the Brazos River in Bosque County; no detail of his death exists, either. In the meantime, Sam, whose property in Blanco had been assessed at $15,000 in 1871, had moved out of Blanco, away from the Pedernales, down to Lockhart on the plains near his father-in-law, Robert Holmes Bunton, and then, after a short stay there, to a small farm near Buda, on a low ridge just on the edge of the Hill Country. This farm appears—the records are unclear—to have been purchased by his wife, with money given her by her father.

Sam and Eliza Johnson lived on this farm for fourteen years, raising nine children, trying to live on a reduced scale, running a few score cattle, planting about a hundred acres of the farm in cotton, corn and wheat. But the trap had closed. "About this time," Speer writes, "it began to be said, 'the range is broken, played out,' and we must now depend on farming." But the land was no longer so good for farming, either; there were good years mixed with the bad, but the trend was inexorable. The Buda farm had once yielded a bale of cotton per acre; by 1879, four acres were needed to produce that bale. And by 1879, a bale of cotton wasn't worth nearly as much money as it had been when Sam and Eliza first moved to the farm: 18 cents per pound in 1871, cotton was selling for 10 cents in 1879. In 1879, Sam Johnson sold his crops for $560—five hundred dollars for a year's work, for a man who had ridden the trail with pouches of gold! (Of the $560, he had to pay a hired hand $200 for help in harvesting.)

The Hill Country, meanwhile, was up to its old tricks. 1881 was a good year, and as for 1882, well, that was a year, Speer writes, that reminded him that "some years Texas floats in grease"—"this was emphatically a greasy year. Grass was fine, fruit and most kinds of grain good, and cotton —well, cotton just outdid itself." 1883 was a good year, too—and three good years in a row made men hope. In 1884, Sam and Eliza began selling off parts of their Buda farm to get money to move back to their beloved "mountains." They couldn't raise enough; there was only one thing left to sell—and they sold it, or rather Sam's wife did. Eliza Bunton Johnson, who had kept for twenty years the silver-mounted carriage that had been her wedding present, sold it, and the matched team of Sam Bass and Coreen that she loved, and with the money made a down payment on a 433-acre farm on the Pedernales, near the ranch she and her husband had owned when they were young. They moved there in 1887—just in time for the terrible drought of 1888, the worst drought that anyone in the Hill Country could remember.

NOT ONLY THE JOHNSONS had been young when they moved away from the Pedernales. So had the land. When they moved back, it was still fairly good for farming, by Hill Country standards, but its primal richness was gone.

As for grazing, it now took several acres to support a single cow. The Johnsons arrived back on the Pedernales poor, and lived there almost thirty years—during which they grew poorer.

There are glimpses of their life—photographs of a home that was little more than a shanty, or, rather, two shanties connected: a "dog-run" with a sagging roof and a sagging porch surrounded by a yard, fenced with barbed wire, that was only dirt spotted with tufts of grass and weeds; a daughter's recollection of a long sideboard with a marble top, a Bunton heirloom, stored in the smokehouse because there was no room in the home. Eliza, it is said, kept her egg-and-butter money in an old purse in "the depths of the big zinc trunk, which held her treasures and her meeting clothes." When one of her children needed money,

> she would bring out [the purse], holding the egg-and-butter money carefully saved for the purchase of a new black silk dress, and count out the exact amount needed by the child temporarily financially embarrassed. Sometimes the purse was left empty, but she eagerly assured the recipient of . . . her own lack of present need. . . . All references to the handsome clothes and the elegant furniture of more prosperous days were casual, never complaining nor regretful.

Sam had lost none of the Johnson temper. Once, when his son George "belittled the scriptures, his father . . . knocked him across the room." And he had lost none of the Johnson interest in topics beyond the state of the weather. The Austin paper was still delivered every other day; every other day he would spur his horse, Old Reb, into the Pedernales to ford it to the mailbox on the far side; he would sit in Weinheimer's Store in Stonewall all evening discussing politics and government. In later years, it is recalled, he would often sit on his front porch, reading his Bible or his newspaper, chatting with passersby—or just sitting, an aging man with a snowy beard and a thick mane of white hair, gazing in the evening out over the Pedernales landscape that was dotted here and there with a few lonely cows wandering through hills that had once been covered with great herds.

2

The People's Party

DURING SAM JOHNSON's thirty years back on the Pedernales, there was one brief interruption in this round of life. During a two- or three-week campaign in 1892, he talked about his theories of government not just at Weinheimer's Store but at barbecues and public "speakings"—as the Populist Party candidate for the State Legislature. Although he lost, by almost a two-to-one margin, Populist candidates for statewide office carried the district, and the Hill Country as a whole.

This was fitting. All through the South and West, a belief had been rising among men who felt themselves trapped by forces beyond their control, a belief that, faced by forces too big for them to fight, they needed help in fighting them. This feeling had been rising—slowly but steadily—since the Civil War. Farmers would sweat and slave over their land, and sow and plow and pick a crop, and then, when they brought the crop to market, they would find that because of prices in the East, or prices in Europe, or railroad freighting charges, or grain-elevator storage charges, their crop wasn't worth what they had thought it was worth—they would find, often, that what they might receive for the old crop wasn't enough even to buy seed for a new one, and that, when they tried to borrow money to buy the seed, interest rates were so high that they knew even before they began to plant the new crop that it couldn't possibly pay out. If the 1870's and '80's and '90's were a desperate time for farmers, nowhere were times more desperate than in the Hill Country. In other areas, farmers might believe that railroads were fleecing them; the Hill Country didn't have railroads—because laying tracks through hills was too expensive in a sparsely populated district—and the cost of getting crops to market by wagon (crops that often spoiled because of the length of the trip) ate up farmers' profits. In other areas, farmers might groan under interest rates; in the Hill Country, rates were a moot point; its banks, as poor as their depositors (cash on hand in the Johnson City Bank in 1890: $1,945), had little money to lend at *any* rate. In other areas, farmers felt the price for their crops was too low; in the Hill

Country, the problem was trying to get crops to grow at all. And it was in the Hill Country that America's great agrarian revolt began. In 1877, a handful of impoverished farmers gathered at a tiny cabin in Lampasas County, Texas, about fifty miles north of Johnson City, and founded the Farmers Alliance, which became the National Farmers Alliance and Industrial Union, and then the People's Party (the "Populists")—the party which was the greatest mass popular movement in America's history.

Out of the letters mailed to the Alliance journal, the *Southern Mercury*, from those scattered farmhouses along the Pedernales River glares bitterness and resentment.

"Our lot is cast here in a rough portion of the land where but a small per cent of the land is tillable, hence farmers are thinly settled," wrote J. D. Cady of Blanco County's New Chapel Alliance. "We number only about eight male members in good standing. But if we do live away up here on the Pedernales River, amid rocks, cliffs and waterfalls, cedars and wild oaks, we are not varments, but have hearts just like men."

The letters were written by men and women who seldom wrote letters. "I will try to scratch a few lines to the brethern," said sixty-year-old Larkin Landrum of Blanco. "If I could spell good enough so I could interest them I would like to write, but I never got to go to school in my life, nor learned my letters till I was 35 years old. If I knew that I could do the Alliance cause any good I would like to try. . . . If this is printed and I can read it, I will write once more; for if I can read it I know other people can, who have been to school and worn shoes." They wrote out of a sense of injustice at the way farmers were fleeced by merchants ("Now, Mister Laboring Man, don't buy anything you can do without till you get out of debt, and then not buy till you have the money to pay for it, for when you buy on time you pay from forty to 100% more than you should")—by, it sometimes seemed, everyone who wasn't a farmer: "I see someone put in a piece about professional men. Let me have a say about him. . . . The lawyer, for instance, will pay you $1 for a load of wood and charge you from $5 to $20 for a little writing. Study about this and see if there is any justice in it. I don't speak of the lawyer alone, but all who do not work. I am an Alliance man. Yes, and I am not ashamed to own it." They wrote out of desperation. "I see so many letters from the brotherhood in different parts of the state all aglow with the good news of prosperous condition of the Alliance that it grieves me to chronicle the sad condition of this section," said James Blevin of Dripping Springs. "We are worse than lukewarm, we are cold, almost to heart, and unless we can get a remedy soon, we are gone. . . . Without a remedy, all is lost that we hoped for." And they wrote because the Alliance gave them hope, because it was a hand—the only hand—held out to help the people of the Hill Country. In their isolation, its newspaper gave them a sense of brotherhood. "I consider myself related to all who correspond to the generous old *Mercury*. . . . Remember the *Mercury*," wrote Minnie M. Crider. "If we help the *Mercury,* it will help us to throw off this yoke of bondage and be free people," wrote Minnie's sister Sarah. The famed Alliance lecturers, who criss-crossed the South and West, spreading the word, brought them hope. The farmers pleaded with the Alliance to send more of them to the Hill Country: "Brethern, in sending out lecturers, please remember our isolated corner, and send us in time of need." When none arrived, they were all too ready to feel the slight. "As we live way down here, we are in the dark a good deal in regard to the business of our noble order. . . . We are afraid you have never learned that we have a real cute alliance here. . . . We had an 'encampment' and honestly expected the presence of a 'Big Gun' with it, but, no we were sadly left, as usual. . . ." But when a lecturer did make the journey, hope was rekindled and these poorest of farmers scraped together their dues, or as much of them as they could. "We are in a drouth-stricken district and find it hard work to keep the wolf from our doors," wrote Mrs. Emma Eppes of Blanco County. "But we have a prospect for good crops this season. . . . some have paid up while others have been found wanting the means, but all will pay just as soon as possible."

At first, the hope was embodied in cooperatives: Alliance warehouses to which all the farmers of a district would bring their bales and pool them in a single lot on which bids would be taken not only from the local buyers who previously had been able to bid without competition but from cotton buyers all over the South; Alliance purchasing agents who could deal directly with manufacturers of plows and other farm implements and sell them directly to individual farmers, thereby eliminating not only the middleman's profits but also the enormously high interest the manufacturers charged for selling on credit. Although it proved impossible, even after warehouses and purchasing centers had been established throughout the rest of Texas, to establish them in the Hill Country—one mass sale that was held at Fredericksburg proved a disaster; without a railroad, the buyers said, the cotton could be shipped out only at prohibitive cost—the Hill Country farmers brought their cotton in long caravans of wagons sixty, seventy, a hundred, miles to Austin, and when their bales brought at the Alliance warehouse there prices a dollar or two above what they had expected, they rode home with their empty wagons flying the blue flags that had became the symbol of victory in the Texas Alliance. (In Fort Worth and Dallas, too, the blue flags were flying. By 1885, the Texas Alliance had 50,000 members; by 1886, 100,000; by 1890, 200,000. A spokesman exulted that the Alliance had become "a power in the land." Alliance lecturers began to fan out from Texas to farm counties in other states with a simple message: Join the Alliance, build a county cooperative, a county general store if need be, and get free of the credit merchant. Observers in a dozen farm states echoed the words of one in Mississippi, who said the Alliance has "swept across" that state "like a cyclone.")

Outside forces broke the cooperatives. The big Eastern manufacturing houses refused to sell to them, insisting on retaining their middlemen. Not only Eastern manufacturers and banks but local merchants and banks refused credit to members of cooperatives. Railroads and grain-elevator companies used all their power against the farmers—and won, because farmers could not escape the simple fact that they could not sell their crop if they did not own it; and it was the furnishing merchant who owned it. The Alliance then attempted to free the farmer from the merchant by establishing a central state exchange in Texas to market the state's entire cotton crop from one central point while giving the farmers the money they needed for the next year at bearable rates. (The Southern Exchange planned to get the money from banks, using notes given by the farmers as collateral.) The Exchange opened in Dallas in September, 1887, and the bankers tried to break it by refusing to accept the notes as collateral—by refusing, in fact, to give the Exchange money "upon any terms or any security." And when the Alliance, in desperation, was forced to turn to its own members for money, the Hill Country gave all it could—the thirty-four members of the New Chapel Alliance of Blanco County assessed each of its members a dollar; the assessment would be paid, the secretary wrote Alliance headquarters, "as soon as the cotton comes in." The Hill Country Alliance men stood firm behind their leaders. The banks, and the press they dominated in Texas, tried to smear the head of the Exchange, Charles W. Macune, by blaming its financial crisis on him; the farmers of Hays County in the Hill Country chipped in their pennies for a telegram which said their Alliance "loves Dr. Macune for the enemies he has made." Bankers in other states, determined to break the Exchange, joined the Texas bankers in cutting off credit. Alliance leaders proclaimed June 9, 1888, as "the day to save the Exchange," and asked the farmers to demonstrate their solidarity. Early on that Saturday morning, long caravans of farm wagons—including some from the Hill Country—began to clatter into almost two hundred county seats throughout Texas. The farmers stood for hours in the blazing summer heat. They stood silently. They held banners—lettered by their wives—which said: THE SOUTHERN EXCHANGE SHALL STAND.

The Southern Exchange fell; its members pledged enough for it to survive, but couldn't pay their pledges. The Alliancemen had tried—through cooperatives and boycotts, and endless wagon treks to distant markets, and contributions that came out of their wives' butter-and-egg pennies—to help themselves, and had failed, and the lesson they had learned was that they *couldn't* help themselves. The forces they were fighting were too big for them to fight. They turned to a force that was big enough to fight—and win—on their behalf, if only it could be motivated to do so: their government.

It was only right, the farmers believed, that their government do so. Government was a basic cause of their troubles, they felt, and government must be the means to redress those troubles. Government, through its vast subsidies of land and money and its biased laws, had made it possible for railroads to become powerful, and now railroads were strangling the farmers; should not government, on their behalf, now regulate railroads? Government had protected manufacturers at their expense by high tariffs; should not government now lower tariffs? Government had, by abrogating much of its effective control over the currency, allowed bankers to regulate it, forcing farmers to pay off their liens and mortgages in dollars worth more than the dollars they had borrowed; should not government now take back control of currency and make repayment easier, not harder, for debtors? Government had, by forcing the country onto the gold standard, caused the constant, unending fall in the price of cotton and all the farmers' other crops; should not the gold standard be ended in favor of silver? Government had acted against their interests in so many ways (the first platform of the Populist Party seemingly laid *all* wrong to government: "Corruption dominates the ballot-box, the legislatures, the Congress. . . . From the same prolific womb of governmental injustice, we breed two great classes—tramps and millionaires."). Should not there be now a broad-scale enactment of laws redressing this imbalance? Government had acted to oppress the farmers in a thousand ways; shouldn't it now stretch forth its hand to help them—in a thousand ways? (Some of the ways being suggested were new to America: the march of Jacob S. Coxey's pitiful little "army" of unemployed on Washington in 1894 was an attempt to dramatize his theory that the government should help the unemployed with a system of federal public-works relief.) "The powers of government—in other words, of the people—should be expanded," said the 1892 platform of the People's Party, ". . . to the end that oppression, unjustice and poverty shall eventually cease in the land."

For a while, their hopes were very high. The Alliance lecturers who had brought the word out of Texas had fanned agrarian revolt into flames. In 1890, taking command of the Democratic Party in a dozen states, the Alliancemen won control of their legislatures, elected six Governors and sent to Washington four Senators and more than fifty Congressmen (including Davis H. Waite of Colorado, known as "Bloody Bridles" Waite because he had declared that it was better "that blood flow to the horses' bridles rather than our national liberties should be destroyed"). In Kansas, the third party was known as the People's Party, and in 1892 that name was adopted by the new national party—and its candidate polled more than a million votes, and twenty-two electoral votes (because in the South the Populists, as they were becoming known, refused in general to play white-supremacist politics, all twenty-two were in the mountain states, where they not only elected two Governors but captured twice as many counties as both major parties combined and in a single election established themselves as the majority party). Except for the Republicans, no new party had ever done so well in its first bid for national power. In the Congressional elections of 1894, the Populists rolled up more than a million and a half votes, making heavy inroads into the Democratic vote in the South and West, and it appeared likely that the increasing number of Democrats who saw silver as the crucial issue would desert the Democratic Party in 1896 and make the Populists a major party in America—after all, an analogous situation in the 1850's had resulted in the demise of the Whigs and the creation of the Republican Party.

Instead, there was Bryan. As trainload after trainload of cheering delegates arrived at the Democratic convention in Chicago, silver badges gleaming from their lapels, silver banners fluttering in the breeze, the *New York World* said, "They have the principle, they have the grit, they have the brass bands and the buttons, they have the votes. But they are wandering in the wilderness like a lot of lost sheep, because no . . . real leader has yet appeared among them." Then, when one after another of the silver movement's would-be leaders had proved, during the debate on the party platform, that the *World* was right, young Democrat William Jennings Bryan nervously made his way up the aisle and, speaking on behalf of farmers against Eastern interests, said, "We have petitioned, and our petitions have been scorned; we have entreated and our entreaties have been disregarded; we have begged, and they have mocked when our calamity came. We beg no longer; we entreat no more; we petition no more. *We defy them!*" Suddenly the mighty throng of 20,000 sweltering men and women were on their feet, cheering each sentence with a roar—even before the last sentences:

> Burn down your cities and leave our farms, and your cities will spring up again as if by magic; but destroy our farms and the grass will grow in the streets of every city in the country. . . . Having behind us the producing masses of the nation and the world, supported by the commercial interests, and the toilers everywhere, we will answer their demand for a gold standard by saying to them: You shall not press down upon the brow of labor this crown of thorns, you shall not crucify mankind upon a cross of gold!

The silver Democrats did not leave the Democratic Party but took it over instead; "the Boy Orator of the Platte" became the party's Presidential nominee.

Ironically, however, this development was to mark the doom of the People's Party: the Democrats had stolen the Populists' thunder; at their own convention three weeks later, the Populists had little choice but to nominate Bryan, too, and thus lose their identity as a separate party. And the party with which they had allied themselves lost the election. The Bryan race for President was more a cause than a campaign. "A religious frenzy" was what William Allen White of Kansas called it. "Sacred hymns were torn from their pious tunes to give place to words which deified the cause and made gold—and all its symbols, capital, wealth, plutocracy—diabolical. At night, from ten thousand little white schoolhouse windows, lights twinkled back vain hope to the stars." But the hope *was* vain; the cause was as lost as the one for which many of the Populists had fought thirty years before—Bryan's campaign was gallant but underfinanced, and the Republican Party, run by Mark Hanna, who shook down railroad corporations, insurance companies and big-city banks for campaign contributions on a scale never before seen, won what one historian calls "a triumph for big business, for a manufacturing and industrial rather than an agrarian order, for the Hamiltonian rather than the Jeffersonian state." In the 1898 elections, the disorganized Populists were all but wiped out. In 1900 Hanna's President, McKinley, was able to push through the Gold Standard Act. The Populists ran a candidate for President as late as 1908, but by then there were few surviving Populist officeholders. Some were in Texas, one of the last states where Populism remained strong, but even in Texas, after the debacle of 1896, the spirit was out of it.

Perceptive historians find great significance in the campaign of 1896—"the last protest of the old agrarian order against industrialism"—but in the Hill Country, life remained as mean and meager as before. It was worse, in fact. For a while after 1900, conditions improved for farmers throughout most of the rest of America, but that prosperity didn't penetrate into the Hill Country; the land was too far gone and the weather too dry for any lasting improvement. More and more Hill Country farmers lost their land; each census—1900, 1910, 1920—showed an increase in the number of farms being operated by tenant farmers. The People's Party was all but dead in the Hill Country—by 1904, there would be only twenty-three voters registered in the party in Blanco County—and the things the party had asked for seemed, if mentioned at all, only unrealizable dreams. The People's Party seemed, in the hills, just another legend that old men talked about as they talked about the cattle drives.

BUT WHAT, really, had the People's Party—the farmers who called themselves "Alliancemen"—asked for? Only that when men found themselves at the mercy of forces too big for them to fight alone, government—their government—help them fight. What were the demands for railroad and bank regulation, for government loans, for public-works projects, but an expression of a belief that after men have banded together and formed a government, they have a right, when they are being crushed by conditions over which they have no control, to ask that government to extend a helping hand to them—if necessary, to fight for them, to be their champion?

They had asked too early, that was all.

Franklin Roosevelt wasn't their President yet.

Lyndon Johnson wasn't their Congressman.

3

The Johnson Strut

AMONG THE NINE CHILDREN of Sam Ealy Johnson and Eliza Bunton Johnson were three sons. In the opinion of Hill Country ranchers—convinced, as ranchers, of the importance of breeding—all three were basically Buntons, not only in their height and other striking physical characteristics but in the fierceness of their passions, in their soaring ambition and in the capacity for leadership that was described in the hero John Wheeler Bunton as "commanding presence." In the ranchers' opinion, however, all three sons possessed also a fatal taint of the Johnson blood line: Johnsons, they said, had all the Buntons' temper, pride, arrogance and idealism, together with dreams even more ambitious, but they had none of the Bunton hardness, the canniness and pragmatism, that alone could keep idealism and ambition from bringing ruin in a country as hard as the Hill Country. All three sons, it was noted, were idealists, romantics, dreamers—and unfortunately, in the adjective the ranchers applied to them, "soft" inside. One son fled the Hill Country: if his life was not particularly successful, it was at least not tragic. The other two—one of whom was Lyndon Johnson's father, Sam Ealy Johnson, Jr.—stayed.

Sam Ealy Johnson, Jr., was born in 1877 (his father was relieved to see he was a boy; because his first four children had all been girls, his friends had begun calling him "Gal" Johnson) and was ten years old when his family moved from Buda back up to the Pedernales.

Already the family could tell he had the "Bunton strain." His mother, a family memoir relates, "looked with great tenderness on this child whose dark eyes, black curls and white skin were a Bunton inheritance. . . ." As a boy, he was always tall for his age—he would eventually be an inch over six feet—and he had the Buntons' large nose, huge ears, thick, bushy, black eyebrows and piercing eyes.

When he was a little boy in Buda, it was already apparent that he was very intelligent. "He had a quick mind, keen perception and an amazing memory," the memoir says. "An elder sister memorizing a poem of thirty-two verses for recital the last day of school was astounded to hear the child, Sam, far below school age recite it in its entirety." He was conspicuously mature: "at an early age [he] acquired an unusual poise and assurance." When the family moved to the Pedernales farm, another quality—burning ambition—became noticeable in the eleven-year-old boy. "The tasks and delights of farm life presented a challenge to Sam; he must ride faster; plow longer, straighter rows; pick more cotton than his companions." ("This sense of competition," his wife was to write, "was a strong urge throughout his life.")

As he grew into his teens, Lyndon Johnson's father became ambitious to become something more than a farmer. It was hard for Hill Country families to send their children to school, because they were needed to help work the farms and because even public schools charged tuition, and low though it was—only a few dollars—most Hill Country families couldn't afford to pay it. But Sam was grimly determined to go to school. "Once," the family chronicler relates,

> his father gave him some cattle saying, "This is all I can do on your schooling this year." Each weekend the young high school student turned butcher, slaughtered and cut up a steer and sold steaks and soupbones to tide him over until next "butchering day."

Then the barber in Johnson City, a small town fourteen miles down the Pedernales that had been named for its founder, Sam's cousin James Polk Johnson, became ill and retired. Buying the barber's chair and tools on credit, Sam taught himself to cut hair, practicing on friends, and thereafter went to school during the day while earning his tuition by giving haircuts in the evening.

There are hints that the strain was too much for his health. What his wife later described as "indigestion" forced him to quit high school. His parents sent him to West Texas, where his uncle, Lucius Bunton, had moved —being a Bunton, he had already built up the largest ranch in Presidio County—"hoping that on the ranch . . . he might regain his health."

"After a few months," the memoir relates, the teen-ager came home, "determined to teach school." Realizing this ambition was difficult in the Hill Country—in its 24,000 square miles, there was not a single college and not a single state-accredited high school whose graduates would be admitted by a college. But it was possible to obtain a state-issued teacher's certificate without graduating from high school—by passing a special state examination. "With thirteen books, the required subjects for examination for a teacher's certificate, a bottle of pepsin tablets and a sack of dried fruit (doctor's recommendation)," Sam moved in 1896 to the nearby home of his Grandfather and Grandmother Bunton—having accumulated enough money to retire, Robert Holmes Bunton had moved to the Hill Country; he could therefore enjoy it without having to make his living from it—so that he could have a quiet place to study. Passing the examination ("In later years he often recalled with pleasure that he made 100% in both Texas and United States history; he always loved history and government"), he taught for the next three years in one-room Hill Country schoolhouses. During the year in which he taught in a community named Rocky, he boarded with a family which had as a frequent visitor Captain Rufus Perry, the legendary Indian-fighter and Texas Ranger; years later, the family remembered how intently the young teacher sat listening, his dark eyes gleaming in the firelight, as the old man told stories of great adventures.

Teaching did not satisfy Sam Johnson's ambitions. He wanted to be a lawyer; "he had the type of mind for it and he loved law," his wife was to write. "But," she wrote, "he found it necessary to make a living immediately"; he returned to his father's farm on the Pedernales, working it together with Sam Ealy, Sr., for a year or two, and thereafter, when his father grew too old to work, renting it from him and working it himself. He may not have wanted to be a farmer, but a farmer was what he was.

For a few years, he was successful. Rain was plentiful and winters mild; "Little Sam," as he was called to differentiate him from his father, earned enough to hire several hands and even to start trading in cotton futures in Fredericksburg.

He cut quite a figure in that beaten-down country. Tall, skinny, gangly, considered handsome despite those huge ears because of his pale skin and dark hair and eyes, he had the Bunton arrogance and air of command; a Johnson City resident old enough to remember Sam and his two brothers, Tom and George (and their six sisters) says, "All the Johnsons strutted, except George. And he strutted a little. Hell, the Johnsons could strut sitting down." He dressed better than the other Hill Country farmers and ranchers; in the evening, after work, he would put on a suit and tie. And he was invariably well mounted; he often said something that older Hill Country residents remembered his father and his father's brother Tom saying—when the original Johnson boys had been young: "You can tell a man by his boots and his hat and the horse he rides." And he occasionally carried a long-barreled Colt six-shooter—one of the few guns still worn in the Hill Country.

But the air of command came naturally to him, and he was open and friendly. The rutted dirt track that was the only road between Austin and Johnson City and Fredericksburg ran along the Pedernales, right by the Johnson farm, and travelers tried to schedule their trip "to make it to little Sam Johnson's by nightfall in order to spend the night and enjoy a good time." It was, however, noticeable that although Hill Country men were farmers or ranchers, Sam's best friends were three men who weren't: Jay

Alexander was an engineer; Dayton Moses and W. C. Linden were lawyers. Sam Johnson was a farmer, but he was a Bunton, and he burned to be something more.

After six years on the farm, a chance came along. By unwritten agreement, representation in the Texas House of Representatives was rotated among the four Hill Country counties that constituted the 89th District, and 1904 was the year for Gillespie County, the county in which the Johnson farm was located, to send a man to Austin. Urged on by Judge Clarence W. Martin, a former Representative who had married one of Sam's sisters and moved to Gillespie to practice law, Sam filed for the Democratic nomination—and won it unanimously. His acceptance speech, delivered from the back of a wagon at a barbecue held in a grove of live-oak trees near Stonewall, revealed that he had inherited the Buntons' "eloquent tongue."

"I am aware that by many persons, it is considered in the nature of a joke to become a candidate and to be elected as a member of the Legislature," he said. Yet, he said, when he considered what "the duties of that office are . . . when properly and conscientiously" performed he felt himself handicapped by the lack of a formal education. "I . . . hesitate as to whether my ability and attainments are such that will enable me to properly perform that duty." Being awarded the nomination hadn't removed those doubts, he said; "I take it, that it is an act of kindness upon your part . . . a testimonial that you are willing to aid me to reflect your desire and purposes by giving to me your help and assistance. . . . In application and faithfulness to duty, I shall hope to in a measure make up for any shortcoming that I may possess in qualifications."

The Populist Party may have been dead, Populist principles weren't— at least not to the gangling young man on the wagon. He saw his campaign as part of a national cause. "This is a momentous eve in the history of our nation, and the question has been presented to us in a clearcut form— Whether the principles and tradition of a Republic shall be longer perpetuated, or whether we shall meekly surrender to the great trust combines the interests of the nation." The power of big business, he said, "has assumed proportions that even the wildest fanatical dreamer could not have anticipated, and it is now up to the people what their verdict shall be. We have the Republican Party on the one hand, the champion of the Federalist tendencies of government, while the Democrats are striving for a return to fundamental principles and a return to the Constitution as taught by Jefferson, Jackson and their followers—which is clearly the only hope for the perpetuity of our government. If I can be the means in my own feeble and humble way to assist in a slight degree even of bringing about such results, then I shall feel that my duty has been performed."

Running ahead of the rest of the Democratic ticket, with his largest margins coming from Johnson City and the small towns along the Pedernales that knew him best, Johnson easily defeated his opponent, a German-American lawyer from Fredericksburg, who won only heavily German—and heavily Republican—Gillespie County. His mother pointed out that he had won his first public office even younger than had his famous forebear; John Wheeler Bunton had been twenty-eight, she noted; Sam was only twenty-seven. And when, in January, 1905, he arrived at the towering red-granite Capitol in Austin and walked into the House of Representatives Chamber, he had suddenly found a home.

The young man who had hated the cornfields found that he loved the cloakrooms. Loved them—and knew how to maneuver in them. Relatively uneducated and thoroughly unsophisticated, he seemed to know instinctively the steps of the legislative dance. He seemed, in fact, born to the roll call and the Rules of Order. And he had the unteachable gift for the persuasion that is so integral a part of the legislative life; he roamed the rows of desks as if he had spent his life among them instead of among rows of cotton. He gave few speeches, but he was talking constantly in the cloakrooms and on the floor—with a distinctive mannerism: when trying to win another member to his point of view, the tall, gangling young man would grasp the Representative's lapel and lean very close to him, face right up to face, while he talked.

Several influential Texans, among them his brother-in-law Clarence Martin, had been trying for several years to persuade the Legislature to purchase and restore the Alamo; the old mission had fallen into disrepair, and part of it was being used as a warehouse. But previous attempts had foundered on the question of financing—legislators were outraged that the owners had raised the price to $65,000—and disputes over jurisdiction. Johnson drafted his own Alamo Purchase Bill, providing that it would be administered by the Daughters of the Republic of Texas, and then persuaded more influential legislators to sponsor the measure—he let one of them, an elderly Confederate hero, sign it first, so that it bore his name—and it passed. (Wrote a local newspaper: "Santa Anna took the Alamo—that was 1836. Sam Johnson saved the Alamo—that was 1905.") Johnson wanted a bill passed banning calf-roping contests, a competition he had long felt was brutal to the animals as it was practiced by cowboys at local fairs; although many anti-roping bills were introduced in 1905, it was his that was selected as best and passed. On many issues, Johnson wasn't on the winning side, in a Legislature dominated by "the interests," for he stuck to his Populist ideals, advocating, for example, a franchise tax on corporations and an eight-hour day for railroad workers. But on the bills he personally introduced (for example, one exempting Blanco County from a state law requiring counties to pay a fifty-cent bounty for every wolf shot—the *Blanco News* said the county was so poor it would be bankrupted if it was forced to pay) he had a remarkable record: he was, a newspaper reported, one of the few legislators "who did not fail on a single measure." He worked as a team with two other

Democratic legislators identified with Populist causes—"Honest Buck" Gray and Claud Hudspeth, "the Cowboy from Crockett County"—and a newspaper reported: "Mr. Gray, Mr. Johnson and Mr. Hudspeth are . . . a trio that command the respect and confidence of their fellow members." Johnson had a gift not only for making men go along with him but for making them like him. He was famed for his practical jokes, such as the one he played on Representative J. J. Blount, who not only took frequent naps at his desk in the Chamber but kept a big alarm clock on it to wake him up. Once Blount set the alarm to allow himself a two-hour snooze. As soon as he fell asleep, Johnson walked over to his desk, moved the alarm forward and walked away. A minute or two later, the alarm went off. Blount jumped to his feet, saying, "It's time to go to work! What are we here for?" as the House roared. Decades later, men who had served with Sam Johnson in the Legislature would remember him with fondness; one, Sam Rayburn, on receiving a letter from him in 1937, would reply: "I am mighty glad to get a letter from you and in this wise renew friendships of years ago. You are one man that I served with in the Legislature of Texas that I have always remembered with interest and kindly feeling."

Sam Johnson was a born legislator. He had never displayed much enthusiasm for mending wire fences, but he mended his political fences industriously. He made a point of becoming good friends with the editors of the local newspapers back in the Hill Country, even the editor of the Gillespie *County News,* which had supported his opponent, and after the 1905 legislative session, the *News* editorialized:

> Hon. S. E. Johnson . . . has succeeded in passing more bills, probably, than any other member of the present Legislature. Mr. Johnson accomplishes his ends by quiet and consistent attention to duty, by unfailing attendance on committee meetings and the sessions of the House, and consistently refraining from the making of speeches. His businesslike idea of legislation and uniform courtesy has won him a host of friends, who stand by him when votes are needed. . . .
>
> He is one of the most active and influential of the younger members of the House, and is an ideal Representative in that he works much and talks little.

When, in 1906, he decided to try to break the county-rotation tradition, even the newspaper in Llano County, which according to tradition was entitled to the seat next, supported him. Llano nevertheless put up its own candidate—the closest the county could come to a big businessman, David Martin, owner of the Martin Telephone Company—but Johnson, with the *Blanco News* urging, "Boys, get out and shell the woods, and let the people choose . . . whom they will send to Austin to help make our laws," won even Martin's county in the Democratic primary, rolling up a four-county margin so large that the Republicans did not bother to run an opponent against him in the November elections.

BUT SAM wasn't only a Bunton. He was also a Johnson, and he possessed none of the Buntons' tough practicality that enabled them to realize their dreams—or at least not to be destroyed by them. And the Johnsons' dreams were even bigger than the Buntons'—and suffused with a romantic unreality. 1906 was a year of political victory for Sam Johnson, but it was also a year of financial disaster. Having gambled and won on the cotton-futures market in 1902 and 1903 and 1904, in 1905 he had gambled more, buying on margin, overextending himself—as his father, having gambled and won on the cattle drives of 1868 and 1869 and 1870, had gambled too much and lost on the cattle drive of 1871. Few details are known except for his son Lyndon's statement that "My daddy went busted waiting for cotton to go up to twenty-one cents a pound, and the market fell apart when it hit twenty." Sam lost everything he had invested—and more. And when, in 1906, he borrowed money and bought on margin, he lost again. When he went back to the Legislature after his re-election in November, 1906, he went as a man several thousand dollars in debt.

The Legislature was not the place for a man like Sam Johnson to get out of debt. Texans' early distrust of the federal government—nourished by Washington's indifference to its new state, and particularly by Washington's failure to protect the frontier against Indians—had been extended to their own state government during Reconstruction, when the openly corrupt Carpetbagger Legislature looted the state and imposed heavy taxes on its people to pay for the liberality. "The more the damn Legislature meets, the more Goddamned bills and taxes it passes," one Texan put it—and when Texans regained control of their state government, their new state constitution, essentially an anti-government document, tried to ensure that the Legislature would meet infrequently; it provided that sessions be held only every other year and, as an inducement to legislators to keep even these sessions short, that the legislators' salary of five dollars per day be paid only for sixty days; if the sessions ran longer, they were to receive two dollars per day.

Low salaries didn't bother many of the legislators, for it was not legislators but lobbyists—lobbyists for oil companies, railroads, banks, utilities—who did the presiding in Austin: in the capital's bars and brothels, where they dispensed "beefsteak, bourbon and blondes" so liberally that some descriptions of turn-of-the-century legislative sessions read like descriptions of one long orgy; in its backrooms, where decisions were made; even on the floor of the Legislature, which lobbyists roamed at will, often sitting at legislators' desks and sometimes even casting votes on behalf of absent Representatives. Many of the elected representatives of a generally impoverished people, representatives who had come to Austin poor themselves, went home poor no more, and even most of those who refused to trade votes for cash generally accepted—because they considered their salaries too low to cover their expenses—lobbyists' offers to pay for their Austin meals and hotel bills.*

But Sam Johnson accepted nothing. It was not that he shunned the whorehouses and the bars; he didn't—he is remembered as an enthusiastic participant in the wildest of Austin's parties. He is remembered, in fact, as being a loud and boastful reveler—somewhat foolish when in his cups. But if he was foolish, he was foolish on his own money; he insisted on paying for his own drinks and his own women. And if he is remembered as being loud, he is also remembered as being honest—conspicuously honest; a rather quixotic figure, in fact, in the Austin atmosphere. Once, finding a lobbyist sitting at his desk in the House, he angrily ordered him up; when the lobbyist, thinking he was joking, was too slow to obey, Johnson reached down, grabbed his jacket and pulled him out of his chair. Thereafter, he either introduced or was one of the few supporters of—the legislative record is not clear on the point—a bill to regulate lobbyists' conduct. (It never got out of committee.)

The most controversial issue before the Texas House of Representatives in 1907 was the re-election of United States Senator Joseph Weldon Bailey.

Bailey, an imposing figure in his "dull black frock coat, flowing tie, and big, black slouch hat," was one of the great old Populist orators. His thundering speeches against Eastern capitalists, wrote one who had heard them, "were phrased in the best English, though he was prone to draw on his imagination for history when required to make his point. His voice was melodious. . . ." As Minority Leader of Congress during the 1890's, "he dominated the Democratic minority like an overseer and conducted himself like a conqueror." A close friend of Bryan's, he had "influenced the Great Commoner in the formulation of his most celebrated doctrines, among them the Bryan metal theory."

But according to his enemies, Bailey was a Populist who had sold out. In 1906, he was accused of having accepted huge legal fees from railroads, the big East Texas lumber interests and the Standard Oil Company—from

---

* The use of blondes to influence the Legislature was so widespread that one legislator, a preacher, introduced a bill that would have made adultery a felony. The joke in Austin was that its passage would result in the immediate jailing of most legislators. So, one by one, almost every legislator stood up and proposed an amendment, which the House laughingly passed, by prearrangement, exempting residents of his own district (including, of course, himself) from the bill.

Standard Oil alone, he later admitted, his annual retainer was $100,000 (four times as large as the budget, including the Governor's salary, of the entire executive branch of the State of Texas). His term as Senator ran out in 1907, and some members of the Legislature—Legislatures still elected Senators—were talking of getting a new one, or at least of postponing the vote while the House investigated Bailey's affairs.

When the Legislature met, however, Bailey was in Austin "to drive into the Gulf of Mexico the peanut politicians who would replace me with someone who would rattle around in my seat like a mustard seed in a gourd!" Backing him were the railroads and oil interests, who had a big stake in keeping him in the Senate. They wanted a vote before any investigation began—and they wanted the vote unanimous. The pressure they brought to bear—combined with the power of Bailey's name; the Senator was, at that time, possibly the most famous and powerful politician in Texas—brought, sooner or later, almost all of the 133 members of the House over to their point of view. When the vote on his re-election was held, following a series of pro-Bailey speeches greeted with roaring cheers by most of the members, only seven refused to go along. Sam Johnson, who had been one of the first to call for the investigation, was one of the seven.

To some Austin observers, Sam Johnson's stand—not only on Bailey but on all the Populist positions that he refused to surrender—made him something of a hero. The House Chaplain, who described him as "a quiet worker" whose "pleasant, gentlemanly ways secure to him the friendship of all the members," said he "will bear gentle reproof, but will kick like a mule at any attempted domination." Others put it more simply. A saying about Sam Johnson was widespread in Austin at this time. "Sam Johnson," it went, "is straight as a shingle." But the legislative session dragged on. On five dollars a day—and then two dollars a day—Sam had to pay his expenses at Austin as well as the salaries of the laborers he had to hire to work the farm when he was away. He couldn't do it. And his creditors were dunning him for the money he had lost on the cotton-futures market—and for smaller amounts, too. In August, 1905, for example, he had filled a forty-cent prescription at O. Y. Fawcett's drugstore in Johnson City. In November, he still hadn't been able to pay the forty cents, and when he came in for another prescription, Fawcett made him pay cash. At the end of the year, Fawcett asked him if he could pay up so that the account could be balanced, and Sam said he couldn't. He began to get a bad reputation with some of the local merchants, bad enough, in fact, so that when, in 1907, he asked a Johnson City girl, a schoolteacher named Mabel Chapman, to marry him, Mabel, at the insistence of her parents, refused and instead married another suitor. And then in August, 1907, he did get married, and by 1908, he and his wife were expecting a child. He may have felt at home in that paneled, high-ceilinged House of Representatives, but it was a house he couldn't afford to stay in. All four counties in the 89th District wanted him to run again in 1908, for an unprecedented third term, but he decided not to do so. State jobs—better-paying than legislative seats—were available to many retiring legislators, as were jobs with the railroads and the oil companies and the banks, but Sam Johnson, who had refused to go along with the railroads and the oil companies and the banks—who had refused to come to terms with the reality of Austin—was offered no job. By the time his first child, Lyndon, was born, on August 27, 1908, Sam Johnson had lugged his dreams and ideals back to the Hill Country.

4

The Father and Mother

SAM JOHNSON HAD, moreover, married someone as romantic and idealistic as he.

Rebekah Baines had been raised, on the outskirts of the little Hill Country town of Blanco, in a large two-story stone house painted a smooth and gleaming white. A house of Southern graciousness, it should have been set behind a long green lawn, among tall and stately trees; instead, it towered over the stunted mesquite around it, and over the spindly little fruit trees in the recently planted orchard on one side. Grass grew in its front yard only in brown, scattered clumps. It seemed very out of place near Blanco's rickety wooden stores and dog-run log cabins.

For a while, Rebekah's father was the area's most prominent attorney. Descended from a long line of famous Baptist preachers—his father, the Reverend George Washington Baines, had been president of Baylor, the Texas Baptist university—Joseph Wilson Baines had been a schoolteacher and then a lawyer, a newspaperman (founder of the influential *McKinney Advocate*) and Secretary of State under Governor John ("Old Oxcart") Ireland. Moving to the Hill Country in 1900, he was elected to the Legislature—to the same seat Sam Johnson would later hold—and practiced law and rented land to tenant farmers, accumulating "quite a fortune." But the qualities most remarked about him were his piety ("A Baptist, strict in doctrine . . . he was the chief pillar in the Blanco Church"; "for clean speech and morals, he could hardly have been surpassed"); his love of beauty in literature and nature; and his principles, both as a legislator "public-spirited, profoundly concerned for the welfare of the people . . . high in ideals," and as a lawyer who, his law partner said, "was always more concerned about doing right and acting honorable than he was about the success of the suit." A Hill Country historian wrote of Joe Baines: "He loved the good and the beautiful."

Rebekah was devoted to her father. It was he, she was to recall, who taught her to read, and "reading has been one of the great pleasures and sustaining forces of my life. . . . He taught me the beauty of simple things. He taught me that 'a lie is an abomination to the Lord.' . . . He gave the timid child self-confidence." As an elderly woman, looking back (with some exaggeration) on her girlhood, she would write:

> I am grateful for . . . that simple, friendly, dearly loved town, Blanco. I love to think of our home, a two-story rock house with a fruitful orchard of perfectly spaced trees, terraced flower beds, broad walks, purple plumed wisteria climbing to the roof, fragrant honeysuckle at the dining room windows whose broad sills were seats for us children. Most of all I love to think of the gracious hospitality of that home, of the love and trust, the fear of God, and the beautiful ideals that made it a true home.

But Blanco was in the Hill Country. "On account of disastrous droughts, protracted four years," and "by over-kindness to farm tenants and by overconfidence in men," as his brother put it, Baines' farming operations "brought financial ruin." He lost his home, moving in 1904 from "dearly loved" Blanco to the German community of Fredericksburg, where he built a smaller house for his family and tried to establish a new practice. But his health had fled with his fortune, and he died in November, 1906; his wife had to sell the house, move to San Marcos, and take in boarders.

Rebekah later wrote that she had "adjusted readily and cheerfully to the financial change"—she worked in the college bookstore to earn enough money to graduate from Baylor—but that she had experienced greater difficulty adjusting "to life without my father, who had been the dominant force in my life as well as my adored parent, reverenced mentor, and most interesting companion." Shortly before he died, while Rebekah, having graduated, was back in Fredericksburg teaching elocution and working as a "stringer" for the Austin newspaper, he had suggested that she interview the young legislator who had won the seat he himself had once held. She would recall that when she did—in 1907, shortly after Sam had been turned down by Mabel Chapman—"I asked him lots of questions but he was pretty cagey and I couldn't pin him down; I was awfully provoked with that man!" but she also recalled that he was "dashing and dynamic," with "flashing eyes"— and, however unlike her father he may have been in other respects, the two men were similar in the one she thought most important: she could talk with him, as she had with her father, about "principles." As for Sam, she said, "He was enchanted to find a girl who really liked politics." Soon, in what she called a "whirlwind courtship," he was riding the twenty miles to Fredericksburg to visit the slender, blonde, blue-eyed elocution teacher, and taking her to hear political speeches at the Confederate Reunion and in the Legislature—"We heard William Jennings Bryan, who we both admired extravagantly"), and on August 20, 1907, they were married and he brought her to the Pedernales.

NOTHING IN HER LIFE had prepared her for life there.

As they rode away from comfortable, bustling Fredericksburg and its neat green fields, the land faded to brown, and then gray. It became more and more rocky, more and more barren. The farmhouses were farther and farther apart. Dotting the hills were hulks of deserted farmhouses, crumbling rectangles of logs out of which reared tall stone fireplaces which stood in the hills like tombstones—monuments to the hopes of other couples who had tried to earn a living there. And then, finally, they came to the house in which she was to live.

It was a small shack on a long, shallow slope leading up from the muddy little river.

A typical Hill Country dog-run, it consisted of two boxlike rooms, each about twelve feet square, on either side of a breezeway. Behind one of the rooms was the kitchen. One end of the porch had been enclosed to form a tiny "shed-room"; the roof was sagging as if pulled down a little by the added weight on that side, and the porch slanted down, too. The walls of the house were vertical boards. Out back were a barn—little more, really, than a lean-to shelter for animals—and the toilet facilities, a pair of flimsy, tilted "two-holers." In front of the house was a swinging wooden gate, set not in a wooden fence but in a fence made of four strands of barbed wire which enclosed the front yard. The yard was mostly dirt with a few clumps of grass or weeds stuck up here and there. Sam had painted the house a bright yellow to welcome her.

Rebekah's father had created a niche in the Hill Country, and had raised a daughter who fitted into that niche: a college graduate, a lover of poetry, a soft-spoken, gentle, dreamy-eyed young lady who wore crinolines and lace—and broad-brimmed, beribboned hats with long veils; "She had a flawless, beautiful white skin and never held with this business of going out in the sun and getting tan; she felt that women should protect themselves from the sun," recalls one of her daughters. Now, overnight, at the age of twenty-six (Sam was almost thirty), she was out of the niche—a fragile Southern flower suddenly transplanted to the rocky soil of the Pedernales Valley.

Transplanted, moreover, to a world in which women had to work, and work hard. On washdays, clothes had to be lifted out of the big soaking vats of boiling water on the ends of long poles, the clothes dripping and heavy; the farm filth had to be scrubbed out in hours of kneeling over rough rub-boards, hours in which the lye in homemade soap burned the skin off women's hands; the heavy flatirons had to be continually carried back and forth to the stove for reheating, and the stove had to be continually fed with new supplies of wood—decades later, even strong, sturdy farm wives would remember how their backs had ached on washday. And Rebekah wasn't strong. With no electricity in the valley, all cooking had to be done on a wood stove, and the wood for it—and for the fireplace—had to be carried in from the pile outside, and just carrying those countless loads of wood was hard for a frail woman who had never in her life done physical labor. The pump on her back porch made it unnecessary for Rebekah to lug buckets of water up from the Pedernales as most of the women in the valley had to do, but even working the pump was hard for her. Rebekah was a good cook, but of what the other farm wives called "fancy" foods: delicate dishes, for elegant meals. Now, at "the threshing," the fifteen or twenty men who came in to help expected to be served three huge meals a day. The farm wife had a hundred chores; Sam hired girls to help Rebekah with them, but the girls were always quitting—no girl wanted to live out there in those lonely hills—and even when there was a maid in the house, there was so much work that Rebekah had to do some of it. When, in later years, Rebekah Johnson wrote a memoir, she painted her life on the ranch in terms so soft that it was all but unrecognizable to those who knew her. But seeping through the lines of one paragraph is emotion they believe is true:

> Normally the first year of marriage is a period of readjustment. In this case, I was confronted not only by the problem of adjustment to a completely opposite personality, but also to a strange and new way of life, a way far removed from that I had known in Blanco and Fredericksburg. Recently my early experiences on the farm were relived when I saw "The Egg and I"; again I shuddered over the chickens, and wrestled with a mammoth iron stove. However, I was determined to overcome circumstances instead of letting them overwhelm me. At last I realized that life is real and earnest and not the charming fairy tale of which I had so long dreamed.

Years later, in a statement that may have been more accurate, she would write to her son, Lyndon: "I never liked country life, and its inconveniences. . . ."

It was not, however, the work that was the most difficult aspect of farm life for her.

From Rebekah's front porch, not another house was visible—not another human structure of any type. Other houses were scattered along the Pedernales—and some not far away; Sam's parents now lived just a half-mile up the road, and not much farther away lived two of Sam's sisters, with their husbands. And there was his brother Tom—it was a Johnson valley again; there were Johnson brothers, again named Sam and Tom, working on the Pedernales as there had been forty years before. But the Johnsons were a boisterous crew. They told jokes—the kind of jokes Rebekah's father had so disliked. They might pass around a bottle—and her father had taught her what a sin that was. Going to church on Sundays was great fun for them; they would all meet at Grandfather Johnson's, each family behind its own team, and race, shouting back and forth, pulling up in front of the Christadelphian church in a flurry of dust and laughter. That wasn't the way to go to church! After services, they would gather around the piano in the church and sing—all the Johnsons could sing; Sam had once won a medal in a singing contest. It was not at all like the quiet, reflective Sundays in the Baptist church in Blanco that had been so important to Rebekah's father and to her.

In other ways, too, she couldn't fit in. She was a college graduate, and a college graduate who loved what she had learned, who loved to recite poetry, and to talk about literature and art, and who had spent her life in a home filled with such talk. The other Johnson women were farm wives, raised on farms; when necessary, they worked in the fields beside their men; Rebekah's sister-in-law, Tom's wife, was a sturdy German girl quite capable, if Tom fell behind in the plowing, of hitching up a second team and handling a whole quarter-section by herself. In conversation, the Johnson women were as earthy as Rebekah was ethereal. Many of them "had their letters" and that was all; they could sign their names and laboriously pick out words in a newspaper, but they didn't read books, and didn't talk about them. Some of the women on nearby farms in the valley, and in the rolling hills that stretched away from it, didn't have even their letters; the German women didn't even speak English. Without a telephone, Rebekah could talk only with the people in the valley, and there wasn't a person in the valley with whom Rebekah enjoyed talking.

Sam was "opposite"—loud and boisterous, impatient and cursed with a fierce temper—but he and Rebekah were very much in love. "She was so shy and reserved all the time," says a girl who lived with them on the Pedernales for several months. "Then she'd hear Sam coming home. Her face would just light up like a little kid's, and out she'd go flying down to the gate to meet him." They loved to talk together—long, serious talks, usually about politics; the girl recalls the two of them sitting beside the coal-oil lamp late into the evening, talking about "things I couldn't understand." But when Sam was away, Rebekah had no one to talk to.

And Sam was often away, traveling to Austin on legislative business or to Johnson City to deliver cotton to the gin or pick up supplies, or all over the vast Hill Country to buy and sell farms—in 1908, he had decided to try to supplement his farm income by going into the real-estate business. And it wasn't always possible to come straight home when his business was concluded; more than once, having spurred a mount or whipped a team through the sixty miles of mud that constituted the only road between Austin and Stonewall in a wet spell, he would come to a creek too high to ford.

When Rebekah walked out the front door of that little house, there was nothing—a roadrunner streaking behind some rocks with something long and wet dangling from his beak, perhaps, or a rabbit disappearing around a bush so fast that all she really saw was the flash of a white tail— but otherwise nothing. There was no movement except for the ripple of the leaves in the scattered trees, no sound except for the constant whisper of the wind, unless, by happy chance, crows were cawing somewhere nearby. If Rebekah climbed, almost in desperation, the hill in back of the house, what she saw from its crest was more hills, an endless vista of hills, hills on which there was visible not a single house—somewhere up there, of course, was the Benner house, and the Weinheimer house and barn, but they were hidden from her by some rise—hills on which nothing moved, empty hills with, above them, empty sky; a hawk circling silently high overhead was an event. But most of all, there was nothing human, no one to talk to. "If men loved Texas, women, even the Anglo pioneer women, hated it," Fehrenbach has written. ". . . In diaries and letters a thousand separate farm wives left a record of fear that this country would drive them mad." Not only brutally hard work, but loneliness—what Walter Prescott Webb, who grew up on a farm and could barely restrain his bitterness toward historians who glamorize farm life, calls "nauseating loneliness"—was the lot of a Hill Country farm wife.

Loneliness and dread. During the day, there might be a visitor, or at least an occasional passerby on the rutted road. At night, there was no one, no one at all. No matter in what direction Rebekah looked, not a light was visible. The gentle, dreamy, bookish woman would be alone, alone in the dark—sometimes, when clouds covered the moon, in pitch dark—alone in the dark when she went out on the porch to pump water, or out to the barn to feed the horses, alone with the rustlings in the trees and the sudden splashes in the river which could be a fish jumping, or a small animal drinking, or someone coming, alone in the storms when the wind howled around the house and tore through its flimsy walls, blowing out the lamps and candles, alone in the night in the horrible nights after a norther, when the freeze came, and ice drove starving rodents from the fields to gnaw at the roofs and walls, and she could hear them chewing there in the dark—alone in bed with no human being to hear you if you should call.

SHE TRIED TO MAINTAIN her standards. Her favorite quotation, she said, was one from Browning: "The common problem, yours and mine, everyone's/ Is not to fancy what were fair in life/Provided it could be—but finding first/ What may be and how to make it fair up to our means." She refused to use the customary oilcloth on her table; she used tablecloths, no matter how much work it was to wash and iron them. "She made a ritual out of little things, like serving tea in very thin cups," one of her daughters says. Never— even in her old age—was she able to reconcile herself to the fact that three of her five (they came at two-year intervals) children were delivered by a midwife: when labor pains began for her first child, Lyndon, her husband sent for a doctor, but the nearest one was twenty miles away, and the creeks were on the rise; as morning approached, and the pains came closer together, it became obvious that he wouldn't arrive in time. Sam Johnson, Sr., sixty-nine years old, saddled his most reliable horse, Old Reb, rode along the Pedernales until, half a mile above the usual ford, he found a low spot, and then spurred the horse into the raging water to bring back a German midwife, Mrs. Christian Lindig, and it was she who presided at the delivery; when, in 1951, Lyndon asked his mother to jot down some family reminiscences, she did not mention Mrs. Lindig as among those "present at his birth," but credited as "the attending physician, Dr. John Blanton of Buda"—who actually didn't arrive until quite a few hours later. (Says Sam's sister Jessie: "Rebekah was always, always dignified, you know, in everything. . . . I don't think Rebekah would have ever wanted anybody to say that Lyndon came with a midwife instead of a real doctor. I don't think she would have ever said.")

(There was one other character-revealing note in the episode. As old Sam—the gallant, unselfish Johnson—saddled his horse, his wife, Eliza, who was a Bunton and believed that "Charity begins at home," tried to stop him from going, shouting, "You will be drowned!" as he rode off.)

IN 1913, after Lyndon and two girls had been born, Sam and Rebekah moved into Johnson City, into a snug, three-bedroom white frame house with lacy Victorian "gingerbread" scrollwork on the gables and with trellises on which she soon had wisteria growing. But gingerbread and wisteria couldn't make Johnson City into Blanco or Fredericksburg. Stella Gliddon, who moved there from Fredericksburg about the same time as Rebekah, says: "When I came to Johnson City, I thought I had come to the end of the earth."

She couldn't believe the primitiveness of the living conditions she found there, Mrs. Gliddon says. Registering at the only hotel in town—already appalled at its rickety shabbiness—she asked where the bathroom was, and was told there wasn't any, not even a sink to wash in. Nor, she was told, did most homes in Johnson City have indoor plumbing: "I don't think there were three bathrooms in the whole town," she recalls, meaning, by bathrooms, rooms with sinks and bathtubs; *no one* in Johnson City had a toilet in the house. When she asked where she could eat, she was told that there was one café in town, but that it was only open when the proprietors, King and Fannie Casparis, felt like opening it, and that they hadn't felt like it for some time. (Another visitor recalls going to Casparis' Café at noon one day and finding on its door a sign he considered somewhat unusual for a restaurant: CLOSED FOR LUNCH.) Since there was, therefore, no place in Johnson City where a meal could be purchased, Mrs. Gliddon decided to make herself a sandwich, but when she went shopping, she learned, to her astonishment, that no local store stocked bread because there wasn't enough demand for it; "you couldn't buy a loaf of bread in Johnson City."

Fredericksburg was a town with only 4,000 residents, but its homes were solid German rock houses with arbors and orchards (and indoor plumbing); it had handsome churches and a large, sprawling hotel and a long Main Street lined with bustling shops. Johnson City looked like the set for a Grade-B Western. Its single commercial street, Main Street (unpaved, of course), was a row of a few one-story stores, each with a wooden "awning," supported by poles, extending over the rickety wooden sidewalk that ran in front of them. It was almost wholly a one-story town: the only larger structures were a rickety water tower; a corrugated-tin cotton gin; the bank; Doc Barnwell's "Sanitarium," which had four or five beds upstairs over his office; and two square two-story stone buildings: the school and the court-house. Scattered around that Main Street were a few homes—very few. About 1916, two of the Redford boys, Cecil and Emmette, climbed into the school belfry, from whose platform they could see about five miles in every direction; counting children and hired hands—"because," Cecil says, "we knew every person in every house anywhere around"—the total population of the area, as far as the eye could see, was 323.

The sense of isolation—of being cut off from the rest of the world—was overwhelming, Mrs. Gliddon remembers. From the top of Lookout Mountain, about four miles away, it was possible to see farther than from the school belfry, and from its crest, the hills, ridge after ridge, rolled endlessly away in an awesome, empty landscape. And then one looked down and saw Johnson City—a tiny cluster of houses huddled together in the midst of immense space.

Cars and roads would one day bridge that space, but when Sam and Rebekah moved to Johnson City, there were almost no cars—three or four in the town—and no paved roads for cars to travel on. Even by car, it took long hours to reach Fredericksburg or Austin—when the roads and creeks were passable. Often they weren't, and then someone who wanted to go to Fredericksburg or Austin had to be "brought out" of Johnson City as if out of darkest Africa. "Once I wanted to go home to Fredericksburg for Christmas," Mrs. Gliddon recalls. "I had to have a man with a hack and horse take me out to Stonewall, and a car was able to come out from Fredericksburg to there and take me the rest of the way." Johnson City was, she says, "an island town," a town surrounded by—and cut off by —an ocean of land.

Rebekah saw it the same way. And its people, while friendly—"the people [in Johnson City] were the friendliest, warmest people I met any-where," Mrs. Gliddon says—were not people who could provide Rebekah with the things so important to her. "She was probably the best-educated woman in the whole county," her son Sam Houston has written, and she probably was; she was the only woman with a college degree in Johnson City; no more than two or three residents of the town—of either gender—had spent any time at all in college; Johnson City was, in fact, a town with hardly any books except for the textbooks used in school. One farmer, Robert Lee Green, was so desperate for something to read that when there was some evening event at school, he would sneak out of the auditorium and down to the high-school classroom and sit there reading a history textbook until it was time to go home. Worst of all for Rebekah, the schools were terribly inadequate; her children, she believed, were getting hardly any education at all. Once, when her mother came to visit, she said to her with desperation in her voice: "I don't want to bring up my children in Johnson City!"

Shortly after they moved to Johnson City, their fourth child, Sam Houston, was born. Rebekah had wanted to have her confinement in the Sanitarium, but Doc Barnwell told her that its handful of beds was needed for patients more seriously ill. Although the doctor was present this time, the birth was hard; recuperating from the delivery took several weeks, and for years thereafter, Rebekah Johnson would periodically take to her bed for days or weeks at a time. She had always hated the drudgery of routine housework, and now she all but stopped doing it. Her mother came to visit more and more, staying for weeks at a time to help out, and Sam hired a local girl to come in and clean—Rebekah's neighbors said that what the mother and the maid didn't do remained undone.

Nor, the neighbors said, was Rebekah thrifty. In this desperately cash-poor country, where pennies mattered, women watched them. "Make, or make do" was the saying. The reason there was no bread for sale in Johnson City was that the baker in Marble Falls, who had to cart it in by wagon, wanted five cents a loaf; rather than spend that money, Johnson City women baked their own bread—although that task required them to spend the entire day adjusting the fire in their stoves, continually putting in wood to keep it at the correct temperature. Johnson City women scrubbed their floors on their hands and knees; "brooms," Ava Johnson Cox, Lyndon's cousin, remembers, "were too expensive, so you didn't dare use them every day." Rebekah didn't live like that; in the opinion of her neighbors, she couldn't. Says Ava, whose mother received ten dollars from her husband, Tom, every month for household expenses and, by making or making do, always had two dollars left at the month's end: "Our mother learned as a girl how to can, how to preserve, how to do all the things that a farm woman had to do. She [Rebekah] had never been taught that, and she didn't want to learn. And a woman like Rebekah, even if she had wanted to learn—she just would never fit in to the life that we had. She couldn't learn that around here every penny mattered."

But at the time, Rebekah Johnson's neighbors didn't think badly of her for not working the way they did. They saw that she had other qualities—and that she was generous in their use.

By volunteering her services, she persuaded the school board to start a "literary society," in which she taught poetry, and "elocution," which to her meant the whole art of public speaking. Teaching public speaking to these shy country girls and boys—many of whom came to school only occasionally from their isolated farms and ranches—was difficult. She started the younger students on spelling bees and " 'rithmetic matches," which gave them their first chance to stand up in front of an audience. Then they progressed to "declamation" of poems, to "pantomimes and dialogues," then to debates, and, finally, the high-school pupils would have to speak extemporaneously on subjects they would study in the books, pamphlets and magazines Rebekah ordered from the extension library at the University of Texas in Austin. The girls felt keenly that they were "country"—that they lacked social graces—so Rebekah expanded the curriculum to include dancing: fifty years and more later, one of her pupils, asked what kind of dancing, suddenly became lost in reverie and then, all at once, began humming, very softly, with her wrinkled old face smiling in reminiscence, "Little red wagon painted blue, little red wagon painted blue, little red wagon painted blue, skip to m'Lou, my darling." To records played on a Victrola, which she brought to school—the school couldn't afford one—Rebekah taught not only square dances but waltzes and Virginia reels, and then, in the words of another elderly Johnson City resident, "she teached girls how to stand, . . . how to sit down properly." She did the work without pay—there was no money to give her, and she didn't ask for any—and her students were grateful to her. "We didn't have *anything* before," one recalls. "Before Lyndon's mother came to school and got this going, school was only sitting in class and not raise your finger or say a word or you got spanked. We didn't think they'd let her do the literary society; that was *play,* that was taking your mind off your books."

They were grateful also for the lessons Lyndon's mother gave in private—in the living room of the Johnson home. "Those lessons were the highlight of my young life," says Doc Barnwell's daughter, Gene.

Those lessons *changed* lives, in fact.

One girl who received them was Lyndon's cousin Ava. Ava's sister, Margaret, was beautiful and lively and outgoing. Ava was not. She was very shy, a little stout, and although she wasn't homely, she considered herself so. Rebekah was taking one grade at a time in her literary society, working her way toward the older pupils, and Ava dreaded the day she would get to her grade.

When Mrs. Johnson did, and began assigning speech topics, Ava recalls, "I said I couldn't do a speech.

" 'You come over to the house this afternoon.'

"At the house, I said, 'I just can't do it, Aunt Rebekah.' And she said, 'Oh, yes, you can. There's nothing impossible if you put the mind to it. I know you have the ability to deliver a speech.' And I cried, and I said, 'I just can't do it!'

"Aunt Rebekah said, 'Oh, yes, you can.' And she said, 'Pretty is just skin-deep, darling.' Ooooh, I'll never forget her saying that. And she repeated that Browning poem to me. And she never let up, never let up. Never. Boosting me along, telling me I could do it. She taught me speaking and elocution, and I went to the state championships with it, and I want to tell you, I was one scared chicken. And I won a medal, a gold medal, in competitions involving the whole state. And she still kept boosting me along. I wanted to be a teacher, but I never thought I could: I just didn't think that I could ever get it over to a child. I had *always* wanted to be a teacher, but I couldn't sell myself. I had an inferiority complex that wouldn't quit. She told me, 'You have everything that it takes to make a good teacher. Just make up your mind to do it.' She never let up, telling me I could do it. And I did. And I became a teacher, and taught for eighteen years. I owe a debt to Aunt Rebekah that I can never repay. She made me know that I could do what I never thought I could do."

Many children owed a similar debt to Rebekah Johnson. Her patience in teaching English to German-American children who spoke no English at home and often not in school, either (classes in Fredericksburg and the Hill Country's other German communities were often conducted only in German), became so legendary throughout the area that German families brought their children long miles to the Johnson home. Asked years later why he had done so, one man—from San Marcos, thirty miles away—said: "I had heard praises of Mrs. Johnson since the time when I was a child."

Her husband adored her. Their marriage was a "miss fit," says Ava, pronouncing that last word as two words to give it the emphasis she feels it needs for accuracy. "It was a miss fit, but she wanted to make the best of it because she loved him. And he loved her. Oh, he adored her. He worshipped the ground she walked on."

A miss fit it was, in the sense that their personalities were indeed as "completely opposite" as Rebekah wrote. "Mrs. Johnson was always cheerful, kind and considerate. . . . She was a gentle, gentle woman," Mrs. Gliddon wrote. "Quite the contrary was her husband, Mr. Sam." If nothing could ruffle her calm, so nothing could tame his temper. The Buntons burned without matches, and his fuse was terribly short. And often his anger was directed at his wife.

But it was a temper as quick to die out as to blaze up. As his wife wrote: "Highly organized, sensitive, and nervous, he was impatient of inefficiency and ineptitude and quick to voice his displeasure; equally quick, however, in making amends when some word of his caused pain to another." Once, recalls Louise Casparis, daughter of one of the poorest families in

Johnson City, who worked in the Johnson home, "Mr. Sam lost his temper at me—really got mad about something I had done wrong." But when she arrived at the house the next day, "there on the mantelpiece was a beautiful box of candy for me." He never said a word of apology to her, but she learned he had driven all the way to Fredericksburg to get it. Louise—and other women who worked (and, in some cases, lived) in the Johnson home— agree with neighbors and relatives that the attempts of some biographers to portray the Johnson home as one of unending and bitter conflict between husband and wife are incorrect. "That's not the home I saw," says Cynthia Crider. What most of them recall most vividly is the way Sam would kid Rebekah—about the house he had bought for her ("He used to grumble, kiddingly, about all that gingerbread and all"), about the fact that while she liked to boast of her Baines ancestry, she never mentioned her maternal— Huffman—line ("When she got stubborn over something, Sam would say, 'That's your German blood again. German blood! Look at your brother's name. Huffman! Probably was Hoffmann once—in Berlin!' And Rebekah would say, 'Sam, you know it's Holland Dutch.'"). They recall how "You could see that underneath the kidding he had so much respect for her, for her learning and—well, just for *her.*" And they recall how Sam and Rebekah would sit and talk—for hours. If he had been yelling at her one minute, the next he would be making amends in his own way—telling a funny story. "One minute he'd be shouting, and the next minute she'd be laughing at something he said. He could make her laugh and laugh and laugh." Sam loved to talk politics with Rebekah. She herself was to write that "In disposition, upbringing and background, these two were vastly dissimilar. However, in principles and motives, the real essentials of life, they were one." And that was true: they were both idealists. "The Baineses were always strong for high ideals," she would say, years later. "They talked about high ideals. We felt that you have to have a great purpose behind what you do, or no matter what you do, it won't amount to anything. Lyndon's father always felt the interest of the people was first." Says Louise Casparis: "It was something to see how glad she always was to see him when he came home. There was never any question in my mind that these were two people who . . ." Louise's voice fades away at this point, and she expresses what she saw of their feelings by making a gesture with her arms—an embracing motion.

And for a while, it didn't seem to matter that Rebekah couldn't help Sam as his brother's wife helped *him.*

For a couple of years out in Stonewall, the cotton crop was good, and Sam got good work out of his hired hands. "Men who worked for him used to joke that if they could have been anywhere else, they would rather have been," Ava says. "He was a driver, Uncle Sam was. He was a hard worker, and he wanted everyone else to work hard, too." And he did well in "real-estatin'." In at least one case, where he purchased a ranch for about $20,000 and quickly sold it to Emory Stribling for $32,375, he made a huge profit by Hill Country standards. He hired girls—Louise Casparis and Addie Stevenson and others—to come in and clean the house; and Louise's mother would take the Johnson wash home—lugging it on her back in a bedsheet—and when she returned it, Old Lady Spates would come in and iron it. He even hired a "chauffeur" to take Rebekah and the children for rides in the big Hudson he had purchased: the "chauffeur" was only Guy Arrington, a local teen-ager, but no one else in the Hill Country had one. Rebekah's health was still not good—she had to stay in bed a particularly long time after the birth of her fifth and last child, Lucia, in 1916, and the next year she had two "minor" operations from which she was slow recovering—but she had plenty of leisure to do what she enjoyed and was gifted at: the Literary Society at school, elocution lessons; her needlepoint was much admired. She "put on" plays at school, and, to raise money for local organizations, in her front yard, with the townspeople paying admission; her favorite was *Deacon Doves of Old Virginia*. Sam was always bringing home surprise presents for her, and one day in 1916 he arrived home to announce that Gordon Gore was leaving for Arizona because of ill health and had sold him two items which Sam was sure Rebekah would like: a new Victrola and his newspaper, the *Johnson City Record*, an eight-page weekly. That didn't work out too well—people in Johnson City were so short of cash that many couldn't afford subscriptions; Sam had to take cigars, cabbages, and, on one occasion, a goat, in payment; and Rebekah was unable to cope with the mechanical intricacies of the old hand press; after four months she asked Sam to sell the paper; for years thereafter, Sam would laughingly tell the new owner, Reverdy Gliddon, "I'll tell you, Gliddon, that was one time I got into something I didn't know anything about." But Rebekah's interest in writing had been reawakened. She became the Johnson City correspondent for the Austin and Fredericksburg newspapers, mailing in local news items once a week, and wrote poetry, none of which was ever published. Sam saved little; everything he made, he used to buy more: more ranches; the little auditorium (derisively called the Opera House) over the Johnson City bank where movies were occasionally shown; the town's only hotel. He almost seemed to be trying to achieve, on a much smaller scale but still the largest available to him, what the original Johnson brothers had tried to achieve: to build a little business empire in the Hill Country.

He did a lot of strutting. "You can tell a man by his boots and his hat and the horse he rides," and Sam Johnson's boots were hand-tooled in San Antonio, and his big pearl-gray Stetsons were the most expensive that could be purchased in Joseph's Emporium down the street from the Driskill Hotel in Austin, and his Hudson—his chauffeured Hudson—was the biggest and most expensive car in the whole Hill Country. He dressed differently from the other men in Johnson City—that was very important to him. "You never saw my father go out of the house in shirt sleeves," his daughter Rebekah recalls.

But people didn't take the strutting amiss then, for, as Stella Gliddon puts it, "Sam Johnson had a good heart." On the day she arrived in Johnson City, Stella recalls—on that terrible day when she felt she had come "to the end of the earth"—the nineteen-year-old girl was sitting on the porch of the hotel in the fading evening light, dreading the moment when the light would be gone and she would have to go up to her shabby little room, and thinking that she "could never live in a town like this" and would have to give up her new job and go back to Fredericksburg in the morning, when Sam Johnson came by, and seemed to see at once how she was feeling. "Sam knew my father real well, and he knew me, too," she recalls. "He came right up on the porch and said, 'Stay the night with Rebekah and me, and we'll find you a place tomorrow.' And I did—I slept in the room with the girls—and the next day, he found me a place. And I was real grateful for that. And that was the way Mr. Sam Johnson was. He was good for helping people. If you needed money and he had one dollar, he'd give you half of it—that's the kind of man Mr. Sam was."

People in the Pedernales Valley turned to "Mr. Sam"—that was what he was called, as a mark of respect; no one ever referred to him without the "Mister" then—when they were in trouble, and if they didn't turn to him, he sought them out. Once, he heard that an impoverished German who had done odd jobs for him, a man named Haunish, was in jail in Fredericksburg. Convinced that Haunish had been convicted only because, unable to speak English, he didn't know the law, Sam drove to Fredericksburg, hired a lawyer, went with him to see the judge, and got Haunish released. (A few days thereafter, there was a knock on the Johnsons' front door; it was Haunish, who had determined to repay Sam by doing any odd jobs that needed doing. He painted the house, laid sidewalks, put up more trellises; he wouldn't leave until he was convinced that he had done every bit of work for Sam that he could.)

And Sam was always friendly—laughing and joking; when he walked into the Fredericksburg bank, a teller recalls, he soon had all the tellers laughing; even the bank's stern old president, whom Sam would have come to see because he was constantly paying off old loans or making new ones to buy more property, would sit there laughing with Mr. Sam. And he loved to talk—to discuss politics or world affairs. If, strolling along the wooden sidewalk of Main Street in Johnson City, he bumped into a friend and began talking, he would sit down with him on the edge of the sidewalk and continue the conversation there. Robert Lee Green's daughter recalls that Green was "in hot water with the church-going people in town" because "he believed in the Darwinian theory, so they accused him of being an agnostic." But, she says, "Sam Johnson was broad-minded. He would come by and they'd sit there by our fire spitting tobacco juice into the fire and talking about Darwin and other things all night. My father loved to talk with Sam Johnson. There were a lot of people who loved Sam Johnson then." He was not only friendly but respected. When, in April, 1917, America entered the war, Blanco County farmers, who desperately needed their sons to help work the farms, were very much concerned that decisions of the draft board be just, and they picked Mr. Sam as one of its three members. And when, in November of that year, a special election was announced to fill a vacancy in the district's legislative seat, the seat Sam had been forced to give up ten years before, and Sam, able now to afford the job, announced for it, no one even bothered to run against him.

AFTER HIS ELECTION, Sam was very happy. As he swung open the front gate, coming home in the evening, he would be met by what his daughter Lucia was to call "a flying mass of children." (Lucia, the baby, always beat the others to him.) Swinging her up on his shoulders, Sam would put his arms around his other children and they would walk to the kitchen, where Rebekah would be cooking, and then demand of her and the children—in a ritual the children remembered fondly decades later: "I've brought a bag of sugar" (or a loaf of bread, or some candy) "and what will you give me for a bag of sugar?" "A million dollars," the children—or Rebekah—might shout. "A million dollars isn't enough!" Sam would reply, refusing to surrender the package until he had been paid in kisses.

Supper at the Johnsons' long, narrow table, at which the children sat on benches down the sides, was like supper in no other home in Johnson City. "The first time I ate there, I was a little shocked at how loud it was," recalls a friend of Lyndon's. "The laughing—and the arguments that went on, arguing and fussing. Back and forth with everyone joining in. Mostly about politics—that was the thing that dominated his [the father's] conversation. But about everything under the sun. Every time it calmed down, he would start it up again on some new topic. And then as the meal was ending and the kids were getting up, Lyndon's father, he sort of winked at me, and said: 'I argue with them to keep their wits sharp.' And that was a revelation to me. That he was doing this all on purpose."

After supper, with the light flickering in the painted glass kerosene lamp which hung from the high ceiling on long chains—the lamp swung gently in a breeze, the glass pendants which hung from it tinkling softly—Sam Johnson might open a blue-backed speller and "give out" words in an informal, but fiercely contested, spelling bee. Or he might stage debates: Stella Gliddon was present one night when the topic was: "What's better, sorghum or honey?" Or the whole family might go into the front parlor, a warm room with its two horsehide sofas and pink flowered wallpaper and the big portrait of Grandfather Baines in its gilt frame, and the two bookcases—small, but they contained far more books than any other home in Johnson City—on either side of the fireplace, and, while Mrs. Johnson sat doing needlework, listen to records (or "Edison discs," as they were called); "Red Wing" by Frederick

Allen Kerry, was a favorite, and so was a recording of William Jennings Bryan's speeches—largely because hearing Bryan's voice would move Sam to tell stories about him, and the children loved to hear Sam's stories.

"They loved their father," says Wilma Fawcett, who, as one of Lucia's closest friends, spent many evenings at the Johnsons'. "When I see that family in my mind, I see him laughing, laughing with the kids. It was harum-scarum—not like my house, where everything was decorum. But it was fun. We had such hilarious good times together. I see them as a warm, happy family."

On this point, the people who know—the people who were *there*, who were in the Johnson home with the Johnsons—agree. Ask a score of them, and a score agree: it *was* a warm, happy family.

Except, they also agree, for one of its members: the eldest son.

5

The Son

LYNDON JOHNSON got his name from his father's ambition. His mother wanted him named for a hero in a book; his father, who had wanted so desperately to be a lawyer, wanted him named for a lawyer. For three months after his birth on August 27, 1908, therefore, he was called only "the baby," until, as Rebekah recalled it, "one cold November morning" she refused to get up and cook breakfast until a name was agreed on.

Sam was close friends with three lawyers: Clarence Martin, Dayton Moses and W. C. Linden. "How would you like 'Clarence'?" he asked. "Not in the least," Rebekah replied. Then, she wrote, he asked,

> "What do you think of Dayton?" "That is much better but still not quite the name for this boy," I said. He thought of the third of his three lawyer friends and said, "Would you call him Linden?" There was a long pause and I said, "Yes, if I may spell it as I please, for L-y-n-d-o-n Johnson would be far more euphonious than L-i-n-d-e-n Johnson." "Spell it as you please," said Sam. "I am naming him for a good smart man. . . . We will call the baby for him and for your father." "All right," I responded, "he is named Lyndon Baines Johnson." I got up and made the biscuits.

Relatives felt that naming the baby for the other side of the family would have been more appropriate. Its father, even as an infant, had had the "dark eyes, black curls and white skin"—and the large ears and heavy eyebrows—that were "a Bunton inheritance," and it was soon apparent that that inheritance had been passed on undiluted to the son. The observation Aunt Kate had made bending over Lyndon's cradle on the day he was born was repeated that same day by the baby's grandmother, Eliza Bunton Johnson; she "professed to find marked characteristics of the Buntons (her family) in the boy," Rebekah wrote. And before the day was over (for Sam, friendly and exuberant as always, waited only to see that his wife was all right before leaping onto Fritz and riding around the valley, reporting that he had a son and inviting everyone over to see him, so that people began crowding into the house before Rebekah had recovered enough strength to sit up in bed), the observation was being repeated by neighbors and by relatives who weren't Buntons. Ava, Lyndon's cousin, remembers her mother returning from the Johnson home and announcing, "He has the Bunton eye."

His parents were thrilled with the baby. When he was six months old, his father brought a photographer to the farm to take his picture, and while he went to pick up the prints a few days later, Rebekah waited eagerly. Years later, she was to recall how her husband "raised his hand holding the package as he saw me waiting on the porch and began to run. I ran to meet him and we met in the middle of the Benner pasture to exclaim rapturously over the photograph of our boy." Rebekah suggested ordering ten prints, for members of the family; Sam ordered fifty, and sent them to all his friends in the Legislature as well. While Lyndon was still very young, his mother began telling him stories—from the Bible, history and mythology—every day after lunch and at bedtime. "She taught him the alphabet from blocks before he was two; all the Mother Goose rhymes and poems from Longfellow and Tennyson at three; and when he was four he could spell many words beginning with 'Grandpa' down to 'Dan,' a favorite horse, and 'cat,' and could read." When his father carried him to a picnic at Stonewall in the Spring of 1909, neighbors hurried over to Sam—people always hurried over to Sam then—as he entered the picnic grounds, and Lyndon kept reaching out his arms to each newcomer, and trying to scramble out of Sam's arms to reach them, and everybody exclaimed over the bright-eyed baby. According to his mother, one man said, "Sam, you've got a politician there. I've never seen such a friendly baby. He's a chip off the old block. I can just see him running for office twenty-odd years from now." And neighbors remembered how Sam beamed as his boy was praised.

But Lyndon was an unusually restless baby. His mother made light of this aspect of his character in the careful phrases of the *Family Album* she wrote after her son became famous. "Lyndon from his earliest days possessed a highly inquisitive mind," she wrote.

> He was never content long to play quietly in the yard. . . . He must set out to conquer that new unexplored world beyond the gate or up the lane. He . . . would be playing in the yard and if his mother turned away for a minute, Lyndon would toddle down the road to see "Grandpa."

But she didn't make light of it at the time. Because often, when she would get to "Grandpa's," Lyndon wouldn't be there.

Rebekah was frightened of the snakes and the other dangers that could befall a little child wandering alone. She would run first down to the

Pedernales—she was most afraid that Lyndon would fall into the river—and then up to the top of a hill to look for him, and then she would ask her father-in-law to saddle a horse and find him—and she would wait anxiously until he was found. Then she would scold the little boy, and Sam, when he got home, would scold him, or, as he got older, spank him, and they would sternly forbid him to leave the yard again.

But they couldn't stop him. "Every time his mama turned her back, seems like, Lyndon would run away," his cousin Ava says. And as he grew older, his trips grew longer.

Relatives who lived a half-mile—or more—away would suddenly notice that tiny figure toddling along with grim determination—a picture of Lyndon Johnson at eighteen months is striking not only for his huge ears but for the utter maturity of his expression; the face of the child in that picture is not the face of a child at all—across the open country or up one of the long dirt tracks that branch off to the various farms from the main "roads." They would take him back to Rebekah—and the very next day, or, if Rebekah wasn't careful, the same day, the tiny figure would appear again.

Soon, a further aspect of Lyndon's "running away" became apparent. Once, at threshing time, when twenty or thirty men were working with Sam in the Johnsons' cornfields, Lyndon, then about four years old, disappeared. After searching for him for a while alone because she didn't want to disturb the men (Rebekah had learned that time was precious on threshing days), his mother summoned help—by now, Lyndon was running away so frequently that his father had hung a big bell on the front porch so Rebekah could more easily call for help in finding him—and first his father came in from the fields and then, when he couldn't find Lyndon, the other men came in and fanned out over the hills in a full-scale search. It was a search that proved unnecessary, because Lyndon was near the front gate of the house all the time, hiding in a haystack. "Everyone was looking for him for a long time, and everyone was upset, and he must have been able to hear them," recalls Jessie Lambert, the maid who was living with the Johnsons at the time, "but even though he wasn't asleep, he didn't come out for the longest time. His mother was standing right by the haystack, crying, but he didn't come out." On another occasion, he disappeared for several hours; his father located him only because Lyndon's dog, "Bigham Young," was moving around in the cornfield in which the boy had been hiding and making the tassels wave. "Why did you run away?" Sam demanded. (Lyndon replied, according to his sister, who reported this story, that "he wasn't running away. He was going to the pasture to check on his horse.") If Sam didn't know the answer to the question he asked, his relatives and maids thought they did. "He [Lyndon] wanted attention," Jessie Lambert says. "He would run away, and run away, and the minute his mother would turn her back, he would run away again, and it was all to get attention."

At school, this aspect became more noticeable still.

Lyndon got to go to school by running away. Children weren't supposed to start until the age of five, and his mother didn't want Lyndon going to the local school anyway; the "Junction School," a mile down the road that ran along the river, was only a one-room box with a roof on it, and most of the thirty pupils, scattered through eight grades, were German, so that much of the teaching—by the only teacher, a strapping teen-ager almost six feet tall, Kate Deadrich—was done in that language. Rebekah and Sam were already intending to move into Johnson City the next year so that Lyndon could go to school there. But Lyndon, at four, began running away to the Junction School every day, showing up at recess to play with the children; and, short of tying him up, which they were unwilling to do, his parents were simply unable to stop him. "He'd run off to school and they would bring him back, and he'd run off again," his Aunt Jessie Hatcher recalled. His mother was particularly frightened because the route between the farm and the school was along the river. Giving in, she asked "Miss Kate" to let him start a year early, and, the teacher recalls, "I told her one more wouldn't make any difference." Thereafter, Lyndon as President would recall, "My mother used to lead me from our house to the schoolhouse. . . . With a baby in her arms, she would lead me down here, afraid I would get in the river and drown. She would lead me down and turn me over to the teacher at the side door." After a few months, Sam's brother Tom decided that his seven-year-old daughter, Ava, was old enough to ride a donkey to school, and since her route led past Sam's place, she would pick Lyndon up and take him along with her.

Although he could read better than most of the other children at the school, Lyndon refused to read at all—unless Miss Kate held him on her lap in front of the class. Most of the children were a little awed by their tall teacher, but Lyndon teased her and showered her with affection. "Lyndon used to come up to me and look so shy and cute and then he'd say, 'Miss Kate, I don't *like* you one bit!' I would be so shocked. Then he would laugh and say, 'I just *love* you!' " His mother dressed him in red Buster Brown suits or white sailor suits or in a cowboy outfit, complete to a Stetson hat, and Lyndon not only didn't object to being dressed differently from the other boys, who wore farm clothes—he insisted on it. "He wanted to stand out," Ava explains. When Miss Kate excused one of her students to use the privy out back, the student had to write his name on one of the two blackboards that flanked the back door. The other students wrote their names small; whenever Lyndon left the room, he would reach up as high as he could and scrawl his name in capital letters so huge that they took up not one but both blackboards. His schoolmates can remember today—seventy years later—that huge LYNDON B. on the left blackboard and JOHNSON on the right.

Relatives as well as schoolmates recognized this desire to get attention —to stand out. Once, he bought a little china clown as a Christmas present

for an aunt, but because he didn't want his gift to be just one of many under
the Christmas tree, he gave it to her weeks in advance, informing her
loudly: "It cost me a dime and it's worth every penny." Trying to explain
his behavior, Ava says: "He wanted attention. He wanted to *be* somebody."

HE WANTED MORE.

His cousin Ava would ride by the Johnson farmhouse on her donkey,
Molly, to take him to school. Not only did Molly belong to her, but Ava, at
seven, was three years older than Lyndon. Nevertheless, after just a few
days, Lyndon began demanding that he ride in front and hold the reins—
and when Ava imitates Lyndon demanding, her voice grows harsh and
insistent.

" 'Ah wanta ride in front!'

" 'No, ah'm older, Lyndon, and it's mah donkey.'

" 'No, ah'm bigger! Ah wanta ride in front! Ah wanta ride in front!' And
in the front he got."

A few weeks later, Lyndon was given his own donkey, and on that
donkey there was never any question who would ride in front, not even when
boys older than Lyndon were riding with him. "Well," recalls his Aunt
Jessie Hatcher, "there'd be four or five boys in the neighborhood, and they
all came. They'd all ride that donkey. All got on the donkey, but Lyndon
was in the forefront, he was the head. And he had the quirt to make the
donkey go."

Furthermore, Mrs. Hatcher says, even when the boys were participating
in other activities, Lyndon was still in the forefront. "Whatever they were
doing, Lyndon was the head. . . . He was always the lead horse. Made no
difference what come nor what went, he was the head of the ring."

He had to be the head—and he had to make sure everyone knew it.
The adjective most frequently used to describe him in the recollections of
friends and relatives is "bossy"—and their descriptions of his relationships
with other children make that adjective seem too pale. Ava, who even as a
girl was motherly, and who loved her little cousin (Lyndon called her Sister), nonetheless recalls how Lyndon liked meringue pie, and how another
little boy at the Junction School, Hugo Klein, said he had a piece in his
lunchbox, and she recalls how, during recess before lunch, while Hugo was
playing outside, Lyndon ate Hugo's pie, and calmly walked out to play "with
pie all over his face." And when Hugo started crying, and Ava asked Lyndon,
"What have you been doing?" Lyndon replied calmly, "Ah was just hungry,
Sister. And ah got me some pie."

In Johnson City, where the Johnsons moved in September, 1913, when
Lyndon was five, there were more children—and Lyndon's behavior grew
more striking.

He didn't want to play with children his own age. Boys much older were in school with him, and even in his grade, because some boys had missed whole years of school helping on their families' farms, and some had been very late starting. Ben Crider, whose father had said, "I ain't gonna have no educated sonofabitch in my family," had finally defied him and started the first grade at the age of fourteen. Although Ben was six years older than Lyndon and mature for his age—a big, gruff, friendly ranch boy —Lyndon small, scrawny, awkward, soon became his friend. The Crider and Johnson families had long been friends, Ben explains, "ever since Indian time," and "Lyndon took a liking to me. One thing about Lyndon—he wouldn't run with anyone his own age. He wanted to run with older people, usually about five to ten years older." And on the whole, it wasn't a case of a little boy tagging along after older boys. It was almost a case of him leading them.

"He was a very brilliant young man," Ben Crider says. "The boys his age just wasn't his class mentally." And, some of the older boys felt, neither were they. They let Lyndon play poker with them, and—his father had taught him how to play—he more than held his own. The older boys saw that he talked—and thought—faster than they did. Ben and the others stood guiltily tongue-tied when the owner of the land on which they had earlier that day illegally shot and killed a baby deer—one whose antlers had not yet grown any "points"—suddenly appeared and asked them if they had shot any deer, but Lyndon said they sure had—a big "five-pointer"— and made up an elaborate story which cooled the owner's suspicions.

It was, in fact, more a case of his *insisting* on leading them. When the older boys were discussing what they wanted to do that day, Lyndon always had a suggestion, and, surprisingly often, he persuaded them to go along with it. "Lyndon Johnson was a natural born leader," Ben Crider would say. ". . . And if he couldn't lead, he didn't care much about playing, it seemed like." "Lyndon was a good boy, but he was overpowering if he didn't get his own way," says another of the older boys, Bob Edwards. "He had a baseball, and the rest of us didn't have one. We were all very poor. None of us had a ball but him. Well, Lyndon wanted to pitch. He wasn't worth a darn as a pitcher, but if we didn't let him pitch, he'd take his ball and go home. So, yeah, we'd let him pitch."

HE DIDN'T HANG AROUND only with boys. As he grew older—nine or ten— he started to give shoeshines in Cecil Maddox's barbershop across from the new courthouse, not only, his friends believe, to earn money, but because the barbershop was the place where men gathered. "Lyndon always had to be in on everything," Emmette Redford says. "Every time someone came to town—a drummer, a politician running for something, whatever— Lyndon was there quicker than anyone could be, and invariably he was in the front row, right in front of the fellow. And, of course, the barbershop was the center of gossip and talk." The men delighted in asking Lyndon questions, because, as Stella Gliddon put it, they liked the way that "He just shot the answers right back at them." And it wasn't only boys that he tried to lead. By the time he was ten or eleven, his father, embarrassed to have a son doing such work, had made him stop giving shines, but he still spent a lot of time in the barbershop. Only one newspaper was delivered to Johnson City each day—a single copy of a daily newspaper, two or three days old, that arrived early every afternoon with the mail from Marble Falls. Lyndon always tried to be the first person in town to read that paper, so that he would know the news first, Joe Crofts recalls. "Lyndon would make a bee line from school down there to the barbershop, and he'd get up there in the [barber] chair and read that paper from cover to cover." And sitting up there in that chair, he would not only tell the customers or hangers-on in the barbershop what the news was, but would pontificate on it as well, a twelve-year-old holding court on Courthouse Square. And if one of the men disagreed with him, Lyndon would not hesitate to argue, arguing with somewhat more deference than he showed Emmette Redford, but with no less perseverance, refusing to stop arguing, attempting to win the man to his view. He wanted men as well as boys to defer to his opinions.

Trying to describe the fierce, burning ambitions that drove his father, his mother used the word "competition." Trying to describe the young Lyndon Johnson, who was starting to shoot up now into a tall, very skinny, gangling boy with long, awkwardly dangling arms, white, pale skin, black hair and piercing eyes—and who looked so much like his father that many Johnson City residents, in describing him, still say simply, "He looked like Sam"—the same word is often repeated. "Everything was competition with Lyndon," his cousin Ava says. "He had to win."

He was happiest, his relatives say—the only time he was happy, they say—when he was, in the Hill Country phrase, "politicking" with his father.

Politics was an important part of the table talk in Sam Johnson's house —just as it had been in *his* father's house. For Sam still believed in what he had first believed. At least one copy of a weekly Populist newspaper, the *Pathfinder*, was sent to Blanco County, to Sam Johnson's house. "Uncle Sam got ideas from that," Ava recalls. "I remember one was government ownership of railroads. Another was the Socialist Party. Eugene Debs. He said that it was going to be one of the leading parties in the United States and we'd better learn what it was."

Sam's children and nieces and nephews didn't have to agree with his views, his niece Ava recalls, "but they had to think. Oh my, yes. At dinner, whenever I was over there, he would throw out questions. The government ownership of railroads—we didn't have any railroads, but we had to know. He said, 'What do you think of it?' And the League of Nations—Uncle Sam believed that the League of Nations was going to end war, and we had to know about it." And after dinner, Sam would pull out his blue-backed speller and there would be spell-downs, with Lyndon and the other children lined up in front of the fireplace until they missed a word, and "We'd have arithmetic contests to see who was the fastest in mathematics." And, of course, there were Sam's after-dinner "debates." Says Stella Gliddon: "I have been in that Johnson home when he lined those kids up in front of the fireplace—even Lucia, who was just barely big enough to stand up, she could hardly talk, she was just a baby." Trying to hide his smile, Sam would say gruffly: " 'Now, we're gonna have us a debate here. Now we're gonna get down to *business.*' "

"He was very much a father," Ava says. "He wanted us to be the best. Not only his kids, but I and my sister and brother, too, because we were his brother's kids, and we were Johnsons. He wasn't satisfied with having a bunch of Johnson kids just growing up."

Sam's eldest son was very quick at firing back answers, even if he didn't know them. "Where does snow come from?" Sam asked once. "What's it made up out of?" "It's made out of frozen ice," Lyndon piped up. Sam laughed: "Well, that's sort of right. That's sort of right."

And in politics, quite often, he did know the answer.

Emmette Redford says that Lyndon's intense interest in politics was in part due to the lack of any laboratory equipment, or so much as a single science course, in the Johnson City school. "There was no way anyone could have cultivated an interest in science even if he had wanted to, but we had first-rate history and civics teachers," he says. And, Redford says, it was in part due to the town's lack of other activities. "There were no movie houses then, no nothing. There wasn't anything in the community except the three churches and the courthouse, and Lyndon was more interested in what happened in the courthouse." But there was something in Lyndon Johnson when it came to politics that went deeper than either of these explanations. At the age of six or seven, friends recall, he would drop out of a game he had been playing with them in Courthouse Square if he heard a group of men discussing politics nearby, and would walk over and stand on the fringes of the group, listening intently. After his father re-entered politics in 1917, when Lyndon was nine, politicians, state and local, began dropping by the Johnson home for chats and strategy discussions. Usually, these were held on the porch. Behind that porch was a bedroom, with a window opening onto the porch. Lyndon would hide in the bedroom, sitting on the floor, craning upward so that his ear was almost against the window, listening. In 1918, the Governor, William P. Hobby, came to Johnson City for a Fourth of July speechmaking, and had dinner at the Johnsons'. So many local politicians were invited that the children were relegated to the kitchen. But Lyndon hid under the dining room table all through the meal to listen to the talk.

It was probably in 1918 that Sam Johnson first took Lyndon, then ten years old, to a legislative session in Austin, and thereafter he took him frequently. Doris Kearns relates Johnson telling her (and this Johnson recollection is corroborated by other sources):

> I loved going with my father to the legislature. I would sit in the gallery for hours watching all the activity on the floor and then would wander around the halls trying to figure out what was going on. The only thing I loved more was going with him on the trail during his campaigns for re-election. We drove in the Model T Ford from farm to farm, up and down the valley, stopping at every door. My father would do most of the talking. He would bring the neighbors up to date on local gossip, talk about the crops and about the bills he'd introduced in the legislature, and always he'd bring along an enormous crust of homemade bread and a large jar of homemade jam. When we got tired or hungry, we'd stop by the side of the road. He sliced the bread, smeared it with jam, and split the slices with me. I'd never seen him happier. Families all along the way opened up their homes to us. If it was hot outside, we were invited in for big servings of homemade ice cream. If it was cold, we were given hot tea. Christ, sometimes I wished it could go on forever.

Sam's neighbor August Benner was running against him (largely, some people thought, because he resented Sam cutting through his pasture as a shortcut to the road) and Sam felt that although Benner was regarded as ill-tempered and slow-witted, he would be a formidable opponent because he was German, and the German voters of Gillespie County were by far the largest bloc vote in the district. Learning that about seventy related German families in a valley of one of the Pedernales' tributary creeks were all planning to vote for Benner, Sam asked a friend to go to the valley, look up the head of the German clan and "Tell him that the sitting judge ain't in good health and that lots of us are thinking that he [the head of the clan] will be succeeding the judge before too long." Returning from his errand, the friend reported that he had found the potential judge sitting on a bucket milking his cow: "His wife was in the loft throwing hay down for the cattle. I told him what you said, Sam, and he came up off that bucket like it was hot. And she nearly fell out of the loft."

Whether or not Lyndon actually heard these conversations between Sam and his friend—Lyndon says he did; the quotes are from him—he must have heard many concerning the type of political promises and arrangements that Sam made. He also remembered his father giving him many little pieces of political advice; one was, "If you can't come into a room and tell right away who is for you and who is against you, you have no business in politics." "And if Lyndon learned politics from his father, he learned it from someone who really knew what he was talking about," a friend says. "He learned it from a man who was, in his rough way, a master of politics." In politics, moreover, Sam was a winner. He never lost an election, running for the Legislature six times and winning every time. In the election against Benner, Sam won handily. Benner claimed that fraud had been involved, but his charges were not taken seriously; he did not even show up at the legislative hearing scheduled in Austin to discuss them. And to celebrate, Sam took his son the sixty miles to San Antonio, the largest city Lyndon had ever been in, where they ate tamales at the stands on the streets near the Alamo, which now housed paintings of Travis and Bowie and Crockett and the other heroes of the great battle, and also photographs of the legislators who had saved the Mission from destruction—and one of the pictures Lyndon saw there was of his father.

Sitting in the swing on the big, screened back porch of the Johnson home, Sam and Lyndon Johnson would have long conversations now. Sometimes, children who were playing in the back yard would call to Lyndon to come and join them, but when he was talking with his father, he never would. "I remember them sitting on that swing, talking away," Truman Fawcett says. "We would be playing out back, and they'd be out there talking. They looked like they were having friendly conversations. Those were the only times that I ever saw Lyndon quiet and relaxed."

As a child, he had imitated his father. Of all the outfits in which his mother dressed him, he was fondest of the one that made him look like his father; his favorite item of apparel was a scaled-down version of his father's big Stetson hat. Says Mrs. Hatcher:

> He was right by the side of his daddy wherever he went. When he was little, two years old, he used to go with his daddy down to get a shave. They had to shave him, too. They put him up in that stand, and they put stuff all over his face and took the back of the razor, you know, and shaved it off. Washed his face, set him down, off he went with his daddy.

His father would sometimes bring back from Austin a printed compendium of bills, either the *Congressional Record* or the official *Journal* of the Texas House of Representatives. Once he gave Lyndon a copy; for weeks, the boy carried it everywhere with him, holding it in as conspicuous a fashion as possible.

As Lyndon grew to be eleven or twelve, the imitation became quite noticeable. Sam Johnson, always friendly, always stopping to talk with everyone he met, was very physical in conversation. The man he was talking to would feel Sam's arm around his shoulder, or Sam's hand on his arm or his lapel, and as they talked, Sam's face would bend closer and closer to his own in an onslaught of friendliness. In the words of Wright Patman, who shared a two-man desk in the Texas House Chamber with the Gentleman from Blanco County, "He would get right up to you, nose to nose, and take a firm hold." Now, back in the Legislature, Sam brought his son to Austin, bringing him into the Chamber so frequently that some legislators thought he was one of the page boys. By this time, Lyndon, six feet tall, looked very much like his father. "He was a gangling boy, very skinny," Patman recalls —and he had the same huge ears, the same big nose, the same pale skin, and the same dark eyes. When the mannerisms were added to the picture, the resemblance became remarkable. "They looked alike, they walked the same, had the same nervous mannerisms, and Lyndon clutched you like his daddy did when he talked to you," Patman says. "He was so much like his father that it was humorous to watch."

But there was a difference between father and son.

Patman, who was friends with both—he served with Sam in the Texas House and with Lyndon, for ten years, in the nation's—saw the difference in political terms. "Sam's political ambitions were limited," he says. "He didn't have any aspirations to run for Congress. He wanted only local prestige and power, and the Texas House was fine for him as his limit, because it was close to home and made him feel important." But Patman saw Sam and Lyndon only in Austin and Washington. Those who saw father and son in their home town saw the difference in human terms.

By these people, the difference is often described in terms of that conversational technique that father and son shared. Both grabbed arms and lapels, shoved faces close, but as Truman Fawcett says, in Sam Johnson's case, "there was a friendliness underneath it. Sam wouldn't try to come over you." That is not what these people say was "underneath it" in Lyndon's case. About the father, Stella Gliddon says, "His eyes were keen, but it seemed like he always had a smile—he had a happy face." About the father, Emmette Redford says, "He was always friendly—laughing and joking." About the son, Emmette Redford says: "If there was an argument, he *had to* win. He *had to*. He was an argumentative kid—if he'd differ with you, he'd hover right up against you, breathing right in your face, arguing your point with all the earnestness. . . . I got disgusted with him. Sometimes, I'd try to just walk away, but . . . he just wouldn't stop until you gave in."

Other Johnson City residents—relatives, friends and neighbors of the Johnsons—make the same distinction as Redford: Sam, they say, liked to argue; Sam's son liked to win arguments—*had to* win arguments. Sam wanted to discuss; Lyndon wanted to dominate.

Patman is only partially right about their ambition. Sam's may not have been as big as Lyndon's, but that may have been a function only of education: a function only of the fact that Sam hardly went to school, and Lyndon did, and that even when Lyndon was a boy, the world, through the radio particularly, was impinging more on the consciousness of the Hill

Country than it had when his father was a boy; a function only of the fact that Lyndon's horizons were broader. And Sam's ambition was, in terms of the Hill Country, big enough—huge, in fact. The difference between Sam and Lyndon lay not so much in what they wanted, but in the intensity with which they wanted it.

An example that many who knew him give to illustrate what they are talking about is Lyndon and the ear-popping.

Money—cash money—was very important to Lyndon even at the age of ten and eleven, even, in fact, when he was several years younger than that.

Cash was short for almost everyone in Johnson City, and especially so for children, and any boy or girl who had a few nickels was looked up to by the other children. But Lyndon was no shorter on nickels than his playmates; as a matter of fact, he had more than most of them, for Sam was always generous with his children. "He had a lot more [money] than most of us did," Milton Barnwell says.

But he wanted still more.

Boys in Johnson City would "pop ears" then. Popping ears meant grabbing an earlobe and yanking it—hard. Generally this was done as a trick, one boy coming up behind another and taking him by surprise, for it hurt—"it hurt," says Barnwell, "a lot."

> But Lyndon had very big ears [Barnwell says]. Harold Withers had more money than the other kids because his dad had a store. He used to say to Lyndon, "I'll give you five cents to pop your ears five times." Lyndon would always say yes. Harold would start. Tears would run down his [Lyndon's] face—"Ooooh, Harold, not so hard, Harold!"
>
> "Okay, then, give me my five cents back."
>
> And every time, Lyndon would say, "Go ahead," and he'd be all scrooged down crying, and every time Harold popped him, he'd go Ow. But he always let Harold do it. And after Harold did it five times, if he asked Lyndon if he would let him do it five more times for another five cents, Lyndon would say yes.

Says another one of the boys who would stand watching, Payne Rountree: "You would give him a nickel, and he'd stand there, and tears would come into his eyes, and he'd still stand there.

"Because he wanted that nickel."

TRYING TO EXPLAIN, Stella Gliddon says: "Let me tell you what I think was in Lyndon Johnson. First, his father was politically minded—you have to say that first. But with Lyndon, there was an incentive that was born in him to advance and keep advancing. Oh, Sam had that. More than anyone else around here. Sam had that incentive, he had it fierce. But he didn't have it anywhere near like Lyndon did."

Born in him. To the people of the Hill Country, those are the crucial words. "Don't you understand?" asks Lyndon's cousin Ava. "He was a *Bunton!*"

6

"The Best Man
I Ever Knew"

BUT HIS FATHER was also a Johnson.

In the Legislature—where he was greeted with "warm applause" by those Representatives who remembered him when, in 1918, after a nine-year absence, he rose to be sworn in—he hadn't changed. He was still, at the age of forty-one, tall and skinny, and he still clomped into the House Chamber in his hand-tooled boots, and he still wore his pants tucked into the boots, and a big Stetson hat, and sometimes a gun, a long-barreled old-style Colt six-shooter (although he may have been the only legislator who still did, and he looked more than a little foolish doing so; Edward Joseph would regularly take it away from him on Saturday nights when Sam was roaring drunk, afraid he'd hurt somebody with it). He still played practical jokes in the House Chamber, and was a leading customer of the bars and whorehouses along Congress Avenue, and he was still loud and boastful when he was sober ("Sam was the cowboy type, a little on the rough side . . . he shouted slogans when he talked," Wright Patman says) and very loud and boastful when he was drunk, and sober or drunk, he loved to talk about how his father had driven cattle to Kansas and about the days of the old frontier, which made him seem very foolish in the eyes of some of the legislators.

And he was still "straight as a shingle."

A small band of legislators didn't live at the Driskill, where the bills were routinely picked up by lobbyists, but at small boardinghouses below the Capitol; the members of this band didn't accept free lodging from the lobbyists, and they didn't accept the "Three B's" ("beefsteak, bourbon and blondes") which the lobbyists provided to other legislators—several lobbyists maintained charge accounts at Austin whorehouses for their legislator friends. And they didn't accept anything else, either. Says one of them,

W. D. McFarlane: "The special-interest crowd controlled the Legislature. We people down under formed the opinion that the legislators—most of them were lawyers—were taking fees from the special interests. We were taking the people's fees." The ranks of this band were thin—very thin— and were constantly growing thinner. McFarlane remembers to this day how one legislator, a friend who often ate dinner with him and Wright Patman— the three of them joking, a little bitterly, about the huge steaks that were being consumed at the Driskill while they ate the hash or chili that was all they could afford on their five-dollar per diem (two dollars after sixty days) —suddenly grew a little reticent during their conversations, and then stopped eating with them altogether, and then cast some votes that shocked them, and then, as soon as the session ended, "moved to Houston—he had hired out to them." But when Sam Johnson arrived, the members of the little band knew they had a new recruit. The slogans he shouted were the old Populist slogans. The People's Party had been effectively dead for twenty years—but Sam Johnson still believed in the party's slogans. He shared with the other members of this little band an almost mystical belief in "The People," and he believed that it was the duty of government to help them, particularly when they were, as he put it in a speech once (Sam Johnson may have been uneducated, but he had a gift for a phrase), "caught in the tentacles of circumstance." Shortly after he arrived, there was a vote that showed McFarlane that, as he put it, "Sam wasn't part of the special-interest majority." Sulphur had been discovered in Texas—in such abundance that three Texas counties were already producing eighty percent of all the sulphur produced in the world. Companies that mined it were determined to keep as much of the profits as possible for themselves, and their chief lobbyist, Roy Miller, once the legendary "Boy Mayor of Corpus Christi," who wore a pearl-gray Borsalino instead of the customary Stetson, kept his silver hair long and waved, and possessed the mien as well as the mane of a Southern Senator, dispensed the "Three B's" with the most liberal hand in Austin. Miller's strategy was to accept a state tax on sulphur production, but at a token rate. Only a handful of legislators fought—in vain—for a higher tax, and Sam Johnson was one of them. This in itself wasn't conclusive evidence to McFarlane and others who had seen men start out like Sam only to be gradually lured by the "interests," but they noticed something about Sam that convinced them he never would. While Sam would drink with Roy Miller and the other lobbyists who held court every afternoon at the huge Driskill bar, he would insist on "buying back"—for every drink Miller bought him, they recall, Sam insisted on buying Miller one in return.

He wasn't afraid to stand alone in a hostile House, as he had ten years before, against Joe Bailey. In 1918, anti-German hysteria was sweeping Texas. Germans who showed insufficient enthusiasm in purchasing Liberty Bonds were publicly horsewhipped; bands of armed men broke into the homes of German families who were rumored to have pictures of the Kaiser on the walls; a State Council of Defense, appointed by the Governor, recommended that German (and all other foreign languages) be barred from the state forever. Hardly had Sam Johnson arrived in Austin in February, 1918, when debate began on House Bill 15, which would make all criticism, even a remark made in casual conversation, of America's entry into the war, of America's continuation in the war, of America's government in general, of America's Army, Navy or Marine Corps, of their uniforms, or of the American flag, a criminal offense punishable by terms of two to twenty-five years—and would give any citizen in Texas the power of arrest under the statute. With fist-waving crowds shouting in the House galleries above, legislators raged at the Kaiser and at Germans in Texas whom they called his "spies" (one legislator declared that the American flag had been hauled down in Fredericksburg Square and the German double eagle raised in its place) in an atmosphere that an observer called a "maelstrom of fanatical propaganda." But Sam Johnson, standing tall, skinny and big-eared on the floor of the House, made a speech—remembered with admiration fifty years later by fellow members—urging defeat of Bill 15; although its text has been lost, the theme of the speech was that patriotism should be tempered with common sense and justice, and its peroration centered on the fact that the first American boy to die on the bloody battlefields of France was of German descent. Sam's speech didn't hurt him politically—it could only increase his popularity among the Germans of Gillespie County, and in the other three counties of his district he was so popular that nothing could hurt him—but he went beyond what was politically necessary for him by privately buttonholing members of the committee considering the bill to urge its defeat—and, almost singlehandedly, he succeeded in persuading the committee to delete from it the section that would have given any citizen the power of arrest. Germans who followed his efforts on the scene felt themselves in his debt; the editor of Austin's German-language newspaper, *Das Wochenblatt*, later wrote: "At a time when hate propaganda . . . was at its worst . . . he showed courage and fidelity to the trust which [we] put in him. [He] proved himself a true friend in those dark days when so many who had owed their success in public life to their German fellow citizens proved to be their worst enemies."

Sometimes he seemed almost to relish standing alone. He fought— against the powerful Texas Medical Association—for the right of optometrists to practice in Texas, and his son would later say that the fact that optometrists had "little money and influence" and were "opposed by a powerful enemy at the time my father took up their cause was—for me— a sufficient explanation of why he chose to stand beside them. Those were the kinds of causes Sam Ealy Johnson enjoyed." One night at dinner, the small band of legislators was discussing whether or not it was silly for them to fight battles that they couldn't possibly win; Johnson said it wasn't. "It's high time a man stood up for what he believes in," he said. And these legislators saw that he was willing to do so. "He was not an educated man, anything like that," one of them was to recall, but "he was a good man, and he was highly respected by his people and the members of the Legislature. When he said something, it was that way—no mealy-mouth business, no ifs, ands or buts."

The larger causes for which Sam fought in the Legislature were lost before the fight began; the efforts to force producers of sulphur, oil and natural gas to pay through taxes enough to ameliorate the living conditions of the people of the state from whose earth they were mining such immense wealth never even came close to realization. Efforts to regulate banks, railroads—any of what the little band called "big interests" —never even got out of committee. Their speeches and slogans were hopeless exercises, irrelevancies when the reality of legislative action was considered. In more narrow fights, however, fights which did not affect the interests, Sam Johnson was, in a quiet, behind-the-scenes way, still as effective as he had been during his earlier career.

Being in the Legislature was no longer considered a joke, for the people of the Hill Country were coming to understand how much they needed government—and how much they needed a Representative who could put its power on their side. The symbol of their need was a road, the highway linking the Hill Country to Austin that alone could make feasible the importation of commodities at prices they could afford and allow them to get their produce to market fast enough and in good enough condition to make a profit on its sale. And Sam Johnson got them their road.

Work on the highway had been begun in 1916, but had since been abandoned. Johnson was the prime mover in getting it resumed. CONCERTED EFFORT GETS FEDERAL AID RESTORED, the *Blanco County Record* headlined. HON. S. E. JOHNSON RENDERS VALUABLE ASSISTANCE. By the time he left the Legislature, he had a reputation as one of its "leading good-roads men"— and State Highway 20 had been opened all the way from Austin to Fredericksburg.

But Sam believed government should do more than build roads. His ideals were as shiny as his boots. McFarlane vividly remembers him saying at dinner one night, his face very earnest: "We've got to look after these people—that's what we're here for." He was talking about "lower-middle-class people," McFarlane says, about "poor people"—about all people who were caught within "circumstance's tentacles." When drought hit West Texas hard in 1919 and 1920 and the farmers scattered across its vast, naked plains pleaded for help, Sam was a leading figure—perhaps *the* leading figure—in persuading the Legislature to take the step, unprecedented for Texas, of providing it. Recalling how he obtained a $2 million legislative appropriation for seed and feed, the seed "to be planted by those who are too poor and unable to obtain seed," the feed "for the work stock of such people," the *Blanco Record Courier* said years later:

Because of his influence and insistence, Texas was one of the first states to recognize the public emergency which arises from a long series of private disasters—the foundation stone upon which has been built the modern conception of government as exemplified in the administration of President Roosevelt.

Impressive as was the West Texas relief bill to his fellow legislators, who knew how difficult it was to win any public-assistance concessions from the business-dominated, philosophically reactionary Legislature, the small, less noticeable measures Johnson pushed through for his own district—for example, the state aid for schools that allowed the free term to be extended to seven months—were more impressive still. Passage of his bill to force the big cattle-buying houses to pay small ranchers for their stock promptly, his colleagues told reporters, "was a great victory for Rep. Johnson." Businessmen, bankers—"there were plenty of legislators constantly looking after *their* interests," McFarlane says. "The farming people and the working people—if somebody didn't speak up and take their point and represent them, unless somebody really had their interests at heart, spoke up and took care of their interests, they had no one to look after their interests. And Sam Johnson did speak up on their behalf. I remember Sam Johnson as a man who truly wanted to help the people who he felt needed help." McFarlane was not the only member of the small band of legislators who felt that way about the Gentleman from Blanco County. Fifty years later, Wright Patman, now a powerful United States Congressman who had met and dealt with the nation's most renowned public figures, would be talking to an interviewer about President Lyndon Johnson, when suddenly he changed the subject slightly.

"Of course," Wright Patman said, "his father, Sam E. Johnson, was the best man I ever knew."

"LOOKING AFTER" PEOPLE was something Sam Johnson did even on his own time.

"He had a kind of idea of government as something that could do things personally for people," Emmette Redford says, and since there was no one else to provide personal service in the Hill Country, he provided it himself, obtaining pensions for elderly constituents who had once been Texas Rangers or Army scouts, or for the widows of soldiers who had served in the Spanish-American War but who didn't know how to apply for pensions, driving to San Antonio or Austin or even Houston to help people (some of whom couldn't even read) find the relevant records or to steer them through the bureaucratic mazes of state or federal agencies. He obtained pensions even for constituents who didn't know they were entitled to them: "He was *always* the person we went to, whenever assistance was needed," Stella Gliddon says.

"If there was some legislation to be passed, it was always to Mr. Sam that people went, and he was always there to do it."

For the work he did in the Legislature, he was paid five dollars—or two dollars—per day. For this "personal service" work he got nothing, not even expenses. And this work cost him not only money but time—because of the distances involved and the condition of the roads, immense amounts of time. He regarded such work, however, as part of being a legislator, and he is remembered in the Hill Country as being, in the words of J. R. Buckner, editor of the *San Marcos Record*, "on the job all the time."

In 1923, Sam Johnson sponsored—and saw passage of—what he regarded as his most notable piece of legislation.

Campaigning for re-election in 1922, Governor Pat M. Neff, in a speech at Johnson City, called for legislation to protect farmers and ranchers in poorer sections of Texas who, anxious to participate in the flood of oil wealth beginning to be pumped out of other areas of the state, were easy victims of "high-pressure salesmen" peddling phony oil stocks. Johnson knew, as he said later, that his own constituents "had been fleeced out of thousands of dollars by the rankest kind of promotion swindles," but he had not known how widespread the swindles were. "The Governor's speech . . . gave me an insight and a grasp of the conditions that had never come into my mind before." Drafting regulations for the advertising and sale of oil stock, he embodied them in legislation creating a Securities Division of the State Railroad Commission to enforce them. Introducing this legislation in January, 1923, he said, "I want to leave this bill on the statute books." "No measure offered before the Legislature has created more comment than the 'Blue Sky' Bill* of Sam E. Johnson," reported the *San Antonio Express*, and the need for the measure was quickly demonstrated by letters he received from "literally hundreds of victims of these nefarious oil sharks"—and by the reaction of the sharks themselves. Money—"The word around the Driskill was that it was quite a sum," McFarlane says—was offered to him; his daughter Rebekah says, "A man offered him a lot of money to let it die—he wouldn't have to do anything; just let it sit in committee." But Sam refused the bribes, and when the bill passed—with his name on it; it would be known as the "Johnson Blue Sky Law"—he was very proud. Wilma Fawcett, his daughter Josefa's best friend, remembers that "Whenever we wanted permission from him to do something, Josefa would say, 'Let's get him talking about the Blue Sky Law; then he'll be in a good mood and he'll say 'all right.' "

Sam Johnson loved being a legislator. The job satisfied his idealism, his need for recognition and gratitude, and as Willard Deason, who came to

---

* State securities-regulating measures were known as "Blue Sky" laws because one legislator said that promoters were unloading everything but the blue sky on gullible investors.

know him very well, says: "He was ambitious to stand in the forefront, not for money, no, but to be in the forefront. He would rather serve in the Texas Legislature than have the largest ranch in Blanco County." And he was very good at legislating. His son Lyndon had wished "it could go on forever," and for a while it seemed it could.

BUT IT WAS NOT in the Legislature that Sam Johnson had to earn his living. He had to earn his living in the Hill Country.

"Real-estatin' " sounded impressive, especially as reported by Reverdy Gliddon's friendly *Blanco County Record* ("Hon. S. E. Johnson . . . recently closed up several big land deals, particulars of which will be given later"), but it wasn't profitable, not when the value of real estate kept going down. And in the Hill Country, while land values sometimes rose—sometimes rose for three or four or even five years in a row, when rain was plentiful and cotton crops good and men's hopes on the rise—the long-term trend was inexorably down. Sam worked hard at real-estatin'—in the intervals when he wasn't in Austin for a legislative session or driving a hundred miles to obtain a deposition that would help a Civil War veteran get his pension; if he received a telephone call about some ranch he might be able to buy cheap, no matter how late the hour, how remote the ranch, or how bad the road, he would throw on his suit jacket, crank up his car, and head out into the night. But, no matter how cheap Sam bought a ranch, all too frequently he had to sell it cheaper. His agile, restless mind was constantly conceiving new, non-real-estate, business ventures, but they, too, often turned out badly; his brother Tom, who went into several with him, commented ruefully: "If you want a business to be jinxed, just go into it with Sam." When Sam did make money, moreover, he didn't save it; sometimes it went into a new venture, sometimes into ostentation—new boots, new clothes, a new, expensive car ("You can tell a man by his boots and his hat and the horse he rides"); sometimes, because he had the Johnson extravagance, the gift for the grandiose gesture, into an expensive present for his wife; always into maids and laundry women—or into a fiver to tide over a veteran until the pension started coming. And, most importantly, Sam Johnson either didn't understand the reality of the land itself, of the soil on which all enterprises in the Hill Country (which had no oil wells, no manufacturing to speak of, nothing but farming and ranching) rested; or, perhaps more likely, he refused to accept that reality as he had refused to compromise with the realities of Austin, stubbornly shouting Populist slogans when Populism had been dead for twenty years, stubbornly holding to ideals in an arena in which ideals were largely irrelevant, and so exerting, despite his seniority, no significant influence on major legislative decisions. In Austin—in the Legislature—idealism was irrelevant; in the Hill Country, it was fatal.

His father died in 1915, his mother in 1917. The principal asset of her estate was the Johnson farm, those 433 acres up on the Pedernales. Dividing it up among the eight surviving children was obviously impractical, and when Sam refused to consider selling it to an outsider, John Harvey Bright of Houston, who had married one of Sam's sisters, offered to buy out the other heirs.

Sam wouldn't hear of that. He suspected that once Bright owned the ranch, he would sell it. This was the *Johnson Ranch* they were talking about. It was the family place, the place where they had all been raised. The Pedernales Valley was "Johnson Country," he said, always had been; it had been in that valley that the original Johnson brothers rounded up their great herds. Were they going to sell the Johnson's stake in that valley? Bright made an offer to the other relatives; Sam raised it. Bright made a new offer; Sam raised again. Sam's attitude was the old Johnson attitude, the attitude of the original brothers, who had disdained to haggle and bargain over every last penny because haggling and bargaining was beneath them. Whatever Bright offered, Sam said, he'd offer more. And finally, to get this tiresome bidding over with, he offered considerably more. He offered $19,500. The bid was accepted.

There was pride behind Sam's bid, the old Johnson pride—and there was ambition, vaulting ambition, big dreams on the old Johnson scale; Sam talked, in fact, about making the whole Pedernales Valley "Johnson Country" again; about restoring the once-grand Johnson fortunes. He persuaded Tom, who loved him (and who in this one instance ignored the remonstrances of his practical German wife, whose frugality and ability to lend a sturdy hand with the farm work kept him solvent), to purchase a smaller 125-acre ranch on the Pedernales, and to join with him in leasing the adjacent Klein ranch so that they would have enough land to really work with. The first Sam and Tom Johnson had had bad luck; maybe this Sam and Tom Johnson wouldn't.

But there was also in Sam's bid a failure to see—or to accept—reality; the old Johnson failure—or refusal—to understand what had been happening to the land in which he was investing so much money. Not seeing was easy, of course; the Hill Country always made not seeing easy. The land's decline, an historian says, was "gradual enough that men could lull themselves into not seeing it until too late." The land along the Pedernales had hardly been worked at all during the six years since Sam had moved to Johnson City, and Sam assured his brother that six years of lying fallow must have restored much of the land's original fertility. Once, in the old days of which Sam loved to talk, the land had been rich; Sam apparently believed, or made himself believe, that it could be rich again—maybe not as rich as in the old days, but rich enough. Maybe it would never be possible to raise cattle on it again (although Sam did not really believe that; he talked about one day starting up a herd again), but when he had last worked it, six years ago, he had gotten a respectable cotton crop out of it; now, he felt sure, he would be able to get a larger crop out of it. And—and this was apparently the crucial factor in his thinking—ever since the Armistice, cotton prices had been soaring. By 1919, when Sam was bidding against Bright, it was fetching an unprecedented forty cents per pound, and Texas newspapers were filled with speculation that it would soon soar to fifty cents per pound, or sixty.

The price of the land was only part of the expense of starting up the farm after a six-year lapse. The house had to be fixed up so that he and Rebekah and the children could live in it. Sharecroppers had to be hired, and their houses had to be fixed up. Tractors and other farming equipment had to be bought or rented—naturally, because it was Sam, good, modern equipment so that he could raise the maximum amount of cotton and take maximum advantage of those high cotton prices that were soon going to be much higher. Such expenses cost as much again as the land; by the time Sam moved onto the farm in January, 1920, he had invested slightly more than $40,000 in it. To raise this amount, he sold the little hotel in Johnson City. He sold a two-story stone store that he had been leasing to storeowner Withers for a steady monthly income. He sold every piece of property he owned—and then, since he still didn't have enough, he placed on the 433 acres a mortgage of $15,000, and borrowed additional money from at least three banks, going deeply into debt.

And the trap which had closed around the first Sam Johnson closed around the second.

HE STRUGGLED AGAINST its jaws. The man who had never wanted to be a farmer was a farmer now, and it was going to be as a farmer that he worked out his destiny: the mortgage, combined with the bank loans, was so big that it was a mortgage not just on his farm, but on his fate. And if he had possessed the lawmaker's courage, he possessed the farmer's courage, too. The stand he made now in a cotton field was as gallant as any he had made in a cloakroom. He battled that farm on the Pedernales, trying to make its soil pay out the dreams he had planted in it.

But it couldn't.

A single gully symbolized Sam Johnson's struggle, the struggle that he made, not in a suit and hand-tooled boots beneath the painted dome of the Capitol, before applauding galleries, but in sweat-reeking work clothes and mud-smeared work shoes, alone except for a couple of Mexican share-croppers, or, sometimes, completely alone, a lonely figure in the empty Hill Country landscape, under that empty Hill Country sky. The gully was a long, wide gash that rains had, over decades, cut into the ground all the way from the hill pastures that Sam had rented from the Kleins, across the Johnson fields and down to the river, a gully, in Ava's words, "deep enough to walk elephants in." A lot of cotton could be planted in that gully. Taking a team and wagon down along the Pedernales toward Fredericksburg, Sam filled the wagon with the richest river-bottom soil he could find, heaving it up into the wagon in hours of labor that must have been difficult for a forty-two-year-old man who hadn't done farm work for years. Then he drove the wagon home, and shoveled the soil into the gully. And he repeated the trip over and over until there was soil enough in the gully to plant cotton. And then the first spring rainstorm of 1920 was a "gully-washer"; a flash flood roared down the gully and swept the soil away. Sam needed that gully, needed the cotton that could be grown in it, and by now he knew he needed it badly. He filled it up again, again planted cotton seeds in it. If only the next few rains could be gentle, if only the seeds could be given a chance to put out roots that would hold the soil in place until cotton plants could flower, and then drop more seeds, which would put out more roots—and bind the soil fast. But before the seeds could sprout, there was another gully-washer; seeds and soil were washed away again. That gully symbolized Sam's hopes, and what happened in it symbolized what the Hill Country did to hopes. "He planted it, and planted it," a relative recalls. "And he never got a crop out of it. Not one."

The story of Sam and the farm is the story of the Hill Country. Six years of lying fallow would indeed revitalize most farms—but not Hill Country farms; arid Hill Country limestone turned into soil too slowly, and, being on hills, washed away too easily. When, in the spring of 1920, he and his hands began plowing his hilly fields, they found that the topsoil was terribly thin: on the average, not more than two inches deep. Beneath the soil was "hardpan"—harder, less fertile, soil mixed with clay—and even the hardpan wasn't very deep. Sam had to set his plows so that they dug no deeper than eight inches; any deeper, and the plows would be hitting rock. The farm's "bottom land" along the Pedernales and its tributary creeks was deep and fertile. But that first gully-washer—and the ones that followed it—sent the Pedernales on a real tear. When it receded, it sucked the bottom land back with it. And not only the bottom land. "Sam's land all drained toward the river," Ava explains. "That was part of the reason the topsoil was so thin: because it had kept getting washed away in the rains. And because it was so thin, what there was of it was just barely holding on. If you left it alone, it would have very slowly built up. But the minute you put a plow in it, it would wash away in the next rain. After Sam started to plow it, you could see his land running away. Every time rain hit it, you could see the topsoil running down the hills and into the river."

Still Sam fought. The only way to grow cotton in hardpan is to plow it after every rain. After every rain, Sam plowed it. During his earlier years on the farm he had spent a lot of time at the cotton gins in Albert and Stonewall, playing cotton futures; he was never at the gins now. He drove his hands, and he drove himself. "Uncle Sam was just not a farmer type," Ava says. "He was not a man of the soil. Not physically, and not in his head neither. But he tried very hard to be a farmer then," Ava says. "I still remember how hard he tried."

But trying didn't count in the Hill Country, just as hoping didn't count, just as wishful thinking didn't count, just as a belief that you should hold on to the family place and a willingness to fight for that place didn't count. What counted in the Hill Country was the reality of the soil. "He had seen his daddy make good on the land, at least fairly good," Ava says. "But the soil had been okay then. Now it was just wore out. It was just plain too thin."

The summer of 1920 was a hot summer. That blazing Hill Country sun burned all the way down through that thin soil, scorching away the nutrients in it. The cotton plants weren't as strong as they should have been, therefore, and not as resistant as they might have been to the sun—and some of them burned, too. "They came up just so high, and then the hot sun would get on them, and the leaves would curl up," Ava recalls. They didn't produce nearly as many pounds of cotton as Sam had expected to sell at forty or fifty or sixty cents per pound.

That didn't matter much, though. For all through that summer and fall of 1920, as Sam Johnson's cotton was dying, so was the cotton market. Wall Street speculation was part of the cause, as was an unforeseen world-wide deflation in the price of manufactured goods; moreover, while cotton prices had been driven up immediately after the war by heavy demand from Europe, in 1920, European countries began growing their own cotton again. When Sam went to sell his cotton in the fall of 1920, the price was no longer forty cents per pound. It was eight cents per pound.

The trap had closed. The Hill Country was a land that broke romantics, dreamers, wishful thinkers, idealists. It broke Sam Johnson.

It broke him financially—beyond hope of repair. The yearly interest on the $15,000 mortgage he had placed on the farm came to $1,050; by 1922, with cotton prices still low, he couldn't make the quarterly interest payments. And in 1925 half the principal would be due, and in 1927 the other half; by 1922, it was clear even to Sam Johnson that there was no hope that he would be able to make those payments. He had to sell the farm for whatever he could get, which was $10,000 from a thrifty German named Ove J. Striegler.

Sam didn't get to keep the $10,000; it all went to the mortgage holder, the Loan and Abstract Company of Fredericksburg. Sam had tried to save the family place, the place that symbolized so much to him. Instead, he had lost it. There was no Johnson Ranch any more. It was the Striegler Ranch now.

And the mortgage was only part of what Sam owed. He still owed banks the money he had borrowed to pay for tractors, horses, seed and fertilizer, and for refurbishing three houses. He still owed merchants for the grocery and clothing bills run up over two years by his two sharecropper families, bills they were unable to pay because their share of the cotton proceeds was too small—bills he had guaranteed. He moved off the farm owing money to banks and merchants the whole length of the Pedernales Valley. The total amount of his debt cannot be determined. His daughter Rebekah puts the amount at $40,000, his son Sam Houston puts it at $30,000, and it doesn't really matter which of the two amounts is accurate: in the Hill Country, one would be as impossible to pay as the other. Sam Johnson was in debt so deeply that he would be in debt until he died. He almost didn't have a place to move to: he had mortgaged the Johnson City house for $2,000, and had been unable to meet the $160-per-year interest payments, and now the principal was due. The only reason that the Citizens Bank of Fredericksburg, with whose president Sam had once joked so cordially, didn't foreclose on the house was that his brothers, Tom and George, persuaded the bank to extend the mortgage by co-signing it and by paying the back interest themselves. Had they not done so, their brother, and his wife and five children, would have had no home.

The Hill Country broke Sam Johnson's health. He sold the farm in September, 1922, moved back into Johnson City, and took to his bed with a long-drawn-out illness. The closing was in November; Sam had to get out of his sickbed to place his signature on the documents which formalized the dissolution of his dreams. He got out of bed again to go to the legislative session which began in January, 1923—where he introduced the Johnson Blue Sky Law—but collapsed in Austin and spent most of the session in bed there. Returning to Johnson City thereafter, he had to spend still more weeks in bed. The precise nature of his illness is not known; it has been called both "pneumonia" and "nervous exhaustion." Visitors to the Johnson home recall that he was white and gaunt, and that there was a severe outbreak of boils or "carbuncles" on his face. Many of the visitors were bringing covered plates of food—not just for the sick man but for his family, for by this time, it was common knowledge: there was no food in the Johnson house—and no money to buy any.

It broke him in other ways, too. His face, despite those piercing eyes, had always been friendly and smiling. Now it was grim and bitter, his mouth pulled tight and down. And his temper was worse. Sam had always had a violent temper, but its eruptions had been infrequent and short-lived. Now he would fly into a rage, particularly at his wife and children, at the slightest provocation. What people thought of him had always been so important to Sam. Even during that first terrible year, even as he was going broke out there on that farm, he had tried to keep up the front whenever he came into town: "Hon. S. E. Johnson and his little son Lyndon, of Stonewall, were among the prominent visitors in Johnson City on Wednesday of this week," the *Record* had reported in 1920. "Mr. Johnson has one of the largest and best farms in this section of Texas, and has been kept quite busy of late supervising its cultivation." In August of that year, when the doom of his dreams must have been clear to him, he saw editor Gliddon and spoke of more "big land deals." Now there was no point in trying to keep up a front any longer. When he got out of bed, he still wore suits and high, stiff collars, and his voice and laugh were still loud. But the air of "great confidence" was gone. There was something defensive about him now.

UNDERSTANDABLY DEFENSIVE. For Sam Johnson, who could walk into a room and know in an instant who was for him and who was against him, was a man who knew what people were thinking. And what they were thinking about him had changed—rapidly and completely. In a span of time that seems to an outsider remarkably brief, he had been transformed in the eyes of his home town from a figure of respect to a figure of ridicule.

Perhaps such a transformation would have occurred to any man who fell from high to low estate so rapidly—and so publicly and dramatically—in a small town where everyone knows everyone else's business, particularly when the town had for years believed that he was a shrewd and successful businessman, always negotiating "big land deals" that enabled him to buy big cars and to hire a chauffeur, and then suddenly the town learned that it had all been a bluff, that the deals and the cars were nothing but a front. But the gossip about Sam Johnson was harsh and ruthless even for a small town.

In part, this was because of the nature of Johnson City. Gossip was so powerful a force in many small towns partly because of their isolation: there wasn't much for people to be interested in except each other's lives. Johnson City—this tiny huddle of homes in the midst of the vast, empty Texas hills, this "island town"—was unusually isolated. It was a town which, as late as 1922, still possessed neither a movie house nor a single radio, a town very deficient in things to do, and its residents' interest in each other was, as more than one visitor remarked, very intense. Especially their interest in their most famous neighbor, the only resident of their town with even the slightest claim to fame: Hon. S. E. Johnson.

Johnson City was, moreover, a religious town—hard-shell, hellfire, revivalist, Fundamentalist, Old Testament religious. In most of its little houses, no matter how meagerly furnished, there lay on the dining-room table or on the mantelpiece a big black, leather-bound Bible, its front cover flapping up from frequent use. In few of those houses could be found a deck of cards or set of dominoes. "They were tools of the Devil," says John Dollahite, one of Lyndon Johnson's classmates. "My father wouldn't allow a deck of cards in the house." No dancing was allowed, of course, not in the house or out, and as for drinking—John's father, Walter Dollahite, could scarcely bear to look at the little saloon that was, from time to time, open in Johnson City; its swinging doors were the passage to Hell. Not even a drink of beer was permitted; "sneaking a beer by Jesus is like trying to sneak daylight by a rooster," Dollahite was fond of saying. Half the town was Baptist, and most of the other half—members of the Methodist Church or the Church of the Disciples of Christ—was trying, in Stella Gliddon's words, to "out-Baptist the Baptists." Lest legs show, girls were required to wear long, thick stockings—black until a girl reached her teens, when white was permitted. The fierceness of the town's prejudices and the rigidity of its intolerance led Stella Gliddon to call it "almost a Puritan town. In those days, people were considered bad for things that we take for granted now. They were the friendliest people, but they were very religious people, too." Such people had never forgiven Sam Johnson for believing in the Darwinian theory, or for admiring Al Smith, or for voting against Prohibition. The irregularity of his attendance at church—it was rumored, correctly, that he went at all only to please Rebekah—had been noted, as had the fact that his daughters had more than once appeared in public in knee socks. As for the fact that he was known to drink—well, these people knew what would come of that. Sam Johnson was the kind of man who in a town like Johnson City would ordinarily have been held up to children as an example of what they must avoid; ordinarily, people would have long predicted that he would follow in the path of his father and uncle, who had gone broke and failed to pay their debts. But in a town so impoverished and, because it was so religious, so conditioned to believe that worldly success betokened divine favor, Sam's apparent success in business outweighed all other factors, and as long as the townspeople thought he had money, they respected him despite his faults. But as they realized the truth, they turned on him with a fury made all the harsher because it had been so long pent up.

Their condemnation was harsher still—vicious, in fact—because of the way Sam acted now, in his time of adversity. Humbleness was called for now, and humbleness was not a Johnson trait. Sam's "Johnson strut," in fact, had lost none of its arrogance. The Johnsons—Sam and Rebekah, too —had considered themselves better than anyone else; now it turned out they were worse, but they still acted as if they were better, and people who had always resented this attitude no longer had reason to hide their resentment. One of the bankers who had once been proud to have Sam greet him on the street was now heard to sneer that he was always "playing cowboy and stomping in boots into the bank." Bankers at least had—in Sam's unpaid loans—reason for their new attitude toward him. The rest of the Hill Country had no such reason. What it had reason for was gratitude—for the pensions he had arranged, for the loans he had given, for the highway he had gotten built. Instead, there was relish and glee in the Hill Country's reaction to Sam Johnson's fall. John Dollahite's grandfather was one of those for whose pension Sam had worked. In discussing Sam today, however, John Dollahite does not mention the pension until asked. What is mentioned—at length—is Sam Johnson's illness, for Dollahite has it all diagnosed. "Due to drink," he explains. "You see, too much liquor thins your blood and you don't have the resistance to throw off things." Sam Johnson, he says, "was nothing but a drunkard. Always was." Shortly after Sam's downfall, O. Y. Fawcett, proprietor of Johnson City's drugstore, coined a remark which soon gained wide circulation. "Sam Johnson," he said, "is too smart to work, and not smart enough to make a living without working." The disparagement even became public. At a barbecue at Stonewall in the spring of 1923 (which Sam was too ill to attend), one of the speakers, August Benner, who was planning to run again against Sam in the elections that fall, said: "I tell you, ladies and gentlemen, Sam Johnson is a mighty smart man. But he's got no sense." People who were present at that barbecue still recall how the audience roared with laughter at this *mot*.

Sam didn't run in the next election, which was won by an old enemy, Fredericksburg lawyer Alfred P. C. Petsch. He announced that he was leaving politics "for business reasons"—how people snickered at that! One reason Sam didn't run again could indeed be called "business": he could no longer afford to give up months of each year at inadequate salary. But another reason may have been fear that if he ran again, he would lose: that Benner's gibe and the laughter which greeted it were indications of how low he had slipped in public esteem. And from that standpoint, his decision may have been correct. Just how low he had slipped would be revealed a little more than a year later, when the Austin-Fredericksburg Highway was completed, and a barbecue was held to celebrate the official opening of the road for which Sam Johnson had worked for so many years. A dozen prominent Hill Country citizens were invited to speak. Sam Johnson was not among them.

FOR A TIME, he was in the real-estate and insurance business, but he couldn't earn enough to live on. He went to Austin and tried to get a job in government. Many retired legislators—those who didn't go to work for "the interests" at sizable retainers—were given well-paid sinecures in the state bureaucracy. But Sam had fought the interests, and the bureaucrats who did their wishes. Although, with ten years in the Legislature, he had retired as one of its senior members, there was no sinecure for him. For some weeks, it appeared there might be no job at all. When, finally, he was offered one, it was a one-year appointment at a salary of only two dollars per day. He had no choice but to accept. Thereafter he served the district he had served as State Representative—as a part-time game warden.

He was unable to pay off his back bills at Johnson City stores, and storeowners began writing "Please!" on their monthly statements. Afraid of antagonizing—and losing the business of—his brother and the rest of the large Johnson clan, they hesitated to cut off his credit, but he kept falling further and further behind. "My Dad was liberal-like," says Truman Fawcett, "but he [Sam] finally owed him over two hundred dollars. He had to cut him off." After a while, Sam had to pay cash not only at O. Y. Fawcett's drugstore but at every store in Johnson City. "After a while he owed everyone in town," Truman Fawcett says. "They all cut him off."

Sometimes he didn't have cash. He took to patronizing stores in Fredericksburg or Dripping Springs—or in towns even farther away—where he could charge his purchases. "He'd change towns," Fawcett explains. "And while he was charging at these other towns—until they cut him off, too—he'd save a little cash money and put down some money on his bills here. But he couldn't ever catch up." Fawcett says that he himself believes that "He had intentions of paying his bills, Sam did." But then he adds dryly, "At least, I think he did." And Fawcett is kinder than other merchants who reminisce about Sam Johnson. Some of his debts were, by Hill Country standards, quite large; there is not only contempt but anger in the phrase the other merchants use about him: "He was a man who didn't pay his bills."

Eventually, he ran out of towns. The Buntons—who always had cash money—lent him some, but not enough. In 1925, he had to go back to Austin, hat in hand, to ask for another government job. He was given one. His work to obtain better roads for the Hill Country finally paid off for Sam Johnson. Rough stretches of the Austin-Fredericksburg Highway were being regraded. Sam was given a job on the highway of which he had been the leading sponsor: a job building it—with his hands. He was made foreman —working foreman—of a road-grading crew. The job paid fifteen dollars per week. Stella Gliddon recalls the first day Sam Johnson went to work on his new job. "Until that day, I never saw Sam Johnson without a tie on," she says. "He always wore a nice shirt and suit. But then when he went to work on the road gang, he wore khaki pants like everyone else."

REBEKAH JOHNSON had never been able to do much housework. And now she had no maid to do housework for her. The daughters of other Johnson City women helped their mothers keep house, but Rebekah's didn't—at least not to any appreciable extent. "She could never raise her voice to them," says Wilma Fawcett. "Her whole life was for the welfare of her children. And she was just too sweet to discipline them."

As each birth seemed to cost Rebekah more of her health and energy (after Lucia's, in 1916, she would frequently have to spend weeks in bed) and as the reality which she had always found so harsh grew harsher, she seems to have slipped further into romantic dreaming, giving up the job as newspaper stringer to write poetry, talking more and more about her ancestors, the illustrious Baineses and the even more illustrious Deshas of Kentucky, who had produced, in the eighteenth century, a Governor of

Kentucky—emphasizing that they were aristocratic Southerners. More and more, and to a striking extent, her life centered on her children, particularly on her eldest. She had always been a proud woman; now, as pride became harder to maintain, it took on a somewhat strident quality. She said, often enough so that her children's friends recall her saying it: "Some children are born to follow. My children were born to lead." No one could criticize her children to her, or even venture a hint that they had done anything wrong. "She was like a tiger sticking up for her children," Wilma Fawcett says. Particularly for Lyndon. "She really had everything tied up in that fellow." Says Louise Casparis, who worked in the Johnson home until they could no longer afford to pay her, "She loved her other children, but not to the extent which she loved him." In her eyes, he couldn't do anything wrong. Once, her sister-in-law Kitty told her about a fib in which several children, including Lyndon, had participated. Rebekah said she was sure Lyndon hadn't, because he never told fibs. When Kitty said, "All children tell stories," Rebekah replied, more shocked and angry than anyone had ever seen her: "My boy never tells a lie."

Yet, however much she loved her children and stuck up for them, Rebekah was, in the view of Johnson City, unable—utterly unable—to take care of them. When her mother visited—which she did often now that Rebekah needed help in the house, sometimes staying for weeks at a time—she did the housework, but Johnson City housewives who visited the Johnsons when "Grandmother Baines" wasn't in residence were shocked. Ava still remembers seeing in the Johnson sink something she had never, in all her life, seen in the sink in her own home—dirty dishes piled up, unwashed, so many that Ava felt they hadn't been washed for several days. Rebekah had always dressed her children differently from the other children in Johnson City: Lyndon and Sam Houston in sailor outfits or linen suits, Rebekah and Josefa and Lucia in dresses and pinafores and lace bonnets. Now the clothes were still different—but they weren't pressed, and after a while Johnson City found out why. Wilma Fawcett says that "when the laundry came back, honest to God, they'd just dump it in the bathtub and every child picked out what they wanted to wear to school that day, and it was never ironed unless they ironed it." Sometimes, now, the fancy clothes of the Johnson children—especially the younger ones—would appear to be not only unpressed but unwashed, too.

As finances got tighter and tighter, it sometimes seemed as if the children didn't have enough to eat. Children in Johnson City were continually eating at one another's houses; children who ate at the Johnsons' remember very small meals. Recalls Ohlen Cox: "I remember sausage and eggs—and that was for dinner. That was all there was, and there wasn't a lot of that." Clayton Stribling says, "We were poor, but we always had enough to eat. But once I ate over at the Johnsons', and there was just bread and a little bit of bacon, and the bacon was rancid, too." Often when

Rebekah wasn't feeling well, she wouldn't cook dinner, and now there wasn't much cash to buy dinner at Johnson City's lone café. Other children vividly remember the younger Johnson children, Josefa, Sam and Lucia, eating there—"a little dab of chili for the whole bunch." Sometimes—not often, but sometimes—there was no cash in the house at all. The time that Sam lay ill after he lost the farm wasn't the only time that relatives and neighbors brought meals to the Johnson house out of charity. One Christmas, there was nothing to eat in the house until Sam's brother Tom arrived with a turkey and a sack of Irish potatoes.

The women of Johnson City, who scrimped to save every penny, who baked their own bread to save the nickel cost of a store-bought loaf, might understand why Rebekah didn't scrimp ("She just wasn't brought up the way the other women were"), but they still felt that spending cash money for food from a café was the most wanton kind of waste. They were, many of them, as poor as the Johnsons, but their children had enough to eat. "She lived above the means of what they had—that was the only reason her children were hungry." And they therefore resented helping her. Tom's daughter Ava remembers that every time her mother made preserves or canned corn, her father would insist that she can or jar enough to take some to his brother and his family. "Sam's kids are hungry, Kitty," Tom would say. "We've got to feed them." And Ava remembers that sometimes her mother, that frugal German lady, would protest. Once, Ava vividly recalls, Kitty Johnson and Vida Cammack were canning corn together in the kitchen. When Tom insisted they can some for Sam's kids, Kitty replied, "I don't see why I have to do this every time, Tom. It seems like she could can her own stuff." Mrs. Cammack, Ava recalls, pointed out that Sam had a garden, and that there was plenty of corn ripe in it if only Rebekah would can it. "I think we've done enough for them," Mrs. Cammack said. And, Ava recalls, while the two women canned a hundred cans for each of their own families, for Sam and Rebekah "they canned twenty cans, and called it good [enough]."

That the Johnsons weren't "resented" even more than they were was because no one took them seriously any more. Some pitied them, Sam in particular. "People pitied him because of his wife," Ava says. "She was such a swell person, and smart—but she was not a helper. She was not a person to get up of a morning and get the kids dressed and off to school." Everyone knew how Mabel Chapman had turned him down, and, Wilma says, "I used to think at the time it was a shame he hadn't married her, because she would have managed his house and managed his children. And Rebekah just couldn't manage at all." But most ridiculed them. They weren't disliked so much as laughed at. August Benner's description of Sam had been sharpened: people said about him: "Sam Johnson's a smart man, but the fool's got no sense"—and that was the definitive word on him, that and the word "drunkard." Tears may come to Stella Gliddon's eyes when she tells about the first time Sam Johnson didn't wear a tie, but she is the exception; there is a glint of amusement and pleasure in the eyes of others who talk about Sam and the highway, even if not many are as blunt as John Dollahite, who says, chuckling: "He did a lot for that road, all right, Sam did."

As for Rebekah, when the women of Johnson City heard her remark that "Now is the time to put something in children's heads," they said, "Maybe she ought to try putting something in their stomachs." The Johnson home, these women say—in adjectives an interviewer hears over and over again—was "filthy, dirty. It was a *dirty* house!" And the Johnson children, these women say, were just little dirty ragamuffins. Sam and Rebekah Johnson had always been resented for their pretensions. Now, with those pretensions exposed in all their hollowness, the Johnsons were ridiculed. In Johnson City terms, they did, indeed, appear ridiculous. They were the laughingstock of the town.

7

"The Bottom of the Heap"

WITH THE CHANGE in the Johnsons' fortunes, their relationship with their son Lyndon changed as well. The change was dramatic—so dramatic that it is possible to date it.

Descriptions of Sam Johnson's relationship with his son in Austin—from fellow legislators, legislative staffers and others who saw them together there—provide two contrasting descriptions of that relationship. And the contrast is, in fact, as sharp as if there had been two Sam Johnsons in the Legislature, and hence two different sons. Some of these men vividly describe a son who idolized his father, who not only imitated him—his lapel-grabbing, his nose-to-nose conversational technique—so closely that "it was humorous to watch," but who also tried, as one legislator put it, to "stand or sit as close to his father as he could get," who, in another's words, "stuck as close to Sam as his shadow," and who, when Sam sent him on an errand, ran eagerly to obey. Others describe—just as vividly—a boy who not only refused to run errands for his father ("Whenever Sam wanted him to do something, Lyndon was always interested in doing something else") but who refused to listen to his father or to obey him, who, in fact, defied him so blatantly that one legislator says that "There wasn't a very friendly feeling between them at all. To tell you the truth, he wouldn't pay much attention to anything his father wanted him to do."

The difference in descriptions is explained by a difference in dates. The men who remember a son who loved and respected his father were those who observed the Johnsons in 1918 or 1919 or 1920—when the father was successful. Those who remember a different son were those who observed the Johnsons in 1921 or 1922 or 1923—when the father was a failure.

HAD THE LEGISLATORS visited the Johnson home, that shabby ranch in Stonewall at which the family lived "just long enough to go broke," they would have seen the contrast etched in acid.

Lyndon Johnson had been so close to his parents—imitating his father, dressing like him, talking with him, politicking with him, listening to his mother's stories, learning his alphabet and his spelling at her knee, choosing as his favorite poem "I'd Rather Be Mama's Boy." Now his father was still a father who went off to the Legislature and fought for "The People" and wouldn't take any favors from the "the interests," but he was also a father who was the laughingstock of the county. His mother still read poetry and told her children that "principles" were the important thing, and that "a lie is an abomination to the Lord," but she was also a mother who didn't iron, so that he often had to go out in rumpled clothes, and who didn't cook, so that sometimes he went to bed hungry.

And he wouldn't obey them. When Sam left on legislative or real-estate business, he would assign Lyndon various chores around the farm. Instead of doing the chores, Lyndon would parcel them out among his sisters and brother. He was a hard taskmaster with them—so "bossy" and domineering that, Wilma Fawcett says, "I had always thought I wanted to have an older brother—until I met Lyndon." If the younger children didn't do the chores, they weren't done, for Lyndon wouldn't do them; the woodbox on the back porch, which he was supposed to keep filled, would remain empty unless his mother lugged the wood herself. If his father found out what had been going on in his absence, he would lose his temper, particularly when he learned that Lucia or Sam Houston, who were, after all, little more than babies, had been doing heavy physical work, and he would spank Lyndon (he didn't spank him more frequently only because Rebekah, hating the scenes between father and son, would often conceal Lyndon's derelictions), and order him to do the chores himself. But the next time Sam left, Lyndon would again order the other children to do them. Lyndon's attitude during Sam's absences was striking; in the evenings, he would read the newspaper as his father did, and would lounge on his parents' bed to do it. It is, of course, possible to place a Freudian interpretation on his behavior toward his father and some biographers do—but one complication must be taken into account: he was as hostile, defiant and cold to his mother as to his father. Her tears could make him sit sullenly through the violin lessons she had arranged for him, but nothing could make him practice; Rebekah finally told the teacher not to bother coming again. Meals were scenes of daily conflict, for to Rebekah table manners were as important as the tablecloth she insisted on using instead of oilcloth, as one of the last remnants of her cherished gentility. Lyndon's manners now grew so bad that it was apparent to other children that he was deliberately trying to annoy his mother. He ate with loud, slurping noises, violently cramming huge spoonfuls of food into his mouth. Nothing she could do could make him stop; if he was sent away from the table, his manners would be the same when he returned. More than once, watching him eat, his mother began to cry.

His defiance of his parents was sharpest in the area they considered most important for their children: education. School was a painful experience for Lyndon during the family's time back on the ranch. The nearby Junction School, which he had attended years before, had only eight grades. For the ninth, Lyndon had to attend the school in the tiny community of Albert, four miles away; most of the children there were German, and many of the classes were taught in that language. An outsider because he spoke little German (and that with an accent the other children found funny), Lyndon was mocked because, although he was twelve years old, he still rode a donkey instead of a horse to school—in part because he was physically very awkward and hence an unsure rider, in part, possibly, because his father was by this time in no mood to give him a horse of his own. After a while Sam relented and gave him a pony, but he would always remember the humiliation; "It helped a little when my mother told me that Jesus rode into Jerusalem on an ass," he would recall. (Rebekah knew how best to appeal to her son: Lyndon's desire to be "in the forefront"—to stand out, to be somebody—was as strong as ever; about this time, Lyndon got his first pair of long pants; he arranged for a photographer to come to the ranch to record the occasion—a trip his parents could ill afford. It was at the Albert School, moreover, at about this time—the time when his father was failing on the ranch—that he first made a remark that one of his schoolmates there, Anna Itz, remembers quite vividly. A group of children was sitting under the big hackberry tree near the school during recess, Mrs. Itz says, and "All of a sudden, Lyndon looked up at the blue sky and said, 'Someday, I'm going to be President of the United States.' We hadn't been talking about politics or the Presidency or anything like that. He just came out with it." The other children laughed at him, and said they wouldn't vote for him, Mrs. Itz recalls. "He said, 'I won't need your votes.' ") Lyndon would not do his homework, and he became so boisterous in school that the teacher complained to his parents.

Nine was all the grades that the Albert School had; the next year (1921, when Lyndon was thirteen), he went to school in Johnson City, boarding during the week with his Uncle Tom and Aunt Kitty. One evening, Tom came out to the ranch and told Sam that he and Kitty "couldn't handle Lyndon"; they couldn't get him to do his homework. When his teachers hinted to his frantic mother that he might not be allowed to "pass on" to the next grade, she and Sam scraped together the tuition to send him, in the Summer of 1922, to the private San Marcos Normal School, thirty miles away, to make up his work. There he spent the allowance that his hard-pressed father had expected to last him through the whole eight-week session within a week, buying candy and ice cream for other students. Hitching a ride back to Johnson City, he joked about the matter with the Gliddons, and the next issue of their paper carried the following social item:

Linden Johnson, who is attending the San Marcos Normal School, passed through Johnson City to visit his mother and ask "Dad" for another "raise" for incidental expenses.

But it was no joke to his father. Enraged, he yanked Lyndon into his car, drove him straight back to San Marcos—and left him there without giving him a penny. "He cut Lyndon off and told him never to ask him for anything again," Sam Houston says. Beneath the polite phrases of a letter his mother sent at this time to a teacher at San Marcos Normal, Flora Eckert, is a note almost of pleading for help.

> Lyndon is very young, and has been considerably indulged, so finds the present situation very trying, I am sure. To be away from home and to be compelled to really study are great hardships to him. . . . Anything you do for our boy will be deeply appreciated by Mr. Johnson and myself, and should he require much of your time and service we should be glad to remunerate you as you think right. We are very desirous of his completing the work he had begun as it is necessary, as I am sure you realize. . . .

The letter has a one-line postscript testament to mother love: "Miss E— When L. is homesick please pet him a little for me." Lyndon made up the necessary work—but barely. And when he went back to Johnson City High School in the fall of 1922—his father, having sold the ranch for whatever he could get, had moved back to town—the clash of wills continued. His marks were somewhat better (mostly B's)—not because he worked harder, but because he was so much quicker and more articulate than most of the other students in the little school (there were only ninety students in its eleven grades, and many attended only when farm chores permitted) and he had developed the ability to dazzle his teachers, some of whom did not have much education themselves. As Joe Crofts recalls:

> Lyndon had a very brilliant mind. In fact, I don't think Lyndon ever knew what it was to ever bring a book home. . . . In history, . . . he could run in after recess or after the lunch hour and just glance through the lesson, and he would really know more about it than his teacher. And if by some chance he couldn't, and figured that he didn't know very much about the class . . . he'd come up with just any number of different things and even have the teacher so interested that before you'd know it, the period had gone by, and the rest of us would sit there like a bunch of birds on a telephone line wondering what was taking place.

At home, his mother was less easy to fool, and she developed a stratagem to help her son absorb knowledge. To a reporter, years later, she confided with a smile:

> Many times, I would not catch up with the fact that Lyndon was not prepared on a lesson until breakfast time of a school day. Then I would get the book and place it on the table before his father and devote the whole breakfast period to a discussion of what my son should have learned the night before, not with Lyndon but with my husband.
>
> Of course Lyndon was too well trained to interrupt this table talk, and forced to listen, he would learn. That way, and by following him to the gate nearly every morning and telling him tales of history and geography and algebra, I could see that he was prepared for the work of the day.

But while Mrs. Johnson would indeed, in later years, "confide" the story "with a smile," smiles are not what Lyndon's siblings and friends remember of the constant struggle to get him to do his schoolwork; they remember his father shouting angrily: "That boy of yours isn't worth a damn, Rebekah! He'll never amount to anything. He'll never amount to a Goddamned thing!" And if Mrs. Johnson paints a pretty picture of following him to the gate "telling him tales," the other children recall something else that occurred near the gate; his mother, of course, insisted that Lyndon wear shoes to school, but Lyndon would kick them off as soon as he got out of the gate, and leave them lying in the dust.

Rebekah's recourse was tears. Her own mother was a tougher customer. Discovering that Lyndon's brother, assigned to milk the cow, had bulked out the yield with water from the back-yard pump, Grandmother Baines said angrily, "Bend over, Sam Houston. I'm going to teach you a good Christian lesson right here and now." When she was in residence at the Johnson home, the girls even cleaned up their room. But Lyndon, already resentful of her presence because he had hoped to be in charge during his father's absences, would not accept any "Christian lessons." Between the strict Baptist widow, who would never appear out of her room without every hair in place and her cameo pin precisely centered on her bodice, and the boy whose shoes were defiantly untied, there was, in his brother's words, a constant "battle of wills." Infuriated to see eight-year-old Sam Houston staggering under a heavy load of wood that Lyndon had assigned him to carry, Grandmother Baines would order Lyndon to bend over for a spanking, but he would defiantly dance out of her reach, or run out of the house. "More than once," Sam Houston recalls, "she told my folks and anyone else who would listen, 'That boy is going to wind up in the penitentiary—just mark my words.' "

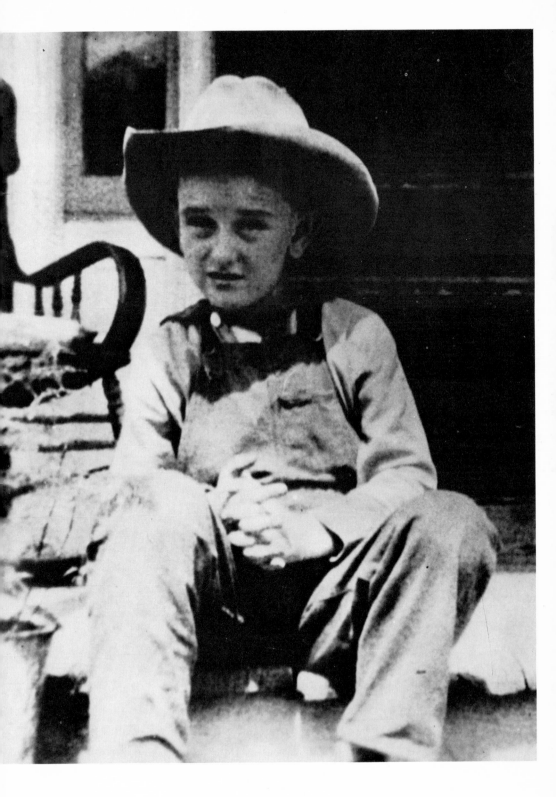

John Wheeler Bunton

Opposite, above: Eliza and her husband, Sam Ealy Johnson, Sr. (with, left, her mother, Jane Bunton), in front of their "dog-run" on the Pedernales, c. 1897

Opposite, below: Sam Johnson, Sr. (left), Eliza (fourth from left), and the Buntons in front of her father's home in Stonewall, c. 1914

Eliza Bunton Johnson, Lyndon's grandmother

arting to meeting, Sunday
orning: Sam Jr., and
ebekah Baines Johnson
eft); Sam Sr., and Eliza
niddle). The Johnsons would
eet at Sam Sr.'s house in
onewall and race to church.

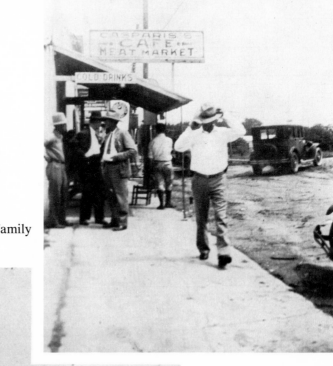

Johnson City, where the family
moved in 1913

Lyndon's parents: Rebekah Baines
Johnson, 1917; Sam Ealy Johnson, Jr., at
home in the Texas House of Representatives, in 1905, the first of his six legislative
terms.

Lyndon at eighteen months,
1910

Lyndon, with cousins Ava and
Margaret Johnson, behind
Kitty Clyde Ross, 1913

Lyndon "in the forefront"—at a family picnic in 1913

Right: Before Lyndon's graduation, at fifteen, from Johnson City High School. First row: Second from right, cousin Margaret. Second row: Third from right, his sister Rebekah; far right, Kitty Clyde Ross (with whom he was "in love"). Back row: from left, Clarence Redford, John Casparis, Otto Crider, John Dollahite, Lyndon, —, —, Principal Arthur K. Krause (with tie), —, Tom Crider, —, —, George Crofts.

Lyndon's first long pants. Lucia, Josepha, Rebekah, Lyndon, and Sam Houston, in 1921. Lyndon himself arranged for the photographer to come to the ranch to record the occasion.

Lyndon, 1924

In California: Cousin Thomas Martin (an attorney in whose office Lyndon worked), Lyndon, Fritz Koeniger, Otto Crider

Lyndon in 1925, and in December, 1926, in the snow with his sister Rebekah

"Old Main" at Southwest Texas
State Teachers College, San
Marcos, 1927

President Cecil E. Evans, with his
little Redbook

The president's garage, over which Lyndon and Boody Johnson lived rent free, and which, to earn money, they painted four times in one term.

Cotulla, 1928

Carol Davis, whom
Lyndon courted at
college

The *Pedagog*'s opinion of the new politics on
campus created by Lyndon Johnson

Lyndon B. Johnson
Alfred "Boody" Johnson

Willard Deason
Wilton Woods
Fenner Roth

Vernon Whiteside
Horace Richards
Albert Harzke

Hollis Frazier
Clayton Stribling
Ella So Relle

Henry Kyle
Medie Kyle
Edward Puls

Joe Berry
Mylton Kennedy
Ruth Lewis

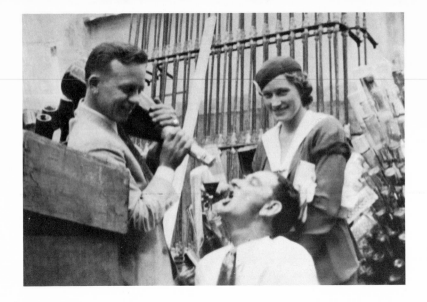

The "wonder kid" of politics and Welly Hopkins celebrating
Welly's election to the Texas Senate, 1930, in Mexico

He refused to obey his father's most direct orders: to do chores or schoolwork—or to stop using his shaving mug. Lyndon didn't need to shave yet, but he liked to show off to his friends by pretending to shave with Sam's shaving mug and ivory-handled straight razor. His father forbade him to use them, but if his father wasn't home, he would do so anyway. "No one could boss him or persuade him to do anything he didn't want to do," Sam Houston says.

In his relationship with his father, moreover, there became apparent now an unusually violent strain of competition. "There was a kind of tension between them," Sam Houston says. "Even in small, unimportant matters, they seemed to be competing." When Rebekah was ailing, she would sleep in the girls' room, and her husband would be alone in their big double bed. On cold winter nights, he would call into the boys' room, where Lyndon and Sam Houston would be sleeping in a double bed, "Sam Houston, come in here and get me warm."

"I would crawl out of bed and scramble into his room like a little puppy, snuggling my always-warm body against his," Sam Houston says. "Pretty soon he'd fall asleep and start snoring, with me right next to him, holding mighty still and afraid to squirm even a little because it might awaken him." But then, he remembers, "I'd hear Lyndon calling me: 'Sam Houston, come on back, I'm getting cold.'

"Back I'd go," Sam Houston says, "moving away from Daddy quiet as a burglar and snuggling up to my big brother." But, he says, "that might not be the end of it." Later on, "Daddy might get cold again and would call me back to *his* bed"—and then Lyndon would call again, his tone superficially sleepy and friendly, but with a note in it that Sam Houston knew as a note of command, and throughout the night, to avoid trouble between his father and his brother, the little boy would shuffle sleepily back and forth between their beds.

To outsmart his father, to get the better of him, Lyndon would go to considerable lengths. Once, in fact, he displayed an insight into his father's weakness, and an ability to do the planning and preparation necessary to take advantage of it and use it for his own ends, rather unusual for a fourteen-year-old boy.

During the 1923 legislative session, Sam telephoned Lyndon to come to Austin so that he could buy him a suit. Lyndon asked Milton Barnwell to drive him—but to make two trips instead of one, to take him to Austin not only on the day Sam had specified but on the day before as well. Lyndon knew that his father was planning to buy him an inexpensive seersucker suit. He wanted a more expensive model. And he had thought of a way of arranging things so that his father, concerned as he always was with appearances and anxious not to seem to appear poor, would be too embarrassed not to buy it for him.

At the store, Barnwell watched Lyndon's arrangements in awe. Selecting a cream-colored Palm Beach suit—a twenty-five-dollar suit, as Barnwell remembers it—he tried it on to make sure that it looked good on him and that there was one in his size. Then he told the salesman that when he and his father came in the next day, the salesman should pretend that he had never seen Lyndon before. And he told the salesman what to say. The next day, the boys drove back to Austin and went to the store with Sam. When Sam told the salesman he wanted to buy his son a suit, the salesman said he had one that might look nice on the young man and would the young man like to try it on? He brought out the Palm Beach suit—which of course turned out to be the right size. It was not in Sam's nature to ask to see a less expensive suit. "Sam like to have a fit," Barnwell recalls. "But he went ahead and bought Lyndon that suit."

As the reality of what had happened to him began to sink in on Sam Johnson, as he had to walk every day past stores that had cut him off, and stop and talk in the street every day with people who knew he had been cut off, his temper became more and more frayed. His mouth, day by day, pulled tighter and grimmer; his eyes, which had always been so piercing, now, often, glared defiantly back at the world. When he came home now, he would sometimes go straight into his bedroom without stopping for his old happy greeting to his children. The door of the bedroom might remain shut for hours, recalls one of his children's playmates, but "if the kids were making noise or she was having trouble with one of them, he might come storming out," and Sam Johnson in his rage, a big man with a loud, harsh voice and those glaring eyes, could be a fearsome sight to a child. "We were all afraid of Mr. Sam," another playmate, Bob Edwards, testifies. One of his daughter Rebekah's beaux refused to come in the house if Mr. Sam's car was out front. "He could say ugly things if he was angry," Louise Casparis says.

With his younger four children, Sam's anger never outlasted his wife's soft "Now, Sam, I'll take care of that." "You could see that a minute after he had said these things, he would be sorry he had said them," Louise Casparis says. His children knew it. If they were misbehaving, Louise says, Mrs. Johnson would say, " 'I'll tell your father,' but that didn't scare them one bit." He was, in fact, very close to his children, particularly Sam Houston, who would get up before sunrise to have an hour alone with his father, to watch him while he shaved in the flickering light of a kerosene lamp hung over the kitchen sink, to eat the breakfast he cooked—"fried eggs, smoked ham, hominy grits or huge servings of pan-fried potatoes, all of them freely sprinkled with tabasco sauce"—and to listen to his wonderful stories, the stories Lyndon would no longer listen to. "Sitting there in the half-light of dawn, my feet not quite reaching the floor, I would listen hours on end to Daddy's stories about the Legislature in Austin, about colleagues named Sam Rayburn, Wright Patman and Jim Ferguson, that great Populist who later became Governor. Naturally, I couldn't really understand most of what he told me, but I could sense it was all very important and sometimes very funny. My daddy had a way of poking fun at even the most serious things. . . ."

With his older son, however, Sam's anger had a different quality. Once, Lyndon, learning that Sam Houston had, by months of diligent saving, managed to accumulate eleven dollars, suggested that his little brother—who, unlike their sisters, idolized him—"go partners" with him and buy a second-hand bicycle "together." Sam Houston was thrilled. "My favorite and only big brother—six years older than me—offering to be partners with me! Of course, I accepted." But the bike, which Lyndon chose, turned out to be the right size for Lyndon—but far too big for eight-year-old Sam Houston, whose feet couldn't even reach the pedals. Trying to ride it, he crashed. "When my daddy came home that night and heard about my accident and our partnership, he gave Lyndon a lecturing he never forgot. I had seldom seen him so angry. 'You give Sam Houston his money back,' he said in a low, threatening voice." While on that occasion, Lyndon obeyed, his defiance of his father's orders on most occasions continued, as did his refusal to do chores or schoolwork, and Sam's bitterness and frustration at his own life would often flare into rage at his eldest son. Returning home unexpectedly one day to find Lyndon, his face covered with lather, using his razor and mug against his wishes, Sam snatched the razor strop out of Lyndon's hand, marched him off to the back porch and spanked him with it. There were many spankings—at least one of which was undeserved. Irritated by Lyndon's posturing while holding court in Cecil Maddox's spare barber chair, several of the barbershop hangers-on decided to teach him a lesson. Knowing he would soon be coming, they smeared the seat of the chair with a fiery oil of mustard solution. It took only a moment to soak through the seat of Lyndon's pants, and he began first to squirm, and then, yelling, "I'm burning! I'm burning!" he jumped out of the chair and started pulling his pants down. Recalls Crofts: "He was on fire, and he began to cry and holler—we were just big ol' kids—and he got his pants down, but he didn't take them completely off, and he ran out on the sidewalk." His father, whose little real-estate office was also on Courthouse Square, "heard him hollering out there" and came running over, "and I never will forget, I always held that against Mr. Johnson, he took his belt off, and he grabbed Lyndon by the hand, and one of the pants legs came off, and ol' Lyndon was going around there, and Mr. Johnson was holding him by one hand, and every so often, why, he'd pop him one across the seat with the belt." Maddox kept trying to tell Sam what happened, but Sam was so angry he "wouldn't listen to him." When, finally, he did, he growled, "Well there isn't any kid of mine going to run up and down the street with his bare butt hanging out."

. . .

BUT SPANKING, or even a more emphatic form of corporal punishment, wasn't an unusual method of discipline in Johnson City; it was, in fact, standard, and generally accepted as such. Lyndon's friend Bob Edwards, for example, says: "My daddy had a razor strop, and he never sharpened a razor on it—he wore it out on me. My daddy had a pair of cowboy boots, and he just wore them out on the instep kicking my heinie. But he didn't do it out of meanness at all. My daddy was just trying to raise me the way his daddy raised him." And Sam Johnson's spankings were not unusually severe; quite the opposite, in fact. His car—his "T Model" Ford—had become the crux of his battle of wills with his son, who, against his repeated orders, would sneak it out of the Johnson barn at night after his parents were asleep, pushing it, often with his cousins Ava and Margaret and friends like Truman Fawcett, down the slope from the barn and out to the road so that the noise from starting it wouldn't wake them up. Not infrequently, Sam would find out the next day what had happened. Once, Lyndon's cousin Ava recalls, he and his brother Tom "came up to school, and they marched us right back over to Sam's house and out on that back porch and whipped our heinies with their razor strops." Truman, she says, had been "real scared" of Sam, but while the children were being marched along from school, "Lyndon had whispered to us: 'When he hits the first lick, scream like it's killing you, and he'll go easy.' We all hollered and screamed, and afterwards Truman whispered, 'He hardly hit me at all.' That was the way Uncle Sam was, you know. We knew we could get away with murder. Uncle Sam would never really hit anyone."

What was unusual was Lyndon's reaction to spankings. He would indeed scream—scream so loudly and hysterically and piercingly that the screams would echo from one end of the quiet little town to the other. Spankings usually occurred around dinnertime, when Sam would come home and be told about Lyndon's misdeeds by Grandmother Baines, or would see for himself that the chores hadn't been done again, and at dinner tables all over Johnson City, the conversation would suddenly be interrupted by those high-pitched yells, and people would say, "Sam's whipping Lyndon again."

Johnson City's children knew Lyndon wasn't really being hurt—some, like Truman Fawcett, because they had once been present at a "whipping," others because of physical evidence; when the boys went swimming in the buff in the Pedernales, quite often little rear ends would bear strap marks, but Lyndon's never did. "I've seen him right after we had all heard him hollering and yelling, and he wasn't hurt at all. He didn't have a bruise spot on him," says one playmate. Some adults—like the Fawcetts, who lived diagonally across the street from the Johnsons and could observe them closely—knew this, too. Their son Truman recalls that "We'd be sitting at the table and you could hear Lyndon hollering, and my parents would say, 'Oh, he's not hurting him.'" But not all adults understood—and many, ready to believe the worst of a man who "drank," would tell biographers years later that Sam had been physically brutal to Lyndon. Sitting at their dinner tables, they would say, when they heard Lyndon's cries, "Sam's been drinking again, and he's beating his boy." And families who lived outside town, and hence were out of earshot, would be notified by "Ol Miz" Spaulding, the telephone operator and a Baptist pillar, who would ring them up and report that "Sam's killing that boy again." Lyndon, in fact, sometimes seemed to be going out of his way to reinforce the impression of his father's brutality. Once, he ran out of the house to hide in a tree—and not only picked one right in Courthouse Square, where there were plenty of people around, but told them he was hiding from his father, acting terrified of Sam, begging them not to tell him where he was. "He always seemed to be trying to make people think that his father was mistreating him," Emmette Redford says.

Did he want people to know that his mother was mistreating him, too? He was constantly "borrowing" food from other families, even when there was no shortage of food in his own home. Recalls Barnwell: "We could hardly sit down to breakfast without Lyndon standing there with a cup wanting to borrow a cup of flour or a cup of sugar or some coffee. And he made such a *production* out of it!" He was continually going into the café saying he was hungry and there wasn't anything to eat at home—and at least once this statement surprised two boys who were sitting, unseen by Lyndon, in the rear of the café, because they had just come from the Johnson home, where they—and Lyndon—had just finished eating. "I think probably he was hungry sometimes," says one of them. "But nowhere near as often as he said he was."

Did he want people to know that his little sisters were mistreating him? He was constantly telling people how difficult it was for him to keep his house clean, particularly because his sisters wouldn't tidy up their bedroom, which was the largest room in the house—"He said they had to have a big room because they'd never keep their clothes up off the floor," Ava recalls. "He said he had to be after them all the time about how sloppy their room was"—a statement which fell somewhat strangely on the ears of people who visited the Johnsons, and who saw that Lyndon's room was by far the messiest of all.

His reaction to injury—or imagined injury—at the hands of people outside his family was just as striking. Once, when he was only ten years old, he and Clarence Redford had been fighting in the Redford front yard, rolling around in the dust, when Emmette Redford came along. Because his father was dead, Emmette says, "I regarded myself as the protector of my brothers, and I yanked them apart and picked up this little shovel that was lying there and turned Lyndon over my knee and whacked him." It was just an ordinary whack, Redford says, and he was utterly astonished by its consequence: "Lyndon let out a wail so loud I can still remember it. I can still see Lyndon. He was standing there—he had knee britches on and one leg was still up, but the other had fallen down around his ankle, and he was dirty, all covered with dust. And he stood there just *screaming*—you could hear him from one end of town to the other." As Lyndon grew older, the pattern of his behavior remained the same. After a male teacher spanked him and Luke Simpson for splashing water on girls in the schoolyard, Luke simply went back to playing. Lyndon raced home, crying, and burst into the house with a story of injustice and mistreatment that brought his father rushing to school for an angry confrontation with the teacher. Sometimes, he would get into fights—just ordinary scuffling and wrestling matches. In the memory of friends, he always lost—he was physically quite uncoordinated; "he threw a baseball like a girl," one classmate says —and as soon as he started losing, he would run home crying, a tall, skinny, awkward, teen-aged boy with dusty cheeks and tears sliding down them, running through the streets of that quiet little town sobbing loudly. "All anyone had to do was touch Lyndon, and he let out a wail you could hear all over town," Emmette Redford says. "He wanted attention. He wanted everyone to know someone had injured him. He wanted everyone to feel sorry for him."

His demeanor was unusual in other ways, too. Except for the extent of its isolation, Johnson City was such a typical little Texas town: a courthouse, a little bank, a cotton gin with walls and roof of dingy tin, a water tank on rickety stilts, a café beside which, at a rickety wooden table, old men in faded shirts played dominoes to fill endless hours, a few stores, not so many as a dozen, lined up along a raised wooden sidewalk on whose edge younger men sat desultorily in a row, and beneath which dogs curled up and slept. Straggling away from the courthouse and the street of stores, set down among vacant lots grown over sometimes with corn and sometimes with weeds, were small boxlike houses behind picket fences. Through its dusty streets occasional Model T's chugged and horses ambled, slowly pulling wooden wagons. But through these streets roamed one boy who wasn't typical at all. His clothes were different from the other boys' clothes—sometimes more elegant than their weekday overalls or knickers or even than their Sunday suits, sometimes outlandishly elegant for such a town; by his senior year in high school, he had acquired not only the Palm Beach suit but the only straw boater in Johnson City; on some occasions, he wore blue jeans, but wore them tucked into brightly polished boots laced up to the knee, and the shirt he wore with them was a bright yellow silk crepe de Chine, the neck of which he kept open to display either a turtleneck dickey or an ascot; to school (in whose graduation picture he is the only boy wearing a necktie) he sometimes wore, on black hair that was painstakingly pompadoured and waved, and sometimes slicked dramatically flat with Sta-comb, a dapper English tweed cap. And sometimes his clothes were less elegant than other boys'—so dirty and full of holes that even in comparison with them he looked shabby, shabbier than he had to, as if he were dressing for some deliberate effect.

When he approached other boys, he would run up to them and begin to talk, gesturing violently with his arms, grasping their lapels, putting his arm around their shoulders, shoving his face close to theirs. He would hug them—this, in the memory of his childhood companions, was a conspicuous aspect of his behavior. "He was always laying all over my brothers," says Cynthia Crider. "The thing I remember about him was how he used to hang all over people. Just hang all over them."

But it was with adults—particularly women, the housewives of Johnson City—that his behavior was most striking. He would flatter women, play up to them. Recalls Stella Gliddon: " 'Miz Stella,' he would say to me, 'I love your fried chicken better than *anything!* Better than anything in the *whole wide world!* ' " And when she invited him to have some, he would say, "Why, Miz Stella, I thought you'd *never* ask!"—say it with such expressiveness that the sentence became a byword in the Gliddon household, so that whenever Mrs. Gliddon asked her own four children if they would like something to eat, they would reply: "Why, Miz Stella, I thought you'd *never* ask!"

He would hug women, and kiss them. Into the voice of Professor Emmette Redford, former president of the American Political Science Association, talking at the age of seventy-two, comes, astonishingly, a definite note of jealousy when he says: "He'd put his arm around my mother and kiss her repeatedly. We used to ask, 'Mama, do you love Lyndon more than you do us?' "

The other children were almost in awe of the way Lyndon acted with adults. "He would put me to shame," Redford says. "We and the Galloways were really close, but I would be too shy to go down and visit Grandma Galloway unless my mother took me. But he'd visit Grandma Galloway. He'd hug and kiss her. He'd hug and kiss all the mothers, and the grandmothers, too. And all the women in town just *loved* him." And the children were in awe of the results he obtained. When Redford had caught him fighting in the dust of the Redford front yard with his brother, and had spanked him, and Lyndon had let out the "wail you could hear all over town," Redford's mother had appeared in the doorway—clad, he remembers, in a freshly starched white dress. She asked what had happened, and when told, said, "Well, Lyndon, I guess you'd better go home for the day." And, recalls Redford: "He stepped up to her—all dirty—and hugged her, and said, 'Oh, Miz Redford, we didn't mean any harm. Why don't you let us play?' And of course she did." She didn't even seem to mind, Redford adds, that the dust had rubbed off Lyndon's clothes onto her white dress. "My mother kept us on a pretty tight leash," he says. "But Lyndon could get whatever he wanted from her." Other children say he had the same effect on *their* parents. "Whenever we wanted to do something that we thought our folks wouldn't like, we'd let Lyndon do the asking," Bob Edwards says. "He could get them to let us do things that ordinarily they'd say no to."

It wasn't just the flattery and the hugging that did it, say the children who grew up with him. It was the quality that underlay his technique. The precise nature of that quality they are unable to define, but they try—hard— to make a researcher understand that it was something very rare. "You see," Truman Fawcett tries to explain, "it didn't embarrass him to just go up and talk to anybody, not like I would be embarrassed, not like anyone would be embarrassed. And the way he did it was like nothing I've ever seen. I've never seen anyone else who could put it over. But Lyndon could put it over. He'd go up to the old ladies and call them Grandma, and they'd just love him for it. He called my ma and pa 'Cousin Melissa' and 'Cousin Oscar,' and they had been all prepared not to like him, and they just loved him, too. Lyndon Johnson was a very unusual boy. He wasn't unusual in smartness. He was smart, but he wasn't smart like Emmette Redford, or like some others, either. He was unusual in this other thing."

What was the reason that he acted this way? That he screamed and sobbed over spankings that didn't hurt, and cried hunger when he wasn't hungry, and made public complaint about the sloppiness of his sisters' bedroom? What was the reason that he seemed almost to be trying to turn people against his own family? Was it, as Emmette Redford believes, because "he wanted people to feel sorry for him," to pity him? And if so, why did he want pity? Was it because, for this boy who had, from his earliest years, needed attention, needed to be somebody, needed to stand out, needed public distinction—for this boy who was now a member of an undistinguished, poor, family, and was himself awkward in athletics and only average in schoolwork—pity was now the only distinction possible?

Was it something deeper? He was the same boy, after all, who had had to ride on the front of the donkey, who had had to be at the "head of the ring," who had taken his ball and gone home if he couldn't pitch—who had needed not only attention but respect, deference; who had needed to lead, to dominate. When his parents had been respected, he had been unusually close to them, especially to the father who was a leader. He had dressed like his father, talked like his father, campaigned with his father (and wished the campaigning "could go on forever"). Did he now feel that his father, by his failure, had betrayed him? Did he act the way he did because now that his parents were looked down on, he wanted to show that he was different from them? Better than them?

What was the reason for the intensity, the feverishness, of the way he acted, the way he worked so frantically to convince people he was right in every argument, worked so frantically to ingratiate himself with them, not with some of them but with all, down to the crustiest, most unapproachable old matriarch? What was the reason that, as Clayton Stribling put it, "The more someone disliked him, the harder he'd try to be his friend"—try by fawning, by smiling, by wheedling, by hugging, by abasing himself, by doing whatever he had to do until he succeeded? What was the reason that he didn't only *want* his way with people, adults as well as children, not only his friends but their mothers as well, but *had to have* his way? Was it because of the depth of his shame, because, as Wilma Fawcett speculates, "he was embarrassed because of his father," and because of the depth of his insecurity, because he had been yanked—in an instant, it must have seemed, so rapid was his father's fall—from security into an insecurity that included continual worry about whether the very house he lived in was going to be taken away from him; because his family had been yanked in an instant not just out of public respect but into something close to contempt; because where once he himself had been able to charge more in stores than other children, now he could charge nothing at all, and had to stand watching while his friends put purchases on their parents' accounts? Lyndon Johnson understood the transformation in his father's fortunes quite clearly: "We had great ups and downs in our family," he would recall. "One year things would go just right. We'd all be riding high in Johnson City terms, so high in fact that on a scale of A–F, we'd be up there with the A's. But then two years later we'd lose it all. . . . We had dropped to the bottom of the heap." Was it, in short, the rapidity of the change in his life—the violence with which he was hurled from one extreme to the other—that made him act the way he did?

Or was it something deeper? Something not just in his circumstances but in his nature? Did he act this way because there was something in him—"born in him," "bred in him"—that *demanded* of him that he be in the A's, that demanded of him as it had demanded of his father, of his grandfather, of all that mighty Bunton line, that they be in the forefront? Lyndon Johnson's father had not, after all, been poor when little Lyndon let Harold Withers pop his ears for nickels no matter how much it hurt. Lyndon Johnson's father had not been despised when Lyndon had hidden in the haystack to get attention, written his name on the blackboard in capital letters, taken his ball and gone home—had displayed so strong a desire to be somebody, to lead. Whatever it was that made Lyndon Johnson act the way he acted—that made him try to dominate people, to get them to defer to his opinion, to get his way with them by any and every means—heredity as well as humiliation plays a role in the explanation. The transformation in his family's fortunes merely emphasized these needs in his temperament—by making it harder, almost impossibly hard, for him to satisfy them had given his efforts to satisfy them that feverish, almost frantic quality. His family's fall had added a powerful dose of insecurity and humiliation to the already powerful inherited strain that formed the base of the complex mixture that was Lyndon Johnson. In many ways, it was not what he did that made Lyndon Johnson so unusual, but the intensity with which he did it. What was it he wanted—attention? sympathy? respect? dominance? Whatever it was, he was desperate to have it.

YET HIS DESPERATION couldn't get for him whatever it was he wanted. He could make adults, particularly women, pity him, sympathize with him, let him have his way (in large part because he *was* desperate and they realized it; ask the women who were fondest of the gangling, awkward youth why they treated him so gently, and they all reply in almost the same words: "I felt sorry for him"). But he could not make them stop thinking of him as a Johnson—and in a small town like Johnson City, family was the significant identification. Moreover, his was a family that had, in Hill Country terms, been steeped in scandal; fifty years before, the original Johnson brothers had gone broke and left a trail of debts across the Hill Country. Now, in the hard and uncharitable opinion of the Hill Country, history was being repeated by another pair of Johnson brothers named Sam and Tom— not so much by Tom, perhaps, although he was unsuccessful in business and going broke, but certainly by Sam, who "owed everyone in town" and plenty of people in other towns besides. Truman Fawcett clearly remembers sitting on a porch with his uncle, Frank Fawcett, while Lyndon Johnson walked by; his uncle's eyes followed Lyndon down the street, and then he said, in a tone of flat finality: "He'll never amount to anything. Too much like Sam." Lyndon may not have wanted to be thought of as Sam Johnson's son, may have been desperate not to be thought of as Sam Johnson's son— but that was how he *was* thought of.

And if he had any doubts that this was so, they must have been erased shortly after his graduation from high school.

All during the spring of 1924, Lyndon and his classmate Kitty Clyde Ross were, their friends said, "in love." It was a spring of picnics beside the Pedernales and ice-cream-and-cake socials given by Johnson City women's clubs in honor of the six-member graduating class, and Lyndon and Kitty Clyde, a bright, pretty girl, sat together at all of them. In class, they passed notes, arranging to meet after school, and at snap parties they tried to kiss only each other. When Lyndon dropped her off at her house after an evening social, she would lean out her window and watch to make sure that he went straight home, and didn't talk to any other girl. Their classmates wondered if they would get married someday—although Lyndon wouldn't be sixteen until August (he was, the *Record* reported, "believed to be the youngest graduate of the school"), Kitty Clyde was a year older, and Johnson City girls married young.

But Kitty Clyde's father was E. P. Ross, "the richest man in town." He was a merchant (the *Record*'s front page often carried a large ad for Ross' General Merchandising store), one of the merchants who was writing "Please!" on the bills he sent to Sam Johnson every month. He was, moreover, a pillar of the Methodist church and strong for Prohibition—and his views of the Johnson clan were no secret; he was known to feel that it had been very lucky for his wife, the former Mabel Chapman, that, twenty years before, her family had forbidden her to marry Sam Johnson and that she had married E. P. Ross instead. When, shortly after graduation, the principal of Johnson City High School, Arthur K. Krause, asked Ross' permission to court Kitty Clyde, he gave it—encouraged the courtship, in fact, though Krause was almost thirty. "It was unusual in those days for a girl to go with someone so much older," Ava says. "But the Rosses were so afraid Kitty Clyde was going to marry Lyndon they were glad for her to go with anybody just to break her up with him."

Kitty Clyde's parents, in fact, ordered her not to spend time with Lyndon, and made sure she didn't have much time to spend—not that she would have disobeyed them, Ava says; "in those days, in towns like Johnson City, girls didn't disobey their parents." Krause was frequently invited for dinner at the Ross home. After dinner, Kitty Clyde and Krause would go for a drive—in the Ross car, a fancy new Ford sedan, with Mr. and Mrs. Ross along as chaperones. Often, in the evenings, Lyndon would be talking or playing with friends in Courthouse Square. He would see the Ross car pass by.

His cousins Ava and Margaret saw how he felt then. Trying to cheer him up, the vivacious Margaret made up a new verse to a popular tune, to mock the fact that Krause couldn't see Kitty Clyde without her mother along, and would sing it after the Ross car had passed: "I don't like the kind of man/Does his lovin' in a Ford sedan;/'Cause you gotta see Mama every night/Or you can't see Baby at all." Quiet, shy Ava never said anything to Lyndon. But sometimes, after she had gone home, she would, she says, "cry for him."

"It was so unfair," she says. "It [the Rosses' attitude] didn't have anything to do with Lyndon. He had never done anything wrong. It was because they thought Lyndon was going to be just like Sam. And what made it even sadder was that it was history repeating itself. Sam hadn't been allowed to marry Kitty Clyde's mother. And now Sam's son wasn't allowed to marry Kitty Clyde. I was a Johnson, and it was very unfair to the Johnsons, and it was very unfair to Lyndon. And I saw how it made Lyndon feel when that big car drove by with Kitty Clyde in it with another man. And I cried for him."

Once, Ava says, Lyndon told her and Margaret that he "was working up his nerve" to ask Kitty Clyde for a date anyway—he guessed, he said, that he would ask her to go with him to the annual Johnson City–Fredericksburg baseball game and picnic. Kitty Clyde said she'd have to ask her parents. She came back and said she wouldn't be able to go. After that, Lyndon never asked her again.

(SOME TIME THEREAFTER, Kitty Clyde and Krause broke up. Her father thereupon sent her to the University of Texas, insisting she live in the Masonic Dormitory, whose tenants were not allowed to have dates. She returned to Johnson City after college, but never dated Lyndon again, and eventually married another local boy, who her father thought had good prospects, but who worked in the Ross store until it was sold. When Lyndon became President, he invited Kitty Clyde and her husband to Washington and took them for a flight on Air Force One.)

WHAT WAS IT LIKE to grow up in Johnson City? On the surface, life was idyllic, as idyllic as the scenery in which the town was set, those rolling hills and that sapphire sky. Listening to the friends of Lyndon Johnson's youth who stayed in Johnson City, Texas, who lived out their lives there, is like reading *Penrod and Sam*; their description is of picnicking and "Kodaking" (taking snapshots with "Brownie" cameras by the Pedernales), of long, lazy days sitting by the river with a cane fishing pole, of swimming in that clear, icy water, of playing croquet on Doc Barnwell's front lawn, of baseball outings when all the kids in town would pile onto a flatbed truck and drive to play a team from Blanco or Marble Falls, of chatting quietly with friends in Courthouse Square as a beautiful Hill Country sunset faded in the wide sky, and twilight fell, of gentle maturing in a quiet, serene, beautiful little town. The children who stayed speak of the friendliness of the Hill Country, "where," as a local saying went, "they know when you're sick and care when you die." More than one says flatly, "There's no place else on earth that I would rather live." More than one says, of growing up there, "it was Heaven."

But, listening to the friends of Lyndon Johnson's youth who didn't stay, to those who—like Lyndon Johnson—left Johnson City, the picture takes on darker shadows.

Poverty shadows the picture. Cash money was in such short supply that Joe Crider once rode a horse twenty miles across the hills at a slow walk, gingerly holding several dozen eggs, in order to sell them—for a nickel a dozen—in Marble Falls. Dolls were a luxury in Johnson City: Joe's daughter Cynthia had only one; it had a china head, on which, "every Christmas, my mother would put a new body," and many Johnson City girls made do with corncobs wrapped in scraps of cloth. Baseballs were a luxury: Lyndon's threat to take his ball and go home was effective because sometimes his was the only ball—after Sam Johnson went broke, sometimes there was none;

when there was a ball, it was usually ragged; "when someone had one, boy, we played with it until it just fell apart," Bob Edwards says. Books, even schoolbooks, were a luxury: ragged, too, because they were handed down from one class to another; there were never enough to go around. "You just can't imagine how poor people in Johnson City were," says Cynthia Crider, whose brothers were Lyndon's closest friends. "You just can't imagine how *little* we had." Sometimes the Criders couldn't buy enough food for their cattle and goats; they would feed them on prickly-pear cactus from which they had burned off the nettles. Sometimes they couldn't buy enough food for their children; then the entire dinner would consist of "Crider Gravy," which was nothing but flour and milk flavored with bacon drippings, on top of bread. For Christmas decorations, the Criders made paper chains out of pages from Big Chief writing pads and colored them with Crayola crayons, and they glued the pages together with the sticky "white" of eggs—because they couldn't afford a bottle of glue.

As dark as the poverty was the consciousness of poverty. The children of Johnson City were not only poor, they *felt* poor. "I sure did," says Louise Casparis, whose father, the town blacksmith, made fifteen cents for shoeing a horse—a three-hour job. "Many times I'd go to the store with just a dollar to spend. That wasn't enough, not to buy food for a whole family. But a lot of times that's all I'd have. I still remember going into the store with just that one dollar."

They realized, moreover, not only that they were poor—but that they were getting poorer. The Depression came early to farmers, and nowhere did it come earlier than in the Hill Country. 1924 and 1925 were years as bad as anyone could remember; the drought in 1925 was so bad that on the Dollahite farm, John Dollahite recalls, "we made no crops at all." And in the Hill Country hard times had a special significance for teen-agers. When farmers' crops didn't bring them enough cash money to pay their taxes and mortgage, they had no choice but to take the step which many of them had vowed never to take: to send their children to work "off the farm," earning cash wages—pitifully small though they were—doing day labor for other farmers. Such labor was brutal in the burning Hill Country sun. Cotton, as William Humphrey has written, "is a man-killing crop." Plowing it, pointing and holding the plow blade in the rocky ground "while the horse or the mule strains at the traces" is hard; thinning it, chopping out every other plant with a hoe, is hard, and when picking times comes,

> you strap on knee-pads and a long sack of cotton duck and you are in the field stooping and crawling and pulling that sack after you before daybreak, out until dark, beneath a searing sun. After just one day of it you cannot straighten your back at night to lie in bed, and your hands, even your work-hardened hands, are raw and bleeding from the sharp-pointed hulls.

Not only men and women were working in the Hill Country in 1924 and
'25. Teen-age boys and girls were out in the fields, too. And even the girls
had to work like men.

The picture is shadowed not only by poverty but by fear. Johnson
City teen-agers understood why they had to work. "Looking back now on
those days, it seems as if everyone, just about, was worried about meeting
the payments on their mortgage," one says. "I know *we* sure were." Not
having a home—being forced to take your possessions and move, to get
into your rickety car, and drive off, God knows where, with almost no money
in your pocket—that was the abyss. And in 1924 and '25, many Hill Country families were on the very edge of that abyss, and their children knew it.
"We had a sense of insecurity," Emmette Redford says. "With very few
exceptions—*very* few—a sense of insecurity hung over everyone around
there."

Poverty, fear—and a sense of hopelessness. For there seemed no way
out of the poverty. A dentist couldn't make money in Johnson City; the
only dentist had long since left (the town's dental needs were met by a
traveling dentist who came through every few months). A doctor couldn't
make money; Doc Barnwell was always complaining that "Half the town is
walking around and I haven't been paid for [delivering] them yet." A lawyer
couldn't make money. As for men who sold insurance or real estate, "I used
to wonder," Redford says. "How much real estate could you sell in that
country?" Most of the people in the Hill Country made their living from the
land, and those teen-agers who thought about the land understood that, as
Redford says, "You go ten, fifteen miles east of Austin and you begin to
see black soil and prosperous cotton farms, and big houses on the farms. But
there was no black soil around us. And there were no big houses. I had a
feeling even as a boy: in this town, there were no opportunities."

When, moreover, Johnson City teen-agers used the phrase "No opportunities," they were talking about more than career opportunities. The
lack of money was not the lack they felt most.

The roar of the Twenties was only the faintest of echoes in those vast
and empty hills—a mocking echo to Hill Country farmers who read of
Coolidge Prosperity and the reduction in the work week to forty-eight hours
and the bright new world of mass leisure, while they themselves were still
working the seven-day-a-week, dawn-to-dark schedule their fathers and
grandfathers had worked; a mocking echo to Hill Country housewives who
read of the myriad new labor-saving devices (washing machines, electric
irons, vacuum cleaners, refrigerators) that had "freed" the housewife. Even
if they had been able to afford such devices, they would not have been able
to switch them on since the Hill Country was still without electricity.

America—confident, cocky, Bull Market, hip-flask, Jazz-Age America
—was changing in the Twenties, changing with furious and exciting speed;
even much of Texas, still geographically isolated from the rest of the country,

was changing, as oil made a boomtown out of Beaumont and war-born industries stayed on to turn Houston and Dallas and even Austin into fast-growing cities. But little of the excitement managed to penetrate those hills. It was the Age of Radio; even the poor had radio; forests of antennas had sprung up on tenement-house roofs; even the rural poor had radio, which was ending the isolation of many rural areas by, in the words of historian David A. Shannon, "bringing the world" not only to "the middle-class home" but to "the tar-paper shack with an immediacy never before known. . . . By the middle of the decade, few people were out of earshot of the loud-speaker." But the Hill Country did not have radio; with the exception of a few crystal sets whose operators sat hunched over the needle they kept maneuvering to bring into their earphones sounds from New York almost two thousand miles away, no one in the Hill Country heard the voice which, during the Democratic National Convention of 1924, became familiar to the rest of America as it bellowed over and over, "Alabama—twenty-four votes for Underwoo---ood!" It was the Age of Movies; by the time "the boys . . . came trooping home" from the war in 1919, Shannon says, "the movie had set up its flickering screen in every crossroads village." But the man who wrote that had never headed west out of Austin: movies in Johnson City, shown on the whitewashed wall of the second floor of Harold Withers' "Opera House," as Harold, Jr., provided background music by playing the same scratchy phonograph record over and over, were shown very infrequently; people couldn't afford to pay the fifteen-cent admission charge too often. To the extent that the 1920's were the age of radio and the movies, and of country clubs, golf, joy-riding and cheek-to-cheek dancing— of a new mass culture—the Hill Country was not a part of the 1920's.

And the children of the Hill Country knew it. Not only were they not current on events, they knew they weren't current—and they were ashamed. During Lyndon Johnson's high-school years, the school's students held a debate on the League of Nations. They sent away to the University of Texas extension service for articles, and studied them, and the students felt they understood the subject. But, they recall, it was the only international—or national—subject they understood. "You know, you couldn't *get* any information out here, even if you wanted it," Louise Casparis says. "In bad weather, even the newspaper wouldn't come in—maybe for a week at a time. We were completely cut off out here. We knew about the League, but that was all we knew about. That was the pathetic thing." Truman Fawcett remembers that, during the years when Sam Johnson was still a politician, Lyndon would bring posters of the Democratic candidates for Governor and other state-wide offices around to shops and ask shopowners for permission to put them in the window. "And we had never even heard of most of them," Fawcett says. "Their names were names we had never even *heard!*" Says Louise Casparis: "You just would hardly understand the situation back there that we grew up in, because, you know, we had no radio, no newspapers to amount to anything—no *nothing!* We were just what you would call back in the woods, compared to the rest of the world."

They felt poor, they felt "back in the woods"—and they felt bored. "It was a rather drab little city," Lyndon Johnson's sister Rebekah says. Says Emmette Redford:

About all there was out there was three fundamentalist churches, a school with six rooms in it, and the courthouse. Occasionally, there would be a case for the Justice of the Peace Court, which handled traffic violations and minor offenses. And three or four times a year, the District Court, which handled the big cases then, would come into town, and would meet for a week, and the town would fill up with visiting lawyers, and the district attorney and the district judge would come in. And occasionally drummers would come in, or outside preachers for revival meetings at the churches, and in political campaigns, candidates for office would come through—not too often, though. Aside from that, the contact with the outside world was very limited. There was no movie, no form of paid entertainment whatsoever. My God, there wasn't even a café half the time. If you were a kid, you went to school five days a week. On Saturdays, everybody comes into town. The kids play with each other. On Sundays, you go to church. Now, that was about the round of life.

There seemed no way out of that round. Once there had been excitement in Blanco County, but that excitement had ended when the last Comanche had faded away to the north. In the half-century since then, the round of life had changed hardly at all. If a teen-ager wanted to see what lay ahead of him, all he had to do was look across Courthouse Square—at the old men, once youths who had stood chatting in the square as they themselves were doing now, who appeared promptly at noon every day (they had, after all, nothing else to do) and sat playing dominoes for matchsticks until it became too dark to play anymore.

And what of the unusual teen-ager, the one more interested in the outside world, more intellectually active, more ambitious or, perhaps, simply more restless than the other teen-agers in Johnson City? Few Johnson City teen-agers—no more than a handful, really—graduated even from the eleventh grade, which was the last grade in its high school. Fewer still went off to college. And of those who went to college, almost none came back to their hometown. "So what was left in Johnson City," says one who did come back, "were people who didn't have much education, and weren't much interested in current events or in the larger world. It wasn't just that we didn't have anything to read—we didn't have anyone to talk to."

And what, specifically, of the one teen-ager most interested in the outside world, the teen-ager who put up the political posters? How did he feel about living out his life in the Johnson City round? Was that last high-school spring, so idyllic on the surface, an idyll for him?

The contemporary most like Lyndon Johnson, in the opinion of Johnson City residents, was a youth three years older, Emmette Redford. "We had two boys who grew up here who became presidents," they say—and indeed Professor Redford, whose presidency was of the American Political Science Association, is the only other person who came out of Johnson City in the 1920's to achieve any substantial measure of nationwide prestige even in a limited field. What were Redford's feelings about Johnson City?

"Well," he says slowly, "I had no resentment. I liked the people out there. They were friendly, good people." He pauses, for quite a long time. Then he says, in a very different tone: "My feelings were *escape,* you see. It was a dull kind of life. It was boring. My God, it was boring! And there was always this feeling of insecurity, that you'd never have any of the comforts of life. And I couldn't see any way of ever obtaining any security in Johnson City. I couldn't see any way of accomplishing anything at all there. There were no opportunities in Johnson City. So my feelings were I had to get out of that town. I had to escape. I had to get out!"

Emmette Redford was a member of a family respected in Johnson City. What was it like to live in Johnson City and be a member of a ridiculed family—a family like the Johnsons?

During this period of his life, Lyndon Johnson was to say, he dreamed —over and over—the same terrible dream. In it, he was sitting alone in a small cage, "bare except for a stone bench and a pile of dark, heavy books." An old woman walked by, holding a mirror, and, catching a glimpse of himself in it, he saw that he had suddenly turned from a teen-age boy into a gnarled old man. When he pleaded with the old woman to let him out, she would instead walk away. And when he awoke, dripping with sweat, he would be muttering in the night: "I must get away. I must get away."

Many of Lyndon Johnson's "dreams" were related to interviewers for a carefully calculated effect, but this dream, real or invented, seems to reveal true feelings, for these feelings are corroborated by outside, independent sources—the recollections of people who knew him—as well as by his actions. Emmette Redford wanted to get out of Johnson City. Lyndon Johnson was desperate to get out.

HE REFUSED TO GET OUT by the road his parents had mapped for him, though. And by refusing to take that road, he gave them one of the most painful wounds it was within his power to inflict on them. They had always assumed—this couple to whom their children's education was so terribly important—that he would go to college. But now he said he wouldn't.

His mother kept trying to reason with him, telling him, in the words of Ben Crider, the older boy whom she enlisted in the struggle, that without an education "you couldn't get anywhere in life," that "she knew he had the qualifications, and she wanted him to be important, . . . to make good." She never, in the memory of Lyndon's friends and siblings, raised her voice or lost her temper, just kept trying to persuade him to go, telling him that he had a good brain and should work with it, instead of his hands, to get ahead, telling him that if he didn't go to college he would never learn to appreciate the beauties of literature or art, would never really learn the history in which he was so interested—kept trying to persuade him and encourage him, telling him she knew he would do well there. "Her big struggle was to get Lyndon" to go to college, Crider says—and she never gave up. Describing the struggle, Louise Casparis says: " 'Hope springs eternal' was written about her." Sam at first tried to reason with him, telling him that without an education all he could look forward to was a life of physical labor. Then he flatly ordered him to go. When Lyndon flatly refused, he tried insulting him, shouting, "You don't have enough brains to take a college education!"

Neither his mother's pleading nor his father's shouting moved him, however. His need to stand out, to "be somebody," to dominate, hadn't abated; now, more than ever, his friends recall, "Lyndon was always talking big"; once, when he said he would be a Congressman one day, and Fritz Koeniger laughed, Lyndon said, " 'I'll see you in Washington'—and he wasn't kidding at all." But, according to a girl who went to the only college in the Hill Country—Southwest Texas State Teachers College at San Marcos—to whom he confided some of his feelings during the summer following his graduation from high school, he was afraid he couldn't be somebody at college. Academic standards were much lower at Southwest Texas than at the University of Texas, but Lyndon was afraid they were too high for him: Johnson City High wasn't an accredited school; before a Johnson City graduate could be admitted, in fact, he had to take examinations to prove he was up to college level in his courses. Says the girl, Lyndon's cousin Elizabeth Roper Clemens: "He didn't have a full education, and he knew it." And, Mrs. Clemens says, although tuition at Southwest Texas was low—much lower than the university, for example—he would have to work while at school, "and going to school as just another poor boy—well, that wasn't something Lyndon wanted to do."

But perhaps there was something else behind Lyndon's attitude. College, the world of books, of Truth and Beauty, of the poetry his mother loved, of the ideals and abstractions so dear to his mother and father both, was the very essence of his parents' way of life—of everything important to these two people. He had seen what their way had got them. He had seen what it had got *him*. And he refused to go to college.

. . .

IF HE WOULDN'T GO to college, his father said, he'd have to go to work.

The state was gravel-topping six miles of the highway between Johnson City and Austin with gravel from the banks of Miller Creek. First, so rocky were those banks, the gravel had to be loosened with pickaxes. Then it had to be shoveled into mule-drawn wagons. The boards that formed the beds of the wagons had been loosened, and after the mules had hauled the wagons into position on the highway, the boards would be turned so that the gravel fell through onto the road, where it was smoothed out with rakes. Only the pickaxing was easy. For what the axes loosened was not soil but that hard Hill Country rock, so that the shovelfuls that had to be lifted up into the wagons were heavy. And the wagon boards had to be turned by hand, turned with piles of rock on top of them.

The hands turning those boards—and lifting those shovels, and tugging those rakes through rock—were young hands, for most of the workers were Johnson City teen-agers. Some of the hands were callused, the hands of boys accustomed to farm work. But the hands of fifteen-year-old Lyndon Johnson weren't. Nor was Lyndon strong, or physically coordinated, or accustomed to working; one night, the foreman, Floyd Ferrell, came home and sarcastically told his wife: "That boy can't even hold a shovel." For Lyndon, the work was almost as brutal as it was for the girls working beside him; in that Summer of 1924, two dollars a day, the wage the state was paying, was precious in the Hill Country, and any pair of hands that could bring it home had to do so—"We had to work like *men*," says Ava (her pretty sister, Margaret, was working, too, during their school vacations; despite their mother's thriftiness, their father was on the verge of losing his farm to the bank that Summer). "That was work I'll never forget." Lyndon had always hated physical labor—Ava remembers him, at the age of no more than nine or ten, whispering to her as they and their friends picked cotton in someone's stony fields, a score of skinny little backs stooped over in the burning sun: "Boy, there's got to be a better way to make a living than this. I don't see that there's any future in this." This road work—the only work available in a drought-stricken Hill Country—was even harder than picking cotton, and Lyndon hated every minute of it. Ava remembers him tugging at a wagon board beside her and grunting, "There's got to be a better way." But he did it—rather than do what his parents wanted.

More and more frequently now, he wouldn't get up on time. Coming into his room, his father would say harshly: "C'mon, Lyndon, get up—every boy in town's got an hour's start on you. And you never *will* catch up." He continued to sneak the car out at night, and his father grew angrier and angrier. Then, one night, while driving a group of older boys to a bootlegger's still, he ran the car into a ditch and wrecked it, and, standing there on the lonely country road, said: "I just can't face my father."

"Money was scarce," recalls one of the boys present, "but we put in our nickels and dimes and got Lyndon enough money" so that he could run away from home; he slept in the wrecked car, in the morning hitchhiked to Austin, and from there took a bus 160 miles south to Robstown, in the cotton country near Corpus Christi on the Gulf, where his cousins, the Ropers, lived. When he arrived, his cousin Elizabeth recalls, he said that "working on that highway was just too much for him, and he wanted to find a job where he could use his brains instead of his hands."

But the only job he could find in Robstown was in a cotton gin. The Roeder & Koether Gin Company was a long, low building filled with the clank of pulleys, the roar of machine belts, the whine of the high-speed saws that cut the cotton lint away from the seeds, and the heavy thuds of the huge hydraulic pump press that hammered the cotton into bales and pounded steel belts around them. Hot as it had been out on that highway in the Hill Country sun, it was hotter inside the gin, with the Gulf Coast sun beating down on its tin roof and fires roaring under the big steam boiler. The air in the gin was so thick with the dust and lint that drifted up in clouds from the cotton as it was pounded into bales by the pump press that men working in it sometimes found themselves gasping for breath. And Lyndon, working amid the roar and the whine and the pounding that must have been very loud to a boy from the Hill Country, where the gins were tiny, almost toylike devices compared to this, was put to work—eleven hours a day— keeping the boiler supplied with wood and water. And it was explained to him that if he ever let the water run out (or if the pop-off valve for some reason failed to work, and too much steam was kept pent up inside), the boiler would explode. Several had exploded in Robstown gins that summer; he was terrified.

"The work was hot and he wanted to come home," a Johnson City friend, Fritz Koeniger, recalls, "but he didn't want to come home and be punished. So he wrote to Ben Crider, and Ben told his brother Walter to bring it up with Mr. Sam. Walter asked him: 'Have you heard anything from Lyndon, Mr. Johnson?'

" 'No. His mother is worried to death about him.' (Pause.) 'And so am I.'

" 'Well, Ben's got a letter from him,' Walter says. 'And he says he's working on a steam boiler down in Robstown. Those old steam boilers are mighty dangerous. The people down there won't work on those boilers.'

"Sam got up and walked down the street in a deep study. Then he swung around and walked back, and said, 'Walter, here's ten dollars for gas. You drive down there just as fast as you can, and get Lyndon, and bring him home!' "

Then Sam went home and telephoned Robstown, telling Lyndon to come home with Walter. But Lyndon wouldn't let his father know he wanted to. Pretending that he was having a good time where he was, he said he would come home only if Sam promised never to punish him for the car wreck—or even to mention it. And when his father finally agreed, Lyndon insisted that his mother come to the phone and say she had heard the promise, so that in the future he would have a witness. And thereafter, whenever Sam, angry at Lyndon, would start to bring up the car wreck, Lyndon would say, "Mama, you remember, he said he wouldn't do it"—and Rebekah would say, "Now, that's out, Sam. You promised." And Lyndon's father would always drop the subject.

Lyndon could always outsmart his father.

But if Lyndon's car accident was a topic banned from the Johnson household, Lyndon's college career was not, and conflict flared again and again as September approached. Johnson City was abuzz over the fact that five children from a single graduating class, the most in the city's history, were going to college—and the parents of the sixth felt very bad. In September, Lyndon drove to Kyle to visit the last of the original Buntons, his Great-uncle Desha, who, tended by a former slave, old Uncle Ranch, who was almost as feeble as he, was dying—on the same ranch he had founded almost sixty years before and had managed to hold on to ever since, and would be able to pass on, unencumbered by mortgage, to his sons. But if Lyndon was offered any financial assistance for his higher education, it was not sufficient to change his mind. On the day that four of his former classmates went to San Marcos to enter college—Kitty Clyde, of course, went to Austin—Lyndon went, too, in response to a direct order. But he returned to Johnson City without registering, and stood sullenly under the lash of his father's tongue. And, a week or two later, he ran away again.

THIS TIME, he ran not south but west—to California.

Four older boys, discouraged by the lack of work in Johnson City, were planning a job-hunting trip to the coast in Walter Crider's old "T-Model," which they had purchased for twenty-five dollars. When Lyndon asked his parents for permission to accompany them, Rebekah became hysterical, and Sam flatly forbade him to go. Lyndon boasted that he was going anyway. Told about the boast, Sam said, "Weeelll, I'm just gonna wait until they're all loaded up, and then I'm gonna yank him out of that car." One Wednesday in November, however, Sam heard of a farm for sale near Blanco at a cheap price, and drove down to investigate. The boys had been planning to leave that Friday, but, Lyndon's brother says, "The minute he [Sam] took off, Lyndon ran into his room, pulled his already-packed suitcase from under the bed, and quickly called his fellow travelers together. In less than ten minutes, they . . . zoomed out of town at close to thirty miles an hour." Returning some hours later, Sam

> exploded in several different directions. I had never heard such rich, inventive language. . . . Cranking the phone as if it were an ice-cream machine, he called the sheriff of nearly every county

between Johnson City and El Paso on the far western border of
Texas, asking them to arrest his runaway son,

but for some reason no one did.

After Lyndon Johnson became President, he would frequently enthrall
reporters—and biographers—with his dramatic description of this California trip, which he said he took because "it meant one less mouth for my
poor daddy to feed." In a typical description, he said the five travelers had
been so naïve and frightened ("None of us had been off the farm for a trip
longer than the road to town") that

> We'd camp out along the railroad tracks at night, and always our
> first chore would be to dig a hole in which to bury our money. The
> heaviest member of our party always slept over our cache. We
> didn't propose to be robbed. Finally we came to a place where a
> hole in the ground was no longer necessary. The money we had
> just trickled away. When we were broke and job hunting, we
> separated.

He remained in California for two years, he said, and during this time,

> Nothing to eat was the principal item on my food chart. That was
> the first time I went on a diet. Up and down the coast I tramped,
> washing dishes, waiting on tables, doing farm work when it was
> available, and always growing thinner.

When finally he returned to Johnson City—hitchhiking the entire fifteen
hundred miles—he said,

> The trip back home was the longest I've ever made. And the
> prettiest sight I ever saw in my life was my grandmother's patch-
> work quilt at the foot of my bed when I got home.

Lyndon Johnson's description of the trip, however, no matter how
enthralling to biographers—a passage in a typical biography reads: "Johnson was barely able to survive on the grapes he picked, the dishes he
washed and the cars he fixed. . . . [He] lived the vagabond life"—is no more
accurate than the reason he gave for taking it.

Once California had been the frontier, the land of opportunity to the
west, and in the Hill Country it was still thought of as the land of opportunity. "Everyone in Johnson City wanted to go to California," Louise Casparis
says. "They thought you could make money out there"—and the five boys
believed they were on the trail of fortune; they named their car "the Covered

Wagon." Arriving in El Paso (population 74,000), they were thrilled by it because it was the first time any of them had been in a "big city." Traveling up through New Mexico and then across Arizona on plank roads, crossing the Colorado River on a ferry, they felt very much like explorers. "We had a lot of fun," Rountree says. And when they arrived in Tehachapi, California, where a number of Johnson City boys, including Lyndon's close friends Ben Crider and Fritz Koeniger, were working in a cement plant, while only two of the travelers could obtain jobs in the plant and two others did indeed pick grapes and do other farm work in the San Joaquin Valley, if Lyndon Johnson picked any grapes, he picked very few. His cousin Tom Martin, son of the well-known attorney Clarence Martin, had become a prominent attorney himself in San Bernardino, and what Johnson actually did as soon as he arrived in California was to telephone Martin and ask if he could work as a clerk in his law office. Martin, after calling the Johnsons and obtaining their consent, agreed. He drove to Tehachapi to pick Lyndon up and took him straight to the best men's shop in San Bernardino, where he bought him two expensive suits, and then brought him to his home, a four-bedroom ranch house. And what Johnson actually did, from beginning to end of his fabled stay in California, was not tramp up and down the coast, "with nothing to eat," "washing dishes, waiting on tables, doing farm work," but work in his cousin's paneled office and live in his cousin's comfortable home.

YET IF THERE WAS no poverty or hunger on the trip, there were terrors nonetheless.

Martin had given Johnson hope: he promised to make him a lawyer. In California as in Texas, he explained, admission to the bar required passing a written examination, which he felt—and Lyndon said he agreed—Lyndon wouldn't be able to pass, even after studying law in Martin's office; not without more education than had been provided at Johnson City High. In neighboring Nevada, however, no written examination was required, and the oral examinations were very informal, especially when the candidate came recommended by a prominent attorney. Martin was friends with several prominent attorneys in Nevada, he said, and if Lyndon studied law in his office—no more than a few months would be needed—he would arrange with one of his friends to have Lyndon admitted to the Nevada bar. Practicing in Nevada wouldn't be a good idea, Martin said; that state was still sparsely settled and rather impoverished. But once he was a lawyer in Nevada, Johnson could be admitted to the California bar under a provision which made such admission all but automatic for any lawyer from another state. And as soon as he was admitted, Martin would take him into his own profitable practice.

To Lyndon, this seemed a chance—his first real chance—to be someone without bowing to his parents' wishes and going to college. Fritz
Koeniger was rooming with Lyndon, who had persuaded Tom to let Koeniger work as a clerk in his office, and, Koeniger says, "Lyndon wanted to be
a lawyer, wanted it very badly." He threw himself into his work with an
energy he had never displayed before. If at home he had had to be shouted
out of bed, now he jumped up and dressed in an almost frantic haste—so
anxious to get to work, in fact, that he developed a habit Koeniger had never
heard of: instead of untying his necktie at night, which would have required
him to spend half a minute or so retying it in the morning, Lyndon would
loosen the knot enough to pull it over his head and hang it, still tied, on a
doorknob, so that he could just pull it over his head and tighten the knot
in the morning. And when he got to the office, he not only raced to do whatever work Martin assigned him, but in every spare minute bent over Martin's
big lawbooks with a fierce concentration. "He had always been ambitious,
even back in Johnson City," Koeniger says, but there was a new level of intensity about that ambition now. "He wanted to get ahead in the world,
wanted to be something, and he wanted it so bad that he was aggressive,"
Koeniger says. "He was very aggressive." Martin, as renowned an orator as
his father, was active in Democratic politics in San Bernardino, and had
been invited to speak at a Labor Day picnic. But the night before, he, Lyndon and Koeniger had driven over to Los Angeles to a party for two Johnson City newlyweds who had come to California, and they had slept over.
As soon as they started driving to San Bernardino the next morning, they
saw that the holiday traffic was so heavy that they might not get to the picnic
on time. The road had only two lanes, one in each direction, and both lanes
were crowded, so that Lyndon, who was driving, had to get cars in his lane to
pull off to the side of the road if he wanted to pass them. And the horn on
Martin's car didn't work. "And then," Koeniger says, "and this is what I've
thought of many times to show how aggressive Lyndon was—he'd pull right
up behind some car and bang the side of his door, just smash it—hard—
with his open palm so it sounded like a crash, almost, over and over until
they'd pull over. Chauffeur-driven cars, some of them. Rich people out for
a holiday. But that long arm would just reach out the window and just smash
and smash. And the other car would swerve over and we'd go by and they'd
glare at us. I wouldn't have done that, but Lyndon was just *determined* to get
there on time." He did—they arrived just as the master of ceremonies was
asking, "Is the Honorable Thomas J. Martin in the audience? He is scheduled to speak at this time." Martin shouted up, "Here I am!" Koeniger was
never to forget that long arm beating—smashing on the car door.

For a few months, Lyndon's hopes seemed on the way to realization.
Martin's practice was booming. He had impressed Cornelius Vanderbilt, Jr.,
and did legal work for him, and he also did a lot of divorce work, some for
movie actresses from whom he received fees that sounded wonderfully large

to the two Hill Country youths. He had a knack for publicity—once, recalls Koeniger, he "saved up" his divorce cases for several weeks, and then gave them all to his two "assistants" in a bunch; "Lyndon and I took them down and filed them in the courthouse all at once, and we got a big headline in the *San Bernardino Sun* because it was the most divorce cases ever filed in one day." And Lyndon was doing more and more of the paperwork in the office, and, Martin said, making good progress in his law reading.

But there was more than one facet to Martin's character. He had blighted a brilliant career in Texas before coming to California. Elected to the Legislature at twenty-one, he had resigned to enlist (it was his seat that Sam took in the special election of 1917), and returned as a war hero with a lieutenancy and a silver star, awarded, the citation read, for his bravery in going "into the front line, which was under severe artillery and machine gun fire, in order to encourage . . . his regiment." He was named police chief of San Antonio, and had been nominated for district attorney when he became involved in a series of escapades (on one occasion, drunk, he and some friends drove around the city shooting out streetlights). He resigned and left town while a grand jury was considering an indictment against him. When, during the summer of 1925, his wife, Olga, took their little son back to Texas for a visit, "she hadn't more than left San Bernardino on the train" when Martin organized a "party" that was to go on ("more or less continuously," Koeniger says) for more than two months.

The key participants were Martin and his actress girlfriend, Lottie. Martin had, in Koeniger's words, a "great capacity" for Gordon's gin, and a bootlegger client—whom he had been keeping out of jail for years—to supply it. "Any time you need anything, just call," the bootlegger told the two youths, and, on Martin's behalf, they called frequently during the ensuing two months, during all of which, Koeniger says, Martin remained "pretty much drunk."

While present at the party—it took place, after all, at the house in which they were living—Lyndon and Koeniger were more spectators than participants. They each had a "girlfriend," but only to have someone to go to the party with; Lyndon's was Martin's secretary, who would come over from the office with him; their relationship was platonic. What the two young men mainly did that summer—Lyndon with feverish earnestness—was try to hold Martin's law practice together, for, with the onset of the "party," Martin completely abandoned it.

At first, the task was fun. When a client telephoned, Koeniger says, he or Lyndon would in turn telephone Martin, "and he'd tell us what to tell the client, and to cover up for him not being there." When Martin was too much under the weather to be of assistance, they would decide themselves what "legal advice" to give—"Lyndon and I were practically running the office."

But it wasn't fun for long. "We had to pay filing fees and other expenses that lawyers have," Koeniger explains. "And we had to pay the office rent. Several times Lyndon mentioned to Tom, 'We've got to raise some money.'" The first few times, Martin gave him some, but then he grew evasive, and his two clerks realized he no longer had any to give. Lyndon and Koeniger had never been on salary—"we had just kind of been sharing with Tom on anything that came in." They paid some filing fees themselves, and then some of the back rent—and found themselves, Koeniger says, "flat broke." And the landlord began coming around to demand the rest of the rent. Then they learned that a mortgage payment was coming due on Martin's house. Lyndon Johnson, who had for years watched his father, broke, worry about losing his home, realized with a start that he was in the same position. And Lyndon had an additional worry. He suddenly realized that in advising clients when Martin was unable to, he had in fact been practicing law without a license. If one of the clients found out, he could be arrested. He could go to jail! And several clients for whom legal papers hadn't been filed as they had expected—because there was no money to pay the filing fees—were beginning to ask suspiciously what was going on. Whether or not jail was a real possibility, it loomed very real indeed for the two unsophisticated youths. Lyndon was terrified—they both were. Years later, with real feeling in his voice, Koeniger would say: "This was a *terrible* experience."

And then Lyndon Johnson found out that he wasn't going to be a lawyer after all. In assuring him that he would be able to obtain a Nevada license, Martin had overlooked the fact that Nevada had an age requirement; a lawyer had to be at least twenty-one. In this summer of 1925, Lyndon was only seventeen; he would have to wait four years! Koeniger isn't sure whether or not Lyndon had known this earlier, but he is sure—for he remembers his friend's shock and dismay when he found it out—that he hadn't known about another requirement. Martin had assured him that once he obtained a Nevada license, it would be easy for him to obtain a California license. California law, however, required that such reciprocal licenses go to attorneys who had been practicing in another state for at least three years. It wouldn't be four years before Lyndon could practice in California—it would be *seven!* And at the same time that Lyndon learned this dismaying fact, Koeniger says, he learned another one: Nevada was in the process of tightening up its previously slack requirements for obtaining a license to practice law; it was going to be much more difficult to obtain one without a college degree, so difficult that it might be all but impossible to obtain one with only a Johnson City High School education.

In September, 1925, Martin received word that his wife was on her way back from Texas, driving back with his father, Clarence Martin. "When we got the word that Olga was coming home—of course Lottie understood that; no trouble there—Tom said, 'Now, you take the car and take Lottie back to Hollywood, and Lyndon and I will clean up. We've got to remove any trace of any woman being here.' Olga never did find out, and when she came back, Tom said, 'Now, boys, we're going to straighten up and practice law.' " But the young men had been too scared. "We hadn't wanted to desert Tom, but we had resolved that when Olga came back, we'd leave," Koeniger says. "After this terrible experience, we had resolved that we didn't want to go on any more." As soon as Olga arrived, they left. Koeniger took the first job he was offered—in a box-making factory in Clovis—and couldn't leave San Bernardino fast enough, so thoroughly frightened had he been. And when, a week later, Clarence Martin started driving back to Texas, Lyndon went with him. In October or November, 1925—less than a year, not two years as he later said—after he had run away from Johnson City, Lyndon Johnson came back home. Just as his stay in California was not at all as he described it, neither was his trip back. He said he hitchhiked home; in fact, he was driven to his front door in Clarence Martin's big Buick.

But coming back, while it may have been in luxury, was still coming back. Lyndon Johnson had gone to California in the hope of finding a way to achieve the security and respect he wanted without following the course laid out by the parents with whom he was in such violent conflict. For a few months, sitting behind Tom Martin's big desk in that paneled law office, acting like a lawyer—believing, because of Martin's promise to him, that he would *be* a lawyer, would be one, moreover, without having to go to college as his parents wanted—he had been sure that he had found the way. He had been given hope. Now he had had to come back. The hopes had been smashed. Before he went to California, Stella Gliddon says, he had been over at her house almost every day. Now she heard he was back, but for some weeks she never saw him. And then, when he finally came around again, she says, "I saw a changed person. Before he went to California, he was just a happy-go-lucky boy. When he came back, well, I saw a serious boy then. I saw a man. I saw what disappointment had done."

HE BEGAN RUNNING AROUND with what Johnson City called the "wild bunch," a group of young men older than he—he was eighteen—who prowled the countryside at night, seizing whatever pathetic opportunities for mischief the Hill Country afforded. Waiting until their fathers were asleep, they took the family cars and held drag races outside of town, or rendezvoused in the hills with bootleggers to buy a jug of moonshine. When they went to the weekend dances, they would pick up a jug first, and at the dance they would get drunk and start fights. They put Eugene Stevenson's buggy up on the roof of his barn, and broke into henhouses and stole a few hens for whiskey money.

While most of their escapades were harmless, some began to skirt closer to the law. When Lyndon and his friends heard that a German farmer, Christian Diggs, had made his annual batch of grape wine, they pried loose boards from his barn and stole a fifty-five-gallon barrel, worth a not inconsiderable amount of money in Hill Country terms—and Diggs was persuaded only with difficulty not to go to the sheriff. They hung a few sticks of dynamite in trees in Johnson City, and ignited them to scare the townspeople—that was just a prank, but it stopped being funny when it was learned that they had obtained the dynamite by breaking into the State Highway Department storage shed. That was a state offense, and the sheriff passed word around Johnson City that whoever had done it had better not do it again. "I always hated cops when I was a kid," Johnson was to say, and on this occasion he defied them; a few nights later, they stole more dynamite and shattered the large mulberry tree in front of the school. The Highway Department put a watchman at the shed; after he fell asleep one night, Lyndon and his friends broke in, stole more dynamite, and hung it from the telephone line that ran across Courthouse Square. Then, Bob Edwards says, "we lit the thing and got in the car and ran like hell"—and the ensuing explosion knocked all the windows out of the Johnson City Bank. The sheriff let it be known that the next time something like this happened, he would make arrests. Lyndon's Grandmother Baines repeated her prediction that "That boy is going to end up in the penitentiary," and Johnson City, which had always known that he was going to come to no good, felt that he was well on the way to fulfilling her prophecy. And, perhaps, so did Lyndon Johnson himself. Recalling his boyhood, he once said: "I was only a hairsbreadth away from going to jail."

His parents were terrified of what was going to become of him. His mother would hear no criticism—"No matter what they came and told her Lyndon had done, it was always the other boys' fault for persuading him to go along," a friend says—but she could not blink the fact of who the other boys were. The Redfords and Fawcetts were in college, and Lyndon was hanging around with the Criders and other young men who weren't ever going to go to college, who were going to spend their lives working on the highway or on the ranches—who were going to spend their lives at manual labor. His father understood why Lyndon was acting this way. "If you want to get noticed," he would say, "there are better ways." Sam Johnson made other attempts to get through to his son. In May, 1926, Lyndon again wrecked his father's car on a nocturnal drive, this time smashing it beyond repair, and again ran away, this time to the New Braunfels home of an uncle. His father telephoned him there, and, Lyndon was to recall:

> My daddy said: "Lyndon, I traded in that old car of ours this morning for a brand-new one and it's in the store right now needing someone to pick it up. I can't get away from here and I was wondering if you could come back, pick it up, and drive it home

for me. And there's one other thing I want you to do for me. I want you to drive it around the Courthouse Square five times, ten times, fifty times, nice and slow. You see there's some talk around town this morning that my son's a coward, that he couldn't face up to what he'd done, and that he ran away from home. Now I don't want anyone thinking I produced a yellow son. So I want you to show up here in that car and show everyone how much courage you've got. Do you hear me?"

"Yes sir," I replied. I hung up the phone, shook hands with my uncle, and left right away.

For a while after this episode, tensions eased between Lyndon and his father, but soon he began to sneak out at night and take the new car without permission. Then, in September, his father grew sick, and had to lie in bed for months—since he was unable to work, bringing no money at all into the house. When he got up—got up to put on his khaki work shirt and go back to the road gang—his emotions were noticeably rawer than before, and tensions rose. On weekends, Lyndon liked to sleep most of the day; his father, awakening him, would shake his bed violently. And when, one morning after Lyndon had sneaked out the car, Sam ran out of gas on the way to work, he came raging back to confront his son; when Lyndon, lying, denied that he had used the car, Sam slapped him in the face—"just with his palm, not his fist, but hard; Mr. Sam was a big man," says Edwards, who was present. Lyndon started to run away, Edwards says, but "Mr. Sam yelled, 'C'mere, Lyndon! Goddamn, you all come here!' And Lyndon had to come back. And his daddy slapped him again. Lyndon was crying, 'Oooh, Daddy, that's enough, Daddy. I won't do it any more.' But the next night, he stole the car again." When, now, Sam stood talking with Rebekah about Lyndon, knowing he would overhear, there was a harsh tone in the voice in which he spoke harsh words. "Nope, Rebekah, it's no use," he would say. "That boy's just not college material."

The strategy hurt Lyndon, but it didn't have the effect Sam had hoped. "If you want to get noticed," he had said, "there are better ways." But his parents' way was going to college—and over and over again during this year, he said defiantly that he wasn't going to go.

But Lyndon Johnson was going to go to college. Had he been as much a Johnson as his father, he might—like his father—never have gone. He might—like his father—have spent his life fighting the realities of the Hill Country and being crushed by them. But he wasn't primarily a Johnson. Beneath the foppish silk shirts was a Bunton. People might call Sam Johnson impractical. No one ever called a Bunton impractical. If there was only one way to accomplish their purpose, the Buntons found that way and took it. Once Lyndon Johnson fully understood the reality of his circumstances, he wouldn't go on fighting them. He may not have wanted to go to college, he may have been determined not to go to college—but if going to college was the only way to accomplish his ends, to escape, to get out of the Hill Country not as a laborer but as something better, go he would. And after he returned from California, the Johnson who was also a Bunton was taught—the hard way—that there was indeed only one way to accomplish his ends.

After he returned from California, he worked for the State Highway Department.

The work started at dawn. Six a.m. sharp was the time the State Highway Department cars left Courthouse Square for the job site, with the road gang on board. And this time the job wasn't merely gravel-topping, or smoothing off, a road. This time the job was building a road.

Because little mechanical equipment was available, the road was being built almost entirely by hand. It wasn't being paved, of course; in 1926, Hill Country roads were still made of that rocky Hill Country "caliche" soil that was as white as the limestone of which it was composed, and as hard. For a while, to earn his two dollars a day, Johnson "drove" a "fresno," a two-handled metal scoop pulled by four mules. He would stand behind the scoop, between its handles. Because he needed a hand for each handle, the reins leading to the mules were tied together and wrapped around his back, so that man and mules were, really, in harness together.

Lifting the handles of the scoop, Johnson would jam its front edge into the caliche. Urging the mules forward, he pushed as they pulled—pushing hard to force the scoop through the rocky soil. When the scoop contained a full load, he pressed down on the handles, straining with the effort, until the scoop rose free of the ground. Then, still pressing down on the handles with all his might, the reins still cutting into his back, he directed the mules to the dumping place, where he would pull up the handles to dump the heavy load. "This was a job which required . . . a strong back," says one description of the work. "This, for a boy of . . . seventeen, was back-breaking labor."

When he wasn't operating the fresno, Johnson worked with Ben Crider, who had come back from California, as a pick-and-shovel team. "He'd use the shovel and scoop the dirt up, and I'd pick it up out of the ground, or vice versa," Crider recalls. And, Crider says, such work was "too heavy" for Johnson. He would come home at night—work started at daybreak, it ended at dusk—exhausted. His skin—that soft white Bunton skin—refused to callus; blister formed on top of blister on his hands, which were often bleeding. He still tried to impress the other workers—at lunch hour, one says, he "talked big . . . he had big ideas . . . he wanted to do something big with his life"—but if he had ever had any difficulty seeing the reality of his life, it must have been clear to him now. He was down in that hated Hill Country rock, down in that rock for two dollars a day, down working beside youths who knew that Kitty Clyde had jilted him because her father had predicted he was going to end up doing work like the work he was in fact doing. And the home he went to at night was again a home to which people brought charity; Sam fell sick again, and stayed sick for months, and without income, there was, again, no money in the house for food, and other families would bring cooked dishes to the Johnsons.

He had started work in Winter. "It was so cold," Ben Crider recalls. "That was the worst part of it—getting so cold you had to build a fire to thaw out your hands before you could handle a pick and shovel. And we have done that many a day—build us a fire and thaw and work all day." Spring was more pleasant, but Spring was followed by Summer, the Hill Country summer where laborers toiled beneath that almost unbearable Hill Country sun with their noses and mouths filled with the grit that was the dried soil the wind whipped into their faces. And Summer became Autumn and then Winter again; the first cut of the wind of this new Winter may have slashed into Lyndon Johnson's consciousness the realization that this wasn't his first year on the road gang any more, that he had been working on it for an entire year, and now a second year was starting, and he was still on the road gang. He had boasted to his cousins in Robstown that he was going to work with his brains and not his hands. That had been in 1924. Now it was 1927, and he was still working with his hands. The boy who had wanted so desperately to escape from the cage that was Johnson City had not done so.

So many others had, moreover. The streets of the little town were empty now of many of the faces he had grown up with. Not only Kitty Clyde but all his classmates were away at college. All three Redford boys were at college, as were his cousins Ava and Margaret. Even Louise Casparis, who had been his mother's maid, was going to college now. But, almost three years after he had graduated from high school, Lyndon wasn't going to college. All during his boyhood, he had boasted to his friends that he wouldn't work with his hands. Well, his friends weren't working with their hands any more. But he was.

Still he wouldn't go. Instead, determined not to continue his education as his parents wanted but desperate to stand out, to be somebody—born with a flaming ambition but born in an area that offered ambition no fuel; driven into desperation by the conflict between lineage and landscape—he flailed frantically, trying to stand out every way but their way.

He was seizing now on anything that might offer prestige. He took to talking frequently about the Baineses' "Southern blood"—which, he emphasized to Ava and Margaret, they possessed, too; once, Ava recalls, Lyndon warned her sternly not to dance with a certain young man because "he's common." At dances, Lyndon dressed differently from other men—and acted differently. Entering a small, bare Hill Country dance hall with his friends, wearing a brightly colored silk shirt, his hair elaborately pompadoured and waved and glistening with Sta-comb, he would walk in front of them, swaggering and strutting—or, rather, so awkward was he, trying to swagger and strut; when his friends attempt to imitate the way he looked, they stick their stomachs far out, pull their shoulders far back, and let their arms flap awkwardly far away from their bodies, so that they look quite silly—and that is how they say Lyndon looked. Even Ava, so fond of him, says, "A lot of times he looked smart-alec, silly-like." His "big talk" grew bigger; he was frequently predicting now that he would be "the President of the United States" one day.

But, always, there was reality. Dress as he might at night, every morning at six o'clock he had to be in Courthouse Square, wearing work clothes. The job he hated was the only job available. And then even that was not available. Ferguson man Sam Johnson had worked for "Ma" Ferguson in the 1926 Gubernatorial campaign, but she had been defeated by Dan Moody. And no sooner was Moody inaugurated, on January 18, 1927, than he began replacing all the Ferguson men in the Highway Department with his own followers. Sam Johnson and his son were notified that they wouldn't have their jobs much longer. The "sense of insecurity" which Emmette Redford says "hung over everyone" certainly hung over the Johnsons then; there were the taxes on the house, and the mortgage, to be paid—over all of the Johnsons now hung the knowledge, every time they looked at their house, that it might not be theirs much longer.

Then, one Saturday night in February, 1927, Lyndon Johnson went to a dance.

It was held in Peter's Hall in Fredericksburg, a big, bare barn of a building undecorated except for benches ranged against the walls—music was provided by a German "Ooom-pah-*pah*" band—and most of the men were wearing plain shirts and trousers, with here and there a suit. But Lyndon was wearing a shirt of white silk crepe de Chine (he had been saving for weeks to buy it; he boasted to his friends that it cost "more than ten dollars") with broad lavender stripes and big French cuffs in which he had inserted a pair of huge, gleaming cufflinks he had "borrowed" from his father. At the dance was a pretty, buxom Fredericksburg girl with big blue eyes and blond hair whose father was a well-to-do merchant. She was "going with" a young German farmer whose first name was Eddie, but as soon as the group from Johnson City arrived—Lyndon, his cousins Ava and Margaret, Harold Withers, Cora Mae Arrington, and Tom and Otto Crider—Lyndon told his friends, "I'm just going to take that little Dutch girl away from that old boy tonight, just as sure as the world." And, Ava says, "He just sauntered across the hall—he looked so silly, I can't keep from laughing; you don't know how funny it was; really, you can't imagine; I can just see him *swaggering* up to this little old country girl; he'd been to California, he had a lot of new airs—and he just sauntered across the hall, just smiling like the world was his with a downhill pull," and pulled her out on the floor.

Eddie, who was standing talking with some friends, didn't pay any attention at first, but Lyndon bent over and put his cheek against hers, and the Johnson City group could see the farmer get angry. And after Lyndon had brought her back to her seat after one set, the music started again, and he pulled her back onto the floor and repeated his actions. "They had up on the wall, NO CHEEK-TO-CHEEK, and Lyndon of course was a lot taller than she was, and he bent down and put his cheek next to hers, and he had made this ol' boy so mad he like to have died." And he was acting, Ava says, "like 'I've got it made—she'll be mine in no time.' Smart-alec." When the third set began, he started to dance with Eddie's girl again, but Eddie walked over and tapped him on the shoulder and asked him to step outside.

"Nice" Hill Country girls wouldn't "go outside" dance halls then, so for a while Ava and Margaret and Cora Mae Arrington could only speculate about what might be happening, but finally Margaret said, "Well, I'm going to see," and all three ran out. And when they did, they saw that, as Ava puts it, "Lyndon was getting *really* beat up!

"Lyndon was so awkward and this boy was so big and fast," Ava says. "He'd knock Lyndon down, and Lyndon would get up, and shout, 'I'll *get you!*' and run at him, and he never got to hit him once that I can recall. He didn't even get close to him. He'd yell, 'I'll *get you!*' and run at that Dutch boy, and the Dutch boy would hit him—whoom! And down Lyndon would go again." Blood was pouring out of Lyndon's nose and mouth, running down his face and onto the crepe-de-Chine shirt. The Criders, afraid he was going to be badly hurt, started to interfere, but Fredericksburg's old, tough sheriff, Alfred Klaerner, had been present at the dance, and Sheriff Klaerner had had, for some time now, more than enough of Lyndon Johnson. "We'll just stand back and let them have it out," he said, stepping in front of the Criders, and when Otto kept coming, the sheriff knocked him backward and said: "If you try that again, I'll stick the whole bunch of you in jail." The Johnson City group stood silent, and the beating went on.

"Lyndon never got in a lick," Ava says. "It was pitiful. Every time he got up, that old boy knocked him down—he had fists like a pile-driver. Lyndon's whole face was bloody, and he looked pretty bad." And finally, lying on the ground, he said: "That's enough."

When Lyndon had recovered a little, Ava says, he realized that one of his father's cufflinks was missing, and he got "very upset." After a while, someone found it and gave it back to him, but there was nothing anyone could do about the shirt; it was thoroughly bloodstained. But it wasn't Lyndon's injuries that most impressed Ava, it was his demeanor. "Lyndon was always so talkative, so lively," she says. He had lost fights before— "Lyndon *always* lost"—but as soon as they were over, he would always be chattering away in no time. But all the way home to Johnson City, he didn't say a word. The group stopped at Flatt's Creek to clean him up, and he still didn't say anything. "He was very subdued," Ava says. "He acted like

a guy who had had all the wind taken out of his sails." When they took up
a collection and gave him enough money to pay his fine—while he had still
been lying on the ground, Sheriff Klaerner had bent over and handed him a
summons for disorderly conduct—Lyndon thanked them, but in a voice so
low that Ava had never heard it before. Possibly his depression was due to
the beating he had taken—"He'd had fights before, but he'd never gotten
walloped like this," she says—but his cousins didn't think so. After they
had dropped him off at his house, he walked inside without a word, and
Ava and Margaret agreed that they had seen Lyndon in a similar mood only
once before: when he had come back from California. And, Ava says, she
and Margaret agreed that the reason for the depression was the same both
times: "Something had made him realize that he wasn't cock of the walk."

WAS AVA RIGHT? Did the dance teach Lyndon Johnson the same lesson that
his California experience had taught him? Was he silent and depressed by
the realization that his hopes were doomed? Realizing how hard it was to
be somebody in the Hill Country, he had tried twice, in running away to
Robstown and California, to escape from it, but to escape without following
the course his parents wanted him to take. But both attempts had failed. On
his return from the second, had he tried to be something *in* the Hill Country—
and had he had pounded into him, every morning that he put on the work
shirt, that he couldn't be? Hadn't there been an increasing desperation in
his actions during the past year; hadn't the boasting become wilder, the
shirts brighter and more expensive, the nighttime pranks more and more
frenetic? And had, then, his beating by the hard fists of the Hill Country
farm boy, his humiliation before his friends, been a final pounding into him
of the reality about the Hill Country, where the physical was all that mattered. Had the beating been a final confirmation of the realization that he
was never going to be somebody as long as he stayed in Johnson City—
that even at a dance in a bare hall he couldn't be somebody—that there
was no choice for him but to get out, even if the only way out was his
parents' way? Is it possible to read into his "That's enough" a surrender
not just in a dance-hall fight but in the larger fight he had been waging for
years: the fight to be somebody without following the course his parents
wanted him to take? No one can say. No one knows what Lyndon Johnson
thought that night, on the way home and lying in bed, and no one will ever
know. But the next morning, he told his parents he would go to college.

WHEN, HOWEVER, he left for college the following week, he did not leave in
a spirit of reconciliation with his parents. He would not, in fact, even
permit his father to drive him to San Marcos, preferring to hitchhike the
thirty miles, carrying a cardboard suitcase, rather than accept a favor from

him. And he didn't attend college in that spirit, either; the values he took from college were not at all what his parents had envisioned, as was perhaps symbolized following graduation by his lifelong reluctance—a reluctance so strong that it was seldom broken—to read books. They wanted him to go to college to learn about literature and art, Beauty and Truth. He wanted to be somebody, to stand out, to lead, to dominate. He may not yet have known how to accomplish *that*, but he certainly knew how *not* to accomplish it: his parents—the lesson of their lives—had taught him. In Austin, he had seen the legislators who accepted the beefsteak, the bourbon and the blondes, who lived at the Driskill while his father lived at the boardinghouse. His father had refused to be like them, and he had seen what happened to his father. His mother had believed that poetry and beauty were the most important things in life, and she had refused to ever stop believing that, and he had seen what happened to his mother. The most striking characteristic of both his parents was that they were idealists who stuck to their ideals. They had been trying ever since he was a little boy to teach him that what mattered was principle, and sticking to principle.

Lyndon Johnson's college career—and his career after college, from beginning to end—would demonstrate what he thought of their teachings.

Part II

ESCAPE

8

"Bull" Johnson

IN ALL THE 24,000 square miles of the Hill Country, there was only one college.

It wasn't much of a college. Its Main Building—surmounted by four spires and by layers of arches, gables, pinnacles and parapets—had been built to impress, and had been placed on the highest hill in the San Marcos area, so that its red spires, trimmed with gold paint, glittered for miles across the hills as if Camelot had been set down in dog-run country. But "Old Main," as it was known, and three other buildings lined up on the steep stairstep campus—a library so rickety that when, the year before, it had enlarged its reference department on the second floor, that floor had begun to cave in and all encyclopedias had had to be hastily moved downstairs; a rough, wooden, barnlike "gymnasium"; and a squat, unadorned class-room structure—were, except for a few frame houses, converted to class-rooms, the extent of the campus of Southwest Texas State Teachers College at San Marcos. Because there were no dormitories, its students boarded in shabby frame houses that clustered around the foot of College Hill and, al-though concrete walks would shortly be laid, they still trudged to school up dirt paths that had been cleared through scrubby cedar patches, and around sagging wire fences that defined back yards. The college had been opened, in 1903, as a normal school, most of whose classes were at the high-school level and whose catalogue stated: "It should be kept in mind that this school is not a university, or even a college. . . . It may lead its students to see the advantages of higher education, and it may hope to influence them to seek these advantages in college or university, but it cannot undertake itself to give them." Academic standards had only recently improved; as late as 1921, its president had admitted that, in some respects, "We know very well that . . . we are not meeting acceptable college standards"; it was only in 1923 that the school had been allowed to change its name from Normal School to Teachers College—1927, the year Lyndon Johnson arrived, was, in fact, the year the college would graduate its first fully accredited class. And the improvement was limited because Texas still classified teachers' colleges as "third-class" colleges, and professors were therefore paid less than high-school teachers—which made attracting first-rate faculty members difficult; in 1919, the president had succeeded in persuading one teacher with a doctorate to join his faculty; ever since, he had been trying in vain to get another Ph.D. to come to San Marcos; several of the fifty-six faculty members had no degree at all. It was a common saying in Texas educational circles that men who taught at "San Marcos" (as the college was commonly known) were there because they couldn't find a job anywhere else; some of the professors had not bothered to update their lectures for so many years that their lecture notes were literally yellow with age. And the students attending San Marcos had few illusions about the quality of education they were receiving. "The reason I went?" says one. "I had saved four hundred dollars, and I looked at the catalogues of different schools, and this was the only place I could get a year of school for four hundred dollars." "It was a poor boy's school," its alumni say; "most of the kids were there because they couldn't afford to go anywhere else."

But to many of these young men and women from the land of the dog-run, Old Main was the largest building they had ever seen, larger even than their county courthouses; its spires loomed over them, taller by far than the spires of their churches. The crowd of students in which they stood in front of Old Main on Registration Day was the largest crowd they had ever been in—the most people they had ever seen gathered together in one place. And some of them had another reason for being nervous as they stood there dressed in new suits or dresses (or, because some of them were very poor, in clothes that weren't new; there were sunbonnets on some of the women, and overalls on some of the men in that crowd): many Hill Country high schools were considered so inadequate by the state that some of their courses weren't accredited, and they weren't sure they would be admitted. It had been a desperate struggle for many of them to raise even the tiny San Marcos tuition; they had made the struggle because they felt the education they could obtain at San Marcos was their only chance of escaping a life of physical toil, and they were worried that San Marcos wouldn't give them that chance. Professor David F. Votaw, who was in charge of admissions, would never forget those young farm men and women coming into his office with their transcripts clutched in their callused hands. "Very frequently," Votaw says, "they came into my office with fear in their eyes. Considerable fear."

Lyndon Johnson, who had been to California and roamed the halls of the huge Capitol in Austin, wouldn't have been awed by Old Main. But he had other reasons to be nervous. Almost three years before, he had said that, coming from Johnson City High School, "he didn't have a full education." Now, after not attending school for three years, what education he had, had faded. So inadequate was Johnson City High School considered, moreover, that none of its graduates were admitted to San Marcos until they had "proven" their credits by taking a six-week course in the San Marcos "Sub-College" and then passing qualifying examinations. There would be examinations in algebra and geometry, which he had managed to pass in high school only with considerable help from his cousin Ava. How, after three years away from school, was he going to pass algebra and geometry now? Was he—after finally consenting to go to college—not going to be able to get into college? And with his father able to give him no financial assistance at all, he was standing on the registration line with barely enough money in his pocket for the registration fee, and he was going to have to start paying for room and board almost immediately. Within two weeks, in fact, he would be vainly asking one of his father's friends for a loan: "I am unable to make sufficient money to cover my expenses. . . . Unless I can arrange in the next ten days for a loan, I am going to be compelled to leave school. . . . I know of no relative to whom I can go for assistance." If he got in, how was he going to get the money to stay in? "I knew Lyndon," Ava recalls. "I could always tell how he was feeling. I was standing on line with him that day when he was waiting to register, and he was one scared chicken."

And then his turn came, and he went into Votaw's office.

He knew he had to prove credits, he said, and he was ready to do so. He was ready to do anything necessary to obtain a college education. He had had a "little bit of a roving disposition" when he was younger, and had "gotten out" and seen "some of the world, and hit against some of its rough edges." Now he wanted to improve conditions in the world, and he had realized that in order to do this, he needed an education, to be better equipped to deal with them. "Lyndon sat down there and talked to me for thirty or forty minutes," Votaw says. "He outlined a program which he expected to follow. He had planned long in advance. He just about told me everything he was going to do. . . . I have always thought that a boy who knew where he was going would be more likely to get there than one who didn't. And he certainly appeared to know where he was going. I don't believe I ever met anyone with more plans that appeared reasonable, workable plans than Lyndon. . . . I was very much impressed." Impressed in particular, Votaw says—and if he appears to remember too well, to have re-created a conversation in the light of this boy's later fame, other faculty members remember him telling them that same day in 1927, "I've just met a boy who's going places"—because so many of the applicants came with "considerable fear," and this applicant was such a refreshing contrast: "There was absolutely no fear."

Admitted to the Sub-College, Lyndon needed a room. His cousin Margaret, a student at San Marcos, had been dating a fellow student who was also named Johnson but was no relation, and when, several months earlier, this student, Alfred ("Boody") Johnson, had visited her in Johnson City, she had asked him to persuade her recalcitrant cousin to go to college. Boody, the captain of the San Marcos football team, and, according to a student poll, the most popular student, was the biggest man on campus, and, a friend would say, "he had the biggest heart, too"; he was a very generous young man. When, during Boody's visit to Johnson City, Lyndon had said he couldn't afford room rent, Boody had invited him to share the rent-free apartment—two tiny rooms above the president's garage—that had been given to him because he was the football captain. Now, appearing at Boody's door, Lyndon reminded him of his invitation. Whether or not Boody remembered issuing it, circumstances had changed during the intervening months: Boody now had another roommate, halfback Clayton Stribling, who would also have to agree to let Lyndon move in, and Stribling, who had gone to high school with Lyndon, despised him. But when Stribling showed no disposition to agree, Lyndon—to his surprise—didn't take umbrage. "He said, 'Won't you help a poor boy?' I said, 'Do you have the president's permission?' Of course, he didn't, and he didn't answer. But he said, 'Won't you help a poor boy?' What could I say? I asked, 'How long do you want to stay?' and he said, 'Thirty days,' so I let him move in."

Stribling's feelings toward him only intensified, and "at the end of thirty days, I just said: 'Lyndon, get out.' He said, 'I thought you were going to help a poor boy.' I said, 'I said you could stay for thirty days. You stayed thirty days. Now just get out.' " But a short time thereafter, Stribling's father, who was ranching 1,200 acres near Marble Falls, suffered a hernia, and had to ask Stribling to drop out of school and help him. And as soon as Stribling moved out of the apartment, Lyndon, who had become very friendly with Boody, moved back in—and shortly thereafter arranged for a third roommate, star athlete and Student Council President Ardis Hopper. Within a short time after he had arrived at college, freshman Lyndon Johnson was a permanent resident of the college's only free lodgings—and living with two Big Men on Campus.

He needed a job. Jobs were hard to come by at San Marcos, for so many of the students needed them, but, unknown to Lyndon, no sooner had he left for school than his father, who had a nodding acquaintance with the college president, Cecil Eugene Evans (Sam Johnson had fought for increased legislative appropriations for teachers' colleges), had written him asking him to give Lyndon one. He did—but it was a job picking up trash and "chopping weeds" and working on the "Rock Squad," raking small rocks off the campus and lugging away larger ones.

Crusty, dignified "Prexy" Evans, as he was called, was an awesome figure on the little campus. He held himself aloof; although he would greet students by name when he saw them, he would almost never stop to talk. He never got "too close to the students," one recalls. "There seemed to be" around him an "invisible wall . . . which we didn't dare go beyond." But while the other members of the Rock Squad raked and lifted, Lyndon Johnson, whenever he saw the president coming, would run over and talk to him, smiling broadly. And soon the other boys noticed, with astonishment, that

Evans was talking, too—and smiling back. The conversations, they noticed, were getting longer and longer.

Johnson had discovered the chink in Evans' wall. The chink was politics. Negotiating for funds with legislators and bureaucrats was part of the job of a president of a state-supported institution, of course, but politics was more than work to Evans: the fascination the field had held for him as a boy working for his father, an Alabama judge, and dreaming of becoming a politician himself, had never waned. He carried with him everywhere a small notebook in which he was constantly writing. On campus, where the notebook was known, because of its color, as "Prexy's Redbook," it was assumed that it dealt with college activities, but when, after his death, thirty years of legendary Redbooks were opened by friends, many of the notes were discovered to be observations on local, state and national politics. Opportunities to talk about this subject he loved had been limited on a campus on which even state affairs seemed remote, and on which no one possessed a level of sophistication that made talking interesting, but Evans found he enjoyed talking to this tall, skinny boy with the rake, this boy who knew so many legislators, so many stories about legislators, so many stories about the Governor, who had visited his home, so many behind-the-scenes stories about Austin. And if the young man somewhat exaggerated his involvement in state politics, he nonetheless was always respectful of Evans' greater knowledge and wisdom, always exceedingly deferential, in fact. He began, moreover—unasked—to run little errands for the president: down College Hill into town early in the morning to get a newspaper so that Evans could read it over breakfast; into town with Mrs. Evans to carry her groceries. Then he told Evans that on the Rock Squad pay scale—twenty cents per hour for a limited number of hours; seven or eight dollars per month was all that could be earned—he would be unable to stay in school. He asked Evans for a job mopping and sweeping classrooms and corridors, which paid thirty cents per hour, or about twelve dollars per month. Such coveted "inside jobs" were, at a college which could not afford athletic scholarships, generally reserved for athletes, but Evans gave Johnson an inside job—mopping the floors in Old Main.

Lyndon's jurisdiction included the hallway outside Evans' office, and that was where he always seemed to be mopping when the president came by. Their conversations continued. And then Lyndon asked if he could work directly for him. Evans had only one assistant—an instructor, Tom W. Nichols, who served part-time as his secretary. Lyndon said that Evans should have another—an office boy, who could carry his messages (the campus had no internal telephone system) and run other errands so that Nichols wouldn't have to run them, and who could mind the office when Nichols was teaching. The assistant registrar, Ethel Davis, who worked across the hall from Evans' office, remembers her amazement at the young man's effrontery. "He was so sure of himself; he just told Dr. Evans he wanted a job there."

She was even more amazed at the result. "Evidently, Evans approved of his attitude, because he gave him the job," she says. The salary was fifteen dollars per month. Within five weeks of his arrival at the college—before, in fact, he had even been admitted to it—he was working in the president's office, in a job which hadn't even existed before he got there.

LYNDON JOHNSON did prove his credits—just barely, and thanks to his mother ("I remember the night before I took my college entrance exams, she sat up all night trying to teach me plane geometry and I had had difficulty with it all through Johnson City High School—and the minimum grade required to get into college was seventy and I made seventy—perhaps with some generous treatment on the part of the grader")—and was admitted to college on March 21, 1927. But he became more and more discouraged and depressed.

Easy as the schoolwork was, it was hard for him. He knew he was weak in grammar; about this time he wrote a vivid description of himself as "a tired homesick freshman . . . foundering in a sea of sentences in English 101." He had thought he was strong in debate—he considered it his strongest subject—but during the first term of his freshman year he received a "D" in debate; "he was very upset about this," a girl in the course recalls. Yet it was not scholastic but financial problems that preyed most on his mind. Rooming with Boody meant that he didn't have to pay rent, but he had to eat. To save money, he arranged a two-meal contract, "noon" and "supper," at Mrs. Gates' boardinghouse, the cheapest he could find, at sixteen dollars a month. At night, he would sometimes be very hungry. The Bobcat, the students' hangout at the bottom of College Hill, charged ten cents for an egg sandwich and twenty cents for a ham-and-egg sandwich; years later, he would remember that "he'd always have the egg, and he'd always wish for the ham." And there were the little expenses of college life— little but so large to him that, decades later, he could recall them down to the nickels and dimes: "I had only two meals—that was sixteen dollars —and my laundry cost seventy-five cents a week, about three dollars a month, and then you had all your books and stuff. . . ." Looming always ahead of him was the tuition bill, which came due every three months: "I just never did have it. . . . Every time it came tuition-paying time, I would [just about] get evicted—I would just about [have enough to] get home. It was seventeen dollars, and I just never did have the money to pay my tuition." He had borrowed money, "and I couldn't pay it back." He had shot up to his full growth now, six-foot-three-and-a-half inches, and he was embarrassed to go to class with his ankles and wrists sticking out of his clothes. During the Spring or Summer of 1927, he wrote his friend Ben Crider, who had returned to California and a job in a cement factory, saying, as he later recalled it, "I just can't make it, and I've got to drop out. I'm in debt forty-fifty dollars. And I got tuition time. And I want to come and get a job. Can you get me one?"

He had also been writing his mother of his discouragement, and, unknown to him, Rebekah, realizing how close he was to the gruff older boy, had written to Ben, begging him to encourage Lyndon to continue in school. The two letters—from Lyndon and from Lyndon's mother—were received at about the same time by the man who had once been half of a two-man pick-and-shovel team. He went to the factory superintendent and arranged for a job for Lyndon. But on his way back to his room to write his young friend, he stopped and thought for a while. And then he turned and walked in a different direction, to his bank, and asked the teller how much money he had in his account, and when the teller told him (the amount is recalled variously as $81 or $103 or $106), he said he'd like to withdraw it all. And when he wrote the letter, it said:

> Well, I can get you a job. Five dollars a day. I've talked to the superintendent, and he said I've got a job waiting for you. But I hope you won't come. They're breathing this dust that goes into your lungs, and a lot of them are getting lung disease from it. I hope you don't have a future like that, because it's Hell out here. I'm sending you all the money I got in the bank, hoping that you'll stay in college.

"Eighty-one dollars!," Lyndon Johnson, reminiscing decades later, would recall. "I was the richest man on the campus! And I took that eighty-one dollars, and I paid all my debts, and I paid my next term's bill."

THE RELIEF FROM DEPRESSION was only temporary—and not just because the eighty-one dollars soon ran out. The doubts and fears that tormented him manifested themselves in silence. "Normally, Lyndon was so outgoing, so bubbling, so loud," Ethel Davis says. "But sometimes he would turn quiet, and stay quiet all day, and when Lyndon was quiet like that, you could see he was *really* down." Sometimes these "down" periods began with a mail delivery that did not include an envelope addressed in Rebekah Johnson's beautifully rounded script. He wrote his mother several times a week, and she wrote him almost every day—letters of effusive encouragement and endearment ("My dearest love"; "My splendid sweet son"); there had begun a torrent of mail from his mother that would not end until Rebekah's death thirty years later. And now, in San Marcos, when she missed a day or two, the silence would come over him, and he would tell her how much he needed her letters. "Dearest Mother," he wrote once, "Have all of my books arranged before me in preparation for a long evening of study. You can't realize the difference in atmosphere after one of your sweet letters. I know of nothing so stimulating and inspiring to me as one of your encouraging, beautifully-written letters. . . . Mother, I love you so. Don't neglect me. . . ." His relationship with his father had not improved—Lyndon's letters were all addressed, "Dearest Mother"; not one bore a salutation to his father, and although Rebekah asked him at least to put in a line sending his love to Sam, he could not make his fingers write those words. Years later, he would recall that his father had said, "You don't have enough sense to take a college education." "Damn I wanted to show him!" he would recall, and when, during his second term at college, he received fairly good grades, "I took them home—they were on a little yellow card—and I threw them down in front of him and I said, 'Does that look like I've got enough sense to take a college education?' " But his relationship with his mother, the mother who had never ceased encouraging him and believing in him, had been transformed during the week she spent with him in San Marcos getting him through his "proving" exams; at every opportunity, he would catch a ride home to Johnson City, and more than once, so deeply did he need her reassurances of his ability and of her love, he would, unable to get a ride, head out on the lonely San Marcos–Johnson City road on foot, hoping to hitchhike the thirty miles home; years later, in a letter to her son, Rebekah Johnson would recall "the long confidential talks we used to have when you would come in from San Marcos and sit on the bed and tell me all your hopes, disappointments and dreams."

But no one in San Marcos saw anything more than the occasional silences.

Lyndon Johnson organized a Blanco County Club for students from his home county. He wasn't elected president—or vice president, secretary or treasurer—but he was given a job that no one else wanted: writing articles on the club's meetings for the campus newspaper, the *College Star*. And when he wrote the article on its first meeting, its lead was not about the election—or the officers' names; the first sentence of the article read: "The students of Blanco County were called together by Lyndon Johnson Thursday afternoon." And in his articles on later meetings, in the list of "students attending," his name led all the rest. Soon his name came first on the *Star*'s own masthead. Sometime during the Spring of 1927, Ben Crider, back from California on vacation, visited Lyndon in San Marcos, and Lyndon took him to the *College Star* offices and said, "Ben, I would like to edit this." The editor-in-chief, Crider recalls, "poked fun at Lyndon making a remark like that. Lyndon hadn't had a haircut in probably two months and was just a kid." But that Summer, back in California, Crider, returning to his room after a day in the cement factory, found an envelope from San Marcos. It contained a copy of the *Star,* and on top of the masthead, underlined in red so that Crider couldn't miss it, was "Lyndon B. Johnson, Editor-in-Chief." All the paper's regular editors had left school for the summer. Johnson, who had had no newspaper experience, had said he had, and, aided by the fact that no one else wanted the job in the Summer, had been given it. He asked his mother to write the first editorial, which he printed as written. But soon he was making his first innovation on the *Star*: using larger headlines—blaring full-page streamers for even ordinary events—than any editor had used before.

JOHNSON'S EDITORSHIP and later stints as editorial writer presented him with an opportunity to express admiration for college officials. He took full advantage of the opportunity—so full, in fact, that some students felt that his articles and editorials bore little resemblance to reality. Dean of Women Mary C. Brogdon, guardian of campus morals, for example, was the campus Gorgon, a stout, stern spinster with a smile as rigid as her corsets, who was merciless to the coed who tried to shorten her skirts to the flapper length popular in the East or to the male student who kept one of her girls out five minutes past the 10:30 p.m. curfew; she had been known to insist on the expulsion of a boy who had failed to obtain her written permission before taking a coed for a drive in his new automobile. But in an article on a meeting of the college literary society, Johnson wrote: "After the meeting, the group had the best time of all, when Miss Brogdon invited the members down to the Cafeteria, where she had refreshments—lemonade and cakes— waiting for them. The refreshments idea of Miss Brogdon's proved to be the best part of the whole evening and the boys think she is one of the best sports on the Hill." Dean of Faculty Alfred H. Nolle was described by the new editor in a stream of adjectives: "alert, experienced, specially trained, just, capable, interested . . . strong and vital." And when Johnson turned his pen to the most important college official, his enthusiasm soared still higher, not only in articles (the pedantic dullness of Evans' speeches was a source of amusement to most students, but this student, reporting on an Evans speech, wrote that it was "very interesting . . . he made his talk bristle with interesting facts") but in an editorial which he made sure no one could miss by placing it on the front page:

> Great as an educator and as an executive, Dr. Evans is greatest as a man. Here we find a man who cherishes a fellowship with the humanities of life. He plans for deeds that live, leaving indelible impress on the lives of the youth of the college. With depth of human sympathy rarely surpassed, unfailing cheerfulness, geniality, kind firmness and friendly interest in the youth of the state, Dr. Evans has exerted a great influence for good upon the students of S.W.T.S.T.C. He finds great happiness in serving others.

Previously, the *Star* had displayed a penchant for sly digs at administration and faculty members, to the point where strict censorship by Nolle and the Dean of Students, H. E. Speck, had been instituted. ("Not with Lyndon, though," Nolle says. "Lyndon had exceptionally good judgment of what was appropriate, and there was no need to censor, to edit, any of Lyndon Johnson's writing.") Now some of the students remarked at the change, not favorably. The college yearbook, the *Pedagog*, mentioned "Lyndon Johnson, editorial writer, whose outbursts in that line gained wide comment."

Comment might have been wider still had the students known about Johnson's private outbursts—notes placed in the most strategic location possible for a student concerned about his grades: at the end of his examination papers. These notes were targeted for maximum impact on the individual at whom they were aimed. Mrs. V. S. Netterville, for example, was not only an English professor but a devout Baptist. Johnson had previously displayed no interest in the Baptist or any other religion, but that was apparently not the tenor of his note to Professor Netterville; she was so moved by it that she wrote him a letter in reply:

> May I thank you for the note you wrote me at the close of your examination. To have led you through your study of Robert Browning in such a way as to have strengthened your faith is the best reward I could ask for the labor and time I have given the course. . . .
>
> May God continue to bless you and keep you always a firm believer.

Nor did Johnson confine his compliments to the written word. Dropping in to chat with Ethel Davis, the forty-year-old assistant registrar, he would tell her how much he loved and respected his mother. Then he would tell Miss Davis that she reminded him of his mother. Or he would ask her advice on some matter; when she replied, he would tell her, she recalls, that "what I said was like what his mother had said. . . . I was sort of flattered." When dealing with members of the administration and faculty in person, in fact, Johnson displayed an admiration so profound that fellow students say that if they described it fully, "no one would believe it." If, for example, a professor held an informal bull session on the "quadrangle" and Johnson was attending, he could be found sitting at the professor's feet. "Yes, literally sitting at his feet," a classmate says: if the professor was sitting on a bench, students might be standing around him, or sitting next to him, but one student, Lyndon Johnson, would often be sitting on the ground, his face turned up to the teacher, an expression of the deepest interest and respect on his face. "He would just drink up what they were saying, sit at their knees and drink it up, and they would pour out their hearts to him."

Many students doubted the sincerity behind the compliments and the admiration, because, they noticed, no matter what the professor was saying,

Johnson would never disagree. "That was what got me," says Joe Berry, who, having succeeded Ardis Hopper as president of the Student Council, was often involved in quadrangle discussions about campus issues. "He never took a strong position—you never knew where Lyndon stood." Says another student leader, Mylton Kennedy: "He would never disagree with anything a faculty member would propose. Having enough knowledge [of how the professor felt], he would make a statement he knew the faculty member would agree with." Says a third, Vernon Whiteside: "I have heard Lyndon agree enthusiastically with one point of view that a professor was saying, and the very next day, if another professor was giving the opposite point of view, I have heard Lyndon agreeing with *that* point of view—just as enthusiastically."

As for Lyndon's front-page panegyric on Dr. Evans' "unfailing cheerfulness" and "geniality," Evans' secretary, Tom Nichols, had reservations about the editorial's sincerity. The president would frequently unleash a fearsome temper on subordinates, and Johnson could tell when a storm was brewing. At first sign of worsening weather, he would find a hasty excuse to get away, and he wouldn't come back until he had ascertained that Evans had left—usually by sticking his head in the front door of the outer office and whispering to Nichols: "Has he gone yet?"

THE REACTION OF the targets of this barrage of compliments is documentation of the adage that where flattery is concerned, no excess is possible. Miss Brogdon, so inflexible about her curfew rules, relaxed them for Lyndon Johnson. The professor at whose feet Johnson sat most often was H. M. Greene, a history professor and debate coach; Johnson may have received a D in the debate course taught by another professor, but he made Greene's debating team, much to the surprise of students who, like one member of the team, considered him "very forceful, but really not a good speaker at all."

The key to Johnson's college career—the key, in fact, to whether he would be able to earn enough money so he could *have* a college career— was Prexy Evans. The public flattery was nothing to the private flattery (witnessed only by Tom Nichols) that went on in the president's office, and flattery—a striking humbleness, deference, obsequiousness—was not the only weapon employed; Nichols, a non-competitive man, liked Johnson (Nichols was "red of face, a real country boy whom Lyndon could easily get around," another professor says), but he couldn't resist remarking on the pains the student took not only to carry out Evans' assignments diligently, but to dramatize his diligence. Equipping himself with a large note pad, he listed his assignments on it and, when reporting back to Evans, held it up where Evans could not fail to see it. "I have seen him standing at the president's elbow holding a written list of the items to which he had devoted himself, calling these off and checking with his pencil as the signal that each had been completed," Nichols says. He began to make his own assignments—looking "eagerly" for them, Nichols says, "to make the favorable impression which he was determined to create"—and would include these on the list, telling Evans of each chore, and then placing next to it a big, bold checkmark.

And the impression he wanted to make was the impression he made: Evans mentioned Johnson's efficiency several times in his short talks at the weekly "general assembly" in Old Main's second-floor auditorium. He began to listen to Johnson's suggestions on student job assignments; "He got next to Prexy and . . . he got me promoted to 'inspector of buildings' at twenty-five dollars a month," his roommate Boody Johnson says. Prexy even fell in with a scheme to help Lyndon pay his tuition. "About that time," Lyndon Johnson would recall, "I couldn't get tuition from any other source." He also needed money for food. He asked Evans to allow him and his roommate, who were already living rent-free above his garage, to earn money by painting the garage. Evans not only agreed, but allowed them wages of forty cents per hour—"That was a craftsman's wages," Johnson would recall; other students got twenty cents per hour for similar work. And when one painting did not give Johnson enough money to stay in school, Evans told him to paint the garage again—and again. According to some students, the garage was painted four times that term. Once or twice, Evans even took Johnson with him to Austin.

Evans' references to Johnson in his assembly talks created an impression on campus that the student was close to the president. And the student fostered that impression. When asked where he lived, he replied, "At the president's house." He was only the president's office boy, and to dramatize the difference in status between him and Nichols, his desk had been placed outside the railing in the president's waiting room, not inside it like Nichols'. But Johnson made the position of his desk work for him, jumping up and greeting everyone who came into the office, and doing so in such an expansive manner that, Nichols says, "Some of them probably thought he was running the place. Smooth as silk." Decades later, a woman student would remember how Johnson "opened a swinging gate to admit me to President Evans' office for an interview which led to my [first job]." Leaving the office to deliver messages from the president, he made a production out of it. A pencil would be tucked behind an ear, a huge sheaf of papers would be clutched in one hand, and he would always be in a hurry, bursting out of the office and rushing down the halls of Old Main or along the dirt paths to another building with a long, gangling stride, his arms swinging vigorously if awkwardly out from his sides, too busy to stop and talk—a busy man, on the president's work. No one knew that Johnson's sole responsibility on his occasional trips to Austin with Evans was to report to Evans on what one legislative committee was doing, if the president was tied up before another committee; Johnson talked at every opportunity about how "Prexy and I" worked together in Austin to obtain funds for the college. At every opportunity, moreover, he would try to be seen in public with Evans, and in public he acted so differently from the way he did in private that Nichols was astounded by the contrast with the humble, obsequious Lyndon of the office. Introducing the president to his friends, chatting and laughing ostentatiously with him—even, once, patting him on the back (the campus buzzed about *that* for days)—he created an impression of familiarity. Many faculty members believed he had a far more important job than was actually the case. And Johnson never took advantage of this belief, never listened to faculty members with less deference than before. He still sat "at their knees" and drank in everything they had to say, and, Whiteside says, "Boy, you could see they loved it."

His popularity with the faculty did not, however, carry over to the students.

Mylton Kennedy, who echoes Whiteside's vivid description of Johnson sitting at his instructors' knees and drinking in avidly all they had to say, pauses and finally says: "Words won't come to describe how Lyndon acted toward the faculty—how kowtowing he was, how suck-assing he was, how brown-nosing he was." And if students disliked Lyndon Johnson because of his attitude toward the faculty, they disliked him even more because of his attitude toward *them*. If he was obsequious to those above him, he was overbearing to those who were not.

He had come to San Marcos with the same tendency to "talk big" that he had displayed in Johnson City, and if, when he first arrived at college, he had had little to talk big about, he made maximum use of what he did have. He would introduce himself as "Lyndon Johnson from Johnson City," leaving the impression that he was a member of the town's founding family. If he was asked directly whether he was, he would confirm that impression, saying that Johnson City had been founded by his grandfather, a statement that was, of course, not true. One of the first editorials he wrote for the *Star* made a point of mentioning "my heritage of Southern blood." (In a later editorial, he made a point of expressing admiration for Jefferson Davis.)

Now he had more to talk big about—and he talked bigger. And he wouldn't let anyone else talk. The young man so eager to sit and listen to the faculty seemed determined that everyone else was going to sit and listen to him. Fellow students who ate at Mrs. Gates' boardinghouse remember two things about Lyndon Johnson most vividly: how he grabbed for food and gulped it down and grabbed for more, trying always to get more than his share—"He had those long arms, and he would reach out with that fork and get the last biscuit on the plate, even if it was on the other end of the table, and if there was one pork chop that was bigger than the others, no one was going to get it but Lyndon Johnson," says one of those students— and how he also grabbed more than his share of the conversation. Says another of Mrs. Gates' boarders, Horace Richards: "He was a very good talker. He would tell these stories about his father, and about Jim Ferguson, and about all the things that had happened in Austin. And he was a great imitator. He would imitate these Germans from around Fredericksburg with their accents, and he was very entertaining sometimes, particularly to some of these country boys who really didn't talk very much. But if someone else tried to talk—well, he just wouldn't let them. He'd just interrupt you—my God, his voice would just ride over you until you stopped. He monopolized the conversation from the time he came in to the time he left. I can still see him reaching and talking, reaching and talking."

The dislike of Lyndon Johnson had a particularly sharp edge, moreover, because of a certain lack of accuracy in his conversation. The students didn't know of all the inaccuracies. He told the men at the table that he had an IQ of 145, and they never found out that that was not the case.* He told them he had high marks—years later, most of them would still be under the impression that he was, in the words of one, "a brilliant student, absolutely brilliant—straight A's"—which also wasn't the case.† He had made the college debating squad—not the first team, as he would ever after maintain, but one of three alternating teams—and shortly after he arrived at San Marcos, it was announced that debaters would be awarded school letters as were athletes. At Mrs. Gates' table, Lyndon let it be known that he had persuaded Dr. Evans to make this decision—his auditors, who did not know that the decision had actually been made before he arrived in San Marcos, were greatly impressed. If students didn't know about these inaccuracies, however, they knew about many others. Johnson's debating partner was Elmer Graham, an older student, back in college after teaching four years to make enough money to continue. Graham did most of the preparation for the team—"I was studying to be a minister, and I had been preaching at country churches, so I was used to organizing material"—and most of the debating, too; he would generally lead off with the primary argument, and then, after Lyndon had given the first rebuttal, Graham would give the final rebuttal. But he didn't mind that, and admired Lyndon's instinct for the jugular; "Lyndon's debating was more clever than profound. The one thing I can honestly say about Lyndon is that he had a knack of finding a weak point in the other team's argument, and coming back at it pretty good." He was fond of Lyndon—until he started hearing the reports of the debates with which his partner was regaling diners at Mrs. Gates'. "It was a little bit irritating," Reverend Graham recalls. "I would hear that he had said all these things that were so devastating. Well, he hadn't said them

---

* His actual Intelligence Quotient has been lost in time, but the two faculty members in charge of administering the tests during the time he was at San Marcos both say it was not outstanding.

† His overall average was B–. He frequently remarked that he had taken 40 courses and gotten 35 A's. He actually took 56 regular classroom courses and received 8 A's.

at all. Either I had said them, or no one had said them. Lyndon liked Lyndon, no doubt about that. He bragged quite a bit about the debating."

The exaggerations in Johnson's political stories were also sometimes revealed; as a result, some of Mrs. Gates' boarders agreed with one who said: "I just didn't believe that he was as much on the inside of big decisions in Austin as he claimed." They were ready to laugh when Whiteside, one day, related what had been said when he pressed Lyndon about his father, whom "he was continually depicting as a member of the state's highest political councils."

" 'What does your father do?'

" 'Well, uh, he works for Jim Ferguson.'

" 'Oh, what's he do?'

" 'Well, uh, he's the bus inspector.' "

He talked a lot about girls, too. His brother, Sam Houston Johnson, recalls that more than once, when he visited his brother at San Marcos, Lyndon, coming back into the room naked after a shower, would take his penis in his hand, and say: "Well, I've gotta take ol' Jumbo here and give him some exercise. I wonder who I'll fuck tonight."

He devoted to his appearance an amount of time—and, considering his financial situation, money—inordinate even for a college man. He was continually experimenting with new styles for his black, wavy hair, which he considered his most attractive feature: parting it in the middle or on the side, slicking it flat with Sta-comb or working—endlessly, it seemed to his roommates—to get it pompadoured just right. Despite the expense, he was frequently at the barbershop for forty-cent haircuts and twenty-five-cent shaves ("He was very hard to shave," says the barber. "He had that very tender white skin . . ."). Worried that his neck was too long and thin, he would practice scrunching it down between his shoulders—practice endlessly, a roommate recalls. Before a date, he would spend quite a long time dressing. "He'd stand in front of the mirror and comb his hair, and dress, and get everything just *right* when he was going out," Boody says. Then he would scrunch down his neck, and head out for the evening's encounter.

These preparations, combined with his continual, vivid boasting about his sexual successes, gave him a reputation as a ladies' man—except among those students who *were* ladies' men. On a campus where women outnumbered men three to one, it was very easy for most men to get a date, but among the social clique on campus, it was known that getting one was not always easy for Lyndon Johnson. Miss Brogdon would as a matter of course grant him privileges—an extended curfew, permission to drive to Austin—she only grudgingly granted to other students, so couples wanted to double-date with him, but they often had difficulty finding a fourth. His pretty cousin Margaret, who was dating Boody, got him a blind date with her roommate, and, with Boody borrowing a car, the four got to go to a movie in New Braunfels, a considerable treat. Margaret and Boody were looking forward to other trips, but the roommate refused to go out with Lyndon again. His unpopularity with women students would not have aroused particular comment on campus, had it not been for the zealousness with which he tried to retouch reality. "I mean, we all boasted and bragged about girls," says one man. "But Lyndon's boasting and bragging were to an extent that was ridiculous. Nobody believed him."

To some of his fellow students, in fact, it began to seem unwise to believe Lyndon Johnson on *any* subject. In their opinion, he seemed almost unable to tell unvarnished truth about even the most innocuous subject. Some of them took to asking him questions just so they could laugh at his answers. "Once I was sitting next to him in class, and I saw him wearing a new tie and socks," Horace Richards recalls. "I knew where he had bought them, but I asked *him* where he had bought them. He said, 'I got them over at Scarborough's in Austin. I paid a dollar for the socks and a dollar for the tie.' Scarborough's was the fanciest store in Austin, and a dollar was a whole lot of money in those days. I said, 'Lyndon, you're just lying. You were never in Scarborough's yesterday. Besides, I saw them in Woolworth's window yesterday. The socks were ten cents and the tie was twenty cents.' But Lyndon just had to lie and say he was wearing a dollar tie. It just seemed like he had to lie about everything." He had made a great point of describing himself as a tough man in a fistfight—something believable, despite his awkwardness, because of his size. During a poker game, however, he began arguing with another student, and wouldn't stop shouting at him. The other boy jumped up and lunged at him. Johnson, without a single gesture of resistance, immediately fell back on a bed and, as his foe approached, began kicking his feet in the air with a frantic, windmilling motion. The other poker players all remember him lying there and kicking—"like a girl," Horace Richards says—and they remember him shouting: "If you hit me, I'll kick you! If you hit me, I'll kick you!" The other men were astonished. Says Whiteside, one of those present: "He was a coward. You know, every kid in the State of Texas had fights then, but he wouldn't fight. He was an absolute physical coward. And the thing about it was that he had made such a big thing about what a great fighter he was."

But the aspect of Lyndon Johnson's character most remarkable to other students was his lack of embarrassment when caught out in an exaggeration or an outright falsehood. "You could catch him in a lie about something, and it was like he didn't care," Richards says. "The next day he'd be back lying about the same thing again." Says Clayton Stribling: "He never seemed to resent [being found out]. He just didn't care. He wouldn't get mad. He'd be back the next day talking the same as ever."

THE BIGGEST MEN on campus were the athletes. They had formed a "secret" organization called the Black Stars, which met in the big meadow on Barney

Knispel's farm for drinking parties at which these burly farm boys consumed beer by the kegful, frequently vomiting it out on the grass, and held "initiation ceremonies," a highlight of which was convincing a blindfolded initiate that he was kissing a bull's penis, which was actually the bent elbow of the group's president, who was called the "Jupiter." The Black Stars won most of the class offices. They hung around together at the Bobcat, the little shack at the bottom of College Hill run by the Coers brothers, former football stars themselves, and partied together—with the college's prettiest girls. "Everyone wanted to be part of that crowd," recalls Ella So Relle. "That was the 'in' crowd."

Lyndon Johnson wanted very badly to be part of that crowd, and his roommate wanted him to be.

Alfred T. Johnson had been born and reared on a lonely ranch in the empty wastes of West Texas, and had thought he was doomed to that life—until one day, at tiny Lytle High School, someone put a football in his hands. One of the most famous players in Texas high school football history had been a great halfback named Boody Johnson, and on that day at Lytle, as the shy, rangy ranch boy began to run with the ball, someone yelled in awe, "Look at ol' Boody Johnson go!" Word of his ability spread, and one day a coach from Southwest Texas State Teachers College showed up and offered him the San Marcos version of a scholarship—a job sweeping out campus buildings—and he took it; "My dad worked hard all his life, and I had worked hard all my life," he would say. "If I could get me an education, I could let my brain work for me instead of my hands." The Southwest Texas Bobcats were a tough team ("After bulldogging steers all our lives, you think it was tough tackling a *guy?*" Clayton Stribling asks), but during practice scrimmages they had as little success tackling Boody as high school teams had had; a talented athlete—he was a star baseball and basketball as well as football player—he was elected captain. In an age in which, even at faraway San Marcos, football players were lionized, he was the campus hero; under his picture in the *Pedagog* is the caption: "The stalwart Boody Johnson."

But it is not the remembrance of his athletic ability that—fifty years later—makes San Marcos students smile when they remember the stalwart Boody Johnson. "He was the fatherly type," a football player says. "If things were going bad in a game, he'd call a time-out, and gather the team around, and say, 'Now, look, fellows, we're here to play football,' and settle everybody down." He didn't settle down only football players. "You always felt you could go to him with your problems," says one woman. "He was a very kind person. Gruff and tough, but very kind. He was just like a father to everybody." His unselfishness was legendary, and not just on the football field (where, because the other halfback, Lyons McCall, a good runner, was a poor blocker, Boody volunteered to do most of the blocking while McCall carried the ball—if the team was behind in the last minutes of a game, however, the players would growl: "Give it to Boody"). "Boody was the kind of guy who, if you woke him up in the middle of the night and told him your car had broken down, would get out of bed and walk five miles to help you—nothing was too much trouble for him," Vernon Whiteside says. And he was always so soft-spoken and slow-talking and friendly; no campus activity was complete unless Boody was part of it: he played the lead in romantic comedies and sang the solo in "Sweet Adeline" with the campus barbershop quartet. "Old Boody," Ella So Relle would say, fifty years later, smiling and crying a little at the same time. "Gruff old Boody. A sweeter, calmer human being I never met." And, she adds, "a more complete contrast with Lyndon could not be found. You would see them walking around campus together—Lyndon talking, talking, talking, swinging those arms, and Boody so calm and sweet. You just could not *imagine* how two boys so different could be friends."

But friends they were—so close that the campus, seeing them so often together, called them "Johnson and Johnson." Slow-talking Boody admired Lyndon's glibness. "He had a wonderful way about him," he recalls. "Once Lyndon and myself were sitting there on the campus, after Lyndon had gotten himself a pipe, and Dean Speck came by, and he said: 'Lyndon, you know we don't allow any smoking on campus.' 'I'm not smoking, Dean Speck.' 'Well, Lyndon, you've got your pipe in your mouth.' 'Yes, Dean Speck, and I've got my shoes on my feet, but I'm not walking.' I nearly died laughing, and Dean Speck did, too, and he said something like, 'Good boy,' and went on walking. Well, I could never have thought of saying something like that." Shy Boody admired Lyndon's effusiveness. "He was so warm and affectionate," he says. "The first time I brought him home, he grabbed my mother and hugged and kissed her, and my sisters—my father said, 'That boy you brought down here—I thought he was going to kiss *me!*'" And fatherly Boody was touched by something he saw in the skinny boy three years younger than himself. Before dates, he would lend Lyndon money—money he had earned in his campus jobs—and would tie his bow tie. And then, when Lyndon was ready to leave, he would dance around Boody, jabbing out at him with his fists—"he'd make like he was going to fight, punch you and all," Boody says, still smiling at the memory. Just as the fatherly older boy who had been Lyndon Johnson's best friend in Johnson City, Ben Crider, had helped him, so Boody tried to help him. He asked the Black Stars to make Lyndon a member.

Because of the respect in which Boody was held (when one Black Star was asked, "Who was the Jupiter?" he replied, in a tone of surprise that anyone would have to ask: "Why, Boody, of course"), they would normally have admitted anyone he sponsored, even a student who wasn't an athlete. But not when the student was Lyndon Johnson.

Lyndon acted differently toward the athletes than he did toward less-renowned students, but they saw through his attitude. "If he thought you could help him, he would fawn all over you," star end Joe Berry says. "If you couldn't, he wouldn't waste much time with you." In later years, Lyndon would maintain that a single blackball—cast by a student whose girlfriend Lyndon had stolen—had kept him out of the organization, but the truth was otherwise. Black Stars who were present remember seeing the slips of paper on which the votes on Lyndon Johnson's nomination had been cast and seeing, on one slip after another, the same word: *No.*

At the Black Stars' next meeting, Boody brought Lyndon's name up again—this time with arguments uncharacteristic of Boody. The Black Stars guarded the secrecy of their organization with the exaggerated seriousness of college boys. Boody said that he had inadvertently left the organization's constitution, bylaws and membership list out on his dresser, and that his roommate had seen them, and that he should be admitted so that he would be bound by the Black Stars' oath of secrecy. "We figured Lyndon had thought of that business," one Black Star says. "That wasn't Boody's style at all. Boody would never have said a thing like that on his own." Whoever the author of the strategy, it did not succeed. The second vote on Lyndon Johnson was the same as the first: *No. No. No.*

ELLA SO RELLE could see how hurt he was. "He wanted so badly to belong to the 'in' crowd," she says. "He would have loved to be part of that crowd, to be accepted by them. But they wouldn't let him in. He was just not accepted. You had the feeling of climbing and climbing—and then he didn't make it. You see, he was just one of the mass. And he so badly wanted to be more. To tell the truth, I felt very sorry for him."

Her reaction to Lyndon Johnson was more charitable than that of most students, however. A more common feeling was that expressed by a group of his classmates who frequently visited the little "summer lodge" on the Blanco River in nearby Wimberley that was owned by Ethel Davis, the assistant registrar. Fond of Lyndon, who had told her that she reminded him of his mother, she invited him along. "The youngsters would go fishing and swimming," she says. "But I don't remember Lyndon fishing or swimming. He just talked all the time. He told funny stories." The "youngsters," however, were less amused. "Everybody else was always anxious for the meal to be served, but he was never ready to eat. They often said, 'Of course, Lyndon's not ready to eat. He has to finish telling his story.' And he embroidered the stories. I found them interesting, but the boys didn't care to have Lyndon there." They asked Miss Davis not to invite him back. Even Ella So Relle has to admit: "He was not a popular boy."

The feelings about Lyndon Johnson spilled over into print.

Each edition of the San Marcos yearbook, the *Pedagog*, contained a section, "The Cat's Claw," which mocked students' foibles. In the 1928 *Pedagog,* twelve students were selected for such treatment. The treatment of eleven is rather gentle, but the twelfth was Lyndon Johnson.

Instead of a picture of Johnson, the editors used a picture of a jackass. The caption beside it read: "As he looks to us on the campus every day." Johnson, the caption went on, is "From far away, and we sincerely trust he is going back." And, the caption said, he is a member of the "Sophistry Club. Master of the gentle art of spoofing the general public."

The *Pedagog* was not the only publication in which the word "master" was applied to Lyndon Johnson. In the *College Star's* humor column appears the following definition: "Bull: Greek philosophy in which Lyndon Johnson has an M.B. degree."

" 'Master of Bullshit'—that's what M.B. means," says one of Lyndon Johnson's classmates, Henry Kyle. "He was known as the biggest liar on the campus. In private, when there were no girls around, we called him 'Bull-shit' Johnson."

He was given the public nickname "Bull."

"When you saw him, that's what you called him," says Horace Richards. " 'Hiya, Bull.' 'Howya doin', Bull?' Bull Johnson was his name, as far as we were concerned."

"That was what we called him to his face," Edward Puls, another classmate, says. "That was what he was generally called. Because of this constant braggadocio. Because he was so full of bullshit, manure, that people just didn't believe him. Because he was a man who just could not tell the truth."

9

The Rich Man's Daughter

IN JOHNSON CITY, Lyndon Johnson had courted Kitty Clyde Ross, the daughter of the richest man in town. In San Marcos, the richest man was A. L. Davis. Lyndon Johnson began courting Davis' daughter.

Carol Davis, two years older than Lyndon, had graduated the year before he arrived in San Marcos, but although she was not unattractive—a tall, sandy-haired, slender young lady—she was painfully shy, and had never had a serious suitor. Johnson, meeting her early in 1928, became her first, and when she responded to his interest—the only young lady in San Marcos who had done so—he made sure the news got out. The couple was conspicuous anyway, because Carol's father had bought her a big white convertible, and Lyndon, who would drive it when they were together, would honk its horn loud and long when signaling for curb service at Hillman's Confectionery in town or when passing students trudging up College Hill. In the words of one student, Lyndon "made a production" of the romance—a production whose primary theme was not the usual college-boy boasting about his sexual progress with Carol (although there was plenty of such boasting), but Carol's car, and Carol's willingness to pick up checks ("He'd brag about this," a student says. "He'd say, 'We've been to the movies in Austin, and Carol paid.' "), and about the fact that Carol's family had enough money so that she could do so. So incessantly did he harp on this last point that there was a general feeling that the basis of the romance was, in the words of another student, the fact that "She was a rich man's daughter, and Lyndon was always looking for a way to help himself." Says yet another student: "He was hinting: he wanted to find a girl who had a lot of money." So unconcealed was his desire to marry for money, in fact, that it was to become the subject of a joke in the *Pedagog*.

If this was his intention, however, it was to be thwarted in San Marcos as it had been thwarted in Johnson City—and for the same reason.

Carol's father had become one of the Hill Country's few successful businessmen, building a small grocery in Dripping Springs into the Southern Grocery Company of San Marcos, a wholesale house so big that it purchased baking powder by the freightcar load. A large, friendly man who had designed his home so that he could greet passersby from his porch as he sat there every evening, he possessed not only unshakable physical courage (in a Ku Klux Klan parade held in San Marcos at the height of the Klan's power, virtually every prominent local family participated—except the Davises; he had defiantly announced that "No member of my family will be with them") but convictions to match. "A. L. Davis," says a friend, "was a man who made up his own mind," and once he had made it up, "I don't know that anything could ever change it." And among the firmest of his convictions, along with his fierce Baptist faith, was his loathing of men who drank; of politicians—particularly liberal politicians—whom he considered leeches living off the taxes paid by hard-working businessmen (he had served as mayor of San Marcos, but only because the townspeople, during the years in which the town's streets were being paved, had begged him to take the job to ensure that the paving was done right; he had done so by marching, daily, behind the paving machines; as soon as the job was completed, he resigned); and of the impoverished farmers and ranchers of the Hill Country whose poverty, he was convinced, was due to loose morals and laziness. (San Marcos, situated on the very edge of the Hill Country—on the first line of hills above the plain—was served by two railroads, and was more prosperous than other Hill Country towns, with 5,000 inhabitants and several streets of large, gracious homes.) Sam Johnson, of course, qualified on all three counts —and on a fourth: he was a Johnson, a member of that shiftless, no-account clan for which Davis had long had contempt.

Davis' most precious possessions, moreover, were his four daughters. He lavished dresses and automobiles on them; he had a grand piano shipped in from St. Louis so that they could learn to play. He was fiercely possessive about them, and very much afraid they would marry beneath them. Having dreamed one night that his eldest daughter, Ethel (the college's assistant registrar), had married the owner of a local ice-cream parlor, he woke up in a rage at the man—which, Ethel recalls, lasted for months, although she and the man were barely acquainted. Davis had, in fact, moved from Dripping Springs because he was afraid his girls would marry "those goatherders up there." Wanting them to be educated women, he sent them to boarding schools, but none was a particularly good student except Carol, his youngest and his favorite; when she graduated from college with high marks, he was very proud. Like the father of Kitty Clyde Ross back in Johnson City, he had no intention of allowing his jewel to fall into unworthy hands. "Papa did not want Carol to marry Sam Johnson's son, and that was that," Ethel says. When he realized that Carol was serious about Lyndon, he told her: "I don't want you getting mixed up with those people. That's the reason I moved away from the Hill Country. I wanted better for my children."

Lyndon tried to overcome this prejudice, but Davis, whose eyes could glitter coldly behind his gold-rimmed spectacles when he was angry, was not charmed by the approach Lyndon was using so successfully on his professors. "Lyndon was pretty determined to get on his good side," recalls Ethel, and tried to chat with him on his porch, but Davis, after one or two conversations, would leave the porch when his daughter's suitor arrived. "My father always sat on the porch and talked to people," Carol says. "But he wouldn't talk to Lyndon."

For a while, nonetheless, the romance flowered. In May of 1928, Carol visited Johnson City on two consecutive weekends, staying with a college friend. While she says that she and Lyndon did not have much in common —she liked to play the piano and sing, but Lyndon didn't like to listen; "I loved the picture shows, but Lyndon didn't care much about them"; "Lyndon was just interested in politics, which . . . I didn't believe women should get mixed up in"—she also says that "we were very interested in one another." On a picnic with a group of Johnson City friends, Lyndon and Carol went off alone, "hugging and kissing."

But Carol was a very devoted daughter. "I knew I couldn't go against my father's wishes," she says. She had told Lyndon how strongly "my father felt about him," and "it was always hanging over us. All the time we were going together, it was hanging over us. The whole time." During that summer, chaperoned by an uncle, she went to the Democratic National Convention in Houston, to which Lyndon had wangled tickets as a representative of the college newspaper. He was tremendously enthusiastic about the convention, but "I just remember how hot it was and how long those sessions lasted into the night. More boresome than anything." Whether or not her father's opposition was the real reason for these feelings, she began to wonder, she says, whether two people with so little in common ought to marry. In September, she would be leaving San Marcos to become a schoolteacher in the little South Texas town of Pearsall, and she was almost looking forward to the chance to get away and think.

AT ABOUT THIS SAME PERIOD, the Summer of 1928, Johnson's money troubles were growing worse, and no longer from a simple lack of cash.

Ben Crider's $81 was not the only gift Johnson received during his first year and a half in San Marcos. Several relatives (including his aunt Lucy Johnson Price, who on one occasion called him aside and handed him all her laboriously saved egg money: $30) gave him cash presents. And he also received loans: the Blanco State Bank advanced him $75; the deans who administered the Student Loan Fund were, perhaps because of his closeness to President Evans, unprecedentedly liberal with him—by the time he graduated, he would owe the fund $220. His monthly salaries ($15 as Evans' assistant, $30 as *Star* summer editor) were among the highest paid to students, and, of course, Evans allowed him to earn additional money by painting and re-painting his garage at craftsman's wages. If students—many students—were attending Southwest Texas State Teachers College for $400 per year (including rent, which Johnson, of course, did not have to pay), Johnson should have been able to afford to stay in college.

But he spent more than most students: on forty-cent haircuts, on clothes they considered extravagant, and, before he began going with Carol Davis, on dates; although they were none too frequent, each one was "a production"; whether "show-offing" at Hillman's Confectionery or in Austin, he spent money on girls as if such expenditures could give him popularity. Whatever he made—or borrowed—he spent. Once, for example, he conceived the idea of selling "Real Silk Hose" on campus, and, returning from Austin with sample cases well after midnight, walked from boardinghouse to boardinghouse, barging into men's rooms, snapping on the lights and, while they were still growling sleepily, "What're you doin', Lyndon?" trying to sell them a pair or two. The next morning, Dr. Evans, legendarily close-fisted with his money, agreed to buy so many pairs from Johnson—thirteen dozen was the figure the president sheepishly told Dean Nolle—that he was still wearing them years later. Lyndon earned more than $40 from that twenty-four hours' work—and promptly spent it all in another twenty-four, in a spree, on which he took another student as his guest, in San Antonio. As a result of these spending habits, he was continually broke, and continually borrowing small sums of money from Boody and from anyone else who would lend it to him, even the publisher of the *San Marcos Record,* Walter Buckner (" 'Mr. Walter, do you happen to have fifty cents on you? Well, I need it. Could I borrow it?' And I'd always give it to him"). And while Boody never asked for his money back, the others did—and Lyndon could not always pay his debts. "He was always borrowing," says Horace Richards. "And he was always short. He didn't have a pot nor no window."

Then, after some months of driving Carol's car, he bought his own, a used Model A roadster, for $400. The purchase guaranteed him conspicuousness at a college at which no more than a handful of students had cars, and Lyndon would drive up and down College Hill, offering rides to coeds. But he could not make the monthly payments; soon he was several months behind. The automobile agency was threatening to repossess the car, and Lyndon hid it in someone's garage. In September, moreover, the $75 loan from the Blanco Bank would come due. His father had defaulted on a loan from that bank; the thought of being classified with Sam in the bank's books was intolerable to him.

Each Summer, superintendents of school districts all over Texas enrolled in San Marcos Summer school to earn more credits, and Johnson, joining the Schoolmasters Club, became acquainted with W. T. Donaho, school superintendent in Cotulla, a little town in South Texas. Donaho offered him a $125-per-month teaching job in the Mexican school there, starting in September, and he accepted, with the understanding that he would return to San Marcos after a year. Boody urged him not to interrupt his education, but, he says, understood why Lyndon rejected his advice: "The bucket was just dry, and had been dry too long."

10

Cotulla

LYNDON JOHNSON had driven south before—to San Antonio, which he considered a gay, lively city. But Cotulla was south of San Antonio.

South of San Antonio, the land abruptly levels into a great, flat plain that sweeps 150 miles south to the Mexican border. Few houses dotted that plain, few trees. Stretching away from the road on every side was an unbroken vastness of thorny, low brush. Every few hours—for the highway's asphalt surface had ended in San Antonio, and cars made very slow progress through the sand, which was a foot deep on some parts of the road—Johnson would come to a "town," a fringe of stores bordering the highway, from which sandy tracks wound out to scattered little houses half hidden in the brush. Then the town would fall behind, and he would drive hour after hour without seeing another human being, another human habitation—the only assurance that this land was still connected to civilization the railroad tracks that glinted in the sun alongside the road ruts. The land broiled beneath that sun; the very air seemed not only dusty but hot to breathe; the heat of the Hill Country, fierce though it was, was as nothing to this heat; here the temperature could climb to 105, 107, 110, and stay there day after day. The Hill Country's trees and springs and streams—and hills—gave it beauty, moreover, even if that beauty masked a harsh reality. South of San Antonio, there were only these flat, treeless, desolate plains. The twenty-year-old schoolteacher in the Model A roadster had entered one of the great wildernesses of the United States, the emptiness at the end of America that was called the South Texas brush country.

Cotulla, sixty miles above the Mexican border (ninety below San Antonio), was more a Mexican than an American town. Less than a quarter of its 3,000 inhabitants were "Anglos" and thus entitled to live on the west side of the Missouri-Pacific Railroad tracks; the rest, who worked at slave wages on the area's ranches or on the farms that huddled close to the Nueces River or to deep artesian wells, lived on the east, or "wrong," side of the tracks.

Lyndon Johnson was going to teach on the wrong side. The "Mexican school" (its real name was the "Welhausen School," after the county judge), was a handsome, long, low, red brick building that had been completed just two years before, but the houses among which it was located were hovels, street after street of tiny, unpainted, tin-roofed, crumbling shanties without even running water. Some, in which families were still living, were falling down, corners of their walls having been eaten by the hordes of huge termites which swarmed everywhere in Cotulla. On the porches of some of these houses, men sat on rusting metal chairs and stared vacantly straight ahead of them. In front of the school was a debris-littered vacant lot; a group of men were squatting in it; others were sitting on the steps of the school. When he saw the area in which he was to teach, Lyndon Johnson must have realized quickly why, with a glut of teachers in Texas, he, still in college, had not only been offered a job, but one with an unusually high salary.

The Anglo side of Cotulla was better only by comparison. These people were even poorer than the people of the Hill Country. Their tiny, cramped houses sat on stilts three or four feet high to protect them from the termites. The only accommodation Johnson could find was a room—or rather half a room; he would have to share it with another, older boarder—in a small, rather shabby house on stilts next to the railroad tracks on which long trains carrying bawling cattle up from Laredo passed endlessly each night. Near the house in which he boarded, the land sloped up a bit from the tracks. Sometimes, he would walk to the top of this small rise and stand there looking out over the barren land stretching away in all directions. Slanting away to the north, he could see a lighter-colored scar in the brush that was the road leading back to San Antonio. But the road faded in the empty distance.

DONAHO HAD BEEN UNABLE to lure anyone else from outside Cotulla to teach at the "Mexican school"; the five other teachers were Cotulla housewives, and they treated the job with the contempt they felt it deserved, putting in the minimum time necessary, arriving just as classes started and leaving as soon as they ended. Lyndon Johnson arrived early and stayed late—and he was a teacher like Cotulla had never seen.

When he went into the "playground" for recess on his first day (he had already been informed that there was no lunch hour at the Welhausen School; these pupils had no lunch), he found a dirt lot bare of both equipment and other teachers; his colleagues relaxed in the teachers' lounge during recess periods. Donaho, in his joy at seeing a male teacher for Welhausen arrive in Cotulla, had appointed Johnson principal on sight, and the new principal's first order was that all teachers spend recess supervising games. He persuaded the school board to provide volleyballs and a volleyball net, softballs and bats. Then he arranged for activities with other schools—baseball games and track meets like those the white kids had. The school board wouldn't pay for buses to transport his kids to the meets, but a few—a very few—Mexican families had cars. Climbing the rickety porches of hovels to call on families which had never before been visited by an Anglo, he persuaded men to whom every day's work was precious to give up the days necessary to take the children to the track meets.

No teacher had ever really cared if the Mexicans learned or not. This teacher cared. No laughing or joking was allowed in class. "He spanked disorderly boys and tongue-lashed the girls," one parent recalls. Their greatest handicap, he felt, was their lack of familiarity with English, and he was very strict in making them learn it. He instituted a rule that only English could be spoken on school property; if a student forgot and greeted him with a cheery "Buenos dias" when passing him in the hall, the result was a spanking or tongue-lashing. The playground was directly outside his classroom; hearing Spanish words through its windows, he would rush outside and turn the offending boy over his knee or angrily berate the offending girl. He insisted that students not only speak English, but speak it in front of audiences —he instituted schoolwide assemblies at which pupils performed in skits— and even debate in it, first in assembly, then against other schools. Cotulla's Mexican students had never had extracurricular activities; within weeks, the new teacher had arranged interscholastic debating contests, declamation contests, even spelling bees. And he didn't want students reciting speeches or poems by rote; he explained to his students, one of them remembers, that "as soon as we understood what the poem meant, we would be able to speak it correctly," and "He would coach us for hours on how to speak a piece such as 'Oh Captain! My Captain!' "

He displayed scant respect for their own culture. Knowing little Spanish when he arrived in Cotulla, he did not bother to learn very much. His "highly dramatic" lectures on Texas history indicated that he had apparently forgotten "that his swarthy charges were related by blood to those on the losing side" (he depicted Santa Anna, a hero to Mexicans, as a treacherous and cold-blooded murderer). But he was tireless in teaching them his culture. "If we hadn't done our homework, we had to stay after school that day," another student says—and if they were not allowed to leave until the assignment was done, their teacher stayed with them. Teaching them—and telling them that if they learned, success would surely be theirs. Says another of his students, Daniel Garcia: "He used to tell us this country was so free that anyone could become President who was willing to work hard enough." Telling them with an absolute assurance, hammering in the theme over and over, inspiring them with it. He would often begin class with a story about a baby. "The little baby in the cradle," recalls Juan Ortiz. "He would tell us that one day we might say the baby would be a teacher. Maybe the next day we'd say the baby would be a doctor. And one day we might say the baby—any baby—might grow up to be the President of the United States."

Demanding though he was, moreover, he was demanding in a way that made his students like him. "He put us to work," says Manuel Sanchez. "But he was the kind of teacher you wanted to work for. You felt an obligation to him and to yourself to do your work." The children he spanked "still liked him." He displayed toward these children feelings he had never displayed before. Their attendance at school was not regular, and if Johnson sometimes seemed to regard their absences as personal insults to him, he was also to recall lying in his room before daylight and hearing motors and knowing that trucks were "hauling the kids off . . . to a beet patch or a cotton patch in the middle of the school year, and give them only two or three months schooling." In December, he took several of his older students down to the Nueces and cut Christmas trees so the classrooms could be decorated. Although he had never been a teacher before, he displayed as much confidence and self-assurance in assuming command over the other teachers as he did in directing his students, and while one bitterly resented him, the others felt as did Mrs. Elizabeth Johnson, who says: "He just moved right in and took over. . . . We were all crazy about him." And he drove himself as hard as he drove the students and other teachers. "He didn't give himself what we call spare time," Elizabeth Johnson recalls. For a young man, she says, he was a remarkable disciplinarian—the discipline she is talking about, she makes clear, is self-discipline. He became friendly with a calm, quiet Mexican who had been a farm laborer but had become janitor at the school, Thomas Coronado. He told Coronado that he, too, should learn English, and with his own money bought Coronado a book to learn it from. He always arrived at school before anyone else did, and left later, and therefore had time to tutor Coronado. "After I had learned the letters, I would spell a word in English. Johnson would then pronounce it and I would repeat." Friendly though he was with the janitor, however, "He made it very clear to me that he wanted the school building to be clean at all times. . . . He seemed to have a passion to see that everything was done that should be done—and that it was done right."

In California, Lyndon Johnson had displayed the same "passion." Seeing a chance in his law "studies" there to escape the dreaded life of physical labor, the chance, moreover, to be "somebody," to have the respect he wanted so desperately, he had grabbed at that chance with the furious energy of someone fleeing a terrible trap. In Cotulla, he was aware that his job represented another chance, a very important one—not because he wanted to remain in Cotulla, but because teaching jobs were very scarce in Texas, and, no matter where he tried to get one, the recommendation from Cotulla would be crucial. And he threw himself into the job, tried to do the best work possible, to be so good a teacher that his excellence could not but be acknowledged. In Cotulla, unlike California, however, he received an immediate compensation—in the coin he most desired. He had sat behind Tom Martin's desk under false pretenses; here his classroom desk was his legitimately; he had been installed behind it—placed in a dominant position—by outside authority. Of all the students he could have had, moreover, with these students, the impoverished, almost illiterate Mexicans of Cotulla, there was the least possible chance that his authority would be challenged even by children's normal pranks. Because he was a teacher—a principal, in fact; because his students were Mexicans accustomed to taking orders from and acting subservient to Anglos; because they could barely speak the language in which he was teaching them—there was no question that in his relationship with them he was the superior, the "somebody." The thirty-two students in his class were the first people he had ever dealt with of whose respect he could be certain unless he lost it through his own efforts. And he acted differently with them than he had with anyone else—in the assurance that was a feature of his teaching style. And he received in return for his energy and his interest and his beneficence a rich measure of the gratitude and respect he had always craved. In his classroom in the Welhausen School, Lyndon Johnson was, for the first time, the somebody he had always wanted to be. In that classroom, people did what they would never do in Johnson City, where he would always be "a Johnson." They looked up to him. The parents of the children were almost tearfully grateful, and as for the children themselves, "This may sound strange, but a lot of us felt he was too good for us," Danny Garcia says. "We wanted to take advantage of his being here. It was like a blessing from the clear sky." Years later, Lyndon Johnson would say: "I still see the faces of the children who sat in my class. . . . I still see their excited eyes speaking friendship."

ONLY OCCASIONALLY were there small signs that what lay behind the passion and the self-discipline might be something other than self-assurance.

Johnson would march into his classroom in the morning, his stride long, his arms swinging vigorously—and he wanted to march in to music. To a popular vaudeville tune of the day, he composed new words:

> How do you do, Mr. Johnson,
> How do you do?
> How do you do, Mr. Johnson,
> How are you?
> We'll do it if we can,
> We'll stand by you to a man,

How do you do, Mr. Johnson,
How are you?

He was quite insistent that every student learn the words, and sing—and sing loud. At first, some of the boys thought he was joking, but if he saw someone not singing, he would get very angry.

Once, moreover, while Johnson was out of the room, Danny Garcia went to the front of the classroom and began imitating the teacher—a performance easy to make funny because of Johnson's awkward walk. Suddenly the class stopped laughing, and when Garcia turned around, there was the teacher in the doorway. Grabbing the boy by the hand, Johnson took him into an empty room. "I thought I was going to get a lecture," Garcia recalls, but instead, "He turned me over his knee and whacked me a dozen times," and as Garcia felt the force of the blows, he realized that Johnson was angrier than he had ever seen him. And when he re-entered the now hushed classroom, Johnson said something that the students considered quite striking. As Amanda Garcia recalls it, he asked them how they could make fun of him: "He told us we were looking at the future President of the United States."

An unusual remark for someone so sure of himself. With these students —more than with any other group he had encountered—Lyndon Johnson should have been confident of respect, and of the "friendship" he himself said he saw in their eyes. Yet at the slightest sign—even a false sign: a typical schoolboy imitation, someone not singing his song—that that respect and affection might be less than absolute, he reacted so strongly. Was it possible that nothing could convince him that he had respect?

That nothing could make him, deep inside himself, feel secure?

IN THE EVENINGS, there was little to do in Cotulla, and had there been any entertainment available, Lyndon Johnson would have had difficulty paying for it. Out of his monthly salary check, he was paying off his car, and the $75 bank loan, and the other, smaller, debts he had left behind in San Marcos. "He was broke from payday to payday, always borrowing a dollar here and a dollar there," says his landlady, Mrs. Sarah Tinsley Marshall. But he was very gay—"as exuberant," a Cotulla acquaintance says, "as a young boy. He was a happy-go-lucky sort of a fellow."

Johnson made a friend of Mrs. Marshall. "Lyndon confided in me a lot," she says. "Lyndon looked on me sort of as a second mother." His attitude toward illness surprised her: "If he got just a little sick, it scared him half to death," she says. But she was happy to take care of him; whenever he caught cold, she would boil water in a dishpan, and put mustard in it, and have him soak his feet. Her boarder's attitude toward food would have been

familiar to Hugo Klein, the little boy at the Junction School whose pie Lyndon ate, or to Lyndon's fellow diners at Mrs. Gates' boardinghouse in San
Marcos. "Lyndon just took everything for granted in my house," Mrs. Marshall recalls. "One day I baked a coconut cake. He slipped into the kitchen
and started eating it. He was down to one piece when I came in. He looked
up and said, 'Miz Sarah, if you give me this piece, I'll buy you another
cake.'" But Mrs. Marshall didn't mind. "I didn't care, and he knew I
wouldn't care. He just did about like a son would do in his own home." With
another boarder, Marthabelle Whitten, a plump waitress who worked in Cotulla's café, he would joke and twist her arm, trying to force her to say "Calf-
rope"—Cotulla slang for "I give up." And then he would ask her to press a
shirt or tie—"He was always in a hurry; he would run in and say, 'Marty,
won't you please press this tie for me?'"—and Miss Whitten always would,
and would be happy to do so. Sometimes, he would play bridge with the
older man who was his roommate, and two sisters, and then "He was always
the life of the party."

Only occasionally, he would get very quiet, and stay quiet, sometimes
for days. People would see him wandering up the rise in back of town, a tall,
skinny, awkward figure staring into those endless, empty distances. Most
times, he was "light-hearted like most twenty-year-olds," Mrs. Marshall
says. But "Sometimes, Lyndon could be as serious as an old man."

Mrs. Marshall didn't know what was behind the sudden quietnesses.
Only his mother, to whom he wrote almost daily during his months down
in South Texas, knew—his mother and Boody. Boody had graduated while
Lyndon was in Cotulla, but was planning to return to San Marcos for more
courses in the Summer of 1929, when Lyndon would be back in college. He
had agreed to room with Lyndon then, and Lyndon wrote again and again
reminding him of this arrangement, making sure his friend would be there
when he got back. "He was very lonely down there in Cotulla," Boody says.
"*Very* lonely." Perhaps the best indication of how Lyndon Johnson felt
about the nine months—September, 1928, through May, 1929—that he
spent in Cotulla comes from his wife, who saw it mostly through his eyes
when, years later, he told her about the experience. "That was a little dried-
up town," Lady Bird Johnson says. "It was just a dying little town." And
then—in words that startled an interviewer who, during long hours of previous conversation with Mrs. Johnson, had become convinced that *nothing,*
no provocation, no matter how strong, would draw from her diplomatic lips
so much as a single word even faintly derogatory about anyone or anything
—she says: "That was one of the crummiest little towns in Texas."

HIS ONLY GOOD TIMES came when he drove over to see Carol Davis, who
was teaching in Pearsall, another little South Texas town.

Carol was apparently not the only member of the couple who was experiencing qualms about the relationship. Sarah Marshall, in whom Johnson was confiding, recalls that "He was beginning to feel they didn't have . . . much in common." She remembers her young boarder saying: "Miz Sarah, this girl loves opera. But I'd rather sit down on an old log with a farmer and talk." But his qualms didn't prevent him from courting her determinedly, almost frantically, telephoning her, writing her, taking her to see touring opera companies in San Antonio, and other musical events, or movies, or just driving the thirty-three miles to Pearsall to see her almost every evening she said she was free.

And then, suddenly, she was saying that less and less frequently. One evening, when Carol had been playing the piano in the parlor of the house in which she was boarding, a young man had appeared at the front door, which was open because of the heat. He loved music, he said, and would Carol mind if he listened?

The young man, a postal clerk named Harold Smith, was aggressive, as was Carol's other boyfriend, but, unlike the other, he liked not only music but movies. "Lyndon was just interested in politics, which I certainly wasn't," Carol recalls. "Harold was more interested in the things I was interested in."

And her father approved of Harold. One weekend, he accompanied her to San Marcos, and A. L. Davis said he liked him. (Carol's sisters wondered if his approval was based less on his feelings about Smith than on his feelings about Lyndon; they wondered if he didn't feel that marrying anyone else would be better than marrying Lyndon.)

For a while, back in Pearsall, Carol juggled evenings, seeing Lyndon one night and Smith the next. But more and more often, when Lyndon telephoned, she would say she was busy. Her job ended some weeks earlier than Lyndon's, and when she returned to San Marcos, torn between the two young men, her father sent her to California with her sister Ethel to think things out. Waiting for her upon her return were two letters proposing marriage, one from Cotulla and one from Pearsall. "She sat down in the back room, where Daddy used to sit when he thought," Ethel recalls. When she emerged, she had made her decision. While he was still down in Cotulla, Lyndon Johnson was notified that Carol Davis was engaged to Harold Smith.

11

White Stars and
Black Stars

LYNDON JOHNSON returned to San Marcos in June, 1929, and immediately resumed his place not only at the president's side, but at the professors' feet. There was, in fact, an almost frantic aura now about the sycophancy that students called "brown-nosing."

And about the fawning in print as well, for he was again Summer editor of the *College Star*. Despite, for example, widespread student complaint about Registration Day delays that had forced them to wait for hours on queues that wound back and forth across the campus and most of the way down College Hill, the student newspaper lauded the "capable management" of the registrar's office. "The able and efficient manner in which [it] handled the crowd of students Monday created much favorable comment," Johnson wrote. "One can scarcely picture such a task being more expeditiously, tactfully and pleasantly discharged." His popularity with undergraduates—as contrasted with "management"—rapidly resumed its pre-Cotulla level. He had hoped to remain as *Star* editor when the regular session started in September, and to be yell leader for the football season, but the Student Council elected Mylton (Babe) Kennedy to both jobs, demoting Johnson to editorial writer. Soon, moreover, Kennedy and Johnson became involved in a series of increasingly angry shouting matches that erupted in a fistfight—or in what would have been a fistfight had Johnson participated. Instead, when Kennedy swung at him, he fell back on a bed as he had during the poker-game incident two years before and began kicking his feet in the air. And as Kennedy came on, Johnson shouted: "I quit! I quit!" Vernon Whiteside, present during the encounter, was soon imitating Johnson's panicky tone all over campus, and students were laughing at him again.

. . .

THE LAUGHING WAS about to stop, however—to stop and never start again. For Lyndon Johnson was about to enter a new area of campus activity, an area for which he was to prove better equipped than for journalism or jousting. He was about to enter campus politics.

In the opinion of other students, he *began* campus politics.

Interest in elections for class officers and Student Council members had always been slight. "We had few class meetings or activities," says Joe Berry, the tall, quiet star football end who was often elected class president. "There were no issues that people cared about." The Black Stars, who were elected to most offices, cared least of all. Berry, a brilliant student who was to become a renowned microbiologist at Bryn Mawr College, looks back on his teammates with fondness for some of their qualities. "These guys had physical courage, and they were very, very loyal," he says. "They would go to almost any lengths to back you up. They had basically an openness about them—you always knew where they stood. It was a kind of an open integrity of the West, where a man always stood up and was counted." He also saw in many of them, however, an utter lack of "sharpness." Even in a college where academic standards were almost non-existent by Eastern criteria, many of the football players were notably uninterested in course work. Their interests included drinking beer, girls, hunting and fishing—"physical things," Berry says. They would not talk about—because they had absolutely no interest in—campus politics. "Someone might say, 'Who we gonna run for president?' And someone else would say, 'Oh, hell, let's run ol' Joe.' That's how the nominations were decided." Berry himself resigned during one of his terms, in fact, in favor of a friend—just so the friend could say he had been president. No one objected to that; no one cared. "I wanted to give him the honor," Berry says, "and besides it didn't mean very much. Elections were so unimportant."

A few other students—less "country," more interested in making money, better dressed—decided during the 1929 Summer session to form a rival White Stars group. Lyndon Johnson asked to join. But he was disliked by the group's two leaders—fast-talking Vernon Whiteside, whose two earlier years at New York University endowed him with an aura of sophistication on the San Marcos campus, and Horace Richards, the campus promoter (who once stood outside a pep rally and, as the enthused students emerged, held out his hat, yelled, "Kick in for the decorations," and kept the money he collected). "Anyone who talked back to him, he despised," Richards says. "He wanted to dominate everybody." Moreover, they wanted the White Stars to be a secret organization, and Johnson talked too much. When, at the group's first meeting, someone mentioned that Johnson wanted to join, the subject was closed when someone else said scornfully: "Ol' Bull? He'll tell everybody in school." And when the White Stars organized—each one taking his oath in a mystical night ceremony on the bank of a creek, holding a candle and, in lieu of a Bible, a dictionary that was the biggest book available—Johnson was not among them. Denied membership in the "in" crowd, he had been denied membership in the "outs" as well. He would never have become a White Star had not three early inductees been among "those country boys who really didn't talk very much" and who found Johnson "very entertaining." He asked them to bring up his name again, and when they did, at a meeting several weeks later, the two founders agreed to admit him— because they felt sorry for him, and because, in Whiteside's words, "What difference did it make? I mean, the White Stars weren't supposed to be any big deal. We formed it, I suppose, just because we weren't invited to join the Black Stars. The real reason we did it, to tell you the truth, was because it was hard for anyone who wasn't a Black Star to get a date with the pretty girls. We said, 'Hell, if they can have the Black Stars, we can have the White Stars.' We did it because of girls. Hell, we weren't even thinking about elections or politics then."

But Lyndon Johnson was thinking about politics. Hardly had he been inducted into the White Stars when he suggested they run a candidate for senior class president as the Black Stars did. And after he persuaded them to do so, he displayed considerable competence in political tactics.

In "nose-counting," or vote-counting, for example. The other White Stars felt that no one had a chance against the Black Star candidate, Dick Spinn, the popular football and track star who had won an easy victory when the first class elections were held in October. (Class officers were elected— in October, January and April—for three-month terms.) But the other White Stars hadn't counted votes. If most students voted, Johnson admitted, Spinn would win easily. But on a campus so uninterested in politics—a campus, moreover, on which there had never been a closely fought campaign—most students didn't bother to vote. An opposition candidate could win with just a few votes.

He had, moreover, figured out where to get those few. The "in" crowd —the "T" Association of varsity lettermen and the two "literary societies," the Shakespeare and the Idyllic, whose members included the pretty, popular coeds who dated the "T" men—would be solid for Spinn, of course, but there were two other groups on campus: the "townies," students from San Marcos, and the "YMCA" crowd, members of the Young Men's and Young Women's Christian Associations, who were considered the campus intellectuals. Nor were those the only votes available. There were also the students who belonged to no crowd at all. No one had ever thought of these campus nonentities in terms of class elections. But Johnson thought of them, and counted their votes, and counted the votes of the townies and the YMCA crowd—and realized that these "outs" had enough votes among them to defeat the "ins."

And he knew how to get those votes. A popular candidate was needed, he said, and he had one picked out. And when, in the darkness down on the creek bank, a scornful voice said, "I bet it's you, huh, Lyndon?" he said no it wasn't; he had made too many enemies. Bill Deason should be their candidate, he said. "Let's take ol' Bill—he's got no scars on him." Deason, he added, would also be a strong candidate because, smooth-spoken and as handsome as a model in a collar ad, he was very popular with campus coeds; in counting noses, the most obvious fact was that on the San Marcos campus more than two-thirds of them were women's noses.

A popular issue was needed, too. Neither he nor any of the other White Stars had one that they cared about, so, says Whiteside (who, along with Richards, regarded the whole "politicking" idea with cynical amusement), "We'd say anything—we didn't care if the argument was true or not. We kept trying arguments to find one that touched." And, finally, Johnson discovered one that did. Extracurricular activities were funded from the so-called "Blanket Tax," a single all-inclusive fee that each student paid as part of his tuition. The Student Council, which allocated it, had always given the lion's share to the athletic teams. The townies and the YMCA crowd, whose votes Johnson needed, weren't athletes, so he had the White Stars campaign, using the slogan "Brains Are Just as Important as Brawn," for additional allocations of the Blanket Tax to non-athletic activities such as debate and drama.

To his own campaigning Johnson brought the aggressiveness and energy he had displayed in California and Cotulla. None of the other White Stars—not even Deason, who believed he had no chance—did much campaigning. "They made fun of his [Johnson's] enthusiasm," one says. "Their attitude was: if he wanted to organize and pull something off, let him." But Johnson spent evening after evening visiting boardinghouses, talking to students, asking for their votes. When talking to a potential voter, he would place one arm around the voter's shoulders; with his other hand, he would grasp the voter's lapel—or, if there was no lapel available, a shirt collar. "He would do a lot of buttonholing—talking right into their face to make the point," White Star Al Harzke says. This conversational technique had irritated some of his Johnson City schoolmates, but now that he had an issue to talk about, the technique was surprisingly effective. Deason, watching him, saw that "his greatest forte [was] to look a man in the eye and do a convincing job of selling him his viewpoint. In one-on-one salesmanship, Lyndon was the best." Nonetheless, on election eve Deason agreed with the other White Stars that the effort had failed.

> The night before election we caucused and decided we were behind twenty votes and decided to throw in the sponge—all but Lyndon. He said, "Oh, no, if twenty votes is all we need, we've got from now until eight o'clock in the morning to get twenty votes." This was toward midnight. . . .
>
> There was our group, there was the athletes' group, . . . but there was a third group which we called the YMCA group. . . .

And they had been against us because Dick Spinn was also a member of the YMCA and an outstanding student. So there wasn't any reason why they shouldn't support him. But LBJ in his inimitable way said . . . , "Well, if I can change that group, it may change it. The rest of you may be going to bed, but I'm not." So he started making rounds to the dormitories and buttonholing folks. And . . . he switched about twenty votes.

And the next morning, when the votes were counted, Deason had won.

Stung by the defeat—the first ever, so far as anyone could recall, for a Black Star—the athletes determined that Deason wouldn't win again. "The day I won, the war was on," he recalls. "They started cutting me up"—pointing out, during the three months before the April elections, Deason's weaknesses as a student leader. But Johnson used a tactic to counter this campaigning against one man: he saw to it that that man's name didn't appear on the ballot. "This was Lyndon's strategy," Deason recalls. "They were going to beat me pretty good, so we let them think I was going to run again, and then, at the very last minute, it was announced that Al Harzke would be running instead."

He used other kinds of tactics, too.

In that April election, Johnson himself was running for an office: senior class representative to the Student Council. Because of his unpopularity—and the popularity of his opponent, Joe Berry, who was generally considered the best-liked man in school—"we didn't think he had much of a chance," Horace Richards says, "but he wanted to be representative, and he wanted it bad." And when, on the night before the election, the White Stars met on the creek bank, they found, in Richards' words, that "he had planned things" so that he would get it.

Johnson's strategy was based on the confusion that existed at San Marcos—whose students, to earn money, were continually dropping out for a term, or a full year, or several years, and then returning to school—over exactly which class (senior, junior, sophomore or freshman) a student was in at a given moment. His strategy was based on the relaxed atmosphere in which class elections were held: due to the past lack of interest in the elections, the election meetings, held in different classrooms in Old Main, were extremely informal, with hasty nominations, quick voting, rapid adjournment and no set rules of procedure. And, most importantly, perhaps, it was based also on the fact that, because elections had been conducted honestly in the past, no one was prepared for something different.

There was more interest in the April elections than anyone could remember. Johnson had persuaded the White Stars—more receptive to the idea now because of Deason's victory—to run not only Harzke but a whole slate of candidates for class offices and Student Council seats. The aroused Black Stars were also running candidates, and because of the new interest in campus politics aroused by the White Stars' campaigning, there were individual candidacies, most notably that of the brilliant, popular Henry Kyle, the only student who could argue Johnson to a standstill in government classes, who had campaigned on a far-reaching platform of reforms in student government. Since the other candidates were, in general, more popular than the White Star candidates, the White Star candidates would normally have lost, but under Johnson's strategy, this would not necessarily follow— because, while everyone else would be voting only once (in his own class election), each White Star would be multiplying his vote by voting in *every* class election. There were, moreover, refinements to the strategy, refinements designed to further minimize the handicap of limited numbers; that night on the creek bank, the White Stars carefully rehearsed the tactics Johnson proposed, because, with the four class meetings all scheduled to begin at ten a.m. and only one hour set aside for them, their little band would have to work fast.

When they went into action the next morning, they worked very fast indeed. Vernon Whiteside describes what happened. "We took one meeting at a time. There was only a small group of us—maybe a half-dozen or so. But there were so few other kids there. One of us would shout, 'C'mon, let's get going. Let's elect Horace Richards temporary chairman.' We always elected Horace, because Horace had a loud voice and more guts than a burglar. 'All in favor of Horace Richards, say *Aye*.' We'd all shout *Aye*. 'The *Ayes* have it. C'mon, get up there, Horace.' And he'd run the election, and when he called for the vote, we'd all yell loud for our candidate so that we sounded like more than we were. And no matter who sounded louder, he'd say our candidate had won. Then we'd go—Horace, me, Lyndon, the same half-dozen of us—to the next election, and pull the same thing. So each of us, you might say, voted in all four elections."

In the junior class meeting, there was almost trouble because, with time running short and Johnson anxious to get to the senior class meeting where he was a candidate, Richards tried to rush the nominating procedure even faster than he had done previously. As soon as the White Star candidate had been nominated, he shouted "Nominations closed!"

There were still "a lot of guys with their hands up," he recalls with a grin. "Henry Kyle was jumping up and down. He said, 'You can't do that [close the nominations]! I want to nominate someone!' " But Richards was equal to the challenge. "I said, 'Don't tell me what I can do. I'm president [temporary chairman] of this class, and I'm running this election. What I say goes.' And I closed the nominations. The juniors and seniors were meeting in rooms right across from each other. As soon as I closed the nominations, I ran across the hall. The other guys—everyone who could possibly pass for a senior—were already in there voting. They were just closing up their election. I said, 'I want to vote.' They said, 'You can't vote, Horace. You're not a senior.' I said, 'Don't tell me I'm not a senior. I'm taking more senior subjects than junior, and that makes me a senior.' Well, who could tell if I was telling the truth unless they looked up the record, and they didn't have time to do that. I voted for Lyndon, of course. The seniors were voting by paper ballots, and when they counted the votes, all our guys had won, and Lyndon had won—by one vote. I wasn't really a senior, but I voted for him, and it was my vote that won for him, and it was illegal.

"You know," Horace Richards says with a smile, "later on, when everyone got so excited about the election [the 1948 election for United States Senator from Texas] that Lyndon Johnson stole, I felt that I had been in on the beginning of history. Because I was in on the *first* election that Lyndon Johnson stole."*

WERE EVEN SUCH TACTICS inadequate for Lyndon Johnson's purposes? He used others.

The annual voting for the Gaillardians,† the college's seven prettiest, most popular and most "representative" coeds, aroused the greatest interest of any campus election—far more than the class officer elections. And the voting, by secret written ballots deposited in a ballot box in the ground-floor hall of Old Main, was conducted under a strict supervision which would prevent repetition of the multiple-voting technique. Previously, most of the winners immortalized in full-page sepia pictures in the *Pedagog* had been members of the literary society–Black Star "in" crowd, but now Johnson wanted "White Star" girls to win as many of the seven places as possible. Standing in his way were three nominees too popular or pretty to be beaten, but he was confident that his vigorous campaigning would win four places— confident, that is, until Ruth Lewis was nominated.

Unlike the other candidates, Ruth Lewis was not a campus beauty. But although in practice the Gaillardian election was mainly a beauty contest, it was not supposed to be—"representative" was defined as "foremost in college life"—and Miss Lewis had other qualifications. There was always a twinkle in her eye, and in her fingers when she sat down at the old Underwood in the *Pedagog* office, where she was an assistant editor. "She was a terrific writer—brilliant," says *Pedagog* editor Ella So Relle. She wrote for the Press Club, the Scribblers' Club, and was involved in half a dozen campus activities. And she had ideas as novel on the San Marcos campus of that era as the hair she wore short and straight in the defiant and very un-Texan

---

* Johnson's joy in victory was not unalloyed, however. Richards, writing up the elections for the *Star*, wrote that Johnson had won "by a neck's lead"(a narrow margin). Johnson was furious over what he regarded as a slur on his victory. "Boy, that boy was angry at me," Richards recalls. "We sat in a car and talked for an hour about that. He said, 'Horace, it just looks to me like you try to dig me every time you get a chance.'"

† The gaillardia is a Hill Country flower.

flapper style: an enthusiastic tennis player herself, she believed that women should have their own athletic teams; she did not want to get married as soon as possible, preferring a career in journalism, where her writing could help people. But she argued for her ideas with a quiet earnestness and self-depre-catory humor that made her so popular that when she was nominated for one of the seven places, it was generally assumed she would win.

But then, as Ella So Relle puts it, "Lyndon found out this dirty little thing about Ruth."

The "thing" was not really "dirty"—it was not even significant—except in light of the deep feeling of inferiority at San Marcos about the famous University of Texas just thirty miles away, where richer, smarter students went to college. "To understand [what happened], you have to understand how defensive we were about going to San Marcos," Miss So Relle says. Johnson's discovery consisted of nothing more than the fact that when two men had stopped to fix a flat tire on a car in which Ruth Lewis and two friends had been riding, and had asked the young women where they went to college, Miss Lewis, out of defensiveness, or embarrassment, had blurted out that they went to the University of Texas, and only later, with a shamefaced grin, had corrected herself. A more trivial incident can hardly be imagined —except that one of the men was an acquaintance of Lyndon Johnson, and happened to mention it to him.

Johnson told Miss Lewis that unless she withdrew from the Gaillardian election, the whole campus would know what she had done. Unless she with-drew, he said, he would write an editorial in the *Star* revealing the incident and stating that she should not be elected because any woman who was ashamed to say she went to San Marcos was not a "representative" San Marcos coed.

When Johnson left Ruth Lewis, he knew he had won. "He came back [after seeing her] and said we could stop worrying," Horace Richards says. "He had blackmailed her right out of that election, and he knew it." John-son's assessment was correct. As soon as he had left Miss Lewis, Ella So Relle says, "she came to my house in tears—which was very unusual for Ruth. She said, 'I'm going to withdraw from the election.' I was astounded. I wanted her to battle him, but she said he was going to put this in big head-lines in the newspaper, and she just could not face that embarrassment." She withdrew, and the four coeds Johnson wanted to be Gaillardians were all elected.

HIS NEXT TARGET was the Student Council. He himself, as a result of the "stolen" election, was a member, but more than half of the twelve other members, including almost all the seniors and juniors, were athletes and members of the "in" crowd. "I had to rely on the freshmen and sophomores to get the votes to run the Student Council," he would recall in 1970. He

knew how to get them: use the "brains are just as important as brawn" issue
that had "touched" in other elections. But he had to know whom to use the
issue *on*: he had to learn the identities of "bright" underclassmen who would
either be his candidates for the council or would vote for those candidates.
And the inchoate, constantly shifting, nature of the San Marcos student body
made identifying such students difficult.

But Johnson had figured out a way to identify them. As night watchman
in Old Main, White Star Archie Wiles possessed keys to the registrar's office.
One midnight, Johnson was to recall in that 1970 conversation, "We took the
keys and went in there and I . . . got those little yellow (grade) cards, and I
got the names of everyone who had a B average—I took the people with superior intellectual ability." Lining up nominees, nominators and voters, he
saw to it that the freshmen and sophomore places on the council were filled
with students to whom the "brains" argument would appeal.

In selecting women candidates, he took a further precaution. He instructed White Stars to date the freshman and sophomore coeds he was considering as nominees. Says Wilton Woods, a senior, who did a lot of such
dating because his soft voice and tentative manner were attractive to younger
girls, "Lyndon's idea was to get a real nice-looking girl and see if you could
control her. Date her and see how she comes out, see if she'll go along if she
was elected to the Student Council." If Johnson received a report that a girl
would "go along," he would instruct the White Star who was dating her to ask
her to run for the council. "I was dating a little ol' girl, and my sole purpose
in dating her was to get her to run," Woods says. "That was Lyndon's idea.
[He] wanted [me] to tell her how to vote once she was elected." The strategy
worked. Women at San Marcos were not "modern girls," Richards explains:
they were not particularly interested in politics. (Although they outnumbered men three to one, no woman, so far as can be determined, had ever
been a class president.) Johnson's weeding-out process had ensured, moreover, that the women he selected as candidates were even less interested than
most. Women at San Marcos were also not "modern" because, in Richards'
words, "Girls at that time—they'd do what you told them" in areas such as
politics that were considered men's domain. And Johnson's process ensured,
of course, that his candidates were not particularly independent. "And,"
Whiteside adds, "don't forget—these were girls in a school where there were
six girls to every two boys. A lot of the girls were very lonely. A boy was a
prized possession. They didn't want to do anything to get you mad at them."
Says Woods: "Seldom did you have to make an issue of it. You'd say, 'So-
and-so wants to be editor of the *Star*. He's a good ol' boy. You'll vote for
him, won't you?' And almost always, they would."

Johnson employed a similar strategy with at least one woman who was
already on the council, having Woods date her as long as Lyndon needed her
vote. In this instance, the strategy worked particularly well, for the woman,
a lively, dark-haired young lady with dark, glowing eyes, fell in love with

Woods. "And then, of course, as soon as Lyndon didn't need her [vote] any more, ol' Wilton drops her," Richards laughs. "She really liked Wilton, too, and I bet she really used to wonder what had happened. I bet she could never figure out why ol' Wilton dropped her."

PROBABLY SHE NEVER COULD, for, varied as were Lyndon Johnson's political tactics, one aspect was common to them all. This aspect would have been striking no matter who was planning the tactics, but it was all the more striking when the tactician was a young man who had displayed throughout his life—and was, in his other, non-political, activities, displaying still—so notable a tendency for "talking big." Lyndon Johnson was planning many tactics now—a whole political strategy, in fact. And he never talked about it at all.

Occasionally, his little brother got a glimpse of it. On some weekends, fifteen-year-old Sam Houston Johnson visited Lyndon, and he would, he would write, never forget "those wonderful conversations (monologues, really) that ran through the long Saturday afternoons and Sunday mornings. . . . I heard several installments of his campaign against the Black Stars during my periodic weekend visits to San Marcos, always listening with wide-eyed admiration as my brother outlined his strategy for the coming week. Even now, I can still visualize him restlessly moving back and forth in his room . . . sometimes lounging on his bed and then moving on to a rickety wooden chair near the window, his eyes gleaming with anticipation and his deep voice tense with emotion." But even Sam Houston got only a glimpse. At Sunday noon, he had to go home, and when he left, his brother would still be pacing and prowling around his little room, his eyes gleaming, his hands clasping and unclasping, his long fingers, nails bitten down to the quick and into the quick, twisting and twining under the tension of hidden thoughts.

The White Stars understood the necessity of keeping their existence secret. Students were especially susceptible to the "brains are just as important as brawn" argument because they knew that the "brawn"—the college athletes—belonged to a secret organization and, along with their girlfriends, to an exclusive clique into which most students were not invited. Johnson was playing on that susceptibility quite deliberately. "Most of the non-athletic students secretly resented and probably hated the Saturday heroes, no matter how much they apparently enjoyed the games," his brother explains. "Quite obviously, since every practical politician knows that hate and fear offer more forceful tools for organizing than love and respect, Lyndon had a rather fertile field at San Marcos. . . . Lyndon had sized up the situation like an old pro. He had that gut knowledge about the little man's resentment of the big man. . . ." The susceptibility of the voters—the "little men"—to whom Johnson was appealing would be less easily translatable into support for Johnson's candidates if the voters discovered that, in being asked to vote for a Deason or a Harzke, they were being asked to vote for members of another secret organization—also one into which they were not invited.

In forming the White Stars, Richards and Whiteside, not for political reasons but to enhance the feeling of "brotherhood, fraternity" that was so important to them, had formulated strict rules for secrecy. Johnson devised others, which they embraced. No three White Stars could ever be seen talking together on campus, for example; should three find themselves together, meaningful glances would indicate which one should leave. White Star meetings, previously held down at the creek or in members' rooms in their boardinghouses, were now, at Johnson's suggestion, moved to the two-story Hofheinz Hotel, where, Johnson pointed out, no passerby could peep through the windows. There was even an ingenious device to allow a White Star to deny with a straight face that he was one: immediately upon being asked if he is a member of the group, a White Star rule read, the member is—upon the very asking of the question—automatically expelled, so that he can answer "No"; he will be readmitted at the next meeting. These rules and others were incorporated into the White Star Bylaws, which new members had to swear to uphold in that impressive ceremony with the candle and the dictionary on the creek bank—and so seriously did these young men take this oath that, forty years later, asked about the White Stars, Deason declined to go into detail "in order not to violate certain oaths that I have taken," and others declined to talk at all. So successful was Johnson in his insistence on secrecy that even after White Stars had won many campus elections, the campus did not know that there *were* White Stars. "The Black Stars didn't know we were organized—*nobody* knew," Deason says. "They didn't know this was an *organization* working on them. They knew someone was playing havoc with the school, but they didn't know who." Whiteside recalls with glee "all these unsuspecting people we used. . . . We'd say, 'You're not going to vote with the Black Stars, are you? You're not going to help the Black Stars?' And all the time we had another organization that was so secret they didn't know we had one."

Johnson also had reasons for keeping his strategy—and even the fact that he *had* a strategy—secret from the White Stars themselves. Richards and Whiteside, jealous of their leadership, might well balk at a Johnson plan simply because it wasn't *their* plan. Or, if they agreed to it, they might —loudmouths that they were—talk about it, revealing it to the campus at large. Other White Stars might balk at a Johnson plan because of their dislike of him. He couldn't let even his allies know what he was planning. Occasionally, very occasionally—only when it was unavoidable because Johnson needed his help—Bill Deason got a glimpse of the planning. Al Harzke recalls returning to the little room he shared with Deason and finding his roommate and Johnson sprawled across the bed "calling politics, talking as if there wasn't nothing but politics—I used to call Bill 'Senator' and Lyndon 'Governor.' " But Johnson never gave even Deason, his first candidate and closest ally, more than a glimpse. It took Deason quite some time, in fact, to realize something about the White Stars' meetings. They were still informal affairs—loud talk and laughter. And they were still chaired by the group's founders, Richards and Whiteside, who did most of the talking; Lyndon Johnson, in fact, did very little talking at these meetings. But Deason began to notice by a meeting's end the decisions they arrived at—Richards, Whiteside and the rest—would invariably be the decisions Johnson had told him, the night before, that he wanted them to arrive at. "In discussions that five or six of us would have in a room, he would not be the dominant one," Deason says. "But I remember I began to think that he may have controlled the meeting more than we realized, that maybe . . . he was swaying the group. Gradually, we came to realize that. At least I did. I came to realize that he had a very clever mind." Gradually, in fact, Deason came to understand something understood by no one else. Richards and Whiteside, the founders of the White Stars, thought they were still running the White Stars. But they weren't.

THE MOST STRIKING ASPECT of Lyndon Johnson's secrecy, however, was not the success with which he imposed it on others but the success with which he imposed it on himself.

All his life he had "talked big"—had boasted, bragged, swaggered, strutted, tried to stand out, shoved himself into the forefront—so incessantly that he had revealed a *need* to talk big, a desperate thirst for attention and admiration. This thirst had not been quenched; his boasting and bragging on other subjects—any subject but campus politics—was as arrant as ever; it is difficult to escape the conclusion that he talked at length about campus politics to Sam Houston Johnson because he had to talk to *someone,* had to let *someone* know how smart he was, and his hero-worshipping little brother was the only listener who, because he was not part of the college and would go back to Johnson City on Sunday, could be trusted not to reveal his secrets on campus. But much as Lyndon Johnson may have wanted to talk on this subject, he said not a word to anyone but his little brother—and, in his silence, revealed that beneath the skinny, gangling, awkward, big-eared exterior, beneath the rambling monologues and the wild boasting, beneath the fawning and the smiling and the face turned so worshipfully up to the professors, lay a will of steel. Lyndon Johnson was planning to take a tiny group of outsiders and with them snatch student power; not only snatch existing power, but create for them—and him—new power, of dimensions no students had ever had on campus before.

If anyone on campus, even his allies, realized his purposes, he would not be able to accomplish them. If anyone saw what he was doing, he would not be able to do it.

And no one saw.

THE SUCCESS WITH WHICH he cloaked his maneuvers in secrecy was demonstrated most dramatically during the selection, in May, 1930, of the following year's *Star* and *Pedagog* editors.

Merit, not politics, had traditionally been the criterion for filling these posts, not only the highest-paying but the most influential available to undergraduates. In filling them, the Student Council had always accepted the recommendations of the incumbent editors, who nominated their most qualified assistants from the junior class. In May, 1930, the nominees for the *Star* and *Pedagog* editorships, respectively, were a brother and sister who lived in San Marcos, Henry and Medie Kyle, and they were so clearly the best-qualified candidates—as was another "townie," Edward Puls, for *Pedagog* business manager—that there appeared to be no question that they would be selected. "We just assumed they would," says *Pedagog* editor Ella So Relle. "They [the council] had never failed to do this before." Kyle's reforming zeal—he advocated not only less emphasis on athletics and a more equitable distribution of the Blanket Tax, but more independent reading to supplement the almost total reliance on textbook work, and adoption in "honors courses" of the "Oxford Method" of fewer examinations so that students could pursue lines of study without being tied to rigid curricula—had been thwarted during the elections a month before, but he was already planning to resurrect the campaign in the *Star*. While the council was meeting in Old Main, the three friends, who had grown up together in San Marcos, sat together on a bench outside, awaiting notification of their election.

But it was Horace Richards and Wilton Woods who emerged from the building—and as they saw the waiting trio, they started giggling. Puls and the Kyles soon found out what they were giggling about. When a member of the council, a friend, appeared, he told them that there had been surprising developments at the meeting. A new rule had been suggested. He had objected to it, and so had others, but a vote had been quickly called for and, with the council's freshman and sophomore members voting for it— along with a single senior, Lyndon Johnson—the rule had been quickly passed by the margin of a single vote. This rule, the friend said, made residents of San Marcos ineligible for *Star* and *Pedagog* jobs because, since they lived at home, they didn't need the salaries as much as other students, and, with the Depression at hand, jobs should go to students in need. The new rule had made Puls and the Kyles ineligible, the friend said, and the jobs they had expected had gone instead to students who had not previously been considered in the running: the *Star* editorship to Osler Dunn, a junior whose previous role on the paper had been so minor that his picture had not even been included among those in the *Pedagog* section devoted to the newspaper; the post of *Star* business manager to Harvey Yoe, a freshman, the first freshman in anyone's memory to have received such an honor.

Mortified though they were at the injustice of the new rule (far from not needing money, Puls needed it badly; he had been counting on the *Pedagog* salary to pay his tuition; without it, he would have to drop out of college), they had no inkling at first that it had been devised solely to make them ineligible—and they had no inkling that Lyndon Johnson had done the devising. Kyle was especially shocked to learn the truth. He and Johnson were very different young men—the slender, bespectacled, studious Kyle was a voracious reader, a brilliant student who received in reality the A's that Johnson only said he received, a brilliant debater who, undefeated during his junior year, won in reality the debating victories that Johnson only said he won—but they shared an interest in politics (although Kyle was more interested in the science than the practice). They argued constantly in history and social-science courses—Kyle, a professor says, could argue Johnson "to a standstill"; he had read the books that Johnson only said he had read—but Kyle had enjoyed those arguments, had thought the give-and-take of ideas was what college was all about, and he had believed that Johnson enjoyed them, too. During Johnson's pre-Cotulla days at college, Kyle says, "I befriended him when no one else would have anything to do with him," and Johnson had apparently reciprocated, inviting him to his home to meet his parents. During Johnson's post-Cotulla days, he had needed the support of "townies" for Deason's election, and, as Kyle was their leader, had cultivated him. "I thought we were friends," Kyle says. Enraged though he had been by Richards' railroading of the junior class vote, he had thought that Johnson was only one of the group following Richards around that day; he had not the slightest suspicion that Johnson was its leader. Now he had not the slightest suspicion of Johnson's role in conceiving the "Depression" argument that had deprived him of the editorship. And he was as unaware of the existence of a secret organization called the White Stars as he was of how Lyndon Johnson really felt about being argued to a standstill. The previous year, Kyle recalls now, "two of his henchmen [Richards and Woods] asked me . . . would I be willing to be a member of a group that would try to get more money for these literary activities, forensic activities, because the football team was getting too much money. I never got the idea that [it] was a secret group, I never knew that Lyndon was even a member of it." After he declined the invitation ("I said all these people you all are fighting are my friends"), he never again, although he previously had been class president, won another student office. Without understanding how, he felt that Richards and Woods were somehow behind those defeats. Now he felt that, in some way he didn't understand, they were also behind his defeat for the editorship, and as soon as he learned about it, he recalls, "I sought them out, and stopped them on the side of Old Main and cursed them with every name in the book. They just stood and looked at me and grinned." But he never guessed—never had even a suspicion—who was behind Richards and Woods. Not until "the very last part of school," some weeks after the decisive council meeting, was Kyle told that Johnson had been the moving force at the meeting, and that, moreover, "Lyndon had been working for years to keep me from getting any honors at all." Puls also suspected nothing. "All the time this was going on," he says, whenever he saw Lyndon Johnson on the campus, Johnson would smile in a friendly way and "stop and talk just like nothing was happening."

Puls, ironically in light of the argument Johnson had used to sway the council, had to spend "a horrible year" in Bishop, Texas, to earn enough money to return to college. He left for Bishop, he says, with "a bad taste" in his mouth. "He [Johnson] started [the politicking] at San Marcos," Puls says. "He had to start it. If he hadn't done the politicking and maneuvering, he couldn't have been outstanding. He wasn't an outstanding student, and he wasn't outstanding in anything else. He was just the type of character who was snaky all the time. He got power by things you or I wouldn't stoop to. But he got the power, and he cheated us out of jobs we had worked very hard for, and had earned." Kyle and his sister had enough money to continue at San Marcos, but they dropped out, too—and would not return until Johnson had graduated and left. "We left college because of him," Kyle says. "Because of disgust at what he did." The disgust would not fade for years, Kyle's friends say. Says Ella So Relle, who did not herself learn until years later the real reason the council rejected her recommendation for her successor: "Henry was very smart, and he was very idealistic, and he just could not tolerate what he saw as political purposes." Says another student, who has asked not to be identified: "It was as if Henry, who had lived a very sheltered life, found out all at once just how dirty life could really be."

CLASS PRESIDENTS, Student Council members, Gaillardians, *Star* and *Pedagog* editors—when Lyndon Johnson had returned from Cotulla in June, 1929, all had been members of a clique that had scorned Lyndon Johnson. By the time he graduated in August, 1930, all had been replaced by members of a clique led, in fact if not in name, by Lyndon Johnson. His enemies had been supplanted by his allies, and with remarkable speed. In little more than a year, he, a young man with a long-standing interest in politics but absolutely no political experience, had manipulated a campus political structure—*created* a campus political structure—so that he, still one of the most disliked students on campus, exerted over it more influence than any other student.

"Thinking back on those wonderful . . . monologues, . . . I can clearly see that political stratagems have always been my brother's natural vocation and favorite pastime," Sam Houston Johnson writes. *Natural vocation*: the insight of a brother who, throughout his life, would display considerable brotherly insight. Lyndon Johnson had come to his new field already an expert in it.

His brother understood part of the reason for this aptitude. "His penchant for nose-counting comes from Daddy," he wrote. For nose-counting —and for much else. The tall, gangling, big-eared young man with the lapel-holding mannerism and the powerful talent for persuasion was, after all, the son of a man with the same mannerism and the same talent. The young man possessed of an instinctive gift for a campus version of backroom maneuvering was the son of a man who, coming to the State Capitol without experience, had displayed immediately a similar gift.

But there was a crucial difference between father and son—as a single contrast demonstrates. His father's most gallant fight was the one he waged, alone in the Texas House of Representatives except for six forlorn allies, against Joseph Weldon Bailey, the Populist who had betrayed the Populists. Once, in a history class, Lyndon Johnson was asked if he had a particular hero. "Joe Bailey," he replied.

Sam Ealy Johnson, an idealist "straight as a shingle" whose uncompromising adherence to the beliefs and principles with which he had entered politics made him a hero to some, was nonetheless a political failure who didn't accomplish any of his most cherished aims. His son had, in the campus arena which was the only arena in which he had yet fought, accomplished his aims—because the impedimenta which hampered his father did not hamper him. He had won believing in nothing—without a reform he wanted to make, without a principle or issue about which he truly cared ("We didn't care if the argument was true or not."). He had demonstrated, moreover, not only a pragmatism foreign to his father but a cynicism foreign as well: he had persuaded students—had persuaded them earnestly, his arm around their shoulders, looking intently into their eyes —that they should not cast votes that would help a secret organization, without letting them know that he was a member of a secret organization. A cynicism—and a ruthlessness. He didn't merely count votes; he stole them. In what a lieutenant termed "blackmail," he had threatened a frightened girl with the exposure—the exposure and exaggeration, in "big headlines"— of a meaningless, momentary indiscretion. He had exploited the loneliness of women. The son of the man of whom "you always knew where he stood" let no one know where *he* stood. Men like Kyle and Puls, into whose ambitions he was scheming to plunge a knife, thought he was their friend until the knife was in up to the hilt. These tactics had, of course, been employed within the confines of campus politics, so small-scale and insignificant compared to the politics of the outside world. Within those confines, nonetheless, had emerged a certain pattern to the tactics—the politicking—of Lyndon Johnson. Perhaps the most significant aspect of the pattern was its lack of any discernible limits. Pragmatism had shaded into the morality of the ballot box, a morality in which nothing matters but victory and any maneuver that leads to victory is justified—into a morality that is amorality.

AND HOW DID Lyndon Johnson himself feel about the ruthless methods he had employed?

Many years later—forty years later: in 1970, after he had left the Presidency—Lyndon Johnson returned to San Marcos and spent an entire day touring the campus and reminiscing. Late in the afternoon, he sat chatting with four of his former professors, five old men in the shade, and the talk turned to his White Star activities, and to the Student Council, and he made the following statement:

> The freshmen, the sophomores and me—we had a majority. We gave to the Band, the Dramatic Club, the debaters, and we started electing the Gaillardians, and we were still doing it when I left—I don't know what happened after I left, but we were still doing it when I left. It was a pretty vicious operation for a while. They lost everything I could have them lose. It was my first real big dictat——Hitlerized—operation, and I broke their back good. And it stayed broke for a good long time.

The day had been long, particularly for a man with a serious heart condition, and Lyndon Johnson was tired when he made that statement. Perhaps it was the tiredness that let those words—particularly those two words, "dictator" and "Hitlerized"—slip out. But he was not so tired that he didn't realize what he had said as soon as he had said it. Abruptly cutting off the conversation, he rose from his seat, gathered his aides, and strode away. Had not a young man been present with a tape recorder, posterity would not possess Lyndon Johnson's own assessment of his first political activity.

But it was a revealing assessment, and not merely because he had seen himself as a "dictator," a "Hitler," and had not recoiled from the sight. The overall tone of the assessment is more revealing than those two words. *It was a pretty vicious operation for a while. They lost everything I could have them lose. . . . I broke their back good. And it stayed broke for a good long time.* Did he not see the ruthlessness? He saw it. Was he ashamed of it? He was proud of it.

· · ·

"A PRETTY VICIOUS OPERATION"—and sometimes Lyndon Johnson displayed a viciousness that had little to do with the operation. Black Star Frank Arnold was slow academically, but, an immensely strong, quiet and gentle boy, he had other qualities; his courage playing football despite a series of painful injuries had led his teammates to elect him captain and call him Old Reliable; off the field, a friend says, "He was the kind of boy who always had something nice to say to everyone." And sometimes he had a knack, despite his slowness, of seeing to the heart of a situation; during that Student Council vote on the *Star* and *Pedagog* editorships, for example, he had turned on Johnson and said that he didn't believe in giving something to someone who hadn't earned it. "He was the kind of boy that everyone liked—except Lyndon," the friend says. Lyndon didn't like him at all. Arnold, slow though he was, was dearly loved by one of the brightest girls on campus, pert, pretty Helen Hofheinz. Johnson devised a scheme to break them up.

His instrument was Whiteside, the fast-talking, handsome ladies' man. "Lyndon had a Model A," Whiteside recalls. "He'd say, 'Call her up and take her out—take my car . . . just to aggravate him.' He got a real kick out of that. Because he didn't like Frank Arnold." Says Helen: "I had been going with Frank Arnold for years. I was in love with him. And then, all of a sudden, Vernon Whiteside—he just gave me a frantic rush. For two weeks. Meeting me after class and sitting under the trees. I was so naïve I never thought Lyndon was back of it. I just thought I had blossomed out. I never took it serious. I was too in love with Frank Arnold. But it was exciting." Even when she accepted Arnold's ring, Whiteside persisted. "Lyndon would say, 'Whyn't you call her, and get a date tonight, and make her take ol' Frank's ring off?' I'd go up there, and Helen was wearing his engagement ring, and I'd go up there and talk her into taking it off. The next day, it would be back on, but you could see Frank walking around with that worried look on his face. He was so wrapped up in her." Whiteside's courtship ended, he says, "when I finally got ashamed of myself."* Had it been up to Johnson, the false courtship would have continued until the true one had been shattered beyond repair. "That wasn't politics," Whiteside says. "That was just Lyndon."

Sometimes, the viciousness had nothing at all to do with the operation.

One student, a Bohemian farm boy, was generally immune from practical jokes because he was so "slow" and gullible—some students believed he might be slightly retarded—as to be too defenseless a target. This student had a severe case of acne, and one evening, talking with Johnson, Whiteside and another student, he said girls wouldn't go out with him because of it.

Recalls Whiteside:

---

* Arnold and Helen Hofheinz were married; he died in 1955.

Lyndon said to him that the cure was to get fresh cow manure and put it on your face. He said, "Oh, go on," and Lyndon said, "Didn't you ever turn over a cow pile and see how white the grass was underneath, how the manure bleached the grass?"

So Lyndon said, "Let's drive [the boy] out to get some," and we all four of us drove out to some pasture, and he gets out and walks a long ways, and we can't believe he's this gullible, and he comes back [with some, which he had put in a shoebox. When they returned to San Marcos,] Lyndon tells him to take a towel and cut eyeholes in it and wrap it around his face. He . . . came into our room and asked how it was, and Lyndon said, "You don't have enough on to do any good." He made him put more on. In the morning, he smelled so bad, you couldn't go near him. And then Lyndon tells everyone the story, and the next day, when the boy walks in, everyone goes, "Mooooooo." I tell you, that was the worst thing I ever took part in.

JOHNSON'S FLATTERY of President Evans had continued—and so had its results. Prexy now displayed toward Lyndon a friendliness he had never displayed to any other student, or, for that matter, to any faculty member; a friendliness that was almost paternal. So at home was Johnson in Evans' office now that the impression Tom Nichols had noted before Johnson left for Cotulla—"some of them probably thought he was running the place"—was strengthened. Professors, noting that he had Prexy's ear, tried to get his. "As he was secretary of Dr. Evans, I always stopped and had a little chat with him . . . ," one says. Even Deans Nolle and Speck were wary of him, leery of crossing him. The strict Nolle, for example, had never relaxed the rule requiring a student to take six physical education courses. When, before he left for Cotulla, Johnson, embarrassed by his awkwardness and lack of physical coordination, asked Nolle for permission to write a paper on athletics instead of attending physical education class, Nolle had refused, and Johnson had received an F in the course. Now, when Johnson repeated the request, Nolle granted it. The meek Speck, as an ex-officio member of both the Student Council and the publications council, was frequently in Johnson's company—and, says one student, "it was hard to tell who was the student and who was the dean."

Then Evans, in an informal way, let his deans know that he wanted Johnson to have a say in assigning students to campus jobs.

The grip of the Depression, which had started early in the Hill Country, had tightened. A few years before, three bales of cotton would have brought enough money at the gin to send a child to college for a year. Now prices had fallen so low that six to eight bales were needed—six to eight bales of that man-killing labor in the fields so that a man's son wouldn't have to labor in the fields. Talk to a score of Hill Country men, and a score remember their mothers taking the cotton money, and adding it to the pennies they had saved out of the egg money, and hiding it away—and trying desperately not to take it out until tuition time came. Professors tried to help. Some loaned students money. Others, with no money to loan, borrowed money from the bank against their next paycheck to give a young man or woman another term at school. Nonetheless, many students had to pack their cardboard suitcases and turn away from Old Main's spires. Of 1,187 students enrolled at San Marcos during the spring term of 1929, only 906 came back in the Fall (a "good" figure, the *Star* said, "because times in this district are hard; it is known that many sacrifices were made"). Jobs—those twenty-cent-an-hour jobs on the Rock Squad, those set-the-alarm-for-three-a.m. boiler-room jobs—were precious now. "Twenty cents an hour, and you either went to school or you didn't," Horace Richards says. And, Richards says, "If Lyndon would say (to the deans), 'This boy is a good boy—give him a job,' he'd get that job." Evans had handed Johnson what was, at a "poor boys' school," real power.

And what Johnson did with that power was revealing.

He gave his friends jobs—the best jobs. Within a few months after his return from Cotulla, the twenty-five-dollar-a-month part-time "inside" jobs, which formerly had been held almost entirely by Black Stars, were held almost entirely by White Stars. But he didn't give himself a job to supplement his salary as Evans' assistant. The regular paycheck he had received at Cotulla had enabled him to pay his debts, but not to save any money for the year ahead, and, with his spending as free as ever, he still needed money badly. But there were only a few twenty-five-dollar jobs, and he didn't take one; every job he controlled, he gave away. Money had always been important to him, but there was something more important.

In the opinion of some of his allies, the manner with which he gave showed what was important. "He was always willing and ready to do whatever he could. In fact, it seemed to please him for you to ask him to do something for you," one says. But you had to ask. He insisted on it. One White Star was too proud to do so; no job was given to him. When this student told Richards that he was going to drop out of school, Richards, thinking that Johnson must be unaware of the situation, told him about it. Johnson, he found, was fully aware—but adamant. He told Richards, "If he's got too much pride to ask me for a job, I ain't going to give him one. Let him ask me. If he asks me, I'll give him anything I've got, but he's got to ask me." The White Star asked—and was given. "Lyndon wanted to show off his power, see?" Richards says. The opinion is echoed by other White Stars. What was important to Johnson, they feel, was the acknowledgment— the deferential, face-to-face, acknowledgment—that he had the power.

AND WHAT HE wanted from power, power gave him.

His personality hadn't changed. He still strutted, both on wheels (he honked his horn repeatedly as he drove up College Hill to make sure everyone saw him in his car) and on foot ("I can see him now walking up that hill, slinging his arms and talking to everybody with that smile. He was always head-huddling people. He always had something that they had to confer about"). He was still as deferential as ever to professors and as domineering as ever to students—the same mixture of bootlicker and bully. And the reaction of many students to that personality hadn't changed. The "in" crowd still wouldn't accept him—would hardly talk to him, in fact. "Lyndon was always the string-puller behind the scenes," says Joe Berry. "He found those he could use, and used them, and those he couldn't, he worked behind the scenes to put down. And he was just anathema to me." The more idealistic students still noticed that if, when Johnson approached a group of students, he realized they were discussing a serious issue in campus politics, he would hastily walk away. "He'd avoid us because he didn't want to have to take a position," one says. "He never took strong positions, positions where you knew where Lyndon stood. He was only interested in himself and what could help himself." This reaction was still not confined to "ins" and idealists. His campus-wide nickname remained "Bull." He still —on a campus on which women outnumbered men three to one—had difficulty getting dates, so much difficulty that one student says that "After Carol Davis, he never had a real girlfriend."

His involvement in campus politics had, for some students, only intensified the reaction—by piling distrust atop dislike. Says Helen Hofheinz: "He could be very gracious and very pleasant. But I just didn't trust him. He was likable. He was smart. But he would do anything to get his way. He was a very brilliant man. But he'd cut your throat to get what he wanted." Ella So Relle recalls the election that Horace Richards says Johnson "stole." The students were so naïve about politics that no one was quite sure what had happened, she says, "but everybody felt it wasn't straight, and everybody felt that if it wasn't straight, it was Lyndon Johnson who wasn't straight." Thanks to his involvement in campus politics, however, the reaction was no longer universal. Though some students despised his methods, others, more pragmatic, were aware of the power that those methods had gotten him. This recognition complicated their feelings. Richards, who was one of them—a wry, sardonic, self-seeing man—admits that while he didn't like Johnson any more than he ever had, he made considerably more effort to make Johnson like *him*. "It's just like everything else—if you feel this guy can help me if he likes me, you're going to be awful nice to him." Quite a few students were coming to understand that Johnson could help them. "He had power. He was secretary to the president. . . . If there was anything to give away, he would know. It paid to know him." And, understanding, they acted toward Bull Johnson not with disdain but with deference. "It was quite noticeable that quite a few boys who had always said they couldn't stand him started to act now as if they liked him."

In the way of human nature, some *did* like him. His keen eye had found men who enjoyed taking orders as much as he enjoyed giving them— had found, in students like Bill Deason, Wilton Woods and a freshman named Fenner Roth, individuals who related to domination in a way that pleased him, men he was to keep in his service thirty years and more. By the time he graduated, a small clique followed Lyndon Johnson's orders enthusiastically as well as slavishly. Some idolized him. Silent little Woods, for example, not only ran Johnson's errands and did his dirty work with the girls, but wrote his editorials, the editorials in the *College Star* to which "Editorial Writer Lyndon B. Johnson" signed his own name. "Lyndon was always loading me down with work. He'd say, 'Write an editorial on Thanksgiving.' I'd say, 'Where am I going to get the dope?' He'd say, 'Go to the encyclopedia,' "—thereby making Johnson one of the few college students with his own ghost writer (and furnishing material for Johnson biographers who, believing he wrote those editorials, have analyzed them in great depth). And Woods felt honored to be allowed to do so. "We were immature and he was mature. . . . And he was smart. He could talk wonderfully. I could never talk like he could."*

Even some students who didn't like him, respected him now. The respect was grudging—in Ella So Relle's words, it was the respect "you'd give a politician who won a political office you knew he didn't really deserve"—but it was respect nonetheless; Ella herself, for example, campaigned for Lyndon Johnson some years after college. ("Why? Because I also felt that he was very capable, had a lot of energy, and had the ambition to do things that other people didn't.")

The hostility that many of his fellow students felt for Lyndon Johnson is striking in its depth and passion. It does not surface immediately, for not only is it deep, it *lies* deep—deep and hidden. The researcher begins his interviews on Johnson's college years expecting to hear about a popular campus leader—because the Lyndon Baines Johnson Library has collected oral histories only from students who describe him in this way. The researcher's initial round of interviews confirms, in general, this expectation. If, when he interviews men who were not interviewed by the library—an Edward Puls or a Henry Kyle—he gets a different picture, he dismisses it as a biased view,

---

* Woods, who in later life worked for Johnson in many capacities, was, at the age of sixty, to write a paper analyzing Lyndon Johnson the college student ("Here's the way he differed from the other students. He differed in one respect: he always had more energy. His mother had absolute control of him. She protected him from debilitating habits such as drinking and dancing and playing poker. And therefore, his energy wasn't sapped.").

the view of men who lost to Lyndon Johnson and were embittered by the experience. But there are enough puzzling hints even in the interviews with men and women who praise Johnson to make the researcher go back and re-interview them, and when he does, other feelings begin to surface. They surface slowly—because of fear. In some cases, they *never* surface. Joe Berry, at the time of his interview a faculty member at the University of Texas, is not the only San Marcos alumnus who asks the researcher not to quote him by name because of the power he says the "Johnson group" still wields in Texas ("They could punish me, you know")—he is merely one alumnus who at last agrees to allow his name to be used. Others never do. But when at last the picture comes clear, it is far from a picture of a popular campus hero. The researcher had at first dismissed Puls' remark that "He was just the type of character who was snaky all the time" as the bitterness of a man defeated by Lyndon Johnson; now, over and over again, he hears some version of that remark repeated by men who had no defeat to embitter them. The researcher had not even bothered to type up his notes of his interview with Kyle, an interview conducted at the very beginning of his research—so obviously prejudiced and therefore unreliable did he consider that old man. Now he finally persuades other men—a dozen men—to talk about the incidents which Kyle described, and he finds that Kyle described them accurately. By the time the researcher completes his work on Lyndon Johnson's college years, he knows that one alumnus had not been exaggerating when he said: "A lot of people at San Marcos didn't just dislike Lyndon Johnson; they despised Lyndon Johnson." But after Lyndon Johnson, returning from Cotulla, became involved in campus politics, the hostility felt for him by his fellow students was no longer universal, and it was no longer unmixed. To some extent, at least, power had done its work. If there was still disdain, there was at least a leavening of respect.

Respect—and fear. His power over jobs for students was, on that impoverished campus, real power. "By the end of his time in San Marcos," says Ella So Relle, "people wanted to make sure they didn't have his enmity." However he had obtained power—by broad-scale brown-nosing, arrant flattery of the college faculty as a whole and the college president in particular, by the tricking and manipulating of his fellows—obtain it he had. Lyndon Johnson had always wanted attention, and more than attention—he had always wanted people to look up to him, to show him deference and respect. Now, because he had power, he had, at last, a taste of what he wanted.

AND DID THAT TASTE LIGHTEN the gloomy side of his character—the side seen by almost no one, but so striking to those who did see it, the sudden, intense silences that Boody called "loneliness" and that one woman said meant that "Lyndon was really down," the silences that were the outward sign of the doubts and fears that tormented him, of the depression that could be lightened only by the one person in the world of whose love he was sure? In December, 1929, he wrote to her:

> My dear Mother,
>
> The end of another busy day brought me a letter from you. Your letter always gives me more strength, renewed courage and that bulldog tenacity so essential to the success of any man. There is no force that exerts the power over me that your letters do. I have learned to look forward to them so long and now when one is delayed, a spell of sadness and disappointment is cast over me. . . .
>
> I have been thinking of you all afternoon. As I passed through town on my way home to supper, I could see the mothers doing their Christmas shopping. It made me wish for my mother so much.

No matter how busy he was at San Marcos, he still made frequent trips home to sit on his mother's bed and talk. His torrent of letters to her—the testimony of his need for reassurance of his ability—had slackened not at all.

Now THAT HE POSSESSED POWER, he was no longer without recourse against printed expressions of his fellows' enmity—as would be demonstrated, during his final term at college, by two incidents.

Sometime during that term—the month cannot be determined—*Star* editor Mylton Kennedy wrote an editorial satirizing Lyndon Johnson's "relationships with the faculty" and with President Evans. But the editorial never appeared—because, Kennedy says, Johnson "went to Dean Speck." The newspaper had been set in type, and the presses at the Buckner Print Shop were just beginning to roll, when over their rumble, Kennedy heard the telephone ring. When Kennedy answered it, Speck was at the other end. "Have you got an editorial in this issue about Lyndon Johnson?" he asked. And when Kennedy admitted that he did, the dean shouted, "Stop the presses!" (Those were literally the words Speck used, Kennedy says.) He demanded that Kennedy bring him the editorial. And after he read it, he ordered Kennedy to remove it from the paper, and confiscated the few copies already in print.

The feelings about Johnson that Kennedy had attempted to express did see print in the 1930 *Pedagog*, however—those feelings and others. The *Pedagog*'s "Cat's Claw" section is liberally studded with uncomplimentary references to "Bull" (for "Bullshit") Johnson, and while some of these references indicate only generalized dislike ("Lyndon Johnson was recently asked if he was a college man or had a horse kicked him!"), some are more specific. The qualities that his fellows believed they saw in Johnson are, in fact, itemized in his college yearbook. Set down in cold print are his determination to marry money (a fake advertisement to persuade students to join a Lonely Hearts Club entices him with the line: "Lyndon, some of our girls are rich"); his penchant for flattering, or "sucking up to," the faculty ("Believe It Or Not—Bull Johnson has never taken a course in suction"); his loudness and untruthfulness. Two entire pages are devoted to a denunciation of the elections the White Stars stole under his direction—he is depicted hiding behind one of his candidates, and the whole group of White Stars is pictured before a crude drawing of a "nigger in a woodpile"—and those pages include a question which testifies to the distrust with which other students viewed him: "What makes half of your face black and the other half white, Mr. Johnson?" In the 1928 *Pedagog*, which called him a master of sophistry and of "spoofing the public," sophomore Lyndon Johnson had been more harshly ridiculed than any other student at his college. In the 1930 *Pedagog*, senior Lyndon Johnson was again afforded that dubious honor. As his fellows got to know him better, their opinion of him had not softened but hardened. The 1930 *Pedagog* is a detailed documentation of that opinion—the opinion of his peers about the young man who would one day be the most powerful man on earth.

The *Pedagog* was published in June, 1930. Lyndon Johnson graduated in August, and the yearbook did not mar his graduation day. For by August, the copies still available on campus no longer contained the pages in which he was so harshly ridiculed. They had been excised from the volume—by the man who had been his benefactor all through college. "Although probably little worse than other editions of the *Pedagog*, the 1930 'Cat's Claw' section was particularly loathsome to President Evans," his secretary, Tom Nichols, was to write; Evans himself was to write that "a number of pages . . . aroused bitter resentment among our students." In fact, only one student was particularly resentful—but he was Lyndon Johnson. Johnson had a talk with the president—and following it, Evans ordered Nichols, Deans Nolle and Speck and several trusted professors to cut out the section in every copy they could lay their hands on; it was removed from several hundred copies.

His benefactor made graduation day a triumph for Johnson, in fact. Evans often said a few personal words about some student to whom he was handing a diploma. But his words about Johnson were unusually complimentary. When the tall, gangling young man strode across the rough wooden stage that had been erected near the bank of the San Marcos River, Nichols says, "there was . . . a smile on Prexy's face before the youth came to a halt." Giving him his diploma, he put a hand on his arm to detain him, turned to the audience, and said: "Here's a young man who has so abundantly demonstrated his worth that I predict for him great things in the years ahead. If he undertakes his tasks in the future with the same energy, careful thought and determination that he has used in all his work in the classroom, on the campus picking up rocks, or as an assistant in the president's office, success to him is assured." The student's father, sitting next to Nichols, leaned over and whispered: "We shall never forget what President Evans has done for our boy." His mother wept for pride.

TWENTY-FIVE YEARS LATER, Vernon Whiteside, a tourist in Washington, was sitting in the visitors' gallery of the Senate of the United States when, below him, the doors of the Senate cloakroom swung open, and the Senate's Majority Leader walked into the Chamber. As he began restlessly roaming the floor, a few of the more knowledgeable tourists nudged each other and whispered as the tall man, talking to each Senator, draped a long arm around his shoulder, seized his lapel and bent into his face, eye to eye, for they recognized these characteristics from articles in newspapers and magazines.

Whiteside recognized the characteristics, too, but not from an article. The man grabbing lapels and peering into eyes was a heavy man, clad in a suit of rich fabric, and he was grabbing and peering in a setting grave and noble, but so familiar were the gestures to Whiteside that these differences faded away, and he was seeing again a scene he had seen before—many times before—on a dusty campus on a hill in San Marcos, Texas. "To me, he was just like he was," Whiteside says. "He was the same Lyndon he always was, exactly."

Whiteside was right. All the characteristics of Majority Leader and President Lyndon Baines Johnson that were so unique and vivid when unveiled on a national stage—the lapel-grabbing, the embracing, the manipulating of men, the "wheeling and dealing"—all these were characteristics that the students at San Marcos had seen. And the similarity extended to aspects of the man less public. The methods Lyndon Johnson used to attain power on Capitol Hill were the same ones he had used on College Hill, and the similarity went far beyond the stealing of an election. At San Marcos, power had resided in the hands of a single older man. Johnson had begged that man for the opportunity to run his errands, had searched for more errands to run, had offered that man an audience when he felt talkative, companionship when he was lonely. And he had flattered him—flattered him with a flattery so extravagant and shameless (and skillful) that his peers had marveled at it. And the friendship of that one older man had armored him against the enmity of hosts of his peers, had given him enough power of his own so that it no longer mattered to him what others thought of him. In Washington, the names of his patrons—of older men who bestowed power on Lyndon Johnson—would be more famous: Rayburn, Russell, Roosevelt. But the technique would be the same.

So were techniques more complicated than reliance on a single, older individual. The penchant for vote-counting and vote-changing that, during

Johnson's Majority Leadership, was to entrance a nation—that penchant was there at San Marcos. The passion for deception, the obsession with secrecy—they were there, too. Johnson's entire career, not just as a Congressman but as a Congressman's secretary, would be characterized by an aversion to ideology or to issue, by an utter refusal to be backed into firm defense of any position or any principle. That characteristic was evident at San Marcos. And the same also, of course, was the talent that was beyond talent—the natural genius for politics—that animated all these techniques. From the day he arrived in Washington, Lyndon Johnson's rise would be spectacularly rapid; yet in relative terms, what achievement was more spectacular than his achievement at San Marcos, where, within little more than a year after returning from Cotulla, not only did he create a political organization on campus, he created *politics* on that campus— created it and, unpopular though he was, reaped power from it?

The man behind the methods was the same, too. In Washington, his fellows would be astonished by his frantic, almost desperate aggressiveness— that aggressiveness would have been familiar to his college classmates. The desire to dominate, the *need* to dominate, to bend others to his will—and the manifestation of that need, the overbearingness with subordinates that was as striking as the obsequiousness with superiors—had been evident at San Marcos. The tendency to exaggeration—to untruthfulness, in fact—the sensitivity to the slightest hint of criticism, the energy, the fierce, unquench-able drive that made him a man who worked harder than other men— his college classmates would have found those qualities familiar, too. Other qualities of Lyndon Johnson less immediately evident to others were present not only in Washington but at San Marcos: the viciousness and cruelty, the joy in breaking backs and keeping them broken, the urge not just to defeat but to destroy; the iron will that enabled him, once his mind was set on a goal, to achieve it no matter what the obstacles; above all, the ambi-tion, the all-encompassing personal ambition that made issues impediments and scruples superfluous. And present also was the fear—the loneliness, the terrors, the insecurities—that underlay, and made savage, the aggressiveness, the energy and the ambition. He himself saw this. On the day he returned to reminisce at his old college, he said: "The enduring lines of my life lead back to this campus." The Lyndon Johnson of Capitol Hill was the Lyndon Johnson of College Hill; to a remarkable extent, nothing had changed him.

Nothing could change him. Some men—perhaps most men—who attain great power are altered by that power. Not Lyndon Johnson. The fire in which he had been shaped—that terrible youth in the Hill Country as the son of Sam and Rebekah Johnson—had forged the metal of his being, a metal hard to begin with, into a metal much harder. In analyses of other famous figures, college, being only part of the formulating process that cre-ates character, deserves only cursory study, but the years Lyndon Johnson spent at college are revealing of his character as a whole—all the more revealing, in fact, because at college there are no complications of national or international politics or policy to obscure character. All the traits of personality which the nation would witness decades later—all the traits which affected the course of history—can be seen at San Marcos naked and glaring and raw. The Lyndon Johnson of college years was the Lyndon Johnson who would become President. He had arrived at college that Lyndon Johnson. He came out of the Hill Country *formed*, shaped—into a shape so hard it would never change.

12

"A Very Unusual Ability"

EVEN BEFORE HE GRADUATED from college, Lyndon Johnson had demonstrated that he was a master of politics beyond the college level.

Pat Neff, the former Governor of Texas who in his new post as State Railroad Commissioner had given Sam Ealy Johnson his bus inspector's job, was campaigning for re-election to the commission, and was scheduled to speak at a political barbecue and "speaking" in the live-oak grove outside the town of Henly in July, 1930. Lyndon, eager to hear the only orator in Texas who bore comparison to the mighty Joe Bailey, accompanied his parents. But when, with darkness falling after a long procession of candidates for local offices had followed one another to the speaking platform—the bed of a wagon under an old oak—the master of ceremonies, Judge Stubbs of Johnson City, called Neff's name, no one responded. The judge asked for a substitute to speak on Neff's behalf, but there was still no response. Once, Sam Johnson would have spoken, but Sam Johnson didn't give speeches any more. "Lyndon," he said, "get up there and say something for Pat Neff."

Stubbs, reports one of the earlier speakers, Welly K. Hopkins, a young State Representative who was running for State Senator, was "in the act of declaring a default" when a voice called out, " 'Well, I'll make a speech for Pat Neff.' And here through the crowd came this tall, brown-haired, bright-eyed boy, kind of, with a bushy-tail attitude of vigor. And he repeated it. He would make a speech for him, so the master of ceremonies handed his hand down to him and pulled him up on the tailgate." "Sam Johnson's boy," Stubbs said—*that* made the crowd sit up—and Lyndon made his first political speech.

"He talked in the dark," recalls Wilton Woods, who was sitting with the Johnsons. "The only light was the light from the barbecue fire, a big fire. He talked loud and a little bit squeaky like an adolescent. But I was impressed." So was Hopkins: "He spoke maybe five to ten minutes in a typical fashion, a little bit of the oratorical effect, and a good one, some of the arm-waving that I guess I'd indulged in some, too. But he showed pretty good cause why Pat Neff should be re-elected, and was favorably received." Approaching Johnson after he had returned to his family, he asked him why he had made the speech. "His reply I've never forgotten," Hopkins says. "It was, in substance, 'Governor Neff once gave my daddy a job when he needed it, so I couldn't let it go by default.' We became friendly-familiar, you might put it, within a very short time." Hopkins asked Johnson if he would help in his campaign, and "he very readily consented."

Hopkins had expected a tough campaign, but he was to win by more than 2,000 votes, a large margin in the Hill Country. And the reason, he was to conclude, was the lucky chance that had led him to meet Lyndon Johnson. Johnson provided him with campaign literature; when Hopkins ran out of money to print his own, Johnson, because one of his White Stars was night watchman in Old Main, was able to use the college mimeograph machine and stationery supplies. He provided him with campaign workers; some White Stars—Woods, Deason, Richards, Fenner Roth—were persuaded, "just for the fun of it," as one recalls, to drive with Johnson to the little towns in the six-county Senate district; they would pile out of his Model A roadster on Main Street, press literature on every passerby, and talk up the candidate's virtues. He provided him with a claque—a loud one; arriving at a "speaking," before Hopkins, the White Stars would quietly spread out through the crowd; Hopkins, a renowned stump orator, began his speeches by ostentatiously rolling up his shirt sleeves as if preparing for a hard job ahead; at that signal, Richards recalls, "We'd start cheering, and get the whole crowd cheering." And provided Hopkins' campaign with the same fierce, driving, driven energy he had given to Deason's. In so sparsely populated a district, every vote counted, and, it seemed to Hopkins, every vote was courted. "Lyndon knows every man, woman and child in Blanco County, and has wide acquaintance in Comal, Kendall and Guadalupe Counties," he was to write, and no acquaintance lived in a homestead too isolated, or at the end of a road too rough, to be paid a personal visit. "We worked Blanco in and out," he recalls. "I guess I was up every branch of the Pedernales and every dry creek bed there was. . . . I rode all the byways . . . with Lyndon." Once, at Lyndon's insistence, he found himself not merely visiting but giving a speech to an audience of three persons. And, Hopkins saw, Lyndon Johnson was providing him with something else, too. Over and over again, he would recall in later years, he saw the tall, gangling college boy put his arm around a dour farmer, pump his hand, talk to him earnestly, smile winningly into his eyes. And over and over again, he saw the farmer smiling back at Lyndon before the conversation had ended. Writing to a friend about the campaign worker he had found at the Henly barbecue, Hopkins said that he was "gifted with a very unusual ability to meet and greet the public." To meet, to greet—and more.

Not a month after he had seen a gangling college boy scrambling up onto a wagon tailboard, he was to recall, "I kind of turned my campaign over to him" in four counties. "I followed his lead completely." For election eve— August 1—Hopkins had planned a big rally in New Braunfels. Johnson said he should hold another one as well in San Marcos. When Hopkins said he couldn't get from one to the other in time, Johnson said he could, barely —he had timed the route. And when, at the end of a wild ride through the black Hill Country night in Johnson's roadster, Hopkins arrived in San Marcos, he found a rally like none he had ever seen in the Hill Country. It was being held in the auditorium of Old Main—that in itself was unusual, for President Evans, leery of becoming embroiled in partisan politics, did not generally allow the use of college facilities for political rallies. And sitting on the platform was Evans himself—and that was unprecedented; somehow Johnson had persuaded Prexy Evans, the most respected man in the area, to lend silent support to Hopkins' candidacy. The audience was, by Hill Country standards, huge, jamming the auditorium—flyers had flooded the campus and town for days to ensure that. And it was enthusiastic—when Hopkins strode out on the stage, a cheer went up, a cheer led by the familiar voices that he had been hearing, at picnics and barbecues, for weeks, and when he rolled up his sleeves for the last time, it grew even louder. And as the audience filed out after his speech, student volunteers, standing at the door polite and respectful under the eye of his new young friend, passed out more flyers, mimeographed by his new young friend, summarizing the speech's main points; he had just had his campaign climaxed, Welly Hopkins realized, with a rally planned down to the last detail. "He did a magnificent job for me," Hopkins says. "I always felt that he was the real balance of the difference as to whether I'd be elected."

Other politicians felt the same way. Bill Kittrell recalls coming to Austin and hearing, over and over again, about "this wonder kid in San Marcos who knew more about politics than anyone else in the area." Kittrell was in Austin to organize Edgar Witt's campaign for Lieutenant Governor. Believing that Witt had no chance in the Hill Country counties, and feeling that there was nothing to lose in turning them over to a novice, he drove out to San Marcos and put the young man he met there in charge of "eight or ten" counties. Witt carried every one. Hopkins, active in Witt's campaign, said, "Never have I seen better work." He had become not only professionally but personally fond of Johnson. Shortly after Johnson's graduation, he took him on a week-long spree in Laredo and Monterrey that cost a hundred dollars—"a pretty good-sized sum of money in those days."

BUT WHILE HOPKINS could give Johnson a good time, he couldn't give him a job. Johnson had decided by now that he wanted to make a career in politics rather than teaching, but, with the Depression forcing the state government into staff cutbacks, there was no state job available. And he had already found out that there was no teaching job available either. His father's brother George, who had remained an idealist but, having fled the Hill Country, had escaped the worst of idealism's consequences, was chairman of the history department at Sam Houston High School in Houston. (A tall man with big ears and piercing eyes, he was very popular with students, despite their tendency to mock his "reverence for figures such as Andrew Jackson and William Jennings Bryan," who, he believed, had fought for "the people.") When, some months before graduation, Lyndon had asked him for a job at his school, he had agreed to get him one—although because the Depression was forcing the Houston School Board to restrict hiring, the job, which paid $1,600, was contingent upon the occurrence of a vacancy. Months passed without such an occurrence. Lyndon tried other school boards. By now there was almost a note of desperation in his efforts: a talk by President Evans to his seniors during the Spring of 1930 was entitled "All Dressed Up and No Place to Go," and his sober listeners knew exactly what he meant; the diploma which had cost them so many bales of hand-picked cotton, so many hours on the Rock Squad was rapidly turning into worthless paper; Ella So Relle, perhaps exaggerating slightly, says that only three August graduates of San Marcos had jobs waiting for them. When Lyndon, who wasn't one of the three, heard of an opening in Brenham, he deluged the Brenham board not only with letters but with telegrams of recommendation from every top administrator and faculty member at San Marcos. The warmth of these missives was all he could have asked for— impressive testimony to the opinion of his elders (Mrs. Netterville, who believed, because of his examination-paper note, that she had "strengthened" his "faith" during her Browning course, called him "a young man of . . . great spiritual force"; another professor noted that Johnson "has a habit of making friends of the best people wherever he goes"). But the Brenham board sent them back—with regrets. The position he finally obtained was in South Texas, not far from Cotulla—in Pearsall, the other town which broke the bleak flatness that stretched south from San Antonio. Pearsall was even smaller than Cotulla; its single hotel had so little business that, residents believed, it was the only self-service hotel in the United States; guests selected their own rooms, put a dollar in an envelope and dropped it into a box at the unmanned front desk. Carol Davis had taught in Pearsall, but Carol was married now (had been married in June in what the *San Marcos Record* called an "impressive ring ceremony in the spacious Davis home" with the bride very beautiful in a long white dress as she swept down the long stairway). There is no direct evidence of Lyndon Johnson's feelings after, in September, 1930, he left San Marcos and drove back down to South Texas. None of the letters he wrote to his mother survive. But his brother and his sister Rebekah remember that there seemed to be one every day; and every weekend, as soon as he had finished his last class, Lyndon Johnson drove home.

NOT MANY SUCH TRIPS were necessary. In October, a position opened in the speech department in Houston. Johnson had assured his uncle that "In the event that I can secure the place in Houston I can resign this place at any time." That had not been the precise understanding of the Pearsall superintendent, George Barron, who says that he was in fact "a bit stunned" to lose a teacher in the middle of a term, particularly a teacher of such promise; Johnson, he says, "took on the task as though the future of America depended on what he taught those children." But, he says, "Lyndon took a seat on the corner of my desk and, abandoning all formality, he said, 'George, I look upon you as an older brother. I feel somehow that you have a kindred feeling toward me. If I didn't feel that way toward you, I wouldn't make this request.' " And, he says, Lyndon had a replacement ready; his sister Rebekah. Barron agreed to release Johnson from his contract, and near the end of October, Johnson arrived in Houston, where he moved into a two-story white frame house, owned by other relatives, on a tree-shaded street; he shared a room with his uncle.

Houston must have looked huge to Lyndon Johnson as he drove toward it across the flat Gulf plains in his battered little car; from miles away, the setbacks of its skyscrapers, thirty stories high and more, cut right angles out of the blue Gulf sky; the long lines of factory smokestacks before them belched out plumes of smoke like banners announcing a new age for Texas, and the last miles before he reached the city were covered with forests of oil derricks. With its population closing in on 300,000, Houston dwarfed the cities of his youth; the high school in which he was to teach, with its 1,800 students, was twice as large as his college (and its faculty had more advanced degrees than the San Marcos faculty). But if he felt intimidated or unsure, he gave no sign of it; while informing Lyndon that he would not only be teaching public speaking but coaching the debating team, his new principal mentioned that the team had never won the city championship, and Lyndon announced that it would win this year—and would win the state championship as well!

Public speaking at Sam Houston High School had been taught by a mild-mannered gentleman whose classes were rigidly decorous. On the first day with Lyndon Johnson, every student had to stand up in front of the class and "make noises" for ten seconds. Any noises, Johnson said: "Ow, ow, ow," or "Roaw, roaw, roaw"—just any noises at all. The next day, it was thirty seconds, and the noises had to be animal noises: roar like a lion, quack like a duck. "You were sort of encouraged to be silly," recalls one of his students. "He was trying to get people to feel comfortable on the podium, to make the whole thing such a game that no one would feel embarrassed. He'd do it with smiling and laughter to make you feel at ease. 'Everybody's going to do it, so don't worry about it—just have fun.' And we did. Even the shy kids did. There was a feeling that we're all comrades, we're all going to be doing these silly things, so we were all together in it. And everyone would laugh." Then came speeches—first, thirty seconds, "very short, and on so limited a topic that you wouldn't be scared." Then a minute, and then five minutes. Speeches no longer extemporaneous but prepared, and prepared thoroughly. "I have a memory of an *enormous* number of assignments," says one student. "And he was terribly strict about you doing them." Says another: "We had to do more reading for Mr. Johnson's course than all the rest of my courses combined. You really had to *know* your stuff." Then came the heckling. "No kidding—heckling," one student says. If the heckling wasn't fierce enough, the teacher would join in. Students could try to pick holes in a speaker's arguments, or simply insult him, or shout nonsense to try to drown him out. "The idea of that was so you could keep your head clear and think logically of the arguments, no matter how much pressure you were under," a student says. Always the teacher was picking out flaws not only in arguments but in appearance. "Mr. Johnson wanted you to stand straight, but not stiff, to move your eyes around, no silly gestures but make some gestures to show you're alive. And he'd shout at you, 'C'mon, Gene, stand up! Stop slouching! Who're you talking to, Gene—the ceiling? Look at the audience! C'mon, Gene, look at them!' Boy, he wanted you *perfect.*"

In general, his students didn't resent the shouting or the insistence on perfection. One of them—William Goode, later a renowned sociologist—says this was partly *because* of the insistence: "He made you feel important just because he's nagging at you so much. He's throwing his whole self into improving you." Partly it was because the students could see that he was working himself as hard as he was working them. When they handed in written assignments, the assignments were handed back the following day, always. And they were handed back with their margins filled with comments. For some months, another teacher, Byron Parker, roomed in the same house as Johnson. He remembers that sometimes when he went to sleep, Johnson would be sitting at a little desk piled high with his students' papers, and sometimes when he woke up the next morning, Johnson would still be sitting there, correcting the last of the papers; he had not slept that night. "He did that job as if his life depended on it," William Goode says. His classes were "very exciting, and everybody thought so. He wasn't a sit-down teacher—he strode back and forth and harangued. He was overpowering as hell."

Out of his public-speaking classes, the new teacher had to select a debating team. The two youths he chose were both, in those Depression years, delivery boys, but there the similarity ended. Luther E. Jones, seventeen (known as "L.E."), was tall, handsome, brilliant, but stiff and aloof—

"smart as hell, but cold as hell," a student says. "And so reserved, I remember thinking, 'How the hell is he going to get up on a stage and sell himself?' " Gene Latimer, a short, stocky, sixteen-year-old whose hair never stayed combed, was, this student says, "an Irish charmer, with a cocky, wonderful smile and a marvelous gift of gab." But he was rebellious, insolent, notorious for not doing his assignments, always in some kind of mischief. "They were not the ones people expected Mr. Johnson to pick," a student says.

But Mr. Johnson was a reader of men. "At first he is not my favorite teacher," Latimer says.

> He impinges too much on my hours of leisure. . . . In practice he has no reticence in cutting me off in the middle of a sentence to comment on its inadequacy, and to make pointed suggestions for improvement.

Soon, the rebellious, independent Irish boy who had never willingly obeyed any teacher was waiting anxiously for an expression of approval in this teacher's eyes.

> In competition he sits at the back of the auditorium and has an unsettling habit of frowning and ruefully shaking his head just when I think I am on the right track. But once in a while he opens his mouth in amazement at how clearly I am making a point. He sits up very straight and looks around in wonderment at the audience to make sure they're not missing this. And it is then he makes me think I have just personally thought of, and am in the process of enunciating, an improvement on the Sermon on the Mount.

Johnson had somehow seen in Gene Latimer—as he had in Willard Deason, another man not easily led—someone who would accept his leadership, totally and unquestioningly. Latimer would work for Johnson off and on for much of his life as, in the words of another Johnson staff member, "his slave—his totally willing slave." In his oral history, Latimer says of Johnson: "He [is] the best friend I shall ever have."

Having picked his men, he trained them. No one at Sam Houston High had ever witnessed training like this. Day after day, teachers passing the auditorium late in the afternoon—hours after classes had been dismissed—would hear voices and, looking in, would see Jones or Latimer (or Margaret Epley and Evelyn Lee, the two women debaters) or one of the "declaimers," five or six students who had lost out for the debate team but represented the school in declamation contests, up on the stage, practicing. And seated in the audience, commenting on their delivery, was their coach. Delivery was only part of what he was teaching. William Goode, one of the declaimers, says: "He picked out your suit for contests, [or] how much lipstick and what dress you wore. Nothing was too small. Everything had to be made perfect. . . . It was a total enveloping process." And the work in the auditorium was only part of the work. Day after day, the debating team polished its delivery; night after night, it polished its arguments. The topic for the Interscholastic League Debates—the state championships—was: "Resolved: That the Jury System Should Be Abolished." In the evenings, Johnson and his debaters read everything they could find on the jury system. But, other teachers noticed, the debaters didn't seem to mind the work their coach loaded on them. "He worked the life out of them, but they would do anything for him," one says.

Then the schedule of practice debates began. No one in Texas had ever seen a schedule like this. In informal, "no-decision" contests, the Sam Houston High School team faced every team in Houston that would debate them. Then the team left Houston: writing letters to scores of high schools, arranging without any assistance all the complicated logistics involved, the new debating coach had, in his first year as coach, arranged a tour—hundreds of miles long—of a magnitude beyond any ever before scheduled by a Texas high school debating team.

The time spent driving those hundreds of miles could not be wasted; as they drove, Lyndon Johnson's debaters practiced. The debates themselves were learning experiences: a telling point or anecdote used by another school had to be incorporated into their own presentation. They debated one school on their way west from Houston, and a week or two later, on their way back, they debated the same school again—and its coach heard the Sam Houston High team using the very arguments his team had used on them in the first debate.

Nonetheless, the trip was fun. A certain barrier between the coach and his team, between the teacher and his students, was never lowered. "Lyndon was always the teacher, and I was the pupil," L. E. Jones says. "He was always in a position of command, and he acted like that." But they *were* pupils, and they understood and accepted that. And as long as that understanding existed in the Model A roadster, there could exist also laughter. Assured of his position, Johnson may not have been more relaxed, but he was more jovial. He regaled the four debaters with stories—most of them about politics ("He talked about Welly Hopkins incessantly, about the campaign he had won for Welly Hopkins; he was proud of himself"). They were so fascinated by his stories that they would remember some of them in detail forty-five years later. The hundreds of miles sped by—and not just because of the speed at which Johnson drove. "Though we practice even as we drive, we also sing and joke with the Chief leading," Latimer recalls. "With the Chief leading the singing and the joking. And these are days to cherish and remember."

And the trip—and the whole debating season—was fun because they

were heroes. The high schools they visited held dances in their honor, and
back at Sam Houston High there were honors, too, for their coach was not
only training his team but promoting it, relentlessly and aggressively. Following a visit from Johnson, the editor of the *Houston Press* wrote in his
weekly column: "How to talk is being taught in the Houston public schools.
There is a course in public speaking. . . . It should be encouraged." To help
encourage it, the editor offered a $100 prize to the best public-speaking stu-
dent at Sam Houston High, to be awarded at Coach Johnson's discretion.
San Jacinto High's coach, J. P. Barber, angered because he had never succeeded in obtaining such a prize for *his* school, became angrier still when
the *Press*—and the *Houston Post* and the *Houston Chronicle*, both of whose
editors Johnson had also visited—gave the Sam Houston High team more
coverage than his own four-time champions received. Johnson had been
helping to lead pep rallies for the football team, with an enthusiasm and a
storytelling gift that made his appearances popular; now he began holding
rallies for his own team. The publicity began to get results. Debates early
in the year had been held in an auditorium almost as empty as it had been
for practice sessions; at one, only seven persons were in the audience. But as
the team's undefeated streak rolled on, the big, balconied room began to fill
up for debates. The rewards he had promised his boys and girls began to
materialize. Says Goode: "His attitude was, all the minor details must be
taken care of, everything must be taken care of, and of course we must win.
But the thing was: if you took care of all the minor details, you *would* win.
If you stayed up late, if you did just absolutely everything you *could* do—
well, from it would grow everything. The world's going to open. God, he made
you believe, man—you weren't just [debaters]. You were people who were
going to succeed. And we began to see that was true. He was sending you
out in the world, where other people are applauding you. I'd be sent to an
elementary school or Kiwanis Club, for example, to talk to them about some
topic, and you'd be applauded, so you never had the feeling that he was a
con man. And then the debates came—and we won, for Christ's sake." Latimer, Jones, Epley and Lee found their pictures in the papers—not just in
the school paper but in the *Press* and the *Post* and the *Chronicle*—under
headlines like one that appeared in the *Post*: SILVER-TONGUED STUDENTS. At
rallies, they were cheered by name, with cheerleaders cartwheeling in their
honor as they did for football heroes. In April, the city championships were
held. They had been won by the San Jacinto team for four consecutive years
and had *never* been won by Sam Houston High; this year Sam Houston won
them easily. At a general assembly, Latimer and Jones stood on stage as
silver loving cups were presented to the school, and heard their principal,
William J. Moyes, call them "two of the best high school debaters ever heard
in this city." The next hurdle, the district meet, "is almost too easy," Latimer
says. In an auditorium so jammed that students were unable to find seats and
crammed into window alcoves and stood in the halls to hear, both the men's

and the women's teams won. The school newspaper ran their pictures—on a page which contained a drawing of a crowing cock and the words: " 'Nuff said."

During the two weeks before the state championships were to be held in Austin, preparations intensified. With the school caught up in the excitement, whole classes researched the jury system and its alternatives to find new material, and Johnson scheduled still more practice debates. "In Austin," Latimer recalls, "it is evident that a few other teams had been practicing, too." Epley and Lee were defeated in one of a series of elimination debates, but Latimer and Jones advanced to the finals. After sixty-seven consecutive victories, one more would give Sam Houston High the state championship Johnson had promised.

For that final debate, Johnson's team drew the affirmative. "I just almost cried," Johnson was to recall. "We had no trouble on the side that it shouldn't be abolished. But when we had the affirmative," although his boys had always managed to win anyway, "we always had trouble." Waiting for the judges' verdict, the two young men and their coach thought they had won again. Johnson was to remember for the rest of his life the suspense as the judges announced their votes. "They drew it out, and they said affirmative and that brought smiles and then negative and then affirmative and then negative and then they waited a long time and it was negative and we lost it by one vote, 3–2." Latimer looked first for his coach. "The look on [his] face is one of disbelief, and my worst reaction is that in some ways we have let him down." But that look passed quickly. "He tells us that we have done well and he comforts us," Latimer says. And Latimer and Jones never knew that when he was done comforting them, their coach went behind the stage and vomited.

Despite the defeat which ended their months of effort, the debaters were still heroes—and so was their coach. Accepting the trophies the team had won, Moyes, after praising Jones and Latimer, had said that credit for their victories "is due to the splendid work in all lines of public speaking done by Lyndon B. Johnson, who is making a great record in his first year as a teacher in a Houston school." Now, at a banquet on May 23 in the Lamar Hotel attended not only by faculty and students from Sam Houston High but also by delegations from Houston's four other high schools, and by the city's business and political leaders, the principal repeated his praise of the young teacher, which was echoed by a parade of other speakers, including one who had been invited at Johnson's request, Welly Hopkins. The following day, at a meeting of the Houston School Board—a meeting at which which many teachers' salaries were again lowered—Johnson's salary was raised by $100 as he was rehired for the next year.

Students tried to change their course schedules so that they could attend "Mr. Johnson's speech class"; in his first year at Sam Houston High, enrollment in his courses increased from 60 to 110. "He was a handsome

guy—a tall, lean, handsome, attractive guy who was full of excitement,"
one student says. "And he was always up there leading assemblies—he was
a charismatic figure at that school." As for the feelings of the faculty, a
reporter was talking to a mathematics teacher, Ruth Daugherty, one day
when he saw "a tall and strikingly handsome young man" rushing down a
corridor during a break between class periods, towering "above the milling
students." He recalls Miss Daugherty saying: "That man is going to be a
big success someday. He'll be ahead of everybody. Nobody can keep up
with him." He was, in fact, as popular at Sam Houston as he had been
unpopular at San Marcos. Describing him as "pleasing in personality, inde-
fatigable in his labors, zealous in all of his undertakings," the school newspaper added, "Although one of our newest faculty members, he has carved
for himself a place in Sam Houston as one of the outstanding teachers."

He enjoyed teaching and coaching. He would recall his pride in his
debaters—"to see them stand up there . . . without a note in their hands on
a subject with such basic fundamental importance as maintaining a jury
system. Children just in high school with no constitutional history backgrounds, with no governmental backgrounds"—and in their victories:
"Every time they brought in the judges' decision I would just look at [them]
and smile like I stuck in my thumb and pulled out a big plum and say my
how proud am I." To supplement his salary, he taught at night: a businessmen's course in the Dale Carnegie method. And he enjoyed that, too. Ella
So Relle, his San Marcos classmate who was now teaching at Houston's
Galina Park High School, would sometimes drop in on his businessmen's
class and watch him make each member of his class stand up and try "to
sell something silly, like a picture frame," and Johnson recalls that "I used
to stand along the side wall and heckle these successful businessmen to
death while they gave their talks, so they'd gain some confidence," and she
says, "I saw at that time a little more self-confidence than he had had in
San Marcos. He was in charge, and there was no question he was in charge.
And they liked him."

A LITTLE MORE SELF-CONFIDENCE. Not, to this woman who had known
Lyndon Johnson longer than the faculty and students of Sam Houston High,
a lot. In fact, she emphasizes, sometimes, despite Lyndon's new popularity,
she felt as "sorry for him" as she had in San Marcos. He didn't have a girlfriend; in fact, she believes, during the year he taught in Houston, he never
asked a girl for a date. Another old friend was in Houston, coaching at
Galina Park: Boody Johnson. Boody and Lyndon spent a lot of evenings
together; Boody confirms that "old Rattling Bones" didn't have any dates
in Houston. And to Boody it was obvious that Lyndon needed to be with
someone—needed it so badly that Boody sometimes wondered if his former
roommate was afraid to be alone. His new popularity had not reduced his

dependence on the one person he felt would always be there to listen to him, a dependence expressed not only in seven-hour weekend drives home to San Marcos (where his family was now living) but in letters. His sister Rebekah recalls that every time *she* came home, her mother would chide her for not writing more frequently, and show her how many letters her brother had written during the same period. "There were whole *stacks* of Lyndon's letters," his sister says. And when told that his Houston colleagues describe him as self-confident and cheerful there, she is surprised. "Lyndon was very lonely in Houston," she says. "Quite down-hearted and blue."

If Miss So Relle recognized the same insecurities in Lyndon Johnson in Houston that she had seen in San Marcos, she recognized also, in long talks they had together, the same ambition—not just the general ambition ("climbing and climbing") but the specific. "He had this job, it was a good job," she says. "But he was always thinking, 'What can I do next?' 'What should my next job be?' " And he didn't want the next job to be in teaching; much as he liked that field, he had no intention of staying in it. He had known for a long time what he wanted. He was constantly talking politics. A fellow teacher remembers sitting around after debating practice, "drinking Cokes . . . with a group of Sam Houston High kids, and you [Johnson] analyzed the political technique of Joe Bailey for us; and we argued about Jim Ferguson, . . . and you said, 'When I go into politics I am going to use these fellows' effective methods and avoid their mistakes—I'm learning from them.' " Talking politics—and thinking politics. He was constantly referring to *Battle for Peace*, a collection of the speeches of Pat Neff. Some years later, he would give Neff's book to L. E. Jones, and Jones found the margins filled with Johnson's handwriting: he had not only read the speeches of one of his state's greatest speech-makers, but had analyzed them—and decided how they could have been improved.

He had moved fast during his first year in Houston. He began his second year moving even faster. Teams of "declaimers" were dispatched to Kiwanis and Rotary clubs, and to other high schools and junior high schools, to talk on "timely civic topics"; assemblies at his own school began revolving more and more around his debaters ("I don't think there was one at which Mr. Johnson's boys or girls weren't speaking"); there was not enough room in his public-speaking courses for all the students who wanted to take them. And by November the debate season was gearing up: repeating his promise to win the state championship, he had arranged a series of elimination contests to select a new team. On November 25, however, while he was chatting in the school's administration offices, a secretary said there was a telephone call for him. On the line was Richard Kleberg, whom Johnson had never met but who had just won a special election to fill a vacancy in Texas' Fourteenth Congressional District. He said that he would need a private secretary in Washington (that was then the title of a Congressman's Administrative Aide), and that Johnson had been recommended to him by his political ally Welly Hopkins—and he asked Johnson when he could come to Corpus Christi for an interview. A fellow teacher who was present in the administrative offices recalls that, for a moment, Johnson "was so excited he didn't know what to say"; then he told Kleberg he would call back in a few minutes, and when he did, he said he could come immediately. At the interview, he was offered the job, and when the new Congressman personally telephoned Principal Moyes, an immediate leave of absence was arranged. Five days after the telephone call, Lyndon Johnson left for Washington with Kleberg, clothes packed in a cardboard suitcase, aboard the crack streamliner, the *Bluebonnet*. Arriving in Washington late the following evening, they checked into the luxurious Mayflower Hotel, where they shared a room. About seven o'clock the next morning, Kleberg telephoned room service for a large pot of coffee—which was, as Johnson wrote in a letter a few days later, "an eye opener and a good excuse for the secretary to get his shave and bath and be on his way."

Part III

SOWING

13

On His Way

AFTER A SINGLE NIGHT sharing his boss' room, he lived in the basement of a shabby little hotel, in a tiny cubicle across whose ceiling ran bare steam pipes, and whose slit of a window stared out, across a narrow alley, at the weather-stained red brick wall of another hotel. Leaving his room early in the morning, he would turn left down the alley onto a street that ran between the red brick walls of other shabby hotels. But when he turned the corner at the end of that street, suddenly before him, at the top of a long, gentle hill, would be not brick but marble, a great shadowy mass of marble—marble columns and marble arches and marble parapets, and a long marble balustrade high against the sky. Veering along a path to the left, he would come up Capitol Hill and around the corner of the Capitol, and the marble of the eastern façade, already caught by the early-morning sun, would be a gleaming, brilliant, almost dazzling white. A new line of columns—towering columns, marble for magnificence and Corinthian for grace—stretched ahead of him, a line, broken only by the pilasters that are the echoes of columns, so long that columns seemed to be marching endlessly before him, the acanthus leaves of their mighty capitals hunched under the weight of massive entablatures, the long friezes above them crammed with heroic figures. And columns loomed not only before him but above him—there were columns atop columns, columns in the sky. For the huge dome that rose above the Capitol was circled by columns not only in its first mighty upward thrust, where it was rimmed by thirty-six great pillars (for the thirty-six states that the Union had comprised when it was built), but also high above, 300 feet above the ground, where, just below the statue of Freedom, a circle of thirteen smaller, more slender shafts (for the thirteen original states) made the *tholos*, a structure modeled after the place where the Greeks left sacrifices to the gods, look like a little temple in the sky, adding a grace note to a structure as majestic and imposing as the power of the sovereign state that it had been designed to symbolize. And as Lyndon Johnson came up Capitol Hill in the morning, he would be running.

Sometimes, the woman who worked with him, coming to work in the morning, would see the gangling figure running awkwardly, arms flapping, past the long row of columns on his way to the House Office Building beyond the Capitol. At first, because it was winter and she knew that he owned only a thin topcoat and that his only suits were lightweight tropicals suitable for Houston, she thought he was running because he was cold. "We weren't used to weather like they had in Washington," Estelle Harbin recalls, "and Lyndon couldn't afford any warm clothes. When I would get to the office, his cheeks would still be all rosy." But in Spring, the weather turned warm. And still, whenever she saw Lyndon Johnson coming up Capitol Hill, he would be running.

THE DAY Lyndon Johnson first entered the Capitol—December 7, 1931, the opening session of the Seventy-second Congress—was the day on which the first order of business was the election of a new Speaker of the House of Representatives, and after the election, as the House rose in applause (applause mingled with Indian war whoops and the Rebel yell), a committee escorted to the triple-tiered white marble rostrum a short, red-faced man with fierce white eyebrows, dressed in a cheap, rumpled brown suit and a rancher's heavy, blunt-toed brogans: John Nance Garner, "Cactus Jack" Garner—Garner of Texas.

Later that day, the great Standing Committees of the House met to select their chairmen. For twelve years, these chairmen had been Republicans; under Coolidge Prosperity and Hoover Prosperity, Democratic rolls had dwindled until one Democratic Congressman was heard to mutter, "We're going the way of the Whigs." The Crash had changed the situation; the election of Lyndon Johnson's new boss, in fact, had sealed the change. The 1930 congressional elections had reduced the Republican majority in the House from 104 to two. By October, 1931, special elections to fill the seats of Representatives who had died had given the Democrats their first majority in the House since 1919. But the majority was only two, and with two seats still vacant and a third held by a member of the Farmer-Laborite Party, three votes were uncertain, and the Democrats could not be sure they would be able to organize the House when it reconvened in December. Then, on November 6, 1931, Harry Wurzbach, the only Republican Congressman from Texas, died. It was the election of Richard Kleberg, a Democrat, in Wurzbach's district on November 24 that made the Democrats' majority 218 to 214, and assured them of enough votes to control the House. Within the parties, seniority determined chairmanships, and Democratic Texas had for years been sending Congressmen to Washington and keeping them there. And after the Standing Committees met on December 7, the chairman of the House Committee on Interstate and Foreign Commerce was Garner's right-hand man, Samuel Taliafero Rayburn—Rayburn of Texas. The chairman of the Rivers and Harbors Committee, overseer and dispenser of funds for the nation's great public works, was Joseph Jefferson Mansfield—Mansfield of Texas. The chairman of the Judiciary Committee was Hatton W. Sumners of Texas, of the Agriculture Committee Marvin Jones of Texas, of the Committee on Public Buildings and Grounds Fritz Lanham of Texas. Texans were elected on December 7, 1931, not only to the Speakership of the House but to the chairmanships of five of its most influential committees. Lyndon Johnson's first day in the Capitol was the day Texas came to power in it—a power that the state was to hold, with only the briefest interruptions, for more than thirty years.

But the coming to power of Texas had nothing to do with Lyndon Johnson then. *His* Congressman had no power; in a body in which power was determined almost solely by seniority, his Congressman, the last one elected, had the least seniority of any of its 435 members.

His Congressman, moreover, had little interest in *being* a Congressman.

Richard Mifflin Kleberg was one of the wealthiest men in Texas, owner of a full twenty percent of the King Ranch, that colossal empire which had been founded by his grandfather, Richard King, and expanded by his father, King's son-in-law, Robert Kleberg, into a 2,000-square-mile empire—a domain so large that automobiles crossing it had to carry compasses to navigate and there was a full month's difference in seasons between its southern and northern boundaries. Extending the Ranch's influence beyond its borders, founding colleges and banks, building railroads, harbors, whole towns, in fact, Robert Kleberg turned much of South Texas into "Kleberg Country." And when, in 1922, Kleberg suffered a stroke, his son Dick, then thirty-six, was put in charge of the empire's affairs.

But Richard displayed little interest in his inheritance. During his youth, he had loved to play polo and golf, and to spend his time outdoors (he was renowned even among the King Ranch's hundreds of hard-riding Mexican *vaqueros* as a great rider, a great roper, a great marksman). In his forties, he still bulldogged steers in rodeos, sat up all night drinking and playing poker, and, accompanying himself on the accordion, singing Mexican songs to the adoring *vaqueros*, who called him "Mr. Dick"; he still vacationed in Mexico City for weeks at a time. He was an easy-going, affable, considerate man. "A sweeter man than Dick Kleberg never lived," a friend says. "But," the friend adds, "he was a playboy. As for work, he had no interest in that *whatsoever*." By 1927, he had let the affairs of the great ranch slide until, almost unbelievably, it was in financial difficulties, and the executors of his father's estate removed him from authority and turned the administration of its affairs over to his younger brother (who soon had it back on sound footing). Dick didn't seem to mind; business, he said, was not for him.

Neither, it turned out, was politics. His views on government were strong, if a trifle simplistic. The cause of the Depression, he felt, was Al

Capone. "The trouble with the nation's economy," he declared, was simply Prohibition, which "makes it possible for large-scale dealers in illicit liquor to amass tremendous amounts of currency"; the "present economic crisis," he explained, was due to the "withdrawal of billions of dollars from the channels of legitimate trade" by these bootleggers. His passions were also aroused by Herbert Hoover—not because, as some felt, Hoover was not doing enough to fight the Depression, but because he was doing too much. Kleberg's first speech in the House, in January, 1932, urged Congress to begin "whittling down . . . government interference in business and society and the expenses of maintaining these interfering agencies." Not long thereafter, he sharpened his attacks, calling Hoover's policies "un-American" because of their "enormous expense." He had had, however, no interest in entering politics, becoming a candidate as a favor to a friend, the legendary Roy Miller, the onetime "Boy Mayor of Corpus Christi," whose lobbying activities for the gigantic Texas Gulf Sulphur Corporation were making his pearl-gray Borsalino and silvery mane as familiar in Washington as they had been in Austin. Miller was a Garner ally; when Wurzbach died, the paramount qualification necessary for the Democratic nominee in the Fourteenth District was, in Miller's view, electability—since his election would give the Democrats the previously Republican seat, and with it the vote that would ensure Garner's election to the Speakership. And, in Kleberg Country, who was more electable than a Kleberg?

Playing his accordion and singing in Spanish to San Antonio's thousands of Mexican-American voters, waving a big sombrero as he led rodeo parades (and, at the Robstown Rodeo, roping and throwing a calf in a respectable fourteen seconds), telling funny stories, Kleberg won easily. But campaigning was the extent of his interest in his new job. At Lyndon Johnson's request, he had, on their first day in Washington, taken his secretary around to introduce him to his influential friends ("Hello, Dick, you old cow-puncher," Garner said; he had a word for Dick's secretary, too, as soon as he caught his name: "You Sam Johnson's boy?" he asked), but had done little thereafter to help him with his work. Kleberg had given Miller what Capitol Hill called "carte blanche": permission to use his office—Room 258—as if it were his own. The lobbyist "was in there every day," says one congressional secretary, dictating letters to Miss Harbin (not only letters Miller signed with his own name but letters he signed with Kleberg's), telephoning for appointments with departmental and Cabinet officials (always in Kleberg's name rather than his own—but when Kleberg went, Miller always went with him). The House convened at noon; most Congressmen spent mornings in their offices handling their district's "casework"—individual requests from constituents—either taking care of it themselves or calling bureaucrats to tell them that their secretaries would be calling, thereby smoothing the secretaries' way. Kleberg, however, spent his mornings sleeping off the previous evening's poker-and-bourbon session, and his afternoons indulging another passion—golf—at Washington's famous Burning Tree Golf Club. On his trips to Capitol Hill, his first stop would be the congenial House cloakroom—not his office, in which the work bored him. He seldom appeared in Room 258* before the House adjourned in the late afternoon—when he would show up to welcome friends, his own and Miller's, dropping by for a drink. On many days, he never showed up at all. Room 258 was a Congressman's office without a Congressman. The work of the Fourteenth District was left to the Congressman's secretary.

In some districts, this might not have mattered much. With air travel still in its infancy, distances insulated Congressmen—and their secretaries —from their constituents; few came to Washington to be greeted, entertained, and taken on tours of the capital. Because the national government touched the lives of its citizens only occasionally, there was little communication between them and the Representative who was their link to it; the office of a Congressman representing a typical Western district might receive only ten or fifteen letters a day, most of them from job-hunters or from veterans needing assistance to obtain or increase government pensions. Many Congressmen therefore employed only one of the two secretaries allowed them by law; many—by one estimate, more than half—paid the rest of their $5,000 "clerk-hire" allowance to a relative who never bothered to show up in the office. Some secretaries were, moreover, elderly spinsters who had spent a lifetime working for one or another "Member" and who were notably slow in the performance of their duties. Life was leisurely on Capitol Hill; the House Office Building—there was only one House Office Building then, the one now known as the Cannon Building; each Congressman's office consisted of a single room—was a place of open doors; in the late afternoon, members and secretaries would drop in on each other, desk drawers would be opened, and bottles would be pulled out for a friendly drink.

But Texas' Fourteenth was not a typical district. Included in its half-million residents—twice as many as the average Texas district—was one of the nation's largest concentrations of servicemen and veterans, the constituents who made the most demands on a Congressman, for San Antonio was the site of Fort Sam Houston, the nation's largest Army post, and the center of a ring of military aviation fields. Tens of thousands of men had trained in the city (31,000 at Kelly Field alone during World War I), enough had married there so that San Antonio was jocularly known as "the Mother-in-law of the Army"—and enough had made their homes there after their enlistments were up to ensure that the district's congressional office would have an outsize share of mail about pensions, disability benefits, and the new issue that was agitating ex-servicemen in 1931: pre-payment of their bonus for World War service. Kleberg's predecessor had been ill

---

* Offices in the Cannon Building have been renumbered. Kleberg's office is the room—now unnumbered—next to the present Room 244.

for more than a year, so that his office had fallen behind in its work even before his death; when Lyndon Johnson opened the door to Room 258 for the first time, gray sacks bulging with months' accumulation of mail were heaped before him.

And the new Congressman's new secretary didn't know the district. Its northern end was the Hill Country, including his home county, Blanco, but from the southernmost ridge of the familiar hills, the district stretched more than 200 miles farther south. On his first trip through it, Lyndon Johnson drove south to San Antonio as he had on his way to Cotulla and Pearsall, but then turned not southwest on a sandy track across treeless, desolate plains toward Mexico, but southeast, on a broad, well-paved highway that ran past pastures of lush grass filled with fat cattle, and cotton fields that stretched to the horizon. This land, beneath its grass and cotton, was not the parched whitish soil of the Hill Country, but the rich black loam of the coastal plain, loam with an average depth of four feet; the Fourteenth District included some of the richest land in all Texas. And when Johnson reached the southern border of his new responsibility, he was looking at palm trees and fishing boats and freighters and the great half-moon shoreline of the Gulf of Mexico.

Johnson didn't know the problems of this district—not of teeming San Antonio, not of gracious Corpus Christi and humming Port Aransas, the district's two port cities, not of the farmers and ranchers in the little towns he had passed in between. He had never even *heard* of some of those towns. He didn't know the problems, and he didn't know the people. Since Kleberg's predecessor had been a Republican, there were a lot of patronage jobs to be filled by a newly elected Democrat. As Johnson opened the mail bags, there spilled out on his desk requests to the Congressman for postmasterships and assistant postmasterships and rural-route mail-delivery assignments, for jobs with the federal government in Washington and for recommendations that would help to obtain jobs with the state government in Austin, for appointments to West Point and the Naval Academy, for help in obtaining contracts to supply food or to pave roads at Fort Sam Houston or Kelly Field. The new secretary didn't know the names signed to the letters or mentioned in them, much less the names' political significance. There were scores of jobs to be filled; he had no idea who should be getting them.

And he didn't know Washington.

The hundred new Congressmen who had come to Washington in December, 1931, had brought with them a hundred new secretaries, but few were less sophisticated than twenty-three-year-old Lyndon Johnson. When Estelle Harbin, a twenty-eight-year-old secretary from Corpus Christi who had been hired to assist Johnson, met him for the first time in January, 1932—at the Missouri-Pacific Railroad station in San Antonio; Johnson had gone home to Texas when Congress recessed for Christmas, and now was returning to Washington—she saw "a tall, real thin boy" who couldn't stop talking about the wonders of train travel; he asked her excitedly, "Have you ever ridden in a Pullman? I never did until I went up with Mr. Kleberg. Have you ever eaten in a dining car? I never did." When Johnson received his first monthly paycheck, he told Miss Harbin that he wanted to deposit it ⸱ in a bank, but that he didn't know how to open a bank account; he had never had one. And as for the intricacies of government, "That," says Miss Harbin, "was a whole new world to us." The mail sacks contained letters from secretaries of farm cooperatives asking for the Congressman's support of an application for a loan from the Division of Cooperative Marketing of the Bureau of Agricultural Economics, or for assistance from the Department of Agriculture's Federal Farm Board, and hundreds of letters from veterans seeking assistance on pension and disability problems, each one with individual problems, each one complicated—mailbags full of requests requiring action from some federal agency or department or bureau. The new secretary didn't even know *which* agency or department or bureau— and when, after a day or two of fruitless telephoning, he decided to go to the Veterans Bureau in person, he found himself standing in front of a building a block square and ten stories high, each floor filled with hundreds of offices.

"We didn't know which bureau to go to, to ask about something, or to try to get something done," Estelle Harbin recalls. "We didn't know you could get books from the Library of Congress—and, my God, we never even *thought* of asking them for information. I wanted a plant for the office, but I had no idea you could get one by calling up the United States Botanic Garden. My God, we didn't know *anything!* The first time we heard that there was a little train that Senators could ride [from the Senate Office Building] to the Capitol—well, we just couldn't believe *that!* Lyndon didn't know how to type, and he didn't know how to dictate a letter—he had never dictated one. We were two ignorant little children." Kleberg gave them his two complimentary gallery tickets to President Hoover's address to a joint session of Congress, but when they arrived, all the seats had been taken, and they sat, Miss Harbin recalls, "on the two top steps," not saying a word. "Lyndon was there beside me as scared as I was. We sat there like two scared field mice."

Johnson could not persuade his boss to read the mail, much less dictate replies. If he asked the Congressman to call a government bureau on behalf of a constituent, Kleberg would always agree, but he never seemed to get around to doing it. When Johnson asked him to call an official so that he, Johnson, would have an easier time dealing with him, that call never seemed to be made, either. Johnson realized that he would have to handle the mail himself. And three times each day, the mailman would arrive with another bundle of it. "The mail really dismayed him at first," Miss Harbin recalls; Johnson was to describe his own feelings about it: "I felt I was going to be buried."

. . .

SOME OF THE INFORMATION he needed could be obtained from the Hill's elderly spinster secretaries; with them, he displayed the same gift with elderly women that had awed his boyhood friends back in Johnson City. "He was always so courteous," Miss Harbin recalls, "and there was never a little favor that was too much trouble for him to do." Soon—"in nothing flat," Miss Harbin says—in every office along those long cold corridors on the first floor of the House Office Building, there was a warm smile for Lyndon Johnson. But he needed more knowledge—more tips on how to get things done in Washington's bewildering bureaucratic maze—than the elderly women could give him. And he was living in the right place to get it.

Once the Grace Dodge Hotel had been a "ladies' hotel," with its name in Old English gilt lettering above its door, the most elegant of the cluster of eight-story red brick hotels at the foot of the long north slope of Capitol Hill near Union Station. With the Depression emptying its rooms, however, its management had decided to cater also to young men whose paychecks were small but, coming from the government, regular. The two basement floors were divided into cubicles, and rented out at $40 per month for rooms on the "A" floor, just one level down from the lobby, with bathrooms that had to be shared only with the tenants of the adjoining room; and $30 for the smaller rooms on the bottom, or "B," floor, where a single communal bathroom served all rooms, and, since this level was partly below ground, the only daylight came from half-windows, high up on the walls, facing on a back alley. Basement tenants were forbidden to mingle with the Dodge's upstairs guests—who included two United States Senators and a Supreme Court Justice—or, in fact, to set foot in its lobby, which badly needed painting but still boasted a grand piano, a fireplace, Oriental rugs and glittering chandeliers; they were required to enter and leave by the back-alley door. But the lodgings were cheap and convenient—most of the basement tenants were, like Lyndon Johnson (who lived on "B"), congressional aides whose offices were right up Capitol Hill—and the tenants were young: the Dodge's basement was crammed with camaraderie, as well as with enthusiasm, ambition and, because many of the aides had several years' experience, with the expertise Lyndon Johnson needed on how to get things done in Washington. Since they couldn't afford to eat in the Dodge dining room, the young men walked down to the All States Cafeteria, decorated with plaques of state seals, on Massachusetts Avenue, for a meal that Southern secretaries called the "Fo-bitter" because it cost fifty cents—or, just before payday, to Childs' Cafeteria, where, one secretary recalls, "you could do pretty well on two bits." A lot of joking and horseplay went on among the young men standing on line for their food, but Johnson didn't wait on line. After walking over to Childs' with the other secretaries, he would, as they entered the cafeteria door, dart ahead, grab a tray, hurry to choose his food, rush to the large table where they usually sat and wolf down his meal. One of the older secretaries in the group—Arthur Perry, a Capitol Hill veteran then secretary to Senator Tom Connally of Texas—was a shrewd observer of young men. Johnson, he saw, rushed through his food because he wanted to be done with it before the others got to the table —so that eating wouldn't interfere with his conversation. "That left him free to shoot questions at us while we ate," Perry would recall. The questions were all on a single theme: how to get things done in Washington, how to get ahead in Washington, how to *be somebody* in Washington. "He'd say, 'But how did he do it?' (Whatever it was.) 'Did he know somebody? Is he a nice guy? What's his secret of getting ahead?' " The simple answer—the shallow answer—didn't satisfy him. If one of the other men at the table replied, "I don't know as he has any special secret—maybe he's just lucky," Johnson would say, "I don't believe in luck. You look into it and you'll find it's always a lot more than just luck." He himself would not stop looking into it until he was satisfied. "If he didn't like the answers he got, he would argue" on all sides of a question, worrying it from every angle, Perry says. "It took a long time" for Perry "to catch on" to what Johnson was doing, he says, but finally he realized "that most of his arguing was done simply to bring out every possible answer to his arguments. He wanted to be sure he knew all the answers."

ONCE HE KNEW HOW to do things in Washington, he started doing them—with the same frenzied, driven, almost desperate energy he had displayed in Cotulla and Houston, the energy of a man fleeing from something dreadful.

Estelle Harbin, accustomed to the early-rising ways of Texas, would arrive at the House Office Building before eight o'clock, saying good morning to the guard at the desk inside the New Jersey Avenue entrance, and then turning down the corridor to her right. The corridor, which was silent and dark, for congressional offices didn't open until nine, was longer than a football field, so long that the light from the window at its far end reached only a little way toward her, and so high that the lighted globes on its ceiling did little to dispel its dimness. And when she reached the far end, she would turn left into another corridor, unwindowed and even darker—except that, halfway down it, from the twelfth door on the right, a single shaft of light would always be falling across it from the open door of Room 258.

Often, Lyndon Johnson would be writing when she walked into 258. Because of his difficulty giving dictation, he wrote out the letters he wanted Miss Harbin to type—writing and rewriting them until he was satisfied—and he wanted to finish that work before eight o'clock, because at eight the dollies carrying the new day's mail began clattering down those long corridors. "The minute the mail arrived, we would start opening it together, and decide what to do about it," Miss Harbin says. "Then I'd start [typing] the letters he had written out before I got there, and he would get on the phone."

He knew whom to call now, and he knew how to talk to the people he was calling. "He had charm to burn," Miss Harbin says. "He would get someone to do something for him, and then he would hang up and we would laugh about it. Very soon, he had a real pipeline to all the bureaus. And he wouldn't take no—he would pursue these things like it was life and death. And when he got something for somebody—when we could write and tell somebody that they could look forward to getting something—that was a real victory. He'd put down the phone—'Stelle! Yay!' He'd just practically jump up and down."

Work not only began unusually early in Room 258 (other secretaries say that no matter how early they arrived, the light in 258 was always on) and was not interrupted by lunch (Johnson and Miss Harbin would eat sandwiches at their desks) but also ended unusually late. The offices that, in those leisurely days, opened at nine, closed at four or four-thirty. Miss Harbin's boardinghouse stopped serving dinner at eight, she recalls, "so, often, I couldn't get there in time for dinner." Generally, the Kleberg office staff would dine at Childs'. "Lyndon knew the price of every dish in that restaurant," she says, "and a lot of times, we had to put our money on the table and count it to see what we could afford to order. We'd do this in the office [before leaving]. He'd say, 'This is Wednesday, and on Wednesday they have so-and-so.' We always had to leave me [bus fare] to get home." Occasionally their boss would take them to dinner at the Occidental ("Where Statesmen Dine"); "that was a big deal," Miss Harbin says; "we saw people we recognized from magazines, and we might have oysters on the half-shell." Soon an unusually heavy stream of letters "telling somebody that they could look forward to getting something" was pouring out of Room 258. But repetition did not dull the thrill Johnson received from each "victory." And it didn't dull the edge of his effort. When Spring came, Miss Harbin would sometimes persuade him to take a brief stroll on the Capitol grounds. But although the stroll might begin at a relaxed pace, inevitably, Miss Harbin recalls, she would have to begin trotting, because her companion would be walking faster and faster. "He was so tall and he took such long steps, and I couldn't keep up with him. I would say something, and he'd slow down, but soon he'd be going faster again. I'd skip to keep up with him, and then I'd have to run." And when they turned back toward the office he would begin striding faster and faster, "and then he would take my hand, and we'd run, literally run, across the Capitol grounds. He just couldn't wait to get back to that office."

．　．　．

THOUGH he no longer had time to eat dinner with the Dodge boys, he was still a participant in their late-evening bull sessions—but the tone of his participation had rapidly changed. Coming in late from work, he would walk into a discussion in one of the crowded little basement cubicles, and begin at once to dominate it. He didn't want to talk about anything but politics, and steered every conversation onto that subject. And while only a week or two before he had been asking questions at the Dodge, now he wasn't asking any more, he was telling—talking as if he knew all the answers. "We used to have discussions," one of the young men was to say. "Now we were having lectures—lectures by Lyndon."

His demeanor had changed not only in a basement but in a balcony. In January, he and Estelle Harbin had sat on the steps of the gallery of the House of Representatives like "two scared field mice" during President Hoover's address to Congress. In February, the President addressed Congress again. Several Congressional secretaries, sitting in the gallery reserved for them, remember Johnson coming in late, pushing aggressively to get to an empty seat, and introducing himself to everyone around him in a very loud voice. One secretary sitting in a front row of the gallery remembers people hunching down a little in embarrassment, and says that he was doing so, too, when he felt a tap on his shoulder and, turning, found the tall young man who was making all the fuss leaning down toward him, and stretching out his arm for a handshake. "Lyndon Johnson from Johnson City, Texas!" the young man said loudly. "Dick Kleberg's secretary."

His demeanor had also changed in the halls of the House Office Building. When he wasn't working the telephone in 258, Johnson had begun roaming those corridors with the air of a successful politician. Says a secretary to a Pennsylvania Congressman: "I remember him bounding in the door every day with a big smile, and saying, 'Hi! How's everyone from Pennsylvania today?' He just *radiated* self-confidence."

He acted like a successful politician in other ways, too. Despite the thinness of his suits, his first paycheck went not for warm clothing, but for a formal portrait—and a hundred prints—by Washington's most expensive photographer. Inscribing and autographing the pictures ("To Gene and the members of the Sam Houston High debating club. I love you all— Lyndon B. Johnson"), he mailed them back to Texas, as if he were a Congressman responding to constituents' requests for an autographed picture. Recalling this mailing, one secretary says: "What I remember about Lyndon Johnson was his fantastic assurance in everything he did."

CONFIDENCE? Assurance? The photographs weren't the only communications that Lyndon Johnson sent to Texas. No sooner had he arrived in Washington than he began writing to Gene Latimer, Luther ("L.E.") Jones and other former students at Sam Houston High. These letters were not the conventional letters from a teacher to former students. Though he wrote them late at night after a grinding day in Kleberg's office, they were not brief notes but detailed descriptions of his life in Washington that often ran four handwritten pages. And in them, he didn't merely ask his former pupils to stay in touch; he pleaded with them to stay in touch. The happy-go-lucky Latimer was not a faithful correspondent; Jones was, but on one occasion he didn't reply promptly. "Dear L.E.," said the next letter from Washington, "Have you forgotten me?" And when Jones wrote back, Johnson replied: "Thanks for your letter. . . . I had almost begun to think you had quit me too. Haven't been able to get a line out of Gene et al for weeks. . . . It's now after 12 and I've just finished work. Must drop Gene a note also. Love and for goodness sakes write me a long letter now." Johnson's letters reveal not only a penchant for secrecy rather surprising in personal notes (on one, entirely innocuous, he wrote: "Burn this—others probably won't understand the personal references"), but also concern about how his own letters were being received ("Hope you won't be bored with this long letter"), and an urgent need to be reassured that these two young men to whom he had once been close still wanted to be close to him. Pouring out affection, he asked— over and over, in every letter, in fact, that survives—that the affection be reciprocated. In a letter written on a Sunday night ("Have not been out of the office all day. Didn't get up until late this morning so I was forced to rush to work and have been at it until only a few minutes ago. I never get time to do anything but try to push the mail out"), he told Jones: "You are a real boy. I love you and Gene as if you were my own." The letter ends: "Thanks for your . . . letter. I'm waiting for another . . . letter."

Other letters were needed even more. If a few days went by without the mailbags containing a letter in Rebekah Johnson's carefully rounded script, Estelle Harbin says, "you could see him get quiet and homesick."

Sometimes, even when the letters from Texas were regular, he would get quiet, Miss Harbin says. As he had done with Mrs. Marshall in Cotulla and with Ethel Davis in San Marcos, he made a confidante of this somewhat older woman, and, in a maternal way, she was very fond of him and felt she understood him—as perhaps she did, working beside him all day, day after day, the two of them alone in an office. And she had a very different picture of him than did the young men in the Dodge or on Capitol Hill. "Now, Lyndon had a side to him," she says. "He could get very low. When he got real quiet, it was bad." She even devised a strategy to cheer him up. Johnson was very proud of working for a Kleberg; he never tired of repeating to acquaintances that the King Ranch was so big that the entire state of Connecticut could be dropped into it and never touch a fence. In these first months, a friendly word from his boss meant a lot to him, Miss Harbin saw, so whenever Kleberg (who, with golf in season, was now coming to Capitol Hill less and less frequently) asked Lyndon to deliver papers to him at his red-carpeted Mayflower Hotel suite, "I'd wait until Lyndon cleared the building, and I'd call Mr. Kleberg and say, 'Lyndon is real low—I think he's real homesick. And he needs some cheering up.' And Mr. Kleberg would say, 'Don't say another word. I'll take care of it.' And as soon as Lyndon would get there, Mr. Kleberg would say, 'Now put those things down, boy, and we're just going to talk.' And every time, Lyndon would come back a different person. When he hit the door, his hat would just be on the back of his head with the brim turned up, and he'd be smiling, and he'd say, 'I'll tell you, that Mr. Dick is the most wonderful man in the world.' "

But the quietness would return, and sometimes, Estelle Harbin says, "it was *very* bad." She felt she understood why he ran—not only physically but "in his mind, too": because "he had a burning ambition to be somebody. He didn't know what he wanted to be, but he wanted to be *somebody*." He ran, she says, because "he couldn't stand not being somebody—just could not *stand* it. So he was trying to meet everyone, to learn everything—he was trying to gobble up all Washington in a month." Dining with him at night she sometimes felt that even after the long day's work, "he was still running in his head." Walking toward her bus in the dark, watching him running awkwardly down Capitol Hill toward the Dodge, she would hope that he would relax when he got there. But often, when the next morning she turned into the only open door in the House Office Building and his pale face looked up at her, he would say something that told her he had been running all night, too. When he got quiet, she says, it was because he was doubting himself, because he was afraid he would never get to be somebody. Or, she says, it was because he had been hurt—deeply hurt—by some off-hand remark. "He was very sensitive to the other person, and he was very sensitive himself," she says. "And he was very, very easily hurt." Because she felt she understood him, "sometimes," Estelle Harbin says, "I felt very sorry for him."

HE RAN HARDER. In June, 1932, Miss Harbin, for personal reasons, returned to Texas. Johnson had the opportunity to hire a new assistant—two, in fact, since among the information he had acquired at the Dodge was the fact that a $130-per-month patronage job as mailman in the House Post Office traditionally "belonged" to the Fourteenth District. And he had his new assistants already picked out. He brought Gene Latimer and L. E. Jones to Washington.

Latimer, the little Irish boy with the "wonderful smile"—"the best-natured little guy you ever saw," says one of the Dodge residents—came for love. His fiancée's family had moved there, and Latimer was anxious to be near her and to earn enough money to get married, and the only job he had been able to find in Depression-racked Houston had been as a delivery boy. Johnson told him a job was waiting for him in Washington. "L.E."

came for ambition. The son of an impoverished druggist, he had spent his childhood in a Houston slum from which he was desperate to escape; he had worked his way through two years at Rice University, but was afraid he would have trouble getting a job when he graduated. Johnson wrote him, "I know you are going places and I'm going to help you get there," and said the place to start was a government job in Washington.

He got them cheap. So that he could keep for himself the balance remaining for 1932 in the district's $5,000 annual clerk-hire allowance, Johnson had arranged for Latimer, who arrived several months before Jones, to be given the $130-per-month mailman job, which put him on the payroll of the House Post Office instead of the district. Since that job was not yet open, he had arranged for Congressman Kleberg to pay Latimer out of his own pocket: $25 per month. He would not need much money, Johnson assured him; he could share Johnson's room at the Dodge and therefore have a place to sleep for only $15 per month, leaving $10 to spend as he pleased. After a month, Latimer told Johnson that he simply could not live on $10. Johnson arranged to have Kleberg pay him $57. For several months, that was Latimer's total salary.

When he finally began receiving his $130, Latimer found that to be a low wage even in Depression Washington, too low to enable him to save enough money so he could get married. It was, however, a higher wage than Jones received. Johnson had persuaded Kleberg to increase his own share of the $5,000 allowance for 1933 to the maximum permitted by law: $3,900. Jones' annual salary was therefore the remaining $1,100, or $91.66 per month.

And he got his money's worth. Many Congressmen required House patronage employees—mailmen, elevator operators, gallery doorkeepers—to work an hour or two each day in their own offices after getting off work. But an hour or two was not what Johnson had in mind. He asked the House Postmaster to assign Latimer to the earliest shift, which began at five a.m. and ended at noon. Johnson allowed Latimer to take a half-hour for lunch but no more: at twelve-thirty sharp each day, Latimer was to be in Room 258—ready for work.

This work might be over at eight or nine o'clock in the evening, Latimer says, "but often I would stay until eleven-thirty or midnight." During much of this time, Johnson would be out of the office, cultivating bureaucrats or other congressional secretaries. Latimer would be alone in 258, an eighteen-year-old boy working eighteen-hour days. Soon Johnson found a way to get even more work out of him. "My job in the Post Office was sorting the mail, pitching it into different bins, and we made two or three deliveries [each day]. He urged me to pitch the mail faster, and I got so I did it faster than any other clerk, and then between deliveries I might have ninety minutes free at a time. And I'd run over to the office [Kleberg's office] and do ninety minutes of typing" before heading back to the Post Office for more mail-sorting and delivering. And "then, at the end of the shift, I'd rush over to that little corner place and eat that fifteen-cent stew and rush over to the office so I could be at work at twelve-thirty."

By the time Jones arrived in Washington—a third bed was moved into the little room at the Dodge—Kleberg had been given a two-room suite, Office 1322, in the new House Office Building (now known as the Longworth Building) which had just been opened alongside the old one. A routine was soon established for the staff of that office. It began before five, when Johnson shook Latimer awake and started him on his way up Capitol Hill. Not long thereafter, he would awaken Jones. Pulling on their clothes —Johnson had taught Jones his trick of taking off his necktie still knotted so he wouldn't have to waste time tying it in the morning—Johnson and Jones would hurry out of the Dodge and up Capitol Hill in the dark, past the shadowy mass of the Capitol and into the Longworth Building. To avoid wasting time awakening the napping night elevator operator, they ran up the winding stairs, dimly lit from eagle sconces, to the third floor. Having raced through his mail-sorting and delivering, Latimer would arrive at about the same time—at Johnson's request, he had been assigned to a route which included 1322, so he brought the mail himself.

Ripping open the mail sacks, Johnson began sorting through the mail— "reading it so fast that you couldn't believe he was reading it, but he was," Latimer says. At first, Johnson had dictated replies to every letter, but he had discovered that his former debater had a gift of Irish blarney with not only the spoken but the written word. Johnson wanted to flatter "important people" with whom he was corresponding, Latimer says, "to butter them up," and "he liked to have the butter laid on thick. It was almost impossible to put too much on. If he wanted to tell someone he liked him, he didn't want to say, 'I like you.' He wanted to say, 'You're the greatest guy in the world.'" Latimer says, "I did get to be a master of laying it on, all right," and he is not exaggerating; a typical letter refers to Sam Fore, a newspaper publisher from Floresville, as "The Saint Paul of Floresville." Soon Johnson, riffling through the mail as rapidly as if he were dealing a deck of cards, would hand many letters to Latimer with only the briefest of instructions—"Say yes. Say no. Tell him we're looking into it. Butter him up"— and Latimer would expand those instructions exactly as Johnson wished; Johnson had, in fact, discovered a genius in a minor art form: the letter to constituents. When the last letter had been dealt, Latimer sat down at his desk, in front of a heavy Underwood typewriter, and began typing. To dictate replies to letters on which more detailed instruction was needed, Johnson would lead Jones, carrying a stenographer's pad, into the adjoining room, so that, as Latimer explains, "his dictating wouldn't distract me, because my typewriter was supposed never to stop."

When the dictating was finished, and Jones had sat down at *his* Underwood, Johnson would "mark up" district newspapers, the big San Antonio and Corpus Christi dailies and the scores of small-town weeklies, putting checkmarks next to the articles (a wedding, a birth, the opening of a new business, a local Kiwanis Club election) which merited a letter of congratulation. "He insisted on getting every paper in the district, no matter how small," Latimer says. "And some of those papers would just be *filled* with checkmarks." By the time most congressional offices opened and began sorting mail, Kleberg's staff had finished sorting it and were well into answering it.

By this time, government agencies were open, and Johnson would get on the phone to them—while the two typewriters clattered away. No coffee was allowed in Kleberg's office, because Johnson felt making it and drinking it would distract Latimer and Jones from their work. Less ominous distractions also were frowned on. "If he caught you reading a letter from your mother, or if you were taking a crap, he'd say, 'Son, can't you *please* try a little harder to learn to do that on your own time?' " If Latimer asked if he could go out to buy cigarettes, Johnson would say, "What am I paying you for? Buying cigarettes? Buy them on your own time." "Our job was to keep those typewriters humming," Latimer says. "He would come down the hall—I could hear his heels clicking—and if he didn't hear both those typewriters going ninety miles per hour, he wanted to know what the hell was going on." The natural competitiveness of young men was used as a spur. "The Chief has a knack, or, better said, a genius for getting the most out of those around him," Latimer recalls. "He'd say, 'Gene, it seems L.E.'s a little faster than you today.' And I'd work faster. 'L.E., he's catching up with you.' And pretty soon, we'd both be pounding for hours without stopping, just as fast as we could."

The Depression was swelling the mail now, as more constituents asked for jobs and new government programs, and as veterans appealed more urgently for bonus pre-payment. With only one or two staffers in each congressional office, many offices answered more and more of the mail with mimeographed form replies, or with *pro forma* promises, or simply didn't reply at all—and still fell further and further behind. Kleberg's office answered personally every letter that could possibly be answered. For Lyndon Johnson, the mail possessed almost a mystique. At that time government programs touched the lives of few constituents, so the mail—the only means by which a Congressman could keep in touch with his district almost 2,000 miles from Washington—was a key to a Congressman's power; Johnson could hardly have avoided hearing, over and over, about one former Congressman or another who had "lost touch with his district"—and who was a Congressman no longer. But although other congressional staffers heard the same stories, they didn't answer every letter. For Lyndon Johnson, the mystique of the mail went beyond the political. He had always done every job "as if his life depended on it." Believing that "if you did just absolutely everything you *could* do, you would succeed," he had tried to perform—

perfectly—even minor tasks that no one else bothered with. For such a man, congressional mail, which consisted so largely of minor details—of small, unimportant requests—was a natural métier. Doing everything one *could* do with the mail meant answering *every* letter—and that was what he insisted his office must do. And not only must every letter be answered, he told Latimer and Jones, it must be answered the very day it arrived. "The only excuse that was accepted for not answering the same day was that you had lost a file, and, boy, there had better not be too many of those: not being able to find a file—that was some sin!" Latimer says. "And if your reply said, 'We have asked the Veterans Administration to look into this,' you really had to ask—that same day. So that the next day, you could write another letter about it." The early-morning mail delivery was only the first of three—and then four, and then five—made during the day, and still the bundles of each delivery grew heavier. Johnson would sort through the bundles, writing brief instructions on each letter about its handling and dividing the letters between his two aides. After typing his way for hours through a pile of letters, Jones or Latimer would finally be almost to the bottom—and then Johnson would smack down on his desk another pile, "a pile that," Jones says, "might be a foot high." And before he would be allowed to leave the office that night, the pile would have to be gone.

There was no escape from the mail. Small bundles meant not less but more work for the two young men. "It was important to get mail," Gene Latimer explains. "That was the most important thing. You had to have people writing you. So if the mail got light, we had to generate mail. Any day when we didn't get a hundred letters was a terrible day. And we had to do something about it." Letters were solicited, by scanning the weekly newspapers more closely than ever for any conceivable good or bad news that might justify a message of congratulation or condolence—a message in which the Congressman would solicit a reply by asking, in Latimer's words, " 'How am I doing in Washington? What government programs would you like to see passed?'—that kind of question." Then came the ultimate refinement of the congratulatory broadside. At some point, Latimer recalls, the "mail fell off" to a point at which

> we were receiving perhaps no more than double that of the usual member. This condition was intolerable for the Chief, and . . . he decided that each boy and girl graduating from high school in the Fourteenth District that year should have a personal letter of congratulations from his Congressman, commenting on his glorious achievement. There were literally thousands of such graduates each year. So began the production of lists and concurrently the production of forty or fifty letters, different, so the graduates would not receive the same letter. . . . We had only to take the names in order and write each a personal letter from the Congressman. We

whacked away harder and harder, and faster and faster, until we could recite those letters from left to right and from bottom to top.

After the typing came the retyping. No letter was going out of the office unless it was perfect, Johnson said, and to ensure perfection, he read every one. "And if he didn't like a letter," Latimer says, "he would just make huge, angry slash marks across it." No explanation would be vouchsafed. "You had to figure out what was wrong," Latimer says. "He wouldn't tell you." A single error in spelling or punctuation, and the letter was slashed. "He had no compunction at all about making you write them over . . . even if you had to stay past midnight," Jones says. "You handed him fifty, sixty letters . . . and he might mark out every one of them."

Sometimes Latimer and Jones would be finished with work by eight or nine o'clock, and would head back to Childs' for dinner and then to the Dodge for the evening bull sessions. But usually they wouldn't be finished until 11:30 or midnight. Then they would return to their room to fall exhausted into their beds, to grab a few hours' sleep—for no matter how late they had worked the night before, they would be dragged from those beds at five o'clock the next morning. Recently completed on the long slope between the Dodge and the crown of Capitol Hill was an elaborate fountain illuminated by colored lights that were turned on only between sunset and sunrise. "I almost never saw that fountain without the lights on," Latimer says. Returning from his work in the dark, he went back to his work while it was still dark.

THE WILLINGNESS of the two teen-agers to adhere to so brutal a routine—a seven-day routine: Kleberg's office did not close on weekends—was based in part on admiration for their boss. Listening to him "work the departments" over the telephone, they heard him tailoring his approach to the individual he was talking to, bullying one bureaucrat with a threat of bringing down Congressman Kleberg's displeasure on his head (or, with increasing frequency, masquerading as the congressman himself), pleading with another: "Look, I've got a problem. I've got to get you to help me"—and obtaining results that they felt other secretaries could never have achieved. Listening, for example, to Johnson talking to the Veterans Administration about a veteran's request that a disability be considered "connected" to his war service, which would make the veteran eligible for a pension, Latimer and Jones would be awed by his glibness. "Damage-suit lawyers have a jargon, you know," Jones says. "Johnson was adept at rationalizing like that. He could sit there and talk like a great lawyer or a doctor." And they were amazed by his persistence. "He took each case personally," Latimer says. "He wouldn't take no." While congressional offices routinely endorsed a veteran's request to the VA, denial of the request generally marked the end of the office's interest in the case. If the veteran was from the Fourteenth District, however, the congressional secretary would react to the denial by taking up the case personally over the telephone. If the telephone appeal did not succeed, the secretary went to the VA in person. If the request was still denied, the secretary, without the veteran asking, filed a formal, written appeal, and procured him a lawyer. When the lawyer appeared before the Board of Veterans Appeals, the secretary of the Fourteenth District was also present. And if the case seemed to be going against his constituent, the secretary did not remain a silent observer. When Lyndon Johnson took a personal hand at a Veterans Board hearing, he displayed his obsession with secrecy, asking that the stenographer be instructed not to take down his remarks, but he also displayed considerable persuasiveness. Reading the typed minutes of the hearing later, Latimer would invariably see the same sentence: *Mr. Johnson spoke off the record.* "I'd say to myself, 'Here it comes!' And sure enough, when they went back on the record again, the attitude would have changed. It was almost unheard of to get someone 'service-connected' after it had been denied, but the Chief did it. Many times."

The two teen-agers' willingness to work so hard was based in part on their boss' ability to inspire enthusiasm. To Johnson, Jones says, "every problem had a solution. . . . He was completely confident, always optimistic. . . . And this was contagious. It would absolutely grab ahold of you." Casework was, moreover, not only a crusade but a crusade complete with triumphs, in which the whole office shared. Jones echoes Estelle Harbin: "He would get ecstatic. I mean, we had won a real *victory.*"

They were also willing to work long hours because they were not working alone. If they awoke at five, it was because their boss was awake at five, and if they trudged up Capitol Hill before daylight, their boss trudged beside them. The days they spent chained to typewriters, he spent chained to the telephone—bullying and begging on behalf of their constituents. And often, after they had returned to their little room and were falling asleep, they would hear their boss still tossing restlessly on his narrow bed. "He worked harder than anyone," Latimer says. "His head was still going around when the rest of us had knocked off."

OTHER FACTORS, however, were also involved.

Sometimes, Latimer rebelled. Rebellion was generally related to his fiancée. Although Johnson had brought him to Washington ostensibly so that he could be near her, the work schedule that Johnson had set up for him left little time for romance. He was allowed time off from the office to see her on Sundays after three p.m.—and only on Sundays after three p.m.

Johnson's response to rebellion might be a sneer: a sneer with a particularly telling point. Once, when Latimer had requested an evening off and was being viciously tongue-lashed by Johnson for his temerity, "I couldn't stand it, and I packed the little wicker suitcase I had come up with, and said I was leaving." Towering over the little Irish boy, Johnson said, sneering, "How are you going to get back?" When Latimer, sobbing, said, as he recalls it, that he would rather hitchhike all the way to Texas than remain, Johnson said: "What are you going to do when you get there? How are you going to get a job? If you leave, how are you ever going to marry Marjorie?"—questions which enunciated an aspect of the Johnson-Latimer relationship that was generally unmentioned but that was one of the realities that underlay it: that Latimer had no money, that his only source of money was Lyndon Johnson, that, without Johnson, he would not have a job, in a time when jobs were hard to come by; that, in short, he needed Johnson so badly that he had little choice but to do whatever Johnson wanted. The suitcase was unpacked, and Latimer remained.

But rebellion was rare. To so skilled a reader of men, Gene Latimer was an easy text. Revolt could be anticipated, and headed off. "He wouldn't really have a talk with you for months," Latimer says. "And then he would hug you, and he might spend an hour talking about your problems. He didn't do it very often, so you might think he was getting a hell of a lot for not very much, but if he did it very often, it wouldn't mean very much, you know." The way Johnson did it, it meant so much that the hug and the talk generally ended even the hint of revolt.

He could deflect any of Latimer's desires. The youth was always broke during his years in Kleberg's office—as might be expected on so low a salary. He was always falling behind in his bills for clothing and dry cleaning, and he relates with gratitude how Johnson consolidated his bills, and then collected his salary himself, and paid the bills out of it, putting Latimer on a $10-per-week allowance. But he also relates how once, "when the pain had been severe for some time, I summoned up the considerable courage it took to ask [him] about the possibility of a small increase in salary. He listened with sympathetic concern, commented at some length on the shortage of money and jobs all over the country at the time and especially in our own office, then told me he had been thinking for some time on how to reward the excellent work I had been doing. He had finally decided that I merited having my name put on the office stationery as assistant secretary. As he described the prestige and glory of such an arrangement, I could see the printing stand out six inches." Latimer accepted the title instead of a raise; "I never questioned the procedure," Latimer says. "Indeed, it just seemed to follow as a matter of course."

In general, he never questioned Johnson at all. Ask Latimer why he was willing to work so hard, and he replies first, "I guess I didn't know there was any other way to do it. He was the only guy I had worked for. And he keeps the pressure on you all the time. . . ." But Latimer himself knows this is only part of the explanation, and he soon goes on. For Gene Latimer—sixty-five years old at the time he spoke, sitting alone in a little apartment in a little town in Texas, a tiny Irish elf with sad eyes that often spill over with tears as he describes his life as an employee of Lyndon Johnson, so that he periodically excuses himself and goes into the bathroom to wash them off—understands, even if he was unable to cure, his own psychological dependence on Johnson: to listen to him talk is to hear a man who is fully aware that during his sixteenth year, he surrendered—for life—his own personality to a stronger personality. To listen to him talk is to hear a man who is fully aware that he has been used as a tool. Once, during the long days he spent with the author in his little apartment—difficult days for both men—he said: "He never talked *to* me too much, because with someone like me, all he wanted was to keep me busy. When he saw me: 'Where's your [stenographer's] book? I want you to take this down.' When he saw me, he just wanted to know what orders he could give me." But the awareness is accompanied by acceptance, not resentment. Johnson called him "Son"; he called Johnson "Chief." Asked if he ever called Johnson by his first name, he replied, shocked: "I would never have *dreamed* of calling him by his first name. He was *The Chief!*" Lyndon Johnson had found a man who liked taking orders as much as he liked giving them. Gene Latimer speaks of Lyndon Johnson with idolatry. "I don't think he's ever been scared in his life." And he talks of him with fear. "He can be mean. He can make people cry. He can make you feel so bad that you could go out and shoot yourself." And he talks of him with a feeling deeper than idolatry or fear. "I had such tremendous respect for the man," he says. "I don't know any other man I had such respect for. And, hell, you just had faith—hell, he could talk you into *anything* and make you feel it was right, and absolutely necessary and proper. He can make you cry, he can make you laugh—he can do anything. And if you like him, then he puts things on such a personal basis, you know. You felt like I belong to him, and he belongs to me. Whatever you do, you do it for *him.*"

He did a lot for him. Gene Latimer would work for Lyndon Johnson for the next thirty-five years, as "his slave—his totally willing slave." This term of service would not, however, be continuous. In 1939 began the first in a series of many nervous breakdowns; Latimer spent a substantial portion of his life recuperating from them—and from recurrent, severe, bouts of alcoholism. He understood their cause. "The work broke me," he says. But as soon as he recuperated, he would always return to the same work. Because the work was for Lyndon Johnson.

JOHNSON'S RELATIONSHIP with L. E. Jones was more complex. The tall, handsome Jones was a very different type of personality. A brilliant young man who would later be known as the "finest appellate lawyer" in Texas, a "lawyer's lawyer" consulted by even its most famous attorneys ("He is," one magazine stated, "the man with probably the finest technical legal knowledge in the state"), L.E. was as precise as Latimer was easy-going ("His shorthand looked like it was printed in a book," Gene says), as stiff and cold as Latimer was warm. And he was very ambitious. He was willing to work the killing hours that Johnson demanded because Johnson had played on that ambition: "You work hard for me, and I'll help you." Jones would remember "being awakened at five a.m. and walking to the office in the snow, and wondering was it worth it." But he concluded it *was* worth it because "I always had the feeling that if I worked for Lyndon Johnson, goodies would come to me. . . . I was on the make, too. . . . I wanted to improve myself." He was, however, also very independent—as independent as Latimer was dependent. In later life, he would never join a law firm, because he did not want partners; at the peak of his career, when he was earning impressive legal fees, he worked alone in a converted, book-lined garage behind his house in Corpus Christi. His willingness to work endless hours for Lyndon Johnson did not include a willingness to surrender his personality to him. He was afraid of surrendering his personality. "Lyndon was always in a position of command," he says. "I never felt equal. Ordinarily, I'm aggressive and belligerent. My nature is such that if I can't be an equal, I will not remain in a situation, and he was so demanding that— well, you lose your individuality if you allow someone to be too demanding for too long." A struggle—never stated but, Jones feels, understood by both men—went on. Johnson ridiculed the college education Jones had obtained with such effort, and of which he was so proud. Letters Jones wrote would be rejected, slashed across, and if Jones asked for an explanation, Johnson would say they were "too literary"—"Is that what they taught you at college, L.E.? Dumbest goddamned thing I ever read." A mistake in spelling in an L. E. Jones letter, recalls another man who spent some time in Kleberg's office, "was a very rare thing, but whenever there was one," Johnson "made quite a point of it—'My God, L.E., aren't you *ever* going to learn how to spell? Don't they teach you *anything* in college?' " For some time, Jones refused to surrender. If Johnson was discussing current events over dinner and Jones saw a parallel to something that had happened in Rome or Greece, he would mention it, despite Johnson's displeasure. If he disagreed with Johnson, he would express his disagreement; if he had an opinion, he would state it.

A surrender of sorts was to occur, however. Strikingly neat and clean— invariably well scrubbed, his hair carefully slicked down, every button buttoned on his double-breasted suits, his shirts highly starched—Jones was as aloof and reserved, almost prim, in physical matters as about everything else. "Any kind of coarseness or crudeness just disgusted him," a friend says. Johnson began making Jones take dictation from him while Johnson was sitting on the toilet.

The toilet in Kleberg's office suite was set in a short corridor between its two rooms. Johnson would sit down on it, and, Latimer says, "there would come a call: 'L.E.!' L.E. would say, 'Oh, God,' because he hated this." He would take his pad, and go to the bathroom. At first, he attempted to stand away from the door, but Johnson insisted he come right into the doorway, so he would be standing over him, and "L.E. would stand with his head and nose averted, and take dictation."

In later years, Johnson's penchant for forcing subordinates to watch him defecating would be called by some an example of a wonderful "naturalness." Others would find it, as one journalist put it, "in part, a method of control. Bring Douglas Dillon into the bathroom with you, and he has a little less independent dignity." This tactic was, indeed, "a method of control." The first person on whom it was employed was L. E. Jones—and those who observed it, knew it was being done to humiliate him, and to prove to him who was boss.

Jones had little choice but to accept the humiliation; the job was his only chance to realize his ambition. He continued working for Johnson for more than two years, until, in 1935, he had saved enough money to pay tuition at the University of Texas Law School, and then he left for Austin. He and Johnson were on friendly terms when he left—Johnson told him that when he finished law school, he would keep his promise and help him get a government job—but leave he did. To a friend who asked him why, he said he felt that if he stayed, "He'd be devoured."

(THE LATER Johnson-Jones relationship reveals the quality Johnson considered indispensable in a subordinate. He did indeed help Jones obtain a government job—as an attorney with the Justice Department in 1938—and kept in touch with him thereafter, when Jones was in private practice. In his most desperate crisis—the legal battle that climaxed the 1948 Senatorial election—he turned to him, asking Jones to join his legal team for the duration of the crucial appeal, and Jones did, indeed, join it. The end of the appeal, however, signaled the end of any working relationship.

The Johnson-Jones relationship contrasts sharply with that between Johnson and Latimer. Jones was the more intelligent of the two assistants— and Johnson's awareness of his brilliance is proven by the fact that Johnson turned to him in time of crisis. From four years of personal observation, moreover, Johnson must have realized that Jones would have been the hardest-working of aides. But, except for two brief periods of part-time employment, Jones would never again be on his payroll—and Latimer would be on it for much of his life.

What are the implications of this contrast? Was brilliance not enough to qualify a man for permanent work for Lyndon Johnson? Was hard work not enough? In fact, as would be demonstrated as soon as Johnson began hiring men on a large scale, the crucial qualification was subservience. Dignity was not permitted in a Johnson employee. Pride was not permitted. Utter submission to Johnson's demands, the submission that Jones called "a surrender of personality," a loss of "your individuality to his domination," was required. Otherwise, no matter how brilliant or hard-working, a man or woman could not work for Lyndon Johnson.)

14

The New Deal

For almost a year and a half after he went to work for Richard Kleberg, veterans were, in general, the only constituents for whom Lyndon Johnson could win victories. Though the mail sacks might be bulging with pleas for help, he had no help to give.

Outside San Antonio, the Fourteenth District was farming country, and for farmers the Crash had come long before 1929—with the resumption after the war of the great harvests of Europe; the 1920's had been one long bad decade for farmers. After Black Thursday, times grew worse. Prices fell, and fell, and fell again, until they reached levels "not seen in generations or even in centuries." By 1932, farmers were being paid twenty-five cents for a bushel of wheat, ten cents for a bushel of oats, seven cents for a bushel of corn—prices below what they had been in Colonial days; the prices of some farm commodities were, in actual value, at the level of the Middle Ages. While farmers were forced to sell low, they were also forced—in part by tariffs which kept high the price of manufactured goods—to buy dear. By 1930, it took a farmer almost three wagonloads of produce to buy the manufactured goods that one wagonload would have purchased in 1920. War-inflated crop prices had lured him into debt to buy more land and new machinery to work it, so that he could raise more crops. The plunge in crop prices made paying off that debt impossible; he was, in fact, forced to go deeper into debt just to purchase seed for another crop: the mortgage load on American farms, $3 billion when the war began, was $10 billion in 1930. The interest on those mortgages was so high that farmers could not pay it. During a five-year period ending March 1, 1932, one out of every eight farms in the United States would be up for forced sale because of mortgage or tax delinquencies.

All during the 1920's, farmers held out a hand to their government, but the administrations of Harding and Coolidge were deaf to their pleas. Seeing the industrialists of the Northeast prospering behind a wall of protective tariffs—tariffs that helped the Northeast at their expense—farmers asked for tariff reform. But when, in 1927, Congress finally passed the McNary-Haugen Bill for tariff reform, Coolidge vetoed it, claiming it violated the sacred principle of *laissez-faire*—"although," as the historian Frank Freidel notes, "on the very day of his . . . veto, he signed an order increasing by 50 percent the tariff on pig iron." In 1928, Congress passed McNary-Haugen again; Coolidge again vetoed it. In 1929, Herbert Hoover, Coolidge's Secretary of Commerce, builder of the immense Department of Commerce Building that was a temple to American business, became President, having carried forty of the forty-eight states. A new tariff bill was introduced; Hoover said that if it was passed he would veto it, so Congress didn't bother to pass it. Farmers asked for debt relief; Hoover's reply was that federal mortgages were already available, and so they were—from a federal agency whose directors seemed to feel they were running a company store, so onerous were the terms of its loans. By 1931, one out of every four of its borrowers was delinquent—and the agency was busily foreclosing: during 1931 alone, almost 4,000 American families were thrown off their farms by their government. Hoover's solution for falling farm prices was the creation of a Federal Farm Board empowered to stabilize farm prices by buying a farmer's produce for more than it was worth. While the Farm Board's right hand was working to implement this solution, however, its left hand was working against it. Even farmers, traditionally among the most independent and conservative of Americans, now were coming to understand that the heart of the problem was overproduction, that, as one writer put it, "surplus is ruin"; there was a surprising amount of agreement among farm groups that some kind of government limit on production was necessary. But the Farm Board, by paying high prices for crops while refusing to limit the amount grown, encouraged farmers to grow more rather than less; the funds Hoover committed to the Board, inadequate to begin with, ran out without even a dent being made in the agricultural crisis; the net result of its policies may, in fact, have made it worse. (Hoover's solution was to ask farmers—many of whom were unable to survive on what they were presently raising—to voluntarily raise less.)

By the time congressional secretary Lyndon Johnson arrived in Washington in December, 1931, the American farmer's long slide toward ruin had become a headlong plunge. Foreclosures on farms—many by rural banks which themselves were teetering on the brink of failure—had reached a rate of 20,000 per month. By the end of that year, one-quarter of Mississippi had been auctioned off, one-third of Iowa. Moreover, as William Allen White wrote, "Even though a man has no mortgage on his farm, even though he is not in immediate danger, he is, as a matter of fact, running behind. Every farmer, whether his farm is under mortgage or not, knows that with farm products priced as they are today, sooner or later he must go down. . . ."

The southern part of Texas' 200-mile-long Fourteenth Congressional

District had been insulated throughout the 1920's from the despair roaming the American countryside. The fall in cotton prices was cushioned by the quantity of the crop that could be produced in that four-foot-deep loam— in 1929, Nueces County, hub of the southern part of the district, produced 424,000 bales of cotton, more than any other county in the United States— and by the ease in getting it to market; since ships heading for Europe and the East Coast could dock, at Corpus Christi, within a few miles of the cotton fields, freighting costs and the cost in time were reduced to a minimum. "In many instances," exulted the *Corpus Christi Caller*, "cotton has been picked and ginned in the morning and compressed and loaded for export the same day." Even during the first year of the Depression, cotton buyers continued to crowd the seaport city with its row of tall office buildings along the bluff. But when the white bolls opened on the Gulf plain in 1931, warehouses throughout the world were still choked with unsold bales from the 1930 crop; few ships came, prices plummeted to six cents per pound, a level at which it didn't pay to grow cotton, and even at that price, there were few buyers. Only 330,000 bales would be picked along the Gulf in 1931—and 56,000 of these bales remained unsold. Prices for the onions and tomatoes and watermelons produced by the area's thousands of small truck farms dropped so low in that year that farmers let them rot on the vine.

Human evidence of the Depression's existence had begun to filter into Corpus Christi early, for railroads had laid tracks to the very beaches of the Gulf, and despite the railroads' diligence—the Southern Pacific boasted that its dicks threw 683,000 vagrants off its trains in 1931—the long lines of freight cars from the north now often carried, huddled in corners, or riding the rails underneath, human cargo which debarked when it reached Corpus Christi because that was the end of the line. For a while, local residents seemed to regard the Depression as something that couldn't happen to them; when it proved impossible to ignore the transients because of their number and importunity, they set up soup kitchens "for strangers seeking food . . . to keep [them] out of residential areas"; their attitude toward people who couldn't earn a living was condescending.

By 1931, however, with cotton unsold in the warehouses and tomatoes rotting in the fields, the lines at the soup kitchens were no longer composed entirely of strangers. Even prosperous Gulf Coast farmers were going into debt; by the end of the year, more than half of the 20,000 farms in the Fourteenth District were under mortgage. And now the debts were being called. Farmers saw SHERIFF'S SALE notices being tacked up on neighbors' houses—on the houses of men who worked as hard as they did; they saw neighbors loading their cars high with their possessions and driving away with their wives crying and their babies looking bewildered, and their older children's faces averted in shame. Some they never saw again; some they did, and wished they hadn't: they saw former neighbors, friends, living in shacks in Corpus Christi or Robstown or Alice, and seeking day work. So desperate were these men that they were willing to pick cotton even in the rain and mud; in the past, because a man must pick cotton on his knees, picking had never been done—at least not by white men—when the fields were muddy. And evicted South Texas farmers couldn't earn enough to support their families even by working in the mud; "My boy and I worked full nine hours Saturday and made ninety cents, or five cents per hour each," said one man who referred to himself as a former member of the middle class. More and more had to go on relief; so hard was it for these proud Texans to seek charity that they did not do so until they had sold everything they could sell. Many showed up at the Red Cross or Salvation Army staggering from weakness; they had refused to come in until they were literally starving. (Some of the men, a Salvation Army worker reported, would never have come in at all had it not been for their inability to watch their wives starve.)

With the approach of the winter of 1931–1932, the families living in the shacks needed heat and warm clothing as well as food. Appealing for donations of old stoves, Mrs. L. D. Berry, director of the local Red Cross, made clear that she meant wood stoves; "there is no need for gas stoves, as none of the families can afford gas," she noted. The families in the shacks were luckier than some families: they at least had shelter. A growing number of evicted farm families did not; elderly men and women, afraid they would die of exposure during the winter, advertised their services in exchange for room and board. The Salvation Army set up fifty cots in an empty warehouse that would once have been filled with cotton; hundreds of persons lined up to use them. Not only the elderly but the young were in need: children were growing out of their clothes and their shoes. Then Mrs. Berry started asking children in school what they had had to eat that day; as a result of their answers, she announced that the Red Cross must immediately begin providing at least one meal a day for 500 schoolchildren.

But the Red Cross had no money to do so. Relief funds were running out. Since President Hoover felt that any involvement in relief by the federal government would weaken the national character, relief remained the province of local municipalities and private agencies, and as winter approached, not only the municipalities of the Fourteenth District but its Red Cross and Salvation Army chapters and local relief committees were all running out of money. Bacon and onions were no longer ingredients in soup-kitchen meals; beans—plain beans—were what the hungry were given to eat. The Salvation Army had reduced its allocation for feeding each client to a penny per day. Its funds were virtually exhausted. And each day the soup-kitchen lines grew longer.

By the time Lyndon Johnson arrived in Washington, the district's arrogance was gone; its people were asking the government for help now—for government participation in relief funding; for government refinancing of farm mortgages; for government support of crop prices; and, more and more, because "surplus is ruin," for government-enforced crop controls. There was desperation in the mail sacks he opened each morning.

There was desperation in the mail sacks of almost every Congressman, it seemed. Americans everywhere were asking their government for help. Despair was stalking city streets as well as the countryside. In Chicago, 600,000 persons were unemployed, in New York, 800,000; the total of unemployed men in America's cities was between 15 million and 17 million, and many of these men represented an entire family in want. Witnesses were telling congressional committees that private charities had run out of money, that states and local municipalities which had attempted to shoulder the burden had run out of money—that, for want of federal assistance in relief, growing numbers of America's people were, literally, starving. During that session of Congress, there were reminders of the nation's plight not only in Washington's committee rooms but in Washington's streets—25,000 reminders: the penniless World War veterans who, in May, 1932, marched up Pennsylvania Avenue, their faces set in concentration as they tried to march in step as they had marched when they were young, and who then encamped with their wives and children in abandoned warehouses and empty stores, and in tents set up in parks, so that "Washington, D.C., resembled the besieged capital of an obscure European state."

But little help came from the government. When its legislative branch, which had, in December, 1931, turned a deaf ear to suggestions that it forgo its usual two-week holiday, returned in January, it was to begin seven months of wrangling and delay, enlivened only by Congressmen's near panic when they encountered Bonus Marchers; some Congressmen broke into a run when the ragged men approached. When Congress finally adjourned in July, 1932, the only substantial aid that had been given to farmers was a $125 million increase in the capital available for federal mortgages—an increase so far below the amount needed as to be all but meaningless, particularly since it was not accompanied, despite the pleas of farm organizations, by even a token easing in the onerous interest and repayment schedules. Despite the urgency of witnesses' pleas for help with relief funding, the Congressmen who had heard those pleas squabbled over minor details for weeks that turned into months—and the provisions of the bill that finally passed were so niggardly that the average relief stipend for a family of four would be fifty cents per day. As for the vital tax and tariff reform bill, special interest blocs squabbled over its provisions, and states traded tariff proposals back and forth until, in May, one Senator was moved to shout: "Have we gone mad? Have we no idea that if we carry this period of unrest from one week to another, a panic will break loose, which all the tariffs under heaven will not stem? Yet we sit here to take care of some little interest in this state or that. . . . 'My state! My state!' My God! Let's hear 'My country!' What good is your state if your country sinks into the quagmire of ruin!" For months, the *Forum* magazine said, "the country [has] been looking on, with something like anguish, at the spectacle of the inability of the national legislature, in a time of desperate need, to take any action— good, bad or indifferent—for dealing with the crucial problem of national finance." A columnist, more succinct, called the House of Representatives "The Monkey House," and his sentiment was echoed by some of the congressmen themselves; declared McDuffie of Alabama: "representative government is dead."

As FOR THE leader of the government's executive branch, when the Bonus Marchers begged Herbert Hoover to receive a delegation of their leaders, he sent word that he was too busy. Reinforced police patrols surrounded the White House; barricades were erected to close nearby streets to traffic; a *New York Daily News* headline proclaimed: HOOVER LOCKS SELF IN WHITE HOUSE. And in July, the President had the Army, with fixed bayonets and tear gas, drive the veterans out of Washington.

He handled the Depression with equal firmness. In December, 1929, he had said, "Conditions are fundamentally sound." In March, 1930, he said the worst would be over in sixty days; in May, he predicted that the economy would be back to normal in the Autumn; in June, in the midst of still another market plunge, he told a delegation which called at the White House to plead for a public works project, "Gentlemen, you have come sixty days too late. The Depression is over." In his December 2, 1930, message to Congress, he said that "the fundamental strength of the economy is unimpaired." Asked why, then, so many unemployed men were selling apples on street corners, he said: "Many people have left their jobs for the more profitable one of selling apples." His secretary noted that the President was beginning to regard some criticism as "unpatriotic." In 1932, his tune had not changed; in April of that year, a visitor was authorized to report that "Conditions are getting better. The President was in high spirits over the economic improvement." When delegations came to the White House begging him to endorse direct federal aid for relief, or increased spending on public works, he refused; "As long as I sit at this desk, they won't get by," he said. He couldn't bear to watch suffering, so he never visited a breadline or a relief station; as his limousine swept past men selling apples on street corners, he never turned his head to look at them. Even *Time* magazine, after more than two years of maintaining a façade almost as cheery as Hoover's, noted in 1932 that "the nation's needy have gone through three hard winters without a dollar's worth of direct aid from the Federal Treasury." Said Hoover: "Nobody is actually starving. The hoboes, for example, are better fed than they have ever been. One hobo in New York got ten meals in one day."

He wasn't starving. Having decided that economy in the President's kitchen would be bad for the country's morale, he continued eating at the most elaborate table ever set in the White House. Even when the only other diner was his wife, Lou, dinners were always seven courses; while Hoover, dressed always in black tie, ate his way through them, the dress blues of the Marine duty officers in the doorways provided ceremonial trappings, and butlers and footmen—all of them the same height—stood as rigid as statues, "absolutely silent, forbidden to move unbidden."

When, after months of haggling, Congress finally passed a public works bill, the President called it "an unexampled raid on the public treasury," and warned, "We cannot squander ourselves into prosperity." When Congress attempted to add to his request for $25 million for the relief of animals in Southern drought regions another $35 million so that humans as well as livestock might be fed, he refused to allow the measure, saying: "Prosperity cannot be restored by raids on the public treasury." When, finally, he became convinced that *some* government action was necessary, the action he selected was the creation of the Reconstruction Finance Corporation, which critics called a "breadline for big business," because of its emphasis on bailing out corporations, railroads, insurance companies and banks (big banks; in general, it would not help smaller institutions); the RFC's attitude toward suffering on a human scale was revealed when Congress in 1932 pushed through against the administration's wishes an act authorizing the agency to advance the states $300 million for relief; it deliberately dragged its feet, so that the states actually received only $30 million—exactly one-third of the amount the RFC's president had loaned his own bank. Herbert Hoover, said Breckenridge Long, "has set his face like flint against the American government's giving one cent to starving Americans." And when, in the Autumn of 1932, Hoover went to the country to campaign for another term, crossing states he had never visited since he had been elected four years before, the reception that greeted him was one that had been afforded no previous American President—not even Lincoln in Richmond in the last days of the Civil War; as the President's train was pulling into Detroit, the men on it heard a hoarse, rhythmic chant rising from thousands of throats; for a moment they had hopes of an enthusiastic reception—and then they made out the words of the chant: "Hang Hoover! Hang Hoover! Hang Hoover!" Mounted police charged the crowd, and the Secret Service hustled the President into a limousine for the four-mile drive to Olympic Stadium. And as the Presidential caravan sped past, those inside his limousine saw, through its thick windows, that the route was lined, block after block, with tens of thousands of men and women who were, in Gene Smith's words, "utterly silent and grim save for those who could be glimpsed shaking their fists and shouting unheard words and phrases." When, in St. Paul, the President defended his treatment of the Bonus Marchers, saying, "Thank God we still have a government in Washington that still knows how to deal with a mob," the crowd responded with one vast snarl, a snarl so vicious that the Secret Service chief suddenly found himself covered with sweat. As the President's train moved across his country, its people pelted the train with eggs and tomatoes. Four years before, he had carried forty of the forty-eight states; in 1932, he carried six.

DESPITE HIS REJECTION by the people in November, 1932, Hoover was going to be President until March, 1933—March which lay on the far side of the winter ahead. Although no fewer than 158 Congressmen had been defeated in November, they were going to be Congressmen until March.

That was a winter of despair. When, on December 5, 1932, the lame-duck Congress reconvened, those of its members who had hoped that the tear-gassing of the veterans had frightened the jobless away from Washington received a surprise; crowded around the Capitol steps were more than 2,500 men, women and children chanting, "Feed the hungry! Tax the rich!" Police armed with tear gas and riot guns herded the "hunger marchers" into a "detention camp" on New York Avenue, where, denied food or water, they spent a freezing night sleeping on the pavement, taunted by their guards. Thereafter, Congress met behind a double line of rifle-carrying police, who blocked the Capitol steps. And behind these body-guards, as the weeks of the terrible winter turned into months, Congress dawdled and wrangled as it had been dawdling and wrangling ever since the Depression began; sullenly, it deadlocked over the scores of competing relief proposals, while spending hours and days squabbling over whether to legalize beer and what percent of it should consist of alcohol. As for the man in the White House, he spent the interregnum maneuvering to tie his successor to his discredited policies. The program of the "President-reject," as *Time* called him, had the virtue of consistency; his State of the Union message called, as had his previous three messages, for economy in government and a balanced budget; the lone new proposal was for a sales tax that would fall hardest on those least able to afford it. With conditions worsening as rapidly as the weather, with the welfare rolls growing longer and longer, and the relief structure, so long crumbling, beginning to dis-integrate, he continued to withhold federal help.

As the people saw that their government was going to give them no leadership, there began to be heard throughout America the sound of hungry men on the march. In Columbus, Ohio, 7,000 men in ranks tramped toward the Statehouse to "establish a workers' and farmers' republic." Four thousand men occupied the Lincoln, Nebraska, Statehouse; 5,000 took over the Municipal Building in Seattle; in Chicago, thousands of unpaid teachers stormed the city's banks. A Communist Party rally in New York's Union Square drew an audience of 35,000.

.   .   .

IN THE CITIES, such outbreaks, while violent, were brief. It was in America's countryside that rebellion began to flare with a flame that, while fitful, did not die out—in the countryside, among the descendants of the People's Party, among the descendants of the Alliancemen. For half a century and more, America's farmers had been asking for tariff reform, for railroad and bank regulation, for government loans, for silver remonetization—for help in fighting forces too big for them to fight—and for half a century, their government had turned to them a very deaf ear. Now, starving, they asked again—often in words that echoed those spoken in Chicago thirty-six years earlier before an audience bearing silver banners that fluttered in the breeze; an Oklahoma rancher told a House subcommittee: "We will march eastward, and we will cut the East off. We will cut the East off from the West. We have got the granaries; we have the hogs, the cattle, the corn, and the East has nothing but mortgages on our places. We will show them what we can do." And this time, when their pleas were, as usual, unanswered, the House passed farm legislation; Hoover, calling it "wholly unworkable" (his *Memoirs* reveal that he had not taken the trouble to understand it), let it be known that he would veto it, and it died in the Senate—farmers reached for their pitchforks and their guns.

The previous summer, under the leadership of sixty-five-year-old Milo Reno, who had in fact been one of the early Populists, Iowa farmers, singing, "Let's call a farmers' holiday,/A holiday let's hold;/We'll eat our wheat and ham and eggs/And let them eat their gold," had refused to deliver milk to Sioux City, where distributors who bought it from them for two cents were selling it for eight cents—and, to enforce the strike, blocked every road leading into the city with spiked telegraph poles and logs. Warned by sympathetic telephone operators of the approach of police and sheriffs, they disarmed them and threw their pistols and badges into corn fields. The movement had spread—soon Des Moines, Council Bluffs and Omaha were isolated; when sixty insurgents were arrested in Council Bluffs, a thousand farmers marched on the jail and released them. That revolt had died away, but now, in the desperate interregnum winter, rebellion flickered and flared all across America's countryside. In Iowa, a mob of farmers, flourishing a rope, threatened to hang a lawyer who was about to foreclose on a farm. In Kansas, the body of a lawyer who had just completed foreclosure proceedings was found lying in a field. In Nebraska, the leaders of 200,000 debt-ridden farmers announced that if they didn't get help from the Legislature, they would march on the Statehouse and raze it brick by brick. A judge who had signed mortgage foreclosures was dragged from his bench by black-shirted vigilantes, blindfolded, driven to a lonely crossroads, stripped and beaten. And in scores of county seats in America's farm belt, the same scene was repeated: when a foreclosed farm was to be auctioned, crowds of armed farmers would appear at the courthouse; prospective bidders would be jostled and shoved until they left, and the farm would be "bid in" for a dollar or two, and returned to the original owner. The respect for institutions and public authority that holds societies together was beginning to vanish.

IN FEBRUARY, 1933, the country's banks began to close. Some 5,500 had already closed in the three years since the Crash. Few of the remaining 13,000 were healthy; they had a total of $6 billion in cash to meet $41 billion in deposits; should a wholesale run begin, they would have to cover the balance by selling securities and mortgages which had by now declined to a fraction of their previous value. And now the run was beginning. On February 14, 1933, Governor William A. Comstock of Michigan was told that Detroit's Union Guardian Trust Company was tottering, and that if it fell, every other bank in the city would go down with it. He was asked to declare a banking moratorium throughout Michigan, and at midnight he agreed, and issued a proclamation closing the state's 550 banks.

With the collapse in Michigan, suddenly there were long lines—of depositors withdrawing their savings—in front of tellers' windows in banks all across the country. On Monday, February 20, the Baltimore Trust Company paid out $1 million, on Tuesday $2 million; on Friday, February 24, it paid out in a single day more than $6 million. Governor Albert C. Ritchie closed Maryland's 200 banks; another state had gone under. On February 26, banks in Indianapolis and Akron announced that withdrawals would be limited to 5 percent of balances; by the next day, that policy had been adopted by a hundred Ohio banks. In neighboring Kentucky, banks began imposing similar restrictions. By March 1, frantic Governors had declared bank "holidays" in seventeen states. By noon on March 3, every bank in Kansas and Minnesota had closed, and closings had begun in North Carolina and Virginia. And in New York, opposite Grand Central Station, depositors had formed long lines to withdraw their money from the Bowery, the world's largest savings bank; in Chicago, bankers totaling their shrinking reserves realized that their institutions had paid out $350 million in two weeks. The nation's two great financial strongholds were at the brink of chaos.

CHAOS WAS THREATENING even those farm areas that had once seemed most secure—areas such as the one that Lyndon Johnson's Congressman represented. Revolt was flaring down on the Gulf. As the desperate winter of 1932 finally drew near its end, farmers applied to local banks for the usual seasonal loans for seed for the Spring planting—and were told that the banks had no money to lend. Soon the truth of that statement was demonstrated to them the hard way: a farmer who still had money in a bank would suddenly hear that the bank had closed.

To the farmers of South Texas, it was as if the very fabric of their society was ripping apart. One of the shuttered banks was the depository of the Corpus Christi School District; with the bank's doors closed, the school doors closed. Other school districts, dependent on property tax payments, found that with tax payments so sharply down, there was no money for teachers' salaries. Many children weren't going to school, anyway; they had to work "off the farm," work like field hands, for a nickel an hour. The education of their children had been so important to these farmers; now the children were no longer receiving an education.

Few farmers were free now from the dread of losing their homes. In 1933, only 38 percent of the farmers—about one out of every three—in once-prosperous Nueces County were able to pay their taxes; many were three years behind now, so penalties and interest had been piled atop the debt. And the abyss that gaped before them seemed bottomless. Farmers who had lost their land the year before had been able to go on relief, so that at least their families would not starve. Now relief organizations were all but out of funds. In February, the Corpus Christi branch of the Salvation Army announced that the last of its funds would be exhausted by the end of May.

Government couldn't, or wouldn't, help. Their local government was poor because they were poor. Their state government was dominated by what Populists called "the Interests." In January, 1933, Nueces County farmers joined farmers from all over Texas in asking the Legislature for passage of a bill authorizing the issuance of bonds to raise money for relief funding; the bill was defeated. Eleven bills providing for a tax moratorium were introduced in the Legislature in January and February, 1933, by its small group of Populists; lumping all eleven bills together for easy handling, the Legislature defeated them on February 11—although, just a few days before, it had been informed that without a moratorium, tens of thousands of Texas families would shortly lose their farms. Hope for assistance from the national government had long since faded. And when the farmers realized that there was going to be no help from government, they decided to help themselves—even if it meant breaking the law. The first Tuesday of each month was "foreclosure day" in Corpus Christi: the day on which foreclosed farms were auctioned off on the steps of the Nueces County courthouse. Twenty-five farms were scheduled for auction on Tuesday, March 7. At a rally on February 25, more than 1,500 grim farmers, after being told by a speaker, "I know you are here to see that the masses of the land get justness and fairness and right," vowed to be at the courthouse on March 7—with guns. Similar vows were being taken that week in county seats all across rural America. An entire nation was going up in flames, and its government seemed paralyzed; as James MacGregor Burns has written: "Crisis was in the air—but it was a strange, numbing crisis, striking suddenly in a Western city and then in the South a thousand miles away. It was worse than an invading army; it was everywhere and nowhere, for it was in the minds of men. It was fear."

ON MARCH 2, as his train pulled into Washington, two of his sons lifted Franklin Delano Roosevelt to his feet and snapped his heavy iron braces into place so that he could stand. Resting his full weight on his sons, he swung his legs, so terribly thin under his trousers, forward in the motion—so hard for him that after only a minute of it, sweat stood out on his brow— that made people think he was walking, and came off the train in Union Station as the flashbulbs popped. And on March 4, he jerked those crippled legs onto the high white platform that had been erected before the Capitol— and told the nation that all it had to fear was fear itself. (During the speech, his face had been set and grim—"so grim," reported Arthur Krock, "as to seem unfamiliar to those who have long known him." But when it ended, he threw back his head and suddenly he smiled his great, confident smile.)

First, he ended the banking crisis.

Although every bank in America had closed in the early-morning hours before the Inaugural, most could reopen safely if only their depositors' confidence was restored. In part, their confidence was restored by legislation. The Roosevelt administration's first bill provided for the reopening of banks under Treasury Department licenses that in effect guaranteed their soundness; if a specific bank did not have sufficient funds, the Federal Reserve Board would lend funds against the bank's assets. But mostly, their confidence was restored by *his* confidence. When he smiled on the crisis, it seemed to vanish. After the legislation had passed—in a single day —Franklin D. Roosevelt held, on March 12, his first "Fireside Chat." "I want to talk for a few minutes . . . about banking," he said. "When the people find out that they can get their money—that they can get it when they want it—the phantom of fear will soon be laid. . . . I can assure you that it is safer to keep your money in a reopened bank than under the mattress." When the banks began reopening the next morning, the long lines were gone. Depositors put back their money so quickly, in fact, that in a single day the excess of deposits over withdrawals was more than $10 million in the Federal Reserve Districts alone.

Then he turned to the farm crisis.

That crisis was not weeks old, but decades—except for a few periods of prosperity such as that caused by the World War, the condition of America's farmers had been worsening steadily for more than a century. But Roosevelt turned to it not reluctantly but with a will. On March 16, twelve days after he had taken office, he sent farm legislation, accompanied by a special message, to Congress.

The words of the message, five paragraphs long, were words that farmers—and their fathers and grandfathers—had been waiting all their lives to hear. "At the same time that you and I are joining in emergency action to bring order to our banks," he told Congress, ". . . I deem it of equal importance to take other and simultaneous steps. . . . One of these . . . seeks to increase the purchasing power of our farmers and . . . at the same time greatly relieve the pressure of farm mortgages. . . ." *Of equal importance*—of equal importance to *banks!* For generations, farmers had been begging their government to recognize their problems as it recognized those of institutions such as banks; they had been pleading for acknowledgment that they were as important to their government, as worthy of its help, as the institutions in which they deposited their money. Now, in a phrase, the recognition and the acknowledgment had been conferred.

Embodied in the bill were concepts for which farmers had long been pleading. It made provision at last for the reduction of the surplus that was ruin: farmers would be paid to take acreage out of production, the money for the payment to be raised by a tax on the processors and distributors and speculators who had grown rich off farmers. It made provision for "parity" (a synonym for "justice"). Said the bill's Section 2—in words some elderly Populists could hardly believe they were reading: *"It is hereby declared to be the policy of Congress to establish and maintain such balance between the production and consumption of agricultural commodities . . . as will re-establish prices to farmers at a level . . . equivalent to the purchasing power . . . in the pre-war period. . . ."* Even more significant than the specific provisions was the tone of the five paragraphs, which contrasted so strongly with the pomposity of Hoover, and of Coolidge and Harding. He didn't know whether what he was going to try would work, the new President said: "I tell you frankly that it is a new and untrod path." But he was going to try. "I tell you with equal frankness that an unprecedented condition calls for the trial of new means." And if these means didn't work, he said, he would be the first to admit it. And then he would try something else.

And three weeks later, there was another message. Convinced by Progressives, the spiritual heirs of the People's Party, that the first bill was not sufficient, Roosevelt sent up another. "I ask the Congress for specific legislation relating to the mortgage and other forms of indebtedness of the farmers of the nation," he said. The proposed legislation was revolutionary in concept; it would use federal credit agencies to drive down the high interest rates that farmers were paying by refinancing their mortgages at 4½ percent, and it would give them longer to pay. The legislation was revolutionary—monumental—in scope: $2 *billion* would be allocated for the plan. The legislation was ingenious; through a complicated arrangement that would ease the burden on the Treasury, banks and other mortgage holders could exchange unpaid mortgages for Federal Land Bank bonds paying interest at 4 percent, an exchange the banks would be happy to make, since it would guarantee them a 4 percent return, while at the moment they

were guaranteed only possession of farm land that no one would want to
buy from them. And the legislation was only just:

> That many thousands of farmers in all parts of the country
> are unable to meet indebtedness incurred when their crop prices
> had a very different money value is well known to all of you . . .
> [Roosevelt said].
>
> The Federal Government should provide for the refinancing
> of [such] indebtedness so as to accomplish a more equitable re-
> adjustment of the principal of the debt, a reduction of interest rates,
> which in many instances are so unconscionably high as to be con-
> trary to a sound public policy, and, by a temporary readjustment
> of amortization, to give sufficient time to farmers to restore to them
> the hope of ultimate free ownership of their own land.

Some of the Progressives felt he still hadn't done enough. After all,
the Populist Party had in 1892 asked also for currency inflation and for
remonetization of silver; now Senators Elmer Thomas of Oklahoma and
Burton K. Wheeler of Montana and others who had picked up the Populists'
fallen banner and had fought as the "farm bloc" all through the 1920's took
up those demands again. The tall, earnest Thomas, who had campaigned for
William Jennings Bryan, said,

> Agriculture does not demand a fifty-cent dollar or an unsound
> dollar, but does protest the retention of the 200-cent dollar. A
> dollar which fluctuates in purchasing power from 50 cents in 1920
> to 200 cents in 1933 is neither sound nor an honest dollar.

At first, Roosevelt balked. ("Burt," he said to Wheeler, "Bryan killed the
remonetization of silver in 1896.") Then he compromised, accepting amendments providing for remonetization and a mild inflation. For five long weeks,
the Senate tried to stall, but it couldn't stand before him: said one Senator
from a traditionally Republican state, "We gave Franklin D. Roosevelt a
160,000 majority. We had confidence in Franklin D. Roosevelt. We still
have confidence in Franklin D. Roosevelt." On May 10, the omnibus Farm
Relief Act passed the Senate. On May 12, the President signed it into law.
For decades, while their fortunes fell and fell, farmers had been asking for
the measures embodied in that Farm Relief Act, and in all those years no
action of lasting significance had been taken in their behalf. It hadn't taken
Franklin D. Roosevelt a Hundred Days to give them that action. He had
needed only sixty-nine.

And on May 13, when Lyndon Johnson opened the usual letters from
constituents asking for help, there was help available for him to give them.

. . .

THERE WAS a desperate urgency to the task of the new Agricultural Adjustment Administration. Its mission was to reduce crops, and with every passing day, more crops were being planted as Spring spread north across America —the AAA was working against the sun. All the organizational problems that might be anticipated in a gigantic administrative machine created in such haste were present in the Agriculture Department's huge South Building, where clerks were struggling to reduce a nation's agriculture to millions of punched cards running over and over through automatic tabulating machines, each card representing a farmer, his farm, and his complex crop-reduction agreements with the government. Not even in existence in April, by the end of May the AAA had 5,000 employees; the seven-story South Building, as big as three city blocks, was a sea of desks, its miles of corridors crowded with delegations of cotton growers, wheat growers and dairymen, with packers and processors, with farm leaders and reporters. So bitter was an ideological split at the new agency's upper levels between its traditionalist farmer-agrarians and its new visionary reformers and urban lawyers that both sides, as one observer noted, were using "that saddest and shabbiest of tricks employed by zealots within any organization—the trick of holding up papers or decisions at bottlenecks, or of burying them in details, or of trucking them out with such bureaucratic harness or baggage as delays or kills actions." Power struggles were also virulent because the AAA was not under civil service, and a large number of politicians had found places in it. In the daily skirmishes, bureaus were shifted from one agency to another, or abolished entirely overnight, their work parceled out among other bureaus, which might or might not be informed of their new responsibilities. The AAA was "the despair," in another's words, "of everyone having to do with it," a monstrous bureaucratic maze.

Assistance from his Congressman would have been helpful to Lyndon Johnson in finding his way through this maze, but in the Spring Dick Kleberg spent his time at Burning Tree. ("Mr. Dick" was not disposed to cooperate with the AAA anyway. He would, in fact, have voted against the AAA, which he called "socialistic" and "radical," even after Johnson told him that mail from his district was running thirty to one in favor of the measure, had not Johnson, and the pragmatic Roy Miller, assured him that his vote didn't matter because the bill was going to pass by an overwhelming margin.)

So Johnson found his own way—found it himself, after he had paved it himself. Telephoning an AAA bureaucrat, he would introduce himself as "Congressman Kleberg—from the Agriculture Committee," and ask the bureaucrat to give all assistance possible to his secretary, Lyndon Johnson. Not long thereafter, Secretary Johnson would show up at the bureaucrat's office.

Other secretaries similarly used their Congressmen's names on the telephone to gain entrée, although not as brazenly (or as frequently; it was almost matter of course for Johnson to introduce himself as Congressman Kleberg now). But what he did with that entrée was not at all usual. "He was smiling and deferential," Tommy Corcoran, a keen observer of the Washington scene, was to say of Johnson, "but hell, lots of guys can be smiling and deferential. He had something else. No matter what someone thought, Lyndon would agree with him—would be there ahead of him, in fact. He could follow someone's mind around—and figure out where it was going and beat it there. . . ." And he touched every base; leaving a bureaucrat's office, he smiled and chatted with his assistants and his secretaries until, soon, he had entire bureaus, top to bottom, willing to help him.

He was pushing farmers as well as bureaucrats. Confused by the complexity of the new programs and distrustful of government promises that they would actually receive money for plowing up crops, farmers all across America were hesitating to sign AAA applications and plow-up contracts. Many of the Agricultural Extension Service's county agents, whom the AAA had been counting on to educate farmers about the new programs, didn't understand the programs, and others, Republican-appointed, long in their jobs and deeply conservative, were unwilling to cooperate with "socialism." Lyndon Johnson educated his district himself; hour after hour he sat in Room 1322 telephoning his county agents; when he heard about an influential farmer who was balking, he telephoned the farmer. The nationwide progress of the cotton sign-up program was so slow in 1933, despite two appeals by Roosevelt for cooperation, that on July 11 Secretary of Agriculture Henry Wallace was forced to announce that the program would be canceled if the sign-up rate did not double. At the time Wallace made that announcement, the sign-ups from the Fourteenth Congressional District of Texas had already far exceeded the district's quota. Applications and plow-up contracts from other districts became stalled or lost in the South Building because the bureau to which they were addressed no longer handled them, and no one seemed to know who did. Johnson knew—and he saw to it that applications from his district were sent to the right office. After they arrived, he would show up at that office and get them moved to the top of the huge piles awaiting action. With approval from a dozen different bureaus required for each contract, contracts from other districts might be stalled for months. Johnson would show up at each bureau—and contracts from the Fourteenth District were approved and back in the mail within days. In a White House ceremony on July 28, 1933, President Roosevelt presented the first AAA check for plowed-under cotton. Its recipient was farmer William E. Morris—of the Fourteenth District's Nueces County.

. . .

THE COTTON PLOW-UP PAYMENTS enabled South Texas farmers to make their monthly mortgage payments, but were insufficient to enable them to pay their arrears. The machinery established by Roosevelt for assistance with these arrears—the mortgage-refinancing Federal Land Bank—was not yet in gear. Not only was refinancing more complicated than plowing up crops, refinancing required an appraisal of each individual farm, and during the first three weeks of September alone, 2,631 desperate Texas farmers applied for refinancing to the Federal Land Bank's Houston office—whose appraisal staff consisted of nine men. Before the machinery could get in gear, many farms would be lost. Banks and mortgage companies, already overstocked with farms they could not sell, did not want more farms if they could instead get the money they were owed on them, but, by Fall, they had decided they could wait for it no longer. In October, sheriffs tacked up foreclosure notices on sixty-seven farms in the Fourteenth District, farms for which the Roosevelt rescue operation was going to come too late.

With Congress in recess, the district's Congressman was home in Corpus Christi. The farmers appealed to him for help, asking for a meeting. The Congressman was not disposed to grant them one, seeing no way in which he could help them, but his secretary said the meeting should be held. He had thought of a plan.

Only the furnishing of new collateral would persuade the mortgage companies to wait for their money. The farmers felt they didn't have any collateral, and in the traditional sense they didn't: their savings, even the butter-and-egg money, were long gone; not only every acre of land but every piece of machinery was already mortgaged. But Lyndon Johnson had thought of new collateral: crops that hadn't been planted yet. The farmers, he thought, should each agree to give their mortgagor a landlord's share—a third—of the 1934 crop in exchange for a year's extension on the mortgage. The mortgage companies might not normally agree to this, but Johnson felt they would now if they could be given assurances that the extension would enable them to get their money, not only current interest payments but the arrears as well. And Johnson had conceived an innovation that would give farmers enough money to pay their arrears. The richness of the black loam of the Gulf Coast had made its farmers prosperous in good times. Johnson wanted to use the richness of the soil to help them in bad times as well. He wanted the Federal Land Bank to agree to take soil productivity into account in deciding how much to lend on a farm. Such an innovation would mean considerably more money for each farmer than the Federal Land Bank had previously been willing to lend—enough money to pay the mortgage arrears. The mortgage companies would also, he knew, want assurances that they would get their money on time—within the year's extension. At the present slow pace at which the Federal Land Bank had been moving, no one could be assured of that. So he wanted the pace accelerated. He wanted the Land Bank to promise the mortgage companies that it would give priority to loan applications from the Fourteenth District. He needed, in other words, commitments both for a new policy and for speed in implementing it.

He got them. To obtain the commitments, two requirements had to be met. A Federal Land Bank official had to be persuaded to come to Corpus Christi and meet personally with the farmers; Johnson was sure that a face-to-face meeting with these desperate men could not help but win the official's sympathy. And the official had to be high enough in rank to give commitments on the Land Bank's behalf, so that his sympathy would be translated into the immediate action needed. In dealing with the Land Bank, he had a weapon available: the deputy governor of the bank's parent body, the Farm Credit Administration, was W. I. Myers, an old friend of Dick Kleberg. Tracking down Myers, who was visiting Dallas, Johnson put Kleberg on the phone with him—and the old friend agreed to come to Corpus Christi himself for the meeting, and to bring with him the president of the Federal Land Bank's Houston office, A. C. Williams. Then Johnson began telephoning; all day, he telephoned bankers and mortgage-company representatives; at night, when they were in from the fields, he telephoned farmers. And on the evening of October 27, sixty-seven farmers—sixty-seven men who had given their lives to their land, and then had received notices saying that the land would be taken away from them—trooped onto the broad, shady porch of Dick Kleberg's enormous home overlooking the Gulf in Corpus Christi to meet there with the men who had sent the notices—"the largest gathering of farm credit leaders ever held in South Texas," the *Caller* termed it—and with the two men who could provide the money to save their land. Kleberg's tall, skinny secretary explained his proposal, and everyone accepted it: the farmers agreed to write letters to the mortgage companies promising them a third of their crop; the government promised to speed—and to liberalize—mortgage refinancing; and the mortgage holders agreed to accept the letters and the promises, and to take down the foreclosure notices. Myers went off to the King Ranch for a few days of hunting—after first, at Johnson's discreet urging, telephoning the head of the Land Bank appraisal division in Houston. Within a week, all sixty-seven farms had been appraised and refinanced; by the end of the year, Federal Land Bank mortgages, stretching out amortization payments from five years to fifteen, and reducing interest payments from 8 percent to 4, had been given to every endangered farm in South Texas.

DURING THAT SUMMER of 1933, as farmers plowed up tens of millions of acres of cotton (whipping their mules, which had been trained not to step on plants, to make them pull the plows over the cotton rows), farm prices rose to ten cents a pound, but by Autumn they were falling again. Because of bureaucratic difficulties, moreover, many farmers had not received their first AAA payments.

If what he was trying didn't work, the President had promised, he would try something else. In October, he tried something else: to offset the drop in prices, he established a Commodity Credit Corporation to lend ten cents a pound on cotton to farmers who agreed in advance to participate in the 1934 crop-reduction program. This shored up prices, and as Winter began, the AAA and Farm Credit Administration programs began to take hold: benefit payments, commodity loans and mortgage refinancing contracts began to flow out to farmers, the currency expansion they had so long demanded at last took place—for American farmers, the long, desperate decades were finally over. For the first time, moreover, farmers could plan ahead without the fear that forces beyond their control made planning senseless; for the first time they possessed a measure of meaningful control over their destiny: beyond its immediate benefits, AAA programs gave farmers what they had thought they could never have—a kind of insurance against ill fortune: As the *Corpus Christi Caller* put it: they can "know almost to the cent how much money they will receive in benefit payments during the year [despite] the vagaries of the weather. . . ."

Whatever the New Deal program, Johnson reaped for his district every dollar it could provide. He urged district farmers to repay their 1933 crop-reduction loans as quickly as possible, so that they could get new loans—so that, as a press release from Congressman Kleberg's office put it, "the record for this section would remain on the favorable basis established and so that this section would be in a position to ask for consideration on any farm matters which might arise in the future." On November 19, 1933, the AAA announced that the Fourteenth Congressional District of Texas had the best loan-repayment record of any of the nation's 435 congressional districts. And in 1934, the district received the type of "consideration" Johnson had had in mind; it was the first congressional district to have every one of its crop-reduction loan applications approved by the AAA. (Eighty-five percent of its farmers had applied for these loans, a figure that may itself have been the highest for any congressional district in the nation—the figures are unclear on this point.)

Most Congressional offices closed during the five-or six-month congressional recess; during the recess, Johnson returned with Kleberg to Corpus Christi—but kept either Latimer or Jones in Washington, so that the office of the Fourteenth District never closed. Assistance was always available with applications for loans from the AAA, or the Federal Land Bank, or the new Homeowners Loan Corporation that was established to provide urban homeowners with the same protection against foreclosure as farmers. So effective was this assistance that, by the end of 1934, the *Caller* said that "Corpus Christi and the South Texas area [are] suffering less under the business depression than any other section of the nation." This statement may have been an exaggeration, but specific figures are impressive testimony to Johnson's diligence. The Fourteenth District was the first of the nation's 435 congressional districts to have all its AAA loan applications approved; as for Federal Land Bank applications, during the first ten months the program was in operation—the only ten months for which this figure is available—not a single loan request from the Fourteenth District was turned down. Although district-by-district figures are not available for the Home-owners Loan Corporation, 450 HOLC loans were made in Corpus Christi alone, a figure which appears to be the highest in the United States for a city of its size. As other New Deal programs—CWA, PWA, WPA—were inaugurated, the district received more than its share of these, too—so many CCC camps (one, at Floresville, was named for Kleberg), for example, that when, in 1936, the government established limits to the number in any one district, the Fourteenth was a distinct embarrassment.

Four hundred and thirty-five Congressional districts: among them districts represented by Congressmen of long seniority whose favor even a President had to court; among them districts represented by Congressmen who chaired powerful committees; among them districts represented by Congressmen who were allies of the New Deal; among them districts represented by Congressmen who worked hard for their districts. Few districts fared better under the New Deal's programs than this district with a junior Congressman who opposed the New Deal, a Congressman who seldom visited his office—this district whose only asset on Capitol Hill was a young secretary who worked for it with a frantic, frenzied, almost desperate aggressiveness and energy.

15

The Boss of the Little Congress

A VETERAN TEXAS POLITICIAN, watching Lyndon Johnson, at the age of twenty-one, ramrodding eight tough districts in a Lieutenant Governor's race, had called him a "wonder kid" of politics. Welly Hopkins, watching him work "all the byways" of Blanco, Comal, and Guadalupe counties, had spoken of his "very unusual" political ability. The same ability had been evident even earlier—in San Marcos, where Lyndon Johnson had not only captured campus politics, but had created campus politics. Now what his brother called his "natural vocation" was to be seen on a larger stage.

There existed in Washington an organization called "The Little Congress."

It was a moribund organization. Formed in 1919 to provide congressional secretaries with experience in public speaking and a knowledge of parliamentary procedures, it was modeled on the House of Representatives and held debates under House rules. But it had degenerated into little more than a social club, whose desultory meetings, held in the Cannon Building's chandeliered Caucus Room, were attended by no more than a few dozen secretaries.

But the White Stars of San Marcos had also been considered a social club. In April, 1933, Johnson approached a few carefully selected fellow residents of the Dodge Hotel and asked them to help him become the "Speaker," or presiding officer, of the Little Congress.

As in the House of Representatives, seniority and line of succession had determined the selection of previous Speakers: at each election, only one new officer, a sergeant-at-arms, always an older man with long Washington tenure, was chosen; the other officers each simply moved up one notch, the former sergeant-at-arms being nominated for clerk and the clerk being nominated for Speaker; there was never any opposition. Johnson, however, had a plan to sidestep this practice.

The plan depended on secrecy. By counting votes, says William H. Payne, who ran for sergeant-at-arms on the Johnson ticket, Johnson had determined that so many new secretaries had been brought to Capitol Hill in March by the new Congressmen elected in the Roosevelt landslide that their votes would give him the Speakership—if the older secretaries, who still far outnumbered the newer ones, did not realize what he was planning and turn out in force at the April meeting. To minimize chances of discovery, he waited to launch his campaign until only a day or two before the election, and when he campaigned, he campaigned not in person but by telephone—remaining in Kleberg's office and calling new secretaries in other congressional offices to ask for their votes—so that there would be as little activity visible as possible. He had discovered another cache of votes: although only congressional secretaries had attended past meetings of the Little Congress and there existed a general impression that only secretaries were eligible for membership, the organization's bylaws actually made any person on the "legislative payroll"—which included Capitol Hill mailmen, policemen and elevator operators appointed under congressional patronage —eligible, so long as he paid his two-dollar dues. Johnson told Latimer to round up his mailmen friends, and bring them to the meeting—and he told Latimer not to tell them about the meeting until the last possible moment. He asked a friendly elevator operator to do the same with the other elevator men—and repeated the enjoinder of secrecy. And on the night of April 27, 1933, as a few handfuls of Little Congress regulars sat all but lost in the rows of seats in the spacious Caucus Room, they were taken completely by surprise when, just as the meeting was about to begin, there suddenly burst into the room enough people with unfamiliar faces to elect as Speaker a tall, thin twenty-four-year-old from Texas, whom few of the older men even knew. "Who is that guy?" one asked as Johnson came forward to take the gavel.

(When, the next day, the older men collected their wits, they had other questions: about the honesty of the election. Many of the votes that had elected Johnson, they said, had been cast by men not eligible to vote. Many of the mailmen and elevator operators who had shown up for the first time had not paid their dues, they said, and hence were not members of the Little Congress. Moreover, they said, many of the new voters could not *be* members even if they paid dues: Johnson's supporters, they charged, had simply rounded up every Capitol Hill employee they could find, whether or not the employee had been appointed under congressional patronage. There were complaints that, as Lucas puts it, "He stole that election." If the charge was true, the election was, of course, the second he had stolen.)

· · ·

JOHNSON'S ACCEPTANCE SPEECH was somewhat derivative from a speech delivered a month before by another man lately come to Washington. "My election," he said, "will mark a New Deal for all Little Congresses." (He also promised to "be mindful" of the "forgotten man," by naming committees on "an equitable basis of membership and seniority.") Derivative or not, however, a new deal was what he delivered: he transformed the Little Congress of Capitol Hill as he had transformed the White Stars of College Hill. He turned a social organization into a political organization—into an organization, moreover, to serve his own ends.

One of those ends was entrée—the entrée a congressional staffer needed but found so hard to obtain. Henceforth, Johnson announced, meetings would be held not every month but every week, and would include not only debates but speeches by "prominent figures." And although the new Speaker declared that the reason for this innovation was to make the meetings livelier, his teen-age assistants knew that there was another reason as well: says Latimer, "It gave him an excuse to go and see Huey Long or Tom Connally or a Texas Congressman who was head of a committee he thought he might need for something, and invite them to speak, and once he got in to see somebody, the Chief, being the way he was, would make them remember him."

Another end was publicity. First, he organized the Little Congress debates. Previously, anyone who wished could speak; now only assigned speakers could take the floor during the sixty minutes allotted to each side. He made the assignments, naming teams to represent both sides of an issue currently before Congress (one "floor leader" would generally be the aide of the Congressman who had introduced the bill, the other the aide of a Congressman who opposed it); kept checking with the leaders to make sure they were actively organizing their teams; further formalized the atmosphere by assigning speakers places at the long witness table that ran across the front of the Caucus Room. Sitting at the center of the long, raised horseshoe dais, used by congressional committees, he ran the debates strictly. Says Payne: "The first time he presided, everyone knew: by George, here was a man who was running the show. The Little Congress was run by the same rules as the House of Representatives, and he knew those rules. He was his own parliamentarian, and there wasn't anyone who could argue with him about whether the proceedings were proceeding according to the rules, because he *knew* them. He was in *command.*" At the end of each debate, the Little Congress voted on the "bill." Once he had the debates organized, he asked newspapers to cover them. Congressional aides generally reflected their bosses' feelings, he told reporters, and Little Congress votes on pending legislation were therefore previews of upcoming votes in the Big Congress. Moreover, since the Little Congress floor leaders were the same men who were helping their bosses prepare to lead the upcoming fights in the House, the debates would provide a preview not only of votes but of maneuvers to come. The reporters came—and were impressed; "one of the most interesting forums in Washington," the *Washington Post* said. Finding that House votes could indeed be predicted on the basis of voting in the Little Congress, they began to cover it fairly regularly. Payne recalls: "Every week there'd be a meeting, and every week there would be stories in at least a couple of the Washington papers"—and stories on the Little Congress generally contained a statement from, or at least a mention of the name of, its Speaker. The chance for press coverage made even the most famous political figures receptive to Johnson's invitations to address it. When Johnson said he was inviting the colorful and controversial Huey Long to speak, recalls another Little Congress member, Wingate Lucas, "none of us thought he could pull it off." But sure enough, Long came—the Caucus Room was, another member says, "just crowded with newsreel cameras. Pathé News and Metro News and all that. . . . There were lights all over the place, these movie lights. A tremendous number of reporters were there." And when Long came into the room, surrounded by a phalanx of tough-looking bodyguards, the Speaker of the Little Congress was there to welcome him, shaking his hand and smiling at him as the flashbulbs popped and the cameras rolled.

Soon, 200 or more Congressional aides were crowding into the Caucus Room every week. Johnson organized other events—including a three-day trip, which many secretaries remember vividly forty-five years later, on which 293 secretaries toured New York City with a motorcycle escort provided by Mayor La Guardia, and, in the evening, were the Mayor's guests at Radio City Music Hall. Then the Congressional aides went on to West Point, from which they returned to Washington by train. "I remember Lyndon roaming up and down the aisles, from car to car, eyes flashing, smiling, too excited to sit still," Payne says. The annual banquet, held at the Mayflower Hotel, became an elaborate affair, with prominent speakers and formal dress. Says Lucas, who, some years later, would be Speaker himself: "Little Congress became *quite* a big thing. When we had a debate, members of Congress would show up. To hear the points on each side and to get an indication of how the members themselves would vote. Members [of Congress] wanted their bills debated by the Little Congress for publicity, and because it would help prepare them for debate on the floor. A Congressman would come to you and say, 'I'd like to get the Little Congress to debate one of my bills.' I remember one Congressman from California doing this. He had a copy of his bill in his pocket, and he gave it to me, and he gave me a pitch for it. So if you were Speaker, you were respected by members of Congress, and *called upon* by members of Congress." In a remarkably short time—taking into account congressional recesses which he spent back in Texas, in less than a year spent on Capitol Hill—Lyndon Johnson had, through an organization in which advancement had previously depended upon longevity on the Hill, lifted himself dramatically out of the anonymous crowd of congressional aides.

Little Congress bylaws allowed a Speaker only a single term. While Johnson made no attempt to change the bylaws—in the opinion of at least one ally, because there had already been too many rumors about the circumstances under which he had been elected—he kept control of the organization through hand-picked candidates. He never campaigned publicly for them. "Word just circulated around that so-and-so was Johnson's candidate," Payne says. "He did everything behind the scenes." But behind the scenes he was very effective. A half-dozen Johnson allies—all distinguished by their willingness to defer to his orders—would telephone other members before each election to suggest who should be supported. Members who, in the open balloting, failed to follow the suggestion did not thereafter receive invitations to speak, and it became understood that antagonizing Lyndon Johnson was not a good idea for anyone who wanted to advance in the only organization in which, for congressional secretaries, advancement was possible. "He had a machine," says secretary Lacey Sharp. "And if you wanted to run, you had better have the blessings of Lyndon Johnson." The machine's existence had become an acknowledged reality in the self-contained little world of Capitol Hill. Another secretary, newly arrived on the Hill, recalls seeing Johnson for the first time. Struck by his appearance—his height, his huge ears, his flashing eyes and smile, the confidence with which he walked, arms akimbo, down a House Office Building corridor—the secretary asked a friend who he was. Replied the friend: "That's the Boss of the Little Congress."

DID HIS VOCATION—his "very unusual ability"—work only with contemporaries? Only with the congressional secretaries who were his equals in rank? The Speakership of the Little Congress may have furnished him entrée to officials other secretaries never got to talk to; it was the use he made of the entrée that awed those contemporaries who had a chance to see him use it.

At the Department of Agriculture, for example, the hundreds of patronage jobs created by the new AAA programs were dispensed by three tough Tammany politicians: Julien N. Friant, special assistant to the Secretary of Agriculture and Jim Farley's personal representative in the department, and Friant's assistants, Vincent McGuire and Lee Barnes. Even Congressmen had difficulty getting these men on the phone; for most congressional secretaries, personal communication was all but impossible. But congressional secretary Lyndon Johnson wanted another assistant to help with his district's mail, and, with no more room on the district's payroll, he wanted the assistant, Russell M. Brown, a young law student from Rhode

Island, put on Agriculture's. Aware of the inaccessibility of Agriculture's personnel trio, Brown was startled when Johnson said casually that they would run over and see them. He was even more startled by the reception Johnson received. When Johnson told McGuire, whose office they went into first, "Mac, I got to have a job for Russ here," Mac replied simply, "I can arrange it, Lyndon." ("That's great," McGuire added with a smile, "Texas helping Rhode Island.") Then McGuire asked Johnson, "Would you like to say hello to the boss?" and they all strolled down to Friant's office, where the reception was equally warm. ("The Chief and Friant got along fine," Latimer remembers. "I don't even know how they got to know each other, but anything Friant could do for the Chief, he was happy to do.")

Brown was to receive a larger shock. While they were chatting in Friant's office, the door opened, and in walked Friant's boss, the great personnel director himself, chief patronage dispenser of the New Deal, Postmaster General James A. Farley. Brown stared almost speechless at this living legend, but Farley, he says, "was very affable and shook hands." And Lyndon Johnson, who had met Farley when the Postmaster General had accompanied Vice President Garner to the King Ranch some months before, was affable right back. "This is my friend Russell Brown from Rhode Island," he said. Farley, who never forgot a name—or a political affiliation —remembered something McGuire and Friant hadn't. He asked Brown if he was Charles Brown's son, and then said to Friant: "What are you doing helping a Republican?" A moment of tension ensued, but it evaporated when Johnson, putting his arm around Brown, said expansively: "He's *mah* Republican." Everyone burst out laughing, Brown recalls, with the Postmaster General, beaming at Johnson, laughing loudest of all.

Other Capitol Hill aides witnessed similar scenes. Not only, they came to realize, did Lyndon Johnson know powerful officials who were in a position to help him, these officials knew *him*, knew him and liked him—and *wanted* to help him. A measure of this feeling was the number of patronage jobs Johnson obtained in the AAA and other newly formed New Deal agencies such as the Homeowners Loan Corporation and the Federal Land Bank. Such jobs were generally rationed by the New Deal on the basis of a Congressman's importance. The office of the average Congressman might be given four or five, the office of a senior or powerful Congressman perhaps twenty, the office of a committee chairman as many as thirty, or, in rare cases, forty. The office of Richard Kleberg, a Congressman with neither seniority nor power, was given fifty.

DID HIS ABILITY with the powerful consist merely of the capacity to make friends with them?

One Texan notably unmoved by Johnson's charm was Vice President Garner, whose desire for new friendships was limited. "Me and my wife," tough old Cactus Jack explained once. "My son and his wife. We four—and no more." As for his paternal instincts toward bright young men, even his son was able to obtain a loan from him only after he had agreed to pay a very high rate of interest. In May, 1933, the Texas Legislature redrew the state's congressional districts. Seeing Garner's hand in the redistricting, Texas Congressmen feared it would be present as well in the confusion that was bound to follow. During the year-and-a-half interim before the redistricting went into effect in January, 1935, federal patronage in counties that had been shifted from one district to another would be in dispute between the old Congressman they had elected and the new one into whose district they had been shifted. In some counties, moreover, a vacuum would exist: three new districts had been formed by taking counties away from old districts; these counties would have no opportunity to elect a new Congressman until November, 1934. Aware of Garner's ruthlessness and appetite for power— and of his long and close friendship with patronage dispenser Farley—Texas Congressmen feared he would step into the vacuum by claiming, as the state's highest federal official, the patronage power in counties in which it was in dispute. Despite a number of secret caucuses among themselves, however, they still didn't know how to meet this threat.

One of their secretaries did. Lyndon Johnson had not, of course, been present at the caucuses, but Kleberg had told him about them, and Johnson had a suggestion. If, instead of fighting among themselves, all twenty-one Congressmen, plus Senators Connally and Sheppard, agreed on a division of patronage powers, both vacuum and confusion would be eliminated. In the absence of a vacuum, Garner's maneuvers would become more difficult to carry out; without confusion to cloak them, they would be revealed as a naked grab for power. A united front among the Congressmen would deter Farley, too, since he would be interfering in a state's internal politics against the wishes of its entire congressional delegation. Such a united front, Johnson said, should take the form of a non-legal but signed "gentlemen's contract" between all Texas Congressmen and Senators stating that patronage power in every Texas county should remain in the hands of its present Congressman until the redistricting went into effect. And when Kleberg asked how Connally and Sheppard, who might themselves see confusion as an opportunity for patronage gains, could be induced to go along with the Congressmen, his secretary had an answer for that, too: since the two Senators, jealous of their statewide powers, would be as worried as the Congressmen about the Garner threat, only a small inducement would be necessary: the right, previously reserved to the local Congressman, to name the postmaster in their hometowns.

Johnson drafted the agreement: "Until January 1, 1935, present representatives of the district shall control in counties of their present existing districts. . . . We ask that this agreement be respected by all [federal] departments and offices." Kleberg was reluctant to engage in a fight, particularly with his old friend Garner, but Johnson told him that the existence of a clear agreement was the best way to avoid one—and when he reminded Kleberg, to whom personal honor was very important, that in return for support in his last election, he had promised federal positions to supporters in Bexar County, which had been removed from his district in the redistricting, and that if the right of appointment was given to Garner, he would be unable to live up to his promises, Kleberg agreed to circulate the "contract" to the whole delegation. Everyone signed it. And when, in January, 1934, Garner made his move—Texas Congressmen who submitted recommendations to Farley on federal postmasterships in the redistricted counties were told to clear them with the Vice President—Johnson knew how to use the weapon he had forged. He leaked the agreement to the press—not to a local Texas newspaper, but to the Associated Press. Huge headlines (REVOLT AGAINST PATRONAGE ARRANGEMENT) and angry editorials ("Postmaster Farley's insistence upon giving Garner control . . . will make political orphans of dozens of Texas counties") in Texas, combined with nationwide publicity, produced precisely the effect Johnson had calculated. Within the week, Garner had beaten a hasty retreat. In the presence of a "grievance committee" of Texas Congressmen, he dictated a document of unconditional surrender—a letter of his own to Farley: "Dear Jim: . . . a committee representing the Texas delegation are in my office at this moment. They are very much worried about the proposal that I pass on qualifications of postmasters in the new districts in Texas, and, to be frank with you, Jim, I am worried about it myself because of the friction that might arise between the Texas members of Congress and myself. . . . I want to ask you if you won't relieve me of the burden of saying anything about the qualifications of any postmaster anywhere in Texas." Farley agreed to Garner's request, dashing off a letter of his own telling Texas Congressmen to submit their recommendations directly to him as in the past. William S. White, then an Associated Press correspondent in Washington, recounts that "for days [Garner] went among fellow Texans with a scowling, half-amused demand: 'Who in the hell is this boy Lyndon Johnson; where the hell did Kleberg get a boy with savvy like that?'" Others familiar with the episode say White's description is accurate except for the hyphenated adjective; Cactus Jack Garner was not even half amused. Garner's question, moreover, was a natural one. "This boy Lyndon Johnson"—a twenty-five-year-old congressional assistant—had defeated, in a small but bitter skirmish, the Vice President of the United States.

16

In Tune

FEW—if any—congressional secretaries implemented New Deal programs more successfully than Lyndon Johnson. His assistants were, therefore, surprised when they realized what Johnson thought of the New Deal.

The man with whom he was "most in tune," says L. E. Jones—and Gene Latimer and Russell Brown agree—was Roy Miller, the legendary lobbyist who had made the district's office his own.

With his wavy silver mane, his suits and waistcoats of rich fabric, the small but perfect diamond in his lapel, and, of course, his pearl-gray Borsalino, Miller looked to the three admiring young assistant secretaries like the very model of a Southern Senator. Erect and dignified ("He didn't even *own* a short-sleeved shirt," says his son, Dale), he strode through the Capitol as if he owned it—which, some said, in the areas in which he was interested, he did; for legislators like Sam Johnson, who had refused to accept a drink from Roy Miller without buying him one back, were apparently almost as rare in Washington as in Austin, and, with the seemingly unlimited funds at his disposal for "campaign contributions," he bought national legislators as easily as state. Echoing the *Austin American-Statesman*'s judgment that he was "perhaps the most effective single lobbyist Washington has ever known," the *Saturday Evening Post* commented that "perhaps no one outside official life has a wider acquaintance among congressmen. . . . For twenty years he has had the status of a quasi-public figure." The Congressman most important to Texas Gulf Sulphur, which needed deep harbors for the freighters carrying away the sulphur it mined along the Gulf Coast, was Rivers and Harbors Committee Chairman Mansfield. Precisely at noon each day, Miller arrived at Mansfield's office and closeted himself with the crippled Congressman for half an hour. Precisely at 12:30, a House page arrived to push Mansfield's wheelchair— with Miller striding alongside it, somewhat in the manner of a Roman emperor displaying a captive in a triumphal procession—through the underground passageway between the Longworth Building and the Capitol, and

into the House Restaurant, where it was placed at a large round table just
inside the door known as Roy Miller's Table, in honor of the man who
picked up the checks at it. "A surprising number of representatives," the
Saturday Evening Post reported, "knew his hat and coat, when it hangs
on its accustomed peg in the House restaurant"—a discreet reference to
the fact that many Congressmen checked to see that he was present before
they entered the restaurant, lest they be forced to pay for their meals themselves. Nor was Miller's generosity confined to the House dining room. So
awed was Jim Farley by Miller's munificence during Farley's trips to Texas
that the mimeographed advice given by the normally discreet Postmaster
General to a group of Congressmen leaving for a Miller-sponsored Texas
junket began: "Carry only what money you need before you get to Texas.
You will not be able to spend a dime in the State of Texas." The consummate lobbyist, Miller did not confine his friendships to the powerful.
"He knew policemen, he knew the elevator operators, and he knew everybody in the offices," Latimer says. "He would come in and talk to them,
and never mention the Congressman. He'd come by if you were working
ten, eleven o'clock at night: 'Can I take you all out and buy you a drink?'
And then he would buy you a wonderful dinner." The objects of these
attentions might be aware of his motives (as Latimer puts it, "When he
wanted to see a Congressman, he could ask the secretary, 'You reckon
the Congressman's busy?' And they'd break a leg getting him in to see
him"), but they were flattered and charmed nevertheless. The three young
assistant secretaries in the Fourteenth District office admired Miller and
were awed by him—by his manner ("He was so suave and smooth,"
Jones says); by his salary ("He was making $80,000 a year, and this was
during the Depression!" Latimer says); by his luxurious suite at the Mayflower; by the ease with which, in those days before regular air service, he
seemed to stride around the country as easily as he did around the Capitol
("Roy Miller would call from Texas . . . and say, 'I'm going to be in the
office in the morning,' " Brown recalls. "It was always quite a thing that he'd
call from Texas on Monday and be in the office on Tuesday, because he
would come up with his private airplane"). And so, they say, was their immediate superior. "Lyndon hero-worshipped Roy Miller," Jones says.

If in public Miller seemed the archetypal Southern Senator, in private
he might have been the model for another caricature: the wealthy businessman venomously ranting and raving in Peter Arno's *New Yorker* cartoons,
about That Man in the White House. Miller and a group of friends would
often gather in Kleberg's inner office for a late-afternoon drink. These men
were Roosevelt-haters, who saw in the President's programs the erosion of
the power and the privilege so dear to them, and their hatred was made
more bitter by the President's popularity, which forced them, for the sake
of expediency, to keep their feelings hidden. (Expediency dictated con-

cealment of their feelings on many subjects. One of the Miller group was Martin Dies, later chairman of the House Committee on Un-American Activities; Jones vividly remembers Dies coming off the floor of the House in 1935 after making a speech supporting a new bid by the veterans for payment of the bonus. "There, that'll sound good back home," Dies said, and then, unable to contain his true feelings any longer, snarled: "God-damned Reds!") So in the privacy of Kleberg's office, their laughter at the latest scatological joke about Franklin's physical disabilities, or about Elea-nor, was all the louder, and their railings against "Reds" and about the "dictatorship" being foisted on the American people, and about the "social-ists," "communists," "Bolsheviks" and—worst of all—college professors who surrounded the dictator were all the more vehement. Of that group—Dies, Kleberg himself, Horatio H. ("Rasch") Adams, a Kleberg golfing partner and reactionary lobbyist for General Electric, other ultra-conserva-tive Texas Congressmen such as Nat ("Cousin Nat") Patton, James P. ("Buck") Buchanan and Hatton W. Summers—no one laughed louder or railed more vehemently than Miller. Lyndon Johnson was always invited in for a drink. And since the door between the suite's two rooms was open, Jones, Latimer and Brown could hear what their Chief was saying.

His tone with these powerful men was very different from the tone he used with *them*; he was as obsequious to those above him as he was over-bearing to those below. "In talking with these guys," L. E. Jones says, "Lyndon was very much the young man, very starry-eyed, very boyish. It was very much the junior to the senior. 'Yes, sir.' 'No, sir.' " Even if there was a vacant seat in Kleberg's office, Johnson would often be sitting on the floor, his face upturned to whoever was speaking, an expression of the deepest interest and respect on his face, in the manner that had led Vernon Whiteside to say he would "drink up what they were saying, sit at their knees and drink it up." Says a fellow congressional secretary who observed Lyndon in this type of situation: "With men who had power, men who could help him, Lyndon Johnson was a professional son." (The reaction would have been familiar, too: proof that, on Capitol as on College Hill, where flattery is concerned, excess is impossible. These men were very fond of Lyndon Johnson—and the fondness had strongly paternal overtones; Rasch Adams, for example, gave Lyndon Johnson advice not only about women but about culture; feeling that his cultural horizons needed broadening, he bought him theater and opera tickets.) And the flattery that Johnson's three assistants overheard was no stronger than the philosophy. To their surprise, their Chief agreed with Miller, agreed en-thusiastically. "Miller just *hated* Roosevelt," Jones says, "and Lyndon was in tune with Miller. Hell, sometimes he was louder against Roosevelt than Miller was." Johnson used Miller's arguments in dealing with Kleberg. Opposed to the AAA program as "socialistic," Kleberg said he was going to vote against it. Johnson, like Miller, told the Congressman he must vote for it—not because the program was sound, but because his constituents were overwhelmingly in favor of it, as was Congress; his vote didn't matter, they said; the bill would pass anyway. This scene was repeated. Kleberg would return to his office from meetings of the Agriculture Committee "just shocked at" new Roosevelt proposals. Johnson agreed that the proposed programs were "terrible," but, Jones recalls, told Kleberg that he "had to" vote for them "because it was just good politics."

And Johnson did not—for a while at least—espouse a conservative philosophy only in the company of conservatives. During bull sessions at the Dodge, Johnson, echoing one of Miller's pet phrases, would say of Roosevelt: "He's spending us into bankruptcy." The President's first priority, he would repeat emphatically, should be to "balance the budget." A hot topic at the Dodge was Huey Long's recently published *Every Man a King*. Johnson admired the Louisiana populist, but not for his populism. His admiration was for Long's speech-making ability and his growing political power; he was critical of his proposal to redistribute the nation's wealth. And Long shared the President's fault. "Lyndon was critical of the part [of Long's book] about spending so much money—you know just spend, spend, spend," Jones says. Discussing the book with Jones, he dictated several sentences which he told L. E. to write inside its cover—sentences, Jones says, to the effect that "Roosevelt is spending too much money. If we're not careful, he'll lead the country into disaster." Most of the young men of "A" and "B" floors were liberal; Lyndon Johnson was the basement conservative.

He was "in tune" with Miller not only in talk but in action. His closest associate among Texas politicians was Welly Hopkins, who, between trips to Washington to obtain RFC loans for clients of his law firm (he always spent his free time on these trips with Johnson; once, they went to New York together to see the Empire State Building), was distinguishing himself back in Texas as one of the state's most vociferous Red-baiters (he was also leading the fight in the Texas State Senate against attempts to regulate the use of child labor). When Kleberg's bid for re-election was challenged in the Democratic primary by a more liberal candidate, Johnson, Miller and Hopkins orchestrated a campaign to turn back the challenge in the time-tested method of Texas reactionaries: refusing to discuss the liberal's positions, they tarred him as a "communist," guilty of "radicalism" and "similar filth and slime." Although it is difficult to ascertain the precise stands of Kleberg's opponent, Carl Wright Johnson, because in a district so completely controlled by the King Ranch, no newspaper would give Carl Johnson more than cursory coverage, he was, in general, attacking Kleberg for advocating a federal sales tax which would fall hardest on the poor—while at the same time advocating other federal legislation which would largely exempt Texas Gulf Sulphur from paying any federal taxes at all. Johnson imported the fiery little stem-winder ("Lyndon called me from Corpus Christi and said, 'Dick's in trouble down here' ")—who used his customary strategy, with its customary success. Turning to Carl Johnson at the end of a county-fair debate, Hopkins recalls, "I said to this guy: 'Your heart's black, and your mind's Red. . . .' And he was finished." (Roy Miller issued a formal denial of the charge. "The company I represent has absolutely no interest in federal legislation," he said.) Miller's son, Dale, already a knowledgeable lobbyist in his own right, had, in a brief first meeting with Johnson, gotten the impression that he was a New Dealer. "His manner personified the New Deal," he says. "He looked the part. He was young, dynamic, outgoing—the new wave of the future." Dale Miller was, therefore, surprised that "my father, who was very, very conservative in his political philosophy," was "comfortable" with Kleberg's secretary. But his father, Dale recalls, assured him that Johnson "was not a wild-eyed liberal," and as Dale himself got to know Johnson better, he understood what his father had been trying to tell him. "He [Johnson] gave the impression of being much, much more liberal than he actually was. He gave a lot more impression of being with the New Deal" than was actually the case.

Jones had realized this, too—and the realization never ceased to astonish him. Watching Johnson's constant display of thank-you letters from constituents, Jones had seen in his Chief a deep "need for gratitude," and, as Jones puts it, "For someone who needs gratitude, the New Deal is the natural philosophy, because it lets you do things for people, and therefore gives you the greatest opportunity to get gratitude." He was seeing, at the closest range, how effectively Lyndon Johnson was translating the new government programs into action; not one of the thousand Congressional aides, Jones says, could possibly have been better at implementing the philosophy of the New Deal. And yet, Jones says—and Brown and Latimer and other contemporaries who knew Johnson at the time agree—he was implementing the philosophy without believing in it.

BUT IF IN THE OPINION of these congressional secretaries, Lyndon Johnson's true feelings were in harmony with those of reactionaries such as Roy Miller, the secretaries also heard him singing quite a different tune when he was in the company of powerful older men of a different persuasion. The same young men who had heard him denouncing the New Deal when with Miller heard him praising it when talking with Congressmen such as Wright Patman, who had not yet abandoned the Populism he had espoused in the Texas Legislature. Once, a congressional aide, who had just heard him "talking conservative" with Martin Dies, came across him, "not an hour later," "talking liberal" with Patman—espousing a point of view diametrically opposite to the one he had been espousing sixty minutes before. When talking with older men, men who could help him, Lyndon Johnson "gave them," this aide says, "whatever they wanted to hear."

Younger men he gave nothing. The shift in his behavior at the Dodge was quite sudden. For a time, he had been "B" Floor's conservative; then, abruptly, he started, in the words of another "B" Floor resident, "shifting gears," drawing back from his position. Other residents noticed that on two consecutive nights, Johnson would argue on opposite sides of the same issue. And then, in a very short time, he stopped arguing about issues at all. He would no longer, in fact, even discuss them.

His silence in this area was especially conspicuous because of his volubility in all others. If political tactics, for example, were being discussed, Johnson would be the center of the discussion; if the discussion concerned political issues—philosophy, principles, ideas, ideals—Johnson would not even be part of it. Realizing, as he entered a room in which a bull session was being held, that its topic was a serious issue, he would try to duck back out of the room before he was seen. If he was already participating in a bull session and it turned to such an issue, he would quietly slip out of the room, or, if he remained, would refuse, even if drawn into the discussion, to allow himself to be pinned down to a specific stand. He would refuse to take a stand even when directly challenged to do so, turning aside the challenge with a joke, or a Texas anecdote. Pressed to the wall, he would say he simply hadn't yet made up his mind on the issue. During those first exciting years of the New Deal, discussion of great issues swirled through Washington, and nowhere was discussion more animated than in that basement home of a hundred bright young men in government. Amidst the swirl of ideas, Lyndon Johnson seemed unmoved. The son of the man who had said, "It's high time a man stood up for what he believes in" seemed ready to stand up for nothing.

At San Marcos, it was assumed this behavior stemmed from ambition. "He never took strong positions, positions where you knew where Lyndon stood," one student had said. "He was only interested in himself and what could help himself." The feeling in Washington was the same.

THE YOUNG MEN at the Dodge saw the ambition expressed in other ways as well. The Texas State Society, composed of all Texans in Washington, held monthly dances in various hotels. At these dances, young men danced mostly with young women, but not Lyndon Johnson. He danced almost exclusively with older women. "I don't remember his ever taking a girl [to a dance], but he would dance with all the wives of all the Congressmen and Cabinet officers," Brown recalls. Even the adoring Latimer felt he knew why: "because the wives would introduce him [to their husbands]," he says. Other aides held the same opinion. Brown recalls standing with a group of friends from the Dodge and watching Lyndon dancing, and one of them saying: "Do you notice he ignores the young, pretty, single women? He's dancing with all the wives." Another said: "Lyndon's campaigning for something." And a third chimed in: "He never quits campaigning. He's always campaigning." The young men commented to each other on remarks he made; once one of his three assistants drafted for his signature a letter to Secretary of the Treasury Henry Morgenthau, Jr., on behalf of a constituent. The salutation in the draft was "Dear Henry," and Johnson crossed it out, writing "Dear Mr. Secretary" in its place, saying, "Look, I can't call him Henry." There was a pause, and then Lyndon Johnson added: "There's going to come a day when I will, but it's not now." And Brown recalls that once, after Johnson had been introduced to someone as an assistant to Congressman Kleberg, "he kind of objected to being classified as an assistant because, he said, 'I'm not the assistant type. I'm the executive type.' "

Ambition was not uncommon among those bright young men in the Dodge, but they felt that Johnson's was uncommon—in the degree to which it was unencumbered by even the slightest excess weight of ideology, of philosophy, of principles, of beliefs. "There's nothing wrong with being pragmatic," a fellow secretary says. "Hell, a lot of us were pragmatic. But you have to believe in *something*. Lyndon Johnson believed in *nothing,* nothing but his own ambition. Everything he did—*everything*—was for his ambition." A saying about Johnson had gained wide currency among these young men because they felt it described him accurately: "Lyndon goes which way the wind blows."

To those closest to him—the three assistants who worked in the same office—the statement that "Lyndon Johnson believed in nothing" is an oversimplification, and not merely because during the discussions with the Roy Miller clique which they could overhear, their Chief "was always as conservative as ever." Lyndon Johnson, they feel, did possess beliefs— quite conservative beliefs. His "earliest orientation," Brown says, "was on the conservative side." Says Jones: "Intrinsically, he was conservative." But, they feel, the crucial point is that this statement has no relevance in any discussion of Johnson's career. Having spent years in close proximity to Johnson, they are certain that any beliefs of his, regardless of what they may have been, would have not the slightest influence on his actions. In his actions, Jones says, "I don't think Lyndon was either a conservative or a liberal. I think he was whatever he felt like he needed to be. . . . Winning is the name of the game. I have no doubt that he could have become either an ultra-liberal or an ultra-conservative, if that would have brought victory. Now that suggests hypocrisy, doesn't it? But, well—winning is the name of the game.

"Lyndon was a trimmer," he says. "He would be guided by no philosophy or ideals. He would trim his sails to every wind."

SOON THERE WAS symbolic proof of this.

During the 1933 redistricting, San Antonio (Bexar County) and its 240,000 inhabitants had been split off from the Fourteenth Congressional District and placed in a new—Twentieth—District. In 1934, it would elect its own Congressman. One of the candidates had been impressed, during a visit to Washington, by Kleberg's "very efficient" secretary, with his "ready entrée into all of the government departments"; upon his return to Texas, he told reporters that "Lyndon B. Johnson . . . is considered to be the brightest secretary in Washington." He asked Johnson to work for him during the 1934 Democratic primary, which would be held during Congress' Summer recess. Johnson, with Kleberg unopposed in the primary, agreed— although the candidate was Maury Maverick, the fiery radical whose utopian schemes and fierce defense of Communist organizers in Texas had already caused an opponent to charge him with a desire to "supplant the American flag with the Red flag of Russia." (Sam Johnson was very proud at praise for his son from such a source; mailing him a newspaper clipping containing Maverick's quote, he wrote on it: "Breaking into front-page space. Mighty fine, and worthy of it all. Them's my sentiments—Sam.")

Arriving in San Antonio with Latimer and Jones in tow (he had persuaded the genial Kleberg to "donate" all three of them to the Maverick campaign), Johnson put them to work mailing out brochures. He himself began writing them. Maverick saw that this young secretary understood without being told what many politicians never understand: that voters' reluctance to do extensive reading makes simplicity the key to successful political prose. As the worried opponent—San Antonio's corrupt and long-entrenched "City Machine"—stepped up its advertising, Maverick asked Johnson for help writing his own advertising, as well as his speeches. Soon Johnson was not only a writer but an adviser—one of Maverick's inner circle. "The significant thing was—and you could see this very clearly —that the older men trusted him," Jones says. And he was a campaigner as well—a campaigner whose "very unusual ability to meet and greet the public" was as effective in San Antonio's teeming Mexican-American ghettoes as in the isolated little towns of the Hill Country. The *abrazo*, or embrace, was a key element in campaigning among Mexican-Americans, and Lyndon Johnson had always been addicted to hugging and kissing. Towering above swarthy men in bright-colored shirts and old women in black *rebozos*, the tall, skinny, pale young man with big ears and long arms was a conspicuous figure as he abrazoed his way enthusiastically through the crowded, pushcart-jammed San Antonio slums. Maverick won the June primary, but not by the requisite plurality, so a second primary, in August, was required. Johnson spent most of the intervening two months handling Kleberg's affairs in Corpus Christi, but on weekends he would race back to

San Antonio; during the Summer of 1934, therefore, Lyndon Johnson was working simultaneously for one of the most reactionary members of Congress—and for a man who would, immediately upon his arrival on Capitol Hill a few months later, be one of the most radical.

THE 1934 MAVERICK CAMPAIGN also marked Lyndon Johnson's first involvement with one of the more pragmatic aspects of politics. Awakening early one morning a day or two before the election, in the big room in San Antonio's Plaza Hotel that he shared with Johnson, L. E. Jones experienced an awakening of another sort. Johnson was sitting at a table in the center of the room—and on the table were stacks of five-dollar bills. "That big table was just *covered* with money—more money than I had ever seen," Jones says. Jones never learned who had given the cash to Johnson— so secretive was his boss that he had not even known Johnson *had* it—but he saw what Johnson did with it. Mexican-American men would come into the room, one at a time. Each would tell Johnson a number—some, unable to speak English, would indicate the number by holding up fingers—and Johnson would count out that number of five-dollar bills, and hand them to him. "It was five dollars a vote," Jones realized. "Lyndon was checking each name against lists someone had furnished him with. These Latin people would come in, and show how many eligible voters they had in the family, and Lyndon would pay them five dollars a vote."

"EVERYTHING WAS FOR HIS AMBITION." "Elective office," Johnson was starting to say now, was what he wanted. "You've got to be your own man if you're going to amount to anything," he told Russell Brown. He knew *which* elective office he wanted. Once, Brown recalls, "he was talking about somebody who . . . had run to succeed his boss . . . and he said: 'That's the route to follow.' "

A few adjustments began to be made in the physical arrangement of Suite 1322. In most congressional offices, the senior aide placed his desk as far as possible from the front door, so that subordinates would "handle" —and shield him from—casual visitors, who would be mainly tourists from the district. Now Johnson moved his desk immediately inside the entrance door, "so that," in Latimer's words, no visitor could "possibly advance further without his interception." In part, Latimer says with his wry, knowing grin, the purpose of the shift was "to keep the typewriters humming. If anyone talked to L.E. or me, we'd have to stop typing. And that typing was supposed never to stop." But Latimer began to suspect there were other reasons as well. Johnson did not want to be shielded from visitors from the district; visitors were voters. The new position of his desk ensured that he met voters. A favor routinely bestowed by Congressmen's offices—

passes to House and Senate galleries—frequently impressed visitors and made them grateful. Johnson wanted visitors—voters—to receive that favor from him, and the position of his desk ensured that they would. "The casual visitor who just 'happened to be in town' was weeded out" by Johnson, who "talked with him thirty seconds, and had him out of the office and on his way in another thirty, happily clutching" his passes, Latimer says. ("All the while, the typewriters never lost a beat.") Sometimes, moreover, a casual visitor would turn out to be what Latimer calls "an important person" back home. "The Chief would steer him into Mr. Kleberg's [vacant] private office," sit down—behind the Congressman's desk—chat with him, ask if there was any favor he could do for him, strike up a friendship—which would be cemented a few days later by a "buttering up" letter from Latimer.

Noticing that such private audiences were held not only with "important persons" but with any visitor who happened to mention an interesting piece of district political gossip, Latimer felt there was still another reason for the change in the position of Lyndon Johnson's desk: "He didn't want anything concerning his district, no matter how small, going on without him knowing about it." Positioning himself right at the door was Johnson's best defense against such a contingency, Latimer understood.

This defense contained one loophole. Each of the two rooms in a Congressional suite had its own door to the corridor outside, and, in the casual atmosphere of the 1930's, those doors were both generally kept unlocked. Visitors—particularly knowledgeable late-afternoon visitors who were aware which door led to Kleberg's private office, and who wanted to see the Congressman without being cleared by his staff—were therefore able simply to walk in that door, knowing they would receive his invariably pleasant welcome.

Now that loophole was closed. Johnson locked his boss' door—and kept it locked. Kleberg never objected to this new development—he may not have noticed it: he customarily entered and left the two-room suite through the anteroom so that he could chat with his staff. If he did notice it, he did not understand its significance. But Latimer understood. Johnson did not want even his boss doing anything without him knowing about it. "He didn't want anyone to see Mr. Kleberg without going through him first; he didn't want anyone seeing Kleberg that he didn't know about." Locking Kleberg's door was an effective device to prevent that. Another effect of this device was in a small but not insignificant way (since a visitor knowledgeable enough to know the right door was probably an important visitor) to isolate the Congressman from his district, to give a tighter hold on it—at his expense—to his secretary.

Latimer and Jones began to notice some other changes.

Johnson had always been so diligent in grabbing for his boss the credit for federal projects—a PWA sewer or a CCC camp—in the district.

Now he still grabbed the credit—still raced for Western Union and got the wire off to the mayor of the lucky town before Senator Connally or Senator Sheppard—but not always for his boss. More and more now, the releases he dictated began: "Congressman Kleberg's secretary, Lyndon B. Johnson, announced yesterday that . . ."

As was, of course, the custom in all congressional offices, letters advising individuals that they had received federal favors—pensions, visas, private bills—had always gone out over the Congressman's signature, to ensure that the gratitude was directed to him. Now the letters being mailed out of this office were beginning to have a different signature, as well as a different opening phrase: "In the Congressman's absence, I am advising you . . ."

And more and more of a certain portion of the district's business—its political business—was no longer transacted by letter.

In Kleberg Country, all chairmen of county Democratic organizations had been Kleberg men: personal friends of Dick and his relatives, or men economically in thrall to the King Ranch, either as employees of Ranch-controlled enterprises or as businessmen dependent on its favor. Persuading Kleberg that a tighter organization was needed in the district (not much persuading was needed; says Latimer: "Anything the Chief wanted, Mr. Dick would just say, 'Sure, go ahead.' He didn't care"), Johnson began to tour its nineteen counties*—in a new car that he had persuaded Kleberg to buy (and to which Johnson possessed the only set of keys): an expensive Ford roadster with big balloon tires and seat covers of steerhide stitched together in the King Ranch saddle shop to display the Ranch's famed Running W brand that was South Texas' ultimate status symbol. Driving into sleepy cow towns in that car, dressed in an expensive blue suit, "he must have made quite an impression," Latimer says. He met the Democratic leaders—but he also met other leaders, the local banker, the local lawyer, the editor of the local weekly newspaper, the farmer who, his sharp eyes observed, was the man other farmers listened to at meetings of the local grange or the county AAA crop-control committee. Upon his return to Washington, he asked county chairmen to send in regular reports on local political conditions. Those chairmen who responded found themselves in correspondence with Johnson, who replied to their letters the day they were received, and asked for another letter in return. Failure of a chairman to respond regularly was the excuse Johnson needed to have a co-chairman appointed—and these co-chairman were not Kleberg men but men with whom Johnson had, during his tour, established a personal rapport. He made certain, moreover, that each of these new appointees understood that he owed his appointment not to Kleberg but to him.

---

* Nine rural counties—most in "Kleberg Country"—had been added to replace Bexar.

In communicating with these men, he used the telephone. The office's telephone bills had always been enormous by congressional standards (they were paid not out of the meager congressional telephone allowance but by the King Ranch), but now, each month, when Latimer opened the bill, the list of long-distance calls to Texas grew longer and longer.

One explanation for Johnson's increased use of the telephone was his desire for secrecy. The door between Kleberg's private office and the staff's anteroom had always been open. Now, more and more, it was closed, for when the private office was vacant, Johnson would go into it to telephone—and shut the door behind him, for hours at a time. When he was forced by Kleberg's presence (or, more likely, Roy Miller's) to use his own telephone in the anteroom, he would often cup his hand around the mouthpiece to prevent Latimer and Jones from overhearing his words. Other clues about these conversations were also kept to a minimum. In the past, Johnson's invariable practice during telephone calls had been to jot down lists of things to be done as a result of the call, so that Latimer and Jones could do them. Now—on these calls made with his hand shielding the mouthpiece—nothing was put in writing. "Once we had known just about everything that was going on in the district," Latimer says. "Then we started to realize that there was starting to be a lot going on that we didn't know about."

Latimer began to wonder whether use of the telephone was providing Johnson with an advantage beyond secrecy. From the few words he overheard, he knew that the telephone calls to these new friends in the district often concerned favors, including the obtaining of federal patronage jobs, that Johnson was doing for them. Written communications—press releases and letters—were, more and more, bearing Johnson's name as well as Kleberg's. In these oral communications, Latimer wondered, was one of those names being omitted entirely? "In a letter," Latimer says, Johnson "would have to sign the Congressman's name," or, even if he signed his own name, he would have to make clear that he was only acting for his boss. "The letter would have to say, 'At the Congressman's suggestion, I am doing such-and-such. . . .' It might have been dangerous for him otherwise. But on the telephone, it was *him*—Lyndon Johnson—speaking, not Dick Kleberg." Latimer had, in fact, discerned an overall pattern in his Chief's behavior. "Before, he had been making friends for Mr. Dick. Now he was making friends for himself instead."

A Johnson-arranged boat trip also fit into this pattern. He persuaded Kleberg that a group of district leaders, in Corpus Christi for an American Legion Convention, should have a day's outing on his big cabin cruiser. Foreseeing a boring day, Kleberg was more willing to give his boat than himself. And Johnson's urgings that Kleberg should come along were quite noticeably *pro forma*—which made them, predictably, unsuccessful. Wright Patman, one of the guests, recalls that, on the "wonderful outing on Dick

Kleberg's big boat," not Kleberg but Johnson "was the host when we came on board, and he impressed everyone."

Lyndon Johnson was using his boss' boat, his boss' car, to pay the enormous telephone bills his boss' money, to make friends—but he was making friends not for his boss but for himself. A new political organization was being created in the district, an organization which was coming, more and more, to be centered not on the district's Congressman but on the Congressman's secretary. The purpose of Johnson's creation was not to take Kleberg's seat away from him—there was not the slightest chance of anyone defeating a Kleberg in Kleberg Country—but to place him in position to take the seat should it become vacant.

And he was working to make it become vacant.

The minimum age at which a person could become a Congressman was twenty-five, and Johnson would become twenty-five on August 27, 1933. During that year, a quiet movement began to float the name of Richard M. Kleberg for the post of Ambassador to Mexico. Leaks were planted in Texas newspapers; one went out on the Associated Press national wire—no one was quite sure who was planting them. There began to be some talk about the possibility in Washington; no one was quite sure who had started it. The Texas State Senate even passed a resolution formally proposing him for the post; the introducer of that resolution was State Senator Welly Hopkins. Kleberg loved the idea; he had little interest in being a Congressman, and, he often said, of all the cities he had ever visited, Mexico City was his favorite. For a while, Miller and other Texas insiders thought he was going to get the Ambassadorship. He didn't—it went instead to Josephus Daniels. But periodically thereafter, whenever any hint was received in Washington that Daniels was tired of the post, the quiet push for Kleberg would begin again. Having determined the route he wanted to follow, Johnson was paving it.

BUT WAS HE ALSO PAVING a longer one? One that only he saw? One that he, who talked so much, never talked about at all?

Since he was not a resident of the adjoining—Twentieth—Congressional district, in which Maury Maverick had won election, he was not planning to run for one of that district's elective offices. But his interest in the Twentieth district did not cease with Maverick's election.

The key appointive post in that district was the San Antonio postmastership, which controlled 600 postal-service jobs. Since the incumbent postmaster's four-year term was to expire during 1934, before Maverick took office, under the "gentlemen's contract" which Johnson had devised earlier that year, Kleberg, as the area's former Congressman, had the right to name the new postmaster. "Kleberg didn't care" about the successor's

identity, Russell Brown says, but Johnson cared. He had his postmaster all
picked out, in fact: Dan Quill, a tough young Tammany-type Texan from
the San Antonio stockyards and a power in the city's labor circles. "You see
Dan Quill, and you see five thousand votes," Latimer says.

Kleberg's nomination of Quill evoked demands from the old-line San
Antonio machine for intervention by Garner, a longtime ally, but the Vice
President, having lost one skirmish over the "gentlemen's contract," declined
to participate in a second, and when the machine nonetheless persisted in
its opposition, Brown remembers, "Lyndon put on a first-class war. I mean
he went all out, with all guns blazing" and "got the appointment" for "Kleberg's" man. To cement Quill's allegiance to him, he got Quill's sister,
Eloise, a job with the Department of Agriculture in Washington and made a
point of being in San Antonio on Saturdays, when Quill's mother (whom the
postmaster adored) made cornbread and roast beef with brown gravy:
"That's what brought him out to the house a great deal," Quill says; "he
was very fond of her cooking." Had Johnson devised and promoted the
"gentlemen's contract" in anticipation of the San Antonio postmaster fight—
because he already had his candidate for the job picked out? No one
knows—Johnson never said. But the appointment that resulted from the
contract was to prove important to Johnson over not only the long run—
Quill would be his staunch ally in San Antonio for thirty-five years—but the
short. An extravagant admirer of Lyndon Johnson (from the first time he
met him, Quill says, he knew "he was . . . way above the average man of
his age. He grasped things easily, and the political thing—he just took it
over"), Quill was immediately handling small but vital political favors for
Johnson in San Antonio and giving jobs to at least a few of Johnson's San
Antonio friends.

Johnson and Maverick became fast friends when Maury arrived to be
sworn in; shortly to enter a hospital for an operation to ease the effects of
a crippling wound he had suffered in the Argonne, he could hardly walk,
and Brown remembers him holding on to Johnson's arm for support as the
two men walked from the Dodge to Childs' for breakfast on New Year's
Day. The friendship was based partly on Johnson's ability to talk as liberal
with the liberal Maverick as he could talk conservative with his own
conservative Congressman. Discussing a New Deal bill coming up in
Congress, he would demand: "You're not going to throw down the President
on this, are you?" Partly it was based on Maverick's admiration for what
he had called Kleberg's "very efficient" office set-up; at his request, Johnson
showed Maverick's secretary, Malcolm Bardwell, a newcomer to Washington,
how to set up the Twentieth District office. (Maverick autographed a
photograph: "To Lyndon Johnson, who got me started.") And partly it was
based on admiration for Johnson's political as well as secretarial skills. "I
remember Maury calling the office after he was in Congress" and picking
Johnson's brain, "about legislation and what the effect of it was going to

be and what the sentiment of the House was," Brown says. And Johnson cemented the friendship. Maury's younger brother, Albert, a resident of Kleberg's Fourteenth District, was given a coveted patronage post there. Johnson was only a congressional secretary, but he had influence now—influence on a level that most congressional secretaries never achieved—not just in one congressional district but in two.

AND NOT JUST IN TWO.

Among the more popular of the rubber stamps provided by the office of the House Stationery Clerk was one that read: RESPECTFULLY REFERRED TO _____. Most congressional offices routinely employed that stamp on all out-of-district requests. A staffer would smack the stamp down on the letter, fill in the name of the proper Congressman to see, and drop the letter in the OUT file. "The normal man working for a Congressman doesn't care about people living in other districts," Latimer points out.

In the office of the Fourteenth Congressional District of Texas, however, the use of that stamp was more selective. "We would not do what was normally done," Latimer says. "Not if the person needing something was important, not if he knew other people who were important, not if he had money." If a person needing something was "important," Johnson would work for him—and have his assistants work for him—no matter where he lived.

More and more important businessmen needed "something"—specifically, entrée—in Washington as government regulation of and participation in business escalated. They needed guidance through the immense jerry-built maze of bureaucratic regulation; they needed introductions to officials who could help them circumvent those regulations: they needed someone who could tell you whom you should see—and who could get you in to see him.

Businessmen from Richard Kleberg's district learned that his office could provide them with that entrée—and, because Johnson was making friends now not for Mr. Dick but for himself, the shrewder of them learned that it was not Mr. Dick who was providing it. Becoming exasperated over his inability to reach Kleberg on the telephone, former Texas State Senator Alvin J. Wirtz, an attorney for a score of Nueces County clients, asked Russell Brown one day, "Do you suppose if I called the Burning Tree Golf Club I could get our Congressman?" The embarrassed Brown said, "Well, I just don't know where he is, Senator Wirtz." "I know. I know," Wirtz said with a grim chuckle. And then, Brown recalls, Wirtz said, "Lyndon isn't there, is he?" And when Brown said no, Wirtz asked to have Johnson, not Kleberg, call him back, and said, "I know *he'll* call me." And after that, Brown says, "He stopped asking for Congressman Kleberg and he always called for Lyndon."

Johnson, of course, always *did* call back—and provided influential district residents not only with the assistance they requested, whether it was hard-to-obtain hotel reservations on their trips to Washington, or aid of a more significant nature, but also with assistance they had never thought of requesting. For example, a Corpus Christi businessman named Elmer Pope wanted introductions to the staff of the House Interstate Commerce Committee in connection with a bill that would provide federal aid for Corpus Christi; Johnson provided him with the introductions—and, unasked, with a detailed memorandum on the need for the legislation which Pope could present to the staffers.

Attempting to impress these influential men with his entrée and competence, to make them feel secure in his hands, he was careful not to let them realize what young and low-level hands they were; he tried to never let them see his living quarters (one prominent visitor from Texas who saw the Dodge basement—Welly Hopkins—was shocked: "They were living just like youngsters, like in a dormitory," he recalls). When they asked for hotel reservations, he provided them—as if it were easy for him to do so; they never suspected that because he possessed in fact no influence with hotels, he was often forced to frantically telephone one after another until he found a room—and, sometimes, when he had been turned down everywhere, to make a trip in person to see a reservation manager, and spend his own money on a big tip. He never gave them even a hint of the difficulties he might encounter in attempting to secure interviews for them with high-ranking officials—difficulties which occurred frequently with officials who did not need Congressman Kleberg's support on a pending bill, and who had never even heard of Congressman Kleberg's secretary. His care was rewarded. Businessmen from the Fourteenth District were as impressed as he could have wished. And when businessmen from other Texas districts complained to them that *their* Congressman couldn't provide much help with the Washington bureaucracy, they would suggest that they contact Dick Kleberg's secretary.

The newly formed Lower Colorado River Authority, for example, was planning to operate not in South but in Central Texas. But its counsel was Alvin Wirtz, and he told the board members that it was to the Fourteenth District office that the Authority should look for help in Washington. The board member who accompanied Wirtz to Washington, Thomas C. Ferguson, saw that Wirtz was correct.

Entrée was vital to the LCRA, whose planned construction of a series of flood-control dams required not only funding from the PWA but permits from a dozen federal agencies. Provisions of the legislation under which the State of Texas had created the agency, moreover, made it necessary to obtain the funding and permits without delay. "We needed to see people quickly," Ferguson says. "We were pressed for time." Some of the officials they needed to see, Ferguson says, were "high officials"; one was Jerome N.

Frank, then chief attorney of the Federal Power Commission. "And we couldn't get in to see them. Senator Wirtz said, 'Let's go over to Kleberg's office and see Lyndon. Maybe he can help.' " Ferguson was surprised to see how friendly the powerful Wirtz was with this young secretary. "They had a love fest there, for a few minutes," Ferguson says. Then Wirtz told Johnson whom he needed to see. Johnson made an excuse not to call Frank and the other officials while Wirtz and Ferguson were present; he didn't want them to witness the shifts to which he would be put to arrange the appointments. When, that night, he telephoned the two Texans at their hotel, he simply told them the appointments had been arranged, as if it had been no trouble at all. And he created the image he had wanted to create. "Johnson called over there, and got us in to see them real quick," Ferguson recalls. "He helped us a whole lot. Senator Wirtz was very much impressed, and so was I. He knew Washington. He could get you in to any place."

That was the word on Lyndon Johnson. That he "knew Washington," that he could "get you in to any place." And now that word was beginning to circulate in wider and wider circles; it was beginning to be heard in conversations of wealthy and influential men across the length and breadth of Texas. John Garner, they said, was a good man to know in Washington. Certain senior and powerful Texas Congressmen were good men to know. Certain senior and powerful Texas lobbyists were good men to know. And so was a young man who was only a secretary to a Congressman. More and more, in Houston and Lubbock and El Paso, businessmen who needed help in Washington were turning not to the offices of their own Congressmen but to Dick Kleberg's office, and to Dick Kleberg's secretary. Although he was the secretary for only one congressional district, he was creating an acquaintance—the kind of acquaintance that matters—in twenty congressional districts, across the entire huge state.

HE WAS CREATING—across that state—more than an acquaintance.

As the New Deal's new programs resulted in new bureaucracies, and as the bureaucracies swelled and swelled again, thousands of new federal jobs were created, jobs that could be filled with minimal reference to merit, since Congress, in approving the new agencies, had thoughtfully exempted many of them from civil service requirements. The choice jobs were out of the reach of Lyndon Johnson's Congressman, junior and inactive as he was, not to mention the reach of his secretary. But the secretary secured quite a few jobs in the lower echelons: in government mailrooms (Gene Latimer was still working in the House Post Office, and now Latimer's best friend, his former Houston High classmate Carroll Keach, was working in the mailroom of the Federal Housing Administration); and in government galleries (a rotating succession of young men served as doorkeepers in the House

visitors' galleries); at the endless banks of desks in the Department of Agriculture's South Building (where Eloise Quill had been joined by several
other young women from the Fourteenth Congressional District of Texas),
and in the immense federal warehouse on D Street, Southwest, that was the
temporary headquarters of the Treasury Department's vastly expanded Pro-
curement Division (where at least one of its 2,000 clerks, Ivan D. Bell,
addressed Lyndon Johnson as "Chief"); and in nooks and crannies of federal service ranging from library stacks on Capitol Hill (several Kleberg
constituents, including Johnson's oldest sister, Rebekah, were researchers
at the Library of Congress) to border-crossing stations on the far-off Rio
Grande (federal customs officers along the Mexican border came under
Kleberg's patronage, and by 1935, Latimer says, "Johnson just about had
the final say on who got hired to the Border Patrol, and who got promotions.
He had quite a few fans down there"). He also plucked a few plums in
Texas state agencies, for a telephone call from Roy Miller carried consider-
able weight in Austin.

Low-ranking and low-paying, these jobs were nonetheless precious, in
the Depression, to the persons for whom Johnson obtained them. They included fellow White Stars who had graduated from the teachers' college at
San Marcos only to find teaching positions all but unavailable; other young
men from the Hill Country, who had, against long odds, managed to put
themselves through not only college but law school—only to find that hanging out a small-town shingle meant starvation, and that joining a big Houston
law firm meant a salary of $75 per month—and other young men from the
Hill Country who, without a college education, had been able to find no
job at all. "Lyndon didn't make you rich," says one of them. "But he got
you a job." Ben Crider, who had once loaned his young Johnson City
friend money to help him stay in college, now received a $145-per-month
job as an appraiser with the Federal Land Bank's Houston office—and
could hardly believe his luck: "The best job I ever had," he exulted. They
were very grateful.

And they knew whom to be grateful to. Although the federal jobs were,
as the phrase went, "on the Congressman's patronage," the people being
placed in them were not the Congressman's friends, but Lyndon Johnson's.
Driven to Southwest Texas State Teachers College by his dread of spending
his life on a farm, White Star Ernest Morgan was to find that the degree
he had sacrificed so much to earn was no shield from that dread, for it could
not get him a job. But Johnson could. "I was very appreciative of what
Lyndon Johnson did for me," Morgan says.

Reinforcing the gratitude, in some cases, were self-interest and ambition.
The ability of a contemporary, a young man with whom they had gone to
school, to distribute jobs reinforced their belief that he was "going somewhere, somewhere UP." And, says one of them, "I had sense enough to tie
on [to him], because I wanted to go up with him."

Gratitude—and other aspects of the quality he considered most important, the unquestioning obedience that he called "loyalty"—was, in fact, the prime qualification for a man receiving a Johnson job. Although one White Star recipient of a job, Horace Richards, possessed an independent cast of mind, all the others were men like little Wilton Woods, who had been willing to write editorials for Lyndon's signature and to date women for his designs; Fenner Roth, who had been willing to run his errands; and Willard Deason, who had, as his candidate for class president, served as his principal front man in his campaign to attain campus power—men who had demonstrated at college a willingness to follow his leadership. Meeting them for the first time, L. E. Jones observed that they were all slow-talking, good-natured country boys, and that they shared another quality: all, he says, were "yielding" in nature, men willing to take orders.

Some, in fact, now demonstrated that quality anew. Deason, for example, allowed Johnson to order his postgraduate life as he had allowed him to order his undergraduate life. He had been studying law at night while teaching in San Antonio's Alamo Heights High School, but when, in 1934, he obtained his law degree, school officials "sort of halfway promised me the principalship if I stayed on." That prospect, with its prestige and its annual salary of more than $4,000, made him ecstatic. Johnson had obtained for him a Summer job as a junior attorney with the Federal Land Bank's Houston branch, but, dissatisfied both with the job—"little more than a clerk"—and its $125-per-month salary, Deason was planning to return to Alamo Heights in September. Johnson, Deason recalls, "said to me, 'So you get to be a principal—what's that? If you're a lawyer, you can get ahead in the world.'" Johnson "was very insistent that I . . . stay at the Federal Land Bank." He stayed.

Loyalty—the Johnson brand of loyalty—was the quality he looked for in new recruits, too. In determining whether or not it existed in a potential recruit with whom he had had no personal experience, he sometimes had to be guided by what he saw in a single meeting. But he had very sharp eyes. His relationship with these recruits over the years to come was to demonstrate that if Lyndon Johnson was not a reader of books, he was a reader of men—a reader with a rare ability to see into their souls. Nothing was to prove this more dramatically than his selection to receive the best job he had to give—a high-level administrative post with the State Department of Education, obtained through Roy Miller—for the man he chose was regarded by other men as a giver, not a taker, of orders.

The toughness—viciousness—of slim, wiry Jesse Kellam was legendary in oil fields, where he had worked as a roustabout to earn college tuition, and on football fields. At San Marcos, from which he had graduated a year before Johnson arrived at the school, he had been a 140-pound fullback who scorned to wear a helmet, and who once deliberately broke an opponent's leg. On another occasion, when a huge opponent had persisted in illegally battering a 200-pound San Marcos tackle, Kellam had beaten him mercilessly until he could no longer rise, and then, standing over him, had said in his low, hard voice: "Now, you quit beatin' on this little tackle of mine." The other quality for which he was known was leadership. Although he was the fullback, he called signals, and, a teammate recalls, "In the huddle, Jesse spoke and we listened. He had command presence."

But the reader of men had read Jesse Kellam. Despite his toughness and command presence—and a fierce, consuming ambition—when Lyndon Johnson met him for the first time in 1933, he was football coach in the dusty backwater town of Lufkin, Texas, earning little more than $100 per month. He had been stuck in that job for eight years; at the age of thirty-three, he had all but lost hope of ever finding a way out of the dead end his life seemed to have hit. Johnson arranged for him to get the state job. When the state Superintendent of Education attempted to renege on his promise to Roy Miller, Kellam, seeing his last hope disappearing, made a desperate telephone call to his young patron. Johnson was in Corpus Christi, but he jumped into his car and raced the 200 miles to Austin (and 200 back) that day to force the Superintendent to deliver on the promise. For almost forty years—starting a year or two thereafter—Jesse Kellam would work directly for Lyndon Johnson. Although he was the older by eight years, he called Johnson "Mr. Johnson." Johnson called him "Jesse." Although Kellam liked giving orders—in a coldly domineering fashion (he made a point of never bestowing the courtesy of his full attention on a subordinate; when one was talking to him, his invariable, studied, habit was never to stop shuffling through, and at least ostensibly reading, the papers on his desk)—from one man he took orders, took them unquestioningly, with, in fact, a slavish obedience that, increasing over the years, eventually came to remind observers of Gene Latimer's; as the years passed, and Kellam's powerful personality became submerged in a personality more powerful, his gratitude for a word of praise from his master would be almost painful to watch—almost as painful as his reaction to his master's anger. Latimer was not the only employee whom Johnson could make cry. What he said to Jesse Kellam behind the closed doors of his office is not known, but on more than one occasion, when the doors opened, Kellam, outwardly the toughest and most self-possessed of men, was to emerge with tears running down his hard face.

In obtaining and filling patronage positions, Lyndon Johnson worked very hard. In no field were his energy and his willingness to do whatever was necessary to achieve a goal more evident. Hearing that a job—federal, state or county—was opening up, he would spend hours on the telephone talking to men who might be willing to make another telephone call to the official in charge of hiring someone to fill the job, and who might be willing to ask the official to give it to someone recommended by Dick Kleberg's secretary. The 400-mile round trip to save the Education Department position for Kellam was not the only long drive he took in Texas when he felt that his personal appearance might give him a say in the disposition of a job. This work was very important to him. Latimer was with him when he received Kellam's call telling him that the Superintendent of Education was reneging. Hanging up, Johnson shouted, as he headed for his car: "We can't let him get away with that!" And, Latimer says, "The Chief was very, very upset." Patronage was very important to him. "I remember hearing Lyndon say that this business of getting these people jobs is really the nucleus of a political organization for the future," Russell Brown says. In his attempts to obtain patronage, he did not—the secretary to an obscure Congressman—have much ammunition to work with. So he could not afford to let any opening slip away.

And his work paid off.

A network had sprung up, a network of men linked by an acquaintance with Lyndon Johnson, who were willing, because of Lyndon Johnson, to help one another. Johnson had few jobs at his disposal; if one of them was vacated by the friend for whom he had obtained it, he wanted it to be passed on to another friend. White Star Deason's acquiescence to Johnson's insistence that he not return to Alamo Heights High School meant that a job would be vacant there when school reopened in September, 1934. Deason did not notify the school of his change of heart until the very day that classes began in September. And it had been arranged that at the very moment Deason was telephoning a school official to tell him he needed a new teacher, a new teacher was actually standing in the official's office, application in hand: White Star Horace Richards, who was quickly hired. "We always passed jobs on this way," Deason says. Johnson, in fact, had "passed on" his own. Leaving Sam Houston High School to become Kleberg's secretary, he had persuaded school officials, in somewhat of a quandary because of the suddenness of his departure, to hire Hollis Frazier—college debater and White Star—to replace him as debate coach. Frazier, at Johnson's suggestion, later passed on the job to White Star Bert Horne; Richards passed on his to White Star Buster Brown.

Among the significant aspects of this network was its location. More and more of the jobs Johnson was obtaining now were in Texas—all across Texas. Kleberg's secretary had parlayed Kleberg's friendship with Myers, of the Federal Land Bank, into a friendship for himself with the head of the Land Bank's Houston office. That office was to hire 294 appraisers and attorneys in the first two years after its establishment in 1933. Among them would be Ben Crider, Bill Deason, Sam Houston Johnson and a dozen other men hired on Johnson's recommendation. Also in Houston, of course, were Sam Houston High and Hollis Frazier. In San Antonio, there were Horace Richards and Buster Brown—and Dan Quill and his post-office jobs. In Austin, there were Jesse Kellam and, when the Fed-

eral Housing Administration opened a branch office there, an appraiser
or two. And in Corpus Christi, and in many of the little towns of the
Fourteenth Congressional District, there were postmasters and rural mail-
carriers, and WPA and CCC employees. Houston, San Antonio, Austin,
Corpus Christi—the network was beginning to cover a significant part of
Texas.

It was not a political organization. Its members were far too few to
justify that title. It was, however, what Lyndon Johnson said it was: the
nucleus of a political organization. Thanks to his skill in distributing the
meager resources he possessed, the skill with which he had selected the
recipients of his precious jobs, those jobs were held by men bound—by
gratitude, by ambition, by love—to a single leader, even though that leader
was still only a young congressional aide. They were men he could count
on. The road he saw before him—the road to the dim, vast ambition about
which he never spoke—was a very long road. Though its general direction—
elective office—had become clear, he still couldn't see its turnings, still didn't
know which of many paths he would follow. But now, as a result of his
genius in distributing jobs, he could be sure that, whatever the paths he
chose, he would not be without assistance when he trod them. As a far-
seeing and determined explorer caches hidden supplies along a route he
knows he will follow in years to come, so that they will be waiting for
him when he needs them, Lyndon Johnson had cached along *his* route
the resource indispensable to his plans: men. These men were hidden now,
low-level aides in nooks and crannies of large bureaucracies. But they were
ready to march at his command; when he needed them, he would be able
to call them, and they would come.

Geography had always been a barrier to the ambitions of Texas politicians. The state's vastness, coupled with its division into 254 counties,
many more than any other state, each with its own independent political
organization (and coupled also with the strict constitutional limits placed
on governmental powers by a citizenry notably distrustful of government),
had blocked efforts to achieve statewide political power. During the ninety
years since Texas had become a state, only Jim Ferguson had been able
to form an organization responsive in all corners of Texas to the command of a single individual. In ninety years, only one statewide political
organization had been created—by this immensely powerful and resource-
ful Governor. Another was being created now—by a congressional aide,
one of a thousand congressional aides, not yet twenty-seven years old.

HE TRIED to arrange his trips back and forth to Texas so that he drove with
Kleberg or another Congressman rather than with his assistants—"He
wanted to go with someone up, not someone down," Latimer explains—but

sometimes he had no choice but to make the three-day journeys with the two youths with whom, representing Sam Houston High, he had already spent so much time in a car.

Latimer and Jones dreaded these trips. Their chief drove a car as he drove them. "He drove to the limit of the car's ability," Jones says. "If it would go eighty, he would go eighty." Roaring up behind a slower-moving vehicle, he would honk the horn wildly to make it pull over so that he could pass. "He drove like a crazy man," Jones says. If one of them was at the wheel, his concern for his own physical well-being, always so noticeable, was manifested by constant, nervous, criticism. As Latimer came up behind another car, Johnson would reach in front of him to push viciously down on the horn, while shouting, "Get on around, Gene! You're going to kill us!"

Adding to the unpleasantness of these trips was another aspect of Johnson's personality—one that would have surprised those who, knowing only the public Lyndon Johnson, the loud Lyndon of the Little Congress and the Dodge Hotel, thought they knew him. There were times when Johnson would stop criticizing their driving or even noticing it. Slouching down in the seat, he would sink into a kind of reverie. "He would get very, very quiet," Latimer says. "His eyes might be pointed at the window, but you could tell he wasn't sitting over there looking at the landscape. He was thinking, planning. Some people in Washington would say, 'Oh, Lyndon—he's always talking,' but in that car sometimes he would be quiet for a long time—for hours and hours. He'd never close his eyes, and he'd never say a word. He'd just be thinking. And, boy, everyone found out pretty fast not to bother him while he was thinking." He didn't want anyone talking to him while he was "thinking," and, because it disturbed him, he didn't want anyone talking to anyone else, either. As the car roared down the narrow roads to Texas, across the gentle green hills of Virginia, through the winding passes of the Appalachians, down the valley of the Cumberland in Tennessee, and finally onto the flat plains of Texas across which his forebears had trudged behind wagons, Lyndon Johnson stared unseeing out the window, hour after hour; his two young assistants, bored, in the words of friendly, loquacious little Latimer, "through and through," were afraid to break the silence with a single word.

Another aspect of Lyndon Johnson on these 1,600-mile drives would also have surprised those who knew him only in Washington—and who, having been given a short lift home in his car, felt that the speed with which he drove indicated carelessness or recklessness. Pulling into a gas station, he never failed to check the car—the motor and, most conspicuously, the tires. "He was always conscious of the tires," Jones says. "He always bought the best tires available, and whenever we would stop, he always, *always* took the time to check them very, very carefully." Walking around the car, Johnson would kneel on the ground beside each tire, look at its treads, press it to measure the air pressure, test the tightness of each and every bolt holding it on.

Back on the road again, Johnson would be driving "like a crazy man." Because of his behavior at the service station, however, Jones and Latimer felt that behind the "craziness"—the frenzied, frantic, almost desperate aggressiveness and haste—lay thorough, painstaking care. And because of the long, intense silences, they believed that behind the haste lay also the most careful, calculating "thinking, planning." Those who knew only the public Lyndon Johnson saw the energy and the aggressiveness. Those who knew him best of all, the two youths who for years had not only worked in the same room with him but slept in the same room with him, saw the preparation—the long, intense, silent, secret preparation—behind the energy and aggressiveness. They did not know its details—Johnson let them know, as he let others know, nothing. But they knew it was taking place.

And if the two youths were correct, what, exactly, *was* Lyndon Johnson planning? As he sat, hour after hour, staring out at a road without seeing it, what was the road he *was* seeing? What was the road he was paving—paving with such care? What was the road down which he was traveling—traveling so fast? What led him, already working endless hours a day, seven days a week, on the affairs of his own district, to add to that crushing load hours on the affairs of other districts, affairs that he could so easily have respectfully referred to others? He never said. His energy and his talent, the talent that was beyond talent and was genius, were at the service of some hidden but vast ambition. And no one knew what it was.

17

Lady Bird

IN THE 1932 DEMOCRATIC PRIMARY in which Richard Kleberg was challenged for re-election, Kleberg won ten of the eleven counties in his district. The one he lost was Lyndon Johnson's home county of Blanco—although in 1931, before Johnson went to work for him, Kleberg had carried Blanco by a two-to-one margin. Some residents of the county felt that he lost Blanco in 1932 *because* it was Johnson's home; they say that the votes against Kleberg were an expression of dislike for Kleberg's secretary. The dislike was to intensify—even the adoring Latimer, accompanying Johnson on a trip to his home town two years later, noticed it. "He worked hard— he just broke his back—to get those people up there to like him," Latimer says. "But they just didn't." Johnson did not return to Johnson City in his own car, or in the car Kleberg normally put at his disposal. He arrived in the little town in the fanciest car in the Kleberg fleet—a big, bright-yellow Buick with white balloon tires and Running W seat covers. He wore his flashiest clothes—and a manner to match. "Lyndon came back swaggering around, showing what a big shot he was," says Clayton Stribling. "Same old Lyndon."

The same phrase was used at his alma mater. Dazzled though they were by the big Buick, undergraduates who remembered him (and, since so many San Marcos students had to interrupt their college careers to earn money, a considerable number of old acquaintances were still around), and who had disliked his swaggering and boastfulness, discerned beneath the dazzle a familiar figure. Loading them into the Buick, he drove them around, pulled out a bottle of whiskey, and, his head tilted back to address those in the back seat, talked incessantly and pompously, largely about the famous men with whom he was now on intimate terms. Barney Knispel, one of those in the back, recalls him saying (and as Knispel imitates Johnson, he adopts a tone of overbearing pomposity): "You know, that's the kind of people you have to associate with." Says Horace Richards: "I can still see him in that car—talking, holding sway. Same old Lyndon."

One college acquaintance who accompanied him to the King Ranch saw another familiar trait in Johnson, one especially familiar to her. The ultimate power at the Ranch resided in its matriarch, eighty-two-year-old Alice Gertrudis King Kleberg, daughter of its founder (and mother of Congressman Kleberg). Having inherited not only her father's controlling interest in the Ranch but some of his personality as well, she was held in considerable awe; employees who didn't call her "Mrs. Kleberg" never ventured beyond "Mrs. Alice." But her son's secretary called her "Grandma Kleberg." He had taken every opportunity to write her from Washington—when he sent her copies of her son's speeches, he always attached a little note—and soon the fierce old woman was writing back. At the Ranch, she sat in a big rocker on the long porch; he sat at her feet, his face upturned, listening avidly to her stories about Captain King. He asked her advice on personal matters, told her how much she reminded him of his mother, how much he loved her famous prickly-pear jelly. She had inherited from her father an obsession that gates be kept closed to prevent cattle from wandering out of their assigned pastures. One day, after a heavy rainstorm, Johnson drove around the Ranch with her. Hooves had churned the ground around each of the many gates through which they passed into deep, sticky mud. Johnson was wearing an expensive blue suit and expensive, highly polished shoes. But at each gate, although there were two booted ranch hands in the car and, at many of the gates, cowboys standing around, he made a point of leaping out of the car so that he could be the one to make sure the gate was closed after it passed through. The San Marcos acquaintance who had accompanied them on this drive was not surprised by the scene—as she was not surprised by his overall adoration of "Grandma Kleberg." The acquaintance was Ethel Davis, who, years before, had herself been asked by Lyndon for advice, and had been told of her own resemblance to his mother—and who had concluded, in a phrase now being echoed in Washington, "He was a professional son."

Another development in Lyndon Johnson's life would have been found familiar at San Marcos—for the belief that he was determined to marry money had been widespread on the campus. Lyndon Johnson had courted two young women. Each—Carol Davis of San Marcos and Kitty Clyde Ross of Johnson City—had been the daughter of the richest man in town. In 1934, he began courting a third young woman. She was Claudia Alta Taylor of Karnack, Texas, her nickname was "Lady Bird"—and whether or not (and no one can know) her father's position was the explanation, or any part of the explanation, for Lyndon Johnson's interest in her, her father was the richest man in town.

The son of an Alabama sharecropper, Thomas Jefferson Taylor had GTT—to Harrison County in East Texas, an area reminiscent, in the rutted red clay of its low hills, in its fetid swamps and stagnant, muddy bayous lined with the gnarled roots of giant, moss-draped cypresses, and in the servitude in which it kept its Negro sharecroppers (who made up half its population), of the Old South from which he had come. And Thomas Jefferson Taylor might have been type-cast as an Old South small-town furnishing merchant. He had opened a truly general store ("T. J. Taylor— Dealer in Everything"), and then another, and then a cotton gin, and then another. A tall (six-foot-two), fat, ham-handed man, loud and coarse, "he never talked about anything but making money," and he was tireless in its pursuit. He rose at four a.m. to open his stores, and, after a long day behind the counter, returned home at sundown to spend a long evening toting up accounts and checking the dates on IOU's. During harvest time, he never left his gins until the last wagonload of cotton had been baled, but even if the baler didn't stop until one or two a.m., when he went home, he went home to his ledgers. Tireless and ruthless: he loaned money to tenants and sharecroppers at 10 percent interest, and his tactics with those who fell behind on their payments led Gene Lassater, who grew up near his home, to say, "The Negroes were kept in peonage by Mr. Taylor. He would furnish them with supplies and let them have land to work, then take their land if they didn't pay. When I first saw how he operated, I thought the days of slavery weren't over yet." (His own son, Lady Bird's brother, says: "He looked on Negroes pretty much as hewers of wood and drawers of water." White men called him "Cap'n Taylor"; Negroes called him "Mister Boss.") He bought more land, and more—until by the time he married Minnie Lee Patillo of Alabama, he owned 18,000 acres, was "Mister Boss" of the whole northern portion of Harrison County, and lived in the county's most imposing residence, the "Brick House," a two-story white antebellum structure, with columns in front, that sat on a red clay hill about a mile outside Karnack, a town with about one hundred residents that had been named (by someone who couldn't spell) after the temples of Egypt.

When Lady Bird (her nickname was given her at the age of two by a Negro nurse because "She's purty as a lady bird") was born, on December 22, 1912, Cap'n Taylor was still poring over ledgers at night, and Lady Bird's two brothers, both much older, were away at school; aside from Negro playmates, her mother was her only companion. Her mother loved culture—she had come to Karnack with trunkloads of beautifully bound books and every year went to Chicago for the opera season—and loved to read to her daughter, who loved to listen ("I remember so many things," Lady Bird would say. "All of the Greek and Roman myths and many of the German myths. Siegfried was the first person I was in love with.") But when Lady Bird was five, her mother died—and the leitmotif of the rest of Lady Bird's childhood, the sixteen years until, at twenty-one, she met Lyndon Johnson, was loneliness.

Her father didn't know what to do with the motherless little girl. For a while, he took her with him, letting her play around the store in the daytime; at night she slept on a cot in the attic above the store. Stacked near the cot were long wooden boxes that Taylor sold: coffins. Then, when she was six, he sent her, a tag around her neck for identification, on a train ride alone (Cap'n Taylor appears to have been fond of his daughter, but he wouldn't neglect his business) to Alabama, and her mother's spinster sister, Effie.

Aunt Effie, who soon moved to Karnack, raised Lady Bird. She was a slight, sickly woman. "She opened my spirit to beauty," Lady Bird says, "but she neglected to give me any insight into the practical matters a girl should know about, such as how to dress or choose one's friends or learning to dance." Nonetheless, her aunt was her closest companion—her aunt and those beautiful books; the little girl loved to read, memorized poems that she could recite decades later, finished *Ben-Hur* at the age of eight. "Perhaps I had a lonely childhood," she was to say, in her carefully chosen words, "but it didn't seem lonely to me. . . ." But she perhaps affords a more revealing glimpse of her life in the Brick House when, talking about another town in Texas, she says, "I came from . . . a small town myself, except that I was never part of the town—lived outside." At school—a one-room structure atop a red clay hill—there were seldom as many as a dozen students, and few of them stayed long: since they were children of tenant farmers who owed money to Cap'n Taylor, they were constantly moving away. At thirteen, she moved with Effie into an apartment in Marshall, the county seat, where she went to high school, graduating at fifteen, but her high school years do not appear to have been happy ones. Although her eyes were expressive and her complexion a smooth olive, she was not a pretty girl, and her clothes seemed almost deliberately chosen to make her less attractive—although her father would buy her any clothes she wanted, her baggy dresses looked as if they had been handed down from some older, and larger, woman. At dances, she was a wallflower. She appears to have been somewhat of an object of ridicule to the other girls, to whom she had, in any event, little to talk about, preoccupied as they were with dresses and dancing, and boys. In remembering her, they remember a shyness so deep that it seems to have been active fear of meeting or talking to people. One schoolmate, Naomi Bell, says: "Bird wasn't accepted into our clique. . . . We couldn't get Claudia to cooperate on anything. She didn't date at all. To get her to go to the graduation banquet, my fiancé took Bird as his date, and I went with another boy. She didn't like to be called Lady Bird, so we'd call her Bird to get her little temper going. My mother would call her 'Cat.' She'd say, 'All right, pull your claws in, Cat.' . . . When she'd get in a crowd, she'd clam up." Her own recollections of high school are perhaps saddest of all. "I don't recommend that to anyone, getting through high school that young. I was still in socks when all the other girls were wearing stockings. And shy—I used to hope that no one would speak to me. There was one boy who used to try to talk to me. He was real nice, and, what's more, he was real glamorous, being on the football team. But I never knew what to say, and finally it got so that if I saw him coming, I'd leave the room." She loved nature, the winding bayous of Lake Caddo, the moss hanging around her as she walked along the lake or rowed a boat on it, flowers ("drifts of magnolia all through the woods in the Spring—and the daffodils in the yard. When the first one bloomed, I'd have a little ceremony, all by myself, and name it the queen"). But she boated and walked mostly alone. Even her good grades brought her dread; she would never forget her fear at realizing that she might finish first or second in her class, and thereby be valedictorian or salutatorian and have to make a speech at graduation. She prayed that she would finish no higher than third; she prayed, in fact, that if she came in higher, she would get smallpox: she would rather risk the scars than stand up before an audience. She still remembers the exact final grades of the top three students: Emma Boehringer, 95; Maurine Cranson, 94½; Claudia Taylor, 94. When she graduated, the school newspaper joked that her ambition was to be an old maid.

At the University of Texas, to which she transferred after two years at a junior college in Dallas, she was still shy—almost as silent and retiring as she had been in high school—but she began to date occasionally, and two of her beaux received glimpses of qualities beneath the quietness. For a while, says Thomas C. Soloman, "I thought I was the leader." But, he says, he came to realize that this impression was incorrect. "We had been doing what she wanted to do. Even when we went on a picnic, it was she who thought up the idea. This convinced me that it would take a strong man to be the boss. I also knew she would not marry a man who did not have the potentiality of becoming somebody." J. H. Benefield came to realize that the shy, reserved young woman "was one of the most determined persons I met in my life, one of the most ambitious and able. She confided in me her wish to excel." Determination and ambition were also beginning to be manifested in other areas of Lady Bird's life. When she received her Bachelor of Arts degree in 1933, her father and aunt expected her to return to Karnack, but she didn't want to—and she took pains to make sure she wouldn't have to. She had studied to be a teacher, a respectable occupation for a Southern girl in danger of becoming an old maid, and had graduated (with honors) with a second-grade teacher's certificate. But she returned to the university for an extra year, and received a second degree—in journalism, "because I thought that people in the press went more places and met more interesting people, and had more exciting things happen to them." And because a journalist couldn't be shy, she fought her shyness, forcing herself to become a reporter for the *Daily Texan* and to ask questions at press conferences, volunteering to be public relations manager of the university's intramural sports association. And she took other measures to ensure that she wouldn't have to go back to Karnack, or be a teacher.

She studied shorthand and typing, so that she could go into business; she took those courses, she would say, years later, so that she would have "the tools that can get you inside the door. Then, with a little skill and a great deal of industry, you can go on and take over the business—or else marry the boss!"

But if Lady Bird Taylor would make such statements later, she made no statements then; the determination and ambition were well concealed. Despite the "unlimited" charge account her father had opened for her at Neiman-Marcus, she still dressed in flat-heeled, sensible shoes, very plain, and in plain dresses, too big, and of colors so drab that they seemed deliberately chosen to avoid calling attention to herself. During her years in Austin, her only coat was an old coat of her Aunt Effie's.

She was still, as one observer was to put it later, "no glamour girl." If her high school classmates remember a plain girl, almost dowdy in appearance, her college classmates remember a plain young woman. And her battle against shyness sometimes seemed to be a losing one. She had acquired a friend, Emma Boehringer's older sister, Eugenia. "Gene made me feel important for the first time," Lady Bird says. "She was one of those tremendously outgoing people who made everyone around her feel a little more alive. . . . I am a friendlier, more confident person today because of Gene." But Gene herself didn't observe much—if any—confidence in her friend. As for Lady Bird's appearance, after attempting in vain to get her to buy more attractive clothes, Gene called her, in exasperation, "stingy." Gene worked for C. V. Terrell, who, as chairman of the Texas Railroad Commission, was bus inspector Sam Johnson's boss, and Sam had introduced the vivacious, pretty young woman to his son Lyndon. She had turned down his request for a date, but they stayed friends, and in September, 1934, passing through Austin on his way to Washington from Corpus Christi, Johnson telephoned Gene and asked her to get him a blind date, and she did, with Dorothy McElroy, who also worked in Terrell's office. Lady Bird dropped by to talk to Gene that afternoon, and when Johnson arrived to pick up Dorothy, she was there. Lyndon already knew, through Gene, who Lady Bird was; he quietly asked her to meet him for breakfast the next morning in the coffee shop of the Driskill Hotel. She says she didn't plan to, but she was in Austin to consult with an architect about remodeling the Brick House, the architect's office was next to the Driskill, and as she passed the coffee shop, she saw Lyndon sitting at a table at its window. As he realized she wasn't planning to join him, he frantically waved at her until she did. Then he took her for a drive. On it, he first showered her with questions ("I never heard so many questions; he really wanted to find out all about me"), and then—this man whose "mind could follow another mind around and get there before it did"—with answers, answers, as she puts it, to "questions that hadn't been asked. . . . He told me all sorts of things

I thought were extraordinarily direct for a first conversation"—about "his ambitions," how he was determined to become somebody, and was already well on his way as secretary to a Congressman, a Congressman who was, moreover, a Kleberg, about "his salary . . . how much insurance he had . . . his family. It was just as if he was ready to give me a picture of his life and what he might be capable of doing." And then, on this, their first date, he asked her to marry him.

"I thought it was some kind of joke," she recalls. But she was impressed. "He was excessively thin, but very, very good-looking, with lots of black wavy hair, and the most outspoken, straightforward, determined manner I had ever encountered." And he was insistent. The next day he took her to meet his parents, and spoke as though she were already in the family. (Bird's eyes were sharp; describing her first meeting with Lyndon's father, she said, "I felt sorry for him. It was obvious that he had been a vigorous, roaring personality once. Now he had a job—a poor-paying one—only because someone remembered him from back when." Asked if she felt any competitiveness between father and son, she said, "I felt the competitiveness *had* existed" once, but no longer; by the time she met Sam Johnson, she says, "He was an old and ill man, old and ill before his time." As for Lyndon's mother, "As soon as you met them, you were aware that she was a lady. It was obvious that Lyndon just loved her greatly, and I felt drawn to her, and yet I felt like patting her on the shoulder and saying I wasn't going to harm this son on whom she had pinned so many hopes. . . . I just felt like saying, 'Don't you worry.' I had no intention at that time of getting married." Bird also says that "The house was extremely modest. It was obvious that she had done what she could to make it prettier, had bought some furniture and nice bedspreads, but it was extremely modest. Lyndon knew it, and knew I knew it, and was kind of watching me look at it. But he was intensely proud of his family.") He took her to the King Ranch, and she was *very* impressed by that feudal empire, telling her friends later that it was so big that the Klebergs and their retainers used compasses the way other men used watches. And Grandma Kleberg took her aside, and, in her gruff way, told her that Lyndon was a fine young man and that she should marry him. When, a week after they had met, he had to leave for Washington, she invited him and his traveling companion, Malcolm Bardwell, Maury Maverick's secretary, to stop over for a night at the Brick House, which was on the way. Edgy over the impression he would make, Johnson exploded with embarrassment the morning after they arrived when Bardwell appeared downstairs in his pajamas. "He told me, 'I'm going to marry this girl. You're going to ruin my marriage if you run around this way.' " But the man whose opinions counted in the Brick House was not one to be put off by *déshabille*. Ruth Taylor, whom Cap'n Taylor was to marry not long thereafter, says that "My husband liked Lyndon from the first. Both were much alike. Both were big men physically. Both were work-minded and always in a hurry." Says Lady Bird: "I could tell that Daddy was right impressed with him. After dinner, he said in a quiet moment, 'Daughter, you've been bringing home a lot of boys. This time, you've brought a man.'" Before Lyndon drove off for Washington, he asked her to marry him, and again she demurred, but kissed him before they parted (which led a scandalized neighbor to shout at Johnson: "Don't do that! Hurry up, go on—or the Ku Klux Klan will get you!"). Bird was shortly to tell a friend, "I have never felt this way before." Describing her feelings, she says, "I knew I had met something remarkable, but I didn't know quite what. . . . I had a queer sort of moth-and-flame feeling."

AFTER JOHNSON ARRIVED back in Washington, Latimer and Jones received what they regarded as the surest possible sign that his intentions were serious. His morning routine had always been inflexible. "He always had this invariable rhythm," which nothing had ever been permitted to interrupt, Latimer says. "First he would do the mail, then go in the bathroom and go through the newspapers, and dictate to L.E. . . ." Now, however, after he did the mail, he would go not into the bathroom but into Kleberg's private office, shutting the door behind him and sitting down to compose a daily letter to this young woman with the funny nickname whom he had met down in Austin. Latimer, who was to work for Johnson so long, says that during the early years of his career "that was the only time he ever got out of that rhythm—that one time, getting off that letter to Bird. The one and only time."

He took a lot of care with those letters. Finishing a draft, he would summon Latimer, the brilliant letter writer, for corrections, "asking about the spelling and should there be a comma, or was that a dangling participle. He'd say, 'You know, Bird's got a journalism degree.'"

He was as insistent on a fast decision in his letters as in person. He assured her of his ambition ("My dear Bird, This morning I'm ambitious, proud, energetic and very madly in love with you—I want to see people—want to walk thru' the throngs—want to do things with a drive . . .") and pressed her for an affirmative response to his suit ("I see something I *know* I *want*—I *immediately exert efforts* to get it—I do or I don't but I try and do my best. . . . You see something you *might* want . . . You tear it to pieces in an effort to determine if you should want it . . . Then you . . . conclude that maybe the desire isn't an 'everlasting' one and that the 'sane' thing to do is to wait a year or so . . ."). He assured her of his interest in the cultural matters so important to her ("Every interesting place I see I make a mental reservation and tell myself that I shall take you there when you are mine. I want to go through the Museum, the Congressional Library, the Smithsonian, the Civil War battlefields and all of those most interesting places . . ."), and pressed ("Why must we wait twelve long months to begin to do the things we want to do forever and ever?").

And she responded, writing of the interests she evidently had been led to believe they would share. "Dearest: I've been reading *Early Autumn* [by Louis Bromfield] and am enthralled. If we were together, I'd read it to you. . . . There's nothing I'd like better than being comfortable in a nice cozy place and reading something amusing or well-written or interesting, to someone I like. All good things are better shared, aren't they?"

He was also telephoning her almost daily, and early in November, she recalls, "when we were on the phone from Washington, we decided he would come down and we would decide if we would" get engaged. The next day, to her shock, the Ford roadster pulled up the rutted driveway— he had driven from Washington to Karnack without stopping, "and had gotten to my father's at least twenty-four hours before I was expecting it. I hadn't gotten the house quite ready, and I hadn't been to the beauty parlor." No sooner had he arrived than he began arguing, in her words, "Let's go on and get married, not next year . . . but about two weeks from now, a month from now, or right away."

She agreed to let him buy her an engagement ring—they drove together the 300 miles to Austin to pick one out together—but when, in the jewelry store, he proposed buying a matching wedding ring, she refused to allow him to do so. She wouldn't make any decision without going to Alabama and talking to Aunt Effie. "She had concentrated all her life and all her love on me, and I just knew that I had to go and see her." She took the trip while Lyndon drove to Corpus Christi, and her aunt was appalled that Bird would even consider marrying a man she had known less than two months. But when she returned to Karnack, there in the driveway of the Brick House was the Ford roadster, and when she reported Effie's reaction, her father said, "If you wait until Aunt Effie is ready, you will never marry anyone," and added, "Some of the best deals are made in a hurry." She said she wanted to ask Gene Boehringer's advice, but Lyndon insisted on accompanying her to Austin, and hardly had they started driving when he issued an ultimatum: "We either get married now or we never will. And if you say goodbye to me, it just proves to me that you just don't love me enough to dare to. And I just can't bear to go on and keep wondering if it will ever happen." When she agreed to get married at once, she says, he let out a "Texas yip" that she was sure could be heard in the next county.

The engagement lasted as long as it took to drive from Karnack to San Antonio. Worried about making arrangements on such short notice, Lyndon called Dan Quill, whose influence in City Hall procured an immediate marriage license, and who then argued a reluctant Episcopalian minister, who said at first that to marry two people he had never met on such short

notice would be a "justice-of-the-peace ceremony," into making an exception in this case. Johnson was to recall that as he and Lady Bird walked
into St. Mark's Episcopal Church, he was still persuading Lady Bird that
she was doing the right thing. And when, during the simple ceremony attended only by Quill, a lawyer acquaintance, and a hastily summoned friend
of Lady Bird's, it came time to place a ring on the bride's finger, Johnson
had still not bought one, and Quill dashed across the street to a Sears, Roebuck store and brought back a tray of inexpensive wedding bands—the one
she chose cost $2.50—to complete the ceremony. After a wedding supper at
St. Anthony's Hotel—at which, because none of the guests had sufficient
funds to purchase a bottle of the hotel's high-priced wines, the wedding toast
was drunk after the lawyer rushed home to get a bottle of his own—Lyndon
and Lady Bird drove to the Plaza Hotel, where they spent their wedding
night.

The next morning, Lady Bird telephoned Gene Boehringer, who had
been expecting her in Austin, and told her surprised friend: "Lyndon and I
committed matrimony last night."

Lyndon telephoned his mother, who had hoped that when her son
got married, she would be invited to the wedding.

THE TONE of the letters that Lyndon Johnson wrote to Lady Bird before he
married her was not the tone that others heard him using to her immediately
after they were married. The morning after the ceremony, heading for a
brief honeymoon in Mexico, they stopped at the little town of Cal-Allen,
near Corpus Christi, to say hello to William P. Elliott, a reporter for the
Corpus Christi Caller, and his wife, Mary, and as they sat chatting in the
living room, Johnson said, in Mrs. Elliott's recollection, "You've got to
change your stockings, Bird. You've got a run." Embarrassed, Bird did
not immediately obey—and, Mrs. Elliott remembers, he ordered her to,
"just *ordered* her—right in front of us."

Back in Washington, where, after a few days in an upstairs room at
the Dodge, they moved into a furnished one-bedroom apartment at 1910
Kalorama Road, the tone was similarly one of command; it was, in fact,
little different from the tone in which he addressed Latimer and Jones.
Acquaintances who heard it were shocked. If he disapproved of the clothes
his bride was wearing, he would tell her so, in a voice harsh with contempt,
regardless of whether others were present. Across a crowded room—at a
Texas State Society party, for example—he shouted orders at her, and the
orders had to be instantly obeyed.

"Lady Bird, go get me another piece of pie."

"I will, in just a minute, Lyndon."

"Get me another piece of pie!"

Wingate Lucas says, "He'd embarrass her in public. Just yell at her across the room, tell her to do something. All the people from Texas felt very sorry for Lady Bird." Seeing her shyness, her almost visible terror at having attention called to herself, acquaintances were soon making a remark that would be repeated for decades by acquaintances of the Johnsons: "I don't know how she stands it."

The interest in culture—the promises to take her to museums and libraries "and all of those most interesting places" "when you are mine"— was somewhat less apparent once she was, in fact, his. Exploring Washington thrilled her—"I remember a song, 'Walking in a Winter Wonderland,' " she says. "I'd just walk and explore, because it was all so fresh and new." But, because Lyndon worked all day, every day, and she was too shy to make friends, she did the exploring alone. In the evenings, he might not be in the office, but that did not mean he would be in a place that did not interest him. He would not, except on the rarest of occasions, take Lady Bird even to a movie; as for plays, when, in desperation, she purchased two tickets to the Theatre Guild's four-play season at the National Theatre, her husband would take her to the door; he would not go inside. Russell Brown says:

> I was always prepared to see her home, but she never would let me do so. She always went home by herself. . . . But I went to the Theatre Guild that season with her. I remember he used to bring her and say, "Now, I'll see you later." . . . They were fairly expensive tickets, and so on. But he wouldn't go to the theater.

Her hopes of sitting quietly, sharing the joy of a good book with her husband, were not frequently fulfilled. She had, in fact, no more success than L. E. Jones had had in persuading him to look for more than a minute or two at any printed matter less timely than a news magazine or the *Congressional Record*. She then tried to underline paragraphs in books she thought he should read, but even if the subject was politics or government, his lack of interest was so marked that she was soon playing a scene that would have been familiar to residents of Johnson City who had watched Lyndon Johnson's mother following him to the front gate in the morning reading his lessons to him because he would not read them himself; if he would not read an underlined passage, Lady Bird would try to read it to him, sometimes following him about the apartment to do so.

She found it easier to fulfill other functions that Johnson regarded as wifely, however much they may have conflicted with her own training or expectations of married life. Here are her own words on the subject:

> He early announced, "I'd like to have coffee in bed," and I thought, "What!?!? Me?!?!" But I soon realized that it's less trouble serving someone that way than by setting the table and all. . . .

Did she also realize that it was less trouble to bring him his newspaper in bed, so that he could read it as he sipped his coffee? To lay out his clothes, and, so that he wouldn't be bothered with the chore of placing things in pockets, to herself put his pen—after filling it—in the proper pocket, his cigarette lighter—after checking the level of its fluid—in the proper pocket, his handkerchief and money in the proper pocket? To shine his shoes? He insisted that she do these chores, and she did them.

ONE CHORE WAS particularly difficult for her. Hospitality is, of course, a potent political weapon, and Johnson was, of course, planning to employ it. Hardly had they moved into their little apartment when he informed Bird that a Congressman—Maury Maverick—and his wife would be coming for dinner.

Not only her shyness but her upbringing in a house full of Negro servants made entertaining difficult for the young wife; until the day she moved to Kalorama Road, she recalls, "I had never swept a floor, and I certainly had never cooked." Mrs. Maverick says that when she entered the Johnsons' apartment, in which a table had been set in the living room, and met Lady Bird, she felt "as if a little girl had invited me"—and not just because of the obvious nervousness of her small, slim hostess. "One of the first things I saw was a Fannie Farmer cookbook open on the table," Mrs. Maverick says. "Staring at me was a recipe for boiled rice. The menu included baked ham, lemon pie and, of course, the rice. The ham and pie were very good, but I'll never forget that rice. It tasted like library paste. To this day, I connect boiled rice and library paste."

But Mrs. Maverick was also struck by the bride, by her sweetness and graciousness as a hostess, by the way, covering her nervousness with a smile that never wavered, she made both the Congressman and his wife, so much older than the Johnsons, feel at home in the little apartment. Others were struck by the same qualities: Congressmen like Marvin Jones and Ewing Thomason who condescended to accept a staffer's dinner invitation because the staffer's father was Sam Johnson; young reporters ("Get the furniture insured for Friday night," Johnson told Bird one day. "I'm having a bunch of newspapermen out there . . . we'll have a wild evening"); older congressional secretaries like Kate George and younger contemporaries of her husband's—all felt, as she said good night to them at the door with "Y'all come back real soon, hear now?" that she really *wanted* them to. And this graciousness, Lady Bird Johnson's remarkable ability to make anyone feel at home, was, within just a few months of their marriage, to give her husband's career the biggest boost it had yet received.

For one of the guests visiting the Johnsons' little apartment—visiting it more and more frequently; coming regularly, after a while, every Sunday for breakfast, and staying longer and longer each Sunday, sitting always in a straight, hard chair, but, week by week, bending forward more, hands on his knees, to tell stories of Texas, and, more and more relaxed, chatting with Lyndon Johnson hour after hour—was a man who seldom visited anyone, and who had *never* visited anyone regularly, a man as shy in his own way as Lady Bird was in hers, a small, stocky man with a bald head and a face like a rock: Sam Rayburn.

18

Rayburn

RAYBURN. Rayburn who hated the railroads, whose freight charges fleeced the farmer, and the banks, whose interest charges fleeced the farmer, and the utility companies, which refused to extend their power lines into the countryside, and thus condemned the farmer to darkness. Rayburn who hated the "trusts" and the "interests"—Rayburn who hated the rich and all their devices. Rayburn who hated the Republican Party, which he regarded as one of those devices—hated it for currency policies that, he said, "make the rich richer and the poor poorer"; hated it for the tariff ("the robber tariff, the most indefensible system that the world has ever known," he called it; because the Republican Party "fooled . . . the farmer into" supporting the tariff, he said, the rich "fatten their already swollen purses with more ill-gotten gains wrung from the horny hands of the toiling masses"); and hated it for Reconstruction, too: the son of a Confederate cavalryman who "never stopped hating the Yankees," Rayburn, a friend once said, "will not in his long lifetime forget Appomattox"; for years after he came to Congress, the walls of his office bore many pictures, but all were of one man—Robert E. Lee; in 1928, when his district was turning to the Republican Hoover over Al Smith, and he was advised to turn with it or risk losing his own congressional seat, he growled: "As long as I honor the memory of the Confederate dead, and revere the gallant devotion of my Confederate father to the Southland, I will never vote for electors of a party which sent the carpetbagger and the scalawag to the prostrate South with saber and sword." Rayburn who hated the railroads, and the banks, and the Republicans because he never forgot who he was, or where he came from.

Forgetting would have been difficult. He was born, on January 6, 1882, on a forty-acre farm in Tennessee whose worn-out soil could not support so many children—he was the eighth of eleven—and in 1887, the Rayburns moved to a forty-acre farm in Texas, in Fannin County, northeast of Dallas. (The thousand-mile train trip to Texas provided him with one of his most enduring memories; from the train windows, he was to recall, he saw "the people . . . on their trek west, all their earthly belongings heaped on covered wagons, men in plainsmen's outfits with wide-brimmed hats and guns on their shoulders, leading the oxen.") The first year in Texas almost finished the Rayburns: floods covered the fields, and boll weevils feasted on the cotton that survived—and out of the forty acres, only two-and-a-half bales. Although Fannin County soil was deep, rich loam, and the rainfall plentiful, forty acres was inadequate for a large family when the interest on the mortgage was 10 percent and cotton was selling for nine cents a pound. The Rayburns managed to hold the farm year after year only because the whole family, even five-year-old Sam, worked in the fields.

Except for four months each year in a one-room, one-teacher schoolhouse, Sam Rayburn spent his boyhood in the cotton rows. In the Spring, he plowed—plowed while he was still so small that his weight couldn't keep the plow point in the ground and he had to strain to hold it down as the mules yanked it forward. In the Summer, under the searing Texas sun, he worked with a hoe, chopping at the plants to thin them out, going to bed at night with an aching back, knowing that at daybreak he would be out with the hoe again. And in September, he would be in the rows on his knees—crawling down the rows, dragging behind him a long sack, while he picked the cotton—in the rows day after day, knees raw and bleeding from the crawling, hands raw and bleeding from the picking, back aching even worse than from the chopping. "I plowed and hoed from sun till sun," Sam Rayburn was to recall. "If some of our city friends who talk about the beauty and romance of farm life would go out and bend their backs over a cotton row for ten or twelve hours per day and grip the plow handles that long, they would see how fast this romance they have read in the novels would leave, and how surely it would come down to a humdrum life of work and toil." Work and toil—and little to show for it, thanks to the government's tariff and currency policies. The injustice that farmers felt was embodied in these policies—and that made northeast Texas a stronghold of the People's Party —was exemplified by the inclusion of steerhides on the "free" (unprotected by tariff) list, which meant that farmers received little for their steerhides, and the inclusion of the shoes manufactured from steerhides on the protected list, which forced farmers to pay high prices for shoes. Cotton prices were kept low, too. When, after a year's work in the fields by the entire family, its cotton went to the gin, the Rayburns might have left, after paying the furnishing merchant and the mortgage holder and the railroad's cruelly high freighting charges, *in a good year*, as much as twenty-five dollars to show for the year's labor.

And it wasn't the work and toil—or the poverty—from which he suffered most. Except when telling stories about the war (the most prominent object in the living room was a framed picture of General Lee), his father, the bearded Confederate veteran, was a gentle but very silent man, and his mother ("Hard Boss," the family called her because of her rigidity), who loved and was devoted to her children, was careful to conceal her affection; to Sam's parents, a biographer says, "any show of sentiment toward young children was a sign of weakness." All through his boyhood, Sam's life was the cotton fields—the fields and little else. If, Sunday, chores were light, they were supposed to be replaced not by play but by piety. "Many a time when I was a child and lived way out in the country," Sam Rayburn later recalled, "I'd sit on the fence and wish to God that somebody would ride by on a horse or drive by in a buggy—just anybody to relieve my loneliness." Terrible as were the toil and the poverty, the loneliness was worse. Poverty, he was to say, only "tries men's souls"; it is loneliness that "breaks the heart. Loneliness consumes people."

IN THE BLEAKNESS and boredom of Sam Rayburn's childhood, there stood out a single vivid day.

Fannin County's Congressman was Joseph Weldon Bailey, who, as Minority Leader of the House of Representatives, "dominated the Democratic minority like an overseer and conducted himself like a conqueror," and was expected, if the Democrats won control of Congress, to become Speaker. Bailey was one of the greatest of the great Populist orators. When he spoke in the House, it was said, "his tones lingered in the chamber like the echo of chimes in a cathedral." In 1894, when Sam Rayburn was twelve, Bailey spoke in Bonham, the county seat. And Sam Rayburn heard him.

He was to remember, all his life, every detail of that day: how it was raining so heavily that his mule took hours to cover the eleven miles to town; how he felt when he arrived at the covered tent "tabernacle" of the Bonham Evangelical Church, where Bailey was speaking. "I didn't go into that tabernacle. I'd never been to Bonham since we bought the farm, and I was scared of all the rich townfolks in their store-bought clothes. But I found a flap in the canvas, and I stuck there like glue while old Joe Bailey made his speech." And most vividly of all, he remembered Joe Bailey. "He went on for two solid hours, and I scarcely drew a breath the whole time. I can still feel the water dripping down my neck. I slipped around to the entrance again when he was through, saw him come out, and ran after him five or six blocks until he got on a streetcar. Then I went home, wondering whether I'd ever be as big a man as Joe Bailey."

Passing the barn the next morning, his brothers heard a voice inside. Looking through the door, they saw their little brother standing on a feeding trough, practicing a political speech. From the day he heard Joe Bailey, Sam Rayburn knew what he was going to be. Knew precisely. He told his brothers and sisters, and friends; as one recalls his words, "I'm going to get myself elected to the State Legislature. I am going to spend about three terms there and then I want to be elected Speaker. After that, I am going to run for

Congress and be elected." He would be in the House of Representatives, he said, by the age of thirty. And eventually, he said, he would be its Speaker, too. Sam's ambition became a joke on the Rayburn farm; his brothers and sisters would stand outside the barn and laugh at the speeches being made inside. But the speeches went on. And in 1900, when he was eighteen years old, Sam Rayburn, standing in a field with his father one day, told him he wanted to go to college.

His father said that he had no money to send him. "I'm not asking you to send me, Pa," Sam said. "I'm asking you to let me go." The cavalryman's back was stooped from the fields now; he was old; two of his eight sons had already left the farm; the loss of a third pair of strong hands would be hard to bear. "You have my blessing," he said. On the day Sam left, his clothes rolled up and tied with a rope because he had no suitcase, his father hitched up the buggy and drove him to the railroad station. A silent man, he stood there silently until the train arrived and his son was about to board it. Then he suddenly reached out and pressed some bills into his son's hand. Twenty-five dollars. Sam never forgot that; he talked about that twenty-five dollars for the rest of his life. "God knows how he saved it," he would say. "He never had any extra money. We earned just enough to live. It broke me up, him handing me that twenty-five dollars. I often wondered what he did without, what sacrifice he and my mother made." And he never forgot the four words his father said to him as he climbed aboard the train; he was to tell friends that he had remembered them at every crisis in his life. Clutching his son's hand, his father said: "Sam, be a man!"

Tuition at East Texas Normal College, a handful of buildings on a bleak prairie, was twelve dollars a month; to supplement his parents' gift, he got a job sweeping out a nearby elementary school, and became the college's bellringer, running up to the bell tower every forty-five minutes to signal the end of a class period. Unable even with those jobs to stay in school, he dropped out, and taught for a year in a one-room school to earn money, then returned, to take a heavy load of courses and graduate with his class. (He was so ashamed of his only suit and its frayed elbows that he tried to avoid attending the graduation ceremony.) Then he got another teaching job, this one in Fannin County, held it for two years, and in 1906, at the age of twenty-four, announced for the Legislature.

HE CAMPAIGNED on a little brown cow pony, riding from farm to farm. Unable to make small talk, he discussed farm problems, a short, solid young man with a hairline that was already receding, and earnest brown eyes. At each farm, he asked who lived on the next farm, so that when he got there, he could call them by name. Two incidents in the campaign showed that he had not forgotten his father's four words of advice. A man approached him one day and said that a ten-dollar contribution to an influential farmer would ensure the votes of the farmer's relatives. "I'm not trying to buy the office," Rayburn replied. "I'm asking the people to give it to me." He and his opponent, Sam Gardner of Honey Grove, became friends and, near the end of the campaign, rode from town to town together in a one-horse buggy; arriving in a town, they would take turns standing in the back of the buggy and speaking. In one town, Gardner became ill and spent three days in bed. Although Gardner appeared to be leading, Rayburn didn't use the three days to campaign; he spent them with Gardner, nursing him. Gardner was to be a friend of Sam Rayburn's all his life.

The votes were cast on a Saturday, but, because the ballot boxes had to be brought in to the county clerk's office in Bonham, and the ballots counted by hand, the results would not be announced until Tuesday. Sam arranged for a friend with a fast horse to bring the news the eleven miles to the Rayburn farm. On Tuesday, he sat with his family in the living room, waiting for the hoofbeats that would announce his destiny. It was victory, by 163 votes.

In Austin, Sam Rayburn didn't forget where he came from. Enlisting in the small band (which included, of course, Sam Ealy Johnson, then in his second term in the Legislature) which fought "The Interests" and talked of "The People," he introduced bills to regulate railroads and banks. Unlike some of that band, he never sold out. Years later, when someone mentioned that Rayburn's father had not left him much of an inheritance, Rayburn quickly corrected him—his father, he said, "gave me my untarnished name." He kept it untarnished. He wouldn't drink at the Driskill, and wouldn't live there; rooming at a cheap boardinghouse below the Capitol, he shared a small room to save his five-dollar-per-day salary for tuition at the University of Texas Law School. After paying his tuition, he was to recall, he had so little money that once, after offering to buy a soda for a Representative named Pharr, he realized that he had only a nickel to his name; "so when we got to the counter, I told Pharr I wasn't feeling so well and would not take anything. He went on and got his drink and I paid for it. . . . I don't know what I'd have done if he had ordered a dime drink." But when, shortly after he had obtained his law degree and joined a law firm, one of his partners handed him the largest check he had ever seen as his share of a monthly retainer from the Santa Fe Railroad, he handed it back—and added that he would never "accept a dollar of the railroad's money." To his partner's request for an explanation, he replied: "I said to him that I was a member of the Legislature, representing the people. . . ." Legislators were routinely presented with free railroad passes; Rayburn returned his, even though, at the time he refused his pass, he was desperately lonely in Austin and unable to return home because he could not afford the fare. (His mother approved. "We often wish for you to be with us," she wrote, "but we would rather wait a little longer than for you to accept free passes.") It was while he was in Austin, where legislators were bought wholesale, that there was first heard a saying that men would be repeating for fifty years: "No one can buy Sam Rayburn."

He didn't forget where he came from—or where he was going. He discussed his ambitions with his fellow members of the Texas House of Representatives as bluntly as he had done, years before, with his brothers and sisters. He wanted to be Speaker of the House, he said, and he told them quite frankly why: "I've always wanted responsibility because I want the power responsibility brings."

Not only did he know what he wanted, he knew—seemed to know instinctively—how to get it. Like Sam Johnson, he had an instinctive gift for the legislative process, but, unlike Sam Johnson, he was not a romantic or a dreamer. When he helped someone, he insisted on help in return, even when the recipient of his aid was his idol.

Arriving in Austin, Rayburn found his idol on trial there: debate was raging over the threatened legislative investigation of Joseph Weldon Bailey, now a United States Senator accused of selling out to the railroads and to Standard Oil. Rayburn, who throughout his life was to refuse to believe those charges, offered his support to Bailey's legislative lieutenants, pointing out that, as the representative from Bailey's old district, his opinion might carry more weight than that of the average freshman legislator. But in return for his support, he said, he wanted more than might be given the average freshman legislator. He gave his support—and proved, during his first days in the Legislature, a very effective, if quiet, figure in Bailey's defense. And he got what he wanted in return. The backing of Bailey's lieutenants gave him, in his first term in the Legislature, the chairmanship of a key legislative committee.

A committee chairman's power was used to build more power. Legislators who received favors from him were expected to give favors in return. And the favors Rayburn asked for were, like the favors he gave, shrewdly chosen. Hardly had he arrived in the Texas House, it seemed, when he was a power in it, thanks to a gift—a rare gift—for legislative horsetrading.

He had other gifts, too—in particular, a very unusual force of personality.

In part, that force was physical. Sam Rayburn was a short man—five-foot-six-inches—but his body was broad and massive, the chest and shoulders so broad and thick that they bulged through the cheap fabric of his suits. His head, set on a bull neck, was massive, too, and seemed even more massive than it was, for already, in his twenties, he was going almost completely bald, so that the loom of the great bare skull was unsoftened by hair. His wide, heavy face could be pleasant in private, but in public it was expressionless, immobile, grim; so hard were the thin line of the lips and the set of the wide, jutting jaw that, except for the eyes that smoldered in it, it might have been the face of a stone statue—and it exuded an immense, elemental strength.

That aura was not dispelled by Sam Rayburn's character.

Already men were whispering about his temper. When he lost it, and he lost it often, a deep flush would rise along the bull neck and completely cover the great head, and the lips, so grim, would twist in a snarl, and the voice, so low, would rasp. "In dark moods," one observer was to write, "his profanity was shattering," and as he cursed, he spat—and, as the observer tactfully put it, "If a . . . cuspidor was handy, that was fine. If there wasn't, it was too bad." In a rage, "Mr. Rayburn's face blackened in a terrible scowl and his bald head turned deep red. . . . That was the way he looked in a rage, and few cared to see such a mien turned upon themselves." When he lost control of that temper, he was deaf to reason; not even considerations of career or ambition could stand before it. The most feared figure in Austin was the recently retired Governor, Tom Campbell; the ruthlessness he had exhibited in the Statehouse, rumor had it, had not been tempered since he had become lobbyist for the state's banking interests—and the power of those interests still enabled him to punish opponents. Rayburn, fighting bank-sponsored legislation in his committee, and pushing his own, became an opponent. Campbell planted in cooperative newspapers stories that Rayburn was fighting in committee because he was afraid to fight in the open—articles that Rayburn considered an attack on his personal honor. Friends aware of his temper urged him not to lose it; Campbell, they warned him, had destroyed the careers of other men who had opposed him even indirectly. Rayburn thereupon took the floor of the House with a speech that was not indirect. His own bills, he said, "are in the interest of the people, and I will stand here day by day and vote for them. . . . It matters not to me what Mr. Campbell's views are." Pausing, he raised his great head and stared straight at Campbell, who was sitting in the gallery, not speaking again until everyone in the Chamber was staring at Campbell, too. Then he said: "It matters not to me whether Tom Campbell stands for a measure or against it. Tom Campbell, in my opinion, is the least thing to be considered in legislation." The temper, the aura of immense strength, the legislative cunning, the implacable standards: in Austin, men learned that they couldn't buy Sam Rayburn—and that they couldn't cross him.

Nor was his temper the only striking aspect of Sam Rayburn's character. His colleagues talked not only of his rage but of his rigidity.

His standards were very simple—and not subject to compromise. He talked a lot about "honor" and "loyalty," and he meant what he said. "There are no degrees in honorableness," he would say. "You are or you aren't." Harsh though that rule was, he lived up to it—says one of his fellow legislators: "He had a reputation for honesty and fair dealing. You could always swear by anything Sam told you"—and he insisted that others live up to it, too. "Once you lied to Rayburn, why, you'd worn out your credentials," an aide says. "You didn't get a second chance." His colleagues learned, however, that if they paid Sam Rayburn what they owed him, they would never be short-changed; his friendship, they learned, was a gift to be cherished. "If he was your friend, he was your friend forever," one man was to say. "He would be with you—*always*. The tougher the going, the more certain you could be that when you looked around, Sam Rayburn would be standing there with you. I never met a man so loyal to a friend."

He used the words "just" and "fair" a lot, and his colleagues learned that he meant those words, too. "Whether or not he liked an issue was actually immaterial," a friend said. "He kept saying he wanted to find out what was *right*—and after a while, you realized: by God, he was trying to do just that."

He would spend "about three terms" in the Legislature, he had told his brothers and sisters so many years before, and then he would be elected Speaker. During his third term, he ran for Speaker. His speech in the well of the House was to the point. "If you have anything for me," he told his colleagues, "give it to me now." It was a personal appeal, and the response was personal. Bailey's weight was behind him, but that was not a decisive factor—not for a candidate supported by none of the state's major power interests. "Sam Rayburn was elected," says one of his colleagues, "because of the simple respect everyone had for him." (For a moment, the iron façade cracked and the emotion beneath it showed—but only for a moment. When the vote was announced, recalls a friend, "Sam jumped up and gave a cotton-patch yell and then sat down real quick—like he was ashamed of himself." There was another brief crack—during his acceptance speech. "Up in Fannin County there is an old man already passed his three score, and by his side there sits an old woman at whose feet I would delight to worship," he said. "For them also I thank you.")

A Speaker's power was used to get more. That power (the Speaker's "rights and duties") had been undefined; when, at his direction, they were defined now—by a committee of his friends—the definition gave the Speaker unprecedented power. He had no reluctance to use it. He himself recalled that "I saw that all my friends got the good appointments and that those who voted against me for Speaker got none." Even supporters could not threaten him; when he turned down their nominee for a clerkship, their spokesman told him, "If you don't appoint her, I'll get up a petition signed by a majority." "I don't give a damn if every member signs your petition," Rayburn replied. "I still won't appoint her." And he knew what he wanted to use his power for: during his single year as Speaker, the Texas House of Representatives passed significant legislation regulating utilities, railroads and banks—including bills whose passage the Populists had been urging, without hope, for years.

A single year: he had, after all, told his brothers and sisters that he would be in Congress by the age of thirty, and now, in 1912, he was thirty. He appointed a committee to redraw the boundaries of congressional districts, and the committee removed from the Fannin County district the home county of the State Senator who would have been his most formidable opponent. Running for Congress, he evoked his destiny. "When I was a schoolboy," he said, "I made up my mind that I was going to run for Congress when I was thirty. . . . I have reached that age, and I am running for Congress. I believe I have lived to be worthy of your support. I believe I will be elected." He displayed a quiet but effective wit: "I will not deny that there are men in the district better qualified than I to go to Congress, but, gentlemen, these men are not in the race." And he was elected.

DECADES LATER, when Sam Rayburn was a legend, one aspect of the legend, fostered by the brief, almost cryptic terseness of his rare speeches, was taciturnity, at least in public. And the reporters who created the legend, who had not known Sam Rayburn when he was a young Congressman, assumed that such taciturnity had always been a Rayburn characteristic.

It hadn't. He had been in Congress less than a month, in fact, when he took the floor. He was aware, he said, of "the long-established custom of this House, which . . . demands that discussions . . . shall be left . . . to the more mature members," but he was going "to break" that custom—to "refuse to be relegated to that lockjawed ostracism." He was refusing, he said, because he represented 200,000 people, and they needed someone to speak for them —and, in his speech, which lasted for almost two hours, he did indeed speak for them, pouring out all the bitterness and resentment that had, a generation before, made the northeast corner of Texas a stronghold of the Texas Alliance and of the People's Party.

The issue was the tariff. The House, newly Democratic, was, under the spur of the newly inaugurated Woodrow Wilson, debating the Underwood Bill, which would begin to reform the tariff laws that Populists hated by, for example, placing shoes as well as steerhides on the free list.

The Republicans "talk about the hard deal the producer is getting in this bill," Rayburn said. The Republican Party, he said, is always "willing and anxious to take that small rich class under its protective wing, but unwilling at all times to heed the great chorus of sad cries ever coming from the large yet poor class, the American consumer." What's wrong, he demanded, with reducing the price of the shoes a man "must buy to protect the feet of his children?" The system that kept that price high was "the most indefensible system the world has ever known." Under it, "the poor man . . . is compelled to pay more than the rich man," and "manufacturers fatten their already swollen purses with more ill-gotten gains wrung from the horny hands of the toiling masses," from the people who "have forever been ground under the heel of taxation with a relentless tread."

He was especially bitter about the Republicans' attempt, then in full stride, to persuade the farmer that tariffs were really in his best interest. The Republicans "talk about the farmer," he said. What did they know about the farmer? "What consideration have they shown him?" They would find that they underestimated the farmer, he said; they would learn, to their shock, that "they are dealing with a thinking and intelligent class." The Democratic Party, "the party of the masses," was in power at last. Its representatives were "men who came from every walk of life, and who were fresh from the people, who knew their hopes and their aspirations, and their wants, and their sufferings." Its President was "clean and matchless" with "the great heart and mind that he could interpret the inarticulate longings of suffering humanity." The Democrats would pass the Underwood Bill, reduce the tariffs, break up the "swollen fortunes," destroy the "trusts," lift the load from the bending backs, the "stooped and weary backs," of the farmers and laboring class.

Decades later, when Sam Rayburn was a legend and reporters constantly quoted his advice to young Congressmen—"To get along, go along" —one aspect of the legend was the assumption that when *he* was a young Congressman, he had "gone along," that he had subordinated his own views to those of his party and its leaders.

He hadn't. As a young Congressman, he had "gone along" with no one —not even with the President, the President of his own party, whom he idolized.

During his second year in the House, he wrote—himself, with no staff assistance—a bill embodying the old People's Party dream of intensified government regulation of railroads, by giving the government authority over the issuance of new securities by the railroads. Happening, by chance, to see the bill, Louis D. Brandeis, then one of President Wilson's advisors, thought it so good that, says Wilson biographer Arthur Link, it was made one of the three measures that formed the centerpiece of the President's campaign against the trusts. Despite the opposition of the senior member of the Texas delegation, the popular and powerful John Nance Garner, Rayburn pushed the bill to passage in the House; in a note hand-delivered to Rayburn, the President said he had watched Rayburn's fight "with admiration and genuine appreciation," and for some months thereafter invited him frequently to the White House. But the heady moment passed. Railroad lobbyists killed the bill in the Senate, and by the following year, Wilson had had second thoughts; Rayburn was told that the President did not want the bill re-introduced. Although he knew that without White House support the cause was lost—as, indeed, it proved to be—Rayburn refused to stop fighting for it; he introduced the bill anyway. This was an embarrassment to the White House; Rayburn was told the President did not want the bill actively pushed. Rayburn actively pushed it. The President sent the message again— via a messenger whose orders he was sure would be obeyed: the leader of

Rayburn's own state delegation, Cactus Jack Garner himself. Rayburn continued pushing. Then Wilson summoned the obstinate freshman to the White House to give him the order face to face. If Wilson received an answer at all, it was a short one; Rayburn was to recall replying in a single sentence: "I'm sorry I can't go along with you, Mr. President." Turning his back on his "clean and matchless" idol, he walked out of the room without another word.

Angered by his recalcitrance, President Wilson threw the weight of the White House behind Rayburn's opponent in the next Democratic primary. Holding his seat nonetheless, Rayburn, on his return to Congress, introduced half a dozen railroad bills against the President's wishes, secured the passage of several, and was eventually to play a crucial role in winning the eight-hour day for railroad workers. Admiring colleagues gave him a nickname: "The Railroad Legislator." And he was active—defiantly and eloquently active, often against the wishes of party leaders—in other areas, including the creation of the Federal Trade Commission.

One aspect of the legend that *was* true was his personal integrity. Men learned in Washington what they had learned in Austin: no one could cross Sam Rayburn—and no one could buy him. Lobbyists could not buy him so much as a meal. Not even the taxpayer could buy him a meal. Spurning the conventional congressional junket, Rayburn would during his forty-eight years in Congress take exactly one overseas trip—a trip to inspect the Panama Canal that he considered necessary because his committee was considering Canal legislation—and on that trip he insisted on paying his own way. He refused not only fees but travel expenses for out-of-town speeches; hosts who, thinking his refusal *pro forma*, attempted to press checks upon him quickly realized they had made a mistake: the face, already so hard, would become harder; Rayburn would say, "I'm not for sale"—and then he would walk away without a backward glance, as he had walked away from a President. His integrity was certified by his bankbook. At his death, at the age of seventy-nine, after decades as one of the most powerful men in the United States, a man courted by railroad companies and oil companies, his savings totaled $15,000.

Sam Rayburn's blocky figure—pounding along the Capitol corridors with strides that one observer likened to the pumping of a piston—seemed broader now, even more massive, the face beneath the bald skull even more grim and hard. The impression of physical strength was not misleading. Once, two big Congressmen—one was a 230-pound six-footer, Thomas Blanton of Texas, the name of the other has been lost in time—got into a fistfight. Stepping between them, Rayburn pushed them apart. Then, bunching each man's lapels in one hand, he held them apart, his arms rigid. Standing between two men almost a head taller who were thrashing furiously in his grip, he held them, each with one hand, until they had quieted down, as effortlessly as if they had been two crying babies. But it was not his physical strength that most impressed his colleagues. About his integrity, one said: "Amidst the multitude, he was the incorruptible." About his accomplishments when he was still new on the Hill, another said, introducing him on the floor for a speech in 1916, during his second term in Congress, "He is a member young in years, but old in accomplishment." In a body in which seniority or powerful friends ordinarily determined a member's standing, Sam Rayburn, who possessed neither, was already, solely because of the strength of his personality, a formidable figure.

HE WAS GOING to need this strength.

As a boy, he had vowed that he would become Speaker of the House of Representatives. Now, as he stood each day amidst the milling and confusion of the House floor, there loomed above him, so aloof and alone on the topmost tier of the triple-tiered white marble dais, the single, high-backed Speaker's chair. From the day he arrived in Congress, he wanted to be in that chair, wanted the Speaker's gavel in his hand. He knew how he would wield it—just as he knew for whom: for the People, against the Interests. For years, no Speaker had dominated the House, and the result was confusion and ineffectiveness; it was during his early years in the House that Sam Rayburn, in a private conversation, suddenly burst out: "Someday a man will be elected who'll bring the Speakership into respectability again. He'll be the real leader of the House. He'll be master around here, and everyone will know it." He knew himself to be capable of such mastery: had he not, after all, demonstrated it already, in another Speaker's chair? He felt, moreover, that the high-backed chair and the gavel were his destiny; had not every other element of his boyhood prediction—election to the Texas House, to its Speakership, to the national Congress—already been fulfilled?

His first years in the House may have given him the illusion that the fulfillment of that destiny was not far off. During those years, he had dealt with a President and with presidential advisors, had seen his name in the Eastern press, had become somewhat of a figure in the House. Now reality set in—the long reality.

In 1918, the Democrats lost control of the House of Representatives. They were not to regain it for twelve years. For twelve years, Sam Rayburn would be in the minority.

A minority Congressman of insignificant seniority had power to realize neither his dreams for others nor his dream for himself. There was no way of circumventing, no way of battering down, this fact. John Garner had said, "The only way to get anywhere in Congress is to stay there and let seniority take its course." Rayburn had not wanted to believe that. Now he learned that he had no choice. As the prosperity of the Twenties waxed brighter, so did the fortunes of the Grand Old Party, the party identified with the glow: Harding was succeeded by Coolidge, and Coolidge by Hoover, and Republican majorities in Congress grew and grew and grew again—and Democratic Congressmen were allowed little voice in its affairs. Sam Rayburn, who had rushed toward his destiny, was going to have to wait.

The waiting was made harder by the lack of assurance that it would ever be rewarded. Rayburn could remember when, at thirty, he had been the youngest Congressman; he had still been young—thirty-six in 1918—when the waiting began. Now he was no longer so young: he passed forty and then forty-five. And instead of growing closer, his goal seemed to be receding before him. After the 1928 elections, when Hoover beat Smith, there were only 165 Democrats left in the House, to 269 Republicans; never had the party's prospects of regaining control of the House seemed more remote. Nor, of course, would a Democratic victory in itself end Rayburn's waiting. He was not the first Democrat in line for the Speakership; he was not even first within the Texas delegation—if the Democrats turned to Texas for a Speaker, they would turn to the delegation's most powerful and most senior member, the popular Garner, who had been in Congress since 1902.

If a Democratic victory did come to pass, moreover, would he still be in a position to take advantage of it? Would he still be in Congress? He had already had several close primary races, and it seemed to him, pessimistic as he was by nature, inevitable that he would one day lose. "My ambition has been to rise in the House," he wrote to one of his sisters in 1922. "But nobody can tell when the Democrats will come into power and then a race every two years—they will finally get a fellow in a district." So many men had waited patiently for the tides of history to turn—and had been defeated before the turn came. Had been defeated, or had become ill, or had died. So many men who had once dreamed of rising to the Speaker's chair had died without achieving their ambition. Was he to be only one of these?

Waiting was hard enough. He had to wait in silence. Seniority might one day lift him to the chairmanship of his committee. Seniority alone would never enable him to climb the triple dais. The Speaker was elected by a vote of the majority party, a vote based not only on seniority but on popularity, particularly among the party's influentials. He needed friends. He couldn't make enemies. He needed friends not only for his own dreams but for the dreams he dreamed for what he had referred to as "the large yet poor class." Even if he became committee chairman—even if he became Speaker—the forces which would oppose him, the Interests he hated, would be strong. If he wanted not just to hate them but to beat them, he would need allies among his colleagues; he would need, in fact, every ally—every friend—he could get. The savagery with which he fought made enemies. He would have to stop fighting. Sam Rayburn, who had never bided his time, who had rushed to fight the oppressors of "the People," was going to have to bide his time now. This man who so hated to be licked, who said that being licked "almost kills me," was going to have to take his lickings now—take them in silence.

He waited. He had made so many speeches during his first six years in the House; during these next twelve, he made so few; entire sessions would pass without the representative of Texas' Fourth Congressional District taking the floor. And he was hardly more loquacious in private. He took to standing endlessly in the aisle at the rear of the House Chamber, his elbows resting on the brass rail that separated the aisle from the rows of seats, greeting passing members courteously, listening attentively to their problems, but saying very little himself; if he was pressed to say something, his words would be so few as to be cryptic. Those twelve years were the years in which the legend of Sam Rayburn's taciturnity was born. The heavy lips compressed themselves into a thin, hard line, so grim that even in repose the corners of his mouth turned down. The Republicans passed legislation raising the tariffs again, helping the railroads; the lips of the "Railroad Legislator" remained closed. Men who had not known him before had no idea how much strength it took for him to keep them closed. When Silent Cal Coolidge noted that "You don't have to explain something you haven't said," Rayburn told people that that was "the smartest thing he'd ever heard outside of the Bible." He took to quoting the remark himself; he talked sometimes about men who "had gotten in trouble from talking too much." Was he reminding himself what he was doing—and why he had to do it?

There was no more breaking of House customs, no more defiance of party leaders. He had disregarded Garner's advice once. Now he sought it, became the older Texan's protégé. His hotel, the Cochran, was the Washington residence of many prominent members of the House. In the evenings, they would pull up easy chairs in a circle in the lobby and talk; Rayburn made it his business to become part of that circle: a respectful, advice-asking, attentively listening part. If he felt he knew as much as they, they never knew it. In later years, he would frequently quote a Biblical axiom: "There is a time to fish and a time to mend nets." This was net-mending time for him—and he mended them. The House hierarchy came to look upon him with paternalistic fondness. And these older men learned that on the rare occasions on which Sam Rayburn did speak, there was quite a bit of sense in what he had to say. They saw, moreover, that he had what one observer was to call an "indefinable knack for sensing the mood of the House"; he seemed to know, by some intuitive instinct for the legislative process, "just how far it could be pushed," what the vote on a crucial bill would be if the vote was taken immediately—and what it would be if the vote was delayed a week. Asked decades later about this knack, he would reply: "If you can't feel things that you can't see or hear, you don't belong here." He never discussed this knack then—or admitted he had it—but the older men saw he did. And the older men learned they could depend on him —once he gave his word, it was never broken; Garner tendered him his ultimate accolade: "Sam stands hitched." Garner and other Democratic leaders admitted him to the inner circles of House Democrats, "employed him," as one article put it, "to do big jobs in tough fights, and were repaid by his hard-working loyalty." It was during these years that, when some young member asked him for advice on how to succeed in Congress, he began to use the curt remark: "To get along, go along."

He used his growing influence to make friends among young Congressmen, but the alliances thus struck were made very quietly. Recalls one Congressman: "He would help you. If you said, 'Sam, I need help,' he might say, 'I'll see what I can do.' He might just grunt. But when the bill came up, if you had needed some votes changed, the votes were changed."

More and more now, other Congressmen turned to him. Said one, Marvin Jones:

> The House soon spots the men . . . who attend a committee session where there isn't any publicity, who attend during the long grind of hearing witnesses, who day after day have sat there. . . . Men will come in and out of an executive session, but there are only a few men who sit there and watch every sentence that goes into the bill and know why it went in. . . . The House soon finds out who does that on each committee.

A Congressman, required to vote on many bills he knows little about, "learns to rely heavily on those few men," Jones was to say. "I could give you some of the names of those men. . . . There was Sam Rayburn. . . ."

"TO GET ALONG, GO ALONG"—wait, wait in silence. It was hard for him to take his own advice—how hard is revealed in the letters he wrote home. "This is a lonesome, dark day here," he wrote.

> You wouldn't think it, but a fellow gets lonesomer here, I think, than any place almost. Everybody is busy and one does not find that congeniality for which a fellow so thirsts. . . . It is a selfish, sourbellied place, every fellow trying for fame, perhaps I should say notoriety . . . and are ready at all times to use the other fellow as a prizepole for it. . . . I really believe I will here, as I did in the Texas Legislature, rise to a place where my voice will be somewhat potent in the affairs of the nation, but sometimes it becomes a cheerless fight, and a fellow is almost ready to exclaim, "what's the use!"

He wrote that letter in 1919. The cheerless fight had just started. He would have to fight it for twelve more years. But he fought. He took his own advice. He waited in silence, waited and went along, for twelve years, acquiring not only seniority but friends, until on December 7, 1931, the day on which, thanks to Dick Kleberg's election, the Democrats regained control of Congress, the day Lyndon Johnson came to Washington, he became not Speaker —it would be another nine years before Sam Rayburn became Speaker— but chairman of the House Interstate Commerce Committee. One more year of waiting was required, because of the general governmental paralysis during Herbert Hoover's last year in office. But on March 4, 1933, the new President was sworn in—and then, after all those years of waiting, Sam Rayburn showed what he had been waiting for.

At Roosevelt's direction, legislation had been drafted giving the federal government authority to regulate the issuance of securities for the protection of those who bought them. Rayburn, who had seen so many financially unsophisticated farmers invest the little spare cash they had been able to scrape together in worthless stocks or bonds, had fought for similar legislation more than twenty years before—not only in Austin but in Washington; it was, of course, over his attempt to give the federal government authority over the issuance of railroad securities that the freshman Congressman had defied Woodrow Wilson. That attempt had been unsuccessful, as had decades of Populist outcry for meaningful federal legislation; in the face of Wall Street opposition, the most Populists could get was state "Blue Sky" laws (the Texas law had, of course, been authored by the Gentleman from Blanco County). But when he had made that attempt, Rayburn had been a junior member of the Interstate Commerce Committee. Now he was its chairman. There was uncertainty over which committee had jurisdiction over Roosevelt's proposed "Truth-in-Securities" Act, but Speaker Henry Rainey was a friend of Rayburn's. "I want it," Rayburn told him. Rainey gave it to him.

His first difficulty was with the legislation itself, a poorly drafted bill as confusing as the problems it was trying to solve, and almost completely lacking in any effective enforcement measures. Attempts to patch it up had been hamstrung by Roosevelt's reluctance to offend the man he had asked to draft it, an old Wilsonian Democrat, Huston Thompson, and since no one knew what to do, the measure seemed likely to die. Then Rayburn paid a visit to Raymond S. Moley, one of Roosevelt's advisors.

Rayburn knew what to do, Moley was to recall. The bill "was a hopeless mess," Rayburn said, and the patching-up should stop. A new bill should be written from scratch, he said, and it should be written "under [his] direction" by new draftsmen, experts in the complicated securities field.

Moley agreed with Rayburn's analysis, but felt he could not bring in new draftsmen unless he could find a way around Roosevelt's reluctance to ease out Thompson. Moley was unwilling to spell out the problem—but he found that he didn't have to. Before he "went ahead on the draftsmen business," he said, "it would have to be understood that I was acting directly on his, Rayburn's, authorization, not the President's. For all his seeming slowness, there isn't much Sam misses. He laughed appreciatively. 'All right,' he said, 'you've got it.' " On a Friday in early April, three young men began working on a new bill: a Harvard Law School professor, James M. Landis, and two lawyers expert in the securities field, Thomas G. Corcoran and Benjamin V. Cohen. On Monday, they presented their work to the Interstate Commerce Committee.

Questions from the puzzled committee members about the immensely technical draft lasted all day. All day, the committee's chairman sat silent. Trying to read his face for clues, the young men found none. They were discouraged. Moley had learned what lay behind the seeming slowness, but they hadn't, and to them Rayburn seemed, in Cohen's word, a "countryman" —incapable of understanding so complex a subject. At the end of the day, the chairman asked the young men to wait outside; after a while, he came out, and told them that the committee had approved their work and wanted them to turn it into a finished bill. He said no more; only later did Landis learn that "it was Sam Rayburn who decided that this was a bill worth working on."

Rayburn said he wanted them to work with a House legislative draftsman, Middleton Beaman. Beaman was a Rayburn man. "I had thought I knew something of legislative draftsmanship until I met him," Landis was to say. "For days," in his office, "deep in the bowels of the old House Office Building," Beaman, a "rough, tough guy, would not allow us to draft a line. He insisted instead on exploring the implications of the bill to find exactly what we had or did not have in mind. He probed. . . ." This was, Landis recalls, "exasperating." The young men began to suspect "that this delay bore symptoms of sinister Wall Street plotting." Rayburn's demeanor did not alleviate their suspicions. Dropping by Beaman's office, he would pick up a draft paragraph and stand there studying it. He didn't, Landis could see, "know anything about securities," and they felt he didn't understand what he was reading; if he did, he certainly gave no sign of it. Sometimes he gave them a word or two of advice, but it was advice so simple, so unsophisticated, that they could hardly keep from laughing at it. He said that "He wanted a strong bill, but he wanted to make sure it was right, that it was fair, that it was just," Cohen says. He gave no sign of approval, either. The grim face beneath the gleaming bald skull was as immobile as a mask. They didn't know what to make of him, this man of whom Beaman, and Beaman's assistants—and everyone else they talked to—seemed so unaccountably afraid, but he certainly didn't seem to be on their side.

Their suspicions were seemingly confirmed when Rayburn agreed to Wall Street demands that its representatives be given a hearing to present their views on the draft bill. Suspicion turned to apprehension when they heard that the Street's views would be presented by three of its most prominent attorneys, led by the feared John Foster Dulles himself. They would have to rely for their defense on this slow, stolid farmer.

And then came the hearing. "I confess that when I went in that morning to the hearing, I was scared," Landis was to recall. "After all, I was something of a youngster." The hearing was closed, and no records of it exist, but those who were there agree. Two men, John Foster Dulles of Sullivan & Cromwell and Sam Rayburn of Bonham, were the principal antagonists—and the Dulles who stalked into that hearing room slunk out of it. And after the hearing, there came the moment that, Landis was to say, "I'll never forget," the moment when he found out what was behind the mask.

"I went back to my little cubbyhole down in the sub-basement. . . . About twenty minutes later, I got a call from Sam Rayburn, to come up to his office. Well, naturally, I was worried. I thought maybe all our work was down the drain." But Rayburn said that the work was just fine, and that they should get right on with it. For the first time, there was an expression on Rayburn's usually expressionless face. It was a snarl. He began talking about Dulles and about Wall Street lawyers, and he cursed them, "in very obscene language."

"Now Sam didn't know anything about securities," Landis was to say, recalling that meeting, "but Sam was an expert on the integrity of people. . . . He knew when a man . . . was telling the truth. . . . He had no patience for men who were not sincere and honest. And this is what he expressed to me, at that time. . . ." He had not, Landis was to say, known Rayburn "too well up to that time. I got to know him quite well later on. He was an expert in . . . procedure—oh, absolutely an expert in matters of procedure! He was an expert in procedure, and sizing up the motives of what made human beings tick."

An expert on human beings. With the full twenty-four-member committee susceptible to Wall Street pressure, he delegated the Truth-in-Securities Bill to a subcommittee—the right subcommittee; as its chairman, he named himself; as its other four members, he named four Congressmen he knew he could dominate, four who would bow to his personality rather than to Wall Street. When, in the showdown, they did, and reported the young men's bill favorably to the full committee, he told the young men which committee members to approach, and how to approach them. Says Thomas Corcoran, whose expertise in handling men was to become legendary in Washington: "Sam was a genius in handling men. He would send you to see a guy, and he would tell you exactly what the guy was going to say, and in what order, and he'd tell you how to answer each point. And the guy would say exactly what Sam had told you he was going to say, and if you just answered exactly what Sam told you to answer, you could just see these conservative sons-of-bitches coming around right before your

eyes." He told them which committee members not to bother approaching—
because they would never come around. And these he handled in a different
manner; his weapon was the gavel, and, almost half a century later, the
young men can still remember its harsh crash as their champion swung it in
their defense. During the Hundred Days, his chairmanship was a "temporary dictatorship," writes Michael E. Parrish in his *Securities Regulation
and the New Deal*. "Even under normal circumstances a powerful chairman,
[he] dominated the . . . committee as never before." Still other committee
members didn't understand the incredibly complex bill, with its pages of detailed technical regulations governing securities issuance—but they felt it was
not necessary that they understand. Rayburn told them it was a good bill,
and they trusted Sam. The hearings the committee held on the bill—before
reporting it favorably to the full House—were so brief that Moley years later
was to write incorrectly that none had been held.

An expert in procedure—*oh, absolutely an expert in matters of procedure*. The young men had anticipated problems in the full House because
of the legislation's complexities; "If you amended Section 7, it might have
an effect on Section 2 and 13, and so on," Landis was to say. But, thanks
to Rayburn, the complexities made passage easier, not harder. As Landis
recalls: "Because of its complexities, and the danger that an unstudied
amendment, apparently fair on its face, might unbalance the articulation of
its various sections," the bill was introduced under a special rule that "permitted the consideration of amendments only if they had the approval of the
committee chairman." No such approval was forthcoming. Landis, watching with apprehension from the gallery, saw that "Rayburn had complete
control of the situation." To his astonishment, the bill passed "with scarcely
a murmur of dissent."

The young men had anticipated more problems—all but insoluble problems—in the conference committee, in which five-member delegations from
the House and the Senate met to try to reconcile their conflicting versions
of the same bill, for the Senate bill was, in effect, Huston Thompson's original, "hopeless" bill, which was thoroughly approved by the distinguished
chairman of the Senate delegation, Duncan U. Fletcher, of Florida. But
there were procedures for a conference committee also.

Few men knew them. "If they exist, and documentary evidence to that
effect is to be found in *Hine's Precedents*, they are observed as much in
breach as in conformance," Landis was to write years later, after he had
become a veteran of conference committees. But one of the men who knew
them was Sam Rayburn.

Taking advantage of them was made easier because Fletcher, a courtly
Southern gentleman, suggested that Rayburn be chairman for the first meeting. Rayburn said that the first question to be decided was, as Landis puts
it, "what document"—House version or Senate version—"you would work
from, which was a very important issue, really a basic issue." Rayburn

"quietly asked Senator Fletcher if he did not desire to make a motion on this matter." Apparently unaware of the trap into which he was walking, the seventy-five-year-old Fletcher replied that he certainly did so desire: he moved that the Senate bill be made the working draft.

"Motion moved," Rayburn said quickly. "Motion seconded?" It was seconded. "Vote on the motion." The vote was, of course, a tie; all five Senate members voted in favor of the motion; all five House members voted against it. Since it was a tie, Rayburn said, the motion was lost; consequently, the House bill would become the basic draft. Had a House member made the motion, and a tie vote resulted—as, of course, it would have—the Senate bill would have become the basis for negotiations; by luring a Senator into making the motion, Rayburn had won a crucial point before the conferees had more than settled into their seats. "Except for an occasional reference to its provisions," Landis was to reminisce, "that was the last we heard of the . . . Senate bill."

The Senate delegation included not only Fletcher but such big names as Carter Glass of Virginia, James Couzens of Michigan and Hiram Johnson of California. "The House had no such distinguished personalities except for Sam Rayburn," Landis was to say. But that one was enough. While Fletcher had apparently intended that, at succeeding meetings, he and Rayburn would alternate in the chair, he was too much of a gentleman to put himself forward; and, as Landis puts it: "Absent any request from him, Rayburn continued to guide the proceedings."

Aides were guided with an iron hand. Once, desperate because their handiwork was being ignored, two Senate staffers who had worked on the Thompson bill attempted to put their draft in front of the committee members. Rayburn spoke to them, in Landis' phrase, "rudely but firmly"; the attempt was not repeated. Senators were guided with deference: deference in tone, in solicitation of their opinions—in all matters except matters of substance. The atmosphere of most conference committees is tense, Landis was to write: in this committee, "thanks to Rayburn's guidance," and the respect he showed for everyone's opinions, "friendships developed," and the tension dissolved. And so did the opposition. On every crucial point, the final bill was the House bill. On May 27, 1933, Roosevelt signed it into law—and after decades of fruitless discussion, government regulation of the issuance of securities was a reality. In the public mind, Rayburn was associated hardly at all with the dramatic months immediately after Roosevelt's inauguration, during which so much legislation that was to change the shape of American life was rushed through Congress. But to the young men who had seen what he did, he was one of the heroes of the Hundred Days.

The next year brought the introduction of legislation for governmental regulation of the exchanges on which securities were traded. Tough as the fight had been in 1933, the fight in 1934—for the creation of a Securities and Exchange Commission, and an end to the operation of the Stock Exchange as a private club, run by and for the benefit of its members, often at the expense of the public—was tougher. The business community moved against Rayburn in his own committee, and almost beat him there. He had to use every ounce of persuasiveness he possessed—and every lever of power—to break the revolt in the committee. Then, in angry scenes on the House floor, he compromised and compromised and compromised again—and never compromised on the crucial point. He maneuvered like a master in another conference committee. And the Securities Exchange Act of 1934 joined the Securities Act of 1933 on the nation's statute books.

1935 was the year of the Public Utilities Act—the bill to curb the power of giant utility holding companies over their operating subsidiaries. To Populists, these holding companies symbolized the entrenched economic power of the Northeast—and its effect on "The People" throughout the country. Electric rates were unjustly high for consumers—and particularly for farmers—because of the siphoning off of local power companies' cash by the holding companies up in New York; electricity was unavailable to most farmers because the decision-makers in New York, interested only in profit potential, saw too little in rural electrification. For decades, Populist legislators had attempted to enact state legislation to curb utilities—and had been defeated in almost every significant attempt by the utilities' awesome power in state capitals; as a member of the Texas State Legislature twenty years before, Rayburn himself had fought unsuccessfully against them. Rayburn knew now that only the power of the federal government could curb the power of the holding companies, and now, at last, there was a President who knew it, too (as Governor of New York, Roosevelt had fought these giants in their lair, and had lost). The President demanded, and Corcoran and Cohen drafted, and Rayburn and Senator Burton K. Wheeler, the old Populist from Montana, introduced legislation that included a clause—dubbed the "Death Sentence" clause—which gave the Securities and Exchange Commission power to compel the dissolution of holding companies.

The mere mention of lobbyists brought the deep red flush to Rayburn's head; wrote a friend, "He hates [them] with a venomous hatred." 1935 was the year of the utility lobby. "You talk about a labor lobby," Roosevelt said. "Well, it is a child compared to this utility lobby. You talk about a Legion lobby. Well, it is an infant in arms compared to this utility lobby." This was, he said, "the most powerful, dangerous lobby . . . that has ever been created by any organization in this country."

The lobbyists played dirty—it was during the Death Sentence fight that there began the first widespread whispers that the President was insane —and they played rough. The flood of almost a million messages that inundated Congressmen was reinforced by the threat direct: Congressmen were told bluntly that money, as much as was needed, would be poured into their districts to defeat them in the next election if they voted for the

Public Utilities Act. This time, Rayburn's control of his committee was broken. When, after six weeks of bitter hearings, the bill was reported out, it came to the floor with the Death Sentence provision removed, and the bill emasculated.

I hate to be licked. It almost kills me. Three times, against the wishes of congressional leaders of his own party, Rayburn demanded a roll call on the Death Sentence. He had the White House on his side—on Roosevelt's orders, Corcoran was working tirelessly beside him—and Senator Hugo Black's hearings were providing the White House with new ammunition as they revealed that the utilities had spent $1.5 million to generate the "spontaneous" mailings, which had actually been produced by using names picked broadscale from telephone directories. But in Texas, newspapers were calling him a Communist, and accusing him of trying to "murder" a great enterprise. John W. Carpenter, president of Texas Power & Light, asked a banker in Rayburn's district "to estimate how much it would cost to beat Sam Rayburn. . . . He said they had the money to do anything." With a storm of abuse rising about him in the House Chamber (and with Carpenter and other utility executives sitting in the House gallery, their presence a silent warning to the Congressmen), he lost all three roll-call votes by overwhelming margins. But there was still the conference committee. No friends were made in this one; so bitter did feelings run during its two months of meetings that other members barred Cohen and Corcoran, the bill's drafters, from the committee room. But the bill that emerged from the conference—and that was passed—while far short of what Roosevelt and Rayburn had originally hoped for, nonetheless contained the mandate they wanted for the SEC to compel holding companies' reorganization. Sam Rayburn issued a rare public statement: "With the Securities Act of 1933, the Stock Exchange Act . . . of 1934, and this Holding Company bill to complete the cycle, I believe that control is restored to the government and the people, and taken out of the hands of a few, and that the American people will have cause to believe that this administration is trying and is establishing a government of the people, by the people and for the people."

Rayburn received little credit at the time for his role in the passage of this legislation. "Few people, if they depend on the public prints for their information, know much about him," the *New York Times* noted. "It is doubtful if there is any member of his ability who is less conspicuous, less self-heralded, and less known outside the influential group with which he is immediately in contact." And he has received little credit from history, in part because he left almost no record of his deeds in writing; not in memoirs, not even in memos—as David Halberstam says, he "did all his serious business in pencil on the back of a used envelope." (When asked how he remembered what he had promised or what he had said, he would growl: "I always tell the truth, so I don't need a good memory to remember what I said")—in part because, shy, he shrank from publicity: "Let the other fellow get the headlines," he said. "I'll take the laws." It is possible to read detailed histories of the New Deal and find hardly a reference to Sam Rayburn.

Occasionally, when he was old, he would refer to what he had done. In 1955, Drew Pearson was interviewing him about the regulatory commissions when Rayburn suddenly blurted out: "I was in on the borning of every one of those commissions. . . . I wrote the law that passed the Federal Communications Commission and the Securities and Exchange Commission. . . . I wrote the law for the Civil Aeronautics Board. . . ." But the people to whom he was speaking would not usually understand what the old man was talking about. During the Eisenhower administration, a young congressional aide was expounding on the brilliance of John Foster Dulles when Rayburn suddenly said: "I cut him to pieces once, you know." What do you mean? the aide asked. When was that? The old man grunted and refused to answer. But his name is on the Securities Act of 1933 (the Fletcher-Rayburn Act), and the Securities Exchange Act of 1934 (the Fletcher-Rayburn Act), and the Public Utilities Act of 1935 (the Wheeler-Rayburn Act), and on other pieces of New Deal legislation that, for a while at least, took control "out of the hands of a few," and restored it to "the people." And those who fought beside him knew what he had done. SEC Chairman William O. Douglas was to recall that "[We] called it affectionately the 'Sam Rayburn Commission,' since he had fathered [it]." The three great pieces of legislation embodied principles for which the People's Party— the party of the great orators, Bryan and Tom Watson and Old Joe Bailey— had been fighting for half a century. But the Populist perhaps most responsible for the achievement represented by their collective passage was the least eloquent of Populists: the man who had achieved the power to bring their dreams to realization not by speeches but by silence. (Rayburn, of course, gave credit to someone else—in his own, quiet way. Although over the course of his many years in Washington, autographed photographs of many notables had joined the pictures of Robert E. Lee on his office walls, in his home back in Bonham, resting on his desk, there was, after all these years, still only one picture, the picture of Sam Rayburn's first hero. But now, when Congress adjourned and he came home and unpacked his suitcase, he lifted out of the suitcase and placed beside the picture of Robert E. Lee a picture of Franklin D. Roosevelt.)

EVEN BEFORE he had attained power, Sam Rayburn, with his grim face beneath the gleaming bald head, had been a formidable figure. Now there was power behind the presence—substantial power: the committee chairmanship as well as patronage on the grand scale, for he had been given not only the naming of some commissioners and top staff members of the new regulatory agencies,* but a voice in the White House dispensation of patronage to other Congressmen; a columnist noted that while his aversion to publicity made him "a man in the shadows," he was one of the handful of Congressmen "who made the wheels go around" in the House. The full force of his personality, held under check so long, was unleashed at last. On the issues he cared deeply about, he was immovable. "If you were arguing with him and raised a point, he'd give you an answer," says a fellow Congressman. "If you raised the point again, you'd get the same answer again. The exact same answer. You realized, that was the conclusive remark. That was the end of that conversation." He almost never raised his voice, and he never threatened; the most he might say—in a low, mild, almost gentle, tone—was, "Before you go on here, I want to tell you this—you are about to make a mistake, a very big mistake." And he never asked for anything, a vote or a favor, more than once. If you turned Sam Rayburn down once, men learned, he would never ask you again—for anything.

He would never ask a man to do anything against his own interests. "A Congressman's first duty is to get re-elected," he would say, and he would advise young Congressmen: "Always vote your district." If a Congressman said that a vote Rayburn was asking for would hurt him in his district, Rayburn would always accept that excuse. But Rayburn knew the districts. And if the excuse wasn't true, Rayburn's rage would rise. Once, for example, it erupted against a Congressman from a liberal district who took orders from the district's reactionary business interests only because he didn't want to offend them. The Congressman had often used the excuse of public opinion in his district, and, because Rayburn had never challenged him on it, and had stopped asking for his support, was under the misapprehension that Rayburn believed that excuse. One evening, however, after the Congressman had voted against a bill Rayburn supported, he approached Rayburn, who was standing with a group of friends, and with a winning smile said he sure wished he could have voted with him, but that such a vote would have hurt him in his district. Rayburn did not reply for a long moment, while the deep red flush started to creep up his head. Then, says one of the men who were standing with Rayburn, in a recollection confirmed by another, Rayburn said:

"Now, I never asked for your vote on this bill. I never said a word to you about this bill. I knew you wouldn't vote for this bill, and I never said a word to you about it. But you came across the room just now and told me you wish you could have voted with me.

"So I'm going to tell you something now. You *could* have voted with me. I've known that district since before you were born, and that vote

* Roosevelt allowed him, for example, to name one of the commissioners of both the Federal Communications Commission and the Interstate Commerce Commission.

wouldn't have hurt you one bit. Not one bit. You didn't vote with me because you didn't have the guts to."

The flush on the huge head was so dark now that it looked almost black. The men standing with Rayburn backed away. "So don't you come crawling across the room telling me you wish you could have voted for the bill. 'Cause it's a damn lie. It's a damn lie. And you're a damn liar. You didn't vote for the bill 'cause you didn't have the guts to. You've got no guts. Let me tell you something. I didn't raise the issue, but you did. You came across the room. So let me tell you something. The time is coming when the people are going to find out that all you represent is the Chamber of Commerce, and when they find that out, they're going to beat your ass."

A young state legislator who had considered challenging the Congressman for his seat had dropped the idea because he didn't have enough political clout. Not a week after his confrontation with Rayburn, the Congressman walked into the House Dining Room for lunch and saw the legislator sitting there—at Rayburn's table. When the legislator returned home, he had all the clout he needed, and the Congressman's political career was over. Rayburn drove him not only out of Congress, but out of Washington. He tried to stay on in the capital, looking for a government job or a lobbying job, but no job was open to him. And none would ever be—not as long as Sam Rayburn was alive.

The temper—backed by the political power—made men afraid of Rayburn. They tried to gauge his moods. "When he would say 'She-e-e-e-t,' drawing the word out, I knew he was still good-natured," recalls House Doorkeeper "Fishbait" Miller. "But if he said it fast, like 'I don't want to hear a lot of shit from you,' I knew I was in trouble." Some Congressmen, says House Sergeant-at-Arms Kenneth Harding, were "literally afraid to start talking to him." Says Harding: "He could be very friendly. But if he was frowning, boy—stay away. I mean, if he was coming down a corridor and he was frowning, people were literally afraid to start talking to him. They feared to get close to him. They were afraid of saying the wrong thing." And if the great heavy head wore not only a frown but that dark red flush, "when he came down a corridor," it was "a stone through a wave. People would part before him."

BUT IF MEN WHO SAW SAM RAYBURN only in the halls of Congress feared him, men who also saw him outside those halls pitied him.

As a child, loneliness had been what he dreaded most. "Loneliness breaks the heart," he had said. "Loneliness consumes people." Now he was a man, who had attained the power he had so long sought. But he had learned that even power could not save him from what he dreaded.

During the hours in which Congress was in session, of course, he was surrounded by people wanting to talk to him, clamoring for his attention, hanging on his every word.

But Congress wasn't always in session. It wasn't in session in the evenings, or on weekends. And when Congress wasn't in session, Sam Rayburn was often alone.

He had wanted so desperately not to be alone. He had wanted a family—a wife and children. Driving through the Washington suburbs with a friend not long after he first arrived in the capital, he had said, as they passed the Chevy Chase Country Club, "I want a house that big," and when the friend asked him why, he said, "For all my children." Adults, another friend says, "were scared of Rayburn, but children weren't. They took to him instinctively. They crawled all over him and rubbed their hands over his bald head." He would sit talking to a little girl or boy for hours—with a broad, gentle grin on that great, hard face to which, it sometimes seemed, no man could bring a smile. Friends who saw Sam Rayburn with women realized that his usual grim demeanor concealed—that, in fact, the grimness was a mask deliberately donned to conceal—a terrible shyness and insecurity. He was always afraid of looking foolish; he would never tell a joke in a speech because, he said, "I tried to tell a joke once in a speech, and before I got through, I was the joke." And this fear seemed accentuated when he was with women. He had fallen in love once—with the beautiful, dark-haired, eighteen-year-old sister of another Texas Congressman, his friend Marvin Jones; Rayburn was thirty-six at the time. Although he wrote Metze Jones regularly, nine years passed before he asked her to marry him; friends say it took him that long to work up the nerve. And when—in 1927, when Rayburn was forty-five—they finally became engaged, he asked her to make the engagement short; "I was in a great hurry to get married . . . before she changed her mind," he wrote a friend. The marriage lasted three months. Rayburn never spoke of what had happened; so tight-lipped was he on the subject that most men who met him in later years never learned he had been married. (Once, when he was an old man, he was talking to a group of Girl Scouts, one of whom asked why he wasn't married. "Oh, I'm so cranky that nobody would have me," he said. *"I'll* marry you," one of the girls said. Rayburn laughed.) Fishbait Miller, who knew about the marriage—in working with Rayburn for thirty years, he learned things about Rayburn despite Rayburn—says that even after Metze remarried, Rayburn "kept watch over her from a distance"; when her daughter from the second marriage contracted polio, the girl was admitted immediately to the famed polio treatment center at Warm Springs despite the long waiting list. ("It is true that someone can be powerful and you can feel very sorry for him," Miller says. "I felt sorry for Rayburn because he lost the woman he loved.") For years thereafter, Rayburn had not a single date. He may, in fact, never have had more than a few scattered dates; no one really knows.

After Metze left him, Sam Rayburn was alone. He moved into two rooms in a small, rather dingy apartment house near Dupont Circle, where he lived for the rest of his life.

He could, of course, have gone to parties, but his belief that he could not make small talk, his fear that he would make a fool of himself if he tried, made parties an ordeal; he talked for years about the first Washington cocktail party he had gone to, back when he was a freshman Congressman. "I never felt that [the hostess] knew, or cared, whether I was there or not. So I stopped going [to parties]."

He tried to prolong the hours he spent on Capitol Hill. Jack Garner's old "Board of Education" had been disbanded, but a few congressional leaders still gathered for a drink at the end of the day, and Rayburn was always there. But the others would leave rather quickly; they had wives, and families, and social engagements, to go to. (Rayburn tried never to let them see that he did not; he never asked them to stay, often made a point of leaving early himself, as if he too had somewhere else to go.)

"The tough time was the weekends, when everyone went home to his wife," says D. B. Hardeman, who was to become his aide during the 1950's. During those later years, Rayburn's position as Speaker provided him with a staff, and on weekends he would telephone its members, aides like Hardeman and John Holton, House Doorkeeper Miller or Sergeant-at-Arms Harding; he would sound very jovial on the phone, asking them to go fishing with him in some lakes down near the Maryland shore, or to come over for Sunday breakfast and read the Sunday papers with him. Asking was very hard for Sam Rayburn, however, and although the aides would accept his invitations ("Sometimes I had something planned, but I would come because I knew he had nothing to do," one says), he did not ask often. The pride which made it so hard for him to issue an invitation made it hard for him even to accept one: his aides would, of course, invite him to their homes, but he could not accept too often; he didn't want anyone to get the idea that he didn't have anything to do. (His aides knew the truth, however; Rayburn would sometimes instruct Hardeman or Holton to come to the office on a Sunday, on the pretext that there was work to do, but, often, there wasn't; the young men would watch him opening all the drawers of his desk, and taking out every paper, "looking for something to do.") Says Ken Harding: "He had many worshippers, but very few close friends. You held him in awe. You didn't dare get close to him. People feared to get close to him, because they were afraid of saying the wrong thing. And because people were afraid to get close to him, he was a very lonely guy. His life was a tragedy. I felt very, very sorry for Sam Rayburn."

During the 1930's, he did not yet have a staff that he could telephone. For a while, he made an effort to round up weekend fishing parties from among the Texas Congressmen, driving down to the Maryland lakes on Saturday and sleeping over in cabins Saturday night. "Those who went along for the first time were stunned by the change in Rayburn's person-ality," a friend writes. "Solemn, laconic and brief in the Capitol, on the road he was talkative, humorous and a great tease."

But how many times could he ask people to come—and if he was turned down once by someone, no matter how legitimate the excuse, how graciously it was made, how could Sam Rayburn ask again? So if he went to the Maryland lakes, he usually went alone; in a letter to a friend in Texas, these words burst out of him: "God what I would give for a tow-headed boy to take fishing!" And often, during the Thirties, he would spend his weekends in Washington, taking long walks, a lonely figure wandering for hours through the deserted streets, his face set grimly as if he wanted to be alone—as if daring anyone to talk to him.

WHEN LYNDON JOHNSON had first come to Washington, in December, 1931, he had made a determined effort to become friendly with Sam Rayburn. The entrée had been good—as it was with everyone who knew Lyndon's father; "Dear Sam," Rayburn was to write, "you are one member with whom I served in the Legislature who I remember with pleasure"—and Rayburn took a liking to the gangling young man. But his cordiality was limited by custom. A congressional secretary could visit a Congressman in his office only on the rare occasions when he had an excuse—a business reason—to be there. Sometimes, in the late afternoon, Kleberg and Roy Miller would go to Rayburn's office, or to Garner's (where Rayburn would be present). Watching them walk out, Johnson would tell Latimer or Jones, "Well, they're going to have some bourbon and branch water." He wanted to go, but he was never asked. And he had no excuse to see Rayburn outside the office.

After Lyndon and Lady Bird took their little Kalorama Road apart-ment in December, 1934, however, Lyndon could invite "Mr. Sam," as he called him, to dinner.

When he came, Lady Bird recalls, nothing was too good for him. This was, of course, the rule at many homes to which he was often invited—but to which he came infrequently, or, more probably, only once. At this apartment, however, although the hostess' smile never wavered, there was not only nervousness behind it but fear: Lady Bird was very much afraid at first of this fierce-looking man. And Sam Rayburn saw behind the smile, and made an effort for this shy, timid young woman, so small and slim that she looked like a little girl—how great an effort can be measured by the number of more sophisticated Washington hostesses for whom he would not make it—to put her at ease. When he saw—she never told him—how homesick she was, he tried to cheer her up by talking about Texas, and about his boyhood on the farm. He told her his favorite foods ("He liked to eat the things he had had at home as a boy: black-eyed peas, cornbread, peach ice cream, good chili," she recalls), and when he came to dinner thereafter, she cooked them for him, and, she says, as he came more and more frequently, "learned to make them the way he liked them." And her sweetness and graciousness put *him*—this man who was seldom at ease without a gavel in his hand—at ease. He began to accept the Johnsons' invitations not only to dinner but to breakfast—to Sunday breakfast, breakfast on the weekends when he had nothing to do. After breakfast, Lady Bird would suggest that Lyndon and Mr. Sam read the Sunday papers together while she cleaned up, and he began staying longer and longer. Lyndon Johnson was provided with ample opportunity to exercise the talents that had led people to call him "a professional son" on this man who so desperately wanted a son. Other congressional secretaries found one Johnson gesture particularly unbelievable (although it would have been quite believable to San Marcos students who had seen Johnson pat feared Prexy Evans on the back): when, in the halls of Congress, Johnson met Sam Rayburn, he would bend over and kiss him on his bald head.

So strong was the wall that Sam Rayburn had built around himself that it was not easy even for Lyndon Johnson to break it down. But he broke it down. Although the Johnson living room contained a sofa and an easy chair, Mr. Sam always sat instead in a straight-backed kitchen chair, as if afraid to relax. But more and more often now, he would lean forward and put his hands on his knees and tell stories; "he was a great story-teller," Lady Bird recalls. "He remembered Woodrow Wilson and all these other figures." He began to invite Lyndon and Lady Bird to his apartment for breakfast.

And sometime in the late Spring of 1935—the exact date cannot be determined, but it was while Lady Bird, homesick, had returned to Karnack for a visit in May and June of that year—Lyndon Johnson developed pneumonia and was taken to a hospital. And when he awoke, sitting beside his bed was Sam Rayburn, his usually expressionless face twisted with anxiety. He was so agitated that he had forgotten he was smoking, and his vest was littered with cigarette ashes. "Now Lyndon," he said, "don't you worry. Take it easy. If you need money or anything, just call on me."

GIFTED THOUGH HE WAS at arousing paternal feelings—not only Rayburn's but those of Roy Miller and Rasch Adams and Alvin Wirtz—he had been unable to translate affection into advancement. On the very day in 1931 on which he had been appointed to his new job, he had begun planning to leave it. To Ella So Relle's congratulations on that day, he had replied that the post of congressional secretary was only "a stepping stone"—only the bottom rung on the political ladder he was so anxious to climb. Now, however, it was 1935—and he was still on the same rung. For almost four years he had been tirelessly ingratiating himself with Congressmen, agreeing with their views, dancing with their wives, "always campaigning"—and where had the campaigning gotten him? Long aware of what the next rung should be (it had been years now since, hearing about a congressional secretary who had succeeded to his boss' seat, he had said: "That's the route to follow"), he had attempted to set out upon that route the moment he was eligible, subtly attempting, as his twenty-fifth birthday approached, to turn Congressman Kleberg into Ambassador Kleberg. Now the birthday approaching was his twenty-seventh, and the route was still blocked—blocked, since no one could beat a Kleberg in Kleberg Country, by an immovable object that was giving no signs of moving of its own accord. Dick Kleberg's lack of interest in his job had led Johnson to hope that he would tire of being a Congressman. To his dismay, however, he saw that, while Kleberg remained bored by Washington politics, he had discovered the attractive possibilities of Washington social life; with a sinking heart, Johnson was coming to realize that his boss had no intention of leaving his job. A South American Ambassadorship might still have changed his mind, of course, but an Ambassadorship was no longer a realistic possibility for a man whose hostility to the "Bolshevik" in the White House had become obvious.

If there was a longer route—to a higher peak than a Congressional seat —a route that only he saw, he had tried to start along that route too, had worked for the most radical as well as the most reactionary Congressman, had trimmed his sail to every wind, had done favors and created an acquaintance not just in his district but throughout Texas. But acquaintance had thus far borne no more fruit than had affection; he was no closer to achieving his great ambition in 1935 than he had been in 1931.

During his first months in Washington, Estelle Harbin had seen that "he couldn't stand not being somebody—just could not *stand* it." "I'm not the assistant type," he had said. But the little daily humiliations—having to step back when his Congressman stepped into the MEMBERS ONLY elevator, having to wait outside the Congressional cloakrooms because he was not allowed inside—reminded him daily that, after almost four years, an assistant was what he was; that he was not a somebody, but a nobody— just one of the crowd of low-paid, powerless congressional secretaries.

OTHER DEVELOPMENTS, too, were making Johnson's life in Washington less pleasant than it had been.

Among his contemporaries, at least, he had been somebody: "the Boss of the Little Congress." But in 1935, that changed, too.

The whispers about the way in which Lyndon Johnson had won the organization's Speakership had not died away—because, with each succeeding election, invariably won by the candidate of "the Boss of the Little Congress," they started up again. The belief that elections were being, in the word of his fellow secretary Wingate Lucas, "stolen," that the ballot boxes were being stuffed with the votes of mailmen, policemen and postmen who were not members of the Little Congress, and that Johnson was directing the stuffing, was widespread. And so was the belief that if such stuffing did not produce a majority for the Johnson slate, the votes would simply be miscounted by the organization's elected clerk, who was, of course, a Johnson man. "Everybody just knew this," Lucas says; "everybody said it. They said, 'In that last election, that damn Lyndon Johnson stole some votes again.' " This belief—and his domineering manner—had antagonized many of his fellow secretaries. His popularity among his Washington peers had, in fact, descended to a level little higher than it had been among his San Marcos peers. But his fellow secretaries had never challenged the control of the Little Congress by his "machine," the cadre of his supporters who accepted his dominance, in part because of fear of incurring his displeasure and thereby losing any chance of advancement in the only organization in which advancement was possible for a secretary. However, among the new secretaries who came to Washington with Congressmen elected in November, 1934, was a gawky youth, obviously fresh from the country, who arrived in Washington even younger than Johnson had three years before, and who possessed his own considerable "natural vocation" for politics; he was twenty-year-old James P. Coleman, a tall, skinny Mississippi farm boy who would shortly begin a whirlwind political career that would propel him to the Governorship of Mississippi at the age of forty-one. Coleman was sufficiently astute to be impressed by Johnson at the first Little Congress meeting he attended, in January, 1935. "He was a very tall fellow and had a very commanding personality when he stood up to talk. And he was extremely well-informed. He always knew the issues. And—well, he just had something. It sticks out on some folks and not on others."

His astuteness, however, allowed him to see through—and resent— Johnson's attempt to make friends with him by portraying himself in their first conversation as just another country boy. Coleman says he realized quickly that "He was one of those highly adaptable fellows. When he was up on the Hill, he dressed and acted like he came from the city, but when he met up with someone like myself who had come from a small town in the interior of Mississippi, he acted like a fellow who had grown up with me." Moreover, Coleman, who had decided that he wanted to become an officer of the Little Congress, also realized during their first conversation that Johnson would support only those who were "willing to knuckle under" to him—and he was not one for knuckling under. He decided to run for the Speakership at the next election, which would be held in March.

Rounding up support for his attempt to defeat Johnson proved unexpectedly easy—particularly among secretaries from Texas. Coleman was warned, however, that support did not necessarily mean victory; he was told about the alleged miscounting of votes, and about the rumors that votes were cast by mailmen and policemen who were not members of the Little Congress. He and his three closest allies—Texans Lloyd Croslin, Wingate Lucas and Gore Hinzley—decided to demand that the votes be counted publicly, in front of the entire membership, and that ballots be signed, so that each voter's eligibility could be checked. (There was hesitancy among Coleman's supporters about insisting on signed ballots because of Johnson's methods toward beaten opponents; as Coleman puts it, "If people who voted against him could be identified, this, of course, gave the winners a chance for revenge on those who voted against them; I remember Croslin and Lucas and Hinzley telling me, 'You better win. We don't want to lose and have Lyndon Johnson's unhappiness about it.' ")

The March meeting was stormy. Coleman's opponent was William Howard Payne, but Coleman's allies made clear in their speeches in the House Caucus Room that the chief issue was Payne's chief supporter. "It was really Lyndon we were running against," Lucas says. Pointing to Johnson, who was sitting silently in a corner, Croslin shouted: "That's the man we're going to defeat. He's been boss too long. We're not going to be bossed!" Looking directly at Johnson, he said: "You're not going to tell us what to do." (Johnson said nothing.) Then Coleman's supporters proposed the new voting procedures; Lucas said: "We're going to have the ballots counted in the open, and we're going to have a membership list and check the ballots against it." Although Johnson again sat silent, his supporters opposed the new rules. Only after a long, angry debate were they adopted.

Their adoption meant that the March, 1935, meeting of the Little Congress would be the first time that the suspicions which had surrounded elections in which Lyndon Johnson had been involved—elections not only in Washington but at San Marcos—would be given objective scrutiny. And the first time the suspicions were checked, the result proved to be precisely what Johnson's opponents had charged it would be. When the signatures on the ballots were checked against the membership list—by two tellers, one from each side, sitting in front of the audience—a number of votes for Payne did, in fact, prove to have been cast by non-members. With these votes included, Johnson's candidate would have won. With those votes thrown out, Johnson's candidate lost.

JOHNSON'S REACTION to the defeat surprised those who had expected him to attempt a comeback in the next election—although it might not have surprised his boyhood playmates, who had known that "If he couldn't lead, he didn't care much about playing." Having lost the leadership of the Little Congress, Johnson displayed no further interest in it. The Caucus Room had been the only place in Washington in which he had possessed prestige and status of his own. Now he was only one of the crowd there, too.

(Not long thereafter, the old informal voting methods were reinstated, and the checking of votes was abolished. "There was no more need to check," Lucas explains. A later Speaker of the Little Congress, James F. Swist, who came to the organization in 1939, years after Johnson had left it, expresses surprise that checking had ever been considered necessary. "My God," Swist says, "who would cheat to win the presidency of something like the Little Congress?")

IN HIS EFFORTS to "be somebody," he began frantically, almost desperately, to cast about in wider and wider circles. Welly Hopkins, to whom Johnson appealed for help, says, "He wanted to get ahead. He had that burning ambition. He wanted to climb that ladder. But he didn't know exactly how he was going to climb. Just what order he had in his mind I don't think he knew any more."

Despite previous statements to Hopkins that the real political future lay in national politics and that state government was a "dead end," he now asked Welly to get him a state job. "In a vague way, he wanted to come back to Texas, and [Alvin] Wirtz and I talked to Bill McCraw [newly elected State Attorney General], and Bill said he didn't know him, but if Wirtz and I wanted him to, he would find a place for him, and Wirtz and I told Lyndon that." But the job actually offered turned out to be at a level that Johnson considered humiliatingly low.

In his desperation, he even considered leaving politics. Wirtz, paternally fond of Johnson and impressed by his ability, had offered him a partnership in his Austin law firm if he obtained a law degree, and in September, 1934, he had enrolled in evening classes at Georgetown University Law School. At law school, however, his boyhood reluctance—refusal, almost— to study boiled over again. Extremely defensive about his education ("There we go again with that Latin," he would grumble under his breath to Russell Brown, who sat next to him in class. "Why don't they stick to plain English?"), he was nonetheless not prepared to make up his deficiencies by studying. Willing to learn specific rules of law, he was unwilling—defiantly, determinedly unwilling—to learn the historical or philosophical reasoning behind them. Johnson's law school career, during which, Brown says, "Lyndon never recited once in class," was, at any rate, ended after two months by his marriage. "He dropped out of law school to marry Lady Bird," L. E. Jones says.

The next job for which Johnson tried was a somewhat surprising choice, considering this lack of interest in formal education. His target was a college presidency. The thousand students at the ten-year-old Texas College of Art and Industries (Texas A&I) in Kingsville wore black blazers decorated with a golden Brahma bull, symbol of the King Ranch, whose funds had helped found the institution. Like most institutions in Kleberg Country, it was still dominated by the Klebergs, and Johnson persuaded

Dick Kleberg, who had once been chairman of its Board of Trustees, to support his candidacy. The scholarly Jones, who revered education, was "shocked" by Johnson's effrontery, not only because of his attitude toward education but because of his lack of qualifications: "All he had was a B.A. degree." And Jones was "horrified" when Johnson confided to him that he thought he was going to get the job. "There was a period of several weeks when he dreamed, talked about what he would do [as president], talked it all out—how he would revolutionize the college, slant it towards agriculture, make it the greatest college in the United States." In the event, however, cooler heads intervened, and Jones' fears—and Johnson's hopes —turned out to be unfounded.

Then a new path opened. Johnson, who so admired Roy Miller and Miller's fellow big-time lobbyists as "real operators," had often said, "I want to be a big lobbyist like Roy Miller." Now he got the chance. Miller's buddy, the reactionary General Electric string-puller Horatio H. ("Rasch") Adams, paternally fond of Johnson and impressed by his entrée into government departments, formally offered him a job at $10,000 per year (a Congressman's salary) as his assistant—the Number Two lobbying job in Washington for giant GE. But with the chance actually before him, Johnson hesitated. According to those with whom he discussed Adams' offer, his reason for hesitating was not principle, but rather a consideration emphasized by Roy Miller. Speaking in terms of the Texas of that era (times would later change in Texas), Miller told Johnson, in several long, serious talks, that acceptance of the General Electric post might mean the end forever of Johnson's hopes for elective office, and for a career in the public side of politics. A man identified as a corporate lobbyist, Miller said bluntly, could never win a major office in Texas.

The offer was nonetheless a heady one for a twenty-six-year-old secretary then earning an annual salary of $3,000. Accepting it would give him not only a salary equal to that of a Congressman but entrée that might well be superior. "Lyndon had stars in his eyes" at the offer, Jones says. "He was impressed. These lobbyists had the run of the Capitol, you know. For two or three weeks, he was speculating how nice it would be to be a big dog like this." More important, if the path opened to him by Adams was not the path of which Lyndon Johnson had dreamed, it seemed, during these anxious months of 1935, to be the *only* path open to him. All through his life, an indication of a crisis in Johnson's career would be a breakdown in his physical health. His first serious illness—the pneumonia that sent him to the hospital—occurred during these months. He was desperate to be "somebody," and this job would make him "somebody." Although accepting it would force him to leave, possibly forever, the field of politics which was his "natural vocation," he was, aides and friends agree, on the verge of accepting it.

But, as it turned out, he would not have to. His talent at arousing paternal affection in powerful older men would, at the last minute, provide him with opportunity within his chosen field.

The General Electric job was offered in May or June of 1935. On June 26, 1935, with Johnson about to accept the offer, President Roosevelt announced the creation of a new governmental agency. It would be called the National Youth Administration, its annual budget would be $50 million—and it would be administered in each state by a state director.

TEXAS SENATOR Tom Connally would have an important voice in the selection of the Texas NYA director. Sam Rayburn went to see him.

Connally was surprised by the visit. He and Rayburn had never been friends. He was surprised by the purpose of the visit, for he knew, as everyone on Capitol Hill knew, that Rayburn never asked even a friend for a favor. And he was surprised by Rayburn's demeanor, by the face of this man who never let his feelings show. For feelings were showing now.

"One day, Sam Rayburn, who had never been friendly toward me, came to see me," Connally was to recall. "He wanted me to ask President Roosevelt to appoint Lyndon Johnson. . . . Sam was agitated." He was, in fact, so agitated that he refused to leave Connally's office until, Connally says, "I agreed to do this."

Connally agreed, but the White House refused to accept his recommendation. It reacted with amusement to the very thought of entrusting a statewide program to a twenty-six-year-old utterly without administrative experience. It announced that the Texas NYA director would be DeWitt Kinard, a former union official from Port Arthur. Kinard was, in fact, formally sworn in to the post.

Sam Rayburn went to the White House. What he said is not known, but the White House announced that a mistake had been made. The NYA director for Texas was not DeWitt Kinard after all, the announcement said. It was Lyndon B. Johnson.

THE APPOINTMENT made Johnson the youngest of the forty-eight state directors of the NYA. He may, in fact, have been the youngest person to be given statewide authority for any major New Deal program. Was he pleased? Was his ambition satisfied—even for a moment? When his appointment was announced, other secretaries crowded into his office to congratulate him. What was his response?

"When I come back to Washington," he said, "I'm coming back as a Congressman."

19

"Put Them to Work!"

THE NATIONAL YOUTH ADMINISTRATION was the inspiration not of Franklin Roosevelt, but of his wife, who said in May, 1934, "I have moments of real terror when I think we may be losing this generation."

"Lost generation" was a phrase occurring with increasing frequency in discussions of America's youth. Attendance at the nation's colleges had begun falling in 1931, with more and more parents unable to afford tuition, and with students having a steadily more difficult time obtaining part-time jobs to help pay their way. High school attendance had begun falling in 1932 because steadily increasing numbers of teen-agers had to drop out and go to work to help support their families (often at a dime an hour—the prevailing Depression wage for teen-age workers); or because their families couldn't spare them even the money necessary for books, or pencils, or bus fare—or shoes. "Again and again in many states," wrote the historians of the NYA, Betty and Ernest K. Lindley, "we heard the word 'shoes' used as the equation for going to school—'The children can get to school until it's snowtime; they can't go then unless they have shoes.' Underwear can be made from sugar sacks. Clothes can be patched and remade. Shoes seem the insurmountable obstacle to school attendance." While no attempt to collect statistics on the young was comprehensive, every attempt was instructive, as if, as the Lindleys put it, the attempts "sank scalpels far enough into the social organism to expose to view conditions far worse than most people had suspected." The United States had always been proud of its educational system; now, in 1935, with the Depression in its sixth year, a study—one which did not include the Deep South, where educational levels were traditionally low—would disclose that of 35,000 young people employed on NYA work projects, half had never gone to school a day beyond the eighth grade. Out of every hundred such young people, then, only fifty reached high school; out of that fifty, only ten graduated from high school; out of that ten, only three even began college; and out of those three, fewer than two graduated from college—two out of one hundred. As the Lindleys wrote: "The more one sees . . . , the more insistent becomes the question: 'Where is the celebrated American school system?' "

Once out of school, young people found themselves looking for jobs in a world with few jobs to offer. In normal times, some would have been taken on as beginners or apprentices, earning enough to live on while they learned a trade. Now, with even skilled men pounding the pavements, who was hiring apprentices? Of the 22 million persons between the ages of sixteen and twenty-five in the United States in 1935, at least 3.3 million—and perhaps as many as 5 million—were both out of school and out of work, millions of young people drifting through their days with nothing constructive to do.

For such youths, idle, bereft of hope, even coming home at night was agony. Said one: "Maybe you don't know what it's like to come home and have everyone looking at you, and you know what they're thinking, even if they don't say it, 'He didn't find a job.' It gets terrible. You just don't want to come home. . . ." Many of them—more and more of them, in one of the Depression's most disturbing developments—didn't come home. A government investigator watching ragged, bundle-clutching figures jumping off a Southern Pacific freight train as it pulled into the yards in El Paso was shocked to see that "most of them are only boys," but the railroad "bull" standing beside him told him his surprise was unwarranted. "Most of those on the road nowadays are young men," he said, "just young fellows, just boys who don't know where they are going, or why." Many of them were heading west; poignantly, some of them compared themselves with their forefathers, who had headed in the same direction. But, as the Lindleys wrote, "The last frontier disappeared some forty years ago. When young men now want to move on, they find there is no place to go." The hospitable Western "Howdy" had been replaced by the "Keep moving" of law enforcement officials who escorted newcomers to the nearest county line. And when they got as far west as they could—to golden California—they found guards posted on the highway to turn them back at the border, and those of them who made it into the state anyway were placed in forced-labor camps until they could be dumped back over the state line. The youths lived in squalid hobo jungles with thieves, alcoholics, drug addicts and ex-convicts, and the railroad bull in El Paso told the federal man, "The worst thing is that the boys may turn into bums. This year, already, they are tougher than they were last year." Observers with a broader overview held the same opinion. "To workers in the U.S. Children's Bureau and the National Association of Travelers' Aid Societies," William Manchester was to report, "it sometimes seemed that the youth of a nation was being destroyed on the rails."

While the New Deal might be making headway in other areas, it was losing ground on the youth front. Every year, either by graduating or dropping out, some 2.25 million more young people were leaving schools and colleges; and every year the number of young people both out of school and out of work rose. And, even more ominously, by 1935, a substantial number had been in that category for a long time. The Depression was in its sixth year now, and, as one 1935 study put it, "boys and girls who were fifteen or sixteen in 1929 when the Depression began are no longer children; they are grown-ups"—adults who had never, since they left school, had anything productive to do; adults embittered by "years of suffering and hardship." The President's Advisory Commission on Education was to warn of a whole "lost generation of young people."

In thinking of the youth problem, moreover, September always loomed ahead; September when schools opened, and America's children either entered their doors—or didn't. In September, 1934, no fewer than 700,000 boys and girls of high school age had failed to enroll in high school. Now the September of 1935 was approaching, and unless something was done, that number would be even higher; hundreds of thousands more young people would join the ranks of that lost generation.

Eleanor Roosevelt—whose empathy with the young, with those who would rather light the candles than curse, was always so deep—had sat on platforms, many platforms, where lecturers told young people that their problems were their own fault, and she had not agreed.* The plight of youth, Mrs. Roosevelt felt, was the fault of society; "a civilization which does not provide young people with a way to earn a living is pretty poor," she said. Having grasped the dimensions of the problem early—it had been in May, 1934, that she spoke of her "real terror" about it—she had early begun pressing her husband to alleviate it with some program which would help youngsters stay in school and out of the ranks of the unemployed, and which would also give youngsters out of school both jobs and the training for better jobs. Nor was this all she wanted for them. "We have got to [make] these young people . . . feel that they are necessary," she said. And, she said, they should be given "certain things for which youth craves—the chance for self-sacrifice for an ideal." What she envisioned was some sort of youth service for the country on a broader scale, and incorporating more formal education and vocational training, than the immensely popular Civilian Conservation Corps, which had been created during the Hundred Days.

Her husband, whose inventor's pride in the CCC (which was largely *his* personal inspiration) perhaps made him reluctant to concede the need for additional measures, and who saw that a program such as the one his

---

* After one conference at which former Secretary of War Newton D. Baker said there was "plenty of opportunity for young people of initiative and spirit to earn a living," she wrote him, "I confess that my own imagination has been extremely lacking for the last few months! If you have any convincing suggestions . . . I shall be more than grateful." (Baker had no such suggestions.)

wife was suggesting would be bitterly opposed—not only because the education lobby would fear that federal intervention in education would lessen its control of the schools, but because of traditional fears that such a program would inject politics into the schools—did not at once agree. Fulton Oursler witnessed one discussion between them on the subject, a discussion that became rather heated when Eleanor called the CCC "too militaristic." (Franklin: "It's the last thing in the world it really is." Eleanor: "Well, after all, my dear, it is under the supervision of the Army." Franklin: "That does not make it militaristic.") The President made the additional point that there was no specific young people's problem, but only a problem of the whole people ("Another delegation could come to you, representing men over forty who can't get jobs. . . . Such movements as a youth movement seem to be especially unnecessary"). But Mrs. Roosevelt knew how to appeal to her husband; she shifted, Joseph P. Lash relates, "to the political argument. The young people would soon be voters. . . . Franklin relaxed. 'There is a great deal to what you say. . . .' Her husband was a 'practical politician,' she later said. If other arguments failed, he was always sensitive to the 'purely political' argument." Then some of his advisors— even Harry Hopkins and Aubrey Williams—warned him that the establishment of a youth agency in the government might boomerang politically by raising the cry that he was trying to regiment America's youth the way Germany was doing. "If it is the right thing to do for the young people, then it should be done," he replied. "I guess we can stand the criticism, and I doubt if our youth can be regimented in this or any other way." ("That was another side of him," Lash has written. "He was not only the politician.") "I have determined that we shall do something for the Nation's unemployed youth," he declared. "They must have their chance." The National Youth Administration was created to give it to them.

Since, to defuse the "regimentation" charge, it had been decided "that the NYA should operate with . . . a minimum of centralized control," each of the forty-eight state directors was to be allowed "the widest latitude" to create, organize and administer his own program. Even during the period of the NYA's greatest activity, when it was employing half a million youths, its national office in Washington would never grow to more than sixty-seven persons, including secretaries.

The Texas State Director's initial creation was a staff.

In assembling it, Lyndon Johnson's ability to read men was put to the proof—and was proven. The men he wanted were the men he had cached in patronage jobs while he had been Dick Kleberg's secretary. In selecting them to be the recipients of his patronage, he had been gambling that when at some future date he called them, they would come to him. Now he called, and they came—even those who did not want to.

Not a year before, Willard Deason, bowing to Johnson's arguments, had forsaken a promising career in education for a career in law. Now Deason was summoned for another chat.

No more was heard about the beauties of the law. Flying to Austin on July 27, 1935, the day after his appointment was announced, Johnson, meeting with Deason, dwelt instead on the beauties of the National Youth Administration. "I had never heard of it," Deason recalls, and his eagerness to join it was not enhanced by the meager salary—$2,100—he was offered. But Johnson, he says, was "the greatest salesman"; the marching orders had been changed—and Deason obeyed them. Feeling that his job as attorney with the Federal Land Bank was "a real stepping stone," he agreed at the July 27 meeting to leave it only for two weeks: when Johnson pleaded with him to "help me get this thing started," he said he would use his two-week vacation to do so. But during those two weeks, Johnson persuaded him to take a six-month leave of absence from the Land Bank job—and at the end of the six months, Deason left it permanently.

His reluctance was matched by Jesse Kellam's. Kellam, the tough ex-fullback who had been given the State Education Department position that had been the best job at Johnson's disposal, had been promoted to the department's fourth-ranking post, a high-paying, prestigious, secure position as State Director of Rural Aid; and, with his memories of his terrible years in Lufkin still vivid, he had no intention of leaving it. But Johnson persuaded him to take a two-week leave of absence. At the end of those two weeks, he persuaded him to take another two. And at the end of that period, Kellam left his state job for one that paid less than half as much.

Similar scenes were repeated a dozen times—always with success. Even Ben Crider, hardly installed in the federal post that was "the best job I ever had," left it. Lyndon Johnson's appointment had allowed him to bring together, in a single office, the men he had scattered through the federal bureaucracy.

To the nucleus of a staff thus formed, Johnson added new recruits whose personalities documented yet again the fact that what Johnson called "loyalty"—unquestioning obedience; not only willingness but eagerness to take orders, to bow to his will—was the quality he most desired in subordinates. Many of the men he hired now were former White Stars from San Marcos. They were not the brightest of that band of brothers, but rather those who, like Wilton Woods, had demonstrated at college a capacity for subservience. Men who had been leaders of the secret fraternity—and who had revealed a capacity for success in the postgraduate world—were not hired. One of the bright White Stars, Horace Richards, had been given a job while Johnson was Kleberg's secretary, but had insisted on offering, and arguing for, his own opinions. He was not given an NYA job.

The personalities of the new, non-San Marcos recruits documented the

same point. The one young man from the Hill Country besides the malleable
Crider to be hired had, as a boy, demonstrated the greatest willingness to
allow young Lyndon Johnson to assume the place he wanted: "the forefront," "the head of the ring." Sherman Birdwell of Buda had, as a boy, not
only followed Lyndon Johnson around obediently while their parents were
visiting together, but had even attempted to imitate his way of talking and
walking (and who, indeed, continued as a man to do so).

CREATING A STAFF proved easier than creating a program. Directives from
NYA headquarters in Washington mandated the creation of 12,000 public
works jobs for young Texans. Lyndon Johnson's only experience with public
works had been his job on a Highway Department road gang in Johnson
City. Now he had to create—create out of nothing—a public works program
huge in size and statewide in scope. And once it was created, he had to
direct it—to manage it, to administer it. His only administrative experience
was his work as Kleberg's secretary; the only staff he had previously directed
—this twenty-six-year-old who would now be directing scores of men—
had consisted of Gene Latimer, L. E. Jones, and Russell Brown.

Complicating the problems of all forty-eight state directors was the
strictness of the criteria by which NYA headquarters in Washington would
determine the acceptability of proposed "work projects." To avoid dis-
placement of adult workers, for example, the projects could not involve
work that would otherwise be undertaken by state or local government.
To ensure that the limited NYA funds went primarily to young people
rather than to contractors or suppliers, NYA Bulletin No. 11 required that
75 percent of project allocations be spent on wages (this requirement
reduced the amount that could be spent on the materials and equipment
essential for work projects to an unrealistically low level). Complicating
the state directors' problems further was the lack of guidance from
Washington. Recalls one director: "When we asked Washington: 'What
kind of work?' we were told: 'That's up to you. . . .' But we didn't know,
we couldn't possibly have known what kind of work these youths wanted or
needed."

Complicating the problems of the Texas NYA director—the youngest
of the forty-eight directors and one of the few without public works or
administrative experience—was the factor that complicated *every* problem
in Texas: its vast size. Every attempt to establish a statewide public works
program in Texas had been hamstrung by the variations in climatic, cultural,
social and economic conditions in a state 800 miles from top to bottom, and
almost 800 miles wide, a state that, had it been located in the East, would
have covered all the states of New England, as well as New York, New Jersey, Pennsylvania, Virginia, and West Virginia. Since, moreover, the state
was divided into 254 counties, public works programs could not feasibly be

planned on a county-by-county basis, as would be possible in other states. Nibbling at the problem would not solve it. A statewide program, one applicable to all counties, and unaffected by sectional variations, was what was needed. Lyndon Johnson had to find a public works project that no one else had thought of, that required only minuscule expenditures on the materials and equipment that normally were staples of public works projects, and that had huge, sweeping, statewide scope.

It was while discussing Lyndon Johnson's early days with the NYA that his wife first told this author, "Lyndon was not the supremely confident person he seemed, you know." L. E. Jones, who had returned to Austin but worked part-time for the NYA for a few weeks, says, "They had to spend the money, and they had to do it fast. This was a decision that Lyndon had to make. . . . Making the decision was hard. I remember the interminable wrangling over what's going to be our first project. They just couldn't decide. Everybody had a different idea."

Finally, after weeks of discussion, someone—no one remembers who— hit on the idea of building "roadside parks" adjoining the state's many new highways: areas of an acre or two that would be leveled and paved with gravel, and in which would be set a few picnic tables, a few benches and three or four barbecue pits as well as shrubs and shade trees. Without even comfort stations, by Eastern standards such small areas would scarcely justify the name of parks, but in barren Texas, where it was possible to drive a hundred miles with no place to picnic except the ground, they would be welcome. They would, moreover, improve highway safety. Lack of such facilities had caused accidents because motorists had been forced to park on highway shoulders or (because many highways in Texas were built with only narrow shoulders or with none at all) on the edge of the roadway itself while they picnicked or relieved themselves, or, on long trips, slept at night. Only a few months before, a family of five had been killed near San Antonio when a car rammed theirs while they were sleeping under it during a rainstorm.

The State Highway Department enthusiastically agreed to furnish not only the necessary land and materials—mostly cement and wood for the benches and tables—but also the transportation (young workers would be taken to each site in departmental trucks) that was an important considera- tion in so sparsely populated a state. And when the Department also agreed to furnish the supervision (by departmental foremen), the roadside parks became projects which met fully the NYA's requirement that 75 percent of the cost go directly for young people's wages. The little parks met as well the criteria peculiar to Texas; suitable to all climates, they could be built everywhere in the state, and the Highway Department, a statewide or- ganization, was of course the sponsor. Since the Department had had no plans to build such parks, the projects would not displace regular depart- mental employees. One additional criterion, not referred to in NYA bulletins, remained: for political reasons, as Jones puts it, the project "had to not only be good, but look good; it had to be something that would be popular." So important was this to Johnson that he had persuaded Maury Maverick to let him hire his speechwriter, an ex-newspaperman named Herbert C. Henderson, to write up each proposal that had been discussed "to see how it sounded." No previous proposal had seemed right, but when Henderson finished writing up this one, Jones says, it "turned out to be perfect." When Johnson realized that he had a project at last, his relief could not be contained. "He was beside himself with happiness." Jones, the near-perfect typist, had to stay up all night copying Henderson's description to be sent to Washington for official approval. And then, as dawn was breaking over Austin, Johnson walked with Jones to the post office, to see with his own eyes that the precious proposal was placed properly in a mailbox. Within a few days, a handful of young men carrying picks and shovels rode out of Austin on a Highway Department flatbed truck to begin building, on Route 8 near Williamson Creek, the first roadside park in Texas. If there had been desperation to find the right program, once they found it, there was desperation to get it under way. "Lyndon was like a crazy man," Jones says. "He just worked night and day, he just worked his staff to distraction." By June, 1936, 135 parks would be under construction, and 3,600 youths would be earning thirty dollars per month working on them.*

HIS QUOTA, of course, was not 3,600 jobs, but 12,000. Some were created by additional projects connected with the Highway Department. NYA workers built "rural school walks"—gravel paths paralleling heavily traveled highways—to encourage children to stay out of the road while walking to school. They trimmed back trees and shrubs to improve visibility at dangerous intersections and curves. They filled in the erosion-caused ditches that lined many Texas highways and whose slopes were so steep that a car veering even a few feet off the road could overturn in them; and, to inhibit future erosion, they built drainage ditches. They graveled the last several hundred feet of dirt roads which intersected paved highways, because when rain turned these roads to mud, cars dragged the mud onto the highways and made them slippery. They built graveled "turn-outs" by farmers' mailboxes in areas where mailmen had created a traffic hazard when they stopped their cars on the pavement. These were small projects—even smaller than the roadside parks—but they would furnish another 2,800 jobs.

To create more jobs, "local" projects—projects involving only a

* Was there something else that made the roadside park an especially attractive idea to Johnson? The project he selected was one—practically the only one possible—in an area of work with which he himself was familiar. He himself, after all, had once been in a group of youths, riding, picks and shovels in hand, in a flatbed Department truck out to a creek.

single town—were necessary. As with the Highway Department projects, NYA regulations required that the materials and equipment be supplied by an "outside" sponsor. Johnson asked local officials to suggest improvements they wanted to see made in their towns.

In some places, the response was: "We don't want any federal hand-outs," and in other towns, the small "in" group didn't want any innovations that might interfere with its power; one area that particularly resisted the NYA, for example, was Karnack, Lady Bird's home town—because of Lady Bird's father. Cap'n Taylor "ran things in Karnack," Bill Deason recalls, and in the whole northern end of Harrison County. "And he said, 'You just stay out of the north end of the county. I'll take care of the folks up here.' " But such resistance wasn't widespread, because most towns were desperate over the plight of their young people. A more serious problem was the lack of initiative and ability to think along new lines. "Even if they wanted the [federal] money, they didn't have any imagination," Deason says. "We tried terrifically not to have any of that leaf-raking that was being criticized so much elsewhere, but so often they didn't have any worthwhile ideas of what projects might be worthwhile to do." Johnson overcame these problems. "Lyndon Johnson had to *sell*," Bill Deason says. "And I've told you before, he was the greatest salesman I've ever seen. He would say, 'Now, I've got a mission to do, and the money to do it with. Now you've got to get us a worthwhile program.' " Proposals for local "work projects" began to be sent in to the NYA offices on the sixth floor of the Littlefield Building in Austin.

WORK PROJECTS provided income for young men and women who were out of school. The other half of the NYA program was to keep young men and women *in school*—to provide them with jobs on campus that would allow them to earn enough to continue their education. Implementing the student-aid portion of the program required little creativity. The number of students who could be employed—in colleges, 12 percent of the previous year's enrollment; in high schools, 7 percent—had been set by directives from Washington, as had broad guidelines as to the type of job that would be acceptable, and the amount that could be paid: up to twenty dollars a month for an individual student, although the average payments within a single institution could not exceed fifteen dollars. But the program required desperate haste.

September was approaching—September, when tens of thousands of young Texans would have to drop out of school unless they received help. The NYA state directors had not been appointed until late July, the enrollment and salary quotas had not been issued until August 15, and these guidelines had to be interpreted state by state and then explained to the college deans and high school principals who would have to select the jobs that met them. And the size of Texas made explaining more difficult than in other states, even after the NYA allowed Johnson to divide the state into four districts, each with its own District Director. "There was [still] a lot of travel involved," Deason was to recall. "These young district men [directors] we had out there would maybe be setting up a project in one county seat today and trying to get another started a hundred miles away the same day. He might work until eleven-thirty in the morning at one, and just jump in his car and get to the other one by one or two in the afternoon and try to work there."

Attempts to make haste were snarled by a human factor: the reluctance of college and high school administrators to decide which students would be given the precious NYA jobs. Twelve percent of their students might be eligible for NYA aid, but a much higher percentage needed such aid; 29,000 college students would apply for the 5,400 jobs available in Texas. Futures—the chance for an education, the chance to get off the farm—hung in the balance on administrators' decisions, and they knew it. Dean Victor I. Moore of the University of Texas, who during the Spring term, a few months before, had dug deep into his own meager savings to keep a few students in school, arrived at the NYA offices with the list of the 761 students he had selected out of more than 3,500 applicants, and, as he handed the list to Deason, said: "I feel like I have blood on my hands." Shrinking from such decisions, other administrators delayed submitting the necessary lists to the NYA as the precious days passed.

Adding to the snarl was red tape. To ensure that student aid would go only to bona-fide students, the NYA required that all aid recipients carry at least 75 percent of the normal academic schedule. Compliance with this requirement had to be certified by the college for each student, and then by the NYA. To ensure that the jobs provided by the college would not deprive adults of work, the NYA required that NYA jobs not be work that could be done out of the regular college budget. To avoid alienating organized labor, pay scales had to be set at the hourly rates for comparable labor in the area. And to avoid criticism that the students were "boondoggling," the jobs had to be necessary, not "make work." Compliance with these requirements—and with a dozen more—had to be certified. For each student employee, therefore, the college had to fill out long, complicated forms—in quadruplicate, so that while the college kept one copy, others could be sent to the state NYA, the WPA and the State Department of Education. Only after certifications from all three agencies had been received by the Federal Disbursing Office in San Antonio would the desperately needed checks be mailed out—not to the students, but to the NYA office, which would in turn, under national NYA procedures, distribute them to the colleges, which would in turn distribute them to the students. When dealing with high school students, only students whose families were on relief were eligible; no application could be processed by the NYA until certification of such fact was received from either the Texas Relief Commission or the WPA; both these agencies, swamped with their own work, and believing that it was more important to get heads of families certified for their own programs than to certify students, gave low priority to NYA certifications. And if a form was filled out incorrectly, the WPA would simply return it, often after weeks had passed. The NYA's Washington office added to the confusion by continually issuing new sets of regulations which often contradicted one another. By late August, many state directors were telling Washington that they could not possibly implement the programs in time for September registration.

THE NYA'S TEXAS OFFICES had originally been a three-room suite in the seven-story Littlefield Building, one of the tallest buildings in the little city of Austin; now the NYA office expanded into five rooms, and then six and seven, all crammed with people, as the staff expanded and expanded again.

The staff was very young. With few exceptions, its members shared two characteristics: they had gone to college at San Marcos, and they had graduated only recently; of the first twenty-six men Lyndon Johnson appointed to administrative posts in the Texas NYA (women in the NYA offices worked only as secretaries), nineteen were in their twenties.

The director, young himself, drove that staff. "He was very nervous," says Ernest Morgan, San Marcos graduate, White Star, twenty-three years old. "If he wanted you to bring him a letter, he'd be edgy until you brought it." Often he couldn't wait for it to be brought to him; "Tell Morgan to get me that letter!" he'd shout through his office door to a secretary—but a moment later, the shout would be followed by the shouter. Shoving back his chair, he would jump up from his desk, lunge across the room and out the door, and almost run, with that awkward arms-akimbo stride, to Morgan's office, and stand there—"edgy"—while Morgan searched through his files. "He dictated very fast," says one of his secretaries, Mary Henderson. And while dictating, "he just couldn't sit still," striding around the room, acting out the letter, gesticulating with his long arms, jabbing with his forefinger as if making a speech, sometimes, if the phrase he wanted eluded him, waving his arms in the air in a frenzy of frustration. And when he had finished composing an important letter, he "couldn't wait" to see it on paper: *"Where's that letter? How you doin' with that letter, Mary?"* Or a secretary transcribing a letter would look up from her typewriter and see him standing there behind her in a corner of the office, staring at the typewriter. "Everything had to be done NOW!" says another staff member. "And he could get very, very angry if something couldn't be done immediately." Each of thousands of letters—from mayors, county commissioners, school board presidents, college deans, high school principals, students, state and federal officials—was, he ordered, to be answered the day it arrived. In Washington, two typewriters had been at his disposal; here there were twenty—and with twenty, as with two, he "didn't want those typewriters ever to stop." He didn't want the mimeograph machine to stop, either; if, with all available hands busy at other work, he saw the machine standing idle, he would frantically crank the handle himself until dragged away by other business.

He didn't want the people to stop. "The nature of the man," says one NYA staffer, "is to think of a hundred things for you to do during the day that you can't get done. I don't care what the problem is, he'd start looking at it and he'd start asking questions, and he'll have fifty thoughts and fifty things for you to get done in the next hour. And then he'll take off with his shirttail flying and leave you to do it." And then, says another, "Tomorrow he'd want to know why you didn't get through with it."

As he had utilized competition to make two employees work faster in Washington, he used the same spur to make twenty work faster now, telling each man about some other who was working faster. "He would pair us off, or there'd be two or three of us," one recalls. "He would work Ray [Roberts] against Bris [Al Brisban], or C.P. [Little] against Fenner [Roth]," and "you were always behind somebody else. He had it down to a fine point. I don't care how hard I worked. I was always behind."

The mail descended on their desks in tall stacks, and as the day passed into evening, and the evening drew later, the sight of the stacks—the evidence of work not done—seemed to make him wild. Answering often required telephoning some state agency for information, but Johnson, rushing through the office and seeing a clerk on the telephone, would shout: "Goddammit, do you spend all your time on the phone?" In his frustration, he sometimes began cursing someone for no apparent reason. "Listening to him, I heard every curse word I had ever heard, and some combinations I had *never* heard," Morgan says. "God, he could rip a man up and down." Birdwell, soft-spoken, sweet-tempered, "the gentlest man who ever lived," literally cowered before Lyndon Johnson in his rage—stood before him with head lowered and shoulders bent under the lash of Johnson's tongue. Curses were not the only words that hurt. His gift for finding a man's most sensitive point was supplemented by a willingness—eagerness, almost—to hammer at that point without mercy. The brilliant Herbert Henderson, for example, had been an alcoholic; Johnson never let him forget it. Another staff member, unable because of the Depression to find a job in the United States, had for a time worked at a humiliatingly low-level post in an American company's Peru office. He was ashamed of that fact, and was ashamed also of the fifty-dollar-per-month salary he had been forced to accept in private industry in order to return to Texas. Johnson never let this staffer—or anyone else within earshot—forget these facts. "Why don't you go back to Peru?" he would shout. "Maybe you can get by with work like this *there!* Why don't you go to *China?* Why don't I just fire you? Then you can go back to making fifty dollars a month. You know why you were making fifty dollars a month, don't you? Because that's what you're worth!"

Not all the rage was real. Sometimes, at the height of a tantrum—as Johnson stood screaming, flailing the air with his arms as epithets poured from his contorted mouth, seemingly out of control—an important telephone call would come in. Without a moment's pause, he would pick up the telephone—and his voice would be soft and calm, and, if the caller was important, deferential. Then the call would be over, the phone would be replaced in its cradle and without a moment's pause the rage would resume. Lyndon Johnson employed curses as he employed competition: for the control of men.

Sometimes his treatment of his staff seemed colored by cruelty as much for its own sake as for the sake of the work. Once, rushing by a desk with the mail piled high, he snarled at its occupant in a voice loud enough to be heard by everyone in the room: "I hope your mind's not as messy as that desk." The employee, by desperate effort, succeeded in getting to the bottom of the pile before the next mail arrived, and then wiped off the desk so its clear surface would earn the boss' approval. The boss' reaction: "I hope your mind's not as empty as that desk." The staff would joke about his constant practice of keeping a subordinate whom he had summoned to his office standing before him, often for quite a long time, while he silently studied papers on his desk. And the silence might be preferable to what followed when he deigned to look up; men who will talk in detail about every other aspect of the NYA days will not discuss what Lyndon Johnson said to them in private; "I'll never tell you that," one man said, "I'll never tell anyone that."

All days were work days. "There weren't any hours with him; there weren't any days of the week." The days did not include breaks, coffee or otherwise, and lunch was a sandwich at the desk, or a hamburger or a bowl of chili hastily gulped at a six-stool café downstairs. And the days were often nights as well. On their first evening in the Littlefield Building, Johnson, Kellam, Deason and Birdwell had suddenly been plunged into darkness when the lights in the office went off. Opening the door to the hall, they found the entire building in darkness. Groping his way down the six flights of stairs to the basement, Johnson located the building superintendent, who told him that the generator which supplied the building's electricity was switched off every night promptly at ten o'clock. By the time Johnson had groped his way back upstairs, however, there were flickers of light in the NYA office. The building's original gas lights—little tubes sticking out of the walls, with glass bowls around them—had never been removed, and through some oversight the gas had never been turned off; Kellam had discovered that the lights could be lit with matches. Thereafter, because work in the NYA offices was seldom finished by ten o'clock, the work was often finished by gaslight; because the elevators were powered by electricity, the staff became accustomed to feeling their way down the stairs in the dark.

Then, emerging onto Congress Avenue, where their cars were parked, they would usually drive not to their homes but to Johnson's. Half of a small two-family frame dwelling at 4 Happy Hollow Lane, it had a large back yard. It was in that back yard that, in the nights, the work went on.

In 1967, during her husband's Presidency, Lady Bird Johnson would say that in their marriage "Lyndon is the leader. Lyndon sets the pattern. I execute what he wants. Lyndon's wishes dominate our household. . . . Lyndon's tastes dominate our household." This pattern antedated the Presidency. Lady Bird was not told in advance when her husband would be home, or how many guests he would be bringing with him. But, no matter how late the hour or how large the number, she was expected to cook them dinner—and she did, with a graciousness and a smile that made them feel at home. Usually, food was gobbled between talk of work. Then, curtly ordering Lady Bird to bring dessert out to them, Lyndon would lead the group into the back yard.

The discussions there often concerned the latest bulletin from NYA headquarters in Washington. "That was the hardest thing: to understand the regulations," Deason says. "There was a lot of confusion at the beginning." So in the back yard, by lantern light, Birdwell says, "we would go over" those rules and regulations, "paragraph by paragraph, and page by page."

Every paragraph. Every page. "Lyndon would take this book, and he would start reading very carefully, line by line. . . . He would ask us, 'Now, what do y'all think this means?' and we'd discuss it—'It means so and so.' " Sherman Birdwell had thought he knew his boyhood playmate well, but now he realized he had never seen him at work: "He was very, very detailed, far more than I knew Lyndon was. . . . He got down to exactly what Washington was trying to tell us ought to be done and what it meant to us. . . . He wanted things to be absolutely correct." The discussion would be ended not by their exhaustion but by the subject's; as the hours passed, some of the young men sitting there in the dim light would surreptitiously leaf ahead through the booklet to see how many pages were left, because they knew that Johnson would not let them go home until the last page had been turned.

Even after they went home, the work went on, for home for two members of the staff was 4 Happy Hollow Lane; at Johnson's suggestion, Willard Deason and L. E. Jones had rented the Johnsons' spare room. Even after he and Jones had tumbled tiredly into bed, Deason recalls, "We weren't off duty . . . because he could yell upstairs and say, 'What did you do about this?', 'What did you do about that?' His mind was still working." In the morning, it seemed to begin working the moment he awoke—"when he woke up, he was immediately wide awake," Mrs. Johnson says, "and he was likely to immediately reach for the papers or whatever correspondence he brought home with him from the office." And when, after Lady Bird had brought him—along with the newspaper—coffee in bed, and he had showered and shaved and dressed in the clothes (pen, cigarette lighter, handkerchief and wallet already in the pockets) that she had laid out for him, and in the shoes she had shined, and had tightened the necktie he had left hanging, knotted, over a doorknob the night before, he ate breakfast with Deason and Jones, he would often say something that made them realize, as Latimer had realized in Washington, that it had gone on working in the dark.

YET THE STAFF didn't feel driven. In part, of course, this was because he had chosen them so well. His selections—men like Kellam, Deason, Roth and Birdwell—proved, every one, to be men who were not only willing to work all day, every day, but who were also willing to take orders, and curses, without resentment; to be humiliated in front of friends and fellow workers; to see their opinions and suggestions given short shrift. As the staff grew larger, however, its ranks could no longer be filled only from the director's personal acquaintance. He had to hire men he knew slightly or not at all—White Stars who had come to San Marcos after he had left, and whom he hired on the recommendation of Fenner Roth or Deason, for example. Some of these new recruits proved unsuitable, but mistakes were rectified. It was during Johnson's tenure as NYA director that there took place the process Deason calls "the sifting out."

Some new recruits resigned because they weren't willing to work Johnson's hours. "There might be a guy in West Texas [300 or 400 miles from Austin]," Deason says. "Johnson would say to him, 'We're having a meeting Saturday night. Get here six o'clock Saturday.' That would mean he would work until noon Saturday, then get into a car and drive here, and meet from six to ten. And we'd meet again on Sunday, and at four o'clock he'd say, 'Okay, get home and get started Monday morning,' " Some men, Deason says, "quit" because "they couldn't go the pace. . . . They just couldn't gear themselves to go Lyndon Johnson's pace, so they just had to fall by the wayside. They didn't make the team, so to speak." Some resigned because they weren't willing to accept Johnson's abuse; as Deason puts it with his usual discretion, "Lyndon Johnson pushed and shoved and cajoled—and [there were] those who could not bear to be pushed and shoved and cajoled." Or, if they didn't resign, they were fired—not by Lyndon Johnson, of course; Deason understood that: "He couldn't afford to make enemies; he was looking down the road," but by Deason. "He'd say, 'So-and-so just can't cut it. Let him go as easy as you can.' "

Lyndon Johnson liked to call a subordinate "son"—even though the employee might be older than he. He liked a subordinate to call him

"Chief." The recruits who "made the team"—who survived the "sifting out"—were, in almost every case, men who allowed this paternalism full scope. Their distinguishing characteristic (in addition to energy and a striking capacity for hard work) was not intelligence; in decades to come, outsiders in Washington or New York who came in contact with these early "Johnson men" in business or politics, and who assumed from their rank and status a certain level of mental capacity, would be astonished by the reality. Nor was this characteristic dignity or pride; these qualities were, in fact, notably absent in most of these early Johnson men. Their distinguishing characteristic was a remarkable subservience and sycophancy; observers noted that they seemed to *like* calling him "Chief" and being called "son."

Another reason that the staff didn't feel driven was gratitude. Ernest Morgan was from the Hill Country, and, he says, "The Depression really hit this area hard." But because it was farm country, food, while not plentiful, was cheap. The job in a café near the San Marcos railroad station with which he had worked his way through college, where he had been a debater and a White Star—a nine-hour-a-day, six-day-a-week job—paid only five dollars a week, but it included meals, so he had the luxury of feeling pity for "the city people" who got off the arriving trains and begged for food. The café's owner "made a woodpile, and a person who wanted a meal could chop wood for an hour for twenty-five cents, which was the cost of a one-plate meal. And what was really sad was a father would chop wood, and he'd come in with his wife and two kids, and they'd all divide the one plate." But after San Marcos, Morgan went to a city himself—to Austin, to become a lawyer by attending the University of Texas Law School—and learned what hunger was like. To earn money, he typed for a professor for fifteen dollars a month. But at times, "I would run out.

> One time a guy asked me, "How long's it been since you've eaten?" and I said, "Two or three days," and he gave me a dollar, and I went to a café, and I first ordered the dinner, which was thirty or thirty-five cents, and when I got through, I was just as hungry as when I started, so I ordered a hot roast beef sandwich, and then I suddenly got sick, and I had to run out the door and throw up in the street, and I wasted almost all of that dollar.

Fear of living out his life on a farm had brought Morgan to San Marcos, and then to the university, but the fate he had feared loomed ahead of him now. He couldn't go on. "And then I heard—I don't remember how—that Lyndon was running the NYA. I had known Bill Deason, and I applied, and Bill said he would have to check with Lyndon. And the next day he called back, and said, 'Are you ready to go to work?' And I said, 'Yes sir! Right now!' " The next day he began working as an NYA "project supervisor," a part-time job that allowed him to continue at law school—and that paid sixty-five dollars per month. That was, he says, "a big *pile* of money in those days." "I don't believe," he says, "that I would ever have made it through law school without that particular job." And he did not forget who had given it to him. After noting that he was "very appreciative" of Johnson's help, Morgan adds, "I would have done anything within reason that he asked me to do."

Morgan's poverty was not unusual: many of the men who came to work as NYA executives were rescued from circumstances similarly desperate. And they felt as grateful as Morgan to their rescuer.

In some cases, gratitude was reinforced by fear. Morgan could look forward to a law degree—a profession. Most of the men working beside him in the NYA offices had no such prospects; in fact, many natives of the Hill Country were all too aware that they might have difficulty finding *any* other job if they lost the high-paying, prestigious job Lyndon Johnson had given them. Their fear of losing it not only contributed to the energy with which they performed it, but made easier deference to the man who had given it—and who could take it away. Says one of those who declined to give such deference, and who therefore did not "make the team," "He knew he had them by the hairs because where else were they going to go? That's why he knew he could treat them like that, and they had to take it. And you know, once you start taking it, well, you get into the habit, you know, and habits get harder and harder to break. They got so used to taking his abuse that after a while they hardly knew they were taking it."

Reinforcing gratitude and fear was ambition. Deason is not the only one of Lyndon Johnson's NYA "boys" who cites self-interest—"sense enough to try to tie on"—in explaining his allegiance to Johnson. Johnson played on their ambition, of course; his future was a frequent topic of the back-yard discussions. "We knew he was going to run for something," Jones says. And, Jones says, "you felt, knowing him, that whatever he ran for, he would win." If he did, he assured them, his victories would be theirs. They believed that—believed that when he had better jobs to give out, they would get them. So few paths out of poverty existed for a Texas farm boy then. These young men felt they were on one of those paths—perhaps the only one they would ever find—and they were eager to stay on it.

But if gratitude and fear and ambition tied these men to Lyndon Johnson, there were other—less selfish—ties. The Chief made his boys feel like part of a team, almost like part of a family. "Well now, let's play awhile," he would say. Playing was done ensemble; wives and babies would come with their husbands for back-yard picnics, or they and the Johnsons would spend an afternoon picnicking and swimming at icy Barton Springs, or an evening night-clubbing in the Mexican cantinas of San Antonio. And he made them feel like part of history, too. During those long evenings in the back yard, he didn't merely read NYA regulations; he put them into perspective, an inspiring perspective, explaining how the NYA was trying to salvage the lives of young men and women who were walking the streets or riding the rails in despair, who were cold and hungry. Look, fellows, he would say, these rules are a lot of nonsense, but we have to follow them, because we have to put the kids to work, we have to get them into school and keep them there, and we have to do it fast. We can't have Washington sending the forms back because we didn't fill them out right, because every day more of them drop out of school, and we lose 'em forever. "Put them to work; get them into school!" he would say—and as he spoke, his eyes, shining out of that pale face there in the dark, would reflect the glow of the flickering lanterns. "Put them to work! Get them out of the boxcars!" He lit in even the most stolid of his boys a sense of purpose that they remembered decades later. Says the earnest Deason: "It was during the deep days of the Depression. We had a mission to get the young folks to work as fast as we could." Most of them found it impossible to resist the spell. "You can't be around the guy" without falling under his influence, Jones says, trying to explain. "First he fills himself up with knowledge, and then he pours out enthusiasm around him, and you can't stop him. I mean, there's no way. . . . He just overwhelms you."

If he drove men, he led them, too. Once, a long-awaited WPA certification of children whose families were on relief and who were therefore eligible for NYA employment arrived late on Friday afternoon. There were 8,000 names on the list, and Johnson told Deason and Morgan that he wanted those 8,000 teen-agers at work—on Monday morning. Morgan's first reaction was despair; the teen-agers couldn't be contacted by mail over the weekend, and the NYA had already found that many teen-agers didn't respond to letters, anyway. Morgan, whose assignment at the time was nothing larger than supervising a roadside park on which about twenty youths were employed, recalls that his first reaction was incredulity. But Johnson told him to take the twenty youths, divide up the 8,000 names among them, and have them spend the weekend going directly to the teen-agers' homes to speak to them in person. "I got the kids in, and stayed there almost until morning, dividing up the names among them, by streets; I'd shout out an address on Guadalupe, and the kid who had Guadalupe would write it down. And Saturday morning, we hit the streets. We didn't contact all of them, but on Monday morning, we had 5,600 of them down there, and we put them to work. That's the kind of assignments he'd give you—that would seem nearly impossible. But he taught you you could do them."

Cursing his men one moment, he removed the curse the next—with hugs ("I saw him get angry at Sherman Birdwell one time, and he used most of the cuss words and combinations I had ever heard," Morgan says, "and just as soon as he got through eating his ass out, he had his arm around him") and with compliments, compliments which, if infrequent, were as extravagant as the curses: remarks that a man repeated to his wife that night with pride, and that he never forgot. He made them feel needed.

Congressional secretary Lyndon Johnson

Congressman Richard M. Kleberg

Roy Miller, the legendary, consummate lobbyist, who
used Kleberg's office as if it were his own and with
whom Johnson was "in tune"

"The Chief" with L. E. Jones (left) and Gene Latimer

Claudia Alta ("Lady Bird") Taylor, in the summer of 1934

Lady Bird and Lyndon Johnson on their honeymoon in Mexico, November, 1934

Sam Rayburn

"LITTLE CONGRESS" RECEIVES GAVEL

Vice President John Garner presents an historic gavel to "The Boss of the Little Congress"

Maury Maverick and FDR in San Antonio. Johnson helped the fiery radical in his election to Congress in 1934.

On Congress Avenue: Johnson, back in Austin as State Director of the National Youth Administration, with Willard Deason. The Littlefield Building, at right, housed the offices of the NYA and of Alvin J. Wirtz.

Director Johnson inspecting
an NYA project

The Chief with Sherman
Birdwell, who as a boy had
obediently followed Johnson
and as a man continued to
imitate his speech and his stance

NYA officers Willard Deason (left)
and Jesse Kellam

Sam Ealy Johnson and his sons, Christmas, 1936

Alvin J. ("Senator") Wirtz, whom
Lady Bird Johnson called "The
Captain of My Ship, Any Day"

Charles Marsh

Opposite: Suave George Brown
and his fierce brother Herman

VOTE FOR

LYNDON JOHNSON

CANDIDATE FOR

CONGRESS

10TH TEXAS DISTRICT

3

"For Roosevelt and Progress"

The first campaign, 1937: Johnson with a group of supporters

Read the Record!
and Vote Saturday

READ THIS TELEGRAM

D203 74 DL — BH FT WORTH TEXAS 8 1214p
LYNDON JOHNSON
AUSTIN HOTEL AUSTIN TEX

MAY I WISH YOU EVERY SUCCESS AND A GLORIOUS VICTORY IN YOUR RACE FOR CONGRESS. I FEEL SURE THAT WHEN YOU GET TO CONGRESS THE ADMINISTRATION WILL HAVE A YOUNG VIGOROUS AND ARDENT SUPPORTER REPRESENTING THE TENTH DISTRICT FROM TEXAS. YOUR PAST RECORD AS STATE DIRECTOR OF THE NATIONAL YOUTH ADMINISTRATION HAS DEMONSTRATED YOUR ORGANIZING ABILITY AND HIGH FITNESS FOR THIS OFFICE. WITH EVERY BEST WISH, I REMAIN,

SINCERELY YOUR FRIEND
ELLIOTT ROOSEVELT.

LYNDON JOHNSON

Read the Washington Merry-Go-Round

By Drew Pearson and Robert S. Allen

President Roosevelt's court plan will undergo its first real baptism of fire at the ballot box in Texas on April 10. Nine candidates are waging a hot scramble for the seat, but only one of them has pledged himself to support the President's court bill.

He is Lyndon Johnson, former Texas administrator of the National Youth Administration. Johnson is running as a 100 per cent New Dealer, promising to go down the line with the President. On the surface the Administration is keeping hands off the contest, but under cover is quietly boosting Johnson.

If Johnson wins, the Administration can be depended on to make heavy capital of his triumph.

From Washington Again:

By RAY TUCKER

WINNER Major plebiscite on the supreme court will take place in Texas April 10, when 10-galloners will stage a special election to fill the seat and shoes of the late Rep. James Buchanan.

Young Lyndon Johnson, former national youth administrator, carries FDR's judicial colors. Of 9 contestants, he is the most vociferous and aggressive in approving the 15-man court. The district's largest city is Austin, seat of the first legislature to denounce the presidential proposals. The district also presents a typical cross-section of the state; it includes state employes, business and financial interests, students and professors at the University of Texas, small home owners.

Several senators now lukewarm towards the White House scheme may suddenly shift if Mr. Roosevelt wins out there by proxy. And Mr. Farley, who recently addressed the Texas legislature on a surprise post office dedicating visit, expects his champion to land on top.

From The National Whirligig

Johnson's Record

Lyndon Johnson was chosen to represent President Roosevelt in the organization and operation of the National Youth Administration in Texas. He worked under and in cooperation with Harry Hopkins and Aubrey Williams, two Washington officials having most direct and intimate access to the White House. And when Johnson resigned, Williams complimented him for his fine work, and declared Johnson was one of the best administrators they had.

What candidate in this race will be the most welcome in Washington?

What candidate has the best opportunity to serve the Tenth District?

LYNDON JOHNSON
SPEAKS FRIDAY AT 8:30 P. M.
WOAI—HEAR HIM

(Political Advertisement)

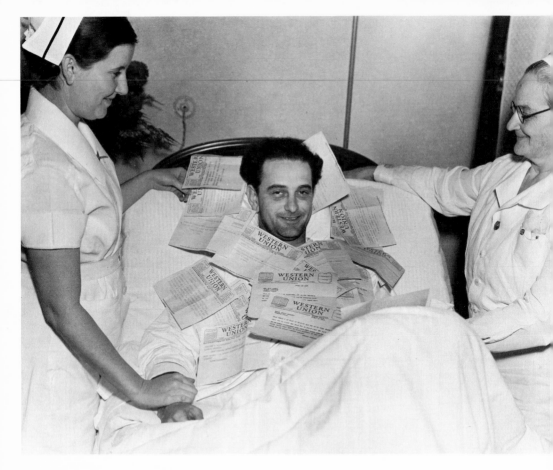

Johnson in the hospital, after his appendicitis attack, surrounded by congratulatory telegrams

Right: Johnson at the depot to return to Washington as a Congressman. A poignant scene, given the father-son relationship. He walked alongside his mother, ahead of his father, who could not keep up, and was aboard before his father arrived. Sam started to climb up, Lyndon bent down: father and son kissed.

The Galveston handshake: The new Congressman, whose platform had been "Roosevelt! Roosevelt! Roosevelt!" meets FDR for the first time. Between them, Governor James Allred (who later would be airbrushed out).

Mary Henderson recalls watching him in a crisis, when he was "absolutely frantic with worry." And she recalls that when the crisis was over, "he said: 'I have never been in need of people, or been in trouble, without looking around and finding your face.' And he put his arm around me. And I was nobody. Oh, you wanted to please him more than anything." He joked with them. On a trip to Houston, he shared a hotel room with Mary's husband, Charles (Herbert Henderson's younger brother). During the night, Henderson was awakened by groans from the other bed. "Charlie! Charlie!" Johnson moaned. "I feel terrible. I need a drink of water." Henderson jumped up and ran to the bathroom. When he returned with the water, however, the light was on, and Johnson was sitting up in bed, smiling. The jokes had an edge—they were designed for the same purpose as the cursing: so that Johnson could display his dominance over his men; Henderson told his wife he understood that Johnson had moaned because he didn't want to have to get up and get the water himself—but the edge was honed differently for each man, differently and precisely. Henderson didn't resent getting up for the water, or said he didn't, and Henderson's fellow workers didn't resent, or said they didn't resent, the jokes played on *them*. He gave each one of his "boys" a precisely measured dosage—of cursing, of sarcasm, of hugging, of compliments: of exactly what was needed to keep them devoted to his aims. He was more than a reader of men, he was a master of men. And these men, the first on whom he had an opportunity to fully exercise his mastery, not only served him, but loved and idolized him.

"I knew that he would be moving into something with a bigger challenge," Deason says. "I had a sense of destiny for him." When young Chuck Henderson had still been engaged to Mary, then a secretary back in Ashtabula, Ohio, he wrote to her, she says, "I'm working for the greatest guy in the world. Someday he's going to be President of the United States. And he's only twenty-seven years old!" Mary found this hard to believe, but when she arrived in Austin to get married—Lyndon Johnson was best man—and to become a secretary in the NYA offices, she saw at once why Chuck believed it. "I find it hard to understand when I talk about it now," she says. "But he had what they call now a charisma. He was dynamic, and he had this piercing look, and he knew exactly where he was going, and what he was going to do next, and he had you sold down the river on whatever he was telling you. And you had no doubts that he was going to do what he said—no doubts at all. You never thought of him being only twenty-seven years old. You thought of him like a big figure in history. You felt the power. If he'd pat you on the back, you'd feel so honored. People worked so hard for him because you absolutely adored him. You loved him." She saw why Chuck—and Chuck's brother, and Chuck's friends: all the men in the NYA offices—wanted so badly to stay on his team. "Working for him was very exciting. Fascinating. History was being made. The country was being turned around. And Lyndon was one of the turners—

one of the makers and the doers and the shovers. And you knew he was going to be doing even more. You knew he was going places. And you wanted to be on his wagon when he went." *Idolized.* "I named my only son after him and in all probability, as far as I know, he was the first boy to be named after Lyndon Johnson," says Fenner Roth proudly. The first, but not the last; there would, among others, be not only a Lyndon Johnson Roth but a Lyndon Baines Crider.

DECADES LATER, Willard Deason would be asked about the genesis of the political machine with which Senator Lyndon B. Johnson controlled Texas. "It all went back to that NYA," he said.

As Dick Kleberg's secretary, Johnson had cached men in bureaucratic nooks and crannies in Washington and all across Texas. His NYA post allowed him to bring these men together under his leadership. Now he could observe them at work, in action; could assess precisely not only personalities but potentialities. He could dispense with those not suited to his purposes.

Moreover, he could, with more jobs at his disposal, add to their ranks, and personally assess the new recruits. The "sifting out" left him with a cadre of men—perhaps forty in number—proven in his service, instruments fitted to his hand. Included in their ranks were specialists: not only the gifted speechwriter Herbert Henderson; but a skilled public relations man: in 1936, he brought into the NYA former *Austin American* managing editor Ray E. Lee. Johnson's ability to see the potential in the most unlikely of raw materials had also provided him with a chauffeur. When Gene Latimer's closest friend, a slow-talking, phlegmatic teen-ager named Carroll Keach, had come to Washington from Houston, Johnson had told him to learn typing and stenography, but, Keach says, "I was very inept. I mean, I was just a beginner." Johnson would not give him a job in his office, placing him in the Federal Housing Administration mailroom instead. But when Maverick was elected, Johnson recommended Keach to the new Congressman, who hired him for *his* office. And on the trip back to Texas, Keach accompanied Johnson. Johnson, who so distrusted other people behind the wheel, noticed that Keach, who didn't talk much anyway, concentrated on his driving. And he noticed that unlike most of his assistants, the calm young man did not become flustered when he berated him. Now he put Keach on the NYA payroll, and used him as his chauffeur.

The significant aspect of his earlier network, its statewide scope, was emphasized now; the NYA operated in every one of Texas' 254 counties. The NYA provided, throughout Texas, contracts to local businessmen who might be politically well connected, and jobs not only for the cadre but for the public. It did so in a minor way. Its total funding—just slightly more than $2 million during Lyndon Johnson's term as director—was only a small fraction of that spent by the state government, or by other federal agencies in Texas. But with forty men personally loyal to a single leader, with a speechwriter and a public relations man, with jobs and contracts to distribute—it was a political organization. *His* political organization.

His NYA job allowed Lyndon Johnson to expand not just his organization but his acquaintance. Austin was a city whose life was dominated by politics as its skyline was dominated by the gigantic pink dome—modeled on (but even larger than) the great dome in Washington—of the State Capitol. A substantial portion of its permanent population, 70,000 in 1935, consisted of state officials and bureaucrats; when the Legislature was in session, the city's hotels and boardinghouses were crowded with legislators and lobbyists. If one spent enough time on Austin's main thoroughfare, Congress Avenue—a street (built wide enough to allow U-turns by prairie wagons pulled by two teams of horses) that began at the foot of the Capitol and ran from it down low hills and wide terraces to the Colorado River three-quarters of a mile away—one would meet most of the men important in Texas politics.

Lyndon Johnson, whose Littlefield Building office was at Congress and Sixth Street, met them. To some he could introduce himself because he was Sam Johnson's son; his young assistants were startled (because he spoke so derogatorily of his father) at how many influential men remembered the Chief's father, and remembered him in such a way that they were disposed to be friendly to this young man who resembled him so closely that more than one elderly legislator, seeing the long, gaunt frame, and the smiling face with the huge ears, white skin and black hair, coming toward him, thought for a moment that young Sam Johnson was walking Congress Avenue again. He knew others through his work, which gave him entrée to the most powerful men in Austin, for, despite his youth, he was, after all, a representative—since most federal agencies had established their Texas headquarters in San Antonio or Dallas, practically the *only* representative—of the central government in this isolated little provincial capital. He was, moreover, a representative of the fabled New Deal, with access to New Deal funds; as much as any man, its representative in the capital of Texas. Influential men with college-age children who needed jobs to help pay their way or with a child who had recently graduated and could use a job on the NYA staff itself, realized that this young man had such jobs to dispense. Lyndon Johnson had no trouble meeting the most influential men of Texas.

Meeting such men, he made friends of them, with the facility and rapidity at winning over older people that had amazed his contemporaries in Johnson City and San Marcos. Nervous about meeting them, worried about the impression he would make, he attempted to disguise the nervousness by appearing totally at ease. Emerging from the Littlefield Building, he would habitually take off his suit jacket and sling it, as if carelessly, over one shoulder. He would turn up the brim of his fedora—turn it up as far as it would go, in fact, so that it touched the crown—in an attempt to add another touch of insouciance. But these attempts at casualness were undermined. Unable to keep from checking his reflection in the windows of the stores he passed, he continually straightened and tightened his necktie. He carried a blue comb clipped to his shirt pocket, and, as he walked, he constantly combed his hair, smoothing its waves and pushing higher his pompadour; even if he was wearing a hat, he would sometimes, staring at his reflection, take the hat off and use the comb—just in case he met someone walking with his wife and had to doff the hat. Despite these preparations, the sight of an influential figure approaching in the distance would precipitate panic. Ducking into the doorway of the nearest store, he would hurriedly tuck in his shirt, recheck his tie, hitch up and carefully adjust his pants and belt and then pat his pompadour into perfection—after which, looking his absolute best, he would saunter, with exaggerated carelessness, toward the man for whom these preparations had been made.

Witnesses to this Congress Avenue toilette could not keep from laughing. Edward A. Clark, then Texas' Secretary of State, says: "Everyone knew about Lyndon's little blue comb." But the laughter was friendly. Listening *at* them, sitting at their knees drinking in their wisdom, following their minds, agreeing with their thoughts before they had uttered them, he made these men like him, and he cemented their affection by hiring their children; many NYA secretaries were daughters of state influentials.

They grew friendly—and, increasingly, respectful. When he had been Kleberg's secretary, Clark says, "everybody in Austin knew Lyndon was a good fellow to see up there if you needed something out of one of the departments." Now, meeting him on Congress Avenue, men who "needed something" in Washington asked him how to obtain it—and found his advice sound. They told their friends he was a good man to talk to.

Good not only on Washington, but on Texas. The state's byzantine politics seemed to hold no mysteries for him. If politics was the dialect of Austin, this young man, these canny politicians realized, possessed a remarkable fluency; his opinions, cloaked though they were in deference, were worth listening to. Lobbyist Bill Kittrell reminded them that he had told them about Lyndon Johnson years before; this, he said, was the "wonder kid" he had been talking about. Now, observing Johnson in person, Austin saw that Kittrell's description had been accurate. Of all the men Johnson met in Austin, Ed Clark was the one who would, over the long years to come, acquire and hold the most power. Only thirty years old in 1936, he was already not only Secretary of State but chief political advisor to Governor James V. Allred—the man you had to see before you could see the Governor. Clark, whose folksy, giggling, story-telling manner concealed a hard, shrewd mind, was an astute observer of politicians, and he rationed the time he gave each one according to the assessment he made of his future. He began to make it his business, when Johnson came to call on the Governor to solicit his advice on an NYA program, to spend quite a bit of time with Johnson, to be friendly with him, to let Johnson know he could, whenever he might need help, call upon Clark for it. He did so, he recalls—and Ed Clark can always recall exactly why he did things—because "He knew Rayburn, and that meant plenty," because "He was the hardest worker I ever saw—he couldn't relax"—and because he had a boundless ability to ingratiate himself with powerful men ("Nothing was too much trouble for him to do . . . for someone who might be able to help him someday"). Accompanying Johnson to cocktail parties, Clark saw his nervousness up close. "He didn't want to be standing there by himself," Clark would recall. "If I started to walk away, he would say, 'Stand with me, Ed, stand with me.' Insecurity. There was a lot of insecurity in Lyndon. He had some kind of inferiority complex. You could see that right away." But Clark, a great reader of men in his own right, saw beyond the nervousness. "I would see him talking to somebody, and I would see what he was doing. He was ingratiating himself. And he could do it so good. I never saw anything like it. He was listening *at* them. He could start talking to a man at a party, or he could stop a fellow on the street, and in five minutes he could get that man to think, 'I like you, young fellow. I'll be for you.' I considered him a comer. I knew the way he was getting around and meeting the people, getting acquainted. I knew he was figuring on running for office. I didn't know what office he was going to run for, but I knew he was going to run for some office, and I knew he was going to run for a big office. And I was willing to buy a ticket on him."

IN 1936, legislator Ernest O. Thompson asked Johnson to manage his campaign for the chairmanship of the State Railroad Commission. The Commission—unique to Texas—was the body empowered to regulate not only railroads but the production of oil and natural gas. Its chairman was one of the state's most powerful men, and the popular Thompson, heavily favored to win the post, promised Johnson a commission post with substantial power of his own. Thompson had thought he was doing Johnson a great favor by offering him, at such an early age, statewide power, but Johnson declined the offer.

The job was a far more attractive post than the one Lyndon Johnson had asked for not a year before when, still Kleberg's secretary, he had pleaded with Welly Hopkins for a post in the State Attorney General's office. But he was no longer a secretary. Not state but national power was what he had always wanted. He had known for so long what he wanted to be, and what "route" would take him to his far-off goal. A state job—no matter how good—was not on that road; state politics was, he had said, a "dead end." In the frustration, almost desperation, of his last months with Kleberg, he had almost decided to abandon his chosen road, but, with the NYA appointment, he was back on it and did not intend to leave it again. The NYA job, attractive as it was, was not the main chance for which he was looking. But if the main chance came, he would recognize it. And he would grab it.

THE FRENZY on the sixth floor of the Littlefield Building bore fruit. Few states met the NYA quotas when schools and colleges reopened in September, 1935. NYA Administrator Aubrey Williams was to admit on October 28 that the youth agency had gotten off to "a very bad start." But the quota was met in Texas. By September, 1936, the Texas NYA program was running with notable efficiency. Returning to campus after the Summer vacation, 7,123 students enrolled not only in college but in the NYA, whose fifteen-dollar monthly stipend was keeping them in college. At every one of the state's eighty-seven colleges—even the state's four Negro colleges, conspicuously excluded from federal and state aid programs of the past*—NYA programs were a smoothly functioning part of campus life. Some 11,061 high school students were receiving smaller, but helpful checks.

The student aid program was, moreover, accomplishing its purpose. In 1935, it had encouraged students to return to school; in 1936, it kept those students in school. The fact that almost 40 percent of the students receiving NYA help in 1936 had received it in 1935 marked the beginning of a trend that would have pleased Eleanor Roosevelt: with the help of the NYA, a substantial percentage of Texas students who would otherwise— with the Depression still gripping the state—have had to drop out of school would make it through, year after year, all the way to graduation; by June, 1939, the NYA's fourth year, more than a thousand graduating college seniors had received NYA aid for each of their four years.

The students the NYA kept in school in Texas were students who deserved to be in school. Of 5,713 NYA-aided college students surveyed during the 1938–1939 school year, the grades of 54 percent were above the school average; 27 percent had average grades; and only 19 percent were below average. If the explanation lies partly in the fact that, to some extent, college administrators selected above-average students for NYA help, these students nonetheless kept their marks above average while holding down NYA jobs.

The Texas NYA was, in fact, accomplishing purposes only vaguely, if at all, envisioned in Washington, where colleges were often thought of as the ivied, lavish campuses of the Northeast. Many Texas colleges, only a few

---

* Lyndon Johnson's relationships with Negro colleges and schools during his NYA directorship—significant in light of his later relationship with civil rights legislation— will be explored in depth in Volume II.

years old and engaged in a continual struggle just to keep their doors open, had been unable to build needed facilities. For example, ten years after the founding of Texas Technological College, its campus was still only a tree-less, barren tract on the plains just below the Panhandle, with inadequate library and laboratories, and with dormitory space for only 600 of its 3,000 students. Falling enrollment from among the children of the plains' strug-gling farmers and ranchers had imperiled its existence. The NYA not only got Texas Tech's students back to school, but put them to work building needed facilities, planting trees and bushes, and sodding the quadrangles.

One NYA program, begun in Texas at the suggestion of Lyndon John-son's old boss, President Cecil Evans of Southwest Texas State Teachers College, was designed to help young people who had never been to college and who—without help—would not be able to go for some time. There were many such youths in Texas who, after graduating from high school, had found that their families, in desperate financial straits, could not spare them from the farm and who had gone to work, intending to resume their educa-tion when the grip of the Depression eased. To educators like Evans—he had watched enrollment at San Marcos falling steadily since the Depression began—this trend spelled tragedy. In sparsely settled rural areas, higher ed-ucation was not an accepted part of life. Once youths from these areas dropped off the educational path, they were all too often off it for good, never to return. What was needed, Evans felt, was a way to maintain in such youths, through desperate times, a link with education—to allow them to keep at least a toehold on the path to the better life that they once had sought. To do so, he suggested creation of a Freshman College Center. At it, students whose families were on relief, and who could not be spared from the farm or ranch, were offered, upon graduation from high school, the op-portunity to take one or two tuition-free college courses while continuing to live and work at home. A college could not afford to pay the professors for such a center, he said, but the NYA could—and if the teachers hired by the NYA were those who had been laid off by colleges and were now on relief, teachers as well as students would be helped. By March, 1936, twenty Fresh-man College Centers were operating in Texas.

Another NYA program used colleges to help young men and women who didn't want to go to college. Some wanted to stay on the farm; the NYA did not attempt to change their feelings, only to show them how life on the farm could be better than they had known it, while giving them a little cash to ease life there. Rural youths were brought to the campus for a four-month vocational course in such areas as animal husbandry, dairy manufacturing, farm-machinery repair; experts taught young men how to build sanitary hog wallows and better chicken houses, young women how to can faster and more efficiently. In return—and in return for a monthly NYA wage—boys working under the direction of foremen hired by the NYA built dormitories, and girls sewed sheets and pillowcases to be used in them.

Some didn't want to stay on the farm—were, in fact, desperate to move
to a city, even without a college education. But they did not possess the
skills that city life required; the farm work they hated was the only work
they knew. Often, even the basic skills of plumbing or electricity or mechanical work were mysteries to them—as were the job discipline and the subtle-
ties that children raised in the industrial world learn without thinking about
them: starting work on time, working set hours, taking orders from strangers
instead of their father, playing office politics. They lacked, moreover, not
only skills but, because of their isolation, knowledge of the world of which
they dreamed. Isolation was all too often unrelieved by reading; their education, in one-room schools, had been meager, and, as the Lindleys put it:
"Theirs are not the homes that have books and magazines." And giving
them skills and knowledge was, as the Lindleys wrote, "a challenge. It is
difficult to provide sound work for isolated boys and girls who have no way
of getting to or from a construction job, a workshop, or a sewing room in
a town twenty miles away from their farms." If the young men and women
from the thinly scattered farms of the Hill Country or the endless barren
plains of West Texas who wanted a different life were to be given a chance
at it—even if the chance was only to become a mechanic—providing the
chance would be very difficult.

To meet this challenge, Resident Training Centers were established.
Texas farm youths were brought together in groups to be taught "useful
[city] occupations" on four college campuses, paying for their instruction by
practicing their newly acquired skills on projects the colleges needed. San
Marcos, for example, had, years before, purchased three white frame houses
on College Hill, intending to turn them into laboratories and classrooms.
The college had never had enough money to do so—but the college had
fifty empty dormitory beds, and fifty youths, paid twenty-one dollars a
month by the NYA, were brought in to work on those houses. Since San
Marcos was in the Hill Country, part of the work had to be with rock:
chipping away at stubborn limestone and digging boulders out of the ground
so that pipes could be laid for plumbing, piling the boulders atop one another and cementing them in place as retaining walls. The young men tore
out walls, built new ones, installed bathrooms, built stone steps to the front
doors, sodded the lawns. This work was done in the mornings; by noon, a
solid six hours' work had been completed by these farm boys who rose with
the sun. In the afternoons, they went to classes. A visitor found that the college's industrial-arts building had "taken on the appearance of an eastern factory going full blast. At a drafting table in one corner is a lad who has long
yearned to know the intricacies of mechanical drawing, [poring over] his
plans and specifications under the eyes of an instructor. Another is at the
forge, his eyes glued to the glowing rod he holds in the coals. A group of
youths are repairing the engines of college automobiles and maintenance
vehicles under the eye of a master mechanic." They learned to read blue-

prints (NYA instructors insisted that no matter how simple the job—building a chair or a cabinet, for example—the trainee work from plans, "because," as one said, "they can't ever expect to earn their livings as carpenters or cabinetmakers if they can't read drawings"); to make the required mathematical calculations; to learn the properties of materials.

The fifty boys went to San Marcos for four months. At the end of that time, work on the three buildings was half completed; the second group of fifty, who arrived the day after the first group left, completed it. And if the college gained three dormitories, what the youths acquired, while less tangible, was nonetheless significant to them, whose world had consisted so largely of their families. The very act of getting beyond the boundaries of their own counties was important; a young woman at an NYA Resident Training Center in Arkansas said, "At first I was kind of homesick. You know how it is when you've never been away from home at all. Not even farther than five miles." Just the feeling of being part not only of a family but of a group—of living and working with people who were not their relatives—was important. At Johnson's insistence, moreover, Resident Centers in Texas elected their own self-governing councils, and colleges provided a "citizenship course": twenty-eight lectures on subjects ranging from the Constitution to proper table manners. As a college president in Arkansas put it, "The associations these boys get from their new environment would be worth this whole thing even if they didn't get a single other thing." (In fact, so poor were some of them that just being fed regularly was important to them; one Texas supervisor says that in their first week or two at an NYA Resident Center, they might gain ten to fifteen pounds.)

The program also helped young women, who were brought in from the farms and taught not only the homemaking skills felt appropriate for young women but secretarial skills. And they, too, received intangible benefits—as is indicated by one description, written by a young woman reporter for the *Brenham Banner-Press* after visiting an NYA Resident Training Center at Washington County Junior College, near Brenham, Texas, at which were studying twenty-eight women, each of whom had been the valedictorian of her high school class—and each of whom had, immediately after graduation, gone back to farm life. "When you were young," the reporter wrote to her audience of farm and small-town readers, "didn't you dream about that grandest of all youthful experiences—the day when you could go to college and live in a dormitory and get an education that would open the portals of the world to you? Certainly we all had that dream and yet, how few of us ever realized it. However, some dreams do come true, and twenty-eight girls are now having their dream of real college life fulfilled. . . ."

THE PROGRAM of the Texas NYA was hailed throughout the state. Declaring that isolated farm families had never before been helped by any government program, the *Dallas Journal* said: "The lads from the forks of the creeks deserve some chance in life. And the NYA is going to give them that chance."

It was hailed beyond the state. Several of its innovations, including the roadside parks, were copied elsewhere. "Similar roadside parks are being built in Oklahoma," the *Oklahoma Farmer-Stockman* commented, "but Texas seems a little further along with the program." NYA Administrator Williams described Johnson's work as "a first-class job."

By the end of 1936, more than 20,000 youths were receiving NYA aid, either at school or work, in Texas. And a huge expansion of the state's entire NYA program was planned for the Spring of 1937. In 1936, the NYA had built a greenhouse, and planted in it more than 6,000 trees and shrubs which, in 1937, were to be transplanted to the scores of new roadside parks scheduled for construction that year. And in 1937, for the first time, the NYA was to begin building not just roadside parks but bigger parks in towns and cities. Still more substantial projects were to get under way. After eighteen months of urging on local officials, a substantial number of proposals for new schools, community centers and halls to house fire trucks of local fire companies had been received, and the blueprints completed. Materials and equipment had been obtained, and construction was about to start on a dozen of these projects.

On February 22, 1937, however, Lyndon Johnson got the chance for which he had been waiting. And, without a moment's hesitation, he grabbed it.

20

The Dam

HE GOT THE CHANCE because of a dam—and because of what that dam meant to two men.

The dam was in one of the most deserted regions of the Hill Country. To reach it, you drove northwest out of Austin on a narrow, unpaved, gravel-topped road. About ten miles deep in the hills, you turned off the road onto an even narrower path that had been hacked through the dense cedar brakes. You bumped along its rough surface for another eight miles, heading deeper and deeper into the empty hills, passing scarcely a sign of human habitation, until suddenly the path ended in a void that was a deep, wide canyon. Walking to the edge of the canyon, you looked down—and far below you were a battalion of rumbling bulldozers, scores of trucks, 2,000 scurrying men, and, rising out of the bed of the river that had cut the canyon, a broad wall of masonry twenty-seven stories high and more than a mile long: one of the largest structures built by man.

The dam (named Marshall Ford* because it was located at the spot at which cattle from the Marshall Ranch had been driven across the Lower Colorado River—before the cedar had covered the hills, gobbled up the last of the grass and ended grazing in the area) was being built by the United States Bureau of Reclamation to control the floods which periodically roared down the 700-mile-long valley of the Lower Colorado, sweeping away the precious fertile soil on its banks. But to the two men most responsible for its construction, the dam had a more personal significance.

To one of them, the significance was simple—as simple as the man. His name was Herman Brown, and he wanted to build big things, and to make big money building them.

He had wanted that for a long time. The son of a Belton, Texas, shopkeeper, he went into the construction business in 1909, at the age of sixteen, earning two dollars a day carrying a rod to assist surveyors. Road-

* Later renamed Mansfield after the Rivers and Harbors Committee chairman.

building—fresno and mule-team road-building—was a rough business in Texas then; the weekend sprees of the building crews, tough ex-cowhands and oil-field roustabouts, generally landed them in jail, from which the contractor would bail them out on Monday morning, and the crews lived next to the mule corrals, in crowded tents.

Herman Brown was to live in those tents for almost ten years. A rather small, slender boy, unexceptional in appearance, he had a way with men; in 1913, when he was twenty, he was made a foreman. When, a year later, his boss went broke, he paid off his young foreman's back wages by giving him four mules and a fresno. At the age of twenty-one, Brown was a contractor.

Contractors had to know how to handle mules, and they had to know how to handle men. Herman knew how to handle both. With the mules he was gentle, with the men he was rough; from his first job, the word about Herman Brown began to get around in the construction industry in Texas: "You either do things Herman's way, or else." And they had to know how to handle politicians, too, in a state where politics centered on a county-courthouse system as corrupt as anything Tammany Hall ever envisioned. Herman had a gift for handling politicians—all the way up the line from the Sheriffs who could facilitate the Monday-morning bailing out of his crews to the County Judges who handed out highway contracts—and an understanding that it was in the pockets of politicians that his slender funds would be most profitably invested. In Texas, political influence was often exerted through lawyers. No matter how tight his finances—and for many years they would be very tight—Herman always found enough for "legal fees." Soon he had a road-building contract of his own. (Having stretched himself to the limit to finance it, he almost went broke when rains turned the road into a sea of mud and forced him to stop work; at one point, when he could not afford to buy feed for his mules, a local merchant, taking pity on him and the mules, gave him credit. Decades later, Herman learned by chance that the merchant had gone broke in the Depression and, old now, was living in poverty on an isolated West Texas ranch. A day or two later, there arrived in the old man's mailbox a check big enough to keep him in comfort for the rest of his life.)

Soon he had many contracts, in counties scattered all across Texas. To oversee these jobs, sometimes hundreds of miles apart, and to bid for new ones in county seats hundreds of miles apart, he spent endless days in a car. For years, he would work all day on one job, and then sleep in the car while his chauffeur (a very low-paid luxury, considering the wage scale for a Negro driver at the time) drove all night to the next job, on which Brown would work all day before getting into the car to sleep while the chauffeur drove all night again to get to the next job. In a single year, Herman Brown traveled, over unpaved, bumpy, rutted roads, more than 75,000 miles.

That figure was calculated by an aide, not by Herman Brown. He measured not his effort but the profit it brought. But the profit was, considering the effort, minimal. In so impoverished a state, public works contracts were very small; as late as 1927, the average road construction contract was only $90,000—a sum out of which the contractor had to pay wages for his men, and buy feed for his mules, materials and equipment, bonding and insurance. And the profit was often not even in cash; contractors were generally paid off in "paving notes," secured by municipal real estate, and due to mature in five or ten years—by which time various tiny Texas towns and sparsely inhabited counties hoped to have sufficient cash to redeem them. Herman Brown had been living in a tent on the job in 1909. He was still living in a tent (when he wasn't living in that car) in 1917, when he married a pert young college graduate, Margaret Root; it was to a tent that he brought his bride for their wedding night, and a tent was their first home. As important to him as profit was the scale of the work he was doing. With the vision of the great builder, he thought in terms of projects that would leave his mark on the face of the earth—for centuries; on his first visit to Rome, he headed straight for the Colosseum, and, with a penknife, chipped away at its stone to collect samples which he could take back to Texas for an analysis of its composition; at last he would know, he said, what the Romans had put into it to make the Colosseum stand for two thousand years. In Texas, however, the scale was as unsatisfactory as the money. The state could not afford public works of the size of which Herman Brown dreamed.

Herman Brown had two partners. He acquired the first because he loved his wife; at her request, he took her brother, Dan (the "Root" of Brown & Root), into the business. He acquired the second—after Dan had died; the name of the firm was left unchanged out of Herman's deference to his wife's feelings—because he loved his younger brother, George.

Having quit college, George was working for Anaconda Copper in its great mines near Butte, Montana. Attempting "to break into the engineering end" of the company, he had advised his superiors where to drill to hit a new copper vein, and, although his shift ended at three a.m., he had risen at six, and had gone alone into the deserted mine to "see if they had hit." He saw—as he was careful to emphasize fifty years later—that "they *had* hit," but in his moment of jubilation, the mine caved in. Falling rock fractured his skull and cut open a vein. "I could see the blood spurting out of my head." The floor started to collapse beneath him, leaving a seemingly bottomless pit below, but "there was a beam there—twelve inches wide— and I got to it as the shaft caved in." Lying down on that twelve inches of steel over the chasm, "I pressed the vein in my head against a rock, with that side of my head down, and when I became unconscious, that shut off the bleeding." Eight hours later, George Brown was brought out of the mine, with fractures not only of his skull but of bones throughout his body. He was sent home to Belton, and when Herman heard how close George had come to death, he let his penniless brother have half of the business he had spent ten years building up, "at terms he could afford."

Herman was still the absolute boss of Brown & Root, and always would be—a situation with which George was perfectly content; asked what *he* did in the business, George would reply, "What Herman doesn't do." But Herman wasn't the only one of the brothers with soaring ambitions, and with a willingness to work as hard as was necessary to achieve them. (A third brother was not willing; after a month in the business he left, telling Herman, "I don't want to work these eighteen-hour days. You'll kill yourself." He returned to his job as a streetcar conductor.) George was sent to supervise the building of a small bridge over the San Gabriel River. He had never built a bridge—had never built *anything*—but he built that bridge, and made a profit on it.

Gradually the desperate days faded away. It was no longer necessary for Herman Brown to live in a tent; he still spent many nights driving back and forth across Texas, but when he got home, it was to a handsome, white-pillared house at 4 Niles Road, in the fashionable Enfield Road section of Austin. Though he was comfortable, however, Herman Brown was not wealthy, or even particularly well off. Texas jobs were still small jobs; the pay for them was still often in paving notes; he was always short of cash. After twenty years of terrible effort, the man who had wanted to build big things had still never built anything big.

In 1927 and 1928, moreover, the Brown brothers began to realize that the paving notes—the paving notes which represented most of their resources—might never be paid. The Depression had already begun in Texas; municipalities couldn't pay their debts; new construction jobs were scarce. Brown & Root's cash shortage became serious. The firm's banker advised Herman to sell the notes at a discount—to get whatever he could for them. George remembers: "Our banker in Houston—in 1927 and '28 and '29, he kept telling us, 'You're going to [have to] sell that paper.' " Herman wouldn't do it; those notes represented years of effort; he could not bear the thought of selling them for a fraction of their face value—for a fraction of what he had earned. "But finally, in 1929, we had to sell it. I went to Chicago and sold it just before the Depression. We had to discount it, but it was a good thing we sold it. Another month or two, and we wouldn't have been able to." And if they hadn't had the money realized from its sale, Brown & Root would have been out of business. By 1930, George Brown says, "everything was broke down here in this part of the world. It was a good thing we sold it. Because we did, we were the only contractors in Texas who could keep men on the payroll." Herman Brown managed to preserve the organization it had taken him so many years to create, although there was little work for it. "We lived off that paper in 1930 and 1931 and 1932—for years, really, during the Depression." And by 1936, the "paper"—to be precise, the proceeds Brown & Root had obtained from selling it—"was running out." After twenty years as a contractor, Herman Brown was almost broke.

And then, in 1936, the Bureau of Reclamation announced that it was taking bids for a $10 million dam at the Marshall Ford. It was the job—the big job—for which Herman had been waiting all his life.

To THE OTHER MAN, the significance of the dam was subtle—as subtle as the man. He was Alvin J. Wirtz, the former State Senator who had come to Washington in 1935 and been helped in his efforts to obtain federal funding for the newly formed Lower Colorado River Authority by Richard Kleberg's young secretary.

Because of the thoroughness with which the life of Franklin Roosevelt has been chronicled, the men who helped him to power—burly, bald, gregarious Jim Farley, for example; wizened, wheezing Louis Howe—have themselves become minor but vivid historical figures, our century's Northumberlands and Worcesters. Because the life of Lyndon Johnson—particularly the early decades of his life, the rise to power—has never been chronicled with either depth or accuracy, the figure of Alvin Wirtz has never emerged from the shadows. Johnson said of him: "Alvin Wirtz was my dearest friend, my most trusted counselor. From him . . . I gained a glimpse of what greatness there is in the human race." Lady Bird called him "the lodestar of our lives," and in the long picture gallery at the Johnson Ranch, his picture hangs prominently and bears the identification written by Mrs. Johnson: "Senator A. J. Wirtz—The Captain of My Ship, Any Day."

There is, however, some aptness in the fact that shadows surround the figure of Alvin Wirtz. For it was in the shadows that he worked.

One would not think it to meet him on Congress Avenue—a big, burly man with a broad, ever-present smile—and be favored with his open, friendly greeting, or to sit across from him, in his unpretentious law office in the Littlefield Building, as he chatted amiably, tilted comfortably back in his low swivel chair, smoking a big black cigar. At his home—a white Colonial mansion off Enfield—he made mint juleps with his own hand, served them on the back porch, and, as one of his guests says, "He was always smiling, and so relaxed that he just made you feel right at home." Virginia Durr, who knew him later in Washington, speaks of his "warmth of personality," of his "funny stories." He "was just such a sweet fellow," she says. He was "terribly amusing," he was "delightful. It just made you feel good to see Alvin."

With young politicians and lawyers who came to him for advice, he was not only friendly but calm and judicious. While they stated their problem or opinion, he sat quietly, never interrupting, speaking only in encouraging monosyllables, until the young man was finished. Often, he did not say much even then. And when he did speak, he spoke softly and very slowly and deliberately. Says Willard Deason: "He never told you what to do. But when you were finished talking to him, you *knew* what to do." His advice was valued. Says Welly Hopkins: "He had a sort of aura of dignity about him—he didn't say a whole lot, but when he said something, you listened." Says Charles Herring, another rising Texas politician: "He would never raise his voice. But you could feel his strength." Although he was no longer in the State Senate, young Austin politicians felt that he was truly senatorial; the title "Senator" seemed to fit him so well that they used it about him without the customary preceding article—"Senator says" or "I'm seeing Senator today"—as if there were no other Senator. His manner was no less impressive to young men, even the smartest young men, in Washington. Says one of the smartest, James H. Rowe: "He was a soft-voiced Texan, which is unusual in itself. He was the summer-up, who would not say anything while everyone else was talking, and then would say, 'Well, I think . . .' Charming, very gentle—If you needed a wise old uncle, and didn't have one, and could have one appointed, he'd be the one."

The image he cultivated so carefully had other aspects as well. He was fond of saying, "I'm only a country boy," and of reminding new acquaintances that he was from a small town, Seguin. Even other Texans who used that camouflage were startled by the thickness with which Wirtz applied it. When, in Washington, he was asked where Seguin was located, he would reply, "Oh, it's a fur piece from Austin." Says one Texan, himself a "professional country boy," who heard that reply in Washington: " 'A fur piece' —my God, they weren't even saying that in *Texas* any more!" The camouflage was used in courthouses, where Wirtz seemed the typical country lawyer, plodding and slow in his presentations. Even his signature was slow and deliberate, "the most deliberate thing I ever saw," Hopkins says. Signing a letter—after taking a very long time reading it—he did so as if reluctant to put his name to it, his hand tracing out the A and J in big, painfully slow circles.

But those who knew Alvin Wirtz well, knew better. Welly Hopkins was his first protégé—the man Wirtz chose to succeed him in the Senate. "Slow in his movements, slow in his speech, but he had a mind as quick as chain lightning," Hopkins says. "I'll never forget the first time I saw [Alvin Wirtz] in a courtroom. [It was] when I was still down in Gonzales . . . in the old Gonzales courtroom. He and the opposition lawyer" were arguing "in front of the Judge, and each would talk in turn, and suddenly I realized that he [Wirtz] was not only thinking even with him, but that he was ahead of him—that he was three steps ahead of him, all the time." Some legislative observers came to the same realization. "On the Senate floor," says one, "you did not want to be opposing Senator Wirtz in a thinking match."

And it was not on the floor—not in the open—that Wirtz was most dangerous. Fighting for passage of bills to regulate the growing oil industry and to curb patronage in state bureaucracy by instituting civil service requirements, a liberal Governor, Dan Moody, called five special sessions of the Legislature in 1929, only to see his program defeated all five times. Moody and his aides were not even aware that Wirtz was active in the fight; says an Austin observer: "They never knew until years later that it was Wirtz who had beaten them every time." As a lobbyist—for the same reactionary oil interests he had been representing unofficially as a legislator—his technique was as soft as his drawl. A threat or an offer was never direct. The most he might say to a legislator was, "I just want you to know that I have been employed by a group to help pass this bill. There is a great deal of interest in seeing that it is passed. I hope you'll vote the courage of your convictions." But a legislator who didn't take the hint would find arrayed against him the power not only of the most politically active oil company in Texas, Humble Oil & Refining (known respectfully in Austin as "the 'Umble") but of Humble's chief competitor, the Magnolia Petroleum Company ("the Magnolia")—for, competitors though they were, Wirtz represented both of them. And in the next legislative redistricting, legislators who had not taken his hint often found themselves redistricted out of the Legislature; they went to their graves never knowing it was Wirtz who had maneuvered them out of their seats. Politics in Austin was as loud and flamboyant a business as it had ever been, but among those few men familiar with the innermost corridors of power in the Capitol there was growing awareness that slipping along those corridors was a silent, smiling figure. Ed Clark, for example, saw that it was not on Wirtz's back porch but in the dimly lit library behind it that he did his real work—silent and alone. Clark, who was to work closely with Wirtz for years, says, "What he wanted was P-O-W-E-R—power over other men. He wanted power, but he didn't want to get it by running for office. He liked to sit quietly, smoke a cigar. He would sit and work in his library, and plan and scheme, and usually he would get somebody out in front of him so that nobody knew it was Alvin Wirtz who was doing it. He would sit and scheme in the dark. He wasn't an outgoing person. But he was the kind of person who didn't want to lose any fights. And he didn't lose many."

Stealth was his style. Ignoring the assistance of secretaries at the law firm of Powell, Wirtz, Rauhut & Gideon ("If you knew Alvin Wirtz," says another attorney, "you would know that his name would never come first"), he wrote many letters in longhand—because he didn't want even a secretary to know what was in them. Nor did he want his partners to know. The only partner in whom he even occasionally confided was the junior, and very young, Sim Gideon; Wirtz's letters to Gideon were often addressed to his home rather than the office because, as he wrote in one letter: "I don't want this in the firm's files." Since wire-tapping was not yet a widespread practice, Wirtz transacted as much business as possible over the telephone; "Senator didn't want anything on paper that didn't have to be," Gideon explains.

Senator's caution was understandable in light of what *was* on paper. As his files show, Alvin Wirtz was the kind of lawyer who would slip into a contract a sentence—a sentence that changed the contract's meaning—in the hope that the opposing lawyer would not notice it. ("My dear Lyndon," he would later write about one such maneuver, after he had sent off the contract to the unsuspecting attorney—an attorney who thought Wirtz was his friend—"I have not called his attention to the fact, but at the end of Article XI is a sentence" which alters the contract's import; with the exception of that sentence, he said, the contract "is the same" as the contract we agreed upon, so he will sign it, "so long as he is not advised" of the alteration.) A San Antonio attorney who often watched him in action calls him "a conniver—a conniver like I never saw before or since. Sharp, cunning." Says another attorney: "He would gut you if he could. But you would probably never know he did it. I mean, that was a man who would do *anything*—and he would still be smiling when he slipped in the knife."

WANTING POWER, power over other men, Wirtz had early seen dams as the way to get it.

The giant utilities—Texas Power & Light, Dallas Power & Light, San Antonio Gas—that controlled the generation of hydroelectric power in Texas were, in those days when the oil industry was still a relative infant, a major political power in Texas; not only did they make use of their revenues to purchase and control politicians, but in an era in which jobs as much as cash were the currency of politics, they were the state's largest employers, with thousands of jobs to distribute. These utilities, with their lawyers and lobbyists, were a tight, closed group into which Wirtz had no chance of breaking. But during the 1920's, a new player entered the field, and Wirtz hastened to attach himself to his team. He was Samuel Insull of Chicago, whose gigantic holding companies already extended from Maine to Florida. Wirtz made himself Insull's man in Texas. The state's rivers were under tight state control, and the Chicagoan learned that the Senator from Seguin was the man to see when permits were needed from the State Board of Water Engineers. After he was retained, Wirtz proved useful in many other ways as well. When farmers along the Guadalupe River near Seguin, where an Insull-backed firm from Chicago was building six small dams for irrigation purchases, stubbornly refused to part with their land, Wirtz's influence with the Legislature procured for the Insull interests the right of eminent domain usually reserved for government. The Chicagoans learned that Wirtz's fee—exorbitant as it was; Wirtz was greedy for money as well as power—saved them money in the long run. When the farmers' land was condemned—by Wirtz-controlled county appraisal boards—the prices set were very low. And when the farmers, believing they had been cheated out of their land, appealed to the courts, they found that Wirtz had considerable influence with courts as well.

Wirtz's main thrust for power came not along the Guadalupe but along the Lower Colorado. The dam Insull had begun building there (in isolated Burnet County in the Hill Country)—named the George W. Hamilton Dam after one of Insull's engineers—was a huge dam, one of the largest in the world, and designed not for irrigation but for the generation of hydroelectric power on a vast scale. In its construction alone some 1,500 men would be employed, and Wirtz was given a say in the distribution of some of these jobs. As attorney for the enterprise, moreover, he expected a considerable voice in the utility's affairs after the dam was completed. The power he wanted seemed within his grasp.

In 1932, however, with the Hamilton Dam half completed, the Insull empire collapsed, and because of the Depression, no alternative method could be found to finance the project. In 1934, with the construction having been stopped for two years, the dam that had been Alvin Wirtz's dream of empire was still only half completed, its steel skeleton glinting dully in the sun.

There had been another development, moreover. Feeling against Wirtz was running very high among the Guadalupe River farmers who felt they had been cheated by a law sponsored by their own State Senator. On February 26, 1934, Tom Hollamon, Sr., a sixty-seven-year-old farmer who had once been a Texas Ranger, strode into Wirtz's office, where he was meeting with Insull representatives, and began shooting; before he could be disarmed, one Chicago financier was dead. Hollamon was arrested for murder, but the Hollamon clan was a large one, and the Hollamons were not the only farmers enraged at the Insull firm, and at Wirtz. His former constituents told him to get out of Seguin and never come back; according to an attorney familiar with the case, the warning was issued in the classic Texas phrase: Wirtz was told, "Don't let the sun set on you in Seguin." Senator took the advice—he "was just run out of town," this attorney says—and removed to Austin.

But if for a while his dream seemed dead, the New Deal gave him a chance to revive it—bigger than ever.

Under the $3.3 billion Emergency Relief Appropriation Act passed during the Hundred Days, a newly formed Public Works Administration (PWA) was empowered to give loans and grants to self-supporting enterprises such as public authorities. The Texas Legislature was basically conservative and, moreover, dominated by public utilities determined to keep their monopoly on hydroelectric power and to resist federal intrusion into the field. Detailing Wirtz's maneuvers to persuade the Legislature to create a public authority—the Lower Colorado River Authority—to take over the Hamilton Dam and receive a grant from the PWA to complete its construction would require a book in itself (no such work exists). But because only in its later stages would the maneuvering involve Lyndon Johnson, the detailing will not be done here. In brief, the maneuvering was based on the techniques—indirection, deceit, secrecy—of which Wirtz was by now a master: at its heart was the lulling of a suspicious Legislature into the belief that the authority's purpose was not power production at all, but flood control. In 1934, the Legislature passed the bill, and in 1935, Wirtz, who had been appointed LCRA counsel, went to Washington to arrange PWA financing; it was on one of these trips that he had the "love fest" with Dick Kleberg's young secretary, by whom he was "very much impressed" because he "knew Washington" and "could get you in to any place." When problems arose in Washington, Wirtz had another maneuver ready. The chairman of the House Appropriations Committee was a Texas Congressman, James P. ("Buck") Buchanan. Buchanan's district did not include the Lower Colorado, or Burnet County, the site of the half-completed dam, but Wirtz remedied that defect. A redrawing of congressional districts by the Texas Legislature was even then under way; when it was completed, the boundaries of Buchanan's district had been changed to include Burnet County, and the dam. Another change took place: the LCRA changed the name of the dam. No longer was it the George W. Hamilton Dam. Now it was the James P. Buchanan Dam. Buchanan was touched; the PWA at first resisted giving a grant to finish the dam, but the Appropriations Committee did, after all, have a not inconsiderable say over Roosevelt's program; and when Buchanan went to confer with the President about several sticky items, during the last week of June, 1936, he mentioned that he had recently had a birthday and—so he later related to Wirtz and LCRA board member Thomas C. Ferguson (Ferguson is the source of this story)—told Roosevelt: "Mr. President, I want a birthday present." "What do you want, Buck?" Roosevelt is said to have replied. "My dam," Buchanan is said to have answered. "Well then, I guess we'd better give it to you, Buck," the President is said to have replied; picking up the telephone, he gave Secretary of the Interior Harold Ickes the necessary order. Whether or not this blunt conversation ever took place, the order was, indeed, given. The problem posed by the utter unsuitability of the Buchanan Dam for flood control was solved by expanding the Lower Colorado River Project. Now it would be not just one big dam, but two.* The second dam, twenty-one miles downstream from the Buchanan, was the Marshall Ford Dam, to be built, at a cost of $10,000,000, not by the PWA, but under a grant from the Department of the Interior's Bureau of Reclamation. Marshall Ford would be much bigger even than Buchanan, and the focus was shifted to it—particularly Wirtz's focus. The contractor who was selected to build it, and who began work in September, 1936, under an initial $5 million appropriation, was Brown & Root, Inc.—which happened to be one of Wirtz's clients.

Since Alvin Wirtz was counsel for both the LCRA and Brown & Root

---

* And several smaller dams, including one that would be completed almost simultaneously with Buchanan, a Roy Inks Dam near Marble Falls.

(and for other clients with interests in the LCRA development) and was court-appointed receiver for the Insull interests, he was collecting legal fees from many sides. He set his schedule of fees high; Ickes considered the ones the PWA had to pay exorbitant, and from that source alone Wirtz received $85,000, an immense fee for a Texas lawyer in those days. But the Marshall Ford Dam represented much more than fees to Wirtz. More than 2,000 men would be employed on that dam, and he would have a voice in their selection. When the dam, or, rather, both dams, together with others already on the drawing boards, were completed and producing electricity—when, in other words, the LCRA had become a gigantic utility—he would, as its counsel, have, he was certain, the dominant voice in its operation. It would provide him not only with money but with power on a big scale.

The Marshall Ford Dam, that structure in an isolated gorge in the Texas Hill Country, was the vehicle that would give both of these men— Herman Brown and Alvin Wirtz—what they wanted.

THERE WERE, however, two problems that even Alvin Wirtz had not been able to solve concerning this dam on which the Bureau of Reclamation had begun spending millions of dollars.

One problem was that the Bureau had not been authorized to build the dam.

Each public work built under the Emergency Relief Appropriation Act had to be separately and specifically authorized by Congress after hearings and, generally, an affirmative vote by the proper congressional committee—which, in the case of the Marshall Ford Dam, was Joseph Jefferson Mansfield's Rivers and Harbors Committee. But the Rivers and Harbors Committee had never voted on the Marshall Ford Dam. It had never even held a hearing on the dam. *No* committee had voted or held a hearing on the dam, and neither had Congress as a whole. Appropriations for a specific project were not supposed to be made until authorization— approval of the project by Congress—was given; otherwise, a congressional committee would be giving money to build a project before Congress had decided whether or not to build it. Authorization was supposed to come first —and in the case of the Marshall Ford Dam, authorization had not come at all.

The genesis of this situation lay in the informal way Buchanan had obtained President Roosevelt's "birthday present" approval of the project— and in the fact that the approval had been obtained, in late June, 1936, after Congress had recessed. The Comptroller General's office had noticed the lack of authorization, and had at first refused to approve the initial first-year $5,000,000 expenditure on the $10,000,000 dam. But Buchanan, in a series of tense conferences with that office, had persuaded it to allow work to begin, assuring it that he would have the dam authorized during the 1937 session of Congress. Because Buchanan's power made such authorization a certainty, the Comptroller General's office reluctantly agreed.

Accepting the contract prior to authorization was, of course, a gamble for Brown & Root—and Herman and George Brown knew it. "The appropriations were for one year at a time—piecemeal," George Brown recalls. "And [because of the lack of authorization] they were illegal. Wirtz was telling us all along that the money was wrong, and that if someone in Congress raised a question they would stop it [would stop paying out money under the contract]." If a Congressman made enough of a fuss over the fact that the Bureau of Reclamation was paying out money for a project that had not been authorized, the money could conceivably even be "stopped" permanently; the Bureau might say it could no longer honor the contract with Brown & Root. Wirtz had told the Brown brothers that in that eventuality the ordinary legal remedies for contractors against the government might not apply in this unusual case. The word that George Brown uses to describe the appropriations—"illegal"—is too strong; the dam was not "illegal" in the sense that anyone connected with it was violating a criminal statute; a more precise word would be "unauthorized." But the consequences to Brown & Root could be as disastrous as if the appropriations *had* been illegal, for what Wirtz was telling the Brown brothers was that they might not be legally entitled to payment for the work they were doing.

This would normally have been a gamble with only a limited risk. Despite the law, the initiation of projects prior to authorization—in the expectation that authorization would come later—had occurred before, and would occur again. But in this case the risk was heightened by another factor. So much larger was the dam than any previous Brown & Root project that the company would have to purchase $1,500,000 worth of heavy construction equipment, including one particularly expensive item—a cableway consisting of two steel towers erected on either side of the river, with, hung between them, huge cables along which ran a trolley from which buckets filled with concrete mixed on the cliffs could be lowered to the men pouring it into the foundations—for which they might never again have a use. "We had to put in a million and a half dollars before we could get a penny back," George Brown recalls. Nor could this investment be recouped from the initial $5,000,000 appropriation. Their estimated profit on that appropriation, without the cost of equipment figured in, was just under $1,000,000; on the first appropriation, in other words, they would be losing $500,000. It was on the second $5,000,000 appropriation that their profit would be made. On this second $5,000,000, Herman Brown had calculated, he and his brother would make a profit of almost $2,000,000—enough to cover the $500,000 and leave them with an overall profit on the dam of $1,500,000, an amount double all the profit they had made in twenty previous years in the construction business.

Ordinarily, of course, a contractor starting work on a $10,000,000 government dam—an *authorized* government dam—could be reasonably certain that he would receive the entire $10,000,000—not only the first year's $5,000,000 but the second year's $5,000,000 as well. But no such certainty could exist here. The Comptroller General, who had approved the expenditure of the first $5,000,000 so reluctantly, had flatly told Buchanan at the time that if for any reason congressional authorization was not forthcoming in 1937, he would never agree to the expenditure of the second $5,000,000, and Buchanan had accepted this. If there was no second appropriation, therefore, Herman and George Brown would lose half a million dollars—or most of what they had accumulated in twenty years of harsh struggle. And since they did not have the $1,500,000 necessary to buy the new equipment, they would have to borrow most of that sum, mortgaging all they owned. Building the Marshall Ford Dam was, therefore, a huge gamble for Herman Brown. If the authorization for the dam did not come through in 1937, he would be virtually wiped out.

But although the Browns were gambling, the power of Buck Buchanan hedged the bet. "Wirtz was telling us that Buchanan would take care of things, that he would arrange it [the authorization] as soon as Congress reconvened [in 1937], and of course we had no doubt of that," George Brown said. "We had already seen what he could do." And there were reasons for taking the gamble—compelling reasons. *The paper was running out.* The Browns needed a job, and there weren't any jobs in Texas—none big enough to help them at any rate. *Everything was broke down here.* If the gamble was huge, $1,500,000 was a stake big enough to justify a man in shoving in his whole pile. And Herman Brown was forty-five now. The Marshall Ford job represented the only chance in sight for him to move up to a higher plateau of construction, one of the big jobs he had been dreaming of for twenty years. He decided to go ahead. Brown & Root bid on the contract, were awarded the contract, mortgaged all they owned, purchased the new equipment and, in September, 1936, built the giant cableway—sank, in other words, $1,500,000 into an isolated gorge in the barren Hill Country.

And then the second problem came to light: not only was the Bureau of Reclamation not authorized to build the dam, it was effectively forbidden to build it.

The prohibition was contained in the Act of Congress that had created the Bureau in 1902, and in interpretations of that Act by the Federal Board of Land Appeals. These interpretations had specifically prohibited the Bureau from building any project on land not owned by the federal government. In 1905, for example, the Board of Land Appeals had stated flatly that the Secretary of the Interior "has no authority under the provisions of the Act of 1902 to embark upon or commit the government to any [Bureau of Reclamation] enterprise that does not contemplate the absolute transfer of the property involved to the United States." The reason for the prohibition was simple. "Well, of course you couldn't build a dam—a dam that costs millions of dollars—on land you didn't own," explains a Bureau official. "If someone else owns the land, you're just a tenant, and what are you going to do if the landlord says: 'I don't want the dam on my land any more. Get it off!'? What are you going to do? You can't move a dam." The prohibition had, moreover, been reaffirmed, without qualification, in every opinion on the subject by a federal court or a federal agency. During the Bureau's three decades of existence, an occasional—very rare—exception to this prohibition had been made, generally through special contractual arrangements between the Bureau and the local body with jurisdiction over the dam. But no such arrangements had been made, or even discussed, between the Bureau and the LCRA. In the case of the Marshall Ford Dam, the prohibition was in force.

In sixteen of the seventeen Western states in which the Bureau was authorized to build dams, this prohibition would have caused no problem. By the terms under which these former Territories had been admitted to the Union, the ownership of all publicly owned lands—which included most of the riverbeds in which dams would be built—was transferred, at the time of admission, to the federal government. But the seventeenth state was Texas, which, before its admission to the Union, had been not a Territory but an independent Republic, a sovereign state. The terms of its admission were different from those for the Territories, and one of the differences was that Texas was admitted to the Union still owning its public lands—including riverbeds.

This difference had apparently been overlooked by the Bureau, possibly because no one was aware of it (the Marshall Ford was the first dam the Bureau was to build in Texas), possibly because of the haste, due to the presidential telephone call, with which the dam was approved. So far as can be determined from the sketchy Bureau files still available today (most of the pertinent records no longer exist) and from the recollections of federal and LCRA attorneys involved, no one in the Bureau had thought to check the title of the land beneath the $10,000,000 dam.

This oversight was, moreover, not correctible easily—if at all. In the Act that had, two years before, created the LCRA, the Texas Legislature had, in the strictest of terms, forbidden it to sell its land to any person or body, including the federal government—or to lease it, to mortgage it, or, indeed, to transfer it in any way whatsoever. And there was no realistic possibility that the Texas statute would be changed in the foreseeable future. These restrictions had been placed in the Act by a Legislature violently jealous of the state's rights and determined that the federal government should never gain control over one of its rivers—by a Legislature that was, moreover, in the grip of the state's politically dominant public utilities, who had specifically insisted on the inclusion of the anti-transfer provisions to ensure that no federal power-generating body like the Tennessee Valley Authority could ever be set up in Texas. The Act as a whole was so strict that it effectively foreclosed the normal contractual remedies to the prohibition in the 1902 federal Act.

Under federal law, then, the Bureau of Reclamation was required to own the land on which its dams were built; under state law, it could *not* own the land on which this dam was being built.

Sometime late in 1936—after Brown & Root had begun construction —the Bureau learned about this second problem. Alvin Wirtz (who assured Herman and George that he hadn't known about it) told the two brothers that some low-level attorney in the office of the Comptroller General had thought to do what no one in Washington had done before: had checked the title for the land under the dam, learned that the federal government didn't own it, and informed his superior. Wirtz also reported that the Comptroller General, in a face-to-face confrontation with Buchanan, had pointed out that he was charged with the responsibility of certifying the legality of public works contracts. This contract, he said, was clearly illegal. Unless the conflict with the federal law was resolved, he said, he would not approve a second appropriation, whether or not Congress authorized it.

Decades later, George Brown agreed to tell a story he had never told before except to a handful of intimates: the story of the Marshall Ford Dam. He would, he said, never forget the day he and his brother discovered that the federal government was required by law to own the land on which the dam was being built—and that the federal government didn't own the land. The words "legal" and "illegal"—referring not to lack of congressional authorization but to lack of federal title to the land—recur frequently as he tells about that day. "We had put in a million and a half dollars in that dam, and then we found out it wasn't legal," he says. "We found out the appropriation wasn't legal, but we had already built the cableway. That cost several hundred thousands of dollars, which we owed the banks. And we had had to set up a quarry for the stone, and build a conveyor belt from the quarry to the dam site. And we had had to buy all sorts of equipment —big, heavy equipment. Heavy cranes. We had put in a million and a half dollars. And the appropriation wasn't legal!"

As he recalls that day, George Brown, eighty-two, almost blind but still physically vigorous and clear of mind, gets up from behind his desk, and begins to pace up and down his long office. Wheeling, he walks back to his desk. It is cluttered with reports, pictures of his wife, memorabilia (including a solid gold ingot, into which his name has been chiseled in Arabic characters, that is a gift from a Shah), but without groping he picks up a small, plain piece of weathered steel; on whatever desk he has had, it has lain in the same place for almost forty years. "There, you see that?" he says. "That's a piece of the cableway." He hands it to his visitor, then snatches it back and replaces it in the same spot on the desk, and begins to walk up and down the room again. Reaching out a hand to feel the back of another chair, he sits down and begins to talk again, much more rapidly than is his wont. "That was one of the pulleys," he says. "One of the pulleys from the cableway. We had put in a million and a half dollars in that dam. Then we found out it wasn't legal. But we had already—by the time we found this out—built the cableway. That cost several hundred thousands of dollars, which we owed the banks. . . . The Bureau of Reclamation had been making the appropriations. They were, under the law, allowed to spend money only on land that was owned by the federal government. They had assumed [that] the land on which the dam was being built *was* owned by the federal government, because that would be the situation in any other state, but in Texas the federal government didn't own any land. The appropriations had all been for one year at a time. AND THEY WERE ILLEGAL!!!"

AFTER A DAY OR TWO, as George Brown recalls, Alvin Wirtz came up with a solution. Congress, Wirtz explained, as the nation's law-making body, possesses the power to make legal what is illegal. What was needed, he said, was not just the usual congressional authorization of a dam, but a law which, ignoring the land-ownership issue, specifically authorized the contract under which Brown & Root had been working. Such validation of the contract would blur the question of their original legality. It would no longer be so clear that a clear provision of another law had been violated. The Comptroller General's office would have an excuse ("something to hang his hat on" is the phrase Brown recalls Wirtz using) for overlooking the fact that, validated or not, the contracts still called for construction of a federal dam on someone else's land.

And, Wirtz said, the Comptroller General's office would be happy to use that excuse. The President, after all, wanted the dam built; so did the chairman of the House Appropriations Committee. If the land title issue became a point of general knowledge and debate, passage of the law might be sticky, but Wirtz saw little chance of that happening. No Congressman would make an issue of it, because no Congressman was opposed to construction of this dam in an isolated part of Texas; with the exception of a few Texas Congressmen, no one in Congress was even aware of its existence. And if some low-level bureaucrat wanted to make trouble over the title, Buchanan's power would keep the trouble to a minimum. Wirtz said he had already spoken to Buchanan about his new idea, and Buck had approved it—had, in fact, said that it would end their problems. Buck had told him not to worry—he would personally see to the passage of the necessary law, and with its passage, everything would be as before. When Congress reconvened in January, 1937, Buchanan was as good as his word. The routine House procedures preliminary to authorization began clicking off. The

Rivers and Harbors Committee was expecting to take up the bill, and approve it, without opposition, in March. There really was no need to worry, Wirtz told the Browns, as long as they had the chairman of the House Appropriations Committee solidly on their side; Buchanan's power would protect the Marshall Ford Dam in the future, as it had in the past.

And then, on February 22, 1937, Buchanan suffered a heart attack and died.

Part IV

REAPING

21

The First Campaign

LYNDON JOHNSON was in Houston on February 23, escorting the Kansas state director of the National Youth Administration on a tour of NYA projects in that city, when he suddenly saw, on a park bench, a copy of the *Houston Post* with the banner headline: CONGRESSMAN JAMES P. BUCHANAN OF BRENHAM DIES. He knew at once, he was to recall, that "this was my chance."

His chance—quite possibly his only chance, for years and years to come. The ladder—elective office in the national government—that he had decided was the only ladder he wanted to climb contained only three rungs: a seat in the House of Representatives, a seat in the Senate, and that last rung, of which he never spoke. The first rung was indispensable; until he was on it, the others would be out of reach. He had to win a House seat, and, because of the impossibility of dislodging Dick Kleberg, only one seat was a realistic possibility: that of Buchanan's Tenth Congressional District, in which, living in Austin, he was a resident. That seat was, suddenly, vacant, but once it had been filled (through a special election called by Governor Allred), it might well remain filled for many years. Once Texas sent a man to Congress, Texas kept him there. Buchanan had himself won the seat in a special election—twenty-four years before. Impressive though that tenure was, it was not at all unusual for a Representative from the Lone Star State. Sam Rayburn and Hatton W. Sumners, for example, had also been in Congress for twenty-four years; Joseph Jefferson Mansfield and Marvin Jones for twenty years; John Nance Garner, prior to his election as Vice President, had served in the House for thirty years; in 1937, the twenty-one-member Texas House delegation had a longer average tenure—fourteen years—than that of any other state. The man who won Buchanan's seat would be in that seat to stay. To the astonishment of the visitor from Kansas, his tour was abruptly canceled; he was unceremoniously bundled into Johnson's big brown Pontiac sedan, which sped the 166 miles back to Austin, roaring across level, far-flung pastures dotted with grazing cattle, and through the town of Brenham, where Buck Buchanan's house was being draped in black.

If, as he drove, Lyndon Johnson weighed his chance of gaining Buchanan's congressional seat, that chance must have seemed very slim.

In the first flush of sentiment over Buchanan's sudden death, the first candidate thought of as Old Buck's successor was Old Buck's wife, shy, unassuming and retiring though she was. Should Buchanan's wife choose not to run, his logical successor would be his longtime campaign manager and friend, chubby, rosy-cheeked C. N. Avery. Not only had Avery been Buchanan's man in the district, his liaison with constituents, for twenty-four years, but he had married into the politically powerful Nelson family of Round Rock and was therefore politically well-connected himself. And, as a successful businessman in his own right (his quarry supplied the stone for the post offices with which Buchanan had dotted the district), his business connections assured him ample campaign funds. And Avery was universally popular. "He liked to sit back and smoke and talk," says one district politician. "He was a good ol' boy." There were, in addition, other logical candidates: the district's State Senator, Houghton Brownlee; Austin's Mayor Tom Miller, the district's single most powerful political figure; ambitious young (thirty-nine) Merton Harris, who after eight years as a District Attorney was now an Assistant State Attorney General who had been busily working barbecues throughout the district in hope of one day succeeding Buchanan.

Lyndon Johnson's candidacy would not be logical at all. His age—twenty-eight—was a drawback (no member of the Texas delegation and only two members of the 435-member House were that young), particularly in a farm district, because farmers, conservative in personal relationships, place a high premium on "experience." And age was only one drawback. Lyndon Johnson had spent four years developing an acquaintance with voters, working with boundless energy and initiative to obtain them pensions, to save their homes, to provide them with a multitude of federal services. But those voters had been residents of the Fourteenth District, not the Tenth. The voters of the Tenth District—the district that held his fate—did not know what he had done, or what he was capable of doing.

They did not know *him*. He had been raised in Blanco County, but Blanco, which had not even been part of this huge, sprawling district until the 1935 redistricting, was its most isolated and remote corner, and the smallest of its ten counties; with a population of 3,800, less than 2 percent of the district's 264,000 residents, it was all but ignored in district politics. As for the rest of the district, he had scarcely ever visited it during the five years prior to his NYA appointment, years he had spent in Houston and Washington and Corpus Christi. Large parts of it he had scarcely visited during his entire life except when driving across them to get somewhere else. As NYA director, he had, of course, been a resident of the

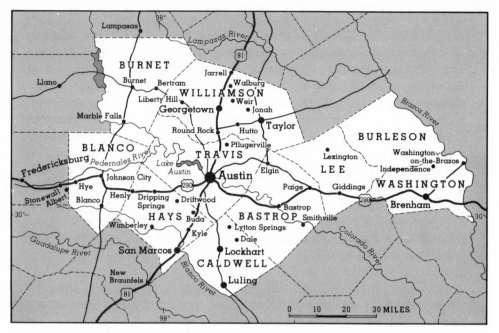

THE TENTH DISTRICT

district for eighteen months, but the directorship was not a job which entailed substantial contact with the public. State officials on Congress Avenue might smile and greet him; on Main Streets in Brenham and Giddings and Liberty Hill and Hutto—in most of the district's scores of small towns—he would be hard put to find a single familiar face. In contrast to an Avery or a Brownlee who was a familiar figure throughout the entire district, or to Mayor Miller, who boasted that he could greet every passerby in Austin by his first name, Lyndon Johnson was, in Dan Quill's words, "not known at all."

Many of the district's political leaders had never heard of him. Having spent almost four years assiduously cultivating rural leaders and county courthouse politicians, Lyndon Johnson had built up, with painstaking effort, a network of such men loyal to him rather than to Dick Kleberg. But that network was in the Fourteenth District, not the Tenth; it couldn't help him now. In the Tenth District, most of the officials he knew were state officials who had little to do with a local election; the county leaders of the Tenth District—the leaders he needed now—were, in the main, men he had never met. Even those leaders with whom he was acquainted (and who were, having talked with him, impressed with him) had no reason to support him. Their alliances were already forged and tested by time. They had been working with Avery and Brownlee and Harris for years. They had never worked with Lyndon Johnson.

Johnson's position was somewhat stronger with a few Austin business leaders and lobbyists—the sources of campaign funds—thanks to his policy of cultivating, as Kleberg's secretary, "important persons" from outside Kleberg's district; in this respect, at least, those four years of effort had not been entirely wasted. But his position with these men, while stronger, would not be strong enough to help significantly. Their gratitude—and contributions—would be limited. Austin businessmen would give their real support to their fellow businessman and longtime friend Avery, who had been obtaining lucrative government contracts for them for years. And businessmen who did not support Avery would support Brownlee or Harris—familiar, trusted faces. They would not support Lyndon Johnson. Indeed, documentation for these pessimistic conclusions had been provided that very day by the district's leading newspaper: the *Austin Statesman*. The *Statesman* had named possible candidates to succeed Buchanan, in a list that included not only the favorites, but long shots as well. The name of Lyndon Johnson had not even been mentioned.

OF ALL THE MEN influential in Tenth District politics, Lyndon Johnson was close to only one. Reaching Austin at the end of his 166-mile drive, he turned not toward his home but onto Congress Avenue, and pulled up in front of the Littlefield Building. The floor to which he went was not the sixth, where his own offices were located, but the seventh, on which Alvin Wirtz worked. And there he asked Wirtz for his support.

Like two other older men who had hitherto played large roles in Johnson's adult life—Cecil Evans and San Rayburn—Alvin Wirtz had no son of his own. Perceptive observers in Washington would find this similarity significant when, later, they saw the young man and the older one together. "Lyndon would always call him 'Yes, sir,' and 'No, sir,' " Virginia Durr says. "It was the junior to the senior, you see. . . . Lyndon had these relationships with older men like Alvin and Sam Rayburn. They both sort of treated him like a son." And, in Austin, Wirtz's secretary, Mary Rather, made a similar observation; she had, in fact, been astonished at her boss' behavior when, one day early in 1935, a lanky young man—"just as tall as he could be, and just as thin as he could be"—whom she had never seen before, "came dashing in" to Wirtz's staid office "with his long, fast steps"; her boss, usually so studiedly unemotional, "rushed out and grabbed him and hugged him. He was tickled pink to see him. . . . After he left, I said to Senator Wirtz: 'Who *was* that young man?' " She was to see a lot more of him. Telephoning Wirtz from Washington to inform him of his NYA appointment, Johnson asked him to find him office space—which Wirtz did, in the building where he himself worked. He named Wirtz chairman of the NYA's State Advisory Board, and they consulted frequently. When Johnson entered Wirtz's reception room, Wirtz would tell Miss Rather: "Here comes m'boy Lyndon." Hugging him, he would say: "Hello, Lyndon, m'boy." After Johnson emerged from Wirtz's private office and went back to his own, Senator would come out, puffing on a cigar, and tell her how quickly Johnson had caught on to a complicated engineering problem; "I just can't get over the young man grasping these things so quickly," he would say. Although Wirtz made himself available as confidant to many bright young men, his attitude toward Johnson, Miss Rather saw, was special. "He was ambitious for him. And he thought he had the ability. And he loved him. Senator Wirtz had a wife and daughter—he was fond of them. . . . But he would have loved to have had a son. And he loved him [Lyndon] like a son." (Wirtz was to inscribe a picture of himself: "To Lyndon Johnson, whom I admire and love with the same affection as if he were in fact my own son.")

Nonetheless, had it not been for the dam in which Alvin Wirtz's dreams were now invested, his paternal affection for Lyndon Johnson might have found forms of expression other than support for Johnson's congressional candidacy. To a businessman-politician like Wirtz, his Congressman's friendship was all-important; he would not ordinarily risk antagonizing the probable winner of the congressional race by backing an opponent; he would want to side with the winner, not with a candidate whose chances were as slim as Johnson's.

Now, however, the dam was all-important. It lay at the point of death; it would, in fact, be effectively dead if the necessary legislation was not rushed through Congress—if it was not, in fact, passed during the congressional session that had already begun, and that would adjourn within a few weeks after Buchanan's successor was sworn in. It could not be revived by Buchanan's shy, politically unsophisticated widow. And, Wirtz felt, it was unlikely to be revived by Buchanan's campaign manager. Friendly C. N. Avery may have been; forceful he was not. An adjective frequently used to describe him is "easy-going"; in Wirtz's opinion, he was rather weak and lazy. Moreover, well-known though Avery was in the Tenth District, Senator had observed on his trips to Washington that Congressmen and bureaucrats effusive in their greetings when they passed the powerful Buchanan in the halls of the Capitol, tendered only perfunctory courtesies to his aide. Says Welly Hopkins, familiar with Senator's thinking on the subject: "He [Avery] didn't have the drive. And he didn't know his way to first base in Washington."

Such drawbacks would not normally be decisive considerations in the selection of a Texas Congressman. He could be expected to remain in Congress long enough to learn his way around all the bases, and to acquire enough seniority to offset lack of drive. He would eventually be a committee chairman himself, a power like Old Buck had been. Had it not been for the Marshall Ford Dam, Wirtz's support might well have gone to Avery. It would probably not have gone to Lyndon Johnson.

Because of the dam, however, the normal course of events would not

help Alvin Wirtz or his client Herman Brown. Slow accretion of knowl-
edgeability and power wouldn't rescue that project; speed—furious speed—
was what was necessary. (If Wirtz and Brown needed confirmation of the
precariousness of their situation, it was shortly to arrive: on March 6, two
weeks after Buchanan died, the Bureau of Reclamation sent to the Bureau
of Budget for processing a routine form concerning the dam; the Bureau
promptly sent it back, marked DISAPPROVED, noting that not only had the
Marshall Ford Dam never been authorized by Congress, but, because of a
question over title, there was substantial doubt as to whether it ever would
be.) The money from the initial $5 million appropriation would, Brown
calculated, run out on September 1—with the Brown & Root balance sheet
for the dam still half a million dollars in the red. As a result of the Budget
Bureau disapproval, moreover, there was no longer any assurance that
Brown & Root would receive even the balance of that initial appropriation;
the Bureau of Reclamation immediately sent to the dam site a team of auditors with unusual instructions: the Bureau customarily audited a contractor's
figures only at the end of the job; henceforth, on the Marshall Ford Dam
project, each bill, however insignificant, that Brown & Root submitted was
to be audited as it came in, so that in the event the Budget Bureau suddenly
placed a Stop Order on the whole project, the Bureau would not have paid
the firm a cent more than was due it for work actually performed. Herman
Brown was face to face with financial ruin, and both he and Wirtz were
faced with the ruin of their dreams. A good ol' boy could never save the
Marshall Ford Dam. And neither could a good young boy—a dynamic
District Attorney such as the thirty-nine-year-old Harris, for example—
without Washington experience. Bright, aggressive and energetic, Harris
could be expected to learn his way around Washington quickly, but not
quickly enough to save the dam. What the dam needed in Washington was
a champion already knowledgeable enough and possessed of sufficient entrée
to find—swiftly—bypasses through the bureaucracy: a champion, for example, able to cut through the endless red tape at the Bureau of Reclamation
by obtaining the personal interest of the Bureau's boss, Interior Secretary
Ickes—or, perhaps, of the Congressman of whom Ickes was particularly
fond, Maury Maverick. What the dam needed in Washington was a champion with entrée to Congressmen powerful enough to roll over those bureaucratic obstacles (the Budget Bureau's quibbling over legalities, for example) that could not be bypassed—a Congressman such as Sam Rayburn, for
example. What the dam needed in Washington was a champion with entrée
to the chairman of the committee with jurisdiction over the dam, Rivers and
Harbors' Joseph Jefferson Mansfield—or, if not to Mansfield himself, then
to the man whose advice Mansfield followed slavishly, the man who pushed
Mansfield's wheelchair through the halls each day at noon: Roy Miller.
And because of his trips to Washington in 1935, Alvin Wirtz was aware
not only that Lyndon Johnson "knew Washington," but that he knew—

possessed entrée to—these very men. The young man sitting across his desk from him now was the champion he needed. When Johnson asked for his support, he agreed at once.

HE ALSO provided Johnson with a strategy. It could be summed up in three words: Franklin Delano Roosevelt.

Roosevelt's Supreme Court–packing plan, announced just two weeks before, had promptly been denounced by a Texas Legislature subservient to the state's reactionary monied interests, but when, on February 20, Harold Ickes, addressing the Legislature during a trip to Texas, had defended the President's proposal, the audience in the packed galleries had leaped to its feet wildly cheering, in a broad hint that the state's people did not agree with their representatives. Nowhere in the state was support for the President more firm than in the Tenth District, whose Hill Country counties had been the stronghold in decades past of the People's Party (the birthplace of the Farmers' Alliance, the Party's precursor, was, of course, the Hill Country town of Lampasas, a bare two miles north of the district line). An *Austin American* poll of the district would shortly reveal a majority of seven to one in support of the President's plan. Johnson should support Roosevelt's proposal, Wirtz said—should, in fact, make support of the Supreme Court plan the main plank in his platform. He should support all Roosevelt's programs. His campaign should be based on all-out, "one hundred percent," support for the President, for all the programs the President had instituted in the past—and for any program the President might decide to initiate in the future.

Behind that strategy lay nothing but pragmatism. Wirtz was not in favor of the Supreme Court plan, he was opposed to it; he had been telling intimates that he was a "constitutional lawyer," and therefore not in favor of any alteration in the Court's composition. In private, his phrases were more pungent. His views—not only on Court-packing but on the New Deal as a whole—were the views of the reactionary Roosevelt-hating businessmen of whom he was both legal representative and confidant. Pragmatically, however, the Roosevelt strategy was Johnson's best chance to win. It would offset his greatest weakness—the fact that he was unknown to the voters—by giving him an instant, popular, identification: "Roosevelt's man." It would give him an instant leg-up on several potential candidates who were anti-Roosevelt: State Senator Brownlee, for example, had voted for the Legislature's condemnation of the Supreme Court plan. And it might obtain for him the support of two passionate New Dealers, Governor Allred and the publisher of the *American* (and of the *Austin Statesman*), Charles Marsh.

Most of the candidates would be pro-Roosevelt, Wirtz said; therefore, Johnson would have to be more pro-Roosevelt than they. If he could identify himself more firmly than any other candidate as the President's champion, he would obtain the support of district voters eager to show their support for the President in general, and for his Supreme Court plan in particular. L. E. Jones, then clerking for Wirtz's firm, was taking dictation from Senator when Johnson rushed in on that fateful February 23. He remained throughout the conversation, and says he recalls it vividly. And Wirtz repeated his views at Johnson's home that evening, with other persons present. They recall Wirtz saying that Johnson's only chance to win was "to get an issue," and that the issue should be the Court-packing plan. "The discussion," Jones says, "was that the Court-packing plan might be a pretty lousy thing, but the hell with it, that's the way to win. Wirtz said, 'Now, Lyndon, of course it's a bunch of bullshit, this plan, but if you'll flow with it, Roosevelt's friends will support you.'"

Jones, of course, was aware that Johnson himself was less than enthusiastic about the New Deal. He never heard Johnson express a private opinion on the Supreme Court proposal, but, he says, "It didn't make a rat's ass [of difference] to him one way or the other." The strategy was accepted in the same spirit in which it was offered.

WIRTZ'S SUPPORT carried with it cash. As attorney for the Magnolia and the 'Umble, he could tap their lobbying funds; although Johnson would not, of course, announce his candidacy until after Buchanan's funeral, that very day Wirtz phoned the headquarters of the two oil giants and obtained the first contributions for the Johnson campaign fund.

Wirtz was also delegated to obtain funds from another source. Asked whether she knew at once that her husband would run for Buchanan's seat, Lady Bird Johnson replied, "We sure did *not* know we were going to run. Looking at it pragmatically, we did not have any right to expect we would win. Lyndon was from the smallest of the ten counties. He was quite young. And finances were a problem."

Wirtz, in his subtle way, enlisted her enthusiasm. "He and I had a talk, and I asked if there was a chance for Lyndon to win. He was a lawyer, and he had all the reasons lined up why we couldn't win. And at the same time he had the reasons why we might never get another chance. He said, 'Yes, there's a very *real* chance, and I'd be quite lacking in my duty if I didn't tell you that it's not a big chance, but there is a chance.' So I called my Daddy. . . ."

The importance of the call was not so much in the money raised— Wirtz himself would eventually raise far more—but in the speed with which it was made available to the campaign. Fund-raising, even by Alvin Wirtz, took time, and time was a luxury this unknown candidate couldn't afford. A large sum of seed money, at least $10,000, was needed immediately to get the campaign under way, and when Lady Bird called Cap'n

Taylor, and he asked, "How much do you need?" she replied, "We need ten thousand dollars."

He said, "Are you sure you can't get by on five thousand?" I said, "No, we need ten thousand." He said, "All right—I'll get it for you." I said, "Can you get it for us tomorrow morning?" He said, "No, I can't." My heart sank. He said, "Tomorrow's Sunday." We had been so busy we had completely forgotten what day of the week it was. "But I'll have it for you Monday morning at nine o'clock."

With his campaign thus made viable, Johnson was able to bring to it the resource he had created with such care: the organization already in place and at work at the NYA. Kellam, who had been appointed acting director when Johnson resigned to run, let the top NYA staffers know they could campaign for Johnson; to a man they flocked to his banner.

Bill Deason, his first follower, who had begun following his banner in San Marcos years before, was in San Antonio when he heard the news of Buchanan's death. "I didn't have to ask anyone what was going to happen," he says. "Within a few hours after his death, Lyndon called me. . . . He didn't mention running. He didn't mention the death. He just said, 'You know what's happened?' I said yes, and he said, 'You'd better come on over here.' . . . So I got into my car and drove to Austin."

The car was Deason's most precious possession: a gleaming, spotless new Chevrolet which he kept polished to a high gloss. He was particularly proud of the fact that he didn't owe any money on the car; he had saved for more than two years so that he could buy it free and clear. When he heard that Lyndon Johnson was running, he realized that a campaign car would be needed, one with a loudspeaker attached to its roof; he donated the car to the campaign, and allowed holes to be drilled into its roof for the bolts that secured the loudspeaker. And before he donated the car, he drove it down to his home town of Stockdale, where they knew him at the bank, and borrowed $500 on it—and when he gave Lyndon Johnson his car, he gave him the $500, too.

Some drove from farther away than San Antonio. Little Gene Latimer was at his desk in the Federal Housing Administration in Washington when he heard that "the Chief" might run. "I called him long distance to ask if he could use any help, and he told me he wished I was there." Less than two days later, he was. He had hung up the telephone, arranged for a leave (his supervisor, he explains, "was an admirer of Mr. Johnson's"), run out to his car, and left on the 1,600-mile trip to Austin—and, except to fill the car with gas, he had not stopped driving until he got there; when he arrived, "I was too exhausted to do anything except pass out."

Like the Chief, his men were unfamiliar with the district. Unlike

Avery's organization, or Mayor Miller's, or Brownlee's or Harris', they had no contacts, no friends. But they had the enthusiasm of the young— and faith in their leader. In part this faith was based on experience. "No matter what anyone said, we felt he had a chance, because we knew he would work harder than anyone else," Latimer says. In part it was blind confidence. Deason says he never had "a doubt in the world" that Johnson would win any contest he entered. "We just assumed if he went into it, he would win."

A STRATEGY, money, an organization—these would give this unknown candidate a slim chance of victory against every opponent but one. Against that one opponent, nothing could give him a chance. Nothing could offset the sentimental appeal of a vote for Old Buck's widow. If Mrs. Buchanan decided to run, Wirtz told Johnson frankly—and Johnson knew he was right—she would win.

And it began to look as if she was going to run. Buchanan's funeral was held on Friday, February 26. On Saturday, the district's most prominent politicians returned to the black-draped house in Brenham to pledge the sixty-two-year-old Mrs. Buchanan their unanimous support. Among them was Avery, who not only said he would not run if she would, but who also volunteered to serve as her campaign manager, as he had served as her husband's. Avery's sentiments were echoed by the other leading candidates, all of whom, the *Austin American* reported, "will stay out of the race" if she entered it. In this article, Johnson's name was included in a list of potential candidates; his candidacy, too, the *American* reported, was "subject to Mrs. Buchanan's remaining out."

All day Saturday, Johnson waited anxiously in his Happy Hollow Lane house as speculation mounted that the widow would run, and then, late on Saturday night, one of Johnson's friends, who had been waiting at the *American*'s printing plant, ran into the house with an early copy of the Sunday paper, which contained an article that seemed to confirm the speculation. Although the article's lead said only that Avery had emerged from a meeting with Mrs. Buchanan's son to promise that an announcement on her candidacy would be made on Monday, farther down in the story—near the very end—was a paragraph that indicated what the announcement was going to be: "Family associates of Mrs. Buchanan said that Mrs. Buchanan has kept closely familiar with all legislative matters affecting the district. . . . They said she is thoroughly conversant with the district's interests in Congress, to carry through the unfinished portions of Cong. Buchanan's program."

Lyndon Johnson's friends would never forget how his face turned white when he read that paragraph. "You could see the color just drain out of it," says one. "He went white as a sheet." Going into his bedroom with Wirtz, he conferred with him behind a closed door, but with this problem, even Wirtz couldn't help him.

So Lyndon Johnson went to see a man who could—the man who was the smartest politician he had ever known. That night, Central Texas was hit by a sudden freeze; when Johnson awoke early Sunday morning, temperatures had dropped to twenty-nine degrees in Austin, and were much lower in the Hill Country; roads were sheeted with ice. But he climbed into his car and drove the fifty miles to Johnson City—alone for once, no one with him on this trip—and pulled up in front of the little white house with the "gingerbread" scrollwork and the wisteria, and went into the shabby front parlor, and asked his father's advice.

Sam Johnson didn't even have to think before giving it. Recalls Lyndon's brother: "Lyndon started saying he was thinking of waiting to see what she [Mrs. Buchanan] does, and Daddy says, 'Goddammit, Lyndon, you never learn anything about politics.' Lyndon says, 'What do you mean?' And Daddy says, 'She's an old woman. She's too old for a fight. If she knows she's going to have a fight, she won't run. Announce now—before she announces. If you do, she won't run.' "

Mrs. Buchanan's announcement was scheduled for Monday afternoon. After driving back to Austin on Sunday afternoon, Lyndon Johnson quickly called in reporters and told them that he was in the race to stay—whether or not Mrs. Buchanan entered it. When Johnson's decision appeared in the newspapers, Mrs. Buchanan's son telephoned reporters. "Mother has just reached the decision not to run," he said.

AFTER LYNDON JOHNSON had left to drive back to Austin, Sam Johnson walked over to the home of Reverdy Gliddon, publisher of the *Johnson City Record-Courier*. Gliddon was eating Sunday dinner with his family when Sam came to the door and shouted in, "Gliddon, I want to talk to you." ("That was Mr. Sam's old booming voice," Stella Gliddon says. "Oh, I hadn't heard that voice in a long, long time.") Entering, he said, "Gliddon, do you know what this silly boy of mine wants to do? He wants to run for Congress against ten seasoned politicians." And he said, "Lyndon just thinks he can conquer the clouds—how can a boy run against ten men?" For some time, Sam went on, listing all the arguments against Lyndon running—until not only Stella (whose fried chicken Lyndon had loved "better than anything in the *whole wide world*") but her husband was moved to come to Lyndon's defense, and point out that his youthfulness was offset by his Washington experience. Steering the conversation ("I only realized later, when I thought about it, what he was doing," Stella says), Sam made them work out for themselves the reasons why his son should be supported; let them convince themselves more firmly than he could have convinced them. Evidence of the success of his strategy was the headline over Gliddon's editorial in the *Record-Courier*'s next issue: JOHNSON FOR CONGRESS.

> We do not wish to praise Mr. Johnson merely because he is a native-born citizen of Blanco County. For the past eight or ten years, the home folks have seen but little of Mr. Johnson, during his absence from this city [because] he has been a very busy man as a congressional aide and NYA Administrator—what an admirable background for a young man. . . . He has made good in all of his undertakings. . . . He enters his political career with "clean hands." No one ever heard of Lyndon Johnson doing anything that was not honorable and straightforward.

Sam also introduced his son before his first campaign speech, which was delivered from the front porch of the Johnson home. Despite unpleasant memories of the "native-born citizen's" boyhood personality and family background, Blanco was predisposed to support him. In the rural counties of Texas—counties in which frontier privations and dangers were so fresh a memory and neighborliness therefore so prized a virtue—it was rare indeed for a county *not* to support its "home man" in a congressional race. Reinforcing this predisposition in Blanco County was the unusual depth of the county's poverty and isolation. Because its residents not only were poor, but *felt* poor—felt poor and isolated and utterly cut off from the rest of the world—the success of a Blanco boy in that world was unusually important to them; it gave them a reason for self-respect. Johnson was at the time the only local boy who they felt had made good in the outside world, the only proof that someone from "our isolated corner," "away up here on the Pedernales River," *could* make good in that world. The "Little Congress" sounded very impressive to them; with his election to its speakership, Johnson City at last had someone to be proud of—something to take pride in. Ava Johnson Cox, Lyndon's cousin, who had so resented the way Johnson City looked down on him, recalls that when his election was reported in the *Record-Courier*, "Well, that was just a *boomerang!* It [the news] just went like wildfire. It went down to the barbershop, and everybody was saying, 'Well, that ol' boy's going places!' " With his NYA appointment, "They were *really* proud of him. Everybody was saying, 'That's my boy. I knew he'd do it. I knew he was coming through!' " Additional reinforcement was, in some cases, provided by gratitude. Ernest Morgan was not, after all, the only Hill Country youth who had been enabled to stay in college by an NYA job; more than a few Blanco families felt personally indebted to the man who had helped their children get an education. And, of course, in the ten years since Lyndon Johnson had spent much time in Johnson City, unpleasant memories had blurred. The crowd standing in front of the Johnson home that day was more than willing to support the young man who had grown up inside.

Sam turned this predisposition into something more. There was little trace of the old Sam Johnson in the man who stood before them now. The last traces of the "Johnson strut" had vanished as heart attack followed heart attack; the eyes that had once been so "keen" were dim now, and sad, and had been sad for many years; he was stooped and gray-faced. So many years had passed since he had been "cut off" by Johnson City merchants that his debts had long since ceased to be news; no one any longer resented a man old and ill before his time; there was even a measure of grudging respect for Sam and Rebekah's decision to move to San Marcos for four years so that their four younger children could finish college. As he stood before them, asking them to vote for his son, some of his listeners may even have remembered debts not owed but owing—for pensions the old man had once arranged for them, for loans he had given them, for the highway he had gotten built. And listening to him speak—this man who once had been so great a speaker—they may have remembered also the ideals for which Hon. S. E. Johnson had stood, for he talked about President Roosevelt and Sam Rayburn, and about how, with men like them in Washington, the farmer at last had allies to fight for the causes in which farmers had so long believed, and about how his boy would help them fight, for his boy believed in the same causes.

He hit the right note, in the Hill Country in which support of Roosevelt was running seven to one, in the Hill Country which had been the birthplace and the stronghold of the Alliancemen of Texas. The causes for which Roosevelt was fighting were causes for which the Hill Country had been fighting for decades; it had, after all, been out of the Hill Country that, almost exactly half a century before, the long line of wagons bearing the blue flags of the Alliance had clattered into Austin.

Sam Johnson had not made a speech for so many years, but he had never made a better speech than the one he made now for his son. Describing it, Lyndon Johnson was to say that while making it, "My father became a young man again.

"He looked out into all those faces that he knew so well and then he looked at me and I saw tears in his eyes as he told the crowd how terribly proud he was of me and how much hope he had for his country if only his son could be up there in the nation's capital with Roosevelt and Rayburn and all those good Democrats. There was something in his voice and in his face that day that completely captured the emotions of the crowd. When he finally sat down, they began applauding and they kept applauding for almost ten minutes. I looked over at my mother and saw that she, too, was clapping and smiling. It was a proud moment for the Johnson family."

. . .

IF IT WAS Sam Johnson the great speechmaker who stirred his county into support for his son, it was Sam Johnson the master politician who mobilized that support. Lyndon Johnson's first major campaign rally would be Friday, March 5, in San Marcos, in the auditorium of Old Main. Sam organized a Blanco County Caravan to go to the rally.

Early that Friday afternoon, Model A's and Model T's and an occasional Hudson or Packard began to pull into the square in front of the courthouse in Johnson City. So many came that the square was filled, and cars began to line the dusty streets of the little town. Most were crammed with people—whole farm families, or two families riding together—and as they waited, they got out and chatted with friends.

Sam had recruited young boys to put big posters bearing Lyndon's picture on each car, in the windows or tied to the radiator grille in front. And as evening drew on, Sam and Rebekah got into his battered Model A and led the caravan out, down Route 66 for sixteen miles before turning onto a bumpy, unpaved road that ran fourteen miles through the hills to San Marcos. And that evening, as San Marcos students and townspeople began to troop toward Old Main, they heard a honking of horns from the hills above the town, and the face of Lyndon Johnson came down out of the Hill Country on a long, long line of rattling old cars—the longest caravan to come out of the Hill Country in fifty years.

THAT RALLY WAS, however, the lone bright spot in Johnson's candidacy for some time to come.

Seven other candidates had entered the election, which Governor Allred had set for April 10.* (He ruled that it would not be a party primary in which a two-man run-off would be held if no candidate received a majority, but rather a "special election"—a "sudden death" election, in Texas parlance—in which the high man would be Congressman with or without a majority.) One candidate was a perennial also-ran not taken seriously, one was a Townsendite candidate who would receive only Townsendite votes. But the others included a handsome young Austin attorney, Polk Shelton, an idealistic conservative (he, like Wirtz, identified himself as a "constitutional lawyer") who had decided to run because he wanted to go to Washington and fight the Supreme Court–packing plan, but who was also a former star athlete at San Marcos, well known and popular throughout the district. And they included four seasoned politicians—not only long-time Williamson County Judge Sam Stone, who could expect the solid support of his county's 45,000 residents, but three politicians who each had a broader base:

---

* A ninth candidate entered briefly, but dropped out; he would receive twelve votes in the election. A University of Texas economist, Robert "Professor Bob" Montgomery, whose possible candidacy had caused Johnson much anxiety because as a recognized New Dealer he would have drawn much of the pro-Roosevelt vote, decided at the last moment not to run.

the district's State Senator, Houghton Brownlee; Merton Harris, the aggressive Assistant Attorney General who had been working the district for years in preparation for the chance that had now presented itself; and, of course, C. N. Avery. Already the heavy favorite because of his district-wide political connections, Avery was also aided by sentimental considerations—on which he played; he was entering the race, he said in his opening statement, only because Old Buck would have wanted him to: "The late Mr. Buchanan . . . told me that [when he died], he wanted me to run for the office he held. He told me I was the only man in the district qualified to carry on his work. . . . Now I feel bound to carry on his work. I feel it is an obligation to my friend." During the campaign's first week, moreover, Mayor Miller, who had decided not to run, announced that he would throw his support, and that of the Austin machine, to Avery. "When Miller came out for Avery," recalls the tough, pragmatic Quill, "why, we thought the race was over. Austin had the votes, you know. It was the largest city in the district. And Miller—he sure was a power, and a very difficult man to oppose. It hardly seemed worthwhile to go on." Political observers were all but unanimous in conceding the election to Avery. And those few observers who thought he might be challenged thought the challenge would come from Stone, or Brownlee or Harris. The candidacy of Lyndon Johnson, "home man" of the district's smallest county, all but unknown in the others, was not taken seriously.

Johnson's limited residence in the district was, moreover, proving to be a major handicap in an area in which the word "carpetbagger" had a particularly distasteful ring. His hometown paper's line—"For the past eight or ten years, the home folks have seen but little of Mr. Johnson"—was quoted out of context by opponents who also noted that, as Avery put it, "He has never voted in the district." And his age was turning out to be even more of a handicap than had been expected. He had attempted to minimize this handicap by confusing reporters and voters about it. The press release announcing his candidacy said, "He will soon be thirty years old." Subsequently, the line adopted was that he was "almost thirty." In the many articles in which a specific age was mentioned, it was twenty-nine; not once during the entire campaign, so far as can be determined, would his actual age—twenty-eight—appear in print. But, whatever they believed his age to be, his opponents emphasized it. "This Johnson is a young, young man," Stone's campaign manager told a Georgetown audience. "Don't let him take off the baby robe and put on the toga." Any illusions that Johnson may have possessed about the effectiveness of this line of attack were dispelled the first time he shared a platform with Avery, at a meeting of the Austin Trades Council. "Now I believe," Avery said, "that every boy by the time he reaches the age of seven develops a burning desire to be a policeman, a fireman. . . . But before we entrust them with such tasks we demand that they gain a considerable amount of experience. We just can't picture a youngster with a pop-gun chasing bandits." As Johnson sat listening on stage, this sally drew laughter from the audience.

But Johnson had men—and he knew how to use men. Divided into teams, they were assigned to towns, and told whom to see in each town and what to say. "We'd go into a little town," Ernest Morgan recalls. "We'd have lists of people to see, and we'd nail up posters. He wanted posters with his picture on them up *everywhere*. And the first thing we'd do was to go to the local newspaper. He would tell us: 'That's the first thing you do— get my picture in the paper. I want it so you can't wipe your ass on a piece of paper that hasn't got my picture on it.' " Although Governor Allred did not announce the special election until March 5, Johnson had announced on March 1 that he was running in the election. And the very next morning, cars crowded with Johnson's young men, the young men who had once been the White Stars of San Marcos, were fanning out across the district, racing across the district; speeding away from Giddings after a long day of electioneering, A. J. Harzke, who in college had been Lyndon Johnson's second candidate for class president, saw roaring toward him on the lonely road to Ledbetter a car that he recognized: it belonged to Bill Deason, Johnson's first candidate for class president. The two men waved as they passed; neither stopped; there was too much to do.

And Johnson had a strategy—and he knew how to use a strategy. The White Stars were told to concentrate on a single, simple point. "When we asked what we should tell people," one recalls, "they told us that the campaign would have many slogans, but that there was only one slogan that mattered: 'Roosevelt. Roosevelt. Roosevelt. One hundred percent for Roosevelt.' " That slogan was the entire content of the posters that, on the day following Johnson's announcement, blossomed, unpunctuated but to the point, on trees and fenceposts throughout the district: A VOTE FOR JOHNSON IS A VOTE FOR ROOSEVELTS PROGRAM. It was the sole theme of the calling cards, printed the same day, that were distributed by the tens of thousands. A vote for Johnson, the cards said, was a vote "For Roosevelt and Progress." It was the message emphasized in the letters that began pouring out of his campaign headquarters. "Dear Mr. Carson: Mr. O. E. Crain has suggested that I send you some literature about my campaign for Congress. I stand wholeheartedly with the President on his program, and I invite the people who favor the Roosevelt program to support me. Yours Sincerely, Lyndon Johnson."

In his initial announcement, Johnson not only stated the theme, but gave it a particular emphasis, one especially appealing in a district grateful to the President for the help he had given it. Because of the timing of the election, he said, a vote for Johnson would not only express generalized support of Roosevelt, it would give the President help—help he badly needed—in the fight in which he was currently engaged. "The paramount issue of this campaign . . . is whether the President shall be sustained in his program for readjustment of the judicial system," he said. "The voters of the Tenth Congressional District, due to the untimely death of Congressman Buchanan, are the first to have a chance to speak on this vital issue and to have an opportunity to speak . . . with such unanimous voice that there will be no doubt throughout the country as to how our people stand on this question." The way to speak, he said, was to vote for him. "I have always been a supporter of President Roosevelt and I am wholeheartedly in favor of his present plan."

This emphasis placed two of his opponents at an immediate disadvantage. Polk Shelton was not a man to compromise his principles. "Roosevelt was Jesus Christ in this area," says his brother, Emmett, "but Polk was Polk—nobody could make him say something he didn't believe in." To a reporter's question about his feelings on the Supreme Court fight, the young attorney replied (in a statement taken as a sneer at Wirtz's about-face), "I am opposed to the court reorganization. I was against it before this election, and I'm no hypocrite." Senator Brownlee tried to compromise, but couldn't —since his vote for the legislative resolution condemning the Court plan was a matter of record.

Furthermore, as Wirtz and Johnson had hoped, the strategy tied in with the editorial stand of Marsh's two daily newspapers, the *Austin American* and the *Austin Statesman*. As for Governor James V. Allred, he was personally fond of Johnson, and had been impressed by his work as NYA director, and by his knowledge of Washington. "He felt Johnson could do the most [of any of the candidates] to get Texas what it was entitled to in Washington," says Ed Clark, the Governor's Secretary of State and the man most familiar with Allred's thinking. Nonetheless, the Governor had originally decided to remain neutral in the congressional race—in part because he believed that Johnson had no chance to win, and he didn't want to antagonize the next Congressman. But Allred was a true liberal—the only truly liberal Governor elected in Texas in the twentieth century, swept into office by the Roosevelt landslide—and he too idolized the President. And Johnson, Clark says, "was just such a real rootin'-tootin' Roosevelt supporter—Jimmy just couldn't stay out." Publicly, he made no statement—reiterated neutrality, in fact—but privately he allowed Clark to go to work for the man on whom the Secretary of State had decided "to buy a ticket," and he put at Johnson's disposal his own campaign manager, veteran Texas political string-puller Claud Wild. Allred could not resist one semipublic gesture: as Johnson was leaving his office after a visit, the Governor impulsively snatched his big white Stetson off a hatrack and gave it to the young man—who wore it, and let it be known whose it was, at every rally.

And Johnson had money—and if, campaigning over unfamiliar terrain, he didn't know how to make the most of it (and he probably did, this wonder boy of politics), Alvin Wirtz knew. Was Johnson unknown to the district's voters? Money could make him known—fast. The printing of posters and calling cards for the typical candidate has to wait on the raising of cash to pay the printer; thanks to the instant cash provided by Wirtz and Cap'n Taylor, Johnson's printings were ready the day the campaign began. The only source of political news for most voters was the twenty-five small weekly newspapers struggling to survive in sparsely populated areas whose residents were so impoverished that many of them paid their $1.50 for a yearly subscription with a chicken or a cord of wood. Few of their publishers were professional journalists—as prevailing practices and ethics revealed. Short not only on cash but on news to fill their pages, some of them were willing to print verbatim not only a candidate's advertisements but "articles" prepared by the candidate's staff—if the articles were accompanied by money. The individual amounts involved were small, as might be expected when dealing with newspapers in which a merchant could purchase an ad for fifty cents or a dollar, but the payments had to be made to perhaps twenty newspapers (some publishers refused to go along with this practice), and they had to be made each week. Johnson had the money to make them. The envelopes containing the announcement of his candidacy—an announcement written in the form of a news story— arrived at newspaper offices containing not only his picture but, although no advertising was being purchased, a check for ten dollars. A covering note from Ray Lee read: "I am enclosing a check for ten dollars which we want you to credit to our account. We shall want to use some advertising space later in the campaign. Here also is Mr. Johnson's statement announcing for Congress. We hope that you will be able to use this statement this week." Many papers used the statement—in the form in which Johnson wanted it used—and four days later, Lee sent a follow-up note: "We appreciate your kind and generous treatment. You will hear from us from time to time."

The times came fast—and with them promises that they would continue; Johnson himself wrote to one editor, "Here are [an] . . . ad for your paper this week, a check for ten dollars for credit against our account, and a news item about one of [my] speeches. I hope you will be able to handle all three. We are planning to have an ad in your paper each week during the campaign, and would like for you to keep us advised how we stand on your books." Some of the checks grew substantially larger, and publishers were not discouraged from asking for more checks larger still; a typical Lee line was "If this is not sufficient to cover the amount due, please render us a bill immediately." The payments paid off for the Johnson campaign. A campaign worker reported that "I called on the 'Marble Falls Messenger' and found that we owe them another $5. . . . He said that he would not add 'paid advertisement' at the end [of a news item written by Johnson's staff] because it would carry more weight this way." From beginning to end of the campaign, not only did the amount of Johnson's paid advertising dwarf that of his opponents, so did the amount of "news coverage"—articles favorable to him written by his aides—that he received.

Money could help with the district's political leaders, too. First, it bought him Claud Wild. The leaders knew the canny old pol, knew him, liked him, had worked with him for years. Wild's first reaction to the Governor's suggestion that he manage Lyndon Johnson's campaign was: "Who the hell is Lyndon Johnson?" After sounding out the leaders he was convinced not only that Johnson had absolutely no chance to win, but that his campaign would be little more than a joke—and that association with it would be an embarrassment. He at first rejected Allred's suggestion that he help the young man, and when, at the Governor's insistence, he finally sat down with Johnson and Wirtz, he was unmoved by their attempt to tempt him with the title of "campaign manager"; he would work for the campaign, he said, only for a fee, payable in advance: $5,000. Although Lady Bird did not know it, that was where half of her father's contribution went.

Wild's enlistment in the campaign could not make the leaders support Johnson, but it would ensure their attendance at—and their permission to hold—the "barbecues" (political rallies highlighted by "speakings") integral to Texas politics. And Lyndon Johnson's barbecues were barbecues such as this impoverished district had never seen. Ed Clark describes them as "all the barbecue you could eat and take home, and all the beer you could drink"—at each barbecue, in other words, beef and beer for hundreds of persons. Emmett Shelton describes them in a more pithy term: a "giving away." "Before then," he says, "barbecues had never been very elaborate around here. And I tell you, we wanted to have one like his [Johnson's] once, and we sat down and started figuring out how much it would cost—and there was no way we were ever going to afford it."

If the barbecues with their drinking and the speaking were the loud side of money in rural Texas politics, there were quiet sides as well: the rural "boxes," or precincts, which could be bought by a payment to a local Sheriff or County Commissioner. There were a few of these boxes in the Tenth District, and Johnson had the money to buy them. The district contained a substantial Negro vote*—located in several small all-Negro settlements in Blanco County; in Lee County, where there were thousands of black sharecroppers; and in the Austin slums. In Austin and Lee County, at least, the Negro community voted the way its leaders wanted it to vote, and the leaders were for sale—cheap. Johnson had the money to buy

---

* Negroes could not vote in party primaries in Texas, but this was not a primary, but a federal election.

them. The Czech vote—several thousand Czechs were grouped together in three or four rural communities—was also for sale; the price for this vote was much higher, but Johnson had enough money to pay it, too.

No one knows, or will ever know, how much money was spent in Lyndon Johnson's first campaign. Mrs. Johnson says, with understandable pride, that her money was virtually all that was needed to launch her husband's career; the deposit slip for the $10,000 she obtained from her father was one of her most cherished possessions; "I kept that deposit slip in my purse until it wore out," she says. "Literally until it just crumpled away." And, she says, while Alvin Wirtz raised some money, "probably" the $10,000 "covered the entire cost of the first campaign." But while Mrs. Johnson no doubt believes this statement, it is not correct. The Sheltons—not only Polk but his brother and campaign manager, Emmett—went broke trying to keep up with Johnson's spending. Emmett vividly recalls raising, at the beginning of the campaign, $1,000 from one friend, and $1,500 from another, "and thinking it was so much," and then realizing that it was nothing. "We would not have started had we known how much the campaign was going to cost," Shelton says. "Because we didn't have it. By the end of the campaign, we had borrowed everything we could borrow. It took us years to get out of the [financial] hole we dug for ourselves." Their expenditures totaled $40,000; Avery and Brownlee, observers agree, each spent considerably more than that figure.

Johnson's expenditures dwarfed those of any of his opponents. Ed Clark, the homespun political genius who in later years would become perhaps Texas' greatest campaign fund-raiser, was exercising his talents on Johnson's behalf. The Governor's trusted advisor telephoned state employees: "If I said to someone, 'The Governor would like you to support his friend Lyndon Johnson,' they knew I was authorized to make the call." Their contributions were small—twenty dollars or ten or even less—Clark says, but there were a considerable number of them. More money came to Johnson from Austin businessmen—suppliers of Camp Mabry, a United States Army base, for example—who, in Clark's words, "thought it would help them to be friends with a Congressman." These contributions were not so small—"these would be one hundred dollars to five hundred dollars," Clark says—and there were a considerable number of these, too. And his money came from men who were used to contributing far larger sums to politics: from not only Alvin Wirtz but Roy Miller, for example, and from lobbyists who contributed where Wirtz and Miller told them to contribute. Although *pro forma* reports on campaign spending were filed (Johnson's shows contributions of $2,242.74), they are not reliable, Clark says. Only three men—Lyndon Johnson, Alvin Wirtz and Ed Clark—had even a vague idea of the total amount spent. Johnson and Wirtz are dead. Clark says that he does not know the actual figure. "There wasn't too much reporting then," he says. "No one knew how much money was spent." But he estimates the

cost of Lyndon Johnson's first campaign at between $75,000 and $100,000
—a figure that would make the campaign one of the most expensive congressional races in Texas history up to that time.

AND, MOST OF ALL, Johnson had the qualities of personality and temperament that he had been displaying most of his life.

All his adult life, because of the agonies of his youth, the insecurity
and shame of growing up in the Hill Country as the son of Sam and
Rebekah Johnson, he had grasped frantically at every chance, no matter
how slender, to escape that past. In Washington, and before that in Houston
and Cotulla, he had worked so feverishly, driven himself so furiously,
forced his young will to be inflexible—had whipped himself into the frantic,
furious effort that journalists and biographers would call "energy" when it
was really desperation and fear. He had tried to do everything—*everything*
—possible to succeed, to earn respect, to "be somebody." "There was a
feeling—if you did *everything*, you would win."

The feeling had been reinforced—in Washington and Houston and
Cotulla—by experience. In each of those jobs, he *had* done "everything"—
had lashed himself into the effort in which "hours made no difference, days
made no difference, nights made no difference," into the effort in which
he worked weekday and weekend, day and night. And he *had* "won," had
made the most of each of those slender chances.

Now had come the main chance, the real chance, quite possibly the
only chance.

And the effort that Lyndon Johnson had made before was nothing
beside the effort he made now.

HE COULD NOT, he felt, win in the city; Austin, home of 88,000 of the district's 264,000 residents, was controlled by Mayor Miller, and Miller was
for Avery. So he had to win in the countryside.

But that countryside covered almost 8,000 square miles. The Tenth
Congressional District of Texas was one of the most sparsely populated
areas of the United States; its 176,000 residents who lived outside Austin
were scattered across ten huge Texas counties, across an area larger than
Delaware, larger than Connecticut—larger than Delaware and Connecticut
combined. Austin, of course, was situated at the very edge of the Edwards
Plateau, near the fateful 98th meridian; to the west of Austin, the district—
3,000 square miles of district—was the vast and empty Hill Country,
through which it was still possible, in 1937, to drive for miles without seeing a human habitation; the 62-mile drive west from Austin through Johnson City to the district's border, for example, was still one of the loneliest trips it was possible to take in the United States. The 111-mile trip from

Austin to the district's eastern border lay across prairies whose black soil
was more fertile than the Hill Country's limestone, but whose population was
almost as sparse.

And in political terms—the terms that mattered to Lyndon Johnson
—it was not the sparseness of the district's population that was most intimi-
dating but the pattern in which it was distributed. With the exception of
Austin, the district contained not a single large community; only six towns
—Brenham, San Marcos, Lockhart, Luling, Taylor and Georgetown—had
even 3,000 inhabitants. Many of the district's country people lived in towns
too small to be marked on any map. Most of the district's country people
didn't live in *any* town—or *near* any town. The voters Lyndon Johnson
would have to convince to vote for him—voters most of whom had never
even heard the name of Lyndon Johnson—were scattered on their isolated
farms and ranches so thinly across those immense spaces that a candidate
could drive miles between one voter and the next. Difficult miles. Two major
highways ran through the district: east-west U.S. Highway 290, and north-
south U.S. Highway 81. Most of the district's other roads were unpaved;
in 1937, the fifty-eight miles of "State Highway 66" between Johnson City
and the northern boundary of Burnet County, for example, were largely
unpaved. And most of the district's voters did not live on 290 or 81—or
even on 66. Their homes, the farms and ranches on which lay the votes
which alone could enable him to take advantage of his great chance, lay on
a thousand separate, long, winding, rutted roads that were little more than
paths or cow trails.

These roads were, moreover, the only way to reach these voters. Newspapers could reach them with only limited impact. Almost none of them
received a newspaper more than once a week; the circulation of the daily
newspapers read in the district, the *Austin American* and *Statesman* (combined circulation 30,000), the *San Antonio Light,* the *Dallas News,* was
limited almost entirely to Austin. Many of them received no newspaper at
all, either because their homes were too isolated to make delivery even of a
weekly feasible, or because they simply could not afford a subscription.
Radio could reach them hardly at all; by now an established political tool in
other areas of the United States, it was a tool with limited use indeed in rural
precincts few of whose residents owned one; the first survey of the use of
electrical appliances in rural areas of the Tenth District, conducted in 1939,
would disclose the presence of a radio in exactly one out of every 119
homes. Out of reach of the media, these voters were—most of them, at
least—out of reach also of personal influence. Here and there a local influential—a "lead man," in Central Texas parlance—wielded influence beyond
his immediate family, either because of the local power he might exercise,
if he was the town banker or the town lawyer or the County Judge, or
simply because people so isolated from news media relied for their political

opinions, to an extent unthinkable in a city, on men whose opinions they respected: a successful farmer, for example. Here and there was a crooked "box," or election precinct, whose votes could be purchased wholesale by a payment to an election judge or local Sheriff. But in this district, lead men and crooked boxes were few. There was no way to persuade these voters *en masse* to support a candidate of whom most of them had never heard. The only way to obtain the votes Lyndon Johnson needed was the hardest way: one by one.

HE STARTED EARLY. The announcement of his candidacy had appeared on Monday, and he was on the road before daylight on Tuesday, March 2, with forty days to go before Election Day, as his chauffeur, Carroll Keach, headed out along 290 on the 111-mile trip to Washington-on-the-Brazos, a score of ramshackle frame buildings huddled on a bluff above the muddy yellow river that marked the district's eastern border. The Texas Declaration of Independence had been signed in the little town on March 2, 1836 (Johnson's hero ancestor, John Wheeler Bunton, had been one of the signers); every March 2, farmers and ranchers flocked there to celebrate—and Johnson wanted to be there to greet them. And when he left the town, he didn't head straight back to Austin. About fifteen miles to the southwest was a junction with a dirt road, muddy, rutted, almost impassable because of deep puddles left by recent rains. But nine miles down that road was the town of Independence. Johnson had heard that morning that some of its 319 residents, deterred by the road conditions, had not attended the celebration. So he ordered Keach to turn off on the dirt road and drive to Independence —so that he could greet them, too.

His opponents, accustomed to the leisurely pace normal in Texas elections, had not expected the campaign to start until Allred set a date for the election; on the day—March 5—that the Governor set the date as April 10, Johnson had already completed a tour of the entire district, and was holding his rally in Old Main. Not having begun preparations until after the Governor's announcement, the other candidates were some time completing them. When Avery opened his campaign on March 9, Johnson had already been in the field for a week. Merton Harris promised a "very active" campaign in the opening statement he issued on March 11, but he actually did not begin until March 18, only a little more than three weeks before the election. Senator Brownlee said that he would not campaign until after the Senate adjourned, so that he could attend to his duties—and adjournment did not come until March 27.

Johnson didn't need an alarm clock; during their thirty-eight years of married life, Lady Bird says, "I don't ever remember Lyndon when something important was afoot ever oversleeping"—what woke Lyndon Johnson was more insistent than any bell. And since he had given Carroll Keach a room over his garage, the big brown Pontiac would be already idling at the curb when, at daybreak or before, Johnson walked out to it.

First, Keach would drive him downtown to his campaign headquarters, a big room on the mezzanine of the Stephen F. Austin Hotel, where he would be handed his itinerary for the day, and a list of the influential men he would meet. Keach would head out of the city while Johnson sat reading beside him on the front seat.

The reading could not have been encouraging. Lyndon Johnson had spent four years learning a district—the hardest type of district to learn; a rural district in which there was little formal political organization with identifiable officials; in a rural district, a newcomer could ascertain the identity of a town's true leaders—which storekeeper was respected, which farmer was listened to by other farmers—only through endless hours of subtle probing of reticent men. He had spent four years learning not only which men to talk to, but what to say to them: who was proud of a daughter, and who ashamed; who was really for Roosevelt, and who only said he was. And he had learned a district well. But that had been another district. The knowledge he had worked so hard to acquire was useless to him here, in rural precincts he had never even visited.

Sometimes, no one in Johnson's campaign headquarters even knew how to reach the tiny communities to which he was traveling that day. The itinerary he was handed would contain directions that were sketchy, incorrect, or simply non-existent. During the early days of the campaign—until he himself had written out directions (typical notation made by this future President of the United States: "Grassyville—5 mi below Paige back over same road. To Schwertner, back to Jarrel, Jarrel to Theon, second left out of town, then to Walburg, Walburg to Weir, Weir to Jonah, Jonah to Georgetown"), he had to stop constantly and ask directions, and, even so, often spent a precious hour jolting over a cowpath into the hills only to find it was the wrong cowpath—a lost candidate in a lost cause wandering around a huge district he didn't know. Often, his aides didn't even know the correct name of the community's "lead man"; the memorandum he was handed on the Walburg precinct informed him that its "about 110 votes all go one way," at the direction of G. W. Cassens—or was it C. W.? Unfamiliar even with the names of the lead men, his aides were of course unfamiliar with the men themselves: he had to win them over unarmed with even a clue as to their politics or their prejudices. A typical daily memo told him that at his first stop, Lytton Springs, he should "See Mr. Frank Gomillion, who may or may not be for you"; three key farmers in the next area—Dale—were listed; not only was he given no hint of where, in the Dale area's 200 square miles, their farms might be found, he was given no hint of their views: "Who these men stand for is unknown," the memo said.

Traveling to these isolated communities was no more discouraging than the reception he received when he arrived.

Johnson had spent four years not only learning a district, but helping a district: working with boundless energy and ingenuity to solve its people's problems. He had earned a district's gratitude. But that had been another district—this new district had no idea of what he had done. What must Lyndon Johnson have thought, after four years of tirelessly obtaining pensions for hundreds of veterans, when, heading out to Red Rock one morning, he read a memorandum advising him that it was necessary for him to "get on record concerning veterans' pensions"?

The district's ignorance about his accomplishments magnified the misgivings aroused by his age. Claud Wild had dispatched a veteran Texas politician, "Hick" Halcomb, to reconnoiter some towns before Johnson visited them to ascertain their initial reaction to his candidacy, and Halcomb's confidential memos to Wild contained, over and over again, an ominous phrase: "too young." Addressing himself to the voters he met in these towns—the quiet, closed-faced farmers—Johnson could see that Halcomb's pessimism was well founded. Sam Johnson had a favorite saying: "You can't be in politics unless you can walk in a room and know in a minute who's for you, and who's against you." Sam's son possessed the gift to which his father had referred. He could see who was for him—and he saw that very few were for him.

The formal speeches he gave in these towns did not do much to improve the situation.

These speeches were generally delivered on Saturday: traditionally, rural campaigning in Texas was largely restricted to Saturdays, the day on which farmers and their wives came into town to shop, and could be addressed in groups. On Saturdays, two automobiles, Johnson's brown Pontiac and Bill Deason's wired-for-sound gray Chevy, would head out of Austin for a swing through several large towns. On the outskirts of each town, Johnson would get out of the Pontiac ("He thought it looked a little too elaborate for a man running for Congress," Keach says) and walk into the town, while the Chevy would pull into the square, and Deason or some other aide would use the loudspeaker to urge voters to "Come see Lyndon Johnson, your next Congressman," and to "Come hear Lyndon Johnson speak at the square"; to drum up enthusiasm, records would be played over the loudspeaker ("The 'Washington Post March'—I can still hear it ringing now," Keach recalls.) But the crowds who came to hear this unknown campaigner were very small—their size discouraging when compared to those who had come to hear Avery or Harris or Brownlee—and the speeches did not move them to much enthusiasm for his candidacy. Written by Alvin Wirtz and Herbert Henderson, their single theme—all-out support of Franklin D. Roosevelt and the New Deal—was the right one for that district and that year when the Supreme Court fight was constantly on the front page of the Austin newspapers, but Johnson's delivery of his theme lessened its effectiveness. When he read from a prepared text—and if he had one before him, he could not seem to stop reading it—his phrasing was as awkward and stilted as his gestures; he shouted the speech, without inflection. Although he was continually urged by his advisors to look at his audience, he did so infrequently, as if he were afraid to lose his place in the text.

AFTER THE FORMAL SPEECH, however, Johnson would circulate through the town, shaking hands with its people—and suddenly there was no awkwardness at all.

When he saw someone he knew, his lean white face "would," in the words of a Hill Country resident, "just *light* up." He would stride over, ungainly in his eagerness, and call the man's name. "Old Herman," he would say. "How ya comin'?" He would put his arm around Herman's shoulders. "How *are* ya?" he would say. "Ah'm *awful* glad to see ya." Looking up at that face, alight with happiness, even the crustiest, most reserved farmer might be warmed by its glow. And the glow would deepen with fond recollection. "Well, the last time ah saw you was at the horse races up to Fredericksburg," Johnson would say. "We had a *good* time, didn't we? Remember that mare we bet on?" Lyndon Johnson had not seen some of the people he was greeting for ten years, but his memory of good times they had shared seemed as vivid as if the times had been yesterday. And so was his memory of the names of their kinfolk. Recalls his cousin Ava: "He would say, 'It's been a long time. How's so-and-so?' And he'd always know some member of his family to talk about. Listening to him, I realized he had a mind that didn't forget anything. 'Well, how's your boy comin'? Ah remember *him!*' " His questions got the other man talking. In no more than an instant, it seemed, a rapport would be established.

The rapport would be cemented with physical demonstrations of affection. With women, the cement was a hug and a kiss on the cheek. The technique was as effective for him as a candidate as it had been for him as a teen-ager. "Lyndon's kissing" became almost a joke during the campaign—but a fond joke. One elderly Hill Country rancher, annoyed by his wife's insistence on attending a Johnson rally, growled, "Oh, you just want to be kissed." (The rancher agreed to take her, but she was ill on the day of the rally, and he went alone. Upon his return, he told his wife, in some wonder: "He kissed *me!*")

With men, the rapport was cemented with a handshake—and a handshake, as delivered by Lyndon Johnson, could be as effective as a hug.

All politicians shake hands, of course. But they didn't shake hands as Lyndon Johnson did. "Listen," Lyndon Johnson would say, standing, lean and earnest and passionate, before a Hill Country rancher he remembered from his youth. "Listen, I'm running for Congress. I want your support. I want your vote. And if you know anybody who can help me, I want you to get them to help me. I need help. Will you help me? Will you give me your helping hand?" *Will you give me your helping hand?*—it was only as he asked that last question that Lyndon Johnson raised his own hand, extending it in entreaty.

With voters he didn't know, his approach was equally distinctive. He wanted their hands, too, in his, and after a brief "I'm Lyndon Johnson and I'm running for Congress, and I hope that you will lend me your helping hand," he would reach out and grasp them. Then, with his hand entwined with the voter's, he would ask questions: "What's your name? Where you from? What's your occupation?" And then, as Ava says, "there was that memory again. That was the key—he always knew somebody. I know your mother, or your father—or some friend. 'I've met so-and-so. He *told* me about you.' He made a connection." Seven years before, still a twenty-one-year-old undergraduate, Lyndon Johnson had campaigned for Welly Hopkins. That campaign had been Johnson's first. But Hopkins, watching the tall, gangling college boy, had concluded that he had a "gift"—"a very unusual ability to meet and greet the public." Now others saw that gift. They watched Lyndon Johnson's hand reach out to a voter—and they saw the voter's hand reach out in return. They saw that once a voter's hand was grasped in his, the voter wanted to leave it there. They saw that after he had talked to a voter for a minute or two, his arm around him, smiling down into his eyes, the voter did not want the talk to end. "What people saw was friendliness and sincerity, a love of people," Ray Lee says. The instant empathy Johnson created began, in fact, to cause problems for campaign aides trying to keep him on a tight Saturday schedule. An aide would attempt to urge Johnson along, but the voter, still holding tight to his hand, would walk along with him, trying to prolong the conversation. Sometimes, several voters would walk along. Waiting in the Pontiac, Keach would see Johnson coming—and there would be a small crowd behind him, a crowd reluctant to see him go. "Sometimes," says Lee, "it was a problem to get him out of town."

And he didn't campaign only on Saturdays.

On the other days of the week, the other candidates campaigned mainly in Austin, or in a "big" town such as Brenham or Lockhart (or, quite often, did not campaign at all). On those days, Johnson campaigned in the tiny towns that dotted the district. No speech had been scheduled for those towns, and none had been prepared by his speechwriters. But, more and more often now, he had to give one. A voter who had shaken his hand would begin following him, and another would join him, and another—and soon a Tenth District version of a crowd (fifteen men and women, perhaps, or twenty or twenty-five; "twenty-five would be quite a crowd," Deason says) would gather, and someone would shout: "Let's hear a speech," and someone else would shout, "C'mon, Lyndon, let's have a speaking," and he would be pushed up onto the bed of a truck or a wagon.

And if Lyndon Johnson with a speech in his hands was stilted and stiff and unconvincing, Lyndon Johnson without a speech—Lyndon Johnson alone and unprotected on a flatbed truck; no paper prepared by others to hide behind; nothing to look at but the faces of strangers; Lyndon Johnson with nothing to rely on but himself—was, nervous though he was (his cousin Ava, who had known him since he was a child, saw that he was "terrified up there"), gangling and big-eared and awkward though he was, suddenly was also a candidate with gifts—"very unusual" gifts—that went far beyond "meeting and greeting."

When, on such unplanned occasions, he talked about the President, it wasn't in Herb Henderson's phrases, or Alvin Wirtz's phrases, but in his own.

"Don't you remember what cotton was selling at when Mr. Roosevelt went into office?" he would ask.

"Don't you remember when it was selling at a nickel?

"Don't you remember when it was cheaper to shoot your cattle than to feed them?

"Don't you remember when you couldn't get a loan, and the banks were going to take your land away?

"I'm a farmer like you. I was raised up on a farm. I know what it's like to be afraid that they're going to take your land away. And that's why I'm for Mr. Roosevelt.

"What President ever cared about the farmer before Mr. Roosevelt?" he would ask. "Did Hoover care about the farmer? Did Coolidge care about the farmer? The only President who *ever* cared about the farmer was Franklin D. Roosevelt. He was for the poor man. He wanted to give the poor man a chance. He wanted the farmers to have a break. And he gave 'em a break. He gave *us* a break! He's the one who did it for us! He's the one who's *doin'* it for us! And he's the one who's *goin' to* do it for us! AND I'M BACKIN' HIM!"

The people before him were, many of them, people he had seen for the first time only a few minutes before. But as a result of his brief conversations with them, he could attach to their faces not only names but circumstances of their lives—and, in so doing, could make them feel that their destiny was linked to Roosevelt's destiny, and to Lyndon Johnson's.

"John Miller," he would say, "didn't you just now tell me you was goin' under when the soil conservation came in, and they started payin' you to let your land lie out? Well, whose program is it that's paying the farmers to let their land lie out? Roosevelt's program. Take the CCC. Now, it's helping *you*, Herman. Didn't you tell me your boy's over to Kerrville doin' terracing?

Well, whose program do you think CCC is? Roosevelt's. All these programs that have got the farmer out of the hole are Roosevelt's programs. He's the man who's doin' it for you. And I'm behind him. It'll take somebody in Congress to keep pushing for the things he wants. And you need to send a Congressman up there who *knows* this."

Their destinies were linked because of the Supreme Court fight, he told the farmers standing before him. The Court had already struck down one program that had helped the farmer—the AAA; whose fault was it that the government cotton certificates they were holding could no longer be redeemed? Who knew what programs the Supreme Court would strike down next? "Can you afford to risk the loss of your personal progress under Mr. Roosevelt? I tell you, this fight of the President is one that affects you and me right in this district. It means our bread and butter, and our *children's* bread and butter."

That was why, he said, they should vote for Lyndon Johnson. "The eyes of the nation are on us right here," he would say. "The whole country's watching what you do on April 10. This is the first and only test at the polls in all of the United States of the President's program." The other candidates in the congressional race were all alike, he said. Sure, only two of them were openly opposing the Court plan. But the rest, he said, are non-committal, vacillating, temporizing—"They're hanging back like a steer on the way to the dipping vat." Only "one man in this race has taken a positive stance," he said. "I am that man. A vote for me will show the President's enemies that the people are behind him. This is the test. Mr. Roosevelt is in trouble now. When we needed help, he helped us. Now *he* needs help. Are we going to give it to him? Are *you* going to give it to him? Are you going to help Mr. Roosevelt? That's what this election is all about. Don't let anybody kid you. That's what this election is all about!"

No Fundamentalist preacher, thundering of fire and brimstone in one of the famed Hill Country revival meetings, had called the people of the Hill Country to the banner of Jesus Christ more fervently than Lyndon Johnson called them to the banner of Franklin Roosevelt. And, as in revival meetings, passions rose.

Often they began to spill over when Johnson began talking about the NYA. "That was when Lyndon *really* touched people," says his cousin Ava. "Because what people here wanted more than anything else was for their children to have a better life than they had had."

Seeing a young man in the crowd, Johnson would speak directly to him—but in words that touched chords in the parents in the crowd. Calling the young man by name, he would tell him that he knew what it took to get an education if you were a poor boy. He knew, he said, because *he* had been a poor boy—and he had gotten an education.

"There's an education for every boy and girl that wants one," he would say. "It's up to you. You can get it if you want it. You have to work for it. You can do what I did. You can pick up paper. You can pick up rocks. You can wash dishes. You can fill up cars. You can do a lot of things if you want that education. But if you want it, you can get it."

A Roosevelt program—the NYA—would help you get it, he said. And if he, Lyndon Johnson, was elected Congressman, *he* would help you get it. He had already helped others. Turning to a father in the audience, he would demand: "Well, how's *your* boy comin'? I remember *him*. Didn't I get him a job down in San Marcos? How's he comin'?"

Suddenly his voice would not be the only voice. "Oh, yes, you sure did," the father would shout back. "You got him that job. And he's doin' just *fine!* We're sure proud of him." Another voice would shout. "That's right, Lyndon. You tell 'em, Lyndon!" Another voice would shout, "A-men." And all at once many voices would be shouting. "A-men, Lyndon. A-men, Lyndon! You tell 'em, Lyndon!"

And sometimes the response took a form even more impressive than shouting. "Sometimes," Carroll Keach says, "when the Chief would start talking, the people in the crowd would be kidding with him, and laughing. But then he'd really get started, and the crowd would get quieter and quieter, and finally there would be just a group of farmers standing there and listening very hard, without saying one word." Observers less impressionable than Keach started noticing the same phenomenon. On March 16, Johnson was pushed up onto a flatbed truck in Lockhart for an impromptu talk. Hick Halcomb, the old pol who was following Johnson around for Claud Wild, was present; his memo to Wild that night did not have its customary cynical flavor. "Speech was to some 45 men, who listened unusually attentively," it said. Two days later, Halcomb reported from Georgetown: Johnson "made a speech at urgence of group on street corner. Spoke to 64 people. . . . Not a man moved out of his tracks during speech." Another report was filed from Bastrop. "Reaction to Johnson's appearance started folks talking," Halcomb wrote. "I followed him and listened to such remarks as these: 'He's a fine-looking chap. He's a go-getter.' " Halcomb's memos began to have a different tone. It was hard to believe, he told Wild, but he was beginning to think that maybe Lyndon Johnson had a chance.

IF MEN, even men who had long known Lyndon Johnson, now became aware of new dimensions of his "gift"—his ability not only to meet but move the public—they became aware also of new dimensions of the effort he would make in using that gift. The men who knew Lyndon Johnson best— who knew best how utterly unsparing of himself he was willing to be, how "hours made no difference, days made no difference, nights made no difference"—had felt at the start of the campaign that, as Gene Latimer put it, "No matter what anyone said, we felt he had a chance, because we knew he would work harder than anyone else." But even these men had not known how hard he would work.

Very few of the local influentials, the "lead men," were for him. The leaders in the four counties in which Harris had been District Attorney knew Harris; the leaders in the counties Brownlee represented in the Legislature knew Brownlee; the leaders in Williamson County knew Sam Stone; leaders throughout the entire district, because they had needed favors from Buchanan, knew Buchanan's man Avery—when Johnson visited them, they were courteous to him, but they also let him know quite clearly that their allegiances, forged over many years, were not transferable to a stranger, particularly not to some young—too young—stranger who thought he should be a Congressman.

But he didn't stop visiting them. In Brenham, for example, he was, as Keach puts it, "working on an old Judge"—Sam D. W. Low. "His house sat on a knoll," and the Judge sat on the porch. After calling on Low, Johnson would come back to the car, and say, "Boy, I don't know. That was a tough cookie. Well, I tried, anyway." He kept trying. Low told Johnson he was for Avery, and was going to stay for Avery, "but," Keach says, "he [Johnson] kept going back. Many times I sat down on the road in the car watching him take the long walk up that trail to the house where the Judge was sitting on the porch."

"He kept going back" even to the one leader who did not, in dealing with Johnson, observe the tradition of courtesy: Austin's beefy Mayor Miller, an arrogant, hot-tempered man who had taken an instant and deep dislike to Johnson. Johnson humbled himself before him; returning to Austin after a day's campaigning, he would sometimes tell Keach to drive by the Mayor's big house on Niles Road; if Miller's car was parked there, indicating that the Mayor was home, he would ring the doorbell and ask if he could come inside for a talk. Miller never wavered in his views, but Johnson never stopped dropping by.

One "lead man" who was for him (because his daughter was married to Johnson aide Ray Lee) was County Judge Will Burnet of Hays County. But Hays looked bad for Johnson nonetheless: the county was the site of San Marcos—and of Johnson's alma mater, Southwest Texas State Teachers College. As the *Austin American* put it, "Johnson was prime mover in organization of a college secret society known as the 'White Stars' which for some years controlled campus politics. . . . The college days' animosities have carried over into later political life." Johnson needed "Judge Will" not just to support him, but to actively campaign for him. The road to the Burnet Ranch (where the stone ranch house was occupied by the Judge's father; the Judge lived in a log cabin "dog-run") was paved—a County Judge's road was always paved—but it was so isolated, deep in the Hill Country fastnesses, that from the nearest town, San Marcos, it was twenty-four miles to the ranch. Yet, every time Johnson finished campaigning in San Marcos, no matter how late the hour, he would tell Keach not to head back for Austin but to head instead into the blackness of a Hill Country night to see Judge Will.

He kept going back to towns, too, visiting repeatedly not just the district's six "big" towns in which the other candidates campaigned but tiny villages which most of the other candidates never visited at all. Many of these towns did not even have a town square; they consisted of a line of little stores along the road. On a typical day, he would stop in five or six towns, going into each business establishment on the square or along the road, shaking hands, talking for a few minutes wherever he found a group, speaking while leaning on counters ("Made favorable impression on farmers in Beyers Store by eating lunch on counter—cheese, crackers, soda pop," Halcomb reported), and on bars ("The fact that Lyndon talked to old man Pfluger in beer joint and treated nine to beers didn't hurt any"), speaking through swirling lint (in cotton gins whose owners had been persuaded to stop the pounding of the baler long enough so the workers could hear him speak), and in front of blazing forges ("LJ talked informally to a group of about eight in a blacksmith shop. Of this group, John Cowart, farmer, was thoroughly sold. Henry Conlee, Raymond Welsch, Albert Gardner, all veterans, were given sales talk, but they are still uncommittal. LJ recited his record in getting claims through").

If Johnson was to win this election, however, it would not be in towns that he won it. The votes that he needed could not be harvested in groups even as large as nine or eight. So, during the forty days—the forty long days —of his first campaign, towns were only stopping places. His real campaign was waged outside the towns: in the vast empty spaces of the hills and the plains.

Scattered outside the towns along the lonely roads, sometimes paved, usually graveled, were occasional general stores. He stopped at every store, purchasing some small item in each so as to predispose the proprietor toward him—if not cheese and crackers then a can of sardines, which he would open and eat on the counter. If he was lucky, there would be a farmer or two there, and he could talk to several people at once. If no one was inside but the storekeeper, he would talk to the storekeeper, in as casual and un-hurried a manner as if he had nothing else in the world to do. Scattered along the roads were filling stations, and he stopped at every one of these, too. At most of these stations, there was only one pump outside, and one voter—the proprietor—inside. But he chatted unhurriedly with that voter. (To ensure that he would be able to buy some gas at each station, he was careful never to fill his tank completely; Polk Shelton's brother Emmett recalls the lesson in country campaigning that Johnson gave him: "I drove down to Smithville one day; I had been planning to put posters in gas station windows, but every time I would get to one, Lyndon had been there before us. And at each one, he would go in and buy a gallon or two. We didn't need any gas; I had filled up before we left. So they were a little cold to us.")

Between the stores and the filling stations, along the lonely roads, other roads—unpaved, ungraveled, often ungraded—would cut off. These roads led into the hills, or across endless expanses of prairie on which no house or human figure could be seen. He turned off on those roads. The Pontiac might bounce along them for miles. Cutting off from them would be other even narrower roads—mere paths leading up into the hills, no more—which led to individual farms. He turned off on every path. Sometimes, so scattered were homesteads in this district in which forty acres were needed to support a single cow, he had to travel for miles along such a path. At intervals, a gate would bar it, to keep the cattle from straying. Johnson would get out and swing it open, careful to close it after Keach drove through. The path would grow rougher; the big car would lurch along the ruts. The slow progress would continue mile after mile, before finally, sometimes far off in the distance, a farmer would be seen at work in his fields. The car would jolt to a halt. Getting out, Johnson would climb the barbed-wire fence next to the path, and walk toward him. There might be several fields, and several fences, before he reached that tiny figure in the distance, who might have stopped working now and would be standing watching the tall, gangling stranger—wearing a necktie and a white shirt that glared in the sun— clambering awkwardly across the barbed wire. But the stranger's face would be alight with happiness to meet him, and with sincerity. And he would stand and chat with the farmer, one foot up on the wheel of the cultivator or the handle of the plow, as if he had nothing else in the world to do.

Day after day, while his opponents rested for the next Saturday, or delivered a major speech or two, Lyndon Johnson campaigned like this. The district covered 8,000 square miles; there were few sections of it that Johnson didn't visit. The fifty miles of State Highway 290 between Austin and Johnson City were barren miles, but at least at the end of them there was Johnson City, with its 300 or so votes. The district, however, extended twelve miles farther to the west beyond Johnson City. Seven miles beyond Johnson City was the "community" of Hye. When Lyndon Johnson had been a little boy, there had been a cotton gin at Hye, but the land in that area had worn out, and the gin was closed now. The "community" consisted of a one-pump filling station, and a combined general store/post office with a pressed-tin front. Lyndon Johnson never came to Johnson City without heading beyond it, still on paved Route 290, to Hye, where there might be a farmer or two shopping and picking up his mail. At Hye, more- over, an unpaved farm road branched south from Route 290. Along the thirty miles of this farm road were no more than a handful of scattered farmhouses. But Johnson never went to Hye without turning off onto that farm road. When, after visiting those farmhouses, he returned to 290, he did not head back to Austin but instead cut off 290 to the north on a rocky cowpath. Flanking 290 on the north was the Pedernales River. Beyond the river the hills became steeper, higher. From 290, those hills looked utterly empty, but Johnson, who had been raised in this area—the Johnson Ranch on the Pedernales was nearby—knew there were farms in them. If the river was low enough, a car could cross the Pedernales on a "low-water crossing" —a narrow slab of concrete, no guard rails or any other amenities—laid flat across the riverbed near Stonewall (at the ford across which his grandfather had spurred Old Reb to summon a doctor to Johnson's birth). Turning toward the river, the Pontiac bumped and lurched down to it on a rocky path. Johnson studied the water; if it was low enough, Keach drove across, and up into those hills. In this western end of the district, at the very farthest, most remote end of one of the most remote areas of the United States, votes were not measured in quantities so large as a handful; exactly two registered Democrats lived in the last precinct in Blanco County, for example. But Johnson never visited Johnson City without going beyond it to visit those two Democrats. In the eastern part of the district, portions of the plains were as barren of votes as the hills; beyond Paige, a Bastrop County community of perhaps fifty persons, for example, was Grassyville; on a typical trip to Grassyville, Halcomb noted, Johnson had found present "two people—store owner and customer." (And the store owner, he noted, was "a deaf old German strong against change in court and will vote for Shelton.") Johnson never went to Paige without going beyond it to Grassyville. Describing her cousin's first campaign, Ava Johnson Cox says: "He went to the blackland belt, he went to the sandyland people —he went everywhere. He went to the people that no one had ever gone to. He went to the people on the forks of the creeks."

The forks of the creeks. Lyndon Johnson was campaigning not just on the creeks—those tiny tributaries that trickled out of the hills and along the plains to create the little rivers of Central Texas—but on the "forks," mere rivulets of water that flowed into and created the creeks. The people who lived along the forks of the creeks lived in the district's emptiest, most isolated sections. And Lyndon Johnson did not rush through these sections. He spent time there. Years before, Welly Hopkins, riding "all the byways with Lyndon," had spoken of campaigning "up every branch of the Pedernales and every dry creek bed"—and of not merely visiting, but giving a speech to, an audience of only three people in an isolated valley. Now, with Lyndon Johnson campaigning for himself, that scene was repeated over and over. Lyndon Johnson talked of the Supreme Court and of the future of the farmer—talked of Roosevelt! Roosevelt! Roosevelt!—before audiences much smaller than the dozen who might gather on a courthouse lawn. The district's roads—paved roads, graveled roads, dirt roads, cowpaths—were measured in thousands of miles; by the end of the campaign, by the end of Lyndon Johnson's forty days, few of those roads would not bear the big Pontiac's tread marks. Hick Halcomb began to realize that he was hearing, in one town after another, some version of the same phrase. He would be standing in a town's courthouse or general store when a farmer from some isolated area entered. "That boy Lyndon Johnson was to see me," the farmer would say. "That's the first candidate for Congress that I've ever seen."

Days made no difference to him, nights made no difference to him. One scene which Carroll Keach was to recall vividly forty years after that campaign, so often had it been repeated during that campaign, occurred at the end of a day of campaigning. The sun might be disappearing behind the hills; the first stars might be out. Or perhaps darkness would already have fallen—the black darkness of the Hill Country unbroken for miles by a single light. He might have pointed the car back toward Austin; if it was dark, the city would be a glow on the horizon as he sped through the black hills, so tired that he could hardly keep awake, and could think only of falling into his bed. And then Johnson, sitting beside him, rechecking in the fading sunlight or in the light from the dashboard the list of names he had been handed that morning, would realize that somehow they had missed one, that one farm back there in the hills behind them had not been visited. "If that happened," Keach recalls, "we would go back, no matter how hungry and tired we were, no matter how far it was. Sometimes, I could hardly believe we were going back, but we always did." He would turn the car; they would be heading away from the glow in the sky, back into the hills, back along the highway looking for the mailbox, then along the path the mailbox marked, jouncing through the ruts in the dark. While Keach had been resting at each stop all through the long day, Johnson had been shaking hands and making speeches. Keach knew how tired his Chief was. But his Chief was portraying a candidate with youth and energy. "He would be very fatigued, *very*," Keach says. "But he never let a voter see the fatigue." When they reached the farm at the end of the path, all the farmer would see, in the last rays of daylight or in the glow of a kerosene lamp, as Lyndon Johnson strode toward him, was a face—young, eager, enthusiastic—all alight to see him.

JOHNSON'S DAYS out in the countryside might begin before the sun came up. They might end after the sun went down: twelve, fourteen hours later. His aides, waiting for him at campaign headquarters or at his home, were shocked at his appearance when he arrived back in Austin. Always thin, he was thinner now, terribly thin, so thin that his shirt collars gaped away from his neck, and his suits drooped off his shoulders. The customary pale whiteness of his face had turned gray; his burning eyes burned now out of sockets sunk deep in his head and rimmed, top and bottom, with skin so dark it looked smudged. In his cheeks, just a few weeks before smooth and youthful, hollows and harsh lines had been carved; his big ears appeared even bigger—huge—alongside this gaunt, haggard face. His fingers, stained yellow with nicotine—he seemed now always to be holding a cigarette— twisted in each other, and he tore at the skin around his fingernails, which was red and raw. But the days weren't over when he got back to the city— not nearly over.

His first concern in the evenings was money. Substantial as were the funds he was raising, they were not as substantial as the funds he was spending; his outlays for posters, calling cards, mailings, "campaign workers," newspaper ads and articles, and radio time was of a prodigality perhaps unprecedented in a Texas congressional campaign. Recalls Latimer: "When he would come in all tuckered out at the end of a day, he would call a meeting, and his first question would be: 'How's our money?' "

The answer to that question would invariably be disappointing, because Wild, unconvinced by Halcomb's reports of Johnson's effectiveness in the field, still regarded the campaign as hopeless and was only going through the motions as campaign manager. On some days, in fact, the campaign cupboard would be bare. "It would cost three, four hundred dollars just to mail out a day's letters, and we didn't always have that," Latimer recalls. Once, in a late-evening meeting in Johnson's living room, disappointment and frustration almost boiled over. "He came in one night and asked the campaign manager [Wild] how our money was, and the campaign manager said he didn't have enough to do something he [Johnson] wanted to do the next day, and he absolutely couldn't raise any more, and Johnson said, 'I hired you because you were supposed to be the best money-raiser, and now you tell me you can't raise any money!' He said something like: 'Okay, all I've done today is make eighteen speeches. Give me the phone.' " He placed long distance calls to two department store owners in Houston whom he had met while arranging jobs for young people in his capacity as NYA director—two ardent New Dealers who might support him because he was for Roosevelt.

It was important that the Houston businessmen not see the disappointment and frustration. Contributors liked winners. Sitting around his living room, his aides watched Lyndon Johnson as he sat in a big easy chair waiting for the calls to be put through. They saw a man ashen with fatigue, slumped in his chair, his nervous fingers tearing at the flesh around his fingernails. Lighting a fresh cigarette, he bent over, head low as he took his first puff, inhaled deeply—"really sucking it in," L. E. Jones says—and sat like that, head bowed, cigarette still in his mouth, for a long minute, as if to allow the soothing smoke to penetrate as deeply as possible into his body. But the Houston businessmen didn't see that man. They only heard his voice. As he talked on the phone, the watchers before him saw a body hunched and tense, a face drawn and gaunt and haggard—but the voice issuing from that face was a voice confident, almost gay (" 'We're almost over the hump'

—that sort of thing," Latimer says). And the checks it elicited were substantial.

Later in the evening after Wild had left, and he was alone with his White Stars, listening to their reports on the day's campaigning, he would no longer have to bottle up his emotions, and they would boil over. If Johnson felt a White Star had made a mistake in talking to some "lead man," he would rage at him. "Well you lost him all right!" he would shout in a high, shrill voice. "And you lost everybody he knows! You cost me fifty votes today!" In later years, the men who sat with him in his living room during his first campaign would speak of Johnson on the record in terms of his "energy." Off the record, they speak of the fear that sometimes filled their Chief's voice. "He would say things like, 'Well, you can just cross off Bastrop after today. Take a pencil and just cross it off!' Or, 'Well you really put a knife into me in Brenham, didn't you? Just put it in and twisted it!' There was a lot on the line, and he was afraid he was going to lose. He was terribly afraid he was going to lose."

But after the outbursts came the work. Tired though Johnson might have been, no part of it was scanted. Had someone failed to persuade a local leader? Should he try another approach? What should it be? Should someone else try? Who would be best? What should *he* say? What could be done in the leader's box that hadn't been done already?

Midnight would pass. Who was going where tomorrow? What was each of them planning to do, and say? What themes were working in each area? What new themes should be used? The White Stars would think a point had been settled; Johnson would begin going back over it, painstakingly reexamining every angle.

Hours after midnight would pass. Henderson would produce the speeches he had written that day—not only speeches for Johnson but speeches for Johnson supporters to read over the radio. Johnson read every one, made changes; reread them, made more changes. Ray Lee would bring out the copy and mats for the new newspaper ads; Johnson would check every ad.

Then he would hurry off to bed, for the next morning he had to get a very early start. And the next morning, he would be up at the moment he had said he would be—for it wasn't an alarm bell that was jerking him out of bed.

Ed Clark had seen a lot of campaigners. "I never saw anyone campaign as hard as that," he would recall forty years later. "I never thought it was *possible* for anyone to work that hard."

AND CLARK DIDN'T KNOW how hard Lyndon Johnson was *really* working. No one knew—with the exception of Carroll Keach. Because only Keach, alone in the car with Johnson for hours each day, knew what Johnson was doing in the car.

The great distances that had to be covered in Texas political campaigns, and the amount of time that politicians were therefore forced to spend traveling by car, had created a Texas political custom: while their chauffeurs drove them from town to town, most politicians spent considerable time sleeping. Keach would watch Johnson try to sleep. "He would try to rest between people," he says. "He sat in the front seat next to me, and I would see him close his eyes, but never for more than a minute or two, and then he'd just jerk up. He couldn't sleep."

Instead, he worked—in a rather unusual fashion. Leaving a town, Johnson would begin talking, not to Keach but to himself, about the people he had met there, the personal and political likes and dislikes that they had revealed. "It was like he was going over his mental notes," Keach says. "Who the people were, and little things about them, and who their relatives were, or how someone had reacted to some remark he had made. Someone didn't like something he had said—why not? 'I don't understand why she didn't react to such-and-such.' " In this sense, the talking was a review, and a preparation—a review of the people and town he had just visited, and a preparation for the next time he would visit them, so he would know what to say to them. "It was like he was having discussions with himself about what strategy had worked or hadn't worked, and what strategy he should use the next time." But the talking was also a critique of himself: self-criticism that was harsh, merciless. "He would talk about whether he had had a successful day, and if he had made a good impression or not. And lots of the time he felt he wasn't doing too good. And he would tell himself it was his own fault. 'Boy, that was dumb!' or 'Well, you just lost that box. You lost it, and you need it.' " And it was exhortation—self-exhortation that was also harsh and merciless. " 'Well, you'll just have to do better, that's all.' 'You'll just have to do something else.' " And as Keach listened, he would try out "something else," practice different approaches he could use the next time he saw the person, run through—aloud—the names of "people that he thought could talk to him." The two men spent hours in the car together, and hour after hour Johnson would talk this way to himself, lashing himself for his mistakes at the last town, lashing himself into readiness for the next town. And always "like memorizing," going over and over people's names and their relatives and their prejudices as if to chisel them into his mind so that they would spring to his lips the next time he saw them.

Only Keach saw the full extent of his fatigue. "Boy, sometimes he would get *so* tired," he says. "He would just slump there. He would close his eyes, but he couldn't sleep. So he'd start talking again. Maybe he had finished his memorizing about one town, going through all the people. So he'd just start all over again, right at the beginning. And he'd just get more and more tired. But when we'd get to the next town, he'd just bound out of the car, and start walking around like he was fresh as could be. He never let the voters see his fatigue."

DESPITE HIS EFFORT, he seemed unable to overcome the handicaps with which he had begun.

Only his sparsely populated home county was solid for him, and he had been unable to unhitch the leaders of the more populous counties from their "home men." He had spent so much time with Judge Low down in Brenham, but Low now publicly announced that he was sticking with Senator Brownlee; Keach had sat outside Mayor Miller's home so many times while Johnson pleaded his cause inside, but Miller now reiterated, even more emphatically, his support of C. N. Avery. The "carpetbagger" and "youth" issues were still weighing heavily with the voters. On March 25, the *San Antonio Express,* which three weeks earlier had found Avery far ahead of the field, took another poll—which showed Avery even further ahead. This poll, which forecast the final vote totals of the candidates, predicted that Johnson, with an estimated 6,000 votes, would finish in third place, 200 votes behind Merton Harris—and more than 4,000 votes behind Avery, who would, the poll estimated, finish with 10,500 votes. "With two more weeks to come around the bend and down the home stretch . . . [of this] horse race," the *Express* said, "the favorite is leading by four lengths." And, the *Express* said, "the indications are that" Avery's margin was continuing to widen. Another poll, in the *San Antonio Light* (which Johnson promptly dubbed the *San Antonio Blight*), placed Johnson behind not only Avery and Harris but also Brownlee and Polk Shelton. Johnson believed that he was doing better than the polls indicated. He felt he was doing well among the isolated rural voters—who were not included in the polls, in part because the polls were conducted by telephone and many of these voters did not possess telephones, in part because past experience led pollsters to discount the preference of rural families since many of them did not vote; time was far too valuable to an impoverished farmer for him to waste it driving long distances over unpaved roads to the voting box. But Johnson's belief was not shared by the district's veteran politicians; their own soundings confirmed the poll's conclusion. Those of them who had, at the urging of Wirtz or Ed Clark, agreed to remain neutral for a while to see if Johnson had a chance, now began, one by one, to announce for his opponents; several who had agreed to introduce Johnson at rallies in their home towns suddenly found excuses for not doing so; even Governor Allred began dissociating himself from his candidacy. This race was Johnson's chance, quite possibly his only chance. And he was losing the race.

. . .

As HE ENTERED the home stretch, however, he made two improvements in his strategy.

One was his own inspiration. He always enjoyed such great success with elderly people; now he invested a valuable campaign morning in a visit to the Austin home of seventy-three-year-old Albert Sidney Burleson, who had himself been elected to Congress from the Tenth District, in 1898, as a young man of thirty-four, to begin a distinguished career climaxed by a term as Postmaster General of the United States under Woodrow Wilson. The investment paid off handsomely. Burleson, long retired and ailing, was an almost legendary figure in the district, from one of its legendary families (Burleson County was named for his grandfather, a hero of San Jacinto). And Johnson emerged from his home bearing his handwritten statement that "I hope the people of this district will elect a young man who can develop. . . . To elect an old man is for the people to throw the office away." The statement made page one in the Austin newspapers, and, of course, in the weeklies. And Johnson made the most of the statement; at climactic moments during his speeches, one White Star, planted in the audience, would shout, "General Burleson is right!" and another would shout back, "Let's send a young man to Congress!" and a third would shout, "Let's do what General Burleson says!"

The other improvement was his father's inspiration.

Lyndon Johnson was very dejected as he sat, on the day the *Express* poll appeared, in his parents' home in Johnson City after hours of campaigning, talking to his parents, his brother, his Uncle Tom, his cousin Ava Johnson Cox, and Ava's eight-year-old son, William, known as "Corky." The leaders were almost all against him, he said; he had several large rallies scheduled, and he had not been able to persuade a single prominent individual to introduce him.

So, Ava recalls—in a recollection echoed by Lyndon's brother—"his Daddy said, 'If you can't use that route, why don't you go the other route?' "

"What other route?" Lyndon asked—and his Daddy mapped it out for him.

There was a tactic, Sam Johnson said, that could make the leaders' opposition work for him, instead of against him. The same tactic, Sam said, could make the adverse newspaper polls work for him, instead of against him. It could even make the youth issue work for him. If the leaders were against him, he told his son, stop trying to conceal that fact; emphasize it— in a dramatic fashion. If he was behind in the race, emphasize that—in a dramatic fashion. If he was younger than the other candidates, emphasize that.

Lyndon asked his father what he meant, and his father told him.

If no leader would introduce Lyndon, Sam said, he should stop searching for mediocre adults as substitutes, but instead should be introduced by a young child, an outstanding young child. And the child should introduce him not as an adult would introduce him, but with a poem, a very special poem. You know the poem, he told Rebekah—the one about the thousands.

Rebekah knew the poem. And when Lyndon asked who the child should be, Sam smiled, and pointed to Ava's son. In an area in which horsemanship was one of the most esteemed talents, Corky Cox was, at the age of eight, already well known for the feats of riding and calf-roping with which he had swept the children's events in recent rodeos; the best young cowboy in the Hill Country, people were calling him. "Corky can do it," Sam said.

All the next day, Sam trained him. "He wanted Corky to really shout out 'thousands,'" Ava recalls. "He wanted him to smack down his hand every time he said that word. I can still see Uncle Sam smacking down his hand on the kitchen table to show Corky how." And that night, at a rally in Henly, in Hays County, Lyndon Johnson told the audience, "They say I'm a young candidate. Well, I've got a young campaign manager, too," and he called Corky to the podium, and Corky, smacking down his hand, recited a stanza of Edgar A. Guest's "It Couldn't Be Done":

> There are thousands to tell you it cannot be done,
> There are thousands to prophesy failure;
> There are thousands to point out to you one by one,
> The dangers that wait to assail you.
> But just buckle in with a bit of a grin,
> Just take off your coat and go to it;
> Just start in to sing as you tackle the thing
> That "cannot be done," and you'll do it.

The audience applauded the eager young boy, and before the applause had died down, Lyndon Johnson took off his coat, and, with his version of "a bit of a grin" (combined with a nod to Corky to make sure the audience got the point), started in to attack the "thousands"—the *San Antonio "Blight,"* for example—who said that just because he was behind, he couldn't win.

THE HENLY RALLY took place on March 26, Good Friday. It was one of many Johnson rallies that day. Avery, whose campaign had been notably casual even before he had learned the previous day of the *Express* poll, decided that a "four-length" lead justified his celebrating the holy day with a day of rest. Johnson headed out to Hays County. Hard as he had run before, now, with the race seemingly lost, he ran harder.

The weather, mild and springlike the previous week, had changed overnight; when he awoke Friday morning, the temperature had dropped to thirty-two, and as he dressed, a hard, driving rain began to fall. He and his aides arrived in San Marcos, at the edge of the Hill Country, to be greeted by the news that an outdoor rally scheduled there had been canceled. Pulling on a slicker, he walked through the rain for hours, going from store to store, entering each store smiling through the water running down his face. By the time he left San Marcos, he was wet through despite the slicker.

"From San Marcos," a reporter wrote, "the fast-moving party" of "mud-speckled campaigners . . . went into the hill country, stopping first at Wimberley, then at Driftwood, before swinging west at Dripping Springs and on to Henly"—speeding ("C'mon, Carroll, let's *go!*") through the rain that rolled across the hills in blinding sheets. The temperature continued to drop. The rain turned to freezing sleet. Late-Spring northers like this had destroyed so many hopes in the Hill Country; this storm was, in fact, destroying hopes that day, killing corn and fruit that had been lured out of the ground by the previous week's warmth. Johnson's aides feared for a while that the storm would deal still another blow to Johnson's hopes. Large rallies had been scheduled in those Hill Country towns; the storm, they feared, would cut attendance. Arriving in each town, however, they found the courthouse or general store packed with farmers and their wives; these towns were in Will Burnet country, and Judge Will had finally emerged from his dog-run to "put his might behind" Johnson; during this "hard-driving day in Hays County, in which the candidate swept on through driving rains . . . and braved chilling cold winds," another reporter wrote, "the people came out to meet Johnson and to hear him talk."

And he talked. At each stop, he would hoist Corky onto the judge's bench or onto the store counter, and the boy would tell him that "There are thousands to prophesy failure." Pulling off his dripping jacket, the candidate would wipe his hand across his dripping face and grin around the room. His voice was very hoarse—because he shouted his speeches, his throat had been hurting almost since the campaign began—but he shouted now. If he felt he was losing, he let none of his listeners know how he felt. "Everywhere I go, the people declare I'm the high man," he said. "Second place is entirely a local matter. It's Johnson and Avery; Johnson and Brownlee; Johnson and Shelton; Johnson and somebody. We've got this race won, and now it's a matter of how big the plurality. . . . We have two weeks to go and we're building up the total every day." He talked of Burleson. "Why don't you write to the General and ask him how he feels?" he shouted. "He'll tell you that you ought to send a young man to Congress." And he talked of Roosevelt, and of the Supreme Court, which, he told these farmers, had stepped in and told the President, "Stop! You can't help the farmers!"

"The people know that you are either for Mr. Roosevelt or against him on this proposition," he said. "You can't be halfway. You can't be indifferent. You can't be for the farm program and against the Supreme Court reform."

With the exception of the references to Burleson, Johnson had been giving virtually the same speech for weeks, winning an enthusiastic response from handfuls of voters but only a lukewarm response at larger rallies. But on this day, at these large rallies, there was, suddenly, a very different response. Corky's poem ignited the emotions of the audience, and the White Stars' reminders of Burleson's statement fueled those emotions, and Johnson's hoarse shouts whipped them into blazing flame.

A White Star might be the first to shout, "General Burleson is right!" but then a farmer, his sun-and-wind-reddened face grim and earnest, would shout back: "Let's do what the General says!" "Amen, brother!" another farmer would yell. "A-men!" another would yell. Soon the whole crowd would be cheering. "Give it to 'em, Lyndon!" "Roast 'em, Lyndon!" And, over and over, punctuating the candidate's words: "A-men, brother! A-men, brother! A-men, brother!"

And now, also for the first time, there was another cheer, one that must have been music to the candidate's ears. In Henly and Wimberley and Driftwood and Dripping Springs and Buda and Kyle (and Uhland and Niederwald, too, for before this day was over, Johnson would campaign on the plains as well as in the hills), Johnson spoke, in a reporter's phrase, "to a group of farm people." And when he shouted "Roosevelt! Roosevelt! Roosevelt!," the farm people shouted back: "Roosevelt *and Johnson!* Roosevelt *and Johnson!* Roosevelt *and Johnson!*"

DURING THE CAMPAIGN'S final two weeks, not only Johnson's voice, rasping and shrill, but the tone of his attacks became more and more strident; those who opposed the President were no longer "in the dark"; now they were "back-stabbers." When, for example, Brownlee tried to tell voters that "I love, admire and praise our great President," Johnson replied: "How much did the State Senator 'love, admire and praise our great President' when he voted for the Senate resolution condemning the President's Court-reform plan? . . . He stabbed the President in the back." He was going into Burnet, the Senator's home town, he said, and in Burnet "I shall read the Senator's record. I shall cite the book, the page and the line. We'll have the evidence right out in the open."

During those final days, desperate, he nerved himself to do things he had shied from doing.

Emmett Shelton was campaigning hard for his brother Polk—the Shelton campaign was the only one at all comparable to Johnson's in energy, although Polk's dogged refusal to change his stand on the Court proposal kept him continually on the defensive—and Emmett Shelton was what Johnson only claimed to have been: a great debater at San Marcos. Whenever, during the campaign, his path had crossed Johnson's, he had attempted to shame Johnson into debating him. Arriving in a town to find Johnson's campaign car there, he would park his own right alongside, and would use his loudspeaker to challenge Johnson to debate. Johnson, aware of his weakness in debating, had refused to do so. In one particularly painful incident, Shelton had parked directly outside a store in which Johnson was shaking hands and had stayed there, blaring, over and over, a challenge to Johnson to come out and debate, for quite some time—and Johnson had not come out, refusing to leave the safety of the store until Shelton had driven away. Now, however, their paths crossed again—in Smithville on a Wednesday on which hundreds of farmers had come into town for a prize-drawing set up by the merchants—and, this time, when Shelton repeated the challenge, Johnson at last turned on his tormentor. To Shelton's sorrow.

Shelton, speaking first, said Johnson was not only too young for the post he sought but too "new in the district," and "comes from the smallest county, Blanco." He accused him of trying to buy the race with large campaign contributions from the "Interests." Stepping up to the microphone to reply, Johnson said, "I am not going to attempt to answer all the wild charges made here this afternoon by a dying, desperate candidate, but there's one I have to plead guilty to—and gladly. Sure, I was born in the small county of Blanco. But I can't believe that's against me. I didn't have any jurisdiction in the matter." The crowd chuckled at that, and laughed outright at his next sally, which reminded these country people that Polk Shelton wasn't one of them; "If my mother had known that you wanted a city slicker or a ward boss for a candidate, maybe she'd have been able to do something about it." His reply to the charge that he was too young subtly reminded the audience where Shelton stood on the Court issue: "I'd rather be called a young whippersnapper than an old reactionary," he said. "And as for buying the race, I do want you to know that my campaign is financed by my own meager savings, and that I am not getting a dime from special interests." Then he briskly stepped down. "Although given only five minutes," the *Austin Statesman* reported, he "won the crowd so well he received four spontaneous bursts of applause and drew two heavy laughs."

DESPITE HIS DENIALS, money—the ingredient with which his campaign was so plentifully supplied—added additional impetus to his dash down the homestretch.

Although most of it was spent on traditional campaign devices, during the last two weeks of the campaign, more and more of it was spent on radio time. Early in the campaign, Johnson had purchased fifteen minutes every evening for a week on Austin's only station, KNOW, and had raced back to the capital every evening to speak over the air. But since few voters owned radios, few heard his speeches. Federal Communications Commission regulations, moreover, required that political speeches be written, and delivered verbatim from the text, and Johnson's delivery of prepared addresses proved even more stilted and pompous over the air than in person; listening to them in his living room, Sam Johnson would chew his cigar in dismay, and Rebekah, the public-speaking teacher, would frantically make notes in her little notebook. For some time thereafter, Johnson had given radio only cursory attention.

Now, however, searching for any means of pulling up on Avery, he bought more air time. And he began to notice that voters who approached him the next day to tell him they had heard him on the radio did so with smiles that were both shy and impressed. An aura of celebrity, he realized, could help to offset an aura of youth. Johnson had the funds to take advantage of this discovery. He purchased time—a lot more time, hour-long blocks of time—not only on KNOW but on the more powerful San Antonio stations that reached into the district. During the campaign's final ten days, in fact, Johnson was on the radio more than the other seven candidates combined.

Prominent supporters, reading fifteen-minute speeches written by his staff, and rewritten, line by line, by him, were also put on the air. The response to this tactic was immediate and gratifying—and it did not come only from listeners. More than one "lead man" who had refused to commit himself to Johnson was lured into his camp by the chance to appear on radio. And as one Johnson supporter followed another to the microphone, some proved surprisingly effective. His father's onetime real estate partner, old Judge N. T. Stubbs (who began his talk by saying, "I come tonight as one who . . . could be classed among the pioneers of this section"), was very persuasive as he replied (in words Johnson himself wrote) to charges that Johnson was trying to "buy" the campaign with huge outlays of cash: "We home-folks know how ridiculous that charge is. . . . We know that Lyndon Johnson's campaign has been financed by his own small savings, by contributions of his family and friends, received a few dollars at a time." Purchasing still more time, Johnson put the old Judge on the air again and again. His opponents' charges about Johnson's unprecedented expenditures were buried under Johnson denials, broadcast thanks to Johnson's unprecedented expenditures.

HIS MOST PRODIGAL EXPENDITURE, however, continued to be not of money but of himself.

The steadily worsening weather—the norther that had begun on March 26 was to rage for four days, with such fury that the *American* called it a "blizzard"—turned the district's roads into mud. Most of the candidates curtailed their campaigning. Avery, for example, was to venture outside Austin only once during the campaign's final two weeks. Brownlee, belatedly realizing that he had waited too long to begin, had scheduled a "blitz" of the district beginning the day the Senate adjourned. That day turned out to be March 27, when the storm was at its height. Brownlee postponed the blitz to March 30, and then to April 1. Johnson stepped up his campaigning, running harder and harder, covering large sections of the district in a single day—speaking, each day, in as many as a dozen little communities, visiting, between speeches, scores of farms and ranches.

On the evening of April 2, eight days before the election, a Johnson speech in Brenham was broadcast over a San Antonio radio station—and one listener in San Antonio heard something in his voice that worried her. Sitting alone in her apartment, Estelle Harbin, who knew Johnson so well, suddenly felt that he was "worn out" in a way he had never been before; "seemingly limitless" though his energy appeared, it had limits nonetheless, she knew—and, listening to his voice, she began to wonder if he was pushing himself beyond them.

The same thought was worrying others who knew Johnson well. "He was very tired," Gene Latimer says. "He had *been* tired for a long time. He had stayed tired ever since the beginning of the campaign. I had seen him tired before, but this was beyond that. I was getting a little concerned."

Desperate for sleep now, Johnson bought a black mask to cover his eyes in the car, but that didn't help; it wasn't light that was keeping him awake. The piercing eyes sank deeper into their sockets. He grew thinner and thinner; the flesh seemed to be almost melting off his face now; gaunt and cadaverous, he might have been a candidate by El Greco. Lady Bird blamed his loss of weight on improper eating habits: "He ate very irregularly and very unbalanced meals, which made me very angry because I'm a great believer in nutrition. He would just stop at some country store and buy a can of sardines and some crackers, or some cheese. . . ." But when she gave him a "proper meal," he would gag on it. He didn't get much down, and what he did eat, he sometimes couldn't keep down. He seemed to be vomiting more and more frequently. He kept complaining about stomach cramps, but he had always complained so much about physical ailments (and, of course, had vomited before in moments of tension, as at the finals of the state debate championships) that the complaints weren't taken seriously, even though he sometimes doubled over in pain. His complaints were further discounted, moreover, because he was not curtailing his activities; he was working more, not less. On April 3, for example, he lost his voice completely, and though it returned the next day, it returned as a croak, so rasping that it was almost painful to hear. But he didn't cancel speeches, only scheduled more.

On Tuesday, April 6, four days before the election, at a rally in a courtroom of the Travis County Courthouse in Austin, he stood during his speech behind the railing which separated the court from the spectators' benches, and some of the spectators said he almost seemed to be holding the railing for support, as he leaned far over it, his hand outstretched to them, appealing for their votes. That his efforts—combined with his opponents' lack of effort—were bearing fruit was obvious now. The editor of Brownlee's home-town newspaper told an *Austin American* reporter that Brownlee "has waited too long to get his campaign into action, and his friends feel he has already lost the race." And when the reporter asked who was winning, the editor said he didn't know, but that Johnson had spoken in the county the night before "and he gained many votes by the speech." The *American* had published a new poll on April 4, and politicians in Austin could hardly believe its findings: Avery wasn't in first place any more. Two other candidates were ahead of him: Merton Harris and Lyndon Johnson. Now, on Wednesday, April 7, three days before the election, another *American* poll showed Harris and Johnson running "neck and neck" in "as closely fought a political race as central Texas has ever seen." A large bloc of "sideline votes"—votes still undecided—would probably decide the outcome, the article said. Lyndon Johnson awoke Thursday morning, with two days to go, nauseated and in pain. At eight o'clock he paid a call on Mayor Miller, to ask again for the mayor's support with Austin voters, and to receive in reply only another rude rebuff. During the rest of the day, Johnson cam-paigned in Austin himself, "reaching," as the *American* put it, "as many voters personally as possible."

Thursday evening at eight o'clock, Johnson was scheduled to address another rally in the Travis County Courthouse. Before the speech, Ray Lee recalls, "Mr. Johnson was drooping about his apartment in Austin, saying he didn't feel good. We didn't attach enough importance to it. He was tired and withdrawn. So we urged him to rest awhile and go to sleep if possible." Keach was off on another assignment, and Lee volunteered to drive Johnson to the auditorium. "I got back to his house about a quarter to seven and he was in the bathroom. He said that he was in pain and that he had taken purgatives but he couldn't get any relief" but "after a few minutes we got in the car and went down to the courthouse." The crowd of 400 persons was perhaps the biggest of the campaign, and it was applauding and cheering the familiar lines ("There is only one issue the voters of the Tenth District face. That is, whether they stand with the President . . .") when Johnson, who again had been supporting himself on the rail while speaking, doubled over, white-faced, and sat down, with his arms across his stomach. Some of the audience came up and, after hearing about the pain, told him he must have appendicitis, but he got up, and after apologizing to the audience for the interruption, finished the speech. Then, as the audience filed past him, he began shaking hands. Sherman Birdwell, coming up to congratulate him, noticed that "he was covered with perspiration and he was constantly wiping his brow." He whispered to Birdwell: "I'm sick. Stand here beside me." He had shaken almost all the hands when he had to sit down again. This time, he couldn't stand up, and, Lee, with Birdwell helping him, got him out to the car, and drove him home, and then to Seton Hospital; doctors there said, Lee and Mrs. Johnson recall, that "his appendix was on the point of rupturing." They operated almost immediately.

"THERE HAD BEEN such mad rushing for so long," Lady Bird Johnson recalls. "And then everything came to a sudden dead stop. There was this dreadful day of hiatus, and then the election."

Shortly after the polls closed on Saturday evening, Sam Stone's Williamson County vote—3,180—was announced, putting him some 2,400 votes ahead of Johnson. But outside Williamson, Stone did very poorly, and, as the votes came in from other counties, Johnson soon passed him. He soon passed all the other candidates, and pulled steadily ahead throughout the evening. The official totals for the major candidates showed Houghton Brownlee with 3,019 votes; C. N. Avery with 3,951; Stone with 4,048; Polk Shelton with 4,420; Merton Harris with 5,111—and Lyndon Johnson with 8,280, 3,000 votes more than his nearest opponent.

"When I come back to Washington," Johnson had vowed, "I'm coming back as a Congressman." Now, less than two years later, he was coming.

22

From the Forks
of the Creeks

ANALYZING IN DETAIL the results of the special election for Congressman in the Tenth Congressional District of Texas in 1937—breaking it down by ethnic groups or age brackets or educational levels—is an unrewarding exercise, for the results are both too small and too fragmented to have much significance.

Although the district's population was estimated at 264,000, only 29,948 persons, one out of every nine residents of the district, went to the polls. And of those voters, only 8,280 cast their votes for Lyndon Johnson. Johnson won the election, in other words, with less than 28 percent of the vote—with only one out of every four votes cast. He won, moreover, with the votes of little more than 3 percent of the district's population; he was Congressman from a district in which only one out of every thirty-two persons had voted for him.* Johnson had been elected with the fewest votes— by far the fewest votes—of any of the nation's 435 Congressmen.

In a broader context, however, the election was significant for two reasons. One, of course, was that it set Lyndon Johnson on the path of elective office that would lead him to the Presidency, and that would lead America to the Great Society and to Vietnam. The other was the identity of the people who set him on that path.

They were not the people of the plains. Half the district consisted of prairies, and Johnson lost that half; in the district's five plains counties, in fact, Johnson finished not first but fourth, trailing Harris by a total of more than 800 votes. Johnson's support came from the hills, from the five counties in the district that lay on the Edwards Plateau. Not only did he

---

* Some 41,000 votes had been cast in the 1936 Democratic primary, which Buchanan won.

win four of those five counties, losing only in Stone's Williamson County, but he won them by overwhelming margins. If his home county, Blanco, gave him 688 votes to 82 for his nearest opponent, Hays County's support was also impressive: 940 votes for Johnson, 270 for his nearest opponent.

And within those five counties, the distribution of his votes was striking. Although—to the surprise of all forecasters (and Mayor Miller)—he won Austin on the edge of the plateau, it was the precincts west of Austin, the boxes in the hills, that gave him a substantial margin in Travis County. The votes he received in Williamson County came, in large proportion, not from Georgetown and Taylor, the two "big" towns just below the plateau, but from the hills to the west. And in Blanco, Burnet and Hays counties, the other Hill Country counties, the results followed, in general, an identical pattern: the deeper in the hills a precinct, the more isolated and remote— and poor—its people, the stronger the showing that Lyndon Johnson made in it. He was the candidate of the Hill Country, of one of the most remote, most isolated, most neglected—and most impoverished—areas of a wealthy nation. His 3,000-vote plurality—a plurality whose dimensions had been utterly unsuspected—came principally from the farmers and the ranchers he had visited one by one, from the people in whom he had invested time no other candidate for Congress had ever given them, from the people who had, on Election Day, repaid that investment in kind, giving up their own time—the time so valuable to them—to make the trip, sometimes quite a long trip, to the polling place to cast their votes for Lyndon Johnson.

His very willingness to travel to these people may have been an important reason that they supported him. Not only were they neglected, they felt neglected—they had always felt neglected; the people of the Hill Country had had to plead even to the People's Party. *"If we do live away up here on the Pedernales River, amid rocks, cliffs and waterfalls, cedars and wild oaks, we are not varments, but have hearts just like men."* "Brethern, *in sending out lecturers, please remember our isolated corner, and send us in time of need."* "We had an 'encampment' and honestly expected the *presence of a 'Big Gun' with it, but, no we were sadly left, as usual."* When, finally, a candidate for Congress made the effort to come to them, muddying his shoes to walk across fields to talk to them, they were grateful for his coming.

But his effort was no more important than the philosophy he expressed. Saying he was a poor man like them, he also said he was fighting for the President who was helping the poor—for the only President who had ever helped the poor, for the President who, with bank regulation and railroad regulation and government loans and public works projects, had held out government's helping hand to the poor instead of the rich. The people of the Hill Country had been asking for such programs for a long time. In half a century, only two long caravans had come out of the Hill Country. One had borne pictures of Lyndon Johnson. The other had borne blue flags.

"He won that election in the byways," Bill Deason says. Ava Cox says: "That's what made Lyndon Johnson be elected the first time. . . . He told them: 'I *know* what you people are up against. Because I'm one of you people.' And it wasn't the people of the cities who elected him, but it was the people from the forks of the creeks."

That was indeed the reason he won—and the reason no politician had thought he could win. The polls had not shown his strength at the forks of the creeks, for no poll bothered with the people at the forks of the creeks, as no candidate visited them. But Lyndon Johnson had visited these people. And they had sent him to Congress.

NOTHING ABOUT HIS VICTORY, however, was as significant as his reaction to it.

"I'm coming back as a Congressman," he had vowed, and he had kept that vow. And he had done so fast—as he had lived his entire life fast: he had been perhaps the youngest state director of any New Deal agency, now he was, at twenty-eight, although not "the youngest Congressman" he now claimed to be, one of the youngest. He was the same age as his hero ancestor John Wheeler Bunton had been when Bunton had first been elected to public office, only a year older than his father had been when he had first been elected. Was he content? Was he happy now—even for a day?

He was desperately weak—not just because of the appendicitis but because of the effort that had preceded it. He was later to say that during the campaign's forty days, he had lost forty pounds. When the campaign began, 181 pounds had been stretched thin over his six-foot-three-inch frame. His weight when he entered Seton Hospital is not known, but when he left the hospital two weeks later—after two weeks of bed rest, and a hospital diet designed to fatten him up—his weight was back up only to 151 pounds.

On the day after the election, congratulations had arrived in stacks. (Phrases in the letters from people who had known him as a boy or as a college student or as a congressional secretary provided a panorama of his life. Marsalete Summy, who had heard him talk of his ambitions in a Johnson City schoolyard, wrote: "You have always had a vision ever since I have known you and I am most happy to see that it is being fulfilled for you." Vernon Whiteside wrote reminding him of "the day at San Marcos" when "I separated you and Babe Kennedy." Arthur Perry, the older secretary who had taken him under his wing when he got to Washington, wrote: "My dear Congressman!!! Do I get a kick out of that!—Well, sir, when I used to see you wearing those summer suits in the winter time, and skimping on lunches until pay day, the prospect of your becoming Congressman in the immediate future, I must confess, appeared a little indefinite." Remembering that, when he had found himself in trouble, he had turned for help to the younger man, Perry also wrote: "On the other hand, when I recall your presentation before the Civil Service Commission . . . I might have known I was in the presence at that moment of a budding 'People's Choice.' " And, aware that Johnson was not quite as wholeheartedly a New Dealer as the campaign had made him appear, he also wrote: "We will be expecting you to make a 'balance the budget' speech in the House.") Early on the morning after Election Day, Johnson sent for his aides, and told them that all the messages had to be answered at once—that very day. Sitting up in bed, smoking one cigarette after another, he began to dictate replies. Many people had expressed a desire to see him so that they could express their congratulations in person, he was told; he wanted to see *them*, he replied; a schedule of visits should be set up at once; he had a lot of people to see before he left for Washington—and he wanted to leave for Washington fast.

The first letters to be answered, moreover, were those not from friends but from enemies: the concession messages from his opponents. And while their congratulations had been strictly *pro forma*, his replies were not.

You didn't lose, he told Avery, just as I didn't win. "It was a victory for President Roosevelt." He repeated that to Sam Stone—"My dear Judge: Thank you very much for your kind telegram. The people voted to support President Roosevelt and his program, and the victory is his"—and, since the Judge would be a more dangerous future opponent than Avery, went on at more length: "You warned me you would show us how to carry Williamson County, and I congratulate you upon the support the homefolks gave your candidacy. Please tell your and my friends there that I admire the way they stood by you." And to the opponent he considered most dangerous of all—Polk Shelton, who had campaigned with energy, and whose strong beliefs Johnson feared would impel him to run again—his reply went even further: "Thank you for your kind telegram and your pledge of support. . . . I hope you will always feel that my efforts are at your disposal. Whatever service I may be able to render will be cheerfully and gladly done."

Letters were not the only means by which he dealt with the men who had been his enemies just twenty-four hours before. The powerful Mayor Miller, so hostile during the campaign, was leaving for Washington the next day on a long-planned visit. Because Johnson did not yet have a secretary in Washington to show the Mayor around, he telegraphed his brother, now Congressman Kleberg's secretary (Sam Houston had returned to Washington a week before) to do it—and to go all out in doing it, to "give him all the privileges and courtesies of the office." Johnson would have to run again in eighteen months, and, this time, he would be running not in a special election but in a regular primary in which victory would require not the 28 percent of the vote which he had received, but 51 percent. Any prudent politician would take steps to try to make friends out of enemies, but even very prudent politicians were amazed by both the rapidity and the extent of the steps Johnson took. The eminently pragmatic Dan Quill had spear-headed the ward-by-ward fight against Miller in Austin; he knew the bit-terness of the fight, and the depth of Miller's dislike of Johnson; he knew that Johnson had visited Miller's house many times to beg for a truce, and he knew how rude Miller had been in denying him one. Quill, by coincidence, left for a Washington visit on election night, and when he arrived, dropped in to see Sam Houston Johnson, and saw the telegram. Pragmatic though he was, Quill could hardly believe that Johnson had sent it. When he had left Austin, Miller had been Johnson's most bitter enemy, "and here he had sent a telegram to take care of him. . . . I never saw anything like it. . . . When I got in a fight with a fellow in an election, I didn't forgive him so quickly. . . . I don't know how he did it. I wouldn't have had the nerve to have been nice to those kind of people, but he was. That was just three days after the election, and he wanted to be nice to Tom Miller. . . ." Quill recalls saying to Sam Houston: "I'll tell you, Washington is a big city, but it's not big enough for Tom Miller and me at the same time." To avoid bumping into the Mayor, "I came back home."

(Quill did not know the extent to which Johnson had gone to "take care of" Miller. Because he was afraid his brother would not carry out the task with sufficient diligence, he had asked not only Kleberg's office but Maury Maverick's to put itself completely at the Mayor's disposal.)

No effort had been spared to defeat these men; no effort would be spared to win their friendship. One day, before Johnson left for Washington, Emmett Shelton would step out of his office building to walk up Congress Avenue to the Travis County Courthouse, and would see Johnson getting out of his Pontiac, having apparently just parked it. Johnson said hello to Shelton, asked him where he was going, and then insisted that Emmett join him; he would be glad to give him a lift, he said. As they were driving up Congress Avenue, Shelton realized that he had left some papers in his office. Johnson drove him back. Shelton said he would be a few minutes, and said it was no trouble for him to walk to the courthouse. No, no, Johnson said, I'll wait. Glad to. Take your time. And the Congressman waited there for Shel-ton as if he were his chauffeur, and as they talked during the brief drive, "He [Johnson] was gracious, very gracious." Though he had disliked Johnson, "now," Shelton says, "he was just nice. He was humble." More than humble, in fact. "He made you feel he was dirt under your feet." (Shelton didn't know the full extent of the trouble Johnson was taking to become his friend; Johnson had not, in fact, just parked his car when Shelton came out; he had parked it an hour before, and had been sitting in it for an hour waiting for Shelton to come, to take advantage of the "chance" meeting.) Shelton was not the only opponent thus disarmed; Tom Miller gave Johnson a post-election contribution of $100 to meet any campaign deficit he might have.

What might prevent a Dan Quill or another man from behaving to his enemies the way Lyndon Johnson behaved would be pride or embarrassment —or any one of a hundred conventional emotions, such as a natural desire to gloat, even for a day or two, over a fallen, and vicious, foe. But Lyndon Johnson had determined many years before the emotion that would govern his life—the emotion that, with "inflexible will," would be the only emotion that he would *allow* to govern his life. "It is ambition," he had written, "that makes of a creature a real man." Pride, embarrassment, gloating: such emotions could only hinder his progress along the road he saw so clearly before him—the "vision" he had indeed held for so long. They were luxuries in which he would not indulge himself.

THE ADDRESSES to which he was sending those letters were not all within the district. Just as he had, as a Congressman's secretary, encouraged influential persons from other districts to come to him for help, now, as a Congressman, he replied to congratulations from out-of-district influentials with similar encouragement, as in his reply to the publisher of a weekly newspaper in Vernon, near the Oklahoma border, almost 300 miles away. (R. H. Nichols to Johnson: "Congratulations . . . I remember with gratitude your many services to our family while you were with Mr. Kleberg"; Johnson to Nichols: "Thank you . . . Any time I can be of some service to you I want you to call on me.") Influential or not, moreover, anyone who wrote to Johnson was to receive a reply—as fast as it could be typed and mailed. Sitting propped up in his hospital bed, his face still gray with the shock of the operation, he dictated fifty different form letters to be sent out, so that recipients wouldn't realize that the letter they received was a form letter.

Among the first letters he wrote were letters to officials of the National Youth Administration in Washington. He wanted them to make permanent Jesse Kellam's temporary appointment as the NYA's Texas director. He wrote, in addition, to Sam Rayburn, to Senator Morris Sheppard, to anyone whose intercession with the NYA hierarchy might conceivably be helpful. Keeping control of the NYA was very important to him; it was, after all, a statewide agency—and thus a potential statewide political organization. Just one day after he had become Kleberg's secretary, Ella So Relle had seen that "he was thinking this was a stepping stone. As soon as he got a job, he thought, now that I'm in this, how can I use this job for the next step?" Nothing had changed. Johnson already knew what the next step was going to be—and for it he needed a statewide organization.

ON ONLY ONE GROUP of letters did he delay putting his signature. These were replies to congratulatory letters which mentioned his father.

Writing to congratulate Johnson on April 12, for example, William P. Hobby had mentioned his admiration for Sam Ealy Johnson. Although Hobby was one of the most powerful men in Texas—a former Governor who was now publisher of the *Houston Post*—and although Johnson immediately dictated a reply to his letter, he did not sign the typed reply for almost a month.

Quite a few letters mentioned Lyndon Johnson's father, and his record in answering them is striking, considering the promptness with which all other letters were answered. Some of these letters must have recalled painful memories—E. B. House, for example, wrote, "Your father served as road foreman under me in 1925–26"—but others had a very different tone: A. R. Meador, for example, wrote that

> I was raised in Buda, and it was a very happy day to me when Sam Johnson would come to our house and stay all night. My brothers and myself would unhitch the horse from that ol buggy.
>
> My mother who was a friend of your grandfather is now 83 years of age. [She] was so anxious to cast her ballot for you but was not able to get out of the car. So she had someone drive her to the polls and the ballot was brought to the car, "So she could vote for Sam Johnson's little boy."

No matter what the tone of the letter mentioning his father, the replies were delayed, sometimes for quite some time. The Meador letter, for example, was not answered for more than three weeks. (Johnson's reply, moreover, contained no mention of his father.) Sometimes the same letter would be presented to Johnson for signature over and over, and each time would remain unsigned—as if he could not bear to sign it.

THE DOCTORS HAD TOLD HIM he would be out of the hospital a week after the operation—by April 15 or 16. A send-off dinner was being planned for the new Congressman, and he told the planners to hold it on April 26, because he was very eager to be off. But he suffered a setback. The doctors told him he would have to rest, but after a day or so, he tried to resume working from his hospital bed—and this time there was a more serious setback. Its precise nature is unknown—in referring to it, Johnson aides and relatives use two adjectives: "nervous" and "exhausted." Talking to an old friend, Edna Frazer, on the telephone on April 20, eleven days after her husband had entered the hospital, Lady Bird said that he "was not progressing as [he] should." Writing to Mrs. Frazer the following day, L. E. Jones reported that: "Two or three times in the last day or two, the Chief has tried to do a little dictating. Every time it seemed to have a bad effect. So now the doctors won't let him write any letters. We all expected he would be out of the hospital by now. The delay no doubt has been caused by the excessive number of visitors." On that day, all Johnson's appointments were abruptly canceled —as were plans for the dinner. He remained in the hospital until April 24 or 25, and his doctors allowed him to leave then only after he and Lady Bird told them that he would be able to rest more quietly someplace out of the district, and that he would go not to Washington but to her father's home in Karnack, to spend at least another two or three weeks resting there. On April 27, the new Congressman went down to the depot of the Missouri-Kansas-Texas Railroad with his wife and parents, his face, still thin, very white above his dark blue suit. He had told reporters he was going to Washington, and the train did in fact go to Washington. But Johnson and Lady Bird were to get off when the train stopped in Marshall; her father would be waiting there to take them to his house, where they would rest until Johnson was better.

On the long platform, there took place a scene somewhat poignant to those who knew something of Lyndon Johnson's relationship with his parents. He walked ahead of his father, alongside his mother; his father was so ill (he would, in fact, be dead within the year) that he could not keep up, and fell behind. Lyndon climbed aboard the train before his father arrived at the door. Sam Johnson, however, started to climb up after him, and turned up his face. Lyndon bent down, and father and son kissed.

23

Galveston

EVER SINCE HIS BOYHOOD in Johnson City, Lyndon Johnson had displayed a remarkable talent for making a favorable impression on older men who possessed power—and for making it with startling rapidity. So keen-eyed a connoisseur of politicians as Ed Clark says, "I never saw anything like it. He could start talking to a man . . . and in five minutes he could get that man to think, 'I like you, young fellow. I'm going to help you.'"

At San Marcos, Lyndon Johnson's talent had worked with the president of the college. Now he was to try it on another president.

Within a few minutes after he had passed Stone in the balloting and knew he had won, he had telegraphed his friends among the wire service reporters in Washington, informing them not only of his victory, but of the manner in which he hoped they would identify the victor—for what had helped him in the Hill Country could help him in Washington, too. He got the identification he wanted. The Associated Press story flashed across the United States that Saturday night—by Ed Jamieson (who sent a copy to Johnson with the inscription: "Hope it suits your Honorable Highness")—began, "Youthful Lyndon B. Johnson, who shouted his advocacy of President Roosevelt's court reorganization all over the tenth Texas district, was elected today. . . . [He] said he considered the result a vote of confidence in Mr. Roosevelt and his program." With news scanty on a Saturday night, the story made front pages of newspapers all across the country—including newspapers in Washington. TEXAS SUPPORTER OF COURT CHANGE APPEARS ELECTED, a *Washington Post* headline read. Encouraging news was in rather short supply at the White House just then, with Roosevelt's court plan reeling under blows from both House and Senate; two days after Johnson's election, the Supreme Court would, by upholding the New Deal's Wagner Act, deliver its own body blow. To reinforce the identification, Johnson asked local supporters to telegraph it to the White House; said one telegram addressed to Franklin D. Roosevelt: "Election of Johnson to Congress . . .

was a high testimonial of your great leadership. . . . Your reorganization of the Supreme Court was made the main issue. . . ." This strategy produced the desired effect, and at a timely moment, for the President, who was shortly to leave for a fishing vacation in the Gulf of Mexico, had just announced that he would disembark in the Texas port of Galveston at the conclusion of his cruise, and would begin his return train trip to Washington by traveling the length of the state. On April 20, someone in the White House placed a memorandum in the President's "Trip File": "When we get down to Texas, we have to arrange to have the Congressman-elect, who ran on a pro–New Deal, pro–Court Reform platform, to see the President."

Before leaving Austin for Karnack, Johnson had asked Governor Allred to do all he could to make sure that the meeting would actually take place, to make sure that it would be photographed—and to ask the President to use his influence to secure him a place, coveted by all Congressmen from farming districts, on the House Agriculture Committee. During the eleven days in which the presidential yacht *Potomac*, escorted by Navy destroyers, cruised off the Texas coast, where the big silver tarpon were running, it touched in at Port Aransas for an hour, and Allred went aboard to arrange details of the Galveston reception. After meeting with Roosevelt, he wrote to Johnson, who was recuperating at Karnack, that the President "will be very happy indeed to see you when he lands at Galveston. . . . He was intensely interested in the details of your campaign, and himself brought up the committee matter which you and I discussed. I suggested to him that you all should have your picture made together next week, and this was entirely agreeable." (The Governor, fond of Johnson, had been disturbed by his haggard condition when he visited him after the campaign; he suggested now that "it might be well for you to come on down" two days early, "and spend Saturday and Sunday there resting.") And when, on May 11, the *Potomac* and its escorting destroyers, their crews lining the rails in dress whites, stood into Galveston Bay and a gangplank was run down from her deck to the pier, Johnson, still very thin, but with a white oleander (Galveston's symbol) cheerful in his lapel, was standing at its foot, along with the Governor and a beribboned Major General from nearby Fort Crockett, in a three-man group at the head of the assembled dignitaries.

They waited almost an hour. Then there was a stir on deck, and sideboys began their shrill piping, and suddenly at the top of the gangplank, just a few feet away, was the massive head, the heavy, confidently tilted jaw, the broad smile that Lyndon Johnson had seen only in newsreels or newspaper photographs or, during a speech, from a distant gallery—the face, bronzed by the Gulf sun, of the man whose banner he had carried for forty days. The gangplank was narrow enough so the President could rest his weight on both handrails at once, and he swung himself down it. When his foot hit the dock, cannon roared in salute from Fort Crockett across the bay, a drum major's baton flashed in the downbeat to "Hail to the Chief,"

Governor Allred said, "Mr. President, I'd like to present our new Congressman," and Franklin Roosevelt shook Lyndon Johnson's hand.

THE PHOTOGRAPH SESSION was all Johnson could have desired: the President stood patiently as the cameras clicked, smiling broadly as his big bronzed right hand clutched Johnson's (Roosevelt's body concealed his left hand, which was clutching the gangplank railing for support; the next day, a typical newspaper report said, "The President . . . chuckled happily as he went unassisted down the gangplank"). Johnson had not been assigned to ride with Allred and Galveston Mayor Adrian F. Levy in the President's open touring car; he rode in one of the trailing cars assigned to lesser dignitaries as the presidential motorcade, thunderous cheers rolling behind it, wound through streets packed with the largest crowds in Galveston's history to a specially constructed ramp, up which the President's car was driven so that he could speak while sitting in it. (Introducing him, the Mayor said, "As we were driving along, I told our President that it must be a wonderful thing for a man to know that he is so universally loved. . . . Just as the time of Pericles was called the Golden Age of Athens, so President Roosevelt's time will be called the Golden Age of Democracy.") Johnson was, however, on the open rear platform of the President's special train as, at ten a.m., it pulled out of the Galveston station with Roosevelt standing on the platform smiling and waving—with his other hand clutching the rail. (There were, in fact, two hands on that rail; the other one was Johnson's. Separated from the President by Allred, he reduced the distance between himself and Roosevelt—and thereby kept himself from being cropped out of newspaper photographs—by a subtle little maneuver. The President, beyond Allred, was on his right. Johnson had been holding his white Stetson in his right hand, the hand closest to the President; as photographers began shooting, he shifted the Stetson to his left hand, placed his right hand on the rail, and slid it a few inches toward the President, so that he could shift his body slightly in front of Allred without blatantly leaning into the picture.) And he, together with Allred, had been invited to ride in the President's private railroad car; when the President left the platform and went inside, the three men, together with White House aides Marvin McIntyre and Edwin M. ("Pa") Watson, chatted throughout the three-hour trip to College Station, where the President was to review 3,000 khaki-clad ROTC cadets from Texas Agricultural and Mining College.

Only one specific detail of that conversation is known: after his election, Johnson had visited General Burleson to thank him for his support; the old man had given Johnson part of a brown paper bag on which, after Johnson's first visit, he had jotted down a predicted order of the finish in the congressional race, with Johnson's name in first place. President Roosevelt, of course, had been Assistant Secretary of the Navy in the Wilson administration during the years in which Burleson had been Postmaster General in that same administration; if Roosevelt did not know Burleson, he knew who he was, and Johnson showed him the wrinkled piece of brown paper. The conversation's other particulars are not known (although back in Washington, the President would talk about the young man who had defied every entrenched political leader in his district to run—alone among eight candidates—in support of the court-reform bill, and who was, incidentally, interested in the Navy, as he had himself been as a young man). But the results of the conversation are known. Although Johnson had expected to leave the train at College Station, Roosevelt invited him to stay aboard all the way to Fort Worth, more than 200 miles away. When the train pulled into that North Texas city at nine p.m., the newly elected Congressman had spent an entire day with the President. Before they parted company, the President said that the Agriculture Committee seat was Johnson's if he wanted it, but that he would suggest the Naval Affairs Committee instead; he liked to see a young man like Johnson taking an interest in that field; powerful as Naval Affairs was now, he said, world trends might well make it more powerful still. When Johnson accepted his suggestion, Roosevelt was delighted and said he would personally see to the matter as soon as he got back to Washington. And he told Johnson that if he needed help in any other matters, he should call "Tommy"—and, scribbling "Tommy's" telephone number on a piece of paper, he handed it to Johnson.

"Tommy" was, of course, "Tommy the Cork," Thomas G. Corcoran, thirty-six, the stocky, ebullient, accordion-playing political manipulator who was at that moment, as one of the President's key strategists in the Supreme Court fight, at the very peak of his power and influence.

Roosevelt, traveling by special train, reached Washington before Johnson. He telephoned Tommy himself. As Corcoran recalls the President's words: "He said, 'I've just met the most remarkable young man. Now I like this boy, and you're going to help him with anything you can.' "

And he helped him himself. On one of Johnson's first days on the floor of Congress—the floor on which, as a congressional secretary, he had never been permitted to step—Representative Fred M. Vinson of Kentucky, a Democratic power on the Ways and Means Committee, whose Democratic members determined committee assignments, approached him and said, "Young man, I'm indebted to you for a good dinner and an excellent conversation." He explained that he had been invited to the White House for dinner, and, while "the President was, as always, a most delightful host, I kept wondering just what it was he wanted from me. I knew it was something. Finally he said casually—oh, very casually—'Fred, there's a fine young man just come to the House. Fred, you know that fellow Lyndon Johnson? I think he would be a great help on Naval Affairs.' "

The President also helped Johnson along avenues less formal than a congressional committee assignment (which, of course, Johnson received) but, to a young politician, more important. He talked about him to men much more powerful than Tommy the Cork, or even Fred Vinson—to Harold L. Ickes of PWA and Harry L. Hopkins of WPA; talked about this "remarkable young man," ordered them to meet him, and to help him. A young man from the Southwest would need connections in New York, the President said to Hopkins, who had excellent New York connections, including not only those who sprang from the same social work background he did, but Edwin Weisl, a New York political financier.

Corcoran, even before he met the young man, had been impressed by the speed with which he had won the President's favor. "That was all it took—one train ride," he says. The achievement earned Johnson Corcoran's highest accolade: whoever the young man was, he said, he must be "an operator." Now, meeting him, and watching him operate on Ickes and Hopkins, he was even more impressed. Lyndon Johnson's college classmates had thought that his talent with older men was nothing more than flattery, "kowtowing, suck-assing, brown-nosing" so blatant that "words won't come to describe it," but Corcoran, a King of Flatterers himself, knew it was much more. He knew a master of the art when he saw one. "He [Johnson] was smiling and deferential, but, hell, lots of guys can be smiling and deferential," he says. "Lyndon had one of the most incredible capacities for dealing with older men. I never saw anything like it. He could follow someone's mind around, and get where it was going before the other fellow knew where it was going. I saw him talk to an older man, and the minute he changed subjects, Lyndon was there ahead of him, and saying what he wanted to hear—before he knew what he wanted to hear."

Fanning out from Ickes and Hopkins and Corcoran, branching down from the White House, was a network of New Deal insiders, men of immense power and influence. Soon, all along the hidden pathways of Washington power, a new name was flashing, sent out so rapidly that sometimes it was garbled in transmission—but sent out from the highest sources. Eliot Janeway, a young political economist from New York who had already become part of this network, was lunching with Ickes in Washington one day when he heard it for the first time. "Ickes told me Roosevelt had said he was frustrated about that boy, that if he hadn't gone to Harvard, that's the kind of uninhibited young pro he'd like to be—that in the next generation the balance of power would shift south and west, and this boy could well be the first Southern President." Ickes said he had met him, and Janeway should, too. "You'll like him." After lunch, Janeway says, "I took the Congressional back to New York." And no sooner had he arrived home than the telephone rang. Ed Weisl was calling to say, "I just had a funny kind of a call from Harry [Hopkins]. Did you ever hear of some kid in Congress named Lydie Johnson?"

· · ·

BELOW HOPKINS AND ICKES, field marshals of the New Deal, below Ben Cohen, one of its principal theoreticians, and Tommy Corcoran, for a time not only its principal recruiting officer but one of its principal strategists, were the lieutenants of the New Deal—the able young liberals, fired with a fervent idealism, who had poured into Washington from all over the United States to enlist in the great crusade. These men, not Cabinet-level Secretaries or even Undersecretaries but their subordinates, possessed no independent power of their own—no official title of significance, no White House access, no discretion over the distribution of funds—but they could be important to a Congressman. "What is a government?" Corcoran once asked. "It's not just the top man or the top ten men. A government is the top one hundred or two hundred men. What really makes the difference is what happens down the line before—and after—the big decisions are taken." Having met the field marshals and taken them into camp, Johnson repeated his triumph with the lieutenants.

He concentrated his efforts on a particular handful of them.

One link between these men was the issue of public power. They were all veterans of the fight for either the crucial Public Utilities Holding Company Act of 1935 (the Rayburn-Fletcher Act) or of the subsequent battles to administer the Act, or of the battles to build the huge dams which, by creating new hydroelectric power, would destroy the utilities' monopoly. A dam—the Marshall Ford Dam—was the first problem Johnson had to confront when he got to Congress, and it was during his efforts to solve this problem that he met and dealt with most of these young lieutenants.

Another link was intellect. The hundred or two hundred key young New Dealers included many brilliant men. Johnson's handful was among the most brilliant. Their leaders were the drafters of the keystone act, Corcoran and Cohen—or, to be more precise, Corcoran, for the kindly, gentle Cohen, who, a friend wrote, "looks and talks like a Dickens portrait of an absent-minded professor," was too shy and dreamy to be a leader; his genius was the genius of the lone and pure intellect. Corcoran's performance at Harvard Law had so impressed Felix Frankfurter that he gave him the best job then at his command: the secretaryship to Supreme Court Justice Oliver Wendell Holmes. But even so, men who knew them well had learned that Corcoran's mind was not the equal of his silent partner's; after one meeting at which Corcoran did almost all the talking, Sam Rayburn confided to a friend: "Cohen's the brains."

The handful included one of Corcoran's successors as Holmes' secretary, James H. Rowe, a tall, studious, bespectacled young attorney (in 1937, twenty-eight years old, the same age as Lyndon Johnson) whose path to Washington had led from Butte, Montana, through Harvard University and Harvard Law School. While serving as one of several low-level assistants who were helping Corcoran and Cohen in the drafting of the

Holding Company Act and in defense of the PWA against power company lawsuits, Rowe had caught Corcoran's eye, and Corcoran had placed him in a low-level White House job—secretary to the President's son James— where he would shortly catch the President's eye.

This handful of men included William O. Douglas, thirty-eight, a sandy-haired former Yale Law School professor who as an SEC Commissioner was a key figure in the administration of the Holding Company Act ("The Holding Company in the utilities field had become a monster," he was to write), and it included the first man Douglas had brought to Washington to assist him, a short, slight, silent young Jew from Memphis with olive skin, large, liquid eyes—and, another Yale professor says, "the most brilliant legal mind ever to come out of the Yale Law School": twenty-six-year-old Abe Fortas. It included Janeway, at twenty-four a Washington-based business writer for *Time, Life* and *Fortune* magazines, and twenty-seven-year-old Arthur E. Goldschmidt, known as "Tex" because he came from San Antonio, who had been brought to Washington after graduating from Columbia University, and who worked under Harry Hopkins. With the exception of Janeway, these men—Corcoran, Cohen, Douglas, Rowe, Fortas, Goldschmidt— often saw each other at work; for a time, in fact, three of them—Cohen, Fortas and Goldschmidt—occupied adjoining offices in the suite used by the Division of Public Power on the sixth floor of the Department of the Interior. And they saw each other after work—Corcoran and Cohen shared an apartment and the younger men—Rowe, Fortas and Goldschmidt—all lived within a block or two of each other in small, rented houses in the Georgetown section of Washington that had until recently been a Negro slum but was rapidly being taken over and refurbished by young white New Dealers. "We were a kind of a group," Goldschmidt says. "We were not organized. But we knew each other, and we saw a lot of each other."

And they began to see a lot of Lyndon Johnson.

He met them in the course of his work for the Marshall Ford Dam. He would telephone and ask them to lunch. He would invite them for Sunday afternoon cocktails at the small, one-bedroom apartment he and Lady Bird had rented in the Kennedy-Warren Apartment House on Connecticut Avenue.

And soon they were inviting him back. The little group would often get together for informal dinner parties or for back-yard cookouts, and Lyndon and Lady Bird became regulars at them.

He cultivated them. He was—in the beginning, at least—deferential, attentive to their opinions. He listened with what seemed like awe as Tommy Corcoran talked about how the lights had burned all night in the Treasury Department when, back in 1933, they had been trying to work out a plan to save the banks. He gave them small presents—a locket for a baby daughter, for example—small but appreciated; "At that time we were not so used to getting presents," Jim Rowe says. "Though you have warned me about pestering you with mash notes," Elizabeth Rowe wrote him, "I can't allow anything as lovely as your little locket to go unnoticed. Really, you do spoil our daughter. . . . I can't think of anything nicer to wish for my daughter than that you would be an honorary uncle. So . . . from now you shall be Uncle Lyndon." Small and large—the largest being Texas turkeys that, beginning in 1937, were hand-delivered by Johnson's secretaries every Christmas to all the members of this group; when she received her first turkey, Mrs. Rowe was astonished by its size; "I had never seen such a big turkey," she recalls. "I didn't have anything big enough to cook it in." Telephoning Johnson to thank him, she said, "You must have had a turkey crossed with a beef." When they were promoted, they received his enthusiastic congratulations. Johnson wrote Rowe when he was made one of President Roosevelt's six administrative assistants, "My dear Jimmie: If I owned a big truck such as the movers use and get in front of me with when I'm in a hurry to go places, I couldn't send you more congratulations on your elevation today than you will find borne by this note. I rejoice with you. And I rejoice with our President that he has such an able pair of shoulders as yours and such a fine mind as you to relieve him of some of the crushing load. . . ."

He helped them. On the day, May 13, on which he had arrived in Washington as a newly elected Congressman, the first office he had visited had been that of the newly elected Majority Leader, and in that office he stooped down and kissed a bald head, and the grim face beneath it had broken into a smile. Sam Rayburn was very glad to see Lyndon Johnson back in Washington. When Johnson asked him to stand beside him at his swearing-in in the well of the House, as his sponsor, he was very touched. The furniture in the Johnsons' apartment was a little worn from use by previous occupants, but, starting on the very next Sunday, their apartment was frequently adorned with the short, broad figure that was, in the catalog of Washington power, a more prized ornament than ever. And Rayburn returned the hospitality in a very significant manner. One of his first acts after his election as Leader had been to reinstitute Jack Garner's "Board of Education," and each day after the House had adjourned, a handful of Congressmen met in a room on the ground floor of the Capitol to "strike a blow for liberty" with a late-afternoon drink. The men invited to this hideaway—which was furnished only with dark leather easy chairs, a long, dark leather sofa, a fireplace, a desk at which Rayburn presided, and a picture of Robert E. Lee—were almost all leaders of the House; the single exception was Wright Patman, who possessed a qualification that was, in Rayburn's eyes, more important than seniority: he had been one of the little band of Populists in the Texas Legislature who never sold out. One day, Rayburn invited Johnson down for a drink after the session. Thereafter, leaving the floor at the end of the day, the Leader would frequently growl to Johnson: "Come on down." Behind the hideaway's tall, narrow door, the twenty-eight-year-old freshman was drinking with Speaker Bankhead, and Minority Whip McCormack, and Rules Committee Chairman Sabath, and as a result he knew quite a bit about the inner workings of the House. The young New Dealers from the White House end of Pennsylvania Avenue were in constant need of information about the Capitol Hill end, about the chances of passage of some bill vital to their agency, about the status of the bill: where, precisely, it was stalled—in committee or subcommittee or the bill-drafters' offices—and why, and who could get it unstalled. Their bosses were constantly asking them to find out some piece of information about Congress.

Obtaining such information was no trouble for Corcoran, who could get it through the White House liaison men (in some matters, *he* was the liaison man), or for SEC Commissioner Douglas. But the more junior Rowe and Fortas and Goldschmidt had to get the information themselves, and hard information—not rumor but fact—was difficult to obtain from the closed, confused world of Capitol Hill. But Johnson, thanks to his attendance in Rayburn's hideaway, often had the information. Moreover, they had seen with their own eyes that he knew Rayburn well; the Leader, with his immense power and fearsome mien, was an unapproachable figure to them. Loving the company of men young enough to be his sons, Rayburn had begun, after he had spent enough time with Corcoran and Cohen so that he could relax a little with them, to invite them occasionally—perhaps once every six weeks or two months—to his little apartment for a Sunday stag breakfast, which he would cook with a big apron tied around his chest. Even on such social occasions, however, the Leader's reserve never melted more than slightly; none of the young men ever felt close enough to him to ask the questions they needed to ask. But these young men saw—with the same amazement with which Lyndon Johnson's San Marcos classmates had watched him pat the feared Prexy Evans on the back—Lyndon Johnson lean over and kiss the Leader's bald pate. They knew that if Johnson didn't himself have the information they needed, he could get it from Rayburn. On minor matters, he might even, on their behalf, ask the Leader not just for information but for assistance. Furthermore, he was learning his way very quickly through the maze that most Congressmen never master. "He learned the levers in Congress very fast," Rowe says. And he was willing to place this knowledge at the service of this small group of men. "I would call and say, 'How do I handle this?'" Rowe says. "He would say, 'I'll call you right back.' And he would call back and say, 'This is the fellow you ought to talk to.'" Says Fortas: "He was close to Rayburn, and an ever-widening coterie of friends on the Hill, and he helped us. He ran errands for us on the Hill. He was very useful to us."

And he made them like him.

"At parties, he was *fun*," Elizabeth Rowe says. "That's what no one understands about Lyndon Johnson—that he was *fun*."

He was, in fact, the life of these parties. Quick wits flashed at them, and none flashed quicker than his. "When I think of the old Lyndon, I think of old-fashioned joshing, kidding around," Goldschmidt's wife Elizabeth Wickenden says. "The small talk was great," Jim Rowe says. "He always had a good Texas story that was in point." He knew three worlds—the world of Congress, about which they knew little, and two worlds about which they knew nothing: the world of Texas politics, and the world of the Texas Hill Country, the world from which he had come. He spoke to them about those worlds—with an eloquence they never forgot, his voice now soft and confiding, now booming—the voice of a natural storyteller. He was always ready with the latest inside stories about Congress, stories on which they hung because such information was important to them, but also because in the telling he mimicked accurately and hilariously the characters he was talking about; pacing back and forth, a tall, gangling figure in those small living rooms, he filled those rooms with drama.

"His greatest stories," Mrs. Rowe says, and the rest of the group agrees, "would be about Texas." He told them about political figures of whom they had hardly heard—Ma and Pa Ferguson, Big Jim Hogg, Jimmy Allred—but whom he painted in colors so vivid that they wanted to hear more. And when he talked about the Hill Country, "then," Mrs. Rowe says, "he could be very eloquent indeed." He talked about the days of the cattle drives, and about the poverty of the people. Bill Douglas, a great talker himself, frequently talked about soil conservation; even Douglas' stories paled before tales of the rampages of the Pedernales or the Lower Colorado. And when Johnson was talking of the poverty of the Hill Country—and about what New Deal programs meant there—then, even Tommy Corcoran, customarily the life of every party himself with his Irish chatter and his accordion, might stop talking for a while.

And it wasn't just his stories that made them like him. He was a great player of practical jokes. On the morning after a cookout at the Fortases' at which the Johnsons and George R. Brown of Brown & Root had been guests—and at which Brown had had a bit to drink—a bouquet of flowers from Brown arrived for Carole Fortas, with the note: "Sorry if I misbehaved." Since he hadn't, the Fortases were puzzled. When Fortas asked Johnson what Brown meant, Johnson said that the next morning he had told Brown, whose memory of the evening was hazy, that he had dropped a steak, liberally covered with Worcestershire sauce, on the Fortases' living-room rug.

He entertained. At a Spanish restaurant one evening, flamenco music was playing. Johnson, so tall, grabbed little Welly Hopkins, and the two of them jumped up on a table and began dancing together. "There was never a dull moment around him," Fortas says. "If Lyndon Johnson was there, a party would be livelier. The moment he walked in the door, it would take fire. Maybe in a different way than the party had been going when he came in, but it would take fire. . . . He was great fun, a great companion." Says Elizabeth Rowe: "He enjoyed living so much that he made everyone around him enjoy it more. He could take a group of people and just lift it up."

As they got to know him better, their fondness was, more and more, tinged with admiration. Politics was their profession, and they were, most of them, very good at it; this little group included men who were already, or would be, among the master politicians of the age. A master of a profession knows another when he sees him, and they knew they were seeing one now. Rowe, asking Johnson more and more frequently for information on Congress, came to realize that the information was invariably correct; following this freshman Congressman through the maze of Capitol Hill, one would make very few wrong turns. They all came to realize this. "He knew how things happened, and what made things happen," Fortas says. "He knew the nuts and bolts of politics. We were all more or less technicians, and he was the best technician, the very best." Counting Congress—estimating the votes on bills important to them—was a frequent pastime at the parties. "He was a greater counter," Rowe says. "Someone would say, we've got so many votes, and Johnson would say, 'Hell, you're three off. You're counting these three guys, and they're going to vote against you.' " "He was the very best at counting," Fortas says. "He would figure it out—how so-and-so would vote. Who were the swing votes. What, in each case—what, exactly—would swing them." Fortas pauses for a moment. Then he says: "I may not have adequately explained to you how good a politician he was. He was the very best."

They admired his thoroughness, his tirelessness—the way he threw himself into every aspect of politics, into everything he did, with an enthusiasm and effort that seemed limitless. He already possessed an amazing store of knowledge about individual Congressmen and their districts through his capacity for absorbing and retaining information. "He was a pack rat for information," Fortas says. "And he was very, very intelligent. He never forgot anything. He would work harder than anyone else. I have never known a man who had such a capacity for detail." Recommendations were the order of the day for these canniest of the young New Dealers; all of them were working to insert friends and allies into key positions in government agencies. Lyndon Johnson was doing this, too—"He was always pushing someone for some appointment or other," Rowe recalls—and a Johnson recommendation had special quality to it. Rowe recalls one of the first vacancies he was put in charge of filling after he became a White House administrative assistant: an Assistant Attorney Generalship. "One of the names on the list was Welly Hopkins." Rowe thought he might casually ask Johnson for information about him, "just because he was from Texas, too" —he had certainly no intention of giving Johnson, a freshman Congressman, any input into the appointment. But, Rowe recalls, "I called Lyndon up, and he said, 'Ah'll be up!' " Startled, Rowe asked, "What do you mean?"

"I'll be up in ten minutes!" replied Johnson. And ten minutes later, Johnson, having run out of his office in the Cannon Building, jumped into his car and roared up Pennsylvania Avenue, was in Rowe's office in the old State, Navy and War Department Building next to the White House, "pounding on my desk—in a nice way—and saying: 'The best man!'" ("Lyndon," Rowe pointed out, "you don't know who the other men are"—but Hopkins got the job.)

Rowe and Corcoran, disciples of Justice Holmes, called the tirelessness and enthusiasm that they admired "energy." "Holmes used to say that in the last analysis the only thing that mattered was energy," Corcoran says, "and Lyndon just bristled with it." Fortas, more precise, says, "It was a matter of intensity more than anything, an intense concentration on whatever was being talked about, or on whatever was the problem in hand." But however they defined it, they admired it—admired it to such an extent that while they might feel that they themselves were, in Fortas' word, "technicians," some of them were beginning to feel that Johnson might be something more. Fortas customarily cloaked himself in reserve and an air of gravity that he may have considered necessary for a man who was very young indeed for the posts he held, and who looked even younger. Or his reserve may have been natural: "I was born old," he once told Goldschmidt, almost ruefully. Sometimes, he seemed to be measuring every word he spoke —he had already adopted the mannerism of stroking his chin slowly before answering a question—and he seemed determined never to let himself reveal enthusiasm; Eliot Janeway was astonished, therefore, when Fortas expressed his feeling about Johnson to him and added, "The guy's just got extra glands." Listening to Jim Rowe speak about Johnson, one can hear beneath the words the struggle of a strong personality to avoid becoming submerged in a personality stronger still. "Listen, I mean, I worked for Roosevelt and Holmes. They were the two perfect people. Johnson was never going to [become one of my idols]—he and I were of an age—but he didn't bore me for one minute. He never bored anyone. He was a magnetic man physically, and you never knew what was going to happen next. He was a remarkable man."

In this little group of remarkable young men, he was becoming not merely one of the group, but its center. Soon the small Johnson apartment was the scene of more and more parties: in honor of Maury Maverick (Harold Ickes, who had decided to attend Johnson's party instead of "a big garden party at the British embassy," was glad he did; "practically everyone was in his shirt sleeves. I am sure that I enjoyed it more than I would have the formal doings . . ."); for Ickes himself, on his birthday— Johnson asked Fortas, then PWA general counsel, to make a little speech in Ickes' honor. ("That shows how smart he was," Welly Hopkins says. By giving the party, but allowing "Abe to make a birthday speech for his boss," he "kept his foot in the door—with both of them.") The parties didn't have to be formal occasions. "He was a great one for spur-of-the-moment parties," Elizabeth Rowe recalls. "He'd call up and say, 'I'm about to leave the office. Get old Jim and come on out.'" When the Rowes arrived at the Johnson apartment, they might find two or three other couples also invited by a last-minute telephone call.

More and more, wherever the parties were held, he dominated them.

His size was one factor in this dominance. He was, of course, over six feet three inches tall, and his arms were very long, and his hands very big, and the sweeping, vigorous gestures he made with those long arms seemed to fill those little rooms. His awkwardness was a factor—the clumsy, lunging strides as he paced back and forth telling his "Texas stories," the ungainly flailing of his arms to make a point—as was his restlessness, which kept him always in motion: sitting down, jumping up, walking, talking, never still. The drama of his appearance, which went beyond size and awkwardness, was a factor, too: the vivid contrast of the coal-black hair and heavy black eyebrows against that milky white skin; the outsized nose and huge ears; the flashing smile; the flashing eyes.

But the dominance went beyond the physical. Although he was only twenty-eight, he had been giving orders for a long time now—to L. E. Jones and Gene Latimer and the rest of the staff in Kleberg's office; to scores of NYA officials. He was accustomed to being listened to, and the air with which he carried himself was in part the air of command.

And it was also the air of belief. He was more than a natural story-teller. The subjects on which he dwelt—the subjects his anecdotes all illustrated—were the poverty of his constituents, and the need to do something about that poverty. And in describing Lyndon Johnson, the words the members of this little group use are "vibrancy," "vitality," "urgency," "intensity," "energy"—and *"passion."* "His belief in what he was fighting for just poured out of him," says Elizabeth Rowe, "and it was very impressive." As he strode back and forth in those little living rooms, he was, in their words, "eloquent," "spellbinding"—and, often, they were spellbound.

Not always, of course. And when they weren't, his behavior was also striking. Even as a boy, of course, he could not endure being only one of a group—in a companion's phrase, "could not stand, just could not *stand* not being the leader," not only of boys his own age but of older boys. "If he couldn't lead, he didn't care much about playing." The need to dominate was as evident in Georgetown living rooms as in the vacant lots of Johnson City, as evident with Abe Fortas and Jim Rowe and even Tommy the Cork as it had been with Bob Edwards and the Crider brothers. Most of the group—Fortas and Rowe and Goldschmidt, and their wives—gave him their full attention during his monologues, but sometimes they wouldn't. And sometimes there were other guests—guests not under his spell. In Washington, the amount of attention a man could command was often in proportion to the amount of power he commanded, and a junior Congressman commanded none at all. As Rowe puts it, "He was somewhat of a young Congressman, and he was interesting, but eventually people would drift off and start having their own conversation," or would interrupt him and hold the floor themselves. And if he was not the center of the stage, Lyndon Johnson refused to be part of the cast at all. He would, quite literally, go to sleep. In a group of people in a living room, he would be talking, someone else would begin talking, and Johnson would put his chin down on his chest, his eyes would close—and he would be asleep. He might stay that way for quite some time—twenty minutes or half an hour, say; he probably wouldn't wake up until Lady Bird nudged him. And when he woke up, as Rowe puts it, "he woke up talking." And if he was not then afforded the attention of the group around him, he would go back to sleep again. Elizabeth Rowe describes the sequence this way: "He'd put on a performance, and then pull the curtain down, and then pull it up again."

The members of the little group forgave him this behavior. Fortas excuses it as a result of what he feels was understandable fatigue: "a man who lives at this intensity . . ." Elizabeth Rowe doesn't attempt to explain it; she just forgives it. Asked whether she, as a hostess, didn't resent one of her guests going to sleep in her living room, she replies, "Anything he did was all right with me. . . . Because he was such a good friend." And because, she adds, when he was awake, he was "such a marvelous, scintillating guest." Says Welly Hopkins' wife Alice: "He demanded attention. He demanded it—and he got it." He was demanding it now, and getting it, from men who gave it to few men—generally, only to their superiors and to other older men with power, not to men their own age without power (and Lyndon Johnson, their own age, had no power at all). Summing up Lyndon Johnson's relationship with Fortas, Rowe, Douglas, Goldschmidt, Corcoran and Cohen, Rowe says, in words echoed by most of the group: "Roosevelt and Rayburn liking him—that gave him the in. And the personal force did the rest. That had to be it, because there was nothing else. He didn't have power, or money or anything. He just had this personal force—a huge, unique personal force."

AND HE USED THESE MEN.

Hawthorne said of Andrew Jackson that "his native strength . . . compelled every man to be his tool that came within his reach; and the more cunning the individual might be, it served only to make him the sharper tool." These were very cunning men, and Lyndon Johnson made very sharp tools of them.

They didn't realize this, of course. In fact, they vehemently deny it. They felt that they were using Lyndon Johnson at least as much as he was using them, and this feeling was important to them; they were clever men, and proud of their cleverness, practical men and proud of their pragmatism;

it was important to them that the upper hand in any relationship be theirs; the thought that someone might be taking advantage of *them*, getting more from them than they from him, would have been difficult for them to swallow (the thought was, in fact, difficult for them to swallow forty years later; the author learned quickly that one way to bring a frown to their faces was to so much as hint that Lyndon Johnson might have been using them more than they were using him).

But he was using them. An element of mutuality did exist, of course; Johnson was, in Fortas' words, "running errands" for them on the Hill, giving them information on what Congress was doing, and tips on how to get something done by Congress. But the mutuality was very heavily weighted in Johnson's favor. He was performing essentially minor chores for them. But what he got from them in exchange was not minor: it was, in fact, the largest thing in his political life during his first years in Congress. What he got from them was the Marshall Ford Dam.

To get the dam completed, he not only used every one of these razor-sharp weapons; he used them with consummate judgment, putting each to the specific use for which it was best suited.

HE DIDN'T NEED THEIR HELP on Capitol Hill, not with Rayburn, the grim power of his personality reinforced now with the power of the Majority Leadership, on his side, and with Roy Miller still wheeling Joseph Jefferson Mansfield through the Capitol corridors.

Time to obtain congressional authorization for the dam was very short. Mansfield's Rivers and Harbors Committee was scheduled to issue its report on the project on May 24, just eleven days after Johnson's arrival in Washington. But in those eleven days, Johnson obtained what was needed: not merely authorization but the type of authorization Alvin Wirtz had devised. Noting that the Marshall Ford Dam "has never been specifically authorized by Congress and its legality has been brought into question," the report said that therefore Section 3 of the House Rivers and Harbors Bill would read, "The project known as 'Marshall Ford Dam,' Colorado River project, in Texas, is hereby authorized . . . and all contracts and agreements which have been executed in connection therewith are hereby validated and ratified. . . ."

Validated and ratified—the contracts under which Brown & Root had been working may have been unauthorized; with passage of the bill they would be authorized.

But Johnson needed the help of the young New Dealers at the other end of Pennsylvania Avenue—and he needed it badly.

While the first step toward congressional authorization had been taken, many other steps—approval of the committee report by the full House; approval of a Rivers and Harbors Bill by the Senate; reconciliation of the two bills by a conference committee—remained before authorization was a fact. And Herman Brown, half a million dollars in debt and with his cash running out, couldn't wait for them. He needed fresh infusions of cash. Such cash was available under the original appropriation made the previous year—but the Comptroller General's office and the Bureau of the Budget were delaying approval of new allocations under that appropriation until these steps had been taken. Even more important, while the ex post facto validation and ratification contained in the House bill made Brown & Root's contracts legal as far as congressional authorization was concerned, it did not solve, but only blurred, the question of the possible deeper illegality posed by the fact that the dam was being built on land not owned by the federal government. Puzzling rumors about the dam were beginning to circulate among bureaucrats, and had reached the ears of one or two Republican congressmen. An investigation would focus attention on the land ownership question, and would make it difficult for the Comptroller General's office and the Budget Bureau to justify new allocations. The delays had to be ended, and the growing bureaucratic curiosity about the dam dampened—and this could be done only by help from the top.

In obtaining this help, Johnson employed his bluntest weapon. This was Corcoran, the broad-shouldered, bouncy, brash Irishman who in 1937 stood, Joseph Alsop and Turner Catledge wrote, "closer to the throne than any" of the young New Dealers, and who was already a Washington legend for his enthusiasm in using that closeness to bludgeon officials into compliance with his wishes. If a fond President had nicknamed him "Tommy the Cork," the rest of the capital called him "White House Tommy" because of his predilection for beginning his telephone conversations: "This is Tommy Corcoran, calling from the White House." And when he called, Alva Johnston wrote, "Cabinet officers, senators, commissioners stand at attention. . . . Smart people who want to get action at headquarters ignore the regular secretariat, overlook the Cabinet and cultivate the acquaintance of White House Tommy. He can get things done."

Despite the favorable impression he had made on Roosevelt, Johnson found that it would not secure a freshman Congressman entrée to the White House. So Johnson used Corcoran's entrée, asking him to raise the subject of the Marshall Ford Dam with the President. Corcoran found the right moment to do so, and Roosevelt's response was all Johnson could have wished. Corcoran recalls that "Roosevelt said, 'Give the kid the dam.' "

With Johnson urging him on, Corcoran made the most out of the President's words, and out of the President's name. Roosevelt probably was never made aware of the legal problems involved—Corcoran himself may not have been aware of all of them—but, whatever the problems, the President's order, as implemented by Corcoran, was enough to settle them. The precise nature of Corcoran's dealings with the previously recalcitrant

Comptroller General's office and the Bureau of the Budget are not known—Corcoran will not discuss them except to say, "I made a hell of a lot of calls on that dam"—but the refusals by these two offices to authorize additional allocations out of the first appropriation abruptly ended, and the previously growing curiosity about the dam abruptly vanished. The President's casual word, hammered home by Corcoran, painted approval on the Marshall Ford Dam with a brush so broad that minor points were buried—forever—beneath the paint.

Even with the authorization finally in hand, the second appropriation—the second $5,000,000 (of which Herman Brown would get to keep $2,000,-000)—proved difficult to obtain. The money was supposed to come out of work relief funds, the $1,500,000,000 Emergency Work Relief Bill that even then was wending its way through Congress. But Work Relief Administrator Harry Hopkins pointed out that since the Marshall Ford Dam was being built not by a government agency but by a private contractor; since the cost of materials far exceeded that allowed for "non-labor" items; and since the labor involved was highly paid skilled labor, the appropriation would violate at least three fundamental work relief provisions.

These objections were registered in July—less than two months before the initial appropriation would be used up, with Herman Brown still half a million dollars in debt. A letter from Brown's banker, Thomas H. Davis of the Austin National Bank, told Johnson that Brown was already beginning to close down. "Activity on the Marshall Ford Dam . . . is practically at a standstill." On July 20, Brown and Wirtz—accompanied, for window dressing, by the rest of the LCRA board—flew to Washington. Tom Connally was attempting to circumvent Hopkins' objections by placing an amendment in the Senate version of the Work Relief Bill, but objections arose in the conference committee over a provision so obviously contradictory to the bill's intent; Connally, despite the power he was beginning to accumulate in the Senate, could find no way around the problem. But White House Tommy could—with an assist from Bill Douglas. Johnson asked Corcoran and Douglas to intercede. The precise nature of their maneuvers are not known, but Jimmy Roosevelt (James H. Rowe, Jr., secretary) began making telephone calls, and Connally was asked to withdraw his amendment—because it was no longer needed. Hopkins quietly withdrew his objections, and on July 22, Johnson, Wirtz and the LCRA directors were invited to the White House. There the President's son handed them the papers approving the additional $5,000,000 appropriation, making a point of telling them that the President was "happy to do this for your Congressman." In case they didn't grasp the point, it was reiterated by Hopkins, when the group was ushered over to his office. "We are doing this," he said, "for Congressman Johnson."

The dam—the dam that represented so much to Alvin Wirtz and Her-

man Brown—was secured. Alvin Wirtz's investment in Lyndon Johnson had
paid off.

TOMMY CORCORAN was Johnson's bluntest weapon. Abe Fortas, too young
to have entrée but gifted with that lawyer's mind at which other lawyers
marveled, was the sharpest. And this weapon, too, was to be called into use.

Herman Brown had his dam now—so he wanted the dam to be bigger.

On November 30, 1937, just four months after Johnson had rescued
him from financial disaster by obtaining the vital congressional authorization for a $10,000,000 Marshall Ford Dam, Brown's construction super-
intendent, Ross White, speaking at an Austin Rotary Club luncheon in the
Driskill Hotel, urged that the dam be made higher, at the cost of an additional $17 million. The next speaker, Howard P. Bunger, who was super-
vising construction for the Bureau of Reclamation, said that the dam *must*
be made higher, for its present height would be "inadequate to control
large floods," and he urged "all interested persons to contact the Congressman representing this district and urge . . . construction of the high
dam." When the *next* speaker moved that the club's board of directors
prepare a resolution endorsing the dam, it was obvious that Brown, who was
sitting quietly in the audience, had orchestrated the meeting. Ray Lee wrote
Johnson that evening: "It seems definitely that a carefully staged coup was
pulled to get the thing into the public demand stage."

Johnson's first reaction, and Wirtz's, was fury, both political (the
statement that the dam was "inadequate" to provide flood control was
embarrassingly accurate; Wirtz, of course, had never intended it to provide
flood control; despite his statement to the contrary, he had always intended
its primary purpose to be the production of hydroelectric power which
could be translated into political power) and personal (the two men felt
that Brown had taken advantage of them to obtain a bigger profit). Wirtz's
anger was also fueled by fear; the first interest payments on the LCRA's outstanding bonds were due on January 1, 1939, and the only way to meet the
payments was by the sale of power from the LCRA dams; power could not
be sold until the dams were completed, and Brown's proposal would mean
that the Marshall Ford Dam, at least, would not be finished in time. Under
the terms of the bond indentures, the bondholders could foreclose and take
over the project if an interest payment was not met, and the holder of the
bonds was the Reconstruction Finance Corporation, whose director, Jesse
Jones of Houston, was a longtime enemy of Wirtz who would be only too
pleased to snatch his project away from him. Wirtz urged Johnson to see
federal officials immediately to make sure that the dam would not be enlarged. (Even before the Rotary meeting, the alliance between the Browns
and the two politicians had grown shaky. Wirtz's plan to use the 2,000 con-

struction jobs at Marshall Ford as the payroll of a Wirtz-Johnson political organization had been defeated by Brown's refusal to cooperate; Bunger had received quiet instructions from his superiors at the Bureau of Reclamation not to hire anyone unless they bore a "paper from [Wirtz and Johnson] saying they were approved," but Brown refused to accept this; "he moved 'em off," Bunger would recall. "Herman could be rough. On a Herman Brown job, you earned your money.")

But a dispute with Herman Brown would not be in Johnson's interest; his ambition dictated the avoidance of a dispute, and, as always, his passions were at ambition's command. By the time—a week after the Rotary luncheon—that he wrote his first letter on the subject of the high dam (a reply to T. H. Davis of the Austin National Bank, who had written him to "wonder . . . why the present Dam, now well under way, if it be so inadequate, was ever contracted for"), his anger was banked, the letter diplomatic. Had he already realized that the support of Herman Brown was necessary for the attainment of his great goal?

Seemingly insurmountable problems stood in the way of a high dam, however. The additional $17 million could not come from the LCRA; for not only had the Authority used up all its authorized borrowing power, even if it was authorized to borrow more, it would not be able to pay the interest on new bonds; every cent of possible revenue that could be generated from the sale of power was already pledged to pay the interest on the existing bonds. And how could the money come from the Bureau of Reclamation? The Bureau could build, out of its own funds, only the flood-control part of the dam; any money spent on a dam, or that part of a dam, designed to provide power, had to be reimbursable. And how could the Bureau maintain that the high dam was *not* for the purpose of providing power? It had said the low dam was for flood control—and the low dam was funded. Any additional funds would have to be for power, would have to be reimbursed —and there was no possible source of reimbursement.

The wily Wirtz was working on a solution. Under it, the existing 190-foot-high dam would no longer be a flood-control dam; it would, with a stroke of a pen, be designated a power dam. The flood-control portion of the dam would be the part not yet built—the additional 78 feet—and therefore the Bureau of Reclamation could legally pay for it. But Wirtz's solution, while ingenious, did not provide a rationale for changing the nature of the 190 feet already built, and it left unsolved another major problem—a result of the fact that the dam was in reality meant primarily for power production. This reality could not be blinked because there was a recognized, accepted, standard formula for determining what portion of a dam was to be allocated to flood control and what portion to power production. By the most generous estimate possible under this formula, no more than $14,850,000 of the cost of the Marshall Ford Dam could be allocated to flood control; the rest had to be chargeable to power production. But it could not be charged to power production, because the power-production portion was reimbursable, and the LCRA had no further capacity for reimbursement beyond the $9,515,000 it had already agreed to pay. And the two figures—$14,850,000 plus $9,515,000—totaled $24,365,000. The dam would cost at least $27 million, so there was at least a $2,635,000 gap that could not be filled by either of the two agencies connected with its construction. Standing in the path of Herman Brown's ambition was an intricate legal tangle. Brown could see no way to cut through that knot. Nor could Wirtz or Corcoran. So, Corcoran says, "it [the problem] was turned over to Abe Fortas."

Johnson telephoned the Browns to report on the situation. As George Brown recalls it, "On his [Fortas'] desk was where the Reclamation thing [had] landed. . . . He was the key to the whole thing. . . . If he said it [Wirtz's scheme] was illegal, it was dead." Aware of the weaknesses of his case, Brown felt it would be "touch and go," but Johnson told him that if any lawyer in the world could solve the problem, Fortas could.

And, in fact, Fortas did. He worked out an elaborate rationale for Wirtz's plan, and he bridged the $2,635,000 gap. Since that money could not be provided by either of the two agencies building the dam, Fortas proposed that it be provided by a third agency: the Public Works Administration. At first glance, legal barriers stood in the way of this solution, too. The PWA was not authorized to build flood-control structures. And it was not authorized to build dams for the production of power, either. But Fortas reasoned—in an elaborately structured memo to PWA Administrator Ickes—that it could build a portion of the dam whose purpose might be defined as neither flood control nor power, because its purpose would be *both* flood control *and* power. This dual purpose would be accomplished by designating 33 feet of the dam—the first 33 feet to go atop the original 190 feet—as a "joint-use pool." The water entrapped by these 33 feet would be available for power use until the floodgates were opened. But since the floodgates would not customarily be open, that water could be used most of the time for power. The 33 feet of dam—the 33 feet whose cost just happened to be about $2.5 million—would, therefore, be built for power production—but the LCRA would not have to pay for its construction. As LCRA board member Tom Ferguson explains: "The Bureau of Reclamation said it would pay for the top forty-five feet [of the 268-foot dam]. But it couldn't pay for any more, and the LCRA didn't have enough money to get up to that top forty-five feet. So the PWA would build the part in between, and the Bureau of Reclamation would build it from where the PWA's money ran out."

Ickes bought it. He had already discovered Fortas' legal abilities—Fortas would be only twenty-eight years old when Ickes appointed him general counsel, chief legal officer, of the PWA—and while Ickes was not yet prepared (he would be soon) to grant intimacy to a man younger than his own sons, he had already learned to put his faith in that man's mind. Fortas told Ickes that the solution was legal. "I don't think it was a matter of persuading [Ickes]," Fortas says. "It was a matter of working out the legal theory."

The Browns understood the significance of what Fortas had done for them. "If it hadn't been for Abe . . . ," George Brown says. "He was the first hitch we had to get by. If he didn't say it was legal, it wasn't. [But] Abe wrote the memo to Ickes and he put it in the right light."

And George Brown, who had seen Johnson and Fortas together, felt he understood why Fortas had done it. He touches on a number of reasons. "He [Fortas] came to Washington wanting to help people," he says. And, he says, there was also a friendship ("Friendship plays so big a role in these things. . . . We used to go to his house and take off our shoes and socks and drink some"). But it was not Fortas' friendship for him that played the crucial role, he says, but Fortas' friendship for Lyndon Johnson. "He liked Johnson," Brown says. "Johnson *made* him like him."

Goldschmidt was not the sharpest tool; he would not rise to great heights in Washington. But, easy-going and not as intensely fired by personal ambition as the other members of this group, he was malleable material in Johnson's hands. He was, in addition, passionately idealistic, and the focus of his passion was public power. When Johnson put the case for the Marshall Ford Dam in those terms, Goldschmidt believed him—and was willing to do anything he could to advance the cause of the dam.

Johnson knew how to make the most of such willingness. He had been assiduously cultivating Clark Foreman, director of Interior's Division of Public Power—the agency whose approval on a thousand pieces of paper was necessary for so large and complicated a project. Painting for Foreman a harrowing picture of how the LCRA's programs were being snarled in bureaucratic red tape, he asked Foreman to assign a single official to handle and be familiar with LCRA problems. And Johnson said he knew just the man: "Why don't we get Tex over there?" he asked. Foreman agreed. Construction of the dam would take almost three more years; during that time, many rulings from Interior on LCRA requests would be expedited by the malleable Goldschmidt.

The little group of which Johnson was a part was an unusual group. Two of its members—Douglas and Fortas—would sit on the highest court in the country. Others—Corcoran and Rowe—would be part (as, indeed, Douglas and Fortas, too, would be part) for decades to come of the nation's highest political councils. In the years immediately after Johnson came to Washington as a Congressman, they were already young men on the rise. But, as one of them—Corcoran—says with a smile, "Gradually, these guys found they were working for Lyndon Johnson." Working for

Johnson, Corcoran says, "on projects for his district"—and, in particular, on one project: that huge dam being built in that isolated gorge in faraway Texas.

FOR THE HIGH DAM, Johnson needed help on Capitol Hill—help of a dimension far greater than any of the young New Dealers could provide. For the dichotomies in the project's financing that Fortas had managed to paper over for Harold Ickes—because Ickes was disposed to favor the project—could not be papered over for Congressmen who had no feelings about it one way or the other. As soon as the necessary legislation was brought before a subcommittee of the House Appropriations Committee, the lack of logic—or legality—in the arguments became apparent. And when the subcommittee's chairman, Representative Charles H. Leavy of the state of Washington (who had apparently been enlisted in the dam's cause without fully understanding its problems), introduced the necessary amendment, to increase the Marshall Ford allocation, and make the increase non-reimbursable, before the full House of Representatives, which was sitting as the Committee of the Whole, members of the subcommittee attempted to make these issues public.

The amendment was to the Rivers and Harbors Bill, which stated clearly that all projects built by the Bureau of Reclamation were "to be reimbursable under the reclamation law." The clerk droned out the words: "Amendment offered by Mr. Leavy after the word 'reimbursable,' insert, 'except to the Colorado Project, Texas.' "

Immediately, there was an objection, from the conservative Republican John Taber of New York. "Mr. Chairman," he said, "I make a point of order against the amendment. . . . It excepts the Colorado River project from reimbursing its cost to the Government. It is a general provision of these reclamation acts that these things shall be reimbursable to the Treasury."

Leavy replied that "it is not a reclamation project in any sense; it is a flood-control project. It is authorized in the Flood Control Act."

Others were ready to jump in. Robert F. Rich,* a Pennsylvania Republican, started to ask the questions that would expose the contradictions. Hadn't the government given $10 million for the Colorado River Project "with the expectation that [the] money was to be paid back out of the sale of power . . . ?" Leavy said that was true. Well, Rich demanded, wasn't the government now being asked to provide $2 million more for the same

---

* Lyndon Johnson was later to write to George Brown that, had Brown been present at the hearing, "I suppose Mr. Rich's comments would have cut you to the quick."

project? "If this [$10 million] money that was lent has to be paid back from power so generated, then tell me why they should not pay this $2,050,000 added to the [$10 million] that they have previously agreed to pay back? If the gentleman can explain that to the House and to the Members of this Congress, then I would like him to do it."

"I do not know whether I can do it in the limited time I have left at my disposal," Leavy said. In fact, he could not do it at all, for the amendment violated not only law—under the law, every Bureau of Reclamation project was reimbursable—but logic. As Leavy attempted to explain it, he floundered.

But Johnson had prepared for this situation. In case of a demand for a roll call, he was to tell Wirtz, "I had at least nineteen members of the Texas delegation with me." If "any questions were raised, Judge Mansfield was going to tell of the dangerous floods in past years on the Colorado River." Texas' amenable Marvin Jones was in the chair. These preparations might not have been sufficient, given the violations of law and logic involved in the amendment, but law and logic could not stand on Capitol Hill against raw power—and Johnson had power on his side.

Years later, another Representative, Richard Bolling of Missouri, would describe the crucial moment in the fight he had had to make—in 1951, during the first months of *his* first term in Congress—for a dam in his district. The dam had been defeated in committee. Bolling had brought the proposal up again before the full House, but knew he didn't have the votes there, either. Although Rayburn, at the instance of his friend, Harry Truman of Missouri, had been friendly to Bolling, the new Congressman hadn't understood what Rayburn's friendship could mean, and he had not asked him for help on the dam bill. But, Bolling says, as he was sitting nervously on the House floor, "I felt someone sit down beside me. I didn't pay any attention to who it was," but when Bolling stood up to speak in support of the dam, the figure beside him stood up, too—and it was Sam Rayburn. Rayburn didn't say a word, Bolling recalls. He didn't have to. The fact that he was standing beside Bolling meant that Sam Rayburn wanted the bill passed—and the House passed it.

In 1951, Sam Rayburn would be Speaker of the House. In 1938, he was only Majority Leader. But he was Sam Rayburn. As Leavy fumbled for an explanation, Rayburn stood up and walked forward to stand beside him. As Leavy finished a sentence, Sam Rayburn said: "The gentleman is correct, yes." He stood there beside Leavy until Marvin Jones banged down his gavel and called the question, and the House agreed that Leavy was correct.

"After . . . Marvin Jones, who was acting as chairman, ruled," Johnson exulted in a letter to Wirtz that night, "we knew we had won and the less we said, the better. We got Sam Rayburn to answer one of Rich's questions in order to indicate to all Democrats that the Majority Leader favored the amendment and when Sam got in the Record we took a vote and called it a day." A jubilant Wirtz wrote back that Johnson had accomplished "the impossible." (Wirtz received another letter as well. "Dear Alvin," Sam Rayburn wrote, "I am mighty glad that Lyndon could get through the additional appropriation for Marshall Ford Dam. Whatever little help I was able to give him was given freely and gladly, as I think Lyndon is one of the finest young men I have seen come to Congress. If the District will exercise the good judgment to keep him here, he will grow in wisdom and influence as the years come and go.")

24

Balancing the Books

DECADES LATER, Tommy Corcoran, reminiscing, would say that "Lyndon Johnson's whole world was built on that dam."

Corcoran was referring to the effect the dam produced on the relationship between Johnson and Herman Brown. In Brown, Johnson had found an older man with a rare immunity to his charm. With his genius for sniffing out political realities, soon after his arrival in Austin as NYA director, he had divined Brown's importance in the capital, and had taken every excuse to drop by the big white house on Niles Road for advice. But advice was all he got; flattery, even Lyndon Johnson's flattery, was too cheap a coin for the purchase of Herman Brown's friendship. Although in the congressional campaign the contractor's support of Avery had been *pro forma*, providing him only with money and not with the full weight of his influence, and although he had hedged even this small bet with a token contribution to Johnson, he had done so only out of deference to Wirtz's opinion. Brown did not share that opinion. A firm believer in experience, he had never seen Johnson in action in Washington, and didn't believe Wirtz when Senator told him that a youth still in his twenties could fill Old Buck Buchanan's boots. Moreover, Herman Brown was a hater. He hated Negroes and he hated unions—in part, for the same reason. Having worked so hard all his life, he hated laziness and he believed that Negroes were lazy, and that unions encouraged laziness in white men; after World War II, he would, with the assistance of Alvin Wirtz and Ed Clark, ram through the Texas Legislature some of the most vicious anti-labor laws in America. And Brown hated the man—that Man in the White House—whose policies were helping unions and Negroes. He had coined his own word for New Deal programs: "Gimme's." Lazy men, he said, were always saying "Gimme," and now the country had a President who was giving them the handouts they were demanding. The very thought of programs that gave people benefits they hadn't earned brought to Brown's narrow, hard face that red flush that men feared. He saw, too, that these programs would lead to increased taxation. The very thought that government—politicians who never worked (Herman Brown, who had bought so many politicians, despised politicians) —was going to take *his* money for which he had worked so hard and give it to people too lazy to work—"well," George Brown says, "Herman really *hated* that idea." His feelings toward Roosevelt had made him ill-disposed toward a candidate who was shouting "Roosevelt, Roosevelt" up and down the district, and in the face of such shouts, Alvin Wirtz's assurances about Johnson's private dislike of the New Deal had a somewhat hollow ring. Johnson, so eloquently mouthing the phrases of the despised New Deal, had seemed, in fact, to epitomize everything Brown disliked. Every time Johnson left after one of his visits, George Brown recalls, "Herman would be saying how he'd never do—how impractical he was." And Johnson wasn't made to feel particularly welcome in Brown's home.

But Herman Brown was a man with his own code of honor. "He always paid his debts," Ed Clark says. "He would always find a way to balance his books. He would never let a man do more for him than he did for that man." And he knew how big a debt he owed Lyndon Johnson for obtaining the authorization that made the dam—and Brown & Root's contracts—legal. When, after Congress adjourned in August, 1937, Johnson returned to Austin, Brown told Clark to bring Johnson along to the house on Niles Road, and soon, Clark says, "Lyndon was over at Herman's house every night."

For a while, the atmosphere was still tense because of Herman's wife, Margaret. A pert, fiery woman with a good education and mind, she liked a chance to display them. She argued with her husband as an equal, and received equal time, and she resented Johnson's practice of talking only to her husband and all but ignoring her. Moreover, Margaret Brown was, in George Brown's words, "a very refined person." Certain of Johnson's habits— his gobbling down of food and his constant combing of his hair, even in her living room—disgusted her. "Margaret really didn't like him," Clark says.

Driving away from Niles Road after one tense evening, however, Johnson said to Clark: "I'm not getting along well with Mrs. Brown, am I?" Recalls Clark: "I said, 'I'm glad you asked me that. I didn't want to bring it up, but now that you asked, it's my duty to tell you.' At that time, Lyndon had a little blue comb . . . and he was *constantly* pulling it out and combing his hair, and constantly jumping up and looking in the mirror. Margaret couldn't stand that, and I told him so. And I said, 'If you'd stop talking all the time, and listen a little, you'd get along with her better.' And he did what I told him. No one ever saw that little blue comb again, and he got along better with Margaret" (although the more she talked with him, the more appalled she was at his lack of education; how could anyone be a Congressman, she sometimes commented after he had left, with so little knowledge of history?).

As for Margaret's husband, Johnson had learned to read him, and had realized that he had to be treated differently from most other men—because, unlike most men, flattery was not what he wanted.

Herman Brown liked to talk politics and government; those subjects fascinated him. And when he talked politics, he didn't want agreement or deference—that was why he never tired of talking to Margaret, because she, liberal in political philosophy like her father, *never* agreed with him. ("Oh, you learned that from some damned radical professor!" Herman would shout at her. "No, dear," she would reply, quietly but firmly, "I learned that at my father's breakfast table.") He wanted argument—hot, violent argument—and it was difficult for him to get what he wanted; in Texas, men interested in politics knew the role that Herman Brown played in Texas politics—and were, those smart enough to give him a good argument, smart enough to be afraid of him.

Lyndon Johnson gave him what he wanted. "They'd have serious fights," recalls George Brown. "Dare each other to get up and hit 'em." One of the two men would ask the other "what'd he think about the Mayor, or this legislator or that one. And they'd argue about it. Herman would say"—and as George imitates Herman, he shows a man pounding a table with angry, heavy blows of his fist—"Herman would say, 'Now, *Goddammit*, Lyndon, you *know* that's not so!' "

Sometimes even George thought his brother and Johnson were going to come to blows; "I'd intervene, and have them make up." But George also knew that Herman acted that violently only with someone "he really liked. If Herman liked yóu, he'd talk a lot, and pound the table. If Herman didn't like you, he'd just smile and not say anything." ("That's right," says one of Herman's lobbyists. "And, boy, when you saw that smile—watch out!") The very violence of Herman's reactions, George says, was an indication of how much he liked Lyndon Johnson.

Liked him—and, more and more, respected him. Johnson, after all, was not the only one of the two who was a reader and manipulator of men. Often they discussed legislators, and, says Frank C. Oltorf, who would later, as one of Herman Brown's lobbyists, witness many such discussions, "you could see they both knew what the other was talking about."

When their discussions centered on legislation rather than legislators, there was also a considerable area of common ground. Brown had been afraid that Johnson was not "practical" enough, but now he learned that Wirtz had been correct. "Basically, Lyndon was more conservative, more practical than people understand," George Brown says. "You get right down to the nut-cutting, he was practical. He was for the Niggers, he was for labor, he was for the little boys, but by God . . . he was as practical as anyone." And his brother soon realized this; even Johnson's defense of Roosevelt was couched in terms with which Herman had no quarrel. "Herman would be ranting and raving about New Deal spending, and Lyndon would say,

'What are you worried about? It's not coming out of *your* pocket. Any money that's spent down here on New Deal projects, the East is paying for. We don't pay any taxes in Texas. . . . They're paying for our projects.' " About this time, George started visiting Johnson in Washington, and he reported back to his brother that indeed many Southern Congressmen were going along with Roosevelt for this same reason; George says, "Lyndon would take me to these meetings of the Southern Congressmen, and that's the way they'd be talking. That the South would get these dams and these other projects, and it would come out of the other fellow's pocket. The Presidents before Roosevelt—Coolidge, Hoover—they never gave the South anything. Roosevelt was the first one who gave the South a break. That's why he had more plusses than minuses, because he was getting them all this money." The relationship between Herman Brown and Lyndon Johnson, George Brown says, was based on the same equation: "He [Herman] felt that Lyndon had more plusses than minuses."

Plusses, moreover, other than philosophical.

Herman Brown was a poor boy from a small town who had, as a youth, worked on a road gang, with mules and a fresno. So was Lyndon Johnson. "He [Johnson] would joke about building roads and shoveling gravel," George Brown recalls. "The stories he would tell were about what a hard time he had growing up. About how poor he had been. About how poor the Hill Country was. They were both poor boys. So there was a kinship there." Johnson had also "gotten his brother and sisters out of there"; Herman Brown, who had gotten one of his brothers out—who would have gotten the others out, had they only been willing to work—liked that, too.

Herman Brown was a poor boy with vast ambitions. Ambition was the wellspring of his character, at least in his brother's view. "We were always reaching. We never had any walking-around money, because we were always reaching above our heads. We never felt we had it made. We were always reaching for the next plateau. We were just always reaching, that's all." Lyndon Johnson's ambitions were different, but their size wasn't. "Hell, running for Congress when he had a good job, and no one thought he could win—that was a gamble," George Brown says. "He was a gambler. He wasn't afraid to take a gamble. He was just reaching all the time, like Herman and me. Herman could understand him."

And poverty and ambition were not all that Herman Brown and Lyndon Johnson had in common. Many poor boys have ambitions—even great ambitions. Few are willing to make the sacrifices necessary to achieve them. Herman Brown, who had, year after year, lived in a tent, and then, year after year, practically lived in a car—slept in a car, ate in a car —had made the sacrifice; and the sacrifice—the work, the effort—had become very important to him. A man who had worked as hard as Herman Brown could tell exactly how hard another man was working. He may not have liked what Lyndon Johnson was saying in the 1937 campaign, but when someone told Herman Brown how Johnson was not only making a dozen speeches a day, but driving hundreds of miles to do it, Herman Brown, better perhaps than any other man, could appreciate the sacrifice, the effort, the work—and, in his grudging, tough way, admire it.

Herman's decision, signaled by the Rotary Club speeches of November, 1937, to launch a campaign for a bigger dam created a rift in the budding friendship. Another source of friction was Johnson's proposed Austin Public Housing Authority, which would condemn slums, raze several blocks of tenements in the city's Negro slum and replace them with modern apartments. Many of the tenements were owned by Brown, who was making a tidy profit from them. Herman didn't want to lose the profit, and at the first hint that condemnation procedures might be invoked if he refused to sell, he erupted into rage at the thought that government might take away *his land*. But it was at this point that the suggestion "Give Herman the dam and let Lyndon have the land" was made and led to a compromise. Johnson began pushing for the high dam. And George's reports, each time he returned from Washington, on how hard Johnson was working for the dam—how successfully he was cultivating Fortas and the others—convinced Herman of the sincerity of his efforts.

Lyndon Johnson's work for Brown & Root did not end with his success in obtaining the appropriation for the dam's enlargement.

Because Brown & Root's equipment, including the massive cableway, was already in place at the remote Marshall Ford dam site, while any other contractor would have to include in his bid the cost of transporting and installing equipment and building a cableway, bidding on the enlargement of the dam was cursory; Herman Brown had considerable leeway in setting a price—$27,000,000—on the work. And once he had the contract, he began working to maximize the profit he would make under it.

Nor was his first price his last. Rather, as soon as he had his price, he wanted the price to be higher.

The order of the day on the Bureau of Reclamation's "Colorado River Project" was the change order, that magical device by which favored contractors are permitted, once they have been awarded a contract, to quietly change its details to increase their profits. Other contractors, particularly in those pre-war days, when government leniency with contractors was not yet a fact of construction life, might find a request for a change order disapproved; with top officials at Interior and Reclamation, including Harold Ickes himself, so obviously committed to the dam, lower-ranking bureaucrats and engineers were reluctant to delay the project by disapproving Brown & Root's stream of requests for changes in specifications and unit prices. And when they did disapprove, for sometimes Herman Brown's requests were so large that the engineers and bureaucrats could not choke them down, Lyndon Johnson got on the phone to them—or to their superiors. On the contract for the low dam, the Bureau of Reclamation had audited the work closely to keep the lid on profits. Now the lid was off. In auditing Brown & Root's requests, and the firm's compliance with contract provisions, in fact, Bureau engineers used Brown & Root's own figures. The delays—caused by government caution and evaluation of work done, or by bureaucratic red tape—which cut into other contractors' profits were substantially eliminated for Brown & Root through Johnson's manipulation of Goldschmidt and his cultivation of other key bureaucrats. Officials telephoned him the moment necessary approvals were signed, and he then made sure the forms were rushed to the next agency—and began pushing there.

He worked with Brown & Root as closely as if he were one of the firm's employees, an employee anxious to impress his boss with his diligence; a typical letter assured Herman: "It is needless for me to tell you that we are humping ourselves on the jobs we have to do here and that this little note . . . is being knocked off between conferences." George rather than Herman was the Brown with whom he was in day-to-day contact—Herman was out on the Colorado, ramrodding the work—and Lyndon Johnson and George Brown reported to each other in detail, exulted with each other over each success. "Finally got together with government engineers, Puls, Moritz, McKenzie on the prices for the new work at Marshall Ford," Brown wrote Johnson on one occasion. "Cut us from $50,000 to $20,000 for flood hazards, and cut concrete 50¢ a yard; we had asked it be cut only 25¢. The rest of the prices are the same as the original contract. Puls, who is out of the Denver office, left that night to return to Denver and write up the change order." After being written up, the change order was sent to Washington, where Johnson took over. Approval by the Comptroller General, then by Interior, and then by Reclamation, was necessary; Johnson obtained these approvals for Brown & Root in a single day, as a telegram from him to George Brown reported:

CONFIDENTIAL. COMPTROLLER-GENERAL SIGNED DECISION THIS MORNING AT 11:30 APPROVING USE OF CHANGE ORDER 67 MARSHALL FORD DAM AS REQUESTED BY THE DEPARTMENT. . . . I GOT DECISION SENT BY SPECIAL MESSENGER TO INTERIOR AND WILL CHECK RECLAMATION LATER THIS AFTERNOON.

George Brown was afflicted with a lisp. Very slight, it affected his pronunciation of only a few words. But because one of those words was "million" (he pronounced it "mee-yon"), the lisp was now to begin proving troublesome to him. For the Marshall Ford Dam was to make that word an essential part of his vocabulary. On the original $10 million Marshall Ford contract—the contract drawn up, and largely carried out, before Lyndon Johnson had begun working on Brown & Root's behalf—the firm, so recently all but broke, had earned a profit of a million dollars. The firm's profit on the subsequent Marshall Ford contract—the contract which brought the total for the entire dam to $27 million—is unknown, but out of a single $5 million appropriation for the high dam, George Brown wrote Lyndon Johnson that Brown & Root's profit was about $2 million ("which," Brown added, "is a nice bit of work . . ."). That appropriation, moreover, was for construction; contractors generally made a higher percentage of profit on excavation contracts. Brown & Root had made a million dollars out of the first contract for the Marshall Ford Dam. Out of subsequent contracts for the dam, they piled, upon that first million, million upon million more. The base for a huge financial empire was being created in that deserted Texas gorge.

Herman Brown was a businessman who wanted value for money spent. His relationships with politicians were measured by that criterion. George Brown, who echoes his brother's thinking, says, "Listen, you get a doctor, you want a doctor who does his job. You get a lawyer, you want a lawyer who does his job. You get a Governor, you want a Governor who does his job." Doctor, lawyer, Governor, Congressman—when Herman "got" somebody, he wanted his money's worth. And with Johnson, he was getting it—and more.

Herman Brown was a man who always balanced his books. When he had been asked for a significant contribution to Johnson's 1937 campaign, he had refused to make one. Now, in 1938, Johnson would be running again. Herman Brown let Johnson know that he would not have to worry about finances in this campaign—that the money would be there, as much as was needed, when it was needed. In Ed Clark's words, "Herman gave Lyndon his full weight."

Herman Brown's full weight meant the support not only of Brown & Root, but of Brown & Root's subcontractors, of the banks in Austin with whom Brown & Root banked, of the insurance brokers who furnished Brown & Root performance bonds, of the lawyers in Austin who received Brown & Root's fees, the businessmen in Austin who supplied Brown & Root with building materials, and the local politicians, not only in Austin but throughout the Tenth Congressional District, accustomed to receiving Brown & Root campaign contributions in return for road-building contracts. These men had followed Herman's lead during the 1937 campaign, and had supported Avery. Now they would follow Herman's lead again. When Lyndon Johnson ran for Congress in 1938, he wouldn't have to raise money from Houston merchants, and he wouldn't have to raise money late at night, after a long day on the road. All the funds he needed would be available at his command—more funds, in fact, than he could possibly use.

25

Longlea

IF HERMAN BROWN was the behind-the-scenes force in the Tenth Congressional District, the public force was the district's influential daily newspaper, the *Austin American-Statesman*.*

The *American-Statesman*'s owner did not share Brown's immunity to flattery. His susceptibility, in fact, was acute.

Charles E. Marsh, who had earned a Phi Beta Kappa key at the University of Oklahoma while working his way through college stoking furnaces, had made money early—while still in his twenties, he had purchased, for a few hundred dollars, a small North Dakota newspaper, had promptly sold it to the Scripps-Howard chain for $10,000, and, with a partner, E. S. Fentress, had headed for Texas to create a chain of his own. And he had made it fast. By 1930, either alone or in partnership with Fentress, he owned newspapers not only in Austin but in fourteen other Texas cities, and in another dozen cities in other states. Thanks to his guarantee of Sid Richardson's bank loans, he was Richardson's partner in some of the most profitable oil wells in West Texas, and the sole owner of other profitable wells of his own. And in Austin, he owned the streetcar franchise and the largest single bloc of stock in the Capital National Bank, as well as vast tracts of real estate. Having made money, he liked to play the patron with it. A tall man—six-feet-three—he had the broad, high forehead and the beaked nose of a Roman emperor, and a manner to match. Tips to headwaiters were dispensed with a gesture reminiscent of a king tossing coins to subjects. Gifts were on an imperial scale: the newspaper he gave to a young reporter as a "tip" was only a weekly, but he was almost as generous with a profitable daily, selling the *Orlando* (Florida) *Sentinel* to Martin Andersen for what Andersen says was "nothing down and at a price which enabled the paper to be paid out over a comparatively short number of years." Richardson

---

* The *American* was the morning edition, the *Statesman* the afternoon; on Saturday and Sunday, they were published as a single newspaper, the *American-Statesman*.

was only one of many young wildcatters he bankrolled. The dividends he wanted from his munificence were gratitude and deference: he wanted to be not only the patron but the seer; "he always had to be the pontificator, the center of attention," Welly Hopkins says, adding, in words echoed by other men who knew Charles Marsh, "he was the most arrogant man I ever met."

Lyndon Johnson, meeting him for the first time in May, 1937, just after arriving in Washington as a newly elected Congressman, gave him what he wanted. Says Marsh's secretary: "The first thing I noticed about [Johnson] was his availability. Whenever [Marsh] would ask Lyndon to come by for a drink, no matter that Lyndon was a busy man, he would always come. He was always available on short notice." The second thing she noticed was his acquiescence. If Marsh wanted to talk, Johnson—seemingly, at least—wanted to listen, and to agree. Marsh liked to pontificate; Johnson drank in what he was saying, and told him how perceptive he was. Marsh liked to give advice; Johnson not only seemed to be accepting it, he asked for more. Marsh had become fascinated by politics; he wanted to feel he was on the inside of that exciting game. Johnson made him feel he was. Marsh may have been a genuine expert in some fields, but politics was not, in Johnson's opinion, one of them. Among themselves, he and his *real* political advisors—Wirtz, Corcoran—laughed at Marsh as an amateur. But no one would have guessed Johnson's feelings from seeing him and Marsh together. He asked Marsh for advice on political strategy, asked him what he should say in speeches—let Marsh *write* speeches for him, and didn't let Marsh know that these speeches were not delivered. And, always, in soliciting and listening to Marsh's opinions, "he was," Marsh's secretary says, "very deferential. Very, *very* deferential. I saw a young man who wanted to be on good terms with an older man, and was absolutely *determined* to be on good terms with him."

And he was. His first conversations with Marsh had taken place in Marsh's Washington townhouse, or in the suite in the Mayflower Hotel that Marsh used as an office. Now Marsh invited the young Congressman and his shy wife to his country home for the weekend, and in the Autumn of 1937, Lyndon Johnson, accompanied by Lady Bird, drove for the first time to Longlea.

"Longlea," set on a thousand acres in the northern Virginia hunt country, was named for the eighteenth-century Sussex manor house on which it was modeled, but it could have been named for its setting. The roads toward it, toward its blue-slate roof and its great chimneys that rose above the soft Virginia hills, led across long, rolling meadows, and the meadows before it were nothing to the meadow behind it. The broad flagstone terrace at the rear of Longlea—a terrace 110 feet long—was bordered by a low stone parapet. Beyond the parapet, the land dropped steeply down to a narrow river. And beyond the river, before the first of the foothills of the Blue Ridge Mountains, a vast, empty meadow (or "lea") stretched on for miles. But, however appropriate the name, knowledgeable visitors to the Charles Marsh estate did not refer to it by that name. They called it "Alice's Place."

Alice Glass was from a country town—sleepy Marlin, Texas—but she was never a country girl. She had been twenty years old when, six years before, she had come to Austin as secretary to her local legislator. Some small-town girls brought to the capital as legislators' secretaries became, in its wide-open atmosphere, their mistresses as well, but Alice Glass was not destined for a mere legislator. "Austin had never seen anything like her," one recalls. She stood, graceful and slender, just a shade under six feet tall in her bare feet, and despite her height, her features were delicate, her creamy-white face dominated by big, sparkling blue eyes and framed in long hair. "It was blond, with a red overlay," says Frank C. Oltorf, Brown & Root's Washington lobbyist and a considerable connoisseur of women. "Usually it was long enough so that she could sit on it, and it shimmered and gleamed like nothing you ever saw."

Bearing as well as beauty impressed. "There was something about the way she walked and sat that was elegant and aloof," Oltorf says. "And with her height, and that creamy skin and that incredible hair, she looked like a Viking princess." Legislators attracted to her at the roaring parties at the Driskill Hotel had sensed quickly that they had no chance with her—and they were right. Charles Marsh had lived in Austin then, in a colonnaded mansion on Enfield Road; at the Driskill parties, he held himself disdainfully aloof, as befitted a man who could make legislators or break them. On the same night in 1931 on which he met Alice Glass, they became lovers; within weeks, Marsh, forty-four, left his wife and children and took her East. He lavished jewels on her—not only a quarter-of-a-million-dollar necklace of perfect emeralds, but earrings of emeralds and diamonds and rubies. "The first time she came back to Marlin and walked down the street in her New York clothes and her jewels, women came running out of the shops to stare at her," recalls her cousin, Alice, who was also from Marlin. And in Washington and New York, too, men—and women—stared at Alice Glass as they stared at her in Texas. "Sometimes when she walked into a restaurant," says another man who knew her, "between those emeralds and her height and that red-gold hair, the place would go completely silent."

And Longlea *was* her place. She had designed it, asking the architects to model it on the Sussex country home she had seen when Marsh had taken her to England, working with the architects herself for months to modify its design, softening the massiveness of the long stone structure, for example, by setting one wing at a slight angle away from the front, enlarging the windows because she loved sunlight, insisting that the house be faced entirely with the native Virginia beige fieldstone of which she could see outcroppings in the meadows below; told there were no longer stonemasons of sufficient skill to handle the detail work she wanted, she scoured small, isolated towns in the Blue Ridge Mountains until she found two elderly master masons, long retired, who agreed, for money and her smile, to take on one last job. She furnished it herself, with Monets and Renoirs and a forty-foot-long Aubusson rug that cost Marsh, even at Depression bargain prices, $75,000. And she had designed the life at Longlea, which was, because she loved the outdoors, an outdoor life. She organized a hunt—the Hazelmere Hunt, named after Longlea's river, the Hazel—and even on weekends on which no hunt was held, horses were always ready in Longlea's stable, and there would be morning gallops; as Alice took the fences ("The only thing Texas about Alice was her riding," a friend says. "She could *really* ride!"), the little black derby she wore while riding would sometimes fall off, and the hair pinned beneath it would stream out behind her, a bright red-gold banner in the soft green Virginia hills. Warm afternoons would be spent around a pool (built, since Alice liked to swim in a natural setting and in clear, cold water, entirely out of native stone in a tree-shaded hollow); as Alice sat in her bathing suit with her hair, wet and glistening, falling behind her, her guests would try to keep from staring too obviously at her long, slender legs.

The focus of life at Longlea was not its magnificent interior but the terrace behind it. Breakfast would be served on that broad, long expanse of flagstone, as the morning sun slowly burned away the mist from the great meadow and the mountains behind it. In the evenings, after dinner, it was on the terrace that guests would sit, watching the mist form and the mountains turn purple in the twilight. Life at Longlea was as elegant as its designer. Champagne was her favorite drink, and champagne was served with breakfast—champagne breakfasts with that incredible view—and, always, with dessert at dinner, dinners under glittering chandeliers imported from France. Served by her favorite waiter: the most distinguished of the Stork Club's headwaiters was a former Prussian cavalryman, Rudolf Kollinger; at Alice's request, Marsh had hired him to be *major domo* at Longlea—even though, to entice Kollinger to private service, Marsh had had to hire as well not only his wife but his mistress. Witty herself, Alice loved brilliant talk, and at Longlea the conversation was as sparkling as the champagne, for she filled the house with politicians and intellectuals—Henry Wallace and Helen Fuller and Walter Lippmann—mixing Potomac and professors in a brilliant weekend salon. She had wanted to create her own world at Longlea—she had wanted a thousand acres, she said, because she "didn't want any neighbors in hearing distance"—and she had succeeded. "Alice Glass was the most elegant woman I ever met," says Oltorf. "And Longlea was the most elegant home I ever stayed in." Arnold Genthe, the noted New York society photographer, who for years came regularly to Longlea, first as a guest and then to practice his profession—to spend day after day taking pictures of Alice because, he said, she was the "most beautiful woman" he had ever seen —asked that his ashes be buried at Longlea after he died because it was the "most beautiful place" he had ever seen.

ALTHOUGH ALICE GLASS resembled a Southern belle—an exceptionally tall and lovely Southern belle—her friends knew that appearances were deceiving.

"She was a free spirit—very independent—in an era when women weren't that way," says her sister, Mary Louise. She didn't believe in marriage, and she had refused to marry Marsh, even though she had borne him two children. (Her sole concession to convention was made to spare the feelings of her parents in Marlin. She wrote them that she had married an English nobleman named Manners. Visitors from Texas would be told that "Lord Manners" was "away" in England on business; she would finally announce that he had been killed fighting for the Loyalists in Spain, and would thereby become a respectable "widow.") And, possessed of brains as well as beauty, she did not, like many Southern girls, try to hide the fact that she was as intelligent as the men she was talking to. She expected them to listen to her opinions as she listened to theirs—and if one was reluctant to do so, she could make him regret that reluctance. A concert pianist from New York, who had monopolized the dinner conversation one evening at Longlea, was gratified, after dinner, to hear one of his recordings playing on the terrace phonograph. As he and the other guests sat there listening, however, Alice suddenly walked over and switched off the machine. "That's the nice thing about having someone on a record," she said. "You can turn him off." Men who listened to her opinions found them worth listening to; Wallace liked to try out his more visionary proposals on Alice, because, he said, "She seems to be the only person with enough imagination to know what I'm talking about." And men with a more political turn of mind found Alice worth talking politics with (Herman Brown was moved to say she had "quite a bit of horse sense—for a girl"), except that her politics contained what to practical men was a rather unfortunate streak of idealism.

"Above everything else," says her sister, "Alice was an idealist." She admired politicians who, in her view, tried to "help people," and detested those who were interested solely in their own advancement, or, worse, in using public office to make money. She herself wanted very badly to help people. "She had a very particular view of the kind of place the world should be," her sister says, "and she was willing to do anything she had to do to make things come out right for people who were in trouble. She was the kind of person who understood very well that she couldn't do much to help—Alice could be very realistic—but she was also the kind of person who wasn't willing not to do anything because she couldn't do it all. She felt you had to try."

IT WAS ALICE'S "IDEALISM"—her desire to "help people"—that first drew her to Lyndon Johnson. In 1937, people in trouble included European Jews. Attending the Salzburg music festival that year, she and Charles made a side trip to hear a speech by Adolf Hitler, and thereafter they understood, earlier than most Americans, how serious a threat he was. When she returned home, she began making money available to help Jews who were fleeing Hitler, and she made Longlea a way station for these refugees when they arrived in the United States; guests sat entranced on the long terrace listening to the stories of their escapes. Max Graf, who at the time of his escape had been one of Vienna's leading music critics and a professor at the Vienna Conservatory, told one evening how he had been afraid to make his true feelings known until his last day in Vienna. On that day, however, when he was leaving his office for the last time, his visa and other necessary papers safely in his breast pocket, a colleague had given him the Nazi salute and said, "Heil, Hitler!" "Heil, Beethoven!" Graf had replied.

One of these refugees was a promising young conductor from Vienna, twenty-five-year-old Erich Leinsdorf, whom Charles and Alice had met in Europe; Leinsdorf was to recall vividly his first meeting with the towering, "immensely rich" couple—the "impressive man" and his consort, "she too quite tall and very handsome." After he had completed an engagement with the Metropolitan Opera in 1938, they invited him to "spend as much time as I wanted" at Longlea, "a large farm, dominated by a magnificent house . . . a great house with eighteen servants, over whom a German butler and his wife, a superlative cook, held sway." Leinsdorf was relaxing there ("There was a constant stream of guests. . . . The accents were new, the lavish and easy life with martinis served at eleven in the morning was new . . . the eighteen black servants were new—I just sat goggle-eyed") when, he recalls, he suddenly remembered, "with a terrific shock," that he had received no reply to his application, submitted months before, for an extension of his temporary visa—and that the visa would expire in just eight days.

When he told his hosts his problem, Alice, who had met Johnson only a few times, suggested that Charles have the young Congressman from Austin try to help.

The next day—a Sunday—Marsh drove Leinsdorf to Washington, and they went to Marsh's suite at the Mayflower, to which Johnson had been summoned ("A lanky young man appeared. He treated Charles with the informal courtesy behooving a youngster toward an older man to whom he is in debt"). He listened "impassively" to Leinsdorf's problem, but on Monday telephoned to say he had begun solving it. The Immigration Department had in fact rejected Leinsdorf's application, but, he told the conductor, due to some clerical oversight the rejection had not been mailed—and this oversight had allowed him to obtain what Leinsdorf describes as "a welcome breathing space." Leinsdorf recalls Johnson saying that he had "exerted his pressure to have the customary phrase 'You have seven days to leave the United States' changed to 'You have six months.' "

The next step, Johnson explained, was to have Leinsdorf's status changed to "permanent resident"—a change which could be accomplished only if he went abroad and returned as a regular immigrant. Johnson arranged for him to go to Cuba, and provided all the necessary documents for his return to the United States. To ensure that there would be no slip-up, he telephoned the United States Consul in Havana to make certain that his quota of Austrian immigrants had not yet been exhausted, and that Leinsdorf would be included in it. "It all went like clockwork," Leinsdorf says.

Marsh was impressed by Johnson's efficiency. Alice was impressed by something else. The young Congressman had brought Leinsdorf's documents to Longlea personally, and had brought with him also a letter to the Consul in Havana. The letter said, Leinsdorf recalls (no copy has been found), "that the United States had a holy mission to provide a peaceful haven for musical geniuses nervously exhausted from persecution and racial bias"; it was, he says, a "moving piece." It had been written by a member of Johnson's staff (probably the gifted Latimer), but it was Johnson who, without mentioning that fact, read it—in a quiet, eloquent voice—that evening on the terrace. The listeners, including Alice, were moved.

As Johnson began coming to Longlea more frequently, she was moved by further manifestations of what she considered the same spirit.

Those stories about the poverty of the people from whom he came—the people of the Texas Hill Country—those stories, told so eloquently, that could bring a hush even to a Washington dinner party, were dramatic indeed told in the stillness of a Longlea evening, and so was his determination to help his people, to bring them the dams and federal programs that would change their lives. Alice Glass, who wanted to help people, believed that Lyndon Johnson shared the same desire. She believed that he was unlike the other politicians who came to Longlea, and whose conversation revealed, before a weekend was over, that their only interest was personal advancement. She believed that she had finally met a politician who was not constantly scheming on behalf of his ambition, a politician whose dreams were for others rather than for himself. Listening to his stories of how he was getting the dams built and the programs implemented, she came to believe, moreover, that he possessed not only the desire but the ability to help people. She told her sister that she felt the young Congressman had limitless potential; recalls Mary Louise: "She thought he was a young man who was going to save the world." And she admired also what she considered his indifference not only to political but to financial advancement. The talk surrounding the immensely wealthy man with whom she lived dealt largely with money, particularly when their guests were close friends like Herman and George Brown. "She was just sick of money, money, money," her sister says. Johnson, with his seeming total lack of interest in the subject, was a refreshing change.

AT FIRST, her relationship to Johnson was that of patroness to protégé. Although he was three years older than she—at the time of the Leinsdorf episode, he was twenty-nine, Alice twenty-six—she, so widely traveled and read, so sophisticated in dress and taste, seemed much more worldly than this man from Texas. He fostered this impression. "He was always asking her for advice," her sister says. She had such perfect taste in clothes, he said; he wanted to ask her what to do about the way his long, skinny wrists stuck out of his sleeves. (She told him that he should have his shirts custom-made, and should wear French cuffs so that if attention was drawn to his wrists, they would look elegant rather than awkward; it was at this time that his lifelong fascination with cufflinks began.) He told her he didn't like the way he looked in photographs; she noticed that one side of his face—the left— photographed much better than the right; for the rest of his life, he would try to allow only the left side to be seen in photographs. He said he realized he didn't know anything about literature and wanted to learn; she read him poetry. "Her favorite was Edna St. Vincent Millay," her sister says; "when she read Millay, you could see Alice in the poetry." She tried to improve his table manners—for a while, he even stopped gulping down his food. She proved his patroness—a very useful patroness—even in politics; when Johnson and Herman Brown seemed on the "collision course" over the condemnation of Brown's real estate, it was she who said to Marsh one night: "Why don't you fix things up between them? Why don't you suggest that they compromise—give Herman the dam and let Lyndon have the land?"— thereby suggesting the compromise that ended the threat to Johnson's political career.

But the relationship changed. Her cousin, Alice, with whom she had grown up in Marlin, now married to Welly Hopkins and living in Washington, was her closest friend. Sometime late in 1938 or early in 1939, Alice Glass told her cousin that she and Lyndon were lovers, and had been for some months. When her sister, Mary Louise Glass, arrived in Washington later in 1939 to become one of Marsh's secretaries, Alice told her, too, and Mary Louise would have known anyway; her offices—first in the Mayflower Hotel and then in the Allies Inn—were right down the hall from the apartments Marsh maintained in those hotels, and she could not help being aware that during Marsh's frequent absences from Washington, Lyndon and Alice spent many afternoons alone together in those apartments. And, more and more, Lyndon and Alice were together at Longlea. On some of his visits to Longlea, Johnson came with Lady Bird, but frequently he would come alone; "he would leave her on weekends, weekend after weekend . . . ," Mary Louise says. "Sometimes Charles would be there—and sometimes Charles wouldn't be there." Johnson had become very much at home at the estate; alone among the guests, he would take off his shirt in the sun on the terrace—"He had this very white skin, but he was always sunning," Mary Louise says—would lead the horseplay at the swimming pool with boundless enthusiasm, and when, on the long terrace in the evenings, the far-off mountains vanishing in the purple mist, Alice put records on the phonograph, he was always the first to jump up and dance.

ATTEMPTING TO ANALYZE why Alice was attracted to Lyndon Johnson, the best friend and the sister who were her two confidantes say that part of the attraction was "idealism"—the beliefs and selflessness which he expressed to her—and that part of the attraction was sexual. Marsh, Mary Louise says, was "much older" than Alice—he had turned fifty in 1937, when Alice was twenty-six—and, she says, "that was part of the problem. My sister liked men." Moreover, they felt that Johnson, for all his physical awkwardness and social gaucheries, his outsized ears and nose, was a very attractive man, because of what Alice Hopkins calls that "very beautiful" white skin, because of his eyes, which were, she says, "very expressive," because of his hands—demonstrating with her own hands how Johnson was always touching, hugging, patting, she says, "His hands were very loving"—and, most of all, because of the fierce, dynamic energy he exuded. "It was," she concludes, "his animation that made him good-looking." Whatever the combination of reasons, the attraction, they say, was deep. "Lyndon was the love of Alice's life," Mrs. Hopkins says. "My sister was mad for Lyndon—absolutely mad for him," Mary Louise says.

Alice Glass believed that her passion was reciprocated. According to her intimates, she told them that Johnson and she had discussed marriage. In that era, a divorced man would be effectively barred from a political career, but, she said, he had told her that he would get a divorce anyway. He had several job offers as a corporate lobbyist in Washington, and he had, she said, promised to accept one of these. Whether or not this was true, the handful of men and women who were aware of her relationship with Lyndon Johnson—including men and women who were to know Johnson over a long period of time—agree that this relationship was different from other extramarital affairs in which he was to be a participant. His conduct at Longlea was striking. One of them, seeing Lyndon and Alice together for the first time, says he could hardly believe his eyes. As Alice sat reading Millay in her quiet, throaty voice, he recalls, Johnson sat silent, not saying a word, just drinking in the beautiful woman with the book in her hands. "I don't believe that Lyndon ever held still for listening to poetry from anyone else," he says. And although Johnson generally ate, even at Washington dinner parties, as he had always eaten—scooping up heaping forkfuls of food and cramming them into his wide-open mouth—at Longlea he made an effort, the first such effort these men and women had ever seen him make, to eat in a more normal manner.

There were, in addition, other telling indications of the strength of Lyndon Johnson's passion for Alice Glass. One is the fact that his love affair with her juts out of the landscape of his life as one of the few episodes in it and perhaps the only one that ran counter to his personal ambition. Charles Marsh, as owner of the only district-wide organ of public opinion, was perhaps the individual in Johnson's congressional district most important to his continuation in office. His love affair with Marsh's lover was, in the words of a man familiar with the relationship, "taking one hell of a chance." And, this man adds, "Knowing Lyndon, I could hardly believe he was taking a chance like that. It just didn't fit in with the Lyndon Johnson I knew. In my opinion, that was the only time—the *only* time—in Lyndon Johnson's whole life that he was pulled off the course he had set for himself."

Johnson, moreover, was silent about the physical side of their relationship.

In later years, such delicacy would not be one of his more striking characteristics. Displaying the same coarseness that, at college, had led him to exhibit his penis and call it "Jumbo," he would show no reticence whatever about the most intimate details of extramarital relationships. His descriptions of his amours were not only exhibitionistic but boastful; particularly with cronies, he would seem almost to need to make other men acknowledge his sexual prowess. There was, seemingly, no aspect of an afternoon in bed —not even the most intimate details of a partner's anatomy—that he did not consider grist for his vivid storytelling ability.

About the physical aspect of his relationship with Alice Glass, he spoke not at all. About her, he was as reticent as a young man in love.

BUT IF HIS RELATIONSHIP with Alice Glass in some respects "didn't fit in" with the rest of Lyndon Johnson's life, in other respects it fit in snugly— emphasizing familiar traits.

His gift for secrecy, for example, had never been more strikingly displayed.

Charles Marsh did not learn of the affair; the lord of Longlea was deeply in love with the woman for whom he had built it, and was more anxious than ever to marry her. "He was asking her and asking her and asking her to marry him," her sister says. But whereas her resistance to the proposal had seemed once to be weakening, now she was adamant. "She wouldn't marry Marsh after she met Lyndon," Mary Louise says. "She wanted to marry Lyndon." Those of the regulars at Longlea who did know dreaded the day when Marsh would find out. His temper was so monumental, his pride so intense, that these younger people, who were somewhat in awe of him, couldn't imagine what his reaction would be when he discovered the truth. And they felt that discovery was inevitable. "They went to great lengths to deceive him," Mary Louise says. "It was all so undercover. But sometimes I would be sitting there when the three of them [Charles, Alice and Lyndon] were together, and I would just be"—and here Mary Louise covers her ears with her hands to demonstrate, figuratively, the way she was inwardly bracing herself for the explosion she was sure must come.

But it didn't come. So guardedly did the two lovers act that even Alice's best friend had not known the truth until Alice told her. "They were unbelievably discreet," Mrs. Hopkins notes. "They were never seen together" in public, and when they were together at Longlea, "they were so discreet" that, she says, no one could have guessed that they were lovers. Until Alice told her, she says, "I had seen them both many times at Longlea, and I never knew." Says Mary Louise: "Nothing showed. Nothing at all."

What did "show," in fact, would have tended to disarm even the most suspicious of men. During his weekends at Longlea, Lyndon Johnson not only displayed his gift for secrecy, he displayed another gift; his capacity for the cultivation of an older man who was important to him, with utter disregard of his true feelings.

He was still at Marsh's beck and call; on scores of occasions like the Sunday on which Marsh brought Leinsdorf to Washington, all Marsh had to do was summon him, and he was there—willing, anxious, eager to be of service. He still agreed fulsomely with Marsh's political analyses and prognostications on world affairs, and was the first to point out that Charles had been right again on some prediction. He still asked Marsh for advice—and was so grateful when Charles gave it that the older man gave more and more. Harold Young, who had watched Johnson "play" many an older man, felt he had never played one better that he did Charles Marsh; never, he felt, had Johnson been more "humble," more the "great flatterer."

Marsh had to be away from Washington frequently on business, but these trips did not interrupt the courtship of the older man by the younger, for he continued it by telegram, wiring Marsh in New York or Chicago or Baltimore to ask for advice: "NEED VISIT WITH YOU. WIRE WHERE CAN REACH YOU OR CALL ME AT HOME TONIGHT"; on another occasion, when Johnson was planning to go to Texas, he wrote the publisher, "I do hope you will be back this way before we leave. I need the inspiration and stimulant that a couple of hours with you always gives me." Or he would give congratulations to Marsh on his perspicacity; on December 15, 1939, for example, while Marsh was checking on business investments in New York, he received a telegram from Johnson in Washington which stated: "SOME IN-TERESTING AND RATHER AMUSING DEVELOPMENTS HERE YESTERDAY WHICH CONFIRMED A PREDICTION YOU MADE IN AUGUST."

Marsh's response was all Johnson could have wished. To his telegrams requesting advice came back telegrams giving it—advice on how to place an ad in country newspapers so that it would receive prominent display, for example ("MERELY ENCLOSE A CHECK FOR $20.00. . . . I DO NOT THINK YOU WILL FIND THAT ANY OF THEM WILL RETURN THE CHANGE. . ."). When Marsh felt that Johnson needed advice in more detail than was feasible for a telegram, an "Extra Rush!" wire would tell the Congressman: "SUGGEST YOU TELEPHONE COLLECT . . . TONIGHT." And sometimes he felt Johnson needed advice in person—"ARRIVE WASHINGTON SEVEN FORTY-FIVE TUESDAY MORN-ING IF PLANE ON TIME WOULD BE PLEASED HAVE BREAKFAST WITH YOU MAYFLOWER HOTEL." The advice was on personal as well as political mat-ters, and it reveals not only the paternal feeling Marsh had toward Johnson, but his total ignorance of the relationship between Johnson and Alice; some of the advice, in view of that relationship, can be read with a certain feeling of irony. On April 9, 1940, during a period when the affair between Lyndon and Alice was at its most torrid, Marsh, who had left Longlea the previous evening on a business trip, telegraphed Johnson: "I DID NOT LIKE THE WAY YOU LOOKED LAST NIGHT. YOU WERE NOT WELL SHAVED. PLAY AS MUCH GOLF AS POSSIBLE WITH ALICE. . . ."

Marsh became, in fact, more and more fond of the young man he con-sidered his protégé. Sometimes, lonely on his travels around the country, he would be moved to telegraph Johnson his affection; from the Stevens Hotel in Chicago, he wired Johnson on September 16, 1940: "DEAR LYNDON: WAKING UP THIS MORNING WITH A GREAT DISTASTE FOR MID-WEST SENA-TORS, I FOUND IT MORE PLEASANT TO WRITE YOU A NOTE."

Marsh's increasing fondness for Johnson disturbed Alice more and more; her own inclination would have been to reveal the truth to Marsh; she had agreed to wait until the time was ripe, but she felt there was some-thing more dishonorable than she had bargained for in the situation as it was evolving. But Johnson seemed to find it completely feasible to have the relationship he wanted not only with the man's mistress but with the man.

And he proved to be right. His discretion gave him rewards. During the same years in which he was making love to the woman Marsh loved, Marsh was giving him more than advice and affection.

He was concerned with Lyndon's financial future because he had no-ticed that, despite his $10,000-per-year Congressman's salary, Johnson was always short of cash. The publisher saw that Lyndon was worried about money, and he didn't want Lyndon to worry about money: a great future lay ahead of him, and he should be freed from sordid cares. In 1939, there-fore, Marsh took his first step toward placing Johnson on a sounder financial footing. With his gift for making money on a grand scale, he had seen, several years before, how to make it in Austin. Standing on a hill above the small but growing city, he had forecast the direction in which most of its growth would occur, and had promptly purchased large tracts of land there. Now the land was worth considerably more than he had paid for it, but Marsh said he would sell Johnson a nineteen-acre tract for the same price he had paid: $12,000. "It was a marvelous buy, and we knew it," Lady Bird says. She borrowed the money from her father, Brown & Root chipped in by building a road out to the land, and by grading and landscaping it—and, for the first time, the Johnsons owned property.

The older man helped the younger man not only financially but politically. Although he owned so many newspapers, Marsh's interest in them was financial rather than journalistic. "Charles just had newspapers to make money with them," says Mary Louise Glass, his secretary. "Making money did not require editorial quality, and there was no concern with that." On the rare occasions on which some local issue or individual captured Marsh's interest and led him to formulate a position on it, he wanted the position expressed not only on the editorial page but—without regard to journalistic ethics—in the news columns. And he left no doubt as to the precise nature of the position he wished taken; making a rare call to the paper's editor (he usually talked only to "the business people," Mary Louise says), he would bark unequivocal instructions over the telephone. And after Lyndon Johnson became his protégé, the instructions to Charles E. Green, editor of the *Austin American-Statesman,* often concerned Lyndon Johnson. Marsh would sometimes dictate pro-Johnson editorials—and articles—himself. His newspapers took one position that was particularly pleasing to Johnson: that no one run against him in the next election. As early as January, 1938, an *American-Statesman* editorial, lauding Johnson's work on the LCRA and other projects, said that he "ought . . . to be unopposed, and thus freed of the burden of a campaign, so as to give his undivided time to his services in the session that will run almost until primary election day." This theme was echoed by *American-Statesman* reporters. Wrote one, in the paper's "Town Talk" column, "I had a nice visit with Cong. Johnson. He looks tired, but I suppose any man who has done as much for his district in the short time that Johnson has, should be tired. Fortunately, I don't think there's anyone in his district foolish enough to announce against him. So that will give him some rest." Potential opponents realized that in 1938, Johnson would have not only overwhelming financial support, but enthusiastic press support.

THE REACTION of the audience—Mary Louise Glass, Welly and Alice Hopkins, and others—to the drama, the drama that Mary Louise calls "Charles and Alice and Lyndon," being played out before them, month after month, against the beautiful setting of Longlea (without, of course, the knowledge of one of the three leads), varies from person to person, and their reactions are colored by their attachment to one or another of the participants.

An unequivocal opinion is obtainable from another observer, who has asked not to be quoted by name. This observer's opinion is colored by the fact that she had reason to be keenly aware, more keenly aware than the other watchers, of a detail almost never mentioned by the others: the fact that not only the principals but two little children of whom Charles Marsh was very fond, and who were very much attached to their father, would be affected by the drama's denouement.

Watching Lyndon Johnson fawn over the children's father when he was present, knowing all the time that Johnson was sleeping with their mother when he was absent; watching Johnson praise the older man to his face, knowing all the time that behind his back he was taking from him the woman he loved; seeing how unshakably deferential, how utterly humble, he was in playing upon Marsh's affections, this observer, a lover of Charles Dickens, was reminded forcefully of a character in *David Copperfield*—a character who, she felt, lacked only a Southern drawl to be Lyndon Johnson in the flesh. "Every time I looked at Lyndon," she says, "I saw a Uriah Heep from Texas."

AND WHAT of the other person who had a stake in the drama—a person so lightly regarded by the spectators that most of them all but ignore her when they talk of it?

Lady Bird Johnson was easy to ignore.

Her husband insisted that she wear makeup and high heels, and, more and more, she did so, but he could not, except on rare occasions, force her to wear dresses of any but the dullest colors, and her appearance was still drab. And nothing, it seemed, could ease her terrible shyness.

During her husband's campaign for Congress, she had been, as always, pleasant and uncomplaining in serving hot meals to him and his aides at all hours of the night; men who worked for him had come to accept as a matter of course a warm, welcoming smile at the door, no matter when they arrived. But when, occasionally, someone—someone who didn't know her well—raised, however gingerly, the possibility that she herself might campaign, the very suggestion that she might have to face an audience and speak brought such panic to the face of this woman who had once prayed for smallpox so that she wouldn't have to speak at her high-school graduation ceremony that the suggestion was always quickly dropped. Following the campaign, an Austin women's organization had held a party in honor of the wife of the new Congressman; she had been able to avoid making a speech at the party, but she could not avoid standing in a receiving line— and while she had shaken hands and chatted with the strangers filing by, she had done it with so obvious an effort that her friends winced inwardly

as they watched; the bright smile on her face had been as rigid as if it had
been set in stone. At Longlea, with so many brilliant raconteurs only too
anxious to hold the stage, no such effort was required; she was able to sit
for hours, just listening, absolutely silent. And, of course, often Lady Bird
was not *at* Longlea. As 1938 became 1939 and 1939 became 1940, with
increasing frequency Lyndon Johnson would arrive alone, having left her
back in Washington. Sometimes, in fact, he would have dispatched her to
Texas. It was necessary for the Johnsons' car, filled with household possessions, to be driven back and forth at the start and finish of each congressional session, and, often, Johnson had her make the 1,600-mile trip to
Austin accompanied by the wife of one of his aides, saying that he had to
stay behind in Washington on business; later, he would fly down. "For
years," Lady Bird would say, "my idea of being rich was having enough
linens and pots and pans to have a set in each place, and not have to lug
them back and forth."

The attitude of the Longlea "regulars" was, of course, influenced by the
attitude her husband displayed toward her: the brusqueness of the orders he
gave her, insisting they be instantly obeyed; the short shrift he accorded her
infrequent, timid comments. Seeing that in her relationship with Lyndon, her
opinion didn't count, they gave it little consideration themselves. Marsh, in
fact, seems to have been in some doubt as to her name; he was constantly
referring to her as "Lyndon's wife." To Alice's adoring sister and her best
friend, moreover, she was an obstacle to Alice's happiness, and when they
did discuss her, there was more than a hint of mockery in their voices; says
Alice Hopkins: "Everybody was trying to be nice to her, but she was just
. . . out of place." And the attitude of the regulars was influenced also by
the attitude she herself displayed; Lady Bird Johnson herself appears to have
felt that she was out of place at Longlea. Decades later, describing the estate
to the author, she said: "My eyes were just out on stems. They would have
interesting people from the world of art and literature and politics. It was
the closest I ever came to a salon in my life. . . . There was a dinner table
with ever so much crystal and silver. . . ." She appears to have felt herself
that she had little to contribute to the scintillating conversation there; she
felt that her host, for example, not only "looked like a Roman emperor"
but was "one of the most fascinating men I have ever met. He knew all sorts
of things. He went all over Europe, he went to Salzburg and places like
that. . . . He was the first one who introduced Lyndon to the danger of
Hitler. . . . I think he saw a Nazi rally. He made my blood run cold. But he
also made us see why the German people would be for him [Hitler]—that
they would be respected and all." She appears, in fact, to have felt keenly the
contrast between herself and her hostess: "I remember Alice in a series of
long and elegant dresses, and me in—well, much less elegant," she says. In
a voice with a trace of heroine-worship, she notes that they had known each

other slightly years before in Austin when she was a University of Texas undergraduate and Alice was working in the Capitol, and even then, Lady Bird says, "she was quite an intellectual girl and, you felt, destined for more exciting things than being a legislator's secretary." And then, when "we saw them again in Washington, she was even prettier, and just dressed so beautifully. She was very tall, and elegant—really beautiful, in a sort of Amazonian way." Once, during a Marsh discourse on the Hitler threat, her admiration for Alice moved her to a rare attempt at a witticism—"Maybe Alice can help us fight him," she said. "She's so tall and blond she looks like a Valkyrie"—an attempt which was, of course, ignored.

Had they been more observant, however, the Longlea regulars might have noticed qualities in the drab woman as well as in the elegant one. During the loud arguments to which she sat quietly listening, books would be mentioned; Lady Bird would, on her return to Washington, check those books out of the public library—check them out and read them. Because of Marsh's preoccupation with Hitler, she checked out a copy of *Mein Kampf*, read it—and learned it. She never attempted to talk about it at Longlea, even though when Hitler's theories were discussed thereafter, she was aware that, while Marsh knew what he was talking about, no one else in the room did—except her. And she read other books, too; one Summer is still remembered by the Longlea regulars as the "Summer that Lady Bird read *War and Peace.*" They snickered at the way she carried the big book with her everywhere—even though, by the end of the Summer, she had finished it, and, because she felt there was something to be gained by a rereading, had promptly begun at the beginning to read it through again.

And there were other qualities—which the regulars note, even though they don't realize the significance of what they are saying. Alice Hopkins, while saying that "She was just . . . out of place," says immediately thereafter that "If everyone was just trying to be nice to her," she would be nice right back, calm and gracious—"She was self-contained." Even Alice's sister noticed that there was something "quite remarkable in her self-discipline—the things she made herself do. She was forever working" not only on her reading, but on her figure—she had always been "dumpy," but now the extra weight came off, and stayed off.

AND SOME of the Longlea regulars even began, after a while, to wonder if there were not still greater depths to the "self-discipline" of Lady Bird Johnson.

"Of course" Lady Bird must have known of her husband's affair with Alice Glass, Frank Oltorf says. "Oh, I'm sure she did." Why else, the regulars point out, would she think that her husband was going—without her—on so many weekends to Longlea when, as she could easily have determined,

Charles Marsh was not at home? Says Mary Louise: "The thing I could never understand was how she stood it. Lyndon would leave her on weekends, weekend after weekend, just leave her home. I wouldn't have stood it for a minute."

But stand it she did. "We were all together a lot—Lyndon and Lady Bird and Charles and Alice," Mary Louise says. "And Lady Bird never said a word. She showed nothing, nothing at all."

———————

THE PASSION eventually faded from Johnson's relationship with Alice Glass. She married Charles Marsh, but quickly divorced him, and married several times thereafter. "She never got over Lyndon," Alice Hopkins says. But the relationship itself survived; even when he was a Senator, Lyndon Johnson would still occasionally dismiss his chauffeur for the day and drive his huge limousine the ninety miles to Longlea; the friendship was ended only by the Vietnam War, which Alice considered one of history's horrors. By 1967, she referred to Johnson, in a letter she wrote Oltorf, in bitter terms. And later she told friends that she had burned love letters that Johnson had written her—because she didn't want her granddaughter to know she had ever been associated with the man responsible for Vietnam.

26

The Tenth District

WHEN JOHNSON RAN AGAIN, he would have not only financial and press support but a record as well—quite a remarkable record.

On Saturday, May 15, 1937, two days after he had been sworn in as a Congressman, Sherman Birdwell and Carroll Keach arrived in Washington, having driven up from Texas. When they pulled up in front of the Old House Office Building, late Saturday afternoon, Johnson was waiting for them on the sidewalk. "Let's go up to the office," he said. "I think we have a lot of mail."

Inside the door of his temporary office, Room 118 on the first floor, gray sacks of mail—from constituents of a district without representation since Buchanan's death almost three months before—were piled high. Although Birdwell and Keach had put in a long day on the road, the three men started working on the mail that night, and worked until well after midnight. Johnson left then—to bunk down with his brother, since the Kennedy-Warren apartment wouldn't be vacant until Monday—but he told Birdwell and Keach to sleep at the office; that would make it more convenient for them to resume work early Sunday morning. Keach left in a few days to return to his job with the NYA, but Birdwell stayed on. A newcomer to Washington, he worked seven days a week, and such long hours that, he recalls, "even though the House Office Building is just across the street from the Capitol, I was there for over a month before I ever saw the Capitol from the inside." The only reason he got to see it then, he says, was that Mayor Tom Miller telephoned from Austin with an urgent message for Johnson: "I went over there to find him, and that was the first time I was even in the Capitol of the United States." Birdwell's wife, Dale, was recruited to help—without pay; "we just all worked, it was just family," Birdwell says. Gene Latimer, back in Washington at his old, full-time, job with the Federal Housing Administration, worked for Johnson in the evenings and on weekends—out of "his love for Mr. Johnson," Birdwell says.

Hard though Johnson's staff had worked when he was a congressional secretary, it had to work harder now. "There was much more work than there had been when we were with Kleberg, because he [Johnson] wanted an organization built overnight, the same type of organization that it had taken him four years to build with Kleberg," Latimer says. Birdwell, who hadn't worked in Kleberg's office, had thought at first that the workload would ease when the backlog of letters was eliminated, but when they had caught up, the load seemed to get heavier; the mail, Birdwell saw, was the best way to make people feel "they had a close personal relationship, a close personal rapport, with their Congressman," so if there wasn't enough mail, "we had to generate mail." No matter how hard they worked, Birdwell was to say, "we never did get caught up"—and, he came to realize, they never would.

Johnson seemed unable to meet the demands he was making on himself. His insistence on overseeing every detail, because he "never could really be sure that things would go right unless he was in control of everything—*everything!*" had not diminished with success. Birdwell saw now what Latimer and Jones had seen years before: "He signed every letter," no matter how brief, or how unimportant the subject matter. "No one rubber-stamped his name on a letter. He looked at and read every letter. If we wrote something that didn't sound right, why, it was rewritten." Success seemed only to have increased his tension: he smoked constantly now, about three packs a day, often lighting one cigarette while another was still burning in the ashtray, taking those deep puffs, head bent toward the floor, as if to draw the last bit of relaxing smoke into his lungs. He was not as gaunt as he had been, but he stayed thin, and a new physical symptom developed: a rash on his fingers; his hands became very dry and scaly, and the skin cracked painfully. Doctors prescribed a salve, but told him the cause was nervousness. The problem kept getting worse. At night, signing the hundreds of letters that his aides had prepared for his signature, his right hand would begin to bleed through the cracks in the skin. Wrapping a small towel around his hand so that the letters wouldn't be stained with blood, he would nonetheless sign every one. Had he been fearful, worried, almost desperate before his victory in the election? No more fearful, worried and desperate than he was after his victory.

The gifted Herbert C. Henderson was the one assistant with a special place on the Johnson staff because Johnson considered his speechwriting talent too important to be wasted. He had his own office in which he kept files on all relevant political topics of the day, and wrote speeches for Johnson to deliver on his trips back to the district. Birdwell and Latimer handled the rest of the work.

Birdwell couldn't stand the pace. "Lyndon said, 'You've got to speed up your typing, and you've got to get shorthand down,' " he recalls. "So after working ten or twelve hours in the office, I went to typing and shorthand class. I was pretty fagged out, and I never did get my shorthand down too well." His weight had dropped from 165 pounds to 130 pounds, and, he says, "I was about ready to crack up." And he simply couldn't learn to take shorthand as fast as Johnson wanted it taken. Johnson sent him back to Texas to work for the NYA.

Latimer, of whom Johnson now wrote, "I think he is the best [secretary] in the Capitol," wasn't so lucky. In August of 1938, Johnson asked him to work for him full time, and Latimer agreed. Once Johnson had hugged and talked to the young man with a "wonderful smile," "the best-natured little guy you ever saw," who was so dependent on him; now there was no time for such interludes. There was only work—work of an even greater intensity than before. "I felt I was literally working myself to death," Latimer says. "I never drew a breath." He says: "Almost a year to the day later —in August of 1939, I believe—nature took its toll and I had what is commonly called a breakdown." Crying now as he speaks, he says: "I just told him, 'You never said I did anything wrong, but you never said I did anything right. Seems like in a year you might have said. . . .' " He "resigned," and left Washington to recuperate at his parents' home in Texas.

New men were brought in, one after the other. Two were to stay: twenty-two-year-old John B. Connally, who had been student body president at the University of Texas and who was within a few years to display a political aptitude of his own; and Walter Jenkins. The method of Jenkins' recruitment reveals the caution and secretiveness with which Lyndon Johnson approached the hiring even of a secretary. Johnson had asked a UT dean to recommend a student for a job on his office staff, and the dean had recommended Jenkins, but Jenkins didn't know this. He didn't know what job he was being interviewed for. He assumed it was a post with the Texas division of the National Youth Administration because his first interview was with its deputy director, Willard Deason, and his next was with its director, Jesse Kellam. But neither Deason nor Kellam mentioned a specific job, and Jenkins was then interviewed by Austin's Postmaster, Ray Lee. The next call came from an official of the Office of Government Reports, and for the first time a job was mentioned; "He said it was for a job in his office," Jenkins recalls. Only after he had passed screening by these four Johnson aides was the true purpose of the interviews revealed. "I got a call from John Connally, and he said, 'Would you like to drive out to Johnson City tonight and meet Lyndon Johnson?' I said, 'Who's Lyndon Johnson?' I was from Wichita Falls and had never heard of him." Jenkins had dinner with Johnson at the Casparis' Café, and after hours of answering questions, the young student was asked, "Would you like to work for me?" Jenkins was to come to understand this circuitous approach: "Because if they decided not to offer me a job, my feelings wouldn't have been hurt"—in other words, Johnson wouldn't have made an enemy. In Jenkins, Johnson found a true successor to Latimer: a young man similarly willing to work hard, and similarly dependent on him psychologically. A friend of Jenkins who would in 1941 visit Washington and board with him for a few nights recalls the young man returning to his room so tired that he fell asleep in the bathtub; "Johnson was working him like a nigger slave," he says.

Johnson seemed determined to learn every program, and get the most possible out of it for his district. By December 17 when Congress adjourned and he and Lady Bird began the drive home, he had obtained not only the $5 million in federal funds for the Marshall Ford Dam, but PWA appropriations for projects ranging from a grandstand for the Smithville High School football field to a new firehouse in Austin and a new "Federal Building" in Elgin. He was able to get more for the district than had the veteran Buchanan—to the astonishment, in particular, of Austin's Mayor Tom Miller. In 1933, Miller had submitted an application to the PWA for a combined grant and loan ($112,500) for additions to the Austin City Hall. The grant had several times been rejected, and the disappointed Mayor had not resubmitted it in 1937. On August 26, 1937, however, Miller received a telephone call from Washington. His new Congressman—the Congressman he had thought would not be able to get things done in Washington—was on the line to tell him that PWA Administrator Ickes had just approved the project—and not as a combined grant and loan, but as a full grant the city would not have to pay back. Soon new PWA grants—for a new wing on the municipal hospital, for a new building at the municipal airport, for new streetlights—were flowing into the city at a rate that, the Mayor told friends, he would never have believed possible.

On September 1, 1937, President Roosevelt had signed an act creating the United States Housing Authority, which could make loans for low-cost slum-clearance projects. An Austin Housing Authority—E. H. Perry, an elderly retired cotton broker, chairman, but Alvin J. Wirtz, vice chairman and key figure—had been quickly established at Johnson's urging, and had proposed a $714,000 project to tear down the squalid shacks in Austin's three slum areas and replace them with three modern garden-apartment projects, one for whites, one for blacks and one for Mexican-Americans. Herman Brown's opposition had dissolved with the compromise Alice Glass had suggested, but many details remained to be solved. Arriving in Austin on December 20, the new Congressman set about resolving them. Austin's loan application would be the first from anywhere in the country to arrive on the desk of Federal Housing Administrator Nathan Straus; Austin would be one of the first five cities to receive FHA approval.

When Johnson returned to Washington in 1938, the pace only accelerated. In 1933, sixteen municipal projects suggested by the city of Austin—their cost would total $2,566,400—had been turned down by the PWA; now Johnson told Mayor Miller to re-submit all sixteen. Not long thereafter, the Mayor was summoned out of a City Council meeting: Congressman Johnson was on the phone from Washington. Miller returned to tell the Council that three of the sixteen projects (a tuberculosis sanitorium, a municipal incinerator, an automatic fire-alarm system in public buildings) had been approved—and that the other thirteen would be approved shortly. One project had long been a particular dream of the Mayor's: the reconstruction of a low dam in the Colorado River at Austin. The dam had been built in 1900, and destroyed that same year by a flood—and ever since the city had been trying, without success, to find the money to restore it. For thirty-eight years it had stood as a useless heap of masonry in the capital; now Johnson persuaded the PWA to finance its rebuilding, at a cost of $2,300,000, and at his suggestion it was renamed: the Tom Miller Dam.

IT WAS NOT, however, in the city that Lyndon Johnson made his greatest impact in his district. It was in the countryside—in the Hill Country where he had been born.

The New Deal's effect on the Hill Country had been more limited than its effect on more prosperous Texas counties such as the Fourteenth District's counties down on the Gulf Coast. The reason—as always in the Hill Country—was the land. The AAA paid farmers to take land out of cotton cultivation. But up on the Edwards Plateau, much of the land had been taken out of cultivation decades before—by the fast-spreading brush which had gobbled up so much of the ground that whole sections of the country as far as the eye could see were covered with the cedar and scrub oak and mesquite whose fierce roots had drained the ground of moisture and fertility, and whose low, wide branches had interlocked in a canopy that cut off from grass the sun it needed if it was to live. The fertility of much of the rest of the land had been so thoroughly drained by erosion and over-cropping, and by the aridity of the climate, that it didn't pay to plant seed in it anyway. In Blanco County, for example, only about 35,000 acres—less than 10 percent of the land—had been under cultivation in 1933. This land was divided among 708 farmers, so that the average farmer was working only about fifty acres, perhaps thirty in cotton. The 40 percent reduction required by the AAA and its successor acts meant a reduction for the average farmer of only twelve acres. And AAA crop-reduction payments were based on the amount of cotton that would have been grown on acres taken out of production; Hill Country land was so unproductive that twelve acres produced perhaps two bales, and the typical Hill Country farmer therefore received a government check for about sixty dollars. Sixty dollars would help—but not enough. And in 1934, 1936 and 1937, there was drought on the Edwards Plateau—which reduced the production of cotton still further, to a point at which, the *Blanco County News* reported in 1937, "The cotton quotas are of very little interest in Blanco County. Only two gins ran there last year, and they didn't do much more than pay the overhauling cost of repairing the gins." The government was buying cattle for about twelve dollars per head. This could translate into a substantial sum in a fertile blackland county where a rancher

might be running hundreds, or thousands, of head; it did not mean much
to the Hill Country rancher attempting to graze a few cows among the
cedar. Truman Fawcett, whose father had "five or six" head, recalls: "The
people were glad to have the, the—twelve dollars, I think it was. They
couldn't sell the cattle [privately], and they were glad to get it, but that
wasn't much cash."

The people of the Hill Country were grateful for what the New Deal
had done for them; little as had been the help they had realized from its
programs, it was far more help than anyone had ever given them before.
But their lives were not changed by the New Deal. The Hill Country was
a country in which there was unbelievably little cash. In 1937 as in 1932, the
Johnson City High School nearly missed basketball season—because the
school could not afford a basketball; after several weeks of fund-raising, the
News reported that "collections are coming in too slow on the basketball."
Store owners found that any item costing more than a dime was likely to
go unsold. "People couldn't pay for anything," says Lucille O'Donnell of
Burnet. "The people bought everything on credit. Whatever you bought, you
would pay for it when the cotton came in. And whatever your cotton crop
brought in, the storekeeper took off your bill. No money changed hands. I
remember I didn't have three cents to send a letter." Their poverty forbade
them most modern improvements. In the more prosperous counties of Texas,
gasoline-driven tractors were in widespread use; in a typical Hill Country
county—Kendall—there were, in 1933, three tractors. Hill Country farmers
plowed their fields with mules and hand-held plows—plowed their fields as
European peasants had been plowing fields for centuries. The people of the
Hill Country lived at a level so low that the New Deal could not reach far
enough down to reach them. A very long arm would be necessary if they
were ever to be helped.

JOHNSON DISPLAYED AGAIN the ingenuity and energy in obtaining benefits
for his constituents from the federal bureaucracy that he had displayed as
a congressional secretary. Though some of these benefits were relatively
small, and available only once, they provided a sorely needed lift to those
who received them. In one area, floods had destroyed the crops of hundreds
of farmers for the second successive year. In December, 1938, Johnson
arrived at a meeting with the farmers accompanied by a second car full of
men. When the farmers told him that the Farm Security Administration had
responded to their pleas for emergency loans by refusing to make an exception to the requirement that loans be secured by collateral—a requirement
impossible for most of them to meet because their land and possessions
were already mortgaged—their Congressman pointed to the back of the
room, where the men who had accompanied him were standing. They were
officials of the Farm Security Administration, he said. He had brought them

along so they could hear the plight of the Tenth District for themselves. Two days later, on Christmas Eve, the farmers' leaders received telephone calls from their Congressman. The FSA had just agreed to waive the collateral requirements for 400 Tenth District families because of "unusual conditions," he told them. Each family would receive fifty dollars—enough to tide them over until federal seed loans became available in the Spring. At that very moment, he said, four FSA supervisors, accompanied by stenographers, were on their way to the area to speed the processing of the loans.

And some of the benefits Johnson obtained were not small—and were quite long-lasting.

One Agriculture Department program—"Range Conservation"—had the potential to be particularly helpful in this land of brush. Instituted in 1935, it was designed to encourage the removal of various varieties of brush by paying farmers to cut it down. But the program was not helping the Hill Country. In part, this was because the farmers and ranchers of the Hill Country simply did not know that their land *could* be made better; it had been arid and infertile, after all, for three generations. But there were other reasons as well. Some varieties of brush prevalent in the Hill Country were not covered by the program, and in addition the payment-per-acre schedule was low. This did not matter in more prosperous areas, where the work was done by hired hands receiving low wages, whose employers were amply reimbursed by the increased fertility of the cleared land. But the typical Hill Country farmer had no hired hands; his only resource was his own time, every minute of which seemed necessary for his very survival, and payments were too low to justify him using any for some possible future gain. Besides, to most Hill Country farmers, the possibility of future gain seemed very faint. Many didn't even know about the program. The isolation of the Edwards Plateau—the distances (and inadequate roads) that separated its farms and ranches from Austin and San Antonio, their lack of radio and daily newspapers; the inadequacy of the amateurish weeklies—prevented its inhabitants from learning about developments with which farmers in other areas were familiar. The county agents of the land-grant colleges' Agricultural Extension Service were supposed to explain new programs, but the Hill Country's poverty made even explanations difficult; the federal government matched a county's allocation for a county agent and his assistants; because most Hill Country counties couldn't afford any contribution for assistants, its county agents had to spend much of their time on paper work—and much of the rest of it making veterinary calls in counties too poor to support a veterinarian. To the farmers, moreover, the county agents were merely "book farmers" whose theories would not work in the Hill Country's harsh conditions. The experience of the few Hill Country ranchers who had signed up for the Range Conservation program did not encourage others to follow suit; the red tape involved was discouraging as was the slowness of the payments: in March, 1937, some payments still had not been received for acreage that had been cleared in the Summer of 1936.

After May, 1937, county agents in the Tenth Congressional District began to receive frequent telephone calls from the district's new Congressman. Gently at first, and then more and more firmly, he pushed them to call meetings of the farmers, and to educate them to the advantages of the Range Conservation program. Those who did not respond began to receive inquiries from their superiors, who said *they* had had a telephone call from the Congressman. This effort was not sufficient to get the job done, so Johnson took a more direct hand: his constituents were bombarded by repeated mailings from his office about the advantages of the program. And when this proved still not enough, he toured the district, and educated the farmers himself. "He'd come to the meetings and take off his shoes and loosen his tie," recalls Camm Lary, an inspector for the program. He told the farmers that he had been a farmer like them. He had learned farming in the hard Hill Country soil, not out of some book, he told them, and he knew that if they removed the cedar, the land would get better. And he did more: he persuaded the Agriculture Department to include in its program the varieties of Hill Country brush not previously covered. He persuaded it to increase its payments to five dollars for each acre of brush removed, a figure high enough so that a Hill Country farmer could see a real cash reward in the job —whether or not it was successful in its purpose. He persuaded the Department to release enough funds so that the agent in Blanco County, the enterprising, dedicated Ross Jenkins, could hire outside cedar-choppers to come in and clear scores of acres on one farm, which was made a demonstration farm. The land was cleared, and after some months, truckloads of farmers from all over the Tenth District were brought to see hills which had been covered with cedar so dense that it had seemed almost a solid mass. Now the little trees with the voracious roots were gone, but the hills were not bare. Pushing up out of the hard caliche soil were new green shoots. Says Lary: "You could see that the grass was coming back." A total of only 31,000 acres of cedar had been cleared in Blanco County during 1936 and 1937, the two years before Lyndon Johnson became Congressman. In 1938 alone, 63,000 acres were cleared; in 1939, 70,000 acres. In the Tenth District as a whole, hundreds of thousands of acres of brush were chopped away. By the end of 1940, the amount of land under cultivation in the district had been increased 400 percent.

And more than the grass came back.

Emil Stahl tightened his grip on the reins automatically every time his horse neared a certain spot in a cedar-infested pasture on his Albert farm. The ground was soft and damp there, and his horse would inevitably shy. Stahl had never thought much about it; the pasture had been covered with cedar for at least forty years that he could remember, and, anyway, the ground was too dry for growing or grazing. In 1938, however, he participated in what the Hill Country was coming to call the "cedar eradication program," and the acreage he cleared was the pasture around the soft spot. Within weeks after the cedar—and its voracious, moisture-gulping roots— had been chopped down, a spring broke through the soil on that spot, flow- ing faster and faster, with clear, cool water for his cattle. That year there was a nine-month drought in the Hill Country. All during those nine months, the spring kept his cattle alive. It never dried up.

As more and more brush was cut down, and more and more roots with- ered away, and no longer sucked water out of the ground, other farmers had experiences similar to Stahl's. Warren Smith's ranch contained a whole sec- tion that was, he says, "a solid cedar brake. . . . As soon as I cut the cedar, there was a stream running [through that section]. It used to be dry as dust." Scott Klett lived on a ranch near Johnson City that had been owned by his father. The man from whom his father had bought the ranch seventy years before had mentioned to him that a spring had once been there, but in seventy years it had never flowed. Klett cut the cedar—and, he told the county agent, "the spring is running now."

It had taken fifty acres of Warren Smith's ranch to support a single cow, he says. Now, he told the county agent, "I'm running a cow to fifteen acres." Al Young of Cypress Mill had been running a cow to thirty acres; now it was a cow to six acres. All over the Hill Country, there were more and more cows. The amount of cotton and other crops that the soil could produce steadily increased. The land of the Hill Country had once been lushly fertile. It would never be lush again, but after decades—generations—in which the land had been all but worthless, some of the fertility had begun to return, largely because of the efforts of one man.

He helped the Hill Country through his implementation of a score of New Deal programs. One improvement he made seems rather poignant when one remembers his father: in 1938 alone, 135 miles of paved farm-to-market roads were completed in Travis County, thanks to WPA grants Lyndon Johnson obtained; farmers were able now not only to grow more on their land, but to get produce to market before it spoiled. And roads were only one improvement. The Hill Country was soon dotted with new public works: public libraries, for example, and schools (including a new Johnson City High School, an agricultural school there, and new classroom buildings at San Marcos). Some families that had lost their homes, and were working as tenant farmers on land they had once owned, were able to buy back their land—thanks to the government-supported, low-interest loans the new Con- gressman obtained to enable them to pay out the purchase price over forty years at low interest. Lyndon Johnson didn't invent any of the programs that provided this help for a people of a section of America which so badly needed help. He just got as much out of the programs as he could. "He got more projects, and more money for his district, than anybody else," Corcoran says. By Johnson's own estimate, he got $70 million. "He was," says Corcoran, "the best Congressman for a district that *ever was*."

27

The Sad Irons

OBTAINING THE FINANCING and the authorization for the four dams being built along the Lower Colorado had been difficult. Now Lyndon Johnson undertook a task more difficult still. By ensuring completion of the dams, he had ensured the creation of electric power, which would be generated by the fall of water through dam penstocks. Now he was going to try to get the power to the people. He was going to try to bring electricity to the Hill Country.

Electricity had, of course, been an integral part of life in urban and much of small-town America for a generation and more, lighting its streets, powering the machinery of its factories, running its streetcars and trolleys, its elevated trains and subways, moving elevators and escalators in its stores, and cooling the stores with electric fans. Devices such as electric irons and toasters (which were in widespread use by 1900), refrigerators (which were widely sold beginning in 1912), and vacuum cleaners, dishwashers, hot plates, waffle irons, electric stoves and automatic washing machines for clothes had freed women from much of the drudgery of housework. In the evenings, thanks to electricity, there were the movies, and by 1922, forests of radio antennae had sprouted on tenement roofs. By 1937, when Lyndon Johnson went to Congress, electricity was so integral a part of life that it was hard to remember what life had been like without it.

It was not a part of life in the Hill Country. In Lyndon Johnson's congressional district, the sole source of power had been Texas Power & Light, a subsidiary of the New York–based utility holding giant, Electric Bond & Share. TP&L had, in 1927, agreed to "electrify" a handful of Hill Country towns (Johnson City was one), but not with power from its central generating station at Marble Falls; according to TP&L, which put the cost of building electric lines at $3,000 per mile, the limited use such small communities would make of electric power would never justify the investment required to build lines across the wide spaces of the Edwards Plateau. The TP&L "power plant" in each of these towns was, therefore, no more than a single thirty-horsepower diesel engine; it generated only enough voltage for ten-watt bulbs, which were constantly dimming and flickering—and which could not be used at all if an electric appliance (even an electric iron) was also in use. Since the "power plant" operated only between "dark to midnight," a refrigerator was useless. To most of the residents in these towns, such problems were academic: so high were TP&L's rates that few families hooked up to its lines. And in any case, the diesel engine was constantly breaking down under the strain placed on it. On the rare occasions on which a movie was shown, there was as much suspense in the audience over whether the electricity would hold out to the end of the film as there was in the film itself. Recalls Lucille O'Donnell of Burnet: "I'd be watching *The Perils of Pauline* and I'd just be about to see whether or not the train was going to run over her and the lights would go out." And the residents of these towns were the only inhabitants of the Hill Country with any electricity at all. TP&L refused even to consider building lines to the area's tens of thousands of individual farms and ranches.

As a result, although the electric milking machine had been invented almost two decades before, the Hill Country farmer had to milk his cows by hand—arising at three-thirty or four o'clock in the morning to do so, because milking was a time-consuming chore (more than two hours for twenty cows) and it had to be finished by daylight: every hour of daylight was needed for work in the fields. Milking was done by the dim light of kerosene lanterns; although Sears, Roebuck was boasting in 1937 that a new, deluxe kerosene lamp provided as much illumination as a forty-watt electric bulb, the lamps in use in the Hill Country furnished—at most—twenty-five watts of light. Or it was done in the dark. And there was a constant danger of fire with kerosene lamps, and even a spark could burn down a hay-filled barn, and destroy a farmer's last chance of holding on to his place, so many farmers were afraid to use a lantern in the barn. "Winter mornings," recalls one, "it would be so dark . . . you'd think you were in a box with the lid shut." Because without electricity there could be no refrigerator, the milk was kept on ice. The ice was expensive and farmers had to lug it from town at enormous cost in time. Though they kept it underground—covered with sawdust—it still, as farmer Chester Franklin of Wimberley puts it, "melted away so quick." And often even the ice didn't help. Farmers would have to take the milk out of their pit and place it by the roadside to be picked up by the trucks from Austin dairies, but often—on those unpaved Hill Country roads on which flat tires were a constant occurrence—the trucks would be late, and the milk would sit outside in the Hill Country heat. Even if it was not actually spoiled, the dairy would refuse to accept it if its temperature was above fifty degrees Fahrenheit—and when the truck driver pulled his thermometer out of the milk, a farmer, seeing the red line above fifty, would know that his hours of work in the barn in the dark had been for nothing.

Because there was no electricity, moreover, a Hill Country farmer could not use an electric pump. He was forced not only to milk but to water his cows by hand, a chore that, in dry weather, meant hauling up endless buckets from a deep well. Because he could not use an electric auger, he had to feed his livestock by hand, pitchforking heavy loads of hay up into the loft of his barn and then stomping on it to soften it enough so the cows could eat it. He had to prepare the feed by hand: because he could not use an electric grinder, he would get the corn kernels for his mules and horses by sticking ears of corn—hundreds of ears of corn—one by one into a corn sheller and cranking it for hours. Because he could not use electric motors, he had to unload cotton seed by hand, and then shovel it into the barn by hand; to saw wood by hand, by swinging an axe or riding one end of a rip-saw. Because there was never enough daylight for all the jobs that had to be done, the farmer usually finished after sunset, ending the day as he had begun it, stumbling around the barn milking the cows in the dark, as farmers had done centuries before.

But the hardness of the farmer's life paled beside the hardness of his wife's.

Without electricity, even boiling water was work.

Anything which required the use of water was work. Windmills (which could, acting like a pump, bring water out of a well into a storage tank) were very rare in the Hill Country; their cost—almost $400 in 1937—was out of the reach of most families in that cash-poor region, and the few that had been built proved of little use in a region where winds were always uncertain and, during a drought, non-existent, for days, or weeks, on end. And without electricity to work a pump, there was only one way to obtain water: by hand.

The source of water could be either a stream or a well. If the source was a stream, water had to be carried from it to the house, and since, in a country subject to constant flooding, houses were built well away from the streams, it had to be carried a long way. If the source was a well, it had to be lifted to the surface—a bucket at a time. It had to be lifted quite a long way: while the average depth of a well was about fifty feet in the valleys of the Hill Country, in the hills it was a hundred feet or more.

And so much water was needed! A federal study of nearly half a million farm families even then being conducted would show that, on the average, a person living on a farm used 40 gallons of water every day. Since the average farm family was five persons, the family used 200 gallons, or four-fifths of a ton, of water each day—73,000 gallons, or almost 300 tons, in a year. The study showed that, on the average, the well was located 253 feet from the house—and that to pump by hand and carry to the house 73,000 gallons of water a year would require someone to put in during that year 63 eight-hour days, and walk 1,750 miles.

A farmer would do as much of this pumping and hauling as possible himself, and try to have his sons do as much of the rest as possible (it was Lyndon Johnson's adamant refusal to help his mother with the pumping and hauling that touched off the most bitter of the flareups with his father during his youth). As soon as a Hill Country youth got big enough to carry the water buckets (which held about four gallons, or thirty-two pounds, of water apiece), he was assigned the job of filling his mother's wash pots before he left for school or the field. Curtis Cox still recalls today that from the age of nine or ten, he would, every morning throughout the rest of his boyhood, make about seven trips between his house and the well, which were about 300 feet apart, on each of these trips carrying two large buckets, or more than sixty pounds, of water. "I felt tired," he says. "It was a lot of water." But the water the children carried would be used up long before noon, and the children would be away—at school or in the fields—and most of the hauling of water was, therefore, done by women. "I would," recalls Curtis' mother, Mary Cox, "have to get it, too—more than once a day, more than twice; oh, I don't know how many times. I needed water to wash my floors, water to wash my clothes, water to cook. . . . It was hard work. I was always packing [carrying] water." Carrying it—after she had wrestled off the heavy wooden lid which kept the rats and squirrels out of the well; after she had cranked the bucket up to the surface (and cranking—lifting thirty pounds fifty feet or more—was very hard for most women even with a pulley; most would pull the rope hand over hand, as if they were climbing it, to get their body weight into the effort; they couldn't do it with their arms alone). Some Hill Country women make wry jokes about getting water. Says Mrs. Brian Smith of Blanco: "Yes, we had running water. I always said we had running water because I grabbed those two buckets up and ran the two hundred yards to the house with them." But the joking fades away as the memories sharpen. An interviewer from the city is struck by the fact that Hill Country women of the older generation are noticeably stooped, much more so than city women of the same age. Without his asking for an explanation, it is given to him. More than once, and more than twice, a stooped and bent Hill Country farm wife says, "You see how round-shouldered I am? Well, that's from hauling the water." And, she will often add, "I was round-shouldered like this well before my time, when I was still a young woman. My back got bent from hauling the water, and it got bent when I was still young."

The Hill Country farm wife had to haul water, and she had to haul wood.

Because there was no electricity, Hill Country stoves were wood stoves. The spread of the cedar brakes had given the area a plentiful supply of wood, but cedar seared bone-dry by the Hill Country sun burned so fast that the stoves seemed to devour it. A farmer would try to keep a supply of wood in the house, or, if he had sons old enough, would assign the task to them. (Lyndon Johnson's refusal to chop wood for his mother was another source of the tension between him and Sam.) They would cut down the trees, and chop them into four-foot lengths that could be stacked in cords. When wood was needed in the house, they would cut it into shorter lengths and split the pieces so they could fit into the stoves. But as with the water, these chores often fell to the women.

The necessity of hauling the wood was not, however, the principal reason so many farm wives hated their wood stoves. In part, they hated these stoves because they were so hard to "start up." The damper that opened into the firebox created only a small draft even on a breezy day, and on a windless day, there was no draft—because there was no electricity, of course, there was no fan to move the air in the kitchen—and a fire would flicker out time after time. "With an electric stove, you just turn on a switch and you have heat," says Lucille O'Donnell, but with a wood stove, a woman might have to stuff kindling and wood into the firebox over and over again. And even after the fire was lit, the stove "didn't heat up in a minute, you know," Lucille O'Donnell says—it might in fact take an hour. In part, farm wives hated wood stoves because they were so dirty, because the smoke from the wood blackened walls and ceilings, and ashes were always escaping through the grating, and the ash box had to be emptied twice a day—a dirty job and dirtier if, while the ashes were being carried outside, a gust of wind scattered them around inside the house. They hated the stoves because they could not be left unattended. Without devices to regulate the heat and keep the temperature steady, when the stove was being used for baking or some other cooking in which an even temperature was important, a woman would have to keep a constant watch on the fire, thrusting logs—or corncobs, which ignited quickly—into the firebox every time the heat slackened.

Most of all, they hated them because they were so hot.

When the big iron stove was lit, logs blazing in its firebox, flames licking at the gratings that held the pots, the whole huge mass of metal so hot that it was almost glowing, the air in the kitchen shimmered with the heat pouring out of it. In the Winter the heat was welcome, and in Spring and Fall it was bearable, but in the Hill Country, Summer would often last five months. Some time in June the temperature might climb to near ninety degrees, and would stay there, day after day, week after week, through the end of September. Day after day, week after week, the sky would be mostly empty, without a cloud as a shield from the blazing sun that beat down on the Hill Country, and on the sheet-iron or corrugated tin roofs of the boxlike kitchens in the little dog-run homes that dotted its hills and valleys. No matter how hot the day, the stove had to be lit much of the time, because it had to be lit not only for meals but for baking; Hill Country wives, unable to afford store-bought bread, baked their own, an all-day task. (As Mrs. O'Donnell points out, "We didn't have refrigerators, you know, and without refrigerators, you just about have to start every meal from scratch.") In the Hill Country, moreover, Summer was harvest time, when a farm wife would have to cook not just for her family but for a harvesting crew—twenty or thirty men, who, working from sun to sun, expected three meals a day.

Harvest time, and canning time.

In the Hill Country, canning was required for a family's very survival. Too poor to buy food, most Hill Country families lived through the Winter largely on the vegetables and fruit picked in the Summer and preserved in jars.

Since—because there was no electricity—there were no refrigerators in the Hill Country, vegetables or fruit had to be canned the very day they came ripe. And, from June through September, something was coming ripe almost every day, it seemed; on a single peach tree, the fruit on different branches would come ripe on different days. In a single orchard, the peaches might be reaching ripeness over a span as long as two weeks; "You'd be in the kitchen with the peaches for two weeks," Hill Country wives recall. And after the peaches, the strawberries would begin coming ripe, and then the gooseberries, and then the blueberries. The tomatoes would become ripe before the okra, the okra before the zucchini, the zucchini before the corn. So the canning would go on with only brief intervals—all Summer.

Canning required constant attendance on the stove. Since boiling water was essential, the fire in the stove had to be kept roaring hot, so logs had to be continually put into the firebox. At least twice during a day's canning, moreover—probably three or four times—a woman would have to empty the ash container, which meant wrestling the heavy, unwieldy device out from under the firebox. And when the housewife wasn't bending down to the flames, she was standing over them. In canning fruit, for example, first sugar was dropped into the huge iron canning pot, and watched carefully and stirred constantly, so that it would not become lumpy, until it was completely dissolved. Then the fruit—perhaps peaches, which would have been peeled earlier—was put in the pot, and boiled until it turned into a soft and mushy jam that would be packed into jars (which would have been boiling—to sterilize them—in another pot) and sealed with wax. Boiling the peaches would take more than an hour, and during that time they had to be stirred constantly so that they would not stick to the pot. And when one load of peaches was finished, another load would be put in, and another. Canning was an all-day job. So when a woman was canning, she would have to spend all day in a little room with a tin or sheet-iron roof on which a blazing sun was beating down without mercy, standing in front of the iron stove and the wood fire within it. And every time the heat in that stove died down even a bit, she would have to make it hotter again.

"You'd have to can in the Summer when it was hot," says Kitty Clyde Ross Leonard, who had been Johnson's first girlfriend. "You'd have to cook for hours. Oh, that was a terrible thing. You wore as little as you could. I wore loose clothing so that it wouldn't stick to me. But the perspiration would just pour down my face. I remember the perspiration pouring down my mother's face, and when I grew up and had my own family, it poured down mine. That stove was so hot. But you had to stir, especially when you were making jelly. So you had to stand over that stove." Says Bernice Snodgrass of Wimberley: "You got so hot that you couldn't stay in the house. You ran out and sat under the trees. I couldn't stand it to stay in the house. Terrible. Really terrible. But you couldn't stay out of the house long. You had to stir. You had to watch the fire. So you had to go back into the house."

And there was no respite. If a bunch of peaches came ripe a certain day, that was the day they had to be canned—no matter how the housewife might feel that day. Because in that fierce Hill Country heat, fruit and vegetables spoiled very quickly. And once the canning process was begun, it could not stop. "If you peeled six dozen peaches, and then, later that day, you felt sick," you couldn't stop, says Gay Harris. "Because you can't can something if it's rotten. The job has to be done the same day, no matter what." Sick or not, in the Hill Country, when it was time to can, a woman canned, standing hour after hour, trapped between a blazing sun and a blazing wood fire. "We had no choice, you see," Mrs. Harris says.

EVERY WEEK, every week all year long—every week without fail—there was washday.

The wash was done outside. A huge vat of boiling water would be suspended over a larger, roaring fire and near it three large "Number Three" zinc washtubs and a dishpan would be placed on a bench.

The clothes would be scrubbed in the first of the zinc tubs, scrubbed on a washboard by a woman bending over the tub. The soap, since she couldn't afford store-bought soap, was soap she had made from lye, soap that was not very effective, and the water was hard. Getting farm dirt out of clothes required hard scrubbing.

Then the farm wife would wring out each piece of clothing to remove from it as much as possible of the dirty water, and put it in the big vat of boiling water. Since the scrubbing would not have removed all of the dirt, she would try to get the rest out by "punching" the clothes in the vat—standing over the boiling water and using a wooden paddle or, more often, a broomstick, to stir the clothes and swish them through the water and press them against the bottom or sides, moving the broom handle up and down and around as hard as she could for ten or fifteen minutes in a human imitation of the agitator of an automatic—electric—washing machine.

The next step was to transfer the clothes from the boiling water to the second of the three zinc washtubs: the "rinse tub." The clothes were lifted out of the big vat on the end of the broomstick, and held up on the end of the stick for a few minutes while the dirty water dripped out.

When the clothes were in the rinse tub, the woman bent over the tub and rinsed them, by swishing each individual item through the water. Then she wrung out the clothes, to get as much of the dirty water out as possible, and placed the clothes in the third tub, which contained bluing, and swished them around in *it*—this time to get the bluing all through the garment and make it white—and then repeated the same movements in the dishpan, which was filled with starch.

At this point, one load of wash would be done. A week's wash took at least four loads: one of sheets, one of shirts and other white clothing, one of colored clothes and one of dish towels. But for the typical, large, Hill Country farm family, two loads of each of these categories would be required, so the procedure would have to be repeated eight times.

For each load, moreover, the water in each of the three washtubs would have to be changed. A washtub held about eight gallons. Since the water had to be warm, the woman would fill each tub half with boiling water from the big pot and half with cold water. She did the filling with a bucket which held three or four gallons—twenty-five or thirty pounds. For the first load or two of wash, the water would have been provided by her husband or her sons. But after this water had been used up, part of washday was walking—over and over—that long walk to the spring or well, hauling up the water, hand over laborious hand, and carrying those heavy buckets back.* Another part of washday was also a physical effort: the "punching" of the clothes in the big vat. "You had to do it as hard as you could—swish those clothes around and around and around. They never seemed to get clean. And those clothes were heavy in the water, and it was hot outside, and you'd be standing over that boiling water and that big fire—you felt like you were being roasted alive." Lifting the clothes out of the vat was an effort, too. A dripping mass of soggy clothes was heavy, and it felt heavier when it had to be lifted out of that vat and held up for minutes at a time so that the dirty water could drip out, and then swung over to the rinsing tub. Soon, if her children weren't around to hear her, a woman would be grunting with the effort. Even the wringing was, after a few hours, an effort. "I mean, wringing clothes might not seem hard," Mrs. Harris says. "But you have to wring every piece so many times—you wring it after you take it out of the scrub tub, and you wring it after you take it out of the rinse tub, and after you take it out of the bluing. Your arms got tired." And her hands —from scrubbing with lye soap and wringing—were raw and swollen. Of course, there was also the bending—hours of bending—over the rub boards. "By the time you got done washing, your back was broke," Ava Cox says. "I'll tell you—of the things of my life that I will never forget, I will never forget how much my back hurt on washdays." Hauling the water,

* Because so much water was required in washing, the introduction of a gas-operated washing machine by the Maytag Company in 1935 did not help the farm wife much, even if she could afford to buy it, which most Hill Country wives could not: she still had to fill and refill the machine with water.

scrubbing, punching, rinsing: a Hill Country farm wife did this for hours on end—while a city wife did it by pressing the button on her electric washing machine.

WASHDAY WAS MONDAY. Tuesday was for ironing.

Says Mary Cox, in words echoed by all elderly Hill Country farm wives: "Washing was hard work, but ironing was the worst. Nothing could ever be as hard as ironing."

The Department of Agriculture finds that "Young women today are not aware of the origin of the word 'iron,' as they press clothes with light-weight appliances of aluminum or hollow stainless steel." In the Hill Country, in the 1930's an iron was *iron*—a six- or seven-pound wedge of iron. The irons used in the Hill Country had to be heated on the wood stove, and they would retain their heat for only a few minutes—a man's shirt generally required two irons; a farm wife would own three or four of them, so that several could be heating while one was working. An iron with a wooden handle cost two dollars more than one without the handle, so Hill Country wives did their weekly loads of ironing—huge loads because, as Mary Cox puts it, "in those days you were expected to starch and iron almost every-thing"—with irons without handles. They would either transfer a separate wooden handle from one iron to another, or they would protect their hands with a thick potholder.

Since burning wood generates soot, the irons became dirty as they sat heating on the stove. Or, if any moisture was left on an iron from the sprinkled clothes on which it had just been used, even the thinnest smoke from the stove created a muddy film on the bottom. The irons had to be cleaned frequently, therefore, by scrubbing them with a rag that had been dipped in salt, and if the soot was too thick, they had to be sanded and scraped. And no matter how carefully you checked the bottom of the irons, and sanded and scraped them, there would often remain some little spot of soot—as you would discover when you rubbed it over a clean white shirt or dress. Then you had to wash that item of clothing over again.

Nevertheless, the irons would burn a woman's hand. The wooden handle or the potholder would slip, and she would have searing metal against her flesh; by noon, she might have blister atop blister—on hands that had to handle the rag that had been dipped in salt. Ironing always took a full day—often it went on into Tuesday evening—and a full day of lifting and carrying six- or seven-pound loads was hard on even these hardy Hill Country women. "It would hurt so bad between the shoulders," Elsie Beck remembers. But again the worst aspect of ironing was the heat. On ironing day, a fire would have to be blazing in the wood stove all day, filling the kitchen, hour after hour, with heat and smoke. Ironing had to be done not only in the Winter but in the Summer—when the temperature outside the kitchen might be ninety or ninety-five or one hundred, and inside the kitchen would be considerably higher, and because there was no electricity, there was no fan to so much as stir the air. In a speech in Congress some years later, Representative John E. Rankin described the "drudgery" a typical farm wife endured, "burning up in a hot kitchen and bowing down over the washtub or boiling the clothes over a flaming fire in the summer heat." He himself remembered, he said, "seeing his mother lean over that hot iron hour after hour until it seemed she was tired enough to drop." Rankin was from Mississippi, but his description would have been familiar to the mothers of the Edwards Plateau. The women of the Hill Country never called the instruments they used every Tuesday "irons," they called them "sad irons."

Washing, ironing—those were chores that were performed every week. Then, of course, there were special occasions—harvest time and threshing time, when a woman had to cook not just for her family but for a crew of twenty or thirty men; the shearing, when, because there was no electricity and her husband had to work the shears, she had to crank the shearing machine, pedaling as if she were pumping a bicycle up a steep hill, pedaling, with only brief pauses, hour after hour; "He was always yelling 'Faster, faster,' Mrs. Walter Yett of Blanco recalls. "I could hardly get up the next morning, I was so tired after that." Washing, ironing, cooking, canning, shearing, helping with the plowing and the picking and the sowing, and, every day, carrying the water and the wood, and because there was no electricity, having to do everything by hand by the same methods that had been employed by her mother and grandmother and great-great-great-grandmother before her—"They wear these farm women out pretty fast," wrote one observer. In the Hill Country, as many outside observers noted, the one almost universal characteristic of the women was that they were worn out before their time, that they were old beyond their years, old at forty, old at thirty-five, bent and stooped and tired.

A Hill Country farm wife had to do her chores even if she was ill—no matter how ill. Because Hill Country women were too poor to afford proper medical care, they often suffered perineal tears in childbirth. During the 1930's, the federal government sent physicians to examine a sampling of Hill Country women. The doctors found that, out of 275 women, 158 had perineal tears. Many of them, the team of gynecologists reported, were third-degree tears, "tears so bad that it is difficult to see how they stand on their feet." But they *were* standing on their feet, and doing all the chores that Hill Country wives had always done—hauling the water, hauling the wood, canning, washing, ironing, helping with the shearing, the plowing and the picking.

Because there was no electricity.

· · ·

THE LACK OF ELECTRICITY meant that the days of the people of the Hill
Country were filled with drudgery; at night they were denied the entertainment—movies, radio—that would have made the drudgery more bearable.
The radio could, moreover, have ended the area's isolation. The feeling of
the Hill Country youngsters of the 1920's—Lyndon Johnson's generation—
that "we were completely cut off out here," that "we were back in the woods,
compared to the rest of the world," that "everything had already happened
before we found out about it," was the feeling of the 1930's generation as
well. Because there was no electricity, the only radios in the Hill Country
were the occasional crystal sets with earphones and poor reception. Amos
'n' Andy, Lum 'n' Abner, Ma Perkins—theirs were voices familiar to most
of America; it was a rare inhabitant of the Edwards Plateau who had heard
them even once. "What we missed most was the fireside chats," says Mary
Cox. "I mean, we loved Franklin D. Roosevelt in this country, and we kept
reading about these wonderful fireside chats. But we never got to hear them."

Even reading was hard.

Evening was often the only time in which Hill Country farm couples
could read ("There was no other time," says Lucille O'Donnell. "There was
never a minute to read during the day, it seemed"), but the only light for
reading came from kerosene lamps. In movies about the Old West, these
lamps appear so homy that it is difficult for a city dweller to appreciate how
much—and why—some farm dwellers disliked them so passionately.

Lighting the kerosene lamp was a frustrating job. "You had to adjust the
wick just right," says Curtis Cox of Bryan. "If you turned it too high, it
would flame up and start to smoke. The chimney—that's the glass part—
would get all black, and your eyes would start to smart." Keeping it lit was
even more frustrating. It burned straight across for only a moment, and
then would either flare up or die down to an inadequate level. Even when
the wick was trimmed just right, a kerosene lamp provided only limited
illumination. The approximately twenty-five watts of light provided by most
such lamps was adequate for children doing their homework—although sur-
veys would later find that the educational level of rural children improved
markedly immediately upon the introduction of electricity—but their parents, whose eyes were not so strong, had more difficulty. Mary Cox says that
she couldn't read with their lamp for more than a short period: "I always
loved to read," she recalls. "But I couldn't enjoy it on the farm. It was hard
on the eyes, a strain on the eyes. I had to force myself to read at night." Lucille O'Donnell came to Burnet from Virginia, where she had liked to read
in bed; she couldn't do that on her farm, she says, because she couldn't
afford the kerosene. When she did read at night, she couldn't read in bed.
Her husband, Tom, "would be asleep," she recalls, "and I would put the
lamp beside him on the bed, and sit on that little stool and read in the most
awkward position." Pointing to deep vertical lines between her eyebrows,

more than one Hill Country farm wife says: "So many of us have these lines from squinting to read."

The circle of light cast by a kerosene lamp was small, and there were seldom enough lamps in the home of an impoverished farm family. If a family had so many children that they completely surrounded the one good lamp while studying, their mother could not do her sewing until they were finished. And outside the small circles of light, the rooms of a farmhouse were dark. "The house looked scary," says Mary Cox. "If I was alone at night, it was awfully lonely." And, of course, there were no lamps in the outhouse. Many a Hill Country farm wife echoes the words of Betty Mac-Donald: "I had a horrible choice of either sitting in the dark and not knowing what was crawling on me or bringing a lantern and attracting moths, mosquitoes, nighthawks and bats."

NO RADIO; no movies; limited reading—little diversion between the hard day just past and the hard day just ahead. "Living was just drudgery then," says Carroll Smith of Blanco. "Living—just *living*—was a problem. No lights. No plumbing. Nothing. Just living on the edge of starvation. That was farm life for us. God, city people think there was something fine about it. If they only knew . . ."

So many conveniences taken for granted in American cities were unknown on the Edwards Plateau: not just vacuum cleaners and washing machines but, for example, bathrooms, since, as a practical matter, indoor plumbing is unfeasible without running water, which requires an electric pump. In the Summer, bathing could be done in the creek (when the creek wasn't dry); in the Winter, it entailed lugging in water and heating it on the stove (which entailed lugging in wood) before pouring it into a Number Three washtub. Because bathing was so hard, "you bathed about once a week," Bernice Snodgrass says. Children went barefoot, so "we'd make them wash their feet [at the pump outside] you know. We [adults] would wash our face and hands and ears in washpans but we didn't take a bath but once a week." There were few toilets, and most Hill Country outhouses were the most primitive sort. Many had no pit dug under them. "It would just drop on the ground," Guthrie Taylor recalls. "No, it wouldn't be cleared away"; every so often the flimsy little shelter would just be moved to another spot. Since toilet paper was too expensive, pages from a Sears, Roebuck catalogue, or corncobs, were used. And some families did not have outhouses. When the Snodgrasses moved to Mount Gaynor from Austin, Bernice Snodgrass says, "We were the only people in the neighborhood that had one. You know what everybody else did? They went out behind the barn, or behind a tree, or something." Frederick Law Olmsted had found the same situation—houses at which there was "no other water-closet than the back of a bush or the broad prairies"—on his journey through the Hill Country in 1857. He had been shocked then, because the America he knew had advanced beyond such primitive conditions. Now it was 1937; four more generations had been living in the Hill Country—with no significant advance in the conditions of their life. Many of the people of Lyndon Johnson's congressional district were still living in the same type of dwelling in which the area's people had been living in 1857: in rude "dog-run" shelters one board thick, through which the wind howled in the winter. They were still squatting behind a bush to defecate. Because of their poverty, they were still utterly bereft not only of tractors and feed grinders, but of modern medical assistance—and were farming by methods centuries out of date.

ALTHOUGH THEY UNDERSTOOD that, as Louise Casparis says, "we were behind the rest of the world," natives of the Hill Country did not realize how *far* behind the rest of the world.

How could they be expected to realize? Without many books to read—or, in general, newspapers, either, except for those pathetic four-page local weeklies; without radio to listen to, with only an occasional movie to watch—how was news of advances in the rest of the world to reach them? Since many of them never saw that world for themselves—an astonishingly high proportion of Hill Country residents would never visit even Austin or San Antonio—the Hill Country's awareness of the outside world was dim. The life of Hill Country natives was, moreover, the same life that their mothers and fathers—and grandmothers and grandfathers—had lived; how were they to know, except in general, vague, terms, that there was another kind of life? When they heard about the wonders of electricity, they thought electricity was the electricity they saw in Johnson City, the dim, flickering lights hardly better than lamplight; the wonders they imagined were the electric iron and the radio, little more; "I remember when someone started telling me about these washing machines," recalls Ava Cox. "A machine that *washed?* I couldn't picture that *at all!*" Even the concept of the toilet was difficult for them to accept completely; when Errol Snodgrass, newly arrived in Mount Gaynor, began not only to build an outhouse but to dig a pit underneath it, a neighbor asked him: "What do you want that pit for?" And when he explained, Bernice Snodgrass recalls, the reaction of the neighborhood was, " 'They're so highfalutin that they have to have a toilet.' They thought an outhouse with a pit under it—they thought that that was what people meant when they spoke about a toilet!" Natives of the Hill Country couldn't understand why families that had moved away from the Hill Country never returned. It is not, therefore, by lifelong residents of the Hill Country that the contrast between life there and in the outside world is most clearly enunciated, but by newcomers: from families which, due to economic necessity, moved to the Hill Country in the 1930's.

The Depression had cost Brian and Mary Sue Smith their home and their once-profitable automobile-repair shop in Portland, Texas, a town near Corpus Christi. In 1937, they moved with their three children to the Hill Country—to a fifty-three-acre farm near Blanco—because "that was the only place where land was cheap enough so we could buy a farm."

Portland had electricity—had had it for years. "You never even thought about electricity," Mrs. Smith says. "I just accepted it. I mean, if I thought about it, I suppose I would have thought, 'Doesn't *everyone* have electricity?'"

Now she found out that not everyone did.

The Smiths had brought their radio, a big black Atwater Kent with an amplifying horn on top, to their new home, but it could not be played. "You know, it was very lonely on that farm," Mrs. Smith says. "The quiet was nice sometimes. But sometimes it was so quiet it hurt you." They had brought their washing machine, but that could not work, either. Mrs. Smith loved to read, but "The light was hard on your eyes. My eyes just weren't good enough to read at night." In Portland, she had crocheted at night, but she found the light was too dim for her to do that at night. And, of course, there was no time to do it during the day; what time wasn't consumed by her household chores was taken up husking, shelling and grinding corn by hand for feed for the 150 hens whose eggs she was selling; by cranking the sheep-shearing machine. Soon after she arrived on the farm, her husband became very ill, and for more than a year she had to care for the livestock too, and to plow behind a pair of mules—although she had never plowed before. "Up before daylight. Build the fire in the wood range. Put on the biscuits. Go out and milk the cows. Breakfast. Work was all there was. It was a bare existence."

Getting the water, from a well some 200 yards from the house, was the chore that bothered her most. "The children had had running water in Portland, of course, and they acted like they still had it," she says. When she started meeting other Hill Country women, she noticed that many of them were round-shouldered, and they told her it was from carrying heavy buckets of water. She didn't want to be round-shouldered. But there seemed no solution. "Carry and carry. Back and forth. Sometimes I would get awfully discouraged. When I first moved there [to the Hill Country], I felt like a pioneer lady, like one of the women who had come here in covered wagons. I said, if they could do it, I could, too. But it was very hard. After you spent all morning lugging those big buckets back and forth, you felt more like an ox or a mule than a human being. Portland was just a little town. It was no great metropolis. But moving from Portland into the Hill Country was like moving from the twentieth century back into the Middle Ages."

28

"I'll Get It for You"

As LATE AS 1935, farmers had been denied electricity not only in the Hill Country but throughout the United States. In that year, more than 6 million of America's 6.8 million farms did not have electricity. Decades after electric power had become part of urban life, the wood range, the washtub, the sad iron and the dim kerosene lamp were still the way of life for almost 90 percent of the 30 million Americans who lived in the countryside. All across the United States, wrote a public-power advocate, "Every city 'white way' ends abruptly at the city limits. Beyond lies darkness." The lack of electric power, wrote the historian William E. Leuchtenberg, had divided the United States into two nations: "the city dwellers and the country folk"; farmers, he wrote, "toiled in a nineteenth-century world; farm wives, who enviously eyed pictures in the *Saturday Evening Post* of city women with washing machines, refrigerators, and vacuum cleaners, performed their backbreaking chores like peasant women in a preindustrial age."

For two decades and more, in states all across the country, delegations of farmers, dressed in Sunday shirts washed by hand and ironed by sad iron, had come, hats literally in hand, to the paneled offices of utility-company executives to ask to be allowed to enter the age of electricity. They came in delegations, and they came alone—an oft-repeated scene was that of the husband whose wife had been taken seriously ill, and who had been told by the doctor that she could no longer do heavy work, begging the "power company" in vain to extend electricity to his farm; an Arkansas rural leader, "Uncle John" Hobbs, would, even years later, begin to cry remembering the day "he pleaded with the Arkansas Power & Light Company in vain to build a line to his home, a short distance from one of their lines, when his wife was ill and desperately needed the help electricity could provide." But in delegations or alone, the answer they received was almost invariably the same: that it was too expensive—as much as $5,000 per mile, the utilities said—to build lines to individual farms; that even if the lines were built, farmers would use little electricity because they couldn't afford to buy electrical appliances; that farmers wouldn't even be able to pay their monthly electricity bills, since, due to low usage, farm rates would have to be higher —more than two times higher, in fact—than rates in urban areas.

Studies had long disproved the utilities' figures. A 1925 survey in Wisconsin found that the cost of lines would be not $5,000 but $1,225 per mile. As for the argument that farmers wouldn't pay their bills, as Clyde Ellis, then a young spellbinder in the Arkansas Legislature, was to comment bitterly, "There may have been an element of truth in this, considering the exorbitant rates the companies quoted." Why, rural leaders such as Hobbs and Ellis demanded, wouldn't the power industry learn from Henry Ford, who had proved that the cheaper you make a good commodity, the higher will be your returns; if the power companies kept farm rates low, farmers would buy more electricity. If they kept rates high, the effect would be an endless circle: farmers would use little power because of high rates, and utilities would continue charging high rates because of low usage. Experiments—notable ones had taken place in Red Wing, Minnesota, and in Alabama—had conclusively proved that within two or three years after farmers had obtained electricity and seen the savings possible from its use (the increased value of their milk and eggs once spoilage was reduced by refrigeration paid many times over for the cost of using refrigerators), their usage of electricity soared—to a point where there was substantial profit for the utilities.

When the utilities ignored these studies their true attitude became clear: not that rural electric service could not be profitable, but that it would not be as profitable as urban service. Or as surefire. Waiting two or three years for usage to build up was what industry called a "capital risk"; why take a risk for a profit when there existed, in the urban market, profit without risk? "It hardly seems fair that the farm wife had to wait for electricity so much longer than her counterpart in the city for she needed electricity much more," an historian was to write. But fairness—or social conscience—was not the operative criterion for the utilities; their criterion was rate of return on investment. As long as the rate was higher in the cities, they felt, why bother with the farms? Their attitude was reinforced not only by their political power but by their contempt for country people. Whenever the utilities' mask was stripped away, the arrogance showed through. Alabama Power & Light refused to reduce its rates more than a token amount even after it was allowed to buy electricity at a very low cost from the government-owned dam at Muscle Shoals. When a farmer offered to pay the cost of building a power line to his house, the utilities said they would allow him to do so—but that when it was built, they, not he, would own it. Their policies were quite firm, because they did not want to establish any precedent that might be used as an argument against them. If they once began to lower rates, who knew where such reductions might lead? If they once began to extend lines into rural areas, there would be no end to the demands for more extensions. So no exceptions were permitted. In Lyndon Johnson's own district, Texas Power & Light policy governing the one electric line permitted only farms within fifty yards of the line to hook up to it. Several scores of farmhouses were near the line, but farther away than fifty yards. Some were not much farther away, and these farmers offered to pay the additional cost involved. TP&L was quite firm in its refusals to allow them to do so; if the company made an exception for one farmer, it was explained, it might have to make exceptions for others in other areas of the state as well. Farmers whose homes were just beyond the fifty-yard limit, farmers who could see those lines every day of their lives, were unable to use them, while they had to watch their wives year by year slaving at tasks that electricity would have made so much easier. Some of these farmers, in desperation, said they would move their houses so that they would be within fifty yards. TP&L said that it still would not hook them up. Moving houses would set a precedent, a company spokesman explained: Who knew how many farmers would try to move houses near electricity? Where would it all end?

ATTEMPTS TO UTILIZE GOVERNMENT to bring electricity to America's farms had begun decades before, fueled by the argument that most of America's power was hydroelectric, generated by the water of its rivers; that this power was, therefore, a natural resource; and that such a resource belongs to the people as a whole, and not to any vested interest. As John Gunther was to ask: "Who and what should own a river, if not the people as a whole?" But these attempts had been stymied by the powerful utilities lobby and by the Republican Party which embodied its principles. Much of the battle had centered on the 40,000-square-mile valley of the Tennessee River, because during World War I the government had built there, at Muscle Shoals in Alabama, a dam to produce the power required for the production of the synthetic nitrates used in explosives. The dam, with its associated factories, cost a total of $145 million, and after the war the question arose as to who was to get the permanent benefits of this government investment: private utilities or the valley's impoverished inhabitants, of whom only two in a hundred had electricity. All through the Twenties, Senator George W. Norris of Nebraska fought to keep Muscle Shoals from being transferred to private ownership. Twice he had guided legislation authorizing government ownership and operation through Congress, only to have one bill vetoed by Coolidge and one by Hoover, who said that the legislation was "the negation of the ideals upon which our civilization is based." All through the Twenties, therefore, the dam at Muscle Shoals remained idle, a symbol of the lack of success of all attempts to break the private monopoly of electric power in America. In 1933—as late as

March 3, 1933—attempts to give ordinary citizens some control over the power generated by their rivers had been crushed by the utility lobby.

Then came Roosevelt. The vision of men like Norris (and Roosevelt's cousin Theodore) was his vision, too. As a young State Senator twenty years before, he had been concerned with cheaper electric power. The hydroelectric power of the United States, he had said, should be developed "for the benefit of the people of the United States." As Governor, his vision had been thwarted; it was intolerable, he said, that the "stupendous heritage" of the power of the St. Lawrence River should be monopolized by utility holding companies (it was on a typed copy of a speech assailing the utilities that he scribbled a new introduction: "This is a history and a sermon on the subject of water power, and I preach from the Old Testament. The text is 'Thou Shalt Not Steal' "). He had sought to allow the people—through a state authority—to develop their own power, but the proposal was defeated by the barons who controlled the state's Republican Party and the State Legislature. His vision was, in fact, in some ways, more sweeping even than Norris'. Discussing the Tennessee Valley, he leaped from electric power to broader questions, which he saw as associated: "Is it possible?" he asked an expert on the valley, to relate the question of electric power at Muscle Shoals to the prevention of floods, to erosion, to soil conservation through retirement of marginal farmland, to reforestation, to diversification of industry, to a general improvement in the standard of life of the valley's impoverished people? During the interregnum between his election and inauguration, he and Norris visited the Tennessee Valley together. Upon Norris' return to Washington, someone asked him: "Is he really with you?" Answered the old man: "He is more than with me, because he plans to go even farther than I did." Two months after his inauguration, the Tennessee Valley Authority was created—to build twenty-one dams, and bring electricity to tens of thousands of farm families.

In 1935, the monopolization of the nation's hydroelectric power was being attacked on three fronts. Regulation of private utilities had been strengthened by revitalizing the Federal Power Commission. The Rayburn Utilities Holding Company Act had begun breaking up the giant monopolistic systems which had so tightly controlled—and limited, in the interest of profit—the production and distribution of electricity. And great government-financed dams, such as Marshall Ford and "Big Buchanan," were being built across rivers throughout the West.

Roosevelt wanted the electricity generated at these dams to be made available not to utility companies but to farmers, and to be available so inexpensively that it would "become a standard article of use . . . for every home within reach of an electric light line." On May 11, 1935, he signed an executive order establishing a Rural Electrification Administration. For a year, rural electrification went slowly, partly because of the difficulty of meeting requirements of the relief act, partly because REA Administrator Morris Cooke wanted to enlist power companies in the rural-electrification effort—and felt the lure of government loans would draw them in. For a while, Cooke was optimistic on this score. The companies agreed to form a committee to study the subject. Then the committee issued its report: farmers, it said, were already the "most-favored" class of consumers, "There are very few farms requiring electricity for major farm operations that are not now served." In January, 1936, therefore, the Roosevelt administration introduced a bill that would remove REA from the relief set-up and make it an independent agency, and that would allow it to make self-liquidating loans to cooperatives established by the farmers themselves. Provision was also made for small loans to individual families, to enable them to wire their homes and purchase appliances.

The bill, drafted by Corcoran and Cohen, was introduced in the Senate by Norris. Agriculture Chairman Marvin Jones expected to introduce it in the House. But Sam Rayburn knew that the REA measure would face bitter opposition from the power lobby that, just a year before, had almost beaten his Holding Company bill, and he very much wanted it to pass. "Can you imagine," he was to say, "what it will mean to a farm wife?" And, he told the House, there were other arguments in favor of rural electrification. "We want to make the farmer and his wife and family believe and know that they are no longer the forgotten people, but make them know that they are remembered as part of—yea, they are the bulwark of the Government." To the utility lobbyists' argument that farmers were too "unsophisticated" to organize cooperatives or handle complicated legal questions, and too poor to pay electric bills, Rayburn replied that "the lobbyists did not take into account the spirit and determination of the people who form the backbone of this nation." He felt that Jones was not tough enough to force the bill to passage. Pounding into the office of House Parliamentarian Lewis Deschler, he laid the bill on Deschler's desk. "Give it to me," he said, and left without waiting for a reply.

Rayburn was needed. Although the REA bill had sailed through the Senate, in the House, more susceptible to pressure from the utilities, there was trouble. Members of his Interstate Commerce Committee— Corcoran's "conservative sons-of-bitches" who a year earlier had gutted the Holding Company bill—objected violently to the provision that made private companies ineligible for REA loans. Hostile though he was to the power companies, Rayburn was willing to compromise on this issue; what he wanted was electricity for farmers; he didn't care who gave it to them; he felt, furthermore, that it was silly to exclude from so difficult a task as rural electrification the only organizations that had equipment and trained personnel. The bill was reported out of his committee by the margin of one vote. On the floor, Rayburn had less trouble; his quiet, terse remarks cut to the heart of an argument; to the free-enterprisers, he replied by citing statistics on Texas: "When free enterprise had the opportunity to electrify farm homes—after fifty years, they had electrified three percent," he was to say. But the speech that mattered most was one given not on the floor of the House but in a Capitol corridor—to one man.

The man was Norris. Old now—seventy-six—and somewhat rigid in his long-held views, full of hatred, moreover, for the utilities he had fought so gallantly, he was also full of pride of authorship in the REA legislation and was reluctant to agree to any changes when the House-Senate conference committee met under his chairmanship. "It was in the conference committee . . . that the real battle developed," he was to recall. "I discovered at the very first meeting I had a stubborn, embittered fight on my hands. . . . Days and weeks passed. We held many conferences, and while in those deliberations discussion always was courteous, conducted in a high moral tone, the issue was sharply joined and exceedingly bitter." Rayburn, whose efforts were chiefly responsible for maintaining the courtesy and the high moral tone, was working, member by member, point by point, to effect a workable compromise, but after weeks of meetings, he was still short of his goal. And then Norris flatly said that compromise was impossible. He would take the issue of rural electrification to the voters in the next congressional campaign, he said; he had no doubt it would be a very effective issue. "I am going to quit the conference," he said. "I will not call another meeting of the conference committee."

Rayburn had managed to get the bill out of his Interstate Commerce Committee by a single vote. If it went back to committee, he might not ever be able to get it out again. If Norris carried out his threat, rural electrification might be dead. Sam Rayburn's people didn't need a campaign issue, they needed electricity. Hurrying after Norris, he caught up to him in the hallway, and pleaded with him—Sam Rayburn who hated to ask for anything—to reconsider. "Now Senator, don't be discouraged. I think we are going to reach an agreement. After that little speech of yours, I believe we will come together. . . . Just let it rest awhile." After Rayburn had taken the edge off the old man's anger, Rankin talked to him, and Norris agreed not to quit the conference. Rayburn kept working in his quiet way. When, after some weeks, the conferees returned to the bargaining table, writes the most thorough historian of the affair, "a mood of compromise was apparent." The conflict over inclusion of the utilities was compromised by allowing them to be eligible for REA loans, but giving preference to non-profit bodies such as cooperatives. On May 11, 1936, Congress passed the new REA bill. Within the next eighteen months, electricity was brought to half a million American farms. Hundreds of thousands of other farmers were forming cooperatives so that they could get electricity, too—and rural electric rates were beginning to drop in many areas. The times were changing—and they were changing fast.

· · ·

THEY WEREN'T CHANGING for the Hill Country.

The hopes that had been raised there by the creation of the REA had been dashed when the REA announced the minimum requirements for electrification.

The REA Act required loans to be self-liquidating; before a farmers' electrical cooperative could obtain a loan, therefore, the REA had to be satisfied that the cooperative would be able to repay it, together with annual interest of about 3 percent, within twenty-five years. The crucial criterion the REA established to ensure this was population density: the agency said it would make no loan in any area in which the electrical lines to be built would serve an average of less than three farms per mile.

Even so low a figure was dangerous, critics said; not three but seven customers per mile—seven *good* customers, heavy users of electricity, not poor farmers but farmers equipped with electrical appliances—was the bare minimum necessary to repay a 3 percent loan, they said. And the REA—all too aware that failure to comply with the Act's self-liquidating provision might give congressional conservatives ammunition to use against the agency—would go no lower. Approaching the REA late in 1936, a delegation from the Hill Country was told that the three-per-mile criterion would not be waived; even the powerful Congressman Buchanan, intervening on their behalf, had been unable to persuade the new agency. Developments in other parts of Texas proved that the agency was, in fact, determined not to waive the three-per-mile minimum even for wealthy ranchers who might be expected to be heavy users of electricity: in one area of West Texas, for example, prosperous ranchers guaranteed the REA a minimum payment of seventy-five dollars per month per ranch; their application was turned down "on the ground that it could never pay out."

The REA would not even consider electrifying areas as sparsely populated as the Hill Country—because it simply could not afford to do so. The REA's first administrator, Morris Cooke, had estimated that an investment of a billion and a half dollars—a figure far beyond the agency's anticipated budget—would be necessary to bring electricity to even "fifty per cent of all rural [homes]" within ten years. As for the rest: "Of course, there are many farms which cannot be reached for many years. There are farms in neighborhoods too sparsely settled to afford power. . . ." Early in 1938, representatives of five Hill Country counties—Barnet, Blanco, Llano, Gillespie and Hays—who were planning to form a "Pedernales Electric Co-operative" met in Austin with an REA representative, Russell Cook. Cook put it to them straight: "You have too much land and not enough people." Says one of the men at the meeting: "He was just very discouraging. He said, 'You want to go [lay lines] to one of the most remote areas of the whole country. We simply can't do that. It's impossible.' "

The words were familiar to the people of the Edwards Plateau. The Plateau's implacable geography had always been too strong for men. The distances; the hilly terrain; the lack of rainfall; the rocky sparseness of the limestone soil—these forces, forces over which they had no control, had kept the population small and had condemned them, and their parents and grandparents before them to isolation and poverty. These factors had kept them from getting a railroad. Why shouldn't these same factors keep them from getting electricity? They had not been able to persuade even the People's Party—the party which had been spawned on the Plateau—to send them lecturers because they were "too thinly settled . . . away up here on the Pedernales River." Why should the New Deal be any different? New Deal programs that had helped farmers in other areas hadn't helped the Hill Country much. More important, perhaps, the New Deal had given other farmers hope. After five years of the New Deal, hope in the Hill Country was still in almost as short supply as cash. Why should REA be any different from AAA?

And then other words began to be heard in those hills.

One of the first men to whom they were spoken was a rancher named E. Babe Smith who had, by coincidence, been raised in Lampasas, birthplace of the People's Party, before moving to northeastern Burnet County, an area so isolated that it was known as "The Dark Corner of Burnet County"; Smith's grandmother had lived there for fifty-five years, and had never during that time visited even once the town of Marble Falls, forty miles away. In Lampasas, Smith had had electricity—from a diesel engine—from sunset to ten o'clock every evening ("when it wasn't breaking down"), and when in 1936, he had heard that the Rural Electrification Administration was organizing a cooperative in Bell County, and that lines would be built to Bartlett, only forty miles away from his ranch, he had gone to the Bell Co-operative office to see if the lines could be extended into his area. But, he recalls, "They said there was no way I could be served, that we were just too sparsely populated; they said, 'You're just too thin'; they said there was no hope." Smith, a slender man, six-feet-three-inches tall, a man of considerable determination—he had managed to earn a degree from Southwestern University in Georgetown—was a rancher other ranchers respected, and when the Pedernales Electric Co-operative was being organized, he was asked to join the Burnet County delegation to the PEC meeting in Johnson City. He refused, however. "I said, 'No sense my going. I been to Bartlett. No hope for me.'" His corner was the dark corner; he felt it was going to stay dark.

Then Roy Fry, a Burnet druggist and politician, asked Smith to meet with the district's new Congressman.

The meeting took place in Fry's Rexall Drug Store. The three men sat behind the prescription counter, Fry on a stool, Babe Smith and Lyndon

Johnson on packing cases; when a customer entered, Fry would interrupt the conversation to wait on him.

The Buchanan and Roy Inks dams were almost completed, and would be producing power shortly, Johnson told the two men. With REA help, that power could be brought to the dark corner. Smith demurred, the area would never get an REA loan, he said. Johnson replied: "I'll get it for you. I'll go to the REA. I'll go to the President if I have to. But *we will* get the money!" On June 20, 1938, the PEC held a second meeting, in the Courthouse in Johnson City, for county agents and community leaders. Although the 108-mile round trip took five hours because "there was not a foot of paved road between here and Johnson City," Smith went to this meeting. "Lyndon Johnson had inspired me," he says. "He had made me feel there was a chance."

DESPITE JOHNSON'S EFFORTS—"He had been talking to other people all over the area just like he had me," Babe Smith says—only sixty persons came to the PEC meeting. "And not all of them were believers," Smith says. The Gillespie County Agent, Henry Grote, delivered an angry lecture to the young Congressman, telling him that in attempting to obtain electricity for farmers, "You're not doing farmers any favor." They would not be able to pay their electric bills, would sink into debt, and would lose their farms. Other men at the meeting were not enthusiastic because of their lack of understanding of electricity's many uses on a farm. "A lot just felt it meant the light bulb and that was all," Smith says. "And they weren't sure that that was worth the expense." Even those who were in favor of electricity felt, as Smith felt, that "We cannot meet the three-to-the-mile."

Standing in front of the Judge's bench, Johnson explained that electricity could run farm equipment as well as lights. He said that if lines were laid out carefully, and every person along them was signed up, he believed that a three-per-mile average could be obtained. Most important, in Smith's words, "He inspired everyone with the feeling that there was at least a chance." If you get the people signed up, he told them, he would get the REA loan. "And he made us believe it." They agreed to try to get as many signatures as possible, and the REA-required five-dollar deposit, on applications for electric service, and on easements to allow the REA to string lines across their land.

In that sparsely populated area, these signatures had to be obtained the same way votes were obtained—one by one. And they were harder to get than votes.

The reluctance of the people sprang from simple poverty—"It cost five dollars, and a lot of people didn't have five dollars," says Guthrie Taylor. And it sprang from fear.

They were afraid of the wires. The idea of electricity—so unknown to them—terrified them. It was the same stuff as lightning; it sounded dangerous—what would happen to a child who put its hand on a wire? And what about their cows—their precious, irreplaceable few cows that represented so much of their total assets? "They were so worried," Lucille O'Donnell recalls. "They would say, 'What'll happen if there's a storm? The wires will fall down and kill [electrocute] the cattle.' " Or they were worried that the wires would attract lightning—which would kill the cattle. Or that the crews that came to repair downed lines would leave the gates open, and let their cows loose. "They simply could not afford to lose their livestock," Mrs. O'Donnell says. And they were afraid of the papers—the papers that they were being asked to sign. The people of the Hill Country were leery of lawyers: lawyers meant mortgages and foreclosures. Legal documents—documents they did not understand—turned them skittish: Who knew what hidden traps lay within them? Were they signing something that would one day allow someone to take their land away? In vain, the county agents and community leaders tried to explain to the farmers that they were not being asked to surrender control of their land. Many farmers, as one report put it, "had the idea that in signing an easement they were mortgaging their property to the U.S. Treasury." Thousands of easements were required—not only from farmers who wanted electricity but from farmers who didn't, because the lines had to cross their land—and it was difficult to persuade the farmers to give them. They were afraid of debt—terrified of debt, for in the Hill Country it was felt that once you went into debt you never got out, that once you went into debt it was only a matter of time before you lost your land. At meetings, Smith recalls, "people would say, 'How much is it going to cost to run that line to my farm?' 'Five hundred dollars.' 'You're not going to convince me that when I sign that application, I'm not going to be responsible for that five hundred dollars. You're not going to convince me that I'm not going to be putting a debt on my farm.' I tried to explain to them that this [the Pedernales Electric Co-operative] was a corporation, and that the government was going to look to the corporation to pay back, but they couldn't accept the idea of corporate responsibility." (For families so afraid of debt, the minimum monthly charge for the electricity—$2.45 for twenty-five kilowatts—was also a source of concern.)

And there was the suspicion, generations old, of a people who felt that they had been victimized by railroads and utilities. The first letter sent out on behalf of the PEC—by secretary-treasurer Hugo Klappenbach—sought to allay those suspicions in a rallying cry that might have been sounded by a lecturer of the old Farmers' Alliance. "This line is being built by the consumers it serves and they are the owners," he said. ". . . It will not try to cover up the investments it has either." The management is local people, "and does not have to wait for some group of New York financiers to grant permits or concessions." "Let's stand together and build our own electric distribution lines and then have the voice in the control." Creation of the

PEC, he said, would free the Hill Country from dependence on the Northeast: "We may see the opening up of manufacturing interests here where the raw materials are grown. Why should we continually send our wool to Boston? Why not manufacture it here or anyway . . . get it ready to spin right where it is grown?" But many Hill Country residents could not believe that they would really keep the "voice in the control." Lyndon Johnson was sitting on the porch of his cousin Ava's home one afternoon, talking about the PEC, when Ava's husband, Ohlen Cox, suddenly burst out: "I don't believe it's going to work, Lyndon. The Northerners will pull the strings, and buck you down." And the reluctance sprang from ignorance about the potential benefits of the product they were being asked to buy. To many Hill Country families, electricity meant light bulbs—a benefit, to be sure, but not, in the view of many, a benefit worth risking losing one's farm for. "Something you had never had or experienced—are you going to miss it?" Babe Smith asks. The county agents and community leaders were not having much success in the sign-up campaign. Babe Smith remembers a meeting in the Kempner schoolhouse attended by perhaps one hundred farmers and their families. At the beginning of the meeting, Smith passed out PEC applications; only two of the farmers signed them. So Johnson tried *his* hand at persuasion. "He played on the emotions of the women," Smith says. He talked about his mother, and how he had watched her hauling buckets of water from the river, and rubbing her knuckles off on the scrub board. Electricity could help them pump their water and wash their clothes, he said. When they got refrigerators, they would no longer have to "start fresh every morning" with the cooking. "You'll look younger at forty than your mother," he told them. Because he was the Congressman—and, to rural people, therefore an object almost of awe—and because he was "very persuasive," they listened to him attentively. But they didn't sign up. On the Fourth of July, 1938, he drove with Smith from picnic to picnic—Smith had brought along a Sears, Roebuck catalogue to show them the washing machines and refrigerators that they could use if they had electricity—but collected only a few handfuls of signed applications. "In the car going to the next town, he [Johnson] would say: 'What's the matter with these damned people? You offer them something . . .' He'd get discouraged." Despite months of effort, the county agents had collected nowhere near the number required—not three per mile, but fewer than two. The Pedernales Electric Co-op appeared stillborn. Johnson warned the farmers that if they didn't establish a cooperative to purchase the electricity created by the dams, TP&L might buy it —and offer it only at rates they could never afford. In a speech entitled "Our South," he said, "I believe we should use that power. I believe that river is yours, and the power it can generate belongs to you."

"So," says one of the PEC's first directors, "we went back to Lyndon. The only man who could talk for us."

He had tried to talk to the REA, going all the way up to the new

Administrator, John Carmody, but had had no luck. There was only one man left to talk to. Johnson asked Corcoran to get him in to see the President.

In later years, Johnson told many stories—each different—of what he said to the President, and what the President said to him when Corcoran finally, after considerable difficulty, obtained an audience for him. According to his story on one occasion, Roosevelt picked up the telephone while Johnson was still in the room, called Carmody and said, "John, I know you have got to have guidelines and rules and I don't want to upset them, but you just go along with me—just go ahead and approve this loan. . . . Those folks will catch up to that density problem because they breed pretty fast." On September 27, 1938, a telegram arrived at the temporary Johnson City office of the Pedernales Electric Co-operative: the REA, it said, had granted the PEC a loan of $1,322,000 (shortly to be raised to $1,800,000) to build 1,830 miles of electric lines that would bring electricity to 2,892 Hill Country families.

IN SO IMPOVERISHED AN AREA, the very existence of a large-scale—and government-financed—construction project was significant. The average wage in the Hill Country had been about a dollar or $1.50 per day, but workers on government projects were paid the minimum wage in the area: forty cents an hour or $3.20 per day. Three hundred men would be employed on the PEC project, but when Babe Smith arrived to open the PEC's first hiring office, in Bertram, several times three hundred men were standing in line to apply for these jobs. Many were given to men who had wanted electricity but had not been able to raise the five-dollar deposit; they paid it out of these wages. Herman Brown—Brown & Root had been given the contract to construct the PEC lines—was able to hire men who were known to be very hard workers. They needed to be. The poles that would carry the electrical lines had to be sunk in rock. Brown & Root's mechanical hole-digger broke on the hard Hill Country rock. Every hole had to be dug mostly by hand. Eight- or ten-man crews would pile into flatbed trucks—which also carried their lunch and water—in the morning and head out into the hills. Some trucks carried axemen, to hack paths through the cedar; others contained the hole-diggers. "The hole-diggers were the strongest men," Babe Smith says. Every 300 or 400 feet, two would drop off and begin digging a hole by pounding the end of a crowbar into the limestone. After the hole reached a depth of six inches, half a stick of dynamite was exploded in it, to loosen the rock below, but that, too, had to be dug out by hand. "Swinging crowbars up and down—that's hard labor," Babe Smith says. "That's back-breaking labor." But the hole-diggers had incentive. For after the hole-digging teams came the pole-setters and "pikemen," who, in teams of three, set the poles—thirty-five-foot pine poles from East Texas—into the rock, and then the "framers" who attached the insulators, and then the "stringers" who strung the wires, and at the end of the day the hole-diggers could see the result of their work stretching out behind them—poles towering above the cedars, silvery lines against the sapphire sky. And the homes the wires were heading toward were their own homes. "These workers—they were the men of the cooperative," Smith says. Gratitude was a spur also. Often the crews didn't have to eat the cold lunch they had brought. A woman would see men toiling toward her home to "bring the lights." And when they arrived, they would find that a table had been set for them—with the best plates, and the very best food that the family could afford. Three hundred men—axemen, polemen, pikers, hole-diggers, framers—were out in the Edwards Plateau, linking it to the rest of America, linking it to the twentieth century, in fact, at the rate of about twelve miles per day.

Still, with 1,800 miles of line to build, the job seemed—to families very eager for electricity—to be taking a very long time. After the lines had been extended to their farms, and the farms were wired, they waited with wires hanging from the ceiling and bare bulbs at the end, for the lines to be energized. "It will not be long now until mother can throw away the sad irons," the *Blanco County News* exulted. But month after month passed, for the lines could not be energized until the entire project was substantially completed. As the months passed, the Hill Country's suspicion of the government was aroused again. Brian Smith had persuaded many of his neighbors to sign up, and now, more than a year after they had paid their five dollars, and then more money to have their houses wired, his daughter Evelyn recalls that her neighbors decided they weren't really going to get it. She recalls that "All their money was tied up in electric wiring"—and their anger was directed at her family. Dropping in to see a friend one day, she was told by the friend's parents to leave: "You and your city ways. You can go home, and we don't care to see you again." They were all but ostracized by their neighbors. Even they themselves were beginning to doubt; it had been so long since the wiring was installed, Evelyn recalls, that they couldn't remember whether the switches were in the ON or OFF position.

But then one evening in November, 1939, the Smiths were returning from Johnson City, where they had been attending a declamation contest, and as they neared their farmhouse, something was different.

"Oh my God," her mother said. "The house is on fire!"

But as they got closer, they saw the light wasn't fire. "No, Mama," Evelyn said. "The lights are on."

They were on all over the Hill Country. "And all over the Hill Country," Stella Gliddon says, "people began to name their kids for Lyndon Johnson."

Part V

NEW
FIELDS

29

Mr. Johnson Goes to Washington

LYNDON JOHNSON was so energetic and ingenious a Congressman that a knowledgeable observer called him "the best Congressman for a district that *ever was*." He was, moreover, secure in his congressional seat. In 1938, he would be one of eight Texas Congressmen who did not have an opponent in the Democratic primary, or in the general election in November. In 1940, he would again be unopposed. But a Congressman was not what Lyndon Johnson wanted to be. No sooner had he won the Tenth District seat than he was trying to leave it—as rapidly as possible.

On the day after he had been elected to the House of Representatives, while he was still in the hospital recuperating from his appendicitis attack, he had begun preparing for the next step toward his great goal by writing National Youth Administration officials to urge that Jesse Kellam's appointment as Texas NYA director be made permanent. His success in securing that appointment for his loyal Number Two man had ensured that his state-wide organization would be kept in place, and he worked continuously to build it up and to utilize it. NYA work was only part of what his NYA men were doing all across Texas: whenever one visited a town to check on an NYA project, he was supposed also, says one, "to go to the Courthouse to see the Mayor" and other local politicians, and to see "the school people" and the postmasters, who were often key figures in a local political structure. The NYA man was instructed to put in a good word for Congressman Johnson, and to ask if, although Johnson was not the Mayor's own Congressman, there was any service Johnson could perform for him or for his town. He was also told to keep his ears open for political gossip, and report it to "the Chief." And these reports were not ignored. Says one NYA man, J. J. (Jake) Pickle, "I would write him long letters. And he would call me about them. He would re-explore what I had said. 'Why did he say that? Repeat that.' "

The practice in Johnson's Washington office was, moreover, the same now that he was a Congressman as it had been when he was a congressional secretary: no matter how busy the office might be, requests from "important people"—people with money or political clout—from the other twenty congressional districts in Texas were to be given urgent priority.

Every Wednesday, the Speaker's Dining Room on the ground floor of the Capitol was reserved for a luncheon meeting of the Texas congressional delegation: two Senators, twenty-one Representatives (and, of course, should he want to sit in, Vice President Garner). At one luncheon each month, members of the delegation were permitted to bring occasional guests, either VIP's from their districts who happened to be in Washington or Washington notables. But such invitations were issued sparingly. Says James H. Rowe, who spent a lifetime in the inner circles of power: "It was a great honor to be invited. I think that, in a lifetime, I got there five times or maybe six."

At the other luncheons, guests were generally not permitted—no matter how important they might be. It was understood that these lunches were for business: to plan strategy or to iron out differences within the delegation so that Texas would present its customary united front. "You couldn't bring guests except on that one day," Congressman George H. Mahon of Lubbock recalls. "That was the unwritten law."

Lyndon Johnson did not obey this law, and he violated it in a manner particularly infuriating to the other members of the delegation: he invited to the "closed" lunches not only his constituents—but theirs. On one Wednesday, for example, Amon Carter, Jr., son of the publisher of the *Fort Worth Star-Telegram*, and the paper's editor, James Record, were in Washington, and they asked Fort Worth's Congressman, Wingate Lucas, if they could come to the famous delegation luncheon. But Lucas had once before asked Sam Rayburn for permission to bring an influential constituent to a closed session and had been refused. "There was no one I would rather take," Lucas says. "These were my two key supporters. But it was a closed session. I told them I couldn't take them. I went to the luncheon, and I was sitting there, and Lyndon Johnson walks in, and who do you think was with him?" Seeing Lucas, young Amon waved at him. Lucas sheepishly waved back.

(Johnson was able to violate the law because its enforcer was Rayburn, the delegation's leader. Rayburn was customarily very strict about the "no outsiders" rule because the outsiders were, he knew, likely to be the big businessmen and lobbyists he hated. But when Johnson asked permission to bring a guest, Rayburn frequently gave it.)

Another unwritten but very firm law prohibited a Congressman from interfering in the affairs of other districts. Johnson did not obey this law, either. Asking the White House for an increase in funding for the Reserve Officers Training Corps at Texas A&M University, in Luther A. Johnson's

Sixth District, he wrote that although the university was not in his district, "it is mine by adoption."

And when federal grants were given in other districts—even grants for projects with which Johnson had had absolutely no connection—his tactics could be even more irritating.

Normally, if a project receiving a grant was located in a district with a Democratic Congressman, officials of the federal agency giving the grant would telephone that Congressman so that he could announce it, and thereby get credit for it. If the project was in Texas, however, Johnson's friends in the agencies would often telephone him instead—and it would be Johnson who made the announcement. "I had been pushing for an extension of the Public Health Service Hospital in Fort Worth," Lucas recalls. "Lyndon hadn't had anything to do with it. But when it came about, Lyndon announced it, without even bothering to notify me." And even when agency officials notified the district Congressman, they notified Johnson as well, and the efficiency of his staff, coupled with his long cultivation of the wire-service reporters, ensured that it was his name, not the other Congressman's, that would be attached to the announcement.

"A lot of the delegation was sore as hell," says the AP's Lewis T. ("Tex") Easley. They were, in fact, so sore that Johnson found it expedient to beat a retreat—but only a partial retreat. "He realized it was getting them too mad," Easley says. "So after a while, he would announce it jointly." The shift didn't do much to alleviate tensions. After several "joint" announcements of federal projects in Corpus Christi, Dick Kleberg, his former employer and the friendliest of men, could scarcely bring himself to nod to Johnson when they passed in the halls.

THE ILL-FEELING engendered in the Texas delegation by such tactics was exacerbated by Johnson's personality. His efforts to dominate other men succeeded with one or two fellow Texans (most notably, quiet, unassertive Representative Robert Poage of Waco), but with most of the delegation, tough, successful politicians in their own right, they aroused only resentment —as did his efforts to dominate every room in which he was present. As he strolled through the House Dining Room at lunchtime, acting if he were some visiting celebrity, nodding to left and right, "head huddling" with one man or another, or as he sat at a table, talking too loudly, other Congressmen muttered under their breaths. Albert Thomas of Houston would sit staring at Johnson, snarling *sotto voce:* "Listen to that sonofabitch talking about himself." Other mutters were occasioned by what Lucas calls "insincerity." Johnson "was so insincere," Lucas says. "He would tell everyone what he thought they wanted to hear. As a result, you couldn't believe anything he said." Ewing Thomason of El Paso had served in the Texas Legislature with Sam Johnson, and initially had gone out of his way to befriend Sam's son. Approaching Thomason in the dining room one day, Lyndon Johnson promised him his support on a controversial issue. "Ewing," he said earnestly, "if there's anyone you can believe, it's me." Then he swung across the room and started talking to several Congressmen who happened to be opposing Thomason on the issue. Thomason muttered: "There's that sonofabitch telling them the same thing he told me."

Mutter though they did, however, few cared to raise their voices—for they didn't want Sam Rayburn to hear them. "Rayburn had this very strong feeling for Lyndon," Lucas says. "And that feeling protected Lyndon. Nobody in the delegation wanted to get Rayburn mad."

THE OTHER MEMBERS of the delegation understood why Johnson was making speeches—and friends—all across Texas.

He certainly made no secret of the fact that he wanted to be a United States Senator, says George Mahon, who, without such ambitions himself, was tolerant of Johnson. Chatting with Mahon in the cloakroom, or walking back to the Cannon Building with him, Johnson would frequently pull out a newspaper clipping dealing with local conditions—not conditions in Austin, but in Houston, or Dallas, or Lubbock. "He would always have an editorial from the Dallas paper or the El Paso paper, and he would sit down next to you on the floor [of the House] and tell you or ask you [about it]. . . ." Influential citizens from other districts were cultivated not only when they were visiting Washington, but back home as well. He solicited speaking invitations from cities all across Texas, and, Mahon says, "When he was in town, he would court them, would call them up. And, of course, if someone important, like a Congressman, calls you up, you're flattered." Mahon began to realize that "in my district [which was almost 300 miles from Johnson's], he [had] made friends with the key people. He courted the right people in the right places [all over] the state. He had statewide ambitions from the day he came up here."

But Lyndon Johnson's fellow Texans saw no possibility that those ambitions would be realized—at least not for years and years. Neither of the state's two Senators, Tom Connally and Morris Sheppard—both in their early sixties—was considering retirement, and their immense popularity made remote indeed the possibility that either would *be* retired by the electorate. Should one of the two seats become vacant for some reason, Lyndon Johnson would not be the first choice to fill it. That would be Governor Allred, who wanted the job, or any one of several other state officials with a statewide reputation. Johnson would not be first even among the state's Congressmen; several would be more logical choices—most notably Maury Maverick, a White House favorite, or the energetic and ambitious Wright Patman, who was widely known for his authorship of the Patman Bonus Bill and several pieces of Populist legislation. There was, in the view of the Texas delegation, no realistic chance of a junior Congressman competing with such figures—particularly not a junior Congressman from the Tenth District. The isolation of that district—the expanse of empty plains that surrounded it and cut it off from the rest of Texas—had kept its Congressman unknown in most of the huge state. Says a Dallas political figure: "I had never even *heard* the name of Lyndon Johnson at that time."

None of the Texas delegation saw the real ambition—the goal toward which a Senate seat, like a congressional seat, would be only a stepping-stone. Had they seen it, they would have scoffed at it, and not only because of Johnson's youth and lack of power. While Texans would later maintain that their state was more part of the West than the South, during the pre-war years they regarded themselves as Southerners, and among Southerners on Capitol Hill it was an article of faith—bitter faith—that no Southerner would ever be President of the United States. When, in 1946, his congressional colleagues gave Sam Rayburn a car, the plaque on it would read: "To Our Beloved Sam Rayburn—Who would have been President if he had come from any place but the South." But no member of the delegation saw the true goal, none got even a glimpse of it. When, in fact, his congressional colleagues were discussing the possibilities of a Southerner obtaining national office, Johnson would aver that there was no chance of that, and that a Southerner would be foolish to leave a secure seat on Capitol Hill to try for national office: "*This* is our home; this is where we have our strength," he would say.

Others did see the real goal—despite him. George Brown, of course, knew after that day on the blanket at the Greenbrier when Johnson turned down wealth in the interests of some unstated ambition. Rowe, who was keenly observant in his quiet way—and who spent more time with Johnson than any of the other young New Dealers—says, "From the day he got here, he wanted to be President." And one time, at least, Johnson did reveal himself. One evening, alone with Welly Hopkins, he burst out: "By *God,* I'll be President someday." But even the few who guessed the goal at which Lyndon Johnson was really aiming could not imagine how he could ever realize it. A Senate seat was not the only path to it—national power of another type, behind-the-scenes power, might help him along the road—but men conversant with such power—the young New Dealers he had cultivated—could not see how he could possibly obtain some of it, at least not in any foreseeable future. They were his friends, but they were only young and junior members of the Administration. The fact that he was also young and junior was emphasized by the difficulty Corcoran had experienced trying to get him even a few minutes with the President to obtain approval of the Pedernales Electric Co-operative loan.

As soon as he had arrived in Washington in May, 1937, Johnson had attempted to capitalize on the glow of the Galveston meeting, using every possible opening, no matter how slim; during 1937, he requested auto-graphed pictures not only from the President but from the President's son, James, from presidential secretary Marvin McIntyre, from every White House staffer he had met, however briefly—and the requests were accom-panied by reminders of the circumstances of his election (sending a copy of the Galveston photograph to "My dear Marvin," Johnson noted that "This photograph was taken . . . shortly after my election to Congress in the hot fight over reorganization of the Judiciary"), and by reminders of his loyalty; his letters referred to Roosevelt as "the Chief." On Christmas Eve, 1937, he had delivered to the President, to his son, to McIntyre, and to other White House staffers the huge turkeys (so big they seemed to have been "crossed with a beef"), accompanied by carefully composed notes. "Dear Mr. Mc-Intyre," one said, "The other day I went up into the hills of Central Texas where I was born to pick out the finest turkey I could get my hand on for the President. . . . I'm asking my secretary to deliver this turkey to you at the White House, for the President. . . . And I want to tell you that one of the reasons my own Christmas is so pleasant and joyous is due to the fact that with a million things to do, you have also had time to take a young-ster on the hill under your wing when he needed it and to give him a lot of help, encouragement and advice. I am very grateful. Most sincerely yours, Lyndon."

McIntyre, who was fond of Johnson, was his soft spot on the staff, and he worked on him, but while Mac may have been flattered by a request for an autographed picture, he could do nothing for him without his boss' approval and, whatever the reason—whether the President had been irri-tated by Johnson's boasts of intimacy (one Texas newspaper said that the President "regarded the Texan as one of the banner-carriers of the adminis-tration"); whether he felt that Johnson was pushing his slim acquaintance —the President appears to have felt he had done quite enough for a freshman Congressman. In September, 1937, McIntyre agreed to try to do some small favor for Johnson—its exact nature is unclear—but had to write him, "I regret very much that I have been unable to accomplish your desire. . . ." Replies to Johnson's recommendations on presidential appoint-ments—for Governor Allred as United States Solicitor General, for example —were form letters, perfunctory and non-committal, letters not even from the President but from one of his secretaries. Flatter though he might, Johnson could not flatter his way into the presidential presence; as late as June, 1938, a year after he had come to Washington as a Congressman, he still had not seen Roosevelt personally; when, at that time, he attempted to secure through McIntyre his first appointment—for "five minutes" in "the next five or six days" to see the jovial companion of his Texas train trip— McIntyre apparently had to tell him that his request had been turned down. Worried—for Allred had asked him to present in person an invitation to Roosevelt to attend the dedication of a public works project in Texas, and

Johnson did not want to confess to the Governor that he had no access at all to the President—he made, on June 8, a formal, written request to Roosevelt for "ten minutes on Thursday or Friday"; he was given an appointment—for August 15. And before that date arrived, the appointment was canceled. The PEC audience, in September, 1938, did not improve the situation. In succeeding months, Johnson, despite requests, did not get through the door of the Oval Office again. During his first two years in Washington, that was his only audience with Roosevelt.

ON CAPITOL HILL, developments were very discouraging. He might be a member of Rayburn's "Board of Education," but in the world of Congress, where seniority ruled with an iron hand, without seniority even admittance to that select drinking society meant little—as Johnson learned the very first time he attended a meeting of the Naval Affairs Committee.

The committee's chairman, Carl Vinson, was from the little town of Milledgeville in Georgia's red-clay hill country. He had not yet been nicknamed "the Swamp Fox" in tribute to a mastery of legislative stratagems which Southerners compared to Francis Marion's mastery of guerrilla warfare, but he had already been nicknamed "the Admiral" in recognition of his autocratic manner in dealing with the Admirals of what he called "My Navy" (whom he humiliated by pretending he didn't know their names while ordering them around like cabin boys); with members of the hated "quote Upper House unquote"; and with the twenty-six members of his committee. Slouched down in the center of the two-tiered horseshoe of committee seats in the committee room on the third floor of the Cannon Building, his glasses teetering on the very tip of his long nose, chewing on the shredded remains of a ten-cent cigar, spitting at the spittoon that was always nearby, dressed in a collar two sizes too big and in baggy, food-stained suits, "he looks," one reporter was to write, "like the country lawyer he is, and about once removed from the cracker barrel," but he ran the committee, in the words of another observer, "like a dictator." When, at that first meeting, Johnson, seated on the lower horseshoe among the junior members, began questioning a witness—along with the junior member sitting next to him, young Warren Magnuson of Seattle—Vinson gaveled the hearing into recess and said, as Magnuson recalls the words: "I want to see you two boys in the back room." In his small, bare private office behind the hearing room, Magnuson says, "he let us have it." "We have a rule in this committee," the chairman said. New members were not allowed to ask so many questions; in his first year on the committee, a member was allowed to ask one question; in his second year, two, "and so on."

The Admiral may have been exaggerating the rigidity of his rules—but not by much. "He runs a tight ship," other members warned the two young men, and on that ship, seniority was the standard. Junior members he addressed as "Ensign"; only after some years, and only after the member had pleased him with his deference—and silence—would he be promoted to "Commander." When the Admiral starts calling you "Captain," the other members told Johnson and Magnuson, "you know you've arrived," and no one arrived quickly. Attempting to buck the Admiral's system was useless. If you tried to collect information for independent judgments on naval affairs, the Navy wouldn't give it to you—and neither, without specific permission from Vinson, would the committee's own staff members. If you tried to rally other committee members behind an independent stand, you would find the task all but impossible; the favors Vinson had to dispense—not only the small favors, like the junket to Mexico City on a Navy plane, but the big favors, like the location of a naval installation in your district—were denied, usually forever, to a committee member who had incurred his displeasure. Once a new member, currying favor with Vinson, came up to him after a session and said, "Well, I voted with you." Vinson replied curtly: "What the hell do you think I put you on this committee for?" On "that committee," its members said, "there are no disagreements at all." And if you tried to go outside the committee, and challenge a committee report on the floor of the House, your chances of winning such a vote, from members who might also one day want installations and other favors—a promotion or a transfer for a friend or constituent, for example—and who were, in any case, under the control of other committee chairman, were all but nil. Congress, one observer was to write, had given Carl Vinson "a blank check to operate as a one-man committee" on naval matters; on that committee, only one voice mattered: the chairman's soft Georgia drawl. Lyndon Johnson's voice, in other words, would not matter until *he* became chairman.

Vinson's arrogance was not unique. Most of the great Standing Committees of the House were run by men answerable to no one in Washington—not to the membership of the House (for it was not popularity with their colleagues but only seniority which had given them their chairmanships), not to the leadership of the House (for once the leadership had placed a chairman in his job, it was all but powerless ever to remove him from it), not to the President, and certainly not to the members of their committees. And they ran their committees like men answerable to no one; a little more than a decade earlier, one chairman had faced down a rebellion in his committee by declaring, "I am the committee"; under the rule that one House leader was to call "the strongest and most compelling of all rules, the rule of immemorial usage," that declaration was still true in 1937, as it would be true for decades to come. To observe the House of Representatives was to observe what absolute, untrammeled, unchallengeable power did to men.

The House as a whole was run the same way. The sprawling 435-member body was an oligarchy whose ruling circle consisted of no more than a score of men: the Speaker, the Majority Leader and Whip, the most powerful committee chairmen. And the only qualification that could secure a Congressman admission to this small, select ring of power—even if he was, like Johnson and Patman, allowed to drink with its members— was seniority. Ability wouldn't get you into that select circle. Energy wouldn't get you into it. Only age would get you into it. There was only one way to become one of the rulers of the House: to wait.

And, harshest fact of all about Congress, even waiting was no guarantee. On Naval Affairs, the wait would probably be long, for Vinson, who had come to Congress in 1914 at the age of thirty, was now one of the youngest chairmen—in 1937, only fifty-three years old. As a Southern Democrat, he could probably hold his district indefinitely. As long as the Democrats held Congress, he would be chairman until he died or retired, an event that might be many years away. (In fact, it would be twenty-eight years away: Vinson would be chairman* until 1965, when he retired at the age of eighty-one.) And Vinson's departure would not, of course, make Johnson chairman. If, in 1937, he turned in his seat on the lower horseshoe, he could see above him a whole line of faces—the committee's senior Democratic members, who sat on Vinson's left—that stood between him and the chairman's gavel. Since he was the committee's most junior member—the one last elected, the one with the least seniority—even the Democrats on the lower horseshoe, even the thirty-two-year-old Magnuson, stood between him and the chairmanship. Some of the Democrats would lose their seats, some would die, some might become Senators—but, with the exception of those who left the committee in these ways, he would, in effect, have to survive the chairmanships of all these men, the chairmanships laid end to end, before he became chairman. And, of course, even if he waited out all those chairmanships, he might still not be chairman. The Democrats wouldn't always be in control of Congress, and if, when his turn in the Democratic line finally arrived, the Republicans should be in control, he wouldn't be chairman then, either. Because the Democrats had taken control of the House only five years before, after twelve years of Republican control, evidence of this harsh fact—of what might happen to him even if he waited—was everywhere before Johnson's eyes. He couldn't help being aware of all those Republicans who had waited patiently during the twelve years of Republican rule (and, of course, for long years before that) as the Republicans ahead of them died or retired, who had inched on their committee's dais chair by chair toward the only chair on that dais that mattered, and then—just as they were about to reach it—had, in an instant, had the chair snatched away from them as their party lost control of the House. A young Congressman such as Lyndon Johnson could see such men, old now, pausing for breath

* Of the Naval Affairs Committee and then, after 1946, of a new committee which combined Naval Affairs and Military Affairs, the House Armed Services Committee.

as they climbed the long stairs to the Capitol, or napping in the large, over-stuffed chairs in the cloakrooms after lunch—it was so easy to sink into those big chairs and have lunch brought to you on the solid trays that fit across both arms instead of eating standing up at the counter in the cloakroom so you could get back to work. There were even a few who were turning senile, and who would sit in the Chamber hour after hour, staring into space, refusing to retire gracefully, still hanging on, year after year. Or he could see men —Democrats—who had finally reached the chairmanship, but so late in life that it no longer meant much to them. Another Congressman—Donald Riegle, who, in 1966, came to Congress at twenty-eight, the same age as Lyndon Johnson—would see the same thing: "Some of these [chair] men can't hear very well, can't see very well, have difficulty working a full day." He would muse about what it meant to him: "A man can come to Congress when he's thirty-five, serve here twenty years, and emerge, at age fifty-five, as the ablest man on his committee. But because he has to wait for all the members ahead of him to either retire or die, he may have to wait another twenty years . . . before he becomes a chairman. You will climb to the top of the ladder eventually. The only catch is you may be in your seventies when the big moment comes." And he would describe also his feeling that nothing would change the system, for the men who would have to change it had invested too much of their own lives in it: having waited so long for power, they would, now that they had it, do nothing to dilute it. Congress could be a trap as cruel in its way as the Hill Country—a trap with jaws, the system called seniority, strong enough to hold fast even Lyndon Johnson's ambition.

IN 1938, a year after he came to Congress, Lyndon Johnson made an effort to break out of that trap.

The only House committee in which a junior member was anything more than a cipher was Appropriations, and of all the House committees, only Appropriations had the power to fund government programs. Other committees could authorize a program, but the money for it had to come— in a separate bill—from Appropriations. The Appropriations Committee therefore had unique power. More important to a young Congressman such as Johnson, its members were divided into thirteen subcommittees—each of which had autonomy unique among House subcommittees. Because of the diversity of Appropriations' work—it had to cover the whole range of government operations, not just agriculture, say, or defense—the members of each subcommittee became the experts in the field it covered, and the committee chairman, eighty-year-old Edward T. Taylor of Colorado, customarily deferred to its decisions. Even more important to a young Congressman, these subcommittees were small—in 1937, most had only six or seven members—and their smallness kept the meetings informal, so even an initiate had a chance to contribute something, and members with a few years' seniority often were allowed considerable input. A Congressman —even a junior Congressman—who was named to Appropriations would become automatically, if not a power in the House, at least more than one of the herd.

In 1938, the traditional "Texas seat" on Appropriations fell vacant, and although George Mahon wanted it and had seniority, Johnson tried to step into it, planting newspaper stories hinting that his "close administration contacts" would enable him to use the Appropriations post to obtain more federal projects for Texas.

But he never had a chance. The Texas seat would be filled by the Texas delegation, and on that delegation, Mahon recalls, "Mr. Rayburn had the power." Although Mahon knew of Rayburn's paternal fondness for Johnson, he never worried about the result. "Whatever Rayburn said went," he says. "But Rayburn followed the rules." And the rule that mattered was seniority. "I was the senior Texan who wanted the spot," Mahon says. "I was in line for it. If you were the next man in line, you got it—that was the way the unvarying rule was." Mahon got it—found the immediate rewards he had expected ("Even as a new member of Appropriations," he says, "if you were on Appropriations, you were courted by other members"), and began the climb to greater rewards: in eleven years, he would be chairman of his sub-committee, in twenty-six years, at the age of sixty-four, chairman of the full committee; for his remaining fifteen years in Congress (until he retired at seventy-nine), he would be a power on Capitol Hill. Johnson didn't get it; he remained a member of the Naval Affairs Committee—a junior member of a committee on which junior members were limited even in the number of questions they could ask.

HARDLY HAD HE ARRIVED in Congress, moreover, when an event occurred which apparently convinced him that, even if the long, slow path to power in the House had been the only one open to him, it might not be possible for him.

The speech that Sam Ealy Johnson gave for his son was the last speech he ever made. His heart had been failing for years, and in July, 1937, two months after his son's election to Congress, he suffered another massive heart attack, and doctors told Rebekah it was just a matter of time. He was taken to the Scott & White Clinic in Temple, Texas, where more modern medical facilities were available than in the Hill Country, and he was kept there, often in an oxygen tent, for the next two months. But when Lyndon returned from Washington during the congressional recess of September and visited his father, Sam asked to be taken home to Johnson City. Lyndon protested, but Sam said, "Give me my breeches, Lyndon, I want to go home where people know when you're sick and care when you die." Lyndon checked him out of the hospital, and drove him home, where, on October 23, 1937, twelve days after his sixtieth birthday, Sam Ealy Johnson died.

The next day he was taken to the Johnson burial ground on the banks of the Pedernales, the only acre left to the Johnsons from the Johnson Ranch that Sam had tried so hard to keep in the family. The burial ground was about a half mile upstream from the house to which he had brought Rebekah when they were first married. It was about a hundred yards from the gully —"the gully big enough to walk elephants in"—that Sam had filled and refilled with soil in a vain attempt to grow cotton.

He had asked to be carried to the burial ground not in a modern hearse but in an old-fashioned one—in one of the tall hearses with the carved wooden "draperies" covering the side glass that had been used before the invention of the automobile. One had been found in San Marcos—mounted not on a wagon but on the bed of a Model T Ford—and it clattered out of Johnson City and down the side path to the ford across the Pedernales through which Sam had, as a young man with dreams, so often spurred his horse on the way to the Legislature in Austin. Governor Allred was riding, with Secretary of State Ed Clark, in a car behind the hearse; Clark, anxious to curry favor with Lyndon Johnson, had persuaded the Governor to attend. Since the two men had been told so many times—by Lyndon—that his father was only an impoverished drunk, they had thought that the funeral would be poorly attended and that they would be doing the new Congressman a great favor. Therefore, they were surprised when they reached the river crossing. Across the river, the bank of the Pedernales was covered with people as far as the eye could see.

The cars that had brought these people—pulled up in a long line behind the crowd—were dusty with travel. "Most of the crowd was old people," Stella Gliddon recalls. "You know, people that Mr. Sam had gotten pensions for. Some of them had come a long way." One aged widow, so crippled by arthritis that she hadn't left her house in five years, had insisted that two of her sons carry her out to their car and drive her from their lonely ranch in Marble Falls. Some had come farther. Members of Sam's little band of legislators had come to say goodbye to the man who had fought beside them for "the People." One, R. Bouna Ridgway, lived in Dallas. He had heard of Sam Johnson's death only the previous day and had driven all night— almost 300 hard miles—to be at the funeral of a man he had not seen in years.

There were uniforms on the riverbank, for Sam Johnson had gotten pensions for veterans of the First World War—no one had ever realized for how many until they saw how many elderly men in khaki were standing stiffly at attention as the tall casket rumbled across the river. And not all the uniforms were khaki; it was on the riverbank that afternoon that Ava Johnson Cox saw for the first time, standing at attention, several old men in shirts and light-blue riding breeches holding "funny-looking" hats, "like a Stetson but not quite," and realized she was seeing uniforms that had charged up San Juan Hill. And there were uniforms much older even than those of the Rough Riders. Five Confederate veterans had donned their beloved gray uniforms—and pinned to them medals, bright from decades of shining, of the Lost Cause—to honor the man who had managed to secure the meager monthly stipends that had meant so much to them. "Five, I remember the number," Ava says. "I can see every one in my eye now. You almost never saw those uniforms any more."

The service began, of course, with "Shall We Gather at the River," and the sound of the singing from hundreds of voices carried up and down the lonely Pedernales Valley. And although he cannot remember exactly what was said, one of Allred's aides was to recall forty years later his astonishment when the minister, during the eulogy, listed Sam Johnson's accomplishments. "Why, do you know," the aide said, "he had done a *lot* in the Legislature. And it was him who had gotten built that road we drove on from Austin that day. I had never heard one word about that. I had thought he was—well, you know, to tell the truth—just some old drunk." The service ended with a few words from one of Sam's friends, a rawboned old Texas politician, Railroad Commissioner Lon Smith; the words were taken from *Hamlet:* "He was a man, take him for all in all, I shall not look upon his like again."

A MOMENT OF TENSION occurred after the service when Sam's immediate family, alone in the Johnson home, was sitting around the dining-room table with Lyndon, in his father's chair, disposing of his father's personal effects. Lying on the table was Sam's heavy gold watch and chain, his most prized possession. Lyndon's three sisters and his brother, Sam Houston Johnson, had said hardly a word, but when Lyndon reached out and started to take the watch for himself, Lucia, the youngest and meekest of the sisters, put her hand on his arm and stopped him. "No," she said. "You can't have the watch. That belongs to Sam Houston now. Daddy wanted him to have it. We all know that." Rebekah took the watch and handed it to Lyndon's younger brother.

Sam Houston Johnson was to write, "It was an embarrassing moment for Lyndon, and I felt sorry for him. As a matter of fact, I wanted him to have it because he was the older brother—but I didn't press the point for fear of antagonizing my sisters." On Christmas morning, 1958, more than twenty years later, Sam Houston wrapped the watch and gave it to Lyndon. He recalls telling his brother: "I want you to have the watch. Daddy really wanted you to have it. Anyway, I'm liable to leave it somewhere."

Several years later, Johnson's staff began collecting family mementoes

for the Lyndon Baines Johnson Library. Johnson, who had a keen awareness of his place in history, had carefully saved hundreds of items, including
some very unlikely ones. But his father's watch could not be found.

IF HE DID NOT INHERIT—at least not immediately—his father's watch,
Lyndon Johnson believed he had inherited something else.

He had always been so deeply aware of his remarkable physical resemblance to his tall, gawky, big-eared, big-nosed father, and his father's habit
of grabbing a listener's lapel. A long-standing belief within the Johnson family held that Johnson men had weak hearts and died young. Now his father
was dead, of heart disease, at the age of sixty.

To the heredity and humiliation which had shaped Lyndon Johnson
and had spurred him harshly forward was added the spur of fear. He
entered one of his periods of deep depression, one that lasted for several
months. It was punctuated, as were periods of crisis throughout his life, by
illness; twice in a span of a few months he was hospitalized with what is
variously described as "bronchitis," "pneumonia" or "nervous exhaustion."
During this period, when friends attempted to cheer him up by discussing
with him the topic which was ordinarily of deepest interest to him—his
future—Johnson, whenever reference was made to the possibility that he
might have to make his career in the House of Representatives, would reply,
in a low voice: "Too slow. Too slow." Rayburn had begun trudging along
that path early—he had been only thirty years old when first elected to Congress in 1912, scarcely older than Johnson was now. He had become Majority Leader in 1937—when he was fifty-five; he was still not Speaker. Sam
Johnson had died when he was sixty. And what if the Democrats should lose
control of the House before Rayburn's chance came? The path to power in
the House—the silence, the obeisance—was not too narrow for Lyndon
Johnson, who could follow surefootedly the narrowest political road. But
it was too long. He had managed to break out of the trap of the Hill Country; he might not be able to escape the trap of the seniority system before
he died.

And then, in 1939, Sam Ealy Johnson's younger brother George Desha
Johnson—Lyndon's schoolteacher uncle who had gotten him a job at Sam
Houston High and with whom Lyndon had boarded while he was teaching
there—suffered a massive heart attack. He died a few months later—at the
age of fifty-seven.

WHILE THE SENIORITY SYSTEM might deny a junior Congressman the opportunity to play a significant role in the committee structure of the House of
Representatives, his very membership in the House provided him with an
opportunity to play a different type of role. Unable to contribute significantly

to legislation, he nonetheless possessed the power to bring an issue to the attention of the nation, and to keep that issue before the nation.

Muffled within the institutional structure of Capitol Hill, his voice would be magnified if he chose to address himself to the nation instead of the House. When he spoke in the well of the House, the reporters sitting above him in the press gallery were a sounding board through which his views could reach an entire nation. A Congressman didn't even need the well; the very corridors of Congress, where reporters take down a Congressman's comment on a major development, could be a sounding board. Even a mimeograph machine could be a national megaphone—if the machine was in a Congressman's office; "Any House member can make the news . . . simply by getting a press handout to the [press] gallery early in the morning," Richard Bolling was to say. "When a major subject is on top of the news . . . and the wire services are hurrying to assemble a reaction story, any provocative comment from a member of Congress is likely to get scooped up and given a sentence or two." All a Congressman had to do was speak, and he would be a spokesman. Proof of this fact was readily available to Lyndon Johnson in the careers of three Congressmen with whom he was particularly well acquainted: proof from the past, for one junior Congressman who had declined to stay silent, who had refused "to be relegated to that lockjawed ostracism" because he was the voice of 200,000 persons who needed a voice that would be heard, had been Sam Rayburn; and proof from the present, in the persons of Wright Patman, his father's friend, who had risen to influence in the House on stands that his father would have applauded; and of Maury Maverick, whose district adjoined Johnson's; 1937, the year Johnson came to Congress, was the year of peak influence of Maury and his "Mavericks," thirty-five young Congressmen who met every week in Renkel's Cafeteria to discuss strategies for confounding the House's conservative leadership and advancing causes which, as the *Washington Post* commented, "would have been labeled Bryanesque twenty-five years ago"; Maverick himself had become a national rallying point for such causes. Congressmen such as Rayburn and Patman and Maverick—and, during the Thirties, other Congressmen such as Tom Amlie of Wisconsin and Fiorello La Guardia of New York—had become representatives not just of a district but of causes that affected the welfare of a nation; they had focused America's attention upon significant issues, had prepared the climate for the passage, if not immediately, then eventually, of significant legislation; had become, by introducing what was, in effect, *national* legislation, national legislators. This course carried with it rewards for a Congressman who cared about causes.

Such a course was not invariably quixotic even in terms of immediate results. Anyone who thought a young Congressman's cause was lost before it began to live had only to remember that Sam Rayburn had become the "Railroad Legislator," with significant bills to his credit, by the end of his second term in Congress. Johnson, moreover, had had an opportunity to see this with his own eyes during his years as a congressional secretary, for those years had been the years of Fiorello La Guardia, tiny, swarthy, black-sombreroed, tough enough to face down Garner in the chair and make him like it; La Guardia who fought "the Interests" on behalf of the rural as well as the urban poor ("Fight, farmers, fight. Fight for your homes and your children. Your names will live with Paul Revere"), and who had, in 1932, succeeded in having outlawed (in the Norris–La Guardia Act) the hated yellow-dog contract. Liberal—and radical—stands might eventually destroy a Maverick whose San Antonio constituency, largely military men and Catholics, was conservative. But Lyndon Johnson could have taken such stands with no such fear, for in his district, that stronghold of the People's Party, the New Deal's popularity never waned. Johnson might, in fact, have been expected to take such stands; his victory, after all, had been based on such stands; he had shouted "Roosevelt, Roosevelt, Roosevelt" and promised to support future as well as present New Deal proposals.

Taking stands was not, however, a course which Johnson adopted. He did not take one, in fact, even on the issue on which he had based his campaign. After Johnson took his oath as Congressman on May 13, Maverick had shouted: "Mr. Speaker, the gentleman just sworn in, Mr. Lyndon Johnson, supported the President's judiciary plan and was overwhelmingly elected!" Johnson himself said nothing about the President's plan at the time or—so far as can be determined—at any other time while in Washington. By May 13, Supreme Court–packing had been effectively doomed by congressional opposition. But the fight on the plan was far from over—the Senate Judiciary Committee's crucial 10–8 vote against it would not come until May 18, and maneuvering over the terms of a compromise measure would continue for another two months. But Johnson, who had asked his district to send him to Washington to show support of the President's plan, offered not a single public word of support himself. As for other causes, Johnson's overall record on the introduction of national legislation—legislation which would have an effect outside his own district—was equally striking. Lyndon Johnson became a Congressman in 1937. He did not introduce a national bill in 1937—or in 1938, 1939, or 1940. When he introduced one in 1941 —on December 9, two days after Pearl Harbor—it was a bill to create a job for himself by merging the National Youth Administration and the Civilian Conservation Corps into a single agency which would train youths for war work in factories and to whose chairmanship he hoped President Roosevelt would appoint him, because of his NYA experience. Since he did not introduce a national bill in 1942, that single bill—an attempt to increase his personal power—was the only piece of national legislation he proposed during his first six years in Congress. Was this a function of inexperience? He was hardly more active in this regard at the end of his House career than at the beginning. He introduced one "national" bill in 1943, and two in 1945 —but none in 1946, none in 1947, and only one in 1948. During his more than eleven years in the House of Representatives, he introduced only five bills that would affect the country as a whole.

As striking as the paucity of such bills was their sponsor's effort on their behalf. With a single exception, there was no effort. During his eleven years in the House, only once did Lyndon Johnson appear in support of a national bill he had introduced before the committee to which it had been referred—and, with that one exception, no national bill he introduced received serious (or, indeed, even *pro forma*) consideration from any House committee. Of the five pieces of legislation of interest to more than his own district which, in eleven years, he placed in the House hopper, four were pieces of paper introduced *pro forma*—without genuine interest and enthusiasm from their sponsor. The one fight he made, for a 1943 bill aimed at curbing absenteeism in war plants by requiring the drafting of any worker absent too often, ended in fiasco; he apparently introduced it, in his own Naval Affairs Committee, without the courtesy of consulting with the chairman of the committee that had jurisdiction over such measures, the House Labor Committee. The Naval Affairs Committee reported the measure out favorably, but the angry chairman of the Labor Committee asked the Rules Committee, which controls the flow of legislation to the floor, not to let this bill reach the floor; an embarrassed Carl Vinson had to admit that he had assumed—incorrectly—that the Labor Committee had surrendered jurisdiction; and the bill died in the Rules Committee. During his eleven years as a Congressman, therefore, no national bill introduced by Lyndon Johnson that would have affected the people of the United States became a law of the United States.

He didn't introduce legislation himself—and he wouldn't fight for legislation introduced by others.

He wouldn't fight publicly. He didn't write laws—and he didn't write speeches, at least not speeches to be delivered in Washington. The speeches that the brilliant Henderson kept turning out were delivered only on Johnson's trips home to the district. This was a dramatic departure from the usual practice among Congressmen, who were allowed merely to insert their speeches into the *Congressional Record* without bothering to read them on the floor of the House. All that was required—under the House rule allowing members virtually unlimited freedom to "revise and extend" their remarks in the *Record*—was that a member read the opening words of a speech, and hand it to a clerk for reprinting in the *Record*. Because anything printed in the *Record* can be reprinted at government expense, and then mailed at government expense under the franking privilege, Congressmen used the right to "revise and extend" to have tens of thousands of copies of their statements reprinted and mailed to their constituents, thereby gaining free publicity and creating the impression of deep involvement in national issues. The *Record* was crammed with speeches never spoken on the floor. But, although Johnson made maximum use of other avenues of publicity, very few of the remarks "extended" were extended by him. Entire years went by in which he did not use the device even once.*

His record in regard to "real" speeches—talks of more than a paragraph or two in length that were actually delivered in the House—was even more striking.

On August 8, 1941, after weeks of prodding by Sam Rayburn, who felt it was time, and more than time, for Johnson to raise his voice in the House, Johnson stepped into the well of the House to advocate the extension of the Selective Service Act. The date was noteworthy. He had been a Congressman for four years. With the exception of a brief memorial tribute to Albert Sidney Burleson when Burleson died in November, 1937, this was the first speech he had made.

He didn't make another one for eighteen months. Rising then to argue for his absenteeism bill, he could say, "Mr. Speaker, in the four terms that I have served in this House I have seldom asked your indulgence." After the absenteeism fight, he didn't make another speech for almost another three years. Entire years went by without Lyndon Johnson addressing the House even once.† In fact, until 1948, when the necessities of his campaign for the United States Senate changed his methods, he had, during eleven years in Congress, delivered a total of ten speeches—less than one a year.

He wouldn't fight in the well of the House—and he wouldn't fight on the floor. His demeanor during debates—during the give-and-take argumentation about legislation—was noteworthy. Imitating it, his colleague Helen Gahagan Douglas of California depicts a person sitting slouched far down in a chair, his head in one hand; "He looked the picture of boredom, slumped in his chair with his eyes half-closed," she says. And he seldom stayed long. "He never spoke in the House, you know, except on rare, rare occasions." And, Mrs. Douglas adds, "He didn't spend much time listening to others in the House." He might sit for a while, "the picture of boredom," and "then suddenly he'd jump to his feet, nervous . . . restless, as if he couldn't bear it another minute. He might stop to speak to some member on the floor of the House or to the Speaker. . . . Then he'd leave." As he departed, "loping off the floor with that great stride of his as though he was on some Texas plain," she says, "he always gave the impression of someone in a hurry."

---

* He did not use it in 1940, 1942, 1944, 1945 or 1947. Until 1948, when, after eleven years in Congress, his practice dramatically changed because he was running for United States Senator, he had used this device just fourteen times—a number, like the number of bills he introduced, far below the congressional average.

† 1938, 1939, 1940, 1942, 1944.

The "Mavericks" did a lot of fighting on the floor. When Johnson arrived in Washington, they expected him to enroll in their ranks—a not unnatural expectation, since they had read about this man who had "shouted Roosevelt, Roosevelt, Roosevelt," and had won by supporting the President on the Supreme Court–packing issue. Roosevelt was their hero and the President's causes their causes, and Maverick had assured them that this young man whom he said he knew well held the same views as they. In fact, Johnson enrolled for a time—for several weeks, he attended the dinners at Renkel's. But then he stopped attending, and the Mavericks found that if he held their views, he would not argue for them. Not that he would argue against them. Says one of them, Edouard V. M. Izac of California: "He just simply was not especially interested in general legislation that came to the floor of the House. Some of us were on the floor all the time, fighting for liberal causes. But he stayed away from the floor, and while he was there, he was very, very silent." And Izac's evaluation—which is echoed by others among Johnson's colleagues—is documented, quite dramatically, by the record of Johnson's participation in House discussions and debates. The record is almost non-existent. Whole years went by in which Johnson did not rise even once to make a point of order, or any other point, not to ask or answer a question, not to support or attack a bill under discussion, not to participate, by so much as a single word, in an entire year's worth of floor proceedings in the House.*

His attitude toward comments that would be made public through the press was equally notable. He was not one of the Congressmen who sought out reporters to comment on some national issue. On the contrary, he would go to unusual lengths to avoid having to reveal his opinion. A reporter would be standing in a corridor, soliciting comments from passing Congressmen. Johnson would start to turn into that corridor, see the reporter, whirl on his heel, and hastily walk back the way he had come.

If he didn't fight in public, would he fight in private? Some of the most effective Congressmen, while rather silent in the well of the House or on the floor (although the *Congressional Record* indicates that few were as silent as Johnson), are active in the aisle at the rear of the House Chamber, or in its cloakrooms. Standing in that aisle, one foot up on the brass rail that separates the aisle from the members' seats, these "brass-railers" quietly buttonhole fellow members to argue for or against legislation.

Lyndon Johnson was not one of these Congressmen. Not that he was silent in the rear aisle or in the cloakrooms. He was friendly, gregarious—could, his fellow members agree, even be said to talk a lot.

But he didn't say anything. Congressmen now observed what classmates

---

* The *Congressional Record* records not a single such instance of participation by Johnson in House discussion in 1937, 1938, 1939, 1942, 1943 or 1944.

had once observed: that, while he might be speaking very volubly during a conversation on a controversial issue, he wouldn't take a position on the issue—or, indeed, say anything of a substantive nature. He tried to avoid specifics, and if pinned down, would say what the other person wanted to hear. He did it very well—as discussions with his congressional colleagues reveal. If the Congressman was a liberal, he believes that Lyndon Johnson, as a Congressman, was a liberal. Says the staunchly liberal Mrs. Douglas: "We agreed on so many of the big issues. He basically agreed with the liberals." But if the Congressman was a conservative, he says that Lyndon Johnson, as a Congressman, was a conservative. Says the reactionary up-state New York Republican Sterling Cole: "Politically, if we disagreed, it wasn't apparent to me. Not at all." Great issues came before the House in these years; 1938, for example, was the year in which it was embroiled in bitter battles over President Roosevelt's proposal to reorganize the executive branch and create new Cabinet departments to facilitate the meeting of new social needs—"the dictator bill," angry Congressmen called it. 1938 was also the year of the great battle over the wages-and-hours bill, the proposal to free American workers from the bondage of the early industrial age. It was the year of the battle over the proposal to extend and make more meaningful Social Security benefits. And, most significantly of all, 1938, the year in which the New Deal had to face its own recession, was the year of the great debate in Washington over whether to fight that recession with mammoth new spending programs, or whether a balanced budget—the balanced budget which the President himself so devoutly wished for—was more important: an issue whose resolution was to affect the fundamentals of American life for years, if not decades, to come. Lyndon Johnson did not participate—neither with legislation nor with debate, not on the well of the House or on the floor or in its cloakrooms or committees—in these battles. He had shouted "Roosevelt, Roosevelt, Roosevelt" to get to Congress; in Congress, he shouted nothing, said nothing—stood for nothing. Not only was he not in the van of any cause, he was not in the ranks, either. Lyndon Johnson would later be called a legislative genius. A legislator is a maker of laws. During the eleven years that Lyndon Johnson served in the law-making body that is the House of Representatives, few of its 435 members had less to do with the making of its laws than he.

Some of the more astute of his colleagues felt that they understood the reason for his silence. Mrs. Douglas, who spent a lot of time with him, speculates on his reasons for acting this way. One that she suggests is "caution": "Was it just caution? Just that he didn't want to have a lot of his words come back at him—a more cautious way of working in the Congress than that of many others? . . . He was witty, he would tell stories, he was humorous. But he was always aware of being responsible for what he said. He was always aware that what he said might be repeated or remembered—

even years later. And he didn't want someone to come back years later, and say, 'I remember when you said . . .' " Watching him talk so much—and say so little—Mrs. Douglas began to realize, she says, that Lyndon Johnson was "strong." In Washington, she says, "everyone tried to find out where you stood. But he had great inner control. He could talk so much—and no one ever knew exactly where he stood."

Even years later. By keeping silent, Johnson might, of course, simply be following a proven path to power in the House of Representatives. It was the path that Rayburn had taken—and Rayburn was in power now.

But they were not on the same path. Power in the House was the power Rayburn wanted; the lone chair atop the triple dais was the goal that iron-willed man had set for himself as a boy in a barn. That was his only goal; he had been asked once to run for the Senate, all but assured of success. He had refused to make the race. Although the immense power he wielded as Majority Leader and, after September, 1940, as Speaker, would have allowed him, had he wished to do so, to wield considerable statewide power in Texas, he declined every opportunity to do so. The only interest he ever displayed in the NYA was to obtain Lyndon Johnson's appointment as its head; the only interest he ever displayed in the PWA was to have it build a dam—the Denison Dam—in his own district; he displayed no interest at all in other statewide organizations the New Deal was creating in Texas—the WPA, for example, or the Rural Electrification Administration; most of the big businessmen who wielded so much statewide power in Texas couldn't even get an appointment with him on their trips to Washington. Only the House itself mattered.

But power in the House was not the power at which Johnson was aiming; the triple dais was not high enough for him. The difference between the aims of the older man and the younger had been demonstrated even before Johnson became a Congressman, when, as Kleberg's secretary, he had placed himself at the service of businessmen who were not from Kleberg's district. Had not practically his first move as Congressman—made while he was still in his hospital bed—been to keep the statewide NYA under his control? And now were not the letters from his office going out not just to addresses in his district but to addresses in Houston, and Dallas, and El Paso as well? A House seat had been an indispensable staging area on the long road he saw before him; he had no choice but to come back a Congressman. But the House seat was only a staging area; it was not the destination at the end of that long road. He had needed the seat; he didn't want to stay in it long. So his silence was not for the sake of power in the House; if he was keeping deliberately silent, it was for a different reason. Who could foresee the turnings of so long a road? No matter how safe a particular stand might seem now, no matter how politically wise, that stand might come back to haunt him someday. No matter what he said now, no matter how intelligent a remark might now seem, he might one day be sorry he had made it.

And so he said nothing.

His standing on Capitol Hill—outside the Texas delegation—was, moreover, not improving.

For a while, he was very popular with his fellow Congressmen, for the same reasons he was popular with the young New Dealers: not only because of his charm, his storytelling ability, his desire to ingratiate and his skill in doing so, but because, in George Brown's words, "He was a leader of men. Johnson had the knack of always appealing to a fellow about someone he didn't like. If he was talking to Joe, and Joe didn't like Jim, he'd say he didn't like Jim, too—that was his leadership, that was his knack." And, of course, for a while, congressional liberals thought he was one of them, while congressional conservatives thought he was one of *them*.

But some of them began to catch on. Liberals found it was useless to ask him to speak in support of a bill in which they were interested. Conservatives found it impossible to persuade him to speak in support of *their* legislation. The judgment implied in Izac's statement that Johnson was "very, very silent" on the floor came to be a widespread judgment among Johnson's colleagues. Pragmatism was of course not unknown on Capitol Hill; for many Congressmen it was a way of life—caution was only common sense. But, in the opinion of more and more of his fellows, Lyndon Johnson's pragmatism and caution went beyond the norm: colleagues committed to causes began to regard him with something akin to scorn.

And then, of course, there was the aspect of his personality that had been so noticeable since his boyhood on the vacant lots of Johnson City, where, if he couldn't pitch, he would take his ball and go home—the quality which led one Johnson City companion to say, "If he couldn't lead, he didn't care much about playing." That aspect had been noticeable in Washington, too. "He couldn't stand not being somebody—just could not *stand* it," Estelle Harbin had said. Lyndon Johnson could not endure being only one of a crowd; he needed—with a compelling need—to lead, and not merely to lead but to dominate, to bend others to his will.

At cocktail parties, he could hold the stage when the other guests were young New Dealers, and even for a time, by the force of his personality, when the guests included older men with more power. But in power-obsessed Washington, when older, more powerful men were present, he couldn't hold the stage for long. And on Capitol Hill, where the pecking order was so clearly and firmly established, and he was near the bottom, he was able to hold attention much less. His stories, vivid though they were, commanded much less attention in a congressional cloakroom than in a Georgetown living room.

He wanted to give advice. It was good advice—he had a rare talent not only for politics but for organization, and Congressmen were continually searching for ways to improve the organization of their offices, a skill of which he was the master. But few of his colleagues wanted advice from a junior colleague. He wanted to give lectures—pontificating in the cloakroom or back of the rail as he had pontificated in the Dodge Hotel basement. But his fellow Congressmen resented his dogmatic, overbearing tone at least as strongly as his fellow congressional secretaries had resented it. His skills at manipulating men were useless without at least a modicum of power to back them up, and he possessed no power at all. Says James Van Zandt of Pennsylvania: "When he wanted something, he really went after it. He would say: 'Now, Goddammit, Jimmy, I helped you on this, and I want you to help me on this.' " And, Van Zandt adds, "Johnson kept asking for favors, and he simply didn't have that many to give in return." He tried too hard—much too hard—to trade on what minor "help" he had given. "You can do those things once or twice," Van Zandt says. "He did them too frequently. People would get irritated."

The pattern which had emerged in the Little Congress (and, before that, at San Marcos) was repeated in the Big Congress. The older men to whom he was so deferential were fond of Lyndon Johnson. Among his contemporaries, those whom he needed and to whom he was also deferential —Rowe and Corcoran, for example—were also fond of him. Another few —very few—of his contemporaries in Congress were fond of him, most of them unassertive men such as Poage and Van Zandt. But the feeling of others was quite different. Says O. C. Fisher, whose Texas district adjoined Johnson's Tenth: "He had a way of getting along with the leaders, and he didn't bother much with the small fry. And let me tell you, the small fry didn't mind. They didn't want much to do with him, either." Even Van Zandt, one of his admirers, says: "People were critical of him because he was too ambitious, too forceful, too pushy. Some people didn't like him." As he walked through the House Dining Room, the resentment that followed him did not come only from members of the Texas delegation. Says Lucas: "Guys [from other states] would come [in] and sit down" at a table near where Johnson was sitting; they would greet all their fellow members nearby, except him. "And he would get up and say, 'Well, Joe, why in hell didn't you speak to me?' Well, they hadn't spoken to him because they didn't like him. They wouldn't put up with him." The situation was summed up in a symbolic gesture—a shrinking away. Lyndon Johnson still practiced his habit of grasping a man's lapel with one hand and putting his other arm around the man's shoulders, holding him close while staring into his eyes and talking directly into his face. Some of his fellow Congressmen didn't mind him doing this, even liked having him do it. Recalls Van Zandt: "He would put his hand on my shoulder and say, 'Now, look, Jimmy . . .' I liked him a lot. You always felt relaxed in his presence." But others—many others—did mind. They would draw back from his hand, shrug away from his arm. And sometimes, if he didn't take the hint, they would get angry. Once he took a Congressman's lapel in his hand, and the Congressman knocked his hand away. Without power to back it up, his manner of dealing with his colleagues earned him not the power he craved, but only unpopularity.

His role on the Naval Affairs Committee could hardly have added to his enjoyment of life in Congress. He and Warren Magnuson, a dashing bachelor who sat in the next chair in the committee's lower horseshoe, had, according to one of Carl Vinson's aides, discovered "how to play up to" the chairman by telling him "stories"—stories with a sexual tinge: "humorous dirty jokes and the details of amorous escapades, which he enjoyed with real vicarious pleasure." Devoted to his invalid wife, Vinson, Magnuson says, "went home early each afternoon to take care of his wife, and he never invited anyone to visit him. . . . He was a recluse." But the two young Congressmen began dropping in on him, telling him their "stories," and, Magnuson says, "Before long we were in solidly with the Admiral." Fond though he may have been of them, however, they were still only ensigns on a very tight ship—as Johnson was constantly, and painfully, being reminded. Occasionally, during the questioning of a witness, he would essay a small witticism. "Is the Gentleman from Texas finished?" Vinson would demand dryly. The gavel would crash down. "Let's proceed," the chairman would say. Johnson had become fascinated with tape recorders, which were, in 1939 and 1940, large, clumsy devices just beginning to come into public use. One morning, he brought a tape recorder into the committee room before the hearing began, and set it up at his seat, running the wire over to a microphone which he placed on the witness table. Vinson arrived, slouched down in his seat, lit up a cigar, and then, just as he was about to gavel the hearing to order, noticed the recorder.

Peering over the glasses teetering on the end of his nose, he said, "Now what does the Gentleman from Texas have there?"

"A tape recorder, Mr. Chairman," Johnson replied. "We have a witness from Texas this morning. I'd like to record his statement, and send it to the radio stations down in Texas."

"Well," Vinson said, "the Gentleman is not going to do that. We are not going to record witnesses, and we are not going to send statements back to the district." He curtly ordered Johnson to remove the recorder from the room; to Johnson's humiliation, he had to do so before the eyes of the visitor from Texas.

When Johnson had been sworn in in 1937, only two Congressmen had been younger than he. Now, in 1939, there were quite a few younger. He was no longer even the youngest Congressman from Texas. Newspaper articles on the state's congressional contingent often mentioned "the baby of the delegation," and they were referring to Lindley Beckworth of Gladewater, near Marshall, who had been elected in 1938 at the age of twenty-five. Although Johnson would not be thirty-one until August, 1939, he was no longer a particularly youthful Congressman. He was only a junior Congressman, one of several hundred junior Congressmen.

One of a crowd.

AT THE OTHER END of Pennsylvania Avenue, too, he seemed to be retreating rather than advancing.

Unable to see President Roosevelt in person, he attempted on March 24, 1939, to catch his attention and elicit a response with a rather unusual letter. It was ostensibly a recommendation of an acquaintance for a federal post, but it began:

> Sir:
>   Sometimes as I go about my work for the Tenth District of Texas and the United States as a whole, thoughts come into my mind I feel I just have to talk over with the Chief. I know I can't consume your time with them in appointments, but I am persuaded to do what I am doing now—get out my paper and typewriter and drop you a note. . . .

If Johnson had hoped to thus elicit a response from "the Chief," however, he was to be disappointed. The response came instead from presiden-- tial secretary Stephen Early, and it was distinctly *pro forma:* "You may be sure that your comments will be given careful consideration," it said. (In the event, Johnson's candidate did not get the post.)

During that same month, Johnson wrote Roosevelt requesting increased funding for the Texas A&M ROTC unit. The White House referred the request to the War Department—which cursorily rejected it.

There was, White House aides agree, no particular reason for Johnson's complete lack of success in making contact with the man in the Oval Office. There was, they say, no reason that he *should* have made contact. "You've got to have a reason to see a President," Rowe explains. Johnson had no reason. And Rowe—and other New Dealers who knew of Johnson's unsuccessful efforts—could see no hope that he *would* have a reason, not, at least, in any immediate future. He was after all only a junior Congressman from one of the most remote and isolated regions in the United States.

Those of them who, like Rowe, guessed his ambitions, could see no way that he would get to be a Senator, much less a national power—not in the foreseeable future, at least. How could he possibly transform a political base that consisted of an isolated district in a remote region of far-off Texas into a national base?

How could he possibly—in any foreseeable future—be anything more than an obscure Congressman? Lyndon Johnson could not endure being only one of a crowd. But as the Spring of 1939 turned into Summer, one of a crowd was all he was—and, for long years to come, it seemed, that was all he was likely to be.

30

A Contract
and Three Telegrams

DURING THE SUMMER of 1939, however, he took a desperate step.

This maneuver involved Sam Rayburn. Its backdrop was one of the great dramas of American political history: the blood feud between the President of the United States—and the Vice President.

This feud had been raging since shortly after the two men had run together for the second time, teammates in one of the greatest election triumphs in American history.

Even before the 1936 election, John Nance Garner, perturbed over the direction the New Deal was taking, had been protesting to Franklin Roosevelt. Garner had felt the emergency measures of the Hundred Days were necessary; he felt that the President had saved the country. But by 1934, he felt the emergency was over; the measures should be phased out. As early as October, 1934, in a blunt letter to Roosevelt from Uvalde, he advised him to "cut down as far as possible, the cost of government. . . . Pardon me for mentioning this matter because it is not my 'butt-in,' but it does pertain to the expenditure of federal funds which goes with living within your income and paying something on your debts." The still more liberal measures of 1935's "Second Hundred Days"—measures such as Social Security, the Wagner Labor Relations Act, and, above all, inheritance and stepped-up income taxes—were the very antithesis of the simple, rugged frontier philosophy in which Cactus Jack Garner believed with all his heart. The continued heavy governmental expenditures and annual budget deficits of the "New Deal"—how Cactus Jack hated that phrase!—must inevitably lead, he believed, to another Depression; thirty years later (in 1965, when Garner was ninety-six), a Washington journalist would travel to Uvalde to ask him if he had any advice for government. "Stop the spending!" the old man growled.

His protests had been strictly private. If individualism was one pillar of Garner's philosophy, loyalty was another, loyalty to party and loyalty to his leader; the politician he loathed above all others was Maury Maverick, who stood for everything he detested, and who had, moreover, beaten his friends, the old "City Machine," in San Antonio; but when Maverick ran for re-election in 1936—against the City Machine—Garner arranged for the financing of Maverick's campaign, because Roosevelt had asked him to do so. Sometimes his feelings about the New Deal showed in personal letters to Texas. When, in 1936, an old friend, the wealthy Houston lumberman John Henry Kirby, who was the chairman of the ultraconservative Southern Committee to Uphold the Constitution, demanded: "How long are you going to tolerate the apostasy of the Roosevelt Administration. . . ?" Garner replied tersely: "You can't do everything you want to and I can't do half what I would like to do. You don't control everybody you would like to and I am in a similar fix. I think that answers your question." But his feelings had—before the 1936 election—never showed in Washington. Disagree with administration proposals though he might, he lobbied for them with the conservatives who had been his friends during his thirty years on Capitol Hill. "No man was more influential in the Senate than Garner," Joseph Alsop and Turner Catledge wrote in their detailed and invaluable book on the court fight, *The 168 Days;* "In the President's first administration larger numbers of senators had seen the light on New Deal measures in [Garner's] private office with the well-stocked liquor closet . . . than anywhere else in Washington."

Then, at the end of 1936, just weeks after the election, came the sitdown strikes. Garner's sizable fortune, as well as that of his Texas friends and of his Southern friends in Congress, had been built on cheap labor. In Uvalde, located as it was beyond the 98th meridian, little cotton was grown; instead, Garner grew pecans, and pecans were picked by the Mexican-Americans who made up more than half of Uvalde's population. The work was hard—after the pecans were knocked out of the trees, they had to be shelled, a job which required strong hands—and for it Garner paid one cent per pound; a good man could, his fingers bleeding from a hundred small cuts, pick as many as a hundred pounds in a day—one dollar for a day's work. Mexicans were satisfied with that wage, Garner would explain. "They are not troublesome people unless they become Americanized. The Sheriff can make them do anything." Not that white labor earned much more in Uvalde. Garner built and rented out homes. The union scale for carpenters in Texas was one and a quarter an hour; Garner paid his carpenters the quarter, although there were a few who worked their way up to fifty cents an hour—until they made a mistake ("like sawing a board a mite too short," an Uvalde carpenter explained; "why, back you go first thing to twenty-five cents. Just one mistake, that's all"). To men accustomed to treating laborers like serfs, the very idea of unions was anathema. (There were none in Uvalde.

"Mr. Garner, he don't like unions," another carpenter explained. "The plumbers, they had a union once, but they don't now.") And sitdown strikes were the ultimate outrage, for this form of labor strife, in which workers seized possession of their employer's plant and stayed there, "sitting down" at their jobs, threatened the sacred right of private property. At a Cabinet meeting, Garner said, as he was to recall it, "They permitted men to take over other people's property. In Texas we would call that stealing. That's when I said . . . the federal government owed it to the country to protect the property. . . . I got ugly about it and cussed and raised Cain."

He also went to see Roosevelt personally. As he related the discussion to his lifelong friend and authorized biographer, journalist Bascom Timmons:

> I asked the President, "Do you think it is right?"
> "No," he replied.
> "Do you think it is legal?"
> "No," he replied.

Garner left this meeting under the impression that Roosevelt had promised to immediately issue a statement denouncing the new labor tactic and, if the situation worsened, to take stronger action. But neither statement nor action materialized. This was not the first time that Garner felt Roosevelt had broken his word; he believed the President had repeatedly promised him to balance the budget. John Gunther was to write about Roosevelt's "worst quality," a "deviousness," a "lack of candor" that "verged on deceit." Men who had known Roosevelt longer—when he had been Governor of New York—used stronger words; in Albany it had been whispered that a commitment from the Governor could not be trusted; New York City's ordinarily mild-mannered legislative representative, Reuben Lazarus, told him to his face: "Governor, from now on we deal in writing; and I'm going to demand a bond on your signature." His State Park Commissioner, Robert Moses, not mild-mannered, shouted at him one day: "Frank Roosevelt, you're a goddamned liar and this time I can prove it! I had a stenographer present!" Garner told a friend that the President "was a charming fellow. . . . But he was a hard man to have an understanding with. He would deviate from the understanding." To a man like Garner, no judgment could have been harsher. In the world of Capitol Hill, where a congressional session was round after round of hastily formed alliances, trust in a man's word was all-important; Garner himself was known for honoring his promises, however inconvenient they later proved. In 1937, sitdown strikes were widening, and no presidential action was forthcoming. Alsop and Catledge wrote that Garner, feeling "he had been fooled by the President all through the business," "flew into a fury." Garner in a fury was a man who lost control of his tongue. At a conference with Roosevelt, a conference at which

Majority Leader Joseph T. Robinson was present, Garner was to say that "We went at it hot and heavy"—so hot and heavy that, Alsop and Catledge reported, "Before very long both men had forgotten their self-control and were using such language to one another that Joe Robinson, horrified, shouted them down and forced them to end the conference."

And then, on February 5, 1937, Roosevelt introduced his court-packing bill.

Neither Garner nor any congressional leader had been given so much as a hint that such a measure was being prepared; summoned to the White House, they were informed half an hour before Roosevelt announced it to the press. (Garner was to say, moreover, that Roosevelt had assured him and Robinson not three weeks before that there would be little other than appropriations bills for Congress to consider.)

During his first term, the President had been generally scrupulous in consulting with Capitol Hill; had his second election led him to feel that he no longer needed to consult, "that," as Alsop and Catledge put it, "compliance with his wishes had become automatic? . . . His overconfidence blinded him," Alsop and Catledge were to conclude.*

> There were huge Democratic majorities in both houses. The men who managed the majorities had an all but unblemished record of perfect subservience to the White House; they also had the inconvenient habit of offering advice when their advice was asked. . . . Therefore neither Garner nor Robinson . . . nor anyone else was to be admitted to the secret. The carelessness of congressional feelings was carried so far that the President . . . determined to attach a copy of the bill to the message, as though to suggest that congressional erasure of the merest comma would not be allowed.

The President's lack of courtesy was far from the only reason for Garner's instant distress over the bill. The tough little Texan was not a man given to abstract thought, but there were a few concrete elements of government in which he deeply believed; the Constitution was one of them, and in the instant he first heard the President's proposal, he had no doubt that the Constitution was threatened by it. After the meeting, Garner was to recall, "I loaded my automobile with Senators and Representatives and took them back to the Capitol. We were all so stunned we hardly spoke." According to most accounts, the first reaction came during that ride from Texan Hatton Sumners, chairman of the House Judiciary Committee. "Boys," he said,

---

* During the twentieth century, three of the presidential landslides in America have been followed by a presidential maneuver that might be laid at least in part to overconfidence: Roosevelt's landslide in 1936 by the attempt to pack the Court; Lyndon Johnson's in 1964 by escalation of the Vietnam War; Richard Nixon's of 1972 by the Watergate cover-up.

"here's where I cash in my chips." But it may actually have come earlier—from Garner; as he was leaving the meeting, he was to say, he had a quiet word with Attorney General Homer Cummings, who had secretly drafted the court-packing measure. "General," Garner said, "it will be many, many moons before the boss signs that bill." Capitol Hill was soon left in no doubt about Garner's feelings; a few hours later, while the presidential message was being read in the Senate Chamber, Garner left the rostrum, stalked into the Senators' private lobby behind the Chamber, and there let a group of Senators know his reaction by holding his nose with one hand and making a thumbs-down gesture with the other.

Most congressional leaders agreed with that feeling, but party loyalty led Garner to refuse to oppose the bill publicly and to attempt to arrange a compromise. When, however, he led a group of his colleagues to put their case before the President, Roosevelt "laughed in their faces, so loudly that a number of them were exceedingly annoyed." (So confident was Roosevelt that he was, Alsop and Catledge wrote, "in a laughing mood in those days, when suggestions of compromise were made.")

But by May, with renewed tension over sitdown strikes and general labor unrest, the Vice President was, in Tommy Corcoran's words, "off the reservation . . . almost in open revolt." Soon it was common gossip in the cloakrooms that he had told Senator Wheeler, a leader of the opposition to the Court measure, "Burt, you're a real patriot." When Senator Vandenberg emotionally denounced sitdown strikes as no better than revolution, Garner left the rostrum, went down to the Senate floor and embraced the Republican in full view of the galleries. He was "doing a lot of damage," Corcoran reported. And then Garner took his most dramatic—and effective—step. On June 11, in the midst of the congressional session, he left Washington and went home to Uvalde.

ALTHOUGH GARNER gave no explanation for his departure, the reason was so evident that it exposed to public view the split—the "terrible breach," Alsop and Catledge were to call it—between the New Dealers at one end of Pennsylvania Avenue and the conservatives at the other. It solidified the opposition of wavering and doubtful Senators. By now, moreover, Roosevelt had begun to understand that compromise would be necessary—and that he needed Garner to obtain the best compromise possible. On June 18, Jim Farley, Garner's old friend, found the President "smoldering over the absence of the presiding officer of the Senate."

> "Why in Hell did Jack have to leave at this time for?" he fumed through a cloud of cigarette smoke. "I'm going to write and tell him about all these stories and suggest he come back. . . . He's got to come back."

Roosevelt's letter was packed with Roosevelt charm, but for Jack Garner the charm had long since worn thin. He did not return to Washington until July 19, and he did so aboard the funeral train of his friend Majority Leader Robinson, who had died suddenly of a heart attack. Garner had boarded the train in Little Rock, where the thirty-odd Senators on board greeted him "like a long-lost father." Wrote Alsop and Catledge: "The old Texas fox had made a quick trip from Uvalde, with a purpose spurring him on. He had seen the Democratic party disintegrate in the court fight, and now he had returned to pick up the pieces." During the train ride back after Robinson's funeral, he conferred with the Senators, and the next morning, he arrived at the White House. When, after "a great show of cordiality" by Roosevelt, the subject turned to the court fight, Garner asked him, "Do you want it with the bark on or off, Cap'n?" Roosevelt threw back his head and, with a hearty laugh, said he would have it with the bark off. "All right," Garner said. "You are beat. You haven't got the votes."

Roosevelt empowered Garner to work out a compromise. When it evolved—an agreement to recommit the court-reorganization bill to the Senate Judiciary Committee with the understanding that when it reappeared on the Senate floor, all mention of the Supreme Court would have been removed—it was an almost unmitigated defeat for the President, one which allowed him to save face only in that there would be some reorganization of lower courts. Alsop and Catledge, who did the most thorough job of contemporary interviewing of participants, concluded that Garner "wanted to do the best he could for the President"—and in fact did so, faced as he was with the overwhelming senatorial sentiment against the bill and the desire of some Senators to defeat it outright as a salutary lesson to the President. On one occasion, when he was attempting to bargain with Wheeler, the Montanan told him "with considerable firmness" that the opposition did not have to compromise at all, since it had enough votes to do as it pleased. But Roosevelt, "sore and vengeful," in intimates' words, took the loss hard. Wrote Alsop and Catledge: "He knew there was no way out of an immediate humiliation, but he had made up his mind that if he had to suffer the men in Congress whom he held responsible would suffer doubly later on." And he felt that he knew who was most responsible. To Farley, a "fuming" President said: "He didn't even attempt to bargain with Wheeler. He just accepted Wheeler's terms. If Garner had put up any kind of a fight, the thing could have been worked out differently." Corcoran, one of the President's principal strategists in the fight, said flatly that "it was the Vice President who had betrayed the President."

And the emotion was not one-sided. Garner felt Roosevelt was again "deviating" from "understandings." In the fight to replace Robinson as leader, the two men agreed, in Garner's recollection, not to interfere. In Garner's view, he kept his word, while Roosevelt did not, maneuvering to secure the election of Kentucky's Alben Barkley. Garner had also, in a memorandum, asked the President a question: *"When* was the government going to *balance the budget?"* Garner had asked the question before, and had been given a flat promise in reply: "I have said fifty times that the budget will be balanced for the fiscal year 1938. If you want me to say it again, I will say it either once or fifty times more. That is my intention." But the budget for fiscal 1938 proved to be heavily unbalanced.

The antagonism between the two men could no longer be hidden. At Cabinet meetings, Ickes noted in August, 1937, the President "doesn't overlook any chance to send a pointed barb, albeit with a laugh, in the direction of the Vice President." And if Roosevelt expected Garner to be faced down, he did not know his man. In December of that year, Roosevelt was discussing his upcoming message to Congress when, staring straight at Garner down the length of the long Cabinet table, he said, "Jack, I am going to reassert leadership." He said he had temporarily put it on the shelf because he was tired. Replied Garner: "You were afraid, Mr. President." Roosevelt repeated that he had been tired. ". . . Both scared and tired," Garner retorted. Wrote Ickes: "I have never heard anyone talk like this to the President, and the President did not pursue the subject any further." Now, in 1938, with the economy sliding into a "new Depression," Roosevelt was considering new government pump-priming expenditures—which would further unbalance the budget being prepared for fiscal 1939. In April, 1938, Garner warned the President that such expenditures would meet with considerable congressional opposition—making these statements with "vehemence"; he left Roosevelt's office, the *New York Times* noted, "red-faced and non-committal." In an unusual outburst to a reporter, he said, "We've been trying this New Deal spending orgy for six years, and where has it got us. . . ? I for one refuse to support more reckless spending. It's got to stop." And he apparently told friends that if it didn't stop, *he* would stop it; it is "openly whispered in Texas, among Mr. Garner's home advisers, that he will lead the opposition in Congress to measures not acceptable to many Democrats," the *Times* reported. Among the measures not acceptable was Roosevelt's attempt to reorganize, and expand, the White House staff and the executive branch of government generally; this measure—on its face, as James MacGregor Burns says, "one of the least controversial Roosevelt had ever proposed"—brought to a boil the long-simmering anti-Roosevelt bitterness in Congress, which, despite heroic efforts by Sam Rayburn, and the prodigal use by Roosevelt of patronage to try to bring Congressmen to heel, voted down the "dictator bill." "As the vote was announced," Burns recounts, "wild cheering broke out among representatives in the chamber. Congress was in open revolt."

At this time, Roosevelt took his first public cognizance of the rumors about the rift between him and Garner. He denied that it existed. When

Garner was asked about it, "he merely smiled, then tightened his lips." But then came the purge, a cross-country trip on which Roosevelt attempted to defeat in their district primaries selected Representatives and Senators who had opposed him. John Garner, to whom party unity was so vital, could hardly believe that a President was doing this to members of his own party; in fact, at the time of the court compromise, he had personally promised Senators—his intimates believe on the basis of a commitment given to him by Roosevelt—that there would be no reprisals from the White House. Some of Roosevelt's targets were, moreover, among Garner's oldest friends and closest allies. He no longer bothered to keep his feelings secret. In Texas, where Roosevelt snubbed Garner's friend Senator Tom Connally by announcing from the back platform of his train the appointment to a federal judgeship of a Texan who was a Connally enemy, Garner stayed home in Uvalde, telling reporters he was busy "fishing." The President of the United States had come to the Vice President's state—and the Vice President had refused to meet him! When Garner returned to Washington from Texas, on December 18, 1938, Garner and Roosevelt met privately for the last time. "We didn't get anywhere," Roosevelt told Farley. "Jack is very much opposed to the spending program; he's against the tax program, and he's against the relief program. He seems to be pretty much against everything and he hasn't got a single concrete idea to offer on any of these programs. It's one thing to criticize but something else again to offer solutions." At the next Cabinet meeting, Garner's feelings spilled over. When the hated liberal Henry Wallace began discussing new plans to reduce the cotton surplus, the Vice President, in Ickes' words,

> opened up all along the line on cotton. The Vice President said that people had moved into the South because they liked to be free and the freedom that they wanted was the right to grow as much cotton as they wanted to grow. He believes that restricting crops is bad, both economically and politically. He reminded the President that he had discussed this subject with him at their recent conference.

He "opened up" in his Capitol Hill stronghold, too. A week after the Cabinet meeting, *Time* reported that congressional Democrats were determined to have "economy" in government at last—and that "if they need a leader, John Garner stood ready to lead." The nation was given at last a glimpse of the power he had long wielded: in what *Time* called "an unusual spectacle, . . . a scene that may in fact have been all but unprecedented in American politics," on the same day, two Cabinet members, appointees of the President, had to call, "hat in hand," on the Vice President to plead for congressional approval of the President's policies—Wallace to try to persuade him on acreage restrictions, Harry Hopkins to obtain Senate confirmation as Secretary of Commerce. Roosevelt himself had to go to Garner hat in hand; when Hopkins came close to breaking under the vicious questioning by a Senate committee, Roosevelt asked his Vice President, in Ickes' phrase, "to call off the dogs 'for the sake of the party.' " Garner did. He refused, however, to give in on acreage, and also beat the President on the relief bill. In the Cabinet now, the two men who sat at opposite ends of the table could barely contain their enmity for each other. Sometimes when Roosevelt was talking, Garner would begin talking—not in a whisper— at his end of the table. Sometimes, in what Ickes felt was a "truculent . . . very unpleasant" manner, he would interrupt the President, saying, "Well, didn't I tell you so?" or "You remember that I brought that up two or three years ago." Said Ickes: "How the President takes this from Garner, or anyone else, is more than I can understand. . . . I suspect that there is growing up in the President's heart a hatred of Garner. . . ." Notified during a Cabinet meeting of still another Senate defeat by Garner's allies, Roosevelt, staring down the table at Garner, said, "Well, that is that. Now we will go on to Chapter Two." After the meeting, talking with Ickes, he said, "Do you notice that I am whistling?" (And he was, more or less, from between his teeth, Ickes says.) "Then he added, 'I always whistle when I'm mad.' "

By 1939, Ickes himself, seeing Garner's "old, red, wizened face on the rostrum above the President when the President delivered his message to Congress," found him "disgusting." Even the King and Queen of England were not exempt from his rudeness! At the White House dinner for Their Majesties, "He was as full of life as a kitten. He has no breeding or natural dignity and I doubt if he exercised any more self-restraint than he would have shown at a church supper in Uvalde, Texas. . . . He pawed the King with his hands. . . . To Garner the King was simply a visiting Elk."

Younger New Dealers, including, as one reporter wrote, "those ambitious young intellectuals around Mr. Roosevelt and their journalistic friends, get blue in the face when you mention John Garner's name." *Time* reported in a March 20, 1939, cover story on Garner, titled "Undeclared War," that "John Garner has become to arch New Dealers a symbol of sabotage. They consider him a prairie politician whose archaic notions, plus popular veneration for long public service, accidentally make him the leader of reaction against six years of enlightened reform." The articles of the young New Dealers' "journalistic friends" reflected the intensity of their feelings about the old Texan. Wrote Hamilton Basso in the *New Republic,* "His heart, and most of his mental processes, belong to the America of 1875. . . . As a person, he is not liked. . . . Mr. Garner has taken his personal smallness, his lack of generosity, and forged it into a political principle. The metaphysicians may argue that this, *per se*, is not evil: but on a human plane, it is certainly not good. . . . He has no imagination, no

convictions, and he substitutes political cynicism for social understanding."
In his *Newsweek* column, Raymond Moley, himself long gone from the
reservation, offered a different opinion:

> A good many of the "feature articles" about Mr. Garner
> manage to suggest that he's a kind of glorified clown, spending
> his time thinking up what the next wisecrack should be, what kind
> of funny hat to wear the next time his picture is taken, and what
> he can eat and drink that will look well in the newsreels. The
> trouble with those who write such pieces—and there are a good
> many earning a living in Washington—is that they can never take
> a man for what he is. They have seen so many phonies in their day
> . . . that they automatically conclude that nothing is what it seems
> to be.
>
> It is true that Mr. Garner is picturesque. I have never thought
> of calling him anything but Mr. Garner. . . . Not many people call
> him Jack to his face. There is dignity about the man. . . . He's
> picturesque only because his method of life, which is simple and
> natural, contrasts so weirdly with the sham living that goes on in
> Washington. . . . He's a man who lives his life as he wants to live
> it. . . .

The New Dealers' feelings were reciprocated by the object of their
scorn. He detested what even their journalist friends had to concede was
their "slightly ostentatious intellectualism," and what he saw as a hypocrisy
which made them talk of principles when, as he told a friend, "All they're
interested in is staying in power." They were, in Garner's view, unscrupulous
men who were persuading the President to desert his party, the party
Garner loved.

And now the feud was climaxing, for the presidential election of 1940
was drawing steadily closer.

Historians may puzzle over when Franklin Roosevelt decided to defy
the Third Term tradition and run for the Presidency again, but John
Garner's intimates never had the slightest doubt as to what the decision
would be—"Why, he is panting to run," one of them said as early as the
Autumn of 1938—and neither did Garner, although Roosevelt had assured
him he would not run again. "He has too much power and is continually
asking for more," he had told Timmons; that predilection could lead to
only one decision. Later, he would tell Timmons, "He will never leave the
White House except in death or defeat."

Garner, Timmons wrote, "abhorred even the idea of a third term for
any President," good or bad. The basis for his abhorrence was simple: four
decades in Washington had taught him what power did to men. "No man
should exercise great powers too long," he said. On another occasion, he was

to say: "We don't want any kings or emperors in this country. You have to curb the ambitions of every man, even the best of them, [because] they are human." Often now, there crept into his blunt conversation, when discussing Roosevelt, the word "dictator." Whether or not he wanted the Democratic nomination for himself—whether, as his advisors were to maintain, he was standing for the nomination merely as an anti-third-term symbol —or whether, as the New Dealers said, the seventy-year-old poker player, having long bided his time, had at last found himself holding a royal flush and could scarcely contain his greed at the pot within his grasp—he was determined that the nomination would not go to Franklin Roosevelt.

And Roosevelt, whether or not he had decided to run again, was determined that his successor not be someone who might tear down what he had built; he was determined to deny the nomination to any of the Democratic conservatives who did not believe in the New Deal—in particular, he was determined that the nomination would not go to John Garner.

Nineteen thirty-nine was Garner's year. The war was open now. The "Garner gang" of conservative congressional barons, *Time* magazine said, had long been bound together by "intangible ties of friendship for and trust in the old man. . . . Since Speaker 'Uncle Joe' Cannon, who finally met in Jack Garner his match at poker, no man [has] enjoyed such influence among members on both sides of the aisle in both Houses as this stubby, stubborn, pink & white billiken with the beak of an owl, eyebrows like cupid's wings, tongue of a cowhand." And he was using that influence to the full. During the first months of 1939, Congress defeated several Roosevelt proposals. Then the President proposed a new public works program, for self-liquidating projects, which would include the creation of "a revolving fund fed from the earnings" of these projects which could be used "to finance new projects when there is need of extra stimulus of employment." Garner felt that this proposal would free the executive branch from the need of congressional approval for these projects. "This bill in some particulars is the worst that has come up here," he said. "It gives the President discretion to spend billions where he wants to, how he wants to and when he wants. It is another step away from constitutional government and toward personal government." The House, by a substantial majority, refused even to take it up for debate.

Previously, the President had relied on Garner to kill, or hamstring, potentially damaging congressional investigations. Now, a young Texas Congressman, Martin Dies, Jr. (thirty years before, Garner had served in the House with Martin Dies, Sr.), was given a substantial appropriation for his House Un-American Activities Committee, which, as William Leuchtenberg puts it, "served the purposes of those who claimed that the New Deal was a Red stratagem." And over furious administration opposition, Congress passed—and Roosevelt was forced to sign—the Hatch Act, which would in the event prove ineffective (because, Garner believed, the administration did not enforce it), but which, at the time of its passage, was believed to be a deterrent to political activity by federal employees. The reason for its passage was common knowledge in Washington: at the 1936 Democratic Convention, a majority of the delegates had been made up of postmasters, United States marshals, IRS employees and other federal officeholders, who might be disposed to favor an incumbent President. Garner and his conservative allies wanted to make sure that the incumbent President would have no such advantage at the 1940 Convention.

"A sullen world" was, in Burns' phrase, "girding for war"; a sullen Congress refused to change the Neutrality Act to give the President more room to maneuver on behalf of the embattled democracies. Summoning Senate leaders to the White House, Roosevelt pleaded with them. Then Garner asked them if there were enough votes to change the Act—and summed up: "Well, Captain, we may as well face the facts. You haven't got the votes; and that's all there is to it." He had turned the Vice Presidency, *Time* said, from "a sarcophagus into a throne."

And if 1939 was Garner's year on Capitol Hill, it was his year in the polls, too. In March, the Gallup Poll asked the question: "If Roosevelt is not a candidate, whom would you like to see elected?" Jim Farley received 8 percent, Cordell Hull 10 percent—John Garner 45 percent. And Roosevelt could hardly have been sanguine about the results if his name had been included in the poll: 53 percent of all Democrats were opposed to a third term. As the *New Republic* had to report with chagrin, political prognosticators generally felt that a candidate with so commanding a lead could not be overtaken; pollster Emil Hurja said that "Mr. Garner is so far ahead of all other candidates that he cannot be stopped." If he was to be stopped, certainly, only one man could do it—just as Garner himself was the only man who could stop Roosevelt if Roosevelt chose to run. As the *Congressional Digest* put it, "It is a case of Franklin D. Roosevelt, epitome of the New Deal, . . . against John Nance Garner, to whom much of the New Deal is anathema." Discussing possible candidates with Jim Farley at Hyde Park, Roosevelt said: "To begin with, there's Garner, he's just impossible." Although other names would continually be floated, the contest had, in 1939, narrowed down to two men—each of whom not only hated the other personally but hated also much of what the other stood for.

ROOSEVELT DECIDED to attack Garner in his own state. There was reason to think this bold tactic might have success. While the reactionary "interests" which ran Texas were solidly against the President, the state's people had, at least in the past, been overwhelmingly behind him; they had given him a seven-to-one margin over Landon in 1936. Even if he could not defeat Garner in the state's 1940 Democratic primary, might he not at least poll a respectable number of votes against him, enough to embarrass him? And being forced to fight in his own stronghold might keep Garner on the defensive.

If he was to fight Garner in Texas, however, Roosevelt needed a man in Texas—someone to direct his strategy in the state, preferably someone prominent enough throughout the state to serve as a rallying point for New Deal enthusiasm. The list of potential candidates, however, was very short. A Senator would have been ideal, but one, Tom Connally, had earned the President's bitter enmity by opposing the court-packing proposal. And while the other—mild-mannered Morris Sheppard—was a loyal New Dealer, he put personal loyalties above political, and his personal loyalty belonged to the man who had come to Congress at virtually the same time as he, thirty-six years before. Among the state's Congressmen, Maury Maverick would, a year earlier, have been a logical choice, because his willingness to speak out for liberal causes had not only endeared him to Roosevelt but had made him a statewide name. Another Congressman, W. D. McFarlane of Graham, Sam Johnson's onetime Populist ally in the State Legislature, was an eager volunteer for the job. On the Texas leg of Roosevelt's 1938 cross-country "purge trip," the trip on which Garner had refused to meet him, the President had praised Maverick and McFarlane. But despite the praise, by 1939 both Maverick and McFarlane were no longer in Congress, having lost their congressional seats to conservative opponents.* Garner had had his San Antonio friends support Maverick in 1936; in 1938, the Vice President had quietly passed the word that he wanted Maverick "crushed"—and crushed he was, by Paul Kilday, who stated that his goal was "the elimination from Congress of one overwhelmingly shown to be the friend and ally of Communism."

There was another obvious choice: Sam Rayburn. But this was the Sam Rayburn of whom it was said, "If he was your friend, he was your friend forever. He would be with you—*always*. The tougher the going, the more certain you could be that when you looked around, Sam Rayburn would be standing there with you." In a contest between Roosevelt and Garner, Rayburn's preference was not for Garner but for the man whose picture stood on his desk at home in Bonham. Garner was his friend, but Roosevelt was his hero. Moreover, the philosophy of the New Deal was his philosophy; Garner's was not. "There is much more of contrast than of similarity between the two Texans," wrote Raymond Moley, who knew them both well, and the contrast was deeper than the differences in their bank balances, or the fact that Rayburn would not accept a free pass from the railroads, while Garner rode back and forth to Texas in the luxuriously

---

* Maverick's election as Mayor of San Antonio in 1939 was blighted by his indictment later that year on the charge of using union contributions to pay supporters' poll taxes; although he would later be acquitted, he was hardly in a position to serve as a President's standard-bearer.

furnished private car of the president of the Missouri-Kansas-Pacific line. As Moley explained, Garner "is a big business man" with few "prejudices against financial power" and "limited sympathy for the underprivileged. Rayburn is more likely to suffer for those who fail." Garner's opposition to the New Deal had, Moley says, "opened a fissure" between him and Rayburn. Furthermore, Rayburn had no doubt that Roosevelt would eventually decide to run again—and he had no doubt that if Roosevelt ran, he would crush any other candidate. Garner's campaign for the nomination would not only be one in which Rayburn did not believe, it was, Rayburn knew, bound to be a losing fight. But while Roosevelt was his hero, Garner was his *friend*—had been his friend for a quarter of a century. More, Garner had been his patron. During Rayburn's difficult early years in Congress, it was Garner who had given him the helping hand that enabled him to start climbing the House ladder. In 1937, when Rayburn had been in danger of losing his fight to be Majority Leader (and next in line for his yearned-for Speakership), Garner had rushed back from Texas to throw his weight on the scales and tip them in Rayburn's favor. (Rayburn's reply, when a reporter had asked about the propriety of the Vice President's intervention in a congressional matter, was instructive: "In the first place," he said, "Jack Garner is my friend.") When, in 1939, Garner asked him to manage his campaign for the 1940 Democratic presidential nomination, he agreed. And once he had enlisted in Garner's cause, it didn't matter how tough the going was. Attempting to pry Rayburn away from his fellow Texan, "White House sources" raised the possibility that, despite Rayburn's leadership of New Deal causes, he might not be the President's choice to replace Speaker Bankhead, whose heart disease was rapidly worsening. This threat to Rayburn's long-held dream was a grave one—Roosevelt's potential in Capitol Hill succession battles had been demonstrated by his success in winning the Senate Majority Leadership for Alben Barkley—but Woodrow Wilson could have told Roosevelt what Rayburn's response to a presidential threat would be. Previously, Rayburn had been somewhat circumspect in his remarks on the presidential race. After the first White House leaks appeared, he issued a more pointed statement: "I am for that outstanding Texan and liberal Democrat, John N. Garner, for the presidential nomination in 1940, believing that if elected he will make the country a great President." Roosevelt's reaction to Rayburn's defiance was revealed a month later. Rayburn's district held a celebration in his honor each August. "In previous years," Stephen Early wrote in a memo to the President, "you have sent messages to Sam Rayburn on the occasion of the celebration. . . . Ordinarily I would take care of this without troubling you but in light of Rayburn's recent declarations, I think it is best to leave the decision to you." Roosevelt's decision was not to send a message. During succeeding months—as long as Garner was in the presidential race, in fact—Roosevelt would not even autograph a picture for Rayburn; when, for example, Rayburn's secretary, Alla Clary, sent a photograph taken by one of Rayburn's friends to the White House for a routine presidential autograph, Missy LeHand returned it unsigned.

LYNDON JOHNSON'S APPLICATION for the post of leader of the Roosevelt forces in Texas was at first not considered seriously. A junior Congressman was hardly the ideal leader of the presidential campaign in a pivotal state. Nor did Johnson enjoy White House entrée at this time—a fact which had been forcibly brought home to him during the President's "purge" trip of July, 1938. He was not on the initial list of Texas Congressmen invited aboard the President's train; only a last-minute invitation wangled for him en route by the friendly McIntyre got him aboard. Once aboard, his name was added to the list of Congressmen on whom Roosevelt bestowed public praise, but not to the list of those allowed a private few minutes with FDR— an omission which must have provided a bitter contrast to the hours of intimate conversation with the President he had enjoyed on that other train trip through Texas just a year before.* The Spring of 1939, when the initial jockeying over the Garner nomination was taking place, was the time when Johnson could not elicit a presidential response even to a letter.

But as Spring turned to Summer, Johnson found a role he could play. Because of the leverage its committee chairmen wielded with Congressmen from other states, the Texas congressional delegation was the power base for Garner's presidential bid. The canniness of the delegation's veteran members —augmented, of course, by the political wisdom, and cash, of its "associate member," Roy Miller—and the nationwide political contacts built up during decades of dealing on Capitol Hill, made the delegation in a sense the general staff of the Garner campaign as well; at its weekly luncheon meetings—and whenever, in fact, Texas Congressmen got together—the Vice President's strategy was discussed and planned. The White House needed to know what was going on in those meetings. It needed a spy in the Texas ranks.

Lyndon Johnson volunteered for this mission. No formal enlistment was necessary; he simply began to relay information to members of the White House staff, primarily to Corcoran, and occasionally to Rowe—with his customary assiduity. "He was working at it, I'll tell you that," Rowe says. Johnson was playing a dangerous game, Rowe says, "and sooner or later they would find out, but he could see over the horizon, and he could see that Garner's day was over, and he was playing with our crowd instead of the Garner crowd." Obtaining information on the discussions in the Texas delegation had been "very hard," Rowe says, but it suddenly became much easier. "If we wanted to know something: 'Call Lyndon Johnson.' "

* Johnson was unopposed in the 1938 primary, but other Texas legislators running unopposed were among the invitees.

In July, he took on a new role. There was one asset that only he among the Texas Congressmen possessed: Charles Marsh's friendship. Texas newspapers were overwhelmingly anti-Roosevelt, but Marsh's six Texas newspapers, including the influential paper in the state capital, were for him. The publisher of six pro-Roosevelt Texas dailies had very little difficulty getting in to see the President, and when Marsh requested an appointment, he asked if he could bring Johnson along. On July 14, 1939, "Pa" Watson sent an aide a note: "Put Mr. Charles Marsh down for an appointment with the President on Wednesday. Mr. Marsh is the owner of a large string of papers supporting the President in Texas." And on the note, someone— either Watson or the aide—added in handwriting: "*And Representative Lyndon Johnson.*" At this meeting, Johnson impressed the President with his enthusiasm for the Third Term, and with his political acumen. Something else was at work as well. Marsh and Roosevelt had been acquainted since the President's days as Governor of New York, and they had not gotten along well, at least in part because of Marsh's imperious personality, which allowed him to show deference not even to a Governor. At the White House meeting, strain was again evident. But Marsh, the enthusiastic New Dealer, wanted to support Roosevelt, and Roosevelt wanted his support, and a buffer to make the relationship smoother was available—and Lyndon Johnson thus became the link to the most influential pro-Roosevelt organ in Texas.

Then, two weeks later, came an opportunity for Johnson to dramatize —vividly—his loyalty to the President.

During a bitter hearing on proposed amendments that would weaken wages-and-hours legislation, John L. Lewis exploded to the House Labor Committee: "The genesis of this campaign against labor . . . is not hard to find. [It] emanates from a labor-baiting, poker-playing, whiskey-drinking, evil old man whose name is Garner." As committee members gasped, the lion-maned CIO leader, pounding the table until the ashtrays jumped, went on: "Some gentlemen may rise in horror and say, 'Why, Mr. Lewis has made a personal attack on Mr. Garner.' Yes, I make a personal attack on Mr. Garner for what he is doing, because Garner's knife is searching for the quivering, pulsating heart of labor."

With reporters racing through Capitol corridors searching for comment, Sam Rayburn summoned the Texas delegation to his office to issue a formal resolution denying the accuracy of Lewis' description of the Vice President. But Roosevelt and his advisors did not want that description denied; as Kenneth G. Crawford wrote in the *Nation*, "If they know the church-going public, its reaction will be: where there's so much smoke there must be some firewater." Roosevelt himself was shortly to give emphasis to Garner's drinking with his remark at a Cabinet meeting, "I see that the Vice President has thrown his bottle—I mean his hat—into the ring." Telephone calls were hastily placed to the office of their secret ally within the Texas delegation, Lyndon Johnson. Corcoran was later to say: "*Everybody* called him. I called him. Ickes called him. . . . There wasn't any doubt about what the Old Man wanted."

By the time Johnson arrived in Rayburn's office, a resolution had already been prepared stating, among other points, that Garner was neither a heavy drinker nor unfriendly to labor. Johnson refused to sign it. There ensued what the *Washington Post* later called "considerable discussion." Rayburn finally suggested that he take Johnson into his office and talk to him, but Johnson apparently stood his ground.

The resolution that was finally read to a cheering House by Representative Luther A. Johnson of Corsicana—who said that it had been endorsed by the entire Texas delegation—did not contain a specific repudiation of the allegations about labor and whiskey. It said: "We who know him [Garner] best cannot refrain from expressing our deep resentment and indignation at this unwarranted and unjustified attack on his private and public life. The Texas delegation has complete confidence in his honesty, integrity and ability."

Johnson made the most of his role in this episode. He described it to Roosevelt personally, who "chuckled" as he related it to Harold Ickes. Ickes was later to recount in his *Secret Diary* what Roosevelt said.

> Some grandiloquent resolutions had been drafted in advance and every member of the delegation was asked to sign on the dotted line. Among other things these resolutions declared that Garner was not a whiskey drinker and that he was not unfriendly to labor. The only voice raised in opposition was that of Congressman Lyndon B. Johnson, of Austin. Johnson said that he could not subscribe to any such language and that the delegation would look foolish if such a statement were issued because everyone knew that Garner was a heavy drinker and that he was bitterly opposed to labor. The argument went on for some two hours with Johnson maintaining his ground. Then Sam Rayburn suggested that he take Johnson into his office and talk to him. Of course everyone thought that Rayburn would administer a spanking. However, Johnson still continued to hold his ground and the crestfallen Rayburn led him back to the caucus where he said that he hadn't been able to do anything with him. It was agreed that unless every member signed the resolutions there was no point in issuing them. So the task was given to Johnson to draft such resolutions as he would be willing to sign.

As Johnson recounted the episode to other New Dealers high and low, his extraordinary ability as a storyteller was never in better evidence. "Congressman Lyndon B. Johnson was in to see me," Ickes wrote in his diary. "He told me the very vivid story of the meeting of the Texas delegation. . . . The pressure on Johnson was terrific. Sam Rayburn lost his temper. At one point he said to Johnson: 'Lyndon, I am looking you right in the eye,' and Johnson replied: 'And I am looking you right back in the eye.' Johnson says that he kept his temper and that after it was all over, Rayburn apologized to him. However, Johnson refused to move."

Johnson's depiction of his role in the delegation may have been somewhat exaggerated. On one point, Roosevelt had definitely received a false impression: Johnson was not "given the task" of drafting the final resolution; it was drawn up by Luther Johnson and two other senior members of the delegation, Milton H. West and Charles L. South. And in any case, the resolution—which Johnson did, after all, sign along with the other members —is certainly not a weak statement. His confrontation with Rayburn was apparently not as dramatic in fact as in the telling; other members of the delegation and Texans familiar with its actions would later not recall any confrontation. When newspapermen, intrigued by the stories they were hearing, sought to learn if there was a split in the Texas delegation, its members were surprised; their reaction was summed up by Albert Thomas of Houston, who said, in reply to a reporter's question, "Of course every member of the Texas delegation is for Vice President Garner [for President]." When the *Fort Worth Star-Telegram* two days later sought to pin down members of the delegation as to whom they were supporting for President, Johnson's reply, echoing that of several other members, dodged the issue, in a way that amounted to something less than a ringing repudiation of the Vice President. "My esteem and regard for Vice President Garner, based upon eight years' friendship, was clearly expressed in the resolution of the Texas delegation asserting our complete confidence in his honesty, integrity and ability," he said. "Since the Vice President has not announced his desire to become a candidate for President, I feel an announcement from a new Congressman should await, not precede, his decision." Still, whatever the extent of Rayburn's entreaties or wrath, Johnson had resisted them. If there had been calculation behind his stand ("He could see that Garner's day was over")—a high form of political calculation, given the Vice President's popularity at the time—there was courage behind it, too; given Rayburn's power and personality, considerable courage. And Johnson's portrayal of the confrontation was very convincing. By the time he had finished taking his story around the offices of key administration aides, he was something of a hero to the New Dealers.

Most important, he had impressed, and, apparently, won the liking of, their chief—as was to be proven twice within the next month.

On the first occasion, Roosevelt stepped into a dispute in Johnson's own district to protect the young Congressman from Garner's wrath.

"If a person wronged me," Garner was to say years later, "I never rested easy until I got even." Now Cactus Jack tried to get even with Lyndon Johnson. Still serving as postmaster in Austin was Buck Buchanan's appointee, Ewell Nalle, a member of a family that had long been politically powerful in the city, and an old friend of Garner's. Even before the Lewis-Garner explosion, as suspicions had begun to arise during the Spring of 1939 about Johnson's attitude toward Garner's presidential aspirations, Nalle had received instructions from Garner or Garner's allies to begin stirring up opposition to Johnson—opposition which could pose a threat to him when he had to run again in 1940, since the Austin postmaster controlled more than two hundred jobs. Immediately after Johnson's recalcitrance over the "Lewis resolution," reports from his district told Johnson that Nalle was intensifying his opposition.

During the Spring, Johnson had personally asked Postmaster General Farley to fire Nalle and replace him with his own nominee, Ray E. Lee, the former newsman whom he had hired to do public relations for the NYA. Farley's early benevolence toward an engaging congressional secretary had, however, vanished now that there were doubts about Johnson's loyalty to his old ally Jack Garner. He told Johnson that "enemies" of Johnson had asked him not to fire Nalle, and he declined to do so, citing a number of notably lame reasons to show that such a firing would be illegal. Johnson thereupon managed to have the matter brought to Roosevelt's attention by James Rowe, and the President in fact mentioned it to Farley after a Cabinet meeting. But he did so only cursorily, and when Farley told him, "You can forget it," saying that the dismissal would be illegal, the President apparently did just that; he didn't pursue the matter.

But that had been before the Lewis blast. About a week after it, Johnson raised the matter again, and this time Roosevelt promised to see that Nalle was fired as soon as Congress adjourned. Adjournment brought no action, however, and with the President preparing to leave Washington on a vacation trip, Johnson was becoming increasingly agitated about the matter. On August 10, overcoming Rowe's reluctance to "pester" the President, he prevailed on him to write a memo to Missy LeHand: "I don't know whether in the rush of getting away, the President should be bothered about this, but Lyndon Johnson has been so insistent the past couple of days I will leave it up to your judgment. He says he will not and cannot go back to Texas until the President acts. . . ." When the memo was put before the President, it turned out that his inaction had been due only to oversight. Reminded of his promise, Roosevelt carried through on it—as firmly as even Johnson could have wished. Back to Rowe (in the President's hand) came the message: "Tell the Post Office that I want this done right away for Cong. Lyndon Johnson. That it is legal and to send me the necessary papers. Tell Lyndon Johnson that I am doing it." Before the month was out, so was Nalle, and Lee replaced him, thereby ending the threat to Johnson's re-election chances. In fact, he would be unopposed for re-election in 1940.

During the month following the Lewis episode, Roosevelt not only protected Johnson but tried to promote him.

One of the subjects discussed when, through Charles Marsh, Johnson finally got the opportunity to talk personally to the President was the rural electrification program being carried out in his district. This was a matter of great interest to the President, and he was apparently impressed by Johnson's vivid description of the benefits that the Pedernales Electric Cooperative had brought to Hill Country farmers, and by Johnson's claim (which would have startled officials of Texas Power & Light, enraged at what they viewed as the ruthless use of government power to bludgeon them into a surrender of their properties) that the program had been carried out with un-precedented cooperation between government and a private utility. On the day that Marsh and Johnson met with Roosevelt, Benjamin V. Cohen wrote the President that "As you will see . . . Lyndon Johnson . . . has done an admirable job working out the problems of Texas' little TVA. . . . We are slowly building up a record to prove that cooperation between public and private power is not impossible as Willkie claims." With the post of REA Administrator about to become vacant, Roosevelt added Johnson's name to the list of possible appointees. (When the President asked the opinion of Henry Wallace, who, of course, had spent weekends at Longlea with Johnson, and who frequently relied on Marsh's advice, Wallace replied that "I am so enthusiastic . . . that I am quite ready to recommend his appointment. . . . Lyndon has followed so closely the rural electrification program, has such zeal for it, is so well-rounded a New Dealer, and has such good judgment and general competence, that I think he will make an excellent selection.") Immediately after the meeting of the Texas delegation at which Johnson carried out Roosevelt's wishes—it may have been at the Oval Office session at which Johnson regaled the President with his descrip-tion of the delegation meeting—Roosevelt formally offered him the REA post.

The offer was significant principally because it indicated the strength of the impression Johnson had made on Roosevelt once he got the chance to spend time with him: the directorship of a nationwide agency, particularly one as fast-growing, and politically important, as REA, was not the kind of job offered to many men still short of their thirty-first birthday. The REA post was, in addition, a particularly challenging job, as Roosevelt was well aware; he had two weeks earlier remarked to Ickes that "it was difficult to find the right kind of man for administrator because the man had to be a builder and at the same time a finance man."

However, there was not much chance that Johnson would accept the post. Previously an independent agency, REA was in the process of being transferred into the Agriculture Department, so that its head would report not to the President but to a Cabinet officer. Johnson understood where power came from in a democracy. "You have to be your own man," he had told Russell Brown years before—his own man, not someone else's; an elected official whose position had been conferred on him by voters, not by one man—who could, on a whim, take the position away. Hearing, back in Austin, about Roosevelt's offer, the wily Wirtz wired him: "Think you would be making a mistake which you would afterwards regret for years if you act on proposition," warning Johnson, in a follow-up letter, that he might "be side-tracked or shelved when you get out." Johnson immediately assured Wirtz that he needn't worry. Having fought his way at last onto the road that could lead him to achieve his ultimate ambition, he could not be persuaded by anyone—not even Franklin Roosevelt—to turn off it. "Dear Mr. President," he replied, "Thanks for your offer to appoint me Administrator of the REA. . . . My own job now, however, is a contract with the people of the Tenth District of Texas, which I hope to complete satisfactorily and to renew every two years as long as I appear useful." In a strikingly cordial reply, which, with Roosevelt's permission, Johnson released to the press, the President wrote back:

> Dear Lyndon:
>   I was very sorry that you did not feel that you wanted to accept the proffer of the Administrator of the Rural Electrification Administration, but I do think I ought to tell you that very rarely have I known a proposed candidate for any position receive such unanimous recommendations from all sources as was the case with you.
>   But I do understand the reasons why you felt that you should stay as a representative of your district. I congratulate the Tenth District of Texas.

THEN HE FOUND A MEANS of moving further along the road. The means was money—Herman Brown's money. All through 1939, of course, Johnson had been advancing Herman's interests, working diligently for the enlargement of the Marshall Ford Dam and for the profitable change orders on that project. The Browns were grateful. On May 2, 1939, George, who, of course, did nothing without clearing it with his older brother, wrote, "I hope you know, Lyndon, how I feel reference to what you have done for me and I am going to try to show my appreciation through the years to come with actions rather than words if I can find out when and where I can return at least a portion of the favors." The effort to find out "when and where" the favors could be returned continued; before long George would be writing Lyndon, in response to a Johnson remark about "the ninety-six old men" in the Senate: "I have thought about you often out here and don't know whether or not you have made up your mind about what future course you want to take, but some day in the next few years one of the old ones is going to pass on, and if you have decided to go that route I think it would be 'gret' to do it." No matter what the route, Johnson was assured in letters from Brown & Root headquarters on Calhoun Road in Houston, he could be certain of the firm's all-out support.

In December of 1939, John Garner announced his presidential candidacy. He did so in a terse statement from Uvalde, and then, despite efforts to question him by reporters who had traveled hundreds of miles to do so, he left without another word on a week-long hunting trip with an old friend, a Uvalde garage mechanic. His supporters were more forthcoming. The façade that the Vice President was running only because the President wasn't was stripped away; E. B. Germany, Garner's Texas state chairman, attacked Roosevelt directly, and Roy Miller's son, Dale, already a considerable lobbyist in his own right, wrote in the *Texas Weekly* that "regardless of what anyone may do, Mr. Garner *will* be a candidate, and he will be in the race to the finish." Garner's supporters, Miller wrote, have never believed that a President "could prove so faithless to democratic principles" as to seek a third term, but if Roosevelt should try to "repudiate this cherished American principle," which "is as embedded in our system of government as if it was written in the Constitution itself," Garner was going to stop him. Germany's speech "closes the door to compromise. . . . The Garner-for-President movement has cast the political die. . . . To the President and the third-term apostles, it offers the olive branch of good will if they want it, and the club of resolute and relentless opposition if they don't." Martin Dies and other Garner supporters began using in public some of the words they had been using for years in private—in Dick Kleberg's office, among other places. Railing against the International Ladies Garment Workers Union, and its president, David Dubinsky (spelled Dubinski in the *San Antonio Evening News*), against organized labor in general and the National Labor Relations Board in particular, San Antonio Congressman Kilday said that "Socialists" had infiltrated the Democratic Party, and that only a Garner victory would drive them out. As for the principals themselves, after a Cabinet meeting in January, 1940, Ickes used the words "hatred" and "savage" to describe a Roosevelt attack on "Congress"; in response, "The Vice President's face turned blood red and he retorted angrily. . . . Then he accused the President of attacking our form of government."

A Gallup Poll that month revealed that Garner's popularity had not slipped; if Roosevelt did not run, he was the favorite of 58 percent of registered Democrats. And if Roosevelt *did* run—if President opposed Vice President in Democratic primaries?—the answer to that question seemed, in the first months of 1940, to be far from open and shut. With the economy sagging, and unemployment remaining stubbornly high, with congressional opposition so strong that Roosevelt dared not introduce a single significant new program, and with the "phony war" muddying the international situation and all the President's diplomatic efforts thwarted, March, 1940, was, as James MacGregor Burns wrote, "a low point even for Roosevelt's second term." On March 10, the *Washington Post* stated that "the

Texan is believed to have a good chance to win" when the two men clashed head to head in the California primary in May.

For more than a year, Roosevelt had been pursuing a strategy that Burns calls "broadening the field in order to prevent any candidate from getting too far ahead"—hinting at support for Harry Hopkins or Paul McNutt, for example. The strategy had destroyed the hopes of all other candidates, but it hadn't even dented Garner's. Now the Democratic Convention was close. Garner was immensely popular with many Democratic state bosses. If, when the Convention began, his candidacy was still strong, several "favorite son" delegations—the Alabama delegation pledged to Speaker Bankhead, for example—would fall into line behind him. New Dealers "concede that Garner, with Texas' forty-six delegates, California's forty-four, some Wisconsin, Illinois and probably a few scattered delegates in other states, will aggregate nearly 500" of the 551 delegates needed for nomination, the *Washington Post* reported. Even if this estimate was high, any substantial strength for Garner would do damage. As Burns puts it:

> Roosevelt's basic problem, if he chose to run, was not how to get the nomination—his ability to get a decisive convention majority was never in doubt—but how to be nominated in so striking a manner that it would amount to an emphatic and irresistible call to duty. This party call would be the prelude to a call from the whole country at election time. Only a party summons in July, in short, would make possible a popular summons in November.
>
> Standing formidably in the way of such a call was the very thing that made the call necessary—the anti-third-term tradition. . . . All the polls showed a vast majority opposed to a third term as an abstract matter, and a clear majority opposed to a third term for Roosevelt. . . .
>
> Roosevelt's task—in the event he finally decided to run— clearly was to bring about a unanimous party draft that would neutralize the anti-third-term sentiment. . . . If the President were to run again, everything depended on a spontaneous draft.

The chief obstacle to such a draft was John Garner. Were he to arrive in Chicago with a sizable bloc of votes, the "Stop Roosevelt" movement would be strong enough to preclude a draft. Garner had to be destroyed before the Convention. Roosevelt's earlier inclination to put him on the defensive by attacking him in his home state hardened. Another consideration was expressed in Marsh's *American-Statesman:* "If Roy Miller . . . selects [the Texas] delegation, such a delegation will be used as a trading block for the anti–New Deal group in the convention." New Dealers felt they had to try to at least cut into Garner's strength in the Texas delegation, place on it enough Roosevelt men to prevent it from being the Convention's anti-

Roosevelt rallying point. The odds against an attack in Texas succeeding even in such limited objectives were long—but the attempt had to be made. The decision was taken. Texas was to be made a battleground.

But the battle required money. The state's size made radio the best means of rallying Roosevelt sentiment, but the cost of statewide radio hook-ups was substantial by 1940 standards. Even local rallies were expensive. The price of the permit necessary to hold a rally at the Dallas Fairgrounds, for example, was $300, and the incidental expenses of such a rally might run $1,000 more, even without figuring in the cost of newspaper advertising to attract a crowd. Such costs were multiplied by the system under which the state's delegation to the National Convention would be chosen. The delegates would be selected at a State Democratic Convention. The delegates to this convention would be selected by conventions in all of the state's 254 counties. And the delegates to these county conventions would be selected at precinct conventions—thousands of them—which would be held throughout the state on May 4. Money could play a decisive role in a precinct convention, which might consist of no more than a few handfuls of persons (anyone who had voted in the last election was eligible to attend) gathered in a school or firehouse. Just finding out who was eligible cost money. The names of voters in the previous election were listed in the office of the County Tax Assessor, but these lists had to be purchased. Then there was the problem of finding out which of the eligible voters favored your candidate. This was generally accomplished by telephone calls from a popular local politician or politician's wife. "You'd go to a county clerk's wife and say, 'You're not doing anything. How about taking this seventy-five dollars or hundred dollars, and calling some people,' " recalls Harold H. Young, a burly, brilliant, idealistically liberal attorney who was in charge of the Roosevelt campaign in Dallas and Fort Worth. Then, in Young's words, "it was a matter of who got your folks [voters who favored your candidate] out" to the precinct convention. Direct mailings, which cost money for mimeographing and stamps, were used. And, of course, on the evening of the convention, automobiles—with their drivers given "gasoline and expense money"—were needed. The amount required for a single precinct was not large, but, with thousands of precincts, the total required was considerable.

The Garner campaign in Texas, of course, had all the money it needed. The utilities, the railroads, the major oil companies such as the 'Umble and the Magnolia, the great ranchers and lumbermen and cotton families—the state's monolithic establishment that had long dominated its politics, largely through the use of financial pressure—were united behind the candidacy of the man who had long stood as its symbol. And as soon as the Garner forces realized—to their astonishment and rage—that Cactus Jack was to be challenged on their home ground, they mobilized, in what the *Dallas*

Morning News called "the most painstaking preparations in recent Texas political history."

The Roosevelt campaign's shortage of funds was, in contrast, acute. (Because of his personal friction with the President, and because he was planning to concentrate his political contributions behind the vice presidential campaign of frequent Longlea guest Wallace, Charles Marsh's support for FDR was largely confined to editorials.) When Garner state chairman Myron Blalock declared, "Even here in Texas, there are those small voices who speak out against this distinguished son of the Lone Star State," Young, a gifted political strategist, saw an opening. He wanted to reply, "That's true. Nobody's for FDR except small voices—the people." But because Young had no money, his rejoinder went unheard. Blalock had spoken on a statewide radio hook-up. Young couldn't afford even a local broadcast. Garner, Young reported, had a paid worker in every precinct in Dallas; the Roosevelt forces didn't have a paid worker in *any* precinct. Maury Maverick was leading the Third Term forces in San Antonio, but was all but helpless against the massive outpouring of Garner money in that city.

But Lyndon Johnson was to produce a source of funds.

Success had not diminished Herman Brown's ambitions. His car still roared endlessly back and forth across Texas as he pushed his projects and searched out new work, so that Lyndon Johnson sometimes had difficulty locating him to make his reports; he would send copies of telegrams to two or three towns at once to make sure one of them reached Brown. And even the giant Marshall Ford Dam had not lessened his "obsession" to build giant projects. Now, moreover, the great dam was almost completed. A score of smaller jobs would not enable him to keep on the payroll the organization he had built up with so much effort, and of which he was so proud. Herman Brown wanted—and needed—something *big*.

Something very big was on the horizon. In 1938, Congress, at President Roosevelt's request, had authorized the expenditure of a billion dollars on a "two-ocean" Navy. By early 1939 it had become clear that a substantial portion of that billion would be spent on the construction of naval bases and training stations for a greatly expanded Navy Air Force. On April 26, 1939, Roosevelt had signed into law a bill authorizing the expenditure of $66,800,000 for the first of such bases. Brown's attention was already focused on the Navy because Lyndon Johnson was a member of the Naval Affairs Committee. He decided to bid on one of the bases—in San Juan, Puerto Rico—authorized in the April bill.

In April, 1939, however, Lyndon Johnson still had not yet gained entrée to the President, and his attempt to give Brown & Root a helping hand was rebuffed in a manner suitable to what he was—a Congressman without influence. Within two days of the signing of the naval air base bill, he had to confess to George Brown that "I talked with Admiral Moreell

[Vice Admiral Ben Moreell, in charge of the Navy's shore construction program] and he said there is nothing further that we can do at this time." On May 16, he promised George, "I'll do all I can to get you any information on the Puerto Rico project and will let you know when anything breaks," but added, "You know how hard it is to get any dope in advance"—the statement of a man not on the inside of decisions. Seeking to offset its lack of experience in areas of construction required by this job, Brown & Root took as a partner on its Puerto Rico proposal the W. S. Bellows Construction Company of Houston, and submitted a bid, but the firm was shown no favoritism, as George Brown noted in a letter to Johnson, which stated, "I got some inquiries from the Naval Department for additional data" but added that these inquiries have "apparently . . . been sent to all prospective contractors." The entrée to the President that Johnson gained thereafter may have entitled him to help on a postmastership and the offer of the REA post; it did not involve any say in the awarding of a huge federal contract— as Johnson learned when, after another firm was awarded the contract in November, he demanded an explanation from Moreell. The Admiral brushed him off by sending him a memo from a lower-ranking officer: "Pursuant to your inquiry relative to the reason why Brown & Root, Inc. (and W. S. Bellows Co.) . . . were not selected as the contractors for the San Juan Air Base project . . . ," while both firms had "extensive construction experience," they had no experience whatsoever in the type of construction necessary to build a naval air base.

A naval air base and training station had been proposed for Texas—on the Gulf at Corpus Christi—in the mid-1930's, and indeed its construction had been recommended by the Navy in September, 1938. The city's Congressman, Richard Kleberg, and South Texas' most influential figure in Washington, Roy Miller, had been actively pushing for the project for more than three years. But Kleberg's family was a major Garner financial backer, and Roy Miller was Garner's campaign manager. Herman Brown had been interested in the Corpus Christi base from the first, but he was a Garner financial backer (as, indeed, was fitting, since his views on organized labor, on the balanced budget—and on communists, socialists and liberals—were indistinguishable from the Vice President's. "From what I see in the papers," his brother George happily wrote Roy Miller in May, 1939, "things seem to be moving along all right for the 'V.P.' "). Other big Texas contractors who might have been considered for the job were also identified with Garner—or with Reconstruction Finance Corporation head Jesse Jones of Houston, of whose oft-professed loyalty to the New Deal Roosevelt had become—correctly—suspicious. After Kleberg had been making optimistic predictions for months, he had to admit in September, 1939, that "There has been no intimation as to whether it is intended to build the training station here [in Corpus Christi] in two years or fifteen." The Navy's construction program, surging ahead in other locations, remained stalled in Texas; as late

Alice Glass (above, at Longlea)

Franklin D and Lyndon B during an FDR trip to Texas

Above: Abe Fortas and
James H. Rowe, two of
Johnson's young
New Dealer group

The victors: the men who came
to power in Texas as a result of
the Garner-Roosevelt fight—
Edward Clark, E. H. Perry,
Herman Brown, Lyndon Johnson,
and Austin Mayor Tom Miller

Vice President John ("Cactus Jack") Garner, with Texas
Senators Tom Connally and Morris Sheppard

George Brown, Johnson, Tommy ("the Cork") Corcoran at an airport in Texas, November, 1940

Johnson's habitual greeting to Rayburn: a picture taken in later years

The Congressman of the Tenth District and his staff in his Johnson City office: John Connally, Walter Jenkins, Dorothy Nichols, Herbert Henderson

Johnson at the Santa Rita Housing Project, for which he fought, in Austin

The Mansfield (originally Marshall Ford) Dam. Johnson's first task as Congressman was obtaining authorization for its completion. *Opposite, above*: Johnson, at the dedication ceremonies, kneeling beside Joseph Jefferson Mansfield, Chairman of the House Rivers and Harbors Committee, with Alvin Wirtz at left.

Sign at the headquarters of the Pedernales Electric
Co-operative (Johnson's greatest accomplishment on
behalf of the Hill Country) which in 1939 brought
electricity for the first time to the farmers of the district

Lady Bird Johnson during the 1941 Senate campaign

Left: Lyndon Johnson at the Pedernales Electric Co-operative Building, Johnson City, 1939

Above: Gerald Mann, gaunt and
tired after weeks of touring the
state

Pappy O'Daniel, with his children
Mickey-Wickey and Molly, and
their capitol-dome-shaped sound
truck

The campaigner: bellowing, pleading, shaking hands, reading a telegram of support from Washington, in staged shots with constituents, and his "All-Out Patriotic Revue"

From victory to defeat. Johnson's last speech, election morning, on the porch of his boyhood home. Reading the congratulatory telegrams election night, and elated in his moment of triumph. Bad news starts to come in, and, finally, "It's gone."

Lyndon Johnson, 1941

as January 9, 1940, Moreell told a House subcommittee that the Corpus Christi project was "not viewed as emergent"—testimony that led the subcommittee to reject even a $50,000 request for making surveys of the proposed base site.

Close as he and George Brown had become, Lyndon Johnson may have shied away from suggesting frankly even to him what he felt Brown & Root should do. In October, 1939, with the Corpus Christi base still not included on the list of the Navy's "preferred" projects, George wrote him, "I have been sitting here all week waiting to hear from you. . . . I felt that you had something on your mind last week but did not get around to getting it off." But George may have figured it out for himself. He ended this letter by writing:

> In the past I have not been very timid about asking you to do favors for me and hope you will not get any timidity if you have anything at all that you think I can or should do. Remember that I am *for* you, right or wrong, and it makes no difference if I think you are right or wrong. If you want it, I am for it 100%.

Opposing John Garner would be a huge gamble for a Texas contractor. But it would not be the largest gamble ever taken by Herman Brown, not for the man who had mortgaged everything he had accumulated in twenty years of terribly hard work to begin work on a dam before it had been authorized. And this new gamble, if successful, would give him the chance to build something even bigger than the dam—and to make even bigger money building it. A signal went out. In Houston, where Brown & Root's headquarters were located, Herman Brown's political influence was growing, and the city's Congressman, Albert Thomas, a junior Representative with negligible clout in Washington, was known to take Herman's orders unquestioningly. In August, Congressman Thomas had said, "Of course every member of the Texas delegation is for Vice President Garner." Now, in December, 1939, Thomas made another statement. He was not for Garner after all, he said. He was for Roosevelt.

That signal from Texas was answered by several signals from Washington—from the White House. They involved Lyndon Johnson, and Brown & Root. The first, on January 2, 1940, was a public signal: a presidential appointment. The post involved was a major one: Under Secretary of the Interior. The appointee would be second in command only to Harold Ickes in the giant department. It went to a Texan—"the choicest plum handed out to a Texan in years," said the *Houston Press*. And the Texan it went to was Alvin J. Wirtz, who was not only an attorney for Brown & Root but was identified with Lyndon Johnson.

Lest this latter connection be overlooked, the White House went out of its way to point it out, presidential secretary Early stating that "Rep. Lyndon

B. Johnson . . . presented Wirtz's name," and letting reporters know further that, as the *Press* reported, "Neither Texas Senator was consulted," nor was Sam Rayburn or Jesse Jones. To readers of political signals, therefore, it was clear that Lyndon Johnson had become a key White House ally—perhaps *the* key White House ally—in Texas. In White House inner circles, it was also quickly made clear that the man appointed at Johnson's suggestion was going to play a major role in the Roosevelt campaign in Texas. Roosevelt "told us that Garner had to be sent home permanently to his 6,000 neighbors in Uvalde, Texas, so that he could add to his millions," presidential aide David K. Niles says. "And this crucial task went to Alvin Wirtz." (The Roosevelt campaign in Texas was shortly to be beefed up by the appointment of another Johnson supporter, Austin attorney Everett L. Looney, as Assistant United States Attorney General.)

Another signal from the White House was private. The Navy Department was quietly informed that Lyndon Johnson was to be consulted—and his advice taken—on the awarding of Navy contracts in Texas.

Following this signal, a number of Texans flew up to Washington. One was Herman Brown. Another was Edward A. Clark, who had left his post as Texas Secretary of State to go on retainer for Brown & Root and to begin using his political acumen on Herman Brown's behalf. Still another was an old Brown associate whose qualification for this trip was his ability to know where political money could most profitably be distributed in Texas: Claud Wild, Sr. (While he was in Washington, Herman may have been handed a letter written by Roosevelt. Its contents are not known: no copy of it can be found; the only reference to it comes in a February 9, 1940, letter from Lyndon Johnson to George Brown noting that "Herman came in last night," which states, "Am enclosing the President's letter.")

After Herman's trip to Washington, two alterations in the *status quo* quickly became apparent. First, Brown & Root was, in obtaining coveted Navy Department contracts, no longer just one of a crowd.

The Corpus Christi Naval Air Station, "not emergent" in January, in February was moved abruptly, if quietly, onto the "preferred list" of Navy construction projects with the highest priority. The contract for the air base (which, it was now decided, would be of the "cost-plus" type so profitable to contractors) was not, it was also decided, to be put out for competitive bidding, but was to be awarded on a "negotiated basis." And the only firm with which serious negotiations were held turned out to be Brown & Root; the firm's lack of experience in air base construction, which less than three months before had kept it from getting a contract for a similar base, was no longer mentioned. Because the contract was so big, Brown & Root was to be required to share the profits—if not the work—with another contractor, who had a long association with the New Deal. "The White House said we had to take in [Henry] Kaiser," George Brown recalls. But when George arrived in Washington during either the last week in March or the first week in April to work out the details of Kaiser's participation, "Ben Moreell said, 'You don't have to give him half.'" Moreell probably intended Kaiser's share to be only slightly smaller than half, but the vagueness of the Admiral's instructions gave Brown & Root leeway—and Herman told George how to take advantage of that leeway. Meeting with Kaiser at the Shoreham Hotel, George Brown, an unknown Texas contractor, showed the famous industrialist (famous, among other reasons, for his toughness in negotiations) a little Texas toughness. "I offered him twenty-five percent. He said, 'That's an insult.' I said, 'Henry, we don't need you. We don't need your organization.' So we sat around and talked and then I said, 'Well, I have to be going.' He said, 'Well, what are you going to do?' I said, 'I already told you what I'm going to do.'" And 25 percent was all Kaiser got. (To keep Kaiser's participation in the profits secret—Kaiser's participation in the work itself was almost nil—his share was in the name of the Columbia Inspection Company. The Bellows firm was also a participant. "We needed someone who had done buildings," Brown explains. "We hadn't done many.") To keep other contractors from becoming interested, preparations for the Corpus Christi project were carried on in secrecy. Blueprints and specifications were drawn up by the Navy not in Texas but in Pensacola, Florida. By the time the imminent building of the base was made public, drawings and specifications were almost complete—and, it was revealed, hundreds of acres of the land needed (on Flour Bluff, a point of land at the tip of Corpus Christi Bay) were already under option. Plans for the base became public knowledge on May 15, when the House Naval Affairs Committee opened hearings on a bill that would provide funds for twelve new naval air bases. The Corpus Christi base would be by far the largest, almost twice as large as any of the others. And there were other differences between this and the other bases—most notably the speed with which, now that the plans were public, they were finalized. After a meeting with President Roosevelt, Committee Chairman Vinson announced that "because of the urgency of the project," Corpus Christi would be the only one of the twelve bases for which funds would be provided immediately—in the appropriations bill itself; funding for the other bases would have to wait for the later passage of a deficiency appropriations bill. Lyndon Johnson told the *Corpus Christi Caller* that the bill "would be reported favorably and acted on in the House before the end of the week." That rush schedule was met, and within two more weeks the bill had been passed by the Senate. Shortly after noon on June 13, 1940, President Roosevelt signed a contract for the construction of the base on a cost-plus fixed fee basis. According to the *Corpus Christi Caller*, it was the first cost-plus fixed fee contract Roosevelt had personally signed. The contract fixed a price of $23,381,000 for the base, with the contractors to be paid an additional $1.2 million for doing the work. Even as these figures were being announced, however, those connected with the project knew they would be shortly altered. In fact, before the end of the

year, the authorized cost of the project would be quietly increased to nearly
$30 million. In February, 1941, the appropriation was increased twice, first
by an additional $13 million and then by $2 million more, raising the cost
to $45 million. Each increase, of course, carried with it a proportionate
increase in the contractors' fee. By this time, other contractors, some of them
politically well connected themselves, were anxious to obtain part of the
job, but, says Tommy Corcoran, a close friend of the Under Secretary of the
Navy in charge of such contracts, James V. Forrestal: "Mr. Forrestal twisted
a hell of a lot of tails to" keep the work in the hands of "Lyndon's friends,"
Brown & Root. As war clouds gathered, and then broke in thunder, and the
need for trained fliers—and for facilities to train them—became more urgent,
the increases in funding for the base grew larger; appropriations for the
Corpus Christi base soared to more than $100 million.

The second alteration that followed Herman Brown's trip to Washington was that the Roosevelt-for-President campaign in Texas was no longer
short of cash.

3/4/40   3:30
LBJ: delivered $300.00 in cash to Maury on the floor today.

                                                              jbc*

Three hundred dollars was a minor item in that campaign. Harold Young,
who a week or two before had been so short of funds for running the
campaign in Dallas, was shortly to be able to report:

> I have rented a room at the Adolphus Hotel at $45.00 per
> month, have hired the stenographer [for] $25.00 a week, and I
> have put a publicity man to work at $100.00 per week. Beginning
> tomorrow, I expect to run a small ad in the Dallas *News* each day
> asking those who believe in Roosevelt to write me. . . . We are
> rapidly building up a precinct organization which will be sufficient
> to overpower all opposition by May 4th.

Building up a precinct organization cost money, but the money was available, thanks largely to Herman Brown.

EVEN AS THE FIGHT in Texas was being joined, however, the reason for it
was fading away. 1939 may have been John Garner's year. 1940, the year
that mattered, was Franklin D. Roosevelt's. March was indeed "a low point

* This may not have been the first occasion on which the Browns had, at
Johnson's request, assisted Maverick financially. During his 1939 campaign for the San
Antonio Mayoralty, Maverick asked Johnson for financial help, because on March 30,
1939, Johnson replied: "I've talked with James Rowe, George Brown, et al, and I'm
sure you will hear something before long." On April 7, 1939, Maverick wired: "Have
Johnson send me that five hundred dollars."

for the President," but, although he remained silent as to his intentions, the fox was ready to leave his lair. He had stuck his nose out, in fact, on February 24. That was the last day on which the President could have forbidden the entering of his name in Illinois, whose primary would be held on April 9—and he had not done so. The name of Franklin D. Roosevelt was going to be on a primary ballot. And with every increase in international tension, Americans became increasingly aware that they might soon be at war, and it became more and more evident that the Democratic Convention would select to lead the nation through war the man who had led it through the Depression. Politicians began backing away from Garner's candidacy. Observing him at a dinner in Washington, Ickes gloated that "All his buoyancy seemed to have deserted him. He looked glum and unhappy and did very little talking. I suppose there is no doubt that he realizes he is in for a terrific beating at the hands of the President." His fears were confirmed on April 2, in Wisconsin, where he had once expected to win most of the delegates; instead, he suffered a smashing defeat.

Then, at dawn on April 9, the day of the Illinois primary, German troops struck across the defenseless Danish border, and German destroyers and troopships suddenly loomed out of a snowstorm off the coast of Norway, torpedoing Norwegian gunboats as troops poured ashore. Denmark was overrun in a matter of hours; Norway's main ports were all in Nazi hands—the phony war was over. Roosevelt defeated Garner in Illinois by eight to one. Garner was finished on April 9—and he knew it. If he hadn't known it, clues were promptly furnished. As Columnist Ray Tucker wrote:

> The most down-hearted man on Capitol Hill is Vice President John Nance Garner. His friends have deserted him—left him cold. . . .
>
> When Jack was riding high, . . . his office was the gathering place of . . . Senators. They rushed in every hour of the day to seek advice or to toss off a quick drink. . . .
>
> But . . . his office is no longer a magnet for the politicos. The most popular vehicle on Capitol Hill these days is the Third Term bandwagon.

Refusing to bow out of the race, Garner said defiantly that his name would be presented to the Convention if only as a gesture, but a gesture was all it would be. Although Texas' precinct conventions would be held on May 4, the primary itself, the last in the country, would not be held until May 27—by which time, primaries in other states would have completely eliminated him as a threat to Roosevelt. Roosevelt appears to have seen this—and also to have seen and accepted that while he might crush Garner everywhere else, he could not defeat him in his home state—and he now decided not to wage an all-out war against Garner in Texas. The loudest of the voices for Roose-

velt—Maverick—was abruptly silenced; his statements against the Vice
President ceased, reportedly on a suggestion directly from the President.
Near the end of March, Roosevelt had told Ickes that

> He does not want any fight made for Roosevelt delegates in Texas.
> He thinks that Texans are unusually full of state pride and that
> they would resent an outside candidate coming in, even if that
> candidate were the President himself. He had already sent word
> to others in Texas not to fight for delegates. At the end he became
> realistic and, with a smile said: "Of course, it is not well to go into
> a fight unless we know that we can win."

But while the President's reason for fighting Garner in Texas had faded,
that of Johnson and Wirtz had not—and they apparently persuaded the
President that the fight should go on. During the first week in April, the tall,
eager young Congressman and his calm, cigar-smoking advisor made a series of visits to the White House. What they said is not known, but one
aspect of the situation was revealing. In Texas, politicians knew that Garner's popularity, coupled with his control of the party apparatus, gave
Roosevelt no chance to win the delegation; in Washington, 1,600 miles away,
where Texas sentiment was reported to the White House primarily by Johnson and Wirtz, the impression was given that the President had a good
chance of taking the delegation and completing his enemy's humiliation.
Johnson and Wirtz also may have appealed to other sides of the President's
character. Roosevelt, Joseph Alsop and Robert Kintner were to write, had
earlier told Johnson and "other Texan New Dealers" that "he wanted no
part of" a fight against Garner in Texas, but "then he was shown documents
and other evidence of the character of the Garner campaign in Wisconsin
and Illinois, which was extremely bitter and highly personal in its attacks on
the President. This angered him. . . . [Jesse] Jones again pleaded with him
not to carry the fight into Garner's home state. But the Texan New Dealers
voiced the opposing view, and the President agreed." Whatever the reasons
for Roosevelt's reversal, on April 12 Wirtz was able to write Mayor Tom
Miller of Austin: "The President has not 'called off the dogs,' and you can
take this as authentic. . . . Everything from this end looks good. I asked Ed
[Clark] to communicate with you and [Harold] Young and let me know who
you all could agree on as state organizer with absolute authority to discuss
the campaign, and what such a campaign would cost." The campaign Wirtz
was talking about, Clark was soon informed, was a war in which no quarter
was to be given: a battle in the precinct conventions, in the state convention—a well-financed campaign to take from Garner even the votes of his
own state.

And whatever Roosevelt's reasons for wanting to continue the fight against Garner in Texas, the motive of Johnson and Wirtz was now to become more clear, because of the nature of the campaign they directed. Although it was ostensibly a campaign against John Garner, its real target was not Garner but Sam Rayburn.

Rayburn was determined to save Garner from the humiliation of having to fight to hold on to his own state. For months, he had worked loyally for his old friend. "I do hope," he wrote a Texas ally on March 8, 1940, "that we can keep down any contest in Texas. I am working on the people who I think might lead a third term movement [in Texas] just as hard as I can to keep it down." But as the hopelessness of Garner's candidacy had become evident, he had begun working for a compromise that would save the seventy-one-year-old Vice President from embarrassment, and let him retire from public life with dignity. The solution he devised was to have the Texas convention instruct the state's delegation to cast a first-ballot vote for Garner, while at the same time endorsing Roosevelt's policies,* to make clear that support of its favorite-son candidate did not mean diehard opposition to the President (and to end any hope of a Stop Roosevelt movement, to which Rayburn was, of course, opposed). Going to the White House, he had sued for an honorable peace on behalf of the man with whom he had worked for thirty years—and had for a time thought he had succeeded. Roosevelt, who at the time had decided to drop the fight in Texas, agreed; as one newspaper put it, "His [the President's] first act, designed to re-store friendly political relations with [Garner], was to inform New Dealers in Texas that he has no desire of contesting the Vice President for the Lone Star State's 46 delegates."

After Johnson and Wirtz persuaded the President to change his mind and the campaign for the delegates was resumed under their direction, the direction pointed straight at Rayburn. It was kicked off with a telegram to him. Ed Clark and Tom Miller, two Austinites acting under orders from Johnson and Wirtz, sent a telegram to Rayburn on Thursday, April 12, demanding to know how he stood "as between President Roosevelt and Vice President Garner." The Garner organization in Texas, it said, "has been engaged in a very unwise, cruel and ruthless effort to politically assassinate Roosevelt. We concede your past loyalty to the Democratic Party and trust that you will again evidence this by not trying to stop Roosevelt. . . ."

In his reply to this telegram—and in subsequent events—was given definitive proof of Sam Rayburn's character. The going was to be very tough for his friend now. Wrote columnists Drew Pearson and Robert S. Allen:

---

* "A clearcut endorsement of the policies and accomplishments of the Roosevelt Administration and an unequivocal instruction to the delegates to vote for Mr. Garner for the Democratic nomination for President is what we want," he wrote a friend.

The great Lone Star State of Texas, where Jack Garner was
born and with whose heretofore unfailing backing he rose to fame
and fortune, is today the stage of what, in the opinion of insiders,
will be his last political battle. . . . For the grizzled old warrior, it
is a bitter and ironic clash: bitter because he finds himself on the
defensive in his home bailiwick, where he reigned supreme for
many years; ironic because he actually is only a pawn in a struggle
in which he has no personal stake.

But throughout his last battle, Sam Rayburn stood beside him like a rock.
"Torn between his loyalty to Roosevelt and his close personal friendship
with Garner and the old leaders," the columnists wrote, he is "the unhap-
piest man in the bitter melee. . . . Sam also fears the effect it may have on
his own speakership ambitions . . ." But his reply to the Clark-Miller telegram was unequivocal. "No knowing person doubts my loyalty to the policies and accomplishments of the Roosevelt administration and I shall
advocate that the convention . . . pass resolutions strongly endorsing those
policies and accomplishments," he said. But, he added, "John Garner has
been a distinguished congressman from Texas for thirty years. He has been
the state's only Speaker and Vice President, its most distinguished citizen
since Sam Houston. His fellow citizens of Texas should honor him by sending a delegation to the national convention instructed to vote for him for the
Democratic nomination for President."

A maneuver by Lyndon Johnson's followers had thus forced Rayburn
to take a stand against Roosevelt. But what good was the maneuver if the
stand was not known—and widely known? What good was the maneuver
if the stand did not receive wide publicity—if Rayburn was not portrayed
publicly as a foe of the President, as part of the Stop Roosevelt movement?
The Clark-Miller telegram of Thursday did not find its way into print, and
neither did Rayburn's reply of Saturday. So on Sunday another attempt
was made to get the news out. A discreet leak was made to Paul Bolton, an
INS reporter in Austin friendly to Johnson (he would later work for him).
Approaching Mayor Miller at Austin's annual Dogwood Day Dinner on
Sunday night, Bolton said, in Miller's words, "that he heard from Washington that I had a message from Rayburn." This attempt failed because Miller
had not been informed of the part he was supposed to play. Not realizing
that the exchange of telegrams was supposed to be made public, the Mayor
replied that he considered Rayburn's telegram "a personal message that I did
not care to divulge." That attempt having failed, still another device was
employed to get Rayburn's position publicized. As Miller put it, "Someone
from Washington wired a special story about the telegram to a great many
Texas newspapers." This device worked. Rayburn's stand was on the front
page—and portrayed in the light in which it was supposed to be portrayed.

RAYBURN BACKS GARNER, the *Washington Post* headlined on Monday morning. The device also gave Clark and Miller an opportunity to send another telegram, with guaranteed publicity. As if Rayburn's answer had not been clear enough, they wired: "We concede your past loyalty to the Democratic party and we trust that you will again evidence this by not trying to stop Roosevelt. . . . Are you trying to stop Roosevelt along with Roy Miller [and] Blalock, or do you just want to give Mr. Garner a first-round complimentary vote at Chicago?" These telegrams had their intended effect. As the lead paragraph in the *Dallas Morning News* story put it: "Majority Leader Sam Rayburn of the House of Representatives was brought squarely into the Roosevelt-Garner fight." And he was brought into that fight in the way Johnson intended; the crucial phrase "Stop Roosevelt" had been emphasized. Rayburn was portrayed as a leader not just of the Garner campaign but of the Stop Roosevelt movement.

And the reaction from Roosevelt was all that could have been desired by the men who had conceived these maneuvers. Johnson and Wirtz would, during the week following Rayburn's statement, have three conferences at the White House. After the final one, Wirtz, in a press conference on the White House steps, said that Rayburn's statement "appeared to the President as an attack from within the Administration, and that Roosevelt felt Rayburn had not correctly portrayed his views." Wirtz said he was returning to Texas to lead an all-out fight to take the delegation away from Garner.

In that fight, Rayburn was to continue to be as much a target as the man he was representing. As a young Texas politician wrote Rayburn following an April 24 rally orchestrated by Wirtz: "At the 'New Deal' rally here in Dallas . . . your name was lugged into the discussion mainly by Mayor Tom Miller of Austin. . . . And some of the others tried in a subtle manner to connect you with certain men, who are supporting Mr. Garner. . . ."

Subtle and shrewd, the Johnson-Wirtz strategy gave Johnson what he wanted—as a third telegram would show.

When Wirtz arrived back in Texas, the all-out fight turned out to be something less; after an initial explosion of impassioned rhetoric, Wirtz said that he had no objection to the Texas delegation giving a first-ballot favorite-son vote to Garner, so long as it was not part of a Stop Roosevelt movement. The Garner leaders thereupon expressed understandable puzzlement over the reason for the "all-out fight." As soon as the national sentiment for Roosevelt had become unmistakable, they had repeatedly suggested, they said, the very proposal that Wirtz was now suggesting. Blalock, Garner's state chairman, said: "As heretofore repeatedly stated, we shall advocate that all Texas conventions, precinct, county and state, pass resolutions endorsing the achievements and accomplishments of the Roosevelt administration. Nothing else has ever been in the minds of the Garner advocates." That statement was disingenuous regarding the period—now just a memory

—when Garner had felt he had a chance to win, but it accurately described the feelings of the Garner leaders since the Wisconsin primary. And it had been Rayburn's desire even before Wisconsin.

In the event, Rayburn achieved what he had wanted for Garner. Substantial sums of Herman Brown's money were spent on a campaign to elect at the precinct and county conventions delegates who would vote for Roosevelt on the first ballot.* The Third Term was advertised on radio as well as in newspapers. But the campaign did not shake Garner's control of the party apparatus. A compromise was therefore agreed upon. It was Rayburn's compromise—in effect, it would be almost precisely the proposal he had made weeks before.

Under the terms of the compromise, it would be sealed by a telegram—in the interest of "harmony"—to political leaders in Texas. The telegram said:

> TEXAS ROOSEVELT SUPPORTERS SHOULD ENDORSE NATIVE SON JOHN GARNER AND SEND DELEGATION INSTRUCTED TO VOTE FOR HIS NOMINATION FOR THE PRESIDENCY. . . . GARNER ORGANIZATION AND HIS SUPPORTERS WILL INSIST THAT STATE CONVENTION APPROVE AND ACCLAIM ADMINISTRATION RECORD AND WILL REFUSE TO BE A PARTY TO ANY STOP ROOSEVELT MOVEMENT.
>
> WE THINK . . . BOTH SIDES SHOULD GET TOGETHER AND SEND DELEGATION TO THE NATIONAL CONVENTION WHICH WILL CARRY OUT ABOVE PROGRAM. . . . WE FEEL SURE SUCH AN UNDERSTANDING WOULD NOT BE DISPLEASING TO THE PRESIDENT.

To achieve the compromise, and thus salvage Garner's dignity, however, Rayburn was subjected to embarrassment—embarrassment which was to have profound political consequences. In conferences between Tommy Corcoran, Harold Ickes and Lyndon Johnson in Washington, and, over the telephone, with Alvin Wirtz in Texas, it was decided that the telegram should be signed not only by Rayburn, as leader of the Garner forces, but by a leader of the Roosevelt forces—and that that leader would be Lyndon Johnson. Because the text of the telegram indicated that the compromise, while guaranteeing Texas' votes for Garner, was not a total victory, Rayburn would have preferred that it not be sent, and that if it was sent, it be released to the press in Texas, "so that," as Ickes put it, "it would be less likely to attract national attention." Johnson, Corcoran, Ickes and Wirtz, however, insisted that it be released from the White House, and that Johnson go with Rayburn to show the telegram to the President. "Rayburn balked at this,"

---

* Control of this money was kept in the hands of a very few men: New Dealers whose first loyalty was to Wirtz. The few veteran politicians working for Roosevelt in Texas were given little to spend.

Ickes wrote in his *Secret Diary*. "He did not want to go to the White House, one of his reasons being that he did not want it to appear that in a Texas political matter a kid Congressman like Lyndon Johnson was on apparently the same footing as himself, the Majority Leader." But the compromise gave Rayburn's old friend what Rayburn wanted him to have: the chance to retire with pride, to leave public life with his state's unanimous vote behind him. The compromise also endorsed the accomplishments of the Roosevelt administration, which Rayburn had helped bring about, and in which he believed so deeply. And Johnson and Wirtz held another trump card. With the precinct conventions rapidly approaching, failure to seal the compromise would result in the intra-state fight against Garner that Rayburn had been trying to avoid. For Garner's sake, Rayburn agreed to their terms. "Johnson here and Wirtz in Texas forced the issue until Rayburn reluctantly agreed to go to the White House," Ickes wrote. They were shown into the President's office on April 29. "When Johnson and Rayburn appeared in the President's office that afternoon, he told them benignly that they had been good little boys and that they had 'papa's blessing.' He treated them as political equals, with the malicious intent of disturbing Sam Rayburn's state of mind. I think that he succeeded."

WHETHER OR NOT Rayburn was disturbed by the White House meeting, he was deeply disturbed by subsequent events.

He had assumed that, whatever the causes of the tension with the New Dealers who had once been his allies, the compromise had ended them. "I am sure," he wrote to a friend, "that no one thinks that I am anti-Roosevelt as I think all will agree that I have done about as much to help him carry out his program as anybody in the United States. What I have wanted was to have a delegation from Texas . . . without a fight and representing all elements of the Party in Texas."* But that assumption failed to take into account certain aspects of the President's character. Roosevelt would show an unwillingness to forgive—ever—this man who he believed had been part of a "Stop Roosevelt" movement.

Rayburn was shortly to rise to the place he had envisioned for himself as a boy. Speaker Bankhead died of a stomach hemorrhage on September 15. The hollowness of the New Dealers' threats to deny Rayburn power in the House was revealed by the proceedings to select Bankhead's successor; they

---

* Even at this stage of the fight, however, nothing superseded the protection of his old friend in Rayburn's priorities. Another sentence in the letter reads: "I am sure since the exchange of telegrams between Wirtz, Blalock, Lyndon Johnson and me that everybody will go along with the program and instruct the county delegation to vote as suggested in the telegrams." In rereading this letter after it had been typed by a secretary, Rayburn was evidently afraid that it was not clear enough. After the word "vote," he inserted by hand: "for Garner."

took two minutes and were unanimous—no one even suggested a name other than Rayburn's. The next day, with Bankhead's body lying in state in the well of the Chamber, Rayburn stood above the casket—on the topmost tier of that tripled-tiered dais, in front of that single, high-backed chair —and took the oath that his fellow Texan, Garner, had taken nine years before. He made no speech; except for a brief eulogy to Bankhead, he said only, picking up the Speaker's gavel, "The House shall be in order." To a friend, a few days later, he said, referring to the town in which he had attended a one-room schoolhouse: "It's a fur piece from Flag Springs." And he added: "I still can't realize I'm Speaker." Then he returned to Bonham, where his constituents honored him by coming to a barbecue in a caravan of cars more than a mile long, each bearing his picture; before he went to the celebration, he made another stop: the cemetery, to stand before his parents' grave.

But Rayburn's attainment of his lifelong aim was to bring him only limited satisfaction during the four and a half years that remained of Roosevelt's Presidency. His image of the Speakership had never been limited merely to a gavel and power. "I would rather link my name indelibly with the living pulsing history of my country and not be forgotten entirely after a while than to have anything else on earth," he had written. He had always felt that the House of Representatives, as a sovereign branch of government, had rights and prerogatives, that it should not merely respond to initiatives of the executive branch but should play a role in the initiation of national policy. As its leader, he had felt, he would be entitled to such a role—specifically, since the House as a whole was too unwieldy to initiate policy, he had believed that a strong Speaker would be included by the President in the policy-making process, would, because he understood the will of the House and could represent that will, at least be consulted while policy was being formulated. His ambitions had never been only for himself. He had always thought of himself in the terms he had enunciated in his first speech in the House, so many years before—as a voice for people who had no other voice, as a voice for his beloved farmers. A man who met him for the first time on a train crossing Texas in 1935 saw him sitting "staring in serious reflection across the countryside"; the man introduced himself, and Rayburn, only half shaken out of his musings, said, as if to himself: "Where is the farmer going? Where is America going?" This man, who was to become Rayburn's friend, says that "He was a farmer at heart, but with an ambition to help his own kind." He wanted—wanted passionately—farmers to have a voice in the highest councils of government. And he had always believed that, after he became Speaker, he would be that voice.

He was not—during Roosevelt's Presidency—to have what he had expected to have. He remained loyal, a rock for Roosevelt in the Forties as he had been in the Thirties. The three previous Speakers, Rainey, Byrns and

Bankhead, had been weak—at the time Rayburn picked up the gavel, the potential power of the Speakership had been all but forgotten. Under Rayburn, it was to be remembered. And his strength and personal popularity comprised a key factor in the passage, in that body dominated by anti–New Deal Southerners, of much legislation that otherwise might not have been passed despite Roosevelt's wishes. ("Hell, Sam," said one, "if it wasn't for you, there are about fifty of us from the South who'd walk right out on him.")

His strength was at Roosevelt's service in foreign affairs as well. In August, 1941, the Selective Service Act, which had, a year earlier, established America's first peacetime draft, was about to expire. Unless the Act was extended, not only would most of the men in uniform be discharged, but no new ones could be drafted. And despite Roosevelt's pleas for extension, pressure on Congress to let it die had reached almost a frenzy under the prodding of powerful isolationist organizations and of delegations of mothers.

Rayburn knew the draft was needed. Talking with George Brown, he suddenly fell silent. The grim face turned even grimmer. After a while, he said quietly, "The war clouds are gathering, George." Rayburn didn't stay in the Speaker's chair during the three days of bitter debate; he went back to the spot in which he had stood for so many years, back behind the rail, and he worked the cloakroom, calling in almost thirty years' worth of favors. Wrote a friend: "This was a time when he did not hesitate, all else failing, to make the ultimate plea: 'Do this for me.' "

As he returned to the chair to preside over the vote on the bill—the galleries above him crammed with uniformed soldiers on leave, weeping mothers and isolationist delegations—he knew he had not picked up enough votes. But he had the gavel in his hand. The Republicans were holding back the votes of several GOP Congressmen opposed to the Act, and several others were planning to change their votes from support to opposition as soon as they saw how many votes were needed to defeat the measure—since under House rules a member can change his vote until the result is announced. They never got a chance. Without the new votes and the switches, the slip the tally clerk handed to Rayburn was 203 for the bill, 202 opposed. In the very moment he read those figures Rayburn pounded down his gavel and announced the vote, freezing it. Enraged Republicans, milling in the well of the House, demanded reconsideration; by using, too fast for his opponents to keep up with him, a series of intricate parliamentary procedures —and, finally, when he was cornered, pounding down his gavel to finalize the vote, and grimly defying their leaders to do something about it—he kept the one-vote margin. He had stretched House rules to a point at which they would have broken had not the power of his iron personality stood behind his rulings—"but," a friend wrote, "the end result was that, when . . .

Japanese bombers struck Pearl Harbor less than four months later, the United States had an Army of 1,600,000 men instead of a token force of 400,000."

But if he was to be allowed to push through Roosevelt's policies, he was to be allowed very little voice in their formulation. The charming presidential missives on Bonham's annual Sam Rayburn Day resumed. The two men had been born in the same month in 1882, and each January birthday greetings were exchanged, charming greetings from Roosevelt, admiring greetings from the man who had Roosevelt's picture on his desk at home; "I thank God for you on this day, because at sixty years of age you are ripe and strong for the burden that would crush a less determined man," Rayburn wrote in January, 1942. Real input into policy was not, however, to be among the favors Roosevelt conferred. Each Monday, in meetings highly publicized by the press, Rayburn and McCormack of the House, Barkley of the Senate, and Vice President Wallace would meet with the President, ostensibly to map policy, in luncheons marked by camaraderie and joking. ("Sam Rayburn mentioned that he had been in conference with Mrs. Luce. The President and all the rest of us began to kid him, and Sam turned pink.") But Rayburn was not impressed by such stroking, or by the crowd of photographers who would snap the "Big Four" on the White House steps as they were leaving. These meetings, Henry Wallace was to note, aroused Rayburn's "resentment" because at them "the President never suggests any legislation," so that the meetings amounted to no more than "glad hand affairs of very little significance"; on another occasion Rayburn complained to Wallace "that the President didn't take him sufficiently into his confidence." (Nonetheless, Wallace also noted, Rayburn "was quite loyal to Roosevelt.") Jonathan Daniels saw how easily Rayburn's feelings were hurt. And Daniels saw how often Roosevelt hurt them. "He said he felt he could be much more useful if he could see the President by himself. I asked him if he could not do this and he said of course he could—but—he gave the impression of feeling that his advice was not wanted."

A few of the younger men around the President such as Corcoran and Cohen (and the even younger, more junior, Jim Rowe) admired Rayburn. "Your country owes you a great deal which most of the plain people will never know about," Rowe wrote him. But, after 1940, Corcoran and Cohen faded from the White House scene. To the remaining members of the White House inner circle, men such as Steve Early, Pa Watson and Marvin McIntyre and women such as Missy LeHand and Grace Tully, and to bright young newcomers to that circle, Rayburn was indistinguishable from other Southern conservatives. More important—to this palace guard to whom disloyalty to the President was the cardinal sin—Rayburn had been, they believed, a leader of the Stop Roosevelt movement. This feeling echoed the attitude of their boss, a man to whom a sturdy independence such as Rayburn's was not a prized quality. Their attitude toward this slow-talking Texan was snide; after a Rayburn speech, McIntyre jotted a sarcastic memo to Roosevelt: "Understand Sam was very proud of his literary effort." When Daniels told McIntyre that Rayburn's "pride" had been "worn thin" by his "treatment at the White House," McIntyre replied that "Rayburn, like all other Speakers, has gotten swell-headed." Rayburn told Rowe: "There's nobody in the White House I can talk to."

Because of the size of Texas, and the philosophical as well as geographical diversity among its various regions, there had not been a single person through whom the White House worked in Texas, as there might have been in a smaller, more unified state. Nonetheless, for a long time Garner had been the key link between the White House and Texas, the individual to whom, more than any other, the Roosevelt administration had turned first in matters of patronage and policy affecting the great province to the southwest. Now Garner was gone. With the state's two Senators shunning statewide power, with the hollowness of Jesse Jones' professions of loyalty to the New Deal now apparent, and with Maury Maverick waging a losing fight for his own political survival, Garner's role would, in the normal course of events, have been filled by Rayburn, as the state's senior, and by far most powerful, official in the national government. Once Roosevelt had apparently intended Rayburn to fill that role; he had begun giving him the Texas patronage that would have cemented that position. Normally, Roosevelt would have continued doing so. The new Speaker's advice would have been the first solicited in matters of both policy and politics affecting the state. Normally, Sam Rayburn would have been the President's man in Texas.

But he wasn't. The telegrams to Rayburn from Austin had been cleverly designed to force him into a position which would antagonize the President. Lyndon Johnson's "vivid" description to Roosevelt of the John L. Lewis episode had emphasized Rayburn's anti-Roosevelt role, as had the reports Johnson and Wirtz gave to the President at their private meetings. (Rayburn's statement "appeared to the President as an attack from within the Administration. . . .") And the telegrams—together with the leaked newspaper stories about them, stories that relied on "information" from Johnson—cemented that impression. After those telegrams, the White House had an accurate impression of Sam Rayburn as a Garner supporter, but it also had a false impression of Rayburn as Roosevelt's enemy, as a leader not only of the Garner campaign but of the whole Stop Roosevelt movement, as the enemy of the man he not only idolized but whom he had, on a hundred occasions, loyally served. After those telegrams, Sam Rayburn could never be Roosevelt's man in Texas. He had been tarred beyond cleansing by a brush wielded by Lyndon Johnson. And the tarring gave Johnson what he wanted. By mid-1940, Johnson was Roosevelt's man in

Texas. As Washington columnist Jay Franklin reported, "A virtual freshman Representative . . . is now the acknowledged New Deal spokesman in the Lone Star State."

The most significant aspect of this development involved federal contracts. Before 1940, Jesse Jones had frequently been "consulted" on these contracts. (As RFC head, Jones could of course award RFC contracts himself.) After 1940, Jones was to be largely ignored. Before 1940, Senators Connally and Sheppard had occasionally been consulted—not as often as Connally, in particular, would have liked, but occasionally. After 1940, requests from the Senators for input into contract awards were fobbed off. And before 1940, the Texan most often consulted had been John Garner. Rayburn's lack of interest in this area was already legendary in Washington. Once, following authorization of the Denison Dam in his district, he had been discreetly sounded out on the identity of his favorite contractor; he didn't have one, he replied. But, in the normal course of events, the opinion of the Speaker of the House of Representatives would at least have been asked when a major public works or defense contract was to be handed out in his state. Now it would not be. Freezing Jones, Connally, Sheppard and Rayburn out of major contract decisions in Texas did not, however, result in a vacuum in this crucial area. For even as the vacuum was being created, it was being filled—by the man who had done so much to create it: a "virtual freshman Representative."

Johnson's influence over the Corpus Christi Naval Air Station contract had in itself given him a major role in construction in Texas, for so huge was that $100 million piece of work in that state (the total amount of work let by the State Highway Department in 1940 was only $27 million) that Brown & Root put to work on it subcontractors from all over the state. And with the nation gearing up for war with growing intensity, and with the military bases that already dotted Texas expanding, his influence was to increase, for the word was passed by the White House that Lyndon Johnson was to be "consulted" on expansion contracts. Minuscule though these contracts may have been in comparison with gigantic Corpus Christi, they were important to the firms which received them; in Johnson's own district, for example, a contract for approximately $71,000 to the Taylor Bedding Co. for mattresses for Navy barracks was one of the largest this firm had ever received, as were federal contracts for several hundred thousand dollars of construction work that went to the Ainsworth Construction Co. of Luling. Contractors all across Texas were grateful for REA line-laying contracts arranged by Johnson. The word was out in Washington. Federal contracts in Texas were, as Corcoran puts it, to be given to "Lyndon's friends." "And," Corcoran says, "once he could get public money for his friends, he was made."

He was indeed "made"—by the "public money" represented by federal contracts. He had been able to bring to the Roosevelt re-election campaign a resource which no other Texan could offer: Herman Brown's money. And he had used that resource as a base. Because he could provide that money to the Roosevelt campaign in Texas, he was given a commanding role in that campaign. Because he played that role, he was given input into the awarding of other federal contracts. Because he possessed that input, men who wanted those contracts—and they included some of the most powerful men in Texas—had to come to him.

In a sense, that third telegram had signaled this fact. Lyndon Johnson's name had been placed beside Sam Rayburn's on that telegram; he had been treated by the President as "on the same footing" with the Majority Leader of the House of Representatives. Treating Johnson as Rayburn's equal in the Oval Office, of course, had had merely symbolic significance. Treating him as a full-fledged power in Texas in the awarding of federal contracts had a significance that went far beyond symbolism. Men who could read the map of power understood the significance of the fact that the largest contract ever awarded in Texas—a contract of almost unbelievable magnitude—had been awarded to Lyndon Johnson's friend. Ickes could describe him as a "kid Congressman." "Kid," in some terms, he may have been—a thirty-one-year-old Congressman from a remote and isolated political district. But after that telegram, he was, in terms of power, a kid Congressman no longer. Unknown though his name remained to the public in the state's other twenty congressional districts, it was now not only known but respected by powerful and influential men in those districts. Lyndon Johnson had been maneuvering since shortly after coming to Washington as a congressional secretary in 1931 to obtain statewide power. Now he was able to procure for men who mattered in Texas—all across Texas—not merely hotel reservations and appointments with federal officials, but federal contracts. Thanks to Herman Brown's money, and to the skill with which he had employed it as a political resource, he was much further now along the road he saw stretching before him.

HE WAS ROOSEVELT'S MAN in Texas—but he was not only Roosevelt's man.

The President's popularity with the mass of Texas voters was matched by his unpopularity with the small group of men who ran the state with such a tight grip, as had been proven by the overwhelming roar of acclaim for Garner—and his candidacy—in the state's Democratic Executive Committee, and in precinct, county and state nominating conventions. The President's popularity was, moreover, strictly personal, and could not be taken to include voter support of his policies, as had been proven by the defeat of

Congressmen who supported the New Deal. Only one of the state's twenty-one congressional districts, Lyndon Johnson's Tenth, could be said to be safely "liberal"; in those few districts—no more than three or four—which were represented by Congressmen such as Sam Rayburn who supported the President, the Congressmen had won election by virtue of their personal popularity rather than by their accord with their constituents' views. Even after Garner's last hopes of victory in the presidential nominating race had vanished, the state organization was controlled as tightly as ever by men who had once been bound together by their allegiance to Cactus Jack, but who were now bound, as tightly as ever, by allegiance to a philosophy diametrically opposed to that of the New Deal. Their leader's views would not change (back home in Uvalde, he pinned a Willkie button to his lapel; twenty years later, he would still be railing against the policies of the man with whom he had twice run to great national victories). And neither would theirs. Many of the leaders of the Garner campaign would, in 1944, be the Texas Regulars who deserted the Democratic Party rather than support Franklin D. Roosevelt.

But, however deep their resentment of the New Deal as a whole or of the Texas leaders of the anti-Garner campaign, the objects of that resentment did not include Lyndon Johnson. The reason was simple: they didn't know he was one of the leaders. Johnson's attempt to conceal his views in the Garner-Roosevelt fight had, of course, begun at its beginning. During the very time when he was privately regaling New Dealers with the way he had defied Sam Rayburn to his face in front of the whole Texas delegation, he was dodging every attempt to make him take a public position in the Roosevelt-Garner fight. (His dodging led to an incorrect conclusion, for the AP noted that he had "recently joined in a statement expressing regard for Garner.") And he had attempted to keep his profile low—invisible, in fact—during the whole of that almost year-long battle. When a Roosevelt-for-President Committee was established in Texas, Tom Miller, not Lyndon Johnson, was its president, Ed Clark its secretary. Miller and Clark—and Maury Maverick and Harold Young and, in the battle's concluding stages, even Alvin Wirtz—might be roaming Texas making speeches, but Lyndon Johnson appeared on no speakers' platform.

As much as possible, he did not appear in Texas. The brief trip he made to Austin in March appears, in fact, to have been the only time he ventured within the state's borders during the months in which the Roosevelt-Garner battle was at its height there. The lengths to which he went to stay out of the state were most dramatically demonstrated when Austin's Tom Miller Dam, another LCRA project, was dedicated on April 6, 1940. Johnson had obtained the funds for the dam. At the dedication of other dams on the Lower Colorado, and of every other construction project in his district, he was invariably present, and went to great lengths to assure himself the lion's share of the publicity. When the Tom Miller Dam was dedicated, the only evidence of Austin's Congressman was his name on a plaque and a telegram expressing his regret that he could not be present because of "work yet to be accomplished in Washington."

When he was forced to enter the state, he stayed out of its newspapers. "Johnson was being very cagey," says Vann Kennedy, editor of the *State Observer*, a weekly published in Austin. "Johnson was being very cautious about getting himself exposed to any unnecessary fire." Harold Young, who was receiving so much monetary assistance from Johnson, came to realize— to his shock, for he had heard Johnson railing against Garner privately— that he would not do so publicly. "Lyndon didn't any more want to take a stand on Garner than he wanted to take a stand against the Martin Dies committee," Young says. It was at this time that the Texas liberal and Rayburn man William Kittrell first coined an expression about Johnson: "Lyndon will be found on no barricades."

He may not have been present even at the riotous State Democratic Convention in Waco at which the state's delegation was chosen after fistfights between Garner and Roosevelt supporters. If he was at Waco, he kept a low profile indeed. Asked years later, "Was Mr. Johnson at the state convention?" E. B. Germany, Garner's reactionary, Roosevelt-hating state chairman, was to reply: "I don't think he was there. If he was there—I don't see how he stayed away, but I don't remember seeing him at the state convention." He did not materialize on a speakers' platform where he could be seen by influential Texans until the Democratic National Convention in Chicago—by which time, of course, the battle was over, so he was not called upon to declare his preference.

His efforts at secrecy were successful.

The *Austin American-Statesman*, which took editorial direction directly from its owner, Charles Marsh, almost never mentioned his name in connection with the Roosevelt-Garner fight; as late as March 17, 1940, for example, an article by Raymond Brooks listed the leaders of the Roosevelt campaign in Texas, and Johnson was not mentioned. He stayed out of other newspapers as well. Articles in Texas newspapers identified Tom Miller and Ed Clark— and, later, Alvin Wirtz—as leaders, and included other names—State Democratic Chairwoman Frances Haskell Edmondson, Maury Maverick, railroad Commissioner Jerry Sadler, former Attorney General William McCraw, Harold Young. Seldom was the name of Lyndon Johnson included, and when it was, it was as only a minor figure in the movement to deny the favorite-son vote to Garner; four months after he had summed up the state's political situation without mentioning Johnson's name, Walter Hornaday, chief political writer of the *Dallas Morning News*, added: ". . . The Garner leaders also believe that Representative Lyndon Johnson is active in the third-term movement. . . ."

The fight ended with his anonymity still successfully preserved. The *State Observer*'s June 3 issue, the issue which covered in detail the Waco convention that was the fight's final battle, identified Tom Miller as the "originator of the draft-Roosevelt movement in Texas." As for the movement's other leaders, the *Observer* listed many names. The name Lyndon Johnson does not appear even once in that issue.

One Texas newspaper did attempt at least obliquely to reveal and explain his role—and the reaction to these attempts is instructive. The paper was the *Fort Worth Star-Telegram*, and it may have understood Johnson's role because its publisher, Amon G. Carter, while reactionary in his political philosophy and a longtime Garner supporter (it was Carter's famous Stetsons that Garner always wore in Washington), wanted huge new public works for his beloved Fort Worth and, to get them, had maintained ties with the White House. On March 23, 1940, Carter not only expressed the bitterness of the Garnerites in a long editorial ("Normal Texans are unable to understand those calling themselves Texans who go about urging Texas to desert Garner and to weasel out of its duty to stand by its own") but also attempted to explain the significance to the Roosevelt movement of public works in the state's Tenth Congressional District—and of the district's Congressman. "The whole [Third-Term] outfit gathers round a damsite on the Colorado," Carter wrote. On April 7, the *Star-Telegram* sharpened its attack; in attributing the motives behind the anti-Garner movement in Texas not to philosophy but to greed, it said: "So far no advices have come from Washington . . . that dams of the Lower Colorado River Authority will be abandoned in the event Garner becomes President. But an Austin bloc is alarmed."

Noting past federal generosity for Carter's own pet projects in Fort Worth, Ickes replied by jeering that, after Roosevelt was re-elected, "you and other such 'leaders' will be the first to hie you to the pie counter" for more federal funds. Carter's reaction was to focus his attention more closely on the LCRA dams. Ickes had publicly promised to reveal, when asked, the legal fees paid to private attorneys in connection with all PWA projects. Now Carter instructed his Washington correspondent, Bascom Timmons, to demand from the PWA the total amount of the legal fees paid to Alvin J. Wirtz in connection with LCRA projects.

This figure, paid between 1935 and 1939, was $85,000, a staggering amount in terms of legal fees customary in Texas at the time. And the $85,000 from the PWA was only a drop in the bucket that Wirtz had filled at those dams. Once the question of his legal fees was opened, it might be only a matter of time before it was discovered that he had received for work on the dams fees not only from the PWA but as the attorney for the Insull interests, as court-appointed receiver of those interests in bankruptcy proceedings, and, of course, from Brown & Root. If a spotlight was turned on those dams, moreover, the Congressman responsible for their construction

—the Congressman who had pushed for those legal fees—would be caught in its glare. The light had to be turned off.

The strategy evolved to do so is contained in a memorandum found in Alvin Wirtz's papers. This memo is unsigned, and unaddressed, and its author is unknown. In it, both Wirtz and Johnson are referred to in the third person, although at least one member of Wirtz's staff feels that, because of the secretiveness of both men (and because the wording of the memo reflects Johnson's style), these references do not eliminate either Johnson or Wirtz as the possible author of the memo. In any case, the memo reflects, according to all living members of the Wirtz-Johnson camp, the thinking of that camp: to counter the threat of an attack with a counterattack—a savage counterattack—against not only Garner and Roy Miller, but also Sam Rayburn.

The writer of the memorandum appreciates the significance of the Carter threat; while the PWA feels that $85,000 was a "fair fee," he writes, its disclosure "will have [the] effect of smearing Wirtz." The response should be to let Rayburn know that if the Wirtz fees are to be disclosed, other disclosures will be made: the press will be given "something that will be good nationwide publicity—how much Garner, Mrs. Garner, Tully Garner have received from the Govt. over a period of 40 years; that Ed Clark wants to figure up how much he, Sam, has made, travelling expenses, etc. in 25 years; that Everett Looney . . . has figures on how much Roy Miller paid to try to buy the Texas Legislature. . . ." As significant as the strategy revealed in the memo—the savage attack not only on Garner and Miller, who were used to such accusations, but on Sam Rayburn, who was so proud of his "untarnished name" (which would no longer be untarnished if it was linked in the press with a figure of approximately $225,000, which would represent, of course, only the standard Congressman's salary, but would look bad in the papers)—was the care taken in the memo that neither Alvin Wirtz nor Lyndon Johnson should be linked with that strategy. The threat should be delivered to Rayburn by Maury Maverick, the memo states, not by Wirtz. "Senator ought to be rather independent in the matter, and not be concerned about it. . . . Maury ought to call Sam. . . . Better this way than for Senator to get involved." As for Johnson, the memo goes further in stressing that he had nothing to do with the attacks on Amon Carter that had emanated from Washington. Referring to the "pie counter" missive, the memo begins: "Ickes has replied to Amon Carter, writing a real mean letter," and then hastens to add: "Secretary [Ickes] didn't consult Lyndon, and he didn't know about it." Lyndon Johnson—or his advisors—may have been directing all-out war on the Garnerites, but the Garnerites were not to know. When it became necessary for either Wirtz or Johnson to get publicly involved with the anti-Garner fight—when it was necessary for some key Texan in Washington to return to Texas and publicly lead the fight—it was

Wirtz, always so concerned about the political future of the young man he considered his protégé, who dropped his mask and did so.

Neither Wirtz's fees nor the information about Garner, Miller and Rayburn was ever made public, possibly because the memo apparently was written on Friday, April 26, and Monday, April 29, was the day on which, with Roosevelt's intervention, the "harmony" agreement was drafted and the telegram signed by Rayburn and Johnson was sent, and this most serious threat to Johnson's attempt to keep secret in Texas his role in the Roosevelt campaign died. Amon Carter's newspaper was, moreover, the only newspaper in Texas to make even an attempt to portray Johnson's true significance in the fight. In Washington, his leadership (together, of course, with that of Wirtz) of the fight was an open secret; in Texas, it was just a secret. The only time his name received substantial publicity in Texas was when it appeared on the "harmony" telegram along with Rayburn's—and, because this telegram *was* signed by Rayburn, and because it was seen in Texas as a compromise, the appearance of his name in this context did not anger the Garner leaders.

And Johnson's refusal to take a public stand against Garner even while he was peddling his story about the John L. Lewis episode in the right quarters, his success in keeping his name off the two telegrams to Rayburn (and out of the subsequent press coverage of those telegrams), the care taken to keep his name out of the entire 1940 Garner-Roosevelt fight in Texas ("Lyndon . . . didn't know about it"), paid off. To an astonishing degree, the leaders of the Garner movement never became aware of the true extent of Johnson's role in the fight. Asked, years later, if, during 1940, Johnson brought "any pressure to bear not to have Garner nominated," E. B. Germany replied: "No, as far as I know he [didn't]. . . ." During 1940, two opposing camps were chosen up in Texas, and deep animosity sprang up between them, but surprisingly little of that animosity spilled over onto Lyndon Johnson, because each side appears to have felt that Johnson was on its side.

And after the conventions, when the fight was over, the man who had so carefully stayed out of Texas returned to it—for private talks with many of the Garner leaders. Some of these men had had doubts about Lyndon Johnson, but these talks resolved them; the few minor gaps in his fences were mended. George Brown had known that Johnson could do it. Talking as conservatively with conservatives as he talked liberally with liberals— "that was his leadership. That was his knack." And George Brown was right. He arranged for Johnson to meet in a Houston hotel room with two ultra-conservative, Roosevelt-hating Texas financiers. "He went in there, and in an hour he had convinced them he wasn't liberal," Brown would recall.

"This is a year of strange politics," said an article in the *Austin American-Statesman*. "Texas runs into some of its most amazing contradictions and cross currents. . . . New cleavages threaten a deep and serious break in Texas Democratic solidarity. It is a strange, confused, uncharted field—the field of national politics today." Strange, confused and uncharted it was—a minefield that could easily have destroyed the political future of anyone attempting to build a future in Texas politics in 1940. But through this field, one man—a novice in statewide politics—picked his way, with sure and silent steps.

31

Campaign Committee

AFTER THE ROOSEVELT-GARNER FIGHT in Texas, Lyndon Johnson would always have entrée at the White House. But after the fight ended, in May, 1940, that entrée was again restricted. Lyndon Johnson no longer had a reason to see the President. Impatient—after the death of his father and uncle, almost desperately impatient—to move along the route he had mapped out for himself, he had no means of doing so.

And then this genius of politics found a way.

The way was money. At first, again, the money was Herman Brown's.

Thanks to the profits from the Marshall Ford Dam and the Corpus Christi Naval Air Station contracts, there was plenty of it. However, in political terms, the most significant aspect of Brown's bankroll was not its size but its availability for any purpose Johnson specified. George Brown had promised that Lyndon need only tell him "when and where I can return at least a portion of the favors. Remember that I am *for* you, right or wrong, and it makes no difference if I think you are right or wrong. If you want it, I am for it 100%." Most politicians are forced, in mapping out the next step in their careers, to choose a step that can be financed. Johnson did not have this problem; he could concentrate solely on which step would be best for his career. Whatever road he chose, he could be sure it would be paved by money from Brown & Root. Furthermore, the aims of the Congressman coincided with those of the corporation. The man with the obsession to build—build big—knew that the way to build big was through Washington. Influence within the national government was what Herman Brown needed, and influence within that government—political power that reached beyond Texas—was what Lyndon Johnson wanted. Each of them could obtain what he wanted through the other.

The most obvious use of readily available money for someone aiming at national political power was in the campaign of the man whose strong hands held the reins of national power in such a firm grip. With the great financial resources of the Republican Party solidly behind the campaign of

Wendell Willkie, the President's re-election campaign was in severe financial difficulties, and these difficulties were a prime source of conversation in Washington, and of concern to Johnson's New Deal companions. Around him, in conversations in the cloakroom or on the floor of the House, at cocktail parties and dinner parties, swirled talk of campaign funds, and of where to get them. Furthermore, Johnson could have adduced from his own recent experience with Roosevelt that the President might not prove ungrateful for campaign contributions. Having already provided such contributions to Roosevelt for a state campaign, it seemed the obvious course, the logical course, for Lyndon Johnson to provide contributions for the President's national campaign, and indeed men such as Charles Marsh suggested this course to him.

It was not a suggestion he accepted. No one can know why, but it is possible to list several considerations which may have influenced his decision. In a presidential campaign he would be only one of many contributors—considering the scale of contributions from New York and other financial centers of the Northeast, not even one of the biggest. The President's gratitude would be proportionate. Moreover, any tangible power and patronage that might result from Roosevelt's gratitude would be held at Roosevelt's whim—and could be withdrawn at his whim. Independent power could not result from such a situation, any more than if he had accepted the President's offer of the REA post. Using Herman Brown's money in Franklin Roosevelt's campaign would probably not get Lyndon Johnson what he wanted; it was necessary for him to find another way of using it.

And he did.

One facet of Lyndon Johnson's political genius was already obvious by 1940: his ability to look at an organization and see in it political potentialities that no one else saw, to transform that organization into a political force, and to reap from that transformation personal advantage. He had done this twice before, transforming a social club (the White Stars) and a debating society (the Little Congress) into political forces that he used to further his own ends. Now he was to do it again.

This time, the organization was the Democratic Congressional Campaign Committee.

Like the Little Congress at the moment when Lyndon Johnson's gaze fell upon it, the committee was a moribund organization. Established in 1882 to assist Democratic candidates for the House of Representatives with services and campaign funds, its usefulness had seldom if ever reached a significant level. During the 1930's, under the chairmanship of Patrick Henry Drewry, a diminutive, soft-spoken Representative from the Virginia Tidewater, even that level had been reduced, for Drewry was ill-suited to the role of aggressive fund-raiser, not only because of personal considerations—"He was every inch a country gentleman; he could never ask anyone for a dime," says a friend—but because of moral and philosophical ones as

well: the very concept of the massive use of money in political campaigns
was repugnant to him, and, as a staunch states righter, he saw dangerous
implications for the independence of the nation's elected representatives in
the distribution of money through a monolithic central committee. He had
therefore decreed that the committee's maximum contribution to a Congressman would be $250. Few candidates received even this amount. The
dichotomy within the Democratic Party, with its bitterly antagonistic liberal
and conservative wings, kept the committee's bank account small: big
contributors were unwilling to provide money which might then be channeled
by the committee to candidates with opposing political views; for a wealthy
liberal, the idea that his money might help finance the campaign of a
conservative Midwest Congressman was distasteful—as distasteful as the
idea that his money might help a New York liberal was to a wealthy
conservative. (Drewry's lack of enthusiasm for distributing money was
especially marked when the distributee was to be a Northern liberal.) The
committee's funds had traditionally come primarily from two sources—
contributions from Congressmen themselves, and handouts from the Democratic National Committee—and during Drewry's chairmanship, these
sources had slowed to a trickle. For some decades, the committee had
requested $100 from each Democratic member of the House to fund its
operation; under Drewry, this request had been reduced by 1938 to $25—
and when few members honored it, Drewry made only a token effort to
collect.

Democrats who turned to the committee* for non-financial help were
also likely to be disappointed; although the committee had a speakers'
bureau, headed by E. J. MacMillan, the bureau functioned only in non-
presidential election years; when a presidential election was taking place,
Congressmen who telephoned to ask for a Cabinet member or other "name"
speaker to appear in their districts found MacMillan gone—he was invariably
drafted by the National Committee and sent to New York to help in the
"national" campaign. The committee's other staffer was its capable secretary,
Victor Hunt ("Cap") Harding, a political scientist from California and one
of the House of Representatives' deputy Sergeants-at-Arms. During a
campaign, Harding would take an office—generally only one room—in the
National Press Building at Fourteenth and F streets so that he could accept
whatever contributions happened to come in without violating the law which
forbade the accepting of campaign contributions in a federal building. During campaigns, therefore, when the Congressional Campaign Committee
should have been most active, its office, a dim, green-carpeted room in the

---

* Actually, services were supposedly dispensed not by the Congressional Campaign Committee but by the Democratic National Congressional Committee, but these
committees were actually the same body, operating out of the same office and with the
same staff; the two names had been adopted to avoid various complications of campaign-
financing laws.

basement of the Cannon House Office Building, was often utterly deserted—a condition which sometimes was only slightly improved even on the rare occasions when Drewry scheduled a meeting of the "committee" itself, which consisted of one Congressman from each state; more than once, the only persons who bothered to show up were Drewry and Harding.

In 1940, Democratic congressional candidates were even more desperate than usual for cash. The amounts they needed were, in most cases, small —ridiculously small not only by the standards of later eras but in comparison with the amounts spent during the pre-war era in statewide races and in the presidential campaign. The amounts varied greatly; congressional races in the urban centers of the Northeast could cost tens of thousands of dollars, but in the rest of the nation the situation was far different. In 1928, for example, Ruth Baker Pratt spent $12,000 in her campaign for a House seat from New York City. That was several times the total amount spent that year by all six candidates for the three congressional seats in the State of Oregon. A detailed study of expenditures in House races in that state between 1912 and 1928—the most detailed study available for the pre-war period—showed that of thirty-eight candidates for Congress, only three had spent as much as $3,000. Twenty-four of the 38 had spent less than $1,000. This situation had not changed much in 1938. In that year, the six candidates—three Democrats and three Republicans—for Oregon's three seats spent a total of $12,987, a little more than $2,000 per candidate. In most other Western and Midwestern states, the range that year was the same. "In the great majority of cases campaigning for a seat in the House of Representatives is not an expensive business," wrote Louise Overacker, the era's leading academic expert on campaign finance. Discussions with Congressmen of that era indicate that most campaigns cost less than $5,000. And their recollections are confirmed by insiders who had an overview of the situation, such as Thomas Corcoran and James Rowe. In politics, says Rowe, "Five thousand dollars was a *hell* of a lot of money in those days."

Little as Democratic congressional candidates needed in 1940, however, there was small hope that they would get it from their Congressional Campaign Committee. Because the nation's business community was so overwhelmingly Republican, funds were traditionally in short supply at Democratic National Committee headquarters at the Biltmore Hotel in New York. The party had been outspent by the GOP in every national election since 1920, and the gap had been huge in 1936. And never had the supply of funds been shorter than in 1940. Fueled by rage at Roosevelt and possessed of an attractive candidate to run against him ("For the first time since Teddy Roosevelt," said *Time*, "the Republicans had a man they could yell for and mean it"), the GOP was gearing up—and shelling out— for a supreme effort to put its own man in the White House. After the election, a Senate committee would determine the ratio of expenditures between the two parties as almost two and a half to one. The Democrats, anxious to put such seasoned speechmakers as Harold Ickes on the air, found that they simply "did not have the money to spend" on more than a few such nationwide broadcasts. The five great radio speeches by Roosevelt himself that were to boost his popularity during the last days of the campaign would not have been broadcast had not Richard Reynolds, of the North Carolina tobacco family, appeared on the scene with a last-minute $175,000 loan to pay for the radio time. The National Committee needed every dollar it could raise for the presidential race, and was going to be able to spare very little funds indeed for its poor relation in Washington.

Even had funds been ample at the Biltmore, there would have been little disposition to divert them to the National Press Building. Farley, bitter at the President he believed had deceived him, resigned in August as chairman of the Democratic National Committee. His replacement, Edward J. Flynn, Boss of the Bronx, did not possess Farley's national acquaintance. "I did not know many" Senators and Congressmen, he was to recall. They were aware, moreover, that Flynn's loyalty ran only to the President; "Many of them were suspicious of me and displayed no great enthusiasm over my appointment. They fully realized that the appointment was purely personal on the President's part and that he had not consulted with them before ,he made it. . . ." Flynn was not particularly enamored of them, either: attempting to enlist the fund-raising help of prominent Senators and Congressmen, he found that "few if any" were willing to help. Tensions could not be eased by the National Committee staff, for it was a new staff brought in by Flynn, and it consisted of men he knew—New York men, unfamiliar with the embattled campaigners from Capitol Hill, and hence not particularly anxious to assist them in their campaigns.

For many Democratic Congressmen, raising funds of their own was going to be harder in 1940 than ever before. "The year 1936," Alexander Heard has noted in his landmark study of campaign financing, *The Costs of Democracy,* "was a turning point in the history of political party fund-raising. The policies and methods of Franklin Roosevelt's first term produced political alignments more along economic-class lines than any since the McKinley-Bryan era." Democratic Congressmen from large cities—where burgeoning labor unions were expressing their appreciation for pro-labor New Deal policies with lavish campaign contributions—were aided by these new alignments. Other Congressmen—and that included most Congressmen—were hurt. Once, a Congressman from a rural district or a district that included a small city had been able to rely on contributions from the district's businessmen. By 1940, these businessmen—and their contributions—had turned against the New Deal.

The outlook had not been particularly bright for congressional Democrats even before campaign finances were included in their calculations. In 1938, the Democrats had lost eighty-two seats in the House. Since they had gone into that election with an overwhelming congressional majority from the Roosevelt landslide of 1936, they still held a substantial 265-to-170 margin, but polls early in 1940 showed that about sixty additional Democrats could expect to lose their seats in 1940. And the campaign financial picture added to the gloom. Recent studies had documented the decisive role of money in elections; in one study of 156 state and local elections, all but eleven had been won by the side that reported spending the most money. Politicians had long since reached the same conclusion. Professionals firmly believed that, as Heard put it, "the side with more money has a better chance of winning." In only two of the twenty presidential elections since 1860 had the party which spent less money come out the winner; those were the elections of 1932 and 1936, and the rule had been shattered by the Depression combined with the extraordinary popularity of Roosevelt—but now the Depression was over and so, apparently, was at least some of Roosevelt's popularity, and the old rule could be expected to reassert itself. At the Democratic National Convention in Chicago in July, pols could be heard muttering gloomily about the lack of funds. Some of them turned to Rayburn for help. Nan Wood Honeyman of Portland, Oregon, once the only female member of Congress, had been defeated in 1938, and had learned the necessity of adequate campaign financing. In 1940 she was attempting to win back her seat, and at the Convention asked Tommy Corcoran and Rayburn for help. Corcoran, in his breezy, confident way, "asked how much it would take—'two, three, five thousand?'—indicating a willingness to do the necessary." When the amount needed was set at $5,000, Corcoran said he would contribute $2,000, apparently by tapping private sources in New York, and Mrs. Honeyman said she could raise $2,000 herself from local contributions. That left $1,000, and on the last day of the Convention, Rayburn, in a conversation at which Johnson was present, agreed to find her some funds. As it turned out, however, he was unable to do so. His hope that the Congressional Campaign Committee would be funded by the National Committee more generously than usual was already dimming. When he attempted to convince Flynn to set aside $100,000 for help in congressional campaigns, the reaction was reserved. He repeated his plea by letter ("A great many of these fellows need help"), adding: "Let me say to you again . . . how important it is to re-elect a Democratic House. I remember when President Wilson lost the House in 1918, his path was made rather rough by the Republicans investigating everything that had been done. . . ." Rayburn then threatened "to keep the funds raised by the congressional committee separate from the National Committee treasury and use them for the members of Congress in need of campaign assistance," but the Congressional Committee's lack of fund-raising ability made this threat an empty one. No further word came to Portland from Corcoran, whose time and money-raising abilities were, shortly after the Convention, assigned to the presidential campaign, and when Mrs. Honeyman contacted Rayburn through an intermediary in Washington, he was forced to reply in embarrassment that he would see that she got help "when and if there are funds available to the Congressional Campaign Committee." He was forced to give a similar answer to other candidates who asked for assistance. At a dispirited Democratic caucus on the subject of fund-raising, the only suggestion Rayburn could make was that Congressmen who had ample funds or safe seats should contribute to the campaigns of those of their colleagues who were broke or in danger—but that suggestion would not solve the problem, as Rayburn himself knew even as he made it.

But Lyndon Johnson knew how to solve the problem. He himself could provide the party with substantial funds, and he could provide them fast. And he appears to have been able to generalize from his experience with Brown & Root. Leaving the gloomy caucus with Edouard Izac, another young Congressman, Johnson said, according to Izac, " 'Sam Rayburn's all wet. That isn't the way you raise money for the Democratic Party.' Lyndon's idea was to go to the contractors and get the money."

He knew more. He knew, in fact, of a source of money that was available only to Sam Rayburn—and that even Sam Rayburn didn't know about.

Oil money had long been a factor in politics in the United States. In Texas, oil had come in not long after the century; the Spindletop field on the Gulf Coast, which would eventually prove out at a hundred million barrels, one-tenth as much oil as had been produced previously in America, blew in on January 10, 1901. The robber barons who had tapped the oil fields of the Northeast had been using the sale of black gold to purchase politicians for decades before that; the Standard Oil Company, one historian said, did everything possible to the Pennsylvania Legislature except refine it. But the new oil fields of the Southwest had, through the first three decades of the twentieth century, been controlled by the same companies that controlled the old oil fields of the Northeast; with their control of pipelines, markets and refineries—and the capital needed to explore and drill—they bought out or forced out the discoverers of the Texas fields so thoroughly that in 1930 75 percent of the oil in Texas was owned by Standard Oil and its offshoots and rivals such as Humble, Magnolia, Gulf and Sun, and the owners of the other 25 percent had to sell their oil to these companies, who owned the refineries and pipelines, at prices so low that they were effectively prevented from accumulating capital of their own. The companies, and the families back of them, that poured money into politics in Texas—Gulf Oil (the Mellons), Sun Oil (the Pews), Standard Oil (the Rockefellers)—were the same companies and families who had been financing the Republican Party—and selected Democrats—for decades in Washington and in various states of the Northeast. Their political alliances on the national level had long been made and cemented.

But after 1930, there were new sources of oil money, for 1930 was the year of the great East Texas pool.

The first success among the test wells being "poor-boyed" (drilled on credit, with frequent halts to raise money to go a few hundred feet deeper) by long-broke wildcatters in a poverty-stricken area of East Texas was eight miles east of Henderson. The oil that gushed out of it on October 6, 1930, splashing down on the rusty drill and on the derrick floor set among the pine trees, was believed to come from an isolated pocket, because the major oil companies had been advised by their geologists that there was little oil in the area. The second well that blew in, two months later, was near Kilgore, thirteen miles to the north. That must come from an isolated pocket, too, geologists said. At any rate, being so far from the first well, it certainly couldn't come from the same field. A month later, another well came in, near Longview, twelve miles farther north. Three separate fields, the geologists said: certainly no one field could be that big. But with the major companies uninterested, hundreds of small oil prospectors, men who had been wildcatting for years, most without success, rushed into the area. They found that East Texas was a "poor man's pool," not only because, with the majors not aggressively buying up land, oil leases could be obtained at reasonable prices, but because, at 3,500 feet, the oil was relatively close to the surface and the drilling was relatively inexpensive; since the East Texas oil was a high-grade, light-gravity oil with little sulphur contamination, it could even be refined cheaply; some—very few, but some—of the wildcatters could refine their own oil and sell it to gasoline companies. By the end of 1931, in some weeks, wells were being sunk at the rate of one per hour. And no matter where they drilled, it seemed, not only between Henderson and Longview but to the north and south (and the east and west), when they reached a depth of about 3,500 feet and took a sampling of the sand, it came up resembling brown sugar—sugar that had been dipped in oil. By 1934, it was apparent that underneath those barren, dried-out cotton fields and miles of stunted pine trees was an ocean of oil more than forty-five miles long. By 1935, the East Texas pool was producing more oil than any state had ever produced—more than any nation had ever produced. Spindletop, with its hundred million barrels, had been huge. The East Texas pool had five billion barrels—fifty times as much as Spindletop.

And it was owned not by the majors, but by the independents.

The majors moved in and bought the independents out, of course; Humble alone wound up with 16 percent of the East Texas pool; by 1938, the majors controlled 80 percent of the field. But there was a difference. The East Texas field was unprecedentedly huge, and, to an extent true of no previous field, it had originally been owned by the wildcatters—so that this time, when they sold out, they came away rich. The owner of the first well to hit sold out for a relative pittance, but the owners of the second came away with $2 million, the owners of the third with $2.5 million. Some, like Sid Richardson, took their money and put it into other oil fields—in the Panhandle and in West Texas and down near Houston—and some of these fields came in, too, and this time they didn't have to sell out at all; they could keep the profits themselves. There was by this time so much money that even if they had to share it with the majors, what was left over was millions of dollars. Hugh Roy Cullen, for example, brought in the Tom O'Connor Hill in 1934. He had to share it with Humble—but what he was sharing was half a billion barrels. And, more independent because they now had financial resources of their own, the new owners no longer had to share on the former disadvantageous terms. More and more often, in fact, they didn't have to share at all. "More independent oil fortunes came out of the East Texas field than from any other place in the world," an historian of the industry has written. "This was primarily because of the size of the field. Out of the thousands of tracts and town lots, there was something for almost everyone." And because of this, the East Texas field "became a point of departure from the old pattern of Texans going, hat in hand, out of the state to solicit funds for expansion and development." H. L. Hunt, for example, built his own pipelines, and was soon filling up the tank cars of the Sinclair Oil Company with his own oil.

Little awareness of this development existed among even the shrewdest of politicians in Washington. The names of many of the new rich were not even known, and the wealth of others was drastically underestimated. In August, 1935, Harold Ickes forwarded to President Roosevelt an "interesting document" which Ickes said had been "handed to me by a man in the oil game who thought it ought to reach you." It was a list of oilmen who had contributed that year to the Democratic National Committee—most of the contributions were for $1,000 or less—together with a brief description of the contributors. Of one of them, Herman Brown (Brown had begun buying oil leases), the writer says only: "Do not know of him." One "S. W. Richardson" is described as "in debt and borrows money to develop leases from Charles Marsh. . . ." Of only two names on the list—Clint Murchison and his partner, Dudley Golding—is there an awareness of the size of their fortune ("Golding & Murchison came into the East Texas Field several months after it started with no money and [after] a little over three years . . . sold out . . . for about five million dollars"). Neither the author of the document—nor, apparently, Ickes—had any idea of the true financial circumstances of the men on the list. And this was still the situation in 1940. In part this was due to the rapidity with which their circumstances had changed: Sid Richardson had indeed long been in debt, but at the time the memo was sent, that description of him was out of date by several years—and several millions of dollars. And in 1937, he hit the Keystone Sands in West Texas. By 1940, his income was close to $2 million a year.

But while the politicians had no knowledge of these oilmen, the oilmen had a deep interest in national politics. They enjoyed many federal favors. The most widely known, of course, was the 27.5 percent oil-depletion allowance, the loophole that, as Theodore H. White was to put it, "gives oil millionaires magic exemption from tax burdens that all other citizens must bear" by making 27.5 percent of their income free from tax. But there were many others, also important in oilmen's bookkeeping, if less known—for example, the law that allowed the immediate writing-off of intangible drilling and development costs on successful wells. And the owners were vitally interested in keeping those favors, which were under almost constant attack. Hardly had the Roosevelt administration entered office when Secretary of the Treasury Henry Morgenthau, Jr., called the depletion allowance "a pure subsidy to a special class of taxpayers" that should be eliminated. In 1937, Morgenthau renewed his plea, calling the allowance "perhaps the most glaring loophole," and Morgenthau's boss joined in, calling depletion and other loopholes attempts "to dodge the payment of taxes."

And the wildcatters were concerned with national policy not only because of favor but because of fear. As oil from the East Texas pool glutted the market and the price of oil plummeted, the industry was in turmoil and the positions of majors and independents swirled back and forth in confusion, but in general the wildcatters feared federal regulation. The occasion of the memo to Roosevelt—and of the donations which it reported—was a bill, introduced by the Oklahoma Populist, Senator Elmer Thomas, in 1935, that would have directly regulated the industry. That bill was blocked (in favor of Texas Senator Tom Connally's "Hot Oil Act," which left the setting of production quotas with the Texas Railroad Commission, a body which would be controlled by the wildcatters). Protected by the Railroad Commission from the price-cutting practices of the "majors," the "independents" were soon flourishing, but the threat of federal regulation was a constant cloud on an otherwise limitless horizon. They had plenty of money; they needed a way to make it felt in Washington—they needed a path through which the power of their collective purse could be brought to bear on the federal government.

Of the members of the federal government, the only one they knew well enough to be comfortable with was Sam Rayburn. Richardson was from Fort Worth, and many other wildcatters lived in nearby Dallas. Rayburn's district adjoined Dallas, of course, and he had many close friends among the politicians there. On his frequent visits to the city, he had come to know Richardson and some of the other wildcatters while they were still poor-boying wells, searching for wealth on a shoestring. Becoming rich, other wildcatters moved to Dallas—the nearest large city and also the city whose banks first revealed a willingness to finance the wildcatters' new ventures—and made their headquarters there. Rayburn met these men, too, usually through a pair of old friends who were intimately connected with the wildcatters, former State Attorney General William McCraw and William Kittrell, the veteran Texas lobbyist. Rayburn actively disliked the "old" oilmen, the wealthy shareholders in major companies like the Magnolia, whose

6,000-pound flying red horse atop the Magnolia Building dominated downtown Dallas and, at night, when it was outlined in 1,162 feet of ruby neon
tubing, the plains for thirty miles around; and he disliked the oil-company
corporate executives and lawyers, the lobbyists. And the feeling was mutual;
traditional oil interests disliked Sam Rayburn as much as the utilities; attempting to remove him from Congress, they would fruitlessly pour money into his
district year after year. But Rayburn liked Sid Richardson, whom he had
known for years as a broke young man, and he liked many of Richardson's
friends. And when they had asked him for help, he had helped them. They
had told him that the Thomas bill was a device of the big companies to kill
off the little fellows—little fellows like themselves. If they had very recently
—thanks to the East Texas pool—graduated out of the "little fellow" class
forever, he did not grasp that fact. (He was never to grasp it fully—a fact
that was to have grave consequences for the United States in decades to
come.) The bill was, they said, a device of Wall Street to keep Texans—
them—from ever getting a share of their own state's wealth. They should be
allowed to handle their own problems until it was proved they couldn't, and
since all this oil was in Texas, this seemed like one problem that Texas should
definitely be allowed to handle. Roosevelt at the time was working closely
with Rayburn on the SEC Bill; the President told Ickes (who would, under
the proposed legislation, be given the federal regulatory power), "I do not
want to cross wires with Sam Rayburn about this matter." And the Thomas
bill was tabled.

Rayburn was no stranger to the use of money in politics. As Garner's
campaign manager not only in 1940 but in 1932, he had asked for contributions to his friend's campaign, and had gotten them. But, perhaps
because he was uninterested in money himself, when he thought about
campaign contributions, he had a tendency to think small. When he thought
large, he thought in terms of Texas, and of the kind of Texans who gave
large contributions to politicians, and this old money—cotton money and
cattle money—was, almost entirely, Garner money. He knew how much
Garner's backers hated Roosevelt, and he knew that in 1940 they were contributing to Wendell Willkie, and that their money would not be available
to him.

If there was new money in Texas on the same scale as the old—oil
money, the wildcatters' money—he had not yet come to understand that fact.
Not having even the vaguest notion in 1940 of the extent of the wildcatters'
recently acquired wealth, he could not see its potential for politics. The
scale of contributions they had made in 1935—a scale calculated largely in
the hundreds; a thousand dollars was a generous contribution—was the
scale on which he still thought. And as for using their money on a national
scale—the obtaining and distribution of funds to scores of Congressmen
across the country—what relationship did a task of such a magnitude have

with, say, squat, silent, unassuming Sid Richardson, still wandering around Fort Worth in a rumpled suit and living in the same small, shabby bachelor quarters at the Fort Worth Club where he had always lived? Says Richard Bolling: "He thought that his people were little people. He missed the fact that the independents had become giants. . . . He knew they had money, but he had no idea of the extent of the money."

Rayburn did not, moreover, understand—perhaps because he was a man who could not be bought, and this reputation, and the fear in which he was held, kept anyone from explaining his position to him—how important he was to the wildcatters, how the protection he had extended to them in the past, and the protection they were hoping he would continue to extend to them in the future, was one of the most significant factors in the accumulation of their wealth. The Speaker, according to the unanimous opinion not only of his allies of this period, but of his opponents, had not the slightest idea of the potential of his position for political fund-raising for Congressmen on a national level.

But Lyndon Johnson saw the potential.* Henry Morgenthau and the demands of justice had persuaded Franklin Roosevelt that the oil-depletion allowance should be reduced or eliminated; it was only Congress which had kept it intact. The administration had wanted federal control of Texas oil; it was Congress which had kept that control in the hands of Texas. The wildcatters' strength in Washington was in Congress, yet these men were not acquainted with many Congressmen. The one they did know well enough to talk to frankly, to explain their problems to, was Sam Rayburn; their strength in Washington was, in the final analysis, that one man. Now, as Speaker, Rayburn was the single most powerful Congressman. It was in their interest to keep him in power, to keep him Speaker. And that meant keeping the Congress Democratic. Johnson realized that money could be raised in Texas to keep Congress Democratic. And because Johnson realized the stakes involved, he realized that the money available was big money.

BUT CAMPAIGN CONTRIBUTIONS from contractors (from, that is, all contractors but one) and from the wildcatters would have to be obtained through others. Since they had not previously contributed to the Democratic Congressional Campaign Committee, an element of uncertainty existed as to whether they could be persuaded to give now. More important, there was an element of uncertainty as to whether they could be persuaded quickly; with the

* He appears to have seen it from the beginning. Although no oil had been discovered in his district, a local attorney, Harris Melasky, had begun representing some of the formerly broke wildcatters who owned wells in East Texas; Johnson went to a lot of trouble cultivating Melasky in 1938 and 1939—although none of Johnson's advisors in the district could figure out why.

November election day approaching, it would be difficult to get their money in time. Because of Herman Brown, however, Johnson possessed a source of funds—substantial funds—about which there existed neither uncertainty nor delay. He knew that if he could obtain the position he wanted, he would have—instantly; at his command—substantial sums of money to use in it. If he were put in charge of the Congressional Campaign Committee, he could guarantee that it would have funds. He asked Sam Rayburn to put him in charge.*

Rayburn did not do so.

The relationship between him and Lyndon Johnson during the year and a half following the July, 1939, confrontation over the Texas delegation's resolution on the Garner–John L. Lewis explosion will probably never be charted definitively. Around the Speaker's personal feelings had been erected a wall as impenetrable as the wall with which Lyndon Johnson surrounded himself. But there were hints as to its course.

The confrontation itself had not angered him; if anything, he seemed rather proud of the way Lyndon had stood up to him. "Lyndon is a damned independent boy, independent as a hog on ice," he said when someone asked him about the incident. But despite Lyndon's attempts to conceal the fact that it was really he who was turning Roosevelt and the New Dealers against Rayburn, the Majority Leader may have realized at the last moment the role being played by this young man of whom he was so fond. On the very day on which his secret campaign to undermine Rayburn in Roosevelt's eyes had triumphed—on April 29, 1940, the day the President had forced the Majority Leader to accept as co-signer on the "harmony" telegram "kid Congressman" Lyndon Johnson—Johnson attempted to act as if no reason for a break between them existed. A *Washington Post* article stated that Johnson "praised the work done by Rayburn in achieving the compromise" and "predicted he would lead the Garner-pledged Texas delegation 'with other men of liberal makeup.' " A week later, he made a private overture. Rayburn's roommate during his first year in the Texas Legislature, R. Bouna Ridgway, wrote Johnson a note advocating Rayburn's nomination as Vice President at the upcoming Democratic National Convention (and recalling his roommate's character: "He was so quiet and reserved. Honorable, honest and 100% true to a friend"). Johnson had not written to Rayburn for a year—since the time, in fact, that he had begun his career as the New Deal spy in Rayburn's meetings. Now, perhaps using the Ridgway note as an excuse to resume communications, he sent it to Rayburn with a covering note of his own ("Here is a letter from one of the rank and file boys who I am happy to know is a great admirer of yours . . .") signed, "Your friend,

---

* Whether he asked to be formally appointed chairman in Drewry's place, or whether he would have been satisfied to have Drewry remain, as a figurehead, while he accepted another post, is uncertain; some sources believe the former, some the latter.

Lyndon." Previously, when Johnson had written Rayburn, the Majority Leader's replies had been warm; the three lines of his reply to Johnson this time spoke volumes:

> Thank you for sending me the letter from my old-time, dear friend, Bouna Ridgway.
> With every good wish, I am, sincerely yours,
>
> Sam Rayburn

As part of the compromise that had ended the Roosevelt-Garner fight in Texas, the White House had insisted that Johnson be made vice chairman of the state's delegation to the Democratic National Convention in Chicago. Rayburn was chairman, so at the convention the two men were frequently thrown together, and often heard together of candidates' financial problems. But when Johnson (who of course was himself unopposed for re-election) raised the possibility that the solution to the problems was his appointment as head of the Congressional Campaign Committee, Rayburn gave him no encouragement.

Then Johnson attempted to gain a role in the financing of Congressmen's campaigns by another method. He tried to become the liaison between the Congressional Committee and the Democratic National Committee which furnished much of its funds. Rayburn was not amenable to this suggestion, either. On August 20, Rayburn told a Flynn aide that there would indeed be a congressional liaison man, but neither of the names he mentioned was that of Lyndon Johnson. "I think it will be John McCormack and probably Charlie West," he said.

Johnson continued maneuvering. The young New Dealers who were his friends received from him continuing stories of the desperate straits of Democratic Congressmen, of the likelihood that the Democrats would lose the House, of Drewry's inefficiency, of Drewry's lack of enthusiasm for the candidacies of New Deal Congressmen. These stories were reported at the White House—along with Johnson's interest in being of help in an overall effort to elect Democratic Congressmen—and the suggestion was made, according to some sources, by the President himself, that Johnson should in some vague way be attached to the Congressional Campaign Committee, or to the Democratic National Committee itself, to assist them.

Johnson, however, appears to have had in mind not an assistantship but independent, formal, authority of his own. His next attempt to get it may have been an attempt to circumvent Rayburn: an approach directly to the President, through the malleable Agriculture Committee chairman, Marvin Jones. On September 14, Jones went to see Roosevelt and then sent a letter, drafted by Johnson, suggesting that "If we are to get the results that we desire, Lyndon's work should be supplementary to the regular work done by both the Democratic Congressional Committee and the National Committee rather than an assignment to aid them with their regular functions." A letter drafted by Johnson for Flynn's signature—to be sent out by Flynn to all Democratic members of the House of Representatives—further spelled out the authority he had in mind, and in addition included a reference to the President, which might have thrown the weight of at least a hint of presidential authority behind Johnson's efforts. Had Johnson's draft been sent out by Flynn, Flynn would have been saying:

> Dear Congressman _____:
> . . . The President has discussed with me some of the problems you will face in November and I have assured him that the Democratic National Committee will do everything possible to give you the maximum assistance in your coming campaign.
> In order that we may work most effectively with you in this connection, I have asked one of your Democratic colleagues in the House, Congressman Lyndon B. Johnson of Texas, to act as liaison officer between my office in the Democratic National Committee and the Democratic congressional candidates.

This would, of course, have made Johnson the arm of the Democratic National Committee in dealing with Congressmen.

Roosevelt, however, did not want to give him such formal authority. He eliminated the reference to "liaison officer." All the letter, as edited by Roosevelt, says is that, in order that the Democratic National Committee "may work most effectively with you" in your campaign, Johnson will "assist me [Flynn] and the Democratic National Committee in aiding the congressional candidates."

Roosevelt told Johnson he would give the letter to Flynn, and asked Flynn to see the young Congressman, but Flynn balked at giving Johnson even the informal post. Meeting with Johnson in his room at the Carlton Hotel on September 19, he said he would be glad to send out the letter—if it met with Rayburn's approval.

Rayburn's approval was not forthcoming.

Then Johnson thought he saw an even better opening. On September 23, the National Committee's secretary, Chip Robert, resigned. Johnson pulled strings to obtain this post, using the argument that in it he could serve as a liaison with the Congressional Committee. Influential Democrats such as Claude Pepper, a Longlea visitor, wrote or telephoned the White House to urge the appointment. Johnson persuaded Drewry to write Roosevelt that he would have "no objection" to it. Roosevelt may have considered making it; the possibility was raised with Rayburn, who had become Speaker the week before, but Rayburn's response was that the appointment would be satisfactory to him if it was satisfactory to Flynn—which, of course, Rayburn knew it wasn't. Flynn, who had been less than enthusiastic about Johnson's appointment even to an informal liaison role with the committee, had stronger objections to his being made its secretary. He said, in fact, that if Johnson was appointed, he would resign.

With or without formal appointment, Johnson saw no way around Flynn's opposition, particularly without Rayburn in his corner. He drafted a letter to Roosevelt saying that after discussing

> the matter of my participation in the Congressional campaigns with Ed Flynn and several of my colleagues here on the Hill . . . I have come to the conclusion that because of the shortness of time and the possible resentment of such informal participation in the sphere [of] influence of well-established outfits, it would be inadvisable to make further attempts to work out the suggested arrangement with Mr. Flynn.

He redrafted the letter before sending it to Roosevelt, in the reworking revealing some of his techniques, for the missive's five brief paragraphs contain subtle denigration of the work of the man he wanted to replace ("Certainly the job is there to be done. My own youth and inexperience may be in error, but I feel tonight that we do stand in danger in the lower House"); flattery ("I know in your wisdom you will work it out"); subtle pointing out why he was well suited for the job (the campaign, he said, was "effective in cities" but not "in the fifty per cent remaining"—which, of course, was in rural areas such as the one he represented); and a personal touch (noting that "we lost eighty-two seats in 1938," he said that the present forty-five margin "gives me the night-sweats at three a.m.").

Despite the letter, Roosevelt would agree to Johnson's participation only on the original, very informal, basis. A note from FDR to McIntyre on October 4 said: "In the morning will you call up Congressman Lyndon Johnson and tell him that Flynn strongly recommends that we proceed on the original basis as worked out between him and Congressman Drewry which will give Johnson a chance at once to send out the letters which were agreed on, but which made no reference to the President, and that he should do this right away. . . ." Johnson, however, was still reluctant to accept so informal a role, particularly without Rayburn's support, and that support was still not forthcoming.

But Sam Rayburn was becoming desperate.

If the Democrats lost control of the House, he would lose the Speakership he had just assumed after twenty-eight years of waiting—and every indication was that they were going to lose.

Since 1938, when the Republicans had almost doubled their House holding, from 88 seats to 170, every special election necessitated by the death of a member had confirmed the trend toward the GOP. In 1940, the trend had been accelerating. In the seven special elections held since the first of the year, the Republican share of the vote had risen an average of 6 percent. Democrats had hoped that that trend would be reversed in a presidential election year, but those hopes had been dealt a body blow just three days before Rayburn had become Speaker, for on September 13, in congressional voting in Maine, the Democratic vote in the three Maine congressional districts was down—by the same 6 percent. That 6 percent figure was especially ominous because, in 1938, no fewer than 100 of the 265 Democratic seats had been won by less than 6 percent of the vote. The Republicans needed to gain only forty-eight seats to take control of the House in 1940—and elect their own Speaker. Democrats and Republicans alike felt that the GOP would gain more than that number. "Regardless of the outcome of the Presidential election," the *New York Herald Tribune* reported on September 15, "Republicans are confident and Democrats fearful that the next House of Representatives will be organized and controlled by the Republican Party for the first time in ten years. . . . Those who deal with figures cannot avoid the 'trend' which set in in the congressional elections of 1938 and its continuation in all congressional off-year elections since then. . . ." Democrats couldn't even get back home to campaign. Deepening crisis in Europe and the Far East, and the need for new crisis legislation—the Selective Service Act, funding for new military bases—forced Congress to remain in session all Summer and into September. September drew to a close, and no major new legislation was before Congress, and the gleeful Republicans, backed by the press ("In such a time of crisis the institution through which the will of the American people is expressed ought not to leave Washington," editorialized the *New York Times*), insisted that it stay in session. As Arthur Krock wrote on September 24:

> . . . the Democratic House majority is in real danger whoever may win the Presidency. That is what is disturbing the Democratic members as the time of the session lengthens, and the Republicans, while equally anxious to campaign, count on that to keep the adjournment cake and eat it too. They would then go to the country, crying out against adjournment "at such a time" and making all the political hay which could be gathered in season.

And in to many of the Democratic members, trapped in Washington, poured reports that they were in trouble back home, and that time was growing too short to repair the damage. Sam Rayburn had spent twenty-eight years in Congress waiting to be Speaker; was he to be Speaker for only four months?

Over and over again Rayburn was told that a principal reason for the impending electoral disaster was lack of money. Visiting the Chicago headquarters of the party's Midwest Division, Charles Marsh reported that "Chicago is a skeleton, because no money has trickled from New York West yet. I walked through a graveyard . . . with yawning offices everywhere. Apparently no money for payrolls, no definite amounts to make planning for radio and speaker's bureau." Roosevelt's personal popularity would pull the President through, Marsh predicted, but it wouldn't pull enough Congressmen with him. "I believe the lower house of Congress may be lost by not getting money West now."

And there was no money. In August, Rayburn had asked Flynn to set aside $100,000 to help congressional candidates. At the end of September, the Democratic National Committee had not contributed a penny. On October 2, a letter from Flynn's finance chairman, Wayne Johnson, must have made Rayburn realize how remote was the chance of significant financial assistance to his "fellows" from the DNC: Congressman William D. Byron of Maryland had made a personal trip to National Committee headquarters at the Biltmore to ask for financial help; Johnson wrote Rayburn, "Will you see what *you* can do to help Congressman Byron if his need is as acute as he thinks." As for the National Committee, Wayne Johnson wrote, "We have had such difficulty in getting money to keep things running to date that I don't know how much we will have to help the Congressional Campaign Committee."

Then, over the weekend beginning October 5, premonition turned to panic, for on that weekend, Democrats, desperate over discouraging reports from their districts, began drifting away from Washington; by October 8, when an informal "recess" was finally arranged, more than a hundred members had already left for home on what the *Times* called "French Leave," and others, the *Times* reported, were threatening "to quit the capital regardless of what the body decides to do about . . . remaining in daily session." And when they arrived back in their districts, they found that the reports were all too true. In district after district, Democratic Congressmen who had won by comfortable margins in 1936, and by smaller margins in 1938, returned home in 1940, with less than a month to go before the election, to find that they were behind, and that their opponents' campaigns were well organized and well financed, with plenty of help from Washington—while they were getting no help at all.

Michigan's Sixteenth Congressional District, which included part of Detroit, and adjoining Dearborn, site of a giant Ford Motor Company plant, had once been considered a safe Democratic district. Running for his third term in 1936, Congressman John Lesinski had polled 61 percent of the vote, defeating his Republican opponent by 21,000 votes. But in 1938, the margin had been reduced to 10,000—55 percent. And in 1940, the Republican candidate in the Ford-dominated Sixteenth was a Ford: Henry's cousin Robert. Arriving back in Dearborn to begin his campaign, Lesinski found "hundreds" of ROBERT FORD FOR CONGRESS billboards, and numerous other indications of "unlimited financial backing"—including no fewer than a dozen well-staffed campaign headquarters. Clearly, the district wasn't safe any longer. It contained voters of fifty-eight nationalities, so literature printed in foreign languages was a necessity. In the 1936 and 1938 elections, the Democratic National Committee had sent truckloads of foreign-language pamphlets to the district—100,000 in Polish alone. Now Lesinski was informed that not one piece of foreign-language literature had been received in the district. When he telephoned the Biltmore to find out when some would be arriving, he could not even get through to anyone who could give him a reply. Compiling a detailed list of the minimum needed—50,000 pamphlets in Polish, 5,000 each in Hungarian, Ukrainian, Italian and Russian—he telegraphed it to the Biltmore, and this time he got a reply. The pamphlets had been set in type, he was told, but there was no money available to print them. And he couldn't get campaign buttons. He pleaded for a visit by Roosevelt to his district, reminding Washington of the great crowds the President had drawn in Detroit in 1936, but he couldn't get Roosevelt. That was understandable and standard for any campaign; every Congressman wanted a popular President in his district. But Lesinski couldn't even get a *picture* of Roosevelt! So few posters of the President were available that they were framed under glass to preserve them and carried from one rally to another; not one could be spared, Lesinski was to write, to hang in his own headquarters! John Lesinski knew he was in trouble. He needed all the help he could get. And he couldn't even get a poster.

Lesinski's experience was being repeated, that first part of October, in scores of congressional districts. In 1940, radio was still not the most expensive campaign item for Congressmen; most spent more money on billboards. "When you saw a lot of billboards for your opponent," recalls a man who ran many congressional campaigns in the pre-war era, "you knew that he must have a well-financed campaign in other areas, too." Now, in district after district, the Congressman arrived home to find his opponent's face staring down at him from billboards—and to realize what that meant. And when he wrote or telephoned his Congressional Campaign Committee for help, he found that not only cash but the most basic types of other campaign materials were difficult to obtain. In previous elections, the committee had relayed requests for buttons, posters, bumper stickers, literature, nationally prominent speakers, to the parent Democratic National Committee, and Farley's efficient staff, sympathetic to Congressmen and experienced in solving their problems, had done their best to meet their requests. Now, with Farley and his staff abruptly gone, and with Farley's replacement, Flynn, interested almost exclusively in Roosevelt's election, the National Committee, its resources more limited than ever, was all but ignoring Congressmen's requests.

Overshadowing every other problem for the returning Congressmen was their shortage of campaign funds. Lesinski had pleaded with Drewry for help; what he received was a check for $100, a very small amount of ammunition with which to fight a Ford. That was not an ungenerous contribution by Drewry's standards, particularly given the state of the Congressional Committee's bank account. The long-awaited subvention from the Democratic National Committee finally arrived on October 10. It was not the $100,000 for which Rayburn had asked, but $10,000. Parceled out among seventy-eight candidates in contributions of $100 or $200, it was an amount too small to make a difference in the fight on which hung Sam Rayburn's fate. Not since the New Deal had swept into office in 1932 had Democratic candidates for Congress needed more help—and instead they were getting less help. Tallying the frantic telephone calls from the Congressmen, Democratic congressional leaders realized that the fight was being lost. With Roosevelt's once-substantial lead slipping week by week until Gallup polls in early October showed Willkie pulling into a virtual dead heat, the outlook for the House worsened. "You could have cut the gloom around Democratic congressional headquarters with a knife," Pearson and Allen were to recall. "The campaign committee, headed by Representative Pat Drewry, a charming and dawdling Virginian, had collapsed like the minister's one-horse shay. Activity had so bogged down that hard-pressed candidates had quit even asking for help. For the Republicans it looked like a lead-pipe cinch to regain control of the House."

Sam Rayburn realized the situation, and if he hadn't, a letter misdirected to Congressional Committee secretary Cap Harding would have helped him realize it by giving him additional evidence of the financial odds against House Democrats. Contributions to the Republican Party from A. Felix du Pont, Jr., and his wife, Lydia, had been delivered to the Democratic Congressional Campaign Committee by mistake. The checks were for $3,000 and $4,000, respectively. And they were from just two du Ponts. No fewer than forty-six du Ponts were active Republican contributors. Apparently still unwilling to put Lyndon Johnson in charge of the congressional effort, Rayburn now tried frantically to find someone else. But no one else wanted the job. Recalls one of Rayburn's aides: "It appeared that the Democrats were . . . going to lose the House. No one wanted to risk his political future by being congressional campaign manager for the House." Rayburn talked to "two or three other people," but found "nobody available." Earlier in October, he told Roosevelt what he had told Flynn: "that if this House were lost—even though he was re-elected—it would tear him to pieces just like it did President Wilson after the Republicans won the House in 1918." He asked Roosevelt to appoint Johnson to the post he wanted, Chip Robert's now-vacant National Committee secretaryship. Flynn again refused to accept that appointment, but Johnson now agreed to accept the informal role with the Congressional Committee that he had earlier refused. Apparently changing his mind yet again, Flynn appears to have demurred even at this, but on October 13, Rayburn begged Roosevelt to get Johnson into the congressional campaign in some capacity, formal or informal, and to do it fast. The President agreed to do so. He reportedly said: "Tell Lyndon to see me tomorrow." Lyndon saw the President the next day

—October 14—at breakfast, and that afternoon not only Flynn but Drewry sent out the letters that assigned Johnson a role in the campaign.

The role could hardly have been more informal. Drewry's letter said only that Johnson would "assist the Congressional Committee." No specific position or title was mentioned. While the role may have been informal, however, it was a role not on the district level or the state level, but on the national level. Rushing out of the White House, Lyndon Johnson placed a call to Houston—to Brown & Root.

32

The Munsey Building

THE GREAT POLITICAL FUND-RAISERS—the Tommy Corcorans of Washington, the Ed Clarks of Texas—agree that most businessmen who contribute to political campaigns don't contribute enough to accomplish their purposes. They want Ambassadorships or contracts or input into policy, but they don't give enough to get what they want. Their contributions are grudging, or slow in coming, or too small to place the recipients under sufficient obligation to them. "There's always just a few," says Clark, "only the most sophisticated and the smartest," who give "real money" and who give it eagerly enough, and early enough, so that they can reap the maximum return on their investment. Herman Brown, on top of whose native shrewdness had been overlaid the sophistication obtained from more than a decade of involvement in the financing of state politics and politicians, was one of the few. "When Herman gave," says Ed Clark, "he gave his full weight." When Johnson's call reached Brown & Root headquarters, the response was immediate. Since the Federal Corrupt Practices Act prohibited political contributions by corporations, money could not come directly from Brown & Root. Because of a $5,000 limit on an individual's contribution to a political organization during any one year, not enough of it could come from Herman, or from his brother George. Therefore, Herman arranged to have six business associates —sub-contractors, attorneys, his insurance broker—send money, in their names, to the Democratic Congressional Campaign Committee. And Herman acted fast. Johnson had made his telephone call on Monday, October 14. On Saturday, October 19, George Brown telegraphed Johnson: YOU WERE SUPPOSED TO HAVE CHECKS BY FRIDAY. . . . HOPE THEY ARRIVED IN DUE FORM AND ON TIME. Johnson was able to reply by return wire: ALL OF THE FOLKS YOU TALKED TO HAVE BEEN HEARD FROM. MANY, MANY THANKS. I AM NOT ACKNOWLEDGING THEIR LETTERS, SO BE SURE TO TELL ALL THESE FELLOWS THAT THEIR LETTERS HAVE BEEN RECEIVED. The amount of each check was the maximum contribution allowed under the law: $5,000. The initial Brown & Root contribution to the Democratic Congressional Campaign Committee was $30,000—more money than the committee had received from the Democratic National Committee, which had in previous years been its major source of funds.

Nor was this the only money Lyndon Johnson received from Texas during his first week on the new job, for he had persuaded Sam Rayburn to make some telephone calls to Fort Worth and Dallas, and to stop talking in terms of hundreds. On October 14, Sid Richardson, through his nephew, Perry R. Bass, sent $5,000. On October 16, C. W. Murchison sent $5,000. And another $5,000 arrived from Charles Marsh's partner, E. S. Fentress. By Saturday, October 19, Johnson was able to bring to the offices of the Democratic Congressional Campaign Committee, to be distributed to Democratic candidates for Congress, a total of $45,000. One week after he had taken his job, he was able to write Rayburn aide Swagar Sherley: "We have sent them more money in the last three days than Congressmen have received from any committee in the last eight years."

ONE TALENT that Lyndon Johnson had already displayed in abundance was ingenuity in political tactics. Now he displayed it again. By saying in his letter to the candidates that Johnson was only "assisting" the Congressional Campaign Committee, Drewry had thought he was keeping Johnson subordinate to the committee. All these first checks from Texas, of course, were made out to the committee—Johnson had to turn them over to the committee for deposit in the committee's bank account, and it was on this account that the checks for contributions to individual candidates were drawn. They were signed by the committee's chairman, Drewry, and mailed out, with an accompanying letter by Drewry, from the committee's office in the National Press Building, in the same manner as any other contributions, with no indication that the money that had made them possible had come from Texas, or that it had been raised by the efforts of Lyndon Johnson.

For a man who had pulled political strings to get a dam legalized, authorized and enlarged, Johnson's method of letting the candidates know that he, not the committee, deserved the credit for the contributions was relatively simple—but ingenious, nonetheless. He had had George Brown instruct each of the "Brown & Root" contributors, and apparently had had Rayburn instruct Richardson and Murchison, to send with their contributions a letter stating: "I am enclosing herewith my check for $5,000 payable to the Democratic Congressional Campaign Committee. I would like for this money to be expended in connection with the campaign of Democratic candidates for Congress as per the list attached, to the individual named in the amount specified."

Johnson had, of course, compiled the list, and had determined the amount each of the lucky candidates was to receive. Since the committee would hardly dare to disobey such specific instructions from the "donors," it was Johnson rather than Drewry or Harding (or anyone else) who was determining who would get the Texas money, and how much. And, armed with this knowledge, he had no sooner left the committee headquarters, having handed in his checks, than he sent to each of the recipients the following telegram—which made it abundantly clear to each recipient who was really responsible for the check which he would be receiving from the Congressional Committee the next day: AS RESULT MY VISIT TO CONGRESSIONAL COMMITTEE FEW MINUTES AGO, YOU SHOULD RECEIVE AIRMAIL SPECIAL DELIVERY LETTER FROM THEM WHICH IS TO BE MAILED TONIGHT.

OF THE ELEMENTS in Lyndon Johnson's career, none had been more striking than his energy.

Procuring checks wasn't all he did that first week. Permission to "assist" the Congressional Campaign Committee had finally been given to him on October 14. Election Day was November 5. He had three weeks.

Within three hours, he had rented an office, furnished it, and filled it with a staff: Herbert Henderson, John Connally, and Dorothy Nichols from his congressional office; only Walter Jenkins was left behind to keep that office open. (The furnishings of the room in the five-room suite that would be his private office revealed a distaste for the spartan: the furniture rental order read "1 large Exec. desk, 1 swivel desk chair, 2 arm chairs, 1 club chair, 1 divan . . .") That same day he composed a questionnaire to be sent to congressional colleagues ("1938 votes received?" "Is your present opponent stronger than your 1938 opponent?" "Describe briefly type of campaign he is making and principal issues he is raising," "Where can you or a representative be reached at all times in your district?"), and dictated, to be sent with the questionnaire, a letter announcing his entrance into the campaign.

Although he was ostensibly assisting Drewry's committee, the office he had taken was in another building, the eleven-story Munsey Building at 1329 E Street, Northwest, off Pennsylvania Avenue, away from Drewry's eyes and supervision. He had done more that busy Monday. The letter and questionnaire were not sent to all his colleagues. Conferring over the telephone with Rayburn, McCormack—and with Paul Appleby, campaign manager for vice-presidential nominee Henry A. Wallace and a politician with a detailed knowledge of the political situation in Midwest congressional districts—he had selected from the 435 Democratic candidates for Congress several score who should be helped. His decision was based in part on which districts had had the closest results in 1938, but only in part. One of several lists hurriedly compiled by Henderson and Connally was titled: "The following men received a majority of more than 10,000 over their Republican opponents in 1938." Democrats had considered these seats safe, but only because they had not done a thorough analysis; Johnson did one, analyzing not merely the vote totals and percentages but the type of district, and found that many of them were in danger—and these Congressmen were selected for assistance.

By the end of the first week in his new assignment, he had further refined his lists. One refinement was caused by John L. Lewis. The coal miners' chief was turning against Roosevelt; although speculation was rife about the effect of his defection on the presidential race, no one was thinking about its effect on congressional candidates. Johnson assigned his staff to draw up a list of "Districts Which Produce 1,000,000 Tons or More Coal," and of the 1938 congressional results in those districts. Then, sitting down with a yellow legal pad, he went to work on the list himself. Fifteen districts in six states were involved; in 1938, Democrats had won all of them. Calculating the margin in each district, he added them up and divided by fifteen, and around this average he drew a circle in red, and drew a red arrow to it, for the average was only 8,268. Then he calculated the Democratic percentage of the vote in each district, carrying the long division out to several places, and the percentages confirmed the bad news: the fifteen districts could not be considered safely Democratic this year; their Democratic Congressmen needed help, too. Other lists were compiled—by him, personally; no aide was allowed to do this—compiled with the same painstaking thoroughness ("If you do absolutely *everything* . . ."). He also called a luncheon meeting in a private room at the nearby Hotel Washington. Present were Rayburn, McCormack, Appleby, Alvin Wirtz, and three White House aides, Lowell Mellett, Wayne Coy and Jim Rowe (James Forrestal was invited, but was unable to attend). At this meeting, the lists were further refined, so that when, that first week, the money from Texas having arrived, he began distributing it, the identity of the seventy-seven recipients had been determined by a rather intensive analysis: the type of analysis that for years had been routine for the Republican congressional committee but rare for the Democrats—and that had not been made at all in 1940.

ON THE QUESTIONNAIRE Johnson had sent out, candidates had been asked to "List suggestions as to how, in your opinion, we can be most helpful." Underneath had been left three blank lines, marked "1," "2" and "3." Many of the respondents, of course, asked for a visit to their district by the President, but that was not the reply most frequently made on the first line. The most typical reply was that of Representative Martin F. Smith of the State of Washington's Third Congressional District: "Financially." (Representative John F. Hunter of Ohio's Ninth Congressional District was firmer. "1" was "financial assistance," he wrote. "There is no two.") Others wrote a line or two of elaboration. "The best service that you could possibly render me would be to arrange a campaign contribution of $200 or $300," said Wendell Lund of Michigan's Eleventh CD. "The thing this district needs most of all is money," said George M. May of Pennsylvania's Tenth. And some, as though the mails were not fast enough, made the same point over the phone. Says an inter-office memorandum: "Robert Secrest [of Ohio's Fifteenth] called and talked with John Connally. Said the only help he needed was a little money. . . ."

Candidates who had dealt with the Congressional Campaign Committee in the past had little hope that they would get what they asked for. Secrest wrote on his questionnaire, "Nothing will help except cash, and I know that is scarce." Laurence F. Arnold of Illinois' Twenty-third noted that he had received $200 from the committee in 1936, but nothing in 1938; he had asked for $200 this year, he noted, and had not received even the courtesy of a reply. Emmet O'Neal of Kentucky's Third wrote, "I feel sure that there is nothing that can be done to help." He needed money, he said, "but I know . . . money is not floating around, so this is not meant as an indirect solicitation."

But, to their astonishment, their hopes were answered. Four-term Congressman Martin F. Smith had returned home to find that there was a good chance he wouldn't be re-elected to a fifth. He had stayed in the capital until October 8, and he had stayed too long; stepping off the train after the three-day trip home, he was promptly informed by campaign aides that he was in serious danger of losing his seat. His only hope was to increase his planned advertising in his district's forty-two newspapers, and to reserve radio time—and he didn't have enough money to do either. He left for a week-long tour of the district with no money in sight. And then, when he checked in with his campaign headquarters in Hoquiam one evening, Johnson's telegram was read to him. Naturally, he hoped that the Congressional Committee's airmail special-delivery letter to which the telegram referred would contain funds. Arriving back in Hoquiam several days later, he found on his desk not one but two letters from the committee. Ripping them open, he found in each a check—one for $200, one for $500.

Arriving, weary, at a hotel one evening, Representative Charles F. McLaughlin telephoned his headquarters in Omaha, Nebraska, and was told that a telegram had been received from Lyndon Johnson; when he reached Omaha the next day, the airmail special-delivery letter to which it referred was already there—and it contained a check for $300.

All across the United States, similar scenes were enacted. Slumping into a chair in a hotel room or lying on the bed—shoes still on, too tired to take them off after a long day of campaigning (and worrying about campaign funds)—a Congressman would telephone his headquarters, would be read Lyndon Johnson's telegram, and would realize that funds were on the way.

Others got the news in their campaign headquarters. Representative Edouard V. M. Izac arrived home in San Diego to find, as he wrote Johnson, his opponent's face staring down at him from "hundreds" of billboards. He had no billboards, and, he found to his dismay, "no organization."

Thousands of copies of a hard-hitting pamphlet selling the "Roosevelt-Wallace-Izac" ticket had been printed in an attractive red-white-and-blue color scheme, but there was no money to mail them to voters, and, without an organization, no other way to distribute them; most canvassers who would distribute them door to door wanted to be paid for their work, and even volunteers required reimbursement for lunch money, carfare, gasoline and other expenses. And then the telegram arrived from his colleague from Texas, the telegram and then a check for $500. With it he could pay the necessary expense money to get the pamphlets distributed. And hardly had the workers fanned out from headquarters to, as he put it, "carry the Roosevelt-Wallace-Izac story from door to door" when another letter arrived —with another $500.

Others got the news at home. Nan Wood Honeyman had been campaigning in Portland for months, but was making no headway—largely, she felt, because Sam Rayburn had not been able to deliver on the commitment she believed he had made to her at the Democratic Convention in July. Receiving Johnson's questionnaire, she had responded with a telephone call on October 17, and John Connally's "memo for LBJ" summarizing the call (Connally may have been taking shorthand notes on an extension) began:

> In your conversation of yesterday with Nan Wood Honeyman
> she pointed out the following things which would be helpful to her.
> 1. Finances . . .

Mrs. Honeyman had asked that contributions be sent to her at her house, and the next day there arrived at 1728 S.W. Prospect Drive the telegram (AS RESULT MY VISIT TO CONGRESSIONAL COMMITTEE . . . YOU SHOULD RECEIVE . . .). The first letter from the committee contained the pre-Johnson contribution: $150. She thought that was the airmail special-delivery letter to which Johnson had been referring. She was appreciative, but $150 wasn't going to help much. Her opponent was on the way home, she wrote, and "has sent word to raise an extra $1,500 for him right away in spite of the fact that his literature covers the city, he has been on the radio from Washington once or twice a week for some time and his face and 'One good term deserves another' on huge billboards meets me at every turn." Then, on October 19, the Johnson contribution—$500— arrived. RECEIVED 5 POINT PROGRAM TODAY, she wired back in jubilation.

And they were very grateful. "The text of your thoughtful and kind telegram had been read to me over Long Distance telephone, so that on my return from a thorough tour of four counties of my district, I today found two Air Mail letters," Martin Smith wrote Johnson. "I appreciate your personal efforts in my behalf." McLaughlin said simply: "I am glad you are where you are." When the first $500 arrived from Johnson, Izac had dashed off a letter: "Thanks a million." And before that letter could even be dropped in the mail, he had to add: "P.S. Your airmail letter of the 19th [the letter which contained another $500] just arrived. Again many thanks." "Dear Lyndon," Nan Honeyman wrote, "I have been on the verge of calling you all day instead of writing because it is such fun to hear you. . . . The second contribution from the National Committee arrived on the heels of the first one and the raise of the ante was grand and I know my gratitude belongs to you."

They were to become more grateful. For Lyndon had only begun raising money.

Some he obtained through personal acquaintance. Tom Corcoran, in New York raising money for Roosevelt, arranged for some cash contributions from garment-center unions, which he brought to Washington himself and gave to Johnson (as Corcoran was to relate). Another union with political money to spend was the United Mine Workers. John L. Lewis might be for Willkie, but did the UMW really want a Republican Congress? UMW chief counsel Welly Hopkins recalls that "He hadn't been in place [with the Congressional Campaign Committee] more than twenty-four hours when he called me and said he wanted to see what the mine workers could do toward helping the campaign." Hopkins presented Johnson's case to the union's secretary-treasurer, Tom Kennedy; Johnson went to see Kennedy, and, Hopkins says, "I think he went away satisfied as far as the responses that the mine workers made." Money from New York came not only from Seventh Avenue but from Wall Street, $7,500 arriving from the investment banker brothers Paul and Cornelius Shields through the offices of the wealthy New Yorkers he had met through Ed Weisl. Some he obtained because of his ability to arouse paternal fondness in older, powerful, wealthy men. Charles Marsh did not even have to be asked; no sooner had he learned of Johnson's assignment to save Congress for the Democrats than, busy though he was working on the Wallace campaign, he volunteered at once the two commodities with which he was so free: advice and money. Recalls Alice Glass' sister, Mary Louise, Marsh's private secretary: "Charles said to him, 'Boy, you've got to get some money. You can't do that on good-will.'" Contacting four business associates in Texas, Marsh arranged that each would give him $1,000 per week until the campaign ended, and that he would add to their contributions $1,000 per week of his own, and forward each week a total of $5,000 to Johnson; "I had to keep track of who paid," she says. (Allowing Marsh to know that other men were similarly helping his "protégé" might have dulled the edge of his enthusiasm for the task, so this information was not given to him.) So fast did the money come in that Johnson was able to broaden his assistance. Martin Smith had been so thrilled to receive the Congressional Committee's checks for $200 and $500. Before the week was out, he would receive a second $500 check. A filled-in questionnaire and letter requesting financial help arrived from Representative William H. Sutphin of New Jersey on October 17. Johnson dictated a reply saying, "I am going to make an especial effort to find some way to get you some financial assistance," but before he had had a chance to sign and mail the letter, the influx of funds had enabled him to be more specific. On the bottom, he added a postscript: "Today I'm asking a Texas friend of mine to give me $500.00 for you. If he does I'll take it to the Cong. Committee and ask them to rush it to you tonight." Actually, Johnson had either the money or the assurance of it in hand when he wrote that, and the $500 was sent that night.

He had so much money, in fact, that he was not only meeting requests for funds, but soliciting more requests—*asking* Congressmen to ask for money. On the bottom of Lyndon Johnson's letter accompanying the $300 check for McLaughlin of Nebraska was a scrawled postscript: "If you badly need more funds, let me know and I'll try some more." To one Congressman who hadn't asked for funds, James M. Barnes of Illinois, he wrote: "Do you have desperate need for money, Jim? If so, wire or write me air mail how much and I'll try to get some and send through congressional committee for you."

JOHNSON WAS APPARENTLY anticipating a large contribution from the Democratic National Committee. He had asked its secretary, Paul Aiken, for $25,000, and seems to have felt he had received a commitment for at least a substantial portion of that amount, but when the check from New York arrived, it was for only $5,000, and after Johnson had taken that over to the National Press Building on October 21, he was out of funds. But although Sam Rayburn had not been easily convinced of the efficacy of Lyndon Johnson's fund-raising methods, his doubts must have been ended by the success of his first telephone calls to Dallas. Now the Speaker was going to Dallas in person.

Bonham, his home town, had scheduled a celebration in honor of his becoming Speaker, and Rayburn had left for Texas on October 17. At the celebration (at which bands from the eleven high schools in his district paraded through the streets of his little town), he was presented with a gavel carved by a local carpenter out of bois d'arc wood, and with a gift from Colonel W. T. Knight of Wichita Falls, unofficial spokesman of that city's oilmen, who, Rayburn's friend C. Dwight Dorough writes, "that morning . . . had collected $2,000 from people in Wichita Falls for the National Democratic War Chest, and . . . had come to present the money in person." The need for that gift—and for more like it—would shortly be driven home to Rayburn, for on October 23, he received two communications from Johnson. They were both enclosed in the same envelope. The first had been written, on the twenty-first, as a telegram, but not sent in that form; the secretive Johnson had marked the telegram "Personal & Confidential. Personal Delivery Only," but who could be certain that those instructions would be obeyed? "I started to send you the attached wire yesterday but because I hesitated to send a wire, I am enclosing it in this letter," Johnson wrote. The enclosed "wire" said that a "careful check" of congressional races around the country had disclosed that it was not 77 Democratic candidates who were in trouble, but 105. And, it said, there was no more money available to help them. "Barrel has been scraped." It urged Rayburn to appeal for funds. "Our friends can be helpful now if they want to be by writing me airmail special delivery Munsey Building and directing me to apply as per attached list which I will make up. Hope when you talk to them today and Wednesday in Dallas you will impress importance doing this at once. Hope we can get total at least equivalent to amount I suggested to Paul . . ."

In Dallas, where another celebration was held in honor of his new job, Rayburn rode through its streets at the head of a 200-car caravan. Then he conferred with the oilmen. Some of them had by this time exceeded the $5,000 limit on campaign contributions. Some of their new contributions were, therefore, in cash. William Kittrell, the veteran Texas lobbyist who had, years before, called Lyndon Johnson a "wonder kid," was an intimate of Rayburn and Sid Richardson and other oilmen. Worried that his "Personal Delivery Only" letter to Rayburn would go astray, Johnson wired Kittrell that he had sent the Speaker a letter, adding, PLEASE SEE THAT HE GETS IT. THIS IS URGENT. I AM GATHERING OTHER MATERIAL. ("Material" was the euphemism most frequently used by Johnson to refer to campaign contributions.) Some of the oilmen's response arrived in Washington in envelopes containing cash that were carried by trusted couriers (Kittrell himself was one of them, according to Corcoran and Harold Young), and were handed to Johnson. How much they contained is not known, because no record of these campaign contributions, or of their distribution to individual candidates, has been found. This money did not pass through the committee, or through the Munsey Building office; Johnson arranged for its distribution, in checks or cash, to candidates through outside means, including channels arranged by Marsh, one of which was Young. Only hints about the existence of these channels are contained in letters found in Johnson's office files; one example is a note from Johnson to Congressman Claude V. Parsons of Illinois on October 25: "I am sure that by now you have received all the material I had sent you, both through the committee and otherwise"; Parsons wrote back thanking Johnson both for the checks from the committee and "from Harold Young." There is also an unexplained reference in Johnson's files to money given "on (the) Chicago line." As for money that *did* pass through the committee, Johnson had said on Monday (in a statement borne out at least in general by his records) that he was out of money. On Thursday, he gave the committee $16,500.

. . .

RAYBURN DID MORE in Texas than merely raise money.

The independent oilman perhaps most influential among his fellow wildcatters was Charles F. Roeser of Fort Worth, president of the Independent Petroleum Association; in 1936, Jim Farley had been informed confidentially that Roeser "not only will get money himself, but will raise it from his friends." The contributions Roeser arranged in 1936 had been made through traditional Democratic channels—sent to Democratic National Committee Chairman Farley at the Biltmore. Roeser had planned to contribute through traditional channels in 1940, also; with Farley no longer national chairman, the oilman had asked Elliott Roosevelt, leaving Fort Worth for a trip north, to find out whom he should send the money to. But although Elliott was to wire him to send the money to Steve Early at the White House, those instructions were not followed, for before Roeser heard from Elliott Roosevelt, he heard from Sam Rayburn. The new Speaker "called me from Dallas and advised that I send my contribution to the Democratic Congressional Campaign Committee in care of Lyndon Johnson," Roeser was to recall. Roeser had never met Johnson, but he followed Rayburn's instructions. "Dear Mr. Johnson," he wrote, "After talking with Sam Rayburn, I have decided to send my contribution for this year's campaign to you. . . . I am . . . leaving it up to the Steering Committee, headed by you, to decide in what districts these funds can be best used." And not only Roeser's own $5,000 campaign contribution but the contributions of the independent oilmen who followed his lead went not to the White House or to the Biltmore, as they would have done in the past, but to the Munsey Building. So, moreover, did the contributions of independents who did not follow Roeser's lead—of men such as Richardson and Murchison who followed no man's lead. For however independent they were, these men not only trusted Sam Rayburn, but were aware that now that this grim, unsmiling man was armed with the Speaker's gavel, he was the protector they needed in Washington, and they were therefore willing to follow his instructions—which were to send their money to Lyndon Johnson.

Roeser's terse letter to the young Congressman he had never met was a significant document in the political fund-raising history of the United States (and, it was to prove in later years, in the larger history of the country as well). Sam Rayburn had, on his trip to Texas in October, 1940, cut off the Democratic National Committee, and other traditional party recipients of campaign contributions, from the money of the newly rich Texas independent oilmen. These men had been seeking a channel through which their money could flow to the seat of national power 2,000 miles away, to far-off Washington. After Sam Rayburn's trip to Dallas in October,

1940, they had their channel, a brand-new channel which, ten days before, had not even existed. Sam Rayburn had cut them the channel. A new source of political money, potentially vast, had been tapped in America, and Lyndon Johnson had been put in charge of it. He was the conduit for their cash.

MONEY WAS NOT ALL Johnson was providing for the Congressmen. He wrote to candidates in the same terms in which he wrote to constituents. The letters which carried the welcome news of checks on the way contained also the promise of help in non-financial areas. In the letter he sent to the recipients of the October 24 and 25 checks, Lyndon Johnson wrote: "I want to see you *win*. In order to help you and others of our party out in the front-line trenches, I am devoting my entire time in an attempt to coordinate and expedite assistance to you from this end." Just call on me, he urged them—"call on me, at any hour of the day, by phone, wire or letter. My address is 339 Munsey Building and my telephone number is REpublic 8284." That was a form letter: individual notes expressed in even more emphatic terms his eagerness to help. "I wish you would please keep in close touch with me and let me know if there is any way at all I can possibly help you," he wrote Nebraska's McLaughlin. "My services are available to you day and night on anything."

It was not, in fact, necessary for him to be called on.

He would have read in the newspapers that Senator George Norris, the great old champion of public hydroelectric power, was planning to speak in Portland, Oregon, and visit the Grand Coulee Dam to emphasize the administration's role in its building. On Thursday of that first week—the week during which he was single-handedly raising and distributing to Democratic congressional candidates virtually unprecedented amounts of money—Lyndon Johnson compiled a list of nine Democratic candidates in the Far West who were supporters of public power, and who were engaged in tight races. Then he wrote a memorandum: "I do hope that when Senator Norris gives his address . . . he will say something in support of these people in recognition of the battle they have been carrying on. Just one sentence would be helpful. . . ." No one had asked him to do this; he had just done it—and done it with his usual thoroughness, not merely pleading for "just one sentence," but drafting nine different sentences, each custom-tailored for one of the nine candidates. (That thoroughness, and his capacity for cultivating not only the mighty but their assistants, was also evident in the delivery of the memorandum. He spoke to Norris' assistant, Jack Robinson, about it in advance, and when he sent it to Robinson, he sent with it another memorandum asking him to "Please see to it that this gets the Senator's attention" and adding: "Call on me anytime for anything.") Prodded by Robinson, Norris delivered the endorsements.

Other nationally prominent New Dealers and Cabinet members were heading out of Washington on speaking tours for Roosevelt. Johnson asked them, too, to speak for the local Democratic congressional candidate as well. Labor was strong in the State of Washington, and Senator Claude Pepper was a symbol, because of his vigorous support of the wages and hours bill, of the New Deal's support of labor. SENATOR PEPPER SPEAKING SATUR-DAY IN SEATTLE, Johnson wired his Naval Affairs Committee colleague Warren Magnuson. SUGGESTED TO HIM THAT HE PUT IN GOOD PLUG FOR YOU. CONTACT PEPPER WHEN HE ARRIVES. Magnuson had not asked for the "good plug." He had gotten it without asking—as, all at once, Democratic candidates who had given up hope of obtaining assistance from Washington were receiving help for which they had not even asked.

Suddenly, Democratic candidates all across the country realized that there was someone in Washington they could turn to, someone they could ask for not only money but other types of aid.

And they asked. By his second week in the new job, requests were pouring into the Munsey Building—for voting records of Republican incumbents from the Democratic hopefuls opposing them; for information on the broad scale ("I am debating the congressman in McKeesport Saturday . . . and would like to receive all information about his voting record") or the small, for the little piece of information—difficult for someone unfamiliar with the federal bureaucracy to obtain—that could improve a speech (PLEASE WIRE ME BY WESTERN UNION . . . THE AMOUNT OF MONEY IN SOCIAL SECURITY FUND. I MUST KNOW BEFORE SEVEN O'CLOCK TONIGHT); for a vital, desperately needed, denial (wired Congressman J. Buell Snyder of Pennsylvania: FOLLOWING APPEARED IN PITTSBURGH TELEGRAPH QUOTE A BILL INTRODUCED BY SENATOR WAGNER WOULD COMPEL 81,000 TEACHERS OF PENNSYLVANIA TO TURN OVER INTO THE SOCIAL SECURITY FUND $147,000,000 WHICH THE TEACHERS CONSIDER [THEIR] ACTUAL SAVINGS FUND STOP GIVE ME WIRE ANSWER YES OR NO NO EXPLANATION WILL DO STOP THIS WILL COST 50,000 VOTES IN PENNSYLVANIA STOP GIVE ME WIRE SO IT CAN BE PUBLISHED AS IT COMES STOP BETTER FOR WIRE TO COME FROM WAGNER TODAY); for endorsements (Congressman Franck R. Havenner of California wired: SENATOR CLAUDE PEPPER WILL SPEAK IN SAN FRANCISCO TOMORROW STOP WILL BE GRATEFUL IF YOU CAN WIRE HIM ASKING THAT HE ENDORSE MY RECORD); for speakers ("We are requesting . . . Gifford Pinchot, former Governor and the man who took the county 'out of the mud' with his 'Pinchot Roads' to come into Lancaster County, I feel that his visit would supply the spark needed here. Please join with us in urging him to come").

The requests were answered—with a thoroughness that would have been familiar to Gene Latimer and L. E. Jones, whose high-school debate coach had taught them that if you took care of all the minor details, if "you did everything you could do—absolutely *everything*—you would win."

Buell Snyder had asked that the denial he needed come "today," and it did; his wire was received at the Munsey Building at 1:12 p.m., and a return wire was on its way to Snyder's Uniontown, Pennsylvania, head-quarters that same afternoon, for Johnson had immediately contacted Senator Wagner's secretary. The denial should come direct from Wagner, Snyder had said, and it did; the return wire was signed with the Senator's name. And it should "answer yes or no," and the first sentence of Wagner's wire was precisely what Snyder needed: MY ANSWER TO REPORTED STATE-MENT IS EMPHATICALLY NO. And there followed a wire that could, as Sny-der had requested, be published as it came: a long telegram detailing Wagner's version of the bill in question. That was fast enough service for even a desperate campaigner, but Johnson did not put his trust in Western Union; the next morning he sent his own wire telling Snyder that he should have received one from Wagner: IF NOT RECEIVED, LET ME KNOW. THIS JUST FOLLOW-UP. Answering every request, he did absolutely *everything* he could. The wire that Havenner had requested be sent to Pepper was sent and the endorsement by Pepper was made, and it was not just a *pro forma* en-dorsement, for Johnson had seen to it—telegraphing and telephoning, and then telephoning again, not only to the Senator's aides but to the Senator himself, tracking him down on his cross-country tour—that Pepper was given enough details to make it seem that he really was familiar with the Con-gressman's record.

Among the items of assistance for which Congressmen had been asking in vain were out-of-district speakers with particular appeal to their con-stituents, for oratory cost money—money for the orator's transportation, hotel room and meals (and, in the case of some, honoraria for the rental of their vocal cords)—and the National Committee, which was frantically attempting to scrape up funds to send Harold Ickes and other Cabinet members on cross-country tours for the national ticket, had none to spare for the requests of individual Congressmen.

Touching base only occasionally with the National Committee, John-son had his staff compile lists of "Speaker Requests," and the dates of the meetings for which the speakers were requested; he coordinated them, and soon Congressmen with substantial numbers of Polish constituents were notified that Representative Rudolph G. Tenerowicz, past president of the Polish National Alliance, the Polish Alliance of America, and the Polish Union of America, was on his way to deliver one of his renowned speeches —in Polish, of course. (Having won his own, predominantly Polish, district in Hamtramck, Michigan, in 1938 with a majority of 54,000 votes over all other candidates, Tenerowicz needed to devote only limited time to his own campaign.) Candidates with substantial numbers of Negro constituents were

getting a Negro Congressman who was also a renowned orator, Arthur
Mitchell of Chicago, and many districts of varied ethnic composition were
hearing from little Fiorello La Guardia of New York, who, half Jewish and
half Italian, himself an Episcopalian married first to a Catholic and then to a
Lutheran of German descent, was practically a balanced ticket all by himself
—and could, ranting and shaking his tiny fists, wave the bloody flag in seven
different languages. Democratic nominee Alfred F. Beiter, whose Buffalo district included many Italians—who, as he wrote to Johnson, "are inclined to
be 'off-the-reservation' this year"—had been pleading, in vain, with the
National Committee for a visit by Representative D'Alesandro of Baltimore,
who, Beiter had been told, "makes a very good rebuttal talk to offset the
Republicans' criticism of the President's 'stab-in-the-back' reference to
Mussolini." Johnson could not get D'Alesandro for Beiter, but did provide
Frank Serri, who, he assured Beiter, was a "distinguished Italian Brooklyn
lawyer" and "fine orator." Into melting-pot, multi-ethnic districts whose
candidates had been pleading in vain, before October 14, for a single outside
speaker, now filed a parade of speakers, many with expense money from
Lyndon Johnson in their pockets. Buffalo Congressman Pius Schwert, for
example, got Tenerowicz for his Poles, Serri for his Italians, and La Guardia
for various ethnic blocs—as well as Arthur Mitchell for the district's few
Negroes. Thanks to Johnson, the breadbasket as well as the melting pot was
getting speakers. Oklahoma's Phil Ferguson wrote him that Marvin Jones
"can do more good than anyone. . . . If he could make Guymon the Saturday
afternoon before election [it] would do a lot of good, in fact, it might mean
the difference in my election, and then go to Beaver that night would have
battle cinched." Jones was in Guymon the Saturday afternoon before election, and in Beaver that night—and during the last two weeks of the campaign, the Agriculture Committee chairman, identified by farmers throughout
the United States with the AAA, was in more than forty rural districts to tell
farmers how helpful their local Congressman had been in passing the programs that had saved their farms. Johnson not only dispatched the speakers,
he amplified their voices; when, after he had arranged for a visiting speaker,
a candidate said he hoped the speech could be broadcast on a local radio
station, Johnson provided the funds for the broadcast.

   He was providing other types of help as well. His entrée to Ickes—and
to other high officials of Interior—was put to the use of other Congressmen.
"A lot of projects were approved that Fall," Walter Jenkins recalls. "Mr.
Ickes was very cooperative." Roosevelt had told Johnson to work through
Jim Rowe, and Rowe's entrée to other departments—and the fact that he
could speak in the name of the White House—was put to the use of still
others. After more than a year of struggling with the War Department
bureaucracy, Martin Smith had finally secured the requisite permit for construction of an airport in his district, only to see the project snarled in WPA
red tape. By making him seem ineffectual in Washington, D.C., "this delay

is not doing me any good politically," Smith wrote Johnson on October 26. "If I could get final approval of this project by the WPA, and have it approved by President Roosevelt, before the end of the coming week, it would be a great help." A week later, Smith received a telegram from the Munsey Building: YOUR WPA APPLICATION HAS BEEN APPROVED BY WPA AND IS AT THE WHITE HOUSE AWAITING THE PRESIDENT'S SIGNATURE. WILL DO MY BEST TO GET THIS SIGNED FOR YOU AND WIRE YOU BY MONDAY. Time was running out; Monday was the day before election, but on that day, another Western Union envelope was delivered to Smith:

HAPPY TO REPORT PRESIDENT TODAY APPROVED WORKS PROGRESS ADMINISTRATION PROJECT FIVE OUGHT OUGHT SEVEN TWO, APPROPRIATING THREE HUNDRED EIGHTY TWO THOUSAND SIX HUNDRED FIFTY EIGHT DOLLARS FOR IMPROVEMENT MOON ISLAND AIRPORT

There was help available for Congressmen now not only on projects but on personnel. A "local labor leader" in Scranton was employed by the General Accounting Office, Representative Patrick J. Boland informed Johnson; "will you kindly try to obtain [him] an increase in salary?" Another example of many requests in this area that Johnson handled had been addressed to Drewry first, by Representative John M. Houston of Kansas' Fifth Congressional District. In a casual conversation in a corridor while the House had still been in session, Drewry had assured Houston that if a federal job for one of his constituents would help in his campaign, he would obtain it, but when Houston asked for a job for one W. W. Brown of Wichita, "who swings a lot of votes" because of his membership in a "very strong" United Commercial Travelers local, "and is out of work," the chairman of the Congressional Campaign Committee was unable to deliver. But when his assistant, Cap Harding, appealed to Johnson for help, Johnson was able to deliver. Telephoning a bureaucrat in the Agriculture Department's Office of Personnel, he sounded him out on what was immediately available, and persuaded him to make a call to a higher official who had a $2,400-a-year job open in the Federal Surplus Commodities Corporation. A wire went out to Houston informing him: AT REQUEST OF CONGRESSMAN LYNDON JOHNSON HAVE REQUESTED OUR REGIONAL DIRECTOR IN MILWAUKEE . . . TO FORWARD APPLICATION FOR EMPLOYMENT TO W. W. BROWN.

In other branches of political activity in which similarly urgent appeals came in from Congressmen, Johnson was also able to help. In the same letter in which he thanked Johnson for "sympathetically" helping him with various problems, Martin Smith added: "A new problem has arisen." This problem was a strike that had tied up lumber mills in his district, and was arousing resentment toward the New Deal, which had encouraged the new militancy in organized labor; "As you well know," Smith wrote Johnson, "the President, the Administration and the M.C. [Members of Congress] are given the bulk of the blame for allowing such conditions to prevail." Although this strike could be settled only by the labor leaders in New York, and Johnson didn't know those leaders, Tommy Corcoran did; the introductions necessary for Johnson to get them on the phone were arranged, and the very day he was informed of Smith's "new problem," he was able to assure the Congressman the width of a continent away that he was working on the problem: TALKED TO LUBIN AND HILLMAN TODAY. THEY ARE DOING EVERYTHING POSSIBLE ON STRIKE.

This assistance was also provided with Johnson thoroughness. Every telegram had a "follow-up" (to Kent Keller: AFTER TELEPHONE CONVERSATION WITH YOU IMMEDIATELY WENT TO WORK ON HOSPITAL PROJECT. ASSUME YOU BY NOW HAVE RECEIVED WIRE FROM VETERANS ADMINISTRATION ADVISING YOU THAT PRESIDENT AND BUDGET HAVE APPROVED THIS). Mistakes in numerals were so frequent in telegrams that Western Union policy was to repeat them at the lower left-hand corner of the telegram so that the reader could double-check. This precaution was not sufficient for Johnson. He took his own precaution, insisting that the operator spell out the numerals as words (PROJECT FIVE OUGHT OUGHT SEVEN TWO). He sent two and three copies of some telegrams.

And his assistance was provided eagerly. When a Congressman asked him for help, he thanked him for asking. Replying to Smith's request for help on the Moon Island Airport, Johnson began: "Thanks much for yours of the 26th. It had no more than reached me when I immediately got to work on your project. . . . You can be sure that I will do my best." And he asked them to ask him for more help. "Do you have any other assignment for me?" he asked them. He reiterated his request: "Call on me, at any hour."

No matter how many assignments he was given, he tried, in those frantic three weeks, to carry out all of them—and, in fact, thought of additional help he could give the candidates. His work for Nan Wood Honeyman was an example.

Her telephone call to Johnson on October 17, the call which had been transcribed by John Connally, had asked for money—but for other assistance as well: for letters of endorsement from Rayburn and McCormack, and because "one of her big problems was the Townsend Plan," from a Congressman identified with assistance for the aged, Charles H. Leavy of Washington; and for "Honorable George Norris to speak in [the] district." That very day the Western Union messengers began arriving at the front door of her home—and each yellow envelope contained good news. The telegram that arrived that afternoon, of course, informed her that the AIRMAIL SPECIAL DELIVERY LETTER with a big contribution was coming. The next day two telegrams arrived from LYNDON. The first said that while he had been UNSUC-

CESSFUL ON LEAVY MATTER, the Rayburn and McCormack letters were on the way. The second said that HONORABLE GEORGE NORRIS would indeed SPEAK IN PORTLAND, OREGON. HAVE TALKED WITH HIS SECRETARY ABOUT YOU, AND FEEL SURE HE WILL NOT FORGET YOU. HOWEVER, SUGGEST YOU HAVE SOMEONE CONTACT HIS PARTY AND HAVE HIM REMINDED OF THIS TO PREVENT ANY POSSIBLE OVERLOOKING OF IT. (Johnson had even suggested a sentence that the Senator could include in his speech: "I would like to live in Portland so that I might vote for Nan Wood Honeyman to be my Congressman.") The Rayburn and McCormack letters were warm enough to satisfy even an anxious candidate, and Johnson's work with Norris' staff paid off on the front page of the *Portland Oregonian:* posing before the great dam after his speech, Norris had summoned Mrs. Honeyman to stand beside him, so that she was in the dramatic page-one picture.

In a letter which Johnson wrote on the 22nd, he told Mrs. Honeyman that he had been "thinking about . . . having you back here with us. That's the thing that would really tickle me and the big job I want to do between now and November the fifth. So if you don't write, wire, or phone me any time there is anything—big or little—I can do for you, I am going to be awfully mad at you." Mrs. Honeyman gave him little chance to be mad. If he couldn't get a letter from Leavy, she asked, how about one from Senator Downey, who, she said, "is next to Dr. Townsend in the eyes of his followers. . . . A suggestion from him that the local pensioners support me would carry a lot of weight. . . . I put this up to you as a real job." Johnson was glad for the job, he wrote her on the 23rd; he asked her to give him more jobs: "Nan, I will look into the Downey matter you mentioned and do everything I possibly can to help work this out for you. Please, please let me know if I can do anything else." And the letter of the 23rd brought other good news to Prospect Drive: "I am glad . . . the little financial contributions have helped you some," he wrote. "I talked with them again last night and gave them three hundred fifty more to send you air mail special, so that you should have received that by the time this letter reaches you." The next day, the 24th, there was another letter—and another $350. The extent of the money from Washington had by this time reached levels so unexpected that when, on October 28, Johnson asked her how much more money she needed, she said she had all she could use.

Downey wasn't the only Senator beloved by pensioners; Claude Pepper was, too, and he was at that very moment campaigning on the West Coast. Johnson tracked Pepper down in Los Angeles, and talked to him on the telephone. "I told him to do all he could for you and he heartily agreed," he wrote Mrs. Honeyman. John Rankin was an important name in public power; Mrs. Honeyman was informed that a letter from Rankin was on its way.

Johnson volunteered, in fact, an even bigger favor—one for which she hadn't dared to ask. She had requested letters from Rayburn and Norris; he got her one from a bigger name. He suggested she send a letter to President Roosevelt noting her role in the Bonneville Dam and Columbia River projects—a letter which would give the President an excuse to reply, and emphasize her role. He himself wrote a draft of her letter—and of the President's reply—and persuaded Rowe to arrange to have the letter sent over the President's signature: "My dear Nan: It was good to hear from you again and to receive from one who has fought shoulder to shoulder with me for the Columbia developments a picture of their present usefulness. . . ." Notifying her of this unexpected boon he had arranged, Johnson said: "I just thought this might give you another little push."

IT WAS NOT only Congressmen whom he was assisting.

In an era before the widespread use of political polling, information was a commodity very difficult for a politician to obtain quickly enough for him to make effective use of it. Without computers, even the famous Gallup Poll had to report its results several days after its polling had begun, by which time new political developments might have changed voters' attitudes. And little polling was done on the effect of developments on specific segments of the population. A candidate might wonder—might be desperate to know—how his strategy was working, but it was hard for him to find out.

The Democratic Congressional Campaign Committee had never before been used to fill this gap. But it was used to fill it now.

With many of the checks that went out, there went out also a request for a status report, not only on the Congressman's own chances in his district, but on the President's. And since many of the men Johnson was asking for these reports were veteran Congressmen—seasoned, experienced (and successful) politicians—their replies were often extremely informative. They were especially informative because when Congressmen took their own, local, polls, unscientific and rudimentary in technique though they were, they sent the results to Johnson, and he could pass them along to the White House —and the results of these polls, of course, were hard facts, the kind of facts for which a candidate and his advisors are so anxious. Ohio's Ninth Congressional District, which included Toledo with its large factories, was considered a fairly typical urban, industrialized district, and a good indicator of sentiment in such areas. In mid-October, its Congressman, John F. Hunter, had sent out "blind" postcards, postcards simply asking voters to write in their preference for Congressman and President and send the cards to a numbered postal box. He mailed them to 16,000 voters, and when, a week later, 3,654 postcards had been returned, he could report the figures to Johnson: 2,182 for Willkie, 1,472 for Roosevelt. But Hunter could shrewdly report to Johnson that the figures might not be as ominous as they seemed at first glance, because the return rate from factory districts was so "much less, by percentage, than from the Republican wards, it may be that factory workers are afraid to express their choice."

Most important, Johnson could not only get information for the President, he could get it for him fast. Roosevelt, worried about a Gallup poll which showed Willkie rapidly cutting into his lead, began a series of radio addresses on October 23. Sending out checks to congressional candidates around the country, Johnson had asked them to repay him with a report on how Roosevelt's speeches went over; within a day or two after each speech, he could tell the White House that, as one candidate put it after one speech—in a reaction echoed by other Johnson correspondents—"the President's broadcast of last night has caused [a] definite swing toward the President's candidacy."

John L. Lewis broke his long silence with a dreaded roar on October 25, endorsing Willkie and announcing that he would resign as CIO president if Roosevelt won; not only was the speech shrewdly timed—Lewis had delayed for weeks while press speculation about his intentions aroused interest in his speech, and had finally struck twelve days before the election for maximum impact—but it hit at what was perhaps Roosevelt's weakest point; in his Shakespearean voice, the miners' chief proclaimed that the President was determined to force the United States into war. Initial press reports speculated that Lewis' speech would have substantial impact on the campaign, but no one—including an anxious White House—could know for sure. Johnson, however, soon had specific reports—from the very districts in which the speech would have had the greatest impact. Using his list of "Districts Which Produce 1,000,000 Tons or More Coal"—the fifteen districts in six states, which, of course, contained the greatest concentration of the coal miners who formed the bedrock of Lewis' constituency—Johnson sent telegrams to the Congressmen from these districts asking for a report on the effect of Lewis' speech. The initial responses were surprising: one of the first said that the speech "has not injured us any"; if anything, it had helped; several CIO locals responded to Lewis' threat to resign by asking him to do so immediately. And later responses confirmed the trend: "The coal miners . . . rank and file . . . will stay with Roosevelt," one said. Because the telegraph was too slow for him, Johnson telephoned several of the fifteen whose judgment he particularly trusted (his selection displayed again his keenness as a reader of men; among them were Jennings Randolph of West Virginia and Michael Bradley of Pennsylvania, men who would rise). Their replies confirmed the others' (Randolph, scribbling a note "following up our telephone conversation of a few minutes ago," told him that Lewis' speech would "cut in to the Roosevelt vote in my congressional district" by only about 10 percent, and that the President could still expect to win by 15 percent). Johnson was able to tell the White House that the press reports were wrong; he presented a reassuring district-by-district summary of the limited impact of Lewis' defection—a summary backed by hard facts.

The White House, frantic for information, suddenly realized that there was a new source of it: a young Congressman from Texas.

TEN DAYS TO GO, and there was no time for the mail now. Now almost all requests were couched in Western Union's urgent capitals. For now defeat or victory was staring ambitious men starkly in the face, and so was the realization that just a little money might mean the difference between one and the other—if the money arrived in time.

A single ad might make the difference—just one more ad. MUST HAVE $250 BY THURSDAY NIGHT FOR LAST ISSUE ADVERTISING, wired James E. Hughes of Wisconsin. ADVERTISING PROGRAMS ACCOMPLISHING GREAT RE-SULTS DEADLINE THURSDAY NOON, wired Beiter of Buffalo. On Monday, October 28, James F. Lavery of Pennsylvania wired Johnson asking for $100 for BADLY NEEDED advertising. When he did not receive a reply by Wednesday, he wired again. If Johnson could not spare $100, he asked, could he send $90? CHANCES BRIGHT . . . IF WE GET RIGHT AWAY $14 FOR EACH OF FIVE COUNTY PAPERS AND $20 FOR TITUSVILLE HERALD.

One more mailing. HAVE SET UP MACHINERY TO REACH 11,000 VOTERS BY MAIL IF $250 MADE AVAILABLE BY THURSDAY, Kenneth M. Petrie wired Johnson. In Racine, Wisconsin, J. M. Weisman was staring at stacks of 65,000 circulars—and at the realization that he couldn't get them into voters' hands. URGENCY NEED AT LEAST $500 BY FRIDAY.

One more maneuver of a more informal character. Cap Harding's son, Kenneth, who would succeed him as director of the Congressional Campaign Committee, was running campaigns in California's Eighth Congressional District. "There was a colored minister who controlled the bloc of colored votes in San Jose, and we bought him for fifty dollars. A small amount of money judiciously spent could mean more than a larger amount of money spent on political advertising. Just a few bucks strategically placed could mean all the difference in the world. But those last few days of a campaign—when the deals were being struck—that was when you either had the cash or you didn't. And if you didn't—well, that could mean the end of a man's career."

Election Day itself was looming before these men—Election Day, with Election Day expenses. Arthur Mitchell, returning to his Chicago district from his travels on behalf of other Negro candidates, found to his shock that, as he wired Johnson: PRACTICALLY ALL COLORED BAPTIST MINISTERS HAVE BEEN EMPLOYED BY THE REPUBLICAN PARTY. . . . I CAN AND WILL BEAT THEM IF I CAN GET THE MONEY TO HIRE WORKERS. . . . I NEED A MINI-MUM OF $600. . . . WHATEVER HELP I CAN GET SHOULD BE IN HANDS TOMOR-ROW IF POSSIBLE. Byron G. Rogers of Colorado wired: COULD USE $500 FOR WORKERS IN SPANISH AND ITALIAN DISTRICTS. WIRE TODAY HOW MUCH I CAN EXPECT. Francis T. Murphy of Milwaukee: CAN CARRY DISTRICT BY

2000 BY GETTING VOTE TO POLLS IN KEY WARDS. NEED $300 FRIDAY TO CARRY OUT INTENSIVE WORK. . . . WIRE BY WESTERN UNION. Vernon Sigars of Missouri: NEED $1,000 NOVEMBER 1ST TO HIRE POLL WATCHERS.

There were other Election Day expenses, too, for San Antonio was not the only city and Texas not the only state in which money was piled on tables to purchase votes, just as Mexican-Americans were not the only immigrants whose votes were purchased; in New Brunswick, New Jersey, heavily inhabited in 1940 by first-generation Americans of Slavic descent and controlled by a ruthless city machine (to name just one Northeastern city in which this practice was widespread), the big oak desks of city officials were traditionally cleared of papers on Election Day and covered with piles of cash. In the big cities of the Northeast, votes might cost more than five dollars each; in the slums of New York and Chicago, at least, it was not uncommon for Bowery and Skid Row residents to be handed tens or even, in a close election, twenties for their franchise. And for those candidates who were not planning to buy votes, money might be needed for poll watchers to prevent illegal balloting by voters bought by their opponents. As for rural areas, certain "boxes" in the Tenth District of Texas were not the only precincts which could be delivered for a candidate if a payment was made to a local Sheriff or County Commissioner.

There was no time for circumlocutions now. Money was what was needed, and money was what was asked for. Some candidates, in their anxiety to obtain funds, entrusted to Western Union stratagems usually mentioned only in whispers. Hardy Steeholm of Dutchess County, New York, wired that TWO THOUSAND . . . WILL DO THE TRICK. The trick he had in mind was not, perhaps, a clean one; this Democratic candidate wanted the money for the payment not of Democratic workers, but of Republicans. SUCCESS OF CAMPAIGN NOW HINGES ON FINANCES NECESSARY TO LINE UP REPUBLICAN WORKER IN EACH POLLING DISTRICT. Martin Smith, who had gotten funds from Lyndon Johnson for radio and newspaper advertising, now needed more—for another purpose: I SHALL HAVE TO CONTACT KEY MEN IN THE CIO. . . . THIS IS GOING TO ENTAIL CONSIDERABLE EXPENSE. John E. Sheridan required a cash subvention to offset the use he expected his opponent to make of cash on Election Day. KNOW ATTEMPT WILL BE MADE TO BUY THE ELECTION . . . BY PAYING WORKERS AND VOTERS TO STAY HOME ON ELECTION DAY.

AND MONEY was what they got.

On Sunday, October 27, Sam Rayburn and Lyndon Johnson met with Franklin Roosevelt at the White House. The youngest of the three men reported that eighty-two Democratic Congressmen were in tight contests in which additional financial help—perhaps $1,000 per man—might be decisive. According to a summary of the conversation that Johnson wrote the next day, Roosevelt said that the Democratic National Committee should give the Congressional Campaign Committee at least $50,000 to distribute in these key districts. Johnson relayed his analysis of the situation—along with the President's message—to Rayburn's contact at the Democratic National Committee headquarters at the Biltmore, Swagar Sherley.

> Dear Mr. Sherley:
>
> Unless we are resigned to sizable losses in the House membership which may mean loss of control, the 82 men listed on the attached memo should receive financial help immediately.
>
> If you will notice, 1,000 is to be given to each member unless otherwise designated. . . .
>
> If you could get Ed Flynn to give the Democratic Congressional Committee 50 thousand tomorrow, I will raise the additional 26 [sic] necessary and tomorrow night will get out the funds according to the memo. . . .
>
> The Boss said in his conference with the Speaker and me yesterday that he thought the Committee should get us at least 50 thousand in order to save this situation.
>
> Excuse this hurried note because we are working day and night and am about to go out.
>
> > Sincerely,
> > Lyndon B. Johnson

The money from the Democratic National Committee was not forthcoming, so Johnson raised his own. He went to his original source, obtaining substantial new sums from Brown & Root. (Charles Marsh also sent money, perhaps only the $5,000 a week collected by Mary Louise Glass, perhaps more—it is impossible to be certain because Marsh's money was collected and distributed not by the Congressional Committee but through channels that Marsh arranged and no written record whatsoever of these transactions has been found.) And he went to his new source, working it this time not through Rayburn but by himself. Oilman W. W. Lechner of Dallas was in Washington, staying at the Mayflower Hotel. On October 29, Johnson spoke with him, and Lechner gave him a check for $1,500. On that same day, another $1,500 check arrived in the mail, from oilman Jack Frost of Dallas, who sent a note: "All of us down here want to see Hatton Sumners hold his position at the head of the Judiciary Committee. It would be a shame if Texas lost its chairmanship of this and other powerful committees." D. F. Strickland of Mission, Texas, a powerful Austin lobbyist—and an oilman— sent Johnson a money order for $1,000 also with a message: "I am particularly interested in reelecting a Democratic House so that my friends Lyndon Johnson, Sam Rayburn, Hatton Sumners, Milton West and other Texas congressmen may retain their present positions of honor and influence in the

House." C. W. Murchison, First National Bank Building, Dallas, sent $5,000. Toddie L. Wynne, First National Bank Building, Dallas, sent $5,000. If the pipeline for political oil money from Texas had been opened two weeks before, Monday, October 28, 1940, was the date the flow was stepped up. How much money gushed up from Dallas on that date cannot be determined, because some never passed through the Congressional Campaign Committee, but was distributed, at Johnson's instructions, by others. But on Tuesday, October 29, one week before the election, the anxious Congressmen received a telegram from Lyndon Johnson:

AM ATTEMPTING TO GET ADDITIONAL HELP FOR CONGRESSIONAL COMMITTEE IN ORDER THAT WE CAN GIVE YOU MORE FINANCIAL ASSISTANCE. IF VERY URGENT WIRE ME TODAY ABSOLUTE MINIMUM AND DEADLINE.

A week to go—less than a week. There was desperation in those yellow envelopes now. THERE IS NO ABSOLUTE MINIMUM, George B. Kelly of Rochester wired. ANYTHING WILL HELP THE FIGHT AGAINST ODDS. VERY URGENT. Snatching the envelopes from the messengers, Henderson or Connally would read: WE NEED FUNDS AND NEED THEM BADLY. IMPERA-TIVE. ANY AMOUNT. *Or* WE ARE SIX HUNDRED DOLLARS BEHIND NOW WITH MORE EXPENSE TO COME. ABSOLUTE MINIMUM NECESSARY $350. *Or* APPROXIMATELY TEN THOUSAND MAJORITY FOR WILLKIE IN MY DISTRICT. MORE MONEY NEEDED. *Or* LYNDON URGENTLY NEED AT LEAST FIVE HUN-DRED DOLLARS BY SATURDAY. WOULD ESTIMATE FIFTEEN THOUSAND MAJOR-ITY FOR NATIONAL TICKET IF OPPOSITION MONEY DOES NOT INCREASE OVER WEEKEND. *Or* LYNDON SITUATION IN DANGER HERE. . . . REALLY BELIEVE DISTRICT MAY BE IN TROUBLE DUE TO HEAVY REPUBLICAN EXPENDITURES. ANY SUM WOULD BE MUCH APPRECIATED. COULD USE $1,000. PROSPECTS AND MAJORITY UNCERTAIN.

Some telegraphed repeatedly. Two wires arrived from the new Con-gressman from Washington's Second District. Henry M. ("Scoop") Jackson, elected just a few months before in a special election, saw danger that his career would be over almost before it had begun. SLIGHT SHIFT MY DISTRICT TO REPUBLICANS. . . . THIS WILL BE CRUCIAL WEEK. MY ELECTION WILL BE CLOSE. HAVE RECEIVED NO ASSISTANCE FROM DEMOCRATIC NATIONAL COM-MITTEE. PLEASE WIRE ONE THOUSAND DOLLARS. When he did not receive an immediate reply, Jackson wired again: ABSOLUTE MINIMUM $750 NECES-SARY IMMEDIATELY. . . . MY RACE EXTREMELY CLOSE. AM ONLY NEW CON-GRESSMAN IN STATE. NEED FUNDS NOW. PERSONAL CREDIT EXHAUSTED. WIRE ANSWER. Petrie's 11,000 pieces of mail had been set in type, but the $350 which would enable him to mail them, the $350 for which he had asked Johnson, had not arrived. He sent another telegram: ANXIOUSLY AWAITING REPLY.

Some of his fellow Congressmen were trying frantically to get Lyndon Johnson on the telephone. J. Buell Snyder spoke to one of his secretaries, and her report of his message was to the point: "In trouble. Needs help." Lenhardt E. Bauer of Indiana sent a wire at 1:37 p.m. on October 30: PLEASE CONTACT ME ON TELEPHONE EARLIEST POSSIBLE MOMENT. MUST TALK TO YOU. . . . When, four hours later, he had not heard from Johnson, he sent another telegram: NEED FOUR HUNDRED DOLLARS STILL MUST TALK TO YOU.

In far-off Washington State, Martin Smith had been running hard, but time for him to make up the ground he had lost because of Congress' late recess was running out—and he feared he was still behind. Lewis County was his district's most rock-bed Republican territory, but picking up votes there was his best hope. On the twenty-eighth Smith left for Lewis—with a bullhorn; during the next three days, he was planning to address rallies and speak informally in the county's little towns. But Smith was afraid that, run as hard as he could, he would not be able to reach enough voters with a bullhorn to pull this race out. He could reach more by radio, and had reserved radio time on all five stations in his district, but FCC regulations required that radio time be paid for in advance. He had reserved space for last-minute ads in the district's daily newspapers—but they had to be paid for, too. Johnson had done so much for him, but what he had done wasn't enough. Leaving for Lewis County, Smith wired him: IMPERATIVE EVERY EFFORT BE MADE TO FURTHER ASSIST ME. Then, on the twenty-ninth Johnson's telegram arrived at his headquarters in Hoquiam. Tracking the Congressman down by telephone, his secretary, Robert A. Leroux, read him Johnson's telegram, and Smith told Leroux to reply: MINIMUM SHOULD BE FIVE HUNDRED AND DEADLINE SATURDAY. And the secretary added a sentence showing how hard his boss was fighting—and how much he needed Johnson's help. HAVE JUST SUCCEEDED IN CONTACTING CONGRESSMAN SMITH BY LONG DISTANCE AT ONALASKA LEWIS COUNTY WHERE HE'S HOLDING MASS MEETING WITH LOUD SPEAKER ONE OF TWELVE MEETINGS TODAY IN THIS STRONG REPUBLICAN COUNTY.

Henderson and Connally summarized, state by state, each candidate who replied, the amount he needed, and any additional information he furnished. Lyndon Johnson sat down with this list, and in the left-hand margin wrote the amount each man was to receive.

He wasn't wasting his money. A candidate's assessment of his chances was discreetly checked and rechecked through other sources; evaluations of the races in Illinois' twenty-five districts, for example, were telephoned to Johnson by the dean of the state's congressional delegation, Adolph J. Sabath, chairman of the House Rules Committee. If a report said that the candidate had a good chance to win, the candidate got his money. Assistant Secretary of Agriculture Grover Hill, on a speechmaking tour through rural districts, reported from Kansas' Fifth that, although the race was close, Democrat incumbent John M. Houston "has good chance to win." Houston had responded to Johnson's telegram by asking for $300; that was what he got. But if a report was highly unfavorable, so was Johnson's response; Noel P. Fox, Democratic candidate in Michigan's Ninth District, told Johnson that he was leading by 1,500 votes, but Johnson knew better (Fox in fact was to lose by 12,000); "None," he wrote next to Fox's name. Other considerations might also influence Johnson's response. Montana incumbent James F. O'Connor, who was running well ahead in his district, had apparently antagonized someone in Washington. Johnson had promised him a contribution on the twenty-fourth, but had not sent it, and now O'Connor asked for $300. OPPOSITION USING . . . LOT OF MONEY TO ELECT REPUBLICAN IN MY PLACE, he said. IF HAVE HELP SURE CAN WIN. "None," Johnson wrote next to O'Connor's name. "Out."

Many of the candidates who responded received less than they had requested. Thomas R. Brooks telephoned the Munsey Building, telling one of Johnson's staff that he had a "slight edge," and said a scheduled election-eve visit to his heavily Norwegian district in Wisconsin by the Ambassador to Norway might pull him through—if he received money as well. He asked for $2,000, then lowered his request to $1,000 and, as the staffer noted, "finally came down to $500." Then he sent a wire: WHATEVER YOU CAN DO. "$250," Johnson wrote next to his name. C. Arthur Anderson, who "said he is in midst of a tough fight," had asked for $350. Receiving no immediate answer, he telephoned Johnson and reduced his request to $200. "$150," Johnson wrote beside his name.

Others did not fare that well. Francis T. Murphy said he had a "50–50" chance. He could win, he said, "by getting vote to polls in key wards," but money was needed to accomplish that. "None," Johnson wrote next to Murphy's name. C. H. Armbruster of Ohio asked for $1,000, but said he would take less; "urgent," he said. "None," Johnson wrote. "$1,000 would be a lifesaver," George W. Wolf wrote. "Two counties hold fate. . . . Hard battle." *None.*

Johnson's decision to cut off some candidates was not due to lack of funds. Most of the candidates who replied received at least a substantial portion of the amount they had requested. Scoop Jackson got $500 of the $750 he had requested, George B. Kelly $350 of the $400 for which he had asked. Some got all they had asked for. Rogers had asked for $500; "O.K.," Johnson wrote next to his name, "$500." Mitchell got his $600, Lee Guyer the $200 which enabled him to pay the printer. Some got more than they had requested—Myers of Pennsylvania $700 instead of the $500 for which he had asked, for example; Havenner of California $1,250—and in other instances Johnson did not wait for a candidate's request, but pressed funds upon him. J. Joseph Smith of Connecticut received a Johnson check—and the next day, November 2, a Johnson telegram: IF I CAN BE OF FURTHER HELP TO YOU IN THE LAST MINUTE RUSH, LET ME KNOW. Some, in fact, were given so much money that they asked Johnson to stop sending it. Michael Kirwan, who had told John McCormack on October 18 that he was "hard-pressed for money," had since received so much from Johnson—$200 on October 17, $500 on October 21, $350 more on October 24 (and these, of course, are only the contributions of which there is a written record)—that he replied to Johnson's telegram of the twenty-ninth by thanking him for "your offer of further assistance" but adding, "However, I believe I have sufficient to see me through." Charles H. Leavy of Washington had written on his questionnaire that he didn't need money; "Think I will be able to handle situation without outside help," he had said. Johnson had sent him $600 nonetheless. Now Johnson asked him how much more he needed—and Leavy replied by sending *him* a gift: a box of State of Washington apples.

ELECTION DAY. The day on which information—early information—was most precious, because a candidate, his fate riding on the ballots, is impatient for an early indication of a trend; because if he learns early enough that the vote is close, a last-minute effort to get out his voters can be mounted or intensified; and because, in states in which some portion of the vote is controlled (Illinois, with its controlled Republican votes in downstate counties and its controlled Democratic votes in Cook County, was a prime example), early information is helpful in preparing for the necessary late adjustment in the figures.

Washington's new source of information had geared up for Election Day. Sending out on October 29 his request for information on their finances to 175 Congressmen across the country, Lyndon Johnson had added a request for other information—early returns not only on their own races but on Franklin D. Roosevelt's—and ("if you do *everything* . . .") had followed that up in later telegrams, including one on the day itself.

He had let the White House know he would have information for it. Rowe already knew, of course, but as Rowe himself puts it, Johnson "never did anything through just one person." He was not well acquainted with Missy LeHand, and this was an excuse to communicate with her. He wired her that IF I FEEL THE INFORMATION IS OF SUFFICIENT INTEREST I WILL TAKE THE LIBERTY TO CALL THE PRESIDENT. FOR THAT REASON I AM LETTING YOU KNOW IN ADVANCE OF MY PLAN.

The information for which he had asked arrived—early, as he had asked. By 2:47 p.m. on Election Day, the first flash was in from Detroit. MICHIGAN FIRST DISTRICT VOTING HEAVY INDICATES BETTERING PREVIOUS DEMOCRATIC MAJORITY, Tenerowicz reported. By late afternoon, Western Union messengers were racing to the third floor of the Munsey Building in a steady stream. Other news came over the telephone; James Shanley of

Connecticut telephoned at 6:45 because, as he was to write, "I certainly wanted to give you the first news in Washington."

In the evening, the telegrams bore hard news. The first telegrams from other Detroit districts were less optimistic than Tenerowicz's: the figures in the initial communication from Representative George D. O'Brien were close—too close (104 PRECINCTS OUT OF 222 . . . O'BRIEN 28,700, MCLEOD 24,769), but just twenty-four minutes later, O'Brien could dictate another wire (140 DISTRICTS OUT OF 222 . . . O'BRIEN 39,797, MCLEOD 28,586). Some of the telegrams were tinged with jubilation as well as gratitude. Edouard Izac's last pre-election wire had told Johnson: ROOSEVELT SHOULD WIN BY 10,000 . . . MY PROSPECTS DOUBTFUL, but on election night, the wire from California said: APPARENTLY WINNING BY APPROXIMATELY 8,000. THANKS. . . . Some were not. John G. Green, who had thought up to the last minute that he might beat out incumbent Republican Bernard J. Gehrmann, wired: GEHRMANN APPARENTLY REELECTED. DAMN TIRED. At 2:37 a.m., a single brief line arrived from Ernest M. Miller in Harlan, Iowa: PRESENT PARTIAL RETURNS INDICATE MY DECISIVE DEFEAT. Jubilant or dejected, however, the telegrams, taken together, added up to a great deal of information.

On the evening of Election Day, Johnson wasn't at the Munsey Building, but at the spacious Georgetown home of Jim Rowe's brother-in-law, Alfred Friendly, where a crowded election-night party was in progress. His staff, back at the Munsey Building, was taking the reports as they came in, and telephoning them to Johnson there. Many more reports came in than Johnson had expected so early in the evening, and he telephoned Walter Jenkins and told him to come out to Friendly's house. Jenkins was installed in a bedroom, where he sat on the bed tabulating the incoming information.

Johnson and Rowe bantered back and forth throughout the evening in the easy and—then—quite close camaraderie that existed between them. They had several wagers—twenty-five cents each, as befitted two young men with no money to spare—riding on the returns. Rowe, reflecting the prevalent Washington thinking on the likely outcome of the congressional elections, had bet that the Democrats would lose at least thirty seats in the House; Johnson had bet that the Democrats would lose less than thirty. And the two tall young men, both in their early thirties, also bet on several individual races, while they waited for a call from Hyde Park.

For some hours, no call came.

In the house above the Hudson, crowded with family and friends, the President sat at the dining-room table, with news tickers clattering nearby and big tally sheets and a row of freshly sharpened pencils lined up in front of him.

"At first," as Burns has written in an unforgettable scene, "the President was calm and businesslike. The early returns were mixed. Morgenthau, nervous and fussy, bustled in and out of the room. Suddenly Mike Reilly,

the President's bodyguard, noticed that Roosevelt had broken into a heavy
sweat. Something in the returns had upset him. It was the first time Reilly
had ever seen him lose his nerve.

" 'Mike,' Roosevelt said suddenly. 'I don't want to see anybody in here.'

" 'Including your family, Mr. President?'

" 'I said anybody,' Roosevelt answered in a grim tone."

As the news tickers clattered feverishly, Franklin Roosevelt sat before
his charts with his jacket off, his tie pulled down, his shirt clinging damply
to his big shoulders. "Was this the end of it all?" Burns writes. "Better by
far not to have run for office again than to go down to defeat now." Would
his enemies beat him at last, "and write his epitaph in history as a power-
grasping dictator rebuked by a free people? . . . In the little black numbers
marching out of the ticker, not only Roosevelt but the whole New Deal was
on trial. . . . Still Willkie ran strong. Disappointing first returns were coming
in from New York. . . . The ash dropped from the cigarette; Mike Reilly
stood stolidly outside the door. Was this the end . . . ?

"Then there was a stir throughout the house. Slowly but with gathering
force, the numbers on the charts started to shift their direction. Reports
arrived of a great surge of Roosevelt strength. . . . By now Roosevelt was
smiling again, the door was opened, and in came family and friends. . . ."
And the President made a number of telephone calls—including one to Jim
Rowe and Lyndon Johnson.

The twenty-two-year-old Jenkins had been thrilled by other calls he
had been taking. "It was the most exciting night of my life," he would recall.
"I thought I was in the high cotton. All those big shots, you know," voices
on the telephone that had previously been only names in a newspaper. And
then the call from the biggest name of all. "Mr. Roosevelt called and asked
how many seats we were going to lose, and Mr. Johnson said, 'We're not going to lose. We're going to gain.' " He and Rowe got on extensions and talked
to the President. Recalls Rowe: "Johnson got good, early counts and we
both got on the telephone . . . and told him [Roosevelt] how many Congressmen we had elected, and it *was* impressive—a helluva lot of Congressmen.
And it impressed the hell out of Roosevelt. I remember that."

LESSER POLITICIANS were also impressed. Knowledgeable Democrats in
Washington had reluctantly reconciled themselves to the loss of a considerable number of seats in the House. Instead, they had gained eight (while
losing three in the Senate). "My father expected to lose," Ken Harding
recalls. "We were the most surprised people in the world when we didn't
lose."

Many of the men most directly affected—the Democratic candidates—
gave considerable credit for the surprise to Lyndon Johnson. Despite the
frenzy of the last days before the election, several candidates had taken

time out from their campaigning to write to express appreciation for the help
he had given them. "I want to thank you again from the very depths of my
heart for the interest you have taken in me, because of the confidence which
you have manifested and the effort you have put forth," Arthur Mitchell
wrote. Said Nan Honeyman: "As darling as I think it was of you I still was a
bit perturbed over your taking all the trouble to enlist the interest of the state
of Texas in my welfare. Really, darling, that was too good of you and of
them. How can I thank you? If I am elected I shall really owe the victory
to your efforts." After the election, similar letters were received at the
Munsey Building from scores of men who remembered the yellow rectangles
from Western Union that had arrived with the information, or the money,
they needed, and who wanted to thank the man who had sent them. "Before
you came to my rescue, I was really getting discouraged," John Kee of West
Virginia wrote. Thanking Johnson for the money he sent, John F. Hunter
of Ohio wrote, "We were able to put on some thirty short radio programs in
the last two days." Lansdale G. Sasscer of Maryland said, "I used it among
our colored vote very effectively both for the President and myself." "Certainly I never had such grand cooperation from the Congressional Committee before," wrote Draper Allen of Michigan. "This is . . . the first time I
have ever received any financial assistance from Washington, and I assure
you I deeply appreciate it." And some of the gratitude was expressed in a
form that must have been particularly pleasing to a man looking down a long
road. "Congratulations on your fine and successful work in the campaign,"
wrote Pat Morrison of South Dakota. "We look forward to the date, not too
far distant, when our delegation will be able to be of aid and assistance to
you." Says Walter Jenkins: There was a lot of gratitude among his colleagues
for what he had done. "I saw it in the phone calls and the letters. And the
feeling of respect. It built him up from being just—he was barely a first-term
Congressman—to probably the most . . ." Here Jenkins pauses and searches
for the right word; and finally says, "He was *the* hero." The same feeling was
expressed by observers less impressionable than Jenkins. Wrote Drew Pearson
and Robert S. Allen in their "Washington Merry-Go-Round" column:

> To the boys on the Democratic side of the House of Repre-
> sentatives, many of them still nervously mopping their brows over
> narrow escapes, the hero of the hair-raising campaign was no
> big-shot party figure.
> The big names got all the publicity, but in the House all the
> praise is for a youngster whose name was scarcely mentioned. But
> he left his mark on the battle—as GOP campaign managers will
> ruefully attest.
> Their Nemesis and the Democrats' unknown hero was
> Lyndon Baines Johnson, a rangy, 32-year-old, black-haired, hand-
> some Texan who has been in Congress only three years but who

has political magic at his fingertips and a way with him that is irresistible in action.

How Johnson took over the Democratic congressional campaign, when it looked as if the party was sure to lose the House, and without fanfare turned a rout into a cocky triumph, is one of the untold epics of the election.

Gratitude is an emotion as ephemeral in Washington as elsewhere, but Lyndon Johnson obtained from his work with the Democratic Congressional Campaign Committee a reward more lasting.

During those three weeks in the Munsey Building, his secretaries had compiled lists of Congressmen who had asked for money, and the amounts for which they had asked. And then the lists had been placed before Lyndon Johnson—for decisions. If Sam Rayburn or John McCormack requested a specific amount of money for a specific Congressman, Johnson would honor the request, but these requests were relatively infrequent. And except in those few cases, the decision as to which Congressman got money, and how much he got, would be Lyndon Johnson's decision. His alone. *O.K.*, he wrote next to some requests. *None*, he wrote next to others. "1,000 would be a lifesaver"—*None*. "An additional $300 will, I am sure, get results"—*None. Out.* The words and numbers he wrote on those lists were a symbol of a power he now possessed—over the careers of his colleagues. The power was a limited one—it was the power of the purse, and the purse was not a large one. Small though it might be in comparison to the purse which financed a presidential campaign, however, it was not small to most of the men whose campaigns it *was* financing; it was substantial in terms both of their needs and of their expectations. They needed its contents, needed it badly. What Lyndon Johnson wrote beside their names had played a role—a small role but a definite role—in determining their fates.

Returning to Washington after the election, Congressmen compared notes on their campaigns, and in these discussions the name of Lyndon Johnson kept coming up; when someone mentioned it to a freshman Congressman, Augustine B. Kelley of Pennsylvania, Kelley said: "Oh, Lyndon Johnson! He really had a lot to do with me getting elected. He sent money up to my campaign. He'd call up from Washington to see how we were getting along, and what we needed. 'Gus, what do you need?' And he sent me money, and kept up with my campaign." Listening to his colleagues talk, a Congressman who had received campaign funds from Johnson—funds on a scale unprecedented for a central Democratic congressional financing source—would realize that Johnson had contributed funds, on a similar scale, to scores of Congressmen. Through cloakrooms and Speaker's Lobby spread a realization that, in some way most of them did not understand, this young, junior, rather unpopular Congressman, a scant three years on the Hill, had become a source—an important source—of campaign funds.

For some of these funds—the money from Texas—he had, moreover, become the sole source. The telegrams candidates had received from Johnson announcing that funds were on the way had said they had been contributed by "my good Democratic friends in Texas." By *his* friends. The recipients did not know who those friends were—and even were they to find out, they could hardly ask these Texans with whom they were not even acquainted to contribute to their campaigns. Their only access to this new—and, apparently, substantial—source of money was through Lyndon Johnson. He controlled it. The money they needed could be obtained only through him.

They were going to need money again in 1942, of course, in less than two years. In 1942—and in succeeding years. Whether or not they liked Lyndon Johnson, they were going to need him. Not merely gratitude but an emotion perhaps somewhat stronger and more enduring—self-interest —dictated that they be on good terms with him.

This realization—and the reality behind it—abruptly altered Johnson's status on Capitol Hill. When Congress had left Washington in October, he had been just one Congressman among many. Within a short time after Congress returned in January, the word was out that he was a man to see, a man to cultivate. Harold E. Cole of Boston, a friend of John McCormack, had lost a close race, and was planning to run again. He hadn't learned until late in the campaign of Johnson's role in campaign funding, and he didn't want to make the same mistake again. He wrote Johnson asking if he could come to Washington and drop in and see him. Working closely with Johnson, Jim Rowe had understood what he was trying to accomplish with the money from Texas. "He was really trying to build a power base as a new Congressman," he says. And he succeeded. Ray Roberts, a Rayburn aide, says that Johnson had

> made lots of enemies [in Congress]. . . . He was brash, he was eager, . . . and he wanted people to move out of the way. . . . The thing that really gave him his power was becoming chairman of the congressional campaign committee. . . . There were some thirty or forty people [after the 1940 election] that figured they owed their seat in the House to Lyndon Johnson. Whenever he called on them, he could count on this group being for whatever he wanted.

Roberts' remark is an exaggeration. Lyndon Johnson controlled no Congressman that completely. As an analysis of the alteration in Johnson's status, however, Roberts' remark was in some respects an understatement. For it was not only junior Congressmen with no influence whom Johnson had helped.

During the campaign, John McCormack had been asking Lyndon Johnson for funds for his Massachusetts delegation and for old friends from other states—and for credit for himself from those other Congressmen for obtaining them. And Johnson had given the Majority Leader what he asked for. Now the Majority Leader owed him something. The situation was duplicated with other members of the House hierarchy. The William H. Sutphin of New Jersey who had pleaded with him for funds—and who had received in return $1,500—was the Assistant Majority Leader. Andrew J. May of Kentucky ("I hope you can do something for me, and I will owe you an undying debt of gratitude") was chairman of the Military Affairs Committee. Normally, young Congressmen were suppliants to the Majority Leader, or the Assistant Whip, or committee chairmen, for favors. In the case of this young Congressman, the situation had been reversed. The extent of the reversal was dramatized the first time the House Naval Affairs Committee met following the election. Normally, in a committee, seniority was the determining factor. When the Democrats moved into their seats this time, Johnson was still five seats away from the chairmanship. But three of the five men ahead of him in seniority owed him favors because of his contributions to their campaigns. He had been not only dealing with the most senior members of his party in the House, but dealing with them from a position of independent strength. When he asked Sam Rayburn and John McCormack to come to a luncheon meeting, they came.

Nor, during the campaign, had he dealt only with Congressmen. When he had asked labor leaders in New York to intervene in a strike in the State of Washington, he had been playing a national political role. And his work with powerful political figures across the country had not consisted merely of liaison work. There had been a "Chicago line." Precisely what it was, how Johnson operated through it, or how much he gave through it cannot be determined. But it had a connection with Chicago Boss Ed Kelly. By the end of the campaign, he had become acquainted with, had worked with—had funneled money through—some of the most powerful men in America. There was a New York connection, too. At first, the connection had been Tommy Corcoran; it was he who raised cash from New York garment-center leaders such as Hillman or Lubin or Dubinsky. But by the end of the campaign, Johnson was personally acquainted with them; several of them, in fact, were to become strong Johnson allies and generous Johnson financial backers. Men such as Kelly and Lubin were not without influence on Congressmen; after the 1940 campaign, Johnson was in a position to ask them to use that influence; a Congressman who would not respond to a Johnson request might receive a telephone call from his own home town. He even had a potential ally—if a low-level one—on the staff of the Democratic National Committee. Paul Aiken wrote to Johnson, "One of your chief boosters, Swagar Sherley, has been spending a lot of time with me in the last few days," and as a result Aiken would look Johnson up on his next trip to Washington. All these things combined to radically alter Johnson's status.

The alteration was apparent at Georgetown dinner parties, where he dozed off at table less frequently. His need to be the center of attention at parties had been thwarted by the degree to which, in Washington, attention was a function of power, but now, as Dale Miller puts it, "because of his political power," he was more often the center of attention. The alteration was apparent in the House cloakrooms and dining room, where, before the 1940 campaign, some fellow Representatives would snub Johnson, greeting other colleagues while ignoring him because, as one says, "they wouldn't put up with him." He still acted the same way in the House Dining Room, strolling through it nodding to left and right as if he were a visiting celebrity, "head-huddling," talking loudly. But his colleagues "put up with him" now. Symbolically, the shrinking away was much less evident. The fellow Congressman whose lapel he grasped while staring into his eyes and talking nose to nose was often a colleague who had appealed to him for help, and who had received that help—a colleague, moreover, who not only had needed him once, but who would need him again. A Congressman who was thinking about his next campaign didn't resent Lyndon Johnson's arm around his shoulders—he was all too happy to have it there. Before 1940, Johnson had never been shy about asking for favors, "irritating" colleagues by his insistence when he had no favors to do them in return. He was in position now to return favors—in a big way. And if other Representatives still felt irritated, they no longer allowed the irritation to show. Says one: "A lot of guys still didn't like him, but unlike before [the 1940 campaign], you tolerated his idiosyncrasies. Because you knew this guy was going somewhere. You knew—I don't think most of us knew how he had done it, but we knew he had done it—that he had already started going somewhere. A lot of guys still didn't like him, but they knew they might need him someday. Now he was a guy you couldn't deny any more."

THE NEW POWER he possessed did not derive from Roosevelt's friendship, or from Rayburn's. It did not derive from seniority in the House, nor even —despite the relationship that power in a democracy bears to the votes of the electorate—to his seat in it. His power was simply the power of money. To a considerable extent, the money was Herman Brown's. A single corporation, Brown & Root, may have given Democratic congressional candidates more money than they received from the Democratic National Committee. Lyndon Johnson had been attempting to, as Rowe puts it, "build a power base." He had succeeded. His power base wasn't his congressional district, it was Herman Brown's bank account. Although he was young, he had been seeking national power for years. Now the power of money had given him some.

Simultaneously, it had given a new kind of power to Texas—through him.

This was a significant aspect of his work in the 1940 campaign. Texas had had power in Washington for nine years—since Dick Kleberg's victory had given the Democrats control of the House in November, 1931, and John Garner had taken the Speaker's chair. But that power had been somewhat personal, and therefore in constant danger of vanishing. Much of it had been embodied in, and exercised through, Garner, leader of the Lone Star State's delegation and the key protector of the state's interests in Washington, not only because of his position but because of the power of his personality. The ephemeral nature of power based on individuals was vividly demonstrated by the fact that Cactus Jack was, abruptly, no longer even going to be present in Washington. Sam Rayburn's ascension to the Speakership and Texas' continuing hold on key committee chairmanships in both House and Senate meant that Texas still had power in the capital, but great as this power was, it could disappear in a day—Election Day. Because of Texas' predilection for keeping its Congressmen in office indefinitely, there was little fear that they themselves would lose some November, but their power rested on an overall Democratic majority in the House and Senate that depended on less reliable states. A Democratic loss would cost them their chairmanships and their power. And a Republican victory was not the only way in which Texas could lose power: a chairmanship could be lost through death, as Buchanan's death had cost Texas the key Appropriations post, and the key "Texas chairmanships" in the House were held by elderly men. In the world of the pork barrel and the log roll, Texas had a commanding position because of Joseph Jefferson Mansfield; let that elderly wheelchair-bound man die, and Texas' power over public works would vanish in the instant of his death. A chairmanship could be lost through individual ambitions; arrangements had, in fact, already been finalized for the Agriculture Committee's Marvin Jones to resign his House seat for a federal Judgeship immediately after the election. In 1932, Texas had held not only the Speakership but five key House chairmanships; Jones' departure would reduce the number to three.

Moreover, because, in a legislative body, personal relationships are so important, the effects of increased Republican strength would be for some period of years irreparable. A Republican victory would sweep out of office Congressmen with whom Texans had long and close alliances. The Democrats might return to a majority—but they might be different Democrats.

The power of money was less ephemeral than power based on elections or individuals. It could last as long as the money lasted, exerting its effect not only on an incumbent but on his successors. And there was enough oil in Texas so that it would last, in political terms, a long time. Lyndon Johnson had become the conduit for the oilmen's money. To the extent that he could remain the conduit, his power would endure.

And there was a lot more Texas money available than had been apparent in the 1940 campaign. Lyndon Johnson's base had been Herman Brown's money, but he had expanded that base by adding to Herman's cash, Sid Richardson's and Clint Murchison's. The extent of their wealth made his power base infinitely expandable. It could become a factor in campaigns other than those for members of the House of Representatives. It could exert more influence. To the extent that he remained in charge of its distribution, he could exert more influence. In terms of power in Washington, his power was still quite small, but if the amount of money at his command grew larger, his power might grow with it.

If journalists did not generally understand the reason for Johnson's new status, some of them were aware of it. Wrote Alex Louis, a correspondent for a Texas newspaper chain:

> When the United States Congress convenes for a new session in January, the familiar face of John Nance Garner will be missing for the first time in more than a third of a century. After a brilliant career as congressman, Speaker of the House, and Vice-President, the bushy-eyebrowed Westerner who rose to higher official position than any other Texan in history will be absent.
>
> Yet one of the eternal charms of politics is that as the old political oaks fall before the axe of retirement or death, sturdy new ones are rising in the forest to take their place. To many a Washington and Austin observer this winter, it seems that one of the sturdiest saplings in the forest—a young one which may grow into a mighty pillar of strength not only for Texas but for the American nation—is 32-year-old Congressman Lyndon B. Johnson of Johnson City.
>
> A member of Congress for the past three years, tall, dark-haired, handsome Lyndon Johnson already has won an enviable position in Democratic circles and national affairs.

A symbolic scene had dramatized Louis' analysis. John Garner's last Cabinet meeting—the end of his active political life in Washington—had been held on October 4, and at its conclusion the grizzled Vice President came up to the President and said, "Well, goodbye, Boss." He clapped the President on the shoulder with one hand and gripped him with the other, appearing, in Ickes' description, "to be a very pleasant fellow indeed, saying farewell to a man to whom he was deeply attached." Then he turned and walked out of the room. Ickes was a witness to the farewell because he had been waiting "after Cabinet" to have a word with the President. The word was on behalf of Lyndon Johnson; at the time, Johnson had not yet been given a role in the national congressional campaign, and he had asked Ickes to urge Roosevelt to give him one. Roosevelt had already decided to do so, and he

told Ickes this. In the very moment in which the old Texan was making his
exit from the national political scene, therefore, arrangements were being
made for the entrance onto the national stage of a younger representative
of the great province in the Southwest.

LYNDON JOHNSON'S WORK with Democratic congressional candidates had
in effect added a new factor to the equation of American politics. The concept of financing congressional races across the country from a single central
source was not new, but the Democrats had seldom if ever implemented
the concept on the necessary scale or with the necessary energy. "No one
before had ever worked at it," James Rowe says. "Johnson worked at it like
hell. People running for Congress in those days never had much money; it had
been that way for years, but Lyndon decided to do something about it; he
got in it with both feet, the way he did everything, and he raised a hell of a
lot of money." In effect, says Robert S. Allen, "he was being a one-man
national committee for congressmen"—an apt analogy; although he was
ostensibly "assisting" the Democratic Congressional Campaign Committee,
his connection with that body consisted almost entirely of the checks he
brought to it; otherwise, working out of his own office and with his own staff,
he operated entirely on his own. The scale of money he raised for congressional races was unusually large for his party; his involvement in other
aspects of congressional races—liaison with the White House, and, through
the White House, with other government departments; furnishing candidates
with information—was unprecedentedly active. Almost incredibly—although
confirmed by the surviving Congressmen of that era—so was the coordination
and financing of speakers' tours that he undertook. As to the liaison between
candidates and White House on approval of public works and other governmental projects, this had not been undertaken on a similar scale even by the
better-organized Republicans, possibly because under Republican Presidents,
in the pre–New Deal era, the federal government had not sponsored public-
works projects on the broad-scale basis that existed in 1940. Nor had the
liaison-in-reverse that he undertook: the use of Congressmen as sources of
information, the rapid collecting of their information, its collating and dispatch to the White House. By the 1980's, when Democratic and Republican
congressional committees would be large-scale operations that furnished services and money to candidates, it would be difficult to imagine an era in
which most Congressmen were left to fight their campaigns without significant
help from their national party, but before Lyndon Johnson, that was, certainly in the case of the Democrats and to some extent in the case of Republicans, largely the practice. Discussing what Lyndon Johnson did in the campaign of 1940, James Rowe says flatly: "Nobody had ever done this before."

.   .   .

A HALLMARK OF JOHNSON'S CAREER had been a lack of any consistent ideology or principle, in fact of any moral foundation whatsoever—a willingness to march with any ally who would help his personal advancement. His work with the congressional campaign committee brought this into sharper focus. Because Democratic congressional candidates in the one-party South had no opposition in the November elections, he was providing money only to Democrats in the North—who were primarily liberals. But the money came from men who were not liberals. Some of them, in fact, were arch-conservatives; among the "Texas friends" who had provided funds for Lyndon Johnson to distribute were men who would be bankrollers in 1944 of the "Texas Regulars," Texans who bolted the party rather than support Roosevelt. He was helping New Dealers with the money of men who hated the New Deal.

In dealing with these men, Johnson did not make the slightest effort to paper over this conflict in his fund-raising efforts, nor was it necessary for him to do so. Political philosophy played not the smallest role in his appeals for money. During the next congressional campaign in 1942, after Ed Flynn had again attempted to freeze him out but had again been thwarted by Johnson's control over Texas money (replied oilman G. L. Rowsey to a Flynn plea for funds: "My delay in replying is due to the fact that I expected to be in contact with our congressman, Honorable Lyndon Johnson . . . I desire to know his wishes in this matter and to make my contribution to or through him"), Johnson, exasperated by Rayburn's continued failure to understand the new realities, wrote the Speaker that "these $200 driblets will not get the job done." What was needed, Johnson said, was to "select a 'minute man' group of thirty men, each of whom should raise $5,000, for a total of $150,000. . . . This should be done between now and next Wednesday. . . . There isn't any reason why, with the wealth and consideration that has been extended, we should fall down on this." The logic behind that advice was the logic of Mark Hanna. Mobilizing the business community against the threat of Bryan and the populist philosophy embodied in his candidacy, the Boss of Ohio raised political contributions to a new level in 1896 by transforming campaign financing, in the words of his biographer, "from a matter of political begging . . . into a matter of systematic assessment according to the means of the individual and institution," an assessment in which each great insurance company, railroad and bank would "pay according to its stake in the general prosperity of the country. . . ." "Dollar Mark" made campaign financing, in other words, a political levy upon wealth based straightforwardly upon gratitude. For past government help in acquiring that wealth and upon the hope of future government protection of that wealth, and of government assistance in adding to it. Johnson's fund-raising, not being for a presidential race, was on a much smaller scale than Hanna's, but it was based on the same naked philosophy of pure self-interest: "the wealth and consideration that has been extended." And, as had been true in the case of Hanna, who raised millions more for a presidential campaign than had ever been raised

before, Johnson's logic was irresistible to those—oilmen and contractors—
at whom it was directed. His confidence that the $150,000 could be raised in
five days was justified; it was, and it was distributed just as rapidly to those
candidates Johnson selected.

IF HERMAN BROWN regarded the campaign contributions he funneled
through Lyndon Johnson as an investment, he received a healthy return on it.

Neither Herman nor his brother George had ever seen a ship being
built. "We didn't know the stern from the aft—I mean the bow—of the boat,"
George recalls. Nonetheless, in 1941, at about the time that their Corpus
Christi Naval Air Station contract was rising toward $100,000,000, the
brothers were awarded a lucrative Navy contract to build four subchasers.
(The brothers established a new corporate entity for the purpose: says
George, "They needed a name to put on the contract, and I said, 'Brown
Shipbuilding.' That was all there was to it.") When the Japanese attacked
Pearl Harbor, the four subchasers were not yet completed, but a Navy De-
partment official told the brothers, "We'll put you in the destroyer business."
During the war, Brown Shipbuilding—under contracts with provisions so
favorable that profits were all but guaranteed—would carry out $357,000,000
worth of work for the Navy.

AND WHAT OF THE RETURN reaped by the oilmen on an investment in Lyndon Johnson that, as years passed, was to grow and grow? What did they
want from government?

They wanted a lot: not only continuation of the oil depletion allowance
and of other tax benefits, and of exemption from federal regulation but new
benefits, and new exemptions—and other new, favorable, government policies. As the future will demonstrate, they wanted government favoritism on a
scale so immense that it would become a significant factor in the overall
political and economic development of the United States.

In 1940, they had not yet achieved what they wanted. But they were
asking too early, that was all.

Lyndon Johnson wasn't their Senator yet.

33

Through the Back Door

IN ORDER TO REAP THE FULLEST BENEFITS from his work with the Democratic Congressional Campaign Committee, Johnson kept working after Election Day. Among the implements he employed were letters—letters with the Johnson touch. These letters, written to powerful officials, all shared a single theme: each official was told that it was he—and he alone—who had made it possible for Johnson to participate in the 1940 campaign. Each official was thanked—humbly, gratefully—for giving a young man his great opportunity. And each official was flattered—with flattery custom-tailored by a master of the art.

Johnson had noticed how entranced Henry Wallace had been at Longlea by his stories about Texas. To the Vice President-elect, Johnson wrote:

> When Texas was fighting for its independence there were several squirrel-shooters from the hill country who heard the news and wanted to get into Sam Houston's army.
>
> They couldn't find Old Sam himself, because he was busy outmaneuvering the enemy, leading him into a trap. But they had friends who took them in hand, set them out over the right trails and landed them at San Jacinto where they could witness the action and, in their small way, participate.
>
> I am a successor of some of those squirrel-shooters and in 1940, 104 years afterwards, I was in a similar quandary. Not very strong, but smarting to add my few grains of powder to the battle fire.
>
> I have not forgotten that you showed me the right trail and helped set me out on it.
>
> With congratulations, and assurances of my confidence in and affection for you,
>
> Sincerely,
> Lyndon Johnson

John McCormack had a tradition *he* was proud of—the Massachusetts tradition, which included Bunker Hill—and to the Majority Leader, Johnson wrote: "You helped me get in line and to see the whites of a few enemy eyes. I shall not forget it." ("Until I ran across you," Johnson also wrote, "it looked . . . as if the undersigned Texas boy from the hill country wasn't going to be able to get in with his few rounds. . . . The big guns were all roaring [and] I didn't know whether I was going to find a loop-hole through which to point my muzzle-loader.") The key to Sam Rayburn was the Speaker's protective, paternal feeling for young men who depended on him, and Johnson wrote Rayburn (after telling him that it was only through "your good offices that I had the chance" to participate in the campaign) that some young Congressmen "would have been out in the bitter winter wind without firewood if you and other veteran hands hadn't pitched in, accomplished the necessary and effected their rescue." Letters from this prince of flatterers went not only to men who, like McCormack, had indeed helped him get into the fight, but to men who—as he was well aware—had tried to keep him out of it; to Ed Flynn, he sent a letter of "felicitation and appreciation."

The fighters in the ranks give thanks not only for the victory but for the leadership which brought them the victory. As one of the infantrymen, I rejoice in the victory, and in my officers who arranged it.

And I thank you warmly for your consideration, in the midst of an incredibly busy time—consideration which made it possible for me to get in my few licks.

Call on me at any time I can do anything and remember me. . . .

The most important of these letters began with the simple salutation: "Sir," and told Franklin Roosevelt:

There wasn't much I could do to help when the battle of 1940 was raging, although I smarted to do *something*.

I know I should have been utterly out in the cold except for your good offices. You made it possible for me to get down where I could whiff a bit of the powder, and this note is to say "Thank you." It was grand. The victory is perfect.

During the 1940 campaign, Roosevelt and Johnson had had several discussions. Now they were to have more. The President and the young man talked together in the Oval Office—one can only imagine Lyndon Johnson's feelings during those conversations in that bright, sunny room in which he had for so many years longed to sit. And they talked together in the upstairs, private, quarters of the White House. Johnson had breakfast in Roosevelt's spartan bedroom, the President sitting up in bed with a blue Navy cape around his shoulders. He had lunch in the President's private study, a comfortable room with chintz-covered furniture and walls so full of naval paintings that they seemed almost papered with them, dining with Franklin D. Roosevelt off a bridge table. Johnson, describing the President as a lonely man whose wife was often traveling, is quoted as saying, "He'd call me up" and "I used to go down sometimes and have a meal with him."

External evidence reveals that one subject they were discussing was Texas, for Roosevelt was, more and more, making Johnson his man in that state: the individual through whom political matters relating to Texas were cleared. These included minor details seemingly far removed from Johnson's immediate interest. A note requesting a letter of presidential greetings for an East Texas banker was referred by the President not to Sam Rayburn or Jesse Jones—or to the banker's Congressman, Lindley Beckworth—but to Johnson, with a covering note: "Do you think this is all right to do?" (Johnson's suggested reply was followed exactly.) And they included matters not minor at all, and very close to Johnson's heart. With Garner departed, and Rayburn tarred, Johnson's major remaining rival for the role of the President's man in Texas was Reconstruction Finance Corporation Chairman Jesse Jones. A symbolic confrontation came on Jones' own turf: financing that involved RFC bonds. The bonds in question were those of Alvin Wirtz's Lower Colorado River Authority, $21 million of which had been purchased by the RFC to help the Authority get under way. Superlatively safe investments (because the Authority's now ample revenues were pledged, through unbreakable bond covenants, to pay the interest and amortization), highyielding, tax exempt—these bonds were coveted by investors; "I think every bond house in the United States is waiting to get its hands on the Lower Colorado River Authority bonds," Wirtz was to write to Johnson. Wirtz had his own, favored, bond house in mind, but Jones had another, and he had the power to sell the bonds to whom he chose—and was about to exercise that power when, at a Cabinet meeting, the President handed him a scribbled note:

Private

J.J.

Don't sell the Lower Colorado River Auth. bonds without talking with Father.

                                                            FDR

"What this meant was that some moocher had been to see the President, looking for an inside deal," Jones wrote in his memoirs, "meddlers wanting to muscle in for a little private smoosh." He also wrote that he defied the

President and sold the bonds to the highest bidder, but in fact Roosevelt's intervention dissuaded him from making the sale he had intended, and eventually the bonds, and the "smoosh," went to the firm favored by Wirtz and Johnson. What else Roosevelt and Johnson talked about we don't know, just as we don't know how often they actually talked alone. Did they talk politics—this master of politics who had persuaded a mighty nation to grant him ultimate power for an unprecedented span and this wonder kid of politics who was searching for every possible handhold on the path to power? Did they talk personalities, these two matchless readers of—and manipulators of—men? No one really knows. All we know is their reaction to their discussions, reactions revealed to others. Lady Bird Johnson says her husband saw Roosevelt "often." She says, "I of course know nothing" about what transpired between them at these meetings, "but I know the mood they left him [her husband] in—which was one of high excitement. . . . Every time he came from the White House, he was on a sort of high." As for Roosevelt, he was convinced—quite firmly convinced—that the young Congressman believed in the things he himself believed in. Moreover, Franklin Roosevelt's initial impression of Lyndon Johnson—the feeling that he was "a most remarkable young man"—had evidently been reinforced by familiarity; in the opinion of James Rowe, the presidential aide with the best opportunity to observe the interplay between Roosevelt and Johnson, the principal reason for the growing rapport between the two men was the President's belief that Johnson was not only committed but capable. "Johnson was in many ways just more capable than most of the people Roosevelt saw. We're talking about a very capable man. . . . You've got to remember that they were two great political geniuses." The President told Anna Rosenberg Hoffman, who worked in congressional liaison for the White House: "I want you to work with that young Congressman from Texas, Lyndon Johnson. He's a comer, and he's a real liberal." The President tendered Johnson the ultimate compliment. He told Harold Ickes that Johnson was "the kind of uninhibited young pro he would have liked to have been as a young man"— and might have been "if he hadn't gone to Harvard." And, Ickes recounted, Roosevelt had also said "that in the next generation the balance of power would shift south and west, and this boy could well be the first Southern President."

With older men who possessed power, Johnson had always been "a professional son"—utterly deferential ("Yes, sir," "No, sir"). Was this a technique that he employed on Roosevelt, and that endeared him to the President? "The only man I think he never quarreled with was Roosevelt, and maybe that was because he [Roosevelt] was always President," Rowe says. With older men, moreover, he was always the most attentive of listeners. Was this a quality that endeared him to a man who loved to talk—and who, lonely, needed someone to talk to? Or was the crucial quality ability— that rare ability so many older men recognized? The reasons for the rapport between the President and the young Congressman were, Rowe emphasizes, "complicated." Johnson, Rowe says, "used" Roosevelt "when he could." And, he says, "Roosevelt knew he was being used." But whatever the reasons, the rapport was there—and it was deep.

EVER SINCE HE HAD ARRIVED in Washington nine years before, Lyndon Johnson had, first as a congressional secretary and then as a Congressman, been touching every base: cultivating not only bureaucrats, but their secretaries and their assistants, and their assistants' assistants, and *their* secretaries, until entire government bureaus knew him, liked him—wanted to do things for him. He used the same technique with members of the White House staff.

The basis of their friendliness toward him was their belief that he loved their chief as they did. The White House was "filled with the fierce loyalty and warm affection that he [Roosevelt] inspired," Robert E. Sherwood wrote. "If you could prove possession of these sentiments in abundance, you were accepted as a member of the family and treated accordingly." Marvin McIntyre, the "soft touch" among the presidential secretaries, had long been convinced that Johnson was a devout Roosevelt worshipper, but General Edwin M. ("Pa") Watson, the presidential secretary who was now in charge of appointments and was therefore official guardian of the door to the Oval Office, was, behind his amiable exterior, a much tougher customer, and had for a long time been notably immune to the Johnson charm. Now Pa, too, had been completely won over—as was demonstrated by a remark he made when Jim Rowe was attempting to persuade him to give another Congressman a few minutes of the President's time. "Is he like Lyndon?" Pa asked. "Is he a perfect Roosevelt man?" Friendly with two presidential secretaries, Johnson didn't neglect the third, cultivating Stephen T. Early at every opportunity.

He didn't neglect anyone in the White House. The fight against Garner had certified his *bona fides* with Missy LeHand, Roosevelt's longtime personal secretary. But Missy had an assistant, Grace Tully, who took most of the President's dictation. She was a fortyish spinster, and Johnson had always had particular success winning the friendship of such women; now he devoted a great deal of effort to winning Miss Tully's, sometimes stopping by her apartment on Connecticut Avenue and giving her a lift to work. The effort was successful; so fond was she of him and so convinced of his loyalty to the man she was to call "one of the great souls of history" that she would later suggest (with a rather dramatic misunderstanding of Johnson's ambitions) that he be made a presidential secretary.

This determination to "touch every base" paid dividends. Pa Watson guarded only the front door to the Oval Office. There was a "back door," too. This was the door to the small, cluttered office—on the opposite side of the Oval Office from Watson's—that was shared by LeHand and Tully. Visitors Roosevelt wanted to see without the knowledge of the press—"off-the-record" guests, in the parlance of the White House inner circle—would use this door, entering the White House by an unfrequented side entrance, then going up the back stairs to Missy's office, to be ushered into the President's presence by her. This door was used as well by knowledgeable young White House staffers, because the two personal secretaries possessed virtually unlimited access to the President; "everyone had to go through Pa—except Missy and Grace," Corcoran recalls. If one of these two women knew Roosevelt was alone, she could bring someone in for a quick moment's discussion in which the President could give him the decision or guidance he needed, "so if Pa wouldn't let you in, you went around back to Grace, and she or Missy got you in." A refinement of this procedure was also employed. If Rowe, say, or one of the President's five other administrative assistants (the men with a "passion for anonymity" whose offices were across narrow West Executive Avenue in the old State, War, and Navy Building) asked Watson for an appointment with the President, he might be told that the schedule was filled, but that Watson would try—no guarantees—to fit him in between appointments if he wanted to wait with other visitors in his spacious anteroom. "And you'd sit there," says Rowe, "and if Pa wouldn't let you in fast enough, you'd go out and go around back to Missy [and ask her], 'When do I get in? I've got to talk to the President.' Then you'd go back and sit in Pa's office again, and Missy would tell Roosevelt, and he would tell Pa, 'I need to talk to Jim Rowe. Get him, will you?' And Pa would say, 'He's right here.' It was a game." This version of the game was used frequently by those of the young men the two women were fond of. "I learned —I always went in through the back door," Rowe says. "And Lyndon got in like me—through the back door." Fond though Watson was of Johnson, Pa was a vigilant guardian of the President's time, and had Johnson asked for more than occasional bits of it, he might easily have worn out his welcome with the General. So he used the more informal route—which is one reason his name seldom appears in the White House logs that chronicle the President's official visitors.

Touching every base paid off in another way as well. The arrogant Corcoran habitually had Missy LeHand take him into the Oval Office, and didn't bother paying much attention to other members of the presidential secretariat. But in 1941, for reasons never explained, Roosevelt dropped Tommy the Cork, and because Miss LeHand suffered a stroke, there was no one to get him in through the back door to repair the damage. One of the reasons that the break between the two men couldn't be restored, Rowe suggests, was the fact that Corcoran "always went through Missy, and Missy died." Lyndon Johnson would never make such a mistake. He had taken care to be friends not only with Miss LeHand but with her assistant, and LeHand's illness did not close the back door to him; in fact, it was more open than ever, for Grace Tully was in some ways the easiest mark for the Johnson charm of anyone on Roosevelt's staff, and she was very useful to him.

Not only would he personally hand to her a memo that he wanted the President to see, so that she could put it on top of the pile, but he would, Rowe says, "*tell* Grace something that he didn't want to put in a memo. He would say, 'Grace, will you tell him_____? But don't take any notes, and don't tell anyone else.' "

He didn't work only through Tully, of course; he didn't have to, so long as Rowe was his friend. Often, he would visit Rowe in his office; sometimes —since the President would be more likely to read a memo from Rowe than from him—his purpose would be to obtain Rowe's imprimatur on a Johnson proposal; "he would come over, for example, if there was a memo he wanted to make sure Roosevelt saw; he would say, 'I can't write. You write it. You do it for both of us.' Johnson was a great man for 'Jim Rowe and I think . . .' " Rowe and Johnson were quite close now; their late-afternoon telephone conversations had become almost a custom, one that was not interrupted even when Johnson was in Texas—although when he initiated a long-distance call, he took care to have his secretary reverse the charges. (Once, when a secretary neglected to do so in advance, Johnson told her that if she couldn't make some *ex post facto* arrangement to have the White House pay for the thirty-minute call, she would have to pay for it herself.) When Rowe didn't hear from Johnson for a few days, he missed him; once he dropped Johnson a note: "There has been a deadly silence around here for some time. Miss Gilligan [Rowe's secretary] says it makes this office very dull. I got so worried about it last week I called to see if you had fallen in front of a train. I was relieved to find you were only in Texas." And close as he was to Rowe —and hard as he worked to maintain that closeness—Rowe was not the only one of the President's six administrative assistants he was cultivating. When he ran up the stairs that pierced the forest of columns on the towering, grotesque façade of the State, War, and Navy Building, and then ran up an inside flight of stairs to "Death Row," as the administrative assistants had dubbed their line of offices on the second floor, he might be heading for any of the six offices. And no matter which one he was heading for, he could be sure of a warm welcome in it.

Part VI

DEFEAT

34

"Pass the Biscuits, Pappy"

SHORTLY AFTER DAYLIGHT on April 9, 1941, the telephone rang in the Johnsons' Washington apartment. Walter Jenkins was telephoning from the police desk at the front door of the Cannon Building, where, he told Lyndon Johnson, he had just heard a startling piece of news: during the night, Morris Sheppard, the senior United States Senator from Texas, had died of a stroke.

"Well, I won't be in this morning," Johnson said.

Under Secretary of the Interior Alvin Wirtz was also awakened early that morning. His secretary, Mary Rather, got to their offices at Interior unusually early because she had heard the news, but when she opened the door to Wirtz's private office, there he was, already sitting at his desk. "Are you thinking what I'm thinking?" he asked. Soon he and Johnson were mapping strategy for a Johnson campaign to fill the seat that Sheppard had held for twenty-seven years.

The principal obstacle to Johnson's candidacy was the one that had confronted him in his race for the House four years before: most voters had never heard of him. The voters of his Tenth Congressional District knew him, of course, and so did the voters of the Fourteenth, which he had earlier served as a congressional secretary. But in the state's other nineteen congressional districts, his name was all but unknown. Shortly after Sheppard's death, an East Texas radio station asked its listeners to send in postcards indicating the name of their favorite candidate. Not one of the hundreds of replies bore the name of Lyndon Johnson.

There were, moreover, potential candidates whose names were household words throughout Texas: the state's Governor, W. Lee O'Daniel; its youthful Attorney General, Gerald C. Mann; Congressman Martin Dies, chairman of the House Committee on Un-American Activities. A Belden

Poll—the Texas version of the Gallup Poll—taken shortly after Sheppard's death showed that 33 percent of the state's voters favored O'Daniel in a Senate race, 26 percent Mann, 9 percent Dies—and 5 percent Johnson.

Johnson's best hope of overcoming this handicap was the same strategy that had worked so well in 1937: linking his name with the name that was still magic in the state; just six months before, Franklin D. Roosevelt had crushed Willkie in Texas by a margin of more than four to one. Strong reasons existed for the President's active support of a liberal in the special election that would be held to fill Sheppard's seat. He obviously didn't want either Dies, the Garner protégé whose committee had begun investigating New Deal agencies, or the conservative, isolationist O'Daniel in the Senate; a memo circulating in the White House warned that the election of either is a possibility "too frightful for contemplation." But there was also a reason—a very strong reason—why the liberal should not be Lyndon Johnson but Gerald Mann.

Mann was an ardent New Dealer; although he had never met the President, "Gerry was a Roosevelt *worshipper,*" an aide recalls. He had, in fact, worked for Johnson in 1937 because of Johnson's all-out support of the New Deal. And Mann had a much better chance to win than Johnson did.

A small-town boy who worked on farms and in a local hotel to earn money to attend Southern Methodist University in Dallas, the slender, speedy back was twice named to all-conference football teams and became famous throughout Texas as SMU's "Little Red Arrow." He possessed three enthusiasms somewhat rare among politicians: for God, for poetry and for the law as an abstract force that could promote the general good. Determined to study at the best law school in the country, he took his wife and baby son to Melrose, Massachusetts, where, while commuting to Harvard Law School, he worked two shifts a day in a garment factory—until parishioners of the Congregationalist Church in Gloucester, impressed by the Sunday School sermons of the intense, handsome young man, made him their pastor. Thanks to football, he had entered politics with a statewide reputation, and in public office he had burnished it. Returning to Texas from Harvard, he had become one of Governor James Allred's Assistant Attorney Generals and had produced some notably progressive legislation (including a revision of Sam Johnson's now-outdated "Blue Sky Law"), and then had been Ed Clark's predecessor as Secretary of State. In 1938, at the age of thirty-one, he had run for Attorney General. Finishing second to an experienced and popular politician in the first primary, Mann overtook him in the run-off and beat him by an astonishing 130,000 votes. Replacing the political hacks in the Attorney General's office with bright young lawyers, Mann raised its notoriously low standards, waged what Texas historian Seth McKay calls "continuous war" against loan sharks and usurious finance companies and, most significantly, instituted strict enforcement of the state's anti-trust laws, hitherto all but ignored by state administrations subservient to business interests. During his first two-year term, scores of anti-trust suits were filed, and a substantial portion were won. So popular was he that when, in 1940, he ran for re-election, no one ran against him. Thirty-four years old, already twice elected to statewide office, he was in 1941 by far the best-known and most-respected young public official in Texas. "A brilliant career was predicted for him in Texas politics," McKay writes. And when Sheppard died, several of the state's leading newspapers spontaneously joined in asking him to run for the Senate. O'Daniel had said he wasn't running; if the immensely popular Governor entered the race, Mann had the best chance to beat him. If O'Daniel stayed out, a Belden Poll showed, he would beat Dies, although the vote would be close. The only way Dies could win, in fact, was if another New Dealer—such as Lyndon Johnson—entered the race, and split the New Deal vote.

A little deceit was necessary to offset this reasoning. Roosevelt and the White House staff knew little about the internal politics of Texas, of course—as had been amply demonstrated the year before. In 1941, as in 1940, most of the information given to the President about Texas came from Johnson and Wirtz, and from Johnson's admirers on the White House staff (whose information of course came mostly from him). This information was not strictly accurate. The President was told that Mann possessed neither guaranteed loyalty to the New Deal nor the statewide reputation necessary to defeat Dies (or O'Daniel, should the Governor choose to run); a Johnson-inspired memo told Roosevelt that Mann was "unbranded and unknown."

Several influential Texans, including Senator Tom Connally, tried to explain the true situation to Roosevelt, but the President's fondness for Johnson predisposed him to be convinced by his arguments. Roosevelt, who had, following the 1938 "purge" attempt, re-adopted his pose of never intervening in an intrastate Democratic fight, orchestrated a scenario designed to show—without his actually saying so—that he was intervening in this one. He arranged for Johnson to see him on April 22, just before his regular Tuesday press conference, so that arriving reporters would see Johnson emerging from the Oval Office. While the reporters watched, Johnson announced his candidacy from the White House steps, saying he would campaign "under the banner of Roosevelt." And when the reporters, crowding into the Oval Office, asked the President if he had given Johnson permission to wave that banner, Roosevelt replied: "First, it is up to the people of Texas to elect the man they want as their Senator; second, everybody knows that I cannot enter a primary election; and third, to be truthful, all I can say is Lyndon Johnson is a very old, old friend of mine." Then, as *Time* magazine put it, the "correspondents laughed, and he laughed with them." F.D.R. PICKS JOHNSON TO DEFEAT DIES, said the headline in the *Dallas Morning News*.

In 1941 as in 1937, therefore, the Johnson campaign consisted of a single issue: "Roosevelt. Roosevelt. Roosevelt." That issue was emphasized in the candidate's speeches. What America needed, he said, was "Roosevelt and unity—unity under one management, and for a common purpose: saving America from the dangers ahead; united behind Roosevelt, we'll save America from the threat of slavery by the Axis." If he was elected, he said, he would be "100 percent for Roosevelt," "an all-out Roosevelt Senator," "just a private under my Commander-in-Chief." The issue was symbolized by his campaign emblem: the picture of Roosevelt and Johnson shaking hands on the Galveston dock at their first meeting four years before. In that picture, then-Governor Allred had been standing between the two men, but now he was airbrushed out. What remained was two tall, smiling men shaking hands across the empty space where Allred had once stood. This image was used in countless brochures and campaign newspapers. And, painted larger than life, it was plastered on thousands of billboards along highways the length and breadth of Texas—and not only the busy roads leading into Dallas and Houston and El Paso; the state's great empty spaces were not ignored; before a driver speeding across the vast, flat plains of West Texas or the Panhandle, those two huge figures shaking hands, painted dark against a red-white-and-blue background, would loom up against the sky, miles ahead. The issue was summed up in the campaign's slogan, which had originally been a private password used with a grin among the Chief's NYA boys who were out campaigning for him, but which was so catchy that it quickly became the campaign's public motto as well, appearing in new editions of the brochures and campaign newspapers—and on hundreds of thousands of hastily printed red-white-and-blue bumper stickers, simple and to the point: FRANKLIN D AND LYNDON B!

This time, the man whose name Johnson was invoking played an active role in the race. Ignorance of Texas politics may partially explain Roosevelt's original decision to support Johnson, but it does not explain the extent or the enthusiasm of his support. As if his press-conference hint had not been sufficiently broad, leaks went out from the White House to sympathetic columnists. "Roosevelt has a fatherly interest in young Johnson," Pearson and Allen wrote. Said Alsop and Kintner:

> Although overburdened with the huge war effort and facing the gravest decision in this country's history, the President still takes a personal interest in the campaign of his protégé, Representative Lyndon B. Johnson. . . . Intimates disclose that the President and his small group of advisors are receiving regular reports on the campaign and that the President has lost none of his determination to give Johnson every aid. . . . As much as any candidate in recent years Johnson is running under the White House banner.

The President's support went beyond hints and leaks. Johnson wanted Vice President Wallace's aide Harold H. Young, the burly, brilliant Dallas attorney, seconded to his campaign for its duration. The Vice President refused to let Young go; the President intervened, and when Johnson flew down to Texas to open the campaign, Young was sitting beside him on the plane. Johnson had asked which Department of Agriculture officials could best help him, and Roosevelt apparently said he would find out. Informed that they were Milo Perkins, Maston White and Assistant Secretary of Agriculture Grover Hill, the President sent Rowe a memo: "Will you pass the word on to Lyndon Johnson and do the necessary." The necessary was a direct order to the three men, delivered by Rowe, to give Johnson any help he wanted.

Rowe had been designated liaison between the White House and Johnson's camp. One of his first tasks was to ensure that Johnson received credit for all federal spending in Texas. He says: "Word went out—from me—to all departments, all departments in Washington: no projects approved for Texas unless Lyndon Johnson is notified." In cases in which Rowe did not possess sufficient forcefulness, a more forceful man stepped in. Thomas Corcoran wouldn't be "White House Tommy" much longer, but in April, 1941, he could still use the magic words that had given him that nickname, and he used them on behalf of Lyndon Johnson. On the very day Johnson left for Texas, he requested approval of a certain Rural Electrification project, asking for its approval before he left. An REA official said such rapid action was simply impossible. The phone rang in the official's office: "This is Tommy Corcoran at the White House. Congressman Johnson wants this today, and the White House wants him to have it today." Not only had Rowe, Corcoran and other Roosevelt aides been told to help Johnson, but their fondness for Johnson, and their fear of an O'Daniel (or Dies) victory made them eager to help him; Harold Ickes took the trouble to telephone Dies' hometown himself to check on whether the Congressman had paid his real-estate taxes. "Everybody was helping him," Rowe says. "And I'm thinking of all the liberals, all the way." Their feelings are summed up in a memorandum from Pa Watson, who felt Lyndon was the "perfect Roosevelt man"; on a letter from a Texas politician critical of Johnson, Watson wrote: "Referred to Sec. Ickes for his perusal and then the ash-can."

The on-the-scene beneficiary of all this help was Walter Jenkins, who had been left behind in Washington when John Connally and Herbert Henderson left for Texas to work in the campaign. When Johnson needed something from the federal agencies, it was Jenkins who had to visit the officials involved. The shy twenty-three-year-old had no experience doing this. "I had been answering mail," he says—filling constituents' requests for farming pamphlets—when he wasn't directing tourists around the Cannon Building in his guard's uniform. Suddenly, he had to deal with Steve Early, Missy LeHand, Grace Tully, Jim Rowe and the legendary Corcoran. When Johnson told him his new assignment, he was at first "scared, nervous." But, he says, "I received a wonderful reception—it was just unbelievable to me."

Tommy the Cork couldn't have been nicer: "I talked to him lots of times. He was still very powerful, and when you asked him something, he could do it." Even the Old Curmudgeon was nice. Once, Johnson told Jenkins to see Secretary Ickes personally about some matter too sensitive to be broached over the telephone, "and I remember thinking I couldn't possibly get to see Ickes." But Ickes' office returned his call immediately, and said the Secretary could see him—immediately. ("I was very excited," Jenkins says.) And when he told Ickes what Johnson needed, Ickes said that Johnson would have it. No matter what he asked these officials to do, Jenkins says, they did it. In fact, in many cases he didn't have to ask. The White House would "often" call him about "something we hadn't even asked about. I think that Mr. Roosevelt had put the word out to do anything possible" to help Lyndon Johnson "within reason . . . and sometimes beyond reason. . . . He [Roosevelt] wanted Mr. Johnson to win so bad."

There were other similarities between Lyndon Johnson's first campaign for the Senate and his first campaign for the House. In 1941 as in 1937, only he, among all the candidates, possessed an efficient campaign organization. Although it was of course much larger than the 1937 organization, it was in many respects the same organization, from top (Under Secretary Alvin Wirtz directed campaign strategy from his desk in the Department of the Interior) to bottom (Carroll Keach was again Johnson's chauffeur). The Henderson brothers were on hand again, Herb (the "genius with a pencil") to write speeches, Chuck to write letters as the man in charge of communication with potential voters. The organization came primarily from the National Youth Administration, and many of the key names on the roster of the Johnson campaign workers of 1941—Kellam, Deason, Ernest Morgan, Fenner Roth—were the names of 1937. John Connally took orders from Wirtz and ran campaign headquarters in Austin.

It was an organization not only young, energetic and capable but devoted to its leader. When someone sneered at Carroll Keach for again being only Johnson's chauffeur, Keach replied simply: "Everyone can do something for him. This is what I can do for him." The "weeding out" begun by Johnson when he had been NYA director had continued under Kellam, and the NYA was composed now of men who had proven the hard way that they were willing to work, willing to take orders, and able to get things done. They were bound to Johnson as they had always been by the force of his personality (Fenner Roth had named his son after his Chief), as well as by self-interest; in 1941, their investment in his future was four years greater than in 1937, and this time the stakes were much bigger: J. J. ("Jake") Pickle, perhaps the most capable of the post-1937 recruits, had no hesitation about quitting his NYA job for a lower-paying campaign job, in part because "Well, it was expected that you would get your job back after the campaign," but mostly because "I felt at this time that Mr. Johnson had the prospects of being a state and national figure, and he'd take you along with him. It was a good gamble to do it. It was the best way to get ahead." It was an organization in place—and its individual members knew *their* place. The NYA was, after all, a well-organized, going concern; it was, in effect, shifted virtually *en masse* to the Johnson campaign. And, as in all Johnson operations, there was an iron-clad chain of command, a chain that carried over into the campaign. Superimposed above the NYA boys were Wirtz, Connally and James Blundell, a former Garner supporter who had seen where the future lay, had switched to the New Deal, and was now Connally's assistant. But the organization below—the organization that carried out the daily campaigning—was largely the NYA organization; the state was divided into districts, along the lines of the NYA districts, and an NYA director supervised each, and gave orders to local NYA men, who were familiar with smaller areas. And because the NYA was a statewide organization, Johnson's campaign organization was a statewide organization—the first statewide political organization Texas had ever seen. Johnson's insistence that his NYA workers meet and cultivate local officials would pay off now; the Mayors and County Commissioners whose support he needed would be contacted by men who were already their friends. Within a week after his campaign had begun, twelve two-man teams had fanned out from Austin across Texas to carry the message of "Roosevelt and Unity"—and these teams knew whom to see. Having worked in the 1937 campaign, moreover, they knew many little tricks of the political trade. Wingate Lucas knew he was in the hands of professionals from the moment the Johnson team of advance men arrived in his hometown to oversee his preparations for a Johnson speech; the audience was going to sit on a hillside, and Lucas' aides had been setting up the chairs "right next to each other. And his people said, you never put the chairs so close together at a political rally: you want to make it look like there are more people there." They removed every other chair; "we spread out those chairs across the whole hillside," and the press reported that Johnson had drawn a larger audience than in fact he had. "Now that sounds like a simple thing," Lucas says. "But at the time I didn't know that."

And in 1941 as in 1937, Johnson had money.

Running a statewide campaign had always been expensive in Texas. In part, this was because of the state's size—800 miles from top to bottom, close to 800 miles across, it is bigger than all New England (with several other states thrown in). In part, it was because the state was largely rural: only a third of its 6,450,000 residents lived in cities; a third lived in small towns, and a third still lived on farms. A substantial percentage of the farmers didn't possess radios; some didn't even get a weekly newspaper. In 1941 the only way to reach these people was by the campaigning methods that had been in use in Texas decades before. "You'd put a loudspeaker on some guy's car, load up the back with literature, mark up a road map for

him, and send him out," driving from one "Saturday town" to another to put
up placards, pass out literature and give speeches on the courthouse square,
says D. B. Hardeman. Although the cost of individual items such as gasoline,
hotels and food was low (a good small-town hotel charged no more than
two or three dollars a night, a like amount would pay for a day's food, and,
recalls one campaigner, "You couldn't drive far enough in a day to use up
two dollars' worth of gasoline"), overall this type of campaigning was expensive. The campaigner needed money for car repairs and "to buy fellows a
beer, to be a big shot, to be able to act like an 'important representative of
headquarters.' " Keeping a man on the road cost about $100 per week, and
because of the size of Texas, it was desirable to keep a lot of men on the
road. Just keeping in touch with these men was expensive; long-distance
telephone bills were no small item. Because of the size of Texas, the cost of
every category of campaign expenditure was multiplied; a candidate who
wanted to make a significant impact with highway billboards had to think
not of hundreds of billboards, but of thousands. A candidate considering the
purchase of advertising in weekly newspapers had to consider the fact that
there were more than 400 weekly newspapers in Texas. No daily newspaper
covered more than a small fraction of the state, so a candidate had to try to
buy space in all sixty daily newspapers. And the new (and most effective)
medium of campaign communication—radio—was the most expensive of
all, and since no radio station reached more than a small fraction of the state,
a candidate had to try to buy time on sixty stations.

Money had played a significant role in the 1941 campaign even before
it began. The most logical candidate in Washington was Congressman Wright
Patman. The forty-eight-year-old Patman wanted that Senate seat, had been
dreaming of it for years—and, having earned a formidable reputation as a
crusader for Populist causes, he was qualified for it. But dreams had to surrender to reality. "I wanted to run," he was to say, but "I couldn't afford to
run. . . . Of course I knew that I could do more in the Senate, but I told Mr.
Rayburn, 'Lyndon can be financed. It takes a lot of money for the Senate. . . .
I don't have the money for it in 254 counties in Texas. I don't have the potential of a good organization with funds to support it. Lyndon has. . . .' "
The most logical candidate in Texas was James Allred, now, retired from
the Governorship at the age of forty-two, a federal Judge. Allred, too, wanted
the job, but Allred was faced with the same reality—heightened, in his case,
by the debt into which he had been plunged by two statewide races, a debt
that had proven difficult to erase for an official unsympathetic to the reactionary oil and business interests that financed Texas politics. Publisher Houston
Harte, a New Dealer and owner of the only Texas newspaper chain as large
as Marsh's, sent D. B. Hardeman and another young, liberal, reporter, Alex
Louis, to the ex-Governor's home to promise him the support of the seven
Harte-Hanks dailies and to ask him to run. "We got Allred so excited he was
walking up and down and making campaign speeches," Hardeman says.

"But the next morning, early, he rapped on our door. He asked us to go for a walk with him, and . . . he told us that his wife had just absolutely laid down the law to him. Jo Betsy had said: 'For the first time in your life, you're about to get out of debt. You cannot run again.' " Before the campaign even began, lack of money had eliminated two of the strongest potential candidates.

But Lyndon Johnson had money.

It came from Washington, because of ideology or self-interest. Traditional sources of New Deal funds, prodded by Tommy Corcoran, contributed, as did attorneys such as the one who made a contribution through Welly Hopkins because he "was building up a law practice and he may or may not have had clients who he thought might be benefited." It came from New York, from the garment district, because Corcoran assured Dubinsky and Lubin that Johnson was for labor and a liberal ("You'll be getting a liberal Senator from *Texas!*" Corcoran growled at them. "What do you want for a nickel?"), and because their idolized leader was so interested in the race ("Everybody knew he was Roosevelt's pet"), and it came from Wall Street, and from big corporations. Eliot Janeway had been made to understand that the New Deal considered the election of Lyndon Johnson a matter of the highest priority. ("[Justice William O.] Douglas would call me every third day and say, 'How are you doing for Lyndon?' " Janeway says.) Janeway did well. In 1941, he jokes, he raised so much money for Johnson in New York that he "created a balance-of-payments crisis in New York over that campaign." The funds raised were carried to Texas by trusted couriers. Says Hopkins: "I . . . was able to raise a fairly good-sized sum for those days —a few thousand dollars." He says: "I had checks. And some cash." Carrying the money to Texas was a new experience, he says. "It was certainly novel to me—I had never had that much cash in my personal life." Asked in what form the contributions were made, Rowe replies, "It was *all* cash in those days." In fact, it was not, as Hopkins' statement shows, but a steady stream of couriers carrying cash or checks was soon heading for Lyndon Johnson's headquarters in Austin.

It came from Dallas—from anti–New Deal oilmen who didn't care what Lyndon Johnson's politics were so long as he protected their profits. In 1941, the specter of federal regulation by the hated Ickes was becoming more and more of a possibility, and they needed protection in Washington more than ever, and their trusted advisor, Alvin Wirtz, assured them they would get it from Johnson. Those of the wildcatters who had dealt personally with the young Congressman could assure their fellows that, unlike Rayburn, who was far too independent for their taste, Johnson would take orders. (On April 23, in fact, an exchange of telegrams had occurred which demonstrated the peremptory tone they used to him, and his eagerness to please them. Arch Underwood, the reactionary oil-and-cotton baron, had asked Johnson for some unknown favor in Washington, and Johnson had not replied. At two p.m., Underwood sent Johnson a three-word telegram: TELL ME SOMETHING. Johnson's reply, sent a few hours after he received Underwood's wire, said: TRIED TO GET YOU AT DALLAS BUT WAS TOLD YOU HAD JUST LEFT. . . . [HAROLD] YOUNG LEAVING HERE WITH ME FRIDAY NIGHT. AM GOING TO TRY TO DO JOB IN WHICH YOU ARE INTERESTED BEFORE I LEAVE.) Bill Kittrell, who along with Bill McCraw was Johnson's contact with the oilmen, was able to wire him shortly after he announced that he was running: HAVE TALKED LECHNER, ARCH, ARMISTEAD, BROOKS, PURL AND CLARK. ALL OKAY. They were indeed. A few of the oilmen's contributions to the Johnson campaign are recorded: W. T. Knight, $2,000; Sid Richardson, $3,000; Clara Driscoll, $5,000. But most are not. The oilmen made them in cash through McCraw or Kittrell or Wirtz: on one occasion, Kittrell handed Johnson an envelope bulging with bills; on several occasions, Wirtz, who directed the campaign from a private office away from campaign headquarters, called Wilton Woods over to it. Woods says that Wirtz gave him cash to pay various "office expenses," and that the amount Wirtz gave him totaled $25,000.

It came from Charles Marsh. The alacrity with which Johnson had leaped at this chance for higher political office—after promising Alice Glass that he would leave politics, get a divorce and marry her—had led to a breach in his relationship with Marsh's mistress. (He would repair this breach shortly after the election, and their relationship would enter one of its most intense phases.) But Marsh, of course, was unaware of the relationship. On the day Sheppard died, the publisher had pledged Johnson his support in the race, which he was to point out was for a "25-year senatorship." At first, for reasons that can only be guessed at, Johnson pointedly did not respond, and did not ask for help from this man who liked to be asked. But now, needing him, he asked—so skillfully that Marsh dropped all personal business and rushed to Texas. Marsh liked to write speeches and plan campaign stratagems—it gave him the feeling of being on the inside of politics. He spent the ten weeks of the campaign driving his Buick convertible back and forth across Texas to be on hand whenever Lyndon Johnson arrived in a big city. As he drove (like many wealthy Texans, he refused to use a chauffeur), he dictated speeches and memos to his secretary, Alice's sister Mary Louise, who was sitting beside him, so that he could hand them to Lyndon when they met. With automobile air-conditioning still unknown, some of these long drives, often on narrow, badly paved roads, were memorable for their discomfort. "In one day," Mary Louise recalls, "Charles and I drove from Amarillo to San Angelo—all day long in the heat." But he was perfectly happy doing this for the young man of whom he was so fond. And Marsh was not only writing speeches, he was getting them on the air. FCC regulations required that radio time for political speeches be paid for in advance, and Marsh paid. Although this was a period in which he was, by his standards, somewhat short of ready cash, he donated thousands of dollars to Lyndon's campaign, and raised thousands more; his partner, E. S. Fentress, gave $5,000 himself. Richardson wasn't the only impoverished wildcatter Marsh had helped to hold on to his leases; Jack Frost of the Byrd-Frost Oil Company was another. Frost wasn't interested in politics, but now that he had made his money, he would donate to any politician Marsh asked him to, and Marsh asked him to donate to Lyndon Johnson. Whenever Marsh passed through Dallas, he would, Mary Louise says, "get some fellows in for a meeting." The money raised at such meetings would be pooled with his own, in his own bank account. Arriving in a city, Marsh would drive first to the local radio station, or send Mary Louise, and pay for radio time with his own checks, so that Marsh's checking account became almost an official arm of the Johnson campaign.

But, mostly, Johnson's money came from Brown & Root. Herman Brown had wanted so fiercely to build big things, and to make big money building them. Now, thanks to Lyndon Johnson, he had been able to do so —had, in fact, made money on a scale perhaps as big as his dreams. But the appetite grows by what it feeds on, and now his dreams were bigger. Representative Johnson had brought Brown & Root millions of dollars in profits. What might not Senator Johnson be able to do? On May 5, 1941, a luncheon was held in Houston at which were present thirty-four Brown & Root "subs," the sub-contractors who had gotten a piece of the work on the Marshall Ford Dam or the Corpus Christi Naval Air Station. They were asked for pledges for the Johnson campaign. And Herman Brown did not ask others to take risks he was unwilling to take himself. Brown & Root might be breaking the law if it gave money to the Johnson campaign, but Brown did not let the law deter him from backing his candidate to the hilt. He simply took precautions to conceal what he was doing. These precautions had to be more extensive than the ones he had taken the previous year, for the scale of his contributions was larger now. Corporation checks, entered on its books as "legal fees," were given to attorneys, who were instructed to get the money into the hands of the Johnson campaign. They deposited the Brown & Root checks, made out their personal checks for the same amounts (or, in some cases, for 10 percent less, deducting that amount for the service), or drew cash, and brought or mailed the checks or cash to Johnson campaign headquarters in Houston or Austin, or got it to the campaign through routes more circuitous; one lawyer, given $12,500 in "attorneys' fees," gave part of it to his partner as a "profit distribution." His partner promptly gave it right back to him—and he gave it to the Johnson campaign. "Bonuses" were paid to Brown & Root vice presidents— $30,000 apiece to two vice presidents, $33,800 to another, $40,000 to a fourth—who, Internal Revenue Service agents later came to believe, were instructed to give at least part of the money to the campaign as if it were their own. Within the first few weeks of Johnson's Senate run, Brown had put behind him well over $100,000.

During the pre-war era, the cost of a typical statewide campaign in

Texas was about $50,000; an expensive campaign might run as much as $75,000 or $80,000; says one politician who managed many campaigns during that period: "That was what you figured you'd need to do it right. You seldom got nearly that much, but if you got that [much] money, you could do it right." But thanks to Herman Brown—and Tommy Corcoran and Eliot Janeway and Welly Hopkins and Sid Richardson and Charles Marsh— Lyndon Johnson had a great deal more than that. He could hire talent—the best that money could buy. Soon top political reporters—lured from their newspapers for the campaign—were, under Herb Henderson's direction, writing Johnson press releases and cultivating press contacts (along with, in some cases, their editors). He hired not just public relations men, but the best public relations men, including the legendary PR wizard, Phil Fox of Dallas, whose fee was a reported $300 per week. And Johnson could ensure that his press releases would be played as news stories in those weekly news-papers—and there were hundreds in Texas—whose editorial policy could be influenced by cash. Says one former Texas newsman familiar with the prac-tice: "You'd go and say to the publisher of a small weekly newspaper, 'If your views are sound, we'll take a $25 ad every week.' " Few candidates for statewide office had utilized this practice on a broad scale, because few can-didates possessed the requisite funds—$25 per week for a ten-week cam-paign, multiplied by hundreds of weeklies, ran into tens of thousands of dollars. Johnson could hire typists, after renting chairs and desks and of course typewriters for them to use; one way to make an unknown candidate known—fast—was through letters to individual voters; dozens of volunteers pounded out such letters, but Johnson wanted professionals as well; soon, in a large room on the mezzanine of Austin's Stephen F. Austin Hotel, eighty-two secretaries were working under the direction not only of Chuck Henderson but of experienced directors of corporate secretarial pools. (So big did the Austin mailing operations become that even eighty-two typists couldn't handle it; the students of an Austin secretarial school were commis-sioned to address 7,000 envelopes a week.) Veteran Texas politicians walked down from the Capitol along Congress Avenue—dominated by gigantic JOHNSON FOR SENATOR and JOHNSON FOR ROOSEVELT AND UNITY signs—to take a look at the hotel mezzanine for themselves; no letter-writing operation on such a scale had ever been seen in Texas politics.

In all newspapers, even those whose editorial policy would not be in-fluenced by money, Johnson could ensure the repetition of his name and of his link with the beloved President by purchasing ads. To run an advertise-ment in sixty daily newspapers and hundreds of weeklies cost tens of thou-sands of dollars in a single week; Johnson ran ads on this scale in many of the campaign's ten weeks. He printed his own newspaper; using the facilities of a cooperative local weekly, the journalists on his payroll composed a four-page full-size newspaper. In it, Roosevelt's name appeared in headlines al-

most as many times as Johnson's. There were catchy renditions of the motto
—suitable for singing: "Now all over this state/they're saying/and it's going to be/Franklin D and Lyndon B!" (and, of course, there was only one
front-page picture—the two men shaking hands in Galveston under the
headline: "Old and Close Friends"). And copies of this newspaper were
printed and mailed in the hundreds of thousands. Johnson bought radio time
in huge hunks; one half-hour of air time in enough stations to blanket the
entire state cost approximately $4,000. And then of course there were those
thousands of "handshake" billboards—which in strategic locations cost
$200 or $300 apiece. Johnson's barbecues were the most extravagant in
Texas political history (by now he was employing Ed Clark's device of providing enough meat so that everyone attending could not only eat his fill but
be encouraged to take home enough for several additional meals), his rallies
the most elaborate (with, behind the stage, that huge canvas backdrop of
him and Roosevelt shaking hands and the immense words: ROOSEVELT AND
UNITY).

To speak at barbecues and rallies—and to tour their home areas on his
behalf—Johnson needed local "lead men" and stump speakers. Although
few of them knew him personally, some would campaign for him because
they were persuaded that he represented the New Deal. Many, however,
required other motivation. Buster Kellam, Jesse's brother, reported to Jake
Pickle on the reception he had received from J. Edward Johnson, an attorney
who was reputedly an effective stemwinder, and who had agreed to accompany Kellam on a speaking tour for Johnson in rural counties north
of Dallas.

> Mr. Johnson didn't approve of my coming with just $50. I did my
> best to explain that there would be more as it was needed. That he
> didn't like and made it clear that he wasn't spending any of his
> money, and that since he was neglecting his practice, he was en-
> titled to more. He also said that he hesitated about leaving unless
> he had at least enough money to cover two weeks' expenses. . . . I
> have hopes that by the time you receive this we will be gone, but I
> do know that won't be until he has more money.

The requirements of most of the lead men were satisfied, and soon scores
were out hawking the abilities of a candidate they had never met.

Four years before, campaigning in a district whose voters hardly knew
his name, Johnson had overhauled far better-known and more experienced
candidates partly through the use of money on a scale unprecedented in that
district. Now he was using money on the same scale in twenty-one districts
—all across Texas. Lyndon Johnson, in his first campaign for the Senate,
was using money on a scale Texas had never seen.

FOR A WHILE this campaign seemed to be following the course of Johnson's
1937 race.

It was enlivened by a touch of humor. Because it was a special election
rather than a party primary, any citizen could get his name on the ballot
merely by paying a $100 fee, and twenty-seven candidates besides Johnson
had taken advantage of this opportunity. One candidate was a radio peddler
of various goat-gland concoctions designed to improve, among other things,
virility. Another was a laxative manufacturer (Hal Collins of Crazy Water
Crystals) who attracted big crowds at rallies by giving away a free mattress
to the couple present who had the most children. A third, "Commodore"
Muse Hatfield, felt that Roosevelt had not gone far enough; the Commodore
favored the immediate creation of a five-ocean Navy, to be financed by a
national lottery. The ballot also included "Cyclone" Davis, who lived under
a Dallas viaduct and announced that he didn't have to campaign because
"Providence will place me in the Senate"; a geologist who proposed a $50
monthly pension for everybody over sixty-five and a $5 pension for everyone
else; a chiropractor; an ex-bootlegger; an admitted kidnapper; two bearded
prophets, and two rocking-chair sages (including a wealthy self-styled
"rump farmer" who said he was for "the masses"—by which he apparently
meant his masses of impoverished tenant farmers). There were also two
candidates whose qualifications rested on their kinship with famous Texans
of the past. Joseph C. Bean was a cousin of a pair of legendary Texans:
Judge Roy C. Bean, "The Law West of the Pecos," and Ellis P. Bean,
a hero of Texas' war against Mexico who had gained fame by spending
several years in a Mexican prison with a pet lizard named Bill. Edwin
Waller III had only one famous ancestor, but that one, Edwin Waller I,
had claimed the honor of having begun the Mexican War by committing
that war's first "overt act" (which on closer inspection, turned out to be
an argument between Waller and some Mexicans over the use of a small
boat).

Besides Johnson, there were, during the first six weeks of the campaign,
two serious candidates: Martin Dies and Gerald Mann.

The belief that Dies would make a strong candidate lasted only until he
entered the race. A fiery stump speaker, the Congressman could evoke
hysterical cheers when he addressed the Mothers of Dallas on the prevalence
of Communism within the American Youth Congress. But he spoke rather
infrequently, doing little touring and relying on a few speeches in the big
cities. And even when these speeches were broadcast, the public was often
not aware of them, because, although plenty of money was available to Dies
for advertising, most of it went unused. He displayed an almost total lack of
interest in setting up an organization beyond the boundaries of his own

East Texas congressional district; in most of the state, there was no Dies organization at all. The Communist threat was practically the sole topic of his campaign, and it quickly became apparent that while a hard core of "super-patriots" would vote for him, he wasn't going to be able to add to that base. His strength—which soared to 27 percent the week he announced—declined, week by week, in every poll thereafter.

Mann's candidacy was a different story. The young Attorney General's personal qualities attracted loyalty. The wording on the plaque he had hung on the wall behind his desk—"I sacrificed no principle to gain this office and I shall sacrifice no principle to keep it"—did not strike a false note with those who knew him, and neither did his habit of carrying around a Bible and reciting poetry; the most cynical of politicians had to admit, as one puts it, "There was a guy who you wouldn't *dare* to ask him to do anything even slightly wrong"; D. B. Hardeman, the Austin journalist and an astute observer of Texas politics, says that Mann was "a very deep Christian, a very sincere man, a very clean man—politically, financially. A very gentle man. He had practically the loftiest ideals of any public servant I ever knew." He had, Hardeman says, "assembled an outstanding staff, because men were very loyal to him." When Senator Sheppard died, these young Assistant Attorney Generals asked him to run, and volunteered to resign and campaign for him—which meant that he would have at least the nucleus of a campaign organization.

He also, of course, had a statewide "name"—a very respected one, as had been demonstrated by the unsolicited newspaper editorials that echoed his aides' request that he run, and by his rating in the first Belden Poll: second only to Governor O'Daniel. And he had a fierce, driving energy that resembled Johnson's. Having launched the type of campaign that had given him his upset victory in 1938—a campaign that resembled Johnson's 1937 campaign in the refusal of the young candidate to spare himself—he was driving hundreds of miles each day, and giving dozens of speeches, in every corner of Texas. His intensity and earnestness made him a compelling speech-maker; slender, clean-cut, very handsome, he was an impressive figure in front of a county courthouse. O'Daniel was still saying he didn't plan to run, and a poll taken on May 12 to determine what would happen if he didn't showed that without the Governor in the race, Mann would receive 42 percent of the vote, Dies 40 percent, Johnson 15 percent and all the other candidates a total of 3 percent. Mann felt that Dies was not a substantial threat because of his unwillingness to work, or to organize. As for Johnson, Mann liked him, but felt "the people of the state didn't know Lyndon Johnson." He felt he was going to win.

In two respects, however, Mann's campaign was very different from Johnson's. A score of his former assistants were out enthusiastically working for him—an adequate campaign nucleus by traditional Texas standards. But it was not adequate in comparison with the Johnson campaign. And while Mann's workers were able, trained lawyers, they weren't able, trained campaign workers; they didn't know the local officials, as Johnson's men did. "Johnson had this network of young, aggressive operators from the NYA . . . that Mann couldn't match," says Hardeman (who himself joined Mann's campaign). "They knew more about how to organize a campaign, how to get a campaign manager in each county and city, how to get people to put up placards and pass out literature and ring doorbells . . . Johnson's operation was just a better political operation than Gerald Mann's."

The second—more significant—deficiency in the Mann campaign was in its funding. Although Mann had spent relatively little in his first race for Attorney General, he had spent more than he possessed, and in 1941, three years after the race, he was still paying off debts from it. He told his two campaign managers, his brother, Guy L. Mann, and his former law partner, Sam McCorkle of Dallas, that they were not to place him further in debt for this race. They didn't follow his instructions; strapped for cash, they arranged loans from the Republic National Bank of Dallas. But the amount of money available to Mann from this loan—and from contributions from his backers —was minuscule beside Johnson's. The difference was visible in Austin, where Johnson had eighty-two typists on the hotel mezzanine, and scores of other campaign workers, whereas the Mann-for-Senate headquarters consisted of Hardeman, and a few other volunteers. The same contrast existed in other cities, where Johnson headquarters were filled with paid, trained workers. "We didn't have any big headquarters staff anywhere," Mann says. In Dallas, for example, "my organization consisted primarily of Guy Mann and Sam McCorkle." This lack of staffing hurt in innumerable ways: Johnson's traveling "teams," for example, sent back from each town they visited lists of individuals who might be potential supporters, with a little personal data on each one; when these lists arrived at headquarters, letters with a personal touch carefully added by Chuck Henderson and other expert Johnson letter-writers were sent to these individuals (over the candidate's signature), and repeated "follow-up" letters were sent thereafter to win them to Johnson's side or keep them there. Thousands and thousands of such letters were drafted, typed and mailed. Mann could do nothing comparable.

Nor could Mann's men do much traveling—not when such campaigning cost a hundred dollars per man per week. Johnson had twelve two-man teams out full time; as for Mann, he says, "We didn't have any teams out—it would take all the money we had to keep *me* on the road, and to buy some advertising. We didn't have that kind of money at all."

It was sometimes hard for Mann's headquarters even to keep in touch with his campaigners: "telephoning over an area that was bigger than all New England—just the cost of it was an impossibility," Hardeman recalls.

When Johnson traveled, speechwriters and advance men traveled with him; Mann often traveled alone except for a single aide who had volunteered to be his driver.

The influence of money in the campaign was magnified in the media. When Gerald Mann received an endorsement from a respected daily newspaper, it appeared once—in that newspaper; perhaps, if he was lucky, the paper might repeat its endorsement once. But when Lyndon Johnson received an endorsement, it was reprinted, in ads or in "news stories" written in his headquarters, in scores of weeklies throughout the daily's circulation area—week after week. It was reprinted in brochures mailed—week after week—to voters across the entire state. It was reprinted on the hundreds of thousands of throwaways placed in voters' hands by campaign workers—NYA employees, Brown & Root employees, electric co-operative meter readers and repairmen, FHA mortgage appraisers—who reinforced to the voters, face to face, the message in the flyers they were being handed. The most glowing phrases of such an endorsement were shouted, or recited in honeyed tones, on radio broadcasts over and over, day after day. Mann's speeches might be persuasive to the voters who were actually standing in front of him when he gave them, and, perhaps, listeners to a local radio station, but that was all. Johnson could not speak well, but when he spoke, it was to large areas of the state, for his speeches were broadcast over statewide radio networks. Men—local lead men and stemwinders who had come to admire the young Attorney General—wanted to speak for Mann, but after the first few weeks of the campaign, the money to send them on the road ran out. All too often, Mann's headquarters was handicapped in responding even to a specific request to furnish a prominent speaker for the meeting of some local organization. When such a request came in to Johnson headquarters, the speaker was sent, all expenses paid, often accompanied by a claque to arouse enthusiasm in the audience. Newspaper advertising drummed up attendance. When a similar request came in to Mann's headquarters, expense money would have to be scraped up before a commitment could be made to send a speaker. Often, it couldn't be scraped up, and the opportunity was lost. Hardeman, hardly a prominent Texan, wound up making some speeches himself because he had no money to send anyone else.

Mann was mercifully unaware of the full extent of Johnson's advertising, for traveling long hours every day around the state, he would see only the local newspapers. "I was out campaigning, so I would see only one ad, not hundreds at a time," he recalls. His staff tried to shield him from the truth: "You want to keep the candidate believing he's going to win, so you don't tell him things like that," Hardeman says. But, a perceptive campaigner, Mann knew something was happening, something bad. "I could tell by the crowds," he recalls. "I don't know how to describe this—out on the stump, you can feel if things are going right," and now he began to feel that things were going wrong. "The crowds were just not as large any more, or they were just not as enthusiastic as they should be." And gradually the explanation dawned on him. "As I traveled around, I could just feel the effect of Johnson's money. The advertising, and the employing of people, and in every county in the state there were federal bureaus—they were really putting out so much money I could just feel what was happening." Mann was correct, but, without sufficient funds of his own, he couldn't do anything about it. He was campaigning now as Lyndon Johnson had campaigned in 1937—day and night, weekday and weekend, spending sixteen to eighteen hours a day in a car. He became so exhausted that he could "fall asleep on a moment's notice in a car. If I hadn't been able to do that, I couldn't have been able to keep going. You can look at a map and see how big Texas is, and how far apart these towns are, but you can't imagine it until you try to get from one place to another." He was, he says, "almost automated": he could sleep until his car pulled into a town, wake up and jump out of the car, make a speech, get back into the car—and go right back to sleep. And he was campaigning like this day after day. But even such an effort could not help him against the weight of Lyndon Johnson's money. Mann was running a traditional Texas campaign, and running it brilliantly. But it couldn't compete with the new type of campaign, Lyndon Johnson's type of campaign.

THERE WAS ONE GLARING DIFFERENCE between Lyndon Johnson's 1941 campaign and his 1937 campaign—the candidate himself.

The candidate of 1941 bore little resemblance to the skinny, gawky, nervous youth of four years before. When he took off his suit jacket, it became apparent that the only part of Lyndon Johnson that was still thin was his shoulders, conspicuously narrow in proportion to the middle of his body which had became quite wide. His belt sagged a little around the beginning of a paunch, and his rear end was now quite large. The jacket was seldom doffed, but not through concern over his bulk. His speeches, he instructed his speechwriters, were to be "senatorial"—statesmanlike and dignified—and he wanted his appearance to match, as the handkerchief painstakingly arranged in his breast pocket matched his necktie. His suits, most of them with a vest, were of good materials, mostly dark blue. There was often a carnation in his lapel, and his white shirt was starched and stiff; gold cufflinks gleamed on the sleeves. Bare-headed in 1937, now he often wore a hat, not a Stetson but a fedora, which he would wave to the crowds, and there was frequently a briefcase under his arm from which he would remove the text of his speech as ostentatiously as if it had been papers of state; to read the speech he would fussily put on a pair of eyeglasses. The gaunt face of 1937 was a broad, heavy face now: flesh had filled in the lines and filled out the cheeks; there was a full-fledged double chin, and the big jaw jutted now out of heavy jowls. The candidate of 1937 had looked so young; the candidate of 1941 was not young at all; he looked at least a decade older than his thirty-two years.

The difference was accentuated by his bearing. In 1937, he had been as ineffective reading a prepared speech as he was persuasive speaking extemporaneously. Now he almost never gave an extemporaneous talk, and he was, if possible, even worse now at reading prepared speeches—but in a very different way. In 1937, he had given the impression of being afraid to look at his audience lest he lose his place in the text. He still did not look at his audience nearly as much as his mother, the elocution teacher, would have liked, but fear was no part of the impression he made now. On a stage, he was a dominant, powerful figure, tall, long-armed; the spotlight glittered on his gold-rimmed eyeglasses, glistened off the waves of his black, carefully pomaded, shiny black hair and highlighted the pale whiteness of his skin, the blackness of the heavy eyebrows that the glasses did little to conceal, and the sheen of beard that was present on the jutting jaw no matter how closely he shaved. A powerful figure, but not a pleasant one. The modest tone in the text of most of his speeches (Charles Marsh, who wrote many of them, was constantly urging upon the candidate at least a public humility) was belied by the domineering tone in which they were delivered. Johnson shouted his speeches in a harsh voice almost without inflection except when he was especially determined to emphasize a point, when his voice would rise into a bellow; the tone was the tone of a lecturer uninterested in any opinion but his own: dogmatic, pontifical, the tone of a leader demanding rather than soliciting support. Reinforcing the tone were the gestures, as awkward as ever but now authoritarian to the point of arrogance. He spoke with his big head thrust aggressively forward at his listeners, and sometimes it would thrust forward even more and he would raise his hand and repeatedly jab a finger down at them. Sometimes he spoke with one hand on a hip, with his big head thrown back a little, shouting over their heads. His attitude went beyond mere inability to learn public speaking. His rare smiles were so mechanical that they seemed calculated to let the audience know they were mechanical, as if he wanted to let them know that he didn't need them, that he was the leader and they the followers. Early in the campaign, the ability of his advance men, the skill with which they were organized, and the waves of radio and newspaper ads which preceded each speech ensured large crowds at his rallies, and, spurred on by introductions from the best local orators (only the best were hired) and by the cheers of the Johnson campaign workers and federal and Brown & Root employees with which it was liberally seeded, the audience would welcome him with enthusiasm. As he spoke, though, the enthusiasm would steadily diminish; all too often, by the end of a speech the only cheers would be the cheers of his claque. His speeches were invariably long—too long, not infrequently an hour or more; the audience would begin to drift away relatively soon, and by the end of a speech it would often be embarrassingly smaller than it had been at the beginning. Word about Johnson's lack of speaking ability began to get around: despite the unprecedented publicity, crowds at Johnson's rallies began growing smaller than expected.

The difference was as noticeable after the speech as during it. During the 1937 campaign, a handshake from Lyndon Johnson had been an exercise in instant empathy; circulating among an audience with a face glowing with friendliness, he would keep a voter's hand in his for long minutes while he asked him for his help and told him that he too was a farmer, and wanted to help farmers; he had established rapport with the rapidity of a man who had a "very unusual ability to meet and greet the public." Now, in 1941, that ability was not often in evidence, for Johnson did not often choose to use it. In part, of course, this was because there were so many more voters to meet and greet now, but the difference went beyond that circumstance. When, after a speech, Johnson shook hands with voters lined up to meet him, he did so in a manner so mechanical that a friend from Washington commented on it—Justice Douglas happened to be in Big Spring to make a speech on the night Johnson spoke there. "As LBJ came to the close of his speech, he shouted, 'I want all you good folks of Big Spring to line up and shake the hand of the next Senator from Texas, Lyndon B. Johnson.' " And Douglas noticed that "Lyndon gave each of them two pumps with the arm and one slap on the back before greeting the next comer." The two-pump, one-slap technique was, in fact, one that Johnson had rehearsed; he boasted that, using it, he could, with his aides prodding the voters past him in a fast-moving single line, shake forty-two hands per minute. The method was efficient, but not effective. Far from establishing rapport with voters, he only managed to emphasize the feeling that he was not one of them, and that, while he might be asking for their help, he didn't really need it. And he would not allow a voter more than a hurried word or two, if that; Bill Deason says, "He never missed anybody on the street. . . . He shook hands with every one of them, but he never let them involve him in an argument. He moved fast. . . ." In fact, he seldom let them involve him in a conversation; the candidate moved through crowds in a cordon of officious aides who pushed people aside, none too gently, hurrying him along as he flashed mechanical smiles to left and right. And his aides were around him, and hurrying him along, because he had ordered them to. He wasn't always so coldly mechanical, of course. With "important people"—some local politician he recognized on the line of voters —his face would light up, and his greeting would be warm and unhurried, his handshake again as good as a hug. On some nights, his greeting of the public would also be warm, reminiscent of the campaigning of 1937, but such nights did not occur frequently during the first six weeks of the 1941 campaign. In 1941, his campaigning was as strikingly cold and mechanical as it had been strikingly warm and individual four years before; indeed at times his manner was almost contemptuous, making it clear that the individual to whom he was speaking simply didn't matter.

There was another difference between the two campaigns. Johnson was campaigning hard in 1941, was still putting in long days on the campaign trail, but there was a marked drop in his energy level. The desperation, the frantic, driving work was gone. He wasn't, in fact, even the hardest-working candidate. Gerald Mann in 1941 displayed the willingness Johnson had displayed in 1937: the willingness to do everything—to work day and night, without regard to hours—in order to win. The Attorney General was determined to go everywhere, to shake the hand of every voter who wanted to shake his. Mann had done it twice before, and in 1941, he was doing it again. Johnson's speeches were, thanks to money, reaching more voters, through being broadcast, but Mann was determined to overcome that difference with sheer physical effort. Johnson was making far fewer speeches, visiting far fewer towns. He concentrated largely on the big cities, where, of course, the votes were concentrated, and in the big cities he concentrated on the big men. Arriving, he would huddle, generally in a suite in the hotel in which he was staying, with the city's political and business bosses—in Texas, often the same men. Then he would make telephone calls or rest until the evening's rally. The pace was still grueling—the travel between cities made any campaign in Texas grueling—but it was much slower than the 1937 pace. It was the pace of a man confident of victory. Implicit in Johnson's delivery of speeches, and in his manner of greeting voters, was the feeling that with the mighty President behind him, he couldn't lose.

And, indeed, for the first six weeks of the campaign, the President's support, combined with Johnson's money and organization, suggested that Johnson's confidence was well founded. Although the May 12 Belden Poll showed Mann still far in front of Johnson, 28 percent to 9 percent, both his advisors and Johnson's—and the state's veteran political observers—felt that the poll was not accurately measuring the rapid shift toward Johnson, an opinion that would be confirmed by the May 26 poll, which found that Johnson had narrowed the gap from nineteen points to eight—19 percent for Johnson to 27 percent for Mann. Out on the campaign trail, Mann realized that the shift was continuing—and accelerating. He knew—and Austin knew —that Johnson was going to win.

THEN, HOWEVER, a twenty-ninth candidate, Governor O'Daniel, entered the race—and any resemblance to Johnson's first, victorious, campaign ended on the spot.

Until he had run for Governor three years before, W. (for Wilbert) Lee O'Daniel had never had the slightest connection with politics—not as a candidate, not as a campaign worker, not even as a voter; he had never cast a ballot. He was a flour salesman and a radio announcer. He had turned to radio—in 1927—to sell more flour. At the time, newly arrived in Texas, he was the thirty-seven-year-old sales manager for a Fort Worth company that manufactured Light Crust Flour. An unemployed country-and-western band asked him to sponsor it on a local radio station. The Light Crust Doughboys were not notably successful until one day the regular announcer was unable to appear, and O'Daniel substituted for him; finding that he liked the job, he decided to keep it.

He began whistling along with the band. He began composing tunes, and writing lyrics. Then he began writing little poems that he recited himself.

After a while not all the songs were about flour. They were tributes to Texas ("Beautiful, Beautiful Texas," "Sons of the Alamo") and to cowboys ("The Lay of the Lonely Longhorn"). There were hymns to an old horse and to "The Orphan Newsboy." Many were about motherhood: "The Boy Who Never Grew Too Old to Comb His Mother's Hair" was a particular favorite, as was another which began: "Mother, you fashioned me/ Bore me and rationed me. . . ." The songs were about current events: when the Lindbergh baby was kidnapped, the Light Crust Doughboys sang (to the tune of "My Bonny"), "Please Bring Back My Baby to Me"; when Will Rogers was killed, O'Daniel wrote: "Someone in heaven is thinking of you; someone who always was loyal and true; someone who used to be close to your side, laughed when you laughed and cried when you cried." More and more, the songs and poems were about religion—old-time, Fundamentalist, evangelical religion; "It was good for Lee O'Daniel, and it's good enough for me," the Doughboys sang.

He began giving short talks that were almost sermons. In 1938, most Texans still lived on farms, and even those farm boys who had recently arrived in the state's fast-growing cities were still farm boys, whose customs, tastes, vocabulary and view of life were those of country people. This view was simplistic, homespun, and very, very firm. A country boy himself—he had been raised in poverty on farms in Ohio and Kansas—W. Lee O'Daniel understood country people, and he knew how to appeal to their feelings and prejudices. He talked about how poor people should stick together and help each other, about how they should listen to their mothers; while the Dough-boys played—pianissimo—"Marvelous Mother of Mine," he began one program: "Hello there, mother, you little sweetheart. How in the world are you anyway, you little bunch of sweetness? This is your big boy, W. Lee O'Daniel." And, while the band softly played "Shall We Gather at the River" in the background, he talked about religion: "You young folks who want jobs. You farmers who want crops. All of you folks who want things. How do you expect to get them when you are slapping your Savior in the face?" He urged his listeners to go to church, to love one another, to tell the truth, to avoid sin.

It was not the content of these rambling, informal little homilies that made them so popular, nor the soft violins playing familiar sentimental tunes in the background. It was the voice in which they were delivered. The voice was warm and friendly and relaxed—captivatingly natural. And yet it was also fatherly, soft but firm. It was a voice you could trust. For years, radio experts didn't understand this. As one reporter put it, they "didn't think very much of him. They figured it was the band that was putting the program over." But after a few years, the band broke up, and he replaced it with another, and then another, and the popularity of the show kept growing. In an era in which most radio messages were hard sell, the flour salesman from Fort Worth had, as one chronicler was later to put it, "either stumbled into, or deliberately figured out, that a microphone is an ear and not an auditorium—and you don't make public speeches to microphones, you don't shout into them any more than you would shout into your sweetheart's ear when you wanted to tell her you loved her. O'Daniel learned early that he had Texas by the ear and from that day on he cooed and caroled and gurgled into it." In 1935, he stopped selling flour for others and started selling it for himself. He organized his own company, Hillbilly Flour, and started his own show. It opened with a woman's request to him to "Please pass the biscuits, Pappy," and then, above the fiddles and guitars of the Hillbilly Boys, the voice of a "Pappy," friendly and fatherly, would be heard. On this show, there was less music and more O'Daniel—and the show's popularity leaped. By 1938, it had more listeners than any other daily show in the history of Texas radio. Most advertisers wanted their shows to be heard in the evening, when the men were home from work; O'Daniel wanted his show to go on when men *weren't* home; he wanted to talk to lonely housewives. And when his show went on, a half-hour past noon, he talked to them. He told them how to mend broken dishes and broken hearts. He told them how important families were. He told them how important *they* were—because they were mothers. "He talked to the housewives of Texas," one reporter wrote, "like a big brother and a pal, a guide, philosopher and friend." And "at twelve-thirty sharp each day a fifteen-minute silence reigned in the State of Texas, broken only by mountain music, and the dulcet voice of W. Lee O'Daniel." A newsboy who delivered his papers at midday in the little North Texas town of Decatur recalls that in summer his customers' windows were open, "and you never got out of the sound of the Hillbilly Boys—or of Pappy's voice."

Studio technicians who saw his show up close, and who saw him turn on, in an instant, laughter or tears, said, "He's just a born actor"; at the same moment in which he was bending into the microphone, intoning, in an emotion-choked voice, a tribute to an aged mother or an old horse, he might be imperiously motioning the band into precisely the right distance from the microphone for the background music it was playing. And, indeed, doubts about Pappy's sincerity were occasionally raised in print by commentators who noted that the first of his fervent paeans to Texas had been composed when he had hardly arrived in that state, having previously lived in Kansas, and that even now he was occasionally prone to minor errors about Texas history—such as confusing the Battle of San Jacinto with the Alamo. Those closest to him knew that his country-boy image was a pose; he was actually a business-college graduate and a businessman who dealt not just in Hillbilly Flour but in Fort Worth real estate; by 1937, while he was telling his listeners that he was a "common citizen," poor like them, his net worth had passed half a million dollars. Intimates also had some doubts about the depth of his religious feeling; although he was constantly urging his listeners to go to church, he seldom went himself. (Similar doubts were felt by one visitor to Pappy's radio studio. While the band was playing "That Old Rugged Cross," O'Daniel leaned over to the visitor and whispered, "That's what brings 'em in, boy. That's what really brings 'em in!") But O'Daniel's listeners, mesmerized by that friendly, sincere voice, had no doubts. They bought whatever he was selling. Hillbilly Flour was no different from any other flour; in fact, O'Daniel did not even manufacture it himself, simply buying flour ready-made from other mills and packing it in his bags. (He had designed the bags himself; in huge black letters, they bore the word GUARANTEED [against what, the bags didn't say]; they were also stamped, in vivid red, with the words, "Pass the biscuits, Pappy"; under that motto was a picture of a billy goat and a stanza he had composed: "Hillbilly music on the air/Hillbilly Flour everywhere;/ It tickles your feet, it tickles your tongue;/ Wherever you go, its praises are sung.") Soon, Hillbilly Flour was selling so fast that other millers realized that the surest way to sell their product was to let Pappy sell it as his own— which he was pleased to do, taking a hefty royalty on every bag. Pappy's listeners bought not only his flour but his suggestions; when he urged childless couples to adopt an orphan or two, every orphan asylum in Texas was shortly out of stock. And in 1938, on Palm Sunday, he asked his listeners if he should run for Governor. A blind man had asked him to do so, he said, and he wished they would write and tell him whether or not he should. He received, he said, 54,449 replies. All but three told him to run; these three said he shouldn't—because, they said, he was too good for the job.

O'Daniel's candidacy was not taken seriously by politicians or by the press, which noted his total lack of political experience (since he had not paid his poll tax, he was not even eligible to vote); reporters treated it as a joke, if they mentioned it at all; newspaper articles lumped this "radio entertainer" and flour salesman, who had announced that he would campaign (with the Hillbilly Boys) in a red circus wagon, with the numerous other fringe candidates who regularly people Texas politics. Then the campaign began. O'Daniel's first rally was held in Waco. When he drove up in the red wagon, the crowd waiting for him was possibly the largest crowd in the history of Texas politics—tens of thousands of people. Then the red wagon moved on to San Angelo, where one of Pappy's leading rivals, a veteran of thirty years in politics, was to draw 183 people to the Courthouse lawn. When Pappy arrived, 8,000 people were standing on that lawn.

His opponents, and the state's entire political establishment, concluded, as did the press and indeed most sophisticated and educated Texans, that the crowds had been drawn by the Hillbilly Boys, who were by now a popular country-and-western band starring banjo player Leon Huff, the "Texas Songbird"; for the campaign, a vocalist, "Texas Rose," had been added along with O'Daniel's sons, Pat, a fiddler, whom he called Patty Boy, and banjo-playing Mike (Mickey Wickey). People were coming to Pappy's rallies for entertainment, politicians said; they weren't coming for politics. The politicians were unable to take seriously a candidate who said his only platform was the Ten Commandments, who hadn't paid his poll tax, who was only barely a Texan, and who wasn't even a Southerner—who was, in fact, a carpetbagger from Kansas.

But the crowds weren't coming only for the band, they were coming for Pappy; "for years he's been talking to us on the radio," an elderly farmer explained. "He's been telling us things we like to hear because listening to 'em makes it seem easier to us to be poor folks." He was hours late for one rally, and a thunderstorm was raging at the site; for hours, 20,000 people stood in the rain waiting for him. When the circus wagon pulled in, the band played for a while under a big umbrella they had set up, but when Pappy stepped up to the microphone, he took it down. "If you folks can stand in the rain and listen to me, I sure can stand in the rain and talk to you," he said—and the roar of the crowd drowned out the thunder. And Pappy turned the politicians' attacks against them; if the Ten Commandments didn't satisfy them, he said, he would add another plank to his platform: the Golden Rule. "I didn't pay my poll tax because I was fed up with crooked politics in Austin and hadn't intended to vote for anyone this year," he said. A carpetbagger? Well, he said, he guessed that was true, but it was true for a lot of Texans; almost a million Texans had been born in other states, and the parents of many more had come to Texas from other states. Perhaps his crowning touch was his answer to the charge that he wasn't a Southerner. The reason he preferred to be known by his middle name, Lee, rather than by his first name, he said, was that his middle name had been bestowed on him in honor of the great Robert E. himself. One of his uncles had been a Union soldier mortally wounded in the war; during his final days he had been nursed so tenderly by a Southern family that he had sent a deathbed message to his sister that if she should ever marry and have a son, he should be named after Robert E. Lee. And after he had answered all the attacks, Pappy would say he didn't mind them; remember what the Scriptures say, he would tell his audience: "Blessed are ye when men shall revile you and persecute you and say all manner of evil against you falsely for my sake." The Scriptures were a significant element of all O'Daniel's rallies, along with

sacred music; his appearances resembled revival meetings more than political
rallies. Texas was a wellspring of evangelism, and Pappy O'Daniel was
tapping it. A Baptist minister compared him to Moses, because he could lead
the nation back to the fundamentals of God and home.

If he had opened his campaign without a theme, moreover, he had two
themes now. One of Texas' most knowledgeable political observers, analyzing
O'Daniel's appeal, said that in part "He sensed the fears and the hopes of
people before they actually had them." One fear that wasn't hard to sense—
among the farm people who were O'Daniel's strength—was the fear of old
age, when they would no longer be able to do farm work. O'Daniel proposed
a simple state pension plan: thirty dollars a month to everyone over sixty-five.
When he was asked if he planned to raise the necessary funds for this plan—
approximately $100 million per year, four times the entire state budget—
through new taxes, he said certainly not, and said it to the tune of "My
Bonny":

> *We have builded our beautiful highways*
> *With taxes from city and farm,*
> *But you can't pyramid those taxes,*
> *Without doing our Texas great harm.*

Questions about financing details were drowned out by that tune, by another
he wrote (to the tune of "Let Me Call You Sweetheart")—"Thirty Bucks
for Mama"—and by his Mother's Day speech lamenting the Legislature's
failure to act:

> Good morning, ladies and gentlemen, and hello there, boys and
> girls. This is Lee O'Daniel speaking. This is Mother's Day from a
> sentimental standpoint only. Tired, forlorn, disappointed, and
> destitute Texas mothers several months ago thought they saw
> Mother's Day breaking in the East—but the golden glint preceding
> sunrise faded and faded again and again until today perhaps the
> practical Mother's Day is more obscure than ever before. But from
> the Texas plains and hills and valleys came a little breeze wafting
> on its crest more than 54,000 voices of one accord—we want W.
> Lee O'Daniel for governor of Texas. Why that avalanche of mail?
> Surely each and every one of you 54,000 folks could not have
> known that W. Lee O'Daniel is an only living son of one of those
> tired, forlorn, disappointed, and destitute mothers—a son who had
> played at that widowed mother's skirts, while during each day and
> way into the darkness of the nights she washed the dirt and grime
> from the clothes of the wealthy on an old worn-out washboard—
> for the paltry pittance of twenty-five cents per day—and that by

that honest drudgery she provided corn bread and beans for her children which she had brought back with her from the Valley of the Shadow of Death.

His second theme was, if possible, even more effective. To his opponents' charge that since he had no platform, he had no reason for running, he replied that there was indeed a reason; the reason, he said, was *them*. The principal reason he was running, he said, was to throw them—the "professional politicians"—out of Austin.

This theme touched a deep chord in government-hating Texas, where distrust of politicians had been heightened by the dichotomy between the state's newfound and rapidly growing natural wealth and the poverty of its government. As one writer put it: "Texas was producing more oil, more gas . . . and more of a dozen things than any other state in the Union. It was producing more sulphur than all the rest of the world put together. . . . Under efficient and honest government, it certainly should have had a full treasury." Instead, the state's general fund was more than $19 million in the red. The treasury hadn't been emptied on behalf of its citizens; this state, first in the nation in natural resources, was last, or near last, in almost every significant category—education, library services, pellagra control—of state aid to improve the lives of its citizens. The fault, O'Daniel said, lay in the "professional politicians." He was no politician, he told his listeners, he was a "common citizen"—one of *them*. And if he was Governor, he told them, "we" would be Governor. His victory would be the victory of common citizens over professional politicians; his election he said, would be "the election of *us*. If I am elected Governor of Texas, *we* will be the Governor of Texas—*we* meaning the common citizens, of which I am one."

Press and politicians had predicted that once the novelty of seeing him in person had worn off, O'Daniel's audiences would get smaller. They got larger: crowds unprecedented in Texas politics—20,000, 30,000, 40,000—came to hear him in the cities. Crowds followed him from town to town. They barricaded the highway to force him to stop and speak to them. The man they saw was entirely unexceptional in appearance. He looked like a typical, fortyish Texas businessman, five-foot-ten and just a little portly, with a close-shaven face, and slicked-down hair. He would generally doff the jacket of his suit and speak in a white shirt and necktie. While his smile was broad, it was not often in evidence; his face was rather expressionless. But when he spoke, the voice was the voice of Pappy. A reporter watched its effect on about a thousand Texans gathered near Raymondsville. "It was amazing," he wrote. "They were fascinated. It was a typical summer day in the hottest part of Texas and there they stood, dripping sweat and drinking in [his] words. . . . Next to me . . . stood a young mother with her baby in her arms and her eyes glued to the face of the speaker. The baby squalled; she opened

her dress and put the child to her breast without even looking at it. Every
member of that outdoor congregation was equally attentive." And at the end
of each of O'Daniel's rallies would occur another impressive scene. He asked
his audience to finance his campaign. Saying, "We have not one dollar in our
campaign fund," he told his listeners he was giving them "the opportunity
to join the people's candidate against the professional politicians. You
had better take that old rocking chair down and mortgage it and spend
the money in the manner you think best to get your pension." Then his
sons and his pretty daughter Molly would pass among the crowd holding
little flour kegs labeled "Flour; not Pork," with a slot cut into them. And
the audience crowded around his children, pushing and shoving to give dimes
and quarters to Pappy. According to the press, the leading candidates in
the race were two of the state's best-known politicians, onetime State Attorney General William McCraw and Colonel Ernest O. Thompson, chairman
of the Railroad Commission. McCraw received 152,000 votes. Thompson
got 231,000. O'Daniel got 573,000. Polling 30,000 votes more than the
eleven other candidates combined, he won the Governorship without a
run-off.

With O'Daniel's inauguration, the shape of his true philosophy became
clearer, as did the identity of his true friends. During the campaign, he had
repeatedly promised to fight to the finish any proposed sales tax, which would
fall hardest on the small wage-earners (or "common citizens") whom he was
allegedly championing; no sooner had he been inaugurated than he tried,
unsuccessfully, not only to push through a sales tax (secretly drafted by his
oilmen allies and the state's largest corporations) disguised under a different
name, but to make it a permanent part of state government by incorporating
it in a constitutional amendment (the amendment would also have permanently frozen—at ridiculously low levels—taxes on oil, natural gas and
sulphur). As for his pension plan, he refused to discuss new taxes to pay
for it—lest one of the new taxes turn out to be a tax on oil. And with this
refusal, his pension plan was effectively dead. Almost totally ignorant of the
mechanics of government, O'Daniel proved unwilling to make even a
pretense of learning, passing off the most serious problems with a quip; asked
once what taxes he was proposing to keep the deficit-ridden government's
head above water, he replied that "no power on earth" could make him
say. Ignoring Democratic party machinery, he tried to appoint to key government posts either men with absolutely no experience in the areas over
which they were to be given authority or reactionaries, including members
of the Jeffersonian Democrats, an extremist group that had bitterly opposed
Roosevelt's re-election in 1936. He offered few significant programs in any
area, preferring to submit legislation that he knew could not possibly pass,
and then blame the Legislature for not passing it. He vetoed most significant
programs passed by the Legislature. The Legislature in return rejected many
of his nominees. His problems were exacerbated by his personality: that of a

loner. Walking between the Governor's Mansion and the Capitol, he kept his head down to avoid having to greet passing legislators. (The legislators were not particularly anxious to greet *him*; one reporter, watching the Governor on his walks, called him "the loneliest man I ever saw.") The state's government was all but paralyzed.

But if legislators didn't like him, the voters did—and he knew it. When a reporter asked him, "What are you going to do about delivering the goods?" he held up his hand cupped like a microphone and said: "I've got my own machine. This little microphone." He knew why he had been elected. "Thanks to radio," he said. And he knew how to keep getting elected. He was still on the radio, broadcasting every Sunday morning from the Mansion while his hillbilly band played in the background: "Good morning, ladies and gentlemen, and hello there, boys and girls, this is W. Lee O'Daniel, the Governor of Texas, speaking direct from this beautiful Governor's Mansion in Austin. . . ." He ran for re-election in 1940 because, he explained, he didn't want his pension plan to fall into the hands of demagogues. To the charge that he had betrayed the common citizens, he replied, "How can they say I'm against the working man when I buried my daddy in overalls?" When opponents talked about state financing, he talked about Communists and Nazi fifth-columnists—who he said had infiltrated industrial plants in Texas; he said he had lists of their names, but declined to make them public. Communists and racketeers had also infiltrated the state's labor unions, he said; he coined a phrase, "labor union leader racketeers." Touring the state in his new campaign vehicle—a white bus, with a papier-mâché dome of the Capitol mounted on top, that had been furnished him by one of his secret oilmen backers—he reiterated some version of that phrase over and over; recalls one observer, "He'd just drum, drum, drum with his little catch phrases: 'professional politicians,' 'pussy-footing politicians,' 'labor leader racketeers,' 'Communist labor leader racketeers'—you wouldn't think there would be that many ways to get 'labor leader racketeers' into a sentence. He just got up at his rallies, and said, in effect, 'I'm going to protect you from everything.'" And the people believed he would. In 1938, he had gotten 51 percent of the vote; in 1940, he got 53 percent, winning re-election as he had won election, by beating a field of well-known politicians without even a run-off. He had stormed out of Fort Worth waving a flour sack in one hand and the Decalogue in the other—and had become the greatest vote-getter in the history of Texas, a campaigner who had crushed every opponent he had run against. And during the week of May 15, 1941, the sixth week of the campaign, Lyndon Johnson learned he was running against him.

BEFORE JOHNSON HAD ENTERED the race, he had asked the Governor if he was going to run, and O'Daniel had assured him that he wasn't. The news that he actually was came on the heels of a Belden Poll that said if he ran, he would crush any opponent; according to this forecast, the Governor would get 33 percent of the vote to 9 percent for Johnson. Discounting those figures, Johnson's advisors assured him that the next poll would reflect the rapid increase in his popularity (as in fact, it did), but their Chief was beyond reassurance. He took to his bed. He himself was to recall that the shock "made me feel mighty bad. . . . I know that my throat got bad on me, and I had to spend a few days in the hospital." In fact, he was in the hospital for almost two weeks. Although the illness was described by John Connally as "pneumonia," another Johnson aide called it "nervous exhaustion," and Lady Bird, unknowingly echoing a phrase used by other women who had known Lyndon Johnson when his ambitions were threatened, says, "He was depressed, and it was bad." When doctors told Johnson he would have to be hospitalized, a violent scene erupted at his Happy Hollow Lane house. He insisted to Connally and Gordon Fulcher, an *American-Statesman* reporter working in his campaign, that his illness be kept secret—an insistence that the two aides considered irrational since he wouldn't be able to make scores of public appearances that had already been scheduled; in Connally's words, "He just threw a fit, went into a tirade, ordered us out of the house, said he never wanted to talk to us again." (His hospitalization—not in Austin, but, for reasons of secrecy, at the private Scott and White Clinic in Temple, fifty-seven miles away—was in fact kept quiet for almost a week; fiery stump speaker Everett Looney substituted for Johnson at speaking engagements, saying that the candidate was "busy with organizational work"—an excuse echoed by Marsh's cooperative *American-Statesman*. When, in the second week, the candidate's whereabouts became public knowledge, the *American-Statesman* explained that "the young congressman is getting a much-needed rest from congressional and campaign worries.") The situation became so serious that Wirtz abruptly resigned his Interior Department post and rushed back to Texas to run the campaign on the spot. There may even have been some doubt that Johnson would resume the campaign; there was quiet talk that if he didn't get out of the hospital soon, he might withdraw, using his illness as an excuse. "But," Lady Bird says, "he *did* get out."

He came out—on May 26—much thinner than he had gone in. Whatever had put him in the hospital had melted away most of the fat; although he still had a round little pot belly, he had lost so much weight that the shoulders of his suits slumped down, and his pants bagged away from his body. He came out changed in demeanor, too—as humble with voters now that he feared he was losing as he had been arrogant when he had felt sure he was winning.

And he came out fighting.

In election campaigns in college and for the Little Congress, he had demonstrated a pragmatism that had shaded into the morality of the ballot box, a morality in which any maneuver that leads to victory is justified. Now he displayed the same morality on a larger stage.

There was a ruthlessness to it. Federal loans and grants could give communities and community leaders projects they needed; previously, Johnson had been offering to help communities obtain such grants. Now he changed tactics, using not only the promise but the threat—naked and direct. Communities were told that if they didn't help him, he would see that they didn't get such grants. The threat was used on the leaders of small communities and of large cities alike. Because electricity could transform the lives of farmers, Johnson's influence with the Rural Electrification Administration was a powerful weapon in dealing with rural leaders. His liaison men were told to take off the kid gloves with these leaders. Two Johnson liaison men met, for example, with an influential farmer who was for Mann but whose community was desperate for electricity. Says one of the Johnson men: "We told him straight: 'If your box comes in for Johnson, you'll get the lines.' " If the box didn't come in for Johnson, they made clear, the electric lines that meant so much to the community's people would not be built. (The box came in for Johnson, and the community got electricity.) Fort Worth's leading booster, Amon Carter, publisher of the *Fort Worth Star-Telegram,* wanted a number of federal projects. Stephen Early quoted him the price: support for Lyndon Johnson. (The *Star-Telegram* supported him in a front-page editorial, and Fort Worth got its projects.)

And there was a cynicism. He proclaimed himself the New Deal candidate, running under "the banner of Roosevelt." Few political organizations in the United States hated that banner more than San Antonio's "City Machine," the organization that had been Jack Garner's and that now was dominated by P. L. Anderson, the city's police and fire chief, who wore in his necktie a diamond as big as a peanut, and by the Kilday brothers (Paul, the Congressman, and Owen, the Sheriff), to whom the New Deal was "radicalism" and "Communism." The City Machine's bitter enemy in San Antonio was Mayor Maury Maverick. Maverick was, moreover, one of Johnson's oldest allies; he considered himself Johnson's friend. The day after Johnson emerged from the hospital, however, Maverick was defeated in his bid for re-election as Mayor by the City Machine candidate, C. K. Quin, and abruptly ousted from power in San Antonio. Before the week was out, Johnson had entered into a secret but firm alliance with the City Machine.

Anderson, Quin and the Kildays were not the only Roosevelt-haters with whom the Roosevelt candidate now allied himself. Roy Miller, who as Garner's campaign chief had led the "Stop Roosevelt" movement, is a convenient symbol; the great money-raiser was now quietly raising money for Lyndon Johnson. But at least Roy Miller was an old friend. Needing the power that they could put behind him in their cities and towns, Johnson made new friends. Telling them that in truth he believed as they did, that his campaign rhetoric had little relation to his real feelings, this "liberal" candidate enlisted, while continuing to wage a public campaign based entirely on support for Roosevelt, the private help of some of the most conservative men in Texas, reactionaries such as Dallas millionaire movie magnate Karl Hoblitzelle, who was shortly to organize an anti-labor crusade in Texas; when University of Texas economics instructors sought to speak in support of unions, Hoblitzelle played a leading role in having them fired.

THE CYNICISM was to be demonstrated also in his rallies.

Before O'Daniel had entered the race, Johnson and his advisors had loudly sneered—as did most educated Texans—at the Governor's style of campaigning, with his hillbilly band, his cheap theatrics and his refusal to discuss the issues; O'Daniel's rallies, they said—and Johnson was one of those who said it—were designed to appeal to the lowest common denominator among voters. Now Pass-the-Biscuits-Pappy was in the race, and Johnson no longer sneered at Pappy's rallies. He copied them.

There was one major difference. If the candidate was the centerpiece at an O'Daniel rally, he was not at Johnson's rallies. They were no longer even called "Johnson Rallies." As one newspaper put it, Johnson and his strategists "have at last tumbled to the fact that they can't get anywhere if they don't . . . do something to offset their lack of speaking abilities." The way to offset the candidate's lack of personal appeal, his strategists had decided, was to de-emphasize the candidate. The emphasis was shifted to his issue—Roosevelt—and to a tie-in theme, equally as popular as war grew closer: patriotism. His appearances were called "Patriotic Rallies." Most advertisements for them featured an "All-Out Patriotic Revue"; "a patriotic address by Congressman Lyndon Johnson" was generally in smaller type. And to minimize the candidate's "lack of speaking ability" he was surrounded with pageantry. If Johnson had earlier seemed to be equating Senatorial with "stuffy," that charge could certainly not be made about his rallies once O'Daniel had entered the race.

O'Daniel had made good use of a band. For Johnson's rallies, a six-man swing ensemble was chosen, by audition, from the best musicians in Houston, and named The Patriots. To offset the appeal of O'Daniel's Texas Rose, two-hundred-eighty-five-pound Sophie Parker, "The Kate Smith of the South," was hired, along with a thinner, notably shapely, country and western alto. Blackface comedians were hired, as were dancing girls, Pete Smith and His Accordion, a fifteen-year-old champion harmonica player and the best master of ceremonies in Texas, handsome, golden-voiced Harfield Weedin. These performers—together with a second musical organization, a twenty-four-man "big band" which was used at the largest rallies—were dressed in red, white and blue.

Johnson's rallies were held in civic auditoriums in the larger cities, and outdoors, in the courthouse square or on the bandstand in a park, in smaller towns. No matter what the location, the backdrop was the same: the painting of Franklin D and Lyndon B, larger than life, shaking hands. In a small county seat, the stage and that canvas backdrop would be set up in the square in front of the columns and portico of the old courthouse. As twilight fell, a pair of giant revolving searchlights would be switched on, their circling beams shooting up into the night as a beacon to the surrounding countryside, whose anticipation of the rally would have been honed by radio and news-paper ads. The old Model A's and Model T's would pull into the square, and line up against the far side, and farm families would get out, men in overalls, women in gingham dresses holding babies. By dark, the square would be full. Suddenly spotlights would be switched on, and looming over the people in their glare, framed by big American flags, would be the two huge figures, one, taller and thinner than the other, unfamiliar, but the other, with its heavy head and uptilted jaw, a part of their lives by now, the two figures dark and big against the red, white and blue stripes of the background. Beneath the figures were the words: ROOSEVELT AND UNITY—ELECT LYNDON JOHNSON UNITED STATES SENATOR. A blare of trumpets, and another spot-light would pick out the Patriots, patriotically resplendent in red carnations, white dinner jackets and blue trousers, and the band would swing into "Hail, Hail, the Gang's All Here." And before the dazzled audience would unfold a show such as most of the audience had never seen. The Kate Smith of the South would emerge, all 285 pounds of her, clad in a snow-white evening gown that looked like a great white tent (decorated with red, white and blue ribbons), to sing "I Am an American."

With the patriotism of the evening thus established, it was time for the "jest folks" aspect, which was introduced by the more shapely vocalist, Mary Lou Behn, who would sing "I Want to Be a Cowboy's Sweetheart." Then it was time to bring in the South ("Dixie" by Ms. Parker) and of course Texas ("The Eyes of Texas" and "New San Antonio Rose" by Ms. Behn, "Rancho Grande" by Johnnie Lansy on his harmonica), and a touch of sex in the dancing girls. With these bases covered, the main part of the pageant began.

It was called "The Spirit of '41," and it was narrated by Weedin, who, he recalls, gave "my best imitation of Westbrook Van Voorhis narrating a 'March of Time' newscast." At first, Weedin's wonderfully evocative voice was sad, as he gave a grim recital of America's plight during the Depression. Then it turned dramatic: "On March 4, 1933, we, the American people, inaugurated our thirty-second President, Franklin D. Roosevelt!" (Music: HAPPY DAYS ARE HERE AGAIN—UP TO FULL—THEN SEGUE TO STARS AND

STRIPES FOREVER—ESTABLISH AND FADE TO BACKGROUND) "People were eating chicken and ice cream again. We Americans had again found faith, courage and peace of mind under the leadership of a great Democrat and his *loyal* supporters. . . . We can thank God today that there were enough far-sighted men in Congress, *loyal* men, to see that these social reforms became the law of the land. . . . But [sad music, sad voice] things started to slip again. What did the people do? They re-elected Roosevelt!" (STARS AND STRIPES—SWELL TO FULL) Weedin's voice was happy: "There was more prosperity, more jobs! America was saved! Then [SEGUE TO OMINOUS DRUM ROLL] shadows began to gather over Europe. . . . War clouds gathered— clouds, however, that never hid the monster that raised itself up to gaze with covetous and fiendish eyes upon the democracies of nearby France and England. That same monster now searches out the democracy of the Western Hemisphere! The country needed someone it could trust. What did it do? It re-elected Roosevelt again!"

By this time, Weedin recalls, the audience was cheering and weeping with emotion. "Never have I seen anything other than a religious meeting get an audience so worked up." They were ready for the climax. Roosevelt cannot save Democracy all by himself. He needs "*loyal* supporters in Washington." In particular, he needs a *loyal* supporter from Texas—Texas, which gives America oil, sulphur, metals, wheat and vegetables, the soil for camps and landing fields, and is therefore vital to America's defense. "And, Mr. Roosevelt, on June 28, Texas will make one more contribution to national unity when we show undeniably that we want our President to have a man whose loyalty and cooperation has never been—and *will never* be— questioned. To you, the President, and to the Nation, we give *your* choice for Senator from Texas—Lyndon Baines Johnson!" Another large flag was unfurled on stage, to ripple dramatically in the currents from a small wind machine, the Patriots broke into "God Bless America," the Kate Smith of the South emerged on stage to sing it; as she entered the second chorus, Weedin and the rest of the cast lined up beside her and sang along, hands over their hearts; as they sang, they began marching in place, Weedin's knees enthusi- astically pumping up almost to his chest, Sophie Parker's knees rising as high as they could go—and then Weedin introduced "that dynamic young, native Texan, six-foot-three, that high-riding Texan from the hills of Blanco County . . . ," and as the claque and the rest of the audience roared, out onto the stage bounded the candidate, his arms outstretched high over his head in a useless attempt to stop the cheering, to stand—his chin uptilted as much like Roosevelt's as possible—waving his right arm in an awkward imitation of a Roosevelt wave.

NO LONGER was Lyndon Johnson trying to look Senatorial. Now he was try- ing to win. Except at a few big city rallies, the vest and the carnation were gone; the dark suits of Washington had been replaced by Texas white; the jackets of the suits hung open, or were taken off, exposing sweat-stained, rumpled shirts; his neckties were the ties of the Hill Country again, not of Capitol Hill; they were the ties of his first campaign, the unfashionably short mail-order neckwear of the countryman; their knots, loosened in the heat of campaigning, dangled from an open, sweat-wilted collar.

Unfortunately, however, Johnson's own speeches were usually more anti- than climax. Their theme was the right one before crowds who loved FDR: "I stand for all-out aid to President Roosevelt and his program on every front." Their prose was in keeping with the evening's ambience. Pledging to stand behind the President's efforts to prepare the nation for war, he said:

> We must stop the beast of Berlin before he reaches America. Now if you want your Senator to go up there to Washington to snoop and sneak and snipe at your Commander-in-Chief, don't vote for Lyndon Johnson. Because he'll always support your Commander-in-Chief . . .
>
> The most important job today in our nation is all-out American preparation. We must beat Hitler. We must keep aggressors from American shores. If not, we shall writhe under the dictator's heel as more than a dozen formerly free European nations now are writhing.

All other considerations must bow to the need for preparedness, Johnson said. Strikes by defense workers must be banned, he said; all too often, they were inspired by foreign agitators. "Every fifth-columnist, Communism, Nazism, all proponents of every 'ism' except Americanism must be wiped out." His words were punctuated by shouts from his claque—in the right places. "Do you want another 'no' man like Wheeler or Lindbergh?" (*No! No!*) "Or do you want a man who can say 'yes' to the President, and to whom President Roosevelt can say 'yes'?" (*Yes! Yes!*) "I am proud to be a 'yes man' now, and my critics can make the most of it! I am a 'yes' man because I have placed my flag with the flag of Roosevelt and unity!" (*Applause. Cheers.*) After half an hour or so of speaking, when the candidate would ostentatiously throw aside his prepared speech (which he had finished) and say, "Now let's get down to my country-boy style of talking," the claque would applaud and cheer some more. But the candidate's appearance diminished the effect of his words. Without the concealment of a suit jacket, his little pot belly and his big rear end made him a somewhat comical figure. He had always been very awkward when he ran, and now that awkwardness was on display when he ran out onto the stage as Weedin whipped up the applause. When he had to run up steps to reach the stage, his rear end jutted out so far that small boys in the audience audibly snickered. He practiced end-

lessly trying to wave his right arm as Roosevelt did, but the gesture emerged
so rigid as to be more Hitlerian than Rooseveltian. When speaking, he still
jabbed his finger at the audience, and bellowed at them, and when he wasn't
bellowing, he delivered his text in a harsh, very loud monotone so that
his demeanor was not only awkward but aggressive. During his congressional campaign, he had been able to effect a marvelous empathy with an
audience, as long as it was only a few handfuls to whom he could relate
individually, but utterly unable to do so when the crowd was larger, and
in this Senate campaign all crowds were larger. His problems were especially marked during his "country-boy style of talking." Lyndon Johnson's
real country-boy style was emotional and forceful; the "country-boy" talking he did before these larger crowds was stilted and rehearsed; even the
stories about his father's homilies emerged flat and insincere. Night after
night, the enthusiasm of the crowd—whipped up to fever pitch for the candidate's appearance—crested as he ran out on stage and drained away, moment
by moment, thereafter. In fact, not long after Johnson began speaking,
the audience began leaving; farm families started drifting back to their cars;
small boys started playing tag among the automobiles that remained in the
square.

Another attraction was therefore added to the rallies—one that astonished even Texas political observers who thought they had seen everything.

The attraction was money. It was given away to the audience. In keeping with the "patriotism" theme, it was handed out in the guise of Defense
Bonds and Stamps; every person who attended was given a ticket, and a
drawing was held on stage to determine the winners. Although Johnson's
ads were careful to explain that the lottery would be held in the interest of
the national defense, they emphasized the pecuniary more than the patriotic.
A typical full-page advertisement (this one in the *Williamson Sun*) said that,
at the "Big Patriotic Rally in San Gabriel Park Tuesday Night," not only
would there be "a patriotic review" and "band music" but (in bold black
letters) $25.00 IN DEFENSE TO BE GIVEN AWAY. "12 defense stamps, in the
amount of $25.00 will be given away free to those in attendance by local
citizens who are interested in national defense. Numbered tickets will be
distributed at the rally. Be sure to get yours. Get a ticket for each member of the family. The prizes: One Saving Stamp, $10.00 Value; One
Saving Stamp, $5.00 Value; 10 Saving Stamps, $1.00 Value." If, in rural
areas, as little as $25 was considered sufficient to attract the citizenry, in
cities the amounts were higher: $100 in Port Arthur, for example, $175 in
Austin.

The new attraction worked. Night after night, the *American-Statesman*
commented, Johnson was now "addressing thousands where three weeks ago
he was talking to hundreds." To keep the audience at the rally until its end
—despite the dullness of the candidate's speech—the bonds and stamps were

not distributed until after the speech. The squirrel cage device from which the winning tickets would be drawn was placed in a prominent position on the stage, and it stood there all the time Johnson was talking. Its presence had the hoped-for effect: the crowds stayed to the end. As the *State Observer* noted in a description of a typical Johnson rally, despite the heat and the swarms of bugs attracted by the spotlights, 15,000 persons "stood crowded together" until Johnson had finished speaking. "They all kept their eyes on the speakers' stand. They jealously guarded hundreds of lottery tickets. They were all waiting for the free money."

The reaction of Texas journalists to "free money" was summed up in the *Granger News'* two-word comment: *"Glory be!"* National journalists who came to Texas to watch the campaign were more caustic. "At political rallies, Johnson drew the crowds by handing out defense bonds and stamps, thereby demonstrating his patriotic fervor and simultaneously proving that he was a handy man to have around between paydays," wrote Jack Guinn in the *American Mercury*.

National journalists were somewhat startled by the campaign as a whole. "The current election campaign in Texas to fill the late Morris Sheppard's seat in the United States Senate contains so many elements of the ridiculous that at times it is difficult to take it seriously," wrote Roland Young in *The Nation*. *Time* magazine called the campaign the "biggest carnival in American politics."

But beneath that carnival atmosphere, a grim battle was taking place.

Two Johnson tactics much more subtle than his rallies were proving much more effective.

One was based on the devotion to O'Daniel and the faith in Pass-the-Biscuits-Pappy among the poor people of Texas. Lying in the hospital, Lyndon Johnson had devised a stratagem that made O'Daniel's popularity work against him. Johnson's thousands of workers—not only his teams of paid, expert campaign workers but the REA employees bringing electricity to the farms, the meter readers of the electric co-ops, the soil-conservation experts and county agents and other federal employees who spent their days traveling from farm to farm—were told to use a new argument: Pappy O'Daniel is a great Governor and a great man. We need him in Texas. Let's keep him in Texas.

This argument was particularly persuasive when it was linked to pensions. Dozens of weekly newspapers—the only source of news to so many rural families in Texas—made the link by reprinting a *Fort Worth Press* article sent to them by Johnson headquarters, under a headline suggested by the headquarters: WILL THE OLD FOLKS KILL THEIR GOLDEN GOOSE?

Aesop, the old fable teller, may have called the turn on the Texas Senate race.

Remember the folks who killed the goose that laid the golden
eggs—and then there weren't any more eggs?
. . . If O'Daniel is elected Senator he can't be Governor any
more. He will have to resign. . . . If the people elect O'Daniel
Senator they may be killing their pension hopes. O'Daniel can't be
a pension-giving Governor and a U.S. Senator at the same time.

Pappy is fighting for our pensions, a county agent would remind a farm
family who had invited him to share their dinner. The Legislature is keeping
us from getting those pensions. If Pappy leaves for Washington, there won't
be anyone left in Austin to fight for pensions. We need him in Austin. But
the argument was effective even when it wasn't linked to pensions. For
to many of O'Daniel's faithful, the strongest reason for not electing him to
the Senate was their love for him. They didn't want him to leave them, to
go to faraway Washington; they couldn't bear to lose him. The argument was
working. Recalls one Johnson campaign worker: "I said, 'O'Daniel's
made us a good Governor—let's keep him there.' I said, 'Don't send Pappy
way up there to Washington with all those professional politicians.' And
that argument really touched. They loved Pappy. They didn't want him to
go away."

O'Daniel's campaign manager, his Secretary of State, William J.
Lawson, saw that the argument was indeed "touching." The evidence was
piled on a long table in Lawson's office in the Capitol. On his Sunday-morning broadcasts, O'Daniel was, both before and after he announced for the
Senate, using the tactic that had worked so well for him in his previous campaigns: asking his listeners to write and tell him if they thought he should run
for Senator. As always, the response was immense. It would begin coming in
Tuesday morning, and would keep coming on Wednesday. Each delivery
brought so many letters and postcards to the Post Office branch in the
Capitol that Lawson would have to recruit a crew of porters to haul the big
mail sacks back to his office. Secretaries would go through the mail, dividing
into separate piles on the table the replies urging him to go to the Senate and
those urging him not to.

At first, the piles were very unequal. Lawson, who counted them, says,
"At first, it was maybe ninety to ten that he should run for the Senate. 'We'll
support you. Anything you want, we'll help you.' " This response duplicated
that of 1938 and 1940, and O'Daniel was sure it would continue, and that
the result of those campaigns would be duplicated in 1941. "He got a little
smug," Lawson says. "He didn't think he was going to have to [actively
campaign]." But it didn't continue. The pile urging O'Daniel to run began,
day by day, to grow smaller, the pile urging him not to began to grow higher.
One day, to Lawson's shock, the latter pile was bigger than the former. And,
day by day, this trend continued.

"I didn't see any reason why it should change, in just two or three weeks, like this," Lawson says. Although he had previously taken little interest in the campaign—believing none was necessary—"I went down to the hotel lobbies and the restaurants" frequented by politicians, "and over and over again, I heard the same explanation: 'Well, Bill, here's what's doing it. It seems that Lyndon Johnson's people in all the counties had started this rumor: "O'Daniel is a great Governor. Why send him to Washington? Keep him here. He'll be more valuable here." ' Johnson's previous arguments had been too complicated for the people out there to grasp. But just a little simple lie—'He's doing more for you than any Governor ever did; it'd be silly for us to vote to send him to Washington'—they could grasp that. And that spread like wildfire."

Johnson saw that it was touching. After just a week back on the campaign trail, he had sufficient confidence in the argument to use it publicly. Over statewide radio hook-ups, he pointed out that although the federal government would match a state's contribution to Social Security up to $20 per recipient per month, Texas, because of the state's empty treasury, had been putting up only $4.75. Instead of a possible $40 per month, he told his listeners, "Your pension checks will average $9.50" until the state's contribution rises. "The best thing you can do is to keep your Governor on the job until you get that forty dollars a month, and while he is holding that end up for you here, Lyndon Johnson, as your Senator in Washington, can work with President Roosevelt toward" increased federal pensions. Waving a twenty-dollar bill before the audience at his rallies, he said, "Your Governor can't raise that money in Washington." So effective was the argument that Johnson's strategists considered printing up a new bumper sticker, KEEP PAPPY IN TEXAS, but that tactic was considered too blatant.

Soon there was harder evidence that this argument was touching. In McLennan County, for example, a mass meeting of local pension clubs and "friends of Governor W. Lee O'Daniel" was called "to discuss a resolution urging the Governor's withdrawal from the campaign," in order, a spokesman for the clubs said, "to ensure that 'a friend of the pensioner' would remain in the Governor's chair."

THE GOVERNOR HIMSELF was hardly aware of this threat to his plans. With crucial appropriations stalled by a hostile Legislature, the state government was in disarray, and he had pledged not to leave Austin until the bills were passed and the Legislature had adjourned. At the end of May—two weeks after he had announced he was running—he still had not made a single campaign appearance; his campaigning consisted solely of his Sunday-morning broadcasts. Not out among the people, he was not aware of their feelings. Nor did he see any reason to be; "he had expected to win just by announcing," Lawson said. When Lawson told him he was behind both Johnson and Mann, his reaction was disbelief; it wasn't until he had checked around the state himself that he found that Lawson was correct. "He didn't like to lose," Lawson said. He told his Secretary of State to get the campaign in gear.

But Johnson's second subtle tactic—one quieter (and even more effective) than the first—kept those gears from turning. The legislative session had already dragged on far longer than normal; and O'Daniel, sure it would not last much longer, announced that he would open a statewide speaking tour on June 2 in Waco. But working for Johnson behind the scenes in Austin were two men with a lot of legislators in their pockets: Alvin Wirtz, 1940 head of the Roosevelt campaign in Texas, and Roy Miller, 1940 head of the Stop Roosevelt campaign in Texas. The crucial appropriations bills remained unpassed, and every attempt to have the Legislature adjourn—or recess—was defeated. The Governor brought Molly, Mickey-Wickey, his hillbilly band and his big sound truck with the Capitol dome on top to Waco on the 2nd, but immediately after that one speech, he had to return in it to Austin. Canceling his speaking dates for the following week, he said he hoped he would be able to start his statewide tour by June 9. During the week of the 2nd, however, no fewer than eight separate plans for adjournment or recess were presented—and if one was approved by one house, it was disapproved by the other. The Governor had to cancel the next week's engagements, too—and then the next; the 1941 Legislature was staying in session longer than any other Legislature in the state's history. On June 16, desperate, he announced that he was sending his children out in his place, each with half the hillbilly band; Molly, speaking in Waco the next day, said that "Dad got a raw deal from the Legislature, which for some unknown reason, won't adjourn." But the kids and the band were no substitute for Pappy himself, and "many voters were resentful after he had made engagements and cancelled them." As late as June 18, just ten days before the election, he still hadn't gotten out on the road. Pappy O'Daniel was perhaps the greatest campaigner in the history of Texas—but Lyndon Johnson wasn't letting him campaign.

AND ALWAYS there was the money.

The "free money" given away at the "Patriotic Rallies" was a very minor item in their cost. There were the salaries of Harfield Weedin, and of the two singers, the harmonica player, the accordion player, and the band (or bands). There was the cost of transporting the cast—and the flags and the huge, rolled-up canvas of the Galveston handshake—around the state, which meant the rental of a bus and the salary of a driver. Weedin had been wary when he was approached to put the show together. "I had worked in Texas politics before, so the cash was always in advance," he says. But he had learned quickly that he could stop worrying: the Lyndon Johnson campaign was unlike other political campaigns. There was money available to pay for the talent and the transportation—and for much more besides. Johnson wanted big crowds, so he wanted newspaper advertising before each rally, and soon a Houston advertising agency was "up to their ears with artwork and getting the necessary plates and mats prepared." And when, on May 26, Weedin and his troupe arrived in Wichita Falls for the first rally, he got a better indication of the financial resources at Johnson's disposal. "Full pages had been purchased in each of the Wichita Falls papers," and in every weekly newspaper for a hundred miles around. (Weedin also noticed that in the ads for the "All-Out Patriotic Revue" presented by "Friends of Roosevelt," "not one word was mentioned that there would also be an address by Congressman Lyndon B. Johnson, candidate for Senator from Texas.") And, Weedin adds, "Naturally, Congressman Johnson's words were too important to be wasted upon only the few thousand people assembled at the rally, so his speeches were always broadcast—and on a tremendous number of stations which joined together to form a network for each occasion." For six weeks, the Lyndon B. Johnson Show was on the road ("Big Spring, Eastland, Abilene, Denison, Waco, Dallas, Amarillo, Austin, San Angelo, Corpus Christi, Harlingen, Marshall, San Antonio, and so on, night after night— Man! Texas is a big state! One hop alone, from Harlingen to Marshall, was over eight hundred miles," Weedin recalls), and for six weeks the money never ran out. In fact, more and more was spent. A press agent, an ace reporter from the *Houston Post*, was hired, and advance men were attached to the entourage. And when Johnson's campaign managers realized that Weedin was a celebrity local politicians wanted to meet, he was removed from the bus and flown (along with the press agent) from stop to stop in an oilman's ten-seat Lockheed with built-in bar so that he would arrive in advance of the troupe and could entertain the local VIP's in a hotel suite stocked with whiskey. Weedin was very impressed; campaign funds of unprecedented magnitude "sprang from nowhere," he says.

Every aspect of the campaign was being carried on in a similarly unprecedented scale: the banks of typists and telephoners on the hotel mezzanine in Austin, and in campaign headquarters in El Paso and Lubbock and San Angelo and Houston and Corpus Christi, the posters and placards with which, as one observer put it, Lyndon Johnson seemed to be trying to "plaster the state," the billboards, of which new crops blossomed weekly, the newspaper advertising. The impact of the Johnson money was particularly strong on the airwaves, of course. Radio was rapidly becoming the most potent political weapon, but it was a weapon that could be wielded only by those who could afford it. Although Johnson's radio campaign had already been on a scale new to Texas, he wanted that scale expanded—greatly expanded. Mayor Tom Miller was as strong a speaker as he himself was weak. After hearing Miller make one particularly effective speech, he told the Mayor he wanted it on the air every day "from now until election. Please contact John Connally and arrange to make that speech this week over statewide hook-up." Roy Hofheinz, the young Harris County Judge who was one of his campaign managers, was a great speaker; Johnson wanted Hofheinz on the air more often. He wanted other supporters on the air more often. And he wanted advance advertising for those speeches—plenty of advertising.

So fast was the Johnson campaign spending money that, despite the lavishness with which the campaign had been funded, the money began to run out. At one point in late May the twelve teams almost had to be brought in off the road; so low were funds that the owner of the rented sound trucks sent dunning letters to Johnson headquarters. Therefore more money had to be raised. Some was raised in Washington—with the help of a tactic suggested by Wirtz: a recording was made of an O'Daniel speech criticizing Roosevelt, and it was sent to Washington to be played for Corcoran and Rowe, where it had the desired effect of intensifying their enthusiasm for O'Daniel's defeat. Envelopes stuffed with cash cascaded into Texas. So much money was sent, in fact, that Johnson sometimes lost the personal control of its use that was so important to him. Corcoran "went up to the garment district and raised money for Johnson, and we . . . sent it to Texas" via one of the men active in his campaign, Rowe says. "Johnson called and said: 'Where's that money? I need it!' " Told the identity of the courier, Johnson grew upset, apparently because the man had authority to distribute funds on his own. Rowe recalls Johnson saying: "Goddamn it—it'll never get to me. I'll have to meet him at the plane and get it from him." The fate of one envelope in particular caused the candidate to erupt in wrath. On June 20, Walter Jenkins, who had remained in Washington to run Johnson's office there, left for Texas on Braniff's midnight flight. He was carrying between $10,000 and $15,000. The money, collected by a Washington lobbyist from Texas, was in small bills; "I went down to Texas carrying this money in bills stuffed into every pocket," Jenkins recalls.

When the plane arrived in Austin the next morning, Jenkins immediately went to campaign headquarters, "and the first guy I saw was Charles Marsh." Marsh said: "You got that money? Well, Lyndon has told me to take it."

Aware of Marsh's influential role in the campaign, Jenkins assumed that Johnson did indeed want the publisher to have the money, and he gave it to him. Actually, however, Johnson did not. Marsh wanted to use the money for advertising; Johnson wanted it for other purposes, but knew that if the imperious publisher got his hands on it, he would spend it his way. The realization that he had made a mistake dawned on Jenkins when Johnson asked him for the money, and, informed that it had been given to Marsh, exploded. Jenkins recalls that "I caught hell from Mr. Johnson," who,

Jenkins says, told him that, having been entrusted with a large sum of money, "You turn it over to the first person you see!"*

Conservative lobbyists and New Deal strategists—both groups were sending cash to Texas to help Lyndon Johnson. This unanimity was displayed in New York, too. The liberal garment center leaders sent more money—and so did New York conservatives who were interested in power; men who hated Roosevelt and what he stood for, but who needed an "in" at the White House and who had been told by Ed Weisl that the way to get it was to back Lyndon Johnson. Principle or power—both found expression in cash for Lyndon Johnson.

To obtain most of his new supply of money, however, no tactic was needed. For most of it came from Brown & Root. That firm had made so large an investment in the Johnson campaign already that a further investment was only logical, and it was not only logic that dictated. Herman Brown had thrown himself into the fight, and, as his lobbyist Frank Oltorf says, "Herman didn't want to lose any fights." Yet it was beginning to look as if he might lose this one. He summoned the "subs" again. Describing Herman's demeanor in meetings with contractors, men familiar with these meetings say that he would say, "I'm putting you down for a thousand"—or two thousand, or five. And if someone balked, Herman would look at the man, and say, very quietly, "Now listen, we've made you a lot of money." And he got the sums he wanted. He called in his insurance man, Gus S. Wortham, president of the American General Insurance Company of Houston, and Wortham subsequently gave cash to an American General employee who took it to radio stations, and paid for Johnson political broadcasts with it. He distributed money to men who knew how to use money in Texas: $4,000 to Roy Miller, for example.

Herman Brown didn't ask others to give if he wasn't giving himself, although he appears to have had some qualms about what he was doing. Sometime during these months, a member of the Brown & Root hierarchy called in one of the firm's tax attorneys, and asked him if political contributions were deductible expenses. The attorney told him what he already knew —that they were not. But Brown made the contributions anyway: giving more "legal fees" to attorneys who passed the money on to the campaign, more "bonuses" to executives who did the same thing.

With the campaign roaring to its climax, caution was flung to the winds. Some $7,581 was paid to a sub-contractor, W. L. Trotti, as "rental" for some equipment; Trotti placed the funds in a dormant bank account, and made

* The ultimate disposition of this shipment of cash is unclear. Jenkins says that Marsh used it for newspaper advertising, "and that wasn't what it was supposed to be used for." Marsh's personal secretary, Mary Louise Glass, says that the publisher, after taking the money from Jenkins, gave it to her to hold, "and I put it in a white mesh purse. It just bulged with money. I carried it around two or three days." She says that when Marsh took it back, he used it to purchase not newspaper but radio advertising.

withdrawals to "cash." An IRS agent who later investigated believed the cash was given to the campaign—which would be a more transparent device than any previously used. Herman even drew money himself—$5,000 in one instance—and gave it to the campaign through Austin banker Walter Bremond, Jr. No tactic was necessary for Lyndon Johnson in dealing with Herman Brown. All he had to do was ask. No one knows how much Brown & Root gave to the 1941 Lyndon Johnson campaign for Senator, and no one will ever know, but the amount was in the neighborhood of $200,000. No one knows how much was spent in total in that campaign, and no one will ever know. But in an era in which the cost of a typical Texas political campaign ran in the tens of thousands of dollars, Lyndon Johnson spent hundreds of thousands of dollars—according to one estimate, half a million dollars. Johnson's first campaign for the House of Representatives had been one of the most expensive congressional campaigns in the history of Texas. His first campaign for the Senate was *the* most expensive campaign in the history of Texas. Even in a state in which money had always been a significant factor in politics, his use of money to obtain political office was unprecedented.

More significant than the amount of money was its availability. Asked how much money Johnson was given in 1941, Ed Clark says flatly: "All he needed. If he had $50,000 or $100,000 more, that wouldn't have mattered. He had as much as he asked for."

SOME VOTES for Lyndon Johnson were being purchased more directly, for it was not only the size of Texas that made campaigning so expensive but the ethics that pervaded politics in entire sections of it.

One of these sections was San Antonio, and the area south of it to the Rio Grande. "The way to play politics in San Antonio," as John Gunther was to write, "is to buy, or try to buy, the Mexican vote, which is decisive." The city's West Side was a gigantic slum, containing perhaps 60,000 residents, who were paid, Gunther says, "probably the lowest wages in the United States"—for pecan shellers (San Antonio was the "Pecan Capital of the World) an average of $1.75 per week. It might have been supposed that the support of these disadvantaged people would go to advocates of the New Deal which was attempting to improve the lot of the disadvantaged, but in fact they voted at the direction of their leaders—who were motivated mainly by cash. Some of it they passed out to individual voters: two, three, or, perhaps, five dollars per voter. A single payment might not be enough—which inspired what Gunther calls a "cruel little joke, 'An honest Mexican is one who *stays* bought.'" Explains San Antonio Postmaster Dan Quill: "First [some months before the election] you had to pay their poll taxes. And that was a very dangerous thing to do because they might take your money, and then on Election Day some guy might come along and give them five dollars, and they'd vote the other way—with *your* poll taxes." Constant precautions were therefore necessary; in many of San Antonio's "Mexican boxes" election supervisors would, in violation of law, stand alongside each voter in the voting booths to make certain that each vote was cast as paid for. Even the supervisors might take a candidate's money and deliver the precinct's votes to another candidate, who had paid more (or had paid later); the supervisors had to be watched by other men, more trusted men, usually from the candidate's own staff. On Election Day, careful candidates had men "riding the polls" in San Antonio—driving from polling place to polling place to make sure the candidate was getting what he had paid for. Northern liberals might rhapsodize, as Sherwood Anderson did after one Maverick election victory, that he had, through implementation of New Deal policies, bought the West Side's votes in a "new and legal way," but in fact the use of cash had played a not inconsiderable role in his victories—and in 1941, he had learned again the crucial factor in San Antonio elections the hard way; "Maury Maverick won when he carried the West Side, and lost when he didn't carry the West Side," Gunther was to write; in 1941, this champion of the New Deal had been heavily outspent by the "City Machine" on the West Side, and had lost it and the election.

In 1941, Lyndon Johnson needed the West Side, for he was very unpopular on the North Side, among the city's large, and conservative, Catholic population; the San Antonio Rotary Club had refused even to let him address it during the campaign. He knew, of course, how to get the West Side; he had himself participated in the purchase of votes on the most basic level when, still a congressional secretary, he had sat in a hotel room handing dollar bills and five-dollar bills to Mexicans on behalf of Maury Maverick. Now he had to buy in large lots.

He had a good man handling the West Side. Dan Quill had been handling such jobs for a long time. He had begun in 1931, when Kleberg ran for the first time, and Roy Miller gave him money and told him he was responsible for one of the Mexican "boxes." "It was right in the heart of Mexican Town" in an area dangerous for an outsider even to walk through, the tough little Irishman was to recall forty years later. "That was a real terrible slum." But he moved there "so I could be eligible to be an election supervisor there. I moved into a house there with a school janitor who was also going to be a supervisor. We were scared; we locked the doors. . . ." But on Election Day, he carried his box, and he had been carrying key Mexican boxes for the next ten years. He knew every trick of the trade—and he knew how much money was needed to get Lyndon Johnson San Antonio's West Side vote. "We figured we needed ten thousand dollars," he says—and that sum was provided.

The reason Quill didn't need more—$10,000 was a comparatively small investment in the West Side—was Lyndon Johnson's new alliance with the "City Machine." The alliance was kept secret, so secret that most of Johnson's closest advisors didn't know about it, but the alliance was solid. With the Kildays, Mayor Quin and Sheriff Anderson on Johnson's side, Quill was

excused from responsibility for those Mexican boxes which they controlled—
and which would be delivered to Johnson by them; "If the leader [in a box]
was a deputy sheriff [for example], we figured he'd control his precinct. We
didn't spend any money there." San Antonio, third largest city in Texas, was
a key to any statewide election. Johnson may have been unpopular there, but,
thanks to his foresight when still a congressional secretary years before, now,
running for statewide office, he could be sure of Quill's 1,500 votes "who
ought to follow in the steps of the Postmaster." Now he was confident that
San Antonio would give him about 10,000 more.

South of San Antonio, south even of Cotulla, was "The Valley."

In the counties that bordered the lower reaches of the Rio Grande,
which separated the United States from Mexico, and in the counties which
adjoined them to the north—the counties of the South Texas brush country
—votes were delivered *en masse* to a degree true of perhaps no other region
in the United States.*

Only because of the drawing of a border were these counties part of the
United States. More than half their inhabitants were Mexican not merely by
descent but by culture; they spoke only Spanish, and clung to the customs
of their homeland across the river; their tiny, dozing towns, strung like beads
along it, "bore," one traveler wrote in 1940, "an appearance as foreign as
their names"—San Ygnacio, Santa Maria, La Paloma, Los Indios. Their
houses were thatched adobe huts or *jacales,* one- or two-room structures of
willow branches daubed with mud, around which swarmed goats and chickens
and children. In the larger cities—Laredo, Harlingen—they lived in shacks
in sprawling slums; entering these slums was like entering a foreign city.
Largely illiterate, they had, as V. O. Key, Jr., noted, "only the most remote
conception of Anglo-American governmental institutions." One custom
prevalent in the near-feudalistic regions of Mexico from which they came
was that of dependence on a local leader, the *patron* or *jefe;* "from time
immemorial, they had given obedience . . . to the head or overseer of the
ranch," one observer wrote. They continued this custom in America. In this
region of great ranches, where so many of the Mexicans worked—the King
Ranch, which extended over four of the counties in this region, alone employed more than 700 *vaqueros—el patron* was often the ranch owner. The
cattle barons, Weeks wrote, "established themselves as lords protector of
those Mexicans who became their tenants and ranch hands." The resulting
relationship was feudal, with the *vaqueros* giving "unquestioning loyalty to
the ranch owners and regard[ing] their wishes as law, the only law he knows."
But some of these *patrons* were political bosses—ruthless, in some cases
vicious, men who stalked the streets of the dusty little towns in their domains

* All these counties were lumped together as "The Valley" in Texas political
parlance of that era.

surrounded by armed, unshaven *pistoleros;* politics was violent in the Valley. A reporter from Philadelphia who journeyed there in 1939 found "as hard-bitten a political crowd . . . as Texas ever saw . . . Each [county] has its own iron-fisted boss, who would make Philadelphia's Jay Cooke or New York's Jimmy Hines look like pikers." The most famous among them, the Valley's Boss of Bosses, was George Parr, son of Archie Parr, the legendary Duke of Duval, and now Duke in his own right. The Parrs had ruled Duval County since 1912, when Archie sided with the Mexicans after an "Election Day Massacre" in San Diego, the county seat, had left three of them dead. But others, less well known, had been in power even longer. Among the petty despots who ruled along the Rio Grande—Judge Bravo of Zapata County; Judge Raymond of Webb (a figure, one chronicler wrote, so secretive that "little is known of him except rumor," who ruled Laredo "with an iron hand"), Sheriff Chub Pool of La Salle; the "Guerra boys," four brothers who ran Starr County—were some whose families had held power in their dusty duchies for half a century.

On Election Day, Mexican-Americans were herded to the polls by armed *pistoleros*, sometimes appointed "deputy sheriffs" for the day; each voter was handed a receipt showing he had paid his poll tax (usually these taxes had been purchased by the *jefes* months before and kept in their safes to, as Key puts it, "insure discipline and orderly procedure"). In some precincts, these voters were also handed ballots that had already been marked; according to one description,

> The Mexican voter . . . was marched to the polls, generally by a half-breed deputy sheriff with two six-shooters, a Winchester rifle, and a bandoleer of ammunition, to perform the sovereign act of voting. He entered the polls, one at a time, was handed a folded ballot which he dropped in the box, was given a drink of Tequila, and then was marched out, where he touched the hand of one of the local political bosses or some of his sainted representatives.

In other precincts, matters were managed less crudely: the voters were told whom to vote for, but were allowed to mark their own ballots; of course, the guards accompanied them into the voting cubbyholes to ensure that the instructions were followed. Even if the voter was allowed to cast his ballot in secrecy, he had little chance of escaping unnoticed if he disobeyed instructions; each ballot was given a number that corresponded to the number on a tear-off sheet attached to the ballot, and a voter had to sign his name on the sheet before it was torn from the ballot and the ballot cast. This procedure had been enshrined in Texas law ostensibly to keep a person from voting more than once, but it also allowed the election judges to know—by matching the tear sheet to the ballot—how a citizen voted. Some *jefes* dispensed with all this bother; an attorney for one of them, who let his voters keep their poll tax receipts, recalls his procedure: "Go around to the Mexicans' homes. Get the numbers of their [poll tax] receipts. Tell them not to go to the polls. Just write in 100 numbers, and cast the 100 votes yourself."

The number of votes at the *jefes'* command was not necessarily limited by the number of eligible voters. Another advantage of the poll tax system to the Valley "machines" was that after the age of sixty, a voter did not have to pay the tax. Poll tax lists were checked only irregularly to eliminate the names of those who died after sixty, and, in the words of one expert on the subject, when an election was close in Texas, "in the Valley, the 'machine' votes the dead men." Nor were all voters even American citizens; on Election Day the saloons of the Mexican town of Reynosa, across the Rio Grande from Hidalgo, were cleaned out, and truckloads of Mexicans were brought across to vote in Texas; Starr County was also "an excellent location for bringing voters from across the border," a commentator notes. In Webb County, the small town of Dolores had about 100 American citizens—and in some elections recorded as many as 400 votes. As a result of such tactics, the vote from the Valley (a vote which generally went "all one way": the *jefes* had learned to stick together to maximize their impact—and influence—on Texas politics) rarely displayed the diversity of opinion associated with a democracy; some 15,000 votes were generally believed to be controlled in the Valley, and it was not unusual for them to go to a favored candidate by margins as large as ten to one.

The decisive consideration was cash. The power of these petty despots was matched by their greed. Not content with siphoning off hundreds of thousands of dollars from every aspect of municipal government (the Parrs "treated the county budget virtually as their own personal bank account," says one Texas historian), the Parrs collected a nickel "tax" on every bottle of beer sold in Duval; visitors inquiring why beer, twenty cents everywhere else in Texas, cost twenty-five cents in Duval, were informed that the extra nickel was for "George." To some of these despots, votes were a commodity like any other—a commodity to be sold. According to the best history of politics in the Valley, "The State candidates who have the most money to spend usually carry these machine counties." In 1940, O'Daniel had carried them—with their customary unanimity. George Parr's Duval County, for example, had given the Governor 3,728 votes, to a total of 180 for the other seven candidates. But in 1941, efforts were being made to ensure that these counties would be carried by Lyndon Johnson instead. These efforts had begun almost as soon as the campaign had begun. Brown & Root played a hand in them; on April 23, the firm's "Labor Director" informed Johnson that one bloc vote—the state's captive labor unions—had been secured ("Statewide labor vote assured, but no noise"), and added: "Latin American support in lower counties is next objective. Looks easy." For a while, with Mann refusing to buy votes, and Dies refusing to take an interest in buying them, this assessment proved correct. On May 9, Johnson headquarters was assured by a scout it had sent to the Valley that "this district . . . is for Lyndon Johnson." The George Parr machine, the scout said, is "very active for Johnson." The entrance into the campaign of the Valley's 1940 favorite changed the situation—nor would this be the first time that the Valley's commitment to a candidate had been changed by a later, higher, offer from another candidate. But Alvin Wirtz was an old ally of the Parrs. He had personally negotiated with old Archie, with whom he had served in the State Senate, for the Parr-controlled votes in Nueces County in a 1928 Democratic attempt to defeat Congressman Harry Wurzbach which failed when Wurzbach made charges of election fraud stick. When, with Johnson hospitalized and the campaign in crisis, Wirtz rushed to Texas, he stopped over in Dallas, where he held a meeting with the campaign's treasurer, oilman Lechner. Then he disappeared for several days; only later would puzzled newsmen learn that during these days Wirtz had been in South Texas. No one can say with certainty what he was doing there, although, according to sources whose information on other, more verifiable, Wirtz activities invariably proves correct, he and O'Daniel supporters were engaged in a bidding war for the Valley's votes. Lyndon Johnson himself contacted George Parr on the telephone at least once, in the presence of Polk and Emmett Shelton, two of Parr's attorneys. By June 18, the situation had been resolved. Horace Guerra of Starr County, Parr's principal ally, assured Johnson, "You can depend on my and my friends' wholehearted support. I predict Starr County will give you a substantial majority."

IF O'DANIEL COULD USE the popular revival-meeting tune "Give Me That Old-Time Religion," Johnson could, too—and his lyrics incorporated the name that in Texas was second in potency only to Christ's: "Franklin D and Lyndon B / They're good enough for me." With Pappy having entered the race, moreover, Johnson felt he needed increased support from "Franklin D" —and he got it. Asked at another Oval Office press conference if he had any additional comment on the Texas race, the President "smilingly" replied that "he thought he had done a good job the first time and was quite certain the people of Texas understood him." (Their understanding was facilitated by a description of the press conference written at Johnson headquarters and run verbatim by scores of obliging weeklies under a headline also written at headquarters: FDR ENDORSES JOHNSON.) Roosevelt also decided that Steve Early should reply to a letter from a Texas voter who had inquired if Johnson was indeed the President's choice. Although he was still unwilling to have his support stated flatly, Roosevelt directed Early (and James Rowe, who was helping to draft the reply) in precisely what words to use so that his support would be clear nonetheless. And to ensure that it became public, he told Rowe that if the voter did not release Early's letter, Johnson could release it himself. The letter said:

> . . . At a press conference several weeks ago, the President made his position perfectly clear. He told the newspapermen that he is not taking any part in the Texas primary as that is solely a question for Texas to decide. In answering a question the President stated something which everybody knows to be true, which is that Congressman Lyndon Johnson is an old and close friend of his.

Because of O'Daniel's entry into the race, another presidential letter was requested—this one to help Johnson counter the strength with the elderly that O'Daniel possessed because of his pension plan. Rowe balked at this request. He was continually being pushed by Johnson and Wirtz for greater presidential involvement in the campaign, and he had, over and over again, given them what they asked for. Now he was fearful that he had gotten the President too involved. And he felt that in the suggested wording of this letter, Johnson had gone too far: it attributed to the junior Congressman a totally non-existent role in the fight for Social Security. "I thought he was asking too much. I said, 'Goddammit, Lyndon, I can't do too much. We've done so much for you already—I can't go back" and ask for this. He refused to do so, and even sent the President a cautionary note: "The polls show Lyndon leading at this time (but I suspect they are Lyndon's polls)." But Johnson only used other avenues to reach the President. "Four days later, the letter comes out anyway," Rowe says. "He just went right around me."

> Dear Lyndon:
>
> I have your letter favoring further help for our senior citizens over 60 years of age. As you remember, you and I discussed the problem before the Chicago convention of the Democratic Party last year. Our ideas were incorporated in the party platform, which called for the "early realization of a minimum pension for all who have reached the age of retirement and are not gainfully employed." I agree with you that the implementation of this pledge is the best solution of the problem. I hope you will come in and talk to me about it when you return.
>
> Very sincerely yours,
> Franklin D. Roosevelt

(Johnson made the most of this letter, reading it over a statewide radio network and saying, "As your Senator I can and will continue to take your problems to our President. I have worked with him for years and I shall continue to work with him for you." And Marsh's *American-Statesman*—and many country weeklies—carried the story under the headline: F.D. TO HELP JOHNSON ON PENSION PLAN.)

The wording of this letter made clear to Rowe that he hadn't understood how far the President was willing to go on behalf of the young Congressman. And Rowe was to be reminded of this again and again. Already well on his way to becoming one of Washington's smoothest political operators, he understood very well the seldom stated White House rules that governed Roosevelt's participation in the campaign of even a highly favored candidate, but he became aware that Roosevelt would make an exception to the rules for Lyndon Johnson.

During the last month of the campaign, Roosevelt's "special feeling" for Johnson was documented over and over again.

Much of it was couched in the form of telegrams.

To many Texans, who had never received one, there was a mystique about telegrams, and they were handy props at campaign rallies because they could be pulled from a pocket and read to an audience. A steady stream of telegrams was sent to Texas at the direction of the White House, to be pulled from Johnson's pocket and waved dramatically before crowds at rallies, and read by him (to make sure that the audience would remember the message, he read the telegram twice or even three times), and be printed in Marsh's six papers or in the weeklies that ran the canned stories emanating from his headquarters, and be reproduced in the hundreds of thousands of campaign flyers and pamphlets and brochures that, day after day, poured into homes throughout Texas. Some were endorsements: from Vice President Wallace, from Interior Secretary Ickes and Navy Secretary Frank Knox and other Cabinet members—even from Eleanor Roosevelt, who scarcely knew (and didn't particularly like) Johnson. And there were numerous telegrams from the President himself. One was designed to counter criticism of Johnson's long absence from his duties in Washington during a national emergency. (Roosevelt had declared one on May 27, with the Wehrmacht massing on the Russian front and the Battle of the Atlantic at fever pitch—the German battleship *Bismarck* had just been sunk off the French coast.) Johnson sent a plea for help to Missy LeHand, telling her: I AM BEING CALLED A SLACKER TO AN OLD TRUSTED FRIEND. To ensure getting the reply he wanted, he had Wirtz draft one:

> . . . WE SHOULD NOT LOSE SIGHT OF OUR ULTIMATE OBJECTIVE
> WHICH IS THE DEFENSE OF OUR DEMOCRATIC WAY OF LIFE. . . .
> UNDER OUR DEMOCRATIC PROCESSES THE PEOPLE OF TEXAS . . .
> ARE ENTITLED TO BE INFORMED OF ISSUES BY THE CANDIDATES
> THROUGH PERSONAL APPEARANCE. THEREFORE, MY ANSWER TO
> YOUR WIRE IS, STAY IN TEXAS UNLESS CONDITIONS CHANGE SO THAT

I THINK IT NECESSARY TO SEND FOR YOU, BUT RETURN IMMEDI-
ATELY AFTER ELECTION AS I WILL BE NEEDING YOU THEN. GOOD
LUCK.

FRANKLIN D. ROOSEVELT

Thinking the telegram went too far, Rowe deleted the words after "election," but the rest of the telegram went out over the President's signature with few other changes; the headline in the *Houston Chronicle* read: STAY ON FIR- ING LINE, JOHNSON TOLD IN WIRE—and the attacks ceased. There was a tele- gram orchestrated by Corcoran on parity in farm prices. At Tommy's sugges- tion, Roosevelt, who was about to sign a new farm parity bill, told Wirtz over the phone that if Johnson sent him a telegram before plans for the signing were announced, he would, in Corcoran's phrase, "be willing to respond to" the telegram with one of his own. Since this would foster the (incorrect) im- pression that Johnson had played a significant role in the bill's passage, Johnson jumped at the opportunity. The wily Wirtz attempted unsuccess- fully to sneak past Rowe into the President's "reply" a "Good luck," which could be interpreted to mean that the President was openly supporting Johnson, but otherwise the President's reply, I WILL APPROVE THE PARITY LOAN BILL THAT YOU HAVE SO ARDENTLY SUPPORTED, was all that a candi- date could have desired. (FARMERS GIVEN PARITY—JOHNSON GETS THE JOB DONE, headlined the *Bertram Enterprise*. Unsophisticated rural voters were told that "President Roosevelt, urged to do so by Cong. Lyndon Johnson of Texas, signed into law the farm parity bill. . . . [Johnson] stopped his cam- paigning and wired his friend, Roosevelt, and shortly thereafter . . .") A private exchange of telegrams provided insight into the relationship be- tween the President and the young Congressman. When Roosevelt pro- claimed the May 27 national emergency, Johnson wired him from Tyler, Texas: YOUR VOICE GAVE ME HAPPINESS TONIGHT. WE WHO HAVE WORKED WITH YOU KNOW THAT YOU HAVE NEVER FAILED WHEN THE HIGH LINE CALLED FOR COURAGE. WHEN HITLER'S MAN THREATENED, WE KNEW THE ANSWER BEFORE YOU SPOKE. I HOPE TO BE WITH YOU BATTLING FOR YOUR FRIENDS AGAINST YOUR ENEMIES ON THE SENATE FLOOR. Roosevelt's staff drafted a form reply, but the President, when signing it, added to it by hand three words that made it personal: "Your old friend, Franklin D. Roosevelt."

Roosevelt saved his best shots for strategic moments late in the cam- paign. One was a rumor, planted by Corcoran with friendly reporters in Washington, that the President would go to Texas and campaign for Lyndon Johnson. The Marsh newspapers, and the hundreds of captive weeklies, played up the rumor; so widely was it believed in Texas that the Legislature passed a resolution inviting the President to inspect the state's defense plants during his trip. Another was a word: "preposterous." Some time before,

Governor O'Daniel had suggested that Texas form its own army and navy to protect America's southern border from invasion. Roosevelt had not replied at the time; on the night of June 27, Election Eve, he denounced the plan with that word, which appeared in headlines as Texas voters went to the polls the next day. Tommy Corcoran was often the instrument through which the President intervened in state elections to help candidates he favored; like Rowe, Corcoran tries to explain that Roosevelt's intervention in Texas in 1941 was something special. "In that 1941 race, we gave him everything we could," Corcoran says. "Everything."

JOHNSON'S MANEUVERS in the Legislature had done the job on O'Daniel. Campaigning by his children, and by recorded speeches, had not been the same as the personal campaigning at which he was the master; at one of his rallies, a record of an O'Daniel speech stuck on one of his key phrases. Before it could be unstuck, it had said, "I want to go to Washington to work for the old folks, the old folks, the old folks, the old folks. . . ." The audience laughed. "The Governor's radio speeches have been marked for their note of worry and frantic exhortation, in marked contrast to the previous calm and good humored self-confidence which he has always showed heretofore and which he showed in his announcement speech in May," the *State Observer* reported. "His personal campaigning always raises his strength. People come to see him and go away convinced. . . . There is no doubt that O'Daniel's failure to make a personal campaign over the state has hurt him." But, trapped by the Legislature's refusal to adjourn, he couldn't get away from Austin until the closing days of the campaign. When he did, he found that it was too late to catch up with the argument conceived by Johnson and disseminated by hundreds of campaign workers. "The people who raised Mr. O'Daniel from a hillbilly flour salesman to the heights of the Governor's chair are divided about the wisdom of sending him to Washington as Senator," the *State Observer* reported. "The old age pensioners . . . still love him, but . . . feel that he can help them more in Texas than in Washington." Frantic, Pappy made increasingly bizarre campaign promises: to purge Congress if it failed to pass a bill outlawing strikes; to do away with the federal debt; to force the Legislature to provide the necessary $100 million per year for his pension plan. After assailing Johnson as a "water carrier" for the President, a yes man who would simply carry out Roosevelt's orders, he abruptly switched and said he had always supported the President himself, adding that he wanted to go to Washington so that he could rescue Roosevelt from the "professional politicians" surrounding him. But nothing helped. The *Observer* reported "undisputable evidence that the Governor is weaker than ever before, and that his campaign . . . has not caught the fire which characterized his previous campaigns."

In June, Gerald Mann was still doing what he had been doing in April: touring the state alone except for a driver and, occasionally, a single other aide—each day traveling 300 or 400 miles, making eight or nine speeches, plus a dozen or so impromptu wagon-bed talks in little towns, doing most of his sleeping in the back seat of his car. Without sufficient funds, without any organization to speak of, "he never stopped fighting, not for one day during that whole time," D. B. Hardeman says.

One spur that roweled him forward was indignation. To a man of such deep convictions, there was something almost immoral about the Johnson campaign, with its theatrics, its use of money, the unadorned appeal to selfishness in its argument that Johnson should be elected because he could get more federal contracts for Texas. Moreover, Roosevelt supporter though Mann was, he was disturbed at the brutal use of federal power in a state election. Having won two statewide elections, he was hardly a political *naïf*, but never, he was to say, had he seen anything like this. "They spent so much money in that campaign," he recalls. "And they did it overwhelmingly. And they had no qualms about it. I heard that Corcoran was down here in Texas. And Wirtz. And Harold Young from the Vice President's office. And Grover Hill. There was an invasion of Texas by Washington bureaucrats, coming down here with money, or the ability to raise money. They were people who were in a position to *exact* money."

Finally, on June 19, Mann's feelings spilled over. They did so, he was to recall, almost on the spur of the moment, as he was making his 252nd speech of the campaign, before another crowd that was smaller than it should have been and less enthusiastic than it should have been because, he believed, of the effect of the money behind the Lyndon Johnson campaign. He had been "feeling" the money everywhere; suddenly, he began to talk about it. Standing in the bandshell in the courthouse square in Plainview, in the shadow of the town's huge windmill, he "made his first mention of the campaign tactics of his opponents," the *Dallas News* reported—of his opponents and of himself. With the wind tousling his hair—and turning the blades of the windmill overhead—he grinned and said, "I'm just doing this in the old-fashioned way—just a handshake and a talk. I have no mountain music nor entertainers, nor do I give away money. I have no telegrams of endorsement. All I know is how to go out and see the people of Texas—on courthouse squares, street corners and sidewalks. I'm just looking them in the eye." Then, in detail, he lashed into what he was to call "the invasion of money from Washington."

Instantly, he knew that he had touched a nerve, that he was saying something his audience had been waiting to hear. By the time he finished, the crowd was roaring in encouragement; a supporter said, "Gerry, you keep making that speech and you'll be elected. Don't make any other speech. Make it from now until Election Day."

He did. Two nights later he gave it before a large crowd in Houston. He was appalled, he told his audience, at the Johnson rallies—"political rallies under the guise of patriotic meetings"—and at the lotteries. "These drawings at the congressman's so-called defense rallies have been held at dozens of places all over Texas—always after the crowd has heard what the congressman has had to say. They have been conducted in the presence of little children all over Texas. What kind of conception of a democratic election do you think such practices are instilling in [their minds]?"

The use of "free money" was only one aspect of what enraged him, he said. There was also the federal pressure. In a way, he said, it threatened the state's "independence" by violating Texans' rights "to elect our own officials without interference from Washington"—Washington which was trying to "cram Lyndon Johnson down our throats."

"You know and I know," he told his audience, "what has happened in this race for the Senate.

> We have seen the tremendous power of the federal hierarchy behind the candidacy of Lyndon Johnson. We have felt the pressure brought to bear upon the countless number of federal employees and Texas citizens employed on federal projects. We have seen the power and the influence of official position wielded in an attempt to influence and dominate a free Texas election. We have seen obvious attempts to take advantage of our love and affection for Franklin D. Roosevelt. We have seen enormous expenditures of money on Texas in this election.
>
> You and I know that every form of political pressure, supported by enormous expenditures of money, has been applied to dictate to you whom you should elect to the United States Senate.

"A federal hierarchy," he said, "is undertaking to set up a federal-controlled political machine in Texas." He was appalled at the very idea of a candidate asking voters to elect him as a patriotic obligation—of, in fact, the very use of "patriotism" as an issue. "There is no issue of patriotism in this campaign," he declared. "You are simply choosing a Senator." A candidate who, night after night, tries "to capitalize on the emotion of honest patriotism, cheapens the impulse. . . . It is like playing on the sacredness of mother love for the purposes of promotion."

He was offended by someone campaigning on the ground that he could get more money—in the form of federal projects—for Texas. "The best job is going to be done for Texas in the United States Senate by sending there a man of individual courage, personal convictions and moral stamina to do what he believes is right. . . . Not political pull but personal integrity is the qualification for getting the job done. . . . I have stood by principles. I have talked about principles. And you can always count on me to fight for principles."

The audience rose up and roared. "That new issue really caught on," Mann recalls today. He realized, he says, that "I should have started earlier an all-out campaign on the use of money because a lot of people who were voting for Johnson because they wanted O'Daniel beaten didn't approve of what Johnson was doing or what was being done for him."

Lean—gaunt now, in fact, after ten weeks of criss-crossing Texas—clean-cut, as handsome as an Arrow shirt ad in his starched collars and double-breasted suits, the thirty-four-year-old Attorney General spoke with one hand in a pocket and the other extended to the audience. His movements were the movements of the fine athlete he had been, and his eloquence was not the shouting of a typical stemwinder but the quieter persuasiveness that moved audiences on the stump as he had moved them in church, particularly when coupled with what the *Dallas News* called his greatest asset, "his evident sincerity." He was so tired and tense now that the hand extended to the audience was often as curled as a talon, and he leaned forward to his listeners as he spoke. At most rallies, he had no politicians on stage with him to introduce him; he would walk onto an empty stage alone, say simply, "I'm Gerald Mann, your Attorney General," and give the audience a grin that would win them over. Even veteran reporters were awed by his energy. "Tireless Gerald C. Mann, 12,000 miles behind him, pushed into vast West Texas Monday on the closing laps of probably the most intensive political campaign in Texas history," wrote Felix R. McKnight.

With this new issue, his campaign took on new life. "Mann, despite the absence of pyrotechnics, is attracting surprisingly large crowds," the *News* reported. Says Hardeman: "His sincerity was such that he could win any crowd that heard him."

But not enough people heard him. Scraping up $1,300 for a limited statewide broadcast, his staff put him on the air on June 23, five days before the election, to give his new speech, but that was one of his last financial gasps, and during the campaign's final week, Johnson was on the radio —with fifteen- or thirty-minute broadcasts on network hook-ups that blanketed the state—five times each day. Johnson's supporters—Young, Wirtz, Looney, Hofheinz—had statewide broadcasts, too. Not enough people read about Mann. In the big-city dailies, he got good coverage. But in the weeklies, he didn't. And, of course, he had few ads in weeklies, while, as he puts it, "They filled the newspapers full." Mann knew he had a good issue, but he also knew he didn't have the funds to make it sufficiently effective. His eloquent voice was being drowned out.

As for Johnson, with Roosevelt behind him, with so much money behind him, with the newspapers filled with his name and the radio filled with his voice, with the guarantee of those bulk votes from San Antonio and the Valley (and, most important, with Pappy O'Daniel trapped in Austin, unable to campaign), how could he lose? The Belden Poll told him he couldn't. Week after week, every poll showed a steady, and accelerating, increase in his share of the vote. A week before the election, the polls showed, for the first time, that he was in first place—by a single percentage point over O'Daniel, and by a greater margin over Mann and the rapidly falling Dies. He pulled further ahead with each survey that Belden took during that last week; in the final poll, Johnson had 31 percent of the vote, O'Daniel 26 percent, Mann 25 percent and Dies 16 percent. Joe Belden himself was so confident of the accuracy of his forecasts that he issued a statement saying: "The voters of Texas Saturday will more than likely send Congressman Lyndon B. Johnson to Washington as their junior Senator." "Lyndon Johnson is pulling away," said the *Houston Post* after its last poll of that crucial city. He had 43 percent and O'Daniel 22 percent. Mann and Dies were far behind and fading.

Lyndon Johnson felt he couldn't lose. Before O'Daniel had entered the race, he had been, for the first time in his life, confident of success. Now, with O'Daniel neutralized, his mood soared upward to euphoria as fast as it had plummeted into depression five weeks before. A staff responsive to its master's every mood was euphoric, too. A reporter who visited Johnson's headquarters found his supporters "jubilant. They said the race was over." The young men were congratulating not only the candidate, but themselves, for their foresight in hitching their wagons to his star. That star had risen far faster than even the most optimistic of them had hoped. The Chief was going to be the youngest member of the Senate—a Senator at thirty-two. Old companions—L. E. Jones, Russell Brown—were planning to drive to Austin for the victory celebration. Even the candidate's wife, ordinarily so cautious, was caught up in the elation—as, indeed, she had been caught up in it throughout this campaign in which her husband had seemed to have all the support, of every type, that he could want. "Oh, the adventures we had," she was to recall. "It was in a way the best campaign ever. . . . Perhaps it was the wine of youth—we were never tired. And our troops loved us, and we loved them—it was a *we* campaign: 'We're going to win.' "

But Lyndon Johnson was to make a mistake.

He made it at the very last moment—on Election Day, in fact. Arriving around noon at the Stephen F. Austin Hotel from Johnson City, where he had voted in the morning after making a last speech from the front porch of his boyhood home and kissing all the mothers and grandmothers, as he had kissed them as a teenager, he took a sleeping pill and napped for a while in the bedroom of his suite, while his mother stood guard in the living room to keep anyone from disturbing him. Awakening in the late afternoon, he learned that the news was good; the early returns had put him ahead of O'Daniel, and his lead was steadily widening. Mann and Dies were clearly out of the race. He was also told that George Parr and the other South Texas bosses had been telephoning to find out when they should report their counties' votes—and he told them, either personally or through an aide, that they should report them immediately.

The votes from the Valley came in. Duval County had given O'Daniel 95 percent of its vote just a year before; in that intervening year, O'Daniel's popularity had evidently suffered a remarkably rapid decline; now Duval gave O'Daniel 5 percent of its vote—and gave Lyndon Johnson 95 percent. He received 1,506 votes to 65 for the Governor: George Parr had delivered. In Starr County, the vote was 615 for Johnson, 12 for O'Daniel: the Guerra boys had delivered. In Webb County, it was 978 for Johnson, 257 for O'Daniel: the mysterious Judge Raymond had delivered. In the other South Texas counties controlled by the Anglo *jefes*, the vote was equally lopsided: in Zapata, 273 for Johnson, 21 for O'Daniel; in Jim Hogg, 119 for Johnson, 12 for O'Daniel. In the five South Texas counties that voted as a bloc, in other words, Johnson received more than 90 percent of the vote: 3,491 to 376 for O'Daniel. Mann, Dies and the other twenty-five candidates received only a few scattered votes.

In the South Texas counties in which only part of the vote—the vote in Mexican and Negro areas—was controlled, Johnson's popularity in those areas was even more overwhelming. In "Mextown" and "Niggertown" in Corpus Christi, for example, the vote in one precinct was 411 for Johnson to 26 for the other three major candidates; in another precinct, it was 338 for Johnson to 53 for the other candidates; the Mexican-American and Negro precincts in Nueces County gave him more votes in that county than all the other candidates combined. The vote in the Valley was lighter than usual because of the paucity of paid-up poll taxes in a year in which no statewide election had been scheduled, but the ratios were still impressive. Taking the South Texas vote as a whole, it was 5,009 for Gerald Mann, 5,251 for Martin Dies, 5,364 for W. Lee O'Daniel and 15,423 for Lyndon Johnson.

The abruptness—and thoroughness—of the decline in the Governor's popularity in the Valley startled even politicians who might have been thought to be immune to voting conditions there. "It was nauseous to learn of the returns from such corrupt stinkholes as Duval and Starr Counties," one said. "Money bought every Mexican vote. . . ." Even some independent spirits in the Valley commented; said one: "They simply voted the Mexicans in a body everyplace they could." Said another: ". . . If there is any law to cover it, I think, in common decency, that the ballot boxes of Starr and Duval Counties should be opened and counted. The majority of those voters can neither read or write the English language so . . . they didn't know who they voted for. As a matter of fact, they probably didn't even go to the polls, and the ballots were all placed in the box by the boss."

An observer in Cameron County said: "We have a situation in this State that is worse than the Pendergast, Kelly-Nash and Boss Hague crookedness ever was. How can one expect honest men and clean government to survive under such a system?"

On Election Day, the early reporting of the South Texas returns did not seem like a mistake. They were simply added to votes from other counties, and the Johnson total continued to mount. By 9:30 that evening, Johnson was leading O'Daniel by more than 13,000 votes. Emerging from the room on the sixteenth floor in which John Connally, Tom Miller and Jim Blundell had been tallying returns, he went down to the mezzanine, clutching a fistful of telegrams from county judges reporting results, and was hoisted to his supporters' shoulders and paraded around, waving the telegrams and shouting in triumph, in a wild celebration.

There was reason for the celebration. He had come not only so far, but so fast: from the Hill Country to, it seemed, a seat in the Senate of the United States at the age of thirty-two. Just ten years before, he had headed for Washington with a borrowed suitcase, no warm clothes, and no money to buy any—impoverished, moreover, in education as well as in pocketbook —to live in a basement and be one of a thousand secretaries to Congressmen. He had become a Congressman himself, and now had become the youngest member of the Senate—so young that, even if he was worried by his family's short life span, it must have seemed that there was plenty of time to attain the next, last, rung on the ladder. Even though the size of his margin was reduced later that evening, it remained substantial. Mayor Miller was preparing a statement that he would run for the vacated House seat of "Senator Lyndon Johnson." With 96 percent of the vote in, JOHNSON WITH 5152 LEAD, APPEARS ELECTED, the *Houston Post* headlined the next morning. Said the *Dallas News*: ONLY MIRACLE CAN KEEP FDR'S ANOINTED OUT. Lady Bird, who was "going around with my little camera, clicking," says, "He was announced the winner. The *Dallas Morning News* was even running pictures: 'Lyndon aged six. . . .' We were talking about staff."

But, in Texas, not all the votes were counted on Election Day.

The urban vote was counted on Election Day, of course—by 1941, voting machines were in use in most Texas cities—and most of the rural vote, too, although most rural voting in Texas was still by paper ballot. The results from some rural precincts, however, often didn't trickle in until several days after a statewide election—and the explanation, in some cases, did not lie merely in the isolation of these precincts and the fact that, in some of them, the county judge might not have a telephone with which to communicate with the Texas Election Bureau.

There existed in the upper levels of Texas politics common knowledge about the precincts that were for sale, the "boxes" in which the county judge wouldn't "bring in the box" (report the precinct totals to the Election

Bureau) until the man who had paid him told him what he wanted the total to be, the precincts in which the county judge took the rather flimsy locked tin ballot box (to which the judge had the key) to his home to count the ballots at leisure and in privacy (and, if necessary, to insert some new ones), with confidence that no one would ever be able to discover—and certainly not to prove—what he had done. Unless an election was contested, the ballots were never checked at all; in case of a contest, as one politician puts it, "so many things could happen to keep them [the ballots in some rural precincts] from being checked": if a box arrived at the Election Bureau with its bottom torn off and no ballots inside, the judge would simply swear that when he had sent it off to the Bureau, the box had been intact—it must have been ripped open by some accident *en route,* he would say.

Since in a close election, precinct results could thus be altered, it was a fundamental rule of Texas politics not to report your important precincts —the ones in which you controlled the result—early. By reporting your total, you let your opponent know the figure he had to beat, and in Texas, it was all too easy then to beat it. Even if a judge had already reported the result in his precinct, so long as he hadn't officially certified it, he could change it, saying he had made a mistake in his arithmetic. Johnson had violated this rule, perhaps out of overconfidence, perhaps because his intelligence network had assured him that O'Daniel, his principal opponent, had made no preparations to change any boxes, and would have difficulty doing so now because, except in South Texas, he had alienated the "professional politicians"—the county judges and commissioners whose cooperation he would have needed. But the vote was to be changed nonetheless.

The reason it was changed had nothing to do with Lyndon Johnson.

According to O'Daniel's campaign manager, William Lawson—and Lawson's account of the following events is confirmed by members of Johnson's campaign staff and by disinterested politicians and political observers —during the last week or two before the election, the Governor's increasingly frantic campaign promises had alarmed some of the conservative business lobbyists, the longtime powers behind Texas politics, who had hitherto been his secret supporters. They feared that his new promises to increase pensions might lead to higher taxes on the oil, sulphur and natural gas industries. "He had always gone along with them," an observer says, "but he was just so unpredictable; they couldn't be sure they would always be able to control him." Says another: "O'Daniel wasn't a very dependable man. You couldn't tell what he'd do! They were all scared of him. He was an unknown quantity."

Business lobbyists' worries had been reinforced by their concern over another, more particular pledge made by O'Daniel during the campaign, one aimed at another major Texas industry: the making of liquor and beer. Murky and shifting as were many of Pappy's beliefs, one was crystal clear and inflexible: his conviction that liquor was a tool of the Devil. Even his

intimates were not excused an occasional drink. "He was a rabid Prohibitionist," says Secretary of State Lawson. "I was very careful never to come to
the office with liquor on my breath." On June 6, needing a new surefire issue
to rekindle the enthusiasm of his rural Fundamentalist supporters, O'Daniel,
assailing "booze dives" which he said were "demoralizing fine young soldiers," sent to the Legislature a bill prohibiting the sale of beer or liquor
within ten miles of any military base. Since the military installations springing up throughout Texas were presenting beer and liquor manufacturers
with an immense new market of tens of thousands of young soldiers, this
bill posed a real threat. The beer and liquor industries had long been powerful in Texas politics. The Texas Brewers Institute (more informally known
on Congress Avenue as "Beer, Inc."), which represented the giant Pearl Beer
Company and more than 200 smaller beer-makers, and the hard-liquor
lobby had long been a force in Austin; they had had to be to keep the business flourishing in a state with such strong Prohibitionist sentiment. They
had assumed they could easily defeat O'Daniel's proposal, but just ten days
before the campaign ended something occurred which made them worry.
When, before the start of the campaign, the chairmanship of the state's three-
member Liquor Control Board, whose power over liquor licenses throughout Texas was all but absolute, fell vacant, the Governor had appointed a
crusading Prohibitionist preacher to fill the post. The lobbyists had mobilized the Legislature to refuse to confirm the preacher's appointment, and to
turn down as well other O'Daniel nominees for the post, all of whom seemed
more interested in closing down the liquor business in Texas than in supervising it—they included the head of the Texas anti-saloon league and the
past president of the Women's Christian Temperance Union. Ten days before the election, however, O'Daniel had succeeded in pushing through his
fifth nominee, another Prohibitionist. A second vacancy on the board would
occur shortly, and if O'Daniel succeeded in filling that, too, with another
Prohibitionist, the Board "could just about have ended the liquor and beer
business down here." Equally important, O'Daniel's victory reminded Beer,
Inc., that a powerful Governor might succeed in winning passage of the bill
creating a "dry zone" around military camps. "There were millions and millions of dollars involved now," Lawson says. "They *had* to get him out of
the Governorship."

The lobbyists had thought the problem would be solved by O'Daniel's
election to the Senate, which would remove him to Washington and see him
replaced in the Governor's chair by Lieutenant Governor Coke Stevenson,
a lifelong Wet and an ally of Beer, Inc., and its hard-liquor partner. Now
O'Daniel appeared to have lost the election, but by only about 5,000 votes;
it was at once apparent to these powerful lobbyists that removing the threat
would not be difficult at all—particularly since Lyndon Johnson, by having
his votes reported early, had let them know precisely how many additional
O'Daniel votes would be needed to beat him.

After midnight on Election Day, while Johnson was being paraded around the Stephen F. Austin mezzanine in noisy triumph, across the street, in the Driskill Hotel, a quiet meeting was being held; according to some reports, its *de facto* chairman was Emmett R. Morse, a former Speaker of the Texas House of Representatives and an attorney for the liquor interests, other key figures were lobbyists for Beer, Inc., and fifteen State Senators. And on Sunday, these men headed out of Austin—to visit county judges who had taken ballot boxes to the privacy of their homes.

This maneuver was made easier by another mistake that Johnson had made. The mistake was as untypical of Lyndon as overconfidence, and it was due to overconfidence that he made it. It ran directly opposite to the whole grain of his adult life, and ignored one of its most consistent themes: "If you do *everything,* you will win." During the ten years since his graduation from college, he had lived by that rule, no matter what the personal cost. For ten years, no matter what the price in fatigue or pride or dignity, he had touched every base, taken every precaution. The 1941 campaign, of course, had been—except for the brief period in which he had been panicked by O'Daniel's entry into the race—atypical of his adult life, the single instance in which he had been cheerful, optimistic; after a lifetime of apprehension and anxiety, in this lone instance he had been overconfident. And his overconfidence had caused him to neglect certain basic precautions.

This had already hurt him. San Antonio's West Side had given him more votes than all the other twenty-eight candidates combined—but it hadn't given him nearly what he had expected. The turn-out had been extremely light. Some boxes in the Mexican slums had produced the kind of margin he had been promised: 101 to 6, for example; 115 to 4; 169 to 3. But in most precincts, only about 100 of the 300 or more possible ballots had been cast. His overall edge over O'Daniel in the Mexican slum had been 3,058 to 1,110, but he had been promised many more than 3,000 votes.

The reason for the shortfall was that maximum effort for a candidate would only result if the candidate had men—men he could trust absolutely, men who would give him an all-out effort—"riding the polls" on Election Day, driving from precinct to precinct, exhorting workers who had just brought a carload of voters to the polls to head out immediately to collect another carload, and to keep doing this from the time the polls opened till the time they closed. The Johnson headquarters had done almost none of this—relying on Quill's men, and on the "City Machine." Quill had put forth a maximum effort, but the Machine—the deputy sheriffs and other officials who handled the West Side boxes—had not. They got Johnson's money— but Johnson didn't get the votes. In fact, they took his money and laughed at him. A leader of the West Side, Frank H. Bushick, Jr., was later to tell him that during the campaign, "I went by your headquarters several times

[and] found an atmosphere of smug self-sufficiency." Bushick had enrolled nine of his precinct men—"men who have carried their boxes on the West Side for the past fifteen years"—in the Johnson cause, but on Election Day, they were given "the munificent sum of $5 to cover entire expenses for large precincts and voluntary workers. The result being that most of them got disgusted and went home. I know that a number of your friends subscribed ample funds to meet the necessary expenses on Election Day, but frankly, Mr. Johnson, I am afraid it was not spent. Since the election, several of them [local election officials] have laughingly admitted that they *made some money*."

On Election Day, this shortfall had seemed unimportant—at the time the San Antonio votes had come in, Johnson had been well ahead; it had, in fact, seemed like a triumph that he had carried Bexar County in the face of his unpopularity in the white neighborhoods. But it was to be important now.

So, more serious, was another elementary precaution he had neglected, uncharacteristically, to take. The only way to prevent vote-stealing in crooked counties was by having men on the scene in those counties, to make sure that only voters placed ballots in the boxes, that no illegal instructions were given to voters, that no local politicians looked over voters' shoulders as they cast their vote—and that, when the precinct was closed, the judges sent in the results before taking the boxes home. It was necessary to keep men on the scene in shifts, twenty-four hours a day, for a day or two thereafter until not only the first but the official returns had been filed. Partly because he thought he was so far ahead—and, more to the point, because he knew that, outside of South Texas (which had been switched to the Johnson camp), O'Daniel had no organization and no acquaintance among election judges and could not steal votes (and because he knew that Mann would not steal votes)—Johnson didn't, except in a very few instances, take that precaution. And in some cases where he did have men present, once the election judges reported their totals Saturday night, his men were told they could come in to Austin and join the victory celebration.

On Sunday evening, after some 8,500 additional votes had been counted, Johnson still led O'Daniel by more than 4,500 votes—167,471 to 162,910. Mann had 132,915 votes, Dies 76,714. More than 96 percent of the votes had been counted, only about 18,000 remained "out" and almost all of these were in Martin Dies' East Texas congressional district, where Dies had been garnering the lion's share of the vote. "Barring a miracle," announced Robert L. Johnson, manager of the Texas Election Bureau, Lyndon Johnson was elected Senator.

But arrangements for Monday were being completed. In a suite in the Driskill Hotel where four of the key figures in these arrangements had spent the night on the telephone, one of them made a last call as dawn was breaking on Monday. Apologizing for waking its recipient, he said: "Just thought you'd like to know that we've got it in the bag. The Governor is going to the Senate. . . ."

O'Daniel himself had had nothing to do with the arrangements, but on Monday morning, even he was told about them, and he in turn informed his aides; when one said that Johnson was still thousands of votes ahead, the Governor replied, "Well, that don't make any difference." The "drawn anxious looks of those close to O'Daniel" abruptly disappeared, the *Austin American-Statesman* noted. By noon on Monday, the paper reported, "the news was abroad—Pappy was in. . . . It was noised about in the Senate Chamber." The capital was snickering over what was about to happen to Lyndon Johnson.

Johnson and his aides were among the last to get the news. At noon on Monday, John Connally was still sending off victory telegrams; he wired a friend in Washington that, while the results were not yet official, ELECTION BUREAU CONCEDES ELECTION UNLESS MIRACLE HAPPENS. . . . LOOKS LIKE WE'RE IN.

Johnson himself was spending the day on Alvin Wirtz's shadowy, comfortable back porch. The two men, relaxed and happy, were sipping drinks in tall silver glasses while Lady Bird Johnson, the only other person present, took home movies.

The news may have reached them on that porch; the home movie shows Wirtz on the telephone, and as he listens, his face, relaxed a moment before, changes. But, however the news came, when it started coming, it came fast.

At nine a.m. Monday, clerks in the Election Bureau began opening the envelopes—telegrams and special delivery letters—containing "late" returns that had not been counted Saturday or Sunday. Many of these envelopes were from East Texas counties—and almost every East Texas envelope contained figures that were a dramatic reversal of the previous trend. In earlier returns from that section, its Congressman, Martin Dies, had led handily, with the other three major candidates running far behind. In these new returns, Dies' percentage dropped off sharply. Mann didn't pick up any of Dies' votes, and neither did Lyndon Johnson. They went almost entirely to Pappy O'Daniel.

Shelby County, for example, was considered a Dies stronghold, and the report Shelby County had sent in Saturday night had confirmed that. Out of 2,275 votes reported, Dies had received 1,040, or 46 percent, almost as many as the other candidates combined. O'Daniel received 779 votes, or 34 percent, Johnson 241 votes, or 11 percent, Mann 215 votes, or 9 percent. But now Shelby reported 256 additional votes. These were mostly from the same precincts that had reported earlier. But Dies did not do as well as he had done earlier. He received only 82 of these "new" votes—not 46 percent but 32 percent. Johnson and Mann didn't do as well either: Mann received 6 votes, or 2 percent; Johnson did particularly badly; he received 3 of the new votes: 1 percent. O'Daniel, who had received 34 percent on the first returns, received 64 percent on these later returns: 165 out of these last 256 votes—165 votes to 3 votes for Lyndon Johnson. When Shelby County's new figures were included in the Election Bureau tally, therefore, Johnson's lead was reduced by 162 votes. As Marsh's *American-Statesman* was to comment bitterly, despite the fact that "These last votes were from the same county, the same folks" who had voted earlier, in this "late" vote "O'Daniel bettered his rate against Johnson, 16 times over."

This shift was repeated in Newton County, which now reported 556 additional votes. Dies again received a smaller percentage of these votes, and again the difference went entirely to O'Daniel. In the late vote from Newton County, therefore, the Governor outpolled Johnson, 168 to 32. Johnson's lead was reduced by another 136 votes. This abrupt reversal was repeated in the late returns from other East Texas counties. Still other counties from this section had telephoned in "complete," if unofficial, returns on Saturday, so that they were now precluded from making substantial changes. But now "official"—written—returns were coming in from these counties by letter or telegram, and many of these written figures were different from the telephoned figures—and the difference was seldom in Johnson's favor. There were 32 less votes for Johnson in Angelina County than had previously been reported; 69 more votes for O'Daniel in Hardin County; 85 more for O'Daniel in Colorado County. County by county, Johnson's lead was being sliced away. Jimmy Allred, presiding over a federal court in New Mexico, telephoned Carroll Keach. "I'm listening to the radio," he said. "They're stealing this election in East Texas!"

Johnson's reaction was to try to steal it back. Telephoning George Paar, he asked the Duke of Duval to give him more votes. But Parr refused; he later told friends that he had replied, "Lyndon, I've been to the federal penitentiary, and I'm not going back for you." Johnson got some "corrected" totals from various strongholds: 226 from Austin, for example. But he couldn't get enough. His strength was in South Texas, and due to his mistake, South Texas had already sent in its official figures; there was little more South Texas could do. East Texas was going for O'Daniel, and because *it* hadn't sent in its figures, it could give Pappy whatever he needed. Indeed, as Johnson's effort to improve his total became apparent, his canny opponents held back certain key counties—Trinity County deep in East Texas was one—to see what would be needed at the end; whatever Johnson managed to add, they would be able to add more.

Having rushed back to his headquarters from Wirtz's porch, Lyndon Johnson sat all day Monday next to a telephone, and almost every ring brought bad news. It was about noon on Monday that the trend to O'Daniel began; at the time, Johnson's lead was still more than 4,000 votes. Hour by hour—telephone call by telephone call—he had to watch it being sliced away: by seven p.m., Pappy was less than a thousand votes behind. But there were only perhaps 5,000 more votes to go, and they had to be divided among four candidates—could he hang on? Late in the evening, a bunch of East Texas counties—Anderson, Cass, Panola, Refugio, Van Zandt—reported their "official" returns almost simultaneously. When they had finished, Johnson's lead was only 77 votes. And there were still more East Texas counties to be heard from. O'Daniel knew what Tuesday was going to bring; when a reporter read him the evening's final figures, the Governor smiled and said, "Well, that's looking fine." And Johnson knew, too. Walter Jenkins tried to console him by telling him he was still ahead. "It's gone," Lyndon Johnson replied. Dan Quill was philosophical. "He [O'Daniel] stole more votes than we did, that's all," he says. But Johnson's frustration and rage erupted over hapless aides. One of them, Dick Waters, was taking his wife out to dinner that night, when, as they were leaving the Stephen F. Austin Hotel, they happened to cross Lyndon's path. Although Waters, a low-level campaign assistant, had had no responsibility, or authority, for seeing that votes were not changed, Johnson began blaming him for what had happened, "screaming and hollering, and throwing his arms like Lyndon can do," viciously reviling him in front of his wife. Inside the candidate's suite on the fifteenth floor, Mary Rather sat, hair disheveled, face wan, trying to muster up a smile for Lady Bird's camera; John Connally wept. Their premonitions were borne out on Tuesday. Hardly had the Election Bureau office opened when more "corrections" began coming in. By the end of the day, O'Daniel was more than a thousand votes ahead; the official final count would give him 175,590 votes to 174,279 for Johnson, a margin of 1,311.

Lyndon Johnson's loss had been due to a political fluke. He had been beaten not by his opponent's friends but by his opponent's foes; O'Daniel had won the Senate seat not because these men wanted him to be Senator, but because they didn't want him to be Governor—because they wanted to get him out of Texas. But it was Johnson's mistake that had enabled these men to take his victory away. He had planned and schemed and maneuvered for ten years—had *worked* for ten years, worked day and night, weekday and weekend—had done "*everything*." And, for ten years, he had won.

He had relaxed for one day. And he had lost.

35

"I Want to See Lyndon"

AFTER MAURY MAVERICK, Franklin Roosevelt's devoted follower, lost the San Antonio mayoralty in May, 1941, the President wrote Maverick's sixteen-year-old son to console him for his father's defeat. "I know he feels badly about it but I also know, because I know him, that he is quietly sure his point of view will prevail in the long run. The same thing is true about Lyndon Johnson. . . . The things for which he stands will eventually win. He will tell you that, your father will tell you and I also tell you. . . . Temporary defeats mean nothing as long as our side wins the last battle."

At the moment at which Roosevelt was writing about "our side"—the side he believed Lyndon Johnson was on—Johnson had already joined the other side, the rabidly anti–New Deal San Antonio City Machine that had defeated Maverick. Roosevelt did not know this—and never found out. He never got more than an inkling of Lyndon Johnson's quiet alliance with the New Deal's enemies in Texas.

Nonetheless, sympathy for losing politicians—or, indeed, even tolerance for them—was not one of Franklin D. Roosevelt's most notable qualities. More than one of Roosevelt's Capitol Hill supporters who had been defeated in a try for re-election or for election to the Senate had found, after his loss, that his previous access to the smiling, genial President had been cut off, cut off completely, regardless of the depth and extent of his loyalty to Roosevelt and the New Deal. Among those who had suffered this fate, in fact, was Lyndon Johnson's predecessor in the role of New Deal informant within the Texas delegation: W. D. McFarlane. Ousted from his House seat in 1938 despite a personal appearance by Roosevelt in his behalf, he asked the President to "keep him in mind for any existing vacancies" on the Federal Power Commission, the Federal Communications Commission, or the federal bench. Roosevelt kept him in mind for nothing. McFarlane received a federal appointment—a temporary, low-level appointment as a Special Assistant Attorney General assisting in condemnation proceedings in connection with the Denison Dam—only through the intercession of Sam

Rayburn, who did so because McFarlane had been one of the old group of Populists in the Texas Legislature. White House aides were wondering whether Johnson's loss, with such strong Roosevelt backing, had not proven embarrassing to the President—and they were wondering what Roosevelt's reaction would be.

They were not kept long in doubt. After his defeat, Lyndon Johnson sent a two-paragraph note to Franklin Roosevelt.

Sir:

In the heat of Texas last week, I said I was glad to be called a water-carrier—that I would be glad to carry a bucket of water to the Commander-in-Chief any time his thirsty throat or his thirsty soul needed support, for you certainly gave me support non-pareil.

One who cannot arise to the leadership shall find the fault in himself and not in you.

Sincerely,
Lyndon

In the margin of the note, the hand of Franklin D. Roosevelt wrote, "General Watson—I want to see Lyndon."

The day after the two men met, Johnson wrote Nan Honeyman: "Had a visit with the Boss today and enjoyed it immensely." The enjoyment was understandable. The President had asked Corcoran what he could do to cheer "Lyndon" up, and had accepted Corcoran's suggestion: Roosevelt was to address the national convention of Young Democrats in Lexington, Kentucky, in August; Corcoran suggested that the President put Johnson on the program with him. Roosevelt did so. When Johnson came in to see him, the President told him he had already arranged for him to give a speech preceding his own. The young Congressman's defeat had only strengthened Roosevelt's "special feeling" for him—despite the defeat, the older man had arranged to give him his first national exposure, the national exposure that he craved.

So completely had Roosevelt accepted Johnson's excuse—that he had lost the election only because he had been cheated out of it—that he joked about it, telling him, "Lyndon, apparently you Texans haven't learned one of the first things we learned up in New York State, and that is that when the election is over, you have to sit on the ballot boxes."

FRANKLIN ROOSEVELT'S GREATEST SERVICE to Lyndon Johnson in connection with the 1941 campaign came not during the campaign but long after it had ended.

In July, 1942, while examining the books of Brown & Root, Inc., in connection with other matters, Internal Revenue agents became suspicious of the large bonuses to the firm's officials and of various "attorney's fees," and began following the trail of that money to see where it had ended up— and the trail led to the Lyndon Johnson campaign.

Brown & Root, Inc., had been advised by tax counsel that campaign contributions by the corporation would not be deductible business expenses. But Brown & Root had deducted hundreds of thousands of dollars in "bonuses" and "fees" that IRS agents now suspected were actually disguised contributions. Moreover, while the potential financial liability (payment of additional taxes plus penalties and interest) would be substantial for Brown & Root even at the new level of affluence to which Lyndon Johnson had raised the firm, as the IRS investigation intensified and widened, the dangers were no longer limited to the financial. The agents had begun to wonder if Brown & Root's attempt to avoid taxes by such devices was so blatant that it might constitute an attempt to defraud the government —and tax fraud was a crime that could result in jail terms for those convicted of it. By the Autumn of 1942, Brown & Root's officials knew, as one of their attorneys, Edward A. Clark, puts it, that "they had *big* IRS trouble."

The man to whose campaign the contributions had been made had trouble, too. Charges involving contributions to his campaign—or even the revelation that charges were being considered—would result in highly damaging publicity. Revelation of the astonishing sums involved—hundreds of thousands of dollars when the Corrupt Practices Act limited the permissible expenditure by a candidate to $25,000—could result in a scandal of dimensions that could end a politician's career.

For about four months after the investigation began, all concerned felt it could be deflected because of Johnson's White House connections. Brown & Root retained Alvin Wirtz as its attorney on the matter, but even a former Under Secretary of the Interior might have trouble winning this case; it was Johnson on whom the firm was depending. "They hired Wirtz for the IRS thing because they knew Johnson would be associate counsel on the case," Clark says.

Johnson did not shrink from the role; he was developing a line of strategy to solve the problem. The first step was to convince James H. Rowe, Jr., who was Johnson's liaison to the President, that the Internal Revenue Service investigation of Brown & Root was politically inspired by IRS officials in Texas loyal to the Garner–Jesse Jones group—and was aimed at cutting off vital Texas financial support for the New Deal. Although this was not true, it was not difficult for so persuasive a talker as Lyndon Johnson to convince men who knew nothing about Texas politics that it was. Rowe, who admired Johnson and believed in him, was thoroughly convinced. During the Summer of 1942, he was to recall,

I sent to the President a memorandum telling that Internal Revenue agents were going all through Texas stirring up political trouble for "our crowd." . . .

I sent to the President this memorandum saying that they were after the "third term crowd," who had done the job in Texas, that they were going to all the banks and to the lawyers checking up on political contributions and that if it wasn't stopped we wouldn't have a friend left in Texas.

Rowe was later to tell Grace Tully that the President had responded to the memorandum: "So far as I can determine, and I think it is with accuracy, the President spoke to Marvin McIntyre about it. Mac called John Sullivan [Assistant Commissioner of the Bureau of Internal Revenue]. . . ." Rowe assumed that the matter had been closed.

But it hadn't. The contributions to the Johnson campaign that were being investigated were too large, the manner in which they had allegedly been concealed too blatant.

The next attempt was made with Sullivan's superior, Internal Revenue Commissioner Guy T. Helvering, known to Washington insiders as "the President's man at IRS." Johnson made the attempt himself; he went to Helvering, told him the same story, and asked him to kill the investigation. But this attempt foundered on the invincible integrity of Helvering's superior. Internal Revenue was a bureau in the Department of the Treasury, and the Secretary of the Treasury was Henry Morgenthau, Jr., a man detested by the young wheelers and dealers of the New Deal for his unshakable adherence to the law. The investigation would go right ahead, Morgenthau declared.

Now, Rowe recalls, "the Browns were worried . . . and so was Johnson." Johnson, he says, "was in trouble," and he knew it. In October, 1942, Wirtz and George Brown came to Washington and discussed the situation with Johnson. Then Johnson and Brown talked to Rowe. Johnson and Rowe both realized how thin was the ice they were treading on now. Rowe had been invited to the Washington town house Brown & Root maintained at Sheridan Circle. When Rowe learned what the subject of the discussion was to be, he recalls, "I said, 'I'll talk to you outside on the street. The IRS probably has this house bugged.'" And that is where they talked—three tall young men, the newly made millionaire, the advisor to Presidents, and the future President, standing on a street in Washington.

"Johnson was worried," Rowe recalls. Reiterating that the investigation was a form of political persecution, a reprisal for his support of Roosevelt, he asked Rowe to take further steps to kill it. Rowe tried. He went to see Helvering himself, and they discussed the matter: "just the two of us—no, no, that's not right; he had a witness like those fellows always do. But I said, 'What the hell, I'll talk anyway.' He said Johnson had been to see him to ask him to kill it. 'Well, I can't. I would, but the Secretary [Morgenthau] won't let me.' "

Rowe had made this approach "on my own." Now he knew that a stronger hand was needed. On November 20, he attempted to bring the subject to the attention of Morgenthau's superior, by sending a memo ostensibly addressed to Grace Tully. "Helvering has indicated that he can take care of this Texas situation without any trouble, and fairly, but he won't do it if Morgenthau is going to interfere at the last minute. If Helvering gets told by the President to handle it, and if he is backed up, he will do it." Apparently Morgenthau's superior took an interest in the case. Says Rowe: "Then I— and *this* I would *not* have done without Roosevelt's clearance—I went in to see Morgenthau and I got to thinking, 'Rowe, you'd better be tactful.' Morgenthau taped everything—everyone knew that. And I just mentioned it—vaguely; just brought it up; I mentioned it to see what he'd say, and he didn't say much. And I just faded out."

Morgenthau may not have said much to Rowe, but the Secretary may have issued instructions nonetheless. The IRS agents had, some weeks earlier, been ordered by one of Morgenthau's aides to stop working on the Brown & Root case until further notice. On December 17, 1942, shortly after Rowe's approach to Morgenthau, the agent coordinating the case, E. C. Werner, was told to send the Brown & Root file to Washington, which he did by special delivery. Shortly thereafter, Werner and James M. Cooner, special agent in charge of Texas and Louisiana for the IRS, were summoned to Washington to meet with top IRS officials, who, Werner was to write in his diary, "had me explain in detail the fraudulent items and suspicious items." The next day, they called him back, and gave him his instructions: in Werner's words,

> that the investigation was to continue; that it was to be expeditiously but thoroughly conducted; that no outside persons were to be interviewed but that the investigation was to be conducted from within; that suspicious items found should be brought to his attention and that we were to be diplomatic in our investigation. [Deputy IRS Commissioner Norman D. Cann] said that no criticism was being made of any of us.

And in 1943, the Internal Revenue Service began to close in on the truth behind the financing of Lyndon Johnson's senatorial race.

On January 22, the six agents involved held a conference in Dallas, and decided on their tactics. Some moved right into the Houston offices of Brown & Root and began checking through the firm's records. Others went to banks and began checking the deposits and withdrawals of some Brown & Root officials. Still others began interviewing these officials and began checking their stories against the records.

The largest sums of money the agents were investigating at this point were the "bonuses" totaling $150,800 that had been paid to Brown & Root's treasurer and to four of the corporation's vice presidents. These bonuses had, according to an entry in the company's books dated December 27, 1940, been authorized at a meeting on that date. But now the federal agents tracked down a former Brown & Root bookkeeper, Robert C. Horne, and interviewed him at McAllen, Texas. Horne told the interviewers that, despite the date in the books, the bonuses had actually been authorized not in 1940 but in 1941. The agents investigated further; as a result, Werner was to write in a report to his superiors: "Sufficient evidence is on hand, it is believed, to show minutes authorizing above bonuses to be fraudulent." Other, smaller, bonuses totaling $24,000 had been paid to lower-ranking Brown & Root executives, the agents found. They obtained transcripts and photostats of the executives' bank accounts, and Werner reported that he and his men were tracing the disposition of this money; that they had already found, and taken possession of, one check by which $2,500 had been transferred to the Johnson campaign's bank account; and that a substantial portion of the rest of the $24,000 "is believed to have been used for [Johnson's] Senatorial campaign."

The more they worked on the case—Case No. S.I. 19267-F in Internal Revenue Service files—the more questionable transactions they uncovered. Some of the routes by which, the IRS agents believed, the Brown & Root money had reached Lyndon Johnson's headquarters were extremely circuitous. Some of them, in fact, led not from Brown & Root but from one of its subsidiaries, the Victoria Gravel Company. It had been not Brown & Root but Victoria Gravel, for example, that had paid a total of $12,500 in "attorneys fees" to Edgar Monteith, a Houston lawyer. And further steps, they believed, had then been taken to cloud the ultimate destination of the money. Ten thousand dollars of it was given by Monteith to his partner, A. W. Baring, as a "profit distribution." Then Baring had transferred the $10,000 back to Monteith. And the checks Monteith wrote were not to the Johnson campaign directly, but to pay bills owed by the campaign to radio stations and printers. The remaining $2,500 of the "fee" paid to Monteith was passed on by him to another attorney, and it was through this attorney that the money reached the campaign. The trail of some of the money was made harder to follow because while it may have started out as checks, it was soon converted into cash. When, for example, J. O. Corwin, Jr., was given a Victoria Gravel check for $5,000, he cashed it, stuck half the bills in an envelope, and mailed the currency to Johnson headquarters. And, the agents believed, some of the money didn't even start out as checks; it was cash from the start—large expenditures being made from a "petty cash" fund under the control of Brown & Root Vice President J. M. Dellinger.

Attempting to trace the trail of the various Brown & Root contributions, the Internal Revenue Service agents found themselves encountering evasions and denials from Brown & Root officials and from some of the attorneys involved. Lyndon Johnson himself was not questioned at the time, apparently because of the directive from Washington that "no outside persons" be interviewed. (Years later, when the matter threatened to come to light in a series of columns by columnist Drew Pearson, Johnson was asked about campaign contributions made by Monteith, and he flatly denied that he had received any financial help from him. He also said that he had never even heard of Monteith, although, as Pearson noted, "Monteith's father was the former Mayor of Houston and a well-known personage" in Texas political circles.) But the agents, digging through corporation and bank records, finding—and photostating—checks and campaign bills, were able to uncover facts that contradicted the denials by the Brown & Root officials and the attorneys.

The agents found the checks involved in the various transfers of money revolving around Monteith's "attorneys fees"—including the checks to pay the campaign expenses. As for Corwin, he was interviewed by an Internal Revenue Service agent about his $5,000 bonus. Did you use any of it for political donations? the agent asked him. "Yes, I did," Corwin replied. To whom? the agent asked. "Oh, I probably contributed half of it to one of the Lyndon Johnson clubs," Corwin said. In what form? Corwin replied that he had mailed it to a Johnson club in Houston—"in currency [cash]." And the balance of $2,500? the agent asked. Corwin replied, "Oh, I spent it." But the agents were tracing checks. The $2,500 balance, the agents said, had actually gone to another Brown & Root official, D. G. Young, who was reputedly the corporation's principal "contact man" with politicians. The money had been transferred by, in agent Werner's words, a "circuitous route. Both Corwin and Young gave false testimony on above item." Another bonus—$2,500—had been paid by Victoria Gravel to Randolph T. Mills. Questioned by Werner, Mills was, Werner reported, "very evasive," but Werner finally pinned him down.

Q 118. Did you keep them [the money]? "Yes, I put them in my account."
Q 119. And retained them? "Well, I didn't retain them very long, no; that is, I paid out of course."

. . . . . .

Q 125. Well, you, in other words, the bonus was used by you in connection with your living expenses or obligations, etc.? "Well, I wouldn't say all of it was. It was in connection with my living—I gave $2500 to the Campaign, Democratic Campaign of 1941."

Mills finally told Werner that he had made out a check—either "to Chairman, committee, or Johnson"—"shortly after time of receipt of bonus." He told Werner that he was "pretty sure" he no longer had the check, but

Werner wasn't concerned with that; *he* had a facsimile of it, made out to one of the campaign's finance directors.

The more the Internal Revenue Service team searched, it seemed, the more they found. The transactions of which they were suspicious became larger; previously, the largest single questionable transaction had been the $45,000 bonus paid to Brown & Root Vice President W. A. Woolsey; now Werner, checking the account of Brown & Root Treasurer J. T. Duke at the Austin National Bank, came across another check—and this check, made out to Duke by the W. S. Bellows Construction Company, a firm that was part of the Brown & Root–headed consortium building the Corpus Christi Naval Air Station, was for $100,000. And there were increasing indications that cash as well as checks had been involved in large amounts in Brown & Root's expenditures that the agents believed had found their way into Johnson's election efforts. Durst, a Brown & Root official, for example, told an IRS agent that he had cashed his $5,500 bonus checks, and kept the money on his person, or hidden it in a drawer of his desk, until it was spent on personal expenditures. The IRS, as its investigation continued, was becoming less convinced of the veracity of this account—although Durst insisted that the only donation he might have made to the Johnson campaign was "chicken feed, ten or fifteen dollars, etc." Then the IRS started asking questions about Vice President Dellinger's "petty cash" account. Vice President W. A. Woolsey was asked if he would normally receive monies from Dellinger in checks; "No, he would [give] me the cash," Woolsey replied. "Did he [Dellinger] have some sort of fund? Cash fund?" the agent asked. Woolsey first said, "Well, I don't know," but later said, "When the Naval Air Station was first started, I am sure he kept considerable cash"—which, Woolsey said, was "used" by top Brown & Root officials. In the margin of his notes on this interview, Werner wrote his conclusion about what he was hearing: "Slush fund."

In July, the IRS agents began to focus on the $150,800 in bonuses. They arranged interviews with Brown & Root's top officials—and with Herman and George Brown themselves. At these interviews, as many as three agents would be present, in addition to a stenographer to take down the witnesses' replies. Some witnesses were defiant. Asked if he had donated any of his $17,000 "bonus" to the Johnson campaign, Treasurer Duke replied: "No, we didn't make any—do you think we want to go to the penitentiary by making donations when we have all of these Federal contracts?" Any such allegations, Duke said, were "just plain bull-shit." But clues as to the disposition of the "bonuses" were growing nonetheless. On October 23, Vice President L. T. Bolin admitted that he had made a cash contribution to Johnson's campaign, although he wasn't sure of the amount; it might have been $500, he said. But he admittted paying for, in an agent's words, "some radio time and other things," and the IRS agents determined that Bolin had written two personal checks—for $1,870 for cash, which they found had been given to

Johnson headquarters, and for $1,150 to a printing firm for campaign printing. As for the Brown brothers themselves, their answers under questioning were consistent with their personalities. Asked if Brown & Root ever "directly or indirectly" made any political donations, suave George smoothly replied, "Insofar as I know, they haven't." Asked again about political donations, he replied: "We have certainly not directed anybody to give campaign funds. We knew it was not legal to give any political funds, and if anybody working for Brown & Root gave any political funds, it was without our knowledge. Certainly I don't think it has been charged to Brown & Root. If it has, it certainly shouldn't have been." Of course, he said, since others had the authority to sign checks, he "wouldn't make a sworn statement that nobody has done it."* Werner was to write that George personally drew $2,500 from the company, and that, while the money was "believed paid to Johnson campaign," it had not been traced. As for Herman, fierce and unyielding, who drew $5,000, no notes on his interview can be found, but he apparently made no bones about what had been done with money: "admittedly paid to Johnson campaign," Werner wrote.

All through October, 1943, these interviews went on, and on November 1, Alvin Wirtz, telegraphing from Houston, asked Roosevelt for an appointment to discuss AN IMPORTANT MATTER . . . AT YOUR EARLIEST CONVENIENCE, supplementing the request with a telegram to Pa Watson: ONLY A MATTER WHICH I THINK IS IMPORTANT TO THE ADMINISTRATION, AS WELL AS MYSELF, WOULD IMPEL ME TO MAKE THIS REQUEST. When he was given an appointment, for November 8, Wirtz specified to Watson that it be "off the record."

The matter was apparently being raised with Morgenthau again—with the same result as before. On November 2, Werner was told by Cooner that he had just received a telephone call from Assistant Secretary of the Treasury Elmer L. Irey in Washington. Irey, Cooner said, had relayed a message from Morgenthau: that "the case was to be handled like any other case." And, Cooner said, Irey had added a message of his own: "that it appeared fraud was present in the Brown & Root, Inc. case," and that "if prosecution was in order, then the Government would prosecute." Wirtz was unable, for all his persuasiveness, and for all the compelling political reasons on his side, to get Morgenthau's decision overruled by the only man who could overrule it. The most the President would agree to do was, in Wirtz's words, to leave the matter "open for further discussion."

Further discussion was to be necessary. In compliance with its previous brief, the IRS had thus far not checked "outside," but Morgenthau's message

---

* George Brown made three other statements of particular interest: (1) Brown & Root had never paid to get a contract; (2) he was under the impression that amounts paid for goodwill, whether to a Congressman, president of an oil company, etc., were proper; and (3) Brown & Root had on rare occasions promoted local bond elections— including one in Duval County.

now removed those restraints, and in December, 1943, the agents took their first steps in this direction. They began trying to find out the identity of the individuals in the "Johnson campaign" who had received the possibly illicit contributions, and what they had done with them. Their first approach, on December 6, was to a clerk at headquarters, Mrs. Margarite Kelly, who didn't know enough to be helpful. Their second, on December 15, was to Sherman Birdwell; "He told me nothing," Werner wrote after that interview. Their third was no more productive; Herman Brown had said that he had given $5,000 to Walter Bremond of the Capitol National Bank. Bremond told Werner "he couldn't recall" to whom he paid the $5,000. But the agents had scheduled a fourth interview—with someone who might have told them quite a lot.

He was Wilton Woods, who at college had, on Johnson's advice, dated girls so the White Stars could control them, and had written Johnson's editorials and run his errands—and who had continued to run errands, including the carrying of money, for his idolized Chief ever since.

Internal Revenue agent Werner was particularly interested in several items that involved Woods. One was a sum of $1,000 which the IRS agents believed had been given to him—by "contact man" Young—on June 14, 1941. Another was the sum of $7,500, which had been given to him by Brown & Root. The IRS's curiosity about this item had been piqued by the fact that this was a rather large sum for the company to hand over to an assistant personnel supervisor who at the time was earning $225 per month; by the fact that when the Brown & Root official who had signed the check was asked if Woods had done anything around Corpus Christi to earn it, he replied, "I don't believe so"—and by the fact that, whatever the expenditure might have been for, Brown & Root had not reported it. The IRS agents believed that the $7,500 was linked to a trip Woods had taken to Washington, D.C. They wanted to know to whom in Washington Woods had given the money—and for what purpose. Woods was scheduled to be the subject of a formal IRS interview, at which his testimony would be recorded, on January 6.

By this time, the stakes involved were huge. With the investigation not nearly complete, the amount by which the IRS team calculated that Brown & Root had underpaid its taxes had already mounted to $1,099,944. Since the IRS penalty where fraud could be shown was fifty percent, Brown & Root would owe the government an additional $549,972, for a total of $1,649,916. And money was no longer what was most significantly at stake. Irey's conclusion that "fraud was present" was echoed by Werner, and the penalties for tax fraud, as opposed to tax underpayment, included jail as well as money. Nor were the potential losses only those of Brown & Root. Lyndon Johnson had a lot to lose, too, and not only in terms of career-tarnishing publicity and scandal. Should Herman Brown—and his company, and some of his employees—be found guilty of fraud for the manner in which they had financed Lyndon Johnson's campaign, would Brown be willing to finance other campaigns? Herman's money—Brown & Root money—had been an essential element of Johnson's rise to power, and Johnson was going to need it again. What if it wasn't there for him when he needed it?

A new attempt had to be made at the White House, and it was not to be sufficient for Wirtz to try to make it alone. On Monday, December 27, Werner was working in Austin, preparing for his interview with Woods. Wirtz was working, too. Roosevelt returned to Washington that day after a weekend in Hyde Park, and Wirtz telephoned the White House and asked for an appointment with the President. The appointment had apparently still not been set up when Woods was interviewed by Werner on January 6. He was accompanied by Attorney Everett Looney, and the IRS notes on the interview state that "In re: $7500 in fees from B&R and Washington, D.C. trip," Woods "declined to answer all questions on above fees on advice of counsel on basis that it might incriminate him." He gave the same answer to the IRS inquiries about the $1,000 fee, and when, Werner notes, he was "given opportunity to tell of any other unreported receipts," Woods again "declined to answer on grounds it might incriminate him," although he did say that "at time of preparation of return he thought it was true and correct." And on January 11, 1944, Lyndon Johnson telephoned the White House and asked for an appointment with President Roosevelt. The secretary who took the message for Pa Watson wrote Watson that Johnson "is very anxious to see the President as quickly as he possibly could. He says it is not a 'Sunday School' proposition."

LYNDON JOHNSON AND ALVIN WIRTZ saw President Roosevelt on January 13, 1944, at 11:50 a.m. At 4:30 that afternoon, Elmer Irey telephoned Texas. He had been ordered to be at the White House at ten o'clock the next morning to give a full report to the President on the income-tax investigation into Brown & Root, Inc., he said.

Irey asked Werner to send him, in time for his meeting with the President, "detailed information on political payments made by Brown & Root, Inc., to the Lyndon Johnson 1941 senatorial campaign." So that the information would reach him before he had to leave for the White House, he asked that it be sent over the government teletype in the Houston office of the Bureau of Narcotics. The report was unequivocal: after listing the $150,800 in bonuses, for example, Werner stated: "Sufficient evidence is on hand, it is believed, to show minutes authorizing above bonuses to be fraudulent." Then the report listed specific drawings against those bonuses which had been traced directly to the Johnson campaign—the $2,500 from Randolph Mills, for example, or the $2,500 which "Corwin admits" was donated to the campaign, together with what the IRS team believed was sufficient evidence to prove the case: of the Mills bonus, for example, Werner wrote: "Admitted by Mills. We traced to Johnson Bank Account and have Recordak facsimile of check."

But the opinion of the six agents who had been working on the Brown & Root investigation for eighteen months was not to carry much weight in its ultimate disposition. Johnson and Wirtz had seen Roosevelt on January 13. On that day, a new agent, who had no previous knowledge of the case, was sent to Texas from the IRS bureau in Atlanta, Georgia, to make a "separate investigation" of it. Arriving in Texas on January 17, this new agent began studying the case. He proved to be a quick study indeed. Three days later, he told Werner, "The case as it now stands does not have quite enough evidence, in my opinion, for the Chief Counsel's office to pass it for prosecution but there is ample to sustain the 50% penalty." The next day, he confirmed this, adding that, as Werner put it in his diary, "he would recommend against making a prosecution case in view of Brown & Root, Inc.'s participation in the war effort." Then he left for Washington, D.C.

The Georgia agent had also told the Texas agents that "he could see no reason why we should not be permitted to finish our investigation of certain unfinished work which we had detailed to him." But this work was, in fact, never to be finished. On February 15, IRS Chief of Intelligence W. H. Woolf told Cooner that it had been decided, based on the facts "now in hand," that there was insufficient evidence on the Brown & Root, Inc., case to "sustain criminal prosecution," and that the "likelihood of developing proof adequate for that purpose is too remote to justify further extension of the investigation." The Texas agents were ordered to submit final reports on the "basis of the facts now in hand."

Agents who had actually been working on the case felt that the facts "now in hand" only scratched its surface; because of the earlier orders that "no outside persons were to be interviewed," they had been restricted until recently to interviewing Brown & Root officials; only within the past few months had they begun talking to members of the organization that had received the questionable contributions: the Johnson campaign. In fact, they had talked only to a handful of campaign aides—all low-level. They had not talked to the campaign's higher-ups: Wirtz, for example. They had not talked to the candidate. They did not agree with the Georgia agent's conclusion that the facts "now in hand" were insufficient for prosecution, but even if he were correct, they felt that if they were allowed to investigate the link between Brown & Root and the Johnson campaign thoroughly, much new evidence would be developed.

Werner asked, apparently on behalf of the rest of the team, to be allowed to continue the investigation. On March 2, he received his answer: he was ordered to drop the case—at once, and forever. A letter from Chief of Intelligence Woolf reiterated that the case was to "be reported by the examining agents on the basis of facts *now in hand* with a view to placing the case in line for disposition under routine field procedure. . . . A further extension of the investigation as proposed by Special Agent Werner will be inconsistent with this finding and it is accordingly directed that the case be disposed of as indicated above."

On June 28, Werner submitted his final report on Case S.I.-19267-F, showing tax deficiencies of $1,099,944 and a penalty of $549,972. But even this was to be scaled down. After a series of further conferences between IRS officials and Wirtz, Brown & Root was ultimately required to pay a total of only $372,000. There were of course no fraud indictments, no trial, no publicity. Franklin Roosevelt had already done so much to advance Lyndon Johnson's career. In this instance, it may be he who saved it.

36

"Mister Speaker"

IN THE FLOOD of endorsements from "big names" in Washington on behalf of Lyndon Johnson's senatorial bid, had one name been, for most of the campaign, conspicuously absent?

Sam Rayburn's coldness in October, 1940, when he had been reluctant to endorse Johnson for a post with the Democratic Congressional Campaign Committee, had been thawed somewhat by Johnson's performance in that role; Rayburn knew how much he owed Johnson for helping to preserve the Democratic majority in the House, and thereby helping *him* keep the Speakership. Rayburn was a man who always paid his debts. After the campaign, he was again courteous to Lyndon Johnson on Capitol Hill.

But the thaw was only partial. The greatest favor Rayburn had bestowed on him—entrée to the "Board of Education," where crucial House decisions were made and strategy was discussed—was withdrawn; no longer, when Rayburn left the Speaker's chair in the late afternoon and headed for the room in which the House leaders met, did he invite Johnson to "come on down." Had the Speaker guessed—or learned—how Lyndon Johnson had betrayed his friendship; how, to help his own career, the young man of whom he had been so fond had turned the President against him by falsely portraying him as the President's enemy? To an effusive letter from Johnson in November, 1940, after the campaign had ended, there was no reply. A month later, Johnson arranged to be one of the speakers at an "appreciation banquet" held for Rayburn in Dallas, and played a high card to a man who so desperately wanted a son: Johnson said he had been a young boy accompanying his father to the State Legislature when he had first met Sam Rayburn; ever since, he said, he had regarded Mr. Sam as "like a father to me." When, however, Congress reconvened in 1941, Johnson found the door to the Board of Education still closed to him, and it remained closed all that year; during this year, encountering House parliamentarian Lewis Deschler late one afternoon on the landing of the staircase near the Board room, he said, almost shouting: "I can get into the White House. Why can't I get into that room?"

This was a rare outburst, however. It was not in Lyndon Johnson's interest for Capitol Hill to become aware that he was no longer on intimate terms with the Speaker, so few hints of the true state of affairs escaped his lips. As for Sam Rayburn, whose grim face had turned only harder now that he held at last the gavel—and the power and the responsibility that came with it—no one would have dared to ask him. It was generally assumed, therefore, that the relationship was intact. Johnson's staff hoped the Speaker would come to Texas and campaign for Johnson, and they were sure he would at least endorse him—and they were planning to make the endorsement a centerpiece of the campaign by emphasizing it, over and over, in a series of newspaper advertisements and in brochures. When they learned that Rayburn had, during the week of April 22, helped dissuade Wright Patman from making the race, they were sure he had done so on Johnson's behalf, and that the endorsement would follow shortly.

It didn't, and approaches were therefore made to the Speaker. At first, they were indirect; one was made, still in late April, through Representative Poage of Waco, who told Johnson of Rayburn's response: "He said that he did not feel that he should make any kind of statement in the 'Record,' although he was writing all of those that he had an opportunity telling them that he was definitely for you."

Private letters were not sufficient; what was needed was a public endorsement, and it 'was needed early in the campaign. During the next weeks, Rayburn was pressed harder and harder, but no endorsement was forthcoming. On May 29, Johnson telegraphed John Connally—and one of the significant aspects of this telegram is that Johnson is asking someone else to call Rayburn rather than doing it himself—YOU OR SENATOR [WIRTZ] CALL RAYBURN TODAY AND ASK HIM IF HE WILL RELEASE OR PERMIT YOU TO RELEASE STATEMENT . . . TO THE EFFECT THAT HE IS GOING TO VOTE FOR AND SUPPORT ME FOR SENATOR. . . . TELL HIM THIS OUGHT TO BE DONE TODAY IN ORDER TO HELP US GET ORGANIZED IN NORTH TEXAS. No such statement was released.

Johnson's puzzled aides began to wonder about the enthusiasm of even the private support that Rayburn was supposedly providing. Rayburn was a powerful force not only in his own seven-county congressional district but all across North Texas. The courthouse politicians in the little towns that dotted the prairies north of Dallas awaited only Mr. Sam's word to swing into action for Lyndon Johnson. The word did not come. By June, the puzzlement among Johnson's supporters was finding expression in letters. Warren Bellows wrote Connally expressing concern about the situation in North Texas. Judge Loy in Grayson County is very powerful up there, he said,

and is a personal friend of Sam Rayburn. I have been trying to get
somebody to have Rayburn to phone Loy [but Loy] has not yet
heard from Rayburn, although I made this suggestion nearly a
month ago. . . .
P.S. Can't you get Rayburn down to Texas for a speech? This
would help more than anything else.

Replying on June 3, Connally had to confess that "We tried to get Rayburn
to call him. However, I don't think he ever did. . . . We are trying to get
Rayburn to come to Texas to make a speech, but I don't know what luck we
are going to have."

As Election Day neared with still no word from Rayburn, puzzlement
turned to anger. The arrogant Marsh, the only one of Johnson's supporters
who would dare to express it to Rayburn himself, did so; in mid-June, he
telegraphed the Speaker:

IF YOU DON'T SPEAK OR SEND MESSAGE BY SATURDAY NIGHT AT
DENISON PLEASE DO NOT SPEAK AT ALL, AS I BELIEVE IT WILL BE
POLITICALLY HARMFUL THE LAST WEEK. IT WILL BE INTERPRETED
AS RELUCTANT, TARDY, AND POOR STATEMENT. YOUR POSITION,
WHATEVER IT IS, ALREADY BECOMING UNIMPORTANT, BECAUSE
TIMING COMING TOO SLOW TO BE EFFECTIVE.

Sam Rayburn finally endorsed Lyndon Johnson on June 20, two months
after he had been asked to do so—and just a little more than a week before
Election Day, too late for the endorsement to be of maximum use. Moreover,
the Speaker's public statement was accompanied by little private support.
The definitive statement on the extent of Rayburn's backing of Johnson in
the senatorial race was the result in Rayburn's own congressional district, in
which 31,000 votes were cast. Johnson received only 7,000 of them.

Following the race, Rayburn's true preference in it became clearer. He
had become acquainted with Gerald Mann, whose hometown in Sulphur
Springs was not far from Bonham, and had liked the young man—a feeling
that was reciprocated; "I was very fond of Sam Rayburn," Mann says. Although Johnson was already gearing up for another try at the Senate seat in
1942, Rayburn may have had another young man in mind for the post. On
September 2, 1941, with Mann on his way to Washington, Rayburn tried to
arrange for him to meet the President; the Speaker told Pa Watson that he
thought a "short visit with [the] President would help all [the] way down the
line." Had Rayburn wanted Mann all along—and endorsed Johnson only
after he had become convinced that the under-financed Attorney General
had no chance to defeat the hated O'Daniel? Johnson was able to fend off
this threat for a while. Watson told Rayburn that he was sure there would be
no difficulty arranging for an appointment with the Attorney General of

Texas, but he was wrong about that. On September 11, Watson was informed that "Miss Tully says the President does not want to see Gerald Mann at this time. Mr. Mann ran against Lyndon Johnson for Senator, and Johnson is now in Virginia recovering from a tonsillectomy, and the President wants to see him first." When Rayburn insisted, an appointment was arranged for the next time Mann was in Washington. But the appointment was made for a Sunday, and the Sunday happened to be December 7.

PEARL HARBOR restored—in an instant—the relationship between Sam Rayburn and Lyndon Johnson.

During the senatorial campaign, Johnson had promised, "If the day ever comes when my vote must be cast to send your boy to the trenches, that day Lyndon Johnson will leave his Senate seat and go with him." So popular had that promise proven in hawkish Texas that the candidate repeated it in almost every major speech, and in every form of campaign literature. Though his seat was still in the House, the promise could not be broken—not if he wanted to continue to have a political career in Texas. Johnson had some months previously been commissioned a Lieutenant Commander in the United States Naval Reserve, and on December 11 he was placed on active duty. Rising in the House, he said, "Mr. Speaker, I ask unanimous consent for an indefinite leave of absence."

"Is there objection to the request of the Gentleman from Texas?" Rayburn asked. There being none, Rayburn said, "So be it."

The story of the naval service of Lyndon Johnson was to prove a very complicated one; as his actions during the war, and his own, private, statements to contemporaries were to demonstrate, it was a story motivated by considerations at least as much political as patriotic. But to Sam Rayburn, to whom some things were very simple, there was nothing complicated at all about a brave young man in uniform going off to fight for his country, perhaps to die. Rayburn was a profoundly silent man, determined that no one ever be able to guess his feelings. But as the coldness of a father toward an estranged son melts in a moment when the boy is in danger, so Rayburn's coldness to Lyndon Johnson melted now. Their exchanges of friendly letters had long since dried up—there had been none for more than a year—but Johnson wrote one on December 18, a few days before he was to depart for the West Coast. He was worried about the Speaker's health, he said; he hoped Rayburn would take care of himself. During the next few months, he said, "you must carry a burden that few—if any—men in our country can carry. You have never shirked a duty or failed a responsibility. You won't now— unless the old physical self cracks up. So take this suggestion from one much less experienced than yourself: 'Get fitted.' " The letter was signed: "Just one who respects you and loves you—LBJ." Sam Rayburn folded over that letter several times—until it was small enough to fit into his billfold. He carried it

around in his billfold for a long time. Then he placed it in a special drawer
in his desk: the drawer in which he kept the letters from his mother. When,
eighteen years later, officials of the Sam Rayburn Library itemized the contents of that drawer, the letter was still there.

IF TO SAM RAYBURN Lyndon Johnson was the brave young man going off
to war, there was a brave young wife staying behind, the shy, timid young
woman, when he had first met her almost as lonely in Washington as he was,
to whom his heart had gone out in paternal fondness—and who had repaid
him, and more than repaid him, by making him feel at home in the Johnsons' apartment.

After his initial trip to the Coast, Lyndon Johnson returned to
Washington. In February, he left again—this time, it was reported, for the
South Pacific. He and John Connally, also in Navy uniform, left from Union
Station, and Lady Bird Johnson and Connally's wife, Nellie, went down to
the station to say goodbye.

So did Sam Rayburn. He had abruptly announced that he was going
down to the station with them. The giant terminal was, in Lady Bird's word,
a "hubbub," jammed with sailors, soldiers and marines, their women kissing
them goodbye. Amid the tumult, Rayburn stood alone, square and silent as
he always stood, well behind the young couple of whom he was so fond. As
the Johnsons said goodbye to each other, he said nothing. His face was as
expressionless as ever.

But after the train had pulled out, he came up to Lady Bird and Nellie.
His words were not tender; only if you knew Sam Rayburn would you know
what was behind them. "Now girls," Sam Rayburn said, with the gruffness
of a man who could never be cheerful no matter how hard he tried, and who
knew it, but who was determined to be as cheerful as he could—"Now
girls, we're going to get us the best dinner in Washington."

IN UNDERSTANDING what many perceptive men had so much difficulty in
understanding—the bond that, for the next twenty years, made Sam
Rayburn the ally of a man so utterly opposite to him in both principles and
personality—part of the answer lies in Lady Bird Johnson's sweetness and
graciousness, and in the shyness that made Rayburn so fond of her. While
Lyndon was away during the war, the Speaker hovered over Lady Bird,
paternally protective, smoothing her work as she tried to run her husband's
office in his absence, providing evenings out for her—and for the wives of
other young men who were off to war, not only for Nellie Connally but for
Elizabeth Rowe, Jim's wife, for example.

Of all the proofs of the power of Lady Bird's graciousness, perhaps
none is more convincing than the fact that she made Sam Rayburn feel at

home in her home; for the rest of his life he would come to dinner as often as several times a week; the only stipulation he made was that "that blamed television set" be turned off. She had his favorite recipes down pat, and, with her unfailing warmth, made him feel she was happy to prepare them— when the Johnsons acquired a cook, the cook was taught how to make cornbread and chili the way Mr. Sam liked them. The bond between Lady Bird and Mr. Sam was to become strong. Talking of "the Speaker," she says with a fierceness very unusual for her: "He was the best of *us*—the best of simple American stock." In his times of sorrow—when a brother or sister died—her heart went out to him; on the occasion of one death, she wrote him: "We wish we could put our arms around you today. Your sadness is ours, too." Rayburn was to write her: "Your friendship for me is one of the most heartening things in my life." During Lady Bird's pregnancies, the Speaker's concern about her health was so deep as to amuse those who witnessed it. He was constantly asking Johnson to telephone her to find out if she was all right; once, when Johnson did not immediately do so, he rasped: "Go call her this minute."

Then came the children: Lynda Bird in 1944 and Lucy Baines three years later. Sam Rayburn had wanted a child so badly, but he had had none, and never would. He loved Lyndon's. He would sit for hours with one of the girls on his lap, patiently listening to her gabble; as soon as Lynda Bird could talk, he taught her a sentence: "We are just two old pals." He gave them birthday parties at his apartment, inviting perhaps ten or twelve of their friends; the children's parents stared as they watched the little girls or boys sitting on the Speaker's lap, or reaching up to hug him—this man whom other men only feared. One of these fathers, the lobbyist Dale Miller, says that he realized watching Sam Rayburn what he had never known— that "He was a kind man, but he would be distressed if he ever thought you had found that out." Lyndon Johnson's family became Sam Rayburn's family —the family he had never had.

Also cementing the bond between the two men was Johnson's talent as a "professional son."

He knew now how much he needed "Mr. Sam." For the next two decades, Sam Rayburn held power in Washington. Presidents came and went—Roosevelt, Truman, Eisenhower, Kennedy—but whoever was President, Sam Rayburn was Speaker; he held the post he had dreamed of as a boy for almost seventeen of the twenty-one years after 1940, more years than any other man in American history. Over his branch of government his power was immense, so great that it spilled over into the government as a whole. Johnson needed him not only at the moment, when he was still only a junior member of the body the older man ruled; he needed him for the realization of his great ambition. And he knew it. If you want to be President, he told William O. Douglas during the 1940's, "you've got to do it through Sam Rayburn." And, needing the Speaker as his friend, Johnson devoted his energy and his skill to making him one. He reiterated his version of their first meeting ("My dear Mr. Speaker," he was to write in 1957, "when I was a very little boy in knee breeches and high button shoes, my Daddy told me that 'there's a young fellow from Bonham who's a mighty good friend and don't you go forgetting it.' I promised to remember—and that was the smartest promise I ever made in my life")—reiterated it so often that Rayburn eventually came to believe that he remembered it, too; nominating Johnson for the Presidency in 1960, Rayburn said: "I'm going to present to you today a man that I have known since his babyhood. . . ." As Rayburn grew old, that story came to mean more and more to him; at one banquet, when Rayburn was seventy-six, Senator Ralph Yarborough was to recall, "Lyndon was telling the story about how Sam had first seen him running up and down the aisles [of the Texas House of Representatives] in short pants. He was telling how 'he's been like a father to me.' I saw tears come out of Rayburn's eyes at this banquet and roll down his cheeks."

When Lynda Bird was born in 1944, Johnson telephoned Rayburn with the news and made a point of telling him he was the first person he had called, even before he had telephoned his own mother. He entertained Rayburn's favorite sister, Lucinda ("Miss Lou"), on her annual visits to Washington, and, when she was back in Bonham, wrote her to keep her up to date on the Speaker's health, and sent her presents, including candy in boxes so elaborate that she kept them on her vanity table as decorations. And he did nothing to discourage the bond between Rayburn and Lady Bird. During the first decade of her marriage, Lady Bird was not usually present at dinners at which her husband discussed serious political business—unless the Speaker was present. If he was, she would be brought along—even if she was the only wife there. During the war years, she recalls, sometimes a group of Texans would go out to dinner, at the Occidental, or to Hall's Restaurant for bluepoints and lobster; "This would be the Speaker, and perhaps Wright Patman, and others. . . . The other men would leave their wives home, because they would be talking business. There would be three or four or five men and me—for some reason, Lyndon always took me."

ALTHOUGH THE RELATIONSHIP between Lyndon Johnson and Sam Rayburn was restored, it was to be subtly different than it had been before. Johnson's actions in the 1940 Garner-Roosevelt fight had lifted from Rayburn's eyes the curtain of uncritical affection through which he had hitherto regarded the younger man. If Sam Rayburn loved Lyndon Johnson, the love was no longer blind. Men who sat in the Board of Education during the next twenty years were aware of this even if most Washingtonians were not. Says Richard Bolling: "A constant refrain was about his [Johnson's] arrogance and egotism. He [Rayburn] said to me several times the same words: 'I

don't know anyone who is as vain or more selfish than Lyndon Johnson.' "
He appears to have understood now what drove the younger man; Ramsey
Clark says, in words echoed by other men who knew both, "He understood
Johnson. I've heard him talk about Johnson, and his ambition. I don't think
it was blind love at all."

But Clark also says, and Bolling agrees, and so do Ken Harding and
D. B. Hardeman and other men who sat, afternoon after afternoon, in the
Board of Education as the dramas of power were played out, that while the
"love" may not have been "blind," love it certainly was. Sam Rayburn could
criticize Johnson, but he let no one else do so. Once, after Johnson's 1948
campaign for the Senate, a reporter from Texas was riding in the Speaker's
limousine and remarked that Johnson had stolen the election; Rayburn had
the chauffeur stop the car, and ordered the reporter out of it. Says Hardeman:
"It was a father-son relation, with all that that implies. . . . Johnson would
just infuriate him, but he would defend Johnson against all comers. He loved
him in the way: he'd like to wear the bottom of his britches out."

The most significant difference was that, although the relationship was
restored, no longer did Rayburn give his love and support to Lyndon
Johnson for nothing; he demanded from him, in political matters at least,
the respect, even deference, that he received from other men. The door to
the Board room on the ground floor of the Capitol was open to Johnson
again, but in that room, Rayburn ruled, and Johnson acknowledged that fact.
Even in later years, when Johnson was the leader of one house of Congress as
Rayburn was of the other, he acknowledged that. The acknowledgment was
in the names by which each referred to the other: "It was never 'Sam,' "
says one man. "It was always 'Mr. Sam' or 'Mr. Speaker,' and 'Lyndon.' "
Says another: "There was never a feeling that they were equals. Never. Even
after [Johnson became Majority Leader], Johnson was quite deferential to
him. He would argue with him, but always in such a way that you knew who
was the boss." If there was a disagreement, Johnson would preface his argument by saying, "Mr. Speaker, we're going to do whatever you want, but
here's what I think." If he did it that way, Brown & Root lobbyist Frank
Oltorf says, Rayburn would go along—but he wouldn't go along otherwise.
Even Walter Jenkins, who idolized Johnson, says, "He kowtowed to Mr.
Rayburn unbelievably." What Rayburn demanded, Johnson gave.

Occasionally, Johnson's feelings—his true feelings—about what he
gave became apparent, but he never let Rayburn see them. When he was in
the Senate, he would sometimes say to Jim Rowe, "Oh, Rayburn's so
goddamned difficult—I've got to go over there to the Board of Education
and kiss his ass, and I don't want to do it." But he went over, and did it—
afternoon after afternoon, year after year. In 1957, when he was Majority
Leader, he attended the dedication of the Sam Rayburn Library in Bonham.
While he was talking with several prominent Texans, one of Rayburn's aides,

House Doorkeeper "Fishbait" Miller, came up and told him the Speaker would like to see him. He waved Miller aside twice, and, when Miller persisted, exploded: "Goddammit, I have to kiss his ass all the time in Washington. I don't have to do it in Texas, too, do I? I'm not coming!" But then he ran after Miller to make sure that the message wasn't delivered, and hurried off to see the Speaker.

And in return for giving Rayburn what Rayburn wanted, Johnson got what *he* wanted. For the twenty years after Pearl Harbor, Sam Rayburn was one of the rocks—one of the firmest rocks—on which Lyndon Johnson's career was built.

IN AUGUST, 1961, Sam Rayburn, seventy-nine years old, virtually blind but still Speaker of the House, was dying of cancer, so racked by pain that he was finally forced to curtly inform a shocked and silent House—while giving it no hint of the true nature of his illness, which he had long concealed—that although Congress was still in session, he was going to leave Washington and return to Texas for medical treatment. Vice President Lyndon Johnson was in Berlin, dispatched there by President Kennedy to reassure that city of American support. (On August 17, when Kennedy had telephoned Johnson to ask him to go to Berlin, he had reached him at Rayburn's apartment at the Anchorage, and Johnson had replied that he had been planning to go fishing with Rayburn that weekend. Rayburn had interrupted to tell him to go to Berlin; they could go fishing another weekend, he said.)

On August 21, Johnson returned to Washington. Lady Bird, at Andrews Air Force Base Airport to greet him, suddenly looked around and to her surprise saw Sam Rayburn standing there behind her, as he had stood at Union Station so many years before.

> Dear Mr. Speaker [Lady Bird wrote],
>   As I stood by that airplane in the gray, grizzly morning waiting for Lyndon, I looked up and saw you and my mind went back to so many times and so many trouble-fraught situations when you have stood by our side. You were dear to take the trouble to come out and I wanted to drop you a line and tell you so.
>   Next April is my twenty-fifth anniversary as a wife of a member of Congress. This quarter of a century of our lives has been marked most by knowing you.

On August 30, Sam Rayburn wrote back, stilted and formal even now. "Dear Bird," he wrote, "Your note was very refreshing and highly appreciated by me. You know that no two people are closer to me in friendship and love than you and Lyndon. It has been a great heritage to have known you so intimately and well." Although the pain was very bad that day, the hand that wrote that letter did not shake. There was not a tremor in the name "Sam Rayburn." The next morning, Rayburn went home to Bonham to die. A friend who spent time with him during his last days explained why he did not stay in Washington, where he could have gotten better medical assistance: Rayburn, the friend wrote, thought that "Washington was such a lonely city for a country boy to get sick in."

37

The "Perfect
Roosevelt Man"

PEARL HARBOR was to derail Lyndon Johnson's career.

He had expected to run against Pappy O'Daniel again in just a year—in the Democratic primary that would be held during the summer of 1942 for the full six-year term in the same Senate seat. He hoped for Roosevelt's backing in 1942, and the President's negative response to Rayburn's request for an interview for Gerald Mann was not the only indication that this hope was to be granted. When, in October, 1941, Wright Patman asked for an appointment to solicit the White House support to which he felt his record entitled him, Roosevelt wouldn't even see him. In 1942, moreover, Johnson would be starting not as an unknown candidate but as one whose name had been made—through hundreds of thousands of dollars' worth of advertising—almost a household word in Texas. The statewide Johnson-for-Senator campaign organization established and perfected in 1941 was champing at the bit for 1942. He would have Brown & Root behind him again, which meant that he would again have all the money he needed. He was confident that he would win. But the outbreak of war—and his pledge to serve in it—made running in 1942 an impossibility. It would be seven years before he got another chance.

And when, in 1948, he got this chance, there would be a slight alteration in the platform on which he ran. In 1941, his platform had been "all-out," "100 percent" support of Franklin D. Roosevelt and the New Deal. In 1948, he no longer supported the principles and programs for which Roosevelt had stood.

With a few exceptions, he opposed them.

Even before Roosevelt's death, the change had begun, for even before Roosevelt's death, Johnson had decided that the power in Texas—the power that could enable him to move up to the second rung on his three-rung ladder—lay not with the people of Texas, who loved the President, but with the state's small circle of rulers, who hated him. In February, 1943, Johnson sent them a signal. One of their voices in Washington was House Un-American Activities Committee Chairman Martin Dies, to whom the New Deal was a Communist conspiracy. An effort was under way in Congress to end the Committee's existence. Johnson voted to continue it, and to increase the funding for its work.

Harold Young, a dedicated liberal, was astonished when he heard of this vote by the man he had so ardently supported, and telephoned Johnson, "You mean to tell me you voted for that son-of-a-bitch to get more money?" Admitting that he had indeed done so, Johnson said, "I never claimed to be a liberal." "Well," said Young, "you sure fooled hell out of me." Then and there, he coined a new nickname that he felt epitomized the cowardice before powerful forces of the man he had previously admired: "Lyin'-down Lyndon."

So long as Roosevelt was still alive—in power—the change was muted. The sentiments Johnson expressed in Texas, 1,600 miles from Washington, were not expressed in the capital, except to a small clique which revolved around Corcoran, now ousted by the President from the circles of official power and already transformed, with remarkable speed, into a lobbyist growing rich on fees from some of the country's most reactionary business-men who hired Tommy the Cork to help them circumvent the laws he had written. By 1942, Charles Marsh was to say in dismay that both Corcoran and Johnson had "reached the conclusion that the public is now tired of the New Deal and they must be given something new." Corcoran arranged for Johnson to deliver in Portland, Oregon, a speech that, according to Marsh, "kicks the New Deal into a cocked hat." At the last moment, Johnson edited out most of the anti–New Deal rhetoric, but a few paragraphs remained to give the tone. The speech was delivered—on December 8, 1942—at farewell ceremonies for the obsolete battleship *Oregon*, which was being scrapped to provide steel for the war effort. Johnson said there was other scrapping to be done as well: of a government that, he said, had grown too big. Many Depression-era government agencies, such as "these old domestic museum pieces, the PWA, FHA and WPA," he said, "have now outlived their useful-ness," as have "men who have become entrenched in power without making or keeping themselves fit for the exercise of that power, men who love their country and would die for it—but not until their own dangerously outdated notions have caused others to die for it first.

> What about over-staffed, over-stuffed government that worries along like a centipede? [he demanded]. . . . While we work and fight to end the career of the paperhanger of Berlin, what are we doing about the careers of our artists in paperhanging, who plaster us with forms and blanks and hem us in with red tape? . . . The roll

of candidates, human and otherwise, for our national wartime scrap heap, is too long to be called here. Scrap them we must. End the entrenchment of the unfit we must. Break the hold of dead hands we must. . . . We are wound and wound in little threads like a spider's web.

In 1944, during the anti-Roosevelt revolt by the reactionary Texas Regulars, Johnson sided with his state's New Dealers, but, with Wirtz's help, he tried frantically to keep his role in the fight as minimal as possible, disguising it so successfully that after this battle the disgusted Bill Kittrell, another Texas liberal who had backed Johnson in the belief that Johnson was also a liberal, began telling friends: "Lyndon will be found on no barricades."

Muted though it was during Roosevelt's life, however, the change had come very early—within a few months after the 1941 senatorial campaign, in fact. Even before he sent out public signals with his vote on the Dies Committee, he had, in a series of quiet meetings arranged by Roy Miller and Herman Brown and Alvin Wirtz and Ed Clark, let key figures in the Texas plutocracy know what Miller and Brown and Wirtz and Clark already knew: that, as Roy's son, Dale, puts it: "He gave the impression of being much, much more liberal than he actually was—his manner personified the New Deal—he looked the part: he was young, dynamic, outgoing. But . . . he gave a lot more impression of being with the New Deal than he actually was. . . ." Or as George Brown says, "He [said he] was for the Niggers, he was for labor, he was for the little boys, but by God . . . you get right down to the nut-cutting, he was practical." "Basically," George Brown says, "Lyndon was more conservative, more practical than people understood"—and by the mid-1940's, Brown says, in Texas at least, "people," the people who mattered, *did* understand. "You could see what side he was really on, then."

On the day of Roosevelt's death, Johnson's reporter friend William S. White wrote that he found the young Congressman in "a gloomy Capitol corridor," with "tears in his eyes," and "a white cigarette holder"—similar to Roosevelt's—clamped in "a shaking jaw." He told White that when the news came, "I was just looking up at a cartoon on the wall—a cartoon showing the President with that cigarette holder and his jaw stuck out like it always was. He had his head cocked back, you know. And then I thought of all the little folks, and what they had lost." He told White, "He was just like a Daddy to me always; he always talked to me just that way. . . ." Then, White wrote, Johnson cried out, "God! God! How he could take it for us all!"

But the King was dead. The day after Roosevelt's death, one of Johnson's secretaries, Dorothy Nichols, asked him: "He's gone; what do we have now?" "Honey," Johnson replied, "we've got Truman. . . . There is going to be the damnedest scramble for power in this man's town for the next two weeks that anyone ever saw in their lives."

With Roosevelt dead, Johnson went public with his change of allegiance. Because he had difficulty erasing the earlier pro-Roosevelt image that he had so painstakingly created, in 1947 he called in another friendly reporter, Tex Easley, to correct it, and after an exclusive interview with the Congressman, Easley wrote that while "People all over Texas formed an impression over the years that Lyndon Johnson personified the New Deal . . . it would be an error to tag Johnson now as a strong New Dealer. That may come as a surprise, but it is true." Except in certain limited, specific, areas of governmental action—Johnson mentioned three: "development of water power, REA, farm-to-market roads"—he wasn't a New Dealer, Johnson told Easley; "I think the term 'New Dealer' is a misnomer," he said. "I believe in free enterprise, and I don't believe in the government doing anything that the people can do privately. Whenever it's possible, government should get out of business." As a liberal reporter was later to put it: "Just roads and rural electrification? This could have been Cotton Ed Smith talking, or Jim Eastland. It was certainly no liberal talking." On another, later, occasion, he sought to excuse his early support of the New Deal by saying, "I was a young man of adventure with more guts than brains. . . ."

If in public he was attacking only certain aspects of the New Deal, in private—at least in Texas—he was going much further. He was not a New Dealer, he said, never had been. He had supported Roosevelt, he said, only to get things for Texas. In private, in fact, he was now opposing the New Deal almost as enthusiastically as he had once supported it. During his 1948 senatorial campaign, he supported few, if any, of the programs that had evolved out of, and were carrying forward, the New Deal. He ran not as a New Dealer, but, to the extent possible because of his earlier statements, as an anti–New Dealer. And during the campaign, he attacked much of what was left of the New Deal. The shift in his views can be symbolized in a single issue: labor. In his first campaign for the Senate, he had told Texas labor unions: "I come to you as a friend of labor." In his second, he came as an enemy—open and bitter. In 1948, it wasn't Pappy O'Daniel who attacked the "big labor racketeers" and "racketeering Communist [union] leaders who take orders only from Moscow." Those words were Johnson's words. Nor was the change limited to labor. Once he had said—over and over, in speeches, in pamphlets, in posters and on huge billboards—that he was "100 percent" for Roosevelt and the New Deal. Now, he still said that he had supported a percentage of New Deal legislation—but the percentage he cited was not 100, or even 50; on twenty-seven major pieces of New Deal legislation, he said, he had voted for the New Deal thirteen times. The Dallas Chamber of Commerce, one of the most reactionary business groups in the United States, checked out his record—and found it so satisfactorily conservative that it enthusiastically endorsed him.

The change may have come as a shock to Harold Young and Bill

Kittrell; it might have shocked Pa Watson, who had considered Lyndon Johnson the "perfect Roosevelt man." But it would have come as no surprise to the young men who had lived in the Dodge Hotel with Lyndon Johnson, and who had said, "Lyndon goes which way the wind blows." His relationship with the President and the New Deal demonstrated how well these young men had understood him. Before the paint had faded on the billboards proclaiming his loyalty to Franklin D, Lyndon B had turned against him.

DEBTS,
BIBLIOGRAPHY,
NOTES AND
INDEX

Debts

I SOMETIMES NOTICE, when reading Acknowledgments sections in other biographies, that the biographers have had the assistance of whole teams of research associates, research assistants and perhaps a typist or two. But I never feel envious of them. I have Ina.

My wife, Ina Joan Caro, has been all these things—in spades—during the seven years it has taken to complete this book, as she was all these things during the seven years it took me to write my first book. On the first book, she made herself an expert on great urban public works to help with my research into the life of Robert Moses. On this book, she made herself an expert on rural electrification and soil conservation, and then spent long days driving back and forth over the Hill Country searching out elderly farm wives who could explain to her—and through her, to me—the difference that these innovations had made in their lives after Lyndon Johnson brought the innovations to the Hill Country. Searching through smalltown libraries, Ina has unearthed copies of weekly newspapers of the 1920's and 1930's that the librarians swore no longer existed. Her incomparable knowledge of big-city library facilities in New York and Washington gives her a seemingly magical ability to say in an instant where a piece of information, no matter how recondite, can be found. And these are just some of the many areas in which, with perseverance and ingenuity, she has been invaluable in the research of this work. In addition, she has typed the massive manuscript—typed some chapters over and over—without a single word of complaint. And she has provided as well not only support and encouragement but many keen critical insights. Long years of gracious selflessness—Shakespeare's line on the dedication page expresses better than I can what they have meant to me. She has been my sole companion now on two long journeys. I could not ask for a better one.

The more I learn about publishers, the more I realize how extraordinary mine is. Robert Gottlieb has stood beside me now during two books: a tower of strength in his belief in my work, in his perceptive criticism, in his never-failing encouragement and support. And in an era in which detailed editing of even short manuscripts is rapidly becoming a lost art, Bob Gottlieb not only gave this long manuscript detailed editing, but editing of the unique keenness and brilliance that make him an artist in his field. The grinding pressures of his responsibilities as president of Knopf did not deter him from lavishing on this book his time, his energy and his genius.

Assisting Bob Gottlieb on this book, as she assisted him on *The Power Broker*, is Knopf's Katherine A. Hourigan. Among the assets she brings to an author is a dedication to making even thick books handsome and readable. Her perceptive editorial criticism is characterized as well by an unflinching integrity. For the endless hours she has devoted to this book I shall forever be grateful.

AMONG THE MANY OTHER PEOPLE at Knopf to whom I am indebted, I must thank especially Lesley Krauss, Virginia Tan and my old friends Nina Bourne, Jane Becker Friedman, Bill Loverd and Martha Kaplan.

Perhaps because my books take so long to write, sons as well as fathers work on them. Andrew L. Hughes has long provided me with valued literary as well as legal advice. And on this book, the man handling the ominously large difficulties in production (and handling them impressively indeed) has been Andrew W. Hughes.

OVER THE YEARS, my agent, Lynn Nesbit, has always been there when I needed her. If I have never told her how much her help has meant to me, let me do so now.

I AM GRATEFUL to many members of the staff of the Lyndon B. Johnson Library for their assistance in my research there. In addition to the Library's assistant director, Charles Corkran, they are Mike Gillette, Linda Hanson, David Humphrey, Joan Kennedy, Tina Lawson, E. Philip Scott and Robert Tissing.

Claudia Anderson, a true historian in the thoroughness of her work and in her devotion to the truth, was particularly helpful in guiding me through the Library's collections.

My thanks also to H. G. Dulaney, Director of the Sam Rayburn Library in Bonham, Texas; to Joseph W. Marshall, supervisory librarian of the Franklin D. Roosevelt Library in Hyde Park, New York; to Audrey Bateman of the Austin–Travis County Collection of the Austin Public Library; Paul K. Goode of the James C. Jernigan Library at Texas A&I, in Kingsville; John Tiff of the National Park Service in Johnson City; Linda Kaban of the Barker Texas History Center; and to Susan Bykofsky.

. . .

SCORES OF TEXAS POLITICIANS and political observers gave generously of their time in guiding me through the intricacies of that state's politics in the 1920's, '30's and '40's, but a few deserve special mention. They include Ann Fears Crawford, Vann Kennedy, the late D. B. Hardeman; Arthur Stehling; Sim Gideon and Judge Tom C. Ferguson, who took me step by step through the formation of the Lower Colorado River Authority and the construction of the Marshall Ford Dam, and E. Babe Smith, who taught me much about rural electrification, and its social and political uses.

My deepest gratitude goes to Edward A. Clark. Over a period of more than three years, Mr. Clark, Lyndon Johnson's Ambassador to Australia and a dominant figure in Texas politics for more than a quarter of a century, devoted evening after evening to furthering my political education. They were evenings that I will always cherish.

The town of Marlin, Texas, has produced two persons who observed Texas politics with keen eyes, and can speak about those politics with perception. They are Mary Louise Young and Frank C. (Posh) Oltorf, an historian in his own right, and a most gracious gentleman and host. Thanks to them, and to Ronnie Oltorf, I will always think of Marlin with fondness.

MANY OF Lyndon Johnson's boyhood companions were of great assistance to me, but I want especially to thank Truman Fawcett, Wilma Green Fawcett and Clayton Stribling for many days of help. Above all, I want to thank Ava Johnson Cox. Witty and wise, and very knowledgeable indeed about Sam Ealy and Rebekah Baines Johnson, and about their son Lyndon, her favorite cousin, she has contributed immeasurably to this book.

A Note on Sources

BECAUSE LYNDON JOHNSON would have been only sixty-seven years old when, in 1975, I began my research on his life, most of his contemporaries were still alive. This made it possible to find out what he was like while he was growing up from the best possible sources: those who grew up with him. And it also makes it possible to clear away in this book the misinformation that has surrounded the early life of Lyndon Johnson.

The extent of this misinformation, the reason it exists, and the importance of clearing it away, so that the character of our thirty-sixth President will become clear, became evident to me while researching his years at college. The articles and biographies which have dealt with these years have in general portrayed Johnson as a popular, even charismatic, campus figure. The oral histories of his classmates collected by the Lyndon Johnson Library portray him in the same light. In the early stages of my research, I had no reason to think there was anything more to the story. Indeed, when one of the first of his classmates whom I interviewed, Henry Kyle, told me a very different story, I believed that because Kyle had been defeated by Johnson in a number of campus encounters, I was hearing only a prejudiced account by an embittered man, and did not even bother typing up my notes of the interview.

Then, however, I began to interview other classmates.

Finding them was not easy. For years, Johnson's college, Southwest Texas State Teachers College at San Marcos, had not had an actively functioning alumni association and had lost track of many of its former students, who seemed to be scattered, on lonely farms and ranches, all across Texas, and, indeed, the United States. When I found them, I was told the old anecdotes that had become part of the Lyndon Johnson myth. But over and over again, the man or woman I was interviewing would tell me that these anecdotes were not the whole story. When I asked for the rest of it, they wouldn't tell it. A man named Vernon Whiteside could have told me, they said, but, they said, they had heard that Whiteside was dead.

One day, however, I phoned Horace Richards, a Johnson classmate who lived in Corpus Christi, to arrange to drive down from Austin to see him. Richards said that there was indeed a great deal more to the story of Lyndon Johnson at college than had been told, but that he wouldn't tell me unless Vernon Whiteside would too. But Whiteside was dead, I said. "Hell, no," Richards said. "He's not dead. He was here visiting me just last week."

Whiteside, it turned out, had moved from his hometown and was traveling in a mobile home. He had been heading for Florida, where he was planning to buy a condominium, Richards said, but Richards didn't know which city in Florida Whiteside was heading for. All he knew was that the city was north of Miami, and had "beach" in its name.

I traced Mr. Whiteside to a mobile home court in Highland Beach, Florida (he had, in fact, arrived there only a few hours before I telephoned), flew there to see him, and from him heard for the first time many of the character-revealing episodes of Lyndon Johnson's career at San Marcos at which the other classmates had hinted. And when I returned to these classmates, they confirmed Whiteside's account; Richards himself added many details. And they now told additional stories, not at all like the ones they had told before. I managed to locate still other classmates—who had never been interviewed. Mylton (Babe) Kennedy, a key figure in many of these stories, was found in Denver; I interviewed him in a lounge at the airport there. And the portrait of Lyndon Johnson at San Marcos that finally emerged was very different from the one previously sketched.

This experience was repeated again and again during the seven years spent on this book. Of the hundreds of persons interviewed, scores had never been interviewed before, and the information these persons have provided—in some cases even though they were quite worried about providing it—has helped form a portrait of Lyndon Johnson substantially different from all previous portraits.

This is true of virtually every stage and significant episode in his life. Lyndon Johnson was fond of talking about the young woman he courted in college, Carol Davis, now Carol Davis Smith. He told at length how, stung by criticism of his family from her father (who he said was a member of the Ku Klux Klan), he vowed (despite her tears and pleading) not to marry her; how he had gotten married (to Lady Bird) before Carol married; how, during his first campaign for Congress he attacked Carol's father before taking pity on her "agony" as she listened to his speech; how, when he was hospitalized with appendicitis at the climax of his campaign, he awoke to find her standing in the doorway of his hospital room; how she had proven her love for him by telling him she had voted for him. His version of this thwarted romance—a version furnished with vivid details—has been retold repeatedly in biographies of Lyndon Johnson. But none of the authors who repeated it had interviewed Carol Davis. She was there to be interviewed; she still lives in San Marcos. Two of her sisters and several of her friends, and several of Lyndon Johnson's friends who observed the courtship, were there to be interviewed. When they are, a story emerges that, while indeed poignant and revealing, bears little resemblance to the one Johnson told. (Apart from the central story told in this book, the following minor details in Lyndon Johnson's own account do not appear to have been correct: that her father was a member of the Ku Klux Klan; that it was Lyndon who decided not to get married; that she pleaded with him to marry her; that he got married first; that she visited him in the hospital; that she voted for him.)

Similarly, Lyndon Johnson gave a vivid and fascinating picture of his family and home life. Before they died, his sister Rebekah and his brother Sam Houston both told me that this picture was all but unrecognizable to them. But it is not necessary to accept their word. One can ask others who spent time in the Johnson home—not only daily visitors such as his parents' friend Stella Gliddon and Lyndon's cousin Ava, but three more disinterested witnesses: three women who worked or lived in that home as housekeepers. None of these three had ever been interviewed. Lyndon Johnson's supposed relationship with his mother and father has served as the basis for extensive analysis. The true relationship is also fascinating, but it is not the one that has been analyzed.

Because Lyndon Johnson's contemporaries were alive, I could walk the same dusty streets that Lyndon Johnson walked as a boy, with the same people he had walked with. During his boyhood and teenage years in Johnson City, his playmates and schoolmates were his cousin Ava and Truman Fawcett and Milton Barnwell and Bob Edwards and Louise Casparis and Cynthia Crider and John Dollahite and Clayton Stribling. Many of these people—and a dozen more companions of Lyndon Johnson's youth—are still there in Johnson City, and the rest live on nearby farms and ranches, or in Austin. Together, their stories, and the stories of their parents, who observed gangling young Lyndon through the eyes of adults, add up to a fascinating story—but one which has never been told.

In REVEALING Lyndon Johnson's life after boyhood—his years as a congressional assistant, as the Texas State Director of the National Youth Administration and as a Congressman—interviews are only one basis of the portrait. A rich mine of materials exists in the Lyndon Baines Johnson Library and Museum in Austin, Texas. But although the information is there—in the Library's collection of 34,000,000 documents which, encased in thousands of boxes, four stories high behind a glass wall, loom somewhat dauntingly over the researcher as he enters the building—this mine, too, has gone largely untapped. Because of this source, however, it is not necessary to speculate or generalize about how the young Congressman rose to national power and influence; one can trace precisely how he did it. In this tracing, too, the fact that when Johnson died, on January 22, 1973, his age was sixty-four, and that many of those who knew him were still alive, is significant. Upon first coming to Washington, he became part of a quite remarkable group of young men: Benjamin V. Cohen, Thomas G. Corcoran, Abe Fortas, James H. Rowe, Eliot Janeway and the lesser-known Arthur (Tex) Goldschmidt. These men—once the bright young New Dealers—gave me their time with varying degrees of generosity, but some of them were very generous indeed, and when the meaning of documents in the Library was not clear, they often made it clear. For these men watched Lyndon Johnson rise to power. Perceptive as they are, they understood what they were watching, and they can explain it.

GEORGE RUFUS BROWN, of Brown & Root, Inc., had never previously talked at length to interviewers or historians, but finally agreed to talk with me, out of deep affection for his remarkable brother Herman—an affection which had led George to attempt in several ways, among them the building of the Herman Brown Memorial Library in Burnet, to perpetuate Herman's name. After two years of refusing to respond to my letters and telephone calls, he decided that although Herman's name might be engraved on buildings, in a few years no one would know who Herman Brown *was* unless he was portrayed in a book, and that he could not *be* portrayed because no one knew enough about him. I told him that I could not say that my portrait of his brother would be favorable, but that if he discussed Herman with me in depth, the portrait would at least be full. He told me stories which he said had never been told outside the Brown & Root circle, and told me still more at a subsequent interview, which also lasted an entire day. Taken together, these stories add very substantially indeed to knowledge of the relationship between Lyndon Johnson and Brown & Root, a relationship that has been until now largely a matter not only of speculation and gossip, but of incorrect speculation and gossip. Mr. Brown's account has, moreover, been verified in every substantial detail by others; to cite one example, his account of the extraordinary story behind the construction of the Marshall Ford Dam, and of Lyndon Johnson's role in it, was corroborated by Abe Fortas and Tommy Corcoran, who handled the Washington end of the matter, and by the Bureau of Reclamation official involved on the site, Howard P. Bunger.

THE PERSONS who knew Lyndon Johnson most intimately during his years as a congressional secretary were the assistants who worked in the same room with him: Estelle Harbin, Luther E. (L. E.) Jones and Gene Latimer. (Jones and Latimer also lived in the same room with Johnson.) They had been interviewed before, but never in depth. For a while, Carroll Keach worked with him in the same office; later, Keach became his chauffeur. Still later, in 1939, Walter Jenkins became Johnson's assistant. These persons gave generously of their time, although some of these interviews—particularly those with Latimer and Jenkins—were difficult for both sides, because of the emotional wounds which were reopened. I should mention here that John Connally, who became a secretary to Mr. Johnson in 1939, refused during the entire period of research on this book to respond to requests for an interview.

LADY BIRD JOHNSON prepared carefully for our nine interviews, reading her diaries for the years involved, so that she could provide a month by month, detailed description of the Johnsons' life. Some of these were lengthy interviews, particularly one in the living room of the Johnson Ranch that as I recall it lasted most of a day. These interviews were immensely valuable in providing a picture of Lyndon Jonhson's personal and social life, and of his associates, for Mrs. Johnson is an extremely acute observer, and has the gift of making her observations, no matter how quietly understated, quite clear. The interviews were less valuable in regard to her husband's political life. In later years, Mrs. Johnson would become familiar with her husband's work, indeed perhaps his most trusted confidante. This was not the case during the period covered by this first volume. (The change began in 1942—shortly after this volume's conclusion —when Mrs. Johnson, with her husband away during the war, took over his congressional office, and proved, to her surprise as well as his, that she could run it with competence and skill.) During this earlier period, Mrs. Johnson was not familiar with much of the political maneuvering in which her husband was engaged, as she herself points out. Once, when I asked if she had been present at various political strategy sessions, she replied, "Well, I didn't always want to be a part of everything, because I was never. . . . I elected to be out a lot. I wasn't confident in that field. I didn't want to be a party to absolutely everything."

Although from the first I made it clear to Mrs. Johnson that I would conduct my own independent research into anything I was told by anyone, for some time she very helpfully advised members of the semi-official "Johnson Circle" in Texas that she would have no objection if they talked with me. At a certain point, however—sometime after the interviews with Mrs. Johnson had been completed—that cooperation abruptly and totally ceased.

ONE FURTHER NOTE of detailed explanation on a particular source may be of interest to some readers. When, in the Notes that follow, I refer to the "Werner File," I refer to a collection of papers written by Elmer C. Werner, a Special Agent of the Internal Revenue Service, who in the years 1942, 1943 and 1944 was in effective day-by-day charge of the IRS investigation of Brown & Root, Inc.'s political financing, largely of Lyndon Johnson's 1941 campaign for the United States Senate.

These papers fall generally into three categories. The first is summaries of the investigation: a 14-page "Chronological History of the Investigation of the Case

SI-19267-F and Related Companies" and a five-page report, "In re: Brown and Root, Inc. et al," which Mr. Werner wrote for his superiors and which summarizes the conclusions reached by the team of IRS agents on the case. The second is his office desk calendar, for the year 1943, with brief notes jotted down by day to show his activities. The third is 94 pages of his handwritten, detailed, sometimes verbatim transcriptions of the sworn testimony given by Brown & Root officials and others before IRS agents.

The Werner File was given to the author by Mr. Werner's daughter, Julia Gary.

THE PAPERS dealing with the period covered in this volume are found in a number of collections at the Lyndon Baines Johnson Library and Museum in Austin, Texas. They are:

House of Representatives Papers: The memoranda (both intra-office and with others), casework, speech drafts and texts, and other papers kept in the files of Johnson's congressional office from 1937 through 1948, when he was Congressman from Texas. These papers also include records pertaining to his other activities during this period, records which were originally compiled by his staff in other offices, such as the records compiled in an office he temporarily rented in Washington's Munsey Office Building when he was raising money for scores of Democratic Congressmen in 1940, and records kept in his Austin campaign headquarters during his first campaign for Congress in 1937 and his first campaign for Senate in 1941. These papers, of which there are 140 linear feet, contained in 349 boxes, are abbreviated in the notes as "JHP."

Lyndon Baines Johnson Archives: These files were created about 1958, and consist of material taken both from the House of Representatives Papers and from Johnson's Senate Papers. It consists of material considered historically valuable or of correspondence with persons with whom he was closely associated, such as Sam Rayburn, Abe Fortas, James Rowe, George and Herman Brown, Edward Clark and Alvin Wirtz; or of correspondence with national figures of that era. These files, of which there are 34 linear feet in 61 boxes, are abbreviated as "LBJA" and are divided into four main categories:

1. Selected Names (LBJA SN): Correspondence with close associates.
2. Famous Names (LBJA FN): Correspondence with national figures.
3. Congressional File (LBJA CF): Correspondence with fellow Congressmen and Senators.
4. Subject File (LBJA SF): This contains a Biographic Information File, with material relating to Johnson's year as a schoolteacher in Cotulla and Houston; to his work as a secretary to Congressman Richard M. Kleberg; to his activities with the Little Congress; and to his naval service during World War II.

Pre-Presidential Confidential File: This contains material taken from other files because it dealt with potentially sensitive areas. It is abbreviated as PPCF.

Family Correspondence (LBJ FC): Correspondence between the President and his mother and brother, Sam Houston Johnson.

Personal Papers of Rebekah Baines Johnson (RBJ PP): This is material found in her garage after she died. It includes correspondence with her children (including Lyndon) and other members of her family, and material collected by her during her research into the genealogy of the Johnson family. It includes 27 boxes, as well as scrapbooks.

Papers of the Lower Colorado River Authority (LCRAP): 60 linear feet, contained in approximately 165 boxes (the material is currently being re-filed), this material, invaluable in tracing the early political careers of both Lyndon Johnson and Alvin Wirtz, consists of the office files of the LCRA from 1935 through 1975, as well as material dealing with the authority's two predecessor private companies, Emory Peck and Rockwood Development Company and Central Texas Hydro-Electric Company, which throws great light on Wirtz, and was associated with both of them.

Personal Papers of Alvin Wirtz (AW PP): 25 boxes.

White House Central File (WHCF): The only files in this category used to a substantial extent in this volume were the Subject Files labeled "President (Personal)" (WHCF PP). They contain material about the President or his family, mainly articles written after he became President about episodes in his early life.

White House Famous Names File (WHFN): This includes correspondence with former Presidents and their families, including Johnson correspondence when he was a Congressman with Franklin D. Roosevelt.

Record Group 48, Secretary of the Interior, Central Classified Files (RG 48): Microfilm from the National Archives containing documents relating to Lyndon Johnson found in the files of the Department of the Interior.

Documents Concerning Lyndon B. Johnson from the Papers of Franklin D. Roosevelt, Eleanor Roosevelt, John M. Carmody, Harry L. Hopkins, and Aubrey Williams (FDR-LBJ MF): This microfilm reel was compiled at the Franklin D. Roosevelt Library at Hyde Park and consists of correspondence to and from Johnson found in various PPF and OF files at the Roosevelt Library. Whenever possible, the author has included the file number, by which the original documents can be located at the Roosevelt Library.

Johnson House Scrapbooks (JHS): 21 scrapbooks of newspaper clippings compiled by members of his staff between 1935 and 1941.

Each document from the LBJ Library is cited in the Notes by collection in the Library, by box number within that collection, and by the folder title within that box. If no folder title is included in the citation, the folder is either the name of the correspondent in the letter or, in the case of files kept alphabetically, the appropriate letter (a letter from Corcoran, for example, in the folder labeled C).

Selected Bibliography

A bibliography for this book would be another book in itself, and an exercise in pedantry to boot. The following list includes only those books specifically cited in the Notes, and I include it for one purpose alone: so that I can use abbreviations in the Notes.

ADAMS, FRANK C.: *Texas Democracy: A Centennial History of Politics and Personalities of the Democratic Party, 1836–1936.* Springfield, Ill.: Democratic Historic Association; 1937.

ALBERTSON, DEAN: *Roosevelt's Farmer: Claude R. Wickard in the New Deal.* New York: Columbia University Press; 1961.

ALEXANDER, HERBERT E.: *Money in Politics.* Washington, D.C.: Public Affairs Press; 1972.

ALLEN, FREDERICK LEWIS: *Only Yesterday.* New York: Harper; 1931.

ALLEN, ROBERT SHARON, ED.: *Our Sovereign State.* New York: Vanguard Press; 1949.

ALSOP, JOSEPH, AND TURNER CATLEDGE: *The 168 Days.* Garden City, N.Y.: Doubleday; 1937.

ANDERSON, JACK, AND JAMES BOYD: *Confessions of a Muckraker.* New York: Random House; 1979.

ANGEVINE, ERMA, ED.: *People—Their Power: The Rural Electric Fact Book.* Washington, D.C.: National Rural Electric Cooperative Association; 1980.

BAKER, BOBBY, WITH LARRY L. KING: *Wheeling and Dealing.* New York: Norton; 1978.

BAKER, GLADYS L., WAYNE D. RASMUSSEN, VIVIAN WISER, JANE M. PORTER: *Century of Service: The First Hundred Years of the U.S. Department of Agriculture.* Washington, D.C.: U.S. Department of Agriculture, GPO; 1967.

BAKER, LEONARD: *The Johnson Eclipse: A President's Vice Presidency.* New York: Macmillan; 1966.

BANKS, JIMMY: *Money, Marbles, and Chalk: The Wondrous World of Texas Politics.* Austin: Texas Pub. Co.; 1972.

BEARSS, EDWIN C.: *Historic Resource Study . . . Lyndon B. Johnson National Historic Site, Blanco and Gillespie Counties, Texas.* Denver: U.S. Dept. of Interior, National Park Service; 1971.

BELL, JACK: *The Johnson Treatment: How Lyndon B. Johnson Took Over the Presidency and Made It His Own.* New York: Harper; 1965.

BELLUSH, BERNARD: *Franklin D. Roosevelt as Governor of New York.* New York: Columbia University Press; 1955.

BENDINER, ROBERT: *White House Fever.* New York: Harcourt, Brace; 1960.

BILLINGTON, RAY ALLEN: *Westward Expansion: A History of the American Frontier.* New York: Macmillan; 1949.

BLAIR, JOHN M.: *The Control of Oil.* New York: Pantheon; 1976.

BROWN, D. CLAYTON: *Electricity for Rural America: The Fight for REA.* Westport, Conn.: Greenwood; 1980.

BROWN, GEORGE ROTHWELL: *The Speaker of the House: The Romantic Story of John N. Garner.* New York: Brewer, Warren, and Putnam; 1932.

BURNER, DAVID: *Herbert Hoover: The Public Life.* New York: Knopf; 1978.

BURNS, JAMES MACGREGOR: *Roosevelt:*

The Lion and the Fox. New York: Harcourt Brace, and World; 1962.

CHILDS, MARQUIS: *The Farmer Takes a Hand: The Electric Power Revolution in Rural America.* Garden City, N.Y.: Doubleday; 1952.

COCKE, WILLIAM A.: *The Bailey Controversy in Texas.* San Antonio: The Cocke Co.; 1908.

CORMIER, FRANK: *LBJ, The Way He Was.* Garden City, N.Y.: Doubleday; 1977.

CRAWFORD, ANN FEARS, AND JACK KEEVER: *John P. Connally: Portrait in Power.* Austin: Jenkins; 1973.

CROLY, HERBERT D.: *Marcus Alonzo Hanna.* New York: Macmillan; 1912.

DANIELS, JONATHAN: *The End of Innocence.* Philadelphia: Lippincott; 1954.
——— *Frontier on the Potomac.* New York: Macmillan; 1946.
——— *White House Witness, 1942–1945.* Garden City, N.Y.: Doubleday; 1975.

DAVIE, MICHAEL: *LBJ: A Foreign Observer's Viewpoint.* New York: Duell, Sloan, and Pearce; 1966.

DAVIS, KINGSLEY: *Youth in the Depression.* Chicago: University of Chicago Press; 1935.

DONOVAN, ROBERT J.: *Conflict and Crisis: The Presidency of Harry S. Truman.* New York: Norton; 1977.

DOROUGH, C. DWIGHT: *Mr. Sam.* New York: Random House; 1962.

DOUGLAS, WILLIAM O.: *The Court Years, 1939–1975.* New York: Random House; 1980.
——— *Go East, Young Man.* New York: Random House; 1971.

DOYLE, JACK: *Lines Across the Land: Rural Electric Cooperatives, the Changing Politics of Energy in Rural America.* Washington, D.C.: Environmental Policy Institute; 1979.

DUGGER, RONNIE: *The Politician: The Life and Times of Lyndon Johnson.* New York: Norton; 1982.

DULANEY, H. B., EDWARD HAKE PHILLIPS, MAC PHELAN REESE: *Speak, Mr. Speaker.* Bonham, Tex.: Sam Rayburn Foundation; 1978.

ELLIS, CLYDE T.: *A Giant Step.* New York: Random House; 1966.

ENGLER, ROBERT: *The Brotherhood of Oil.* Chicago: University of Chicago Press; 1977.
——— *Politics of Oil.* New York: Macmillan; 1961.

EVANS, ROWLAND, AND ROBERT NOVAK: *Lyndon B. Johnson: The Exercise of Power.* New York: New American Library; 1966.

FARLEY, JAMES A.: *Behind the Ballots.* New York: Harcourt, Brace; 1938.
——— *Jim Farley's Story: The Roosevelt Years.* New York: Whittlesey House; 1948.

FEHRENBACH, T. R.: *Lone Star: A History of Texas and the Texans.* New York: Macmillan; 1968.

FISHER, O. C.: *Cactus Jack.* Waco: The Texian Press; 1978.

FLEMMONS, JERRY: *Amon: The Life of Amon Carter, Sr., of Texas.* Austin: Jenkins; 1978.

FLYNN, EDWARD J.: *You're the Boss.* New York: Viking; 1947.

FRANTZ, JOE B.: *37 Years of Public Service: The Honorable Lyndon B. Johnson.* Austin: Shoal Creek Publishers; 1974.

FRANTZ, JOE B., AND J. ROY WHITE: *The Driskill Hotel.* Austin: Encino Press; 1973.
——— *Limestone and Log: A Hill Country Sketchbook.* Austin: Encino Press; 1968.
——— *Texas: A Bicentennial History.* New York: Norton; 1976.

FREIDEL, FRANK: *Franklin D. Roosevelt. Launching the New Deal.* Boston: Little, Brown; 1973.
———, ED.: *The New Deal and the American People.* Englewood Cliffs, N.J.: Prentice-Hall; 1964.

GANTT, FRED, JR.: *The Chief Executive in Texas.* Austin: University of Texas Press; 1964.

GARWOOD, JOHN, AND W. C. TUTHILL: *The Rural Electrification Administration: An Evaluation.* Washington, D.C.: American Enterprise Institute for Public Policy Research; 1963.

GEYELIN, PHILIP L.: *Lyndon B. Johnson and the World.* New York: Praeger; 1966.

GILLESPIE COUNTY HISTORICAL SOCIETY: *Pioneers in God's Hills.* Austin: Von Boeckmann-Jones; 1960.

GOLDMAN, ERIC: *The Tragedy of Lyndon Johnson.* New York: Knopf; 1969.

GOODWYN, FRANK: *Lone-Star Land: Twentieth-Century Texas in Perspective.* New York: Knopf; 1955.

GOODWYN, LAWRENCE: *Democratic Promise: The Populist Movement in Amer-*

ica. New York: Oxford University Press; 1976.

GOULD, LEWIS L.: *Progressives and Pro-hibitionists: Texas Democrats in the Wilson Era.* Austin: University of Texas Press; 1973.

GRAVES, JOHN: *Hard Scrabble.* New York: Knopf; 1974.

—— *Texas Heartland: A Hill Country Year.* College Station: Texas A&M University Press; 1975.

GREEN, GEORGE N.: *The Establishment in Texas Politics.* Westport, Conn.: Greenwood Press; 1979.

GUNTHER, JOHN: *Inside U.S.A.* New York: Harper; 1947.

—— *Roosevelt in Retrospect.* New York: Harper; 1950.

HALBERSTAM, DAVID: *The Best and the Brightest.* New York: Random House; 1972.

—— *The Powers That Be.* New York: Knopf; 1979.

HARWELL, THOMAS FLETCHER: *Eighty Years Under the Stars and Bars.* Kyle, Tex.: United Confederate Veterans; 1947.

HARWOOD, RICHARD, AND HAYNES JOHN-SON: *Lyndon.* New York: Praeger; 1973.

HEARD, ALEXANDER: *The Costs of De-mocracy.* Chapel Hill: University of North Carolina Press; 1960.

HENDERSON, RICHARD B.: *Maury Mav-erick: A Political Biography.* Austin: University of Texas Press; 1970.

HUMPHREY, WILLIAM: *Farther Off From Heaven.* New York: Knopf; 1977.

HUNTER, JOHN MARVIN, AND GEORGE W. SAUNDERS: *The Trail Drivers of Texas.* Dallas: The Southwest Press; 1929.

ICKES, HAROLD L.: *The Secret Diary of Harold L. Ickes.* 3 vols. New York: Simon and Schuster; 1953–54.

JAMES, MARQUIS: *Mr. Garner of Texas.* Indianapolis, New York: Bobbs-Merrill; 1939.

—— *The Raven: A Biography of Sam Houston.* New York: Blue Ribbon Books; 1929.

JOHNSON, CLAUDIA ALTA (TAYLOR): *A White House Diary.* New York: Holt, Rinehart and Winston; 1970.

JOHNSON, LYNDON BAINES: *A Time for Action: A Selection from the Speeches and Writings of Lyndon B. Johnson, 1953–64.* New York: Atheneum; 1964.

—— *My Hope for America.* New York: Random House; 1964.

—— *Pattern for Peace in Southeast Asia.* Washington, D.C.: Department of State, GPO; 1965.

—— *The Presidential Press Confer-ences.* New York: Coleman Enter-prises; 1978.

—— *This America.* Photographed by Ken Heyman. New York: Random House; 1966.

—— *To Heal and to Build: The Pro-grams of Lyndon B. Johnson.* Edited by James MacGregor Burns. New York: McGraw-Hill; 1968.

—— *The Vantage Point: Perspectives of the President, 1963–1969.* New York: Holt, Rinehart and Winston; 1971.

JOHNSON, REBEKAH (BAINES): *A Family Album.* Edited by John S. Moursund. New York: McGraw-Hill; 1965.

JOHNSON, SAM HOUSTON: *My Brother Lyndon.* Edited by Enrique Hank Lo-pez. New York: Cowles; 1970.

JONES, JESSE H.: *Fifty Billion Dollars: My Thirteen Years with the RFC, 1932–45.* New York: Macmillan; 1951.

JORDAN, TERRY G.: *German Seed in Texas Soil.* Austin: University of Texas Press; 1966.

JOSEPHSON, MATTHEW: *The Politicos, 1865–1896.* New York: Harcourt, Brace; 1938.

KEARNS, DORIS: *Lyndon Johnson and the American Dream.* New York: Harper; 1976.

KENDALL, GEORGE W.: *Narrative of the Texan Santa Fe Expedition.* New York: Harper; 1856.

KEY, V. O.: *Southern Politics in State and Nation.* New York: Knopf; 1949.

KOENIG, LOUIS W.: *The Invisible Presi-dency.* New York: Rinehart; 1960.

LASH, JOSEPH P.: *Eleanor and Franklin.* New York: Norton; 1971.

LEINSDORF, ERICH: *Cadenza: A Musical Career.* Boston: Houghton Mifflin; 1976.

LEUCHTENBURG, WILLIAM: *Franklin D. Roosevelt and the New Deal, 1932–1940.* New York: Harper; 1963.

LINDLEY, BETTY GRIMES: *A New Deal for Youth.* New York: Viking; 1938.

LINK, ARTHUR S.: *Wilson: The New Freedom.* Princeton: Princeton Uni-versity Press; 1956.

—— *Woodrow Wilson and the Pro-gressive Era.* New York: Harper; 1954.

LONG, WALTER E.: *Flood to Faucet.* Austin; 1956.

LORD, RUSSELL: *The Wallaces of Iowa.* Boston: Houghton Mifflin; 1947.

LUDEMAN, ANNETTE: *A History of La-Salle County, South Texas Brush Country, 1856–1975.* Quanah, Tex.: North Texas Press.

LUNDBERG, FERDINAND: *America's Sixty Families.* New York: Citadel; 1937.

LYNCH, DUDLEY: *The Duke of Duval.* Waco: The Texian Press; 1976.

MACDONALD, BETTY: *The Egg and I.* Philadelphia, New York: Lippincott; 1945.

MAGUIRE, JACK. R.: *A President's Country: A Guide to the Hill Country of Texas.* Austin: Alcade Press; 1964.

MANCHESTER, WILLIAM: *The Death of a President.* New York: Harper; 1967.

—— *The Glory and the Dream.* Boston: Little, Brown; 1974.

MANN, ARTHUR: *La Guardia: A Fighter Against His Times.* Philadelphia: Lippincott; 1959.

MARSHALL, JASPER NEWTON: *Prophet of the Pedernales.* Privately published.

MARTIN, ROSCOE C.: *The People's Party in Texas.* Austin: University of Texas Press; 1933.

MCKAY, SETH: *Texas and the Fair Deal, 1945–1952.* San Antonio: Naylor; 1954.

—— *Texas Politics, 1906–1944.* Lubbock: Texas Tech. Press; 1952.

—— *W. Lee O'Daniel and Texas Politics, 1938–1942.* Lubbock: Texas Technological College Research; 1944.

MILLER, MERLE: *Lyndon: An Oral Biography.* New York: Putnam's; 1980.

MILLER, WILLIAM: *Fishbait: The Memoirs of the Congressional Doorkeeper.* Englewood Cliffs, N.J.: Prentice-Hall; 1977.

MOLEY, RAYMOND: *After Seven Years.* New York: Harper; 1939.

—— *27 Masters of Politics.* New York: Funk and Wagnalls; 1949.

MONTGOMERY, RUTH: *Mrs. L.B.J.* New York: Holt, Rinehart and Winston; 1964.

MOONEY, BOOTH: *LBJ: An Irreverent Chronicle.* New York: Crowell; 1976.

—— *The Lyndon Johnson Story.* New York: Farrar, Straus; 1964.

—— *Roosevelt and Rayburn.* Philadelphia: Lippincott; 1971.

MORISON, SAMUEL ELIOT, AND HENRY STEELE COMMAGER: *The Growth of the American Republic,* Vol. 2. New York: Oxford University Press; 1958.

MORISON, SAMUEL ELIOT, HENRY STEELE COMMAGER, AND WILLIAM E. LEUCHTENBURG: *The Growth of the American Republic.* New York, London: Oxford University Press; 1969.

MOURSUND, JOHN S.: *Blanco County Families for One Hundred Years.* Austin: Nortex Press; 1979.

MOWRY, GEORGE E., ED.: *The Twenties: Fords, Flappers, and Farmers.* Englewood Cliffs, N.J.: Prentice-Hall; 1963.

NEWLON, CLARKE: *L.B.J.: The Man From Johnson City.* New York: Dodd, Mead; 1966.

NICHOLS, TOM W.: *Rugged Summit.* San Marcos: Southwest Texas State University Press; 1970.

NORRIS, GEORGE W.: *Fighting Liberal.* New York: Collier Books; 1961.

NOURSE, EDWIN: *Three Years of the AAA.* Washington, D.C.: Brookings Institute; 1938.

OLMSTED, FREDERICK LAW: *A Journey Through Texas, or, A Saddletrip on the Southwestern Frontier.* New York: Edwards & Co.; 1857.

OVERACKER, LOUISE: *Money in Elections.* New York: Macmillan; 1932.

PARRISH, MICHAEL: *Securities Regulation and the New Deal.* New Haven: Yale University Press; 1970.

PELZER, LOUIS: *The Cattleman's Frontier.* Glendale, Calif.: Clark; 1936.

PERRY, GEORGE SESSIONS: *Texas: A World in Itself.* New York: McGraw-Hill; 1942.

PHILLIPS, CABELL: *From the Crash to the Blitz, 1929–1939.* New York: Macmillan; 1969.

—— *The 1940s: Decade of Triumph and Trouble.* New York: Macmillan; 1975.

PICKRELL, ANNIE: *Pioneer Women of Texas,* 2nd ed. Austin: Jenkins/Pemberton Press; 1970.

PIERCE, NEAL R.: *The Great Plains States of America.* New York: Norton; 1973.

—— *The Megastates of America.* New York: Norton; 1973.

POOL, WILLIAM C., EMMIE CRADDOCK, DAVID E. CONRAD: *Lyndon Baines Johnson: The Formative Years.* San Marcos: Southwest Texas State College Press; 1965.

PORTERFIELD, BILL: *LBJ Country.* Garden City, N.Y.: Doubleday; 1965.

PRESLEY, JAMES: *A Saga of Wealth: The Rise of the Texas Oilmen.* New York: Putnam's; 1978.

PROVENCE, HARRY: *Lyndon B. Johnson.* New York: Fleet; 1964.

RAMSAY, MARION L.: *Pyramids of Power: The Story of Roosevelt, Insull and the Utility Wars.* Indianapolis, New York: Bobbs-Merrill; 1937.

RASMUSSEN, WAYNE: *The Department of Agriculture.* New York: Praeger; 1972.

REDDING, JOHN M.: *Inside the Democratic Party.* Indianapolis, New York: Bobbs-Merrill; 1958.

ROSEN, ELLIOTT A.: *Hoover, Roosevelt and the Brains Trust.* New York: Columbia University Press; 1977.

ROSENMAN, SAMUEL I., COMP.: *The Public Papers and Addresses of Franklin D. Roosevelt.* 13 vols. New York: Russell & Russell; 1969.

SAMPSON, ANTHONY: *The Seven Sisters: The Great Oil Companies and the World They Made.* New York: Viking; 1975.

SCHANDLER, HERBERT Y.: *The Unmaking of a President: Lyndon Johnson and Vietnam.* Princeton: Princeton University Press; 1977.

SCHAWE, WILLIEDELL, ED.: *Wimberley's Legacy.* San Antonio: Naylor; 1963.

SCHLESINGER, JR., ARTHUR M.: *The Age of Roosevelt: The Crisis of the Old Order; The Coming of the New Deal; The Politics of Upheaval.* 3 vols. Boston: Houghton Mifflin; 1957–1960.

—— *The Imperial Presidency.* Boston: Houghton Mifflin; 1973.

—— *Robert Kennedy and His Times.* Boston: Houghton Mifflin; 1978.

SHERRILL, ROBERT: *The Accidental President.* New York: Grossman; 1967.

SHERWOOD, ROBERT E.: *Roosevelt and Hopkins: An Intimate History.* New York: Harper; 1948.

SHOGAN, ROBERT: *A Question of Judgment: The Fortas Case.* Indianapolis, New York: Bobbs-Merrill; 1972.

SIDEY, HUGH: *A Very Personal Presidency: Lyndon Johnson in the White House.* New York: Atheneum; 1968.

SIMON, JAMES F.: *Independent Journey: The Life of William O. Douglas.* New York: Harper; 1980.

SINGER, KURT D., AND JANE SHERROD: *Lyndon Baines Johnson, Man of Reason.* Minneapolis: Denison; 1964.

SMITH, GENE: *The Shattered Dream: Herbert Hoover and the Great Depression.* New York: Morrow; 1970.

SMITH, MARIE D.: *The President's Lady: An Intimate Biography of Mrs. Lyndon B. Johnson.* New York: Random House; 1964.

SOLBERG, CARL: *Oil Power.* New York: Mason/Charter; 1976.

SPEER, JOHN W.: *A History of Blanco County.* Austin: Pemberton Press; 1965.

STEINBERG, ALFRED: *Sam Johnson's Boy.* New York: Macmillan; 1968.

—— *Sam Rayburn.* New York: Hawthorn; 1975.

TAYLOR, C.: *Rural Life in the United States.* New York: Knopf; 1952.

TERRY, RUTH GARMS: *Retired Teacher on Candid Typewriter.* New York: Exposition Press; 1967.

Texas Almanacs, 1939–45. Dallas: Dallas Morning News.

THOMAS, WILLIAM L., ED.: *Man's Role in Changing the Face of the Earth.* Chicago: University of Chicago Press; 1956.

TIMMONS, BASCOM N.: *Garner of Texas.* New York: Harper; 1948.

TUGWELL, REXFORD G.: *The Democratic Roosevelt.* Garden City, N.Y.: Doubleday; 1957.

TULLY, GRACE: *F.D.R., My Boss.* New York: Scribner's; 1949.

U.S. DEPARTMENT OF AGRICULTURE: *Rural Lines: USA: The Story of the Rural Electrification Administration's First Twenty-Five Years, 1935–1960.* Washington, D.C.: Rural Electrification Administration.

—— *Yearbook of Agriculture, 1921.* Washington, D.C.: G.P.O.

—— *Yearbook of Agriculture, 1925.* Washington, D.C.: G.P.O.

—— *Yearbook of Agriculture, 1940: Farmers in a Changing World.* Washington, D.C.: G.P.O.

WEBB, WALTER PRESCOTT: *The Great Frontier.* Boston: Houghton Mifflin; 1952.

—— *The Great Plains.* Boston: Ginn & Co.; 1931.

WEBB, WALTER PRESCOTT, AND H. BAILEY CARROLL, EDS.: *The Handbook of Texas.* Austin: Texas State Historical Association; 1952.

WHITE, OWEN P.: *Texas: An Informal Biography.* New York: Putnam's; 1945.

WHITE, THEODORE H.: *America in Search of Itself.* New York: Harper; 1982.

—— *In Search of History.* New York: Harper; 1978.

—— *The Making of the President, 1960.* New York: Atheneum; 1961.

—— *The Making of the President, 1964.* New York: Atheneum; 1965.

—— *The Making of the President, 1968.* New York: Atheneum; 1969.

WHITE, WILLIAM SMITH: *The Professional: Lyndon B. Johnson.* Boston: Houghton Mifflin; 1964.

WICKER, TOM: *JFK and LBJ: The Influence of Personality upon Politics.* New York: Morrow; 1968.

WILSON, RICHARD W., AND BEULAH F. DUHOLM: *A Genealogy: Bunton—Buntin—Bentun—Bunting.* Lake Hills, Iowa: Graphic; 1967.

WOODWARD, BOB, AND SCOTT ARMSTRONG: *The Brethren.* New York: Simon and Schuster; 1980.

WPA: *Texas: A Guide to the Lone Star State.* New York: Hastings House; 1940.

—— *Washington: City and Capital.* Washington, D.C.: G.P.O.; 1937.

Notes

AA   *Austin American*
AA-S   *Austin American-Statesman*
AS   *Austin Statesman*
BCN   *Blanco County News*
BCR   *Blanco County Record*
CCC   *Corpus Christi Caller*
CR   *Congressional Record*
DCCC   Democratic Congressional Campaign Committee
DMN   *Dallas Morning News*
DNC   Democratic National Committee
FS   *Fredericksburg Standard*
HP   *Houston Post*
JCR-C   *Johnson City Record-Courier*
MF   Microfilm
NYT   *The New York Times*
OH   Oral History
RJB   Rebekah Johnson Bobbitt
SAE   *San Antonio Express*
SHJ   Sam Houston Johnson
WF   Werner File
WP   *Washington Post*

LBJL   The Lyndon Baines Johnson Library
JHP   Johnson House Papers
LBJA CF   Congressional File
LBJA FN   Famous Names
LBJA SF   Subject File
LBJA SN   Selected Names
PP   President (Personal)
PPCF   Pre-Presidential Confidential File
WHCF   White House Central File
WHFN   White House Famous Names File

Introduction

NOTES

Greenbrier scene and Marsh's offer: Described to the author by George Brown. Confirmed by Lady Bird Johnson, who was not on the blanket, but who was at the Greenbrier that week and was present at discussions of Marsh's offer, of which she says: "It certainly would have done a lot for our financial security." She recalls that "Charles was saying that a great future lay ahead of him (Lyndon) and he ought not to have to worry about money, and this would free him from such cares." Also confirmed by two other members of the group at the Greenbrier, Sam Houston Johnson and by Marsh's private secretary, Mary Louise Glass Young. Mrs.

Young says Marsh's offer was worth not three-quarters of a million but a million dollars, and that during the discussions that week of Marsh's offer, people would say to Johnson, attempting to persuade him to accept it: "Lyndon, it's a *million* dollars!" **"Burn this":** For example, on Johnson to Luther E. Jones, Dec. 6, 1931, Jones Papers. **"He loses":** Malone, *Jefferson and His Time,* Vol. I, p. xi.

Buying votes in San Antonio: See p. 277. **Money in Johnson's own campaigns:** See Chapters 34, 35. **His use of money in others' campaigns:** See Chapters 32, 35.

"The greatest electoral victory": Theodore H. White, *The Making of the President, 1968,* p. 22.

One of the richest men: *Life,* Aug. 21, 1964, examined the Johnson holdings in detail, and estimated their total value at "approximately $14,000,000"—even without the assets of what *Life* described as "a somewhat mysterious entity called the Brazos–Tenth Street Company," an Austin firm whose activities were tightly interwoven with the Johnsons'. "If the assets of Brazos–Tenth are added—as many knowledgeable Texans think they should be—the total rounds off at more than $15,000,000," *Life* said.

Public estimates by Johnson's own financial advisors were much lower. In the *Life* article, for example, the principal trustee of Johnson's financial interests, A. W. Moursund, placed the figure at "about $4,000,000." In that same year, the White House released its own financial statement, which placed the Johnson capital at $3,484,000. However, the *Wall Street Journal,* in analyzing that statement, said that "by employing a number of technically accepted accounting devices, it projects a grossly understated idea of the current dimensions of the Johnson fortune." (Kohlmeier, "The Johnsons' Balance Sheet," *The Wall Street Journal,* Aug. 20, 1964.) The true market value of the Johnson broadcasting interests alone is estimated at $7 million, the *Journal* reported on Mar. 23, 1964; "one broadcasting executive who is not associated with the corporation but who has long known the Johnsons indicates that net earnings may now exceed $500,000 annually." Private estimates by some of Johnson's financial advisors are much higher than the publicized estimates. In its Aug. 20, 1964, article, the *Journal* noted that "Some intimates back home in Austin calculate it [the Johnsons' net worth] would be in the neighborhood of $20,000,000." Even

this figure is considered low by the attorney who was for twenty years one of Johnson's most trusted advisors in Texas, Edward A. Clark, partner of the powerful Austin law firm named, at the time of Johnson's Presidency, Clark, Thomas, Harris, Denius and Winters, the firm that handled the bulk of the Johnson family financial interests. The author asked Clark the worth of these interests at the time Lyndon Johnson became President. Several days later he replied, after apparently checking his firm's records: "It would have been—you mean his net worth?—about $25,000,000 at the time."

If these higher estimates are correct, during the twenty-one years following the purchase of the Johnson radio station—twenty-one years during which Lyndon Johnson continually held public office—the Johnson fortune increased at a rate of close to a million dollars per year.

Among the articles valuable for a discussion of the Johnson wealth is the *Wall Street Journal* article quoted above and articles in the same newspaper on Mar. 23, 1964, and Aug. 11, 1964; the *Washington Evening Star,* June 9, 1964; *Newsday,* May 27, 28, 29, 1964.

"Springing up side by side": *Wall Street Journal,* "The Johnson Wealth," Mar. 23, 1964. **Largely fiction:** Among the many articles of the time that showed his connection with the broadcasting business that was in his wife's name are the *Washington Evening Star,* June 9, 1964; the *Wall Street Journal,* Mar. 23, 1964 ("President Johnson, as Well as His Wife, Appears to Hold Big Personal Fortune"); *Life,* Aug. 21, 1964; *Newsday,* May 27, 1964. **Worth $7 million:** *Wall Street Journal,* Mar. 23, 1964; confirmed by Clark; *Life* put the worth of the radio-television interests at $8,600,000.

A "blind trust": When Johnson became President, he announced that he was placing all his business affairs in a so-called "blind trust," with which he said he would have no connection so long as he was President. The principal trustee was A. W. Moursund, who did not respond to the author's requests for an interview. But during much of Johnson's Presidency, Moursund's partner in the Johnson City law firm of Moursund and Ferguson was Thomas C. Ferguson, a longtime Johnson ally in Hill Country politics, a former judge and a former chairman of the State Board of Insurance. Ferguson says that shortly after he became President, Johnson had a direct line installed in that law office that connected it to both the White House and the Johnson Ranch on the Pedernales. Ferguson says that there was on the phones in both his and Moursund's offices "a button that wasn't labeled anything, but when you pushed that, you got the White House's board in Washington." Moursund had a similar line in his home, Ferguson says. The author asked Ferguson if Johnson conducted personal business over these telephone lines. "Oh, yeah," Ferguson replied. "He and Moursund were talking every day." During the Presidency? the author asked. "Oh, yeah. I don't guess there was a— You see, Moursund was trustee of all his property: one of these blind trusts—it wasn't very blind. 'Cause every night he told Moursund what to do. . . ." Often, Ferguson said, the two men talked at night. "Johnson," he said, "would go to bed . . . and lay there in bed and talk to Moursund." Most of the talk, Ferguson says, concerned the many businesses—banking, radio and television broadcasting, ranching—in which the President or his family had financial interests. "A lot of [it] was Johnson saying to Moursund, 'Well, I want to do this,' 'I want to do that'—'I want to get this piece of land,' 'I want to stock certain places and certain things.' And of course at that time anything Moursund said stood up throughout the Johnson properties . . . and he would carry out what the President would tell him he wanted done. . . . It was a very unblind trust as far as that trust was concerned." And did Ferguson himself conduct business for Johnson while Johnson was President? "Myself? Oh, yes," Ferguson said, and gave details of a number of business transactions. He said that the President would also be in frequent communication with Jesse C. Kellam, president of the Texas Broadcasting Corporation, key to the Johnson broadcasting empire whose name had been changed from the LBJ Corporation when Johnson became President, and would give Kellam instructions as to the conduct of that business.

The other law firm involved was Clark, Thomas, Harris, Denius and Winters. Edward A. Clark, Johnson's Ambassador to Australia during his Presidency, had, for twenty years before that, been a key Texas ally of the President, and, since the death of Alvin Wirtz in 1951, his right-hand man in confidential state political matters as well as the attorney through whom he handled much of his personal business. Clark's account of Johnson's business

dealings as President will be recounted in detail in the later volumes; on the subject in general, he said that Johnson sometimes spent several hours a day during his Presidency conducting personal business. The author asked him to check this point. At their next interview, Clark said he knew this because, "Heck, we keep a record of a client's calls." He said he would not allow the author to see that record. He said that only some of this time was spent speaking to him, but that he knew Johnson was spending considerable additional time discussing business affairs with Moursund, because they were affairs in which he, Clark, was involved. And, like Ferguson, Clark said that the President also frequently spent time on the phone with Jesse Kellam. Clark said that the use of direct lines ensured that White House telephone logs and operators would have no record of these calls. Kellam would not discuss these matters with the author.

During Johnson's Presidency, the existence of the private telephone lines was reported in an article by a team of *Wall Street Journal* reporters who conducted an unusually thorough investigation of Johnson's financial situation. On August 11, 1964, the *Journal* reported that Moursund "is linked by private telephone circuit to the LBJ Ranch and the White House. He can pick up his phone and almost instantaneously talk with the President." Nonetheless, Moursund told the *Journal* that because of the trust, "the Johnsons don't know what is going on" in their businesses. The *Journal* said that Moursund was "heated" in "declaring that certain business operations are entirely independent of any Johnson interest—and never mind confusing 'clues' to the contrary"; the *Journal* then detailed many such clues.

1. The Bunton Strain

SOURCES

Books, articles, brochures, and documents:
ON THE HILL COUNTRY:

Billington, *Westward Expansion: A History of the American Frontier;* Fehrenbach, *Lone Star* (of the many general histories of Texas, Fehrenbach's most faithfully reflects contemporary accounts of early life in the Hill Country and views of it given by the children and grandchildren of its founders); Frantz and White, *Limestone and Log: A Hill Country Sketchbook;* Gillespie County Historical

Society, *Pioneers in God's Hills;* Goodwyn, *Democratic Promise;* Graves, *Hard Scrabble* and *Texas Heartland: A Hill Country Year;* Jordan, *German Seed in Texas Soil;* Kendall, *Narrative of the Texan Santa Fe Expedition;* Maguire, *A President's Country;* Marshall, *Prophet of the Pedernales;* Moursund, *Blanco County Families for One Hundred Years;* Olmsted, *A Journey Through Texas;* Pelzer, *The Cattleman's Frontier;* Porterfield, *LBJ Country;* Schawe, ed., *Wimberley's Legacy;* Speer, *A History of Blanco County;* Thomas, ed., *Man's Role in Changing the Face of the Earth;* Webb, *The Great Frontier* and *The Great Plains;* Webb and Carroll, *Handbook of Texas;* WPA, *Texas: A Guide to the Lone Star State.*

Bessie Brigham, "The History of Education in Blanco County" (unpublished Master's Thesis), Austin, 1935.

Darton, "Texas: Our Largest State," *National Geographic* magazine, Dec., 1913; Joseph S. Hall, ed., "Horace Hall's Letters from Gillespie County, Texas, 1871–1873," *Southwestern Historical Quarterly,* Jan., 1959; Jones, "What Drought Means," *NYT* magazine, Dec. 23, 1956; Mary Nunley, "The Interesting Life Story of a Pioneer Mother," *Frontier Times,* Aug., 1927, pp. 17–21; Edwin Shrake, "Forbidding Land," *Sports Illustrated,* May 10, 1965.

William Bray, "Forest Resources of Texas," U.S. Department of Agriculture, Bureau of Forestry, Bulletin No. 47, Washington, D.C., 1904; Henry C. Hahn, "The White-Tailed Deer in the Edwards Plateau Region of Texas," Texas Game, Fish and Oyster Commission, Austin, 1945; A. W. Spaight, "The Resources, Soil and Climate of Texas," Report of Commissioner of Insurance, Statistics and History, Galveston, 1882.

Department of Agriculture, Records of the Federal Extension Service, Record Group 33, Annual Reports of Extension Field Representatives, Texas: Blanco County, Burnet County, Hays County, Travis County, 1931–1941, National Archives.

ON THE BUNTONS:

Harwell, *Eighty Years Under the Stars and Bars;* Hunter, ed., *Trail Drivers of Texas;* Pickrell, *Pioneer Women in Texas;* Wilson and Duholm, *A Genealogy: Bunton-Buntin-Bentun-Bunting.*

Edythe Johns Whitley, "Kith and Kin of Our President, Lyndon Baines Johnson," Nashville, 1967.

Lorena Drummond, "Declaration Signer," *SAE,* March 22, 1931; "h.," "Col. John W. Bunton," *Weekly Statesman,* Sept. 4, 1879; Josephine A. Pearson, "A Girl Diplomatist From Tennessee Who Matched Her Wits With a Mexican Ruler," *Nashville Tennessean,* Jan. 8, 1935; T. C. Richardson, "Texas Pioneer Plays Part in State's Progress," *Farm and Ranch,* June 7, 1924; T. U. Taylor, "Heroines of the Hills," *Frontier Times,* May 1973, pp. 14–24.

Arthur W. Jones, "Col. John and Mary Bunton"; "N.," "Another Veteran of the Republic Gone Home"; Lon Smith, "Col. John and Mary Bunton," "An Address in the State Cemetery at Austin," March 2, 1939, from "Printed Material: Newspaper Clippings," all in Box 25, Personal Papers of Rebekah Baines Johnson.

ON THE JOHNSONS:

Bearss, *Historic Resource Study . . . Lyndon B. Johnson National Historic Site, Blanco and Gillespie Counties, Texas;* Rebekah Johnson, *A Family Album;* also, "The Johnsons—Descendants of John Johnson, A Revolutionary Soldier of Georgia: A Genealogical History," 1956; Moursund, *Blanco County Families;* Speer, *A History of Blanco County.*

Rebekah Baines Johnson gave her son a draft of *A Family Album* in 1954 with a covering letter that begins: "Here are some of the stories you desire." This contains material different in some details from that in the published *Family Album* and is referred to as "Rough Draft."

Hall, ed., "Horace Hall's Letters"; Andrew Sparks, "President Johnson's Georgia Ancestors," *Atlanta Journal and Constitution Magazine,* March 1, 1964.

"Pedernales to Potomac," *Austin American-Statesman* Supplement, Jan. 20, 1965; "*The Record-Courier*–Blanco County Centennial Edition," Aug. 1, 1958.

Interviews:

Ava Johnson Cox, Ethel Davis, John Dollahite, Stella Gliddon, Rebekah Johnson Bobbitt (RJB), Sam Houston Johnson (SHJ), Clayton Stribling, Mrs. Lex Ward.

NOTES

He would say: LBJ repeated this to college classmates and deans, and to residents of the Hill Country. Pool, *LBJ* (p. 50), says, "According to a cherished Pedernales Valley story, a proud grandfather rode through the countryside to announce to the neighbors that 'A United States Senator was born today, my grandson.' " In Singer and Sherrod, *Lyndon Baines Johnson,* p. 87, Lyndon Johnson is quoted as saying: "The story goes that the day I was born my granddaddy saddled up his biggest gray mare, Fritz, and rode into town, looking as proud as if he had won the Battle of The Alamo singlehanded. He announced to everyone that a U. S. Senator had just come into the world. It was kind of a joke with my playmates as I was growing up. . . ." Among other books in which one version or another appears is Mooney, *The Lyndon Johnson Story,* pp. 28–29. Of numerous articles in which it appears, one is "Lyndon B. Johnson, Boy of Destiny," by a Fredericksburg resident, Bruce Kowert (*Boston Globe,* Dec. 15, 1963). But none of the Johnson relatives or their Hill Country neighbors interviewed remembers that episode. In the "Rough Draft" of the family album, which she gave to Lyndon in 1954, his mother wrote (p. 2) that "when Lyndon was about three years old", his grandfather wrote in a letter that Lyndon is "as smart as you find them," and that he expected him "to be a United States Senator before he is forty." **"He has the Bunton strain":** RJB; Cox. In the published *A Family Album* (p. 17), his mother says: "Aunt Kate Keele [said] that she could see the Bunton flavor."

The "Bunton eye" and personality: Among others, Cox, SHJ, RJB, Mrs. Lex Ward. **"Shadow of sadness":** "Joseph L. Bunton," in Harwell, p. 88.

Encounter on the plains: Eli Mitchell, quoted in Pearson, "A Girl Diplomatist." **At the first battle:** *Ibid.*; "N.," "Col. John W. Bunton." **"Towering form":** Captain Jesse Billingsley, quoted in Drummond, "Declaration Signer." **Leader of the seven-man patrol:** Jones, "Col. John and Mary Bunton," p. 3, says he was the leader. Smith, "Col. John and Mary Bunton," p. 3, and Johnson, *Album,* p. 126, say he was "one of the seven men who captured Santa Anna." **"To the present generations":** "h.," "Col. John W. Bunton." **Wild journey:** Smith, "Col. John and Mary Bunton," pp. 3, 4; Pearson, "A Girl Diplomatist." **"Commanding presence"; "eloquent tougue":** Drummond, "Declaration Signer"; Smith, p. 3. **Texas Rangers bill:** Pearson, "A Girl Diplomatist"; Jones, "Col. John and Mary Bunton," p. 3. **Re-**

tirement: Johnson, *Genealogy,* p. 16; "h.," "Col. John W. Bunton," p. 2; Jones, "Col. John and Mary Bunton," pp. 4–5; Cox; SHJ. A further indication of the respect in which he was held, Jones wrote, is that he was chosen to be Administrator of the estate of the legendary hero of the Alamo, Jim Bowie.

"Big country"; "far behind"; the frontier; the "bloodiest years": Fehrenbach, pp. 255–56, 276–86, 298, 302, 313–20, 501. **To the very edge:** See Figure 1, Jordan, p. 23; Fehrenbach, pp. 276, 279–80, 286, 313–20.

Rancho Rambouillet description; arriving with Uncle Ranch; wife scaring off Indians: Pearson, "A Girl Diplomatist." **"A large impressive":** Johnson, *Album,* p. 90. **Robert Bunton's biography:** Wilson and Duholm, pp. 18, 19; Cox; SHJ. **A "substantial planter":** Johnson, *Album,* p. 89. **All over six feet:** Wilson and Duholm, p. 32. **Military career:** *Ibid.,* p. 19. **Raising cattle:** Caldwell County Ad Valorem Tax Rolls, 1870–1880, Texas State Archives. **Philosophical Society:** *Handbook of Texas,* Vol. I, p. 246. **"Absolutely truthful"; "an idealist"; "an excellent conversationalist":** Cox, SHJ; Johnson, *Album,* p. 90. **"Charity begins at home":** Johnson, *Album,* p. 73. **"Leaving a handsome estate":** Brown and Speer, *Encyclopedia of the New West,* p. 575. **Desha Bunton:** Richardson, "Texas Pioneer." **"Very proud people":** Mrs. Lex Ward. **Selling off, but holding on:** Pearson, "A Girl Diplomatist." The ranch was finally sold off on Oct. 10, 1981, but only because the Bunton heirs got a very good price for it.

Cardsharps: Wilson & Duholm, p. 32. They say that it was James Bunton, who owned half the herd, who said nothing, but family lore says it was Robert (Cox, SHJ). **Renting out pastures:** Connolly, in Hunter, ed., p. 190. **Retiring comfortably:** RJB, Cox. The West Texas rancher was Lucius Desha Bunton of Marfa.

The Hill Country was beautiful: Schawe, p. 240 and *passim;* Hunter, *passim;* Fehrenbach, p. 606; Frantz and White, p. viii; Graves, *Heartland,* pp. 12–16, 24 ff, and *Hard Scrabble,* p. 11. Horace Hall, who came to the Hill Country in 1871, called it "a beautiful country . . . high hills wooded with rich valleys, with tall grass over a horse's back," Hall, p. 342. Also, descriptions of early days from Cox, Gliddon, and elderly residents who heard them from their parents or grandparents. **"The cabins became"; "A man could**

see": Fehrenbach, pp. 286, 301. **"Grass knee high!":** Hall, p. 351. **"My stirrups!":** Hunter, ed.; an "early pioneer" quoted in *AA-S,* Nov. 19, 1967.

The grass and the soil: Thomas, ed., esp. pp. 49–69, 115–33, 350–66, 721–36; Graves, *Heartland,* p. 23. **Role of fire:** Thomas, ed., pp. 57, 119–26; Hahn, "White-Tailed Deer," p. 7; Bray, "Forest Resources," p. 28; Graves, *Hard Scrabble,* p. 12. **Failure to understand:** Fehrenbach, p. 606; Graves, *passim.*

The rain: Webb, *Plains,* pp. 17–27; Bray, "Forest Resources," pp. 28, 29; Fehrenbach, pp. 606, 607. **A small shrub; mulberry bushes:** Engelmann, quoted in Bray, "Forest Resources," p. 29. **Cactus; "too low":** Bray, "Forest Resources," p. 4. **"Well-defined division":** Vernon Bailey, "Biological Survey of Texas, 1905," quoted in Webb, *Plains,* p. 32. **"Divided":** O. E. Baker, Agricultural Economist in the U.S. Bureau of Agricultural Economics, in *Yearbook of the U.S. Department of Agriculture* (1921), quoted in Webb, *Plains,* p. 19. **"West of 98":** Graves, *Hard Scrabble,* p. 20. **"Sound and fury":** Fehrenbach, p. 273.

"A conspiracy": Fehrenbach, pp. 605, 607. **"Kendall's victims":** Speer, p. 12; Brigham, p. 9. **"The springs are flowing":** Frantz and White, p. viii. **"Erratic moves":** Richard Blood, the Weather Bureau's climatologist for Texas, quoted in Jones, "What Drought Means."

No realization: It is apparent, even if not stated in Darton, "Texas: Our Largest State": "It has large areas of fertile soil and a climate approaching the temperate."

The Johnsons: Bearss, pp. 1–6; Johnson, *Album, passism;* Johnson, "The Johnsons," *passim.* **"Some historians":** Including the President's mother, in her *Album,* p. 107. **Jesse's migration:** Sparks, "President Johnson's Georgia Ancestors"; Bearss, pp. 1, 2; Johnson, *Album,* pp. 87–88. **"They were prosperous":** Elizabeth Thomas, an Alabama genealogist, quoted in Sparks, "President Johnson's Georgia Ancestors." **Will:** "Last Will and Testament of Jesse Johnson," Aug. 30, 1854, in Johnson, *Album,* p. 88. **Didn't realize enough:** Caldwell County Probate Record Book C, pp. 267–68; Bearss, pp. 4–6.

Indians in the Hill Country: Speer, Taylor, Fehrenbach, *passim.* **"The terror":** Elliott Coues, *On the Trail of a Spanish Pioneer,* p. xxv, quoted in Webb, *Plains,* p. 120. **"They lived along the streams":** R. Henderson Shuffler, "Here History Was

Only Yesterday," in Maguire, p. 22. **Federal responsibility:** Texans' fury as it is shown in Fehrenbach, pp. 496–97, 501, 530, 532–33. **36 and 34 families:** Brigham, p. 9.

"One of the outhouses": Speer, p. 6. **"The back of a bush":** Olmsted, p. 134. **"Most popular use":** Fehrenbach, p. 298. **"At random":** Hayes, quoted in Fehrenbach, p. 298. **"This life"; "a difference":** Fehrenbach, pp. 300, 451.

Colt revolver; "Never again": Fehrenbach, pp. 474–76. **149:** Fehrenbach, p. 497. **Hundreds died:** Fehrenbach, p. 501. **Torture and rape:** Fehrenbach, pp. 450–51, 460. **"A thousand deaths":** Nunley, "The Interesting Life Story of a Pioneer Mother," pp. 17–21.

Formation of Blanco County: Commissioner of Insurance, Statistics and History, "Blanco County," pp. 27–29, Galveston, 1882. **Pleasant Hill:** Gillespie County Historical Society, p. 63. **Swarming with steers:** Hahn, "White-Tailed Deer," p. 9. **The rise of the cattle business:** Pelzer, pp. 45 ff; Hunter, ed., pp. 96–99 and *passim;* Fehrenbach.

The Johnson brothers as trail drivers: Hall, Speer, Moursund, *passim.* **"The largest":** A. W. Capt, in Hunter, pp. 362–63. **"On his return":** Fred Bruckner, quoted in Bearss, p. 31.

"Tall": Johnson, *Album,* p. 73. T. U. Taylor described her as "a beautiful young woman with piercing black eyes, coal black hair, queenly in her carriage, a woman of great refinement and strong family pride" (p. 21). **"Loved to talk":** Johnson, "The Johnsons," p. 71. **"Admonished":** Johnson, *Album,* p. 74.

"The months": Fehrenbach, p. 558. The bitterness Hill Country ranchers felt toward the federal government for its Indian policies is shown in a remark by Capt, in Hunter, p. 36, that "As for chasing Indians, that was out of the question, for at that time they were under the watchful care of government agents." **The only wife:** SHJ, Cox. **"Gently reared":** Taylor, p. 21. **Hiding in the cellar:** Porterfield, pp. 39–40. Although most published accounts say, as Porterfield does, that it was an "extra diaper," Eliza herself, when recounting the story, was, relatives say, less squeamish.

Losing the soil; drought: The most poignant description of the ranchers' feelings come from their children and grandchildren, including Stribling, Cox, and Dollahite. **The brush:** Bray, "Forest Resources," pp. 30–32; Graves, *Heartland,* p. 20; *Hard*

Scrabble, p. 198. **500 square miles:** Bray, p. 30.

"That king cash crop": Graves, *Hard Scrabble,* pp. 20, 21. **Cotton and the soil:** Stribling; Graves, *Heartland,* pp. 20, 21. **Into "the next county":** Graves, *Hard Scrabble,* p. 22. **"Eating down":** Hahn, "White-Tailed Deer," pp. 41, 43; Graves, *Heartland,* p. 23. **Decline in cotton production:** Agricultural Census for 1880, Hays County, State of Texas, Texas State Archives.

"The terms": Fehrenbach, p. 560. **Buying up the land:** Bearss, pp. 29, 34; Speer, p. 48; Hall, pp. 345–46. **"Made a market":** Speer, p. 58. **Action Mill, store:** Hall, pp. 344–47.

"Inner convictions"; "the best-adapted": Fehrenbach, p. 561. **Table talk at the Johnsons'; "He encouraged":** Cox, Gliddon. **Subscribing:** Cox; Jessie Hatcher, quoted in Bearss, p. 51. **"Tenant purchase":** SHJ, Cox. **Interest in religion; becoming a Christadelphian:** Jessie Hatcher, quoted in Bearss, p. 52. **The wedding gift:** Johnson, *Album,* p. 74. **"They took receipts":** Speer, p. 57. **Businessmen:** Fehrenbach, p. 557, for example. **"$20 gold pieces":** Speer, pp. 57–58. **"Wishful thinking":** Fehrenbach, p. 561. **"Great optimism":** SHJ. **Borrowing $10,000:** Bearss, p. 45. **"The Johnson boys":** Hall, p. 341.

"The year 1871": Speer, p. 56. **The 1869 flood:** Speer, p. 52. **Second overflow:** Speer, p. 54. **The Johnsons' 1871 drives:** Speer, pp. 57–58; Capt, in Hunter, pp. 364–66; Hall, pp. 339–41. **"Half the cattle":** Webb, p. 231. **"Cut a fellow":** Hall, p. 340.

Tied up with theirs; "a great loss": Speer, pp. 57–58. **Mortgages, lawsuits:** Bearss, pp. 43–47, 186. **Losing mill:** Bearss, p. 45. **Selling to James Johnson:** Bearss, p. 187.

"Mr. Louis": Hall, p. 344. **"It has been"; Comanche raid:** Hall, p. 346. **Last land sold:** Moursund, p. 210. **Value of Tom's property:** Moursund, pp. 210, 214. **Tom drowned:** Moursund, p. 214. **Value of Sam's property:** Moursund, pp. 214, 217. **Moving to the Buda farm:** Hays County Deed Record Book H, pp. 478–79, quoted in Bearss, p. 49.

"About this time": Speer, p. 60. **4 acres for 1 bale; $560:** Agricultural Census for 1880, Hays County, State of Texas, Texas State Archives. **"Floats in grease":** Speer. **Selling the carriage for down payment:** Johnson, *Album,* p. 74.

Photographs: For example, Plates XXIX and XXX, in Bearss. **Sideboard:** Hatcher,

quoted in Bearss, p. 179. **"She would bring out":** Johnson, *Album,* pp. 73–74. Rebekah also wrote that "She had no pride of earthly possessions . . . ," but that does not fit with other descriptions. **"Knocked him":** Hatcher, quoted in Bearss, p. 52. **Sam in old age:** Johnson, *Album,* p. 71; Cox.

2. The People's Party

SOURCES

Books, journals, and archives:

Goodwyn, *Democratic Promise;* Josephson, *The Politicos;* Martin, *The People's Party of Texas;* Morison and Commager, *The Growth of the American Republic,* V. 2; Morison, Commager, and Leuchtenburg, *The Growth of the American Republic.*

Southern Mercury, 1888–1890.

Barker Texas History Center.

Interviews:

Ava Johnson Cox, Stella Gliddon, Sam Houston Johnson, W. D. McFarlane, Emmette Redford.

NOTES

1892 campaign: Record of Election Returns, 1892, County Clerk's Office, Blanco, Comal, Gillespie, and Hays counties.

Feeling rising: Goodwyn, pp. 26–37. **Didn't have railroads:** From time to time a track would be laid a short way into a more accessible part of the hills, but the line would quickly fail. **$1,945:** *Fourth Annual Report,* Department of Agriculture, Insurance, Statistics and History, 1890–1891, Austin, 1892. **The Lampasas beginning:** Goodwyn, pp. 33–37.

"Our lot": J. D. Cady, Oct. 30, 1888. **"I will try":** Landrum, April 25, 1889. **"I see":** Blevin, June 6, 1889. **"I consider":** Minnie Crider, Feb. 13, 1890. **"If we help":** Sarah Crider, March 13, 1890. **"As we live":** June 27, 1889. **"We are in":** Eppes, April 19, 1888. All from *Southern Mercury.*

Cooperatives: Goodwyn, pp. 34–39, 43–49, 125–39. Many elderly Hill Country residents recall their parents' descriptions of this. **Fort Worth and Dallas:** *DMN* quoted in Goodwyn, p. 47. **Membership:** Goodwyn, pp. 46, 73, 86. **"A power":** Smith, quoted in Goodwyn, p. 86. **Fanning out:** Goodwyn, pp. 91 ff. **"Swept over":** Darden, quoted in Goodwyn, p. 93. **Breaking the cooperatives:** Goodwyn, pp. 125–39. **Dollar assessment:** L. Sellavan, *Southern Mercury,* Aug. 22, 1889. **"Loves Dr. Macune":** Quoted in Goodwyn, p. 132. **Caravans:** The Austin *Weekly Statesman* said that observers were "completely astonished by the mammoth proportions" of the turnout (quoted in Goodwyn, pp. 131–32).

"Corruption dominates": Quoted in Morison and Commager, pp. 240–41. **"Army":** Morison et al., p. 184. **Taking command:** Morison and Commager, pp. 239–56; Goodwyn, pp. 319–23. **Except:** Morison et al., p. 173. **"They have the principle":** Quoted in *ibid.,* p. 188. **Bryan's speech:** *Ibid.,* pp. 188–90. **Losing their identity:** *Ibid.,* pp. 190–96; Goodwyn, pp. 470–92. **"A triumph":** Morison et al., p. 195. **"The last protest":** *Ibid.,* p. 196.

Hill Country was worse: "Farm and Farm Property, with selected items for 1900 and 1910," Bulletin: Agriculture Texas, Statistics for the State and its Counties, U.S. Bureau of the Census, 1920. **23 voters:** *BCR,* Dec. 17, 1904.

3. The Johnson Strut

SOURCES

Books, articles, and documents:
Bearss, Historic Resource Study; Cocke, *The Bailey Controversy in Texas;* Fehrenbach, *Lone Star;* Frantz and White, *The Driskill Hotel* and *Limestone and Log;* Gantt, *The Chief Executive in Texas;* Gould, *Progressives and Prohibitionists;* Graves, *Hard Scrabble* and *Texas Heartland;* Humphrey, *Farther Off From Heaven;* Rebekah Johnson, *A Family Album;* Maguire, *A President's Country;* McKay, *Texas Politics;* Moursund, *Blanco County Families;* Mowry, *The Twenties;* Nichols, *Rugged Summit;* Porterfield, *LBJ Country;* Speer, *A History of Blanco County;* Webb, *The Great Plains, The Great Frontier;* Wilson and Duholm, *Genealogy.*

Emma Morrill Shirley, "The Administration of Pat M. Neff, Governor of Texas" (Thesis), Baylor *Bulletin,* Dec., 1938.

Anita Brewer, "Lyndon Johnson's Mother," *AS,* May 13, 1965; William N. Kemp, "Representative Sam Johnson—1877–1937," *Journal of the American Optometric Association,* Feb., 1968; Bela Kornitzer, "President Johnson Talks About His Mother and Father," *Parade,* Jan. 5, 1964; Bruce Kowert, "Lyndon B. Johnson, Boy of Destiny," *Boston Globe,*

Dec. 15, 1963; Glenn Loney, "Miss Kate and the President," "Exec. PP 13–1," WHCF; Gene Barnwell Waugh, "The Boyhood Days of Our President: Recollections of a Friend," *San Antonio Express-News,* April 25, 1965; "The Man Who Is the President," *Life,* Aug. 14, 1964; "Lyndon Johnson's School Days," *Time,* May 21, 1965; "This is LBJ's Country," *USN&WR,* Dec. 23, 1963.

Blanco County Record, 1903–1925; *Blanco News,* 1905–1906; *Johnson City Record-Courier,* 1925–1926, 1937; *Gillespie County News,* 1904–1906; *Fredericksburg Standard,* 1920–1928; *Llano Times,* 1906; *San Antonio Express,* 1906, 1918, 1922, 1923. *Austin Statesman,* 1905; *Fredericksburger Wochenblatt,* 1920; *Fort Worth Star-Telegram,* 1923.

"Pedernales to Potomac," *Austin American-Statesman* Supplement, Jan. 20, 1965; *"The Record Courier*—Blanco County Centennial Edition," Aug. 1, 1958.

"The Hill Country: Lyndon Johnson's Texas," an NBC News television program (referred to as "NBC Broadcast"), broadcast May 9, 1966.

"Transcript of an Exclusive Interview Granted by President Lyndon B. Johnson to Robert E. McKay on May 21, 1965" (referred to as "McKay Interview").

House Journals (HJ), 29th, 30th, 36th, 37th, 38th Legislatures.

O. Y. Fawcett, Fawcett's Drug Store, "1905 Charge Account Book."

Oral Histories:
Sherman Birdwell, Percy Brigham, Ben Crider, Joe Crofts, Marjorie A. Delafield, Stella Gliddon, Jessie Hatcher, Carroll Keach, Wright Patman, Payne Rountree, Josefa Baines Saunders, Louis Walter.

Interviews:
Milton Barnwell, Rebekah Johnson Bobbitt (RJB), J. R. Buckner, Louise Casparis, Elizabeth Clemens, Roy C. Coffee, Ava Johnson Cox, Ohlen Cox, Ann Fears Crawford, Cynthia Crider Crofts, Willard Deason, John Dollahite, Robert L. Edwards, Wilma and Truman Fawcett, Stella Gliddon, William Goode, D. B. Hardeman, Eloise Hardin, Ugo Henke, Welly Hopkins, Sam Houston Johnson (SHJ), Eddie Joseph, Ernest Klappenbach, Fritz Koeniger, Jessie Lambert, Kitty Clyde Ross Leonard, W. D. McFarlane, Cecil Morgan, Alfred P. C. Petsch, Carl L. Phinney, William C. Pool, Cecil Redford, Emmette Redford, Benny Roeder, Gladys Shearer, Gordon Simpson, Arthur Steh-

ling, Addie Stevens, Clayton Stribling, Fay Withers.

NOTES

Father relieved: Johnson, *Album*, p. 22. **Sam's boyhood:** *Ibid.*, pp. 22–23. **Robert Bunton's retirement:** Cox. **Teaching:** Bearss, p. 56; Pool, *LBJ*, p. 23; Gliddon. The family was named Shipp. **"He had":** *Album*, p. 24.

Successful at first: Johnson, *Album*, p. 24; Cox. **"Strutted":** Ohlen Cox; Gliddon. **Carrying the Colt:** Joseph. **"To make it"; his best friends:** *Album*, p. 24.

Winning the nomination; his acceptance speech: *Gillespie County News*, July 9, 1904. **Running ahead:** *BCR*, Nov. 10, 17, 1904.

Sam Johnson as a legislator: McFarlane, Coffee, Phinney, Simpson, Buckner, Joseph; Patman OH, and quoted in Steinberg, *Sam Johnson's Boy*, p. 3. **Alamo Purchase Bill:** *AS*, Dec. 2, 1928; *BCN*, Oct. 28, 1937; *HJ, Regular Session, 29th Legislature*, 1905, pp. 76, 149, 152, 164, 198. The hero was Ferg Kyle of Hays County. **Calf-roping bill:** *Gillespie County News*, Jan. 28, 1905; *HJ*, pp. 76, 187. **Franchise tax:** Pool, p. 26. **Wolf bounty:** *HJ*, pp. 291, 332; *Blanco News*, April 10, 1905.

"A trio": *Gillespie County News*, Feb. 25, 1905. **Alarm clock joke:** Walter OH, p. 3. **"Mighty glad":** Rayburn to Sam Ealy Johnson, Jr., Feb. 22, 1937, "General Correspondence—Johnson, Sam," SRL. **"Has succeeded":** *Gillespie County News*, April 8, 1905.

Llano newspaper: *Llano Times*, March 1, 1906. *SAE* said, in an article reprinted in the *Blanco News* on March 29, 1906, "Representative S. E. Johnson of Fredericksburg [*sic*] is one of the hard-working members of the House. Although he is serving his first term in the Legislature he has made a splendid reputation for himself and should he return for a second term he would be in a position to render still more useful service to his constituents." **"Shell the woods":** *Blanco News*, July 26, 1906. **Democratic primary results:** *Blanco News*, Aug. 2, 9, 1906.

Losing on cotton futures: Sam himself would say that he had lost only because of the San Francisco earthquake, but the only one who believed this story was his wife, who wrote: "The San Francisco earthquake of 1906 wiped out his cotton holdings and saddled him with a debt of several thousand dollars" (Johnson, *Album*, p. 25). Among the relatives familiar with the

real story are Cox, SHJ, RJB. **"My daddy":** Quoted in Steinberg, p. 565.

"The damn Legislature": Quoted in Fehrenbach, p. 435. **Austin atmosphere:** Among many descriptions, Frantz, *The Driskill*, and Steinberg, *Rayburn*, pp. 17, 19, 21. **An enthusiastic participant:** Joseph. **Ordering out the lobbyist:** McFarlane. **Bill regulating lobbyists:** *HJ, Regular Session, 30th Legislature*, pp. 76, 660, 754.

"Dull black": *SAE*, April 14, 1929. **"Were phrased":** Bower, quoted in Steinberg, *Sam Johnson's Boy*, p. 9. **"Influenced" Bryan:** Pool, p. 148. **The Bailey case:** McKay, pp. 21–24; Steinberg, *Rayburn*, pp. 17, 18. **"Drive into the Gulf":** Cocke, p. 633. **Only seven:** Pool, p. 29; Bearss, p. 64; Steinberg, *Rayburn*, p. 18.

"A quiet worker": Chaplain W. J. Joyce, in *HJ, 30th Legislature*, p. 427. **"Straight as a shingle":** McFarlane; Percy Brigham, quoted in Porterfield, p. 32. **The Fawcett account:** Fawcett, "Account Book," p. 277. **Mabel Chapman refusing:** Wilma Fawcett, Cox. **Offered no job:** RJB, SHJ.

4. The Father and Mother

SOURCES

See Sources for Chapter 3.

NOTES

Rebekah's girlhood: Johnson, *Album*, pp. 28–30. **Her house:** *Album*, p. 29; *SAE*, Oct. 3, 1963. **Her father:** *Album*, pp. 75–87, 29; Moursund, pp. 11–12.

Meeting Sam Johnson: *Album*, pp. 17, 25, 30; Steinberg, *Sam Johnson's Boy*, p. 10.

Their home: Photographs, Bearss, Plates XXIX, XXX; Cox, Gliddon. **"Flawless":** RJB. **Women working:** See Chapters 27, 28. **Girls quitting:** Lambert, who was one of them. **Normally:** *Album*, p. 30. **"I never":** Rebekah to Lyndon, May 30, 1937, "Family Correspondence, Johnson, Mrs. Sam E., Dec. 1929–Dec. 1939," Box 1, *Family Correspondence*.

Going to church; contrast with other women; with Tom's wife: Cox; RJB; Hatcher, OH, pp. 13–14. **"Opposite":** Cox. Rebekah says, "In disposition, upbringing and background [we] were vastly dissimilar. However, in principles and motives, the real essentials of life, [we] were one" (*Album*, p. 25). **"Then she'd hear Sam":** Lambert. **"If men":** Fehrenbach, p. 302.

Quotation: *Album*, p. 32. **Tablecloths:**

Saunders, OH, p. 14. **Teacups:** RJB; Mrs. Johnson. **Sam bringing Mrs. Lindig:** Hatcher OH, pp. 3, 4, and quoted in Bearss, p. 69. **"The attending":** *Album,* p. 17. **"Always dignified":** Hatcher, OH, p. 3. **"You will be drowned!":** Hatcher, quoted in Bearss, p. 69.

"The end of the earth": Gliddon. **"Closed":** Barnwell. **Climbing the belfrey:** Cecil Redford. **"Probably":** SHJ, p. 8. **Only college degree:** Gliddon. **Green sneaking into the classroom:** His daughter, Wilma Green Fawcett. **"I don't want":** RJB.

No room in Sanitarium; her illness thereafter: SHJ, RJB. **Rebekah as a homemaker:** Casparis, Cox, Cynthia Crider Crofts, Wilma and Truman Fawcett, Stribling. **Rebekah as a teacher:** Cox; Crider OH. Ava is the one who hummed. **"She teached":** Crider OH, p. 8. **"We didn't":** Cox. **"The highlight":** Waugh, "The Boyhood Days." Ava's experience: Cox. **"I had heard":** J. R. Buckner, quoted in Pool, p. 56. **"Gentle, gentle"; "quite the contrary":** Gliddon OH. **"Highly organized":** *Album,* p. 27. **"Mr. Sam lost":** Casparis. **"That's not":** Cynthia Crider Crofts. **Most of them recall:** Casparis, Lambert, Stevens. See A Note on Sources. **"He used"; "German blood"; "You could see"; "One minute":** Casparis, Stevens, SHJ, Cox. **"In disposition":** *Album,* p. 25. **"The Bainses":** Rebekah Johnson quoted in *HP,* June 20, 1954, Sec. 6, p. 6. **"It was something:"** Casparis.

"Men who": Cox. **$32,375 sale:** *Fredericksburg Standard,* Jan. 22, 1916. **Putting on the plays:** *BCR,* May 11, 1923; Bearss, pp. 103, 104. **Johnson City Record:** Bearss, pp. 75–76; Waugh, "The Boyhood Days"; Gliddon.

Sam's buying ranches, etc.: *Fredericksburg Standard,* Nov. 28, 1919. **Gliddon's experience:** Gliddon. **Haunish episode:** RJB. **At the Fredericksburg bank:** Walter OH; Petsch. **"Broad-minded":** Wilma Fawcett. **Selected as a member of draft board:** Bearss, p. 76. **No opposition:** *Fredericksburg Standard,* Jan. 18, 1918.

"A flying mass": Lucia Johnson Alexander, in *AS,* May 13, 1965. **"I've bought":** SHJ, RJB. **"I argue":** Deason. **Spelling bees, debates, listening to records:** Gliddon, quoted in Bearss, pp. 103–4; Gliddon; Cox; Wilma and Truman Fawcett.

5. The Son

SOURCES

See Sources for Chapter 3.

NOTES

His mother wanted: RJB, SHJ. **The naming:** "Rough Draft," pp. 4, 5. Besides other, minor, differences, the sentence "He thought of his three lawyer friends" has been edited out of the published *Family Album.* **"Dark eyes":** *Album,* p. 22. **"Professed":** "Rough Draft," p. 2. **"The Bunton eye":** Cox.

"Raised his hand": Rebekah Johnson's notes on first page of photographs following p. 32 in the *Album.* **Ordered fifty:** Kowert, "Lyndon B. Johnson." **Telling him stories:** *Album,* p. 19. **The Stonewall picnic:** "Rough Draft," p. 5. **Neighbors remembered:** Gliddon.

"A highly inquisitive": "Rough Draft," p. 5. **Her fright:** Cox, Gliddon; Mrs. Lucia Johnson Alexander to Bruce, April 14, 1971, quoted in Bearss, p. 72. **Relatives:** Cox; Hatcher OH, p. 11; RJB. **The bell:** Mrs. Alexander to Bruce. **Hiding in haystack:** Lambert. **In cornfield:** Mrs. Alexander to Bruce. **"He wanted attention":** Lambert.

Running away to school: Loney, "Miss Kate and the President," p. 2; Saunders OH, p. 13; *Album,* p. 19; Cox; Hatcher OH p. 12. **"My mother used to lead me":** Johnson, in "The Hill Country: Lyndon Johnson's Texas," quoted in *NYT,* May 8, 1966. **Ava picking him up:** Cox. **Unless she held him on lap:** Deadrich, quoted in Loney, "Miss Kate," pp. 3, 6. **Dressed differently:** Loney, "Miss Kate," p. 3; Cox. **Writing his name big:** Kowert, "Lyndon B. Johnson." **China clown:** Bearss, p. 71; Cox.

On the donkey: Cox. **"The head of the ring":** Hatcher OH, p. 12. **Hugo's pie:** Cox.

"Lyndon took a liking"; a "five-pointer"; "a natural born leader": Crider OH, pp. 2, 17, 13. **"Take his ball and go home":** Edwards. Among others who knew this: SHJ.

In Maddox's barbershop: Emmette Redford, Cox, Gliddon, SHJ; Crofts OH. **Father made him stop:** SHJ. **"Competition"; populism:** Cox. **Debates:** Gliddon. They are also described by Cox, RJB. **"There was no":** Redford. **Dropping out of games:** Pool, p. 58; Cox; see also

Nichols, p. 439, who says, "His father told me that Lyndon . . . would listen to [his father's] conversations with neighbors and friends instead of indulging in play as would the usual child." **Craning his neck:** RJB; Steinberg, *Sam Johnson's Boy*, p. 21. **Hobby visit:** Kowert, "Lyndon B. Johnson." **"I loved":** Kearns, *Lyndon Johnson*, pp. 36–37; Cox, Gliddon. **"Tell him":** Steinberg, p. 26. **"If you can't":** *Dallas Herald*, Nov. 24, 1963. **"Someone who really knew":** McFarlane. **Benner's claims of fraud:** *San Angelo Standard-Times*, March 31, 1968. **Celebration in San Antonio:** RJB. **Sitting in the swing:** Cox, Fawcett. **Liked to dress like his father:** Cox. **"He was right":** Hatcher OH, p. 21. **Carrying the Congressional Record:** Stribling. **Imitating his father:** Patman, in Steinberg, pp. 28, 3, and OH. In the NBC broadcast, his first teacher, Kate Deadrich, said that when he came to school, "He would wear his father's cowboy hat and then would have his father's boots. A little bit difficult for him to have them, but he had them over his little shoes." **Sam's ambitions limited:** Patman, in Steinberg, p. 28. **The difference:** Fawcett, Gliddon, Redford.

Ear-popping: Barnwell; Rountree OH, p. 14. **"Let me tell you":** Gliddon. **"He was a Bunton!":** Cox.

6. "The Best Man I Ever Knew"

SOURCES

See Sources for Chapter 3.

NOTES

"Warm applause": *SAE*, Feb. 27, 1918. **Sam's description:** Joseph, McFarlane; Patman OH. **"The cowboy type":** Patman, quoted in Steinberg, *Sam Johnson's Boy*, p. 3. **"Caught in the tentacles":** *JCR-C*, Oct. 28, 1937. Here the phrase is used without quotation marks, but numerous Johnson City residents say that it is exactly the phrase Sam used. **Sulphur tax:** McFarlane.

Anti-German hysteria: Gould, p. 225; Pool, pp. 36–38; Fehrenbach, p. 644. **Fredericksburg Square; "maelstrom"; Sam's speech:** *Fredericksburg Standard*, March 23, April 6, 1918; *State Observer*, June 10, 1940. **Remembered with admiration:** Phinney. **Privately buttonholing:**

SAE, March 6, 1918. **"At a time":** W.A. Trenckmann, editor of Austin's *Das Wochenblatt*, in a letter dated Aug. 17, 1920, published in *Fredericksburger Wochenblatt*, Oct. 14, 1920.

Sam Johnson was also a leader in the fight against the Ku Klux Klan, although, contrary to the opinion of some Lyndon Johnson biographers that this fight required political courage, it did not. Sam's son, Sam Houston Johnson, has written (*My Brother*, pp. 29–31) that the Klan "threatened to kill him on numerous occasions," and that once Sam Ealy and his two brothers, Tom and George, dared them to "come on ahead," and spent the night waiting on the porch with shotguns, while the women cowered in the cellar below (the Klan never showed up). But both accounts are at least slightly exaggerated. Sam Johnson, with his sympathy for the underdog, detested the Klan's persecution of Mexican-Americans—he used the phrase "Kukluxsonofabitch" so often that, Sam Houston says, "I never realized that 'son of a bitch' was a separate word, standing all by itself, until I got to high school"—and, in the Legislature, he did speak and vote against measures it backed; one plea, for racial tolerance, won statewide notice; Carl L. Phinney, chief clerk of the House at the time, remembers "very vividly" the "powerful statement." But the House was split about evenly on the Klan, and in Johnson's own district, it was not really a force at all.

Optometrists: Kemp, "Representative Sam Johnson." **"High time":** McFarlane. This was a characteristic phrase. In one of his campaign speeches against Benner, he said, as Cox recalled it for Pool (p. 45), "It is high time that a person stands up and lets the world know how he stands." **"He was not":** Patman OH, pp. 2, 3.

Concerted effort: *BCR*, April 22, 1921. A **"leading good-roads" man:** Johnson's work on the highway is detailed in *House Journal, Regular Session, 36th Legislature,* 1919, pp. 308–9; 1920, pp. 196–97, 503. **"We've got":** McFarlane. **Drought:** *BCR*, Oct. 15, 1920. **"Because of":** *BCR*, Oct. 28, 1937; Pool, p. 39. **State aid:** *BCR*, Oct. 15, 1920. **"A great victory":** *BCR*, March 11, 1921. **"Truly wanted":** McFarlane. **"The best man":** Patman OH.

"He had": Redford. **Sam's work in obtaining pensions:** Dollahite, Koeniger, Gliddon, Buckner.

Blue Sky Law: *House Journal, Regular*

Session, 38th Legislature, pp. 34–35, 827; Shirley, p. 100. **"The Governor's speech"; "I want to leave":** *Fort Worth Star-Telegram*, Jan. 11, 1923. **"No measure":** *SAE*, Jan. 14, 1923. **Money:** McFarlane, RJB. **"Whenever":** Wilma Fawcett. **"Ambitious":** Deason.

"Several big land deals": *BCR*, Aug. 6, 1920. **Kept going down:** Cox, Gliddon, Stribling. **"If you want":** Cox.

Buying the family place: *Fredericksburg Standard*, Feb. 7, 1920; Bearss, p. 81. **Offering $19,500:** Gillespie County Deed Book 27, pp. 420–21, in Bearss, p. 170. **Persuading Tom:** SHJ, Cox. **"Gradual enough":** Graves, *Heartland*, p. 29. **Cotton prices:** Gould, *passim*. **Other expenses:** RJB, SHJ, Cox. **Selling hotel and store:** *BCR*, Jan. 23, 1920. Sam received about $5,000 for the store. **Mortgage, bank loans:** Gillespie County Deed Book 27, pp. 420–21, in Bearss, p. 171; RJB, SHJ say the $15,000 mortgage, from the Loan and Abstract Co. of Fredericksburg, at 7% interest, was to pay for the improvements to the farm. **Gully:** Cox, SHJ, Gliddon. **Cotton prices falling:** *Literary Digest*, Nov. 6, 1920. **Selling to Striegler:** *Fredericksburg Standard*, Sept. 23, 1922; Bearss, p. 88. **All went to Loan and Abstract:** Gillespie County Deed Book 34, pp. 624–26, quoted in Bearss, p. 171. **Still owed banks, etc.; his brothers co-signing:** RJB, SHJ, Cox, Fawcett, Gliddon; Bearss, p. 136, says a $2,000 mortgage, when originally taken, was to mature on Dec. 1, 1918, but RJB, SHJ, Cox say a mortgage for this amount was still in effect in 1923.

Sam's illness: RJB, SHJ, Cox. **Going to Legislature:** *Fort Worth Star-Telegram*, Jan. 19, 23, 1923. **"Among prominent visitors":** *BCR*, March 26, 1920. **"Big land deals":** *BCR*, Aug. 6, 1920. **Benner's mot:** Koeniger. **Johnson City's opinion of Sam Johnson:** Dollahite, Gliddon, Fawcett, and all interviews with residents noted in Sources for Chapter 3. **"Playing cowboy":** Brigham OH. **"For business reasons":** *Fort Worth Star-Telegram*, Jan. 11, 1923. **Not invited to speak:** *Fredericksburg Standard*, Aug. 30, 1924.

Real-estate and insurance; game warden: *BCR*, May 9, 1924; RJB, Cox. **"Please!":** Fawcett. **Buntons lent him:** SHJ, Cox. **Foreman:** Gliddon.

"Some children": Among the many residents who quoted this is Wilma Fawcett. **"Never tells a lie":** Cox. Rebekah herself records this exchange in *Album*, p. 19,

and also says, "He had a passion for truthfulness and could be depended on to admit a failure in duty or obedience." **Laundry:** Wilma Fawcett. **"Sausage":** Ohlen Cox. **"Bread and bacon":** Stribling. **"A little dab"; Christmas food; "She just,"** etc.: Cox. **"He did":** Dollahite.

7. "The Bottom of the Heap"

SOURCES

See Sources for Chapter 3.

Also, Marjie Mugno, "Just a Guy," *Highway* (published by the Austin Employees, Texas Highway Department), March, 1964; Carol Nation, "A Rendezvous With Destiny," *Texas Highways*, March, 1964; Wendell O'Neal, "Motor Buses in Texas, 1912–1930," Texas Bus Owners Association, Inc., 1931.

And interview with John Gorfinkle.

NOTES

"Humorous to watch": Patman, quoted in Steinberg, *Sam Johnson's Boy*, p. 28, and he expanded on this: "They sort of looked alike, they walked the same, had the same nervous mannerisms, and Lyndon clutched you like his Daddy did when he talked to you." Patman shared a two-man desk on the House floor with Sam Johnson. **"Whenever"; "there wasn't":** McFarlane. Also, Coffee, Holden, Joseph, Morgan, Phinney. There was no legislative session in 1922, but some of these men saw Lyndon and Sam together in Austin on legislative business.

"Just long enough": Lyndon Johnson quoted in Waugh, "The Boyhood Days." **"Bossy":** Wilma Fawcett. **Woodbox, etc.:** The description of Lyndon's behavior at home comes from RJB, SHJ, Casparis.

At Albert School: RJB; Cox. **Donkey:** Johnson, quoted in Steinberg, p. 699. See also *Time*, May 21, 1965. **Photograph:** *Album*, p. 38; RJB. **"Someday":** Itz, quoted in *USN&WR*, Dec. 23, 1963, "This is LBJ's Country."

"Couldn't handle"; might not pass; scraping up tuition: Cox, SHJ, RJB. **Spending allowance:** SHJ; *BCR*, July 28, 1922. **"Cut off":** SHJ. **"Lyndon is very young":** Rebekah Johnson to Flora Eckert, July 11, 1922, "Family Correspondence" (Mother) Johnson, Sam E. (Rebekah), Box 1, General Correspondence. **At Johnson City High:** Schoolmates Leon-

ard, Cecil Redford, Edwards, Dollahite, Cox; Crofts OH.
"Many times": Rebekah Johnson, quoted in *DMN,* June 30, 1941. **Father's anger, kicking off shoes:** RJB, SHJ.
"Bend over": SHJ, pp. 11–13. **Tension between Sam and Lyndon:** SHJ, pp. 13, 10. **Suit:** Barnwell. **"All afraid":** Edwards. **Beau refusing:** RJB. **"Ugly things":** Casparis.
"You could see": Casparis. **An hour alone:** SHJ, pp. 9, 10. **The bicycle:** SHJ, p. 16. **Spanking over razor:** Crofts OH. **Barbershop spanking:** Crofts OH; Barnwell.
Sneaking out the car: Cox, Fawcett. **"I've seen him":** Fawcett. **Fawcetts knew:** Fawcett. **Spankings:** Fawcett, Cox, Edwards, Emmette Redford, RJB, SHJ. **The telephone operator; hiding in a tree:** SHJ. **"He always":** Emmette Redford.
"Such a production": Barnwell. **The two boys in the café:** Ohlen Cox, SHJ. **His sisters mistreating him:** Cox. **"I regarded":** Emmette Redford. **Spanking at school:** SHJ.
Hugging: Cynthia Crider. **"Miz Stella":** Gliddon. **"Put me to shame":** Redford, Edwards, Fawcett. **"The more":** Stribling, Wilma Fawcett. **"We had great ups and downs":** Lyndon Johnson, quoted in Harwood and Johnson, *Lyndon,* p. 23. **"I felt sorry for him":** Gliddon, for example. **"Too much":** Fawcett.
Lyndon and Kitty Clyde Ross: Kitty Clyde Ross Leonard, Casparis, Cox, Edwards. **"Believed to be":** *BCR,* May 9, 1924. **Air Force One:** A picture of this trip is in the LBJ Library.
Carrying the eggs: Crider. **"You strap on":** Humphrey, p. 55. **"Half the town":** Milton Barnwell.
"Immediacy"; "by the middle": "flickering screen": Shannon, in Mowry, pp. 43, 59, 60. **"Rather drab":** RJB. **"About all":** "so what was left": Emmette Redford. **Lyndon's dream:** He is quoted in Kearns, *Lyndon Johnson,* p. 40.
"You couldn't get anywhere": Crider OH, p. 6. **She never:** Despite Lyndon Johnson's statements to Kearns—that she daily took him to task with "a terrible knifelike voice," or else, in Kearns' words, "closed him out completely." He also told Kearns (p. 40): "We'd been such close companions, and, boom, she'd abandoned me." Among those who never heard a "terrible knifelike voice," or remember Rebekah even losing her patience with Lyndon: RJB, SHJ, Cox, Casparis—and a score of other persons the author interviewed who spent time in the Johnson household. **"Hope":** Casparis. **Father's anger:** RJB, SHJ.
"Always talking big": Koeniger. **"He didn't":** Clemens.
Gravel-topping the road: The description of the work is from a number of Johnson City teen-agers who worked on the job, including Cox. **"Can't even hold":** Casparis. **"There's got to be,"** etc.: Cox.
"C'mon, Lyndon, get up": NBC Broadcast; Kornitzer, "President Johnson"; SHJ. **Wrecking the car and running away:** Koeniger. **Working in Robstown:** *SHJ,* Roeder, Clemens, Koeniger, Fawcett; Keach OH II, p. 30; *Robstown Record,* Dec. 16, 1936; *CCC,* Dec. 16, 1936.
Visiting the Buntons; refusing to register: The visit, and the fact that he spent two days in San Marcos immediately thereafter, are mentioned in the *BCR,* Sept. 19, 26, Oct. 10, 1924. Also SHJ.
"Weeelll": SHJ. **"The minute," "exploded":** SHJ, pp. 21–22. **"One less mouth":** Johnson, quoted in Steinberg, p. 32. **"None of us had been off the farm"; "nothing to eat,"** etc.: This description by Johnson of the trip, a fair sample of the description he gave to other reporters over the years, appeared in *DMN,* June 30, 1941. Johnson, of course, had recently returned from a 200-mile trip to Robstown. The burying-the-money story seems to be an expansion of a practical joke that Johnson played on one of the other boys, Otho Summy. Rountree says that on one occasion "there were car lights showed up behind us and Lyndon commenced to hoorah Otho Summy. Otho, he's a pretty scary type of guy, you know, easy to scare. . . . He was telling him that these guys were following us . . . making him think that" they were going to rob us, "so we stopped and we saw Otho way off down, and he was burying his money. We all gave our money to him, and he was burying the money down there" (p. 8). About the trip as a whole, Rountree says: "We weren't scared" (Rountree OH, p. 11). See also Crider OH, pp. 3–4.
"Johnson was barely able to survive": Kearns, p. 43. **What Johnson actually did:** Koeniger; RJB; Crider OH, *passim;* Otto Crider in *Cloverdale Reveille,* July 2, 1964. Says Koeniger: "I read an article that Lyndon worked at menial jobs, but I don't know anything about that. I never heard about any jobs like that. I venture to say that his grape-picking and all that was very limited if at all. . . . I suspect that Lyndon may have—I hate to say—said that he did

these things when he didn't. He came up there [to Tehachapi] with Otto [Crider, one of his companions on the trip], and they hadn't been very long when they [went] to San Bernardino." And, Koeniger says, neither Otto nor Lyndon "ever mentioned anything about starving or grape-picking or anything like that."

Johnson's attempt to be a lawyer: Koeniger; Gorfinkle; *Laws of Nevada,* Chapter LXIX, Section 2, As Amended, 1907; *Nevada Compiled Laws*—1929, Vol. I, §593. *The Code of Civil Procedure of the State of California, Adopted March 11, 1872, and the Subsequent Official State Amendments to and Including 1925,* Sec. 279. **Martin's career:** *BCR,* May 7, 1920; *JCR-C,* June 20, 1929; Koeniger. **Said he hitchhiked home:** *Time,* May 21, 1965. **Driven to his front door:** RJB. **"A changed person":** Gliddon.

Drag races, moonshine, dances, etc.: Edwards, who was one of the "wild bunch"; Truman Fawcett; Cox; SHJ; Cynthia Crider; *Life,* "The Man," Aug. 14, 1964; Otto Crider in *Cloverdale Reveille,* July 2, 1964. **Dynamite:** Edwards. **"I always hated cops":** Quoted in Kearns, p. 333. **"Only a hairsbreadth":** RJB, SHJ.

"No matter": Gliddon. **"If you want":** RJB, SHJ; Steinberg, p. 34. **Wrecking the car again:** Johnson, quoted in Kearns, p. 38. **Increased tension between father and son:** Edwards, Cox; McKay Interview, pp. 10–11.

On the road gang: Crider OH, pp. 7, 18–20; Newlon, pp. 30–31. **"Talked big":** Arrington, quoted in Nation, "A Rendezvous," p. 6. **Predicted:** Among those who heard the prediction was C. S. Kinney, who is quoted in Nation, "A Rendezvous."

Trying to stand out: Cox, Gliddon. **Replacing the Ferguson men:** Crider OH, p. 7. **The dance:** Cox, SHJ, RJB, Lady Bird Johnson. **Telling his parents he would go to college:** RJB; SHJ. **Wouldn't permit:** SHJ.

8. "Bull" Johnson

SOURCES

Books, articles, transcripts:
Nichols, *Rugged Summit;* Terry, *Retired Teacher on Candid Typewriter.*

John M. Smith, "The History and Growth of the Southwest Texas State Teachers College" (unpublished Master's Thesis), San Marcos, 1930.

Transcript of "John Dailey, Class of 1936, interviewing Professor David F. Votaw about the Early Days of President Lyndon B. Johnson When he Entered SWTSTC," Feb. 6, 1965, in Exec. PP, 3–5, WHCF (referred to as Votaw Transcript).

"Text of a Discussion Concerning the College Years of Lyndon B. Johnson" (between A. H. Nolle, Oscar W. Strahan, David F. Votaw, and Elizabeth Sterry), Dec., 1963 (referred to as Nolle Transcript).

Tape-recording of an informal discussion between Johnson and several professors who had been faculty members or students during his years at college, held in the office of the President of Southwest Texas State Univ., Billy Mack Jones, April 27, 1970. (The recording was made by E. Phillip Scott, Audiovisual Archivist of the Lyndon Baines Johnson Library, and will be referred to as Scott Tape.)

"Transcript of an Exclusive Interview Granted by President Lyndon B. Johnson to Robert E. McKay on May 21, 1965" (McKay Interview).

NBC News Television program, "The Hill Country: Lyndon Johnson's Texas" (May 9, 1966).

The College *Star,* 1926–1931.

The *Pedagog,* 1927, 1928, 1929, 1930, 1931, published by the senior class of SWTSTC, San Marcos.

Oral Histories:
Percy Brigham, Ben Crider, Willard Deason, Thomas J. Dunlap, Fenner Roth.

Interviews:
With College deans and administrators: Alfred H. Nolle, Leland H. Derrick, Ethel Davis (Registrar), Oscar Strahan (Athletic Director).

Faculty members: David E. Conrad, William C. Pool.

White Stars: Willard Deason, Alfred Harzke, Horace Richards, Vernon Whiteside, Wilton Woods.

Black Stars: Joe Berry, Ardis Hopper, Alfred (Boody) Johnson, Robert (Barney) Knispel, Richard Spinn.

Other students: Louise Casparis, Elizabeth Clemens, Mabel Webster Cook, Ava Johnson Cox, Carol Davis, Elmer Graham, Helen Hofheinz Moore, Mylton (Babe) Kennedy, Mrs. A. K. Krause, Henry Kyle, Ned Logan, Edward Puls, Ella So Relle (Porter), Ruth Garms Terry,

Emmet Shelton, Clayton Stribling, Yancy Yarborough.

Townspeople: Walter Buckner, Barton Gill, Hilman Hagemann.

Others: SHJ, RJB, Fritz Koeniger, Emmette Redford.

NOTES

History and description of the college: Nichols, *passim;* Pool, *LBJ,* pp. 67–111; Smith, *passim;* Nolle, Strahan, Derrick, Ethel Davis. Joe Berry, later a faculty member at Bryn Mawr, says that when he got there, "I felt so inadequate—that I had so much to catch up. . . . I could not go to a dinner party, and participate intelligently in the conversation. . . . And this is a terrible feeling. I don't think anyone who hasn't experienced this can understand how horrible it is. . . . [At San Marcos] I got cheated out of an education." Emmette Redford says that there was a considerable gap between academic standards at San Marcos and at the University of Texas in Austin. "The jump from San Marcos to the University of Texas was a pretty big jump," he says. In the freshman and sophomore years at San Marcos, the course level was only slightly above high-school level. And in most junior- and senior-level courses, there was little or no reading of primary sources. And there wasn't very much reading even in the textbooks. Berry says that a chapter a week in history was about the rule. The professor would "take it a chapter at a time, like they do in . . . high school. . . . There was no outside reading, there was no collateral reading, no biographies."

Floor caving in: Nichols, p. 152. **"It should be":** *Announcement of the Southwest Texas State Normal School for the Session Beginning Sept. 9, 1903,* pp. 9, 190, quoted in Smith, pp. 79–80. **"We know very well":** Evans, to Council of Teachers College Presidents, Sept. 16, 1921, in Nichols, p. 181. **On academic standards; low professors' salaries:** Redford, Nolle; Nichols, pp. 114–20; *San Marcos Record,* undated clipping. The holder of the lone doctorate was Nolle, who was Dean of the College during Johnson's years there; Evans would not persuade another doctorate holder to come to San Marcos until 1931. **"The reason I went?":** Yarborough. **"A poor boy's school":** For example, Clyde Nail, quoted in Pool, p. 79. See also Nichols, p. 104.

"Considerable fear": Votaw, in Nolle

Transcript, p. 12. **"He didn't have":** Clemens. **"I am unable":** Johnson to Biggers, Feb. 21, 1927, Box 72, LBJA SF. **"One scared chicken":** Cox. **His interview with Votaw:** Votaw Transcript, p. 3; Votaw, in Nolle Transcript, pp. 12, 13; Pool, pp. 90–91. Among the faculty members who remember are Strahan, Nolle, Derrick.

Getting a room: Boody Johnson, Stribling, Hopper. **"The biggest heart":** Knispel.

His father calling Evans: RJB, SHJ. **Evans' personality and career:** Nichols, *passim;* Pool, pp. 73 ff. **The chink:** Nichols, pp. 347–49. **Opening the Redbooks:** Nichols, p. 347; Derrick. **"An invisible wall":** Deason OH I, p. 6. **Johnson becoming friendly with Evans; running errands; becoming his assistant:** Johnson, on Scott Tape; Pool, pp. 99–100. **"He was so sure":** Ethel Davis.

"I remember": Johnson, on NBC Broadcast. **"A tired homesick":** *Star,* June 29, 1927. A "D"; "very upset": So Relle.

The egg and the ham: Mrs. Johnson. **His lack of money; writing Crider and Crider's reply:** Johnson, on Scott Tape. **Mother writing Crider:** Crider OH, p. 10. **"Eighty-one dollars!":** Johnson, on Scott Tape.

"Normally": Ethel Davis. **"Dearest Mother":** Johnson to Rebekah Johnson, "Family Correspondence . . . Dec. 1929–Dec. 1939," Box 1, LBJL. All the correspondence between Johnson and his mother is here. **Mother asking him:** RJB. **"Damn I wanted to show him!":** McKay Interview, pp. 10, 11. **"The long confidential talks":** Rebekah Johnson to Lyndon, Nov. 15, 1934, Box 1, LBJL.

Blanco County Club: *Star,* June 29, July 6, Sept. 29, 1927. *Star* editorship: Crider OH, p. 20.

Brogdon's personality: Pool, pp. 82–83; Nichols, pp. 230–34. Not only did she want river swimming in San Marcos segregated by sexes, she didn't want female students swimming downstream from male students lest sperm from the men be carried downstream on the current and impregnate female students. **"After the meeting":** Johnson, in *Star,* March 20, 1927. **"Alert, experienced":** Johnson, in *Star,* July 25, 1928. **"Very interesting":** Johnson, in *Star,* July 24, 1929. **"Great":** Johnson, in *Star,* July 25, 1928.

"Not with Lyndon": Nolle Transcript, p. 26. **"Lyndon Johnson, editorial writer":** 1928 *Pedagog,* p. 150.

"May I thank you": Netterville to Johnson, Dec. 19, 1929, "Letters of Recommendation," Box 73, LBJA SF. **Flattering Ethel Davis:** Ethel Davis.

Flattering professors: The description of Lyndon on the quadrangle comes from Whiteside, Berry, Kennedy, among others. **"Sitting at his feet":** Whiteside. And Nolle also uses that phrase, in describing Johnson and one of his professors, H. M. Greene: "Lyndon literally sat at the feet of Professor Greene" (*Houston Press,* Dec. 12, 1963). **"Just drink up":** Whiteside. **"Has he gone yet?":** Derrick. Johnson himself talked about this (Scott Tape).

Miss Brogdon relaxing: Boody Johnson. **"Very forceful, but":** Graham.

Flattery of Evans: Nichols touches on this only gingerly (pp. 436, 439) in his book, but talked to his friends, including Nolle and Derrick, about it at the time. **"Red of face":** Whiteside. **Dramatizing his diligence:** Nichols, p. 436. **Evans mentioning:** Berry. **"He got next"; painting garage; "smooth as silk":** Boody Johnson, quoted in *Houston Press,* Dec. 12, 1963; Nichols. **"Opened a swinging gate":** Mrs. Christine savage to Johnson, Nov. 25, 1966, Exec. PP, 13–5, WHCF. **Acting familiar:** Pool, p. 100. **"They loved it":** Whiteside.

"Words won't come": Kennedy. **"Lyndon Johnson from Johnson City":** Davis, **"My heritage":** *Star,* June 29, 1927. **At Mrs. Gates' bordinghouse:** Whiteside, Richards.

Saying he had 145 IQ: Woods. **His marks:** One place in which his "40 courses and 35 A's" is quoted is *USN&WR,* Sept. 7, 1964. While in residence at San Marcos, Lyndon Johnson took 56 courses, according to a handwritten record of his grades shown to the author by Nolle. He received 8 A's. He also received A's for three terms of "Practice Teaching." While at Cotulla, he took six "extension courses" (which Nolle said were in reality correspondence courses) and received three A's, but Nolle says these would not have been included at the time in his official overall average. Nolle says that his overall scholastic average was .939, which was "just a trifle under B." An A was 1.33; a B, 1.00; a C, .66; a D, .33. **"A brilliant":** Woods. **Letters for debaters:** *Star,* June 8, 1927. **Lyndon as a debater:** Graham. **"I just didn't believe:** Richards. **"He's the bus inspector":** Whiteside.

"Jumbo": SHJ. **Emphasis on his appearance:** Pool, p. 98; Boody Johnson. **"Hard to shave":** The barber, Barton Gill.

Unpopularity with women: Hofheinz, So Relle, Kyle, Richards. **"Boasting and bragging . . . . ridiculous":** Richards.

"Once": Richards. **Fight:** Whiteside, Richards. **"A coward":** Whiteside. **A liar:** Richards, Stribling, Whiteside, Puls, Kyle.

Black Stars the "in" crowd: Pool, p. 103.

Trying to get into the Black Stars: Knispel, So Relle, Boody Johnson, Spinn, Strahan, Stribling, Derrick. **"Stalwart Boody":** 1927 *Pedagog,* p. 237. **Description of Boody:** So Relle, Whiteside. **Boody's feelings about Lyndon:** Boody. **Black Stars blackballing:** Boody, quoted in Pool, p. 105, says there was only one, but to the author he made clear that the dislike was far more general. Stribling, who was present at the Black Star Meetings, says that the only result of Lyndon's seeing-the-Constitution strategy was that "he got even more blackballs" on the second vote. Also, Strahan, Knispel, and Derrick. Black Star Frank Arnold told his girlfriend (later wife) Helen Hofheinz at the time, and she says, when asked if there was only one blackball, "Oh, that's not true. They were *all* against him." **"We figured":** Stribling.

"He wanted": So Relle. **At Ethel Davis' lodge:** Ethel Davis. **Jackass, etc.:** 1928 *Pedagog,* p. 302. **"M.B.":** *Star,* Dec. 17, 1929; Kyle, Richards, Puls, among others.

9. The Rich Man's Daughter

SOURCES

This chapter is based on interviews with Carol Davis (now Mrs. Harold Smith) and her sisters Ethel and Hallie (now Mrs. Charles Bass), and with a friend Emma Beth Kennard. Unless otherwise noted, the information is from them.

See also Sources for Chapter 8.

NOTES

"Made a production": Richards. **"He'd brag"; "She was":** Knispel. **"He was hinting":** Kennedy.

Carol's father: Description from his daughters and Walter Buckner; *San Marcos Record,* Oct. 31, 1919. **"A man":** Buckner. **Dislike of Lyndon:** Boody Johnson, Knispel.

"Hugging and kissing": Koeniger.

Other gifts: Bank president Percy Brigham, Mrs. Johnson. **"Real Silk Hose":** Deason, quoted in Pool, p. 98; Whiteside, Davis. **Borrowing:** Boody Johnson, Buckner, Richards, Whiteside. **Buying car:**

Boody Johnson, Whiteside. **Intolerable:** SHJ. **"The bucket":** Boody Johnson.

10. Cotulla

SOURCES

Books and articles:
Ludeman, *History of La Salle County.* Vulcan Mold & Oil Co., *Pit and Pour,* April, 1964, pp. 1–2; Louis B. Engelke, "Our Texas Towns: Cotulla," San Antonio *Express* Magazine, Sept. 21, 1952; Carol Hinckley, "LBJ—Teacher Turned President," *The Texas Outlook,* March, 1972; *Houston Post,* Jan. 27, 1964.

Johnson's speeches:
"Remarks of the President at the Welhausen Elementary School, Cotulla, Texas," Nov. 7, 1966, PP 1966, Vol. II, pp. 1347-1350.
"Remarks of the President to the National Conference on Educational Legislation," March 1, 1965, PP 1965, Vol. I, pp. 226–31.

Interviews:
Carol Davis, Ethel Davis, Leland Derrick, Boody Johnson, RJB, SHJ, Sarah Tinsley Marshall, Alfred Nolle.

NOTES

Description of Cotulla in 1928: Ludeman, pp. 30–56; Engelke, "Our Texas Towns"; Pool, pp. 137–45; Mrs. Marshall. **Unable to lure:** To persuade Johnson to come, Donaho had offered him an unusually high salary: $125 per month for nine months—a total of $1,125—compared to an annual income of $842 for male teachers in Texas in 1929 (Pool, *LBJ,* p. 141). **Arrived early and stayed late:** Thomas Coronado, janitor at the Welhausen School at the time, says that Johnson was always the first to arrive and the last to leave the school each day, *HP.* **Arranging games at recess and meets with other schools:** Johnson, 1965 and 1966 speeches (they contain some exaggerations); Hinckley, "LBJ"; Mrs. Marshall; Steinberg, p. 47; Pool, pp. 142–43. **No teacher cared:** Johnson, 1965 speech; Mrs. Marshall; Pool, p. 143. **"He spanked":** Hinckley, "LBJ"; Juan Rodriguez, quoted in Vulcan Mold, *Pit and Pour; HP.* **Making them learn English:** Hinckley, "LBJ"; *HP.* **"As soon as we understood":**

Juanita Ortiz, quoted in *HP.* **Scant respect for their culture:** Steinberg, p. 47. **"If we hadn't done":** Juanita Hernandez, quoted in *HP.* **"He used to tell us":** Daniel Garcia, quoted in *HP.* **"The little baby in the cradle":** Juan Ortiz, quoted in *HP.*
"He put us to work": Manuel Sanchez, quoted in *HP.* **Lying in his room:** Johnson, 1966 speech. [Statements of Lyndon Johnson, Box 221.] **Christmas trees:** Ludeman, p. 124. **Johnson's relations with other teachers:** Elizabeth Johnson (no relation), quoted in *HP.* **Johnson's relationship with Coronado:** Coronado, quoted in *HP.*
He was aware: Nolle, Derrick. **"This may sound strange":** *HP.* **"I still see":** Johnson, 1966 speech.
The song: Hinckley, "LBJ"; Steinberg, p. 45. **Garcia's imitation:** Newlon, *LBJ,* p. 37; Pool, p. 144; Garcia quoted in *HP.* **"He told us":** Amanda Garcia, quoted in *AA-S,* Jan. 8, 1964.
"Broke": Mrs. Marshall, SHJ. **"Lyndon confided in me":** Mrs. Marshall. **Lonely in Cotulla:** Mrs. Marshall, Boody Johnson, RJB. **"A little dried-up town":** Lady Bird Johnson interview, March 1, 1976.
Carol Davis relationship: Mrs. Marshall, Carol Davis, Ethel Davis. **"She sat down in the back room":** Ethel Davis.

11. White Stars and Black Stars

SOURCES
See Sources for Chapter 8.

NOTES

Again summer editor: And again using blaring headlines. He was to be the editor for nine issues, the first of which appeared June 12, 1929. Previously, banner headlines across the entire six-column width of the paper had been used infrequently. But he used them in eight of the nine issues of which he was editor, sometimes for subjects that would not normally have merited such attention; for example, COLLEGE THEATER TO PRESENT MEDIEVAL PLAY. **"Capable management":** *Star,* June 12, 1929. **Demoted; fistfight with Kennedy:** Whiteside to Johnson, April 14, 1937, Box 3, JHP; Kennedy, Whiteside, Richards.
Black Stars in politics: Berry, Knispel, Boody, Spinn; Pool, pp. 104–5. **Formation of White Stars; admitting Johnson; the first election:** Interviews with all five of the founding members of the White Stars

—Whiteside, Richards, Deason, Woods, and Harzke—and with Spinn; Deason OH I, p. 9. Also, Johnson, on Scott Tape. For the Blanket Tax, see, for example, *Star*, Jan. 15, April 9, 23, 1930. **"They made fun":** So Relle. **"Buttonholing":** Harzke. **"His greatest forte"; "The night before":** Deason OH II, pp. 5, 6. **"The day I won"; "Lyndon's strategy":** Deason.

Johnson's own election: Richards, Whiteside.

Ruth Lewis episode: So Relle, Richards. **"I had to rely"; "We took the keys":** Johnson, on Scott Tape. **"Lyndon's idea":** Woods, Whiteside, Richards.

"Those wonderful conversations": SHJ, *My Brother*, pp. 27–28; more details furnished by SHJ in interview. **White Stars' secrecy:** Richards, Whiteside, Deason, Harzke; Deason OH.

Star and Pedagog editorships: So Relle, Kyle, Puls, Richards, Hofheinz, Boody Johnson. See *Star* editorial of April 30, 1930, which states that "some of our student legislators are busy angling about for a suitable candidate," and wonders why, since "there are several persons on the campus who are capable of handling the situation and are willing to undertake the job. . . . there is no dearth of capable editors. So why not cut out all the bickering and wire-pulling and elect the best qualified applicant regardless of political whims or party affiliations." **"To a standstill":** Derrick; and see Pool, p. 95. **"I befriended"; "I thought"; "two of his henchmen,"** etc.: Kyle. **"All the time,"** etc.: Puls. **"Very smart":** So Relle.

"Thinking back": SHJ, *My Brother*, p. 28. **"His penchant":** SHJ. **"Joe Bailey":** Nolle, RJB. And see SHJ, pp. 31–2. **Johnson's reminiscences:** Preserved on the Scott Tape. Scott was the young man present.

Frank Arnold episode: Hofheinz, Whiteside. **Acne episode:** Whiteside.

Evans more friendly to Lyndon than to anyone else: Nolle, Derrick, Strahan. **"As he was":** Strahan. **Deans wary:** Nolle.

Bales necessary: Nichols, p. 38. **Professors helping:** Nichols, pp. 39, 92–93; Nolle. **"Sacrifices":** *Star*, Dec. 17, 1929. **"Twenty cents":** Richards.

Giving his friends jobs: Richards; Nail, quoted in Pool, p. 110; Boody Johnson. **"Always willing":** Casparis. **"If he's got too much pride":** Richards.

"Head-huddling": Hopper, So Relle. **"Anathema":** Berry. **"He'd avoid us":** Kennedy. **"After Carol":** Hofheinz, Kyle.

"Cut your throat": Hofheinz. **"Wasn't straight":** So Relle. **"Just like everything else":** Richards. **"He had power":** So Relle. **Editorials:** Woods. **"Why?":** So Relle. **"Didn't just dislike":** Yarborough. **"By the end":** So Relle.

"My dear Mother": Johnson to Rebekah Johnson, Dec. 13, 1929, "Family Correspondence," Box 1, LBJL. **Frequent trips:** SHJ.

"Stop the presses!": Kennedy, confirmed by Richards. **Pedagog references:** 1930 *Pedagog*, pp. 210, 236, 235, 226–27.

Pages excised: Nichols, pp. 214–15, where Evans' letter is also quoted; Nolle, Derrick. Nichols says that the pages were excised from copies sent "to all high school libraries, to the other [college] presidents, and to the members of the board of regents," but Nolle and Derrick, who were among those who cut out the pages, say that they were removed as well from copies remaining on the campus. **Graduation Day scene:** Nichols, pp. 439–40. **Mother weeping:** SHJ. Evans' fondness for Johnson was documented in his Redbooks. For ten years after Johnson's graduation, each year's notebook contains Johnson's current address (Nichols, p. 27). **"The enduring lines":** Johnson, quoted in *Houston Press*, Dec. 10, 1963. His years at San Marcos, he also said, were "the most formative period of my life."

12. "A Very Unusual Ability"

SOURCES

Articles, transcript:
WPA, *Texas: A Guide*.
"The Printer's Devil," student newspaper of Sam Houston High School, 1930, 1931.
"Transcript of an Exclusive Interview Granted by President Lyndon B. Johnson to Robert E. McKay on May 21, 1965" (McKay Transcript).

Oral Histories:
Ruth Booker, Welly K. Hopkins, L. E. Jones, Carroll Keach, Gene Latimer.

Interviews:
Willard Deason, William Goode, Welly K. Hopkins, Boody Johnson, Rebekah Johnson Bobbitt (RJB), Sam Houston Johnson (SHJ), L. E. Jones, Gene Latimer, Horace Richards, Ella So Relle, Wilton Woods, Yancy Yarborough.

NOTES

Lyndon speaking at the barbecue: Hopkins to Craddock, Dec. 3, 1964, WHCF Exec. GI 2-8/M; The scene is described by Wilton Woods and Welly Hopkins in interviews, in Hopkins' OH, and in many Johnson biographies, including Pool and Steinberg. See also "Town Talk," *AS,* April 15, 1938. **"Lyndon, get up there":** Woods; Rebekah Johnson, quoted in undated and unidentified newspaper clipping, "Family Correspondence (Mother): Box 1, LBJL. **Johnson coming to the platform:** Hopkins OH, p. 9; Woods; Hopkins, quoted in Pool, Lyndon B. Johnson, pp. 165–66. **"He talked in the dark":** Woods. **"His reply I've never forgotten":** Hopkins OH, p. 10.

The reason Hopkins won; Johnson's services in the campaign: Hopkins OH, pp. 10–12. **"A very unusual ability":** Hopkins to Miller, Nov. 25, 1931, Box 19, LBJA SN. **"I always felt that he was the real balance":** Hopkins; Richards, Woods, Deason.

"This wonder kid"; enlisting Johnson in Witt's campaign: Steinberg, p. 53. **"Never have I seen better work":** Hopkins to Miller, Nov. 25, 1931, Box 19, LBJA SN. **Spree:** Hopkins OH II, p. 12.

George Johnson's reverence for Jackson, Bryan, etc.: Pool, pp. 147–48. **George trying to get Lyndon a job:** Johnson to George Johnson, May 19, 1930, Box 73, LBJA SF. **Only three graduates:** So Relle. **Lyndon's letters of recommendation to the Brenham School Board:** All these can be found in the folder "Teaching Certificates, Letters of Recommendations," Box 73, LBJA SF.

Description of Pearsall: WPA, *Texas: A Guide.* **Carol Davis' wedding:** *San Marcos Record,* June 20, 1930, p. 10. **Feelings in Pearsall:** SHJ, RJB.

"In the event": Johnson to George Johnson, May 19, 1930, Box 73, LBJA SF, **"A bit stunned":** George P. Barron in *SAE.* Jan. 30, 1966.

"You were sort of encouraged": Goode. **"I have a memory":** Jones. **"We had to do"; "The idea"; "Mr. Johnson wanted":** Latimer. **Parker remembers:** Undated *Houston Press* clipping: "LBJ in Houston," Box 73, LBJA SF.

"Smart as hell"; "An Irish charmer": Goode. **"Not the ones":** Latimer's impressions of Johnson: Latimer OH, pp. 1–2. **"The best friend":** Latimer OH, p. 1.

Training: Latimer, Jones, Goode. **"He

worked the life": Ellana Eastham Ball, quoted in Pool, p. 151.

The practice debates—unprecedented schedule: Pool, p. 164; *Houston Press,* Dec. 10, 1930, p. 3; March 6, 1931, p. 12. Once, a fellow teacher congratulated Johnson on the good sportsmanship exhibited by one of his students who had lost a debate. Johnson replied, "I'm not interested in how they win. I'm just interested in how they win" (Ruth Daugherty, quoted in Pool, p. 151). **The trip:** Jones, Latimer; Latimer OH, p. 2. *The* (Houston) *Aegis,* March 18, 1931, p. 1. **$100 prize:** *Houston Press,* Dec. 10, 1930, p. 1; *The Aegis,* Dec. 19, 1930. **Only seven; auditorium jammed:** Johnson, in McKay Transcript, p. 20. **More coverage:** An example is *Houston Press,* Dec. 10, 1930, p. 8. **"Silver-tongued students":** *HP,* date missing but appears to be Dec., 1930. **"Two of the best":** *Houston Chronicle,* April 3, 1931, p. 34. **"Almost too easy":** Latimer OH, p. 20.

State championships—"It is evident": Latimer OH, p. 3. **Sixty-seven victories:** *HP,* Oct. 4, 1938. **"I just almost cried":** Johnson, in McKay Transcript, pp. 10–11. **"Disbelief":** Latimer OH, p. 3. **Never knew:** Latimer, Jones. **Vomited:** *Time,* May 21, 1965.

"The splendid work": *Houston Chronicle,* April 3, 1931, p. 34. **Banquet:** *Houston Post-Dispatch,* May 24, 1931, Sec. 1, p. 10; Pool, pp. 157–58. **$100 raise:** *Board Minutes;* The Houston Independent School District, Book E, 121, 170, quoted in Pool, p. 158. **Daugherty's opinion:** "Everett Collier, Sidebar #2—LBJ," General PP 13–5, WHCF, attached to Collier to Valenti, January 21, 1964; she is quoted in a draft of a "proposed article" for the *Houston Chronicle* written by Everett Collier. **"Pleasing in personality":** "The Printer's Devil," April 10, 1931. **"To see them":** Johnson quoted in McKay Transcript, p. 18. **"Every time":** McKay Transcript, p. 17.

Dale Carnegie course: So Relle. **Heckling:** Johnson, quoted in Steinberg, p. 700.

Lonely in Houston: So Relle, Boody Johnson, RJB. **"What can I do next?"** So Relle.

Wanted to go into politics: Hopkins, Jones. **"When I go into politics":** Bess Scott to Johnson, July 1, 1941, "Harris Co.," Box 19, JHP. **Notes in margins:** Jones.

Phone call from Kleberg: Hopkins, SHJ. **Johnson "was so excited":** Helen Weinberg, quoted in Pool, p. 159. Weinberg says he said he "would consult with his uncle and call back in a few minutes." Hopkins and SHJ, both of whom had the story from Kleberg, say he agreed without hesitation to come for the interview. **Leave of absence:** Oberholtzer to Hofheinz, May 3, 1931, Box 73, LBJA SF. **The first night in the Mayflower:** Johnson to Jones, Dec. 6, 1931.

13. On His Way

SOURCES

The description of the daily routine in Kleberg's office, and of Johnson's activities as Kleberg's secretary, is based primarily on interviews with the other persons in that office: Estelle Harbin, Luther E. Jones, and Gene Latimer. Unless otherwise noted, the description comes from these interviews.

Johnson's letters to Jones and Latimer are in their respective possession.

Oral Histories:
Russell Brown, Luther E. Jones, Carroll Keach, Gene Latimer.

Other Interviews:
William Goode, Welly K. Hopkins, Dale Miller, J. J. Pickle, James Van Zandt.

NOTES

Running: Harbin.
Garner's election; Texas coming to power: "King Ranch in Garner's House," *Time,* Dec. 7; "The Congress: Sitting of the 72nd," *Time,* Dec. 14; "Work of the Week," *Time,* Dec. 28; Samuel G. Blythe, "How Congress Mixes In," *Sat. Eve. Post,* Nov. 21, all 1931. **Kleberg:** "Richest Cowboy Now Serves in Congress," *NYT,* Dec. 20, 1931; *Time,* "King Ranch in Garner's House," Dec. 7, 1931; "New Faces in Congress," *Washington Herald,* Dec. 9, 1931; "Texas' Kleberg," *Washington Herald,* Oct. 31, 1933; *CCC,* Oct. 11, 1932, Nov. 27, 1933; "Kleberg, Richard M.," Vertical File, Barker Texas History Center, Univ. of Texas; "Texas Kingdom That Blocks a Road," *Washington Sunday Star,* Oct. 15, 1933; "The World's Biggest Ranch," *Fortune,* Dec., 1933. **Kleberg's campaign:** *American Business Survey,* Jan., 1932, p. 3; Harbin, Jones, Latimer, Hopkins, Miller.

"The trouble": Kleberg, quoted in *CCC,* July 21, 1932; Dec. (date unreadable), 1932. **"Whittling down":** *CR,* 72 Cong., 1 Session (Jan. 21, 1932), p. 2446. **"Un-American":** *CCC,* Oct. 9, 1932. In June, 1932, Kleberg declared himself "unqualifiedly opposed to the constant and shameless encroachment of the federal government upon state and local authority, [to] the continued and increasing use of federal authority to control the business as well as the social and private affairs of our citizens" (*CCC,* June 24, 1932).

"Hello, Dick": Johnson to Jones, Dec. 6, 1931. **Miller's carte blanche:** Dale Miller.
Capitol Hill life: Charles McLean, "Typical Day in the Life of a Congressman," *NYT,* Sec. 5, p. 9, April 17, 1932; R. L. Duffus, "Congress: Cross Section of the Nation," *NYT,* April 10, 1932. **Employing relatives:** G. F. Nieberg, "All in the Congressional Family," *Atlantic Monthly,* Oct., 1931; "Nepotism," *Time,* May 30, 1932.
Dodge Hotel description: Hopkins, SHJ; Keach OH, Brown OH. **"Two bits":** Brown, quoted in Newlon, *LBJ,* p. 46. **Johnson shooting questions:** Perry, quoted in Mooney, *LJ Story,* p. 38.
Incident in the gallery: Robert Jackson, quoted in Edwin W. Knippa, "The Early Political Life of Lyndon B. Johnson" (unpublished Master's Thesis), San Marcos, 1967, pp. 10–11. Knippa says this incident occurred in December, but Johnson to Jones, Feb. 26, 1932, puts the date in February. **"I remember":** Van Zandt. **Inscribed photographs:** Johnson to Latimer, Feb. 25, 1932.
"Have you forgotten me?": Johnson to Jones, Feb. 13, 1932. **"Thanks":** Johnson to Jones, Feb. 26, 1932. **"Burn this"; "Hope":** Johnson to Jones, Dec. 6, 1931. **"Have not been out":** Johnson to Jones, April 18, 1932.
Motives of Latimer and Jones for coming: Latimer, Jones. **"I know":** Johnson to Jones, April 18, 1932. **Latimer's salary:** Latimer; Latimer OH, p. 8; "Civil Service Retirement System — Individual Retirement Record—Latimer, Gene"; Latimer to author, Oct. 19, 1978; Johnson to Latimer's parents, "Jan. 31, 1933," and "Tuesday evening," 1933.
"Saint Paul": Johnson to Fore, April 13, 1939 (letter in possession of Mrs. Sam Fore).
"As if his life": Goode. **Graduation congratulations letters:** Latimer OH, pp. 10–

11. **"No compunction":** Jones OH I, p. 6.

Mail swelling: For example, Dirksen, "Mr. Dirksen Goes to Congress," *New Outlook,* March, 1933; Hal Smith, "A Deluge of Mail Falls on Congress," *NYT,* Jan. 21, 1934, Sec. 9, p. 2.

"When the pain had been severe": Latimer OH, p. 9.

"Probably the finest"; "lawyer's lawyer": Bowmer, *Texas Parade,* May, 1968, p. 45, which also said: "As a money earner he is probably in the top five percent of Texas lawyers; as a legal scholar he is second to none. Many colleagues consider him the finest appellate lawyer in the country." **"Any kind":** Latimer. **Making him take dictation:** Latimer, Pickle.

14. The New Deal

SOURCES

Books, articles:

Albertson, *Roosevelt's Farmer;* Burner, *Herbert Hoover;* Burns, *Roosevelt: The Lion and the Fox;* Farley, *Behind the Ballots* and *The Roosevelt Years;* Freidel, *Launching the New Deal;* Henderson, *Maury Maverick;* Lash, *Eleanor and Franklin;* Leuchtenburg, *Franklin D. Roosevelt and the New Deal;* Lord, *The Wallaces of Iowa;* Manchester, *The Glory and the Dream;* Phillips, *From the Crash to the Blitz;* Nourse, *Three Years of the AAA;* Schlesinger, *The Age of Roosevelt: I, The Crisis of the Old Order; II, The Coming of the New Deal; III, The Politics of Upheaval;* Smith, *The Shattered Dream;* U.S. Department of Agriculture, *Farmers in a Changing World.*

Lionel V. Patenaude, "The New Deal and Texas" (unpublished Master's Thesis), Austin, 1953.

Charles A. Beard, "Congress Under Fire," *Yale Review,* Sept., 1932; James E. Boyle, "The Farmer's Bootstraps," *The Nation,* Jan. 11, 1933; Garet Garrett, "Notes of These Times—The Farmer," *Saturday Evening Post,* Nov. 19, 1932; J. H. Kolb, "Agriculture and Rural Life," *American Journal of Sociology,* Nov., 1933; Jonathan Mitchell, "The Farmer is Financed," *The New Republic,* June 30, 1937; William Allen White, "The Farmer Takes His Holiday," *Saturday Evening Post,* Nov. 26, 1932; "Bounty," *Fortune,* Feb., 1933; "Mr. Roosevelt's Man," *For-*

tune, April, 1934; "The Department of Agriculture," *Fortune,* April, 1936.

Corpus Christi Caller, 1931–1935.

Interviews:

Benjamin V. Cohen, Thomas G. Corcoran, Luther E. Jones.

NOTES

"Not seen": Smith, p. 223. **Farm prices in 1932:** Manchester, pp. 36–38; Freidel, p. 84. **Inflation, debt:** Davis, "The Development of Agriculture Policy Since The End of the World War," and Genung, "Agriculture in the World War Period," in U.S. Department of Agriculture, *Farmers in a Changing World;* White, "The Farmer Takes His Holiday." **$3 to $10 billion:** White, "The Farmer Takes His Holiday." **One out of eight:** Freidel, p. 84.

Deaf to their pleas; "on the very day": Freidel, pp. 85–87; Schlesinger, *Crisis,* pp. 107–9. **4,000 thrown off:** *Time,* Jan. 4, 1932. **Federal Farm Board:** Garrett, "Notes of These Times–The Farmer"; Schlesinger, *Crisis,* pp. 239–40; Freidel, p. 88. **"Surplus is ruin":** Garrett, "Notes of These Times." **Surprising agreement:** White, "The Farmer Takes His Holiday." **Hoover's solution:** Freidel, p. 88. **20,000 per month:** Freidel, p. 84. **¼ of Mississippi:** Manchester, p. 37. **"Even though":** White, "The Farmer Takes His Holiday."

Nueces County cotton production and unsold bales for 1930, 1931; "In many instances": *CCC,* Oct. 26, 1934. **683,000:** Manchester, p. 21. **"For strangers":** *CCC,* Feb. 14, 1933; see also Feb. 18. **Gulf Coast farmers in trouble:** *CCC,* 1931 *passim.* **"My boy":** T. W. Newman, in *CCC,* Feb. 15, 1935. **Going on relief:** *CCC,* Nov. 22, Dec. 30, 1932; by Jan. 20, there were 1,795 on relief (*CCC,* Jan. 20, 1933). **"No need":** Mrs. Berry, in *CCC,* Nov. 18, 1931. **500 schoolchildren:** *CCC,* Feb. 25, 1932. **Relief funds running out:** *CCC,* 1931–1932 *passim.*

Unemployed: Manchester, pp. 35–36. **"Washington, D.C., resembled":** Manchester, p. 3. **Congress returning:** "Relief after Recess," *Time,* Jan. 4, 1932. **Situation in Congress; Bonus Marchers:** Schlesinger, *Crisis,* pp. 256–61. **"Have we gone mad?":** Sen. Millard Tydings of Maryland, in "Taxation Time," *Time,* May 30, 1932. **"Looking on":** *The Forum,* Sept., 1932. **"The Monkey House":** In Pearson's "The Washington Merry-Go-Round," quoted by

Charles A. Beard, in "Congress Under Fire," *Yale Review*, Sept., 1932. **"Representative government":** *Time*, May 16, 1932.
"Hoover locks self": Manchester, p. 3. **Hoover's statements:** Schlesinger, *Crisis*, p. 231; Manchester, pp. 26–27. **Visitor authorized:** Rep. Strong of Kansas, in *Time*, April 25, 1932. **"They won't get by":** Smith, p. 80. **Couldn't bear:** Manchester, p. 22. **"The nation's needy":** *Time*, May 23, 1932. **"Nobody":** Manchester, p. 41. **Hoover dining:** Smith, pp. 96–97; Manchester, p. 23. **"Unexampled":** Schlesinger, *Crisis*, p. 232. **"Cannot squander":** *Time*, May 30, June 6, 1932. **RFC:** For example, Manchester, p. 46. **"Set his face":** Long, quoted in Smith, p. 175. **Hoover's campaign:** Smith, pp. 199–201.
   Winter of despair: Schlesinger, *Crisis*, pp. 448 ff; Manchester, pp. 54–55. **Farm revolt:** Schlesinger, *Crisis*, pp. 459–60; Manchester, pp. 58–60; Smith, p. 221. **"Wholly unworkable":** Freidel, p. 100. **Banking crisis:** Manchester, pp. 72–75.
   Revolt on the Gulf: *CCC*, Jan. 27, 1933; Patenaude, p. 259; *CCC*, May 17, Nov. 4, 1932. **38%:** *CCC*, June 10, 16, 1934. **Out of funds:** *CCC*, Feb., March, 1933. **Bonds for relief:** *CCC*, March 6, 1932, Jan. 6, 1933. **Eleven bills defeated:** *CCC*, Feb. 11, 1933. **Although:** *CCC*, Feb. 2, 1933. **"I know"; vowed:** *CCC*, Feb. 26, 1933. **"Crisis":** Burns, p. 161.
   Ended the banking crisis: Freidel, pp. 229 ff.
   AAA's organizational confusion: "Mr. Roosevelt's Man," *Fortune*, April, 1934; Lord, pp. 358–400; Albertson, Nourse, *passim*. **"The despair":** "Mr. Roosevelt's Man," *Fortune*, April, 1934.
   Would have voted against: Newlon, pp. 46–47.
   "Smiling and deferential": Corcoran.
   Wallace announcing: Jones.
Exceeding the quota: *CCC*, July 12, 1933. **White House ceremony:** *NYT*, July 29; *CCC*, July 28, 30, Aug. 1, 4, 6, 1933.
   Saving the farms: *AA-S*, March 11, 1937; *CCC*, Sept. 27, Oct. 26, 28, 29 (editorial), Nov. 5, Dec. 11, 1933; Jones.
   "Almost to the cent": *CCC*, June 17, 1935. **Johnson urging repayment:** *CCC*, Nov. 19, 1933. **Best loan-repayment record:** *CCC*, Nov. 19, 1933. **The first district:** *CCC*, March 21, 1934; see also *CCC*, May 31, 1934. **Federal Land Bank applications:** *CCC*, March 21, 1934. **HOLC loans:** *CCC*, July 30, Aug. 3, 1935. **Other programs:** *CCC*, Sept. 9, Oct. 6, 1932,

1933, 1934, *passim*, esp. Nov. 30, 1933, Jan. 10, March 10, 1934.

15. The Boss of the Little Congress

SOURCES

Books, articles:
   Steinberg, *Rayburn*.
   Edwin W. Knippa, "The Early Political Life of Lyndon B. Johnson, 1931–1937" (unpublished Master's Thesis), San Marcos, 1967.
   Hope R. Miller, "The 'Little Congress' Speaks," *Washington Post Magazine*, Feb. 11, 1934.

Oral History:
   Russell M. Brown.

Interviews:
   James P. Coleman, Jessie Hinzie, Luther E. Jones, Gene Latimer, Wingate Lucas, W. D. McFarlane, William Howard Payne, Lacey C. Sharp, James F. Swist.

NOTES

   History of Little Congress: Miller, "The 'Little Congress' Speaks," p. 6.
   Johnson's plan: Payne, Latimer, **Taken by surprise:** *Washington Evening Star*, April 28, 1933. **Questions:** Lucas, Latimer, Coleman, Payne.
   "A New Deal": *Washington Evening Star*, April 28, 1933. **"An excuse":** Latimer. **"The first time":** Payne. **Persuading newspapers to cover:** Sharp. **"One of the most":** Miller, "The 'Little Congress' Speaks." **"Every week":** Payne. **"None of us":** Lucas. **"Just crowded":** Brown OH, pp. 29–30.
   New York trip: *NYT*, May 6, 1934; Payne. After the stage show at the Music Hall, Johnson and the sergeant-at-arms on his ticket, William Howard Payne, were shown backstage to see the show's star, Jessica Dragonette. Greeting the two young men, she said, "Hello, Oklahoma," "Hello, Texas." **Other events:** Payne, Lucas, Latimer. **Keeping control:** Payne, Sharp; Miller, "The 'Little Congress' Speaks," p. 6. **"That's the Boss":** Coleman, Payne.
   Getting Brown a job: Brown OH, p. 55; Jones. **Fifty jobs:** *CCC*, Aug. 5, 1935.
   "Me and my wife"; his son's loan: Undated clipping, Garner Papers, Box 3L298, Barker Texas History Center. **The redis-**

tricting fight: *CCC,* Jan. 13, 14, 1934.
Johnson had a suggestion: Robert M.
Jackson, quoted in Knippa, pp. 35–36.
The text of the agreement is in *CCC,*
Jan. 17, 1934. **Reminding Kleberg:** *CCC,*
Jan. 16, 1934. **Leaking to the AP:** White,
The Professional, p. 110. **Headlines:** For
example, *CCC,* Jan. 13, 1934. **"Political
orphans":** CCC, Jan. 16, 1934.
Unconditional surrender: *CCC,* Jan. 17,
1934, in which the Garner letter to Farley
is quoted. See also *WP,* Jan. 17, 1934.
"For days": White, p. 110. **"Who in the
hell":** Steinberg, *Rayburn,* p. 159. **Not
half amused:** McFarlane, Young.

16. In Tune

SOURCES

The description of Lyndon Johnson's
activities and philosophy as Kleberg's secretary, and of his relationship with Roy
Miller, is based primarily on interviews
with Luther E. Jones and Gene Latimer.
Unless otherwise noted, the description
comes from these interviews.

Books and articles:
Adams, *Texas Democracy.*
Edwin W. Knippa, "The Early Political
Life of Lyndon B. Johnson, 1931–1937"
(unpublished Master's Thesis), San Mar-
cos, 1967.
Corpus Christi Caller, 1931–1935.

Oral Histories:
Malcolm Bardwell, Mary Elliott Bots-
ford, Russell M. Brown, Ben Crider, Sam
Fore, Welly K. Hopkins, Luther E. Jones,
Carroll Keach, Gene Latimer.

Interviews:
Edward A. Clark, Willard Deason,
Thomas C. Ferguson, Mrs. Sam Fore,
Welly K. Hopkins, RJB, SHJ, Carroll
Keach, Dale Miller, Ernest Morgan, Dan-
iel J. Quill, Mary Rather, Horace Rich-
ards, Emmett Shelton, Wilton Woods.

NOTES

Description of Roy Miller: Jones, Lati-
mer, Dale Miller, Quill; Brown OH; *Texas
Under Many Flags,* Vol. IV, p. 37; Adams,
pp. 65–66; *AA,* undated, 1917; "Miller,
Roy," Vertical File, Barker Texas History
Center, Univ. of Texas; "Roy Miller—
Texas Builder," *Pic-Century Magazine,*

Feb. 1938; Roy Miller, "The Relation of
Ports and Waterways to Texas Cities,"
an address delivered at the Eleventh
Annual Convention, League of Texas
Municipalities, May 10, 1923, *Texas Municipalities,* 1923.
Seemingly unlimited: Miller told the
Texas Board of Tax Equalization in 1936
that he spent $148,000 annually for "good
will." Populist Congressman W. D. Mc-
Farlane reported to Franklin Roosevelt
in 1939 that photostatic copies of Miller's
"expense accounts for 1934–5 show that
Miller spent more than $250,000 from two
sulphur companies before the Legislatures
at Austin and Washington and they are
but one of many employments of such a
nature that he has. His expenses the past
few years according to his increased activities have greatly increased" (McFarlane to Roosevelt, May 15, 1939, OF 300–
12, Roosevelt Papers). As will be seen
later, Miller was also receiving funds from
Brown & Root. **"Perhaps the most effective":** *AA-S,* Dec. 14, 1946. **"A surprising
number":** Miller Vertical File, Barker
History Center. **"Carry only":** *Time,* Oct.
30, 1933. **"Roy Miller would call":** Brown
OH, p. 39. **Adams' advice:** For example,
on Feb. 21, 1934, Adams wrote Johnson: ". . . I am very much interested
in seeing your artistic side developed, and
for this reason am enclosing for you two
tickets for an evening in the Historic
Homes and Gardens of Virginia" ("Public Activities–Biographic Information–
Secretary to Congressman Kleberg," Box
73, LBJA SF).
Child labor: See, for example, *CCC,*
Jan. 28, 1935. **Tarring the liberal:** Hopkins; Miller, quoted in *CCC,* July 22, 1932.
Advocating federal sales tax: *CCC,* July
21, 1932. **"His manner":** Miller.
Dancing only with the wives: Harbin,
quoted in Knippa, p. 28; Brown OH, p. 86;
Latimer. **"I can't call him Henry":** Brown
OH, pp. 7–8. **"Executive type":** Brown OH,
p. 8. **"Lyndon goes":** Brown OH, p. 86.
"Basic orientation": Brown OH, pp. 39–
40. Excerpts from Oral History interviews
conducted by Michael L. Gillette, Chief of
Oral History at the Lyndon Baines Johnson Library, with Jones and Brown are
revealing. Jones OH—Gillette: "He seems
to have been considerably more of a liberal than Representative Kleberg in the
early thirties." Jones: "I know that would
be easy to imagine, but I'm not sure that's
true. Not really more liberal." Brown OH
—Gillette: "Did you get the feeling that
[Roy Miller] was sort of a mentor for

Kleberg?" Brown: "No. He was a mentor for Lyndon Johnson." Gillette: "Oh, was he?" Brown: "Yes . . . He didn't agree with Roosevelt and the Roosevelt policies at all. I would have to say that Lyndon was really getting himself oriented politically at the time. I think Lyndon's earliest orientation was on the conservative side, you know, with Kleberg and Roy Miller and those people. He didn't become a great liberal until quite a bit later." **"I don't think":** Jones OH II, p. 9. **"Winning,"** etc.: Jones interview.

"The brightest secretary": Maverick, quoted in *San Marcos Daily News*, March 5, 1934. Sam Johnson's handwritten note is found on a copy of the clipping, in "Public Activities–Biographic Information–Secretary to Congressman Kleberg," Box 73, LBJA SF.

"Your own man": Brown OH, pp. 57–58. **Moving his desk:** Latimer interview and OH, p. 6. **Grabbing the credit:** For examples of how his press releases were reprinted in the press, see *CCC*, 1933–1934. An article on April 12, 1934, begins: "Information contained in a telegram last night from Lyndon B. Johnson, secretary . . ." **Building up his own organization in the district:** Latimer, Jones, Quill, Mrs. Sam Fore; Sam Fore, in Knippa, p. 29. **Boat trip:** Patman, quoted in Steinberg, *Sam Johnson's Boy*, pp. 80–81.

Ambassadorship resolution: *CCC*, Feb. 28, March 5, 1933. See also *CCC*, Oct. 21, 1933.

San Antonio postmastership: Kleberg to McIntyre, Feb. 18, 1934, Roosevelt to Garner, March 12, 1934, Howe to Farley, March 12, 1934, OF400-Texas, Roosevelt Papers; Quill; *CCC*, June 15, 1934; among the influential persons whom Johnson persuaded to support Quill was Roy Miller. **"A first-class war":** Brown OH, pp. 52–53. **"That's what"; "way above"; immediately handling:** Quill.

Becoming friends with Maverick: Brown OH, pp. 89–90. **Patronage post:** *CCC*, Dec. 7, 1934.

"Do you suppose?": Wirtz, quoted in Brown OH, pp. 64–66. **Elmer Pope:** Brown OH, p. 63. **"Like youngsters":** Hopkins. **Wirtz and Ferguson coming to Washington:** Ferguson. **"Knew Washington"; "could get you in":** Hopkins, Clark, Ferguson.

Getting jobs: Keach, Latimer, Crider OH, RJB; Brown OH. **Bell:** to Johnson, 1937. **"Didn't make you rich":** Deason. **"The best job":** Crider OH, p. 9. **"Very appre-**ciative":** Morgan. **"Had sense enough":** Deason. **Deason's career shift:** Deason, Richards. **Kellam's personality:** Woods, SHJ, Shelton. **Racing to Austin:** Latimer. **Shuffling papers:** Deason. **Johnson's domination:** Clark. **Kellam crying:** Latimer. **"I remember":** Brown OH, p. 59.

Passing on Deason's job to Richards: Deason, Richards. **Federal Land Bank jobs:** Deason, SHJ; Crider OH.

17. Lady Bird

SOURCES

The primary source of information for this chapter is the author's ten interviews with Mrs. Johnson.

Books and articles:
Two biographies—Montgomery, *Mrs. LBJ*, and Smith, *The President's Lady*—present an idealized picture of her life, at variance with that given by other sources.

Helpful is the script of "A National Tribute to Lady Bird Johnson, on the Occasion of Her Sixty-Fifth Birthday," presented at the LBJ Library, Dec. 11, 1977.

Among scores of magazine articles on Lady Bird Johnson, the most revealing are Blake Clark, "Lyndon Johnson's Lady Bird," *Reader's Digest*, November, 1963; Elizabeth Janeway, "The First Lady: A Professional at Getting Things Done," *Ladies' Home Journal*, April, 1964; Barbara Klaw, "Lady Bird Remembers," *American Heritage*, December, 1980; Flora Rheta Schreiber, "Lady Bird Johnson's First Years of Marriage," *Woman's Day*, December, 1967; "The New First Lady," *Time*, Nov. 29, 1963; "The First Lady Bird," *Time*, Aug. 28, 1964.

Oral Histories:
Sherman Birdwell, Russell Brown, Ellen Taylor Cooper, Daniel J. Quill.

Other interviews:
Mary Elliott Botsford, Willard Deason, D. B. Hardeman, Rebekah Johnson, Sam Houston Johnson, L. E. Jones, Gene Latimer.

NOTES

Democratic primary results: 1931, Blanco County Clerk's office; 1932, *SAE*, July 25, 1932. **Because it was Johnson's home:** Among those who report this feeling are Stella Gliddon, Clayton Stribling, Gene Latimer. **"But they just didn't":** Latimer. **"Same old Lyndon":** Stribling. **A familiar figure:** Knispel, Richards.

Johnson at the King Ranch: Ethel Davis. **Johnson's correspondence with Mrs. Kleberg:** SHJ.

Thomas Jefferson Taylor description: *Time,* Aug. 28, 1964. Also Steinberg, *Sam Johnson's Boy,* pp. 83–4. **"But making money":** Wright Patman, quoted in Steinberg, p. 83. **"Peonage":** Eugenia Lassater, quoted in *Time,* Aug. 28, 1964. **"He looked on Negroes":** Tom Taylor, quoted in *Time,* Aug. 28, 1964. **Negroes called him:** Steinberg, p. 84.

Origin of nickname "Lady Bird": Among others, *Time,* Aug. 28, 1964. **Description of Lady Bird's mother:** Smith, pp. 29–30. **"I remember":** Smith, p. 32.

Playing around the store: Montgomery, p. 10; Smith, p. 33. **Being sent to Alabama:** Smith, p. 33.

"She opened my spirit": Smith, p. 35. **Loved to read; finished Ben-Hur:** *Time,* Aug. 28, 1964. **"Perhaps":** Janeway, "The First Lady." To another reporter, she once said of Karnack: "It was a lonesome place, but I wasn't lonely. It's true that I didn't know many youngsters of my own age and background, and that proved difficult later when I had to mingle with others in school. But I had the whole wide world to roam in. And I had Aunt Effie." (*National Observer,* April 24, 1967.) **"I came from":** Interview with author. **Her high school years:** Steinberg, pp. 85–6; Schreiber, "Lady Bird Johnson's First Years," Janeway, "The First Lady" and *Time* articles. **They remember a shyness:** *Time,* Aug. 28, 1964. **"I don't recommend"; "drifts of magnolia":** Janeway, "The First Lady." **Fear of being valedictorian; praying to get smallpox; she still remembers exact grades:** Smith, p. 36; Montgomery, p. 13. **Newspaper joked:** Steinberg, p. 86. This is not the picture of Mrs. Johnson given in the Smith biography, in which Dorris Powell is quoted (p. 34) as saying that Mrs. Johnson was "a thinker even as a little girl. She was popular, pretty and an A-1 student, but she did not run with the herd. She was never identified with any group; she chose her friends because of their individual qualities, how they appealed to her."

At University of Texas: *Time,* Aug. 28, 1964. **Soloman and Benefield:** Quoted in Schreiber, "Lady Bird Johnson's First Years of Marriage." **Taking pains to make sure she wouldn't have to return to Kar-**

nack: Interview with author. **"Because I thought":** Smith, p. 38.

"Unlimited" charge account: Smith, p. 38. **She still dressed:** Steinberg, p. 87. **Her only coat:** *Time,* Aug. 28, 1964. **"No glamour girl":** Hardeman. **Her classmates remember:** Steinberg, p. 87. **"Gene made me":** Steinberg, p. 87; Smith, p. 37. **"Stingy":** Eugenia Lassater, quoted in *Time,* Aug. 28, 1964.

Lady Bird's first meeting with Lyndon: Interviews with author, which expanded on Smith, p. 40; Steinberg, p. 82; and numerous magazine articles. **"Some kind of joke":** Smith, pp. 40–41. **"Excessively thin":** "A National Tribute," p. 3. **Her feelings for his father and mother; "Extremely modest":** Interviews with author. **Exploding at Birdwell:** Birdwell OH, p. 11.

Cap'n Taylor liking Lyndon: Ruth Taylor, quoted in Schreiber, "Lady Bird Johnson's First Years of Marriage." **"I could tell":** Smith, p. 41. **Kissing him, and scandalizing the neighbor:** Smith, pp. 41–2. The neighbor was Dorris Powell. **"I have never":** Ellen Taylor Cooper OH, p. 11. **"Moth-and-flame":** Janeway, "The First Lady"; Smith, p. 40.

"This invariable rhythm": Latimer, Jones. **"My dear Bird":** Johnson to Lady Bird, Oct. 24, 1934, quoted in "A National Tribute," p. 4. **"I see something":** Johnson to Lady Bird, undated, quoted in "A National Tribute," p. 5. **"Every interesting place"; "Why must we wait?":** Johnson to Lady Bird, Sept. 18, 1934, quoted in "A National Tribute."

"Dearest": Lady Bird to Johnson, undated, quoted in "A National Tribute."

"When we were on the phone"; getting engaged: Interviews with author, which expanded on Smith, pp. 42–3, and numerous magazine articles.

The marriage: Smith, pp. 44–5; Quill OH, p. 8 ff. **Telephoning Boehringer:** *Time,* Aug. 28, 1964. **Lyndon telephoned his mother:** Smith, p. 44.

"Just ordered her": Botsford. **Acquaintances were shocked:** A number of Texans in Washington at the time described Johnson ordering around his new wife, but asked not to be quoted by name on this particular subject. **"He'd embarrass her":** Lucas. **"I don't know":** Lucas; other acquaintances.

Exploring alone: Interviews with author. **"I was always prepared":** Brown OH, pp. 71–2. **Couldn't get him to read:** Steinberg, p. 100. **"He early announced":** Interview with author. **And she did them:** Steinberg, p. 255. She was to tell a reporter: "Lyndon is the leader. Lyndon sets the pattern. I execute what he wants. Lyndon's wishes dominate our household." **"I had never swept":** Smith, p. 57. **Maverick dinner:** Mrs. Maverick, quoted in Schreiber, "Lady Bird Johnson's First Years of Marriage." **"Get the furniture insured":** Brown OH, p. 11. **Her graciousness:** Attested to by dozens who knew her.

18. Rayburn

SOURCES

Books and articles:

Alsop and Catledge, *The 168 Days;* Anderson and Boyd, *Confessions of a Muckraker;* Burns, *Roosevelt: The Lion and the Fox;* Cocke, *The Bailey Controversy in Texas;* Daniels, *Frontier on the Potomac* and *White House Witness;* Donovan, *Conflict and Crisis;* Dorough, *Mr. Sam;* Douglas, *The Court Years* and *Go East, Young Man;* Dulaney, Phillips and Reese, *Speak, Mr. Speaker;* Freidel, *Launching the New Deal;* Gantt, *The Chief Executive in Texas;* Halberstam, *The Powers That Be;* Leuchtenburg, *Franklin D. Roosevelt and the New Deal;* Link, *Wilson: The New Freedom* and *Woodrow Wilson and the Progressive Era;* Miller, *Fishbait;* Moley, *After Seven Years* and *27 Masters of Politics;* Mooney, *Roosevelt and Rayburn;* Parrish, *Securities Regulation and the New Deal;* Schlesinger, *The Age of Roosevelt:* I *The Crisis of the Old Order,* II *The Coming of the New Deal,* III *The Politics of Upheaval;* Steinberg, *Sam Rayburn;* Timmons, *Garner of Texas.*

Joseph Alsop and Robert Kintner, "Never Leave Them Angry," *Saturday Evening Post,* Jan. 18, 1941; David L. Cohn, "Mr. Speaker," *Atlantic Monthly,* Oct., 1942; Robert Coughlan, "Proprietors of the House," *Life,* Feb. 14, 1955; Edward N. Gadsby, "Historical Development of the S.E.C.—The Government View," Foreword by William O. Douglas, *The George Washington Law Review,* Oct., 1959; D. B. Hardeman, "The Unseen Side of the Man They Called Mr. Speaker," *Life,* Dec. 1, 1961; Paul F. Healy, "They're Just Crazy About Sam," *Sat. Eve. Post,* Nov. 24, 1951; James M. Landis, "The Legislative History of the Securities Act of 1933," *The George Washington Law Review,* Oct., 1959; W. H. Lawrence, "The Texan Who Rides Herd on Congress," *NYT Magazine,*

March 14, 1943; Dale Miller, "A Requiem for Rayburn," *Dallas Magazine,* Jan., 1962; W. B. Ragsdale, *U.S. News and World Report,* Oct. 23, 1961; R. Tucker, "Master for the House," *Collier's,* Jan. 5, 1935; Jerry Voorhiis, "Mr. Rayburn of Texas," *The New Republic,* July 10, 1944. William S. White, *NYT Magazine:* "Sam Rayburn—The Untalkative Speaker," Feb. 27, 1949; "Then Martin, Now Rayburn, And So On," Feb. 6, 1955; "The Two Texans Who Will Run Congress," Dec. 30, 1956.

Fortune: "The Legend of Landis," Aug., 1934; "SEC," June, 1940. *Time:* "Leader Apparent," Dec. 14, 1936; "Yataghans at 15 Blocks," April 18, 1938; "Mister Speaker," Sept. 27, 1943; "Sam Rayburn, Texan," Jan. 14, 1946.

Bascom N. Timmons, "The Indomitable Mr. Sam," *Fort Worth Star-Telegram* series, Oct. 11–18, 1961.

Oral Histories:

Helen Gahagan Douglas, Marvin Jones, James M. Landis, Wright Patman, Henry A. Wallace.

Interviews:

Andrew Biemiller, Richard Bolling, Emanuel Celler, Benjamin V. Cohen, Sterling Cole, James P. Coleman, Thomas G. Corcoran, Helen Gahagan Douglas, H. G. Dulaney, O. C. Fisher, D. B. Hardeman, Kenneth Harding, John Holton, Welly K. Hopkins, Edouard V. M. Izac, Walter Jenkins, Lady Bird Johnson, SHJ, L. E. Jones, Murray Kempton, Eugene J. Keogh, DeWitt Kinard, Gene Latimer, Wingate Lucas, George H. Mahon, Gerald C. Mann, W. D. McFarlane, Dale Miller, Frank C. Oltorf, William Howard Payne, Elwyn Rayden, Elizabeth Rowe, James H. Rowe, Lacey Sharp, James F. Swist, Harold Young.

NOTES

"The rich richer," etc.: *CR,* 63rd Congress, 1 Session, May 6, 1913, pp. 1247–51. **"Never stopped hating":** Coughlan, "Proprietors of the House." **"Will not forget":** White, "Then Martin, Now Rayburn." **"As long as I honor":** Quoted in Steinberg, p. 84.

Rayburn's youth: Steinberg, pp. 4–9; Dorough, pp. 43–61; Dulaney, p. 10. **"The people . . . on their trek":** Quoted in Dulaney, p. 10. **The first year:** Steinberg, p. 6; Dorough, p. 58; Dulaney, p. 10. **"I plowed and hoed":** Rayburn speech, May

19, 1916, quoted in Dulaney, p. 10.
Picture of General Lee: Dorough, p. 59.
"Any show": Steinberg, p. 38. **"Many a time"; "loneliness consumes people":** Cohn, "Mr. Speaker"; Rayburn speech at 1952 Democratic National Convention, quoted in Dulaney, pp. 10–11.
"Dominated"; "his tones": Bowers, *My Life,* quoted in Steinberg, p. 14. **"I didn't go":** Alsop and Kintner, "Never Leave Them Angry." **Practicing:** Dorough, p. 65; Steinberg, p. 8. **"I'm going":** Steinberg, p. 8.
"I'm not asking you": *CR,* 76th Congress, 3 Session, Sept. 19, 1940, p. 18747; Steinberg, p. 9. **At the railroad station:** Rayburn interview in Ragsdale, *USN&WR,* Oct. 23, 1961. **"Sam, be a man!":** Steinberg, p. 20.
At college: Steinberg, pp. 10–12.
Campaigning: Dorough, pp. 76–77; Steinberg, pp. 16–17; Lawrence, "The Texan Who Rides Herd"; Rayden. **"I'm not trying":** Rayburn speech, 1912, quoted in Dulaney, p. 20. **Gardner:** Steinberg, p. 16; Dorough, p. 77.
"My untarnished name": Dulaney, p. 12; Hardeman. **Pharr's soda:** Rayburn to Ridgway, quoted in Dulaney, p. 18. **Handed check back:** Dulaney, p. 20. **"We often wish":** Mrs. W. M. Rayburn to Sam Rayburn, March 9, 1909. **"No one":** Among many, who knew Rayburn at different periods of his life, who said it to the author: McFarlane, Hardeman, Miller, Mahon. **"I've always wanted responsibility":** Alsop and Kintner, "Never Leave Them Angry."
Bailey episode: Cocke, *passim;* Dorough, p. 79; Steinberg, pp. 17–18. **"In dark moods":** Robert J. Donovan, *NY Herald Tribune,* Nov. 17, 1961. **Campbell episode:** Dorough, p. 106.
"No degrees": Hardeman. **"He had a reputation":** Ridgway, quoted in Dorough, p. 89. **"Once you lied":** Hardeman OH, pp. 116–17.
"Just" and "fair": Dorough, p. 98. **"Whether or not":** Dorough, p. 104; Hardeman.
"If you have anything": Alsop and Kintner, "Never Leave Them Angry." **Election as Speaker:** Dorough, pp. 96–97; Steinberg, pp. 20–22. **"Cottonpatch yell":** Dulaney, p. 19. **"Up in Fannin County":** Rayburn speech, Jan. 10, 1911, quoted in Dulaney, p. 19. **As Speaker:** Dorough, p. 108; Steinberg, p. 23.
Redistricting: Steinberg, p. 25. **"When I was":** Rayburn, July 16, 1912, quoted in Dulaney, p. 23.

His first speech in Congress: *CR,* 63rd Congress, 1 Session, May 6, 1913, pp. 1247–51. **Railroad regulation bill:** Link, *Woodrow Wilson,* p. 68; Steinberg, p. 43. **"With admiration":** Wilson to Rayburn, June 9, 1914, quoted in Steinberg, p. 45. **Confrontation with Wilson:** Timmons, *Fort Worth Star-Telegram,* Oct. 12, 1961; Hardeman; Steinberg, p. 52.
Refusing lobbyists' meals, travel expenses: Alsop and Kintner, "Never Leave Them Angry"; Dulaney, p. 24; Hardeman. **One trip:** Dulaney, p. 24. **"Not for sale":** Dorough, p. 85; Steinberg, p. xii. **$15,000:** Steinberg, p. 346.
Pumping of a piston: Daniels, *Frontier,* p. 58. **Holding the two Congressmen apart:** Miller, p. 242; Hardeman. **"Amidst the multitude":** Sam Rayburn Scrapbooks, Rayburn Library; McFarlane, Hardeman. **"Young in years":** Rep. William C. Adamson, quoted in Steinberg, p. 45.
"Someday": Alsop and Kintner, "Never Leave Them Angry." **"The only way":** Steinberg, p. 33.
"My ambition": Rayburn to Katy Thomas, Feb. 2, 1922, in Dulaney, p. 35. **"Almost kills me":** Alsop and Kintner, "Never Leave Them Angry." **Standing in the aisle etc.:** *Time,* Dec. 14, 1936. **"The smartest thing":** Dulaney, p. 37; Miller, p. 234.
Cochran Hotel: Alsop and Kintner, "Never Leave Them Angry."
Becoming a part of the hierarchy: Timmons, *Fort Worth Star-Telegram,* Oct. 11, 1961. **"Indefinable knack":** Richard Lyons, "Mr. Sam Made History in 48 Years' Service." *WP,* B9, Nov. 17, 1961. **"Sam stands hitched":** *WP,* Nov. 17, 1961. **"Employed him":** Alsop and Kintner, "Never Leave Them Angry." **Began to use:** Hardeman.
"He would help you": Bolling. **"The House soon spots":** Jones OH, pp. 110–12.
"A lonesome, dark day here": Rayburn to H. B. Savage, 1919, quoted in Dulaney, p. 32. **Waiting in silence:** Steinberg, pp. 63–76; Hardeman, Harding.
"Truth-in-Securities" Act: Freidel, pp. 340–50. **"I want it":** Alsop and Kintner, "Never Leave Them Angry." **Problems with the "Truth in Securities" Act:** Schlesinger, *Coming,* pp. 440–42; Moley, *After Seven Years,* pp. 175–84; Parrish, pp. 42–72. **Rayburn paid a visit:** Moley, *After,* pp. 179–81.
Rewriting the bill: Cohen, Corcoran; Landis OH and Landis, "The Legislative History." **"A countryman":** Cohen. **"Rayburn who decided":** Landis OH, p.161. **"I

had thought": Landis, "The Legislative History," p. 37. **"Strong . . . right . . . just":** Cohen. **"I confess"; "I went back"; "very obscene"; "Now Sam":** Landis OH, pp. 165–70. **"A genius":** Corcoran. **"Temporary dictatorship":** Parrish, p. 112. **Moley was to write incorrectly:** In *After Seven Years*, p. 181, and in *27 Masters*, p. 243.

Complexities in full House: Corcoran; Landis, "The Legislative History," p. 41. **In conference committee:** Landis, "The Legislative History," pp. 43–46; Landis OH, p. 169; Corcoran. **On every crucial point:** Freidel, p. 349.

Securities Exchange Commission fight: Parrish, *passim;* Schlesinger, *Coming,* 456–70; Gadsby, "Historical Development"; Hardeman, Corcoran. **In his own committee:** Parrish, p. 132.

Public Utilities Act: Parrish, pp. 145–74; Schlesinger, *Politics,* pp. 302–24; Steinberg, pp. 125–29; Hardeman, Corcoran, Cohen. **"You talk":** Roosevelt, in Schlesinger, *Politics,* p. 314. **Carpenter's threat:** Steinberg, p. 127. **A rare public statement:** Rayburn speech on NBC, Aug. 30, 1935, in Dulaney, p. 59.

"Few people": *NYT,* April 2, 1934. **"He did":** Halberstam, p. 246. **"I always":** Hardeman, "Unseen Side." **"Let the other":** Dulaney, p. 372. **"In on the borning":** Pearson article, March 3, 1955, quoted in Anderson and Boyd, pp. 279–80. **"I cut him":** Miller, pp. 231–32. **"The 'Sam Rayburn Commission' ":** Douglas, *George Washington Law Review,* Oct., 1959, pp. 3–4. **Putting FDR's picture beside Lee's:** Hardeman; *Time,* Sept. 27, 1943.

Given patronage: For example, Steinberg, p. 120. **"A man in the shadows":** R. Tucker, "Master for the House." **"If you were":** Bolling. **"A very big mistake":** White, "Sam Rayburn," *NYT Magazine,* Feb. 27, 1949. **Never ask you again:** Hardeman.

"Always": Hardeman. **"She-e-e-e-t":** Miller p. 230. **"Afraid":** Harding. **Pitied him:** Hardeman, Harding, Rayden, Holton. **"For all my children":** Steinberg, p. 35. **"They crawled all over him":** Hardeman, "Unseen Side." **"I was the joke":** Steinberg, p. 207.

Metze Jones: Dorough, pp. 183–84; Miller, pp. 228–29; Steinberg, pp. 78–79. Miller says that Rayburn later in life saw another woman once or twice a week, but Miller says, "I never found out who she was" (p. 229). Rayburn's other aides do not believe this is correct. **"A great hurry":**

Steinberg, p. 79. **"Oh, I'm so cranky":** Hardeman, "Unseen Side." **"Kept watch"; "It is true":** Miller, pp. 228–29.

"I never felt that [the hostess] knew or cared": Steinberg, p. 37. **Trying to prolong the hours:** Hardeman, Rayden, Harding. **"Sometimes I had something planned, but":** Harding. **"Those who went":** Steinberg, p. 200. **"God what I would give":** Steinberg, p. 151; Dulaney, p. 176. **Walking alone on weekends:** Hardeman, Harding.

"You are one member": Rayburn to Sam Ealy Johnson, Feb. 22, 1937, "General Correspondence" file, Rayburn Library. **Limited by custom:** Latimer, Jones.

Inviting "Mr. Sam" to dinner: Mrs. Johnson. **Sitting beside Lyndon's bed:** Steinberg, p. 159; Hardeman.

Johnson's feelings: Hopkins, Latimer, Jones, Lucas. **Coleman's feelings:** Coleman. **The Coleman election:** Lucas, Coleman, Payne. **"My God":** Swist.

"That burning ambition"; trying to get him a job in Texas: Hopkins. **Wirtz offering a partnership:** Jones.

At Law School: Brown OH, pp. 1, 2, 5, 7, 19–20; Jones.

College presidency: Jones. **"I want to be":** Dale Miller. **The job offer:** Jones, Mrs. Johnson; Corcoran, who heard the story later.

Rayburn going to see Connally: Connally to his biographer, Steinberg; quoted in Steinberg, *Sam Johnson's Boy,* p. 94. **Announcing and retracting the Kinard appointment:** Kinard, Corcoran. **"When I":** McFarlane, SHJ.

19. "Put Them to Work!"

SOURCES

Books, articles, theses, documents:

Davis, *Youth in the Depression;* Lash, *Eleanor and Franklin;* Lindley, *A New Deal for Youth;* Manchester, *The Glory and the Dream.*

Edwin W. Knippa, "The Early Political Life of Lyndon B. Johnson, 1931–1937" (unpublished Master's Thesis), San Marcos, 1967. Deborah L. Self, "The National Youth Administration in Texas, 1935–1939 (unpublished Master's Thesis), Lubbock, 1974.

Federal Security Agency, "Final Report of the National Youth Administration: Fiscal Years 1936–1943," Washington, 1943. NYA, "Administrative and Program

Operation of the NYA, June 25, 1935—January 1, 1937," Washington, D.C., 1937. NYA, "Digest—NYA in Texas," Feb., 1939. NYA, "Facing the Problems of Youth: The Work and Objectives of the NYA," Washington, 1936. Mary Rodgers, "Youth Gets Its Chance," a mimeographed pamphlet of the New York NYA, 1938.

George Creel, "Dollars for Youth," *Collier's,* Sept. 28, 1935; Walter Davenport, "Youth Won't Be Served," *Collier's,* March 7, 1936; "Texas Gets Better Roadsides," *Engineering News-Record,* Sept. 23, 1937; "Government and Youth," *Life,* May 15, 1940; "Texas Tech Again Receives NYA Funds," *Texas Tech Magazine,* Oct. 1937; "Second Start," *Time,* July 27, 1936; "NYA," *The State Week,* Nov. 14, 1935; "NYA—'Marginal' Jobs Developed for Youth," *The State Week,* May 7, 1936.

Barker Scrapbooks, Barker Texas History Center. Birdwell Scrapbooks, LBJL. Johnson NYA Papers, LBJL.

Oral Histories:
Sherman Birdwell, Richard R. Brown, Willard Deason, L. E. Jones, Jr., Carroll Keach, Jesse Kellam, Ray Roberts, Fenner Roth.

Interviews:
Willard Deason, Edward A. Clark, Mary Henderson, Lady Bird Johnson, L. E. Jones, Ernest Morgan, J. J. Pickle, Horace Richards, Vernon Whiteside, one NYA staff member who asked not to be quoted by name.
"NYA Group Interview" conducted by William S. White with Willard Deason, J. J. Pickle, Ray Roberts, Fenner Roth, Albert W. Brisbane, C. P. Little.

NOTES

"Moments of real terror": Eleanor Roosevelt, quoted in Lash, p. 536. **College attendance falling:** Lindley, p. 158. **"Shoes":** Lindley, p. 195. **"Scalpels":** Lindley, p. 12. **A study:** Davis, pp. 18–19. **"The more":** Lindley, p. 193. **5 million:** NYA, "Facing the Problems of Youth," p. 5.
"Maybe": Quoted in Lindley, p. 21. **"Only boys":** Davis, p. 5. **Comparison with old West:** Davis, p. 29. **"The worst thing":** Davis, p. 5. **"To workers":** Manchester, p. 21. **2.25 million more:** Lindley, p. 7. **"Boys and girls":** Davis, p. 44. **"Lost generation":** Quoted in Lash, p. 550. **No fewer than 700,000:** Davenport, "Youth Won't

Be Served." **"A civilization":** Eleanor Roosevelt, quoted in Lash, p. 538. **Early began pressing:** Lash, pp. 536–554 is the best description of Mrs. Roosevelt's catalytic role in the creation of the NYA. The following quotes are from those pages. Discussion between Eleanor and Franklin is Fulton Oursler, *Behold the Dreamer,* quoted in Lash, pp. 539–540. **"That was another side":** Lash, p. 540.
"Minimum": NYA, "Facing," p. 9
Recruiting Deason: Deason OH IV, pp. 17–18; Deason. **Recruiting Kellam:** Knippa, p. 53; Birdwell OH. **Central staff:** Rodgers, pp. 209–210. **White Stars:** Self, p. 20; Deason, Jones, Richards, Whiteside.
Creating the program: Self, "The NYA"; Lady Bird Johnson; Jones, Deason OHs and interviews; NYA "Facing," p. 9. **Roadside parks:** "Texas Gets Better Roadsides," *Engineering News-Record*; Knippa, pp. 58 ff; Johnson to Brown, July 29, 1936, Box 3, JNYA Papers; Griffith to Johnson, Aug. 27, 1936, Box 7, JNYA Papers; Self, "The NYA," pp. 82–85; Deason and Deason OHs and interviews; Jones.
Hiring Henderson: Jones, Jones OH I, pp. 14–15; Mary Henderson. **Williamson Creek:** *AA,* May 25, 1941. **Quota:** Self, p. 35. **Additional projects:** Birdwell Scrapbooks; "Texas Gets Better Roadsides," *Engineering News-Record*; Griffith to Johnson, Aug. 27, 1936, Box 7, JNYA Papers.
Resistance from local officials and Taylor: Deason. **"The greatest salesman":** Deason.
Directives: Lindley, pp. 184–188. **"A lot of travel":** Deason OH V, p. 11. **Dean Moore:** Self, pp. 54–55, 63. **Red tape:** Self, pp. 53–57; Deason; Morgan. **Other state directors:** Rodgers, pp. 22–24, 210–212.
The staff was very young: Analysis of staff résumés in Box 5, JNYA Papers, and interviews cited in Sources. **"Very nervous":** Morgan. **Dictating:** Mary Henderson. **"The nature"; "tomorrow"; competition:** NYA Group Interview, pp. 22, 23, 28. **"Goddammit"; cursing:** Morgan. **Hurting Henderson, other staffer:** SHJ, confirmed by others. **Without a pause:** Jones. **"I hope":** staff member. **Gas lights:** Steinberg, *Sam Johnson's Boy,* p. 97; Deason, Birdwell OH, pp. 14–15.
"Lyndon is the leader": Lady Bird Johnson, quoted by Schreiber, "Lady Bird Johnson's First Years of Marriage," *Woman's Day,* Dec. 1967. **Guests:** Jones; Deason; Mrs. Johnson, quoted in Self, pp. 23–4. **"Hardest thing":** Deason OH IV, p. 25. **"Lyndon would":** Birdwell OH II,

p. 14, OH I, pp. 7–8. **"We weren't off duty"**: Deason OH IV, p. 22; Deason. **"When he woke up"**: Mrs. Johnson.

"The sifting out": Deason. **Morgan's story**: Morgan. **"He knew"**: Richards. **"We knew"**: Jones OH I, p. 12. **"Let's play awhile"**: Deason OH II, p. 22.

Inspiring: Deason, Birdwell OHs; Henderson; Jones. **"Put them to work!"**: Birdwell, quoted in Knippa, p. 55; Deason. **"Deep days of the Depression"**: Deason. **8,000 teenagers**: Morgan. **"I saw him get angry"**: Morgan. **"Absolutely frantic"**; **"Charlie! Charlie!"**: Mary Henderson, Charlie's wife. **"Sense of destiny"**: Deason OH IV, op. 10, 11. **"I'm working"**: Mary Henderson. **"I named my only son"**: Roth OH, p. 12. **"It all went back to that NYA"**: Deason. **"I was very inept"**: Keach OH II, p. 5. **Johnson's reason for making Keach his chauffeur**: Latimer.

Johnson on Congress Avenue: Clark. **"Stand with me"**: Clark.

"A very bad start": Williams, quoted in *Time*, July 27, 1936. **Texas statistics**: Self, p. 49. **Negro colleges**: Self, p. 61. **Kept students in school; deserved to be in school**: untitled form in Box 9, JNYA Papers; Self, pp. 62, 64; *Texas Tech Magazine*, Oct. 1937.

Building facilities: Self, pp. 63–4, 88. **Freshman College Centers**: Self, pp. 36–7, 69–72. **Resident training centers**: Lindley, pp. 86–108; *The Lubbock Avalanche*, June 10, 1938; *HP*, July 26, 1937. **"Theirs are not"**: Lindley, p. 69. **At San Marcos**: *Greenville Morning Herald*, Nov. 22, 1938. **"Kind of homesick"**: Lindley, p. 91. **"When you were young"**: *Brenham Banner Press*, quoted in "Digest—NYA in Texas," Feb., 1939, p. 10. **"The lads from the forks"**: *Dallas Journal*, April 1, 1938. **"Similar roadside parks"**: *Oklahoma Farmer-Stockman*, Oklahoma City, Okla., Feb. 15, 1937. **"A first-class job"**: Williams, quoted in *Texas Outlook*, May, 1937 (in Self, p. 45). **By the end of 1936**: NYA, "Administrative and Program," pp. 28–29. **Greenhouse**: "Texas Gets Better Roadsides," *Engineering News-Record*. **Plans for 1937**: *The Mission Times*, July 28, 1937; Waco *Tribune-Herald*, Feb. 28, 1937; *DMN*, Nov. 19, 1937; *Galveston Tribune*, Aug. 11, 1937.

20. The Dam

HERMAN BROWN

The story of his life is based on the author's interviews with his brother, George R. Brown; with Herman's long-time attorney and Austin political tactician, Edward A. Clark; with another of his attorneys, Herman Jones; with one of Brown & Root's Washington lobbyists, Frank C. Oltorf; with various Texas politicians who knew him, including Emmett Shelton, Harold Young, Welly K. Hopkins; with the Bureau of Reclamation official who worked most closely with him during the construction of the Marshall Ford Dam, Howard P. Bunger; and with a Pedernales Electric Co-operative official, E. Babe Smith.

ALVIN WIRTZ

Wirtz's personal papers are at the LBJL. In addition, his correspondence with Lyndon Johnson is in the LBJA SN file.

The *Seguin Enterprise*, 1925–1936.

Interviews with Wirtz's law partner, Sim Gideon, and his secretary, Mary Rather; with L. E. Jones, who was for a time his assistant; with his political intimates, Edward A. Clark and Welly K. Hopkins; with his client, George R. Brown; with Texas political friends and foes such as Charles W. Duke, Tom C. Ferguson, D. B. Hardeman, W. D. McFarlane, Daniel J. Quill, Emmett Shelton, Arthur Stehling, Tom Whitehead, Sr., Harold H. Young; with New Dealers in Washington such as Thomas G. Corcoran, Abe Fortas, Arthur (Tex) Goldschmidt, James H. Rowe; with Howard P. Bunger of the Bureau of Reclamation; with young men he advised, such as Willard Deason and Charles Herring. With Walter Jenkins and Lady Bird Johnson.

Oral Histories of Russell M. Brown, Willard Deason, Virginia Durr, Welly K. Hopkins, Robert M. Jackson, Henry Wallace, Claude Wickard, Elizabeth Wickenden.

"My dearest friend": Johnson, quoted in *AA*, June 16, 1952. **"Lodestar"**: Mrs. Johnson in *Woman's Day*, Dec., 1967. **Wirtz personality**: Durr, Hopkins, Deason OHs; Deason, Herring, Hopkins, Rowe, Goldschmidt, Hardeman, McFarlane, Clark, Gideon, Duke, Shelton, Young. **"I have not called his attention"**: Wirtz to Johnson, Dec. 12, 1939. "Independent Offices: REA," Box 36, LBJA SN.

THE DAM

The legal problems encountered in the effort to finance and build the Marshall Ford (now the Mansfield) Dam are detailed in the files of the Lower Colorado

River Authority, which are now in the LBJL, particularly Boxes 167, 168, 178, 179, 185. They are also detailed in the Alvin Wirtz Papers in the Library, particularly Box 36, and there are some revealing letters in correspondence between Herman and George Brown and Lyndon Johnson (Boxes 12 and 13, LBJA SN). They were also detailed in interviews with George Brown; with Wirtz's law partner (and his successor as LCRA counsel, Sim Gideon); with the member of the original LCRA board who accompanied Wirtz on his early trips to Washington to try to solve the problems, Tom C. Ferguson; with the Bureau of Reclamation official supervising the construction of the dam, Howard P. Bunger; and with Abe Fortas, on whose desk, as will be seen in Chapter 23, most of the problems landed. Also helpful were interviews with Arthur (Tex) Goldschmidt, Thomas G. Corcoran, and Charles Herring, and with the following present and former officials of the Bureau of Reclamation: Thomas A. Garrity, Frederick Gray, Louis Maurol, Theodore Mermel, K. K. Young.

Record Group 48, Secretary of the Interior, Central Classified Files, Selected Documents Relating to Lyndon B. Johnson, Roll 1, LBJL (Ickes Files), contains memoranda and correspondence relating to the dam, as do the files of the Lower Colorado River Authority (LCRA Files) at the LBJL.

Jones, *Fifty Billion Dollars;* Long, *Flood to Faucet.*

Comer Clay, "The Lower Colorado River Authority: A Study in Politics and Public Administration" (unpublished Ph.D. Thesis), Austin, 1948.

Colorado River Improvement Association, *Improvement of Colorado River from Austin to the Gulf,* Austin, 1915; *Application: Colorado River Project (of Texas),* presented to the Reconstruction Finance Corporation, Jan. 1933, San Antonio, 1933; Minutes, Board of Directors, Lower Colorado River Authority, 1937–1941; *Contract Between the United States of America and LCRA in Regard to Operation and Maintenance of Marshall Ford Dam and Partial Reimbursement of the United States, March 13, 1941,* "Trust Indenture—Lower Colorado River Authority to Chemical Bank & Trust Company as Trustee and the American National Bank of Austin as Co-Trustee," May 1, 1943, Twentieth Century Press, Inc., Chicago. *Report on Allocation of Construction Costs—Marshall Ford Dam*

—Colorado River Project, Texas, Washington, U. S. Dept. of Interior, 1947.

Wirtz's alliance with Insull: *Seguin Enterprise,* 1927, *passim;* Clay, pp. 58–84; Long, pp. 73–86; **Hollamon shooting:** *NYT,* Feb. 27, 1934; Duke, Hopkins. **"Run Out":** Duke. **Redistricting; renaming the dam;** Long, p. 78. **Creating the LCRA:** Clay, pp. 88–130; Ferguson, Clark, Gideon. **"I want a birthday present":** Ferguson; **AA,** Feb. 23, 1937. **Ickes considered:** Foley to Fry, Jan. 11, 1936, "General Information File—Administrative Data . . . Wirtz A J," Cong. Corres., Box 1, LCRA Papers; Foley to Wirtz, April 19, May 4; Wirtz to Foley, March 7, April 13, 26; Wirtz to Johnson, May 7; Foley to Fry, July 15, 1937, Wirtz to Farbach and to Johnson, Jan. 5, 1938, Box 36, LBJA SN; Corcoran, Ferguson, Gideon. **$85,000:** See Chapter 30. **A voice in their selection:** Bunger; Wirtz Letters and Papers, 1937, 1938, 1939, 1940, Boxes 36, 37, LBJA SN.

Lack of authorization for dam: George Brown, Ferguson; Gideon to Gottlieb, Oct. 6, 1978.

Forbidden to build it: Act of June 17, 1902, 32 Stat. 389 (43 USC 421); 33 L.D. 391–1905 of the Federal Board of Land Appeals; Mermel, Ferguson, Maurol; Gideon. **Reaffirmed:** For example, in 34 L.D. 186–1905, the Justice Department ruled: "This act contemplates that the United States shall be the full owner of irrigation works [including dams] constructed thereunder, and clearly inhibits the acquisition of property, for use in connection with an irrigation project, subject to . . . obligation to . . . a landlord holding the legal title." **If someone:** Garrity. **The difference in Texas:** Bascom Giles, Commissioner, General Land Office of Texas, "Disposition of Public Domain," *Texas Almanac,* 1941–1942, p. 338. **No one had thought to check:** Ickes file; Wirtz Papers, *passim;* Ferguson, Gideon, Fortas. **Legislative prohibitions on LCRA:** Chap. 7, 43rd Leg, 4th Called Session; Gideon. **No realistic possibility:** Gideon, Ferguson. **Wirtz's report; Wirtz's solution:** Wirtz Papers, *passim;* George Brown; Ferguson.

21. The First Campaign

SOURCES

Documents and newspapers:
The records of Johnson's campaign headquarters are in Boxes 1, 2, and 3 of the Johnson House Papers (JHP).

Austin American, Statesman, and *American-Statesman, Johnson City Record-Courier, Blanco County News*—February 23–April 14, 1937.

Oral Histories:
Sherman Birdwell, Russell Brown, Willard Deason, Virginia Durr, Welly K. Hopkins, L. E. Jones, Carroll Keach, Gene Latimer, Ray E. Lee, Daniel J. Quill, Claud Wild.

Interviews:
J. R. Buckner, Howard P. Bunger, Edward A. Clark, Ava Johnson Cox, Mary Cox, Willard Deason, Thomas C. Ferguson, Brian Fudge, Sim Gideon, Stella Gliddon, D. B. Hardeman, A. J. Harzke, Charles Herring, Welly K. Hopkins, Lady Bird Johnson, Rebekah Johnson Bobbitt (RJB), Sam Houston Johnson (SHJ), L. E. Jones, Carroll Keach, Gene Latimer, Ray E. Lee, Gerald C. Mann, Ernest Morgan, Daniel J. Quill, Mary Rather, Emmett Shelton, Carroll Smith, Warren Smith, Clayton Stribling.

NOTES

(All dates 1937 unless otherwise indicated)
"This was my chance": Johnson, quoted in Kearns, *Lyndon Johnson,* pp. 85–86. **Longer average tenure:** Cong. Directory, 75th Cong., 1st Session. **Speeding back to Austin:** Keach, Mrs. Johnson. **"A good ol' boy":** Clark.
"Not known at all": Quill OH II, p. 15. Says Birdwell: "Many of the people that were leaders in the ten counties that comprised the Tenth Congressional District at that time were people that he'd just not met" (Birdwell OH II, p. 23). **Not even mentioned:** *AS,* Feb. 23.
"Lyndon would always": Durr OH II, p. 23; OH I, p. 8. **"Just as tall":** Rather. **Wirtz's opinion of Avery:** Hopkins. **"Disapproved"; money would run out:** Brown to Johnson, July 16, 1937, "CRA: Financing (PWA)," Box 169 JHP, Ferguson, Corcoran.
Unusual instructions: Bunger. **Wirtz's reasons for supporting Johnson:** Ferguson, Hopkins, Clark, Brown OH.
Ickes' speech: *AS,* Feb. 20. **7 to 1:** *AA,* March 28. **Wirtz's advice to Johnson:** From Jones, who was clerking for Wirtz's firm and was in the room during this discussion. In his customary fashion, Jones gave a more circumspect version to the Johnson Library in OH II, p. 14. **Wirtz's**

true feelings on Court packing: Shelton, Hopkins, Jones.
Wirtz raising cash: Quill OH I and II. **Wirtz enlisting Lady Bird:** Mrs. Johnson.
Kellam letting the NYA staff know: Deason; Lee. **Deason's car:** Deason. **Latimer's drive:** Latimer. **"No matter what":** Latimer. **"Just assumed":** Deason OH II, p. 26, and see Birdwell OH I, p. 21.
Pledges to Mrs. Buchanan: *AA,* Feb. 28. **Sam Johnson's advice:** SHJ; confirmed by Cox, Gliddon, who heard the story later that same day, RJB. **Johnson and Mrs. Buchanan announcements:** *AA, AS,* March 1, 2. **"Gliddon, I want":** Gliddon. **"Johnson for Congress":** *JCR-C,* March 4.
Sam Johnson's speech: Johnson, quoted in Kearns, p. 87. **Blanco County caravan:** Cox, Gliddon.
"The late Mr. Buchanan": *AA,* March 9. **"When Miller came out":** Quill OH. **Analysis of Johnson's chances:** Shelton, Clark, Ferguson, Quill, Lee, Deason; Wild, Birdwell, Quill, Deason OHs; Austin newspapers.
"He has never voted": Avery, quoted in *AA,* April 7. **Misleading about his age:** "He soon will be 30," in *AA,* March 1. See also *JCR-C,* March 4. **"A young, young man":** Judge Will Nunn, quoted in *AA,* April 8. **Austin Trades Council:** *AS,* March 20.
Using his men: Morgan, Harzke, Deason, Herring, Keach. **"Dear Mr. Carson":** Johnson to Carson, March 10, "Briggs," Box 1, JHP. Or Johnson to Ratliff, March 18: "Dear Mr. Ratliff: My platform is very simple. I am heartily in favor of the entire broad program of President Roosevelt."
"The paramount issue": *AA,* March 1. **"Jesus Christ":** Shelton. **"I'm no hypocrite":** Shelton.
"He felt": Clark. **The Governor's Stetson:** Keach OH I, p. 8
"I am enclosing": Lee to editors, March 2. **"We appreciate":** Lee to editors, March 6. **"Here are":** Johnson to editors, March 15. **"If this is not":** Lee to editors, March 23—all from "Form Letter to All," Box 1, JHP. **"I called on":** Willie Riggs to Johnson, March 11, "Burnet," Box 1, JHP. **Weeklies coverage:** Author's analysis.
"Who the hell": Wild OH, p. 4. **$5,000 fee:** Jones OH II, p. 32. **Lady Bird did not know:** Mrs. Johnson.
"All the barbecue": Clark. **"A giving away":** Shelton. **Negro, Czech votes:** Clark.
"I kept": Mrs. Johnson. **Sheltons spent**

$40,000: Shelton. **Clark raising money:** Clark. **$2,242.74:** Lee to County Judge, Travis County, "Statement . . . of Lyndon Johnson's . . . expenses," April 20, Box 3, JHP; also *AS*, April 23.

He started early: Keach; *AA, AS*, March 2, 3, 5, 6. **Late openings for other candidates:** *AA*, March 9, 19; *AS*, March 28; *JRC-C*, March 25. **"I don't ever":** Mrs. Johnson.

Sketchy or incorrect directions: Found in "General: Campaign Memo, 1937," Box 1, JHP; Keach. **"Grassyville":** Johnson's handwritten notations on "Jarrel." **Cassens:** "Jarrel." **"Gomillion"; "unknown":** "Memorandum—Lytton Springs" —all from "General: Campaign Memo, 1937," Box 1, JHP.

"Get on record": Halcomb to Wild, March 20. **"Too young":** For example, Halcomb to Wild, March 16, March 20, "General: Campaign Memo, 1937," Box 1, JHP. **"Too elaborate":** Keach; Keach OH I, p. 12, OH II, pp. 21–22. **Awkwardnes with a prepared text:** Gliddon, Cox, SHJ.

Shaking hands: Gliddon, Cox, Lee, Keach. **"He kissed me!":** Fudge. **His unprepared speeches:** To reconstruct Johnson's basic impromptu speech—no complete printed text or recording of one exists—the author took paragraphs and phrases from descriptions of this speech that were printed in the district's daily and weekly newspapers. Then he asked some dozen Hill Country residents who not only heard these speeches, but who were familiar with Johnson and his way of speaking—mainly relatives and boyhood friends from Johnson City—and asked them to give their recollection of what he said, and to try to recall the phrases he used. Those phrases which recurred most often were combined with the written material to reconstruct the speech. Particularly helpful in doing this was Ava Johnson Cox. **"When the Chief would start talking":** Keach. **"Listened unusually attentively":** Halcomb to Wild, March 17. **"Not a man moved":** Halcomb to Wild, March 20. **"Started folks talking"; "a go-getter":** Halcomb to Wild, March 18, 19—all from "General: Campaign Memo, 1937," Box 1, JHP.

Visiting Low and Miller: Keach. **"Prime mover":** *AA*, April 8, 1937.

Burnet: Lee, Keach. The description of Johnson's campaigning in the countryside comes from Keach, who was, of course, his chauffeur, from campaign aides such

as Deason, Lee, and Birdwell, who occasionally accompanied him, from Hill Country politicians such as Ferguson, from Halcomb's daily reports to Wild, and from Johnson's schedules, which can be found in Boxes 2 and 3, JHP. **Campaigning in Beyer's Store; in beer joint; in blacksmith shop:** Halcomb to Wild, March 20. **Gas-station campaigning:** Shelton. **"Deaf old German; "That's the first candidate":** Halcomb to Wild, March 18— all from "General: Campaign Memo, 1937," Box 1, JHP. **"He went":** Cox.

"How's our money?" Latimer. **Johnson in the evening meetings:** Jones, Latimer, Keach, Clark.

Visiting Burleson: *AA*, March 26, 28. **His father's inspiration:** Cox, SHJ. **The Henly rally:** *AA*, March 27. **Avery deciding to rest; Johnson's day in Hays County; "Everywhere I go":** *AA*, March 26; *AA, AS*, March 27, 28; Cox.

"Back-stabbers": *AA*, March 31. **"Love, admire":** *AA*, March 31. **Shelton debate:** *AA*, April 8; Shelton.

Use of radio: His schedules are found in the Austin and weekly newspapers, and in his campaign files, Boxes 2 and 3, JHP. "Judge N. T. Stubbs Broadcast, Station KNOW, 8 to 8:15 pm Wednesday," Box 2, JHP. "Small savings" was a phrase of which Johnson was evidently fond. He used it himself. On one occasion, for example, he said that he was paying for radio time "personally out of my own small savings" (*AA*, March 12). SHJ, Cox, Gliddon. Johnson's heavy expenditures repeatedly drew fire from other candidates. Attacking the "young secretary who claims that as a secretary he got things done," Brownlee said: "Some of the candidates in this race are spending too much money. . . . Where is this money coming from" (*AA*, March 23). Avery took an indirect slap at Roy Miller's financial participation in the campaign in *AA*, March 26. *AA* reported on May 24: "Congressman Lyndon Johnson, we're glad to note, still maintains his sense of humor. During his campaign, there were lots of wisecracks made about his speeches saying that his campaign was financed from 'my own meager savings.' We received a package of radish seed from him in yesterday's mail with this note in it: 'Enclosed purchased from my own meager savings.' "

Harbin's reaction: Harbin to Johnson, April 12, "Correspondence A-L," Box 2, JHP. **Latimer's:** Latimer OH, p. 18. **Black mask:** Keach. **"Very angry":** Mrs. John-

son. **Vomiting, other symptoms:** Mrs.
Johnson; Lee; Birdwell OH. **Courthouse
rally:** *AS,* April 6; *AA,* April 9. **"Waited
too long":** in *AA.* **Rebuffed by Miller:**
Keach. **Campaigning in Austin:** Birdwell
OH I, p. 22; *AS,* March 29.
   Appendicitis attack: Lee OH, p. 19;
Birdwell OH I, p. 24; Mrs. Johnson.
   Vote: Official tabulation of the state
canvassing board, reported in *AA,* April
27.

22. From the Forks of the Creeks

SOURCES
See sources for Chapter 21.

NOTES
(All dates 1937 unless otherwise indicated)

   Fewest votes: Cong. Directory, 76th
Cong., 3rd Sess., pp. 251–57. **"In the byways":** Deason OH I, p. 27. **"That's
what":** Cox. Among the newspapers which
made this point: "Capitol Jigsaw" in
Nachogdoches Sentinel, April 20.
   Lost 40 pounds: *AA* reported on May
15: "He weighed 181 pounds" at the start
of the campaign, and "seemed thin; then,
when he left the hospital bed, he weighed
151 pounds."
   Congratulatory letters: Summy to Johnson, April 30; Whiteside to Johnson, April
14; Perry to Johnson, April 12—all from
Box 3, JHP. **His replies:** To Avery, April
13; to Shelton, April 13 and undated; to
Stone, undated—all from "General: Cam-
paign Memo, 1937," Box 1, JHP. **Miller's
visit to Washington:** Quill OH I, pp. 13–
14; Quill; SHJ; Bardwell to Johnson, April
14, "Correspondence A-L," Box 2, JHP.
Giving Shelton a lift: Shelton, Kellam.
Miller's $100: "Statement . . . of Lyndon
Johnson's . . . expenses," April 20, Box 3,
JHP.
   "Congratulations": Nichols to Johnson,
April 13; Johnson to Nichols, April 17,
Box 3, JHP. **50 form letters:** Author's
analysis of letters in Boxes 2 and 3, JHP.
Supporting Kellam: For example, Johnson
to Brown, April 15; Sheppard to Johnson,
April 21, Box 3, JHP.
   "Your father": House to Johnson, April
15, "Correspondence A-L," Box 2, JHP;
Meador to Johnson, April 30, Johnson to
Meador, May 24, Box 3, JHP.
   Setback: *AS,* April 18; *AA,* April 25.
   "Not progressing": Frazer to Johnson,

April 20; Jones to Frazer, April 21, "Correspondence A-L," Box 2, JHP. **Going to
Karnack:** Mrs. Johnson; *Marshall Messenger,* April 28. **Scene at station:** *Austin
Dispatch,* April 28. See also photographic
section following page 358.

23. Galveston

SOURCES
See Sources for Chapter 20, and the
following.

Books and articles:
   Alsop and Catledge, *The 168 Days;*
Burns, *Roosevelt: The Lion and the Fox;*
Douglas, *The Court Years* and *Go East,
Young Man;* Freidel, *The Launching of
the New Deal;* Ickes, *Secret Diary,* Vols. I,
II; Koenig, *The Invisible Presidency*
("Tommy the Cork" and "Lord Root of
the Matter" chapters); Leuchtenburg,
Franklin D. Roosevelt and the New Deal;
Manchester, *The Glory and the Dream;*
Schlesinger, *The Age of Roosevelt:* I, *The
Crisis of the Old Order,* II, *The Coming
of the New Deal,* III, *The Politics of Up-
heaval;* Sherwood, *Roosevelt and Hopkins;*
Shogan, *A Question of Judgment;* Simon,
Independent Journey; Steinberg, *Sam Ray-
burn;* Woodward and Armstrong, *The
Brethren.*

   Blair Bolles, "Cohen and Corcoran:
Brain Twins," *American Mercury,* Jan.,
1938; Blair Bolles, "The Nine Young
Men," *Washington Sunday Star,* Aug. 29,
1937; Walter Davenport, "It Seems There
Were Two Irishmen," *Collier's,* Sept. 10,
1938; Alva Johnston, "White House Tommy," *Saturday Evening Post,* July 31,
1937; "The Saga of Tommy the Cork,"
Saturday Evening Post, Oct. 13, 20, 27,
1945; Cabell Phillips, "Where Are They
Now," *The New York Times Magazine,*
Sept. 26, 1946; William S. White, "Influential Anonymous," *Harper's,* May, 1960.

Oral Histories:
   Robert S. Allen, Ernest Cuneo, Clifford
Durr, Virginia Durr, Abe Fortas, D. B.
Hardeman, Welly K. Hopkins, Carroll
Keach, Gould Lincoln, Elizabeth and
James H. Rowe, Edwin Weisl, Sr.

Interviews:
   Benjamin V. Cohen, Thomas G. Corcoran, Abe Fortas, Arthur (Tex) Gold-

schmidt, Elizabeth and James H. Rowe, Elizabeth Wickenden.

Richard Bollins, George R. Brown, Oscar Chapman, D. B. Hardeman, John Holton, Alice and Welly Hopkins, Eliot Janeway, W. D. McFarlane, Elizabeth Wickenden, Edwin Weisl, Jr.

The description of Johnson's relationship with the young New Dealers is from interviews with them, unless otherwise noted.

NOTES

"I never": Clark. **"Hope it suits":** Jamieson to Johnson, April 16, 1937, Box 2, JHP. **AP story:** In *WP*, April 11, for example. The TEXAS SUPPORTER OF COURT CHANGE headline is in an early edition; the headline in the later edition said, BACKER OF COURT EXPANSION PLAN WINNER IN TEXAS. **Telegram:** Lockett to Roosevelt, April 11, 1937, OF 300-Texas (J), Roosevelt Papers. **"When we get down":** Unsigned "Memorandum for the Trip File," April 20, 1937, 200-LL, Roosevelt Papers.

Johnson asking Allred: Allred to Johnson, May 3, Allred to McIntyre, May 6, 1937, 200-LL, Roosevelt Papers. **Galveston handshake and rally:** *Galveston Tribune, Houston Chronicle*, May 11; *AA*, May 12, 1937; Keach OH; Clark. **"Went unassisted":** *AA*, May 12. **Hands on the rail:** Johnson's subtle maneuver can be seen in newsreels of the occasion in the National Archives. **Texas A&M Review:** *NYT*, May 12. **Conversation with Roosevelt:** Corcoran; Kintner, quoted in Miller, *Lyndon*, p. 63; Steinberg, pp. 119–20. **Showing Roosevelt Burleson's brown bag:** *CR*, 75th Congress, 2nd Session, Nov. 24, 1937, p. 354. **"Young man":** Vinson, quoted in Steinberg, p. 121. **"Remarkable young man":** Corcoran, Weisl, Jr., Janeway. **"What is a government?":** Corcoran, quoted in Schlesinger, *Politics*, p. 227.

Johnson's relationship with the young New Dealers: Cohen, Corcoran, Fortas, Goldsmidt, James and Elizabeth Rowe, Brown, Alice and Welly Hopkins, Wickenden. **"Cohen's the brains":** Holton. **"The most brilliant":** *NYT*, May 16, 1969. **"Honorary uncle":** Elizabeth Rowe to Johnson, Sept. 16, 1941, Box 32, LBJA SN. **"Crossed with a beef":** Elizabeth Rowe. **"If I owned":** Johnson to Rowe, July 13, 1939, Box 32, LBJA SN.

Johnson's relationship with Rayburn: Corcoran, Rowe, Fortas. **Practical jokes:** Fortas, Brown.

Recommendations: Rowe, Hopkins. **"Born old":** Goldschmidt. **Ickes glad:** Ickes, II, p. 643. **Party for Ickes:** Fortas, Hopkins. **Falling asleep at parties:** Fortas, Elizabeth and James Rowe, Alice Hopkins, Corcoran. **"His native strength":** Hawthorne, quoted in Schlesinger, *The Age of Jackson*, p. 42 **"Has never been specifically authorized" . . . and legality in question:** House, 75 Cong. 1 Session. *Report No. 885*, May 24, 1937, p. 41. **"Is hereby authorized":** Act of Aug. 26, 1937, 50 Stat. 850, Sec. 3.

Cash running out: Herman Brown to Johnson, July 16, 1937, "CRA (1) Financing, PWA," Box 169, JHP. **Delaying approval:** Brown. **Rumors—and dampening them:** Corcoran. **"Cabinet officers":** Johnston, "White House Tommy." **"Give the kid the dam":** Corcoran. **The refusal abruptly ended:** Page to Burlew, June 29, 1937, Ickes File; Corcoran.

Second appropriation: (Signature illegible), "Budget officer," to Hopkins, June 30, 1937; Page to Burlew, June 29, 1937, RG 48. **"At a standstill":** Davis to Johnson, July 29, 1937, "CRA: Davis, T.H., Box 169, JHP. **Connally attempting; James Roosevelt intervention:** *AA*, June 22, 23, 30, July 21, 22, 1937; *AS*, July 23; *Floresville Chronicle-Journal*, July 30, 1937; Johnson to James Roosevelt, Aug. 9, 1937, JHP.

Rotary Club maneuver; reaction: Bunger's untitled speech; Bunger; Lee to Johnson, Wirtz to Johnson, Nov. 30, 1937, McDonough to Johnson, Dec. 12, 1937, "#3 (Marshall Ford Dam)," Box 167, JHP; Ferguson, Gideon. Wirtz to Johnson, March 22, 1938, Box 36, LBJA SN. Johnson to Davis (and attachments), Dec. 7, 1937.

Alliance shaky: See, for example, Wirtz to Johnson, Aug. 12, 17, 1937, Johnson to Wirtz, Aug. 13; Bunger.

Fortas the sharpest weapon: Johnson knew it. Said a Johnson aide: "Johnson always said Abe Fortas was the smartest guy he ever knew, for sheer brains" (*Los Angeles Times*, April 7, 1982).

Maneuvers to secure high dam: Bunger, Fortas, Brown, Corcoran, Goldschmidt, Gideon. "Statement of Hon. Lyndon Johnson, A Representative in Congress from the State of Texas," House of Representatives. 75 Cong. 3 Session. Interior Department Appropriation Bill, 1939. Hearings Before House Appropriations Committee, Vol. 92, pp. 916–17. Page to Ickes, Jan. 3, 1938; Ickes to Burlew, Jan. 11, 1938;

Burlew to Foreman, Feb. 7, 1938; Ickes
to Goeth, Feb. 11, 1938; Ickes to Johnson,
undated, but appears to be March 1, 1938;
Burlew to Johnson, Jan. 17, 1939; Williams
to Mansfield, March 9, 1939—all from
RG 48, Ickes file. "Contract Between the
Lower Colorado River Authority of Texas
and the United States Concerning the Operation and Maintenance of Marshall
Ford Dam . . . March 13, 1941"; Bardwell to Johnson, July 5, 1938, JHP. Bunger, however, did not escape unscathed
for his part in the episode. Johnson quietly
moved against him in Washington. "I have
talked to the proper authorities here (this
is quite confidential)," he wrote, "and I
think we can expect a good-bye from our
Reclamation friend before long" (Johnson
to Wirtz, Dec. 3, 1937, Box 36, LBJA
SN); and he was quietly transferred off the
project (Ickes to Burlew, Feb. 23, 1938,
Ickes File). So effectively did Johnson
move in covering his tracks that Bunger
told the author that he did not know why
he had been transferred but was sure that
Johnson, who Bunger was sure was his
friend, had nothing to do with it.
Committee of the whole: *Cong. Record,*
75 Cong. 3 Session (March 2, 1938), pp.
2707–9 (Rich actually used the figure
$15,000,000 instead of $10,000,000 the
second time he mentioned it, but from the
context it is apparent that he meant to
repeat $10,000,000); McFarlane. **"I felt":**
Bolling. **"The gentleman is correct, yes":**
CR, p. 2708. **"I had at least 19":** Johnson
to Wirtz March 5, 1938; **Accomplished
"the impossible":** Wirtz to Johnson, March
8, 1938, **"Mighty glad":** Rayburn to Wirtz,
March 9, 1938—all Box 36, LBJA SN.

24. Balancing the Books

SOURCES

Interviews:
George R. Brown, Howard P. Bunger,
Edward A. Clark, Thomas G. Corcoran,
D. B. Hardeman, Herman Jones, Frank C.
Oltorf, Emmett Shelton, Harold Young.

NOTES

"Whole world": Corcoran.
**Johnson's relationship with Herman
Brown:** George Brown, Clark, Oltorf. **A
hater:** Herman's dislike of Roosevelt, at a
time when he was asking for contracts

from the New Deal, was common knowledge in Austin. When he heard about
Herman's proposal to enlarge the Marshall Ford Dam, *AA* editor Charles
Green said: "Don't you think we've got
enough dams already? Herman Brown
and McKenzie [another contractor] spend
all their time cussing Roosevelt. Why, if
it wasn't for Roosevelt where would we
all be?" [Lee to Johnson, Nov. 30, 1937,
"#3 Marshall Ford Dam," Box 167,
JHP]. Also Young, Hardeman. **"Watch
out":** Oltorf.
Housing Authority dispute: See Chapter 25.
Lid was off: Bunger. **Working closely:**
See, for example, Herman Brown to Johnson, Aug. 3, 1937, Jan. 15, 1938; Johnson
to Herman Brown, Aug. 9, 1937, Jan. 7,
1938 (with enclosures), Jan. 30, March 10,
1938; White to Duke, Oct. 18, 1937; Mc-
Kenzie to Johnson, Jan. 24, 1938; Johnson
to George Brown, Dec. 2, 1937, Jan. 30,
March 10, 1938; George Brown to Johnson, Nov. 29, 1937, Jan. 17, 1938—all
from Boxes 12, 13, LBJA SN. **"It is
needless":** Johnson to Herman Brown,
April 18, 1939, Box 13, LBJA SN. **"Finally got together":** George Brown to Johnson, May 27, 1939, Box 12, LBJA SN.
CONFIDENTIAL: Johnson to George
Brown, Aug. 11, 1939, Box 12, LBJA SN.
Profits: George Brown; Brown to John-
son, May 27, 1939, Box 12, LBJA SN.
"You get": George Brown. **"Full weight":**
Clark.

25. Longlea

SOURCES

The story of Lyndon Johnson's relationship with Alice Glass and Charles Marsh
was told to the author by Alice's sister,
Mary Louise Glass Young; by Alice's best
friend, Alice Hopkins; and by two of
Alice's confidants and friends, Frank C.
Oltorf and Harold H. Young (who later
married her sister). Additional details
were furnished by Alice's daughter, Diana
Marsh, and by Welly Hopkins. Another
source for information on the relationship
asked not to be quoted by name. Alice and
Welly Hopkins were kind enough, because
Longlea has been closed to the public by
its new owners, to take the author to it
over a back road and to show him around
the estate, pointing out where various
scenes had occurred.

NOTES

Marsh biography: Interviews with the above, and with Edward A. Clark; *AA-S*, Dec. 31, 1964; Jan. 1, 1965; *NYT*, Dec. 31, 1964; *WP*, Jan. 1, 1965. **"Tip":** Young. **"Nothing down":** Martin Andersen, "Charles E. Marsh, President-Maker," *Orlando Sentinel*, Jan. 1, 1965. In this article, Marsh lists five other employees of Marsh—"to name but a few"—whom Marsh allowed to buy newspapers at similarly favorable terms. **"Always had to be":** Hopkins. **"The first thing":** Mrs. Young. **An amateur:** Clark. This feeling is evident in correspondence between Wirtz and Johnson. Marsh's letters—often quite long—frequently contain advice opposite to what Johnson actually decided to do; for example, see Marsh to Johnson, Oct. 22, 1947, Box 26, LBJA SN.
Alice's biography: Mrs. Young, Mrs. Hopkins, Oltorf. **"Had never seen":** Hopkins.
The building of Longlea: Mrs. Young, Mrs. Hopkins, Oltorf; "Longlea, Culpeper County Estate," a real estate brochure printed about 1965 by the Roy Wheeler Realty Company, Charlottesville, Va. By this time, Alice had had to sell off several hundred acres. **Genthe:** quoted by Mrs. Young.
"Quite a bit": Oltorf. **"Heil, Hitler":** Mrs. Young, Oltorf. **Leinsdorf episode:** Leinsdorf, *Cadenza*, pp. 56, 75–79; Mrs. Young. **The compromise:** See Chapter 24. **Discussed marriage:** Mrs. Young, Young. **Reticent:** Oltorf, Hopkins, Young.
"Need visit": Johnson to Marsh, undated, but in 1942 section; **"I do hope":** Johnson to Marsh, Aug. 2, 1947; **"Some interesting":** Johnson to Marsh, Dec. 15, 1939; **"Merely enclose":** Undated but in 1941 section; **"Extra Rush!":** For example, July 8, 1939; **"Arrive Washington":** Marsh to Johnson, July 31, 1939; **"Waking up":** Marsh to Johnson, Sept. 16, 1940; **"I did not like":** Marsh to Johnson, April 9, 1940 —all from "Charles E. Marsh," Box 26, LBJA SN.
"A nineteen-acre tract": Andersen, in *Orlando Sentinel*, Jan. 1, 1965, says that Marsh sold it to Lady Bird Johnson for $8,000, and that twenty years later the Johnsons sold it for a huge profit. Mrs. Johnson says that the price was $12,000, and when the author asked her if she was certain, she said: "Of course I know; it was *my* money." Mrs. Johnson says the reason Marsh sold them the land was the same

reason he offered Lyndon his share in Sid Richardson's enterprises: "I think Charles just regarded himself as a sort of modern-day Leonardo da Vinci—sort of a patron of the arts. . . . Charles was saying that a great future lay ahead of him, and he ought not to have to worry about money. . . ." **Brown & Root landscaped:** "The street improvement project on the Johnson Estate," George Brown called it jokingly in a letter to Johnson (Brown to Johnson, May 27, 1939, Box 12, LBJA SN).
"Ought to be": *AA*, Jan. 30, 1938. **"A nice visit":** "Town Talk," *AS*, May 5, 1938. **Opponents realized:** Emmett Shelton, Clark.
"My eyes:" Lady Bird Johnson. **Mein Kampf:** Lady Bird Johnson. "I still remember his chapter on propaganda—which is worth rereading," she said.
Letter to Oltorf: Alice to Oltorf, Sept. 16, 1967. **Burned letters:** Mrs. Young, Young.

26. The Tenth District

SOURCES

Books, articles, and documents:
Baker, Rasmussen, Wiser, and Porter, *Century of Service*; Nourse, *Three Years of the AAA*; Rasmussen and Baker, *The Department of Agriculture*; Taylor *et al.*, *Rural Life in the United States*; U.S. Department of Agriculture, *Farmers in a Changing World*; U.S. Department of Agriculture, *Yearbook of Agriculture— 1935.*
C. Roger Lambert, "The Drought Cattle Purchase, 1934–1935: Problems and Complaints," *Agricultural History*, April, 1971; "The County Agent," *Fortune* magazine, July, 1938.
Blanco County News, 1932–1941; *Fredericksburg Standard*, 1932–1941; *Johnson City Record-Courier*, 1932–1941.
Department of Agriculture, Records of the Federal Extension Service, RG 33, Annual Reports of Extension Field Representatives, Extension Annual Reports, Texas, National Archives (Counties of Burnet, Blanco, Hays, and Travis, 1933–1941); "Record of the Work Projects Administration, Division of Information, Community Appraisal Files, Texas Record Group 69, State of Texas, County of Travis," National Archives; Johnson House Papers, Johnson House Scrapbooks, LBJL.

Oral Histories:
Paul Appleby (Columbia University), Sherman Birdwell, Carroll Keach.

Interviews:
Walter Jenkins, Carroll Keach, Gene Latimer, Edward Puls, E. Babe Smith. **By Ina Caro:** Truman Fawcett, Chester Franklin, Camm Lary, Lucille O'Donnell, Carroll Smith, Warren Smith, Guthrie Taylor, Walter Yett.

NOTES

Scene at Johnson's office: Birdwell OH I, pp. 29–31; II, 29–36; Keach. **"Let's go":** Birdwell OH I, p. 30. **"Even though"; "we just all worked"; "his love":** Birdwell OH II, pp. 32–34. **"More work":** Latimer. **"Generate":** Birdwell OH II, p. 33. **"He signed":** Birdwell OH II, p. 31. **Bleeding hands:** Latimer OH, p. 22; Latimer. **"Speed up"; 165 to 130; "about ready":** Birdwell OH II, pp. 32–36. **"The best":** Johnson to Mr. and Mrs. Gene Latimer, Undated (except "1933"). **Latimer breakdown:** Latimer.
Jenkins' recruitment: Jenkins. **"Nigger slave":** Puls.
$5 million: *AA,* June 19, July 22, 1937. **PWA appropriations:** *Brenham Banner Press,* Sept. 23, 1937; *Burnet Bulletin,* Dec. 1, 1937. **Housing Authority:** *DMN,* Dec. 17, 1939; *AA,* April 29, 1939, June 25, June 26, 1939; *AS,* Jan. 25, 1938.
Pace accelerated: *AA,* April 4, May 21, June 24, 1938; *AS,* Oct. 31, Nov. 2, 1938. **Tom Miller Dan:** *AA,* April 12, 1938.
Effect on Hill Country: The county Extension Agents' reports, submitted yearly by the county agents of Hays, Burnet, Blanco, and Travis counties, for the years 1932 to 1941, provide general and statistical information on the economic and social conditions in this area. **35,000 acres:** Teasdale, Blanco County Agent report, 1933; *BCN,* June 29, 1933. **Crop-reduction payments:** *BCN,* June 29, 1933. **"Cotton quotas":** *BCN,* April 7, 1938. **"People were glad":** Fawcett. **"Twelve dollars":** Lambert, p. 85.
Basketball collection: *BCN,* Sept. 28, 1933. **Store owners:** Fawcett, Taylor. **"People couldn't pay":** O'Donnell. **Their poverty forbade:** Taylor, Lary, W. Smith, C. Smith, O'Donnell, Beck, M. Cox, A. Cox. **Lack of tractors:** Taylor; *FS,* March 21, 1933; *JCR-C,* Jan. 11, 1934.
Meeting with farmers: *Elgin Courier, Giddings News,* Dec. 22, *Taylor Daily News,* 12/29, *Williamson County Sun,* Dec. 31, 1938.
"Book farmers": Lary. **In March, 1937:** Jenkins, Blanco County Agent Report, 1937.
Cedar eradication program: A year-by-year account of the progress of the range program is given in the reports of the county agents for Blanco, Hays, Burnet, and Travis Counties for the years 1933 to 1941. Interviews with participants in the program: C. Smith, W. Smith, Lary, Franklin, Yett. **"He'd come to the meetings"; he persuaded; "you could see":** Lary, E. B. Smith. **Cedar acreage:** Jenkins, Blanco County Agent reports; *BCN* Sept. 21, Aug. 1, 1940.
Emil Stahl; "cedar eradication": Jenkins, Blanco County Agent Report, 1938. **"Solid cedar brake":** W. Smith. **Scott Klett, Al Young:** Jenkins, Blanco County Agent Report, 1938.
Farm-to-market roads: WPA, RG 69, NA. **"He got more":** Corcoran.

27. The Sad Irons

SOURCES

Books, articles, and documents:
Brown, *Electricity for Rural America*; Doyle, *Lines Across the Land*; Dulaney, Phillips, and Reese, *Speak, Mr. Speaker*; Ellis, *A Giant Step*; Garwood and Tuthill, *The Rural Electrification Administration: An Evaluation*; MacDonald, *The Egg and I*; Olmsted, *A Journey Through Texas.*
John T. Flynn, "All Lit Up and Going Places," *Collier's,* Aug. 24, 1935; Willard Luff, "Water Systems and Bathrooms for Farm Homes," *Rural Electrification News,* Sept., 1940; H. S. Person, "The Rural Electrification Administration in Perspective," *Agricultural History,* April, 1950; *Rural Electrification News,* 1936–1948.
LBJL; *Rural Lines U.S.A.: The Story of the Rural Electrification Administration's First Twenty-Five Years: 1935–1960,* REA, U.S. Department of Agriculture, Miscellaneous Publications, No. 811.
Congressional Record, 76th Congress.
Johnson House Papers and Scrapbooks, LBJL.

Interviews:
Ava Cox, Louise Casparis, Stella Gliddon. **By Ina Caro:** For descriptions of life in the Hill Country before electricity, some fifty ranchers and ranch wives in

various counties. Also, group interviews were held at the Johnson City Nursing Home and at the Hillside Nursing Home in San Marcos. Only those people who have been quoted are listed: Art Anderson, Elsie Beck, Ava Cox, Curtis Cox, Mary Cox, Chester Franklin, Gay Harris, Christine Lary, Kitty Clyde Ross Leonard, Lucille O'Donnell, Carroll Smith, Warren Smith, Bernice Snodgrass, Rena Snodgrass, Frances and Clayton Stribling, Bingie and Walter Yett. County agents and community leaders such as Camm Lary and Guthrie Taylor of Burnet and Pedernales Electric Co-operative employees such as Louis Hunnicut were also interviewed.

NOTES

Bring electricity: "LCRA Power Distribution," Box 186, JHP. **TP&L "power plant":** Leonard, A. Cox. **"The Perils of Pauline":** O'Donnell. **Milking:** Anderson, Stribling. **Sears, Roebuck:** MacDonald, p. 75. **"Winter mornings":** Ellis, p. 58. **"Melted away":** Franklin. **Flat tires:** W. Smith, Hunnicut. **Auger:** Taylor, W. Smith.
Federal study: Luff, *Rural Electrification News*, p. 9. **"I felt tired":** C. Cox. **"More than once":** M. Cox. **"Running water":** Mrs. B. Smith. **"With an electric stove":** O'Donnell. **"We didn't have refrigerators":** O'Donnell. **Ash container:** A. Cox. **"You'd be in the kitchen":** R. Snodgrass. **"You'd have to can in the summer":** Leonard. **"You got so hot":** B. Snodgrass. **"We had no choice":** Harris.
Washing clothes: A. Cox, M. Cox, R. Snodgrass, O'Donnell. **"You had to do it as hard"; "by the time you got done":** A. Cox.
"Ironing was the worst": M. Cox. **"Young women today":** REA Pubs., No. 811, p. 24. **"In those days":** M. Cox. **"It would hurt":** Beck. **Rankin speech:** *CR*, 76 Cong., 1 Sess., May 11, 1939.
Shearing: B. Yett. **"They wear":** Flynn, *Collier's*, Aug. 24, 1935.
Perineal tears: "FSA Survey, Williamson County," July, 1946, Box 265, JHP.
"We were completely cut off": Casparis. **"What we missed":** M. Cox. **"There was no other time":** O'Donnell. **Kerosene lamps:** C. Cox. **"Loved to read":** M. Cox. **Read:** O'Donnell. **"So many of us":** A. Cox. **"The house looked scary":** M. Cox. **"Horrible choice":** MacDonald, p. 94. **"Living was drudgery":** G. Smith. **"You bathed":** B. Snodgrass. **Outhouses:** B. Snodgrass. **"It would just drop":** Taylor. **"We were behind":** Casparis. **"Machine

that washed":** A. Cox. **"What do you want that pit for?":** B. Snodgrass.
The family from Portland: unlike the other families interviewed, this family requested that its real name not be used.

28. "I'll Get It for You"

SOURCES

Books, articles, brochures, and documents:
Bellush, *Franklin D. Roosevelt as Governor of New York*; Brown, *Electricity for Rural America*; Childs, *The Farmer Takes a Hand*; Doyle, *Lines Across the Land*; Dulaney, Phillips, and Reese, *"Speak, Mr. Speaker"*; Ellis, *A Giant Step*; Garwood and Tuthill, *The Rural Electrification Administration: An Evaluation*; Gunther, *Inside U.S.A.*; Leuchtenburg, *Franklin D. Roosevelt and the New Deal*; Norris, *Fighting Liberal*; Rosenman, ed., *The Public Papers and Addresses of Franklin D. Roosevelt*; Schlesinger, *The Age of Roosevelt: I, The Crisis of the Old Order; II, The Coming of the New Deal; III, The Politics of Upheaval.*
Roland W. Olson, "LBJ—His Ranch, His Coop," *Kansas Electric Farmer*, February, 1964; H. S. Person, "The Rural Electrification Administration in Perspective, *Agricultural History*, April, 1950. *Blanco County News*, 1937–1940.
National Rural Electric Cooperative Association, *People—Their Power: The Rural Electric Fact Book*, ed. by Erma Angevine, Washington, D.C., NRECA, 1980; *Rural Lines, U.S.A.: The Story of the Rural Electrification Administration's First Twenty-Five Years, 1935–1960*, REA, U.S. Department of Agriculture, Miscellaneous Publications, No. 811. Rural Electrification Administration, Record Group 221, National Archives.
Johnson House Papers, Box 171, folders "Correspondence," "Power Rural Electrification"; Box 173, Folder "CRA: Power: PEC for the Year 1938"; Johnson House Scrapbooks Four, Part One, and Scrapbooks Four, Part Seven, LBJL.

Oral History:
Marvin Jones.

Interviews:
Stella Gliddon, E. Babe Smith. **By Ina Caro:** Ava Cox, Louis Hunnicut, Lucille O'Donnell, Howard Leighton Snow, Guthrie Taylor.

NOTES

30 million Americans: Schlesinger, III, p. 379. "Every city 'white way' "; lack of electric power: Leuchtenberg, p. 157. "Uncle John" Hobbs: Ellis, p. 29. As much as $5,000: Ellis, p. 33.

1925 survey: Brown, p. 11. "Element of truth": Ellis, p. 33. "It hardly seems fair": REA, p. 47. Alabama Power & Light: Brown, p. 11. When a farmer offered: Ellis, p. 28. Texas Power & Light: Smith. "Who and what": Gunther, p. 183. All through the Twenties: Ellis, p. 37. "Negation of the ideals": quoted in Schlesinger, II, p. 322. "Benefit of the people": FDR to Smith, May 20, 1927, quoted in Schlesinger, I, p. 389. As Governor, his vision: Bellush, pp. 208–241. Scribbled new introduction: Rosenman, ed., 1928–1932, p. 44. "Is it possible": quoted in Schlesinger II, p. 323. FDR and Norris: Schlesinger, II, pp. 323–324. "Become a standard article": Ellis, p. 38. "There are very few farms": Person, p. 73. "Most-favored": Childs, p. 56.

Agriculture Chairman: Jones OH, p. 934. "Can you imagine": Dulaney, p. 60. "We want to make the farmer": CR, Vol. 80, part 5, April 9, 1936, p. 5284. "Spirit and determination": Dulaney, p. 59. "When free enterprise": Dulaney, p. 358.

For the Rayburn and Norris episode, see Brown, pp. 64–65. No one knew about this. No historian mentioned it. Rayburn hardly mentioned it, although once he said, "Of all the bills I have helped on, I think I am proudest of being the author of the Rural Administration Act." (Rayburn speech, Oct. 16, 1957, quoted in Dulaney, p. 59.) Rankin took credit for passage of this legislation in the House—and is awarded credit in most history books. Rayburn's role would have gone substantially unknown had not Norris once mentioned it, and had not the mention been documented in REA, RG 221, NA, and been found by Brown. "Let the other fellow get the headlines," Rayburn would say, "I'll take the laws." Norris, who deserved the largest share of the credit for REA, got many headlines, but so did others much less deserving. But the law does bear Rayburn's name. Just as the Securities Act of 1933 was the Fletcher-Rayburn Act, and the Securities and Exchange Commission Act of 1934 was the Fletcher-Rayburn Act, and the Holding Company Bill of 1935 was the Wheeler-Rayburn Act, so the REA Act of 1936 was the Norris-Rayburn Act.

Self-liquidating: Brown, p. 66. Hill Country delegation: Smith. REA would not even consider: Childs, p. 187. "Fifty per cent": Brown, p. 57. "Too much land": Olson.

"And not all of them were believers": Smith. Grote: Letter from Stehling to Grote, Dec. 13, 1939, Box 173, JHP.

Reluctance of people to sign: Taylor, O'Donnell, Smith. "Signing an easement": Smith; Childs, p. 79.

$2.45 for twenty-five kilowatts: Giddings Star, Nov. 15, 1940. "This line is being built": BCN, May 19, 1938. "I don't believe: Cox, "Something you had never had"; meeting in schoolhouse; "in the car": Smith. "We went back to Lyndon": Smith.

Johnson version of meeting with President: quoted in Miller, Lyndon, p. 71. For another version, see Steinberg, Sam Johnson's Boy, p. 132. Telegram: "Power: Rural Electrification," Box 172, JHP.

Laying the lines: Smith, Hunnicut, Snow. "It will not be long": BCN, Feb. 1, 1940. Persuaded many of his neighbors: Smith. "People began to name their kids": Gliddon.

29. Mr. Johnson Goes to Washington

SOURCES

Books and documents:

Daniels, *White House Witness;* Henderson, *Maury Maverick;* SHJ, *My Brother, Lyndon;* R. Johnson, *A Family Album;* Jones, *Fifty Billion Dollars;* Mann, *La Guardia: A Fighter Against His Times;* Schlesinger, *The Politics of Upheaval;* Sherwood, *Roosevelt and Hopkins;* Steinberg, *Sam Rayburn;* Tully, *F.D.R., My Boss.*

Roosevelt Papers.

Oral Histories:

Helen Gahagan Douglas, Warren Magnuson, W. Robert Poage.

Interviews:

Alan Barth, Richard 'Bolling, George Brown, Emanuel Celler, Edward A. Clark, W. Sterling Cole, Thomas G. Corcoran, Ava Johnson Cox, Willard Deason, Helen Gahagan Douglas, Lewis T. Easley, O. C. Fisher, Stella Gliddon, D. B. Hardeman, John Holton, Welly K. Hopkins, Edouard V. M. Izac, Eliot Janeway, Walter Jenkins, RJB, SHJ, Lady Bird Johnson, Eugene J. Keogh, Gene Latimer, Wingate Lucas,

George H. Mahon, W. D. McFarlane, J. J. Pickle, James H. Rowe, Lacey Sharp, James Van Zandt, Harold Young.

NOTES

"The best": Corcoran. **Keeping NYA in place:** See Chapter 22. **"Go to the courthouse"; "long letters":** Deason, Pickle. **Priority to out-of-district VIPs:** Latimer. **"A great honor":** Rowe. **"Unwritten law":** Mahon. **Johnson bringing guests:** Lucas, McFarlane. **"Mine by adoption":** Johnson to Roosevelt, March 21, 1939, FDR-LBJ MF. **Taking credit for grants:** Lucas, Easley, SHJ, Hardeman. **Unpopularity with Texas delegation:** Fisher, McFarlane, Lucas, Mahon, Sharp, Easley, Young, Hardeman, SHJ.

Rayburn's plaque: Steinberg, *Sam Rayburn*, p. 236. **"This is our home":** Among those to whom Johnson said it was Rowe. **Others saw:** Brown, Rowe, Hopkins. **Requested autographed pictures:** Johnson to McIntyre, Nov. 18, 1937, PPF 6149, Roosevelt Papers; Johnson to James Roosevelt, Aug. 8, 1937, FDR-LBJ MF. **"I regret":** McIntyre to Johnson, Sept. 18, 1937, FDR-LBJ MF. **Still had not seen:** Kannee to McIntyre, June 3, 1938; Johnson to Roosevelt, June 8, 1938, PPF 6149, Roosevelt Papers. **Only audience:** "Roosevelt, Franklin D.—Contacts," Box 6, WH FN.

Vinson: Eliot Janeway, "The Man Who Owns the Navy," *Sat. Eve. Post*, Dec. 15, 1945; Beverly Smith, "He Makes the Generals Listen," *Sat. Eve. Post*, March 10, 1952; Izac, Cole; Magnuson OH; Steinberg, *Sam Johnson's Boy*, pp. 137–40. **"He let us have it":** Magnuson, quoted in Steinberg, p. 139. **Appropriations Committee seat:** *AA*, Oct. 8, 1938; *Amarillo News-Globe*, Jan. 22, 1939; Mahon. **Death of Hon. S. E. Johnson:** *JCR-C*, Oct. 21, 28; *FS*, Oct. 28, 1937; Johnson, *Album*, p. 27; Cox, Gliddon, RJB, SHJ, Clark. **Father's watch:** SHJ, pp. 265–66; RJB; SHJ.

Johnson's belief that he would die young: SHJ, Mrs. Johnson. **Uncle George's death:** *AA*, March 12, 1940. **"Too slow":** Johnson used this phrase to numerous people, including McFarlane and Young. **"Any House member":** Bolling. **Congressmen and national causes:** See, for example, Schlesinger, pp. 142–46; Mann, Henderson, Steinberg, *passim*.

Johnson's legislative record: CR, 1937–1948. *AA, AS,* 1937–1948. "Lyndon B. Johnson's Congressional Activities" (compilation by OH Staff), WHCF, LBJL; "Complete House Voting Record of Congressman Lyndon Johnson, By Subject, From May 13, 1937 to December 31, 1948," Book Collection, LBJL. Douglas OH; Douglas, Izac, McFarlane, Fisher, Cole, Lucas.

Standing on Capitol Hill: Based on interviews with Douglas, Izac, Celler, Keogh, Fisher, Mahon, Van Zandt, McFarlane, Cole. See also Ray Roberts, quoted in Miller, *Lyndon,* p. 76. Congressional staff members, such as Wingate Lucas (later a Congressman), Lacey Sharp, Walter Jenkins; SHJ. Also persons who observed Congress, including Barth, Easley, Corcoran, Holton, Brown. **"A leader":** Brown.

Fond of him: Poage OH; Van Zandt, Corcoran, Rowe. **Other feelings:** Izac, Fisher, Van Zandt, Lucas, McFarlane. **Playing up to Vinson:** Magnuson, quoted in Steinberg, pp. 138–39. **Tape recorder incident:** Van Zandt. **"Baby":** For example, *Fort Worth Star-Telegram,* Aug. 29, 1938. **"Sometimes":** Johnson to Roosevelt, March 24; Early to Johnson, March 25, 1939, FDR-LBJ MF. **ROTC rejection:** Johnson to Roosevelt, March 21; Woodruff to McIntyre, April 11, 1939, FDR-LBJ MF. **"You've got":** Rowe. **Feelings of New Dealers:** Rowe, Corcoran.

30. A Contract and Three Telegrams

SOURCES

Books and documents:
Alsop and Catledge, *The 168 Days* (referred to hereinafter as *Days*); Burns, *Roosevelt: The Lion and the Fox;* Caro, *The Power Broker;* Daniels, *Frontier on the Potomac* and *White House Witness;* Dorough, *Mr. Sam;* Dulaney, *Speak, Mr. Speaker;* Farley, *Jim Farley's Story: The Roosevelt Years;* Fisher, *Cactus Jack;* Gunther, *Roosevelt in Retrospect;* Henderson, *Maury Maverick;* Ickes, *Secret Diary,* II and III; Leuchtenburg, *Franklin D. Roosevelt and the New Deal;* Moley, *27 Masters of Politics;* Mooney, *Roosevelt and Rayburn;* Norris, *Fighting Liberal;* Timmons, *Garner of Texas.*

Lionel V. Patenaude, "The New Deal and Texas" (unpublished Master's Thesis), Austin, 1953.

Garner Papers, Roosevelt Papers, Wirtz Papers.

Oral Histories:
E. B. Germany, Marvin Jones, Henry A. Wallace.

Interviews:
George Brown, Edward A. Clark, Thomas G. Corcoran, O. C. Fisher, D. B. Hardeman, Welly K. Hopkins, Vann Kennedy, Dale Miller, James H. Rowe, E. Babe Smith, Arthur Stehling, Harold Young.

NOTES

"Cut down": Garner to Roosevelt, Oct. 1, 1934, PPF 1416, Roosevelt Papers. **Hated that phrase:** Timmons, p. 205. **"Stop the spending!":** Undated clipping in Garner Papers, Box 36295, Barker Texas History Collection. **Garner financing Maverick:** Ickes, II, p. 37. **"How long":** Kirby to Garner, July 5, 1936; Garner to Kirby, July 9, 1936, quoted in Patenaude, p. 50. **"No Man":** *Days,* p. 238.
Garner's use of Mexican-Americans; low pay to carpenters: *Phila. Record,* Nov. 9, 12, 1939. **"Not troublesome":** Garner, quoted in Hamilton Basso, *New Republic,* Feb. 26, 1940.
"They permitted": Fisher, p. 129. **His discussion with Roosevelt:** Timmons, pp. 215–16. **"Worst quality":** Gunther, p. 50. **"We deal in writing"; "Frank Roosevelt, you're a goddamned liar":** Caro, p. 304. For a discussion of these qualities in Roosevelt, see Caro, pp. 283–98, 426–43. **"A charming fellow, but":** Timmons, p. 225. **Angry conference with Roosevelt:** *Days,* pp. 131–32; Timmons, p. 216.
No hint: *Days,* pp. 48, 65–66; Timmons, pp. 217–18. **Overconfidence:** *Days,* pp. 170, 48. **"Boys":** Timmons, p. 218; *Days,* p. 67. **"General"; thumbs-down gesture:** Fisher, p. 131; *Days,* p. 69.
"Laughed": *Days,* p. 78. **"Off the reservation":** Ickes, II, p. 140. **"Burt":** *Days,* p. 237.
Garner's trip and its effect: Timmons, pp. 220 ff; *Days,* p. 236; Ickes, II, pp. 151, 153, 166, 170–71; Fisher, p. 132. **"Why in Hell":** Farley, p. 84. **Train scene:** *Days,* pp. 277 ff. **"Bark":** Patenaude, p. 60; *Days,* p. 279. **The compromise:** *Days,* pp. 284–95; Timmons, pp. 223–25; Farley, p. 94; Ickes, II, p. 171. **Barkley fight:** Timmons, pp. 224–25. **Garner's question, Roosevelt's reply:** Garner to Roosevelt, June 20,

1937, quoted in Patenaude, p. 66; Ickes, II, p. 144.
"Doesn't overlook": Ickes, II, p. 179. **Staring down the table:** Ickes, II, pp. 278–79. **"Vehemence":** *NYT,* April 12, 1938. **"We've been trying":** *Fort Worth Press,* April 18. **"Openly whispered":** R. B. Creager, Texas GOP State Chairman, quoted in *NYT,* Patenaude, p. 68. **"One of the least":** Burns, pp. 344–45. **"Merely smiled":** *NYT,* April 13. **Personally promised:** *Days,* p. 291; Fisher. **Roosevelt's trip to Texas; Garner refusing to meet him:** Patenaude, p. 134. Garner telegraphed the President: "I regret being unable to greet you in the flesh, but I have two good reasons. First, it is too far to walk, and second, I am now working for a living." *NYT,* July 12, in Patenaude, p. 132.
"Didn't get anywhere": Farley, p. 158. **"Opened up":** Ickes, II, p. 543. Patenaude, p. 70, quotes Maury Maverick as saying that Roosevelt now "hated" Garner. **"If they need":** *Time,* Jan. 9, 1939; Ickes, II, p. 557. **In Cabinet:** Ickes, II, pp. 557, 387, 653–54, 570.
"Old, red, wizened": Ickes, III, pp. 18–19. **"As a kitten":** Ickes, II, p. 645. **"Those ambitious":** *DMN,* Jan. 7, 1940. **"His heart":** Basso, *New Republic,* Feb. 26, 1940. **Moley column:** *Newsweek,* April 10, 1939. **"Slightly ostentatious":** *Days,* p. 225. **"All":** Fisher, p. 147.
Garner's views on Third Term: Miller, Fisher; Timmons, *Fort Worth Star-Telegram,* Oct. 16, 1961; Timmons, pp. 246–52 ff; Fisher, p. 145. **Roosevelt's determination it would not be Garner:** Corcoran; Burns, p. 414.
Open war: *Time,* March 20, 1939; Timmons, p. 244. **"Served the purposes":** Leuchtenburg, p. 281. **Hatch Act:** Timmons, pp. 259–60; Miller. **"A sullen world"; "Well, Captain":** Burns, pp. 392–93. **"A sarcophagus":** *Time,* March 20, 1939. **Chagrin:** *New Republic,* April 12, 1939. **Polls:** Fisher, p. 146; *Time,* March 20, 1939; Timmons, p. 253. **"A case":** *Congressional Digest,* Jan., 1939, p. 1. **"To begin with":** Farley, p. 184.
Garner crushing Maverick: Henderson, p. 177. **Maverick's indictment:** Henderson, pp. 196–97; *DMN,* Nov. 28, Dec. 3, 6, 1939.
Rayburn preferred Roosevelt: Jones OH, p. 444; Clark, Young, Corcoran. **"There is much more":** Moley, p. 245. **No doubt that Roosevelt would run:** Farley, p. 205; Dorough, pp. 293–94. **Garner rushing back to help:** Timmons, *Fort*

Worth Star-Telegram, Oct. 15, 1961. **"In the first place":** *Washington Star,* Dec. 2, 1936. **"I am for":** *DMN,* Aug. 13, 1939. **"In previous years":** Early to Roosevelt, Aug. 15, 1939; written on it, in hand, is "Sorry—my absence makes it impossible, etc., FDR."; then Early to Dickson and Sheppard, Aug. 25, 1939, PPF 474, Roosevelt Papers. **No autograph:** Clary to LeHand, Jan. 27, 1940, PPF 474, Roosevelt Papers.

1938 "purge" trip: McIntyre to Johnson, undated; Johnson to McIntyre, July 10, 1938, FDR-LBJ MF; *DMN,* July 10–14. **Becoming a spy:** Corcoran, Rowe.

Marsh's appointment: Watson to Kannee, July 14, 1939, OF-300-Texas 1938–45 (M), Roosevelt Papers. The White House Logs show that Johnson had an appointment with Roosevelt on July 5 as well; whether this was in connection with Marsh or not cannot be determined, but Corcoran says an appointment when Johnson accompanied Marsh was his first with the President during this period. **Impressing; friction between Marsh and Roosevelt, and Johnson the buffer:** Corcoran, Young.

John L. Lewis episode: Ickes, II, pp. 693–94, 699; Corcoran, Rowe; Corcoran quoted in Miller, *Lyndon,* p. 75. Johnson's draft of a statement is on the back of a letter from Gordon Fulcher, July 26, 1939, Box 18, LBJA SN; *WP, HP, DMN,* July 28. Kenneth G. Crawford, "The Real John Garner," *The Nation,* Aug. 3; *Time,* Aug. 7. **"I see":** Ickes, III, p. 95. **West and South drew it up:** *DMN,* July 28. **"Of course":** Thomas, quoted in *HP,* July 28. **"My esteem":** Johnson, quoted in *Fort Worth Star-Telegram,* July 30.

"If": Timmons, p. 288. **Nalle's opposition:** Wirtz to Johnson, May 2, 1939. **Farley's position, Roosevelt's promise:** Rowe to LeHand, Aug. 10. **Roosevelt carrying through:** Roosevelt to Rowe, Aug. 14 (and attached July 18 memo), OF 400-Texas-A, Roosevelt Papers. **Discussing REA:** *Corsicana Sentinel,* July 22, 1939. **"As you will see":** Cohen to Roosevelt, July 19. See also Johnson to Roosevelt, July 18, FDR-LBJ MF. **"So enthusiastic":** Wallace to Roosevelt, July 19. **"It was difficult":** Ickes, II, p. 683. **REA transfer:** Norris, p. 319. **Johnson's thinking:** Hopkins, Rowe, Young. **Exchange of letters:** Johnson to Roosevelt, July 29; Roosevelt to Johnson, Aug. 2, PPF 6149, Roosevelt Papers. **"I hope you know"; "I have thought":**

G. Brown to Johnson, May 2, 1939, March 5, 1940. **"Ninety-six old men":** Johnson to G. Brown, Feb. 27, 1940–all Box 12, LBJA SN.

Garner's statement: *Wichita Daily Times,* Dec. 17, 1939. **"Regardless":** *Texas Weekly,* Dec. 16. **Kilday statement:** In *San Antonio Evening News,* Dec. 20. **Cabinet meeting:** Ickes, III, p. 112.

March, 1940: Burns, pp. 415–17. **"Roosevelt's basic problem":** Burns, pp. 412–13. **"If Roy Miller":** *AA-S,* March 31, 1940.

Decision to make Texas a battleground: Corcoran, Young, Clark.

Money needed: Young, Hardeman, Clark, Kennedy. **"The most painstaking":** *DMN,* July 2, 1939. **Marsh's support:** Young. **"Even here":** *State Observer,* April 15, 1940. **Young's report:** Young to Marsh, April 10, 1940, Box 26, LBJA SN.

Telegrams to two or three towns: For example, Johnson to H. Brown, Aug. 11, 1939 (to which Herman sent this telegraphed reply from Denison, Texas: "Thanks lot for information Dallas tonight Austin tomorrow night")—Box 13, LBJA SN.

"I talked," etc.: Johnson to G. Brown, April 28, May 16, 1939. **Taking Bellows as partner; "I got":** G. Brown to Johnson, May 13, 27—from Box 12, LBJA SN. **Brush-off:** Morell to Johnson, Nov. 21, with attached memo, Nov. 21, Trexel to Moreell, Box 180, JHP.

Air base had been proposed for Corpus Christi: *CCC,* 1936–1940. **Construction recommended:** *CCC,* Sept. 26, 1938. **Kleberg, Miller pushing:** *CCC,* Jan. 16, 1939. **"From what I see":** G. Brown to Roy Miller, May 1, 1939, Box 12, LBJA SN. **"No intimation":** *CCC,* Sept. 24, 1939. **"Not . . . emergent"; subcommittee rejects survey request:** *CCC,* Jan. 10, 11, 24, 1940. **"I have":** G. Brown to Johnson, Oct. 27, 1939. **New Thomas statement:** *NYT,* Dec. 23, 1939.

"The choicest plum": *Houston Press,* Jan. 3, 1940. **Early statement:** *AS,* Jan. 2. See also *DMN,* Jan. 3; *Dallas Journal,* Jan. 4, 5; *AS,* Jan. 7. **Roosevelt "told us":** Niles, quoted in Steinberg, p. 145. **Herman Brown and associates' trip to Washington:** Johnson to G. Brown, Feb. 27, Box 12, LBJA SN; Feb. 9, Box 180, JHP.

Navy Department was informed: Corcoran. George Brown says flatly, "Johnson got us into Corpus Christi." **Corpus Christi Air Base moves ahead:** Corcoran, Brown; *CCC,* May 16, 17, 21, 23, 24, 31,

June 2, 5, 7, 11, 12, 13, 14, 1940. (Thanks to the strict secrecy, the first public mention of the Air Base's new status did not come until the *CCC* article of May 16, but at that time 400 acres had already been put under option, and the Navy, in making the first announcement of the project, said that drawings and specifications for the work, which had been made in Florida, "are nearing completion." Exactly two weeks after bids for the first stages of the work were requested, the contract was awarded to Brown & Root.) **First Roosevelt personally signed:** *CCC,* Jan. 10, 1943. **Authorized cost increase:** *CCC,* Jan. 26, Feb. 14, 27, 1941. **Eventually $100,000,-000:** *CCC,* Aug. 7, 1943.

"**Delivered $300 in cash**": Folder 1 of 4, Box 15, LBJA SN. "**I have rented**": Young to Marsh, April 10, 1940, Box 26, LBJA SN. **Thanks to Brown:** Young, Corcoran, Clark.

International tensions and political effect: Leuchtenburg, p. 299. "**All his buoyancy**": Ickes, III, p. 145. **He knew it:** Miller; Ickes, III, *passim.* "**The most downhearted**": Tucker, "National Whirligig," April 17, 1940, Garner Papers, Box 3L296, Barker Center.

Roosevelt's decision: Ickes, III, pp. 155, 157. **Maverick silenced:** *DMN,* April 11, 1940. **Johnson and Wirtz persuading Roosevelt:** Wirtz to Miller, April 12, Wirtz Papers, Box 6; Clark, Young, Corcoran. And see *NYT,* April 7.

Rayburn trying to save Garner from humiliation: Rayburn to Simmons, March 8, 25, 1940, Rayburn Papers, Series I, Roll 9; "Washington Dispatch," quoted in *State Observer,* April 15; Clark, quoted in *AA-S,* April 12; Clark, Kennedy, Young. "**As between**": Clark and Miller to Rayburn, in *NYT,* April 16, 1940; *DMN,* April 16. "**The great Lone Star**": Pearson and Allen, *Washington Times-Herald,* April 20. "**No knowing person**": Rayburn to Clark and Miller, April 13, quoted in *Fort Worth Star-Telegram,* April 14.

Leak to Bolton. Miller to Wirtz, April 15, 1940, Wirtz Papers, Box 5; Young. Bolton says he does not recall the incident. "**Was brought squarely**": *DMN,* April 16. And see *AA-S,* April 16. **Another telegram:** Clark and Miller, quoted in *DMN,* April 16.

Three conferences: *AA, Washington Times-Herald,* April 19, 1940. "Appeared to the President" is in *AA* story. "**Your name was lugged**": Wade to Rayburn, April 26, Rayburn MF, Series I, Roll 9. "**All-out fight**": *DMN, AA-S, State Ob-*

server, April 19–June 3, 1940; Kennedy, Clark, Young. "**As heretofore**": Blalock in *SAE,* April 19. **Brown's money:** Young, Clark.

The "harmony" telegram: *WP, NYT,* April 30, May 1, 1940. **Embarrassment to Rayburn:** Ickes, III, p. 168; Corcoran. "**I am sure**": Rayburn to Dorough, May 2, 1940, Rayburn MF, Series I, Roll 9. **Rayburn's swearing-in:** Timmons, *Fort Worth Star-Telegram,* Oct. 17, 1961; Dorough, p. 298; Dulaney, p. 76; Dorough, p. 303. "**I would rather link my name**": Rayburn to Thomas, Feb. 19, 1922, in Dulaney, pp. 35, 453.

"**Where is the farmer going?**": Dorough (who was the friend), p. xiv. "**Hell, Sam**": Daniels, *Frontier,* p. 57. **Selective Service Act:** G. Brown; Mooney, pp. 165–67; David L. Cohn, *Atlantic Monthly,* Oct., 1942; Timmons, *Fort Worth Star-Telegram,* Oct. 17, 1961. **Little voice in their formulation:** Rowe, Corcoran; Wallace OH, *passim;* Daniels, *Frontier* and *Witness, passim.* "**I thank God**": Rayburn to Roosevelt, Jan. 30, 1942, PPF 474, Roosevelt Papers. "**Turned pink**"; "**never suggests**": Wallace OH, pp. 815, 1326, 2920–21, and Dec. 14, 1942. "**He said**": Daniels, *Witness,* pp. 44–45.

"**Your country owes you**": Rowe to Rayburn, Nov. 12, 1946, Box 32, LBJA SN.

White House attitude: Rowe, Corcoran. "**Understand**": McIntyre to Roosevelt, Oct. 29, 1940, PPF 474, Roosevelt Papers. "**Swell-headed**": Daniels, *Witness,* p. 55, and see also pp. 44, 48. "**There's nobody**": Rowe.

"**A virtual freshman**": Franklin, *Washington Evening Star,* May 2, 1940. **Connally and Sheppard out:** The fact that "the 'Stop-Garner' movement is also directed against Senators Connally and Sheppard" was reported in *Fort Worth Star-Telegram,* April 17, 1940.

Jones and Garner had been consulted: Evident in Roosevelt Papers; particularly useful is the OF 300-Democratic National Committee file for Texas, 1933–1939. **Johnson becoming Roosevelt's man in Texas:** Corcoran, Clark, Young, Smith, Stehling, Kennedy, Rowe, Hardeman. **Smaller contracts:** PSF Departmental 84, Navy Department, Roosevelt Papers. **REA line-laying:** Smith. "**Once he could get public money**": Corcoran.

Pinning Willkie button: John Nance Garner Papers, Box 3L295, Barker Center. **They didn't know:** At the very height of the Garner-Roosevelt fight in Texas, an AP dispatch reprinted in *Edinburg Valley Review* on April 3, 1940, could also state—in an article typical of many written during this period—that Johnson "has expressed publicly his great admiration for Garner, but has adroitly side-stepped a commitment of support for anyone in the next presidential election." **Not at dam dedication:** *AA-S,* April 7, 1940. **Low profile:** Young, Kennedy. **At Waco:** Germany OH, p. 14. **Hornaday article:** In *NYT,* March 24, 1940.

"Hie you": Ickes to Carter, April 18, 1940, printed in *Fort Worth Star-Telegram,* April 29. **Unsigned, unaddressed memorandum:** Found in Wirtz Papers, Box 5, folder labeled "Wirtz—Democrats"; Jones, Corcoran, Young, Clark. **"This is a year":** *AA,* March 24, 1940.

31. Campaign Committee

SOURCES

Books, articles, and documents:
Alexander, *Money in Politics;* Bendiner, *White House Fever;* Blair, *The Control of Oil;* Dulaney, Phillips and Reese, *Speak, Mr. Speaker;* Engler, *The Brotherhood of Oil;* Fehrenbach, *Lone Star;* Flynn, *You're the Boss;* Heard, *The Costs of Democracy;* Ickes, *Secret Diary,* III; Leuchtenburg, *Franklin D. Roosevelt and the New Deal;* Lundberg, *America's Sixty Families;* Overacker, *Money in Elections;* Presley, *The Saga of Wealth;* Redding, *Inside the Democratic Party;* Sampson, *The Seven Sisters;* Solberg, *Oil Power;* Steinberg, *Sam Rayburn;* Webb and Carroll, *Handbook of Texas.*

Theodore H. White, "Texas: Land of Wealth and Fear," *The Reporter,* May 25, June 8, 1954.

Drew Pearson and Robert Allen, "Washington Merry-Go-Round," *Austin Daily Tribune,* Nov. 18, 1940.

"Statement of Patrick H. Drewry . . . required by law to be filed with the Clerk of the House of Representatives," undated, Box 6, JHP.

Wirtz, Rayburn and Roosevelt Papers.

Oral Histories:
Ray Roberts, James H. Rowe.

Interviews:
Andrew Biemiller, Richard Bolling, George Brown, Edward A. Clark, W. Sterling Cole, Thomas G. Corcoran, O. C. Fisher, David Garth, D. B. Hardeman, Kenneth Harding, Edouard V. M. Izac, Walter Jenkins, Wingate Lucas, George H. Mahon, James H. Rowe, Harold Young.

NOTES
(All dates 1940 unless otherwise indicated)
Marsh's suggestion: Young.
DCCC: Overacker, pp. 101–2. **Drewry's chairmanship:** Harding; Drewry to various Congressmen, form letters, May 11, Aug. 5, 1938, March 28, June 2, 13, 1939; Harding to Johnson, Aug. 10, 1938, "Democratic National Committee," Box 6, JHP. **An office so that he could accept:** Harding.

Pratt's $12,000: Overacker, p. 58. **Oregon expenditures:** Oregon, Secretary of State, Biennial Reports, 1911–1912, 1927–1928; Overacker, pp. 59–60. **Oregon in 1938:** Oregon, Secretary of State, Biennial Report, 1939, p. 109. **In most other states:** Overacker, p. 60, states that "Less complete and accurate figures indicate that in Michigan the average expenditures of congressional candidates in the elections of 1912 and 1914 was about $1,000; and that in Maine in 1924 it was less than $1,000. . . ." **"In the great majority":** Overacker, p. 60. **Discussions with Congressmen:** Among them, McFarlane, Mahon, Fisher, Izac, Biemiller, Lucas, Cole. **Confirmed by insiders:** Corcoran, Rowe, Harding, Hardeman.

Shortage of funds at DNC: Flynn, pp. 164–69. **2½ to 1:** Overacker, *American Political Science Review,* Aug., 1941, p. 713, based on the report of the Gillette Committee. **"Did not have":** Flynn, p. 166. **"Did not know":** Flynn, pp. 164–65. Flynn says that he repaired this situation with "party leaders" on a cross-country trip. If he included Congressmen among these leaders, however, his recollection is not shared by other veterans of the campaign. **Staff:** Flynn, pp. 161, 167. **"Turning point":** Heard, p. 212.

Early polls: For example, *NY Herald Tribune,* Sept. 15. **Study of 156 elections:** Lundberg, "Campaign Expenditures and Election Results," quoted in Heard, p. 17. **"The side":** Heard, p. 16.

Honeyman turning to Rayburn: Honeyman to Wirtz, Aug. 16; Wirtz to Honeyman, Aug. 23, Sept. 19, Oct. 17, Wirtz Papers, Box 6. **Rayburn asking Flynn for $100,000; reaction reserved:** Rayburn to Flynn, Aug. 20, Rayburn MF, Series I, Roll 9; Corcoran.

Caucus: Izac.

Early oil in Texas: Solberg, pp. 56–62, 127–28; Blair, p. 125; Sampson, pp. 37–40; White, "Texas," May 25, 1954; Presley, *passim.* **East Texas pool:** Solberg, pp. 131–32; Fehrenbach, p. 667; Webb and Carroll, p. 536; Presley, pp. 116–36; White, "Texas." **Cullen's share:** White, "Texas," p. 14. **"More fortunes":** Presley, p. 134. **Hunt's pipelines:** Presley, p. 122.

"Interesting document": "Extract from report filed with Clerk of the House of Representatives," attached to Ickes to Roosevelt, Aug. 10, 1935, OF-300, DNC Campaign Contributions, Aug., 1935–Sept., 1936, Roosevelt Papers. **Still the situation:** Corcoran. **Keystone sands:** Presley, p. 218. After the Keystone strike, he was approached by executives of Gulf Oil, who wanted to buy him out. They offered him $80,000,000. "No," Richardson replied. "I want to be *big* rich!"

Oilmen needing protection, and Morgenthau: White, "Texas," May 25, 1954; Solberg, pp. 9, 76–81, 165–67; Presley, pp. 183, 186, 315–16. **"Hot Oil" fight:** Solberg, pp. 134–35; Presley, pp. 137–80.

Rayburn friendly with them: Hardeman, Young, Bolling, Corcoran. **Was never to grasp it fully:** Bolling, Hardeman, Corcoran. **Cultivating Melasky:** Clark.

"A damned independent boy": Steinberg, *Rayburn,* p. 159. **"Praised the work":** *WP,* May 1. **Overture, reply:** Johnson to Rayburn, May 6; Rayburn to Johnson, May 13, Rayburn MF, Series II, Roll 1.

"I think": Rayburn to Aiken, Aug. 20, Rayburn MF, Series I, Roll 9. **Johnson's maneuvering:** Corcoran, Young; Steinberg, p. 152. The stories of Drewry's inefficiency were leaked to sympathetic New Deal columnists, who wrote about it: for example, Pearson and Allen, "Washington Merry-Go-Round," Nov. 18.

Approach through Jones: Jones to Roosevelt, Sept. 14. In Johnson's files are drafts showing that Johnson prepared this letter (Box 6, JHP). **Draft by Johnson for Flynn's signature:** Various drafts, all headed "B." Also Watson to Maverick, Oct. 3; Maverick to Roosevelt, Oct. 8; Johnson to Maverick, "DNC," Box 6, JHP. **Flynn balks; Johnson attempts to get Roberts' post:** Watson to Flynn, Sept. 19, FDR-LBJ MF; Corcoran; Ickes to Roosevelt, Sept. 27; Johnson to Roosevelt, Oct. 1, PPF 6149, Roosevelt Papers; Ickes to Roosevelt, Sept. 23, PSF Interior Department, Box 76, Roosevelt Papers; Drewry to Roosevelt, Oct. 2, PPF 6149, Roosevelt Papers; Johnson to Green, Sept. 30, Box 7, JHP.

Flynn threatens to resign: Johnson to Maverick, Oct. 19, "DNC," Box 6, JHP. **"It would be inadvisable":** Draft attached to Johnson to Roosevelt, Oct. 1, Box 6, JHP. The revised letter is in PPF 6149, Roosevelt Papers. **"In the morning":** Roosevelt to McIntyre, Oct. 4, PPF 6149, Roosevelt Papers. **Still reluctant:** Corcoran, Young.

Trend to GOP: For example, *WP,* Oct. 1; *Washington Star,* Sept. 22; *NYT,* Sept. 18; *NY Herald Tribune,* Sept. 15. **Maine vote:** *Washington Star,* Sept. 10, *NY Herald Tribune,* Sept. 11. **"A skeleton":** Marsh to Young, Sept. 19, Oct. 22, "DNC," Box 6, JHP.

Not a penny: Drewry Statement. **"Will you see":** Wayne Johnson to Rayburn, Oct. 2, Rayburn MF, Series II, Roll 1 (italics added). **Drifting away:** *NYT,* Oct. 9, 11. **In district after district:** See next chapter.

Michigan's 16th CD: Lesinski to Johnson, Oct. 21, 28; Johnson to Lesinski, Oct. 24 (two telegrams), Box 8, JHP. **"When you saw":** Harding. **Lesinski's $100, $10,000 from DNC; Parceled out:** Drewry Statement, pp. 1–3. **Fight being lost:** Pearson and Allen, Washington Merry-Go-Round, Nov. 18; Corcoran, Young.

DuPont contributions: Harding to DuPont, Sept. 27, Rayburn MF, Series II, Roll 1. **"It appeared":** Roberts, quoted in Miller, *Lyndon,* p. 76.

Rayburn asks Roosevelt to make Johnson secretary: Ickes, p. 348; Corcoran. **"Tell Lyndon":** Pearson and Allen, "Washington Merry-Go-Round," Nov. 18. **Flynn and Drewry letters:** In "DNC," Box 6, JHP. **A call to Houston:** Brown.

32. The Munsey Building

SOURCES

Documents, books:
The principal source for this chapter is Johnson House Papers, Boxes 6, 7, 8, and 9, which include the files and inter-office memos written by Johnson and his staff in the Munsey Building office, as well as copies of his correspondence with Congressmen, and their letters and telegrams to him.

The amount of money sent by Johnson in checks to individual Congressmen is indicated in handwritten notations by Johnson and his secretaries on several typed lists found in these boxes. These lists (and the abbreviations used to refer to them) are as follows: "List of Congressmen to Whom Letter Sent by LBJ, October 15, 1940" (Oct. 15 List), Box 6; "Complete Mailing List—Oct. 25, 1940" (Oct. 25 List), Box 7; An untitled, state-by-state summary of requests sent in by Congressmen (State List), Box 7; "Names of Those Who Have Not Replied to the Telegram of October 29, 1940" (Oct. 29 List), Box 6.

Almost all the letters, telegrams, and papers in the following notes are filed either in folders bearing the same name as that of the correspondent (a letter from Andrew Edmiston, for example, being found in the folder titled "Edmiston, Andrew"), or in the folders in Box 6 marked "Democratic National Committee, 1940" or "1940—Democratic National Committee," so individual folder citations are given only when the folders bear another title.

Alexander, *Money in Politics;* Burns, *Roosevelt: The Lion and the Fox;* Croly, *Marcus Alonzo Hanna;* Dorough, *Mr. Sam;* Heard, *The Costs of Democracy;* Ickes, *Secret Diary, III;* Overacker, *Money in Elections;* Redding, *Inside the Democratic Party.*

"Statement of Patrick H. Drewry . . . filed with the Clerk of the House of Representatives during period from October 21 to October 26, 1940" (referred to as "Drewry Statement"). The other statements required for this period are not in the files of the Clerk of the House.

Roosevelt papers.

Oral Histories:
Welly K. Hopkins, Dorothy Nichols, James H. Rowe.

Interviews:
George R. Brown, Emanuel Celler, Edward A. Clark, Thomas G. Corcoran, Kenneth G. Harding, John Holton, Welly K. Hopkins, Edouard Izac, Walter Jenkins, Dale Miller, James H. Rowe, Wilton Woods, Mary Louise Glass Young, Harold H. Young.

NOTES
(All dates 1940 unless otherwise noted.)

Corcoran and Clark on political fundraising: Corcoran, Clark. **Contributions by corporations prohibited:** 18 U.S. Code 241–256 (34 Stat., 1074). **$5,000 limit:** 54 Stat., 640, Sec. 13, July, 1940. **Reason**

Herman did it through six associates: Brown, Woods. **"You were supposed":** G. Brown to Johnson, Oct. 19, Box 12, LBJA SN. **"All of the folks":** Johnson to G. Brown, Oct. 21, Box 12, LBJA SN. **Each check $5,000:** J. O. Corwin, Jr., to Johnson, Oct. 17, "General-Unarranged," Box 7; James L. Melton to Johnson, Oct. 15, and Johnson to Melton, Nov. 1, Box 6. **He had persuaded:** Corcoran. **Richardson sent $5,000:** Drewry Statement, p. 1. **Murchison sent $5,000:** Murchison to Johnson, Oct. 16, Box 3, PPCF. **Fentress:** Fentress to Johnson, Oct. 17, Box 8. **"We have sent":** Johnson to Sherley, Oct. 21, Box 6.

Made out to the DCCC and mailed by it: JHP, Boxes 6–9 *passim.* **A letter stating:** Samples are the Corwin, Melton, Murchison letters listed above. **"As result my visit":** An example is Johnson to Charles F. McLaughlin, Oct. 17, Box 6.

Renting and furnishing the office: "Commercial Furniture–M.E. 46661," Box 6. **Questionnaire:** "Campaign—Oct. 15, 1940," Box 6. The questionnaire was not sent out until the following day so that the candidates would have time to receive Drewry's letter first. **Selecting the candidates to be helped:** The initial lists compiled by Henderson and Connally are in Box 6. **"Districts Which Produce":** In folder with same title, Box 8. **Luncheon meeting:** Untitled list in Box 6. **Seventy-seven recipients:** "Congressmen to Whom the Letter and the Form Should Be Sent and the Manner in Which They Are To Be Addressed," Box 6.

Replies to questionnaires: All Box 6, except O'Neal, which is Box 9. **"Robert Secrest called":** Inter-office memorandum, Box 6. **"Nothing will help":** Secrest to Johnson, Oct. 17, "General-Unarranged," Box 7. **"I feel sure":** O'Neal to Johnson, Box 9.

Their hopes were answered: The amount of the checks in these early letters to Congressmen is determined from individual correspondence with the Congressmen, and from handwritten notations on the October 15 List. (In some cases, as shown by individual communications, these notations include the amounts sent by Drewry before Johnson became associated with the committee; in those cases the amounts shown on the Drewry Statement for the "pre-Johnson" period are subtracted from the amounts on the October 15 List.) **Smith:** Smith to Johnson, Oct. 23, mentions his gratitude at finding "two Air Mail letters from" Harding. See also two letters from Smith to Johnson, Oct. 26, Oct. 28, Box 6. **McLaughlin:** Johnson to McLaughlin, Oct. 17, and McLaughlin to Johnson, Oct. 17, Box 6. **Izac:** Izac. Johnson apparently sent Izac the AS RESULT MY VISIT telegram because in Izac to Johnson, Oct. 17, Izac states that he had already received $200 (from the pre-Johnson contribution), and mentions "your wire," which he evidently felt referred to the $200. The California Congressman was soon to be enlightened. On Oct. 21, he wrote Johnson, "Since writing you the other day I have received another check . . . in the sum of $500." This letter of thanks crossed in the mail with another from Johnson: "I'll try to get another five out your way as I did last week." Johnson's attempt was successful. On Oct. 23, Izac wrote Johnson thanking him for the second $500 (Izac to Johnson, Oct. 21, 23; Johnson to Izac, Oct. 19, 21, Box 6). **Honeyman:** "Memo for LBJ" from "jbc," Oct. 17. **She thought that:** Nan Honeyman to Johnson, Oct. 18. **"Received 5 point":** Honeyman to Johnson, Oct. 19. All in Box 8.

"The text": Smith to Johnson, Oct. 23, Box 6. **"I am glad":** McLaughlin to Johnson, Oct. 17, Box 6. **Izac:** See above. **"Dear Lyndon":** Honeyman to Johnson, Oct. 21, Box 8.

Garment center: Corcoran. **UMW:** Hopkins OH, p. 6. **Wall Street:** Paul Shields to Johnson, Oct. 24, Box 6; Drewry Statement, p. 2. **Charles Marsh:** Mary Louise Glass Young. **Smith check:** Johnson Oct. 15 List. **"Today I'm asking a Texas friend":** Johnson to Sutphin, Oct. 17, Box 9. **Sent that night:** Johnson Oct. 15 List. **"If you badly need":** Johnson to McLaughlin, Oct. 19, Box 6. **"Do you have?":** Johnson to Barnes, Oct. 21, "General-Unarranged," Box 7.

Asked Aiken for $25,000: Johnson to Rayburn, "Airmail and Special Delivery," Oct. 22. **Out of funds:** Johnson to Rayburn, Oct. 22 Telegram. Both from Box 52, LBJA CF.

Knight's $2,000 gift: Dorough, p. 303. **Two communications from Johnson:** They are the two, dated Oct. 22, cited above. **"Please see":** Johnson to Kittrell, Oct. 23, Box 6. **Envelopes containing cash:** Corcoran, Young. The author asked Young how much they contained. Young said he did not know how much, but that the figure was in the tens of thousands of dollars. This estimate does not appear to be exaggerated. The total contributions of the oilmen have been put at $100,000

or more by a number of observers. For example, Robert S. Allen, whose information on Texas politics generally proves reliable, said that "He [Johnson] didn't tell me this, but I got the information from various sources that he had come up with a campaign fund of a hundred or more thousand dollars. . . . His money undoubtedly came from oil sources" (Miller, *Lyndon,* p. 76). Allen's partner, Drew Pearson, whose information was apparently based in part on the Internal Revenue Service investigation discussed in Chapter 35, wrote in a 1956 column when Johnson was "a young congressman . . . he hired a room in the back of Washington's Munsey Building and passed out $110,000 in cash to fellow Democrats . . . It was oil-gas money from Texas" (*Raleigh News and Observer,* Feb. 8, 1956). (Pearson incorrectly gave the date not as the 1940 but as the 1938 congressional elections.) The key figure in the money-raising appears to have been Sid Richardson. Dugger says that "Harold Young, who talked to many Democratic candidates for Johnson, believed oilman Sid Richardson alone ponied up as much as $100,000." Richardson himself said he raised $70,000 (Dugger, *The Politician,* pp. 224–5). Determining the amount Johnson distributed in checks from the DCCC is difficult if not impossible, because the several overall lists of contributions cited in the notes do not square with each other, and there are notations on letters and telegrams of contributions which do not appear on any of the lists. The best estimate the author can make of the amount distributed by checks through the DCCC is $84,950. The total of contributions which were made by check and of which there is a record in Johnson's files is $74,000, which does not equal even the $84,950 figure. And of the money distributed by Johnson through Young and other outside channels there are, of course, only occasional traces such as those mentioned below. (For further details, see the note in this chapter: **Johnson raised his own.**)

Johnson arranged: Young; see Connally to Johnson, Oct. 25, "Pinchot, Governor," Box 9, and undated, Young to Johnson, "Boland," Box 7. **Johnson to Parsons:** Oct. 25, and Parsons to Johnson, Oct. 28, Box 9. **"Chicago line":** Oct. 29 List, p. 1. Also, next to the names of congressional candidates on a list compiled in the Munsey Building office are notations of the amounts they have received. Among those notations are "Has had $300 and Harold";

"Gave extra $100 on Chicago level"; "Sent $200 on Sabath." Congressman Adolph J. Sabath of Chicago was chairman of the House Rules Committee. (Oct. 29 List, pp. 1, 2.)

"Not only": Crowley to Farley, Sept. 14, 1936, OF-300-Texas, Roosevelt Papers. **E. Roosevelt wiring Roeser, but Rayburn calling him from Dallas:** Roeser to FDR, Oct. 28, OF-300-Texas, 1938-45, Roosevelt Papers. **"Dear Mr. Johnson":** Roeser to Johnson, Oct. 23, "General-Unarranged," Box 7. **Other oilmen's contributions:** Young. **Trusted Rayburn:** Corcoran, Young.

Just call on me: Copies of this form letter can be found in Boxes 6–9. **"I wish":** Johnson to McLaughlin, Oct. 19, Box 6. Johnson also wrote to candidates in the same terms of exhortation that he used to his staff, expressing the philosophy that had become familiar to Latimer and Jones. Encouraging Congressman Louis Ludlow of Indianapolis, he wrote, "Don't leave a stone unturned" (Johnson to Ludlow, Nov. 2, Box 6). **"I do hope":** Johnson to Robinson, Oct. 18, Box 6. **"Senator Pepper speaking":** Johnson to Magnuson, Oct. 28, Box 6.

"I am debating": Weiss to Johnson, Oct. 27, Box 9. **"Please wire":** Weiss to Johnson, Nov. 2, "Telegrams (Duplicate copy of each wire sent)," Box 9. **"Following appeared":** Snyder to Johnson, Oct. 28, Box 6. **"Pepper will speak":** Havenner to Johnson, Oct. 27, Box 6. **"We are requesting":** May to Johnson, Oct. 27, Box 6. **Return wire; his own wire;** Wagner to Snyder, Oct. 28; Johnson to Snyder, Oct. 29, Box 6.

Speakers: Previously, Congressmen had been relying on the DNC to furnish speakers, but its shortage of funds made this difficult in 1940. **Tenerowicz:** Johnson to Schwert, Oct. 26, "General-Unarranged," Box 7. **Mitchell:** Boxes 7–9 *passim.* **La Guardia:** Hunter to Johnson, Oct. 27, Box 6. **"Off-the-reservation":** Beiter to Johnson, Oct. 24, Box 7. **Marvin Jones:** Ferguson to Johnson, Box 8. **Johnson arranging radio broadcasts:** Connally to Johnson, Oct. 25, Box 9; Young to Johnson, undated, Box 7; Johnson to Snyder, Nov. 2, Box 7.

"A lot of projects": Jenkins, Rowe, Corcoran. **Smith's airport:** Smith to Johnson, Oct. 26, Nov. 4; Johnson to Smith, Oct. 29, Nov. 2, 4, Box 6. **Boland's local labor leader:** Boland to Johnson, Oct. 19, Box 7. **Houston's labor leader:** Houston to Drewry, Oct. 15; Harding to Johnson,

Oct. 22; Johnson to Houston, Oct. 25; Johnson to Olmsted, Oct. 28; McGuire to Houston, Oct. 31, Box 8. **Smith's new problem:** Smith to Johnson, Oct. 23, Box 6. **Corcoran introduces Johnson to labor leaders:** Corcoran. **"Talked to Lubin":** Johnson to Smith, Oct. 25, Box 6.

"Thanks much": Johnson to Smith, Oct. 29, Box 6. **"Do you have?":** Johnson to Fox, Oct. 25, Box 8. **"Call on me":** For example, Johnson to J. Joseph Smith, Oct. 24, Box 6. **Honeyman:** See her folder, Box 8. **Rowe asking Roosevelt to sign letter:** Rowe to Roosevelt, Oct. 29, 0955A, Roosevelt Papers.

Hunter's poll: Hunter to Johnson, Oct. 27, Box 6. **"The President's broadcast":** Clark to Johnson, Oct. 26, Box 6. **John L. Lewis:** Burns, p. 449. **Johnson asking candidates for report:** On Oct. 26, he wired: "For important use Monday morning, may I have letter immediately giving your judgment political situation your district and any shift that has taken place," Box 7. **"Has not injured":** Larrabee to Johnson, Oct. 27. **Asking Lewis to resign:** Schwinger to Johnson, Oct. 26. **"Rank and file":** Kelso to Johnson, Oct. 26. **"Following up":** Randolph to Johnson, Oct. 28. **Bradley:** To Johnson, Oct. 28. All these candidates' reports are in Box 6. **Able to tell the White House:** Corcoran.

"Must have $250": Hughes to Johnson, Oct. 30, "Campaign—Oct. 15," Box 6. **"Advertising programs":** Beiter to Johnson, Oct. 29, Box 7. **"Chances bright":** Lavery to Johnson, Oct. 30, Box 6. **"Have set up":** Petrie to Johnson, Oct. 29, Box 9. **"Urgency need at least $500":** Weisman to Johnson, Oct. 30, Box 6. **"A colored minister":** Kenneth Harding.

"Practically all colored": Mitchell to Johnson, Oct. 29, Box 6. **"Could use $500":** Rogers to Johnson, Oct. 31, Box 6. **"Can carry districts":** Murphy to Johnson, Oct. 30, Box 6. **"Need $1,000":** Sigars to Johnson, Oct. 30, Box 6. **New Brunswick:** Author's own observation while working for New Brunswick Democratic organization. **"Key men in the CIO":** Smith to Johnson, Oct. 26, Box 6. **"Know attempt":** Sheridan to Johnson, Oct. 28, Box 6.

White House meeting: Johnson to Sherley, Oct. 28, Box 6.

Johnson raised his own—From Brown & Root: Two contributions—both for $2,500—are recorded in Johnson's office records for this week. One is from Carl Burkhart, Brown & Root's office manager, the other is from L. H. Durst, another official of the firm. However, Brown &

Root may have provided Johnson with considerably more money than Johnson's office records show. Wilton Woods, for example, states that he had brought a $7,500 contribution to Washington, and gave it to Herbert Henderson. And various interviews suggest that additional sums were given. The IRS investigation detailed in Chapter 35 raises the question of whether the firm gave still more money to Johnson to distribute to other candidates, but as Chapter 35 shows, the investigation was stopped before this question could be answered. **From Marsh:** Young; Johnson to Parsons, Oct. 25; Parsons to Johnson, Oct. 28, Box 9. **Lechner:** Lechner to Johnson, Oct. 29, Box 6. **Frost:** Frost to Johnson, Oct. 28, Box 8. **Strickland:** Strickland to Johnson, Oct. 29, Box 9. **Murchison:** Johnson to C. W. Murchison, Oct. 29, Box 6. **Wynne:** Johnson to Wynne, Oct. 29, "General-Unarranged," Box 7. **Johnson's telegram:** A sample can be found in "Telegrams" folder, Box 9. Did Johnson go to Dallas in person and pick up cash there himself? The *Austin Statesman* was to report on May 25, 1941, that during the 1940 campaign, "with the aid of his friend Rayburn, Johnson went to Texas and raised more than $60,000." The author has found no evidence of this trip.

Kelly telegram: To Johnson, Oct. 30, Box 6. **"We need funds":** Imhoff to Johnson, Nov. 2, Box 6. **"We are six hundred":** Heyns to Johnson, "Campaign-Oct. 15," Box 6. **"Approximately ten thousand majority":** Secrest to Johnson, Oct. 29, Box 7. **"Lyndon urgently need":** Sheridan to Johnson, Oct. 30, Box 6. **"Lyndon situation in danger":** Hennings to Johnson, Oct. 30, "Campaign-Oct. 15," Box 6.

Jackson telegrams: Jackson to Johnson, Oct. 28 and Oct. 30, "Campaign-Oct. 15," Box 6. **Petrie:** To Johnson, Oct. 29, 31, Box 9.

"In trouble": Memo, "LD" to Johnson, Oct. 30, Box 6. **Bauer:** Two telegrams to Johnson sent 1:37 p.m. and 5:53 p.m., Oct. 30, Box 7. **Martin Smith:** Smith letters to Johnson cited above, all in Box 6. **"Imperative":** Smith to Johnson, Oct. 28, Box 6. **Tracking, etc.:** Leroux to Johnson, Oct. 28, Box 6.

This list: This is the State List, "General-Unarranged," Box 7.

"Has good chance to win": Hill to Johnson, Oct. 22, "Houston," Box 8. The information on Fox, O'Connor, Brooks, Anderson, Murphy, Armbruster, Wolf, Jackson, Myers, is from the State List,

supplemented in some cases by their original telegrams which are quoted or summarized on that list, and by Corcoran. The Havenner and Rogers contributions are shown on "Oct. 29 List," Box 6. The Geyer contribution is found on "Complete Mailing List, Oct. 25." **Rogers:** Also Rogers to Johnson, Oct. 31, Nov. 7, Box 6. **J. Joseph Smith:** Johnson to Smith, Nov. 2, Box 6. **Kirwan:** John McCormack to Johnson, Oct. 18; Kirwan to Johnson, Nov. 4, Box 6. **Leavy:** The $600 total is compiled from Johnson's various lists. **"Think":** Leavy to Johnson, Nov. 4, Box 6.

"Never did anything": Rowe. **"If I feel":** Johnson to LeHand, Nov. 4, "Telegrams (Duplicate copy)," Box 9. **Early information:** Tenerowicz to Johnson, Nov. 5, Box 9; Shanley to Johnson, Nov. 9, Box 6; O'Brien to Johnson, Nov. 5, Box 6; Izac to Johnson, Oct. 29, Nov. 5, Box 6; Green to Johnson, Oct. 30, Box 6; Miller to Johnson, 2:37 a.m., Nov. 6, Box 6. **At Election Night Party:** Rowe, Jenkins. **Betting on the returns:** Rowe to Johnson, Dec. 11, Box 32, LBJA SN. (On the 30-seat wager, Rowe wrote: "Johnson wins. And how! Is my face red! But then, Rowe did not have as high or accurate an impression of Johnson's ability as did Johnson. Maybe I should pay double.") Johnson jokingly proposed charging Rowe a hundred dollars for "doubting LBJ's ability to forecast Congressional election returns" (Johnson to Rowe, Feb. 11, 1941, Box 32, LBJA SN).

Hyde Park scene: Burns, pp. 451–55. **Roosevelt telephoning Johnson and Rowe:** Jenkins, Rowe.

"My father": Harding. **"I want":** Mitchell to Johnson, Oct. 29, Box 6. **Honeyman:** Her folder, Box 8. **Gratitude:** Kee to Johnson, Nov. 8; Hunter to Johnson, Nov. 8, both Box 6; Sasscer to Johnson, Nov. 7, and Allen to Johnson, Nov. 8, both "General-Unarranged," Box 7; Morrison to Johnson, Nov. 21. **"There was a lot":** Jenkins. **"To the boys":** Pearson and Allen, "Washington Merry-Go-Round," *Austin Daily Tribune*, Nov. 18.

McCormack: Unsigned memo "LBJ talked with . . . ," McCormack to Johnson, undated, both Box 6. **"Oh, Lyndon Johnson!":** Kelley quoted by Mary Louise Glass Young, who would become his secretary. **Realization spread:** Among the Congressmen who described this are Celler and Izac. **"A power base":** Rowe. **"Made lots of enemies":** Roberts quoted in Miller, pp. 76–77. **McCormack, Sutphin:**

See citations above. **May to Johnson:** Oct. 27, Box 6. **Connection with Kelly:** Young. **"One of your chief boosters":** Aiken to Johnson, Nov. 6, Box 7. **"Because":** Miller. **"A lot of guys":** Izac.

Brown & Root: Through October 18, the DNC had contributed $25,000, according to the Drewry statement. Brown & Root had contributed at least $30,000, and possibly considerably more (see citations above). Thereafter, the difference appears to have widened. The lack of any further Drewry statements makes it impossible to gauge further contributions from the Committee, but the only one mentioned in the Munsey files is the $5,000 Johnson mentions and there is a constant refrain in Johnson's correspondence of lack of any substantial further support. Brown & Root gave at least $42,500—$2,500 each from Burkhart and Durst, and $7,500 from Woods and possibly substantially more.

Louis column: In *San Angelo Standard-Times,* Nov. 29. **Symbolic scene:** Ickes, p. 348.

Never implemented: Figures found in filed statutory reports. Such overall views of campaign financing as Overacker, Heard, and Alexander differ so widely among themselves—and from statements made by men such as Corcoran, Harding, and Rowe who were actually involved—that no accurate picture of the actual fund-raising activities can be ascertained. But everyone spoken to agrees that Johnson's fund-raising was on a new scale for his party. After he moved on to the Senate, the fund-raising of the DCCC appears to have dropped back for a time to pre-Johnson levels. In 1952, says Jack Redding, the committee's treasurer, "The congressional committee had available a meager $17,000 for campaign funds." At that point, attempts were made to improve the committee's organization and fund-raising capabilities, but as late as 1956, the total amount spent by the DCCC was $188,000, which was, Redding says, "the largest amount ever spent by the Democratic Congressional Committee in a presidential election year." When the inflation rate is factored in, that amount, raised sixteen years after Lyndon Johnson's 1940 effort, was probably less than he raised in 1940. (Redding, p. 298. And see Heard, p. 293, and Alexander, p. 12.) Redding and all observers agree that Republican expenditures consistently outstripped the Democrats.

"No one before": Rowe. "A one-man

national committee": Allen, quoted in Miller, p. 77. **Unprecedented:** Corcoran, Rowe, and all Congressmen interviewed. **"Nobody":** Rowe.

"My delay": Rowsey to Flynn, Oct. 23, 1942, Box 37. [Flynn then appealed again (Flynn to Rowsey, Oct. 26, 1942), and Rowsey agreed to give without Johnson's okay, but only because he had been unable to get in touch with Johnson, and time was growing short (Rowsey to Flynn, Oct. 27, Box 37; Corcoran). Other oilmen refused to send money to Flynn without Johnson's approval.] **"These $200 driblets":** Johnson to Rayburn, Oct. 10, 1942, Box 52, LBJA CF. **Hanna:** Croly, pp. 220, 325.

"Stern from aft": Brown, who is also the source of the subchaser award story.

33. Through the Back Door

SOURCES

See sources for Chapter 29.

NOTES

Letters of flattery: All from "Campaign-Oct. 15, 1940," Box 6, JHP.

Discussions with Roosevelt: Lady Bird Johnson; Mrs. Johnson, quoted in Miller, *Lyndon,* p. 67. **"He'd call me up":** Johnson, quoted by Sidey, in Miller, p. 77. The fact that at least some of these discussions were not at Johnson's request but at Roosevelt's is confirmed at several places in the Roosevelt Papers. On one Saturday not long after the election, for example, Johnson was in Texas when the White House telephoned his office to say that the President wanted to see Congressman Johnson. His office couldn't reach him over the weekend, so no reply was given, and on Monday the White House telephoned again (Johnson to Roosevelt, Nov. 29, 1940, PPF 6149, Roosevelt Papers). **"Do you think?":** Roosevelt to Johnson, Dec. 27, 1940, PPF 3241, Roosevelt Papers. **LCRA bonds:** Jones, p. 180. **"I think":** Wirtz to Lady Bird Johnson, July 28, 1942, Box 37, LBJA SN. **"One of high excitement":** Mrs. Johnson. **"Just more capable":** Rowe. **"I want you":** Hoffman, quoted in Miller, p. 67. **"The kind of uninhibited":** Ickes is quoted by Janeway; Corcoran says Ickes also told him 'of Roosevelt's remark. **"The only man":** Rowe. **"Complicated"; "used":** Rowe.

"Filled with": Sherwood, p. 206. **"Soft

touch": Tully, p. 153. **"A perfect Roose-
velt man?":** Rowe.
　LeHand: And he sent Miss LeHand
nuts and candy, usually Texas pralines
(LeHand to Johnson, Nov. 30, 1940,
FDR-Johnson microfilm, LBJL). **"One of
the great souls":** Tully, p. 2. **Tully's suggesting Johnson be secretary:** Daniels, p.
273.
　Description of "back door" method:
Rowe, Corcoran, Tully, p. 286.
　Personally, hand her: Rowe, Corcoran,
Tully's own description of officials urging
her to put letters on the top of the pile,
Tully, p. 80. He sometimes sent her a note
about a memo: for example, "Dear Grace:
Here is a memorandum I hope the Boss
will read soon. Sincerely, Lyndon," Johnson to Tully, July 27, 1942, OF-300-
Texas, 1933–1945, Roosevelt Papers. **He
would "tell Grace":** Rowe. And after
Missy's stroke, Johnson often sent her
flowers (for example, Johnson to Tully,
and Tully to Johnson, July 21, July 23,
1941: "Miss Tully wrote to Congressman
Johnson telling him that 'Missy' has enjoyed the flowers so much and asked her
to thank him for his constant thought of
her." FDR-Johnson microfilm, LBJL).
　"'Jim Rowe and I'": Rowe. **Late-afternoon conversations; reversing the charges:**
Rather to Rowe, Aug. 24, 1943, Box 32,
LBJA SN, talks of the "usual" late-afternoon chats of about thirty minutes, and
of Johnson's insistence on having the
White House pay for the call. **"A deadly
silence":** Rowe to Johnson, Sept. 21, 1941,
Box 32, LBJA SN.

34. "Pass the Biscuits, Pappy"

SOURCES

Books, articles, and documents:
　Allen, ed., *Our Sovereign State*; Banks,
Money, Marbles, and Chalk; Douglas, *The
Court Years*; Goodwyn, *Lone Star Land*;
Green, *The Establishment in Texas Poli-
tics*; Gunther, *Inside U.S.A.*; Henderson,
Maury Maverick; Ickes, *Secret Diary*,
Vol. III; Key, *Southern Politics in State
and Nation*; Lynch, *The Duke of Duval*;
McKay, *W. Lee O'Daniel and Texas Poli-
tics*; Perry, *Texas: A World in Itself*;
White, *Texas: An Informal Biography*;
WPA, *Texas: A Guide to the Lone Star
State*.
　Edgar G. Shelton, "Political Conditions
Among Texas Mexicans Along the Rio
Grande" (unpublished Master's Thesis,

Austin, 1946). Harfield Weedin, Memoir
(unpublished).
　Walter Davenport, "Where's Them Bis-
cuits, Pappy?", *Collier's*, Jan. 6, 1940;
Walter Davenport, "Savior From Texas,"
The Nation, June 21, 1941; Ralph Mait-
land, "San Antonio: The Shame of Texas,"
Forum, Aug. 1939; J. P. McEvoy, "I've
Got That Million Dollar Smile," *Ameri-
can Mercury*, October, 1938; Douglas O.
Weeks, "The Texas-Mexicans and the Poli-
tics of South Texas," *American Political
Science Review*, Aug. 1930, pp. 606–27;
Owen P. White, "Machine Made," *Collier's*, Sept. 18, 1957; Roland Young,
"Lone Star Razzle Dazzle," *The Nation*,
June 21, 1941. "27 Candidates Seek Senate
Seat in Screwy Texas Race," *Life*, June 30,
1941; "Pappy Over Cyclone," *Time*, Aug.
5, 1940; *Time*, May 5, 1941.
　The basic source of campaign coverage
are the daily stories in the *Austin American-Statesman, Dallas Morning News, Corpus Christi Caller-Times, Fort Worth
Press*; and the clippings from weekly newspapers found in the Johnson House Papers, both in House Scrapbooks, Books 6,
Vols. I and II, and unbound in various
files.
　The Johnson House Papers, Boxes 10–
34, contain the written material—letters,
memoranda, jotted notes, reports from advance men and other campaigners in the
field, etc.—from his campaign headquarters.
　Home movies of the campaign taken by
Lady Bird Johnson; tape recordings of
Johnson and O'Daniel speeches, at LBJL.
　Roosevelt Papers. Werner File.
　The results of all Belden Polls are summarized in McKay, p. 481, which is the
source, unless otherwise noted, for all
figures on those polls.

Oral Histories:
　Robert S. Allen, W. Sherman Birdwell,
Raymond E. Buck, Willard Deason, Sam
Fore, Jr., Gordon Fulcher, Charles Her-
ring, Welly K. Hopkins, Walter C. Horna-
day, Luther E. Jones, Carroll Keach,
Gerald C. Mann, Marshall McNeil, Wright
Patman, W. R. Poage, Daniel J. Quill, Ray
Roberts, Grace Tully, Claud C. Wild, Sr.

Interviews:
　George Brown, Edward Clark, Thomas
Corcoran, Ann Fears Crawford, D. B.
Hardeman, Eliot Janeway, Walter Jenkins,
Sam Houston Johnson, Herman Jones,
Luther E. Jones, Vann Kennedy, William
J. Lawson, Bob Long, Wingate Lucas,

George Mahon, Gerald C. Mann, Frank Oltorf, J. J. Pickle, Daniel J. Quill, James H. Rowe, Emmett Shelton, E. Babe Smith, Arthur Stehling, Coke Stevenson, Jr., Wilton Woods, Ralph Yarborough, Mary Louise Glass Young, Harold Young.

NOTES

(All dates 1941 unless otherwise noted)

Jenkins telephoning: Jenkins. **Wirtz in early and discussing candidacy:** Rather, quoted in Miller, *Lyndon*, p. 81. Sheppard, sixty-six years old, had served on Capitol Hill, in the House and Senate, for a total of thirty-nine years. He had served in the Senate since 1913.
All but unknown: Interviews with many Texas politicians; moreover, the first Belden Poll, taken on April 21, gave Johnson 5.4% of the vote. **East Texas radio poll:** The station was KFRD in Longview: *DMN*, April 18.
Four-to-one margin: *Texas Almanac*, 1941–42, p. 400. **He obviously:** Corcoran, Rowe. **"Too frightful":** Rowe to Roosevelt, April 10, PSF 184, Roosevelt Papers. This memo shows again a number of misimpressions about Texas politics which, thanks to Johnson, Rowe believed. **"A Roosevelt worshipper":** Hardeman. **Had worked for Johnson:** Mann.
Mann biography: McKay, pp. 70–72, 211–12, 411–19; "Mann's the Mann," campaign brochure; Hardeman, Clark, Mann. **"Continuous war":** McKay, p. 414. **"A brilliant career":** McKay, pp. 413–14. **Several newspapers:** An example is *DMN*, April 28; others were in Kilgore and San Antonio. Says McKay (p. 414): "Several of the more substantial newspapers referred to Mann's devotion to principle and fine statesmanship, his ability, his courage and his refusal to yield to political pressure and expediency." **Mann vs. O'Daniel in polls:** McKay, p. 482. **The only way:** *Austin Tribune*, July 6. Senator Tom Connally was one of those who went to Roosevelt and tried to explain this to him, Corcoran says.
A little deceit: The Rowe memo of April 10, for example, told the President, "You may naturally suspect he [Johnson] cannot make it, but . . . newspapers all over Texas are starting a campaign for him." In fact, at the time, the bulk of newspaper support in Texas—outside of Marsh's newspapers—was for Gerald Mann. **"Unbranded and unknown":** Unsigned and unaddressed memo, April 11, 1941, PSF 75-Interior Department, Roosevelt Papers.

And on April 14, Rowe, in a memo to Roosevelt urging him to talk to Johnson about the race, said that Mann "was put in office by the public utilities"—which was not correct (Rowe to Roosevelt, PSF 184, Roosevelt Papers).
Roosevelt orchestration: *Time*, May 5; *WP; NYT*, April 23; wire service story in *Kenedy Advance*, April 24. **"FDR Picks Johnson":** *DMN*, April 23. This story referred to the President's "blessing" of Johnson. The *Taylor Times* headlined "F.D. Tosses Lyndon's Hat for Senate."
"Roosevelt and unity": For example, *AS*, April 23. **"100 percent"; "All-out":** For example, *Houston Chronicle*, June 5. For an example of Johnson's ads stressing this point, see *Williamson Sun*, June 27. **Slogan had been a private password:** Handwritten notes in "M," Box 14, JHP. A typical editorial from *AA-S* (June 24) shows how strongly Marsh's papers stressed the Roosevelt-Johnson link. Under the headline "A Vote for Johnson Is a Vote for Loyalty to Hard-Pressed President," the editorial said: "The president of the United States is the target . . . of the spears of the greatest enemy of freedom the world has ever known. Is it too much to give him Lyndon Johnson, the man for whom he has shown preference, a preference without prejudice for the qualities of most of the other candidates? Is it too much to give him one who will assist him in bearing the weight of his shield?"
"A fatherly interest": Undated column in Johnson House Scrapbooks, **"Although overburdened":** Alsop and Kintner, *DMN*, May 17. They also wrote that Johnson hadn't wanted to run, and that Roosevelt had persuaded him. Kintner was to recall: "You might say the White House had something to do with inspiring that column" (Kintner, quoted in Miller, p. 83). **Young:** Young. **Department of Agriculture officials:** Ickes to Roosevelt, April 25; Roosevelt to Rowe, April 30, OF-300-Texas, Roosevelt Papers. **REA:** Corcoran. **Ickes telephoning:** Ickes, p. 526. **"Everybody":** Rowe, **"Referred to":** Watson, "Memorandum for Record," June 11, OF-300-Texas, Roosevelt Papers. **Jenkins' experiences:** Jenkins.
"Everyone:" Keach, quoted by Mrs. Johnson. **"It was expected":** Pickle. **Ironclad chain of command:** Described vividly by a number of campaign workers, including Long, Woods. **Twelve two-man teams:** Their organization and financing is detailed in the daily reports sent back by the teams to Johnson's Austin headquarters,

Boxes 11–16, 19, JHP. These reports—fascinating documents in rural campaigning in Texas—furnish the basis for many of the general statements made about the Johnson campaign. **"I didn't know that"**: Lucas.

Only a third: *Texas Almanac,* 1941–42, p. 103. **No radios, newspapers:** *Ibid.,* p. 257; Hardeman. **"Saturday town" campaigning:** Hardeman, Clark, Mahon, Pickle. **"You couldn't drive":** Mahon. **"To buy":** Clark. **$100 per week:** Analysis of daily reports of Johnson campaign teams, Boxes 11–16, JHP. **400 weeklies, 60 dailies, 60 radio stations:** *Texas Almanac.*

Patman eliminated: Patman OH I, pp. 12, 25. **Allred eliminated:** Hardeman.

Money—from attorneys: Hopkins in his OH II, p. 32, says, "I was able to help by solicitation among some people up here other than the [United Mine Workers] union, because at that time I felt that the union could not afford to come financially contributing to Lyndon's campaign. . . . I did get to others who were not in the labor movement that I knew in and around Washington and was able to raise a fairly good-sized sum for those days—a few thousand dollars. It wasn't a magnificent sum, but I took it down to Texas and it was appropriately turned over and spent in his behalf. I don't think Lyndon ever personally knew a damned thing about it." Asked by the author for additional details on this point, Hopkins said that part of the money he raised was contributed by a Washington attorney who "was building up a law practice, and he may or may not have had clients who he thought might be benefited. I had checks. And some cash." Carrying the money to Texas was a new experience, he says. "It was certainly novel to me—I had never had that much cash in my personal life." He says, "I carried some monies down—a few thousand dollars—and turned them over to Wirtz at Johnson's headquarters." **From garment center:** Corcoran. **From Wall Street:** Janeway. **"It was all cash":** Rowe.

From oilmen; Wirtz assured them: Young. A Johnson representative, Everett L. Looney, pledged Johnson's opposition to federal control of the oil industry, and his support of retention of the oil depletion allowance, in a speech at Tyler (*AS,* May 16). **Underwood telegrams:** "T" folder, Box 17, JHP. **"Have talked":** Kittrell to Johnson, April 23, Box 16, JHP. **Knight, Driscoll:** *Fort Worth Press,* July 31. **Richardson:** Raymond Buck Papers, noted in Green, p. 239. See also Buck to

Blundell, May 8, "District Office Correspondence," Box 18, JHP. **Kittrell handed Johnson:** Young. **Wirtz handing Woods:** Woods. **Lyndon and Alice:** Mary Louise Glass Young, Harold Young. **"25-year senatorship":** Marsh to Connally, May 27, 1942, OF-300, Roosevelt Papers. **"In one day":** Mrs. Young. **Marsh raising money:** Mrs. Young. Jack Frost also donated his private plane to Johnson in the latter stages of the campaign.

From Brown & Root—May 5 meeting: Bellows to Brown, May 7, with two attached lists "John Connally," Box 330, JHP. **He simply took precautions:** These are described in detail in the Internal Revenue Service investigation of Brown & Root's financing of Lyndon Johnson that is covered in Chapter 35. **"Legal fees:"** See p. 746 and relevant notes. **$12,500 route:** The attorney was Edgar Monteith, his partner was A. W. Baring, and the transaction is described in Werner to Irey, Jan. 14, 1944, p. 2, WF. **"Bonuses":** The $30,000 was to W. A. Woolsey and L. T. Bolin; the $33,800 was to J. M. Dellinger; the $40,000 was to Robert Thomas, *ibid.,* p. 1. **Well over $100,000:** At the time the IRS investigation was stopped, a total of $170,800 in Brown & Root bonuses alone, given in the early weeks of the campaign, was being investigated, in the belief of IRS agents that the money had wound up in the Johnson campaign. (Werner to Irey, Jan. 14, 1944, pp. 1, 2, WF.)

Costs of statewide campaign: Numerous old-time Texas politicians, including Clark, Hardeman, Lawson, Stevenson, Yarborough, Young. But the best picture of the different types of minor costs involved in Texas campaigning comes from scattered bills and receipts in Boxes 10–34, JHP, including, and in particular, in Box 5, "Pre-Presidential Confidential File." **"That was what":** Clark. **Hiring reporters and editors:** Among them was Gordon Fulcher of the *AA-S.* **Phil Fox:** Hardeman, Mann. **"You'd go and say":** Hardeman. **82 secretaries:** Form SS-1a ("Employer's Tax Return") filed by Travis County Johnson for Senate Club, July 1. **Secretarial school:** Von Kalow to Johnson, May 26, "V," Box 15, JHP.

Ads: Author's review of Texas newspapers during campaign. **Hundreds of thousands; radio time; billboards:** Author's analysis of bills, receipts, and memos in Boxes 11–16, 18, 19, JHP. **Barbecues:** Clark.

Kellam report: To Pickle, June 1, Box 15, JHP. Also see Wardlaw to Johnson,

June 7, "District Office Fort Worth," Box 18, JHP, on paying another lead man $100 per week. **On a scale Texas had never seen:** Hardeman, Young.
Twenty-seven candidates: McKay, pp. 430–38; Steinberg, *Sam Johnson's Boy*, pp. 163–64. **Dies:** Young, "Lone Star Razzle Dazzle"; Mann; Lawson; general description of his campaign in McKay, pp. 416–19, 445, 448, 453, 457, 461, 467; *State Observer*, May 19.
Mann's plaque: Steinberg, p. 169. **"There was a guy":** Kennedy. **"A very deep"; assistants asked him to run:** Hardeman. **Johnson-type campaign:** Kennedy. **"The people":** Mann.
Still paying off debts: Hardeman, Mann. **"We didn't":** Mann. **With a single aide; no money for speakers; Mann's campaigning:** Hardeman, Mann.
Johnson description: Partly from home movies taken by Mrs. Johnson of her husband campaigning, partly from still photos in newspapers; partly from recordings of radio broadcasts of his speeches at the Johnson Library. **"Senatorial":** Young. **"As LBJ came":** Douglas, p. 334. **42 per minute:** *AA-S*, June 22. **"He never":** Deason OHR, II, p. 17. Further description of his campaigning comes from articles in *DMN, AA-S, State Observer,* etc. **Not working as hard as in 1937:** Keach. **He knew:** Mann.
O'Daniel biography: Clark, Herman Jones, Lawson, Mann, Hardeman, Oltorf; Gunther, pp. 848–50; McKay, pp. 14, 23; Green, pp. 24–25; Davenport, "Where's Them Biscuits, Pappy?"; McEvoy, "I've Got That Million Dollar Smile." **"Hello there, mother"; "you young folks":** Davenport, "Where's Them Biscuits, Pappy?" **"They figured":** McEvoy, "I've Got . . ."; *Texas Weekly,* July 2, 1938. **"Either stumbled into":** McEvoy, "I've Got . . ." **Organizing his own company:** McKay, pp. 14–23; Green, p. 23. **More listeners:** Green, p. 23. **Lonely housewives; "He talked"; "at 12:30 sharp":** McEvoy, "I've Got . . ." **Newsboy:** It was Herman Jones.
"A born actor": McEvoy, "I've Got . . ."; Lawson. **Minor errors:** Gunther, p. 851. **Half a million:** Green, p. 25; Lawson. **Seldom went:** Lawson; Gunther, p. 848. **Hillbilly Flour:** Goodwyn, pp. 253–54. **Orphans:** Goodwyn, p. 252. **Asking voters if he should run:** "Under the Capitol Dome," *State Observer,* March 2, 1944; Green, p. 23; Goodwyn, p. 254; McKay, p. 32.
Pappy's first campaign: McKay, pp. 32–53; White, pp. 248–53; Green, pp. 22–24.

Poll tax; carpetbagger; "Blessed"; thunderstorm: Goodwyn, pp. 261–63. **"For years":** White, p. 250. **Lee story:** McKay, p. 15. **Tapping evangelism:** Goodwyn, pp. 258–59, is among those noting this. **Compared to Moses:** Green, p. 24. **"He sensed":** Oltorf. **Mother's Day speech:** McEvoy, "I've Got . . ." **"Texas was producing":** White, p. 252. **Last:** Hart Stilwell, "Texas," in Allen, ed., p. 322. **Raymondsville scene:** White, p. 249. **"We have not":** Goodwyn, p. 259.
His true philosophy; broken sales tax and pension plan promises: Gunther, pp. 849–50; McKay, pp. 93–214. **"No power":** Gunther, p. 849. **"The loneliest man":** Kennedy. **"I've got":** McEvoy, "I've Got . . ." **Sunday morning broadcasts:** Lawson; Davenport, "Where's Them Biscuits, Pappy?" **"He'd just drum":** Young. **The greatest vote-getter:** McKay, Preface, unnumbered page.
"Made me": Johnson, quoted in Miller, p. 84. **"Pneumonia":** Connally, quoted in Miller, p. 84. **"Nervous exhaustion":** Young, who was sent to the clinic by a concerned Marsh to cheer him up. **"He was depressed":** Mrs. Johnson. **"A fit":** Connally, quoted in Miller, p. 84. **"Busy with":** *AA-S*, May 18. **"A much-needed rest":** *AA-S*, May 20. **Quiet talk:** Young. **"But":** Mrs. Johnson.
"We told him straight": Smith. **Fort Worth projects:** The key one was an ambitious flood control and navigation project for the Trinity River, which was dear to Amon Carter's heart. In an undated telegram which appears to have been sent in May, 1941, Carter wired Johnson that this project "has been submitted to the President for his final support. Hope we may have your help and support in making it possible for this work to proceed at once" (Carter to Johnson, "C," Box 17, JHP). **Early quoted:** Young. The editorial appeared on June 15. When it appeared, Wirtz knew who to thank. He wrote Early: "Amon's editorial was a knockout. Many thanks. . . . You are giving us wonderful help" (Wirtz to Early, June 16, OF-300-Texas, Roosevelt Papers). **Early** wrote Carter: "Everybody here is very happy and their appreciation to you is very real" (Early to Carter, June 16, OF-300-Texas, Roosevelt Papers).
Johnson's relationship with City Machine: Quill, Hardeman, Jenkins. Jenkins says, "Mr. Johnson had this sort of 'The King is Dead, Long Live the King' attitude, and after Maverick lost . . ." One way that Johnson quickly cemented his relationship with the City Machine was to intercede on

behalf of public works projects it wanted with Harry Hopkins. (For example, Connally to Jenkins, May 10, "C," Box 17, JHP.) **Roy Miller raising money:** Interview summaries, p. 3, WF. **Telling them:** Brown, Clark. **Hoblitzelle:** Janeway.

Johnson's rallies: Lady Bird Johnson's home movies show the flavor, and Johnson's appearance, as do numerous articles in Texas newspapers. The best description is in an unpublished memoir written by their master of ceremonies, Harfield Weedin, pp. 141–58. The script is contained in this memoir. See also Miller, pp. 83–84; Steinberg, pp. 173–75. **"Have at last tumbled":** *Granger* (Texas) *News,* June 19. **Advertisements:** A typical one is in the *Williamson Sun,* June 20. **"We must stop":** Johnson quoted in Miller, p. 85. **"The most important"; "Every fifth-columnist":** *Wichita Falls Record-News,* June 10. **"Do you want?":** Weedin memoir. **Enthusiasm draining away:** One can hear it doing so on recordings of radio broadcasts, and it is described in newspapers and by such observers as Hardeman. **Now "addressing thousands":** *AA-S,* June 23. **"Stood crowded":** *State Observer,* June 23. **"Glory be!":** *Granger News,* June 19. **National journalists:** *American Mercury,* Sept., *The Nation,* June 21.

A new argument: Lawson, Long, Clark. **"Will the Old Folks":** Johnson House Scrapbooks. **One Johnson campaign worker:** Long. **The mail:** Lawson. **"Your pension checks":** *AA-S,* June 7. **Waving a $20 bill:** For example, *Gainesville Free Press,* July 26. **McLennan County Meeting:** *AA-S,* June 7.

O'Daniel's reaction: Lawson. **Keeping the Legislature in session:** Young, Lawson, Kennedy. **"A raw deal":** *DMN,* June 16. **"Resentful":** McKay, p. 469.

He could stop worrying; "up to their ears"; "not one word" etc.: Weedin memoir, pp. 141–45. **"Plaster the state":** *Life,* June 30. **Putting Miller on the air:** Johnson to Miller, May 25, "M," Box 17, JHP.

Money running out; dunning letters: In Boxes 11–19, JHP.

Wirtz's tactic to raise more money: Hopkins OH II, pp. 32–33. "I think some additional assistance came because of that," he said. "I didn't take it." **Corcoran "went up":** Rowe, confirmed by Corcoran. Corcoran's extensive money-raising for Lyndon Johnson was an open secret in Washington at the time. As Cecil Dickson, then an INS reporter, wrote: "Corcoran, moving in his usual mysterious ways, was credited by Johnson's friends with having

raised a lot of money for the New Deal candidate. . . . Tommy had hoped to ride a Johnson victory into the office of solicitor general" (*Austin Tribune,* July 6).

Jenkins took cash to Texas: Jenkins. **Gave it to Marsh:** Jenkins, Mary Louise Glass Young. **Marsh gave it to Glass:** Mary Louise Glass Young. Jenkins arrived in Austin at 11 a.m. on June 21 (Jenkins to Connally, May 29). **New York conservatives sent money:** Janeway. **Brown & Root:** The IRS investigation described in Chapter 35 gives the details and extent of the financial support of Johnson. **Wortham:** Brown; "Testimony of Martin Heater," p. 42, Interview Summaries, WF. **$4,000 to Roy Miller:** "Victoria Gravel Co. Payments," p. 3, Interview Summaries, WF. **Not deductible:** "Testimony of Thomas G. Shelton, Jr.," p. 69, Interview Summaries, WF. **Trotti:** Werner to Irey, Jan. 14, 1944, pp. 2, 3, WF. **Herman drew $5,000 and gave it through Bremond:** *ibid.,* pp. 3, 4. **No tactic:** Herman Brown. **$200,000:** See Chapter 35. **Johnson's total expenditures:** *Life,* June 30, estimated them at $250,000. In *New York Herald Tribune,* July 5, the estimate is "$200,000 to $300,000." **Half a million:** Steinberg, p. 170, quotes a "Wirtz associate" as saying, "The half-million-dollar figure was closer to reality." **Most expensive:** The veteran Texas political reporter Walter C. Hornaday wrote in a summary of the campaign for the *NYT:* "Observers . . . believe that more money was spent in Mr. Johnson's behalf than in any previous Statewide campaign" (*NYT,* July 6, Sec. IV, p. 7). Lyndon Johnson himself, in his official report filed with the Secretary of the Senate, said he had spent $31,965 and received $29,615 in contributions (*AS,* July 30). **"All he needed":** Clark.

"The way to play": Gunther, p. 834. **"Probably":** Gunther, p. 833. **$1.75:** Henderson, p. 199. **Voted at the direction of their leaders:** Quill; Bushick to Johnson, Sept. 25, "1941 Campaign Correspondence," JHP, Box 11; Gunther, pp. 832–35; White, "Machine Made"; Henderson, pp. 177, 180, 181, 185. **"Cruel":** Gunther, p. 834. **Precautions necessary:** Quill. **Johnson needed the West Side:** Quill. **"If the leader":** Quill.

"The Valley": The overall picture of politics in the Valley comes from Key, pp. 271–74; Lynch, *Duke of Duval;* Shelton, "Political Conditions"; Weeks, "The Texas-Mexicans"; Green, pp. 4–5; *Philadelphia Record,* Nov. 2, 1939; interviews with two of George Parr's lawyers—Em-meet Shelton and Luther E. (L.E.) Jones; Clark; Hardeman.

(In his thesis, Shelton states that much of his material comes from "personal interviews with men who know politics," including "ex-Governors, candidates for high state offices, campaign managers, local politicians. . . . For obvious reasons, these men could not be quoted directly. Their identity must remain a secret." This thesis is valuable nonetheless because of the identity of the author. Edgar Shelton, Jr., was the son of Edgar Shelton, Sr., one of three Shelton brothers—the other two were Polk and Emmett—who were three of George Parr's attorneys, as well as attorneys for other financial and political interests in the Valley. Through them, Edgar, Jr., had entrée to the politicians in the state, and the Valley, most familiar with its political machinations. And the only survivor among the three elder Sheltons, Emmett, not only confirms the statements in the thesis, but gives further details of many of the incidents involved. In some of them, he was himself a principal; he knew of others through discussions with his brothers, and with Valley political figures.)

Jacales: WPA, pp. 460–66, 509–12. **"Only":** Key, p. 272. **"From time immemorial":** Weeks, "The Texas-Mexicans," p. 609. **"Lords protector":** Weeks, p. 610. **"As hard-bitten":** *Philadelphia Record.* **"Little is known":** Shelton, p. 44. **Keeping receipts in safe:** Shelton, p. 107. **"Insure discipline":** Key, p. 273. **"The Mexican voter":** Lynch, p. 23. **Description of voting procedures:** Jones, Hardeman; the herding image is used by Weeks, p. 611. **The tear-off sheet:** *Philadelphia Record.*

Checked only irregularly: *Philadelphia Record.* **"The 'machine' votes the dead men":** Shelton, p. 7. **"An excellent location":** Shelton, p. 74. **Dolores:** *Philadelphia Record.* **"All one way"; 15,000 votes; 10 to 1:** Shelton, p. 110; Table 27, in Key, p. 275, shows that in Duval County, "over a 20-year period . . . almost invariably the leading candidate received over 90% of the vote."

The decisive consideration: "In negotiating with some *jefes,* an ample supply of campaign funds is no handicap," Key, p. 273. **Parr's greed:** See "Remarkable conditions in Duval County" (Shelton, pp. 62–63); Lynch, pp. 30, 41, 53. **"The State candidates":** Shelton, p. 113. **3,728 to 180:** *Texas Almanac,* 1941–42, p. 385.

"Looks easy": Brinsdon to Johnson, April 23, Box 16, JHP. **"This district":**

Martins to Looney, May 9, "L," Box 14, JHP. **Nor:** Key, p. 273, says, "Some bosses are fickle, and the candidate who gets there last with the cash or promise of favor sometimes cuts out an opponent who thinks he has already sewed up the vote." **Wirtz an old ally:** Lynch, p. 36. **Wirtz stopping over in Dallas:** Wirtz to Lechner, May 15, Box 16, JHP. **Wirtz goes to South Texas:** *DMN,* May 17; McKay, p. 447; Young. **A bidding war:** Steinberg, p. 172; Young. **Johnson calling Parr:** Emmett Shelton. **"You can depend":** Horace Guerra to Johnson, June 18, Box 16, JHP.

Increased Roosevelt support—"Smilingly"; *Lexington Enterprise,* June 20. **Roosevelt directing Early and Rowe:** Roosevelt to Early, April 30; Early to Edens, June 5, FDR–LBJ Microfilm; Roosevelt to Rowe, June 9; Rowe to Roosevelt, Rowe to McCord, June 21 (on which is noted: "OK–FDR"); all PPF 6149, Roosevelt Papers. **Rowe balking at Social Security letter:** Rowe. **"The polls show":** Rowe to Roosevelt, June 5. **"Went right around":** Rowe to Roosevelt, June 5, shows that the other avenues Johnson used were Corcoran and Wayne Coy, assistant administrator of the FSA, with whom Johnson was also friendly. **The letter:** *AA,* June 7. **Roosevelt would make an exception:** Rowe.

Telegrams—"Slacker": Johnson to LeHand, May 31; Wirtz to Rowe, June 2; Rowe to Roosevelt, June 3—all PPF 6149, Roosevelt Papers. **Headline:** *Houston Chronicle,* June 5. **"Parity":** Corcoran; Rowe to Forster, May 23; "Corcoran telephone message," May 24—PPF 6149, Roosevelt Papers. **Eleanor:** June 11, FDR–LBJ Microfilm. **National emergency:** Johnson to Roosevelt, May 27; Roosevelt to "Dear Lyndon," June 3.

Corcoran's rumor: McKay, p. 447. For typical press coverage of the President's supposedly planned trip, see *State Observer,* May 19; Corcoran. **"Preposterous":** *NYT,* June 28. **"Everything":** Corcoran.

Stuck record: *State Observer,* June 16. The *San Angelo Standard* ran the story under the headline: "The Old Refrain." **Trapped:** Lawson; McKay, pp. 446, 452, 454–55, 464–67; *HP,* June 4. **Increasingly bizarre:** Good summary in McKay, p. 469.

Mann's campaigning: For example, *DMN,* June 22, says that he had to that date traveled 25,000 miles and spoken in 550 towns in 194 counties, and had made 265 formal speeches, "more . . . than his three leading opponents." **"He never stopped":** Hardeman. **Indignation:** Mann, Hardeman. **"His first mention":** *DMN,*

June 20. **Mann's speaking technique:** Home movies. **"Gerry":** Mann. **Houston speech:** *AA*, June 24; *SAE*, June 25; *DMN*, June 27. **"Tireless":** *DMN*, June 17. **"Despite":** *DMN*, June 27. **"Sincerity":** Hardeman. **$1,300:** *AA*, June 25. **Johnson's radio schedule:** Analysis of radio schedules in newspapers. **"They filled":** Mann.

Belden Polls: McKay, p. 481. **"The voters":** Belden, in *DMN*, June 28. **"Pulling away":** *HP*, June 22.

Johnson felt: This description of his mood is from Mrs. Johnson and his campaign aides. **"Jubilant":** *State Observer,* June 23. **Feelings of his staff:** Long, Pickle, other aides. **"Oh, the adventures":** Mrs. Johnson.

Told South Texas bosses to report votes immediately: Jenkins; Shelton; SHJ; Connally, quoted in Banks, p. 85. **Duval vote:** In 1940, O'Daniel had received 3,728 votes to 180 for all opponents in Duval. **"Mextown" and "niggertown" votes:** The precincts cited were Nos. 30 and 46 in Corpus Christi (from a tabulation compiled for Johnson, apparently by Walter Jenkins), Box 18, JHP. The source for all vote totals is the *Texas Almanac*, 1942–43, pp. 259–60.

"Nauseous": Unidentified source quoted in Shelton, p. 72. **"They simply voted":** Shelton, p. 100, states, "After the Special Senate Election of 1941, . . . much comment on the Mexican vote came out of the Valley, Cameron County in particular. One man asserted that the Mexican vote in that election was silent and bought. Another made the following statement: 'They simply voted the Mexicans in a body every place they could,' and of course there is little you can do to offset that kind of campaign down here." Some of the comment was even made publicly: in a letter published on July 2, 1941, by the *Valley Morning Star* of Harlingen (in Cameron County), Paul G. Maher notes the lopsided results in certain precincts. Of the 175 residents—including children—of La Joya, in Hidalgo County, for example—102 went to the polls to vote for Lyndon Johnson. All other candidates received 21 votes. Other sample votes from such precincts: Johnson 66, all others 11; Johnson 92, all others 7. Then Maher comments: "For certain of the voting places in the Valley we find that 'free' Americans went to the ballot boxes and voted thusly. . . . Strange, isn't it" (Maher letter in *Valley Morning Star*, July 2, 1941, quoted in Shelton, pp. 101, 102). **"We have a situation":** quoted in Shelton, p. 25. **"If**

there is any law": The man quoted by Shelton states: "We all know this is true down here, but it can be proved only with legal action." Such action would not be taken until Lyndon Johnson's second campaign for the Senate, in 1948. The discoveries made as a result of that action will be discussed in Volume II. The opinion given by politicians quoted in the Shelton thesis was echoed to the author by such politicians and political observers as Lawson, Clark, Young, Hardeman, and Jones. **Celebrating:** *DMN*, June 29. **Miller's statement:** Steinberg, p. 181. Also expected to announce, according to the *AA* (June 30) were Sherman Birdwell, Thomas C. Ferguson, and Sam Stone. **"Going around":** Mrs. Johnson. **Not all the votes were counted:** This description of vote-counting practices in some Texas precincts is from sources of Texas politicians and political observers, including Clark, Crawford, Hardeman, SHJ, L.E. Jones, Lawson, Long, Oltorf, Quill, Smith, Shelton, Stehling, Yarborough, Young. See also *AA*, July 11.

Conservatives becoming alarmed: Lawson, Clark, Oltorf, Young. **"A rabid Prohibitionist":** Lawson. **"Booze dives":** A typical O'Daniel statement on the subject said that he had introduced the bill to "help keep them [young Army recruits] from falling into the snares of booze dives set up around our Army camps for the enrichment of the booze manufacturers and booze peddlers of Texas" (*DMN*, June 7). See also *AA*, June 7; *Fort Worth Star-Telegram*, May 24; McKay, p. 470; undated memo, Baldwin to Connally, "B," Box 13, JHP. **Liquor Control Board appointments:** McKay, pp. 367–69; *Brenham Banner-Press*, May 31. **The brewers' feelings:** Stevenson, Lawson, Crawford. Former Governor Jim Ferguson, long associated with brewery interests, summed up their feelings this way: "While one dry Senator in Washington might do little harm to the beer and whiskey business in Texas, one dry wartime Governor such as O'Daniel could knock it cold" (Steinberg, p. 181; see also *AA*, July 5). **"Could just about":** Lawson. **The lobbyists' feeling:** Lawson, Hardeman, Stevenson; *AA*, July 6; Green, pp. 36–37; Banks, pp. 83–85.

A quiet meeting; headed out: *AA*, July 6; Blundell quoted in Miller, p. 87; Hardeman.

Shortfall in San Antonio: The three precincts cited are Numbers 16, 15, and 20. **Only about 100:** Author's analysis of results in the city's twenty-two "Mexican boxes," taken from the "Record of Election Returns, General Elections, Nov., 1936–July, 1946," Archives, Bexar County Clerk, and from "List of Poll Taxes, Precincts Nos. 1–85, 1941, P. E. Dickson, Assessor and Collector of Taxes, Bexar County, Texas, March 27, 1942," and from a second volume for precincts 86–195, also found in the Bexar County Clerk's office, San Antonio. **Reason for the shortfall:** Quill, Hardeman; Bushick to Johnson, Sept. 25, "1941 Campaign Correspondence," Box 11, JHP. **Not keeping men on the scene:** Connally, quoted in Banks, pp. 84–85. **"Barring":** Robert Johnson, quoted in *AA*, June 30.

Scene in the Driskill suite; the last phone call: *AA*, July 6. **"Well, that don't":** Lawson. **"Drawn anxious":** *AA-S*, July 6. **Connally still sending:** For example, Connally to Heine, Box 17, JHP. **Wirtz's back porch:** Mrs. Johnson's home movies.

East Texas developments—Shelby County: *AA*, July 7; Mrs. J. L. Walker to Johnson, July 1, Box 18, JHP. **Newton County:** *AA*, July 8. **Other East Texas counties:** *DMN*, July 1 and 2; *AA*, July 8. **"I'm listening":** Allred quoted by Keach in Dugger, p. 234.

Johnson telephoned Parr: SHJ; Shelton; others. **226 from Austin:** *AA*, July 1. **He couldn't get enough:** Young; Hardeman; Connally quoted in Banks, p. 85, says that the South Texas counties had already given "their complete returns to the Election Bureau, and then everybody knew exactly how many votes were down there. . . . Twelve or 15 East Texas Counties kept bringing in returns Monday . . . and we sat there helpless." **Holding back key counties, including Trinity:** *DMN*, July 2. Trinity would, in fact, be the last of Texas' 254 counties to send in its final figures.

Losing the lead on Monday and Tuesday: *DMN*, *AA-S*, *CCC-T*, June 30, July 1–7. **"Well, that's looking fine":** *AA*, July 1. **"It's gone":** Jenkins. **"He stole":** Quill. **Rage:** Long. **Scene in suite:** Home movies. **Connally weeping:** Stehling. **Final count:** Mann finished with 140,807 votes; Dies with 80,653. The other 25 candidates received a total of 4,550 votes.

35. "I Want to See Lyndon"

SOURCES

Documents and articles:
This chapter is primarily based on the

Werner Files (WF, see A Note on Sources), which consist of E.C. Werner's "Chronological History of the Investigation of the Case S.I.-19267-F and Related Companies" (referred to as Chron. History); his day-by-day business diary for the year 1943, in which he wrote his activities and, occasionally, brief notations on their results (Diary); his summaries, numbered in hand and totaling 93 pages, of the interviews he conducted, either alone or with other agents, of the principals in the investigation (Interview Summaries); and the report summarizing the case which he sent to Assistant Secretary of the Treasury Elmer L. Irey, on Jan. 14, 1944 (Werner to Irey).

A memorandum from James Rowe to Grace Tully, November 20, 1942 (PSF 148, Roosevelt Papers), details the maneuverings involved.

Also, three columns, "Washington Merry-Go-Round," by Drew Pearson on the subject, which ran in the *Nashville Tennessean* on March 26, 27, and 28, 1956.

Interviews:
George Brown, Edward Clark, James H. Rowe, Wilton Woods.

NOTES

"I know": Roosevelt to Maverick, Jr., June 4, 1941, quoted in Henderson, *Maury Maverick*, p. 231. **Never found out:** Corcoran, Brown, McFarlane. **"Keep him":** McFarlane to Roosevelt, July 29, 1939, OF-300-Texas (Box 70), Roosevelt Papers. **For nothing:** McFarlane. In fact, after his loss, he couldn't even get in to see Roosevelt, as he pointed out in a letter to Roosevelt, May 15, 1939 (OF-300, Roosevelt Papers). **Job only through Rayburn:** *DMN*, July 18, 1939.

Two-paragraph note: Johnson to Roosevelt, July 21, 1941. **"Had a visit":** Johnson to Honeyman, July 30, 1941, JHP, Box 8. **Young Democrats; Rowe put the suggestion in writing:** Rowe to Roosevelt, July 17, 1941, PSF 184, Roosevelt Papers. **"Sit on the boxes":** Rowe, quoted in Miller, *Lyndon*, p. 88.

IRS became suspicious: Chron. History, pp. 1–3. **Brown & Root had been advised:** "Testimony of Thomas G. Shelton, Jr.," p. 71. Interview Summary. **"Big trouble"; "hired Wirtz":** Clark, Brown.

Developing a strategy: G. Brown to Johnson, Oct. 5, 13, 1942, Johnson to Brown, Oct. 10, 1942, Box 12, LBJA, SN.

Rowe's feelings: Rowe. "I sent"; "So far": Rowe memo to Tully. Johnson went to Helvering: Rowe. Attempt foundered on Morgenthau: Rowe, in interviews, and in memo to Tully, gives the most convincing testimony of Morgenthau's integrity. In his memo, he said: "Morgenthau, to be blunt, has no political sense."
"The Browns were worried"; Johnson "was in trouble": Rowe. Wirtz and Brown to Washington: Brown to Johnson, Oct. 5, 13, 1942, Box 12, LBJA SN. Talking on the street: Rowe. The address of the townhouse, which is now the Turkish Embassy, is 2304 Massachusetts Ave., N.W. "Just the two of us": Rowe. "Helvering has indicated": Rowe memo to Tully. "Then I": Rowe.
Agents had been ordered to stop working: Oct. 28, 29, Nov. 24, 1942, Chron. History. Werner was told: Dec. 17, 1942, Chron. History. "Had me explain"; was to continue": Jan. 13, 14, 1943, Diary, and summary, p. 5, Chron. History. Conference in Dallas: Chron. History, p. 5 and subsequent entries, and Diary entries. "Bonuses": Werner to Irey. Horne told the agents: Interview Summaries, p. 14. "Sufficient evidence": Werner to Irey. $24,000; $2,500 check; "is believed": ibid., p. 142.
Victoria Gravel: "Testimony of Joe Orville Corwin, Jr.," p. 24, "Testimony of Randolph Thomas Mills," pp. 46, 49, "Victoria Gravel Co. Payments," p. 3, "Gravel Royalty Checks," p. 6, Interview Summaries; Chron. History, pp. 2, 3, 8. Monteith and Baring: "Baring Testimony," p. 93; "Testimony of Mills," pp. 50, 51; "Testimony of Robert Thomas," p. 76, Interview Summaries; Werner to Irey, pp. 2, 3. Corwin mailing currency: "Testimony of Joe Orville Corwin, Jr.," p. 24, Interview Summaries; Werner to Irey, pp. 2, 3. "Petty cash" fund: "Testimony of Robert Horne," p. 14; "Testimony of Francis O'Connor," p. 53; "Testimony of W. A. Woolsey," p. 845; "Testimony of James Murphy Dellinger," p. 25, Interview Summaries; Werner to Irey, p. 4.
Johnson's denial to Pearson: Pearson, "Washington Merry-Go-Round," March 27, 1956. Finding the checks: Nov. 19, 1943, Diary. Corwin interview: "Testimony of Joe Orville Corwin, Jr.," p. 24, Interview Summaries; Dec. 15, 1943, Diary. A "circuitous route"; "false testimony": Werner to Irey, p. 3. Mills' bonus: "Testimony of Randolph Thomas Mills," pp. 46–51, Interview Summaries. Werner had a facsimile: Werner to Irey, p. 3.

$100,000 check: Dec. 16, 1943, Diary. Durst's statement: "Testimony of L. H. Durst," pp. 38–41, Interview Summaries. IRS less convinced: Werner includes $2,000 of it among "bonuses paid and believed to have been used for Senatorial Campaign," in Werner to Irey. Woolsey interview: "Testimony of W. A. Woolsey, p. 845," Interview Summaries. Duke's statement: "J. T. Duke," p. 33, and "Testimony of J. T. Duke," p. 37, Interview Summaries. "Some radio time": "Testimony of Frederick Timothy Bolin," p. 20, Interview Summaries. $1,870, $1,150: Werner to Irey, p. 4. "Insofar as I know": "Testimony of George Rufus Brown" p. 22, Interview Summaries. "Believed paid": Werner to Irey, p. 3. "Admittedly paid": Werner to Irey, p. 3.
"An important matter"; "off record": Wirtz to Roosevelt, Wirtz to Watson, Nov. 1, 1943, Wirtz to Watson, Nov. 6, 1943, all PPF 7562, Roosevelt Papers.
"Like any other case"; "it appeared fraud was present": Chron. History, p. 9. "Open for further discussion"; Wirtz to Watson, Dec. 30, 1943, PPF 7562, Roosevelt Papers.
Began trying to find out: Chron. History, p. 9. "Told me nothing": Dec. 15, 1943, Diary. "Couldn't recall": Dec. 16, 1943, Diary. Woods interview: Woods; Woods letter to author, May 18, 1982. $1,000: "Testimony of D. Young," p. 92, Interview Summaries. $7,500: "Testimony of Wilton George Woods," p. 83; "Wilton Woods," p. 19; "Testimony of James Murphy Dellinger," p. 25, Interview Summaries. In fact, it was linked to that trip, as Woods has told the author. He said that during October, 1940, he brought that sum to Washington and gave it to Herbert Henderson in Johnson's Munsey Building Office for use in the Democratic Congressional Campaign.
$1,649,916: In Chron. History, p. 13. It is impossible to tell from the documents available to the author how much of the $1,099,944 represents funds made available by Brown & Root to Lyndon Johnson. Echoed by Werner: Werner stated flatly in Chron. History, p. 9, that "I . . . found that donations had been made [by Brown & Root] and charged as expense to the corporation's expense accounts." In Werner to Irey, Jan. 14, 1944, he wrote, about the $150,800 in bonuses: "Sufficient evidence is on hand, it is believed, to show minutes authorizing above bonuses to be fraudulent."
Werner working in Austin: Dec. 27,

1943, Diary. **Wirtz asks for appointment:** Wirtz to Watson, Dec. 27; Watson to Wirtz, Dec. 30, 1943, PPF 7562, Roosevelt Papers. **Woods interview:** "Testimony of Wilton George Woods," p. 83, Interview Summaries. **"Not a 'Sunday School' proposition":** "LD" to Watson, Jan. 11, 1944, PPF 6149, Roosevelt Papers.

Johnson and Wirtz see Roosevelt: White House Usher's Diary, Jan. 13, 1944. **Irey telephones Texas:** Chron. History, p. 10, states that Irey told Cooner that "Congressman Lyndon Johnson and former State Senator Alvin Wirtz, now counsel for Brown & Root, Inc., had been to see the President of the United States on the income tax matters of Brown & Root, Inc. Mr. Irey as a result of the meeting of Wirtz and Johnson with the President requested detailed information on political payments made by Brown & Root, Inc., to the Lyndon Johnson 1941 senatorial campaign." **"Sufficient evidence":** Werner to Irey. **A new agent:** Chron. History, p. 10. **"Not quite enough":** On Jan. 17, Werner states in Chron. History, p. 11, Werner and three of the other agents who had been conducting the investigation met with the new agent and "acquainted [him] with the history and the background . . . and with the fraudulent features of the case." The "not quite enough" remark was made on Jan. 20. **"He would recommend"; "no reason":** Chron. History, p. 11.

"Now on hand": Chron. History, p. 12. **Only scratched:** WF, *passim.* **Werner asked; ordered to drop the case:** Chron. History, pp. 12, 13.

Final report: Chron. History, p. 13. **Scaled down:** Pearson, "Washington Merry-Go-Round," March 28, 1956.

36. "Mister Speaker"

SOURCES

See Sources for Chapters 18 and 30. Also interviews with Ramsey Clark, Thomas G. Corcoran, H. G. Dulaney, John Holton, Walter Jenkins, Gerald Mann, Dale Miller, Frank C. Oltorf, Ralph Yarborough.

NOTES

Effusive letter: Johnson to Rayburn, Nov. 14, 1940, Series II, Roll 1, Rayburn Papers. **"Like a father":** Dorough, p. 306. Among those who remember the phrase: Hardeman, Young. **Entrée withdrawn:** Hardeman, Bolling, Harding. Hardeman

was among many persons whom Deschler told about Johnson's outburst on the staircase.

Rayburn dissuading Patman but declining to make statement: Poage to Johnson, April 28, 1941, Box 7, JHP. **"You or Senator":** Johnson to Connally, May 28, 1941, Box 17, JHP. **Awaited only Mr. Sam's word:** "One man said Sam R. could swing the tide in North Texas if he would," Ridgway to Johnson, April 30, 1941, Box 15, JHP. **Judge Loy:** Bellows to Connally, May 27, 1941, Box 13, JHP. **"We tried":** Connally to Bellows, June 3, 1941, Box 13, JHP. **"If you don't speak":** Marsh to Rayburn, June 15, 1941, Box 17, JHP. And see also Frank Balwin, editor of *Waco News Tribune*, to Poage, June 16, 1941, Box 13, JHP. **7,000 of 31,000:** *DMN,* July 15, 1941. O'Daniel and Mann both defeated Johnson by sizable pluralities. McKay, in *W. Lee O'Daniel,* p. 489, says that "The seeming lack of influence of Speaker Sam Rayburn in his district, at least in the matter of making a choice for United States Senator, might be considered a factor in the defeat of Johnson. . . . It may be remarked that the O'Daniel lead over the Rayburn-endorsed Johnson in Rayburn's home county, Fannin, was almost exactly the same as the O'Daniel lead over Johnson in the statewide totals."

"I was very fond": Mann. **Rayburn's attempts to get Mann a meeting with Roosevelt:** Rayburn to Watson, Sept. 2, 1941, Watson to Rayburn, Sept. 3, 1941; unsigned to Watson, Sept. 11, 1941—all PPF 474, Roosevelt Papers. **December 7:** Mann.

"If the day": *DMN, AA, AS,* June 17–27, 1941. **Johnson's naval service:** Will be detailed in Volume II. **None for more than a year:** Their last friendly exchange had been in November and December, 1939 (Johnson to Rayburn, Nov. 14, 1939, and Rayburn to Johnson, Nov. 18, 1939 and Dec. 4, 1939, Box 52, LBJA CF). On May 6, 1940, Johnson had written Rayburn a friendly letter and Rayburn had replied coldly on May 13, 1940 (Series II, Roll 1, Rayburn Papers). After the date, Johnson wrote Rayburn three times, twice in reference to his work with the Democratic Congressional Campaign Committee in 1940, and once on Dec. 22, 1940. Rayburn did not reply to these letters, so Rayburn had not written Johnson at all after May 13, 1940. **"You must carry a burden":** Johnson to Rayburn, "Thursday night," Box 52, LBJA CF. **Rayburn kept letter in billfold:** H. G. Dulaney, Director of the Sam Rayburn Library, wrote Johnson on Nov. 3, 1959, enclosing the letter and saying: "The Speaker wants to place this letter in the Library and if you can tell me just when it was written I will certainly appreciate it. You will notice that he has carried it in his pocket for quite a while." LBJL Archivist Juanita Roberts wrote Johnson on Nov. 10, 1959, dating the letter Dec. 18, 1941, and telling Johnson: "I am told that the Speaker carried your letter in his billfold for a long time and then put it in his desk drawer with the letters he kept from his mother" (all in Box 52, LBJA CF); Dulaney.

Union Station scene: Mrs. Johnson. **Helping the young wives:** Mrs. Johnson, Mrs. Rowe, Rowe.

"That blamed television set": Steinberg, *Sam Rayburn,* p. 297. **Rayburn's relationship with the Johnsons; "He was the best of us":** Mrs. Johnson. **"We wish":** Mrs. Johnson to Rayburn, March 20, 1943. **"Your friendship":** Rayburn to Mrs. Johnson, Sept. 25, 1950. **"Go call her":** Steinberg, *Sam Rayburn,* p. 197. **"We are":** Johnson to Lucinda Rayburn, Jan. 16, 1947. **Birthday parties:** Miller.

"You've got to": Douglas, p. 313. **"Knee breeches":** Johnson to Rayburn, March 4, 1957, Box 52, LBJA CF. **"I'm going":** Rayburn's speech, not the prepared text, but the verbatim version, in Box 52, LBJA CF. **Tears:** Yarborough.

Before his mother: Steinberg, *Sam Rayburn,* p. 218. **Boxes of candy:** Johnson to Lucinda Rayburn, Jan. 16, 1947, Box 52, LBJA CF. **"For some reason":** Mrs. Johnson. On Johnson's constant courtship of Rayburn see, in this same box, such letters as "The most inspiring experience of my life has been your friendship and guidance" (Jan. 6, 1955); "I owe so very much to your wise counsel, advice and friendship over the years" (March 5, 1955).

Difference in the relationship: Bolling, Hardeman, Harding, Holton, Ramsey Clark, Rayden, Jenkins, Izac. **"It was never":** Oltorf. **"There was never":** Hardeman. **"Kowtowed":** Jenkins. **"Kiss his ass":** Rowe. Corcoran also vivid on this point. **Scene at Rayburn Library dedication:** William Miller, in *Fishbait,* p. 232, has Johnson saying, in a sanitized version: "Damn it, you tell him I can't come. And another thing, I don't like you bossing me around

in my home state. I don't mind so much in Washington, but when you come around to my home state in Texas and tell me what to do, I think that's the end of the line." But Miller told many people on his return to Washington, including Hardeman, the "kiss his ass" phrase. Walter Jenkins says, "I never heard that, but I know he felt he had reached a place in life where he could be his own man instead of Mr. Rayburn's," and he "really disliked" still having to be Mr. Rayburn's. Jenkins also said that "whatever Mr. Rayburn wanted, he went out of his way to do. And if it was something *he* wanted, he worked his way around. It usually came from someone else. He planned a strategic campaign."

Rayburn and cancer: Dorough, pp. 34–42; Steinberg, *Sam Rayburn,* pp. 241–247. **Kennedy reaching Johnson:** Steinberg, p. 344. **Last letters:** In Box 52, LBJA CF. **"Washington was such a lonely city":** Dorough, p. 35.

37. The "Perfect Roosevelt Man"

The change in Johnson's sentiments is described in interviews with George Brown, Edward A. Clark, Thomas Corcoran, Louis Easley, D. B. Hardeman, Dale Miller, and Harold Young.

NOTES

Patman's attempt: Memorandum for General Watson, Oct. 1, 1941, PPF 3982, Roosevelt Papers. **Dies Committee vote:** *House Resolution 65,* Feb. 10, 1943. **"You mean":** Young. **"Reached the conclusion"; "kicks the New Deal":** Marsh quoted in Wallace OH, p. 2002. **Editing out:** Corcoran, Young. **Speech:** Portland *Oregonian,* Dec. 8, 1942.

"He gave": Miller. **"He was for":** Brown. **White's article:** *NYT,* April 13, 1945. **"Honey, we've got Truman":** Nichols OH II. **Easley's articles:** *AA,* April 23, 1947. Circumstances related by Easley in interview. **A liberal reporter:** Sherrill in *The Accidental President,* p. 109. **"More guts than brains":** Steinberg, p. 237. **In private:** Brown, Clark, Young. **1948 campaign:** will be discussed in detail in Volume II.

Index

A Note on the Type

The text of this book was set on the Linotype in a face called Times Roman, designed by Stanley Morison for The Times (London) and first introduced by that newspaper in 1932.

Among typographers and designers of the twentieth century, Stanley Morison has been a strong forming influence, as a typographical adviser to the English Monotype Corporation, as a director of two distinguished English publishing houses and as a writer of sensibility, erudition, and keen practical sense.

Composed by The Maryland Linotype Composition Corporation, Baltimore, Maryland. Printed and bound by The Haddon Craftsmen, Inc., Scranton, Pennsylvania. Photographic insert printed by Phillips Offset Co., Inc., Mamaroneck, New York.
Typography and binding design by Virginia Tan.
Cartography by Jean-Paul Tremblay.

PHOTOGRAPHIC CREDITS

The Lyndon Baines Johnson Library: Section I, Plate 1, 2 (top), 3, 4, 6, 7, 8, 9, 11, 14 (top); Section II, 1, 2, (top), 3, 4, 6 (top), 7 (top), 8, 9, 10 (bottom), 14, 15; Section III, 1, 3, 5 (bottom), 6, 7, 9, 10, 11, 13, 14, 15, 16

Campaign material from the LBJ Library, photographs by Zigy Kaluzny: II, 12–13; III, 13 (center)

LBJ National Historic Park, Johnson City: Section I, 5

Barker Texas History Center: II, 6 (bottom); III, 5 (top)

Austin–Travis County Collection, Austin Public Library: II, 7 (bottom) C00472); III, 8 (C01657)

Texas State Library Archives: III, 12 (middle, bottom)

Southwest Texas State University: I, 12, 14 (bottom left)

The Franklin D. Roosevelt Library, photo by Maurice Constant: III, 4 (bottom)

Life magazine: III, 4 (top), Myron Davis (1942), © 1968 Time Inc.; III, 12 (top), Francis Miller, © 1941 Time Inc.

Washington Post: III, 6 (bottom)

Photo by Arnold Genthe, courtesy Mr. and Mrs. Welly Hopkins: III, 2 (bottom left)

Photos courtesy Mary Louise Young: III, 2 (top and bottom right)

Photo courtesy Senator Lloyd Bentsen: II, 5

Photo by Chalmers Marving, courtesy Frank Oltorf: II, 11

Photo by Hessler Studio, courtesy Dale Miller: II, 2 (bottom)

Photos courtesy Wilton Woods: I, 16